Studies in the Legal History of the South

Edited by Paul Finkelman and Kermit L. Hall

This series explores the ways in which law has affected the development of the southern United States and in turn the ways the history of the South has affected the development of American law. Volumes in the series focus on a specific aspect of the law, such as slave law or civil rights legislation, or on a broader topic of historical significance to the development of the legal system in the region, such as issues of constitutional history and of law and society, comparative analyses with other legal systems, and biographical studies of influential southern jurists and lawyers.

STATES' LAWS ON
RACE AND COLOR

STATES' LAWS ON RACE AND COLOR

Compiled and Edited by

PAULI MURRAY

Foreword by

DAVISON M. DOUGLAS

The University of Georgia Press
Athens

Paperback edition, 2016
Published in 1997 by the University of Georgia Press
Athens, Georgia 30602
© 1951 by the Woman's Division of Christian Service
Foreword to this edition © 1997 by the University of Georgia Press
www.ugapress.org

Most University of Georgia Press titles are
avaliable from popular e-book vendors.

Printed digitally

The Library of Congress has cataloged the
hardcover edition of this book as follows:

States' laws on race and color / compiled and edited by Pauli Marray ;
foreword by Davison M. Douglas.
x, 746 p. ; 24 cm. — (Studies in the legal history of the South)
Originally published: Athens, Ga : Women's Division
of Christian Service, 1950.
Includes bibliographical references and index.
ISBN 0-8203-1883-3 (alk. paper)
1. African Americans—Legal status, laws, etc.
2. Race discrimination—United States.
I. Murray, Pauli, 1910–1985. II. Douglas, Davison M. III. Series.
KF4757. Z95M87   1997
342.73'0873—dc20

[347.302873]   96-9128

Paperback ISBN 978-0-8203-5063-9

Reprint made possible through the courtesy of the
Otto G. Richter Library, University of Miami, Coral Gables, Florida.

CONTENTS

ix

FOREWORD

DAVISON M. DOUGLAS

The struggle for equal treatment for African Americans and women has been one of the dominant themes in twentieth-century American history. Pauli Murray, a black woman born at the height of Jim Crow segregation in 1910, spent her life challenging the exclusion of both African Americans and women from full participation in American life. Murray was a civil rights activist long before such activism became commonplace in the early 1960s and a feminist long before the feminist movement captured the imagination of American women in the 1970s and 1980s. Murray's book, *States' Laws on Race and Color,* was but one reflection of Murray's lifelong commitment to equality for all Americans.

Murray grew up in the thoroughly segregated world of Durham, North Carolina, and learned at an early age the profound importance of race in America. Following the death of her mother, Murray was adopted by her aunt, Pauline Dame. Dame had earlier been abandoned by her light-skinned husband who, confronted with formidable barriers to successful law practice as a black man, chose to "pass for white" and to begin life anew in another state. Although Dame was also light-skinned, she declined to leave family, friends, and culture to join her husband in the distant world of white America. Dame's pride in her African-American heritage had a profound influence on Murray.

Upon graduation from a black high school in Durham, Murray moved to New York to seek further education away from the segregated world of the South. After taking an extra year of high school in New York to prepare for the rigors of college, Murray entered Hunter College, a distinguished women's college in New York City. Graduating in 1933 in the middle of the Depression, Murray struggled, as did many Americans, to make ends meet in an uncertain world. Remaining in New York, Murray found employment with the WPA Workers' Education Project, became involved with the American labor movement, and flirted with socialist politics.

At the same time, although glad to be removed from the indignities of the southern Jim Crow system, Murray felt a growing desire to return South to her roots and to confront directly the evils of racial segregation. As Murray wrote in her journal in the mid-1930s: "It seems to me that the testing ground of democracy and Christianity in the United States is the South [and] that it is the duty of Negroes to press for political, economic and educational equality for themselves and for disinherited whites."[1] This felt need to return South converged with Murray's desire to secure additional education and to help care for her aging aunt in Durham. As a result, in December 1938, Murray decided to apply for graduate study in sociology at the University of North Carolina in Chapel Hill.

Murray's choice of the University of North Carolina was a natural one. The University was home to two of the nation's leading social theorists on issues of race—Guy Johnson and Howard Odum—and was near her aunt's home in Durham. At the time of Murray's application, however, no black student had ever been admitted to the University, and one prior lawsuit to force integration had failed.[2] Coincidentally, Murray's application arrived a few days before the United States Supreme Court in *Missouri ex rel. Gaines v. Canada*[3] determined that the state of Missouri must either admit an African-American student to the state's white law school or else make other provision for his education substantially equal to that provided white students. Since no southern state—including North Carolina— offered black students any opportunity for graduate study, the *Gaines* decision posed a challenge to racial segregation of unknown proportions. Nevertheless, two days after the *Gaines* decision, the graduate school at the University of North Carolina rejected Murray's application for admission, claiming that "[u]nder the laws of North Carolina, and under the resolutions of the Board of Trustees of the University of North Carolina, members of your race are not admitted to the University."[4]

The exclusion of Murray bore a special irony. Murray's maternal grandmother was the offspring of a slave woman and a white master whose family had been intimately linked to the University of North Carolina for decades. Murray's great-great grandfather, James Smith, had been a trustee of the University and his children had endowed several scholarships. Notwithstanding this legacy, Murray's mixed-race status placed her outside the custom and law of not just the University of North Carolina but of the entire South.

Murray's application received broad coverage in the state press and placed the University's liberal president, Frank Porter Graham, in a difficult position. Recognizing that Graham was generally sympathetic to black claims for educational opportunity, Murray urged Graham to act favorably on her application: "it would be a victory for liberal thought in the South if you were favorably disposed toward my application instead of forcing me to carry the issue to the courts."[5] Graham, however, understood the intensity of feeling in North Carolina about racial segregation. As one contemporary noted, "When Miss Murray submitted her application to the graduate school she was not merely submitting it to President Graham and a few university officials. In reality she was submitting it to the South, and especially to the State of North Carolina. The University administration is powerless to follow a policy [of integration] which is specifically prohibited by the Constitution of the State, unless it were over-ruled by a higher court."[6] Graham eventually rejected Murray's appeal, explaining that he was already "under very bitter attack in some parts of North Carolina . . . for what little I have tried to do in behalf of Negro people" and that he feared a white backlash if Murray persisted with her challenge.[7]

Murray sought the assistance of Thurgood Marshall of the NAACP in filing a legal challenge to her exclusion. Marshall declined to take Murray's case, however, because of concern that her New York residence weakened her claim for admission. Murray's application nevertheless had an immediate effect; shortly thereafter, in reaction to the *Gaines* decision and the Murray application, the state of North Carolina provided graduate education opportunities for black students for the first time in the state's history at the North Carolina College for Negroes in Durham (now North Carolina Central University). As one journalist noted, "every time Pauli Murray writes a letter to the University of North Carolina they get a new building at the Negro college in Durham."[8] No black student would attend the University of North Carolina until a federal court ordered the integration of the University's law school in 1951.[9]

Murray's challenge to segregation at the University of North Carolina had a profound impact on her attitudes toward the intransigence of racial oppression. In some sense, Murray's unsuccessful effort to desegregate the University of North Carolina marked her initiation into civil rights activism, an identity that would define Murray for the rest of her life. Years later, Murray explained:

> Much of my life in the South had been overshadowed by a lurking fear. Terrified of the consequences of overt protest against racial segregation, I had sullenly endured its indignities when I could not avoid them. Yet every submission was accompanied by a nagging shame which no amount of personal achievement in other areas could overcome. When I finally confronted my fear and took a concrete step to battle for social justice, the accumulated shame began to dissolve in a new sense of self-respect. For me, the real victory of that encounter [at the University of North Carolina] with the Jim Crow system of the South was the liberation of my mind from years of enslavement.[10]

Over the course of the next several years, Murray grew increasingly outspoken in her opposition to racial oppression. In 1940, for example, Murray and a companion, Adelene McBean, refused to move to the back of a Greyhound bus while traveling from New York to Durham to spend Easter with Murray's aunt.

As a result, the two were arrested and jailed in Petersburg, Virginia, for violating that state's segregation law. The case attracted considerable attention and Murray and McBean secured legal representation from the NAACP. Many observers extolled the courage of Murray and McBean; black newspaper editor Louis Austin wrote: "Perhaps Miss Murray and Miss McBean are the beginning of a new type of leadership—a leadership that will not cringe and crawl on its belly merely because it happens to be faced with prison bars in its fight for the right."[11] The State of Virginia, fearing a constitutional challenge to its segregation statute, eventually dismissed the charge of violation of the state segregation law and instead proceeded to prosecute Murray and McBean for "creating a disturbance." The two were convicted and were fined ten dollars. Rather than pay, Murray and McBean returned to jail, only to be released several days later when friends of Murray paid the fines. The Petersburg bus incident helped shape Murray's belief in the power of civil disobedience, convincing her "that creative nonviolent resistance could be a powerful weapon in the struggle for human dignity."[12]

Shortly thereafter, Murray assisted the Workers Defense League in its efforts to challenge the death sentence of a black Virginia sharecropper, Odell Waller. The Waller defense attracted nationwide support among both blacks and liberal whites and helped galvanize support for the broader black freedom struggle. When President Franklin Roosevelt declined to intercede with the Governor of Virginia on Waller's behalf, Murray wrote a widely publicized letter to the president in which she described the "complete disillusionment and embittered resentment of the Negro masses" and noted that "Negroes are beginning to express a willingness and determination to die right here in America to attain a democracy which they have never had."[13]

In the meantime, in the fall of 1941, Murray entered Howard Law School with, in her words, "the single-minded intention of destroying Jim Crow."[14] Howard Law School of the 1940s was an institution of enormous vitality, particularly for a student with an interest in civil rights law. The Howard faculty included a number of prominent civil rights lawyers—William Hastie, Robert Ming, James Nabrit, Leon Ransom, and Spottswood Robinson. The NAACP, when preparing a major civil rights case for presentation to the United States Supreme Court, would often conduct mock court arguments in the law school before interested students and faculty.

Living in Washington in the 1940s, however, reintroduced Murray to the world of racial exclusion, as many Washington establishments would not serve black patrons. In response, Murray helped organize sit-ins by Howard students during the spring of 1943 and 1944 at restaurants that denied service to African Americans.

Predating the sit-in movement of 1960 by almost twenty years, the action of the Howard students successfully desegregated two local restaurants and contributed to the increasing use of civil disobedience to challenge segregationist patterns. The hypocrisy of black soldiers dying for their country but denied service in the nation's capitol influenced the protesters. Some Howard picketers carried signs "We Die Together—Why Can't We Eat Together."[15] The Howard administration, however, fearing retaliation by Congress, eventually prohibited the students from engaging in sit-ins thereby thwarting the nascent sit-in movement.

At the same time, Howard introduced Murray to the practice of excluding women from full participation in American life. Murray was the only woman in her entering class who remained through graduation, and was barred from certain law school activities—such as the school's legal fraternity—because of her gender. On her first day of law school, one male professor announced that he did not know why women came to law school. During her years at Howard, Murray developed a deep sense of the evils of "Jane Crow." Thereafter, Murray's activism would increasingly focus on the evils of not just racism but also gender discrimination.

Murray graduated from Howard in 1944 near the very top of her class. Winning a prestigious Rosenwald fellowship to pursue graduate legal education, Murray sought admission to Harvard Law School. However, in 1944 Harvard remained an all-male bastion and hence rejected Murray's application. Murray appealed the denial to the Harvard Corporation, explaining: "[G]entlemen, I would gladly change my sex to meet your requirements but since the way to such change has not been revealed to me, I have no recourse but to appeal to you to change your minds on this subject. Are you to tell me that one is as difficult as the other?"[16] Murray sought the support of her close friend Eleanor Roosevelt; in response, Franklin Roosevelt wrote a letter to Harvard President James Conant on Murray's behalf. Even the President of the United States could not persuade his alma mater to alter its longstanding exclusion of women. Murray eventually took her scholarship to the University of California at Berkeley where she completed a masters degree in law in 1945.

While at Howard, Murray had continued to explore her vocation as a writer, publishing both poetry and essays decrying the poor treatment of African Americans. Murray's best known poem, "Dark Testament," written in 1945 and dedicated to her mentor, poet Stephen Vincent Benet, expressed the aspirations of the emerging civil rights movement and foreshadowed much of the language later used by Martin Luther King, Jr. The closing lines of "Dark Testament" were read at a memorial service for King in 1968:

Then let the dream linger on.
Let it be the test of nations,
Let it be the quest of all our days,
The fevered pounding of our blood,
The measure of our souls—
That none shall rest in any land
And none return to dreamless sleep,
No heart be quieted, no tongue be stilled
Until the final man may stand in any place
And thrust his shoulders to the sky,
Friend and brother to every other man.[17]

Murray understood the profound capacity of words to stir action, later quipping that "one person plus one typewriter constitutes a movement."[18]

Following her year of graduate study at Berkeley, Murray returned to New York City to practice law. Confronted with the limitations facing women attorneys—particularly African-American women—Murray struggled to secure work. She eventually opened her own practice and became involved in New York City politics as an unsuccessful candidate for city council in 1949.

In 1948, the Women's Division of Christian Service of the Board of Missions of the Methodist Church approached Murray about compiling a report of laws requiring segregation. The Women's Division had long been involved in racial issues, having lobbied for antilynching legislation in the South during the 1920s and 1930s. In the 1940s, the Women's Division issued a call for a review of the racial policies of the Methodist Church to make the practices of the church conform to its creed. As part of this call, the Women's Division discovered that a vast number of the institutions run by the church—hospitals, community centers, and settlement houses—operated on a segregated basis. The Women's Division sought to learn whether this widespread segregation was due merely to the church's observance of local custom or whether such segregation was required by law. To answer this question, the Women's Division turned to Murray.

Murray agreed to compile a list of state statutes that compelled segregation, but persuaded the Women's Division to support a broader study that also included a listing of state laws that forbade discrimination. In early 1951, the Women's Division published Murray's work entitled *States' Laws on Race and Color*. Subsequent to publication, a number of human rights organizations recognized the value of Murray's compilation and distributed copies to interested individuals and organizations. The American Civil Liberties Union, for example, secured a foundation grant to purchase and distribute nearly a thousand copies of Murray's book to state law libraries, black colleges, law schools, human rights agencies, and individuals who had displayed particular interest in civil rights. Similarly, the NAACP purchased copies of the book for each member of its staff to be used as a reference tool in the organization's legal campaign against segregation.

For the remainder of her life, Murray engaged in a broad array of activities connected to the cause of human freedom. In the early 1950s, Murray wrote *Proud Shoes*, a poignant history of her own family from slavery to emancipation. After three years of law practice in the late 1950s with the prestigious New York law firm of Paul, Weiss, Rifkind, Wharton & Garrison as its only black attorney and one of only three women, Murray took a position at the Ghana School of Law in Africa. While in Ghana, Murray taught comparative constitutional law at a time when that nation was struggling to establish a constitutional democracy. Murray remained in Ghana for sixteen months, teaching African students and coauthoring a book, *The Constitution and Government of Ghana*. Thereafter, Murray returned to America to enroll in a doctoral program in law at Yale University.

While at Yale, Murray continued to engage issues of civil rights. Having become increasingly involved in the struggle for gender equality, she was invited in 1962 to join the Committee on Civil and Political Rights of the newly established President's Commission on the Status of Women. The committee sought to review differences in legal treatment of men and women in the area of civil and political rights and to make recommendations. Murray, for her part, was charged with examining the applicability of the equal protection clause of the Fourteenth Amendment to state laws that discriminated on the basis of gender. Murray recommended a litigation strategy challenging gender discrimination under the Fourteenth Amendment; the commission embraced Murray's recommendations in its final report in 1963.[19] The following year, Murray drafted a memorandum for an ad hoc group of women favoring the inclusion of a prohibition on gender discrimination in the workplace in civil rights legislation then pending in Congress. Murray's memorandum emphasized that without protection against gender discrimination, the new civil rights act would leave black women vulnerable to a mix of racial and gender discrimination. Title VII of the Civil Rights Act of 1964 eventually did prohibit discrimination against women in the workplace.

In 1965, Murray continued her attack on gender discrimination in an article she coauthored with Mary Eastwood in the *George Washington Law Review* entitled "Jane Crow and the Law: Sex Discrimination and Title VII," which described the ways in which Title VII and the Fifth and Fourteenth amendments to the U.S. Constitution could be used to fight discrimination against women. Claiming that "[w]e are entering the age of human rights," Murray and Eastwood equated the evil of sex discrimination with the evil of racism: "That manifestations of racial prejudice have been more brutal than the more subtle manifestations of prejudice by reason of sex in no way diminishes the force of the equally obvious fact that the rights of women and the rights of Negroes are only different phases of the fundamental and indivisible issue of human rights."[20]

Following her graduation from Yale in 1965 with a doctorate in law—the first black student to receive such a degree from Yale—Murray struggled in vain to secure a teaching post at a law school. Finding no offers despite her substantial qualifications, Murray supported herself by writing a monograph on recent civil rights history for the Women's Division of the Methodist Church entitled *Human Rights U.S.A.: 1948–1966*. At the same time, Murray supported the civil rights activities of several organizations. Murray joined the national board of directors of the American Civil Liberties Union in 1965. During her tenure on the ACLU board, Murray concerned herself primarily with sex discrimination issues, including a successful challenge to the exclusion of women from juries in Alabama in 1966.[21] In 1966, Murray helped found the National Organization of Women and worked as a consultant to the Equal Employment Opportunity Commission on gender issues.

Murray returned to higher education in 1967, teaching for one year at Benedict College in Columbia, South Carolina, before joining Brandeis University in the fall of 1968 to teach in the American Studies program. Murray's Brandeis years brought her into direct contact with the black power movement of the late 1960s. During her first year at Brandeis, the campus exploded with racial conflict as black students occupied a campus building and presented the University administration with several demands. Murray remained skeptical of the black power movement, dismayed by the sexism that it exhibited. In an essay published in 1970, Murray noted:

> Reading through much of the current literature on the Black Revolution, one is left with the impression that for all the rhetoric about self-determination, the main thrust of black militancy is a bid of black males to share power with white males in a continuing patriarchal society in which both black and white females are relegated to a secondary status.[22]

Fearing that the struggle for gender equality might be subsumed in the struggle for black power, Murray argued that "black women can neither postpone nor subordinate the fight against discrimination to the Black Revolution."[23]

In the meantime, Murray became increasingly drawn to the Episcopal Church, of which she had been a lifelong member. Murray openly criticized her church's sexist policies, particularly its refusal to ordain women to the priesthood. Despite the church's posture on ordination, Murray resigned her professorship at Brandeis in 1973 to pursue a call to the priesthood and enrolled in General Theological Seminary in New York. During Murray's time at General, the Episcopal Church struggled with the issue of women's ordination, finally deciding to recognize such ordination in December 1976. A few weeks later, in January 1977, at the age of 66, Murray became one of the first Episcopal women to be ordained to the priesthood. Murray worked as a priest in a number of parishes in Washington, Baltimore, and Pittsburgh until her death in 1985.

Pauli Murray engaged in an extraordinarily broad range of activities during her long life—as activist, author, poet, lawyer, educator, and priest. Throughout this considerable diversity of engagement, Murray consistently sought to advance the cause of human freedom. Although an African-American woman concerned especially with the rights of racial minorities and women, Murray considered herself an advocate for all peoples in the cause of freedom. As Murray prefaced a book of her poetry late in life:

> Friends and countrymen!
> I speak for my race and my people—
> The human race and just people.[24]

Murray's book, *States' Laws on Race and Color*, provides an excellent snapshot of the status of both segregation laws and civil rights laws at mid-century. The timing of Murray's book was propitious. The 1940s marked a watershed in the campaign for racial equality by African Americans. During that decade, many northern states and communities enacted legislation and local ordinances that forbade racial discrimination in education, employment, and public accommodations, and repealed other statutes that required or permitted segregation. By mid-century, eighteen states had prohibited discrimination in public accommodations,[25] eight states had enacted fair employment practice legislation barring racial discrimination in the workplace,[26] and eighteen states had imposed some type of statutory restriction on segregation in education.[27] As Murray's volume demonstrates, some of this civil rights legislation dated back to the nineteenth century, when many northern states sought to protect the rights of African Americans in the wake of the Civil War, but much of it was enacted during the 1940s as several northern states sought with new vigor to eliminate racial discrimination. Murray appropriately notes in her introduction that "[p]erhaps in no other field is the law more unsettled" than civil rights law.

These significant legislative changes took place as a result of an array of political and cultural changes in northern states including the expansion of black political power and the liberalization of white attitudes towards racial discrimination. During the 1940s, due to the migration of hundreds of thousands of southern blacks into northern states since World War I, African Americans enjoyed greater political strength than ever before, causing both major political parties to compete for the black vote. For example, President Harry Truman's recognition of the importance of black voters helped prompt his support for various civil rights measures during his administration, including vigorous support for desegregation initiatives before the United States Supreme Court.[28] At the same time, World War II had a profound impact on the black freedom struggle, as the hypocrisy of sending black men to die overseas while denying them basic civil rights at home energized many African Americans to demand equal treatment.[29]

Yet Murray's compilation demonstrates the limits of legal prohibition in securing racial change. Many state statutes cited by Murray that expressly forbade racial segregation were ignored. For example, the District of Columbia prohibited discrimination in public accommodations in 1872, yet this prohibition was not enforced and eventually deleted from the District of Columbia Code—but never repealed—in the early twentieth century. Murray's discovery of this long forgotten legislation contributed to a successful legal challenge to segregated public accommodations in the District of Columbia culminating in a decision from the United States Supreme Court in 1953.[30]

More significantly, even though most northern states prohibited school segregation by statute during the late nineteenth century, officially sanctioned school segregation persisted in many northern school districts—particularly in New Jersey, New York, Pennsylvania, Ohio, and Illinois—until the late 1940s and early 1950s. For example, in New Jersey, despite an 1881 statutory ban on school segregation, a 1925 report found school segregation particularly widespread in the state's southern counties: "[f]rom the university town of Princeton, including the capital city of Trenton, southward to Cape May, every city or town with a considerable Negro population supports the dual educational system, with a building for its white and a building for its Negro pupils of the grammar grades."[31] Between 1919 and 1935, the number of racially separate schools for African-American children in New Jersey increased by thirty-five percent and these numbers continued to increase until the early 1940s.[32] Many New Jersey school districts retained dual schools in violation of state law until the late 1940s. At the same time, many school districts in other northern states such as Pennsylvania and Illinois—particularly in the southern counties of those states—also operated segregated schools in defiance of state antisegregation laws until the late 1940s and early 1950s.

Thurgood Marshall, legal director of the NAACP, announced in 1947 that his office would expend considerable resources challenging northern school segregation: "In spite of state statutes designed to prevent discrimination or segregation of the races in its school systems, these vicious practices are put into effect in far too many Northern states, and the NAACP shall concentrate within the next few years on breaking down such practices."[33] For the next several years, the national legal department of the NAACP conducted an extensive litigation campaign in northern states seeking to enforce the nineteenth-century antisegregation statutes. The combination of growing political support for school desegregation among many northern politicians and the NAACP's litigation campaign led to a successful assault on school segregation in many northern states in the late 1940s and early 1950s. By the time of the Supreme Court's 1954 decision in *Brown v. Board of Education*,[34] most northern school districts had eliminated dual schools.

Murray's volume also reveals the full extent of legally imposed Jim Crow segregation throughout the nation—even in states outside of the South—at the midpoint of the twentieth century. In 1950, thirty states still had statutes banning interracial marriage,[35] including states with few African Americans, such as North Dakota, South Dakota, Utah, and Wyoming. Twenty-one states and the District of Columbia required or permitted segregated schools for African Americans.[36] Fourteen states required segregated railroad facilities.[37]

Many states had their own peculiar segregation laws. Oklahoma allowed local communities to establish separate telephone booths.[38] South Carolina required textile workers to work in racially separate rooms.[39] Montana prohibited a black person from adopting a white child.[40] Georgia prohibited a black minister from celebrating the marriage of a white couple.[41] By collecting every state statute mandating segregation, Murray's volume permits a fascinating examination of the full extent of de jure segregation in America on the eve of the Supreme Court's 1954 decision banning school segregation.[42]

Murray's volume also reveals the bizarre nature of racial classifications adopted in connection with segregation laws. Given the extent of sexual liaisons between white masters and black slaves during the antebellum era, many Americans had a mixed-race heritage that made racial classification difficult. Indeed, many Americans with some African ancestry possessed physical features that identified them as white. As the obsession with racial separation increased throughout the country in the late nineteenth and early twentieth centuries, state legislators struggled

xxiii

with the issue of how to define a "Negro." Some states—such as Alabama, Georgia, and Tennessee—defined a person as Negro if he or she had "*any* blood of the African race in their veins," notwithstanding the physical features of such person.[43] Other states—such as Florida, Indiana, and North Dakota—were less restrictive, defining a Negro as a person "having one-eighth or more of African or negro blood."[44] Still other states defined a person's race differently depending on the nature of the segregation. For example, Arkansas defined a person as Negro for purposes of segregation on railroads only if "there is a visible and distinct admixture of African blood,"[45] but defined a person as Negro for purposes of the statutory prohibition on interracial cohabitation if he or she "has in his or her veins any negro blood whatever."[46]

The value of Murray's volume is its completeness. Murray has included every state statute as of 1950 that contains any reference to race or color, whether the purpose is to segregate or to prevent racial segregation and discrimination. Murray also includes some material indicating the legislative history of the various statutes in question. In putting together this volume, Murray has provided scholars with a fascinating resource for examining the full array of race laws in America at the middle of the twentieth century. Because the volume was prepared prior to the *Brown* decision in 1954, it provides an excellent opportunity for assessing the extent of racial segregation in America before such statutes were repealed or nullified in the wake of the Supreme Court's decision. Moreover, this volume provides an excellent snapshot of the range of state civil rights legislation enacted during both the nineteenth century and the 1940s as well as an opportunity for assessing the effectiveness of such legislation in securing equal treatment for African Americans. Because the first edition of Murray's volume had a limited print run in its initial publication and then long remained out of print, this republication will hopefully aid scholars in their explorations of the considerable parameters of the American dilemma.

NOTES

1. *Song in a Weary Throat* (New York, 1987), 107–8.
2. For a description of an unsuccessful lawsuit that forced the integration of a pharmacy school at the University of North Carolina in 1933, see Gilbert Ware, "Hocutt: Genesis of Brown," *Journal of Negro Education* 52 (summer 1983): 227–33.
3. 305 U.S. 337 (1938).

4. *Song,* 115.

5. Ibid.

6. Glenn Hutchinson, "Jim Crow Challenged in Southern Universities," *Crisis* 46 (April 1939): 103, 105.

7. Ibid., 105.

8. *Song,* 127.

9. *McKissick v. Carmichael,* 187 F.2d 949 (4th Cir.), *cert. denied,* 341 U.S. 951 (1951).

10. *Song,* 128.

11. "Jim Crow Bus Dispute Leads to Arrest," *Carolina Times,* Apr. 6, 1940.

12. *Song,* 149.

13. Ibid., 174.

14. Ibid., 182.

15. Ibid., 207.

16. Ibid., 243.

17. *Dark Testament and Other Poems,* (Norwalk, Conn., 1970), 27.

18. *Song,* 242.

19. *American Women: The Report of the President's Commission on the Status of Women and Other Publications of the Commission,* ed. Margaret Mead and Frances Bagley Kaplan (New York, 1965), 149–51.

20. Pauli Murray and Mary Eastwood, "Jane Crow and the Law: Sex Discrimination and Title VII," *George Washington Law Review* 34 (December 1965): 232, 235, 256.

21. *White v. Crook,* 251 F. Supp. 401 (M.D. Ala. 1966).

22. Pauli Murray, "The Liberation of Black Women," in *Voices of the New Feminism,* ed. Mary Lou Thompson (Boston, 1970), 87, 92.

23. Ibid., 101

24. *Dark Testament.*

25. California, Colorado, Connecticut, Illinois, Indiana, Iowa, Kansas, Massachusetts, Michigan, Minnesota, Nebraska, New Jersey, New York, Ohio, Pennsylvania, Rhode Island, Washington, and Wisconsin.

26. Connecticut, Massachusetts, New Jersey, New Mexico, New York, Oregon, Rhode Island, and Washington.

27. Colorado, Connecticut, Idaho, Illinois, Indiana, Iowa, Kansas, Massachusetts, Michigan, Minnesota, Nebraska, New Jersey, New York, Pennsylvania, Rhode Island, Washington, Wisconsin, and Wyoming.

28. See Doug McAdam, *Political Process and the Development of Black Insurgency 1930–1970,* (Chicago, 1982), 77–86; Mary L. Dudziak, "Desegregation as a Cold War Imperative," *Stanford Law Review* 41 (November 1988): 61–120.

29. See Peter J. Kellogg, "Civil Rights Consciousness in the 1940s," *Historian* 40 (1979): 18–45; Robert J. Norrell, "One Thing We Did Right: Reflections on the Movement," in *New Directions in Civil Rights Studies,* ed. Armistead L. Robinson and Patricia Sullivan (Charlottesville, Va., 1991), 65.

30. *District of Columbia v. John R. Thompson Co.,* 346 U.S. 100 (1953).

31. Lester B. Granger, "Race Relations and the School System: A Study of Negro High School Attendance in New Jersey," *Opportunity* 327 (November 1925).

32. Eleanor Oak and Vishnu Oak, "The Development of Separate Education in New Jersey," *Education* 59 (1938/1939): 109–12; Marion T. Wright, "Racial Integration in the Public Schools of New Jersey," *Journal of Negro Education* 23 (1954): 282–305.

33. "NAACP Press Release," Sept. 18, 1947, NAACP Papers, Box II-B-146, Library of Congress.

34. 347 U.S. 483 (1954).

35. Alabama, Arizona, Arkansas, California, Colorado, Delaware, Florida, Georgia, Idaho, Indiana, Kentucky, Louisiana, Maryland, Mississippi, Missouri, Montana, Nebraska, Nevada, North Carolina, North Dakota, Oklahoma, Oregon, South Carolina, South Dakota, Tennessee, Texas, Utah, Virginia, West Virginia, and Wyoming.

    Although most of the statutes banning interracial marriage dealt only with whites and blacks, some states, such as Idaho, Montana, Nebraska, Nevada, and Utah, also banned marriages between whites and certain persons of Asian ancestry. Other states took the ban on interracial marriage even further. Mississippi made it a crime to circulate any written material favoring "social equality or . . . intermarriage between whites and negroes." Mississippi Code Annotated, Section 2339 (1942).

36. Alabama, Arizona, Arkansas, Delaware, Florida, Georgia, Kansas, Kentucky, Louisiana, Maryland, Mississippi, Missouri, New Mexico, North Carolina, Oklahoma, South Carolina, Tennessee, Texas, Virginia, West Virginia, and Wyoming. The Wyoming segregation statute, though still on the books, was superseded by a state constitutional provision prohibiting racial discrimination in the public schools. California still had an antimiscegenation statute on the books, but it had been declared unconstitutional in 1948 by the California Supreme Court on the grounds that it violated the equal protection clause of the Fourteenth Amendment. Perez v. Sharp, 32 Cal. 2d 711, 198 P.2d 17 (1948).

37. Alabama, Arkansas, Florida, Georgia, Kentucky, Louisiana, Maryland, Mississippi, North Carolina, Oklahoma, South Carolina, Tennessee, Texas, and Virginia.

38. Oklahoma Statutes, Title 17, Section 135 (1949).

39. South Carolina Code, Section 1271, 1272 (1942).

40. Revised Code of Montana, Section 5856 (1935).

41. Georgia Code Annotated, Section 53-212 (1935).
42. *Brown v. Board of Education,* 347 U.S. 483 (1954).
43. Williams Tennessee Code, Section 25 (1934) (emphasis supplied); Code of Alabama, Title 1, Section 2 (1940); Georgia Code Annotated, Section 79-103 (1935).
44. Florida Statutes, Section 1.01(6) (1941); Indiana Annotated Statutes, Section 44-104 (1933); North Dakota Revised Code, Section 14-305 (1943).
45. Arkansas Statutes Annotated, Section 73-1221 (1947).
46. Arkansas Statutes Annotated, Section 41-808 (1947).

ACKNOWLEDGMENTS

A work of this scope could be made possible only through the cooperation of many correspondents, particularly federal, state and local officials whose kindnesses in answering many inquiries and supplying numerous laws and regulations were indispensable to the completion of this work. I am equally grateful to the attorneys and staff members of the American Civil Liberties Union, American Jewish Congress, Anti-Defamation League, National Association for the Advancement of Colored People and Woman's Division of The Methodist Church for similar kindnesses.

I am especially indebted to Mr. Lawrence Schmehl and Miss Lena Keller of the New York County Lawyers' Library for invaluable library assistance; to Mr. Eric Springer, Mr. Verne Newcomb and Mrs. Dovey J. Roundtree for assistance in research; to Mrs. Jane Wehncke and Mrs. Marian Wynn Perry for their aid in securing local ordinances; to Dr. Paul Hartmann, Dr. Caroline F. Ware, Dr. George M. Johnson, Mr. James N. Nabrit, Judge William H. Hastie, Mr. Henry Spitz, Mr. Franklin H. Williams, Mr. Will Maslow, Mr. Abe Klugsburg and Miss Nancy L. Haney for valuable comments and suggestions; to Miss Lydia P. Singleton and Mrs. Vivian Lemon for technical aid; and to Maida Springer whose inspiration and encouragement pervaded this undertaking from its inception.

1

EXPLANATORY NOTE

The correct usage of the word "Negro" is to capitalize it. However, where the statute is set forth or quoted verbatim in this compilation, the spelling of this word follows the statute.

Brackets are used whenever a statute is digested or summarized and not set forth in full. An attempt has been made, however, to set forth most of the statutes as they appear in the state codes. Summaries were used only when reference to race and color was casual, or when statutes providing for separate facilities for Negroes follow the same pattern as those setting up similar facilities for white persons. Bracketed material within the body of a statute has been added by the compiler. Brackets at the end of a statute contain the year of enactment, in most cases, and the history of the provision as it has appeared in subsequent state compilations.

The state codes vary in their classification of subject matter, hence it would be well for the reader to examine all the laws of a particular state found in this compilation to determine whether a given subject has been covered. The headings under the various states have followed the classification found in the particular state compilation.

SCOPE NOTE
INTRODUCTION

The compilation presented here is intended to serve two functions: (1) as a convenient reference and guide to state legislation on race and color for both lawyers and laymen, and (2) to indicate the extent to which legislative controls have been imposed in this field, whether to enforce racial segregation and other restrictions on the one hand or to insure equal opportunity and equal access to public facilities on the other. It points up the wide variety of approaches to the whole question of race and emphasizes the uneven development of state laws on the subject. Furthermore, it reveals the acute divergencies of state policy and dramatizes the uncertainty under which the individual must labor with respect to racial practices as he crosses state borders.

Perhaps in no other field is the law more unsettled. This is evidenced by the constant revision or amendment of laws relating to segregation, the repeal of restrictive measures in some jurisdictions and the gradual strengthening of civil rights legislation in others. Few legislatures have not spoken on the subject.

The compilation includes segregation and anti-miscegenation statutes, laws relating to public accommodations and which are popularly called "civil rights" laws, fair educational practice acts, fair employment practice acts, statutes directed against lynching and the activities of the Ku Klux Klan, alien land laws, and miscellaneous anti-discrimination measures.

The study was originally conceived as a method of determining the extent to which racial practices were controlled by law throughout the country. Cursory examination of state laws, however, revealed that while race and color were the most common bases of discrimination against which legal protection was sought, increasingly it has been necessary to provide protection against discrimination because of creed, religion, national origin, alienage, ancestry and sex. Wherever these bases were integrated into laws relating to race and color, they have been included. Future compilations of this nature should include exhaustive treatment of each of these classifications so that the picture may be complete.

Secondly, it was discovered that while segregation has been applied primarily to Negroes, yet three states still provide for separate schools for Indians and a number of states have enacted restrictive legislation against Indians, Chinese, Japanese and other Orientals. Such laws seemed properly to belong in a compilation of this nature and were included wherever possible.

The compilation does not purport to be exhaustive, nor does it seek to interpret the laws except for an occasional note directing attention to a judicial interpretation. It does not attempt to indicate how laws are applied through administrative rulings and regulations, except in rare instances. The basis for inclusion of a law was whether or not it is currently found in the state codes or supplements. Even where laws have been declared unconstitutional, they have been noted if they were not repealed.

Undoubtedly omissions have occurred. Many state indexing systems were found to be incomplete with reference to the classification of race and color. It would be necessary to read all the laws of each state code to prevent such omissions. Also, there may be a number of statutes making no reference to race or color but which are administered in such a way as to warrant inclusion here, but have escaped attention because of lack of access to local administrative and court rulings. Election laws of some southern states are an example of this type of omission.

It should be kept in mind that this is the first effort to bring together under one cover the laws of the forty-nine American jurisdictions in the field of race so that a comparative study of the texts is made available. Even so, the texts of the laws do not offer a precise view of racial practices. In the absence of detailed state enactments, many southern states enforce segregation through local ordinances. Segregation is practiced in other states as a result of custom. In a number of states which do not prohibit segregation by law, schools, theatres, restaurants and other public facilities are nonsegregated in varying degree.

SUMMARY OF STATE LEGISLATION

It may be helpful here to summarize briefly the scope of state legislation relating to race and color. In doing this, I have cross-checked my own references with other summaries, compilations and check-lists in this field.[4] Discrepancies between my classification and others are due in part to the advantages obtained by reference to available materials and in part to recent changes in the laws. Because of the widespread interest in the broad field of human rights, many state legislatures were exceedingly active in this area during 1949 and numerous laws were enacted which have direct bearing on the rights of minority groups.

In order to understand state policy on the question of race and color, a few constitutional principles should be borne in mind. As the law now stands, the protection of civil rights in matters of education, public accommodation, intra-state transportation and other public facilities, the regulation of marriage, and employment in fields not in interstate commerce are areas left primarily to state control. Only when the state regulation of such matters is shown to violate the Fourteenth Amendment or to have invaded a field reserved to the Federal Government will state laws be invalidated.

---

[4]See the following references for further study:
"Civil Rights Legislation in the States, January 1 to September 1, 1949," Compiled and published by the American Council on Race Relations, 4901 Ellis Avenue, Chicago, Illinois.
Compilation of Laws Against Discrimination, New York State Commission Against Discrimination, (1948).
Graves, W. Brooke, *Anti-Discrimination Legislation in the American States* (1948), Library of Congress Legislative Reference Service, Public Affairs Bulletin No. 65.
Konvitz, M., *The Constitution and Civil Rights* (1947).
Newman, Edwin S., *The Law of Civil Rights and Civil Liberties* (1949)
To Secure These Rights, Report of the President's Committee on Civil Rights (1947).
State Anti-Discrimination and Anti-Bias Laws — Check List — Prepared by the Commission on

Discrimination by private persons is held not to be within the protection of the Fourteenth Amendment. In the language of the United States Supreme Court, that Amendment "erects no shield against merely private conduct, however discriminatory or wrongful." Private conduct is left to state regulation unless it can be clearly demonstrated that such conduct violates some right guaranteed by the federal Constitution or that the discrimination involved cannot be achieved without invoking state action. In such matters aggrieved persons are left to whatever remedies are provided under state law.

While morally, segregation is synonymous with discrimination, yet segregation by law is not declared to be discrimination *per se*, although several cases are now pending before the United States Supreme Court in which this issue is raised. So long as "separate but equal" facilities are provided for the races involved, constitutional requirements as currently interpreted are fulfilled.

Thus, states may outlaw segregation by statute if they choose, or they may permit or require segregation so long as equal facilities are maintained. Eighteen states have taken steps to eliminate segregation in public facilities. Twenty-two jurisdictions by law require or permit racial segregation in one form or another. Some states have pursued a *lessez-faire* policy and left the regulation of racial practices to private individuals. Nine states have neither segregation laws nor laws requiring equal access to public accommodations,[5] but six of these states prohibit mixed marriages[6] and two others have acted to prohibit discriminatory advertising.[7] Thus, Vermont appears to be the lone state in the Union which has remained completely silent on this issue.

Law And Social Action, American Jewish Congress, 1834 Broadway, New York City (1948). Weintraub, Ruth G., *How Secure These Rights?* (1949) Anti-Semitism in the United States in 1948, An Anti-Defamation League Survey.

Your Civil Rights, Pamphlet prepared by Commission on Human Relations, 54 West Hubbard Street, Chicago 10, Illinois (1947).

See also annual reports of American Jewish Congress, American Civil Liberties Union, National Association for the Advancement of Colored People, and materials prepared by the Anti-Defamation League, American Jewish Committee, American Council on Race Relations, National Community Relations Advisory Council, Woman's Division of The Methodist Church and Young Women's Christian Association.

[5]Idaho, Maine, Nevada, New Hampshire, North Dakota, Oregon, South Dakota, Utah, Vermont.

[6]Idaho, Nevada, North Dakota, Oregon, South Dakota, Utah.

[7]Maine and New Hampshire.

A. State Laws Against Discrimination

1. Public Accommodations

Eighteen states, exclusive of Louisiana, have enacted what is popularly called "civil rights" laws prohibiting discrimination in places of public accommodation and amusement.[8] Fourteen of these statutes outlaw discrimination because of race or color,[9] seven include religion or creed,[10] four specify national origin or alienage[11] (Conn.) and four indicate no specified ground of discrimination.[12]

In all of the states except California, the denial of full and equal accommodations in the places enumerated is a punishable offense. Fines range from $10 to $100 and provision is made for imprisonment in most cases ranging from 15 days to one year. California provides for a civil action for damages only.

Colorado, Indiana and Wisconsin afford criminal or civil remedies, but not both. Seven states — Illinois, Kansas, Massachusetts, Michigan, Minnesota, New York and Ohio — provide for both criminal and civil actions. Damages under the statutes range from $25 to $500. Iowa, Nebraska, Pennsylvania, Rhode Island and Washington provide criminal penalties only.

In addition to criminal proceedings, New Jersey and Connecticut permit the aggrieved individual to file a complaint before an administrative agency which has power to issue orders enforceable in the courts.[13] Illinois also provides that the place of violation may be enjoined as a nuisance.

These statutes generally prohibit discrimination against or denial of full and equal accommodations, advantages or privileges in restaurants, hotels, public conveyances, educational institutions, libraries, parks and other public places. The laws vary considerably in the enumeration of places covered. Illinois, New Jersey, New York and Pennsylvania have the most extensive laws in this respect. Citizens only are protected by the California and Ohio statutes; the other enactments specify all persons.

The District of Columbia presents an interesting problem. In 1872, the Legislative Assembly, which was the law-making body for the District of Columbia at that time, enacted a statute which prohibited exclusion from restaurants, hotels, barber shops, ice

---

[8]California, Colorado, Connecticut, Illinois, Indiana, Iowa, Kansas, Massachusetts, Michigan, Minnesota, Nebraska, New Jersey, New York, Ohio, Pennsylvania, Rhode Island, Washington and Wisconsin.

The Louisiana statute, enacted in 1869 during Reconstruction, forbids racial discrimination by common carriers and in places of public resort. The statute is generally disregarded and exists side by side with laws requiring segregation in public schools, hospitals, prisons, railroads and other public places. (General Statutes, 1939, (Dart), Sections 1070-1073.)

[9]California, Colorado, Connecticut, Indiana, Kansas, Massachusetts, Michigan, Minnesota, New Jersey, New York, Ohio, Pennsylvania, Washington, Wisconsin.

[10]Connecticut, Michigan, Minnesota, New Jersey, New York, Pennsylvania, Washington.

[11]Connecticut, Minnesota, New Jersey, New York.

[12]Illinois, Iowa, Nebraska, Rhode Island.

[13]See Conn. Acts 1949, c. 417, §§1, 2. The aggrieved person may file a complaint with the Connecticut Interracial Commission which also administers the Connecticut Fair Employment Practices Act. See also New Jersey Freeman Law of 1949, Laws 1949, c. 11, which provides that complaints of alleged discrimination may be filed with the Commissioner of Education. Note also that New Jersey provides for an action for damages, but the money recovered goes to the State and the aggrieved party is awarded only costs of the trial and attorney's fee of not more than $100 to be fixed by the court.

cream parlors and soda fountains by reason of race, color or previous condition of servitude. Refusal to serve a "well-behaved person" was made a misdemeanor punishable by a fine of $100 and forfeiture of license to do business for one year. This law was never expressly repealed, but for some reason, it was omitted from the 1901 Code and every subsequent compilation of statutes relating to the District of Columbia. It is arguable that the law is still in force.[14]

2. Innkeepers and Common Carriers

California, Maine, Massachusetts, Montana, New York and Utah have special statutes which forbid innkeepers to refuse to receive or entertain guests without reasonable cause. Common carriers are prohibited from refusing to accept passengers in California, Illinois, Montana and New York.

3. Discriminatory Advertising Prohibited

Nine states have acted to prohibit discriminatory advertisement designed to discourage racial or religious minorities from patronizing places of public accommodation. Seven of these states also have civil rights statutes barring discrimination itself.[15] The other two outlaw the practice of discriminatory advertising but do not prohibit discrimination.[16]

4. Employment
a. Fair Employment Practice Acts

By the end of 1949, eight states had enacted fair employment practice legislation barring discrimination by employers and labor unions in terms and conditions of employment because of race, color, religion or national origin and vesting enforcement powers in a state commission.[17] Indiana and Wisconsin have passed FEPC laws which are chiefly educational and have no strong enforcement powers. By Joint resolution the state legislatures of Kansas and Nebraska have provided for a commission to study discrimination in employment. Local FEPC ordinances are in force in the cities of Chicago, Cincinnati, Cleveland, Milwaukee, Minneapolis, Philadelphia, Phoenix and Richmond, California.[18]

b. Other types of laws

In addition to the prohibition against discrimination by labor unions found in the fair employment practice acts, five states have special statutes forbidding labor unions to discriminate because of race or color in matters of employment.[19]

Twenty-eight states have legislated against religious bias in the field of civil service.[20] Only nine of these include race or color.[20a] Fourteen states bar discrimination

[14]See Compiled Statutes in Force in the District of Columbia (1894), p. 183, Ch. XVI, Sec. 150, Act of June 20, 1872, Legislative Assembly, Sec. 3, pp. 65, 66. See also 42d, Congress, 3rd. Session, House of Representatives: Mis. Doc., No. 25.
[15]Colorado, Illinois, Massachusetts, Michigan, New Jersey, New York, Pennsylvania.
[16]Maine and New Hampshire.
[17]Connecticut, Massachusetts, New Jersey, New Mexico, New York, Oregon, Rhode Island and Washington.
[18]For texts of FEPC ordinances, see Appendix 5.
[19]Kansas, Nebraska, New Hampshire, New York and Pennsylvania.
[20]See "Table of Statutes Prohibiting Religious Discrimination in Civil Service Employment" infra, p. 706.
[20a]California, Connecticut, Indiana, Michigan, Nebraska, New York, Oregon, Pennsylvania, Rhode Island.

9

on religious grounds in the employment of public school teachers,[21] but only two of these prohibit racial discrimination.[22] Delaware, Maryland, Missouri and West Virginia expressly forbid discrimination in the salaries of Negro and white teachers.

A number of states have acted to prevent discrimination in public works,[23] public utilities,[24] public welfare[25] and work relief.[26] It should be remembered, however, that any action by a state agency which discriminates against an individual is violative of the Fourteenth Amendment. Thus, laws forbidding discrimination by public agencies serve to reinforce existing constitutional law.

No person shall be denied a license to practice law by reason of race or color in Colorado, Florida and New York. Illinois, Nebraska, New Jersey and New York enacted legislation during the recent World War barring discrimination in employment of labor under defense and war contracts. Illinois prohibits discrimination in employment in housing construction. California recently repealed a statute which, in effect, denied commercial fishing licenses to alien Japanese fishermen, following a Supreme Court decision which invalidated the statute.

5. Education

Eighteen states, in varying degree, have legislated against racial and religious discrimination in the field of education.[27] Fair educational practice acts were enacted recently by the legislatures of New York, New Jersey and Massachusetts. These acts bar discrimination in educational institutions generally and provide for the enforcement of these prohibitions through administrative agencies similar to the state commissions against discrimination in employment. Illinois and Minnesota have laws against discrimination in specified private schools.

Six states expressly prohibit segregation in the public school system.[28] Iowa bars segregation through judicial decision. The statutes of eight states declare either that no distinction or classification shall be made of public school children on racial grounds or expressly prohibit discrimination or exclusion from the public schools of pupils because of race or color.[29] A few states outlaw racial bias in the state university. Two of these states, Kansas and Wyoming, forbid racial exclusion from the state university but require or authorize separate public schools for Negro and white children.

---

[21] See "Table of Statutes Prohibiting Religious Discrimination in the Employment of Public School Teachers," *infra*, p. 705.

[22] New Jersey and Wisconsin.

[23] California, Illinois, Indiana, Kansas, Massachusetts, Minnesota, New Jersey, New Mexico, New York, Ohio and Pennsylvania.

[24] Massachusetts and New York.

[25] California, Massachusetts and Pennsylvania.

[26] Illinois and Pennsylvania.

[27] Colorado, Connecticut, Idaho, Illinois, Indiana, Iowa, Kansas, Massachusetts, Michigan, Minnesota, Nebraska, New Jersey, New York, Pennsylvania, Rhode Island, Washington, Wisconsin, Wyoming.

[28] Illinois, Indiana, Michigan, Minnesota, New Jersey and Wisconsin.

[29] Colorado, Connecticut, Idaho, Kansas, New York, Pennsylvania, Rhode Island and Washington.

Note also that California, Maine, Nebraska, Nevada, New Hampshire, South Dakota, Ohio, Oregon and Vermont have not legislated against discrimination in the public schools, but mixed schools exist in these states. Montana, North Dakota and Utah provide for public schools for all children of the state free from sectarian control and apparently have non-segregated schools. California recently repealed a statute providing for separate schools for Indian children and children of Chinese, Japanese and Mongolian parentage, following a United States Court of Appeals decision outlawing the segregation of Spanish-speaking children in California schools.

6. Housing

The legal struggle against segregated housing has been one of the most hotly contested issues in recent years, yet few states have legislated on the subject. Local ordinances designed to create racial zoning were common in Southern cities until 1917 when the United States Supreme Court invalidated an ordinance which made it unlawful for Negroes to occupy houses in blocks where the greater number of houses in such blocks were occupied by white persons. In the case of *Buchanan v. Warley*,[30] the Supreme Court declared that such ordinances invaded the civil right to acquire, enjoy and use property and violated the Fourteenth Amendment.

Following the *Buchanan* decision, segregation of minorities was achieved by inserting into property deeds restrictive agreements under which owners covenanted not to sell or rent the property involved to Negroes or members of minority groups the owners wished to exclude. These covenants were upheld generally by the courts as valid restrictions upon property.

In May 1948, however, the Supreme Court ruled that judicial enforcement of racially restrictive covenants by state courts contravened the equal protection clause of the Fourteenth Amendment.[31] In a companion case the Court found that the enforcement of such covenants in the District of Columbia was contrary to the public policy of the United States.[32]

The Court made it clear, however, that "restrictive covenants standing alone cannot be regarded as violations of any rights guaranteed . . . by the Fourteenth Amendment. So long as the purposes of these agreements are effectuated by voluntary adherence to their terms, it would appear that there has been no action by the State and the provisions of the Amendment have not been violated." Under these decisions, a person may not invoke the aid of State or Federal courts to enforce racially restrictive covenants although he is perfectly "free to impose or comply" with such covenants without violating the Federal Constitution.

In line with the policy behind the Supreme Court decisions the Federal Housing Administration announced on February 18, 1949 that the rules of that agency were being changed "to eliminate type of occupancy based on race, creed or color as a determining factor in the approval of mortgages for FHA insurance." On December 2, 1949, Solicitor General Philip B. Perlman announced that the rules of the Federal Housing Administration would be amended further "to refuse to aid the financing of any properties the occupancy or use of which is restricted on the basis of race or creed or color." "Under the amendments to be issued," Mr. Perlman declared, "no property will be eligible for FHA mortgage if, after a date to be specified in the amendment and before the FHA insured mortgage is recorded, there has been recorded a covenant racially restricting the use or occupancy of the property." It was also announced that the Veteran's Administration was taking action to amend G.I. regulations along parallel lines.[33]

Thus, the principle that governmental support of racially restrictive covenants is contrary to the public policy of the United States has been established in theory, at

---

[30]245 U.S. 60 (1917).

[31]*Shelley v. Kraemer,* 334 U.S. 1 (1948).

[32]*Hurd v. Hodge,* 334 U.S. 24 (1948).

[33]Statement by Solicitor General Philip B. Perlman at Luncheon Session of State-Wide Conference of New York State Committee Against Discrimination in Housing, Hotel Martinique, 32nd Street, Broadway, Friday, December 2, 1949. See p. 599 ff. for amendments to housing regulations.

least. The crucial question which remains is what is "governmental support?" In this connection, a recent New York case has attracted considerable attention. In *Dorsey v. Stuyvesant Town Corporation*[34] the plaintiff, a Negro, has challenged the right of the Stuyvesant Town Corporation and its parent body, the Metropolitan Life Insurance Company, to refuse to consider applicants, solely because of race or color, for occupancy of a housing project constructed under the New York Redevelopment Companies Law. The Stuyvesant Town Project was built pursuant to a contract between the City of New York, Metropolitan Life Insurance Company and its subsidiary Stuyvesant Town Corporation, and has enjoyed tax exemptions and certain other advantages granted by the city. The plaintiff contends that the project has enjoyed certain governmental powers and benefits to the extent that its action, in refusing occupancy on the basis of race, is "state action" and is prohibited by the Fourteenth Amendment. In a 4 to 3 decision the New York Court of Appeals rejected this argument and dismissed the plaintiff's case.[35] An appeal to the United States Supreme Court is being planned.[35a]

Short of governmental action, little protection has been afforded by the states against discrimination in this area. Colorado and Kansas expressly prohibit racial zoning by governmental agencies. These statutes, however, merely reinforce the *Buchanan* decision. Minnesota, the only state which outlaws restrictive covenants by statute, has done so on the basis of religion only. Connecticut, Massachusetts and New York bar discrimination on racial or religious grounds in public housing projects. New Jersey, New York, Pennsylvania and Wisconsin have acted to prevent discrimination in veterans' housing.

Four states have taken steps to eliminate discrimination in slum clearance and redevelopment housing. The Indiana Redevelopment Law bars exclusion of any citizen from a zoned area under the slum clearance plan by reason of race, creed or national origin. The Illinois and Pennsylvania statutes forbid the use of deeds of conveyance under the redevelopment plan containing a covenant which prohibits occupancy because of race, creed or color. Minnesota bars discrimination in the use of projects based upon religious or political considerations. Illinois also prohibits the displacement of the dominant racial group in an area to be redeveloped. Pennsylvania outlaws racial or religious discrimination in the rental or occupancy of any housing constructed under its 1949 housing and redevelopment assistance law.

7. Military and National Guard

By the end of 1949, nine states had taken steps to end inequalities in the state land and naval militias and national guard units.[36] New Jersey led the way in 1947 by adopting a constitutional provision that no person should be discriminated against in the exercise of any military right nor segregated in the militia because of race, color, religious principles, ancestry or national origin.

In 1949, California, Connecticut, Illinois, Massachusetts and Wisconsin enacted laws prohibiting racial or religious discrimination or segregation in the state militias. Minnesota abolished segregation in its state militia by an executive order signed by the Governor on November 22, 1949.[37] New York and Pennsylvania statutes do not

[34]299 N. Y. 512, 87 N.E. 2d. 541 (July 19, 1949).

[35]Bromley, Lewis, Conway and Dye, JJ., concurred in the majority opinion; Fuld, J., Loughran, C.J., and Desmond, J., concurred in the dissenting opinion.

[35a]The 1950 New York State Legislature amended its Civil Rights Law to prohibit segregation or discrimination in future publicly-aided housing projects. See N.Y. Session Laws 1950, Ch. 287.

[36]California, Connecticut, Illinois, Massachusetts, Minnesota, New Jersey, New York, Pennsylvania and Wisconsin. On January 1, 1950, Oregon became the tenth state to outlaw racial discrimination in the national guard. See Oregon Statesman, Salem, January 1, 1950.

[37]*New York Times,* November 23, 1949, p. 33.

expressly abolish segregation but provide for equality of treatment and opportunity for all persons in the state militia and other armed forces. In addition, New York has repealed a 1913 statute which provided for a separate Negro regiment in the New York National Guard.[38]

8. Protection Against Mob Violence, Intimidation and Race Hatred.

Although the enactment of a federal anti-lynching law has been under public discussion for nearly thirty years, only three states — Kentucky, South Carolina and Texas — were found to have laws against lynching. The South Carolina law was passed in 1896 to implement a similar provision in the South Carolina constitution of 1895. The Kentucky statute was enacted in 1920 and the Texas law came into being in 1949.

Nineteen states have legislated against the activities of the Ku Klux Klan and other hooded organizations.[39] While none of these statutes expressly mention the Ku Klux Klan, all of them prohibit in some form or other the wearing of masks, or hoods or disguises in public places and some laws outlaw night riding activities and other acts of intimidation. It is interesting to note that most of these laws were enacted during the aftermath of World War I when violence against racial and religious minorities reached an alarming stage throughout the country.

A number of states have revoked the charters of Ku Klux Klan organizations through actions brought by the state's attorney general, notably California, Kentucky, New Jersey, New York and Wisconsin.[40]

A number of states have sought to protect racial and religious minorities against activities designed to stir up hatred, friction and violence. These statutes vary in the extent of coverage and types of action restrained. California makes it unlawful for any textbook used in the schools to contain and teachers in giving instruction to say anything reflecting upon United States citizens because of race, creed or color. New Mexico punishes as a criminal libel publication or circulation of a malicious written statement concerning any fraternal or religious society. Oregon forbids the use of language in election campaign voters' pamphlets which, in the opinion of the Secretary of State, promotes or advocates hatred or hostility toward any racial or religious group. In Connecticut, it is a criminal offense to publish any advertisement holding up to contempt any person or class of persons. In Florida, the publication or distribution of anonymous literature which tends to expose any individual or religious group to hatred, ridicule or contempt is unlawful.

Illinois, Indiana, Massachusetts and New Jersey laws forbid the malicious advocacy or promotion of racial or religious hatred. The New Jersey statute was invalidated in 1942, however, as being too indefinite and uncertain and as a violation of free speech.[41]

A New Hampshire statute forbids the use of any book in the public schools favoring

---

[38]For action taken by the Federal Government, see Executive Order 9981, July 27, 1948, 13 F.R. 4313, President's Committee on Equality of Treatment and Opportunity in the Armed Forces, Appendix 3 and statements issued by Natonal Military Establishments, Appendix 3.

[39]Alabama (1949), Arizona (1923), Arkansas (1909), California (1923), Illinois (1923), Iowa (1924 Code), Louisiana (1924), Michigan (1929), Minnesota (1933), New Mexico (1923), New York (1881), North Dakota (1923), Ohio (1886), Oklahoma (1923), South Carolina (1928), Tennessee (1869-70), Texas (1925), Washington (1909), Wisconsin (1923).

[40]See Newman, *The Law of Civil Rights and Civil Liberties*, Oceana Publications, New York, p. 39.

[41]*State v. Klapprott*, 127 N.J.L. 395, 22 A. 2d. 877 (1941).

any particular religious sect or political party.[42] North Dakota bans from public school libraries sectarian publications devoted to discussion of religious differences.[43]

9. Miscellaneous Prohibitions

Seven states have barred racial discrimination by insurance companies.[44] All of the statutes apply to life insurance carriers. In addition, the Minnesota law includes automobile insurance and the Connecticut and New York statutes apply to accident and health insurance. Most state insurance codes contain an anti-discrimination clause but these provisions do not specify race, color or creed as a prohibited basis of discrimination.

One interesting discovery was that while two states — Illinois and New York — specifically forbid the refusal to sell liquor to a person because of race or color, the laws of fifteen states restrict or prohibit the sale of intoxicating liquors to American Indians.[45]

B. Segregation Laws[46]
1. Education

Segregation by law is found to be most extensive in the public schools. Twenty-one jurisdictions and the District of Columbia permit or require separate schools for Negro and white pupils.[47] Delaware, Mississippi and North Carolina also provide for separate schools for Indians. The Florida, Kentucky, Oklahoma and Tennessee statutes expressly apply to private schools as well as public schools.

While segregation in all phases of education is the general pattern, with few exceptions,[48] actual statutory regulation varies from state to state. Twelve states require separation of deaf pupils, three states specify segregation among dumb pupils, while eleven states provided for separation of Negro and white blind students.[49]

Eighteen states make provision for separation of the races in juvenile delinquent and reform schools.[50] Fourteen jurisdictions provide for segregated agricultural and trade schools.[51] Seventeen states provided for separate colleges and teacher training schools.[52]

The pattern of segregation on the university level has weakened considerably in the Southern states under the impact of recent Supreme Court decisions. For some years Negro students have been enrolled in the graduate school and in certain of the

---

[42]N.H. Revised Laws, Ch. 135, Sec. 26. Not shown on Chart II.

[43]N.D. Revised Code, 1943, Sec. 15-2507. Not shown on Chart II.

[44]Connecticut, Massachusetts, Michigan, Minnesota, New Jersey, New York and Ohio.

[45]See Note 81 below.

[46]See Chart III, Segregation Authorized or Required by Law, for detailed comparative study of state segregation laws. See appropriate headings under state compilations for text of segregation statutes.

[47]Alabama, Arizona, Arkansas, Delaware, District of Columbia, Florida, Georgia, Kansas, Kentucky, Louisiana, Maryland, Mississippi, Missouri, New Mexico, North Carolina, Oklahoma, South Carolina, Tennessee, Texas, Virginia, West Virginia, Wyoming.

[48]See "Note on Regional Compact — Education", Appendix 6.

[49]See Chart III.

[50]See Chart III.

[51]See Chart III.

[52]Alabama, Arkansas, Delaware, Florida, Georgia, Kentucky, Louisiana, Maryland, Mississippi, Missouri, North Carolina, Oklahoma, South Carolina, Tennessee, Texas, Virginia, West Virginia.

undergraduate departments of the University of West Virginia.[52a] Negroes have also attended the University of Maryland School of Law since 1935, although barred to other departments of that institution. Following the United States Supreme Court decision in the case of Ada Lois Sipuel in 1948,[53] Negro students have been enrolled at the Universities of Arkansas, Delaware, Kentucky, Oklahoma and Texas.[54] It is also reported that some private universities in Missouri, North Carolina, Virginia and the District of Columbia have admitted Negro students in recent years.[54a]

One interesting feature observed in the laws of Delaware, Kentucky, North Carolina, Texas and Wyoming was that, while providing for segregation, these statutes scrupulously forbid discrimination or distinction by reason of race or color in the public schools.[55] New Mexico expressly bars segregation of children of Mexican or Spanish decent while authorizing the separation of Negro and white pupils.

Missouri, North Carolina and Texas authorize separate public libraries, while Florida and North Carolina require that separate textbooks be used for Negro and white public school pupils.

2. Transportation

At the present time, at least fourteen states require segregated railroad facilities for Negro and white passengers.[56] Eleven states provide for separation of the races on buses.[57] Eleven states enforce segregation on street cars and street railways.[58] Maryland, North Carolina, South Carolina and Virginia make provision for segregation on steamboats and ferries. Nine states specify separate waiting rooms,[59] while separate sleeping compartments are required in Arkansas, Georgia, Mississippi[60] and Texas. Segregated dining car and restaurant facilities are mandatory in South Carolina. Thirteen states have exempted from the operation of the segregation laws one or both of two situations: a sheriff conducting a prisoner, or a nurse or servant in charge of children

---

[52a]*Journal of Negro Education*, Vol. 19, No. 1, Winter 1950, p.4; *Survey Graphic*, September, 1949, p. 480.

[53]*Sipuel v. Board of Regents of Univ. of Okla.* 332 U.S. 631 (Jan. 12, 1948).

[54]*Journal of Negro Education*, Vol. 19, No. 1, Winter 1950, pp. 4, 5.

[54a]See Note 54. See also "Note on Regional Compact — Education", and sources cited therein, Appendix 6, for more discussion of newer developments in Southern universities.

[55]The Wyoming law is particularly confusing. The Constitution of Wyoming prohibits distinction or discrimination on account of race or color in the public schools and provides that the University of Wyoming "shall be equally open to students of both sexes, irrespective of race or color." Yet there remains on the statute books an 1876 law which authorizes the setting up of separate schools for Negro children when there are more than 15 such children within any school district. See Wyoming Constitution, Art. 7, Sec. 10, Sec. 16; Wyoming Comp. Stats. Ann. (1945) Sec. 67-624.

[56]Alabama, Arkansas, Florida, Georgia, Kentucky, Louisiana, Maryland, Mississippi, North Carolina, Oklahoma, South Carolina, Tennessee, Texas, Virginia.

[57]Alabama, Arkansas, Florida (carriers), Georgia, Louisiana, Mississippi, North Carolina, Oklahoma, South Carolina, Texas, Virginia.

[58]Arkansas, Florida, Louisiana, Maryland, Mississippi, North Carolina, Oklahoma, South Carolina, Tennessee, Texas, Virginia.

[59]Alabama, Arkansas, Florida, Louisiana, Mississippi, North Carolina, Oklahoma, South Carolina, Texas.

[60]By judicial decision.

or invalids.[61] Similarly, in eight states the segregation laws do not apply to freight cars and caboose.[62]

Aside from state laws, many Southern cities through local ordinances or regulations of public service commissions enforce separate seating arrangements on local transportation facilities.[63]

Years of vigorous legal attack upon segregation in interstate travel culminated in the decision of *Morgan v. Virginia*[64] in 1946, in which the United States Supreme Court invalidated a Virginia segregation statute relating to motor carriers as applied to interstate passengers. The Court ruled that the enforcement of such a statute unduly interfered with the power of the Federal Government to regulate interstate commerce, a field exclusively reserved to Congress. Similarly, the rule of the *Morgan* case was held to apply to railroads.[65]

The *Morgan* decision is a limited one. States are still free legally to segregate intra-state passengers traveling to points within a state. Furthermore, the segregation of interstate passengers has not been declared to be a violation of the Fourteenth Amendment, nor has segregation *per se* been outlawed. Railroad and bus companies operating in Southern states where segregation laws exist have evaded the *Morgan* decision through the device of company regulations requiring separation of Negroes and whites. They justify such action on the ground that it is a reasonable regulation and in accordance with local custom and usage. Under the present interpretation of constitutional law, private action by carriers is not within the purview of the Fourteenth Amendment. Some lower federal and state courts have upheld the right of private carriers to adopt rules of segregation of interstate passengers, but a United States Circuit Court of Appeals decision in 1949 declared such rules to be invalid.[65a] Thus, we have the spectacle of interstate carriers being permitted to do what the States themselves are forbidden to do. Until the Supreme Court clarifies the situation, segregation in one form or another doubtless will continue on carriers in the Southern states.

In this connection, the highly important case of *Henderson v. The United States et al.*[66] is now pending before the Supreme Court. In this case the plaintiff has challenged the legality of dining-car regulatons of the Southern Railway, which provide for separate tables for Negroes in the diner set off from other tables by means of a partition or curtain. Such regulations have been approved by the Interstate Commerce Commission. The plaintiff contends that these regulations violate the Interstate Commerce Act which makes it unlawful for any common carrier to subject any passenger to "undue or unreasonable prejudice or disadvantage."[67] The Supreme Court may be called upon to decide the issue of segregation *per se* in the *Henderson* case. In fact the United States has filed a brief in which it urges that the order of the Interstate

---

[61]Alabama, Arkansas, Florida, Georgia, Kentucky, Louisiana, Maryland, North Carolina, Oklahoma, South Carolina, Tennessee, Texas and Virginia.

[62]Arkansas, Kentucky, Maryland, Oklahoma, South Carolina, Tennessee, Texas, Virginia.

[63]For a sampling of segregation ordinances, see Appendix 5.

[64]328 U.S. 373 (1946).

[65]*Matthews v. Southern Railway*, 157 F. 2d. 609 (1946).

[65a]*Whiteside v. Southern Bus Lines, Inc.*, 177 F. 2d 949 (U.S.C.A. -6th), decided Nov. 23, 1949.

[66]U.S. Supreme Court, October Term, 1949, Docket No. 25, on appeal from 80 F. Supp. 32 (1948). See also "The Legal Case Against Segregation", Appendix 7.

[67]49 U.S.C. 3(1).

Commission approving the dining car regulations is invalid and asks that the doctrine of "separate but equal" contained in *Plessy v. Ferguson*[68] be re-examined and overruled.

3. Amusements

Few Southern states have legislated extensively with reference to segregation in amusements. This is generally achieved through local ordinances or through custom. South Carolina and Georgia statutes provide that no license shall be issued to any person of one race to operate a billiard hall or pool room for persons of the opposite race. Missouri authorizes the state board of education to maintain separate public parks and playgrounds for Negroes and whites. Oklahoma provides for segregation in fishing, boating and bathing. South Carolina forbids the joint use of parks, amusement centers and bathing beaches by white and colored persons. Arkansas requires segregation of the races at all racetracks, while Louisiana and South Carolina require separation at circuses and tent shows. Tennessee authorizes owners and operators of places of public amusement to provide separate accommodations for the races, although the same statute provides that "there shall be no discrimination . . . in the admission of persons to such places on equal terms."

4. Hospitals and Penal Institutions

Mississippi and South Carolina appear to be the only states which specifically provide for segregation generally in public hospitals, but thirteen states require separation of mental patients[69] and seven states make provision for separate accommodations for Negro and white tubercular patients.[70]

In Alabama, it is unlawful to require white female nurses to nurse in a hospital ward where Negro male patients are placed for treatment. Mississippi and South Carolina also require the use of Negro nurses for Negro patients.

Ten states provide for segregation of white and colored prisoners in penal institutions.[71] Six of these statutes include a provision that Negro and white convicts may not be chained together.[72]

5. Welfare Institutions

Alabama and West Virginia statutes make provision for racial segregation in paupers' homes; Delaware, Louisiana and West Virginia require segregation in homes for the aged; Delaware, Kentucky, North Carolina, Oklahoma, Tennessee, Texas and West Virginia provide segregated homes for Negro orphans.

6. Employment

Segregation in employment has been legislated in only six states. Four of these— Arkansas, Oklahoma, Tennessee and Texas — require separate wash rooms for Negro and white workers employed in the mining industry. North Carolina provides for the maintenance of separate toilet facilities for Negroes and whites employed in manufacturing or other business. South Carolina has an elaborate statute requiring segregation

---

[68]163 U.S. 537(1896).

[69]Alabama, Georgia, Kentucky, Louisiana, Maryland, Mississippi, Missouri, North Carolina, Oklahoma, South Carolina, Tennessee, Virginia, West Virginia.

[70]Alabama, Delaware, Kentucky, Maryland, Oklahoma, Texas, West Virginia.

[71]Alabama, Arkansas, Florida, Georgia, Louisiana, Mississippi, North Carolina, South Carolina, Tennessee, Virginia.

[72]Alabama, Arkansas, Florida, Georgia, North Carolina, South Carolina.

in minute detail of employees working in cotton textile manufacturing establishments. As a practical matter, segregation in employment in most Southern states is generally established without the aid of statute.

7. Miscellaneous Restrictions

One of the most widespread racial restrictions is found in the field of marriage. Thirty states forbid marriages between white persons and Negroes or mulattoes.[73] Fifteen of these statutes also prohibit marriages between white persons and persons of Mongolian or Oriental descent[74] and five states bar marriages between whites and American Indians.[75]

Some statutes make it a penal offense to enter into a forbidden marriage, punishable by fine or imprisonment, or both. Some state laws provide that mixed marriages shall be void, but do not penalize the contracting parties. California's anti-miscegenation statute was invalidated by the California Supreme Court in 1948,[76] but an attempt to repeal the statute during the 1949 legislature was unsuccessful. Eight states prohibit cohabitation between persons of different races.[77] In Georgia, a Negro minister may celebrate the marriage ceremony of Negro couples only.

Indiana, North Carolina and West Virginia provide for separate Negro and white battallions in the state militia. Texas makes it unlawful for persons to promote boxing matches between Negro and white prize fighters. North Carolina and Virginia prohibit mixed Negro and white memberships in fraternal organizations. Mississippi makes it a criminal offense to publish or distribute any matter advocating social equality between the races. Oklahoma authorizes the use of separate public telephone booths for Negroes and whites. Louisiana, Montana, South Carolina and Texas permit the adoption of a child by a person of the same race only.

Arkansas requires the recording of separate Negro and white tax lists and provides for the alternate use of voting booths by the two races. Alabama, Arkansas and Virginia provide for separate poll tax lists; Georgia, Indiana and Nebraska require separate voting lists of Negro and white electors to be kept.

C. Aliens

No attempt was made to exhaust state laws which apply to aliens, although a number of statutes do appear in the compilation which indicate some of the legal restrictions in this field. As in the case of race and color, no uniformity exists in state legislation relating to aliens. Some states expressly declare that in matters of property ownership and possession, aliens shall have the same rights as citizens. Some states bar the employment of aliens in public works, in positions of public office, or as teachers in the public schools. A number of states bar aliens from certain licensed occupations. Some states expressly prohibit aliens from possessing firearms.

Emphasis was placed, however, upon those statutes which are directed primarily

---

[73]Alabama, Arizona, Arkansas, California, Colorado, Delaware, Florida, Georgia, Idaho, Indiana, Kentucky, Louisiana, Maryland, Mississippi, Missouri, Montana, Nebraska, Nevada, North Carolina, North Dakota, Oklahoma, Oregon, South Carolina, South Dakota, Tennessee, Texas, Utah, Virginia, West Virginia, Wyoming.

[74]Arizona, California, Georgia, Idaho, Maryland, Mississippi, Missouri, Montana, Nebraska, Nevada, Oregon, South Dakota, Utah, Virginia, Wyoming.

[75]Nevada, North Carolina, Oregon, South Carolina, Virginia.

[76]*Perez v. Lippold*, 198 P. 2d. 17; Perez v. Sharp, 32 Calif. 2d. 711(1948).

[77]Alabama, Arkansas, Florida, Louisiana, Maryland, Nevada, Tennessee, Virginia.

against aliens of certain racial origins, particularly the alien land laws of some western and southwestern states. At least five states — Arizona, California, New Mexico, Texas and Washington — prohibit by law "aliens ineligible for citizenship" from owning or controlling real property within the state. The purpose of these statutes is to prevent Chinese, Japanese and certain Oriental groups from acquiring land. While some of the more discriminatory features of the California law have been challenged successfully in the Supreme Court,[78] the restriction against outright ownership of land by ineligible aliens remains. Oregon and Utah repealed their alien land laws in 1949. An Arkansas statute enacted in 1943 prohibits Japanese or their descendants from purchasing or owning land or an interest in land within that state. This statute, however, is believed to be invalid because it appears to be in direct conflict with a provision of the Arkansas constitution which declares that no distinction shall be made by law between resident aliens and citizens in regard to the possession of property. A Nevada statute bars subjects of the Chinese empire from holding real property in that state.

Other laws restricting the ownership of property by aliens generally are found in Indiana, Kentucky, Minnesota, Mississippi, Nebraska, Oklahoma, Pennsylvania and South Carolina. These restrictions either limit the number of acres which may be owned or the number of years the land may be held.[79]

D. Indians

With reference to American Indians, the national policy has been one of federal responsibility for the protection and regulation of the affairs of this minority group.[80] Hence, few states have legislated in this area. The constitutions of some Western states contain provisions forever disclaiming ownership of lands reserved for the use of Indian tribes. A few states have legislated on the right of Indians to vote, to sell land and to hunt and fish in certain areas.

For the most part state restrictions upon Indians relate to the possession of intoxicating liquors and of firearms. In thirteen states, the furnishing or sale of liquor to Indians is forbidden.[81] Arizona, Idaho, Montana, and Nebraska make it unlawful to furnish Indians with firearms. As already noted, three states provide separate schools for Indians and five states forbid the marriage of Indians to white persons.[82]

A number of states have inaugurated an "Indian Day" to commemorate Indian history and tradition. In 1949 North Dakota and South Dakota provided for the establishment of a Commission of Indian Affairs. The purpose of such commissions seems to be the study of problems of the Indian population in those states in order to provide for the integration of Indian citizens into the economy of the state.

---

[78]See *Oyama v. California*, 332 U.S. 633(1948).

[79]For more detailed study of laws affecting aliens contained in this compilation see heading "Aliens" under various state compilations.

[80]For a discussion of American policy toward the Indian, see McWilliams, Carey, *Brothers Under The Skin* (1945), Ch. I.

[81]Arizona, Colorado, Florida, Iowa, Minnesota, Nevada, New Mexico, New York, North Dakota, Oklahoma, Oregon, Utah, Washington. Idaho and Kansas repealed similar laws in 1949. See Idaho Laws 1949, chs. 9, 10; Kansas Laws 1949, ch. 242, §115.

[82]For texts of statutes relating to "Indians" see appropriate headings under various state compilations.

CONCLUSION

The foregoing brief survey of state laws is intended merely as a working classification. The laws vary in scope and interpretation and should be studied carefully by students of the problem. I have purposely presented this compilation with as little editorial comment as possible, in the belief that such a study offers Americans of all shades and opinions an excellent opportunity for self-examination and comparison. I sincerely hope that this initial effort to reflect legislative policy on racial practices, state by state, will stimulate other students and organizations concerned with human rights to supply omissions, correct errors and offer criticisms and comments which can be incorporated into annual supplements and which will contribute to a more comprehensive knowledge of legislation in this field.

New York City   *Pauli Murray*
January 10, 1950.

ALABAMA

CONSTITUTION

Education

Art. XIV, Sec. 256 [Authorizes establishment of a system of public schools for children between the ages of 7 and 21 years and provides "separate schools shall be provided for white and colored children, and no child of either race shall be permitted to attend a school of the other race."] [Const. 1901]

[Note: This section is held to be mandatory. Elsberry v. Seay, 83 Ala. 614, 3 So. 804.]

Elections

Boswell Amendment [Amended section 181 of the Alabama Constitution to provide, among other things, that "the following persons, and no others . . . shall be qualified to register as electors . . . those who can read and write, understand and explain any article of the Constitution of the United States in the English language . . : : provided, however, no persons shall be entitled to register as electors except those who are of good character and who understand the duties and obligations of good citizenship under a republican form of government."] [Proposed by Acts 1945, p. 551, submitted Nov. 5, 1946; proclaimed ratified Nov. 14, 1946; Amendment 55 to Const. of 1901, 1947 Cum. Supp.]

[Note: The above section was enacted to amend the Alabama Constitution after the United States Supreme Court held invalid the white primary system in the southern states in its decision of *Smith v. Allwright* (1944) 321 U.S. 649. While the amendment, by its terms, makes no mention of race, it has been challenged successfully in the federal courts as an attempt to evade the Supreme Court mandate on the right of Negroes to vote.

In the case of *Davis v. Schnell*, 81 F. Supp. 872, decided on January 7, 1949, by the United States District Court for the Southern District of Alabama, it was held that the Boswell Amendment to the Constitution of Alabama, which provides that only persons who can "understand and explain" any article of the Constitution of the United States to the reasonable satisfaction of the Board of Registrars may qualify as electors, attempts to grant to such board arbitrary power to accept or reject any prospective elector and is a denial of equal protection of the law as guaranteed by the Fourteenth Amendment.

Mr. Justice Mullins, in his opinion, pointed out that the Boswell Amendment both in its object and administration "was intended to be, and is being used for the purpose of discriminating against applicants for the franchise on the basis of race or color", and is therefore unconstitutional because it violates the Fifteenth Amendment. The Court declared, "While it is true there is no mention of race or color in the Boswell Amendment, this does not save it." *Affirmed* 336 U.S. 933, Per Curiam (3/28/1949) 93 L.E. 644, 69 Sup. Ct. 749.]

21

Slavery

Art. I, Sec. 32.   That no form of slavery shall exist in this state; and there shall not be any involuntary servitude, otherwise than for the punishment of crime, of which the party shall have been duly convicted. [Const. 1901]

STATUTES

Code of Alabama, 1940

Definition of "Negro"

Title 1, §2 — Meaning of certatin words and terms. — . . . The word "negro" includes mulatto. The word "mulatto" or the term "person of color" means a person of mixed blood descended on the part of the father or mother from negro ancestors, without reference to or limit of time or number of generations. [1927, p. 716.]

Descent and Distribution

Title 16, §13. Slaves, free person of color and their descendants may inherit. — Slaves and free persons of color prior to the abolition of slavery in this state, and their descendants, are capable of inheriting or transmitting property, real, personal, or mixed, the same in all respects as white persons, where the ancestors lived together as man and wife under such circumstances as would constitute a valid marriage at common law. This section shall also apply to and govern all cases heretofore arising and to which it may be applicable. [Code 1923, §7377.]

Education

Title 52, §93 — Free separate schools for white and colored. — The county board of education shall provide schools of two kinds, those for white children and those for colored children. The schools for white children shall be free to all white children over six years of age. The schools for colored children shall be free to all colored children over six years of age. [1927 School Code, §124.]

Advisory Board for Negro Institutions

Title 52, §24. Advisory board for negro institutions. — [Authorizes appointment of an advisory board of not more than five persons from locality in which any institution for Negroes under the control of the state board of education is located. State Board of Education appoints the advisory board and designates its duties.] [1927 School Code; §50.]

Alabama School of Trades

Title 52, §443. [Admission of students restricted to "white boys and young white men."] [1927 School Code, §482.]

Alabama College

Title 52, §466. Who may be admitted to college — Any white girl or woman residing in Alabama, of good moral character . . . [1927 School Code, §510.]

Agricultural and Mechanical Institute for Negroes

Title 52, §§452-455. [Provides for the maintenance of Alabama A. & M.

Institute for Negroes at Huntsville, Alabama, under the direction and control of the state board of education.] [1927 School Code, §§494-497.]

School for Deaf and Blind

Title 52, §519 [Consolidates the "Alabama school for the deaf" and "Alabama school for Negro deaf and blind" pupils into a single institution called "Alabama Institute for Deaf and Blind" to be located at Talladega, Ala. No specific statutory provision for separate schools for Negro and white deaf and blind.] [1927 School Code, §577.]

Title 52, §524 [1947 Cum. Supp.] Object of School; what children may be admitted. — . . . All deaf and all blind children of the state between the ages of six and twenty-one who are of sound mind, free from disease, and of good character, may be admitted to the benefits of this school . . . [1927 School Code, §582; 1931, p. 332; 1943, p. 220, appvd. June 24, 1943.]

Juvenile Delinquents

Title 52, §§613(1) - 613(15). [1947 Cum. Supp.] [Provides for reform school for Negro boys and girls at Mt. Meigs, Montgomery County, Alabama called "Alabama Industrial School for Negro Children." [1947, pp. 373-379, §§1-15, appvd. Sept. 30, 1947.]

Normal Schools and State Teachers Colleges

Title 52, §438 - Control — The state board of education shall have the control and management of several normal schools or teachers' colleges of the state, for white teachers, located at Florence, Jacksonville, Livingston, Troy, and of the state normal for colored teachers, located at Montgomery. [1927 School Code, §474.]

Higher Education Not Available in Alabama State-supported Institutions

Title 52, §40(1). [1947 Cum. Supp.] Authority to provide graduate and professional instruction not available at state supported educational institutions. — The state board of education, under such rules and regulations as it shall determine, may provide for residents of Alabama graduate and professional instruction not available to them at state-supported educational institutions. The state board of education shall, by its rules and regulations, determine the qualifications of persons who may be aided under this section, and the decisions as to qualifications of persons by the state board of education shall be final. The state board of education may provide such graduate and professional instruction at any educational institution, as it deems necessary, within or without state boundaries. The state board of education shall provide such graduate and professional instruction, within the limits of appropriations available for this purpose, at a cost to students not exceeding the probable cost of such instruction to them if it were offered at a state-supported institution. The state board of education, in providing such instruction, may take into account travel, tuition, and living expenses. [1945, p. 61, appvd. June 1, 1945.]

Title 52, §40(2). [1947 Cum. Supp.] Authority of institutions of higher learning to make interstate educational agreements. — Any institution of higher learning which receives all or part of its support from the State of

Alabama, subject to approval by the state board of education and under such rules and regulations as the state board of education shall determine, may contract, with other state governments, agencies of other state governments, or institutions of higher learning of other state governments, to provide educational facilities at such Alabama institution of higher learning to residents of such other states.

Any institution of higher learning which receives all or part of its support from the state of Alabama, subject to approval by the state board of education, and under such rules and regulations as the state board of education shall determine, may contract, with other state governments, agencies of other state governments, institutions of higher learning of other state governments, or private institutions of higher learning within or outside state boundaries, to provide educational facilities to residents of Alabama at an expense to such residents of Alabama not exceeding the probable cost to them if the facilities were provided at such Alabama institution of higher learning. [1945, p. 62, appvd. June 1, 1945.]

Education
Regional Compact

Acts 1949, p. 327

Act No. 227   H. J. R. 42—White (Covington)

HOUSE JOINT RESOLUTION

A JOINT RESOLUTION giving legislative approval to that certain Compact entered into by the State of Alabama and other Southern States by and through their respective governors on February 8, 1948, as amended, relative to the development and maintenance of regional educational services and schools in the Southern States in the professional, technological, scientific, literary and other fields, so as to provide greater educational advantages and facilities for the citizens in the several States who reside in such region; to declare that the State of Alabama is a party to said compact, as amended, and that the agreements, covenants and obligations therein are binding upon said State.

WHEREAS, on the 8th day of February, in the Year of Our Lord One Thousand Nine Hundred and Forty-eight, the State of Alabama and the States of Arkansas, Florida, Georgia. Louisiana, Maryland. Mississippi, North Carolina, Oklahoma, South Carolina, Tennessee, Virginia, and West Virginia, through and by their respective governors, entered into a written Compact relative to the development and maintenance of regional educational services and schools in the Southern States in the professional, technological, scientific, literary, and other fields, so as to provide greater educational advantages and facilities for the citizens of the several States who reside within such region; and

WHEREAS, the said Compact has been amended in certain respects, a copy of which Compact as amended is as follows:

WHEREAS, The States who are parties hereto have during the past several years conducted careful investigation looking toward the establishment and maintenance of jointly owned and operated regional educational institu-

24

tions in the Southern States in the professional, technological, scientific, literary and other fields, so as to provide greater educational advantages and facilities for the citizens of the several States who reside within such region; and

WHEREAS, Meharry Medical College of Nashville, Tennessee, has proposed that its lands, buildings, equipment, and the net income from its endowment be turned over to the Southern States, or to an agency acting in their behalf, to be operated as a regional institution for medical, dental and nursing education upon terms and conditions to be hereafter agreed upon between the Southern States and Meharry Medical College, which proposal, because of the present financial condition of the institution, has been approved by the said States who are parties hereto; and

WHEREAS, The said States desire to enter into a compact with each other providing for the planning and establishment of regional educational facilities;

NOW, THEREFORE, in consideration of the mutual agreements, covenants and obligations assumed by the respective States who are parties hereto (hereinafter referred to as "States"), the said several States do hereby form a geographical district or region consisting of the areas lying within the boundaries of the contracting States which, for the purposes of this compact, shall constitute an area for regional education supported by public funds derived from taxation by the constituent States and derived from other sources for the establishment, acquisition, operation and maintenance of regional educational schools and institutions for the benefit of citizens of the respective States residing within the region so established as may be determined from time to time in accordance with the terms and provisions of this compact.

The States do further hereby establish and create a joint agency which shall be known as the Board of Control for Southern Regional Education (hereinafter referred to as the "Board"), the members of which Board shall consist of the Governor of each State, ex officio, and three additional citizens of each State to be appointed by the Governor thereof, at least one of whom shall be selected from the field of education. The Governor shall continue as a member of the Board during his tenure of office as Governor of the State, but the members of the Board appointed by the Governor shall hold office for a period of four years except that in the original appointments one Board member so appointed by the Governor shall be designated at the time of his appointment to serve an initial term of two years, one Board member to serve an initial term of three years, and the remaining Board member to serve the full term of four years, but thereafter the successor of each appointed Board member shall serve the full term of four years. Vacancies on the Board caused by death, resignation, refusal or inability to serve, shall be filled by appointment by the Governor for the unexpired portion of the term. The officers of the Board shall be a Chairman, a Vice Chairman, a Secretary, a Treasurer, and such additional officers as may be created by the Board from time to time. The Board shall meet annually and officers shall be elected to hold office until the next annual meeting. The Board shall have the right to formulate and establish by-laws not inconsistent with the provisions of this compact to govern its own actions in the performance of the duties delegated to it including the right to create and appoint an Executive Committee and a Finance Committee with such powers and authority as the Board may delegate to them from time to time. The Board may, within its discretion, elect as its Chairman a person who is not a member of the Board, provided such person resides within a signatory State, and upon such election such person shall become a member of the Board with all the rights and privileges of such membership.

It shall be the duty of the Board to submit plans and recommendations to the States from time to time for their approval and adoption by appropriate legislative action for the development, establishment, acquisition, operation and maintenance of educational schools and institutions within the geographical limits of the regional area of the States, of such character and type and for such educational purposes, professional, technological, scientific, literary, or otherwise, as they may deem and determine to be proper, necessary or advisable. Title to all such educational institutions when so established by appropriate legislative actions of the States and to all properties and facilities used in connection therewith shall be vested in said Board as the agency of and for the use and benefit of the said States and the citizens thereof, and all such educational institutions shall be operated, maintained and financed in the manner herein set out, subject to any provisions or limitations which may be contained in the legislative acts of the States authorizing the creation, establishment and operation of such educational institutions.

In addition to the power and authority heretofore granted, the Board shall have the power to enter into such agreements or arrangements with any of the States and with educational institutions or agencies, as may be required in the judgment of the Board, to provide adequate services and facilities for the graduate, professional and technical education for the benefit of the citizens of the respective States residing within the region, and such additional and general power and authority as may be vested in the Board from time to time by legislative enactment of the said States.

Any two or more States who are parties of this compact shall have the right to enter into supplemental agreements providing for the establishment, financing and operation of regional educational institutions for the benefit of citizens residing within an area which constitutes a portion of the general region herein created, such institutions to be financed exclusively by such States and to be controlled exclusively by the members of the Board representing such States provided such agreement is submitted to and approved by the Board prior to the establishment of such institutions.

Each State agrees that, when authorized by the legislature, it will from time to time make available and pay over to said Board such funds as may be required for the establishment, acquisition, operation and maintenance of such regional educational institutions as may be authorized by the States under the terms of this compact, the contribution of each State at all times to be in the proportion that its population bears to the total combined population of the States who are parties hereto as shown from time to time by the most recent official published report of the Bureau of Census of the United States of America; or upon such other basis as may be agreed upon.

This compact shall not take effect or be binding upon any State unless and until it shall be approved by proper legislative action of as many as six or more of the States whose Governors have subscribed hereto within a period of eighteen months from the date hereof. When and if six or more States shall have given legislative approval to this compact within said eighteen months period, it shall be and become binding upon such six or more States 60 days after the date of legislative approval by the Sixth State and the Governors of such six or more States shall forthwith name the members of the Board from their States as hereinabove set out, and the Board shall then meet on call of the Governor of any State approving this compact, at which time the Board shall elect officers, adopt by-laws, appoint committees and otherwise fully organize. Other States whose names are subscribed hereto shall thereafter become parties hereto upon approval of this compact by legislative action within two years from the date hereof, upon such conditions as may be agreed upon at the time. Provided, however, that with respect to any State whose constitution may require amendment in order to permit legislative approval of the Compact, such State or States shall become parties hereto upon approval of this Compact by legislative action within seven years from the date hereof, upon such conditions as may be agreed upon at the time.

After becoming effective this compact shall thereafter continue without limitation of time; provided, however, that it may be terminated at any time by unanimous action of the States and provided further that any State may withdraw from this compact if such withdrawal is approved by its legislature, such withdrawal to become effective two years after written notice thereof to the Board accompanied by a certified copy of the requisite legislative action, but such withdrawal shall not relieve the withdrawing State from its obligations hereunder accruing up to the effective date of such withdrawal. Any State so withdrawing shall ipso facto cease to have any claim to or ownership of any of the property held or vested in the Board or to any of the funds of the Board held under the terms of this compact.

If any State shall at any time become in default in the performance of any of its obligations assumed herein or with respect to any obligation imposed upon said State as authorized by and in compliance with the terms and provisions of this compact, all rights, privileges and benefits of such defaulting State, its members on the Board and its citizens shall ipso facto be and become suspended from and after the date of such default. Unless such default shall be remedied and made good within a period of one year immediately following the date of such default this compact may be terminated with respect to such defaulting State by an affirmative vote of three-fourths of the members of the Board (exclusive of the members representing the State in default), from and after which time such State shall cease to be a party to this compact and shall have no further claim to or ownership of any of the property held by or vested in the Board or to any of the funds of the Board held under the terms of this compact, but such termination shall in no manner release such defaulting State from any accrued obligation or otherwise affect this compact or the rights, duties, privileges or obligations of the remaining States thereunder.

IN WITNESS WHEREOF this Compact has been approved and signed by Governors of the several States, subject to the approval of their respective legislatures in the manner hereinabove set out, as of the 8th day of February, 1948.

STATE OF FLORIDA
By Millard F. Caldwell
Governor

STATE OF ARKANSAS
By Ben Laney
Governor

STATE OF MARYLAND
By Wm. Preston Lane, Jr.
Governor

COMMONWEALTH OF VIRGINIA
By Wm. M. Tuck
Governor

STATE OF GEORGIA
By M. E. Thompson
Governor

STATE OF NORTH CAROLINA
By R. Gregg Cherry
Governor

STATE OF LOUISIANA
By J. H. Davis
Governor

STATE OF SOUTH CAROLINA
By J. Strom Thurmond
Governor

STATE OF ALABAMA
By James E. Folsom
Governor

STATE OF TEXAS
By Beauford H. Jester
Governor

STATE OF MISSISSIPPI
By F. L. Wright
Governor

STATE OF OKLAHOMA
By Roy J. Turner
Governor

STATE OF TENNESSEE
By Jim McCord
Governor

STATE OF WEST VIRGINIA
By Clarence W. Meadows
Governor

BE IT RESOLVED BY THE LEGISLATURE OF ALABAMA

Section I. That the said Compact be and the same is hereby approved and the State of Alabama is hereby declared to be a party hereto, and agreements, covenants, and obligations therein are binding upon the State of Alabama.

Section II. That upon the approval of this Compact by the requisite number of States the Governor sign an engrossed copy of the Compact and sufficient copies be provided so that every State approving the Compact shall have an engrossed copy.

Section III. This Resolution shall take effect upon its approval by the Governor.

Approved July 12, 1949.
Time 5:19 P. M.

I hereby certify that the foregoing copy of an Act of the Legislature of Alabama has been compared with the enrolled Act and it is a true and correct copy thereof.

Given under my hand this 18 day of July, 1949.

R. T. GOODWYN, JR.
Clerk of the House

[Note: See Note on *Regional Compact — Education*, Appendix 6.]

Tuskeegee Institute

Title 52, §455(1). [1947 Cum. Supp.] [Provides for annual appropriation of $100,000 to Tuskeegee Institution "to be used for the purpose of establishing and maintaining a graduate school in agriculture and a graduate school in home economics and such other areas as are deemed feasible and wise in accordance with felt need"; also provides for annual appropriaton of $50,000. to Tuskeegee "to be used for the purpose of establishing and maintaining a graduate school in veterinary medicine."

Provides for appointment of five commissioners as the governing board of Tuskeegee Institute. [1943, p. 202, appvd. June 26, 1943; 1945, p. 86, appvd. June 12, 1945.]

Fair Employment Practices — Joint Resolution against Enactment of F.E.P.C. Legislation

GENERAL ACTS 1945, p. 725

BE IT RESOLVED by the Senate of Alabama, the House concurring: That it has been the boast of Americans that our form of Government permitted local self-government, thereby making it possible for the widely separated sections of our Country to live together in peace and harmony by making allowances for local conditions and situations;

That in Alabama there exist conditions with respect to the relationship between the races which are not general to the Country as a whole as, for instance, that in certain Counties of this State the colored population very greatly exceeds in number the white population;

That the experience of this State in reconstruction times and since has shown that no good can come from changing the normal course of evolution and development of race by arbitrary legal means, and that such attempts lead only to violence, misunderstanding and destruction of the normal and happy relationship now prevailing between the races in this State, and which will continue to prevail here if they are left in peace and harmony to work out their mutual problems;

THEREFORE, BE IT RESOLVED, That we do now call upon our representatives and Senators in the Congress of the United States by every means within their power to oppose the enactment of such Federal Legislation as the so-called Permanent Fair Employment Practice Law, the welfare of Alabama, in our opinion, demanding that they do so.

BE IT FURTHER RESOLVED, That copies of this resolution shall be forwarded to the President of the United States and to the members of Congress from Alabama. (Approved July 6, 1945)

Hospitals

Title 45, §248 — (Mental Deficients) — [Provides that buildings be arranged and equipped so as to facilitate proper classification according to race, sex, color . . .] [Code 1923, §1481.]

Title 45, §4 — (Hospitals for Tubercular Patients) . . . There shall be proper separation of convicts from free persons, whites from blacks, males from females, in such hospital or place of detention. The department [of Corrections and Institutions] shall be given general authority over the reception, care, custody and segregation of such persons . . . [1923, p. 67.]

[Note: No specific statutory provision for segregation in hospitals generally.]

Ku Klux Klan — Masks, wearing of, prohibited.

Acts, 1949, p. 165, Act No. 139, S. 155 — Mize.

AN ACT

To prescribe the wearing of masks in certain cases, and prescribing penalties for violations of this Act.

Be It Enacted by the Legislature of Alabama:

Section 1. No person over sixteen years of age shall appear or enter upon any lane, walk, alley, street, road, public way, or highway of this State or upon the public property of the State or of any municipality or county in this State while wearing a mask or other device which conceals his identity; nor shall any such person demand entrance or admission to, or enter upon the premises or into the enclosure or house of any other person while wearing a mask or device which conceals his identity; nor shall any such person, while wearing a mask or device which conceals his identity, participate in any meeting or demonstration upon the private property of another unless he shall have first obtained the written permission of the owner and the occupant of such property.

Section 2. The provisions of this Act shall not affect the right of any person to appear in public wearing a mask or costume which conceals the wearer's identity while participating in the celebration of a legal holiday.

Section 3. Any person who violates this Act shall be guilty of a misdemeanor and upon conviction shall be punished by a fine of not more than five hundred dollars [$500.00] or by imprisonment in the county jail for a period not to exceed twelve [12] months.

Section 4. The provisions of this Act are severable. If any part is declared unconstitutional or invalid, such declaration shall not affect the remainder.

Section 5. All laws or parts of laws in conflict with this Act are repealed.

Section 6. This Act shall become effective immediately upon its passage and approval by the Governor, or upon its otherwise becoming a law.

Approved June 28, 1949.
Time 12:00 Noon.

Miscegenation

Title 14, §360. **Marriage, adultery, and formication between white persons and negroes.** — If any white person and any negro, or the descendant of any negro intermarry, or live in adultery or fornication with each other, each of them shall on conviction, be imprisoned in the penitentiary for not less than two [2] nor more than seven [7] years. [Code 1923, §5001, as amended Acts 1927, p. 219.]

Title 14, §361. **Officer issuing license or performing marriage ceremony.—** [Penalty for any probate judge who knowingly issues a license for marriage of white person and Negro, and any minister of the gospel, justice of the peace or person authorized by law to solemnize marriage ceremony, who knowingly performs marriage ceremony for white person and Negro — fine of $100 to $1000 or imprisonment for six [6] months, or both. [Code 1923, §5002.]

Nurses

Title 46, §189 (19). [1947 Cum. Supp.] — **White women not to nurse where negro men are patients.** — No person or corporation shall require any white female nurse to nurse in wards or rooms in hospitals, either public or private, in which negro men are placed for treatment, or to be nursed; and no white female nurse shall nurse in wards or rooms in hospitals, either public or private, in which negro men are placed for treatment, or to be nursed. Upon conviction for a violation of this section, the court shall assess a fine of not less than ten ($10.00), nor more than two hundred ($200.00) dollars, and it may also, as an additional punishment, sentence such persons upon conviction, to confinement in the county jail, or to hard labor for the county for a term not exceeding 6 months. [Acts 1915, p. 727; Code 1923, §§5011, 5012; as reenacted Acts 1945, p. 98, §19½, appvd. June 15, 1945.]

Paupers

Title 44, §10 — [Provides for separation of white and Negro inmates of county homes for poor.] [Acts 1927, p. 521.]

Poll Taxes

Title 51, §244. **Separate account by races.** — The tax collector shall keep a separate account of the amount of the poll taxes paid by persons, of each race in each township or separate school district. [Acts 1935, p. 256.]

Prisons

Title 45, §121. **What prisoners kept separate.** — Men and women, except husband and wife, must not be kept in the same room; and white and colored prisoners, before conviction, must also be kept apart, if there be sufficient number of apartments for that purpose. [Code 1923, §4806.]

Title 45, §122 — **Prisoners separated by race and sex.** — It shall be unlawful for any sheriff, or jailer, or other keeper of the jail or the town or city prison, to confine in the same room or apartment of any jail or prison white and negro prisoners; and men and women, except husband and wife, must not be kept in the same room or apartment. [Acts 1911, p. 356; 1923 Code, §4856.]

Title 45, §123 — **Imprisoning together white and colored prisoners before conviction.** — Any jailer or sheriff, having the charge of white and colored prisoners before conviction, who imprisons them permanently together in the same apartment of any jail, or other place of safe keeping, if there is a sufficient number of apartments to keep them separate, must, on conviction, be fined not less than fifty nor more than one hundred dollars. [1923 Code, §3722.]

Title 45, §172. — **Bathing facilities** — [Provision is made for separate bathing facilities for Negro and white prisoners.] [Acts 1911, p. 356; 1923 Code §4866.]

Title 45, §183 **[County jails and City Prisons]** — [Provision is made for separation of Negro and white prisoners at county jails or city prisons.] [1911, p. 356; 1923 Code §4877.]

Title 45, §52. [Convicts] [Unlawful for white and colored convicts to be chained together or to be allowed to sleep together. Provision made for separate prisons for white and colored convicts where possible. [Code 1923, §3643; Acts 1931, p. 166.]

Title 12, §188. County jail; how constructed and arranged. — [Provides for separation of white and colored prisoners at county jail.] [Code 1923, §215.]

Transportation

Title 48, §186. Station Conveniences. — Every railroad company in this state, shall provide . . . adequate depots and depot buildings for the accommodation of passengers . . . and must have sufficient sitting or waiting rooms . . . having regard to sex and race . . . [Code 1923, §9964.]

Motor Transportation

Title 48, §301(31a). [1947 Cum. Supp.] **Separate accommodations for white and colored races.** — All passenger stations in this state operated by any motor transportation company shall have separate waiting rooms or space and separate ticket windows for the white and colored races, but such accommodations for the races shall be equal. All motor transportation companies or operators of vehicles carrying passengers for hire in this state, *whether intrastate or interstate passengers,* shall at all times provide equal but separate accommodations on each vehicle for the white and colored races. The conductor or agent of the motor transportation company in charge of any vehicle is *authorized and required* to assign each passenger to the division of the vehicle designated for the race to which the passenger belong; and, if the passenger refuses to occupy the division to which he is assigned, the conductor or agent may refuse to carry the passenger on the vehicle; and for such refusal, neither the conductor or agent of the motor transportation company nor the transportation company shall be liable in damages. Any motor transportation company or person violating the provisions of this section shall be guilty of a misdemeanor and, upon conviction, shall be fined not more than five hundred [$500.00] dollars for each offense; and each day's violation shall constitute a separate offense.

The provisions of this section shall be administered and enforced by the Alabama public service commission in the manner in which provisions of the Alabama Motor Carrier Act of 1939 are administered and enforced. [1945, p. 731, appvd. July 6, 1945.] (italics added)

Title 48, §§268, 269. [1947 Cum. Supp.] [Repealed by Articles 3 and 4 of Title 48, Chapter 3, §§301(1) to 301(51). This section required separate accommodations for white and colored passengers and provided separate waiting rooms. The provisions of this section, however, were substantially reenacted in Title 48, §301(31a) supra.]

Title 48, §301(31b). [1947 Cum. Supp.] **Operators of passenger stations and carriers are authorized to segregate white and colored races.** — All passenger stations in this state operated by or for the use of any motor transportation company shall be authorized to provide separate waiting rooms, facilities, or space, or separate ticket windows, for the white and colored races but such accommodations for the races shall be equal. All motor transportation companies and operators of vehicles carrying passengers for hire in this state, *whether intrastate or interstate passengers, are authorized and empowered to provide separate accommodations on each vehicle for the white and colored races.* Any officer or agent of such motor transportation company or operator, in charge of any vehicle, is authorized to assign or reassign each passenger or person to a division, section or seat on the vehicle designated by such company or operator, or by such officer or agent, for the race to which the passenger belongs; and if the passenger or person refuses to occupy the division, section or seat to which he is assigned, such officer may refuse further to carry the passenger on the vehicle. For such refusal neither the officer nor agent, nor the motor transportation company, nor operator, shall be liable in damages. (emphasis added.) [1947, p. 40, §1, appvd. July 18, 1947.]

Title 48, §301(31c). [1947 Cum. Supp.] **Failure to comply with rules and regulations as to segregation of white and colored races.** — It shall be unlawful for any person *wilfully to refuse or fail to comply with any reasonable rule, regulation, or directive of any operator of a passenger station in this state* operated by or for the use of any such transportation company, or of any authorized officer or agent of such operator, providing separate waiting rooms, facilities, or space, or separate ticket windows, for white and colored races; *or wilfully to refuse or fail to comply with any reasonable assignment or reassignment by any officer or agent in charge of any vehicle of any such motor transportation company or of any operator of vehicles carrying passengers for hire,* of any passenger or person to a division, section or seat on such vehicle designated by such officer or agent for the race to which such passenger or person belongs; *any person so refusing or failing to comply with any such reasonable rule, regulation or assignment, as aforesaid, shall be guilty of a misdemeanor and upon conviction shall be fined not more than $500.00 for such offense.* (emphasis added) [1947, p. 40, §2, appvd. July 18, 1947.]

[Note on Alabama Motor Transportation statutes: The 1945 Alabama statute on Motor Transportation (General Acts, 1945, p. 731, No. 508) "required and empowered" motor transportation companies operating in Alabama to provide segregated facilities based upon race. This statute, by its terms applied to both interstate and intrastate passengers. Following the enactment of the 1945 statute, the United States Supreme Court decided the case of *Morgan v. Virginia* (1946) 328 U.S. 373, on June 3rd, 1946. The *Morgan* case ruled that provisions of the Virginia Code which *require* the separation of colored and white passengers on both interstate and intrastate motor carriers was invalid as applied to interstate passengers moving interstate. Such statutes were held to be a burden upon interstate commerce contrary to Art. I, Section 8, Cl. 3 of the Constitution of the United States, even though Congress has enacted no legislation on the subject. Mr. Justice Reed, in his opinion, declared, "It seems clear to us that the seating arrangements for the different races in interstate motor travel require a single uniform rule to promote national travel. Consequently, we hold the Virginia statute in controversy invalid." (p. 386.)

Following the *Morgan* decision, Alabama enacted a statute at the

1947 session of the legislature designed to meet the constitutional objections without eliminating segregation of the races. The 1945 statute was not repealed expressly, but was substantially reenacted, except that by its terms it "authorized and empowered" instead of "authorized and required" motor carriers to segregate the races.

While the 1947 statute [§301(31b) *supra*] patently is permissive and not mandatory, yet it would appear to be unconstitutional to the extent that it applies to interstate passengers by virtue of the *Morgan* decision. Similar statutes and state practices permitting carriers by private regulation to segregate Negro and white passengers are being challenged in the federal courts. See *Henderson v. The United States* (1948), 63 F. Supp. 906; 80 F. Supp. 32; (D.C., Md.) on appeal to U.S. Sup. Ct. Docket No. 570, jurisdiction noted March 14,1949; *Day v. Atlantic Greyhound Corp.*, 171 F. 2d. 59 (1948) (U.S. Court of App., 4th Circuit); *Simmons v. Atlantic Greyhound Corp.*, (1947) (75 F. Supp. 166, (D. Court, W.D. Va.) See *Whiteside v. Southern Bus Lines, Inc.* 177 F. 2d 1949 (U.S.C.A.—6th, 1949) which held segregation rule of private carrier as applied to interstate passengers to be invalid.

Railroads—

Title 48, §196 — Separate coaches for whites and blacks. — All railroads carrying passengers in this state, other than street railroads, shall provide equal but separate accommodations for the white and colored races, by providing two or more passenger cars for each passenger train, or by dividing the passenger cars by partitions, so as to secure separate accommodations. [Code 1923, §9968.]

Title 48, §197 — Conductor must assign each passenger a seat in the car designated for his color. — The conductor of each passenger train is authorized and required to assign each passenger to the car or the division of the car, when it is divided by a partition, designated for the race to which such passenger belongs; and if any passenger refuses to occupy the car or the division of the car, to which he is assigned by the conductor, such conductor may refuse to carry such passenger on the train, and for such refusal neither the conductor nor the railroad company shall be liable in damages. *But this section shall not apply to white or colored passengers entering this state upon railroads under contracts for their transportation where like laws to this do not prevail.* (Emphasis added.) [Code 1923, §9969.]

Title 48, §464 — Passenger on railroad riding in coach not designated for his color. — Any person, who, contrary to the provisions of the statute providing for equal and separate accommodations for the white and negro races on railroad passenger trains, rides, or attempts to ride, in a coach, or a division of a coach, designated for the race to which he does not belong, must on conviction, be fined not more than one hundred dollars. [Code 1923, §5365]

Note: This section does not apply to Negro prisoners in custody of white sheriff.

Spenny v. Mobile etc. R. Co. 192 Ala. 483, 485, 68 So. 870.
Mobile etc. R. Co. v. Spenny, 12 Ala. App. 375, 67 So. 740.
The same rule seems applicable to nurse and patient.

ARIZONA

CONSTITUTION

Aliens

Art. 18, §10. [Employment of Aliens.] — No person not a citizen or ward of the United States shall be employed upon or in connection with any state, county or municipal works or employment . . . . [working prisoners excepted] . . . . [Const. 1912]

Indians

Art. 20.

Third. [Sale of intoxicants to Indians.]—The sale, barter, or giving of intoxicating liquors to Indians and the introduction of liquors into Indian country are forever prohibited within this state. [Const. 1912]

Suffrage

Art. 20, §7 . . . The state shall never enact any law restricting or abridging the right of suffrage on account of race, color, or previous condition of servitude. [Const. 1912]

STATUTES

ARIZONA CODE ANNOTATED (1939)

Aliens

Alien Land Law

Secs. 71-201 -71-210. [Alien Ownership] — [Prohibits aliens ineligible to citizenship under the laws of the United States to acquire any interest in real estate unless there is a treaty existing between the United States and the country of which the alien is a citizen which permits such acquisition. Property acquired in violation of the provisions of this statute shall escheat to the state. Conveyances made to avoid escheat are void as to the state, and the taking of property in the name of a person ineligible to citizenship is made *prima facie* evidence of an intent to evade the statute. Persons found guilty of a conspiracy to transfer property in violation of the statute shall be punished by imprisonment up to 2 years or by a fine up to $5,000.00, or both. [Laws 1921, ch. 29, §§1-12, p. 25, rev., R.C., 1928, §§2781-2790a as added by Laws 1933, ch. 58, §1, p. 114.]

[Note: The above statute is almost identical to the California Alien Land Law, 1 Cal. Gen. Laws, Act 261 as amended, which was challenged in *Oyama v. California* (1948) 332 U. S. 633. See note on California Alien Land Law, infra. Such statutes have been enforced most rigorously against alien Japanese residents of the western states.]

Education — Segregation in elementary schools

Secs. 54-416. [Education Code] — **Powers and duties of board of trustees of school districts** — **(Subdivision 2)** — The board shall prescribe and enforce rules not inconsistent with law or those prescribed by the state board of education for their own government and the government of the schools. They shall segregate pupils of the African race from pupils of the Caucasian race in all schools other than high schools, and provide all accommodations made necessary by such

35

segregation. [Laws 1912, ch. 77, sec. 41, p. 364; R.S. 1913, sec. 2733; Laws 1921 ch. 72, sec. 5, p. 144; 1921, ch. 137, sec. 1, p. 304; 1925, ch. 11, sec. 1, p. 26; 1925, ch. 70, secs. 1-4, p. 203; 1927, ch. 88, sec. 1, p. 234; rev., R.C. 1928, sec. 1011; Laws 1933, ch. 18, Sec. 1, p. 30.]

Sec. 54-430. Duration of school — Grouping of pupils. — . . . — [Authorizes Board of Trustees to segregate pupils.] [L. 1912, ch. 77, §54, p. 364; R.S. 1913, §2750; rev. R.C. 1928, §1025.]

[Note: Sec. 54-416 appears to be mandatory with reference to segregation in elementary schools. Under Sec. 54-430 it would appear that segregation of Negro students in high schools is permissive. See below.]

High Schools — Racial Segregation

Sec. 54-918. Racial Segregation. — Whenever there shall be registered in any high school, union high school, or county high school in the state, twenty-five [25] or more pupils of the African race, the board of education of such school shall, upon petition of fifteen [15] per cent of the school electors, as shown by the poll list at the last preceding annual election, residing in the district, call an election to determine whether or not such pupils of the African race shall be segregated from pupils of the Caucasian race. The question to be submitted shall include the estimated cost to the district of such segregation and shall be substantially in the following form: "Are you in favor of segregating the pupils of the African race from the pupils of the Caucasian race on condition that the board of education provide equal accommodations and facilities for pupils of the African race as are now or may be hereafter provided for pupils of the Caucasian race; it being understood that the estimated cost of segregation will be $........................ over and above the cost of maintaining the school without such segregation?" In other respects the election shall be called and conducted as the regular annual school election, except as to the time of holding the election, and that the notices shall state specifically the information necessary for voting intelligently on the question. If a majority of the electors voting at such election vote in favor of such segregation, the board of education shall segregate the pupils of the African race from the pupils of the Caucasian race and provide equal accommodations and facilities for such pupils of the African race as are now or may be hereafter provided for the pupils of the Caucasian race in any such high schools. [Laws 1927, ch. 88, §1, p. 234; rev. R.C. 1928, §1085.]

[Note: Segregation under this statute is dependent upon two factors: (1) a petition by 15 per cent of the voters in each district and (2) a special election at which a majority vote is cast in favor of segregation.]

Indians

43-3101. Furnishing intoxicating liquors to Indians. — Any person who sells or furnishes to any Indian of whole or mixed blood any tulapai, tisiwin or corn beer shall be guilty of a misdemeanor. [Laws 1917, ch. 26, §1, p. 24; R.C. 1928, §4669.]

43-2203. Furnishing firearms to Indians — Penalty. — Any person who sells, gives, rents, barters or furnishes rifles, carbines, pistols or revolvers, or any ammunition or cartridges therefor, or any shot larger in size than standard number six shot, to Indians, shall be guilty of a misdemeanor, and shall be punished by imprisonment in the county jail not less than one [1] nor more than six [6] months, or by a fine not less than fifty [$50.00] nor more than three hundred [$300.00] dollars, or by both such fine and imprisonment. [P.C. 1901, §362; 1913, §409; rev., R.C. 1928, §4710.]

43-5701. Treason — Capacity to commit — Punishment. — Whoever unlawfully levies war against this state or the United States, or the inhabitants of either, or knowingly adheres to the enemies of either, giving them aid or comfort, is guilty of treason against the State of Arizona. All persons, including Indians, who reside in this state are capable of committing treason, and allegiance to the state shall be conclusively presumed from a resident therein upon a trial for treason. The punishment for treason shall be death. [P.C. 1901, §§30, 31, 33; 1913, §30, 31, 33; cons., R.C. 1928, §4492.]

43-5702. Levying war defined. — Levying war against this state or the United States, or the inhabitants of either, may consist of inciting, setting on foot, assisting or engaging in any rebellion, Indian outbreak, or insurrection against the authority of the state or of the United States, or against the authority of the laws of either. [P.C. 1901, §32; 1913, §32; R.C. 1928, §4493.]

Ku Klux Klan — Wearing Masks

43-3701. Wearing mask in intimidating or evading arrest — Penalty. — Every person who shall wear any mask or personal disguise with intent to disturb, annoy, alarm or intimidate any person, or for the purpose of escaping detection or identification in the commission of any public offense, or for the purpose of evading arrest; or who shall organize or assist in organizing, or shall become or remain a member of, any association or organization, the members of which wear masks or personal disguises, whether complete or partial, with the intent or for any of such purposes, shall be guilty of a felony. [Laws 1923, ch. 78, §§1, 2, p. 299; cons. & rev., R.C. 1928, §4729.]

43-3702. Felony to commit misdemeanor while wearing mask — Penalty. — Every act which would otherwise be a misdemeanor, if committed by any person wearing any mask or personal disguise, whether complete or partial, shall be a felony. [Laws 1923, ch. 78, §3, p. 299; rev., R.C. 1928, §4730.]

Miscegenation

63-107 [1947 Cum. Supp.] Void, prohibited and validated marriages. — The marriage of a person of Caucasian blood with a Negro, Mongolian, Malay, or Hindu shall be null and void . . . [R.S. 1901, §§3092, 3093; 1913, §§3837, 3838; cons. and rev., R.C. 1928, §2166; Laws 1931, ch. 17, §1, p. 27; 1942 (1st. S.S.), ch. 12, §1, p. 465.]

> [Note: The 1942 amendment deleted the word "Indians". Prior to the 1942 amendment the sentence read, "The marriage of persons of Caucasian blood, or their decendants, with Negroes, Hindus, Mongolians, members of the Malay race, or Indians, and their descendants shall be null and void."]

ARKANSAS

CONSTITUTION

Equal rights

Art. 2, §3. Equality before the law. — The equality of all persons before the law is recognized, and shall ever remain inviolate; nor shall any citizen ever be deprived of any right, privilege or immunity, nor exempted from any burden or duty, on account of race, color or previous condition. [Const. of 1874.]

Slavery

Art. 2, §27. Slavery. — . . . There shall be no slavery in this State, nor involuntary servitude, except as a punishment for crime . . . [Const. 1874.]

STATUTES

ARKANSAS STATUTES ANNOTATED, 1947.

Aliens

50-301. Capacity of aliens to take and transmit lands. — [Provides all aliens shall be capable of taking, holding and conveying real property by inheritance or otherwise.] [Rev. Stat., ch. 7, §1; Act Dec. 15, 1874, No. 16, §1, p. 60; C. & M. Dig., §258; Pope's Dig., §272.]

50-302. Japanese prohibited from purchasing or holding title to lands.—On or after the effective date of this act, no Japanese or a decendant [descendant] of a Japanese shall ever purchase or hold title to any lands in the State of Arkansas. [Acts 1943, No. 47, §1, p. 74.]

> [Note: The compiler of Arkansas Statutes 1947 Annotated observes that this Act [§§50-302 - 50-305] may be invalid because of Arkansas Const., Art. 2, §20 which provides "No distinction shall ever ˙ made by law, between resident aliens and citizens, in regard to the possession, enjoyment, or descent of property."]

50-303. Prohibition extended to corporations, trustees or agents. — No corporation, trustee, agent or any person whatever shall purchase or own any lands in the State of Arkansas in which a Japanese or a decendant [descendant] of a Japanese is interested directly or indirectly.]Acts 1943, No. 47, §2, p. 74]

50-304. Rentals limited to one year term. — No corporation, trustee, agent or any person whatever shall rent for a term of over one [1] year any lands in Arkansas in which a Japanese or a decendant [descendant] of a Japanese shall be interested directly or indirectly. [Acts 1943, No. 47, §3, p. 74.]

50-305. Sales conveyances or leases in violation void — Ouster. — All sales, conveyances or leases in conflict with this act [§§50-302 - 50-305] shall be absolutely void and of no effect whatever. Provided that any taxpayer in any County in which an attempted sale or lease is located shall have the authority to file suit for the purpose of ousting any pretended purchaser or lessee in violation of this act. [Acts 1943, No. 47, §4, p. 74.]

Concubinage

41-806. — Concubinage — Penalty. — [Concubinage between a person of the Caucasian race and person of Negro or black race is made a felony;

punishable by 1 month to 1 year in penitentiary at hard labor.] [Acts 1911, No. 320, §1, p. 295; C. & M. Dig., §2601; Pope's Dig., §3288.]

41-807. Concubinage — Proof of violation — Definition. — The living together or cohabitation of persons of the Caucasian and of the negro race shall be proof of the violation of the provisions of section one [§41-806] of this act. For the purpose of this act [§§41-806 - 41-810] concubinage is hereby defined to be the unlawful cohabitation of persons of the Caucasian race and of the negro race, whether open or secret. [Acts 1911, No. 320, §2, p. 295; C. & M. Dig., §2602; Pope's Dig., §3289.]

41-809. — Enforcement of concubinage statute. — It shall be the duty of the judges of the several district courts of this State to specially charge the grand juries upon this act [§§41-806 - 41-810], and it shall be the duty of the magistrates of the counties in which the offense of concubinage between a person of the Caucasian race and a person of the negro race has been committed, or where there shall be complaint made to the magistrate that any woman resident in the county who shall have been delivered of a mulatto child, charging on oath any person with being the father of such child, the magistrate shall issue a warrant, in the name of the State, against the accused person to the sheriff or any constable of the county, commanding him forthwith to arrest and bring the accused person before the magistrate to answer such charge and if the magistrate is of opinion that there is not sufficient cause for believing that the defendant has committed the offense as defined by this act, he shall discharge the defendant from custody and make an entry thereof on the minutes, however, if the magistrate be of opinion from the examination that there are reasonable grounds to believe the defendant guilty of the offense charged he shall be held for trial and committed to jail or discharged on bail to answer at the next term of the circuit court. [Acts 1911, No. 320, §4, p. 295; C. & M. Dig. §2604; Pope's Dig. §3291.]

41-810. Delivery of mulatto child as prima facie evidence — Definition.— Any woman who shall have been delivered of a mulatto child, the same shall be prima facie evidence of guilt without further proof and shall justify a conviction of the woman, but no person shall be convicted of the crime of concubinage upon the testimony of the female, unless the same is corroborated by other evidence.

Provided, that this act [§§41-806-41-810] shall apply to cases of concubinage which is here defined to be the keeping and maintaining for immoral purposes persons of the opposite races named in this act. [Acts 1911, No. 320, §5, p. 295; C. & M. Dig. §2605; Pope's Dig., §3292.]

Definition of Negro

41-808. "Person of negro race" defined. — [Statute relating to concubinage, supra, defines "person of negro race" as "any person who has in his or her veins any negro blood whatever."] [Acts 1911, No. 320, §3, p. 295; C. & M. Dig., §2603; Pope's Dig., §3290.]

73-1221 [Railroads] White and African race defined. — Persons in whom there is a visible and distinct admixture of African blood shall, for the purposes of this act, [§§73-1103, 73-1205, 73-1218 - 73-1221], be deemed to belong to the African race; all others shall be deemed to belong to the white race. [Act Feb. 23, 1891, No. 17, §4, p. 15; C. & M. Dig., §996; Pope's Dig., §1200.]

Education

Public Schools — Segregation of races

80-509. Duties and powers of school directors. — . . . The board of school directors of each district in the State shall be charged with the following powers and perform the following duties: . . .

(c) Establish separate schools for white and colored persons.

(d) Employ such teachers and other employees as may be necessary for the proper conduct of the public schools of the district . . .

(d-b) Other employees [other than teachers] may be elected upon written petition of three-fourths of the qualified white electors of the district for white applicants, and upon written petition of three-fourths of the qualified Negro electors of the district for Negro applicants . . . [Acts 1931, No. 169, §97, p. 476; Pope's Dig., §11535; Acts 1939, No. 316, §1, p. 774; 1943, No. 96, §1, p. 139.]

[Note: The above statute is mandatory.]

80-224. Assistant to supervisor. — . . . (A) [Provides that in counties where not less than 30% of the population is colored, the County Board of Education may employ an assistant to the County School Supervisor who shall exercise supervision over the colored teachers and schools in the county.] [Acts 1941, No. 327, §16, p. 838; 1947, No. 332, §1, p. 750.]

Blind and Deaf Pupils

80-2401. [Requires compulsory attendance by blind and deaf minors over 8 years of age at schools provided for them and provides further "that minors of the negro race who come under the requirements of this sction shall be placed in a separate school located at such place or places as may be determined by the State Board of Control."] [Acts 1925, No. 117, §1, p. 354; Pope's Dig., §12900.]

Juvenile Delinquents — Segregation of

46-322. Boys' industrial school for negroes. — [Provides for a Boys' Industrial School for Negroes under the management and control of the Boys' Industrial School of the State of Arkansas.] [Acts 1921, No. 526, §1 p. 559; Pope's Dig., §12939.]

46-323. Separate from white inmates. — Said Boys' Industrial School for Negroes shall be so located, that the inmates thereof shall be separate and apart from the white inmates of the Industrial School, so that the white and negro races shall not associate together, and to that end the same may be located in a different community or a different county from that part of the Industrial School which has already been put into operation for juvenile offenders of the white race. [Acts 1921, No. 526, Sec. 2, p. 559; Pope's Digest, Sec. 12940.]

46-325. Negro Girls' Training School. — [Provides for Negro Girls' Training School for detention and rehabilitation of delinquent Negro girls under management and control of the board of managers of the Negro Boys' Industrial School] [Acts 1945, No. 186, §1, p. 432.]

46-326. Matron and other employees. — [Requires the Superintendent of the Negro Boys' Industrial School to employ a Negro matron and other Negro personnel to operate the Negro Girls' Training School.] [Acts 1945, No. 186, §1, p. 432.]

Colleges, Universities — Segregation of

Agricultural Mechanical & Normal School for Negroes

80-3201 - 80-3215. [Provide for the maintenance and operation of the Agricultural, Mechanical and Normal School for Negroes at Pine Bluffs, Arkansas.] [Act Apr. 25, 1873, No. 97, §§1, 3, 4, p. 231; Act May 8, 1899, No. 145, §2, p. 262; Acts 1927, No. 341, §§2-13, p. 1090; C. & M. Dig. §§9569, 9571, 9572, 9574; Pope's Dig. §§13213, 13215, 13218, 13231 - 13241.]

13-530. A.M. & N. College (Negro) Fund. — The A.M. & N. College (Negro) Fund shall consist of the general revenues provided in section 13[§13-513] of this act, and shall be used for the support, operation and improvement of the State Agricultural, Mechanical & Normal College, and for paying scholarships for Negro students attending institutions of higher learning outside of Arkansas. Provided, that any moneys set aside by law to be used for scholarships of Negro students attending institutions of higher learning outside of Arkansas, may be segregated in the A. M. & N. College (Negro) fund or set aside in a separate account if deemed advisable. The State Comptroller shall have authority to direct the State Treasurer as to the procedure for handling any such funds provided for by the General Assembly. [Acts 1945, No. 311, §30, p. 721; 1947, No. 114, §18, p. 244.]

[Note: §13-513 provides for allocation of $150,000, during each revenue year to A. M. & N. College (Negro) Fund. This statute apparently was designed to meet the requirements laid down in the United States Supreme Court decision of *Missouri v. Gaines* (1938) 305 U.S. 337, which held that if a State furnishes higher education to white residents, it is bound to furnish substantially equal advantages to Negro residents, though not necessarily in the same schools, and that failure to do so is a denial of equal protection guaranteed by the Fourteenth Amendment to the Constitution. However, that case also held that the requirements of equal protection are not satisfied by the opportunities afforded by a State to its Negro citizens for higher education in other states. It would appear, therefore, that this statute does not meet the requirement of equal protection, and can be successfully challenged.

See also *Sipuel v. Board of Regents of U. of Okla.* (1948) 92 U.S. (Lawyers E.) 256, which held that a Negro is entitled

41

to secure legal education afforded by a state institution and that the State must provide it as soon as it does for applicants of any other group.|

Arkansas State Teachers' College

80-2601. [Provides for the establishment and maintenance of the Arkansas State Teachers' College "for the purpose of providing for the preparation and training of white persons, both male and female, citizens of the State and desiring to teach therein."| [Act May 14, 1907, No. 317, §1, p. 762; C. & M. Dig., §9586; Pope's Dig. §13083.|

Employment — Coal Mines

52-625. **Separate wash houses for different races.** — All coal mines operating in this State, shall by partition, or other means, in the discretion of the State Mine Inspector, maintain separate wash houses for whites and blacks. |Acts 1919, No. 134, §5, p. 107; C. & M. Dig., §7291; Pope's Dig., §9347.|

Elections

3-910. — **Voting by different races at certain precincts — Alternate admission** — In precincts in which more than 100 votes were cast at the election next preceding the one then being held, where the electors consist of persons belonging to the different races, the judges of election and the Sheriff in attendance shall, when there are persons of both races present and ready to vote, so conduct admittance to the voting place as to permit persons of the white and colored races to cast their votes alternatively. |Acts Mar. 4, 1891, No. 30, §7, p. 32; C. & M. Dig. §3808, Pope's Dig., §4778.|

3-1501. — [Violation of §3-910 is a misdemeanor] — |Provides that violation of this section |3-910| is punishable as a misdemeanor.| |Act Mar. 4, 1891, No. 30, §44, p. 32; C. & M. Dig., §3889; Pope's Dig. §4883.|

3-227. — [Voting lists] — |Poll tax receipts must state the color of person paying tax. Certified voting lists must record the color of person paying poll tax.| |Init. Measure of 1916, No. 1, §16, Acts 1917, p. 2287; C. & M. Dig. §3777; Pope's Dig., §4745.|

Hospitals

Tuberculosis Sanatorium

7-401. **Establishment of tuberculosis sanatorium for negroes.** — There shall be established at some suitable place in the State of Arkansas, to be selected in the manner hereinafter selected, a tuberculosis sanatorium for the care and treatment of negroes afflicted with tuberculosis. |Acts 1923, No. 113, §1, p. 62; Pope's Dig. 12631.|

7-402. **Name changed to Thomas C. McRae Sanatorium.** — The name of Arkansas Tuberculosis Sanatorium for Negroes be and the same is hereby changed to the Thomas C. McRae Sanatorium. |Acts 1931, No. 50, §1, p. 142; Pope's Dig. 12630.|

7-404. Admission of patients. — Whenever it shall appear to any county judge in the State of Arkansas that a negro residing in said county is afflicted with tuberculosis and has not sufficient funds to provide for his treatment said judge may commit said person to the Arkansas Tuberculosis Sanatorium for Negroes [Thomas C. McRae Sanatorium], provided that such person is accepted by the chief medical officer of such institution. [Acts 1923, No. 113, §9, p. 62; Pope's Dig. 12639.]

Ku Klux Klan — Night Riders

41-2601. Night Riders—Penalty for banding together.—If two [2] or more persons shall unite, confederate or band themselves together for the purpose of doing an unlawful act in the nighttime, or for the purpose of doing any unlawful act while wearing any mask, white caps or robes, or being otherwise disguised, or for the purpose of going forth armed or disguised for the purpose of intimidating or alarming any person, or to do any felonious act, or if any person shall knowingly meet or act clandestinely with any such band or order, be such organization known as night riders, black hand, white caps, or by any other name, they shall each be guilty of a felony, and upon conviction shall be punished by imprisonment in the penitentiary for a term not to exceed five [5] years. [Act April 6, 1909, No. 112, §1, p. 315; C. & M. Dig., §2795; Pope's Dig., §3499.]

41-2602. Acts prohibited—Penalty.—If two [2] or more persons belonging to or acting with any such band or organization as defined in section one [42-2601] of this act shall go forth at night, or shall go forth at any time disguised, and shall alarm or intimidate, or seek to alarm or intimidate, any other person, by assaulting any such person, or by damaging or destroying property, or by seeking to assault or punish any person or by seeking or attempting to damage or destroy property, or who shall deliver, mail, post or leave any letter, notice or other written or printed communication intended to, or which by its nature, contents or superscription would, naturally alarm or intimidate any person, shall be deemed guilty of a felony and upon conviction shall be punished by imprisonment in the penitentiary for a term not to exceed ten [10] years nor to be less than two [2] years, and by a fine of not more than [$5,000.00] five thousand dollars. [Act April 6, 1909, No. 112, §2, p. 315; C. & M. Dig., §2796; Pope's Dig., §3500.]

41-2603. Acts to intimidate — Penalty. — If any person shall by means of any writing, drawing or printed matter, or by any sign or token, such as the delivery of matches or bundles of switches or other things, seek to intimidate, threaten or alarm any person, or shall knowingly be connected either in the preparation or delivery of any such message or token, by saying or intimidating, either in the wording of any such message, or by any signature, or by the nature of the thing left or delivered; or who shall deliver or repeat any verbal message purporting to come from any such organized band or any member or members thereof, which in its substance or nature is intended to intimidate or threaten any person, shall be deemed guilty of a felony and upon conviction shall be confined in the penitentiary for a term of not less than one [1] or more than seven [7] years. [Act April 6, 1909, No. 112, §3, p. 315; C. & M. Dig., §2797; Pope's Dig., §3501.]

41-2604. Death as result of injury or alarm. — If any such secretly organized band, the existence of which is made unlawful by this act [§§41-2601 - 41-2604], or any two [2] or more members thereof acting in the name or authority of any such organization, or any two [2] or more persons pretending to belong to or act for any such organization, shall assault or frighten any person in the night time, or while disguised or armed, or who shall while engaged in any felonious act alarm or injure any person, and such person shall die as a result of such injury or alarm, they shall be deemed guilty of a murder in the first degree and punished as now provided by law; and any person who shall be present aiding, advising, abetting or encouraging any such unlawful act which shall result in the death of any person, as above set out, shall be deemed guilty of murder in the first degree and punished as by law provided. [Act Apr. 6, 1909, No. 112, §4; p. 315; C. & M. Dig., §2798; Pope's Dig., §3502.]

Miscegenation — Marriage and Divorce

55-104. Whites and negroes or mulattoes forbidden to marry. — All marriages of white persons with negroes or mulattoes are declared to be illegal and void. [Rev. Stat. ch. 94, §4; C. & M. Dig., §7039; Pope's Dig., 9019.]

[Note: See §55-110 which provides that "marriages contracted without this State, which would be valid by the laws of the State or country in which the same were consummated, and the parties actually resided, shall be valid in all the courts in this State."]

55-105. Unlawful marriage — Penalty. — [Violation of the above section [§55-104] is a misdemeanor punishable by fine or imprisonment or both. No specific amount of fine or term of imprisonment is set forth in the statute.] [Rev. Stat., ch. 94, §9; C. & M. Dig., §7045; Pope's Dig., §9025.]

34-1206. [Divorces] Race of parties other than caucasian to be shown in complaint — Record. — It shall be the duty of every attorney filing a suit for divorce for any person of a race other than the caucasian or white race, to show upon a complaint the race of the parties to such suit; and it shall be the duty of the clerks of the chancery courts of the State to enter on the record of the proceedings of all divorce cases the race of the parties to such suit. [Acts 1921, No. 179, §§2, 3, p. 246; Pope's Dig. §4387; Acts 1943, No. 145, §1 p. 235.]

55-236. Marriages of negroes and mulattoes validated. — All negroes and mulattoes who are now cohabiting as husband and wife, and recognizing each other as such, shall be deemed lawfully married from the passage of this act, and shall be subject to all the obligations, and entitled to all the rights appertaining to the marriage relation; and in all cases, where such persons now are, or heretofore been so cohabiting, as husband and wife, and may have offspring recognized by them as their own, such offspring shall be deemed in all respects legitimate, as fully as if born in lawful wedlock. [Act Feb. 6, 1867, No. 35, §3, p. 98; C. & M. Dig., §7040; Pope's Dig., §9020.]

[Note: The above statute is typical of statutes passed in the southern states after the Civil War in order to make slave marriages legitimate.]

Prisons

76-1119. Segregation of races. — [Provides "white convicts shall not be required to eat at the same table or sleep with persons of the negro race."] [Acts 1913, No. 306, §20, p. 1238, C. & M. Dig., §5395; Pope's Dig., §7125.]

46-144 — Separation of races — Separate apartments. — in the State penitentiary and in all county jails, stockades, convict camps, and all other places where State or county prisoners may at any time be kept, confined, separate apartments shall be provided and maintained for white and negro prisoners. [Act Mar. 20, 1903, No. 95, §1, p. 160, C. & M. Dig., §9681; Pope's Dig., §12715.]

46-145. Separate furnishings. — Separate bunks, beds, bedding, separate dining tables and all other furnishings, shall be provided and kept by the State and counties, respectively, for the use of white and negro prisoners, and it shall be unlawful for any department of the State penitentiary or any county jail, stockade, convict camp, or any place where State or county prisoners may at any time be kept and confined or for any bunk, bed, bedding or other furnishing, after having been assigned the use of, or having been used by white or negro prisoners, to be changed the one for the use of the other. [Act Mar. 20, 1903, No. 95, §2, p. 106; C. & M. Dig., §9681; Pope's Dig., §12715.]

46-146. Handcuffing white and negro prisoners prohibited. — It shall be unlawful for any white prisoner to be handcuffed or otherwise chained or tied to a negro prisoner. [Act Mar. 20, 1903, No. 95, §3, p. 160; C. & M. Dig., §9682; Pope's Dig., §12716.]

46-147. Separation of races — Penalty for violation. — Any officer, keeper or guard of the State penitentiary or any county jail, stockade, convict camp, or of prisoners kept at any place in this State, who shall violate the provisions of this Act [§§46-144 - 46-147] shall be guilty of a misdemeanor, and upon conviction thereof shall be fined in any sum not less than fifty [$50.00] nor more than two hundred dollars [$200.00]. [Act Mar. 20, 1903, No. 95, §4, p. 160; C. & M. Dig., §9683, Pope's Dig., §12717.]

46-122. [White guards for white convicts] Trusties as guards. — [Provides that in the use of trusties as guards of convicts "none but white men be used to guard white convicts."] [Act June 1, 1909, No. 398, §11, p. 1133; C. & M. Dig., §9696; Pope's Dig., §12728.]

46-128. [Penalty for violation of Sec. 146-122 is fine of $50.00 to $1000.00 and immediate removal from office.] [Act June 1, 1909, No. 398, §10, p. 1133; C. & M. Dig., §9679; Pope's Dig., §12714.]

Race Tracks

84-2724. Track establishments required to segregate races. — [All persons operating race tracks or gaming establishments are required to segregate white and colored races, in seating, betting and all other accommodations.] [Acts 1937, No. 230, §1, p. 826; Pope's Dig. §12473.]

84-2725. Damages not recoverable for ejecting those refusing to sit in designated places. [Where person is ejected for failure to sit in seats so designated, company is not liable in damages.] [Acts 1937, No. 230, §2, p. 826; Pope's Dig. §12474.]

84-2726. Penalty for non-compliance. — [Penalty for failure to comply with statute — misdemeanor punishable by fine up to $500.00.] [Acts 1937, 230, §3, p. 826; Pope Dig. §12475]

Taxes

84-457. Race of taxpayer to be indicated. — [Provides that tax lists and poll tax lists indicate the race of the taxpayer assessed, whether white or colored.] [Act Apr. 19, 1895, No. 122, §1, p. 179; C. & M. Dig. §9917; Pope's Dig., §13679.]

84-458. Compensation withheld for failure of duty. — [Provides that failure of tax officers to comply with provisions of §§84-457- 84-458 is punishable by denial to tax officers the fees and commissions allowed by law.] [Act Apr. 19, 1895, No. 122, §2, p. 179; C. & M. Dig., §9917; Pope's Dig., §13679.]

Transportation

Electric and Street Railroads — Segregation

73-1614. Segregation of races required in cities of first class. — All persons, companies or corporations operating any street car line in any city of the first class, in the State of Arkansas, be and they are hereby required to operate separate cars or to separate the white and colored passengers in the cars operated for both, and to set apart or designate in each car or coach so operated for both a portion thereof, or certain seats therein to be occupied by white passengers, and a portion thereof or certain seats therein to be occupied by colored passengers. [Act Mar. 27, 1903, No. 104, §1, p. 178; C. & M. Dig., §998; Pope's Dig., §1202.]

73-1615. Discrimination in quality or convenience of accommodations prohibited. — No persons, companies or corporations so operating street cars shall make any difference or discrimination in the quality or convenience of the accommodations provided for the two races under the provisions of this act [§§73-1614 - 73-1619]. [Act Mar. 27, 1903, No. 104, §2, p. 178; C. & M. Dig., §999; Pope's Dig., §1203.]

73-1616. Conductor may change seating space or require passenger to change seat. — The conductor or other person in charge of any car or coach so operated upon any street car line shall have the right at any time when in his judgment it may be necessary or proper for the comfort or convenience of passengers so to do, to change the said designation so as to increase or decrease the amount of space or seats set apart for either race; or he may require any passenger to change his seat when or so often as the change in the passengers may make such change necessary. [Act Mar. 27, 1903, No. 104, §3, p. 178; C. & M. Dig., §1000; Pope's Dig., §1204.].

73-1617. Passengers to take designated seats — Penalty for failure. — All passengers on any street car line shall be required to take the seat assigned to them, and any person refusing to do so shall leave the car, or remaining upon the car, shall be guilty of a misdemeanor, and upon conviction shall be fined in any sum not to exceed $25. [Act Mar. 27, 1903, No. 104, §4, p. 178; C. & M. Dig., §1001; Pope's Dig., 1205.]

73-1618. Penalty for non-designation of accommodations. — Any person, company or corporation failing to operate separate cars, or to set apart or designate portions of the cars operated for the separate accommodation of the white and colored passengers as provided by this act [§§73-1614 - 73-1619], shall be guilty of a misdemeanor, and upon conviction, shall be fined in any sum not to exceed $25. [Act Mar. 27, 1903, No. 104, §5, p. 178; C. & M. Dig., §1002; Pope's Dig., §1206.]

73-1619. Extra or special cars for exclusive accommodations of either race. — Nothing in this act [§§73-1614—73-1619] shall be construed to prevent the running of extra or special cars for the exclusive accommodation of either white or colored passengers, if the regular cars are operated as required by this act. [Act Mar. 27, 1903, No. 104, §6, p. 178; C. & M. Dig., §1003; Pope's Dig., §1207.]

Motor Carriers — Segregation

73-1747. Segregation of races in buses. — All persons, firms, companies or corporations operating any motor propelled vehicle for the transportation of passengers over the streets and highways of the State of Arkansas, are hereby required to designate separate seating spaces in such vehicle for the accommodation of white and colored passengers, and shall cause the white and colored passengers to remain segregated in the seats and spaces so designated. [Acts 1937, No. 124, §1, p. 433; Pope's Dig., §6921; Acts 1943, No. 180, §1, p. 379.]

[Note: The compiler notes that this section and §§73-1748 - 73-1753 may be invalid if applied to interstate passengers. See *Morgan v. Virginia* 328 U.S. 373, 90 L. ed. 1317, 66 Sup. Ct. 1050, 165 ALR 574; See also 30 ALR 55.]

73-1748. Designation of seats by posted signs. — Such designation shall be by means of a sign with letters of at least four [4] inches and of sufficient size as to be visible and discernible at all times, which shall be posted in a prominent place at both the front and back of the vehicle and which shall direct that all white passengers shall seat from the front of the vehicle toward the back, and all colored passengers shall seat from the rear of the vehicle forward. [Acts 1937, No. 124, §2, p. 433; Pope's Digest, §6922; Acts 1939, No. 180, §2, p. 379.]

73-1749. Operator may change designation and reseat passengers. — The operator or other person in charge of such vehicle shall have the right and duty, at any time, when it may be necessary or proper in his judgment, for the comfort, convenience or accommodation of the passengers, to change such designation so as to increase or decrease the amount of space or seats set apart for either race, he may request any passenger to change his seat when or so often as the change in passengers may require. [Acts 1937, No. 124, §3, p. 433; Pope's Dig., §6923; 1943, No. 180, §3, p. 379.]

73-1750. Discrimination in service prohibited. — No person, firms, companies, or corporations so operating motor propelled passenger-carrying vehicles shall maintain any difference or discrimination in the quality or convenience of the accommodations provided for the two races hereunder. [Acts 1937, No. 124, §4, p. 433, Pope's Digest; §6924; Acts 1943, No. 180, §4, p. 379.]

73-1751. Passengers to take seat assigned — Penalty for refusal. — All passengers on any motor-propelled passenger-carrying vehicle shall be required to take a seat or space assigned to them, and any person refusing to do so shall immediately leave the vehicle, or if he remains on the vehicle, he shall be guilty of a misdemeanor, and upon conviction shall be fined in any sum not less than $25.00 or more than $500.00, or sentenced to the county jail for not less than one [1] month or more than six [6] months, or by both fine and imprisonment. Upon refusal of any passenger to leave the vehicle as aforesaid, the operator or person in charge shall proceed to the nearest town, city, hamlet, or village, and thereupon it shall be the duty of the operator or other person in charge of such vehicle to make complaint to the first available peace officer, whose duty it shall be to remove said passenger and subject him to arrest. The failure on the part of the operator or other person in charge of such vehicle to cause the white and colored passengers to take and remain in the seats and spaces provided for them, or the failure of such operator or other person in charge of such vehicle to immediately cause the arrest of any passenger refusing to comply with the request to take or remain in the seat and space so designated, shall be deemed a misdemeanor, and upon conviction, such operator or other person shall be fined in any sum not less than $25.00 or more than $500.00. [Acts 1937, No. 124, §5, p. 433; Pope's Dig., §6925; Acts 1943, No. 180, §5, p. 379.]

[Note: This statute was amended in 1943 to increase the maximum penalty from $100 to $500 and to add the words "or space."]

73-1752. Failure to separate races on bus line — Penalty. — Any person, firm, company or corporation failing to designate portions of motor vehicles for separate accommodations of white and colored passengers as provided by this act [Secs. 73-1747 - 73-1753], or who shall fail or refuse to require the operator or other person in charge of such motor vehicle, as their employee, to cause the white and colored passengers to take and remain in the seats and spaces designated for them, or who fails to require the operator or other person in charge of such vehicle in their employ to cause an immediate arrest of any passenger refusing to take and remain in the seat or space assigned to him, shall be guilty of a misdemeanor ,and shall be fined in any sum not less than $25.00 or more than $500.00; any person, firms, companies or corporations failing or refusing to comply with the provisions of this act shall be liable for any damage to persons or property arising out of any disturbance caused by the failure to enforce the segregation of white and colored passengers. [Acts 1937, No. 124, §6, p. 433; Pope's Dig., §6926; Acts 1943, No. 180, §6, p. 379.]

73-1753. [Provides that this statute [§§73-1747 - 73-1753] is not to be construed so as to prevent the use of extra or special busses for the exclusive accommodation of either race. Act does not apply to Motor Coaches operated in lieu of street cars on city streets.] [Acts 1937, No. 124, §7, p. 433; Pope's Dig., §6927; Acts 1943, No. 180, §7, p. 379.]

Railroads — Segregation

73-1218. Separation of white and African races — Equality of accommodations — Street cars excepted — Passengers to occupy seats assigned — Officers in charge of prisoners — Exceptions — Separate sleeping and chair cars — Division by partition on short lines. — All railway companies carrying passengers in this State shall provide equal but separate and sufficient accommodations for the white and African races by providing two or more passenger coaches for each passenger train; provided, each railway company carrying passengers in this State may carry one partitioned car, one end of which may be used by white passengers and the other end by passengers of the African race, said partition to be made of wood, and they shall also provide separate waiting rooms of equal and sufficient accommodations for the two races at all their passenger depots in this State; provided, that this section shall not apply to street railroads; and provided further, that in the event of the disabling of a passenger coach, or coaches, by accident or otherwise, said company shall be relieved from the operation of this act [§§73-1103, 73-1205, 73-1218 - 73-1221] until its train reaches a point at which it has additional coaches. No person or persons shall be permitted to occupy seats in coaches or waiting rooms other than the ones assigned to them on account of the race to which they belong; provided, officers in charge of prisoners of different races may be assigned with their prisoners to coaches where they will least interfere with the comfort of other passengers; provided, further, that it [this section] shall not apply to employees of a train in the discharge of their duties, nor shall it be construed to apply to such freight trains as carry passengers; provided that carriers may haul sleeping or chair cars for the exclusive use of either the white or African race separately, but not jointly; provided further, than [that] on all lines of railway less than thirty [30] miles long, passenger coaches may be divided by partition. [Act Feb. 23, 1891, No. 17, §1, p. 15; Apr. 1, 1893, No. 114, §1, p. 200; C. & M. Dig., §§986-990; Pope's Dig., §§1190-1194.]

73-1219. — [Penalty for entering unassigned accommodation] — [Fine of $10 to $200. Officer of railroad company assigning person to compartment for other race may be fined $25.00. For refusal to occupy assigned coach, person may be ejected and the railroad company shall not be liable in damages for such ejectment.] [Act Feb. 23, 1891, No. 17, §2, p. 15; C. & M. Dig., §§991-993; Pope's Dig., §§1195-1197.]

73-1220. Failure or refusal to comply with act — Penalty — Posting of law. — [Failure or refusal of railroad company to comply with the act is a misdemeanor, punishable by fine of $100 to $500 for every day of failure to comply. Train employee's failure to comply is punishable by fine of $25 to $50 for each offense. All railroad carriers in the State, other than street railroads, are required to post this law up in a conspicuous place in each passenger coach and waiting-room. *Exception*: Officers accompanying prisoners may be assigned the coach or room to which the prisoners belong by reason of race.] [Act Feb. 23, 1891, No. 17, §3, p. 15; C. & M. Dig., §§994-995; Pope's Dig., §§1198-1199.]

73-1221. White and African races defined. — [Definition of white and African race — see above.] [Act Feb. 23, 1891, No. 17, §4, p. 15, C. & M. Dig., §996; Pope's Dig., §1200.]

CALIFORNIA

CONSTITUTION

Aliens

Art. I, Sec. 17, Rights of Aliens. — Foreigners of the white race, or of African descent, eligible to become citizens of the United States under the naturalization laws thereof, while bona fide residents of this State, shall have the same rights in respect to the acquisition, possession, enjoyment, transmission, and inheritance of all property, other than real estate, as native born citizens; provided, that such aliens owning real estate at the time of the adoption of this amendment may remain such owners; and provided further, that the Legislature may, by statute, provide for the disposition of real estate which shall hereafter be acquired by such aliens by descent or devise. [Const. 1879, as amended by amendment adopted November 6, 1894.]

Slavery

Art. 1, Sec. 18. — Neither slavery nor involuntary servitude, unless for the punishment of crime, shall ever be tolerated in this state. [Const. 1879]

STATUTES

Deering's California Codes

Aliens

Alien Land Law [Alien Property Initiative Act of 1920]

1 California General Laws, Act 261 [Deering 1947 Supp.]
§§1-14. — [This statute as amended forbids aliens ineligible for American citizenship to acquire, own, occupy, lease, or transfer agricultural land. It provides that any property acquired in violation of the statute shall escheat to the State as of the date of acquisition. It further provides that every transfer of real property made "with intent to prevent, evade or avoid escheat" shall be void. Where an alien ineligible for citizenship pays the consideration for a transfer of real property, the statute raises a *prima facie* presumption that the transfer has been made with intent to evade the statute.] [Submitted by initiative and approved by electors November 2, 1920, Stats. 1921, p. lxxxiii; Amended by Stats. 1923, p. 1020; Stats. 1927, p. 880; Stats. 1943, ch. 1003, 1059; Stats. 1945, chs. 1129, 1136.]

[Note: The above statute was directed against alien Japanese and other Orientals ineligible for citizenship under the Federal naturalization laws. The statute was successfully challenged in the case of *Oyama v. California*, 332 U.S. 633, decided by the United States Supreme Court on January 19, 1948. In that case it was held that the California Alien Land Law, as applied to the *Oyama* case resulting in an escheat to the State of some agricultural lands recorded in the name of a minor American citizen of Japanese descent because they had been paid for by his father, a Japanese alien ineligible for citizenship, deprived the son of the equal protection of the laws and of his privileges as an American citizen, in violation of the Fourteenth Amendment to the Constitution of the United States and Revised Statutes §1978, 8 U.S.C. §42.

In its opinion the Supreme Court reaffirmed the general rule, "Distinctions between citizens solely because of their ancestry are by their very nature odius to a free people whose institutions are founded upon the doctrine of equality." (p. 646.) See *Hirabayashi v. United States* (1943), 320 U.S. 81, 100.

The Supreme Court did not decide whether the California Alien Land Law denies ineligible aliens equal protections of the laws, but the effect of the *Oyama* case is to weaken considerably the Alien Land Laws directed toward alien resident Japanese and other Orientals ineligible for citizenship in the United States. More recently, the California District Court of Appeals, Division 2, an intermediate appellate court, invalidated the California Alien Land Law on the ground that it was in conflict with and was superseded by the United Nations Charter. See *New York Times,* April 26, 1950, p. 16.]

Commercial Fishing Licenses
[Fish and Game Code, 1949 Supp.]

§990. Persons required to procure license: To whom issuable. — Every person who uses or operates or assists in using or operating any boat, net, trap, line, or other appliance to take fish, mollusks or crustaceans for profit, or who brings or causes fish, mollusks or crustaceans to be brought ashore at any point in the State for the purpose of selling the same in a fresh state, shall procure a commercial fishing license.

A commercial fishing license may be issued to any person. A commercial fishing license may be issued to a corporation only if said corporation is authorized to do business in this State. [As amended by Stats. 1945, ch. 181, §3; Stats. 1949, Ch. 200, §1, Assembly Bill 882, Appvd. May 11, 1949.]

[Note: Before the 1949 amendment, Sec. 990 provided "A commercial fishing license may be issued to any person *other than a person ineligible to citizenship.*" (italics supplied.) In the case of *Takahashi v. Fish and Game Commission*, 334 U.S. 410, decided by the United States Supreme Court on June 7th, 1948, it was held that Section 990 of the California Fish and Game Code which barred issuance of commercial fishing licenses to persons "ineligible to citizenship" and thus prevented a resident alien Japanese from earning his living as a commercial fisherman in the coastal waters off California is invalid under the Constitution and laws of the United States. Following this decision, the section was revised and the prohibition eliminated.]

§990.1. Application: Requisites. — The application for a commercial fishing license shall contain a statement of the applicant's age, height, and weight, a description of his complexion and color of eyes and hair, and a statement as to whether or not he is a citizen of the United States, and, if not, the name of the country of which he is a citizen. [Added by Stats. 1941, ch. 412, §2, p. 1695; as amended by Stats. 1949, ch. 200, §1, Assembly Bill 882, Appvd. May 11, 1949.]

Real Estate Brokers

[Business and Professional Code, 1949 Supp.]

§10150.5 [Licenses] — The commissioner shall not grant an original real estate broker's license to any person who is not a citizen of the United States.

This section shall not affect the right of a noncitizen now holding a real estate broker's license to renewal or reinstatement of his license in accordance with the provisions of this chapter. [As amended by Stats. 1949, ch. 826, §1, S.B. No. 726, appvd. July 5, 1949.]

Civil Rights

See Public Accommodation.

Civil Service

[Government Code, 1945 Supp.]

§19702. **Sex race, or marital status.** — A person shall not be discriminated against under this part because of sex, race or marital status . . . [Added, Stats. 1945, ch. 123, §1.]

§19704. **Political or religious opinions or affiliations.** — It is unlawful to require, permit or suffer any notation or entry to be made upon or in any application, examination paper or other paper, book, document, or record used under this part indicating or in any wise suggesting or pertaining to the race, color, or religion of any person. [Added Stats. 1945, ch. 123, §1.]

Statutes 1949, Chapter 1578

[Assembly Bill No. 2636]

An act to prohibit the inclusion of questions relative to race or religion in application blanks or forms.

[Approved by Governor August 2, 1949. Filed with Secretary of State August 2, 1949.]

The people of the State of California do enact as follows:

SECTION 1. The inclusion of any question relative to an applicant's race or religion in any application blank or form required to be filled in and submitted by an applicant to any department, board, commission, officer, agent or employee of this State, is hereby prohibited.

Any person who violates this section is guilty of a misdemeanor.

SECTION 2. Any provision of law which is inconsistent with this act is hereby repealed.

Education

[Education Code, 1949 Supp.]

§§8003, 8004. — **Schools for Indian children, and children of Chinese, Japanese, or Mongolian parentage: Establishment: Same: Admission of children into other schools.** — [Repealed by Statutes, 1947, Ch. 737, §1, p. 1792. These sections provided for separate schools for Indian children, and children of Chinese, Japanese, or Mongolian parentage, and denied such children admission to other schools.]

[Note: The above sections were enacted in 1943, but were repealed in 1947 following a decision of the United States Court of Appeals for the Ninth Circuit, holding the segregation of children of Mexican descent in California schools to be an unconstitutional act in violation of the Fourteenth Amendment to the Constitution of the United States. See *Westminster School District of Orange County v. Mendez*, 161 F. (2nd.) 774, decided April 14, 1947.]

[Education Code, 1944]

§8271. Reflection upon citizens because of race, color, or creed. — No teacher in giving instruction, nor entertainments permitted in or about any school, shall reflect in any way upon citizens of the United States because of their race, color, or creed. [Enacted 1943. Based on former Sch. C. §3.50; Pol. C. §1666, as amend. by Code Amd'ts. 1880, ch. 44, §30, p. 39; Stats. 1893, ch. 193, §36, p. 254; Stats. 1901, ch. 238, §2, p. 797; Stats. 1925, ch. 276, §2, p. 460.]

[Education Code, 1944]

§8272. Same: In textbook, chart, or other means of instruction. — No textbook, chart, or other means of instruction adopted by the State, county, city, or city and county boards of education for use in the public schools shall contain any matter reflecting upon citizens of the United States because of their race, color, or creed. [Enacted 1943. Based on former Sch. C.§3:51; Pol. C. §1666, as amend. by Code Amd'ts. 1880, ch. 44, §30, p. 39; Stats. 1893, ch. 193, §36, p. 254; Stats. 1901, ch. 238, §2, p. 797; Stats. 1925, ch. 276, §2, p. 460.]

[Education Code, 1944]

§14123. Questions as to, or discrimination because of political or religious opinions, etc. [race]. — No questions relating to political or religious opinions, affiliations, race, color, or marital status shall be asked of any candidate whose name has been certified for appointment, nor shall any discrimination be exercised therefor. [Enacted 1943. Based on former Sch. C. §5.798, 4th sent. 3rd par., as added by Stats. 1935, ch. 618, §1, p. 1748.]

Indians

[Penal Code, 1947 Supp.]

§397. Sale or furnishing of liquor to habitual drunkard, Indian, or person adjudged incompetent. — Every person who sells or furnishes, or causes to be sold or furnished, intoxicating liquors to any habitual or common drunkard, or to any Indian of whole blood, or to any person who has been adjudged legally incompetent or insane by any court of this State and has not been restored to legal capacity, knowing such person to have been so adjudged, is guilty of a misdemeanor. [Enacted 1872; Am. Code Amdts. 1873-74, p. 462; Stats. 1893, p. 98; Stats. 1897, p. 29; Stats. 1901, p. 460 (unconstitutional); Stats. 1903, p. 93; Stats. 1915, p. 341; Stats. 1939, p. 2839; Stats. 1943, ch. 490, §1.]

Innkeepers and [Common] Carriers

[Penal Code, 1949]

§365. Innkeepers and [common] carriers refusing to receive guests and

passengers. — Every person, and every agent or officer of any corporation carrying on business as an innkeeper, or as a common carrier of passengers, who refuses, without just cause or excuse to receive and entertain any guest, or to receive and carry any passenger, is guilty of a misdemeanor. [Enacted 1872.]

[Note: This statute is not strictly a measure directed against discrimination because of race or color, but it may be argued that refusal to entertain a guest or to carry a passenger because of race or color is refusal without just cause and within the prohibitions of the statute.]

Ku Klux Klan — Wearing Mask

[Penal Code, 1949]

§185. [Wearing mask or disguise for unlawful purpose.] — It shall be unlawful for any person to wear any mask, false whiskers, or any personal disguise (whether complete or partial) for the purpose of:

One: Evading or escaping discovery, recognition, or identification in the commission of any public offense.

Two: Concealment, flight or escape, when charged with, arrested for, or convicted of, any public offense. Any person violating any of the provisions of this section shall be guilty of a misdemeanor. [Added by Code Amdts. 1873-74, p. 426.]

[General Laws, Act. 4707.]

§1. Limitation on right to wear masks. — It shall be unlawful for any person, either alone or in company with others, to appear on any street or highway, or in other public places or any place open to view by the general public, with his face partially or completely concealed by means of a mask or other regalia or paraphernalia, with intent thereby to conceal the identity of such person; provided, however, that this act shall not be construed to prohibit the wearing of such means of concealment in good faith for the purposes of amusement, entertainment or in compliance with any public order. [Stats. 1923, p. 316.]

§2. Penalty for violation. — Every person violating any of the provisions of this act shall be deemed guilty of a misdemeanor. [Stats. 1923, p. 316.]

Miscegenation

[Civil Code, 1949]

§60. [Marriages of white and other persons.] — All marriages of white persons with Negroes, Mongolians, members of the Malay race, or mulattoes are illegal and void. [Enacted 1872; Amended by Stats. 1905, p. 554; Stats. 1933, p. 561.]

[Civil Code, 1949]

§69. License . . . — [Requires marriage license to show whether parties are white, Mongolian, Negro, Malayan or mulatto and provides "no license may be issued authorizing the marriage of a white person with a Negro, mulatto, Mongolian, or member of the Malay race . . ." [Am. Stats. 1943, ch. 341, §1, Effective May 5, 1943; Stats. 1945, ch. 602, §1; Stats. 1949, ch. 729, §1.]

[Note: The above sections on miscegenation were declared unconstitutional by the California Supreme Court on October 1, 1948. See Justice Roger Traynor's opinion for excellent discussion of the history of California's anti-miscegenation statutes in *Perez v. Sharp* (also cited as *Perez v. Lippold*), 32 Cal. 2nd. 711, 198 P. (2nd) 17. The court found the above sections to be "not only too vague and uncertain to be enforceable regulations of a fundamental right, but they violate the equal protection of the laws clause of the United States Constitution by impairing the right of individuals to marry on the basis of race alone and by arbitrarily and unreasonably discriminating against certain racial groups."]

[Health and Safety Code, 1949 Supp.]

§10526. Form and contents of certificate. [Marriage Registration] — The form of certificate . . . shall contain . . . (b) The race, color, age, name, and surname, birthplace and residence of the parties married. [Amended by Stats. 1947, ch. 1148, §4; Stats. 1949, ch. 729, §4.]

Military

[Military & Veterans Code, 1949 Supp.]

§130. Members of militia not to be segregated or discriminated against on basis of race or color: Declaration of policy. — Members of the militia of the State shall not be segregated on the basis of race or color, nor discriminated against on such basis in enlistments, promotions, or commissions.

It is hereby declared to be the policy of the State of California that there shall be equality of treatment and opportunity for all members of the militia of the State without regard to race or color. Such policy shall be put into effect in the militia by rules and regulations to be issued by the Governor with due regard to the powers of the Federal Government which are, or may, be exercised over all the militia of the State, and to the time required to effectuate changes without impairing the efficiency or morale of the militia. [Added by Stats. 1949, Ch. 948, §1, A.B. No. 807, appvd. July 18, 1949.]

National Defense

[Joint Resolution No. 3, filed December 22, 1941, (California Statutes 1943, Ch. 19, p. 58), called upon President and Congress of the United States "to prevent any and all racial discriminations in the National Defense Program, including admittance into the armed forces, employment in defense industries and with governmental agencies, and in the vocational training program . . . "]

Public Accommodation

[Civil Code, 1949]

§51. [Rights of citizens in places of public accommodation or amusement.] All citizens within the jurisdiction of this State are entitled to the full and equal accommodations, advantages, facilities and privileges of inns, restaurants, hotels, eating-houses, places where ice cream or soft drinks of any kind are sold for consumption on the premises, barber shops, bath houses, theatres, skating rinks, public conveyances and all other places of public accommodation or amusement, subject only to the conditions and limitations established by law, and applicable alike to all citizens. [Added by Stats. 1905, p. 553; Amended by Stats. 1919, p. 309; Stats. 1923, p. 485.]

§52. [Denial of accommodations; Discrimination; Liability in damages.] Whoever denies to any citizen, except for reasons applicable alike to every race or color, the full accommodations, advantages, facilities, and privileges enumerated in section fifty-one of this code, or who aids, or incites, such denial, or whoever makes any discrimination, distinction or restriction on account of race, or except for good cause, applicable alike to citizens of every color or race whatsoever, in respect to the admission of any citizen to, or his treatment in, any inn, hotel, restaurant, eating house, place where ice cream or soft drinks are sold for consumption on the premises, barber shop, bath house, theatre, skating rink, public conveyance, or other public place of amusement or accommodation, whether such place is licensed or not, or whoever aids or incites such discrimination, distinction or restriction, for each and every such offense is liable in damages in an amount not less than one hundred dollars [$100] which may be recovered in an action at law brought for that purpose. [Added by Stats. 1905, p. 553; Amended by Stats. 1919, p. 309; Stats. 1923, p. 485.]

§53. [Admittance to places of amusement, etc., on presentation of ticket, or price of ticket: Exceptions.] It is unlawful for any corporation, person, or association, or the proprietor, lessee, or the agents of either, or any opera house, theatre, melodeon, museum, circus, caravan, race-course, fair or other place of public amusement or entertainment, to refuse admittance to any person over the age of twenty-one years, who presents a ticket of admission acquired by purchase, or who tenders the price thereof for such a ticket, and who demands admission to such place. Any person under the influence of liquor, or who is guilty of boisterous conduct, or any person of lewd or immoral character, may be excluded from any such place of amusement. [Added by Stats. 1905, p.554.]

§54. [Violation of right of admission to places of amusement; Damages.] Any person who is refused admission to any place of amusement contrary to the provisions of the last preceding section, is entitled to recover from the proprietor, lessee, or their agents, or from any such person, corporation, or association, or the directors thereof, his actual damages, and one hundred dollars in addition thereto. [Added by Stats. 1905, p. 554.]

Public Works

[Labor Code]

§1735. Race color or religious discrimination; Penalties — No discrimination shall be made in the employment of persons upon public works because of the race, color or religion of such persons and every contractor for public works violating this section is subject to all the penalties imposed for a violation of this chapter. [Added by Stats. 1939, ch. 643, §1, p. 2068.]

Welfare and Institutions

Welfare and Institutions Code. [1947 Supp.] §19. **Purpose of Code; Legislative Intent.** — . . . . It is the legislative intent that [public] assistance shall be administered promptly and humanely, with due regard for the preservation of family life, and without discrimination on account of race, religion, or political affiliation; and that assistance shall be so administered as to encourage self-respect, self-reliance, and the desire to be a good citizen, useful to society. [Added by Stats. 1947, ch. 161, §1.]

COLORADO

Aliens

Art. II, §27. Property rights of aliens. — Aliens, who are or may hereafter become bona fide residents of this state, may acquire, inherit, possess, enjoy and dispose of property, real and personal, as native born citizens. [Const. 1876]

Art. IX, §8. Religious test and race discrimination forbidden; sectarian tenets. — No religious test or qualification shall ever be required of any person as a condition of admission into any public educational institution of the State, either as a teacher or student; and no teacher or student of any such institution shall ever be required to attend or participate in any religious service whatever. *No sectarian tenets or doctrines shall ever be taught in the public schools, nor shall any distinction or classification of pupils be made on account of race or color.* [Const. 1876.] (italics supplied)

Slavery

Art. II, §26. Slavery prohibited. — There shall never be in this state either slavery or involuntary servitude, except as punishment for crime, whereof the party shall have been duly convicted. [Const. 1876.]

STATUTES

COLORADO STATUTES ANNOTATED 1935

Attorneys at Law — Chapter 14

§5. Race or sex not to disqualify. — No person shall be denied a license to practice as aforesaid on account of race or sex. [L. '97, p. 115, §3; R.S. '08, §233; C.L., §6001.]

Civil Rights — Public Accommodation — Chapter 35

§1. Equality of privileges of all persons. — All persons within the jurisdiction of said state shall be entitled to the full and equal enjoyment of the accommodations, advantages, facilities and privileges of inns, restaurants, eating houses, barber shops, public conveyances on land or water, theatres, and all other places of public accommodation and amusement, subject only to the conditions and limitations established by law and applicable alike to all citizens. [L. '95, p. 139, §1, R.S. '08, §609; C.L., §4128.]

[Note: This section has been held to include boot blacking stands. *Darius v. Apostolos*, 68 Colo. 323, 327, 190, P.510, 10 A. L. R. 986.]

§2. Penalty and civil liability. — Any person who shall violate any of the provisions of the foregoing section by denying to any citizen, except for reasons applicable alike to all citizens of every race and color, and regardless of color or race, the full enjoyment of any of the accommodations, advantages, facilities or privileges in said section enumerated, or by aiding or inciting such denial, shall for every such offense forfeit and pay a sum of not less than fifty (50) dollars nor more than five hundred (500) dollars to the person aggrieved thereby, to be recovered in any court of competent jurisdiction in the county where said offense was committed; and shall also for every such offense be deemed guilty of a misdemeanor; and, upon conviction thereof, shall be fined in any sum not less than ten (10) dollars, or more than three hundred (300) dollars, or shall be imprisoned not more than one year, or both; provided, further, that a judgment in favor of the party aggrieved, or punishment upon an indictment or information shall be a bar to either prosecution, respectively. [L. '95, p. 139, §2, R. S. '08, §610; C. L., §4129.]

[Note: Aggrieved person may pursue a civil or a criminal remedy, but a judgment in one bars action on the other.]

§3. Jurisdiction of justice of peace. Trial — [Confers jurisdiction on justices of peace in county where civil rights violation occurred to hear civil actions for damage; gives parties right of trial by jury and appeal as in other civil actions.] [L. '95, p. 140, §3; R.S. '08, §611; C.L. §4130.]

§4. Appeal to county court. — [Civil rights case may be appealed from justice of peace to the county court where it shall be tried over again from the beginning. County court may render judgment for an amount exceeding jurisdiction of justice of peace. Plaintiff must file a complaint in the county court within 30 days after the transcript is filed in county court to which appeal is taken and the case shall proceed as an original action brought in such court.] [L. '95, p. 140, §4; R.S. '08, §612; C.L. §4131.]

§5. Appeal not dismissed without consent of plaintiff. — [So provides.] [L. '95, p. 141, §5; R.S. '08, §613; C.L., §4132.]

Civil Rights — Discriminatory Publication — Chapter 35

§6. Public accommodations — Publishing of discriminatory matter forbidden. — No person, being the owner, lessee, proprietor, manager, superintendent, agent, or employee of any place of public accommodation, resort or amusement shall directly or indirectly, by himself or anybody else, publish, issue, circulate, send, distribute, give away or display in any way, manner, shape, means, or method, except as hereinafter provided, any communication, paper, poster, folder, manuscript, book, pamphlet, writing, print, letter, notice or advertisement of any kind, nature or description, intended or calculated to discriminate or actually discriminating against any religious sect, creed, denomination or nationality, or against any of the members thereof in matter of furnishing or neglecting or refusing to furnish to them or any one of them, any lodgings, housing, schooling, tuition, or any accommodations, right, privilege, advantage or convenience offered to or enjoyed by the general public, or to the effect that any of the accommodations, rights, privileges, advantages or conveniences of any such place of public accommodation, resort or amusement shall or will be refused, withheld from or denied to any person or persons or class of persons on account of race, sect, creed, denomination or nationality, or that the patronage, custom, presence, frequenting, dwelling, staying or lodging at such place of any person, persons, or class of persons belonging to or purporting to be of any particular race, sect, creed, denomination or nationality, is unwelcome, objectionable, or not acceptable, desired or solicited. [L. '17, p. 163, §1; C.L. §4133.]

§7. Presumptive Evidence. — The production of any such communication, paper, folder, manuscript, book, pamphlet, writing, print, letter, notice or advertisement, purporting to relate to any such place and to be made by any person being the owner, lessee, proprietor, agent, superintendent, manager or employee thereof, shall be presumptive evidence in any civil or criminal action or prosecution that the same was authorized by such person. [L. '17, p. 164, §2; C.L., §4134.]

§8. **Places of public accommodation resort or amusement.** — A place of public accommodation, resort or amusement, within the meaning of sections 6 to 10 of this chapter, shall be deemed to include any inn, tavern, or hotel, whether conducted for the entertainment, housing or lodging of transient guests, or for the benefit, use or accommodation of those seeking health, recreation or rest, any restaurant, eating house, public conveyance on land or water, bath house, barber shop, theatre and music hall. [L. '17, p. 164, §3; C.L., §4135.]

§9. **Exceptions.** — Nothing contained in the three preceding sections shall be construed to prohibit the mailing of a private communication in writing sent in response to specific written inquiry. [L. '17, p. 164, §4; C.L., §4136.]

§10. **Violation of sections; Penalty.** — Any person who shall violate any of the provisions of the four preceding sections, [§§6, 7, 8, 9,] or who shall aid in or incite, cause or bring about in whole or in part the violation of any of such provisions, shall for each and every violation thereof be deemed guilty of a misdemeanor, and upon conviction thereof, shall be fined not less than one hundred dollars ($100.00) nor more than five hundred dollars ($500.00), or shall be imprisoned not less than thirty (30) days, nor more than ninety (90) days, or both such fine and imprisonment. [L. '17, p.164, §5; C.L., §4137.]

Housing — Buildings — Zoning
Buildings — Chapter 26

§25. **Racial restrictions.** — This article shall not be construed, in the case of any municipality, to confer or enlarge any authority or power to establish any restriction based upon race or color. [L. '23, p. 654, §10.]

Insurance

C. 87, §274. [1947 Cum. Supp.] **Discrimination prohibited.** — [Prohibits discrimination between individuals of substantially the same hazard in premium rates charged for or benefits payable under insurance policies by sickness and accident insurance companies.] [L. 1947, p. 610, §11.]

[Note: While the above section does not refer to race or color, it may be argued that such a statute may be invoked to prevent discrimination by reason of race, color or religion. While not included in this study, most of the state insurance codes contain non-discrimination clauses of the type summarized above.]

Miscegenation — Ch. 107

§2. **What marriages prohibited; Color.** — [Provides all marriages between Negroes and mulattoes; of either sex, and white persons, are declared to be absolutely void.] [G.S., §2248; L. '83, p. 243, §1; amending G.L. §1736; R.S., p. 452, §2; R.S. '08, §4163; C.L. §5548.]

§3. Penalty for violation of above sections. — Whosoever shall knowingly contract marriage in fact, contrary to the prohibitions in the preceding section, and whosoever shall knowingly solemnize any such marriage, shall be deemed guilty of a misdemeanor, and upon conviction, shall be punished by a fine of not less than fifty ($50.00) nor more than five hundred ($500.00) dollars, or imprisonment of not less than three months nor more than two years, or both, at the discretion of the court which shall try the cause. [G.S. §2249; G.L. §1737; R.S., p. 452, §3; R.S. '08, §4164; C.L., §5549.]

[Note: Apparently if persons marry interracially in other states where such marriages are valid, the marriage will be recognized by Colorado.]

CONNECTICUT

CONSTITUTION

Electors

[Article VIII of the Amendment to the Connecticut Constitution, adopted October, 1845, limiting electors to "male white" citizens of the United States, was altered by Article XXIII of Amendments adopted October, 1876, which provided that the word "white" be erased from Article Eight.] [Const. 1843.]

STATUTES

GENERAL STATUTES OF CONNECTICUT (REV. 1949)

Civil Rights

Sec. 8374. Deprivation of rights on account of alienage, color or race. — Any person who shall subject, or cause to be subjected, any other person to the deprivation of any rights, privileges or immunities, secured or protected by the constitution or laws of this State or of the United States, on account of alienage, color or race, shall be fined not more than one thousand dollars or imprisoned not more than one year or both. [1930, S.6065]

Public Accommodation

Sec. 8375. [691a, 1949 Supp.] Discrimination on account of race, creed or color. — All persons within the jurisdiction of this State shall be entitled to full and equal accommodations in every place of public accommodation, resort or amusement, subject only to the conditions and limitations established by law and applicable alike to all persons; and any denial of such accommodation by reason of the race, creed or color of the applicant therefor shall be a violation of the provisions of this section. A place of public accommodation, resort or amusement within the meaning of this section shall include all *public housing projects,* inns, taverns, road houses, hotels, restaurants and eating houses or any place where food is sold for consumption on the premises; railroad cars and stations, street railway cars and stations, public service buses and taxicabs; and theatres, motion picture houses, music halls, amusement and recreation parks. Any person who shall violate any provision of this section shall be fined not less than twenty-five [$25.00] nor more than one hundred [$100.00] dollars or imprisoned not more than thirty [30] days or both. [1930, s. 5985; 1933, s. 1676c; 1941, s. 860f; as amended Acts 1949, c. 417, §1.]

692a. Complaint to Interracial Commission. [1949 Supp.] — In addition to the penalties provided for violation of section 691a of this act and section 8374, any person claiming to be aggrieved by a violation of either section may, by himself or his attorney, make, sign and file with the inter-racial commission a complaint in writing under oath which shall state the circumstances of such violation and the particulars thereof and shall contain such other information as may be required by the commission. The commission may thereupon proceed upon such complaint in the same manner and with the same powers as provided in chapter 371 [secs. 7400 - 7407, infra.] in the case of unfair employment practices, and the provisions of said chapter as to the powers, duties and rights of the commission, the complainant, the court, the

63

attorney general and the respondent shall apply to any proceeding under the provisions of this section. [1930, s.5985; 1933, s. 1676c; 1941, s. 860f; as amended Acts 1949, c. 417, §2., Public Act No. 291, appvd. July 13, 1949.]

Defamation

Sec. 8376. Ridicule on account of race, creed or color — Any person who, shall, by his advertisement, ridicule or hold up to contempt any person or class of persons, on account of the creed, religion, color, denomination, nationality or race of such person or class of persons, shall be fined not more than fifty [$50.00] dollars or imprisoned not more than thirty [30] days or both. 1930, s. 6066.]

Civil Service

Sec. 374. Discrimination prohibited. — No person in the state service or seeking admission thereto shall be appointed, demoted or dismissed or be in any way favored or discriminated against because of his political or religious opinions or affiliations or because of his color. No question in any examination or contained on any form used in connection with the carrying out of the provisions of this chapter shall relate to political or religious opinions or affiliations of any competitor, prospective competitor or eligible person on any employment or re-employment list established and maintained by the director. [1937, s. 697e; 1943, s. 426g.]

Education

Public Schools

Sec. 1349. [Educational Opportunities] . . . Public schools shall be maintained in each town for at least one hundred eighty days of actual school sessions during each year . . . They shall be open to all children over six years of age without discrimination on account of race or color . . . [1930, S. 833, 1931; 1933, S. 185c]

Employment — Fair Employment Practices

Sec. 7400. Inter-racial commission. Appointment. Duties. — The inter-racial commission shall continue to consist of ten persons appointed by the governor. On or before July 15, 1949, and annually thereafter, the governor shall appoint two members, each to serve for a term of five years, to succeed those whose terms expire. The members of said commission shall choose, annually, from their number, a chairman and a deputy chairman. Said commission shall investigate the possibilities of affording equal opportunity of profitable employment to all persons, with particular reference to job training and placement. The commission shall compile facts concerning discrimination in employment, violations of civil liberties and other related matters. Said commission shall report to the governor biennially the result of its investigations, with its recommendations for the removal of such injustices as it may find to exist. The members of the commission shall serve without pay, but their reasonable expenses, including necessary stenographic and clerical help, shall be paid by the state upon approval of the commissioner of finance and control. [1943, S.470g].

Sec. 7401. Definitions. — When used in sections 7402 to 7407, inclusive (a) "court" shall mean the superior court, or, if said court is not in session, any judge of said court; (b) "person" shall mean one or more individuals, partnerships, associations, corporations, legal representatives, trustees, trustees in bankruptcy, receivers and the state and all political subdivisions and agencies thereof; (c) "employment agency" shall mean any person undertaking with or without compensation to procure employees or opportunities to work; (d) "labor organization" shall mean any organization which exists for the purpose, in whole or in part, of collective bargaining or of dealing with employers concerning grievances, terms or conditions of employment, or of other mutual aid or protection in connection with employment; (e) "unfair employment practice" shall mean only any unfair employment practice specified in section 7405; (f) "employer" shall include the state and all political subdivisions thereof and shall mean any person or employer with five or more persons in his employ; (g) "employee" shall mean any person employed by an employer but shall not include any individual employed by his parents, spouse or child, or in the domestic service of any person; (h) "commission" shall mean the inter-racial commission created by section 7400; (i) "commissioner" shall mean a member of the interracial commission; (j) "discrimination" shall include segregation and separation. [1947, S. 1360i]

Sec. 7402. Additional duties of inter-racial commission. — The inter-racial commission shall investigate and proceed in, as provided in sections 7403 to 7407, inclusive, all cases of discrimination in employment because of race, color, religion, national origin or ancestry. [1947, S. 1361i]

Sec. 7403. Hearing examiners. — There shall continue to be ten hearing examiners. On or before July 1, 1949, and annually thereafter, the governor shall appoint two hearing examiners, each to serve for a term of five years, to succeed those whose terms expire. Each such examiner and each commissioner shall receive twenty-five dollars per day for each day on which he conducts hearings, and their reasonable expenses, including necessary stenographic and clerical help, shall be paid by the state upon approval of the commissioner of finance and control. When serving as members of a hearing tribunal as hereinafter provided, each hearing examiner shall have the same subpoena powers as are granted to commissioners by subsection (f) of section 7404. [1947, S. 1362i.]

Sec. 7404. Powers of the inter-racial commission. — The commission shall have the following powers and duties: (a) To establish and maintain an office in the city of Hartford; (b) to appoint such investigators and other employees and agents as it may deem necessary, fix their compensation within the limitations provided by law and prescribe their duties; (c) to adopt, publish, amend and rescind regulations consistent with and to effectuate the provisions of sections 7401 to 7407, inclusive; (d) to recommend policies and make recommendations to agencies and officers of the state and local subdivisions of government to effectuate the policies of said sections; (e) to receive, initiate, investigate and mediate complaints of unfair employment practices; (f) by itself or with or by hearing examiners, to hold hearings, subpoena witnesses and compel their attendance, administer oaths, take the testimony of any person under oath and require the production for examination of any books and papers relating to any matter under investigation or in question. The commission may make rules as to the procedure for the issuance of subpoenas by individual commissioners and hearing examiners. Contumacy or refusal to obey a subpoena issued pursuant to this section shall constitute contempt punishable, upon the application of the authority issuing such subpoena, by the superior court in the county in which the hearing is held or in which the witness resides or transacts business. No person shall be excused from attending and testifying or from producing records, correspondence, documents or other evidence in obedience to subpoena, on the ground that the testimony or evidence required of him may tend to incriminate him or subject him to a penalty or forfeiture, but no person shall be prosecuted or subjected to any penalty or forfeiture for or on account of any transaction, matter or thing concerning which he is compelled, after having claimed his privilege against self-incrimination, to testify or produce evidence, except that such person so testifying shall not be exempt from prosecution and punishment for perjury committed in so testifying. The immunity herein provided shall extend only to natural persons so compelled to testify; (g) to utilize such voluntary and uncompensated services of private individuals, agencies and organizations as may from time to time be offered and needed; (h) with the cooperation of such agencies, (1) to study the problems of discrimination in all or specific fields of human relationships, and (2) to foster through education and community effort or otherwise good will among the groups and elements of the population of the state. From time to time, but not less than once a year, the commission shall report to the governor, making such recommendations as it deems advisable and describing the investigations, proceedings and hearings it has conducted and their outcome, the decisions it has rendered and the other work performed by it. [1947, S.1363i]

Sec. 7405. Unfair employment practices. — It shall be an unfair employment practice (a) for an employer, by himself or his agent, except in the case of a bona fide occupational qualification or need, because of the race, color, religious creed, national origin or ancestry of any individual, to refuse to hire or employ or to bar or to discharge from employment such individual or to discriminate against him in compensation or in terms, conditions or privileges of employment; (b) for any employment agency, except in the case of a bona fide occupational qualification or need, to fail or refuse to classify property or refer for employment, or otherwise to discriminate against, any individual because of his race, color, religious creed, national origin or ancestry; (c) for a labor organization, because of the race, color, religious creed, national origin or ancestry of any individual to exclude from full membership rights or to expel from its membership such individual or to discriminate in any way against any of its members or against any employer or any individual employed by an employer, unless such action is based upon a bonafide occupational qualification; (d) for any person, employer, labor organization or employment agency to discharge, expel or otherwise discriminate against any person because he has opposed any unfair employment practice or because he has filed a complaint or testified or assisted in any proceeding under section 7406; (e) for any person, whether an employer or an employee or not, to aid, abet, incite, compel or coerce the doing of any of the acts herein declared to be unfair employment practices or to attempt to do so. [1947, S. 1364i]

Sec. 7406. Procedure. — Any person claiming to be aggrieved by an alleged unfair employment practice may, by himself or his attorney, make, sign and file with the commission a complaint in writing under oath, which shall state the name and address of the person, employer, labor organization or employment agency alleged to have committed the unfair employment practice, and which shall set forth the particulars thereof and contain such other information as may be required by the commission. The commission, whenever it has reason to believe that any person has been engaged or is engaging in an unfair employment practice, may issue a complaint. Any employer whose employees, or any of them, refuse or threaten to refuse to comply with the provisions of sections 7401 to 7407, inclusive, may file with the commission a written complaint under oath asking for assistance by conciliation or other remedial action. After the filing of any complaint, the chairman of the commission shall refer the same to a commissioner or investigator to make prompt preliminary investigation of such complaint, and, if such commission or investigator determines after such preliminary investigation that there is reasonable cause for believing that an unfair employment practice has been or is being committed as alleged in such complaint, he shall immediately endeavor to eliminate the unfair employment practice complained of by conference, conciliation and persuasion. No commissioner or investigator shall disclose what has occurred in the course of such endeavors, provided the commission may publish the facts in the case of any complaint which has been dismissed and the terms of conciliation when a complaint has been adjusted. In case of failure to eliminate such practice, the investigator or investigating commissioner shall certify the complaint and the results of his investigation to the chairman of the inter-racial commission and to the attorney general. The chairman of the inter-racial commission shall thereupon appoint a hearing tribunal of three persons who shall be members of the commission or panel of hearing examiners to hear such complaint and shall cause to be issued and served in the name of the commission a written notice, together with a copy of such complaint, as the same may have been amended, requiring the person, employer, labor organization or employment agency named in such complaint, hereinafter referred to as the respondent, to answer the charges of such complaint at a hearing before such tribunal, at a time and place to be specified in such notice. The place of any such hearing may be the office of the commission or another place designated by it. The case in support of the complaint shall be presented at the hearing by the attorney general who shall be counsel for the commission; and no commissioner who previously made the investigation or caused the notice to be issued shall participate in the hearing except as a witness, nor shall he participate in the deliberations of the tribunal in such case. Any endeavors or negotiations for conciliation shall not be received in evidence. The respondent may file a written answer to the complaint and appear at such hearing in person or otherwise, with or without counsel, and submit testimony and be fully heard. The tribunal conducting any hearing may permit reasonable amendment to any complaint or answer and the testimony taken at such hearing shall be under oath and be transcribed at the request of any party. If, upon all the evidence, the tribunal finds that a respondent has engaged in any unfair employment practice as defined in section 7405, it shall state its findings of fact and shall issue and file with the commission and cause to be served on such respondent an order requiring such respondent

67

to cease and desist from such unfair employment practice. If, upon all the evidence, the tribunal finds that the respondent has not engaged in any alleged unfair employment practice, it shall state its findings of fact and shall similarly issue and file an order dismissing the complaint. The commission shall establish rules of practice to govern, expedite and effectuate the foregoing procedure. Any complaint filed pursuant to this section must be so filed within six months after the alleged act of discrimination. [1947, S. 1365i]

Sec. 7407. Enforcement of orders. Appeals. — (a) The commission may, through the attorney general, petition the court within the county wherein any unfair employment practice occurred or wherein any person charged with unlawful employment practice resides or transacts business, for the enforcement of any order issued by a tribunal under the provisions of sections 7401 to 7407, inclusive, and for appropriate temporary relief or a restraining order, and shall certify and file in the court a transcript of the entire record of the proceedings, including the pleadings and testimony upon which such order was made and the finding and orders of the hearing tribunal. Within five days after filing such petition in the court the commission shall cause a notice of such petition to be sent by registered mail to all parties or their representatives. The court shall have jurisdiction of the proceedings and of the questions determined thereon, and shall have the power to grant such relief by injunction or otherwise, including temporary relief, as it deems just and suitable and to make and enter, upon the pleadings, testimony and proceedings set forth in such transcript, a decree enforcing, modifying and enforcing as so modified, or setting aside in whole or in part, any order of the commission or hearing tribunal. (b) No objection that has not been urged before the hearing tribunal shall be considered by the court, unless the failure to urge such objection is excused because of extraordinary circumstances. The findings of the hearing tribunal as to the facts, is supported by substantial and competent evidence, shall be conclusive. If either party applies to the court for leave to adduce additional evidence and shows to the satisfaction of the court that such additional evidence is material and that there were reasonable grounds for the failure to adduce such evidence in the hearing, the court may order such additional evidence to be taken before the same hearing tribunal, and to be made part of the transcript. The tribunal may modify its findings as to the facts, or make new findings, by reason of additional evidence so taken, and it shall file such modified or new findings, which, if supported by substantial and competent evidence, shall be conclusive, and shall file its recommendations, if any, for the modification or setting aside of its original order. (c) The jurisdiction of the court shall be exclusive and its judgment and decree shall be final, except that the same shall be subject to review by the supreme court of errors, on appeal, by either party, irrespective of the nature of the decree or judgment. Such appeal shall be taken and prosecuted in the same manner and form and with the same effect as is provided in other cases of appeal to the supreme court of errors, and the record so certified shall contain all that was before the lower court. (d) Any respondent aggrieved by a final order of a hearing tribunal may obtain a review of such order in the superior court for the county where the unfair employment practice is alleged to have occurred or in the county wherein such person resides or transacts business by filing with the clerk of said court, within two weeks from the date of such order, a written petition in duplicate praying that such order be modified or set aside. The clerk shall thereupon mail the duplicate copy to the commission. The commission shall then cause to be filed in said court a certified transcript of the entire record in the proceedings, including the pleadings, testimony and order. Upon such filing said court shall proceed in the same manner as in the case of a petition by the commission under this section and shall have the same exclusive jurisdiction to grant to the respondent such temporary relief or restraining order as it deems just and suitable, and in like manner to make and enter a decree enforcing or modifying and enforcing as so modified or setting aside, in whole or in part, the order sought to be reviewed. (e) Unless otherwise directed by the commission, tribunal or court, commencement or review proceedings under this section shall operate as a stay of any order. (f) Petitions filed under this section shall be heard expeditiously and determined upon the transcript filed, without requirement of printing. Hearings in the court under sections 7401 to 7407, inclusive, shall take precedence over all other matters, except matters of the same character. [1947, s. 1366i]

Insurance

Life Insurance

Sec. 6140. Discrimination against persons of African decent prohibited. — No life insurance company doing business in this state shall make any distinction or discrimination between white persons and colored persons wholly or partially of African descent, as to the premiums or rates charged for policies upon the lives of such persons; nor shall any company demand or require greater premiums from such colored persons than such as are at that time required by such company from white persons of the same age, sex, general condition of health and hope of longevity; nor shall any such company make or require any rebate, diminution or discount upon the sum to be paid on any such policy in case of the death of any such colored person insured, nor insert in the policy any condition, nor make any stipulation whereby such person insured shall bind himself, his heirs, executors, administrators or assigns to accept any sum less than the full value or amount of such policy, in case of a claim accruing thereon by reason of the death of such person insured, other than such as are imposed upon white persons in similar cases; and each such stipulation or condition so made or inserted shall be void. [1930, S. 4183]

Sec. 6141. Affidavit of examining physician. — Each such company which shall refuse the application of any such colored person for insurance upon his life shall furnish him with the affidavit of some regular examining physician of such company, who has made the examination of such person, stating that the applicant has been refused, not because such person is a colored person, but solely upon such grounds as would be applicable to white persons of the same age and sex. [1930, S. 4184.]

Sec. 6142. Penalty. — [For violation of Sec. 6140 or 6141, company or the officer or agent thereof subject to a fine of not more than $100.00.] [1930, S. 4185.]

Accident and Health Insurance

Sec. 6187 — Discrimination prohibited — Discrimination between individuals of the same class in the amount of premiums or rates charged for any policy of insurance covered by sections 6177 to 6190, inclusive, or the benefits payable thereon, or in any terms or conditions of such policy, or in any other manner, is prohibited. [1930, S. 4227.]

[Note: Although the above section makes no reference to race or color, it may be argued that such a provision can be used to prevent racial discrimination in the matter of accident and health insurance.]

Militia

Section 155a. [1949 Supp.] Discrimination. — No person shall be denied membership in the organized militia, the national guard, or the naval militia of this state, nor be discriminated against in the matter of promotion in such organizations, an account of his race, creed or color. No units of such organizations shall be formed, and no separate types of duties nor separate accommodations shall be assigned, in such a manner as to result in the segregation of members thereof on account of race, creed or color. [Acts 1949, ch. 63, p. 60, appvd. March 16, 1949.]

Public Accommodation

See under Civil Rights.

DELAWARE

CONSTITUTION

Education — Segregation

Art. X, Section 2. — [Authorizes establishment of a system of free public schools and provides "no distinction shall be made on account of race or color, and separate schools for white and colored children shall be maintained."] [Const. 1897.]

[Note: Under the constitutional provision above, segregation in the public schools is mandatory.]

STATUTES

DELAWARE REVISED CODE (1935)

Aged and Orphans — Segregation

Laws 1937 ch. 46, p. 130. — [Annual appropriation is made to the Layton Home for Aged Colored People for operation expenses.]

Ch. 70 Art. 8, §2590. Colored Minor Boys committed to Society; . . . [Provides for the commitment of colored boys under 12 years old who are abandoned or orphaned to St. Joseph's Society for Colored Missions of Wilmington.] [Code 1915, §2265.]

Ch. 70, Art. 10, §2598. Poor and Dependent White Children. — [Authorizes commitment of poor and dependent white children between ages of 2 and 10 years, residents of Kent County, to Elizabeth W. Murphy School, Inc.] ['34 Del. Laws, ch. 156; '37 Del. Laws, ch. 85.]

Ch. 70, Art. 9, §§2592-2595. [St. Michael's Home for Babies] — [Provides for the commitment of children under 10 to St. Michael's Home for Babies. §2595 provides, "Children shall be admitted from any part of the State without distinction as to the nationality or religious belief of their parents or custodians."] [Code 1915, §2267; '37 Del. Laws, ch. 186, 1.]

[Note: Under the terms of the above section it is not clear whether Negro children may be admitted to St. Michael's Home for Babies.]

Education

Public Schools

Ch. 71, Art. 1, §2631. Separate schools for white and colored children — Separate schools for Moors or Indians. — The State Board of Education is authorized, empowered, directed and required to maintain a uniform, equal and effective system of public schools throughout the State . . . The schools provided shall be of two kinds; those for white children and those for colored children . . . The State Board of Education shall establish schools for children of people called Moors or Indians . . . No white or colored child shall be permitted to attend such a school without the permission of the State Board of Eduction . . . ['36 Del. Laws, chs. 211, 222.]

Ch. 71, Art. 5, §2684. White Schools and Colored Schools; White Schools free to White Children and Colored Schools free to Colored

71

Children.—All the white public schools of the State shall be free to all the white children of school age, resident in the State; and all the colored public schools of the State shall be free to all the colored children of school age, resident in the State. [32 Del. Laws, ch. 160, 41.]

Colleges, Teacher Training Schools

Ch. 73, §§2793 — 2801. — [Sets up the State College for Colored Students and makes provision for summer school training schools for teachers to be held at the State College for Colored Students. Name changed to "Delaware State College" by 47 Del. Laws, ch. 202, 1, 2] [Code 1915, 2349 - 2356; 32 Del. Laws, ch. 170, 1, as amended by 47 Del. Laws, ch. 202, 1, 2.]

Juvenile Delinquent and Reform Schools

Ch. 70, Art. 3, §§2525-2537. — [Industrial School for Colored Girls of Delaware.] Provision for the control and management of the Delaware Industrial Home for Colored Girls, Incorporated, and for taking over the Home as a state institution. [32 Del. Laws, ch. 155, 1-6, 10, 11; 34 Del. Laws, ch. 159, 1, 3; 37 Del. Laws, ch. 180, 1-4; 37 Del. Laws, ch. 183, 1.]

Teachers' Salaries

Ch. 71, Art. 1, §2630. Rules and Regulations: . . . — The State Board of Education shall prescribe rules and regulations: . . .

(h) Fixing in conjunction with the respective Boards of Education of Special School Districts, a schedule of salaries for superintendents, teachers professional and clerical assistants, in the respective Special School Districts and School Districts; *provided that the schedule so fixed shall be uniform in application, without discrimination on account of race, color or religious belief* . . . (italics supplied.) [1927 Del. Laws, ch. 156, §1, p. 495.]

Hospitals — Segregation

Ch. 25, Art. 5, §825. Hospital for colored persons; . . . — [Authorizes a separate hospital for colored tubercular patients.] [29 Del. Laws, ch. 53, 1.]

Miscegenation

Ch. 85 §3485 . . . Marriage Between White Person and a Negro or a Mulatto. — [Forbids marriage between a white person and Negro or mulatto. Such marriages shall be void. Penalty: misdemeanor, punishable by fine of $100 or upon default of such payment imprisonment for up to 30 days. Applies also to such marriages made outside the State where the parties are residents of the State and live as man and wife within the State.] [32 Del. Laws, ch. 182, 1.]

Prisons

[There appears to be no statutory requirement of segregation of Negro and white adult prisoners.]

Transportation

[No statutory segregation.]

DISTRICT OF COLUMBIA

CONSTITUTION

[See Constitution of the United States.]

STATUTES

Civil Rights — Public Accommodation

Compiled Statutes in force in the District of Columbia (1894), p. 183

Chapter XVI. Crimes and Offenses

Sec. 150. Any restaurant keeper or proprietor, any hotel keeper or proprietor, proprietors or keepers of ice-cream saloons or places where soda-water is kept for sale, or keepers of barbershops and bathing houses, refusing to sell or wait upon any respectable well-behaved person, without regard to race, color, or previous condition of servitude, or any restaurant, hotel, ice-cream saloon or soda fountain, barber shop or bathing-house keepers, or proprietors, who refuse under any pretext to serve any well-behaved, respectable person, in the same room, and at the same prices as other well-behaved and respectable persons are served, shall be deemed guilty of a misdmeanor, and upon conviction in a court having jurisdiction, shall be fined one hundred dollars [$100.00], and shall forfeit his or her license as keeper or owner of a restaurant, hotel, ice-cream saloon, or soda fountain, as the case may be, and it shall not be lawful for the Assessor [Register] or any other officer of the District of Columbia to issue a license to any person or persons or to their agent or agents, who shall have forfeited their license under the provisions of this act, until a period of one year shall have elapsed after such forfeiture. [Act of June 20, 1872, Legislative Assembly, Sec. 3, pp. 65, 66.

[Note: The above Act of June 20, 1872, passed by the Second Legislative Assembly of the District of Columbia, has never been repealed. Nor has it been included in any subsequent compilation or code of the laws of the District of Columbia. The 1901 Code of District of Columbia omitted the statute but contained no provision for its repeal. it is therefor argued by many students of District of Columbia law that the statute is still in force. The United States Supreme Court has not decided the question, although a test case is reported to be now pending in the lower District of Columbia courts. Suit was brought by Mrs. Mary Church Terrell, a Negro, and others as members of an inter-racial party against Thompson's Restaurant in downtown Washington, charging that the defendant restaurant refused to serve them. The District of Columbia Municipal Court has held this Act to be "superceded" by Congressional legislation passed in 1878.]

U.S. Code, Title 18, Ch. 13. [1948 Revision]

§244. Discrimination against a person wearing uniform of armed forces. — Whoever, being a proprietor, manager, or employee of a theatre or other public place of entertainment or amusement in the District of Columbia, or in any Territory, or Possession of the United States, causes any person wearing the uniform of the Army, Navy, Coast Guard, or Marine Corps of the United

States to be discriminated against because of that uniform, shall be fined not more than $500. [June 25, 1948, ch. 645, §1, 62 Stat. 697, eff. Sept. 1, 1948. Based on title 18 U.S.C., 1940 ed. §523 (Mar. 1, 1911, ch. 187, 36 Stat. 963; Aug. 24, 1912, ch. 387, §1, 37 Stat. 512; Jan. 28, 1915, ch. 20, §1, 38 Stat. 800.)]

DISTRICT OF COLUMBIA CODE (1940)

Education — Segregation

§31-1109. Board of Education may accept and apply donations for colored schools. — The Board of Education is authorized to receive any donations or contributions that may be made for the benefit of the schools for colored children by persons disposed to aid in the elevation of the colored population in the District, and to apply the same in such manner as in their opinion shall be best calculated to effect the object of the donors; the board of education to account for all funds so received. [R.S., D.C., §283; June 20, 1906, 34 Stat. 316, ch. 3446, §2.]

§31-1110. Education of colored children. — It shall be the duty of the Board of Education to provide suitable and convenient houses or rooms for holding schools for colored children, to employ and examine teachers therefor, and to appropriate a proportion of the school funds, to be determined upon the number of white or colored children, between the ages of 6 and 17 years, to the payment of teachers' wages, to the building or renting of schoolrooms, and other necessary expenses pertaining to said schools, to exercise a general supervision over them, to establish proper discipline, and to endeavor to promote a thorough, equitable and practicable education of colored children in the District of Columbia. [R.S., D.C. §281; June 11, 1878, 20 Stat. 107, ch. 180, §6; June 20, 1906, 34 Stat. 316, Ch. 3446, §2.]

§31-1111. Placement of children in schools. — Any white resident shall be privileged to place his or her child or ward at any one of the schools provided for the education of white children in the District of Columbia he or she may think proper to select, with the consent of the Board of Education; and any colored resident shall have the same rights with respect to colored schools. [R.S., D.C. §282; June 11, 1878, 20 Stat. 107, ch. 180, §6; June 20, 1906, 34 Stat. 316, ch. 3446, §2.]

§31-1112. Proportionate amount of school moneys to be set apart for colored schools. — It shall be the duty of the proper authorities of the District to set apart each year from the whole fund received from all sources by such authorities applicable to purposes of public education in the District of Columbia, such proportionate part of all moneys received or expended for school or educational purposes, including the cost of sites, buildings, improvements, furniture and books, and all other expenditures on account of schools, as the colored children between the ages of 6 and 17 years bear to the whole number of children, white and colored, between the same ages, for the purpose of establishing and sustaining public schools for the education of colored children; and such proportion shall be ascertained by the last reported census of the population made prior to such apportionment, and shall be regulated at all times thereby. [R.S., D.C., §306; June 11, 1878, 20 Stat. 107, ch. 180, §6; June 20, 1906, 34 Stat. 316, ch. 3446, §2.]

§31-1113. Facilities for education of colored children to be provided. — It is the duty of the Board of Education to provide suitable rooms and teachers for such a number of schools in the District of Columbia as, in its opinion, will best accommodate the colored children in the District of Columbia. [R.S., D.C., §310; June 11, 1878, 20 Stat. 107, ch. 180, §6; June 20, 1906, 34 Stat. 316, ch. 3446, §2.]

§31-109. Assistant superintendents of schools — Duties. — [June 4, 1924, 43 Stat. 374, ch. 250, §12; Repealed July 21, 1945, 59 Stat. 500, ch. 321, title V, §21, eff. July 1, 1945.]

§31-649. [Supp. VI. 1948.] Number of First Assistant Superintendents — Sphere of supervision — duties. — There shall be two First Assistant Superintendents of Schools, one white First Assistant Superintendent for the white schools who, under the direction of the Superintendent of Schools, shall have general supervision over the white schools; and one colored First Assistant Superintendent for the colored schools who, under the direction of the Superintendent of Schools, shall have sole charge of all employees, classes, and schools in which colored children are taught. The First Assistant Superintendents shall perform such other duties as may be prescribed by the Superintendent of Schools. [July 21, 1945; 59 Stat. 498; ch. 321, title V, §12, eff. July 1, 1945.]

§31-115. [Supp. VI. 1948] Principals of schools—Duties.—Principals of normal, high, and manual training schools shall each have entire control of his school, both executive and educational, subject only in authority to the superintendent of schools for the white schools and to the colored first assistant superintendent for the colored schools, to whom in each case he shall be directly responsible. [June 20, 1906; 34 Stat. 320, ch. 3446, §7, as amended July 21, 1945, 59 Stat. 500, ch. 321, title V., §21, eff. July 1, 1945.]

Deaf-Mutes

§31-1011. Education of colored deaf-mute children of District. — [Provides for education of colored deaf-mute children of District of Columbia in the Maryland School for Colored Deaf-Mutes, or some other suitable school.] [Mar. 3, 1905, 33 Stat. 901, ch. 1406, §1; June 27 1906; 34 Stat. 503, ch. 3553; Mar. 4, 1911, 36 Stat. 1422, ch. 285, §1.]

Juvenile and Delinquent Schools

§32-906 . . . Segregation of white and colored. — [Provides "it shall not be lawful to keep white and colored girls on the same reservations" of the National Training Schools for Girls.] [Feb. 28, 1923. 42 Stat. 1358, ch. 148, §1; Mar. 16, 1926, 44 Stat. 208, ch. 58.]

Boards of Examiners

§31-650. [Supp. VI. January 3, 1941 to January 5, 1948] Boards of examiners — Composition — Designation of members. — Boards of examiners for carrying out the provisions of the statutes with reference to examinations of teachers shall consist of the Superintendent of Schools and not less than four nor more than six members of the supervisory or teaching staff of the white schools for the white schools, and of the Superintendent of Schools and not less than four nor more than six members of the supervisory or teaching staff of the colored schools for the colored schools. The designations of members of the supervisory or teaching staff for membership on these boards shall be made annually by the Board of Education on the recommendation of the Superintendent of Schools. [July 21, 1945, 59 Stat. 498, ch. 321, title V, §13, eff. July 1, 1945.]

§31-651. [Supp. VI. January 3, 1941 to January 5, 1948.] Appointment of chief examiners — Compensation. — There shall be appointed by the Board of Education, on the recommendation of the Superintendent of Schools, a chief examiner for the board of examiners for white schools; Provided, That an Associate Superintendent in the colored schools shall be designated by the Superintendent of Schools as chief examiner for the board of examiners for the colored schools. Provided further, That except as otherwise provided in sections 31-638 to 31-658, all members of the respective boards of examiners shall serve without additional compensation. [July 21, 1945, 59 Stat. 498, ch. 321, title V, §14, eff. July 1, 1945.]

Method of Promotion of Employees

§31-646. . . . Division of salaries between teachers in white and colored schools. — [Provides that the number of group B and group D salaries (salaries based upon promotion) "shall be divided proportionately between the teachers, instructors, librarians, and research assistants in the white schools, and the teachers, instructors, librarians, and research assistants in the colored schools on the basis of the enrollment of pupils in the respective white and colored schools on the last school day of the first advisory period of the first semester in each school year or as near that day as practicable."] [July 21, 1945, 59 Stat. 497, ch. 321, title IV, §9, eff. July 1, 1945, as amended July 24, 1945, 59 Stat. 502, ch. 326-A.]

[Note: See §31-638, D.C. Code 1940 Ed. Supp. VII (1949), for Salary Schedules of teachers, school officers and other employees of public schools in Washington, D.C.]

FLORIDA

CONSTITUTION

Education

Art. 12, §12. Separate schools for negroes. — White and Colored children shall not be taught in the same school, but impartial provision shall be made for both. [Const. 1885.]

Miscegenation

Art. 16, §24. Miscegenation. — All marriages between a white person and a negro, or between a white person and a person of negro descent to the fourth generation inclusive, are hereby forever prohibited. [Const. 1885.]

Slavery

Declaration of Rights, §19. Neither slavery nor involuntary servitude, except as a punishment for a crime, whereof the party has been duly convicted, shall ever be allowed in this State. [Const. 1868, Decl. Rights, §18; Const. 1885, Decl. Rights, §19.]

STATUTES

Florida Statutes 1941 and Florida Statutes Annotated.

Attorneys at Law — no discrimination

§39.18. Officers not allowed to practice. — . . . But no person shall be denied the right to practice [law] on account of sex, race, or color . . . [Laws 1925, c. 10175, §18; Comp. Gen. Laws 1927, §4196, Florida Statutes 1949, §454.18.]

Cohabitation

§798.04. White persons and negroes living in adultery. — If any white person and negro, or mulatto, shall live in adultery or fornication with each other, each shall be punished by imprisonment not exceeding twelve [12] months, or by fine not exceeding one thousand [$1,000.00] dollars. [Rev. St. 1892, §§2609, 2610; Gen. St. 1906, §3532; Rev. Gen. St. 1920, §5422; Comp. Gen. Laws 1927, §7565.]

[Note: §798.03, Florida Stat. Annot. provides a penalty for fornication generally of $30.00 fine or 3 months' imprisonment.]

§798.05. Negro man and white woman or white man and negro woman occupying the same room. — Any negro man and white woman, or any white man and negro woman, who are not married to each other, who shall habitually live in and occupy in the nighttime the same room shall each be punished by imprisonment not exceeding twelve [12] months, or by fine not exceeding five hundred [$500.00] dollars. [Laws 1881, c. 3282, §§2, 4; Rev. St. 1892, §§2612, 2613; Gen. St. 1906, §3533, Rev. Gen. St. 1920, §5423; Comp. Gen. Laws 1927, §7566.]

Defamation

§836.11. [1948 Cum. Supp.] Publications which tend to expose persons to hatred, contempt or ridicule prohibited. — [It is unlawful to print, publish or distribute or cause to be printed, published or distributed, any publication which tends to expose any individual or any religious group to hatred, contempt, or ridicule, unless the printed material contains the true name and post-office address of the person, firm, etc., causing the same to be published, printed or distributed. If the name is that of a firm, corporation or other organization, the printed material must contain the name and post-office address of the individual acting in its behalf. Penalty for violation includes up to $500 fine and up to 90 days imprisonment or both.] [Laws 1945, c. 22744, §§1, 2.]

Definition of "Negro"

§1.01. Definition — . . . (6) The words "negro", "colored", "colored persons", "mulatto" or "persons of color", when applied to persons, include every person having one-eighth or more of African or negro blood. [Rev. Gen. St. 1920, §§3939; Comp. Gen. Laws 1927, §5858.]

Discriminatory Publication

Laws 1949, Ch. 26026, p. 1415, S.B. 599.—[Enabling Act to permit the City of Miami Beach to adopt ordinance prohibiting publication or display of any sign or notice tending to discriminate against persons because of race or creed in any public accommodation.]

Education — Segregation
Public Schools

§228.09. Separate schools for white and negro children required. — The schools for white children and the schools for negro children shall be conducted separately. *No individual, body of individuals, corporation, or association shall conduct within this state any school of any grade (public, private, or parochial) wherein white persons and negroes are instructed or boarded in the same building or at the same time by the same teachers.* [§209, ch. 19355, 1939; Comp. Gen. Laws 1940 Supp., §892(29).] (emphasis added)

[Note: This statute is mandatory and applies to both public and private schools.]

§228.10. White teachers may not teach negro schools; negro teachers may not teach white schools — [Repealed. Laws 1941, Ch. 20970, §15.]

§242.25. White children and negro children are not to be taught in same school. [Repealed. Laws 1943, ch. 21989, §17, eff. June 10, 1943; See §228.09 above.]

§242.26. Unlawful for white teachers to teach [in] negro school[s] and for negro teachers to teach in white schools. — [Laws 1913, ch. 6490, §§1, 2; [Repealed. Laws 1943, ch. 21989, §17, eff. June 10, 1943.]

§230.23. Powers and duties of county board. — The county board acting as a board shall exercise all powers and perform all duties listed below: . . . (6) . . . (a) *Schools and attendance areas.* — Authorize schools to be located and maintained in those communities in the county where they are needed to accommodate as far as practicable and without unnecessary expense all the youth who should be entitled to the facilities of such schools, separate schools to be provided for white and negro children; and approve the area from which children are to attend each such school, such area to be known as the attendance area for that school; provided, that only under exceptional circumstances as defined under regulations of the state board may an elementary school be located within four miles of another elementary school and a high school within ten miles of another high school in rural areas for children of the same race . . . [Laws 1939, c. 19355, §423; Comp. Gen. Laws, 1940 Supp., §892(86).]

Scholarships for teachers

§§239.37 - 239.44. [1948 Cum. Supp.] [These sections provide for a summer school scholarships fund for the improvement of qualifications of school teachers. Under the terms of the statute Negro teachers are included.] [Laws 1945, c. 22944, §§1-8, as amended Laws 1947, c. 23726, §§50-52.]

§239.39. [1948 Cum. Supp.] Summer school scholarships; award.—. . . All teachers recommended by county boards to the state board of education, within the quota assigned to each county, who meet the requirements prescribed by the state board of education shall be eligible for such scholarships. [Laws 1945, c. 22944, §3.]

Schools for Deaf and Blind

§§242.33 - 242.40. [Provision is made for "the education, care and maintenance at the Florida School for the Deaf and the Blind of all persons residing in this state between the ages of six and twenty-one years of age, who are blind or deaf or dumb . . . ". There appears to be no statutory provision for segregation of the races at such school.] [Laws 1903, ch. 5209, §§3, 4, 5; Laws 1905, ch. 5384, §20; Laws 1909, ch. 592, §1; Rev. Gen. St. 1920, §§644-650; Comp. Gen. St. 1927, §§816-822; Laws 1933, ch. 15859, §1.]

Juvenile Delinquents — Segregation of

§955.12. [Florida Industrial School for Boys] White and negro inmates to be separated. — There shall be separate buildings, not nearer than one fourth mile to each other, one for white boys and one for negro boys. White boys and negro boys shall not, in any manner, be associated together or worked together. [Laws 1897, c. 4565, §3; Gen. St. 1906, §4169; Rev. Gen. St. 1920, §6310; Comp. Gen. Laws 1927, §8636.]

§956.02 — [Florida Industrial School for Girls.] [Provides for commitment of delinquent girls to Florida Industrial School for Girls in like manner as boys are now committed to the Florida Industrial School for Boys.] [Laws 1915, c. 6840, §4; Rev. Gen. St. 1920, §6326; Comp. Gen. Laws 1927, §8652.]

[Note: While no specific clause in the above statute requires segregation of Negro girls from white delinquent girls, the statute is made referable to the statutes on commitment of delinquent boys, and it would thus appear that segregation of delinquent girls is incorporated by reference.]

Colleges and Universities

§241.41. [Florida Agricultural and Mechanical College for Negroes.] [Provides for the establishment, control and maintenance by the State board of education of the Florida Agricultural and Mechanical College for Negroes at Tallahassee, Florida.] [Laws, 1905, c. 5384, §11; Laws 1909, c. 5925, §1; Rev. Gen. St. 1920, §§642,643; Comp. Gen. Laws 1927, §§814, 815.]

[Note: Name changed from "school" to "college" in 1945.]

§239.01. [1948 Cum. Supp.] **University system defined.** — (1). The system of higher education of this state shall consist of the following institutions, to wit: One university to be known as the University of Florida located at Gainesville, to which shall be admitted both white male and white female students; one university to be known as the Florida State University located at Tallahassee, to which shall be admitted both white male and white female students; and one college to be known as the Florida Agricultural and Mechanical College located at Tallahassee, to which shall be admitted negro male and negro female students; . . . [Laws 1905, c. 5384, §12; Laws 1909, c.5926, §1; Laws 1909, c. 5924, §1; Rev. Gen. St. 1920, §611; Comp. Gen. Laws 1927, §767 as amended Laws 1947, c. 23669, §1, eff. May 15, 1947.]

§241.39 [Florida State College for Women] [Provides for the establishment of the Florida State College for Women and stipulates "none but female white students may be admitted to this institution."] [Laws 1905, c. 5384, §22; Laws 1909, c. 5924, §1; Rev. Gen. St. 1920, §632; Comp. Gen. Laws 1927, §804.]

[Note: The Florida State College for Woman has been superseded by the Florida State University and is now open to white male and white female students. See Laws 1947, c. 23669, §1; §239.01 above.]

§241.03. [University of Florida] — [Limits admission of students to the University of Florida to "white male students" except in certain instances where white women students are permitted to enroll in special courses not obtainable elsewhere.] [Laws 1905, c. 5384, §23; Rev. Gen. St. 1920, §623; Comp. Gen. Laws 1927, §790.]

[Note: University of Florida is now open to both male and female white students. See Laws 1947, c. 23669, §1; §239.01 above.]

Junior Colleges

§242.41. [1948 Cum. Supp.] **When public junior colleges may be organized.** — The county boards of the several counties of Florida having a population of not less than fifty thousand inhabitants according to the last federal or state census may organize, establish and operate junior colleges offering work in the thirteenth and fourteenth grades including not only classical and scientific courses but also terminal courses of a vocational and technical nature as part of their secondary school system or may take over junior colleges already established therein under the conditions set forth herein and support and maintain the same.

The county boards of any two or more contiguous counties having a combined population of not less than fifty thousand inhabitants according to the last federal or state census may also enter into an agreement to organize, establish and operate, or to take over and operate a junior college in one of the counties under the conditions set forth herein; provided that not more than one public junior college for white students and one for negro students shall be established in any county; provided, further, that no junior college may be established or taken over by the county board in any county until the proposed plan of operation and financial support has been submitted to and approved by the state board, said plan to show that provision is being made to serve all eligible students in the attendance area which should logically be served by such junior college; and provided, further, that no junior college for white students or for negro students may be established in any county in which there is located a state institution of higher learning providing educational courses and facilities through and above the fourteenth grade for students of that race. [Laws 1939, c. 19159, §1; as amended Laws 1947, c. 23726, §47, eff. July 1, 1947.]

Education in fields not provided for in state institutions.

§243.13. [1948 Cum. Supp.] **Education in fields not provided for in state institutions.** — The board of control is hereby authorized to negotiate and enter into contracts or agreements with other states or with standard institutions of higher learning in other states for the admission and education of qualified students from Florida in fields in which adequate educational facilities cannot economically be provided in state institutions of higher learning in Florida for Florida students who can legally attend such institutions. [Laws 1947, c. 24124, §1.]

§243.14. [1948 Cum. Supp.] **Determination of qualified students; costs.** — Pursuant to the provisions of §243.13 the board of control may establish regulations to be used in determining students from Florida who are qualified to be sent to an institution of higher learning when such a contact is made, and may agree to pay such institution a sum which shall not exceed one thousand [$1,000.00] dollars per year for the admission and education of each Florida student approved and educated in the institution in accordance with the contract; provided, that the board of control may agree to pay to said institution a minimum sum annually for one or more students, which sum shall not exceed five thousand [$5,000.00] dollars. Said sums shall cover all non-resident fees. [Laws 1947, c. 24124, §2.]

§243.16. [1948 Cum. Supp.] **Appropriations.** — There is hereby appropriated from the general revenue fund of the state the sum of one hundred thousand [$100,000.00] dollars, or such portion thereof as may be necessary for the purpose herein authorized for each of the annual periods beginning July 1, 1947 and July 1, 1948. [Laws 1947, c. 24124, §4.]

Regional Education

Acts 1949, ch. 25017, H.B. 189. Florida Statutes 1949, §§244.01 — 244.01.

[Authorizes Florida to participate in program of Regional Education and ratifies regional compact signed by the governors of fourteen southern states. For text of compact, see under Alabama or Georgia. See also *Note on Regional Compact — Education,* Appendix 6.]

Separate Textbooks

§233.43. Duties of county superintendent relating to books. — . . . (3) STORAGE — To store books . . . as provided by law; to keep separately the books which have been used in white and negro schools. [Laws 1939, c. 19355, §743; Comp. Gen. Laws, 1940 Supp., §892(255).]

Indians

§569.07. Sale of intoxicating liquors to Indians prohibited; penalty. — Any person who shall sell, give away, dispose of, exchange or barter any malt, spiritous or vinous liquor including beer, ale and wine, or any ardent or other intoxicating liquor of any kind whatsoever, or any essence, extract, bitters, preparations, compound, composition, or any name, label or brand which produces intoxication to any Indian, or half or quarter breed Indian in this state, shall upon conviction thereof, be sentenced to a term of imprisonment for not more than one [1] year, or a fine of not less than one hundred [$100.00] dollars nor more than one thousand dollars [$1,000.00]; provided, that this section shall not prevent the administration of whiskey or any other liquor by or on the prescription of any reputable physician. [1937, ch. 18017, §1; CGL. 1940 Supp., §7648(25).]

Inheritance

§731.32. Inheritance from persons of color.—(1) Whenever, upon the death of any person of color seized or possessed of real or personal estate, there are persons in being who would inherit said property or any portion thereof under the several statutes of descent in this state, but who are prevented from doing so on account of the legal incapacity of said persons of color to contract marriage in a state of slavery, (which said estate would otherwise escheat to the state), all the right, title and interest of the State of Florida is vested in and waived in favor of those persons who would have inherited said estate, if said parties would have been competent to contract marriage.

(2) The fact that the said parties shall have failed to obtain a license to marry, or shall have failed to be married according to the forms of law, shall in no case affect the operations of this section, but the same shall be held to apply to all cases wherein the parties are known as husband and wife. [Act. Nov. 20, 1829, §49; Rev. St. 1892, §1829; Gen. St. 1906, §2305; Rev. Gen. St. 1920, §3628; Comp. Gen. Laws 1927, §5492; Laws 1933, c. 16103, §33; Comp. Gen. Laws, Supp. 1936, §5840(10).]

§741.20. Certain cohabitations declared marriage. — [Validates all Negro marriages where the persons involved lived together as man and wife prior to January 1, 1868. Provides that all children of such marriages shall be legitimate and lawful heirs of their parents, as fully as if they had been born in legally recognized wedlock.] [Laws 1899, ch. 4749, §1; Gen. St. 1906, §2586; Rev. Gen. St. 1920, §3945; Comp. Gen. Laws 1927, §5864; amended Laws 1945, ch. 22858, §7.]

Insurance

§635.02. Life insurers not to discriminate between insurants of same class. — [Prohibits discrimination or distinction by life insurance companies doing business in the state "between insurants of the same class and equal expectation of life as to amount or payment of premiums or rates charged for policies of life or endowment insurance, or in the dividends or other benefits payable thereon, or in any other of the terms and conditions of the contracts it makes."] [Laws 1929, ch. 13661, §1; Comp. Gen. Laws 1936 Supp. 6212(1).]

[Note: While the above statute makes no reference to race or color, it may be invoked against discrimination. Similar provisions appear in most state insurance codes.]

Miscegenation

§741.11. Marriages between white and negro persons prohibited. — It is unlawful for any white male person residing or being in this state to intermarry with any negro female person; and it is in like manner unlawful for any white female person residing or being in this state to intermarry with any negro male person; and every marriage formed or solemnized in contravention of the provisions of this section shall be utterly null and void, and the issue, if any, of such surreptitious marriage shall be regarded as bastard and incapable of having or receiving an estate, real, personal or mixed, by inheritance. [Act Jan. 23, 1832, §§1, 2; Rev. St. 1892, §2063; Gen. St. 1906, §2579; Rev. Gen. St. 1920, §3938; Comp. Gen. Laws 1927, §5857.]

§741.12. Penalty for intermarriage of white and negro persons. — If any white man shall intermarry with a negro, or if any white woman shall intermarry with a negro, either or both parties to such marriage shall be punished by imprisonment in the state prison not exceeding ten [10] years, or by fine not exceeding one thousand [$1,000.00] dollars. [Laws 1881, c. 3283, §1; Rev. St. 1892, §2606; Laws 1903, c. 5140, §1; Gen. St. 1906, §3529; Rev. Gen. St. 1920, §5419; Comp. Gen. Laws 1927, §7562.]

§741.13. County judges not to issue licenses for white and negro intermarriages. — All county judges are prohibited from knowingly issuing a license to any person to intermarry against whom the disabilities in §741.11 specified may or do attach, under the penal sum of one thousand [$1,000.00] dollars, to be recovered by action of debt in any court of record having jurisdiction, for use of the school fund. [Act Jan. 23, 1832, §3; Rev. St. 1892, §2065; Gen. St. 1906, §2581; Rev. Gen. St. 1920, §3940; Comp. Gen. Laws 1927, §5859.]

§741.14. Penalty for violation of §741.11. — If any county judge shall knowingly and wilfully issue a marriage license for a white person to marry a negro, he shall be punished by imprisonment not exceeding two [2] years, or by fine not exceeding one thousand [$1,000.00] dollars. [Laws 1881, c. 3283, §2; Rev. St. 1892, §2607; Gen. St. 1906, §3530; Rev. St. 1920, §5420; Comp. Gen. Laws 1927, §7563.]

§741.15. Marriage between white and negro persons not to be performed. — Any of the persons described in §741.07, who shall knowingly perform the ceremony of marriage between any persons who by the provisions of §741.11

are prohibited to intermarry shall in like manner forfeit and pay the penal sum of one thousand [$1,000.00] dollars, to be recovered in like manner as in §741.13 for the use of the school fund. [Act Jan. 23, 1832, §4; Rev. St. 23, 1892, §2066; Gen. St. 1906, §2582; Rev. Gen. St. 1920, §3941; Comp. Gen. Laws 1927, §5860.]

§741.16. Penalty for marrying white and negro persons. — If any judge, justice of the peace, notary public or minister of the gospel, clergyman, priest or any person authorized to solemnize the rites of matrimony, shall wilfully and knowingly perform the ceremony of marriage for any white person with a negro, he shall be punished by imprisonment not exceeding one [1] year, or by fine not exceeding one thousand [$1,000.00] dollars. [Laws 1881, c. 3283, §3; Rev. St. 1892, §2608; Gen. St. 1906, §3531; Rev. Gen. St. 1920, §5421; Comp. Gen. Laws 1927, §7564.]

§741.17. Marriage law to apply to negro persons. — From and after the eleventh day of October, 1866, all laws applicable to or regulating the marriage relation between white persons shall apply to the same relation between the colored population of the state. [Laws 1866, c. 1469, §5; Rev. St. 1892, §2067; Gen. St. 1906, §2583; Rev. Gen. St. 1920, §3942; Comp. Gen. Laws 1927, §5861.]

§741.19. Certain marriages betwen white and negro persons valid. — In all cases where marriages have been contracted and solemnized between white persons and persons of color prior to the twelfth day of January, 1866, and where the parties continued to live as man and wife up to that date, the said marriages shall be held valid to all intent and purpose. [Laws 1866, c. 1468, §5; Rev. St. 1892, §2062; Gen. St. 1906, §2585; Rev. Gen. St. 1920, §3944; Comp. Gen. Laws 1927, §5863.]

Prisons
Jails and Jailers

§950.05. Jails to be constructed so white and colored male and female prisoners may be separated. — The county commissioners of the respective counties of this State shall so arrange the jails of their respective counties that it shall be unnecessary to confine in said jails in the same room, cell or apartment white and negro prisoners, or male and female prisoners. [Laws 1909, c. 5967, §1; Rev. Gen. St. 1920, §6213; Comp. Gen. Laws 1927, §8545.]

§950.06. Unlawful for white and colored prisoners, male and female prisoners to be confined together. — It is unlawful for white and negro prisoners to be confined in the county jails of this State in the same cell, room or apartment, or be so confined as to be permitted to commingle . . . [Laws 1909, c. 5967, §2; Rev. Gen. St. 1920, §6214: Comp. Gen. Laws 1927, §8546.]

§950.08. Officers refusing to comply with law subject to removal. — Any board of county commissioners and any sheriff wilfully refusing to carry out and comply with the provisions of §§950.05 and 950.06 in their respective spheres of duty shall be removed from office by the governor. [Laws 1909, ch. 5967, §1; Rev. Gen. Stat. 1920, §6216; Comp. Gen. Laws 1927, §8548.]

State Convicts

§952.15 — Chaining white prisoners to colored prisoners; penalty. — It is unlawful for any sheriff, constable, bailiff, guard or other officer having prisoners in their custody to chain, handcuff or in any manner fasten white female or male prisoners to colored prisoners in their charge. Any person violating the provisions of this section, upon conviction, shall be deemed guilty of a misdemeanor, and shall be fined not more than one hundred dollars, or imprisoned in the county jail for not more than six months. [Laws 1905, c. 5447, §§1, 2; Rev. Gen. St. 1920, §5369; Comp. Gen. Laws 1927, §7503.]

Transportation — Railroads

§352.02. Passengers conductor to have police powers. — The conductors of any train carrying passengers in this State are invested with all the powers, duties and responsibilities of police officers while on duty on their trains . . . The conductor may cause any person violating any provision of this section, and which are in violation of the laws of this State, to be detained and delivered to the proper authorities for trial as soon as practicable. [Laws 1891, c. 4072, §1; Comp. Gen. Laws 1927, §7782.]

[Note: §901.18 [Stat. 1941 (Rev.)] provides that an officer making a lawful arrest may summon the aid of "as many persons as he deems necessary to aid him in making the arrest." Such persons are required to give assistance when requested and §843.06 [Stat. 1941 (Rev.)] makes failure or refusal to aid peace officers to make an arrest when required to do so an offense punishable by fine up to $50.00 or imprisonment not exceeding one month. These provisions may explain the behavior of train conductors when segregation on trains is challenged by Negro passengers.]

352.03. First-class tickets and accommodations for negro persons. — All railroad companies doing business in this State shall sell to all respectable negro persons first-class tickets, on application, at the same rates white persons are charged, and shall furnish and set apart for the use of such negro persons who purchase such first-class tickets a car or cars in each passenger train, as may be necessary, equally as good and provided with the same facility and comfort as shall or may be provided for whites using and traveling as passengers on first-class tickets.

No conductor or person in charge of any passenger train on any railroad shall suffer or permit any white person to ride, sit or travel, or to do any act or thing to insult or annoy any negro person who shall be sitting, riding and traveling, in said car so set apart for the use of negro persons, nor shall he or they, while in charge of such train, suffer or permit any negro person, nor shall such person attempt to, ride, sit or travel in the car or cars set apart for the use of the white persons traveling as first-class passengers; but female colored nurses, having the care of children or sick persons, may ride and travel in such car. [Laws 1887, c. 3743, §§1, 2; Rev. St. 1892, §2268; Gen. St. 1906, §2860; Rev. Gen. St. 1920, §4554; Comp. Gen. Laws 1927, §6617.]

352.04. Separate accommodations for white and colored passengers. —

All railroad companies and other common carriers doing business in this State shall provide equal separate accommodations for white and colored passengers on railroads, and all white and colored passengers occupying passenger cars which are operated in this State by any railroad company *or other common carrier* are hereby required to occupy the respective cars, or divisions of cars, provided for them, so that the white passengers shall occupy only the cars or divisions of cars, provided for white passengers, and the colored passengers only the cars, or division of cars, provided for colored passengers; provided, that no railroad shall use divided cars for the separation of the races without the permission of the railroad commission, nor any car divided for that purpose in which the divisions are not permanent. [Laws 1909, c. 5893, §1; Rev. Gen. St. 1920, §455 Comp. Gen. Laws, 1927, §6618.] (italics supplied)

[Note: This statute applies to all *common carriers* and it would appear to include bus travel.]

§352.05. Passenger occupying part of car set apart for opposite race; penalty. — Any white person unlawfully and wilfully occupying, as a passenger, any car or part of car not so set apart and provided for white passengers, and any colored passenger unlawfully and wilfully occupying, as a passenger, any car or part of car not so set apart and provided for colored passengers, shall, upon conviction, be punished by a fine not exceeding five hundred [$500.] dollars, or imprisonment not exceeding six [6] months. Nothing in this section shall apply to persons lawfully in charge of or under the charge of persons of the other race. [Laws 1909, §5893, §4; Rev. Gen. St. 1920, §5566 Comp. Gen. Laws, 1927. §7752.]

§352.06. Penalty for violations §352.04. — [Railroad company or common carrier liable to penalty of up to $500.00 for each offense of violation.] [Laws 1909, c. 5893, §3; Rev. Gen. St. 1920, §4556; Comp. Gen. Laws, 1927, §6619.]

§352.07. Separate accommodations for white and negro passengers on electric cars. — All persons operating urban and suburban (or either) electric cars as common carriers of passengers of this State, shall furnish equal but separate accommodations for white and negro passengers on all cars so operated. [Laws 1907, c. 5617, §1; Rev. Gen. St. 1920, §4557; Comp. Gen. Laws 1927, §6620.]

§352.08. Method of division in electric cars. — The separate accommodations for white and negro passengers directed in §352.07 shall be by separate cars, fixed divisions, movable screens, or other method of division in the cars. [Laws 1907, c. 5617, §2; Rev. Gen. St. 1920, §4558; Comp. Gen. Laws 1927, §6621.]

§352.09. Divisions to be marked "For White" or "For Colored". — The car or division provided for white passengers shall be marked in plain letters in a conspicuous place "For White", and the car or division provided for negro passengers shall be marked in plain letters, in a conspicuous place, "For Colored."]Laws 1907, c. 5617, §7; Rev. Gen. St. 1920, §4559; Comp. Gen. Laws 1927, §6622.]

§352.10. [Exception] Not to apply to nurses. — Nothing in §§352.07, 352.08, 352.09, 352.12, 352.13, 352.14, or 352.15 shall be so construed to apply to nurses of one race attending children or invalids of another race. [Laws 1907,

c. 5617, §8; Rev. Gen. St. 1920, §4560; Comp. Gen. Laws 1927, §6623.]

§352.11. Operating extra cars for exclusive use of either race. — Sections 352.07-352.15 shall not so be construed as to prevent the running of special or extra cars, in addition to the regular schedule cars, for the exclusive accommodation of either white or negro passengers. [Laws 1907, c. 5617, §9; Rev. Gen. St. 1920, §4561; Comp. Gen. Laws 1927, §6624.]

§352.12. Separation of races; penalty. — Any person operating urban and suburban (or either) electric cars as common carriers of passengers in this state, failing, refusing or neglecting to make provisions for the separation of the white and negro passengers on such cars as required by law, shall, for each offense, be deemed guilty of a misdemeanor, and upon conviction thereof shall be fined not less than fifty [$50.00] dollars nor more than five hundred [$500.00] dollars. This penalty may be enforced against the president, receiver, general manager, superintendent or other person operating such cars. [Laws 1907, c. 5617, §3; Rev. Gen. St. 1920, §5600; Comp. Gen. Laws 1927, §7787.]

§352.13 Duty of conductors; penalty. — The conductor or other person in charge of any such car shall see that each passenger is in the car or division furnished for the race to which such passenger belongs, and any conductor or other person in charge of such car who shall permit any passenger of one race to occupy a car or division provided for passengers of the other race, shall be deemed guilty of a misdemeanor, and upon conviction thereof shall be punished by a fine of not exceeding twenty-five [$25.00] dollars, or by imprisonment in the county jail for not exceeding sixty [60] days. [Laws 1907, c. 5617, §5; Rev. Gen. St. 1920, §5602; Comp. Gen. Laws 1927, §7789.]

§352.14. Violation by passenger; conductor may arrest and eject; penalty. — Any passenger belonging to one race who wilfully occupies or attempts to occupy any such car, or division thereof, provided for passengers of the other race, or who occupying such car or division thereof, refuses to leave the same when requested so to do by the conductor or other person in charge of such car, shall be deemed guilty of a misdemeanor, and upon conviction thereof shall be punished by a fine of not exceeding fifty [$50.00] dollars, or by imprisonment in the county jail for not exceeding three months. The conductor or other person in charge of such car is vested with full power and authority to arrest such passenger and to eject him or her from the car. [Laws 1907, c. 5617, §6; Rev. Gen. St. 1920, §5603; Comp. Gen. Laws 1927, §7790.]

§352.15. Each day of refusal separate offense. — Each day of refusal, failure or neglect to provide for the separation of the white and negro passengers as directed in this chapter shall constitute a separate and distinct offense. [Laws 1907, c. 5617, §4; Rev. Gen. St. 1920, §5601; Comp. Gen. Laws 1927, §7788.]

§352.16. Separate waiting rooms and ticket windows for white and negro passengers. — All railroad companies and terminal companies in this state shall provide separate waiting rooms and ticket windows of equal accommodation for white and colored passengers at all depots along lines of railway owned, controlled or operated by them, and at terminal passenger stations controlled and operated by them. [Laws 1907, c. 5619, §1; Rev. Gen. St. 1920,

§4562; Comp. Gen. Laws 1927, §6625.]

§352.17. Penalty for refusal to comply with law or regulations. — If any railroad company or terminal company in this state shall refuse to comply with any provision of §352.16, or to comply with any rule, order or regulation provided or subscribed by the railroad commissioners under the authority of §350.21, such company shall thereby incur a penalty for each such offense of not more than five thousand [$5,000.00] dollars, to be fixed, imposed and collected by said railroad commissioners in the manner provided by law. [Laws 1907, c. 5619, §3; Rev. Gen. St. 1920, §4563; Comp. Gen. Laws 1927, §6626.]

§352.18. Penalty for not providing separate cars for white and negro persons. — If any railroad company or any conductor or other employee thereof, or any person whatever, shall violate the provisions relating to the accommodation of white or negro passengers, he or they shall be punished by a fine not exceeding five hundred [$500.00] dollars, unless otherwise provided for.

If any railroad company shall fail to comply with said provisions of law the punishment herein prescribed may be inflicted upon the president, receiver, general manager or superintendent thereof, or upon each and every one of them. [Laws 1887, c. 3743, §§3, 4; Rev. St. 1892, §2686; Gen. St. 1906, §3632; Rev. Gen. St. 1920, §5565; Comp. Gen. Laws 1927, §7751.]

§350.20. Authority to make rules for separation of races in passenger cars. — The railroad commissioners of the State of Florida may prescribe reasonable rules and regulations relating to the separation of white and colored passengers in passenger cars being operated in this State by any railroad company or other common carrier. [Laws 1909, c. 5893, §2; Rev. Gen. St. 1920, §4625; Comp. Gen. Laws 1927, §6711.]

§350.21. May require construction or alteration of depots to scure separation of races; rules and regulations. — The railroad commissioners of the State of Florida may require the building or alteration of any and all passenger depots and terminal stations in this state, in such manner as to secure the separation of white and colored passengers, as required by §352.16, but said commissioners may, for good cause shown, extend the time for the building or alteration of any such depot for such time as may appear reasonable. Said commissioners may prescribe all necessary rules, orders and regulations necessary to carry §352.16 into effect. [Laws 1907, c. 5619, §2; Rev. Gen. St. 1920, §4626; Comp. Gen. Laws 1927, §6712.]

GEORGIA

CONSTITUTION

Education

Art. VIII. §1(6576) Paragraph I. System of common schools; free tuition; separation of races. — The provision of an adequate education for the citizens shall be a primary obligation of the State of Georgia, the expense of which shall be provided for by taxation. Separate schools shall be provided for the white and colored races. [Const. 1877, §2-6601; Const. 1945, §2-6401.]

Endowed Institutions

Art. VII §2-5404. (6554, 6556) Paragraph IV. Exemptions from taxation.— [In providing tax exemptions for endowed institutions of charity, worship and learning open to the general public, the constitution requires that "all endowments to institutions established for white people, shall be limited to white people, and all endowments to institutions established for colored people shall be limited to colored people;" [Const. 1877, §2-5002, (6554) Par. II.; Const. 1945, §2-5404.]

Slavery

Art. I, §2-117. Slavery and Involuntary Servitude. — There shall be within the State of Georgia neither slavery nor involuntary servitude, save as a punishment for crime after legal conviction thereof. [Const. 1877; Const. 1945 1, Art. I, Par. XVII.]

Social Status

Art. I, §1, Par. XVIII. Status of the citizen. The social status of the citizen shall never be the subject of legislation. [Const. 1945]

GEORGIA CODE ANNOTATED (1935)

Aliens

79-303. (2173) Rights of aliens as to realty. — Aliens, the subjects of governments at peace with the United States and this State, as long as their governments remain at peace, shall be entitled to all the rights of citizens of other States resident in this State, and shall have the privilege of purchasing, holding and conveying real estate in this State. [Act 1785, Cobb, 364; Act 1849, Cobb, 367.]

79-304. (2175) Liens, receiving and enforcing. — Aliens may receive and enforce liens by mortgage or otherwise on real estate in this State. [Act 1785, Cobb, 364.]

Billiard and Poolrooms

§84-1603. Qualification of licensees; . . . — No license to operate a billiard room shall be issued to any person who is not 21 years of age and a citizen of the U.S., or who has been convicted of a felony; nor to any person of the white or Caucasian race to operate a billiard room to be used, frequented or patronized by persons of the Negro race; nor to any person of the Negro race to operate a billiard room to be used, frequented or patronized by persons of the white or Caucasian race . . . [Acts 1925, p. 286.]

§84-1604. **Application for license; affidavit; . . .** — [Requires each applicant for license to make a sworn affidavit "that, if a white person, he will not permit Negroes to congregate or play in his place of business; and, if a Negro, he will not permit any white person to remain or play in his place of business."] [Acts 1925, p. 287.]

Definition of "Negro" and "White"

§79-103. **(2177) Persons of color, who are.** — All Negroes, mulattoes, mestizos and their descendants, having any ascertainable trace of either Negro or African, West Indian, or Asiatic Indian blood in their veins, and all descendants of any person having either Negro or African, West Indian, or Asiatic Indian blood in his or her veins shall be known in this State as persons of color. [Acts 1865-6, p. 239; 1927, p. 272.]

§53-312. **"White person" defined.** — The term "white person" shall include only persons of the white or Caucasian race, who have no ascertainable trace of either Negro, African, West Indian, Asiatic Indian, Mongolian, Japanese, or Chinese blood in their veins. No person, any one of whose ancestors has been duly registered with the State Bureau of Vital Statistics as a colored person or person of color, shall be deemed to be a white person. [Acts 1927, p. 277.]

[Note: — See Miscegenation below.]

Education
Public Schools — Segregation

§32-909. [1947 Cum. Supp.] **School term. School property and facilities.** — [Provides for county boards of education and requires that, "It shall also be the duty of said board of education to make arrangements for the instruction of the children of the white and colored races in separate schools. They shall, as far as practicable, provide the same facilities for both races in respect to attainments and abilities of teachers but the children of the white and colored races shall not be taught together in any common or public school . . ."] [Acts 1919, p. 323; 1937, pp. 882, 892; 1946 pp. 206, 207.]

§32-937. [1947 Cum. Supp.] **Free tuition; colored and white children Separate; . . .** — [Provides free schools for children 6 to 18 years of age. Provides further, "Colored and white children shall not attend the same schools; and no teacher receiving or teaching white and colored pupils in the same schools shall be allowed any compensation out of the common school fund . . ."] [Acts 1919, p. 331; 1945, p. 397.]

Schools for Blind and Deaf
Schools for Blind

§§45-701 - 35-709; §§32-2801 - 32-2805. [1947 Cum. Supp.]—[No statutory provision for segregation.]

Schools for Deaf

§§35-801 - 35-810; §§32-2801 - 32-2805. [1947 Cum. Supp.]—[No statutory provision for segregation.]

Juvenile Delinquents

Georgia Training School for Girls

§77-701. [1947 Cum. Supp.] School established. — There shall be established in the State of Georgia an institution to be known as the Georgia Training School for Girls. The colored division of the Georgia Training School for Girls shall be located in Bibb county, Georgia, upon land donated to the State of Georgia for such purposes . . . [Acts 1913, p. 87; 1937, p. 682.]

[Note: The Georgia Training School for Girls (white) is located in Fulton County, Georgia.]

§77-707. [1947 Cum. Supp.] Support and maintenance of colored division.—The Governor as Director of the Budget and the Budget Commission are hereby authorized to support and maintain the colored division of the Georgia Training School for Girls, created and established by section 77-701, and located in Bibb County, Georgia, out of any funds which may be available from the State Department of Public Welfare, and out of any other funds which might be available for the purpose in the discretion of the Budget Commission. [Acts 1943, p. 628.]

Georgia Training School for Boys

§77-613. (1249 P.C.) Separation of races. — The white and colored inmates shall be kept separate and distinct in all work and study. [Acts 1919, p. 376.]
[Note: See also §77-614.]

Colleges and Universities

§§32-101 - 32-103. [University of Georgia System.]—[Provision is made for the consolidation of all branch colleges into the University of Georgia System. The following schools of this system are for Negroes: Georgia Industrial and Normal College, Savannah, Georgia (four-year college); Georgia Industrial and Normal College, Albany, Georgia, (junior college); School of Agriculture and Mechanical Arts, Forsyth, Georgia, (a junior college; name changed to State Teachers and Agricultural College for Negroes).] [Acts 1931, pp. 7, 20; Acts 1931, p. 134.]

§32-123. — [Provides all the branches of the University of Georgia except the Georgia School of Technology at Atlanta and the colleges for Negroes, "shall be open to all white female students of proper age and qualification."] [Acts 1889, p. 123; 1931, pp. 7, 20.]

Regional Education
Georgia Laws 1949, p. 56.

SOUTHERN STATES EDUCATIONAL COMPACT.
No. 4 (House Resolution No. 9-59C).
A Resolution.

Giving legislative approval to a certain compact entered into by the State of Georgia and other Southern States by and through their respective Governors on February 8, 1948, as amended, relative to the development and maintenance of regional educational services in schools in the Southern States in the professional, technological, scientific, literary, and other fields, so as to provide greater educational advantages and facilities for the citizens in the several states who reside in such region; to declare that the State of Georgia is a part of the State compact, as amended, and that the agreements, covenants and obligations therein are binding upon said State.

Preamble.

Whereas, on the 8th day of February, in the Year of Our Lord, One Thousand Nine Hundred and Forty-eight, the State of Georgia, and the States of Florida, Maryland, Louisiana, Alabama, Mississippi, Tennessee, Arkansas, Virginia, North Carolina, South Carolina, Texas, Oklahoma, West Virginia, through and by their respective governors, entered into a written compact relative to the development and maintenance of regional educational services and schools in the Southern States in the professional, technological, scientific, literary, and other fields, so as to provide greater educational advantages and facilities for the citizens of the several States who reside within such region; and

Whereas, the said compact has been amended in certain respects, a copy of which compact as amended is as follows:

The Regional Compact.
(as amended)

"Whereas, The States who are parties hereto have during the past several years conducted careful investigation looking toward the establishment and maintenance of jointly owned and operated regional educational institutions in the Southern States in the professional, technological, scientific, literary and other fields, so as to provide greater educational advantages and facilities for the citizens of the several States who reside within such region; and

"Whereas, Meharry Medical College of Nashville, Tennessee, has proposed that its lands, buildings, equipment, and the net income from its endowment be turned over to the Southern States, or to an agency acting in their behalf, to be operated as a regional institution for medical, dental and nursing education upon terms and conditions to be hereafter agreed upon between the Southern States and Meharry Medical College, which proposal, because of the present financial condition of the institution, has been approved by the said States who are parties hereto; and

"Whereas, The said States desire to enter into a compact with each other providing for the planning and establishment of regional educational facilities;

"Now, therefore, in consideration of the mutual agreements, covenants and obligations assumed by the respective States who are parties hereto (hereinafter referred to as "States"), the said several States do hereby form a geographical district or region consisting of the areas lying within the boundaries of the contracting States which, for the purposes of this compact, shall constitute an area for regional education supported by public funds derived from taxation by the constituent States and derived from other sources for the establishment, acquisition, operation and maintenance of regional educational schools and institutions for the benefit of citizens of the respective States residing within the region so established as may be determined from time to time in accordance with the terms and provisions of this compact.

"The States do further hereby establish and create a joint agency which shall be known as the Board of Control for Southern Regional Education (hereinafter referred to as the "Board"), the members of which Board shall consist of the Governor of each State, ex officio, and three additional citizens of each State to be appointed by the Governor thereof, at least one of whom shall be selected from the field of education. The Governor shall continue as a member of the Board during his tenure of office as Governor of the State, but the members of the Board appointed by the Governor shall hold office for a period of four years except that in the original appointments one Board member so appointed by the Governor shall be designated at the time of his appointment to serve an initial term of two years, one Board member to serve an initial term of three years, and the remaining Board member to serve the full term of four years, but thereafter the successor of each appointed Board member shall serve the full term of four years. Vacancies on the Board caused by death, resignation, refusal or inability to serve, shall be filled by appointment, by the Governor for the unexpired portion of the term. The officers of the Board shall be a Chairman, a Vice-Chairman, a Secretary, a Treasurer, and such additional officers as may be created by the Board from time to time. The Board shall meet annually and officers shall be elected to hold office until the next annual meeting. The Board shall have the right to formulate and establish bylaws not inconsistent with the provisions of this compact to govern its own actions in the performance of the duties delegated to it including the right to create and appoint an Executive Committee and a Finance Committee with such powers and authority as the Board may delegate to them from time to time. The Board may, within its discretion, elect as its Chairman a person who is not a member of the Board, provided such person resides within a signatory State, and upon such election such person shall become a member of the Board with all the rights and privileges of such membership.

"It shall be the duty of the Board to submit plans and recommendations to the States from time to time for their approval and adoption by appropriate legislative action for the development, establishment, acquisition, operation and maintenance of educational schools and institutions within the geographical limits of the regional area of the States, of such character and type and for such educational purposes, professional, technological, scientific, literary, or otherwise, as they may deem and determine to be proper, necessary or advisable. Title to all such educational institutions when so established by appropriate legislative actions of the States and to all properties and facilities used in connection therewith shall be vested in said Board as the agency of and for the use and benefit of the said States and the citizens thereof, and all such educational institutions shall be operated, maintained and financed in the manner herein set out, subject to any provisions or limitations which may be contained in the legislative acts of the States authorizing the creation, establishment and operation of such educational institutions.

"In addition to the power and authority heretofore granted, the Board shall have the power to enter into such agreements or arrangements with any of the States and with educational institutions or agencies, as may be required in the judgment of the Board, to provide adequate services and facilities for graduate, professional, and technical education for the benefit of the citizens of the respective States residing within the region, and such additional and general power and authority as may be vested in the Board from time to time by legislative enactment on the said States.

"Any two or more States who are parties of this compact shall have the right to enter into supplemental agreements providing for the establishment, financing and operation of regional educational institutions for the benefit of citizens residing within an area which constitutes a portion of the general region herein created, such institutions to be financed exclusively by such States and to be controlled exclusively by the members of the Board representing such States provided such agreement is submitted to and approved by the Board prior to the establishment of such institutions.

"Each State agrees that, when authorized by the Legislature, it will from time to time make available and pay over to said Board such funds as may be required for the establishment, acquisition, operation and maintenance of such regional educational institutions as may be authorized by the States under the terms of this compact, the contribution of each State at all times to be in the proportion that its population bears to the total combined population of the States who are parties hereto as shown from time to time by the most recent official published report of the Bureau of Census of the United States of America; or upon such other basis as may be agreed upon.

"This compact shall not take effect or be binding upon any State unless and until it shall be approved by proper legislative action of as many as six or more of the States whose Governors have subscribed hereto within a period of eighteen months from the date hereof. When and if six or more States shall have given legislative approval to this compact within said eighteen months' period, it shall be and become binding upon such six or more States 60 days after the date of legislative approval by the sixth State and the Governors of such six or more States shall forthwith name the members of the Board from their States as hereinabove set out, and the Board shall then meet on call of the Governor of any State approving this compact, at which time the Board shall elect officers, adopt bylaws, appoint committees and otherwise fully organize. Other States whose names are subscribed hereto shall thereafter become parties hereto upon approval of this compact by legislative action within two years from the date hereof, upon such conditions as may be agreed upon at the time. Provided, however that with respect to any State whose constitution may require amendment in order to permit legislative approval of the compact, such State or States shall become parties hereto upon approval of this compact by legislative action within seven years from the date hereof, upon such conditions as may be agreed upon at the time.

"After becoming effective this compact shall thereafter continue without limitation of time provided, however, that it may be terminated at any time by unanimous action of the States and provided further that any State may withdraw from this compact if such withdrawal is approved by its legislature, such withdrawal to become effective two years after written notice thereof to the Board accompanied by a certified copy of the requisite legislative action, but such withdrawal shall not relieve the withdrawing State from its obligations hereunder accruing up to the effective date of such withdrawal. Any State so withdrawing shall ipso facto cease to have any claim to or ownership of any of the property held or vested in the Board or to any of the funds of the Board held under the terms of this compact.

"If any State shall at any time become in default in the performance of any of its obligations assumed herein or with respect to any obligation imposed upon said State as authorized by and in compliance with the terms and provisions of this compact, all rights, privileges and benefits of such defaulting State, its members on the Board and its citizens shall ipso facto be and become suspended from and after the date of such default. Unless such default shall be remedied and made good within a period of one year immediately following the date of such default this compact may be terminated with respect to such defaulting State by an affirmative vote of three-fourths of the members of the Board (exclusive of the members representing the State in default), from and after which time such State shall cease to be a party to this compact and shall have no further claim to or ownership of any of the property held by or vested in the Board or to any of the funds of the Board held under the terms of this compact, but such termination shall in no manner release such defaulting State from any accrued obligation or otherwise affect this compact or the rights, duties, privileges or obligations of the remaining States thereunder.

In witness whereof this compact has been approved and signed by Governors of the Several States, subject, to the approval of their respective legislatures in the manner hereinabove set out, as of the 8th day of February, 1948."

STATE OF FLORIDA
By (s) Millard Caldwell
    Governor

STATE OF ARKANSAS
By Ben Laney
    Governor

STATE OF MARYLAND
By (s) William Preston Lane, Jr.
    Governor

COMMONWEALTH OF VIRGINIA
By (s) William M. Tuck
    Governor

STATE OF GEORGIA
By (s) M. E. Thompson
    Governor

STATE OF NORTH CAROLINA
By (s) R. Gregg Cherry
    Governor

STATE OF LOUISIANA
By (s) Jimmie H. Davis
Governor

STATE OF SOUTH CAROLINA
By (s) J. Strom Thurmond
Governor

STATE OF ALABAMA
By (s) James E. Folsom
Governor

STATE OF TEXAS
By (s) Beauford H. Jester
Governor

STATE OF MISSISSIPPI
By (s) Fielding L. Wright
Governor

STATE OF OKLAHOMA
By (s) Roy J. Turner
Governor

STATE OF TENNESSEE
By (s) Jim McCord
Governor

STATE OF WEST VIRGINIA
By (s) Clarence W. Meadows
Governor

Therefore, Be It Resolved, and it is hereby resolved by the General Assembly of Georgia:

Section I. That the said compact as amended, be, and the same is hereby approved and the State of Georgia is hereby declared to be a party hereto, and agreements, covenants, and obligations therein are binding upon the State of Georgia.

Section II. That upon the approval of this compact as amended by the requisite number of States, the Honorable Herman Eugene Talmadge, Governor of the State of Georgia, is authorized to sign an engrossed copy of the compact as amended, and provide sufficient copies thereof so that every State approving the same shall have an engrossed copy.

Section III. This resolution shall take effect upon its approval by the Governor.

Approved January 31, 1949.

[Note: See Note on Regional Compact — Education, Appendix 6.]

Education — Minimum Foundation Program.
Georgia Laws 1949, p. 1406.
EDUCATION — MINIMUM FOUNDATION PROGRAM.
Code §32-913 repealed.
No. 333 (House Bill No. 140).

An Act to establish a minimum foundation program of education in Georgia so as to equalize educational opportunities throughout the State; to provide a minimum foundation program fund for the support of public education including the University System of Georgia in Georgia; to fix a minimum public school term; to define "local units of administration"; to define the duties of the State Board of Education, the State Superintendent of Schools, and superintendents and boards of education of local units of administration; to prescribe the method to be used by the State Board of Education in distributing minimum foundation program funds to local units of administration; to provide a schedule of minimum annual salaries for teachers; to permit local units of administration to supplement salaries of teachers; to establish a method for determining the financial needs of local units of administration to support the minimum foundation program as defined in terms of salaries for teachers and other school personnel, current expenses, capital outlay, and transportation costs; to provide a method for allotting teaching, administrative, supervisory, library and other instructional units; to permit the State Board of Education to make salary allowances for personnel employed by local units for more than ten months; to permit programs of education for adults, pre-school children, and exceptional children at State and/or local expense; to provide a formula for distributing State aid for pupil transportation; to provide a method for determining amounts to be allotted to local units for current expenses other than instructional salaries, transportation costs, and capital outlay; to provide a method for distributing State funds to be used by local units for capital outlay; to establish a method for determining the ability of local units of administration to support the minimum foundation program in terms of an economic index of financial ability; to require each local unit of administration to exert an equitable effort to meet these needs before being entitled to share in State funds for public school purposes; to provide a method for using State funds to supplement the amounts raised by local units in support of the minimum foundation program; to require the State Board of Education to submit to each local unit of administration certain data needed by those units to prepare their respective budgets; to require local units of administration to prepare annual budgets for submittal to the State Board of Education; to provide for the acceptance and distribution of vocational education funds and such other funds as may be made available to the State Board of Education; to provide for a method of determining the annual State funds needed to provide the public schools of the State with free textbooks, teaching materials and aids, and school library books and materials; to provide for a method of determining the annual State funds needed to provide the public libraries of the State with library books and materials; to require the State Board of Education to annually determine the funds needed to provide for a program of vocational education for out-of-school youth, adults, teacher-training, and area schools and to provide for the distribution of such funds; to require the State Board of Education to annually determine the funds needed to provide for a program of vocational rehabilitation and to provide for the expenditure of such funds; to require the State Board of Education to annually determine the funds needed for State trade schools and to provide for the distribution of such funds; to require the State Board of Education to annually determine the funds needed for the State schools for the deaf and blind and such other special schools as may be established by the State Board of Education and to provide for the distribution of such funds; to provide scholarships for eligible young men and women in the State who desire training for the teaching profession; to provide for the selection and appointment of the recipients of such scholarships, to prescribe the powers, duties and authority by the State Board of Education, the

State Department of Education, boards of education of county and independent school systems, and teacher-training institutions as related to the administration of said scholarships, to require certain reports from the boards of education of said county and independent school systems, and of certified teacher-training institutions relative to rules and regulations governing the granting and administration of scholarships, and to provide the method of financing such scholarships; to provide for the determination by the Board of Regents of the funds needed to support the University System of Georgia; to provide the time and conditions under which this Act is to become operative; to provide for the repeal of the Act entitled "An Act to equalize educational opportunities throughout the State; to provide for the operation of the public schools of the State . . . ," approved February 10, 1937 which is published on pages 882 through 892 of the 1937 Georgia Laws; and to provide for the repeal of the Act entitled "An Act to authorize the General Assembly to make an extra appropriation to the common school fund for the purpose of equalizing educational opportunities to the children of the several counties of the State, and for other purposes," approved March 13, 1926 which is published on pages 39 and 40 of the 1926 Georgia Laws, to repeal Section 32-913 of the Code of Georgia, and for other purposes.

Be it enacted by the General Assembly of Georgia, and it is hereby enacted by authority of the same:

Section 1. It is hereby declared to be the public policy of the State of Georgia that educational opportunities for all citizens of this State shall be equalized throughout the State so as to establish, so far as possible, a minimum foundation program of education in Georgia.

Section 2. There is hereby established a State minimum foundation program fund for the public schools, including The University System, of this State, to be known as the "Minimum Foundation Program Fund." Appropriations in support of this program and such appropriations as have been made, or may hereafter be made, by the General Assembly for public education purposes shall be made available by (1) the State Board of Education in accordance with a plan described in Sections 3 through 28 of this Act and (2) by the State Board of Regents in accordance with Section 29 of this Act. Sections 3 through 28 of this Act are specially applicable to the public schools of less than college grade and Section 29 to the University System of Georgia.

Section 3. From and after July 1, 1949, the public schools of this State, including the public high schools, shall be operated for a period of not less than nine school months during each school year. Twenty school days shall constitute a school month. The school year shall begin on the first day of July and end on the thirtieth day of June of each year.

Section 4. For the purposes of this Act, the several counties of this State and the various independent school systems established by law shall be the local units of administration. The superintendents and the boards of education of these respective local units shall execute the provisions of this Act under such rules and regulations as may be adopted by the State Board of Education. In the local units of administration, the several teachers, principals and other school employees shall be elected by the boards of education on the recommendation of the respective superintendents. Contracts for teachers, principals and other professional personnel shall be in writing, signed in duplicate by the teacher in his own behalf, and by the superintendent of schools on behalf of the board.

Section 5. The State Board of Education shall provide, by regulation, for certifying and classifying the teachers in the public schools of this State.

No teacher, principal, supervisor, or superintendent other than county school superintendents, shall be employed in the public schools unless such person shall hold a certificate from the State Board of Education, certifying to his or her qualifications as such teacher, principal, supervisor, or superintendant, pursuant to the rules and regulations of the State Board of Education. The State Board of Education shall provide, by regulation, for the classification of all the teachers in the public schools of this State upon the basis of academic, technical and professional training and experience, and the certificate issued to each such teacher by the State Board of Education, or pursuant to its authority, shall indicate the classification of such teacher.

Section 6. The State Board of Education shall annually fix a schedule of minimum salaries which shall be paid to the teachers of the various classes prescribed by the State Board of Education, which salary schedule shall be uniform for each of the classes fixed by the State Board of Education with no differentiation being made because of subjects or grades taught. A local unit of administration may not pay to any teacher in its employment a salary less than the minimum salary prescribed by the State Board of Education for the class to which such teacher belongs. A local unit may supplement the salaries of any of its teachers, and in fixing the amount thereof may take into account the nature of the duties to be performed, the responsibility of the position, the experience and the individual worth of the teacher.

Section 7. The amount of funds needed by a local unit to pay teachers' salaries in support of the foundation program shall be determined on a ten-months' basis in accordance with the State salary schedule provided for in Section 6 of this Act. In each local unit, the number of teachers whose salaries are to be considered in calculating foundation program needs shall be determined on the basis of the number of pupils who were in average daily attendance during the preceding school year per square mile of territory served by the unit.

Teacher-pupil ratios shall be determined separately for Whites and Negroes, and shall, subject to such variations as in the discretion of the State Board of Education may be necessary, be in accordance with the following scale:

Density Scale for Determining Teacher-Pupil Ratios by
Density per Square Mile in Average Daily Attendance
for Whites and Negroes.

	Density Per Square Mile	Teacher-Pupil Ratios	
		Elementary	High School
Class I	Above 12.51	30	25
Class II	10.51 - 12.50	29	24
Class III	8.51 - 10.50	28	23
Class IV	6.51 - 8.50	27	22
Class V	4.51 - 6.50	26	21
Class VI	2.51 - 4.50	24	19
Class VII	1.00 - 2.50	22	17
Class VIII	Below 1	20	15

Independent school systems within municipalities having a popula-
iton of 10,000 or less according to the 1940 U. S. census or any future
census shall be classified on a basis determined by the scale which would
apply to the county by adding the average daily attendance of the independent and county school systems.

The State Board of Education shall have authority to make salary allowances for the employment for two additional months of at least 15 per
cent of the teaching personnel allotted to a local unit for ten months of
the school year, provided: (1) that the local unit employing such personnel
submits a program covering the additional month or months which meets
the approval of the State Board of Education, and (2) that teachers who
work more than ten months in one school year shall be paid for the additional time at the same rate received during the first ten months, provided
if a local unit submits a plan in which it is proposed to employ less than
15 per cent of the personnel the State Board of Education may approve
the plan.

Teachers may be allotted local units to provide programs of education
for adults, pre-school children, and exceptional children at State and/or
local expense when such programs have been approved by the State Board
of Education.

Section 8. The State Board of Education shall have power to determine the amount of funds needed under the foundation program by a local
unit to pay the salaries of the visiting teachers, instructing supervisors,
the county librarian, and supplements to principals.

Section 9. The amount of funds needed by a county school system
to defray the expenses of pupil transportation shall be calculated by the
State Board of Education in accordance with a formula which may take
into account the number of transported pupils in average daily attendance
as well as the density of transported pupils per square mile in the county.
In determining the density of transported pupils within a county the area not
served by public school busses shall be deducted from the total area of the
unit and the State Board shall have authority to determine areas to be
served and not to be served. Counties shall be classified according to the
density of transported pupils as follows:

Density of pupils per square mile in average
daily attendance transported

0 to .99
1.0 to 1.99
2.0 to 2.99
3.0 to 3.99
4.0 to 4.99
5.0 to 5.99
6.0 to 6.99
7.0 to 7.99
8.0 and over

Density classifications shall be determined separately for White and Negro transported pupils and the median cost of transportation per pupil in each of these groups shall be determined on the basis of costs during the preceding school year. The amount of funds needed by each unit to support the foundation program shall be determined by multiplying the number of transported pupils in average daily attendance in that county unit by the median cost of transportation per pupil in the particular density groups to which that unit belongs. Funds granted to a local unit of administration for transportation shall be spent only for transportation purposes.

Section 10. The amount of funds needed by a local unit to take care of current expenses not provided for in Sections 7, 8 and 9 of this Act shall be determined by multiplying the number of teachers allowed that unit under the provisions of Section 7 by a sum of money to be determined by the State Board of Education. This sum shall be determined annually and shall be not less than $300.00 per teacher allotted, provided adequate funds are appropriated by law. The State Board of Education shall define current expenses and shall have authority to establish minimum standards to be met by local units of administration in expending funds for current expenses.

Section 11. The amount of funds needed by a local unit to provide for capital outlay shall be determined by multiplying the number of teachers allotted the unit under the provisions of Section 7 by a sum of money to be determined by the State Board of Education. This sum shall be determined annually and shall not be less than $200.00 per allotted teacher, provided adequate funds are appropriated by law. The State Board of Education may, in its discretion, provide additional funds to local units which have exceptional needs for capital outlay from any funds available for the purpose. In determining these additional capital outlay needs the State Board of Education shall take into consideration the total capital outlay needs of the local unit of administration and the ability of the local unit to meet these needs as measured by the bonding ability of the local unit. It shall be the duty of the State Board of Education to establish minimum standards to be met by local units in order to qualify for participation in capital outlay funds and the State Board also shall provide advisory and supervisory services to the local units regarding the expenditure of such funds. Whether any given item constitutes "capital

101

outlay" as provided for in this Act shall be left to the discretion of the State Board of Education. The State Board of Education shall have authority to survey the needs of local units for capital outlay expenditures.

Section 12. The total foundation program financial needs of a local unit shall be the sum arrived at by adding the amount needed for payment of teachers' salaries as provided for in Section 7 of this Act, the amount needed for payment of salaries of school personnel other than teachers as provided for in Section 8, the amount needed for transportation as provided for in Section 9, the amount needed for current expenses as provided for in Section 10, and the amount needed for capital outlay as provided for in Section 11. This sum shall be known as the total calculated cost of a local unit to support the minimum foundation program of education in Georgia.

Section 13. The State Board of Education shall calculate annually the financial ability of each local unit of administration to support the minimum foundation program. The financial ability of each local unit of administration shall be calculated as follows:

(a) Calculate an economic index for each county in the State as follows:

(1) Calculate for each county its per cent of the State total for each of the following items: property tax digest less homestead exemptions, public utilities tax digest, average effective buying power for five years, average retail sales for five years, motor tag taxes paid, and State income taxes paid.

(2) Giving per cent of the total property tax digest less homestead exemptions, a weight of six; per cent of the total public utilities tax digest, a weight of two; per cent of the average effective buying power for five years, a weight of six; per cent of average retail sales for five years, a weight of two; per cent of motor tag taxes paid, a weight of two; and per cent of state income taxes paid, a weight of one; calculate an economic index of the financial ability of each county expressed in per cent of the State total. Data for property tax digest less homestead exemptions, public utilities tax digest, motor tag taxes paid, and State income taxes paid shall be furnished by the State Department of Revenue, and data for average effective buying power for five years and average retail sales for five years shall be taken from the annual survey of buying power conducted by Sales Management. The State Board of Education shall use the most recent data available at the time the index is calculated. The State Board of Education may, in its discretion vary the number and weights to be assigned to the several factors used in computing the economic index when research proves that a better index can be obtained by changing the weight and/or factors.

(b) Calculate the return of a seven-mill tax levy on the State school tax digest. The State school tax digest shall be composed of the actual tax digests upon which the several county and independent school systems and municipalities levy taxes for the local support of education.

(c) Multiply the economic index for each county in the State as derived in accordance with Section 13 (a) of this Act by the return of a seven-mill tax levy on the State school tax digest as determined in accordance with Section 13 (b) of this Act. The sum obtained by this multiplication shall constitute the local financial ability of a county to support the foundation program financial needs of the county. In those counties of the State which have independent school systems within the boundaries of the county, the local financial ability of the several local units of administration within a county shall be determined by multiplying the per cent that the school tax digest of the local unit of administration is of the total school tax digest of all local units of administration in the county by the total local financial ability of the county to support the foundation program financial needs of the county, provided the school tax digest of each independent school system shall be 133 1/3% of the county tax digest of all property located within the territory of the independent school system. In determining the local financial ability of the counties of Fulton and DeKalb the economic index for the two counties shall be combined so long as the boundaries of the independent school system of Atlanta falls in both Fulton and DeKalb Counties.

Section 14. The amount of State-contributed foundation program funds which shall be allotted to each local unit by the State Board of Education shall be the difference between the total calculated cost as determined in Section 12 of this Act less the local ability of the unit to raise funds as determined in Section 13.

Section 15. The board of education of any local unit of administration, as defined in this Act, may operate the schools of such county or special school district for a longer period than nine months during any school year, or may, in its discretion, supplement the State schedule of salaries, and employ additional teachers not provided for in this Act. It is further provided, however, that teachers in such schools shall receive not less than the minimum monthly salary prescribed by the State Board of Education on the State schedule not only during the regular school year but also during any period by which the school term may be extended, unless the State Board of Education, in its discretion, shall otherwise direct.

Section 16. The State Board of Education shall send to each local unit of administration on or before the beginning of that unit's school year, or as soon thereafter as may be practicable, the following information:

(a) The State minimum schedules of salaries for teachers, and other professional personnel.

(b) The number of teachers in that unit whose salaries are to be considered in calculating foundation program salary needs.

(c) The amount of funds which the State Board of Education considers will be needed by the local unit to pay salaries and travel expenses of personnel referred to in Section 8.

(d) The cost of pupil transportation, as calculated in Section 9.

(e) The local unit's needs for current expenses, as calculated in Section 10.

103

(f) The local unit's current capital outlay needs as calculated in Section 11.

(g) The amount of local effort which will be required of the unit, as set forth in Section 13.

Section 17. Within 30 days from the receipt of the information referred to in Section 16, or within such other period as may be prescribed by the State Board of Education, the board of education of each local unit as herein defined shall file with the State Superintendent of Schools, a budget in duplicate, containing such information as may be required by the State Board of Education and showing proposed expenditures for the ensuing school year, the purposes for which it is proposed such expenditures shall be made, and the sources from which such funds will be derived. When the proposed budget of any local unit of administration has been approved by the State Board of Education, or by the State Superintendent of Schools, in the event that the State Board of Education may delegate such authority to him, the same shall become operative and shall be followed in all expenditures made by such local unit of administration during the school year.

Section 18. All budgets submitted in accordance with the foregoing section shall be passed upon by the State Board of Education, or the State Superintendent of Schools when authorized by the State Board to do so, within 30 days after they are received. If any item or items in the proposed budget shall be disapproved, the board of education of the local unit shall be entitled to notice thereof and a hearing thereon. If the budget submitted shall comply with the provisions of this Act, and of the laws of this State, and shall require the disbursement of no more than the equitable proportion of State funds to which such local unit may be entitled and all available local funds, the same shall be approved by the State Board of Education, and shall become the operating budget for the public schools of the local unit for the ensuing school year. One copy of the approved budget of each local unit shall be filed with the State Superintendent of Schools, and one shall be filed with the board of education of the local unit. State funds to meet the operating expenses provided for by such school budgets shall be withdrawn from the State treasury on executive warrants based on requisitions signed by the State Superintendent of Schools, and shall be disbursed to the various local units by the State Treasurer upon the order of the State Superintendent of Schools. Transfers of funds within their budgets may be made by local boards providing such transfers do not conflict with the provisions of this Act.

Section 19. Nothing in this Act shall affect the distribution of Federal funds allotted to Georgia under the Smith-Hughes Vocational Act, or other Acts of Congress appropriating Federal funds for vocational education purposes, or the distribution of State funds appropriated or allotted for such purposes, but all such funds shall be apportioned by the State Board of Education to the various local units for use in maintaining vocational classes or departments subject to such reasonable rules and regulations as may be prescribed by the State Board of Education and in accordance with the State plan of vocational education; nor shall any provision of this Act prevent the State Board of Education from accepting and administering other funds which may be made available to it, or for the use of the schools of the State for educational purposes, subject to such limitation as may be imposed in the grant or appropriation of the same.

Section 19A. It is hereby declared to be the policy of the State of Georgia, (1) to leave teachers of vocational subjects in the public school system of this state under the jurisdiction and control of the local boards of education, (2) to provide for a program of vocational education for out-of-school youth, adults, teacher training and area schools, under the jurisdiction of the State Board of Education, as provided in Section 22 herein, and (3) that Federal funds for vocational education shall be matched and expended in carrying out the State plan of vocational education in keeping with the requirement of Federal laws relating to vocational education which amount shall not be less than six hundred thousand dollars annually and (4) the State Board of Education is hereby charged with the responsibility of inaugurating and maintaining adequate facilities and opportunities for training in trades and skills in accordance with the policy herein declared.

Section 20. The State Board of Education shall annually determine the funds needed to provide the public schools of the state with free textbooks, teaching materials and aids, and school library books and materials by multiplying the total number of persons enrolled in the public schools of the State by a sum to be determined by the State Board of Education. This sum shall be determined annually and shall be not less than three dollars per person enrolled in the public schools of the State, provided adequate funds are appropriated by law.

Section 21. The State Board of Education shall annually determine the funds needed to provide the public libraries of the State with library materials and books by multiplying the total population of the State by a sum to be determined by the State Board of Education. This sum shall be determined annually and shall be not less than sixteen cents per person, provided adequate funds are appropriated by law.

Section 22. The State Board of Education shall annually determine the funds needed to provide for a program of vocational education for out-of-school youth, adults, teacher training, and area schools. Such funds shall be made available for such programs of education in accordance with rules and regulations established by the State Board of Education.

Section 23. The State Board of Education shall annually determine the funds needed to provide for a program of vocational rehabilitation. Such funds shall be made available for the rehabilitation of handicapped persons in accordance with rules and regulations established by the State Board of Education.

Section 24. The State Board of Education shall annually determine the funds needed for State trade schools established by the State Board of

Education. Such funds shall be made available for the operation of such schools under rules and regulations provided by the State Board of Education.

Section 25. The State Board of Education shall annually determine the funds needed for the State schools for the deaf and blind and for such other special schools for exceptional persons established by the State Board of Education. Such funds shall be made available for the operation of these schools under rules and regulations provided by the State Board of Education.

Section 26. The State Board of Education shall have authority to set up a contingent fund for the special purpose of relieving hardships which may be caused by the operation of the Act and to take care of any unusual or unforseen circumstances.

Section 27. The State Board of Education shall administer this Act, with the exception of Section 29, and enforce its provisions. The State Superintendent of Schools shall be the executive and administrative secretary of the State Board of Education for that purpose. In administering this Act, the State Board of Education shall employ upon the recommendation of the State Superintendent of Schools such supervisors or other employees as may be necessary, and shall fix their compensation.

Section 28. In the event that a local unit of administration should fail to comply with one or more of the provisions of this Act, the State Board of Education, in its discretion, may withhold from that unit, or any part, of the State foundation program funds provided for in this Act until such time as full compliance is made by that unit. Any local board of education shall have the right of certiorari to the courts from any decision of the State Board of Education.

Section 29. The Board of Regents of the University System of Georgia shall biennially determine the funds needed for the operation, maintenance and improvement of the units of the University System of Georgia to be filed with the director of budgets and to be transmitted to the General Assembly as a request for appropriations for the biennium.

In computing the amount of the funds needed for the operation, maintenance and improvement of a University System the following guides shall be followed:

(1) The amount of funds needed for instruction, maintenance and operation shall be determined by multiplying the total estimated number of students to be annually enrolled by a figure to be determined by the Board of Regents which in their opinion will provide adequate funds for these purposes.

(2) Not less than one million dollars annually shall be included for the support of research and extension work.

(3) Two million dollars annually shall be included for the construction of buildings and for the purchase of equipment.

(4) The Board of Regents shall allocate to the several units of the University System all funds appropriated according to the needs of each

institution to be determined under rules and regulations promulgated by the Board of Regents.

Section 30. The Act entitled "An Act to equalize education opportunities throughout the State; to provide for the operation of the public schools of the State; to fix a minimum public school term; to provide for the selection of teachers and administrative officials; to prescribe methods of allotting, distributing, and disbursing the common school funds; to define the duties of the State Board of Education and the State Superintendent of Schools; to provide for local units of administration in the operation of the common schools and for the submission of budgets by such local units of administration"; etc., approved February 10, 1937, which is published on pages 882 through 892 of the 1937 Georgia Laws, is hereby repealed.

The Act entitled "An Act to authorize the General Assembly to make an extra appropriation to the common-school fund for the purpose of equalizing educational opportunities to the children of the several counties of the State, and for other purposes," approved March 13, 1926, which is published on pages 39 and 40 of the 1926 Georgia Laws, is hereby repealed.

Section 31. This Act shall become effective when sufficient funds have been realized from taxes as referred to in Section 55 of H.B. No. 116 (General Appropriations Act of 1949). The State Board of Education is required to formally order this Act into effect as soon as sufficient revenue is available as set forth above, provided, however that the operation of this Act shall not cause a reduction in total funds distributed to any local unit under present laws. The Budget Bureau shall authorize the amount of additional funds available within the appropriations authorized by the General Assembly.

Section 32. The section of the Code of Georgia repealed by the Act entitled "An Act to equalize educational opportunities throughout the State"; etc., approved February 10, 1937, and published on pages 882 thru 892 of the Acts of 1937 does not reinstate the Section of the Code of Georgia repealed by said Act and it is hereby specifically declared that said Code Section shall remain repealed as provided in said Act of 1937.

Section 33. That 32-913 of the Code of Georgia be and the same is hereby repealed. Said section read as follows:

"32-913. Employment of teachers. — County boards of education are empowered to employ teachers to serve in the schools under their jurisdiction and the contracts for said service shall be in writing and signed in duplicate by the teacher on his own behalf and by the county school superintendent on behalf of the board."

Section 33A. The policy of the State with respect to the portions of this Act, which will be administered by the State Board of Education, is to provide a minimum foundation program budget to be expended by the State Board of Education on a minimum basis with the view that when adequate funds are available the following budget shall be adopted

by the State Board of Education:

Public Schools	Total Annual Needs	Amount to be provided by: Cities and Co.	Federal	State
(1) Teachers' Salaries*— 10 months for 23,436 classroom units and 700 other $52,390,050		Less amount of required local effort for foundation program based on index of economic ability.		Difference between the cost of the total basic foundation program and the financial effort required of local school systems to be paid by the State.
(2) Teachers' Salaries*— 15% of Staff— 2 months 2,620,670				
(3) Current Operation Expense (23,436 x $300) 7,030,800				
(4) Pupil Transportation 6,000,000				
(5) Current Capital Outlay (23,436 x $200) 4,687,200				
(6) Twelfth Grade Program—417 Additional Teachers .... 1,251,000 (12 grades for 50% of pupils 1945-51)				
(7) Total Basic Foundation Program $73,979,720		$10,000,000		$63,979,720
(8) Textbook, Teaching Aids and School Library 2,200,000				2,200,000
(9) Maintenance of School Plants and Insurance 2,600,000		2,600,000		
(10) Payment of Bonds and Interest.................. 2,912,140		2,912,140		
(11) Vocational Ed.— Cooperative part-time programs for out-of-school youth and adults, teacher training, and area schools 1,200,000			600,000	600,000
(12) State Department of Education 275,000				275,000
(13) Lunchroom Program 6,735,000		4,075,000	2,610,000	50,000
(14) Surplus Commodities 1,998,318		6,318	1,962,000	30,000
(15) Public Library Program 1,500,000		1,000,000		500,000
(16) Vocatonal Rehabilitation 1,500,000			750,000	750,000
(17) State Trade Schools (Americus and Clarkesville) 375,000				375,000
(18) State School for the Deaf 232,000				232,000
(19) State School for the Blind 160,000				160,000
Total Educational Budget $96,067,178		$20,593,458	$5,922,000	$69,251,720

*Items (1) and (2) include salaries and travel for regular vocational education teachers estimated at $4,608,000, and for principals, system superintendents, visiting teachers, instructional supervisors, county and regional librarians and teachers of non-vocational subjects estimated at $50,402,720.

It is contemplated in this Act that a contingent or equalization fund shall be set up as provided in Section 26 herein and that the above suggested budget shall be varied so as to provide for said fund in such an amount as the State Board of Education deems proper. Such funds shall be taken from the items included in the budget on a pro-rata basis.

In the event funds are not available for the adoption of a budget to include as much as the total amount for each item in the above suggested budget, that all items included therein shall be reduced on a pro-rata basis.

Any surplus over and above $50,000 for any of the above stated items in any fiscal year, shall be returned to the State Board of Education to be used as the said Board deems proper.

Any funds necessary for matching Federal funds for any project approved by the State Board of Education, shall be made available by said Board from any available funds.

Section 34. All laws and parts of laws in conflict with this Act be and the same are hereby repealed.

Approved February 25, 1949.

Endowed Institutions

§92-201. (998) [1947 Cum. Supp.] Property exempt from taxation. — The following described property shall be exempt from taxation, to wit: All public property; places of religious worship or burial; all institutions of purely public charity; hospitals not operated for the purpose of private or corporate profit or income; all buildings erected for and used as a college, nonprofit hospital, incorporated academy or other seminary of learning, and also all funds or property held or used as endowment by such colleges; nonprofit hospitals, incorporated academies or seminaries of learning, provided the same is not invested in real estate; and provided, further, that said exemptions shall only apply to such colleges, non-profit hospitals, incorporated academies or other seminaries of learning as are open to the general public; *provided further, that all endowments to institutions established for white people, shall be limited to white people, and all endowments to institutions established for colored people; shall be limited to colored people* ... [Acts 1946, p. 12; 1947, p. 1183.] (italics supplied)

[Note: See above §2-5404.]

Election — Registration and Qualification of Voters
Georgia Laws, 1949 p. 1204, Act No. 297,
H. B. No. 2, approved February 25, 1949.

[Note: This act provides for the complete revision of all laws in Georgia relating to the registration and qualification of voters. While there is no specific reference to race or color, the Act is admittedly directed toward restricting the Negro vote. Those provisions which appear to be most restrictive are summarized below.]

Sec. 1. — [Provides that from the effective date of the approval of this Act, no person shall be permitted to vote in any election in the State for federal, State or local officers "unless such person shall have been registered and qualified as hereinafter provided."]

Sec. 2. — [Provides that except with reference to any special election occurring before the first general election list shall have been prepared, "all registrations heretofore effected are hereby declared null and void."]

Sec. 3. — [Provides that the first registration list under the terms of this Act be prepared in 1950, and requires that "all persons seeking to register and qualify as voters shall be registered and qualified as herein provided."]

Sec. 4. — [Requires electors to vote at least once in every two years in order to maintain their status as qualified voters.]

Sec. 21. — [Requires all applicants for registration as voters to submit to oral examinations to be given by local registrars. Further provides "In order to ascertain whether an applicant is eligible for qualification as a voter in this classification, the registrars shall orally propound to him the thirty questions on the standardized list set forth in the following section. If the applicant can give factually correct answers to ten of the thirty questions as they are propounded to him, then the registrars shall enter an order declaring him to be prima facie qualified. If he cannot correctly answer the ten out of the thirty questions propounded to him, then an order shall be entered rejecting his application."]

Sec. 22. — [Sets forth the standard list of 30 questions to be used in the oral examination of each applicant who seeks qualification as a voter. Provides "The standard list of questions and the present correct answers thereto and the form to be used under this and the preceding Section is as follows:

STANDARD LIST OF QUESTIONS

(To be propounded to those seeking to register and qualify as voters under Article II, Section I, Paragraph IV, Sub-Paragraph 1 of the Constitution.)

Date of Examination...

Name of Applicant...

Address of Applicant...

Questions	Correct Answer	Answer of Applicant
1. Who is President of the United States?	Harry S. Truman	
2. What is the term of office of the President of the United States?	Four years	
3. May the President of the United States be legally elected for a second term?	Yes	
4. If the President of the United States dies in office who succeeds him?	Vice-President	

110

Questions	Correct Answer	Answer of Applicant
5. How many groups compose the Congress of the United States?	Two — The Senate and House of Representatives	
6. How many United States Senators are there from Georgia?	Two	
7. What is the term of office of a United States Senator?	Six years	
8. Who are the United States Senators from Georgia?	Walter F. George and Richard B. Russell	
9. Who is Governor of Georgia?	Herman Talmadge	
10. Who is Lieutenant Governor of Georgia?	Marvin Griffin	
11. Who is Chief Justice of the Supreme Court of Georgia?	Henry Duckworth	
12. Who is Chief Judge of the Court of Appeals of Georgia?	I. H. Sutton	

STANDARD LIST OF QUESTIONS

13. Into what two groups is the General Assembly of Georgia divided?	Senate and House of Representatives	
14. Does each Georgia County have at least one representative in the Georgia House of Representatives?	Yes	
15. Do all Georgia counties have the same number of representatives in the Georgia House of Representatives?	No	
16. In what city are the laws of the United States made?	Washington	
17. How old do you have to be to vote in Georgia?	18 years old	
18. What city is the capitol of the United States?	Washington, D.C.	
19. How many states are there in the the United States?	48	
20. Who is the Commander-in-Chief of the United States Army?	The President of the United States	

(The following questions requiring a different answer according to the localities in which the applicant lives, the registrars in printing this list will insert under the column headed "Correct Answer" the Correct Answer to each question)

111

Questions	Correct Answer	Answer of Applicant

21. In what Congressional District do you live?

22. Who represents your Congressional District in the National House of Representatives?

23. In what State Senatorial District do you live?

24. What is the State Senator that represents your Senatorial District?

25. In what County do you live?

26. Who represents your County in the House of Representatives of Georgia? If there are more than one representative, name them.

27. What is the name of the County seat of your County?

28. Who is the Ordinary of your County?

29. Who is the Judge of the Superior Court of your circuit? If there are more than one, name one additional Judge.

30. Who is the Solicitor General of your circuit?

TOTAL CORRECT ANSWERS ....

The registrars shall keep a reasonable supply of extra copies of the question and answer blanks and distribute them to any member of the public who may request copies."]

Sec. 23. — [Provides that "electors who have qualified shall not thereafter be required to register or further qualify, except as may be required by the board of registrars. *No person shall remain a qualified voter who does not vote in at least one election within a two year period unless he shall specifically request continuation of his registration in the manner hereinafter provided."* (italics supplied).

The section further provides that the tax collector or tax commissioner is required to notify all voters who have failed to vote once in two years, or before March 1st of each calendar year beginning in 1952, and thereafter to cancel the registrations of those electors who have not applied for continuance of their registration and to remove their names from the qualified voter's list.

All those voters whose registrations thus have been cancelled must re-register and requalify in the manner provided for original registrations.]

Hospitals

Milledgeville State Hospital for Mental Patients.

§35-225. (1598) - **Hospital to be divided into apartments.** — The board of Control shall see that proper and distinct apartments are arranged for said patients, so that in no case shall Negroes and white persons be together, nor the penitentiary convicts with inmates of any other class; and males and females shall be kept separate. [Acts 1931, pp. 7, 19.]

Legitimacy of Negro Children

§74-102. (2180) **Colored children legitimate, when.** — Every colored child born before March 9, 1866, is hereby declared to be the legitimate child of his mother, but such child is the legitimate child of his colored father only when born within what was regarded as a state of wedlock, or when the parents were living together as husband and wife. [Acts 1865-6. pp. 239, 240; 1866, pp. 156, 157.]

Miscegenation

§§53-301 - 53-315. [**Registration of Individuals as to Race.**]

§53-301. [Requires the registration of individuals by race with the State Board of Health.] [Acts 1927, p. 272; 1933, p. 12.]

[Note: The official compiler notes that no appropriation was made to effectuate this statute and that it appears to be a dead letter.]

§53-306. **False registration prohibited.** — No person shall wilfully or knowingly make or cause to be made a registration certificate false as to color or race . . . [Acts 1927, p. 274; 1933, p. 12.]

§53-307. **Marriage license, form of application for, provided.** — [Applicants for marriage license are required to give race and color of each applicant and race and color of each parent.] [Acts 1927, p. 274; 1933, p. 12.]

§53-314. **Birth of legitimate child of white parent and colored parent, report of, and prosecution.** — When any birth certificate, showing the birth of a legitimate child to parents one of whom is white and one of whom is colored, shall be forwarded to the Bureau of Vital Statistics, it shall be the duty of the State Board of Health to report the same to the Attorney General of the State, with full information concerning the same. Thereupon it shall be the duty of the Attorney General to institute criminal proceedings against the parents of such child for any violations of the provisions of this Chapter which may have been violated. [Acts 1927, p. 278; 1933, p. 12.]

§53-315. **Attorney General, duty to enforce Chapter.** — [Requires the Attorney General of the State as well as the solicitor general of the superior court where violations occur to prosecute violations of this Chapter.] [Acts 1927, p. 278; 1933, p. 12.]

§53-106. (2941) **Miscegenation prohibited.** — It shall be unlawful for a white person to marry anyone except a white person. Any marriage in violation of this section shall be void. [Acts 1927, p. 277.]

§53-212. (2179) **Colored marriages, who may perform.**—Ordained colored ministers of the gospel may celebrate marriages between persons of African descent only, under the same terms and regulations required by the law for marriages between white persons. [Acts 1866, pp. 156, 157.?

§53-9902. (678 P.C.) **Intermarriage of whites and colored people.** — If an officer shall knowingly issue a marriage license to persons, either of whom is of African descent and the other a white person, or if any officer or minister of the gospel shall join such persons in marriage, he shall be guilty of a misdemeanor. [Acts 1865-6, p. 241.]

§53-9903. **Miscegenation; penalty.** — Any person, white or colored, who shall marry or go through a marriage ceremony in violation of the provision of Sec. 53-106 shall be guilty of a felony, and shall be punished by imprisonment in the penitentiary for not less than one [1] year and not more than two [2] years. [Acts 1927, p. 277.]

§53-9904. **False statement in application for marriage license; penalty.** — Any person who shall make or cause to be made a false statement as to race or color of himself or parents, in any application for a marriage license, shall be guilty of a felony, and shall be punished by imprisonment in the penitentiary for not less than two [2] nor more than five [5] years. [Acts 1927, pp. 272, 277.]

§53-9905. **Performing marriage ceremony, illegally.** — Any civil officer, minister, or official of any church, sect, or religion, authorized to perform any marriage ceremony who shall wilfully or knowingly perform any marriage ceremony in violation of the terms of Chapter 53-3 [§§53-301 - 53-315], shall be guilty of a misdemeanor. [Acts 1927, pp. 272, 278.]

§53-9906. **Refusal to execute registration certificate, etc.** — Any person who shall refuse to execute the registration certificate as provided in Chapter 53-3, [§§53-301 - 53-315] or who shall refuse to give the information required in the execution of the same, shall be guilty of a misdemeanor. Each such refusal shall constitute a separate offense. [Acts 1927, p. 274.]

§53-9907. **False registration.** — Any person who shall wilfully or knowingly make or cause to be made a registration certificate false as to color or race, in violation of section 53-306, shall be guilty of a felony and upon conviction thereof shall be punished by imprisonment in the penitentiary for not less than one [1] year and not more than two [2] years. [Acts 1927, p. 274.]

§53-9908. **Ordinary's noncompliance with Chapter 53-3. Penalty.** — Any ordinary who shall issue a marriage license without complying with each and every provision of Chapter 53-3 [§§53-301 - 53-315] shall be guilty of and punished as for a misdemeanor. [Acts 1927, p. 277.]

Prisons

§77-315. (1201 P.C.) . . . **Separation of races.** — [Provides that it shall be the duty of the Prison Commission with reference to the State prison farm, "where practicable, to employ whites and negroes in separate institutions and locations, and they shall be provided with separate eating and sleeping compartments."] [Acts 1908, pp. 1119, 1123.]

§77-317. (1203 P.C.) **Segregation of classes of prisoners.** — [Requires that white and colored convicts be kept "separate and apart . . . when not at work, and when actually engaged in work to be kept separate as far as practicable."] [Acts 1897, pp. 71, 73.]

§77-9904. (679 P.C.) **Chaining or confining white and colored convicts together.** — No person controlling convicts shall confine white and colored convicts together, or work them chained together, or chain them together going to or from their work, or at any other time. Any person and each member or a firm violating the provisions of this section shall be guilty of a misdemeanor. [Acts 1890-1, p. 213.]

Slander

§105-707. (4434) **Charge of intercourse with person of color; proof of special damage.** — Any charge or intimation against a white female of having sexual intercourse with a person of color is slanderous without proof of special damage. [Acts 1859, p. 54.]

Tax Lists and Tax Returns

§92-6307. (1086) **Entry on tax digest of names of colored persons.** — [Requires names of colored and white taxpayers to be made out separately on the tax digest.] [Acts 1894, p. 31; 1935, p. 476; 1937-8, Ex. Sess., p. 185.]

§92-6308. (1116) **Returns by receivers and collectors of taxes paid by colored people.** — [Requires tax collectors to make a report to the Comptroller General of the character and amount of all taxes returned or paid by colored taxpayers of the State, and Comptroller must include this material in his annual report.] [Acts 1874, p. 109.]

Transportation

Carriage of Passengers — Railroads and Common Carriers

§18-205. (2716; 533 P.C.) — **Duty of carriers to furnish equal accommodations.** — Common carriers of passengers for hire shall furnish like and equal accommodations to all persons, without distinction of race, color, or previous condition. [Acts 1870, p. 398.]

§18-206. (2717, 2720, 2721, 2723; 529, 534 P.C.)—**Separate cars or compartments for white and colored passengers; seats; lights; ventilation.** — Railroad companies doing business in this State shall furnish equal accommodations, in separate cars or compartments of cars, for white and colored passengers, and when a car is divided into compartments, the space set apart for white and colored passengers respectively may be proportioned according to the proportion of usual and ordinary travel by each on the railroad or line on which the cars are used. Such companies shall furnish to the passengers comfortable seats and shall have the cars well and sufficiently lighted and ventilated. Officers or employees having charge of railroad cars shall not allow white and colored passengers to occupy the same car or compartment. [Acts 1890-1, p. 157.]

§18-207. (2718; 535 P.C.) — **Duty to assign passengers to their cars; police powers of conductors** — All conductors or other employees in charge of passenger cars shall assign all passengers to their respective cars, or compartments of cars, provided by the said companies under the provisions of section 18-206 and all conductors of street cars and busses shall assign all passengers to seats on the cars under their charge, so as to separate the white and colored races as much as is practicable; and all conductors and other employees of railroads and all conductors of street cars and busses, are hereby invested with police powers to carry out said provisions. [Acts 1890-1, p. 157.]

§18-208. (2719; 536 P.C.) — Remaining in seat, compartment or car other than that assigned. — No passenger shall remain in any car, compartment, or seat, other than that to which he has been assigned. The conductor and any and all employees on such cars are clothed with the power to eject from the train or car any passenger who refuses to remain in the car, compartment or seat assigned to him. [Acts 1890-1, p. 157.]

§18-209. (2722)—Nurses and servants excluded from operation of law. — The provisions of the preceding three sections shall not apply to colored nurses or servants in attendance on their employers. [Acts 1890-1, p. 157.]

§18-210 (2724, 2725)—White and colored passengers on sleeping cars to be separated.—Sleeping car companies and railroad companies operating sleeping cars in this State shall have the right to assign all passengers to seats and berths under their charge, and shall separate the white and colored races in making their assignments, and the conductor and other employees on the train to which sleeping cars may be attached shall not permit white and colored passengers to occupy the same compartment: Provided, that nothing in this section shall be construed to compel sleeping car companies or railroads operating sleeping cars to carry persons of color in sleeping or parlor cars: Provided, that this section shall not apply to colored nurses or servants traveling with their employers. A conductor or other employee of a sleeping car, as well as a conductor or other employee of the train to which a sleeping car may be attached, shall have full police power to enforce this section. [Acts 1899, p. 66.]

§18-606. (2716)—Failure to supply equal and like accommodations.— Any railroad violating the conditions of section 18-205, by any of its employees, may be sued in the superior court of the county where the offense is committed, and any person so wronged may recover such sum as the discretion of the court thinks right and proper in the premises, not to exceed $10,000. [Acts 1870, pp. 427, 428.]

§18-9901. (533 P.C.).—Failure to furnish equal accommodations to all — Any officer, employee, or agent of a common carrier of passengers for hire, or persons who are common carriers, who shall violate the provisions of section 18-205, shall be punished as a misdemeanor. [Acts 1870, p. 398.]

§18-9902. (2721) — Allowing white and colored passengers to occupy same car or compartment. — Any officer or employee having charge of railroad cars, who shall violate the provisions of section 18-206, prohibiting such officer from allowing white and colored passengers to occupy the same car or compartment, shall be guilty of a misdemeanor. [Acts 1890-1, p. 157.]

§18-9904. (2719) — Passenger remaining in car, compartment or seat other than that to which assigned. — Any passenger violating the provision of section 18-208, prohibiting any passenger from remaining in any car, compartment, or seat other than that to which he has been assigned, shall be guilty of a misdemeanor. [Acts 1890-1, p. 157.]

§18-9905. (2724; 538 P.C.)—Sleeping-car passenger remaining in compartment other than that to which assigned. — Any sleeping-car passenger remaining in any compartment other than that to which he may be assigned shall be guilty of a misdemeanor. [Acts 1899, p. 66.]

§18-9906. (2725; 538 P.C.) — Employee failing to assist in ejecting passenger from sleeping car. — A conductor or other employee of a sleeping car, or of a train carrying sleeping cars, who shall fail to refuse to assist in ejecting a passenger violating the provisions of section 18-210 shall be guilty of a misdemeanor. [Acts 1899, p. 66.]

Motor Vehicles

§68-513. Carriage of colored passengers. — Motor carriers may confine themselves to carrying either white or colored passengers; or they may provide different motor vehicles for carrying white and colored passengers; and they may carry white and colored passengers in the same vehicle, but only under such conditions of separation of the races as the Commission [Georgia Public Service Commission] may prescribe. [Acts 1931, Extra Sess. pp. 99, 107.]

§68-616. Carriage of white or colored passengers, or both. — [Similar provision to 68-513. Applies to motor common carriers.] [Acts 1931, pp. 199, 204.]

Voting — Elections

§34-111. Race to be noted in book. — [Requires the race of each voter to be listed in the voter's book, whether white or colored.] [Acts 1894, pp. 115, 117.]

§34-202. Lists to be filed with county registrars; contents. — [Requires the voter's registration list to show the race of each voter, whether white or colored.] [Acts 1894, p. 117, 1908, p. 58; 1913, p. 115.]
[Note: See also §34-203.]

IDAHO

CONSTITUTION

Aliens

Art. 13, §5. Aliens not to be employed on public works. — No person, not a citizen of the United States, or who has not declared his intention to become such, shall be employed upon, or in connection with any state or municipal works. [Const. 1890.]

[Note: This provision affects primarily aliens who are ineligible for citizenship, i.e. Japanese and certain Oriental groups.]

Elections

[Note: The organic act of the territory of Idaho [12 Stat. L. 808, Ch. 117] §5 limited voters to "free white male" inhabitants, but the original Constitution of Idaho ratified by a vote of the people November 5, 1889 and approved by Congress on July 3, 1890 contained no such provision. [Art. VI, Sec. 2.]]

Art. 6, §3. [Elections] — **Disqualification of certain persons.** — . . . Nor shall Chinese or persons of Mongolian descent, not born in the United States, nor Indians not taxed, who have not severed their tribal relations and adopted the habits of civilization, either vote, serve as jurors, or hold any civil office. [Const. 1890.]

[Note: An amendment to Art. 6, §3 proposed by H.J.R. No. 2 (Laws 1949, p. 597) to be submitted for approval at the general election, November 7, 1950, retains the voting restriction against Chinese or persons of Mongolian descent not born in the United States but omits the phrase "nor Indians not taxed. "See Idaho Code 1947, 1949 Cum. Supp.]

Education

Art. 9, §6. Religious test and teaching in school prohibited. — No religious test or qualification shall ever be required of any person as a condition of admission into any public educational institution of the state, either as a teacher or a student; and no teacher or student of any such institution shall ever be required to attend or participate in any religious service whatever. No sectarian or religious tenets or doctrines shall ever be taught in the public schools, *nor shall any distinction or classification be made on account of race or color* . . . [Const. 1890.] (italics supplied)

STATUTES

IDAHO CODE 1947

Aliens

44-1005. Employment of aliens on public works prohibited — Exception. — No person not a citizen of the United States, or who has not declared his intention to become such, or who is not eligible to become such, shall be employed upon any state or municipal works; nor shall any such person be employed by any contractor to work on any public works of the state or any municipality: provided, that any state prisoner may be employed within the state prison grounds as provided in section 3, article 13, of the constitution. Any person who shall violate any of the provisions of this section, on conviction thereof shall be punished by a fine of not less than ten dollars [$10.00] nor more than $100.00 for each person so employed, or by imprisonment in the county jail until such fine be paid or until discharged as provided by law. [1890-1891, p. 233, §§1, 2; reen. 1899, p. 70, §§3, 4; reen. R.C. & C.L., §1457; C.S., §2323; I.C.A., §43-603.]

[Note: The compiler of the Idaho Code notes that the above statute may be unconstitutional under the ruling *Re Case* (1911), 20 Idaho 128, 116 Pac. 1037.]

Alien Land Law

24-101. Aliens eligible to citizenship — Corporations composed of such aliens — Right to acquire and hold real property. — [Provides that "all aliens eligible for citizenship under the laws of the United States . . . may acquire, take, hold, possess, enjoy, dispose of and inherit real property, or any interest therein in this State, . . . "] [1923, Ch. 122, §1, p. 160; I.C.A., §23-101.]

[Note: See California Alien Land Law and notes thereon, *supra.*]

24-102. Other aliens — Right to acquire and hold real property. — [Provides that ineligible aliens may acquire and hold property for agricultural purposes for the state only to the extent that it is provided for by any treaty existing between the United States and the country of which the ineligible alien is a citizen. In addition, such aliens may lease agricultural land for 5-year periods. Leases for a longer term than 5 years are declared to be illegal, null and void.] [1923, Ch. 122, §2; p. 160; I.C.A., §23-102.]

24-103. Corporations composed of aliens not eligible to citizenship. Right to hold and acquire property. — [Provides that companies or corporations of which the majority of the members are ineligible aliens may hold property only to the extent provided for by treaty arrangements between the United States and the nation or country of which the alien stockholders or members are citizens, and not otherwise.] [1923, Ch. 122, §3, p. 160; I.C.A., §23-103.]

24-104. Guardians for minor citizens — Ineligible aliens not qualified — Removal. — [Prohibits ineligible alien from being appointed as guardian of any real property of a minor citizen which such ineligible alien is barred from holding directly by reason of the provisions of this act. Provides for the removal of such guardian.] [1923, Ch. 122, §4, p. 160; I.C.A., §23-104.]

24-105. Trustee defined — Annual report of trustee — Section cumulative. [Requires any trustee holding title, custody or control of property of an ineligible alien or the minor child of such alien to file a detailed annual report in the office of the secretary of the State of Idaho and in the office of the county clerk in the county in which the property is located on or before January 31st of each year. The trustee's report must show all property held by the trustee of such alien or minor, the date when each item came into his possession or control and an itemized account of all expenditures, invest-

119

ments, rents and profits, cropping contracts and other agreements relating to the property. Violation of this section is punishable as a misdemeanor by a fine up to $300.00 and imprisonment in the county jail up to 6 months.] [1923, Ch. 122, §5, p. 160; I.C.A., §23-105.]

24-106. Heir or devisee incompetent because of alienship. Procedure. — [Provides that in a probate proceeding where an ineligible alien cannot take real property by will or inheritance because of the provisions of this act, the court shall order the property to be sold and the cash proceeds distributed to the alien heir or devisee of such property.] [1923, Ch. 122, §6, p. 160; I.C.A., §23-106.]

24-107. Escheat of fee unlawfully acquired — Exception. — [Provides that any real property hereafter acquired in fee in violation of the provisions of this act by an ineligible alien or company, association or corporation of which the majority of the members or stockholders are ineligible aliens shall escheat to the State of Idaho. An exception is made in the case of real property acquired in the enforcement or satisfaction of an existing mortgage or lien thereon. No alien company or corporation may hold property acquired in the enforcement of an existing lien or mortgage for a longer period than 2 years.] [1923, Ch. 122, §7, p. 160; I.C.A., §23-107.]

24-108. Escheat of interest less than fee — Escheat of shares unlawfully acquired. — [Any leasehold interest in property acquired in violation of the provisions of this chapter shall escheat to the State of Idaho. Any share of stock or the interest of any member of a company or corporation ineligible to hold real property under the provisions of this act shall also escheat to the State of Idaho.] [1923, Ch. 122, §8, p. 160; I.C.A., §23-108.]

24-109. Void conveyances — Escheat — Prima facie presumptions. — [Provides that a transfer of any real property or an interest therein with the intent to avoid or evade escheat is null and void. A *prima facie* presumption that a conveyance is made with an intent to evade escheat shall arise where the consideration is paid for by an ineligible alien, company or corporation, or where a mortgage is executed in favor of such alien and such alien takes possession or control of the property as mortgagee.] [1923, Ch. 122, §9, p. 160; I.C.A., §23-109.]

24-110. Conspiracy to convey unlawfully — Penalty. — [Provides that a conspiracy to transfer real property in violation of the provisions of the statute is punishable by imprisonment up to 2 years or by a fine up to $5,000.00, or both.] [1923, Ch. 122, §10, p. 160; I.C.A., §23-110.]

Education

33-1303. Eligibility to teach or receive certificate. — . . . (d) No person, except in cases of international exchanges of teachers approved by the State board of education, is eligible to teach, who is not a citizen of the United States, or who has not declared his intention to become a citizen; . . . [1947, Ch. 260. §3, p. 758.]

[Note: The effect of this statute is to bar ineligible aliens from teaching in the schools of Idaho.]

Dentists

54-905. Examination — Applications. — Any person who shall desire to begin the practice of dentistry in the state of Idaho shall file an application in his own handwriting . . . , which application shall state . . . his correct name, age, place of residence, color and nationality . . . [1919, Ch. 60, §5, p. 182; C.S., §2120; I.C.A., §53-1305.]

[Note: The above provision was rewritten by Laws 1949, ch. 102, §16, p. 177, (1949 Cum. Supp., 54-916). The new section eliminates the requirement that applicants for the practice of dentistry must state their color in the application filed. Section 15 of the new law (Laws 1949, ch. 102, §15, p. 177; 1949 Cum. Supp. 54-915) provides that no person is eligible to practice dentistry or dental hygiene unless "he or she be a citizen of the United States of America or have declared an intention to become such citizen."]

Indians

33-2710. American Indian Day. — The fourth Friday of September of each year is hereby designated, and shall hereinafter be known, as American Indian Day. [1943, Ch. 9, §1, p. 11.]

Intoxicating Liquor

23-929. Restriction of sales by licensee. — No licensee or his or its employed agents, servants or bartenders shall sell, deliver or give away, or cause or permit to be sold, delivered, or given away, any liquor to: . . .

5. An Indian.

6. Any person under the age of 21 years, Indian or other person, who knowingly misrepresents his or her qualifications for the purpose of obtaining liquor from such licensee shall be equally guilty with such licensee and shall, upon conviction thereof, be guilty of a misdemeanor. [1947, Ch. 274, §27, p. 870.]

18-4201. Selling Liquor to Indians. — Every person who sells or furnishes, or causes to be sold or furnished, intoxicating liquors to any Indian is guilty of a misdemeanor. [1879, p. 31; R.S., R.C. & C.L., §6929; C.S. §8355; I.C.A., §17-2724.]

Firearms

36-2401. Indians connected with United States agency — Restrictions on bearing arms. — It shall be unlawful for any Indian who is connected with any United States Indian agency to have in his possession, or to bear, firearms beyond the limits of any county or counties within which the reservation is situated during the close game season, between the first day of January and the first day of September in each year. [1899, p. 361, §1; reen. R.C. & C.L., §7216; C.S., §8596; I.C.A., §35-1901.] [Repealed, Laws 1949, ch. 9, §1.]

36-2402. Peace officers to disarm Indians. — A violation of the foregoing section shall be deemed a misdemeanor, and it shall be the duty of any sheriff, constable or other peace officer of the county where the offense shall be committed to forthwith disarm such Indian, and to hold such firearm or firearms subject to redemptions, upon payment to the officer of the sum of ten [$10.00] dollars, one-half of which sum shall go to the officer performing the service and the remaining one-half to be paid into the county treasury for the benefit of the school fund of said county. [1899, p. 361, §2; reen, R.C. & C.L., §7217; C.S., §8597; I.C.A., §35-1902.] [Repealed, Laws 1949, ch. 9, §1.]

36-2403. Notification of Indian agent — Sale of arms. — [Provision for the sale of firearms subject to redemption if not redeemed within 30 days after written notice.] [1899, p. 361, §3; reen. R.C. & C.L., §7218; C.S. §8598; I.C.A., §35-1903.] [Repealed, Laws 1949, ch. 9, §1.]

18-3309. Selling firearms or ammunition to Indians. — Every person who sells or furnishes to any Indian any firearm or ammunition therefor, is guilty of a misdemeanor. [1879, p. 31; R.S., R.C., & C.L., §6930; C.S. §8356; I.C.A., §17-2725.] [Repealed, Laws 1949, ch. 10, §1.]

Miscegenation

32-206. Miscegenation . . . — All marriages hereafter contracted of white persons with mongolians, negroes or mulattoes are illegal . . . [1867, p. 71, §3; R.S. §2425; reen. R.C. & C.L. §2616; C.S. §4596; am. 1921, Ch. 115, §1, p. 291; I.C.A., §31-206.]

Optometrists

54-1505. Examinations — Applications. — Any person who shall desire to begin the practice of optometry in the state of Idaho shall file an application in his own handwriting . . . , which application will state . . . his correct name, age, place of residence, color and nationality . . . [1919, Ch. 34, §5, p. 115; C.S., §2159; I.C.A., §53-1705.]

ILLINOIS

CONSTITUTION

Slavery

[Note: Art. VI, Section 1 of the Illinois Constitution of 1818 prohibits slavery, but this section was not included in the Constitution of 1870.]

Suffrage

[Note: Art. VI, Section 1, of the Illinois Constitution of 1848 which limited the rights of suffrage to "white male citizens" was omitted from the Constitution of 1870.]

STATUTES

ILLINOIS REVISED STATUTES 1949

Air Ports

Ch. 24, Sec. 23-96. [Air Ports] — . . . landing field and landing strips shall be available to any person without unjust or unreasonable discrimination . . . [As amended by act approved July 17, 1945. L. 1945, p. 433; Jones Ill. Stats. Ann. [1947 Cum. Supp.], 21.1726.]

Aliens

CH. 38, §153. — [Firearms] [Prohibits sale or gift of firearms which may be concealed on the person to any alien.] [L. 1925, p. 339.]

American Indian Day

Ch. 122, Sec. 27-21. American Indian Day. — §27-21. The Fourth Friday of September is designated as "American Indian Day", to be observed throughout the State as a day on which to hold appropriate exercises in commemoration of the American Indians. [L. 1919, p. 894, §1; Jones Ill. Stats. Ann., 123.1251.]

Civil Rights

Jones Ill. Stats. Ann. 22.19. [Provided that World's Fair Corporation (1931) "shall extend to all persons the full and equal enjoyment of the accommodations, advantages, facilities and privileges of said World's Fair, subject only to the conditions and limitations established by law and applicable alike to all citizens." Denial of such equal accommodations deemed to be the operation of a public nuisance and provision made for the abatement thereof.]

[Note: This section is obsolete. Included for historical interest only.]

Civil Rights — Public Accommodations — Ch. 38.

An Act to protect all citizens in their civil and legal rights and fixing a penalty for violations of same. [Approved June 10, 1885, L. 1885, p. 64.]

Sec. 125. All persons entitled to equal enjoyment of accommodations — Discrimination in price on account of race or color prohibited. §1. — All persons within the jurisdiction of said State of Illinois shall be entitled to the full and equal enjoyment of the accommodation, advantages, facilities

123

and privileges of inns, restaurants, eating houses, hotels, soda fountains, soft drink parlors, taverns, roadhouses, barber shops, department stores, clothing stores, hat stores, shoe stores, bathrooms, rest-rooms, theatres, skating rinks, concerts, cafes, bicycle rinks, elevators, ice cream parlors or rooms, railroads, omnibuses, busses, stages, aeroplanes, street cars, boats, funeral hearses and public conveyances on land, water or air, and all other places of public accommodations and amusement, subject only to the conditions and limitations established by laws and applicable alike to all citizens; nor shall there be any discrimination on account of race or color in the price to be charged and paid for lots or graves in any cemetery or place for burying the dead. [As amended by L. 1935, p. 708, appvd. July 8, 1935; L. 1937, p. 485, appvd. July 8, 1937; Jones, Ill. Stats. Ann. [1947 Cum. Supp.], 22.01.]

Sec. 126. Penalty. — §2. [Any person who violates any of provisions of Sec. 125 or aids and incites such denal shall for every such offense forfeit a sum of $25.00 to $500.00 to the person aggrieved thereby, to be recovered in a court of competent jurisdiction, in the county where such offense was committed; shall also be deemed guilty of misdemeanor and may be punished by fine up to $500.00 or 1 year in prison, or both] [As amended by L. 1935, p. 708, approved July 8, 1935. Jones Ill. Stats. Ann. [1947 Cum. Supp.], 22.02.]

Sec. 127. Jurisdiction — Justice of Peace. — §3. [Confers jurisdiction upon justices of peace in county where violations occurred in all civil actions brought to recover damages under this act. Grants either party right of jury trial.] [Added by act approved June 13, 1891, L. 1891, p. 85; Jones Ill. Stats. Ann., 22.03.]

Sec. 128. Jurisdiction — Trial de novo. — §4. [Where appeal is taken from judgment of a justice of peace to justice of circuit, superior or county court, the action is tried over again from the beginning as if it were an original action. Plaintiff, within 30 days after transcript is filed in the court to which appeal is taken, must file his declaration as in original suit.

Where a declaration is filed, the appeal may not be dismissed without plaintiff's consent.] [Added by act approved June 13, 1891. L. 1891, p. 85; Jones Ill. Stats. Ann., 22.04.]

Sec. 128a. Violation enjoined as a public nuisance. — §5. — Any inn, [enumerates places listed in Sec. 125] . . . wherein any of the provisions of section one [Sec. 125] of this Act are violated, is hereby declared to be a public nuisance, and may be abated as hereinafter provided. The owners, agents and occupants of any such place shall be deemed guilty of maintaining a public nuisance, and may be enjoined as hereinafter provided. [Added by L. 1935, p. 708, as amended by act approved July 8, 1937, L. 1937, p. 485; Jones Ill. Stats. Ann. [1947 Cum. Supp.], 22.04(1).]

Sec. 128b. Proceedings to enjoin. — §6. — Any action to enjoin any nuisance defined in this act may be brought in the name of the People of the State of Illinois by The Attorney-General of the State or any State's Attorney of the County where a nuisance as herein defined exists. Such action shall be brought and tried as an action in equity by the court without a jury. A verified petition shall be filed setting up the essential facts showing that a nuisance, as herein defined exists. If it is made to appear by affidavits or otherwise, to the satisfaction of the court or judge in vacation, that such nuisance exists, a temporary writ of injunction shall forthwith issue restraining the defendant from conducting or permitting the continuance of such nuisance until the conclusion of the trial: Provided, that no injunction shall issue unless a written notice of the application for the same is served upon the defendant or his agent or some person in charge of the alleged nuisance at least two days before such application is made. No bond shall be required in instituting such proceeding. The defendant shall be held to answer the allegations of the petition as in other chancery proceedings. Upon the trial of the cause, on finding that the material allegations of the petition are true, the court shall order such nuisance to be abated, and enjoin all persons from maintaining and permitting such nuisance. When any injunction, as herein provided has been granted it shall be binding upon the defendant and shall act as an injunction in personam against the defendant throughout the State. [Added by act approved July 8, 1935, L. 1935, p. 708; Jones Ill. Stats. Ann. [1947 Cum. Supp.], 22.04(2).]

Sec. 128c. Violation of injunction. — §7. — In case of the violation of any injunction or order of abatement issued under the provisions of this act, the court in term time, or a judge in vacation, may summarily try and punish the offender for contempt of court. The hearing may be upon affidavits, or either party may demand the production and oral examination of witnesses. [Added by act approved July 8, 1935, L. 1935, p. 708: Jones Ill. Stats Ann. 1947 Cum. Supp.], 22.04(3).]

Sec. 128d. State and municipal officers to enforce. — §8. — It shall be the duty of all municipal, county and state officials to cooperate in the enforcement of this act. If any sheriff, deputy sheriff, chief of police, marshal, policeman, constable or other peace officer shall have knowledge or information of any violation of any provision of this act, he shall diligently investigate and secure evidence of the same and shall, before the proper officer, make and sign complaint against the offending person, anything in the ordinance or by-laws of any municipality to the contrary notwithstanding. [Added by act approved July 8, 1935, L. 1935, p. 708; Jones Ill. Stats. Ann. [1947 Cum. Supp.], 22.04(4).]

Sec. 128e. Duty of State's Attorney and Attorney General. — §9. — It shall be the duty of the State's Attorney of every county diligently to prosecute any and all persons violating any of the provisions of this act in his county and he shall be responsible for the proper enforcement of this act, and whenever he shall have any information or knowledge, or have any reason to believe that any of the provisions of this act are being violated in his county, he shall use every legitimate means at his command to secure the necessary and proper evidence of such violation, and immediately upon securing evidence he shall file a complaint or petition for abatement of nuisance, or both, as hereinbefore provided or cause a complaint or petition for abatement of nuisance, or both, as hereinbefore provided to be filed against any person against whom he shall have any evidence of any such violation, and he shall have said person arrested and shall vigorously prosecute said complaints or petitions on said charges to a speedy disposition.

In case the existence of any place where any violations of the provisions of section one [Sec. 125] of this act are disclosed in any criminal proceeding, it shall be the duty of the State's Attorney to proceed promptly to enforce the provisions of this Act against such place as a nuisance.

The Attorney General shall seek through his assistants, agents, or investigators to obtain evidence of violations of this act when information in that regard is brought to his notice, and shall make, or cause to be made complaints against violators whenever such evidence is secured; and he and his assistants are hereby given authority to sign, verify and file any such complaints and papers required under this act. But nothing in this act shall in any way relieve State, County, Municipal or other officers from the responsibility of enforcing laws relating to civil rights. [Added by act approved July 8, 1935, L. 1935, p. 708; Jones Ill. Stats. Ann. [1947 Cum. Supp.], 22.04(5).]

Sec. 128f. Failure of State's Attorney and Attorney General to enforce. — §10. [Duty of Attorney General and State's Attorney to abate nuisance caused by violation of this act whenever called to their attention by affidavit. Upon failure of Attorney General or State's Attorney to act upon affidavit within reasonable time, special assistant Attorney General or special assistant State's Attorney may be appointed by the circuit court or circuit court judges of the county where violation occurred, whose duty it will be to prosecute the proceeding upon the sworn petition in writing of the aggrieved person, showing facts constituting the nuisance. The expenses of such proceeding shall be borne by county where nuisance is alleged to exist.] [Added by act approved July 8, 1935, p. 708; Jones Ill. Stats. Ann. [1947 Cum. Supp.], 22.04(6).]

Sec. 128g. Partial unconstitutionality. — §11. — If any provisions of this act shall be held invalid it shall not be construed to invalidate other provisions of the act. [Added by act approved July 8, 1935, L. 1935, p. 708; Jones Ill. Stats. Ann. [1947 Cum. Supp.], 22.04(7).]

Civil Service

Ch. 24½, Sec. 38b. University of Illinois — Classification of positions . . Qualifications of applicants . . . — (Non-academic employees) . . . No question in any examination shall relate to political or religious affiliations or racial origins of the examinee. [Ill. Laws, 1941, p. 400; Jones Ill. Stats. Ann. (1947 Supp.) 23.038(1).]

Defamation

See under Discriminatory Publication.

Defense Contracts — Discrimination in Employment

[Act approved July 21, 1941, L. 1941, Vol. 1, p. 557]

Ch. 29, Sec. 24a. — Public Policy declared. — §1. In the construction of this act the public policy of the State of Illinois is hereby declared as follows: To facilitate the rearmament and defense program of the Federal government by the integration into the war defense industries of the State of Illinois all available types of labor, skilled, semi-skilled and common, shall participate without discrimination as to race, color or creed, whatsoever. [Jones Ill. Stats. Ann. [1947 Cum. Supp.], 22.12 (4).]

Ch. 29, Sec. 24b. War defense contractors. [defined]—§2. Every person firm, association or corporation and the subcontractor, agent, or employee of the same to whom has been awarded a contract and to whom shall be awarded a contract by the United States government or any agency thereof and every person, firm, association or corporation which has been authorized or directed or is engaged in the training of persons for skilled and semi-skilled positions of labor for the United States government or any agency thereof and every subcontractor of any such person, firm, association, or corporation is designated in this act a war defense contractor. [Jones Ill. Stats. Ann. [1947 Cum. Supp.], 22.12 (5).]

Ch. 29, Sec. 24c. Discrimination because of race or color in hiring or training employees prohibited. — §3. It shall be unlawful for any defense contractor, its officers or agents or employees to discriminate against any citizen of the State of Illinois because of his race or color in the hiring of employees and training for skilled or semi-skilled employment, and every such discrimination shall be deemed violation of this act. [Jones Ill. Stats. Ann., [1947 Cum. Supp.] 22.12 (6).]

Ch. 29, Sec. 24d. Complaints — Prosecutions. — §4. [Provides for filing of verified complaint with Department of Labor, State of Illinois, and requires state's attorneys of respective counties and attorney general to enforce prosecution of any violations of the act.] [Jones Ill. Stats. Ann. [1947 Cum. Supp.], 22.12 (7).]

Ch. 29, Sec. 24e. Punishment for violations. — §5. [Provides for fine of $100.00 to $500. upon conviction.] [Jones Ill. Stats. Ann. [1947 Cum. Supp.], 22.12 (8).]

Ch. 29. 24f. — Display of copy of act. — §6. [Requires Department of Labor to furnish copies of act to be prominently displayed by each war defense contractor in its employment office and room where employment and training applicants are interviewed. Failure to do so punishable by fine of $25.00.] [Jones Ill. Stats. Ann. [1947 Cum. Supp.], 22.12 (9).]

Ch. 29, Sec. 24g. Fine for each day's violation. — §7. [Provides a fine of $25.00 for each day's violation separately.] [Jones Ill. Stats. Ann, [1947 Cum. Supp.], 22.12 (10).]

Discriminatory Publication — Chap. 38

An Act to prohibit the publication and distribution of discriminating matter against any religious sect, creed, class, denomination, or nationality, and to punish the same. [The exemption allows mailing of a private communication in writing sent in response to a specific written or verbal inquiry.]

[Approved June 28, 1919, L. 1919, p. 433.]

Sec. 129. Circulating paper discriminating against religious sect. — §1. That no person being the lessee, proprietor, manager, superintendent, agent or employee of any place of public accommodation[,] resort or amusement shall directly or indirectly by himself or anybody else publish, issue, circulate, send, distribute, give away or display in any way, manner, shape, means or method except as hereinafter provided, any communication, poster, folder, manuscript, book, pamphlet, writing, print, letter, notice, or advertisement of any kind, nature or description intended or calculated to discriminate or actually discriminating against any religious sect, creed, class, denomination or nationality, or against any of the members thereof in the matter of furnishing or neglecting or refusing to furnish to them or any one of them lodgings, housing, schooling, tuition or any accommodations, rights, privileges, advantage or convenience offered to or enjoyed by the general public or to the effect that any of the accommodations, rights, privileges, advantages or conveniences of any such place of public accommodation[,] resort or amusement shall or will be refused, withheld from or denied to any person or class of persons on account of class, creed, religion, sect, denomination, nationality or that the patronage, custom, presence, frequenting, dwelling, staying or lodging at any such place or [of] any person, persons or class of persons belonging to or purporting to be of any particular religion, sect, creed, class, denomination or nationality is unwelcome, objectionable, or not acceptable, desired or solicited. [Jones Ill. Stats. Ann., 22.13.]

Sec. 130. Paper to be evidence. §2. The production of any such communication, paper, poster, folder, pamphlet, manuscript, book, printing, writing, letter, notice or advertisement purporting to relate to any such place and to be made by any person being the owner, lessee, proprietor, superintendent, manager or any other employee thereof shall be presumptive evidence in any civil or criminal action or prosecution that the same was authorized by such person. [Jones Ill. Stats. Ann., 22.14.]

Sec. 131. Place of public accommodation defined. — §3. A place of public accommodation, resort or amusement within the meaning of this Act shall be deemed to include any inn, tavern, hotel, whether conducted for the entertainment, housing, lodging of transient guests, or for the benefit, use or accommodation of those seeking health, recreation or rest, any restaurant, eating-house, public conveyance on land or water, bath-house, barber shop, theatre and music hall. [Jones Ill. Stats. Ann., 22.15.]

Sec. 132. Exemption — §4. Nothing in this Act contained shall be construed to prohibit the mailing of a private communication in writing sent in response to a specific written or verbal inquiry. [Jones Ill. Stats. Ann., 22.16.]

Sec. 133. Penalty. — §5. Any person who shall violate any of the provisions of this Act or shall aid in or incite, cause or bring about in whole or in part the violation of any such provision or provisions shall for each and every violation thereof be liable civilly to a penalty of not less than ($100) one hundred dollars nor more than five hundred ($500) dollars to be recovered by any person aggrieved thereby, and shall also for every such violation or offense be deemed guilty of a misdemeanor and upon conviction thereof, shall be fined not less than one hundred ($100) dollars nor more than five hundred ($500) dollars or shall be imprisoned not less than thirty (30) days nor more than ninety (90) days or both such fine and imprisonment in the discretion of the court. [Jones Ill. Stats. Ann., 22.17.]

Sec. 134. Partial Invalidity. — §6. The invalidity of any portion of this Act shall not affect the validity of any other portion thereof, which can be given effect without such invalid part. [Jones Ill. Stats. Ann., 22.18.]

Ch. 38, Sec. 471. Publication or exhibition engendering race or class hatred. — Punishment.—§224a. It shall be unlawful for any person, firm or corporation to manufacture, sell or offer for sale, advertise or publish, present or exhibit in any public place in this state any lithograph, moving picture, play, drama or sketch, which publication or exhibition portrays depravity, criminality, unchastity, or lack of virtue of a class of citizens, of any race, color, creed or religion which said publication or exhibition exposes the citizens of any race, color, creed or religion to contempt, derision, or obloquy or which is productive of breach of the peace or riots. Any person, firm, or corporation violating any of the provisions of this section, shall be guilty of a misdemeanor, and upon conviction thereof, shall be punished by a fine of not less than fifty dollars ($50.00), nor more than two hundred dollars ($200.00). [Added by L. 1917, p. 362; Jones Ill. Stats. Ann., 37.420.]

Ch. 38, Sec. 472. Publication representing hanging, lynching or burning — Punishment. — §224b. It shall be unlawful for any person, firm or corporation to manufacture, sell, or offer for sale, or advertise or present or exhibit in any public place in the State any publication or representation by lithograph, moving picture, play, drama or sketch representing or purporting to represent any hanging, lynching or burning of any human being. Any person, firm or corporation violating any of the provisions of this section, shall be guilty of a misdemeanor, and upon conviction thereof, shall be punished by a fine of not less than fifty dollars ($50.00) nor more than two hundred dollars ($200.00). [Added by L. 1917, p. 362; Jones Ill. Stats. Ann., 37.421.]

Division for Enforcement of Civil and Equal Rights

Ch. 14, Sec. 9. Division for enforcement of civil and equal rights — Duties. — §1. There is created in the office of the Attorney General a Division to be known as the Division for the Enforcement of Civil and Equal Rights. The Division, under the supervision and direction of the Attorney General, shall investigate all violations of the laws relating to civil rights and the prevention of discriminations against persons by reason of race, color or creed, and shall, whenever such violations are established, undertake necessary enforcement measures.

[§2. Appropriation of $21,000.00 annually for administration of this act. Approved July 1, 1943, L. 1943, Vol. 1, p. 210.] Jones Ill. Stats. Ann. [1947 Cum. Supp.], 22.24, 22.25.]

Education

Ch. 122, Sec. 15-15. Exclusion of children on account of color. — §15-15, Any school officer or other person who excludes or aids in excluding from the public schools, on account of color, any child who is entitled to the benefits of such school shall be fined not less than five [$5.00] nor more than one hundred [$100.00] dollars. [Hurd's Rev. Stats. 1874, Ch. 122, p. 983, §§100, 101; L. 1889, p. 340, §14; L. 1909, p. 342, §261; Jones Ill. Stats. Ann., 123.1004.]

Ch. 122, Sec. 15-16. Preventing colored children from attending school. — §15-16. Whoever by threat, menace or intimidation prevents any colored child entitled to attend a public school in this State from attending such school shall be fined not exceeding $25.00. [Hurd's Rev. Stats. 1874, ch. 122, p. 983, §102; L. 1909, p. 342, §262; Jones Ill. Stats. Ann., 123.1005.]

Ch. 122. Sec. 6-37. [Powers of Board of School Directors] **Assignment of pupils to schools — . . . Race Discrimination. —** . . . No pupil shall be excluded from or segregated in any such school on account of his color, race, or nationality. [L. 1909, p. 342, §115, as amended by act approved July 17, 1945, L. 1945, p. 1593; Jones Ill. Stats. Ann., 123.811.]

Ch. 122. Sec. 7-14. [Powers of Board of Education] **Apportionment of pupils to schools — Race Discrimination. —** §7-14 . . . No pupil shall be excluded from or segregated in any such school on account of his color, race, or nationality. [L. 1871-72, p. 737, §80, as amended by act approved July 17, 1945, L. 1945, p. 1593; Jones Ill. Stats. Ann. 123.844.]

Refusal of State Funds to School District which discriminates
Illinois Statutes 1949, p. 53, H.B. 1066.

[In making appropriations from the Common School Fund for educational purposes, provides "§4. No part of the money appropriated by this Act shall be distributed to any school district in which any student is excluded from or segregated in any public school, within the meaning of 'The School Code', because of his race, color or nationality."] [Appvd. June 30, 1949.]

[Note: The United Press reports that on December 21st, 1949, the East St. Louis Board of Education announced through its president that the Board has unanimously passed a resolution discontinuing segregation in the public schools of that city on January 30, 1950. The action was taken because the East St. Louis School District faced a loss of $677,989 in state school aid funds under the above statute which excludes any school district which practices racial segregation from participation in state school funds. See New York Times, December 22, 1949.]

[Note: The above section implements Ch. 122, Sec. 15-15, 15-16, 6-37 and 7-14.]

Architects

Ch. 101/2, Sec. 4a. Powers and duties of Department of Registration. §4a. The Department of Registration and Education shall exercise, but subject to the provisions of this Act, the following functions, powers and duties: . . . (3) Prescribe rules and regulations defining what shall constitute a school, college or university, or department of a university, or other institution, reputable and in good standing, and to determine whether or not a school, college or university, or department of a university, or other institution is reputable and in good standing by reference to a compliance with such rules and regulations, and to terminate the approval of such school, college or university or department of a university or other institution as reputable and in good standing for non-compliance with such rules and regulations; provided that no school, college or university, or department of a university or other institution that refuses admittance to applicants, solely on account of race, color or creed shall be considered reputable and in good standing. [L. 1937, p. 243.]

Barbers

Ch. 16¾, Sec. 14.40. Functions, powers and duties of Department. — §6 . . . no school or college that refuses admittance to applicants, solely on account of race, color or creed shall be considered reputable and in good standing; . . . [L. 1937, p. 252, §5 (11.42) as amended L. 1947, p. 310, S. B. No. 48, appvd. July 18, 1947; Jones Ill. Stats. Ann. (1947 Cum. Supp.) 11.77.]

Beauty Culture

Ch. 16¾, Sec. 18a. Powers and duties of department. — §4-a. . . . (3) . . . no school, college or university, or department of a university or other institution that refuses admittance to applicants, solely on account of race, color, or creed shall be considered reputable and in good standing. [L. 1935, p. 232 as amended L. 1945, p. 371.]

Chiropody

Ch. 91, Sec. 73a. Powers and duties of department. — §1-a . . . (3) . . . no school, college or university, or department of a university or other institution that refuses admittance to applicants, solely on account of race, color or creed shall be considered reputable and in good standing . . . [L. 1935, p. 958, appvd. July 10, 1935.]

Dentists and Dental Surgery

Ch. 91, Sec. 58a. Powers and duties of department. — §3-a. . . . (3) . . . no school, college or university, or department of a university or other institution that refuses admittance to applicants solely on account of race, color or creed shall be considered reputable and in good standing . . . [L. 1909, p. 277, as amended by act approved May 24, 1945, L. 1945, p. 977.]

Engineers and Engineering

Ch. 48½, Sec. 36. Functions, powers and duties of department.—§5. . . . 3. . . . no engineering college whose requirements for graduation are below those of the College of Engineering of the University of Illinois, or which refuses admittance to applicants solely on account of race, color or creed shall be considered reputable and in good standing; . . . [L. 1945, Vol. 1, p. 845. Appvd. July 20, 1945; Jones Ill. Stats. Ann. [1947 Cum. Supp.] 15.118 (5).]

Optometrists

Ch. 91, Sec. 92a. Powers and duties of department.—§3a. . . . (3) . . . no school, college or university, or department of a university or other institution that refuses admission to applicants, solely on account of race, color or creed shall be considered reputable and in good standing . . . [L. 1945, p. 995, appvd. June 28, 1945.]

Pharmacy

Ch. 91, Sec. 38a. Powers and duties of department.—§3-a. . . . (3) . . . no school, college or university, or department of a university or other institution that refuses admittance to applicants, solely on account of race, color or creed shall be considered reputable and in good standing . . . [L. 1935, p. 982, appvd. July 10, 1935.]

Public Health Nursing

Ch. 111½, Sec. 35i1. Powers and duties of Department of Registration and Education. — §3-a . . . (3) . . . no school, college or university, or department of a university or other institution or organization that refuses admittance to applicants, solely on account of race, color or creed shall be considered reputable and in good standing . . . [L. 1937, p. 998, appvd. July 12, 1937.]

Veterinary Medicine and Surgery

Ch. 91, Sec. 115a. Powers and duties of department.—§2-a . . . 3 . . . no school, college or university, or department of a university or other institution that refuses admittance to applicants, solely on account of race, color or creed shall be considered reputable and in good standing . . . [L. 1935, p. 990.]

Schools, Colleges, Universities

Professions, Trades and Occupations

Ch. 127, Sec. 60. Additional powers conferred in administration of laws, regulating professions, trades and occupations. — §60. The Department of Registration and Education shall, wherever the several laws regulating professions, trades and occupations which are devolved upon the department for administration so require, exercise, in its name, but subject to the provisions of this act, the following powers: . . .

3. Prescribe rules and regulations defining, for the respective professions, trades and occupations, what shall constitute a school, college or university, or department of a university, or other institutions, reputable and in good standing and to determine the reputability and good standing of a school, college or university, or department of a university, or other institution, reputable and in good standing by reference to a compliance with such rules and regulations: provided, that no school, college or university, or department of a university or other institution that refuses admittance to applicants solely on account of race, color or creed shall be considered reputable and in good standing; . . . [L. 1917, p. 2., as amended by L. 1947, p. 1640, appvd. Aug. 8, 1947; Jones Ill. Stats. Ann. [1947 Cum. Supp.], 126.188.]

Good Will Commission

Ch. 127, Sec. 214. Good Will Commission — Good Will Day. — §1. The Governor of this State is authorized to appoint a commission of fifteen [15] citizens of this State, representing as far as possible the various racial and religious groups, to act as a permanent committee to foster racial and religious amity. The members of such commission shall hold office for a term of three years and until their successors are appointed. The commission shall be called the Good Will Commission. It shall have a chairman and secretary chosen from its members. No compensation shall be paid to any members of said Commission.

The Governor shall, upon request of the Commission, proclaim a Good Will Day in each year, and shall request all citizens of this State to join in private and public functions for the observance of this day. [Approved July 16, 1941, L. 1941, Vol. 1, p. 1252; Jones Ill. Stats. Ann. [1947 Cum. Supp.], 126.479.]

History of Negro Race

Ch. 122, Sec. 27-23. History of Negro race. — History of the Negro race may be taught in all public schools and in all other educational institutions in this State supported or maintained, in whole or in part, by public funds. [Added by act approved June 29, 1945, L. 1945, p. 1581; Jones Ill. Stats. Ann., 123.1252(1).]

Hospitals

Public Health Law — Chapter 111½

An act requiring hospitals to render emergency medical treatment or first aid in cases of accident or injury.

Sec. 86. Hospitals to furnish first aid.—§1. No hospital, either public or private where surgical operations are performed, operating in this State shall refuse to give emergency medical treatment or first aid to any applicant who applies for the same in case of accident or injury where the same shall be liable to cause death or severe injury. [L. 1927, p. 403, appvd. July 11, 1927.]

Sec. 87. Penalty for violation.—§2. Any such hospital violating any of the provisions of this Act shall be guilty of a misdemeanor and upon conviction thereof shall be punished by a fine of not less than $50.00 nor more than $200.00 for each offense, which fine shall be paid into the general corporate funds of the city, incorporated town, or village in which the hospital is located, or of the county, in case such hospital is outside the limits of any incorporated municipality. [L. 1927, p. 403, appvd. July 11, 1927.]

Housing Corporations — Chapter 32

Sec. 510. Acts prohibited. — §7. No housing corporation shall . . . (9) Enter into contracts for the construction of buildings or for the payment of salaries to officers or employees, or for the purchase of materials, equipment or supplies, except subject to the inspection and revision of the State housing board and under such regulations as the board may from time to time prescribe.

No housing corporation or contractor employed thereby shall deny employment to any person on account of race, creed or color. [L. 1933, p. 396, as amended by act approved May 3, 1945, L. 1945, p. 570; Jones Ill. Stats. Ann. [1947 Cum. Supp.] 63.26.]

Sec. 531. Mandamus or injunction by board against corporation. — §28. Whenever in the judgment of the board a housing corporation fails or omits, or is about to fail or omit to do anything required of it by law or by order of the board, or does or is about to do, or permits or is about to permit to be done anything contrary to or in violation of law or any order of the board, or anything which is improvident or prejudicial to the interests of the public, its tenants, lienholders, mortgagees, creditors, or the holders of its securities or obligations, the board shall commence an action or proceeding in the Circuit Court of the county in which the premises are situated or in which the principal offices of the corporation are located for the purpose of stopping such act or ommission, or preventing such threatened act or omission, either by mandamus or injunction. [L. 1933, p. 396.]

Housing and Redevelopment

Blighted Areas Redevelopment Act of 1947

Ch. 67½, Sec. 82. Approval of sales by Land Clearance Commission. — Deeds. — §20. . . . Any deed of conveyance by the [Land Clearance] Commission may provide such restrictions as are required by the plan for redevelopment and the building and zoning ordinances, but no deed of conveyance either by the Commission or any subsequent owner shall contain a covenant running with the land or other provision prohibiting the occupancy of the premises by any person because of race, creed or color. [L. 1947, pp. 1072, 1080; Jones Ill. Stats. Ann. [1947 Cum. Supp.], 63.146.]

Neighborhood Redevelopment Corporation Law of 1941.

Ch. 32, Sec. 550.17. Neighborhood Redevelopment Corporations. — §17. (2)(g) [Provides that upon the application of a Neighborhood Redevelopment Corporation to the Redevelopment Commission for approval of its Redevelopment Plan and before the issuance of a certificate of convenience and necessity, the Redevelopment Commission shall determine that "the execution of the Development Plan will not displace the predominant primary racial group of the present inhabitants of the Development Area."] [L. 1941, v.1, p. 431; Jones Ill. Stats. Ann. [1947 Cum. Supp.], 63.95.]

Indians

See **American Indian Day** above.

Insurance

Life Insurance

Ch. 73, Sec. 848. §236. Discrimination Prohibited. — No life insurance company doing business in this State shall make or permit any distinction or discrimination in favor of individuals among insured persons of the same class and equal expectation of life in the amount of payment of premiums or rates charged for policies of insurance, in the amount of any dividends or other benefits payable thereon, or in any other of the terms and conditions of the contracts it makes. [L. 1937, p. 696; Jones Ill. Stats. Ann., 66.911.]

[Note: While the above statute makes no reference to race or color, it may be invoked against discrimination. Similar clauses appear in most state insurance codes.]

Accident and Health Insurance

Ch. 73, Sec. 976. §364. Discrimination prohibited.—[Similar provision to Sec. 848.] [L. 1937, p. 696; Jones Ill. Stats. Ann., 66.1039.]

[Note: — See note to Sec. 848.]

Interracial Commission

Ch. 127, Sec. 214.1. Illinois Interracial Commission.—§1. There is created an Illinois Interracial Commission composed of twenty [20] members to be appointed by the Governor. Each of the members shall serve for a period of two years from July 1, 1947. The Governor shall designate the Chairman of the Commission from among the members thereof. [L. 1947, p. 1680, H.B. 771, appvd. Aug. 8, 1947.]

Ch. 127, Sec. 2142. Compensation—Expenses.—§2. None of the members except the Chairman may receive any compensation for his services, but all members shall be reimbursed for expenses incurred in the performance of their duties. [L. 1947, p. 1680, H.B. No. 771, appvd. Aug. 8, 1947.]

Ch. 127, Sec. 214.3. Secretary. — §3. As soon as practicable, after this Act becomes effective, the members shall meet and organize and designate, by majority vote, some person to act as secretary, who shall keep a record of all proceedings. The Commission shall act officially only in a meeting duly called by the Chairman or at a regular meeting fixed by resolution of the Commission, adopted by majority vote. [L. 1947, p. 1680, H.B. No. 771, appvd. Aug. 8, 1947.]

Ch. 127, Sec. 214.4. Powers and duties of Commission.—§4. The Commission shall have the following powers and shall perform the following duties: (a) investigate the most effective means of affording opportunity in profitable employment to all persons, with particular reference to training and placement; (b) cooperate with civic, religious and educational organizations in promoting tolerance and good will; and (c) report to the Governor and to the Legislature biennially, on or about the third Monday in January of each odd numbered year, the results of its investigations. [L. 1947, p. 1680, H.B. No. 771, appvd. Aug. 8, 1947.]

Ch. 127, Sec. 214.5. Employees—Report to Governor.—§5. The Commission may employ necessary secretarial, stenographic and clerical help, and may submit to the Director of Finance, for publication, its report made to the Governor. Such report shall contain factual findings only. [L. 1947, p. 1680, H.B. No. 771, appvd. Aug. 8, 1947.]

Intoxicating Liquors — Dram Shops

Ch. 43, Sec. 133. Civil rights in licensed premises. — §12b. No licensee licensed under the provisions of this Act shall deny or permit his agents and employees to deny any person the full and equal enjoyment of the accommodations, advantages, facilities and privileges of any premises in which alcoholic liquors are authorized to be sold subject only to the conditions and limitations established by law and applicable alike to all citizens. [L. 1933-34, Second Sp. Sess. p. 57; Jones Ill. Stats. Ann., 63.040.]

Ch. 43, Sec. 149. Revocation of local license.—§5. The local commission may revoke any license issued by it if it determines that the licensee has violated any of the provisions of this Act or of any valid ordinance or resolution enacted by the particular city council, president, and board of trustees or county board (as the case may be) or any applicable rule or regulation established by the local commission which is not inconsistent with law. [L. 1933-34 Second Sp. Sess., p. 57.]

Ku Klux Klan — Anti-Mask Laws — Chapter 38.

Sec. 57a. Assault while hooded, robed or masked. — §22a. Whoever, being hooded, robed or masked so as to conceal his identity, is guilty of an assault or an assault and battery, shall be fined not less than $100 nor more than $1,000, or imprisoned in the penitentiary not less than one [1] year nor more than five [5] years or both. [Added by act approved June 27, 1923. L. 1923, p. 318.]

Sec. 60a. With deadly weapon, while hooded, robed or masked.—§25b. Whoever, being hooded, robed or masked so as to conceal his identity, is guilty of an assault with a deadly weapon, instrument or other thing, with an intent to inflict the person of another a bodily injury, where the circumstances of the assault show an abandoned and malignant heart, shall subject the offender to a fine not exceeding $5,000.00 nor less than $500.00 or imprisonment in the penitentiary for a period of not less than one [1] year nor more than ten [10] years or both. [Added by Act approved June 27, 1923. L. 1923, p. 318.]

Sec. 160. Disturbing the peace and quiet — Displaying deadly weapons in threatening manner — Disturbing the peace and quiet while hooded or masked — Penalties. — §56. Whoever wilfully disturbs the peace and quiet of any neighborhood or family by loud or unusual noises, or by tumultuous or offensive carriage, threatening, traducing, quarreling, challenging to fight, or fighting, or whoever in a threatening manner displays any pistol, knife, sling-shot, brass, steel, or iron knuckles, or other deadly weapon, shall be fined not exceeding $100. However, in case any person being hooded, robed or masked so as to conceal his identity wilfully disturbs the peace and quiet of any neighborhood or family as herein provided he shall be fined not more than $1,000. [R.S. 1874, p. 348, as amended by act approved July 8, 1947, p. 799, H.B. No. 222.]

Sec. 161a. Concealing identity by hood, robe or mask.—56c. Whoever with an evil or wicked purpose, appears in any public place hooded, robed or masked so as to conceal his identity, shall be fined not less than $100 nor more than $1,000.00 or imprisoned in the county jail, not less than six [6] months nor more than a [1] year, or both. [Added by act approved June 27, 1923. L. 1923, p. 318.]

Sec. 384. Kidnapping. Punishment. — §166. Whoever wilfully and without lawful authority forcibly or secretly confines or imprisons any other person within this State against his will, or forcibly carries or sends such person out of the State, or forcibly seizes or confines, or inveigles, or kidnaps any other person, with the intent to cause such person to be secretly confined or imprisoned in this State against his will, or to cause such person to be sent out of the State against his will, shall be imprisoned in the penitentiary for a term of not less than one [1] year and not exceeding five [5] years, or fined not exceeding $1,000 or both.

In case any person being hooded, robed or masked so as to conceal his identity, violates any of the provisions of this section, he shall be fined not less than $500.00, nor more than $2,000.00, or imprisoned in the penitentiary not less than five [5] years nor more than fourteen [14] years, or both.

This section shall not extend to a parent taking his or her minor child, unless such parent is deprived of the right to have the custody of such child by the order of a court of competent jurisdiction. [R.S. 1874, p. 348, as amended by act approved June 27, 1923. L. 1923, p. 318.]

Military

Ch. 129, Sec. 2. Classification of State Militia—Racial segregation.—Sec. 2. The Illinois State Militia shall be divided into three classes, the National Guard, the Naval Militia and the Unorganized Militia. There shall be no racial segregation nor shall there be any discrimination in accepting enlistment in the service of any unit, company, regiment, corps, division, department or any other subdivision of the National Guard or Naval Militia because of race, creed or color. [L. 1909, p. 437, as amended by act appvd. July 30, 1949, L. 1949, p. 1587, H.B. No. 872.]

Public Assistance — Relief

Ch. 23, Sec. 436-11. §1-11. No discrimination on account of race, religion, etc. — There shall be no discrimination and no denial of assistance or general assistance provided for in this Code [Public Assistance Code of 1949] on account of the race, color, religion, national origin, or political affiliation of any applicant or recipient. [Appvd. Aug. 4, 1949. L. 1949, p. 405, S.B. No. 503.]

Public Accommodation

See Civil Rights above.

Public Officers

Ch. 38, Sec. 128k. Denial of equal advantages by public officers. — §1. No officer or employee in the State of Illinois, or of any political subdivision thereof, or of any Country or any Park District, or of any Forest Preserve District, or of any State University or subdivision thereof, or of any State Normal School or of any division thereof, or of any municipal corporation in the State of Illinois, shall deny or refuse to any person on account of race, color or religion, the full and equal enjoyment of the accommodations, advantages, facilities or privileges of his office or services of any property under his care. [Approved July 6, 1937, L. 1937, p. 480; Jones Ill. Stats. Ann. [1947 Cum. Supp.], 22.20.]

Ch. 38, Sec. 128l. Report of violation — Discharge of employee. — §2. Any violation of Sec. 1 [Sec. 128k] may be reported, in writing, to the head of the department or agency in which the officer or employee committing said violation is employed. It shall be his duty to investigate the complaint thoroughly. If he determines that a violation has been committed, the head of the department or agency, if said employee is not employed under Civil Service Law shall immediately discharge the guilty officer or employee; if said employee is employed under Civil Service Law, then the head of the department or agency in which such offending employee is employed shall file or cause to be filed with the proper person the proper and necessary papers, charging such employee with a violation of this act. Said papers filed shall be in conformity with the provisions of the Civil Service Act, under which such employee is employed; if he determines no violation has been committed, he shall so notify the complainant by registered mail. [L. 1937, p. 480 Jones Ill. Stats. Ann. [1947 Cum. Supp.], 22.21.]

Ch. 38, Sec. 128m. Petition to Circuit Court—Hearing.—§3. Where no violation is found by the head of the proper department or agency, the aggrieved party may file a petition in the circuit court of the county wherein the person complained of is employed. Such person and the department or agency shall be named as respondents. The summons, service and return shall be in accordance with the Civil Practice Act. Upon the return day or any day thereafter fixed by the court, the court shall hear and determine the complaint in summary manner, and if the court finds the issues for the complainant it shall order the head of the department or agency to discharge the offending employee forthwith, or if such offending employee is employed under Civil Service Law, the Court shall order the head of the department or agency in which such employee is employed to file or cause to be filed with the proper person the proper and necessary papers, in conformity with the Civil Service Law under which such employee is employed, charging such employee with a violation of this Act. The head of the department or agency shall be bound by the court's decision and may be held in contempt for failure to obey the same. [L. 1937, p. 480; Jones Ill. Stats. Ann [1947 Cum. Supp.], 22.22.]

Ch. 38, Sec. 128n. Violation of court's order.—§4. Whenever any appointed head of a department or agency violates Section 1 [Sec. 128k.] or refuses to abide by the court's decision, he shall be removed from office by the officer who appointed him. [L. 1937, p. 480; Jones Ill. Stats. Ann. [1947 Cum. Supp.], 22.23.]

Public Utilities — Ch. 111⅔.

Sec. 38. Discrimination forbidden.—§38. No public utility shall, as to rates or other charges, services, facilities or in other respect, make or grant any preference or advantage to any corporation or person *to any prejudice or disadvantage*. No public utility shall establish or maintain any unreasonable difference as to rates or other charges, services, facilities, or in any other respect, either as between localities or as between classes of service.

The Commission, in order to expedite the determination of rate questions, or to avoid unnecessary and unreasonable expense, or to avoid unjust or unreasonable discrimination between classes of customers, or, whenever in the judgment of the Commission public interest so requires, may; except in the case of telephone companies, for rate making and accounting purposes, or either of them, consider one or more municipalities either with or without the adjacent or intervening rural territory as a regional unit where the same public utility serves such region under substantially similar conditions, and may within such region prescribe uniform rates for consumers or patrons of the same class.

Every public utility shall, upon reasonable notice, furnish to all persons who may apply therefor and be reasonably entitled thereto, suitable facilities and service, without discrimination and without delay. [L. 1921, p. 702 §38 as amended by act approved July 8, 1933. L. 1933, p. 41.] (italics supplied)

Sec. 77. Civil damages. — §73. In case any public utility shall do, cause to be done, or permit to be done any act, matter or things prohibited, forbidden or declared to be unlawful, or shall omit to do any act, matter or thing required to be done either by any provisions of this Act or any rule, regulation, order or decision of the Commission, issued under authority of this Act, such public utility shall be liable to the persons or corporations affected thereby for all loss, damages or injury caused thereby or resulting therefrom, and if the court shall find that the act or omission was wilful, the court may in addition to the actual damages, award damages for the sake of example and by the way of punishment. An action to recover for such loss, damage or injury may be brought in any court of competent jurisdiction by any person or corporation.

In every case of a recovery of damages by any person or corporation under the provision of this section, the plaintiff shall be entitled to a reasonable counsel's or attorney's fee to be fixed by the court, which fee shall be taxed and collected as part of the costs in the case.

No recovery as in this section provided shall in any manner affect a recovery by the State of the penalties in this Act provided. [L. 1921, p. 702, §73.]

[Note: While the above Statutes (§§38, 77) make no reference to race and color, they may be invoked to prevent discrimination on any ground, racial or otherwise.]

Sec. 79. Mandamus or injunction proceedings at instance of commission. — §75. Whenever the Commission shall be of the opinion that any public utility is failing or omitting or about to fail or omit, to do anything required of it by law, or by any order, decision, rule, regulation, direction or requirement of the Commission, issued or made under authority of this Act, or is doing anything or about to do anything or permitting anything or about to permit anything to be done, contrary to or in violation of law or any order, decision, rule, regulation, direction or requirement of the Commission, issued or made under authority of this Act, the Commission shall commence an action or proceeding in the circuit or superior court or in any other court of concurrent jurisdiction in and for the county in which the case or some part thereof arose, or in which the person or corporation complained of, if any, has its principal place of business, or in which the person complained of, if any, resides, in the name of the People of the State of Illinois, for the purpose of having such violation or threatened violation stopped and prevented, either by mandamus or injunction. The Commission shall begin such action or proceeding by petition to such circuit or superior court, alleging the violation or threatened violation complained of, and praying for appropriate relief by way of mandamus or injunction. It shall thereupon be the duty of the court to specify a time, not exceeding twenty days after the service of the copy of the petition, within which the public utility complained of must answer the petition, and in the meantime said public utility may be restrained. In case of default in answer, or after answer, the court shall immediately inquire into the facts and circumstances of the case. Such corporations or persons as the court may deem necessary or proper to be joined as parties, in order to make its judgment, order or writ effective, may be joined as parties. The final judgment in any such action or proceeding shall either dismiss the action or proceeding or direct that the writ of mandamus or injunction issue or be made permanent as prayed for in the petition, or in such modified or other form as will afford appropriate relief. An appeal may be taken from such final judgment in the same manner and with the same effect, subject to the provisions of this Act, as appeals are taken from judgments of the circuit or superior court in other actions for mandamus or injunction. [L. 1921, p. 702, §75.]

Public Works

Ch. 29, Sec. 17. Race or color discrimination prohibited in contracts for public works. — §1. No person shall be refused or denied employment in any capacity on the ground of race or color, nor be discriminated against in any manner by reason thereof, in connection with the contracting for or the performance of any work or service of any kind, by, for, on behalf of, or for the benefit of this State, or of any department, bureau, commission, board, other political subdivision or agency thereof. [Approved July 8, 1933. L. 1933, p. 296; Jones Ill. Stats. Ann., 22.05.]

Ch. 29, Sec. 18. Deemed incorporated in contract. — §2. The provisions of this Act shall automatically enter into and become a part of each and every contract or other agreement hereafter entered into by, with, for, on behalf of, or for the benefit of this State, or of any department, bureau, commission, board, other political subdivision or agency, officer or agent thereof, providing for or relating to the performance of any of the said work or services or of any part thereof. [Approved July 8, 1933. L. 1933, p. 296; Jones Ill. Stats. Ann., 22.06.]

Ch. 29, Sec. 19. Includes independent contractors, etc. — §3. The provisions of this Act also shall apply to all contracts entered into by or on behalf of all independent contractors, subcontractors, and any and all other persons, associations or corporations, providing for or relating to the doing of any of the said work or the performance of any of the said services, or any part thereof. [Approved July 8, 1933. L. 1933, p. 296; Jones Ill. Stats. Ann., 22.07.]

Ch. 29, Sec. 20. Deduction from compensation. — §4. No contractor, subcontractor, nor any person on his behalf shall, in any manner, discriminate against or intimidate any employee hired for the performance of work for the benefit of the State or for any department, bureau, commission, board, other political subdivision or agency, officer or agent thereof, on account of race or color; and there may be deducted from the amount payable to the contractor by the State of Illinois or by any municipal corporation thereof, under this contract, a penalty of five [$5.00] dollars for each person for each calendar day during which such person was discriminated against or intimidated in violation of the provisions of this Act. [Approved July 8, 1933. L. 1933, p. 296; Jones Ill. Stats. Ann., 22.08.]

Ch. 29, Sec. 21. Recovery by injured person. — §5. Any person who or any agency, corporation or association which shall violate any of the provisions of the foregoing sections, or who or which shall aid, abet, incite or otherwise participate in the violation of any of the said provisions, whether the said violation or participation therein shall occur through action in a private, in a public, or in any official capacity, shall be liable to a penalty of not less than one hundred [$100.00] nor more than five hundred [$500.00] dollars for each and every violation or participation therein with respect to each person aggrieved thereby, to be recovered by each such aggrieved person, or by any other person to whom such aggrieved person shall assign his cause of action, in any court of competent jurisdiction in the county in which the plaintiff or defendant shall reside. [Approved July 8, 1933, L. 1933, p. 296; Jones Ill. Stats. Ann., 22.09.]

Ch. 29 Sec. 22. Criminal Penalty. — §6. Any person who or any agency, corporation or association which shall violate any of the provisions of the foregoing sections . . . [includes same language as Sec. 21] . . . shall also be deemed guilty of a misdemeanor for each and every violation or participation and on conviction thereof [punishable by a fine of $100 to $500, or in case of non-corporate violators, or participators, by imprisonment for 30 to 90 days, or both such fine and imprisonment.] [Approved July 8, 1933. L. 1933, p. 296; Jones Ill. Stats. Ann., 22.10.]

Ch. 29, Sec. 23. To be inscribed in contract. — The provisions of this Act shall be printed or otherwise inscribed on the face of each contract to which it shall be applicable, but their absence therefrom shall in no wise prevent or affect the application of the said provisions to the said contract. [Approved July 8, 1933. L. 1933, p. 296; Jones Ill. Stats. Ann., 22.11.]

Ch. 29, Sec. 24. Partial Invalidity — Construction. — §8. The invalidity or unconstitutionality of any one or more provisions, parts, or sections of this Act shall not be held or construed to invalidate the whole or any other provision, part, or section thereof, it being intended that this Act shall be sustained and enforced to the fullest extent possible and that it shall be construed as liberally as possible to prevent refusals, denials and discriminations of and with reference to the award of contracts and employment thereunder, on the ground of race or color. [Approved July 8, 1933. L. 1933, p. 296; Jones Ill. Stats. Ann., 22.12.]

Transportation
Railroads

Ch. 114, Sec. 77. Must furnish cars and transport passengers and property. — §22. [Every railroad corporation in the state is required to furnish and run cars for the transportation of such passengers and property as are ready or shall be offered for transportation at the several rail-road stations on its lines.] [Act of March 31, 1874, as amended by act approved June 25, 1883. L. 1883, p. 125.]

Ch. 114, Sec. 78. Failure to transport persons or property — Depots — Penalty. — §23. [For failure of a railroad company or corporation to transport persons or property or to keep its depots open, lighted and warm in accordance with provision of Sec. 77, the railroad is made liable to the aggrieved person for treble damages plus the costs of suit. In addition the railroad corporation shall forfeit a sum of $25.00 to $1,000.00 for each offense to be recovered in a civil suit in the name of the People of the State of Illinois, and the forfeiture recovered shall be placed in the school fund for the county in which the offense is committed. [Act of March 31, 1874 as amended by act approved June 28, 1935. L. 1935, p. 1109.]

[Note: While no mention of race or color is found in either of the two sections summarized above, such statutes may be invoked to protect persons against discrimination by railroad corporations.]

Work Relief

[An Act in relation to civil and legal rights of persons in this State] [Approved June 27, 1935. L. 1935, p. 707.]

Ch. 38, 128h. Discrimination in hiring persons for work relief. — Sec. 1. It shall be unlawful for any agent, appointee or employee of any State commission or governmental sub-division of this State or of any county, municipal, or political sub-division thereof or of any Park District or Forest Preserve District to either directly or indirectly discriminate or cause to be discriminated against any person or persons in this State on account of race, color or creed in the matter of hiring persons for work relief projects. [L. 1935, p. 707; Jones Ill. Stats. Ann. [1947 Cum. Supp.], 22.12 (1).]

Ch. 38, Sec. 128i. Discharge for violation. — §2. Whoever violates any of the provisions of Section 1 of this Act [Sec. 128 h] or whoever shall permit or allow any other person under his employ or direction to violate any of the provisions of Section 1 of this Act [Sec. 128 h] shall forthwith be discharged by the appointing authority responsible for his or her appointment. [L. 1935, p. 707; Jones Ill. Stats. Ann. [1947 Cum. Supp.], 22.12 (2).]

Ch. 38, Sec. 128j. Penalty for violation. — §3. And also whoever violates any of the provisions of Section 1 of this Act [Sec. 128 h] shall be deemed guilty of a misdemeanor and upon conviction thereof shall be imprisoned in the County jail not less than 30 days nor more than six months or shall be fined not less than fifty ($50.00) dollars, nor more than one hundred ($100.00) dollars, or both so imprisoned and so fined. [L. 1935, p. 707; Jones Ill. Stats. Ann., 22.12 (3).]

INDIANA

CONSTITUTION

Slavery

Art. I. §37. Slavery prohibited. — There shall be neither slavery, nor involuntary servitude, within the State, otherwise than for the punishment of crimes, whereof the party shall have been duly convicted. No indenture of any Negro or Mulatto, made and executed out of the bounds of the State, shall be valid within the State. [Const. 1851.]

Suffrage

[Note: Art. 2, §2 of the Indiana Constitution of 1851 restricted the right to vote to "every white male citizen of the United States, of the age of twenty-one years and upwards." The words "white" and "male" were eliminated by amendments adopted in 1881 and 1921.]

STATUTES

INDIANA ANNOTATED STATUTES (BURNS 1933)

Aliens

56-505. [13439] Lands escheat to state. — [Prohibits aliens from acquiring land in the state in excess of 320 acres. Land in excess of 320 acres acquired by aliens which remains unconveyed at the end of 5 years from the date of acquisition shall escheat to the state.] [Acts 1905, ch. 130, §2, p. 410.]

[Note: This prohibition applies to all aliens and is not directed solely against ineligible aliens for citizenship as are the Alien Land Laws of the western states.]

Civil Rights

Public Accommodations

Sec. 10-901. [1942 Replacement] Persons entitled to equal accommodations. — All persons within the jurisdiction of said state shall be entitled to the full and equal enjoyments of the accommodations, advantages, facilities and privileges of inns, restaurants, eating-houses, barber shops, public conveyances on land and water, theatres and other places of public accommodations and amusement, subject only to the conditions and limitations established by law and applicable alike to all citizens. [Acts 1885, Ch. 47, §1, p. 76.]

Sec. 10-902. [1942 Replacement] Persons entitled to equal accommodations. Forfeiture and penalty for violation. — Any person who shall violate any of the provisions of the foregoing section by denying to any citizen, except for reasons applicable alike to all citizens of every race and color, and regardless of color or race, the full enjoyment of any of the accommodations, advantages, facilities or privileges in said section enumerated, or by aiding or inciting such denial, shall, for every such offense, forfeit and pay a sum not to exceed one hundred dollars [$100.00] to [any] person aggrieved thereby, to be recovered in any court of competent jurisdiction in the county where the offense was committed, and shall also, for every such offense, be deemed guilty of a

143

misdemeanor, and upon conviction thereof, shall be fined not to exceed one hundred dollars [$100.00], or shall be imprisoned not more than thirty [30] days, or both: And provided, further, That a judgment in favor of the party aggrieved, or punishment or committal upon an indictment, affidavit or information, shall be a bar to further or other prosecution or suit. [Acts 1885, Ch. 47, §2, p. 76.]

Civil Service — State Employees

60-1336. [1949 Cum. Supp.] **Appeals from dismissal or suspension.** — Any regular employee who is dismissed, demoted, or suspended, or laid off may appeal to the board within fifteen [15] days after such action is taken. Upon such appeal, both the appealing employee and the appointing authority whose action is reviewed shall have the right to be heard publicly and to present evidence. At the hearing of such appeals, the proceedings shall be informal. *If the board finds that the action complained of was taken by the appointing authority for any political, social, religious, or racial reason, the employee shall be reinstated to his position without loss of pay.* In all other cases, if the decision is favorable to the employee, the appointing authority shall follow the findings and recommendations of the board, which may include reinstatement and payment of salary or wages lost by the employee. (italics supplied) [Acts 1941, ch. 139, §36, p. 387; 1949, ch. 235, §12, p. 777.]

Defamation

See Race Hate below.

Education

Appointment of Negro to State Board of Education

Secs. 28-401, 28-401a, 28-401b [1947 Cum. Supp.] [Superceded by Sec. 28-405, Acts 1945, ch. 330, §1, p. 1529. These sections provided for the appointment of a Negro to membership in the State Board of Education. The 1945 provision omits provision for such appointment.] [Acts 1941, ch. 182, p. 553; Acts 1939, ch. 82, §§1, 2, p. 474.]

Separate Schools for Negro Children

Sec. 28-5104. **Colored Children — Separate Schools for.** — [Acts 1869 (Spec. Sess.) Ch. 16, §3, p. 41; 1877, Ch. 81, §1, p. 124; 1935, Ch. 296, §1, p. 1457. *Expressly repealed by Act approved March 8, 1949. Laws 1949, Ch. 186, §11, to become effective September 1, 1949*].

28-2803. **Discontinuing schools.** — [This section provides for the discontinuance and temporary abandonment of all schools where the daily average attendance has been 15 pupils or less, with the proviso, that nothing in this act . . . shall authorize the discontinuance of any school exclusively for colored pupils, where the average daily attendance has been twelve [12] pupils or more and where such school is the only school for colored pupils in such school corporation. [Acts 1907, ch. 233, §1, p. 444; 1909, ch. 30, §1, p. 73; 1935, ch. 77, §1, p. 231; 1937, ch. 274, §1, p. 1272.]

[Note: In view of Indian Laws 1949, ch. 186, which requires the abolition of segregation by race in the public schools, the above section as it related to schools "exclusively for colored pupils" would appear to be obsolete.]

Abolition of Segregation in the Public Schools.

INDIANA LAWS, 1949, CH. 186, P. 603

[House Enrolled Act No. 242] [Approved March 8, 1949.]

[AN ACT establishing a public policy in public education and abolishing and prohibiting separate schools organized on the basis of race, color or creed, and prohibiting racial or creed segregation, separation or discrimination in public schools, colleges and universities in the state of Indiana and prohibiting discrimination in the transportation of public school pupils and students.]

[1949 Cum. Supp.]

28—5156. Equal educational opportunities provided — Segregation in Schools and colleges prohibited. — It is hereby declared to be the public policy of the state of Indiana to provide, furnish, and make available equal, non-segregated, non-discriminatory educational opportunities and facilities for all regardless of race, creed, national origin, color or sex; to provide and furnish public schools and common schools equally open to all and prohibited and denied to none because of race, creed, color, or national origin; to reaffirm the principles of our Bill of Rights, Civil Rights and our Constitution and to provide for the State of Indiana and its citizens a uniform democratic system of common and public school education; and to abolish, eliminate and prohibit segregated and separate schools or school districts on the basis of race, creed or color; and to eliminate and prohibit segregation, separation and discrimination on the basis of race, color or creed in the public kindergartens, common schools, public schools, colleges and universities of the state. [Acts 1949, ch. 186, §1, p. 603.]

28-5157. Establishment or continued operation of segregated school prohibited. — The school commissioners, superintendents, trustee or trustees of any township, city or school city or county or state or any other public school, college or university official or officials, shall not build or erect, establish, maintain, continue or permit any segregated or separate public kindergartens, public schools or districts or public school departments or divisions on the basis of the race, color, creed or national origin of the attending pupil or pupils. [Acts 1949, ch. 186, §2, p. 603.]

28-5158. Segregated schools — Conversion to non-segregated Schools. — Where separate public kindergartens, public schools, common schools or school districts, departments or divisions are established, separated or segregated on the basis of the race, color or creed of the pupil or pupils, that said officials of said public kindergartens and public schools, districts, departments or divisions shall at the beginning of the September, 1949 school year and thereafter, discontinue enrollment on the basis of race, creed or color of students entering for the first time the public kindergartens, the first grades of elementary schools and the first year departments of senior high or junior high schools; but said first year pupils shall be permitted to enter and shall be enrolled in the kindergarten within their district, the elementary school within their district, and shall be free to enroll and attend any public junior high school or senior high school of their choice within the limitations applicable alike to all students regardless of race, creed or color; provided that in schools or districts where equipment and facilities are not available for the enrollment and integration of such first year students in September, 1949, the period for enrollment in the schools of their district may be delayed or extended until the September 1950 school year in the case of kindergarten and grade schools, the September 1951 school year in the case of junior high schools, and the September 1954 school year in the case of night schools, and that on and after the beginning of each of such school years, respectively, such students shall be enrolled in the schools of their district, and shall have and receive credit for such school work as has been completed and shall be certified by the transferring school. [Acts 1949, ch. 186, §3, p. 603.]

28-5159. Admission in district without regard to race, color or creed. — All students and pupils attending and enrolled in separate public or common schools, kindergartens, junior high schools, high schools, colleges and universities after the respective dates set out in Section 3 [§28-5158] of this Act applicable to kindergarten, grade schools, junior high schools and senior high schools shall henceforth be admitted and enrolled in the public or common school in their districts in which they reside without regard to race, creed or color, class or national origin; and no student or pupil shall be prohibited, segregated or denied attendance or enrollment to any public school, common school, junior high school or high school in his district, or college or university in the state because of his race, creed, color or national origin, but shall be free to attend any public school, department or division thereof or college or university within the limitations applicable alike to all students regardless of race, creed, color or national origin, and within the limitations and laws applicable alike to non-citizen and non-resident students. [Acts 1949, ch. 186, §4, p. 603.]

28-5160. Segregation or separation forbidden. — That no public school, college or university, supported in whole or in part by public funds of the state of Indiana or any township, town, county or school city or city thereof, shall segregate, separate or discriminate against in any way, student or students therein on the basis of race, creed or color, nor shall admission to any such public schools be approved or denied on the basis of race, creed or color. [Acts 1949, ch. 186, §5, p. 603.]

28-5161. Teachers — Discrimination prohibited. — No public school, college or university supported in whole or in part by public funds of the state of Indiana or any township, town, county or city or school city or any other school official or officials thereof, shall discriminate in any way in hiring, upgrading, enure or placements of any teacher on the basis of race, creed or color. [Acts 1949, ch. 186, §6, p. 603.]

28-5162. Transportation facilities provided for all. — The board of school commissioners, trustees or officials of any public school district or unit may provide suitable transportation, by proper conveyance to transport any and all children, regardless of race, creed, color or national origin from their home to their district school and back to their home or from school to school, under such regulations or rules as said school officials shall set up and establish applicable alike to all regardless of race, creed, color or national origin of said student or students: Provided, That transportation shall in no instance be provided where the distance to be traveled by a student is less than one (1) mile. [Acts 1949, ch. 186, §7, p. 603.]

28-5163. Supplemental nature of act. — The provisions of this act [§§28-5156 - 28-5163] shall be deemed supplemental to any and all existing common law or statutory law or civil rights on the subject of public schools, common schools, colleges or universities, and rights and remedies thereof of the state of Indiana and the people thereof. [Acts 1949, ch. 186, §8, p. 603.]

[Note: The following sections of Acts 1949, ch. 186, were not included in the code. These sections provide:

Sec. 9. [Separability] — If any section, paragraph, sentence or clause of this act shall for any reason be held invalid or unconstitutional by any court of competent jurisdiction, the same shall not affect the validity of this act as a whole, or any part thereof, other than that portion so held to be invalid or unconstitutional.

Sec. 10. [Repeal]. — All laws or parts of laws in conflict with this Act are to the extent of such conflict hereby repealed and the Acts of 1869 (Spec. Sess.), ch. 16, par. 3, p. 41; 1877, ch. 81, par. 1, p. 124; 1935, ch. 296, par. 1, p. 1457, [28-5104.] are hereby specially repealed.

Sec. 11. [Emergency]. — That whereby an emergency exists, all provisions of this Act shall be in force and effect September 1, 1949.]

Employment

40-1014. Discrimination Prohibited. — Proprietors, agents or managers of any manufacturing or mercantile establishment, mine or quarry, laundry, or renovating works, bakery or printing office, are prohibited from discriminating against any person or persons, or class of labor, seeking work, by posting notices or otherwise. [Acts 1899, Chap. 142, Sec. 16, p. 231.]

Fair Employment Practices

[Note: Acts, 1945, Ch. 325. Title of Act: "AN ACT conferring certain powers and duties on the Division of Labor and the Commissioner of Labor concerning discrimination because of race, color, creed, national origin or ancestry, and providing for an advisory board. (S. 75, Approved March 9, 1945.)

Purposes as Expressed in the Act. "WHEREAS, The practice of denying employment to, and discriminating in employment against, properly qualified persons by reason of the race, creed, color, national origin or ancestry, is contrary to the principle of freedom and equality of opportunity, and the denial by some employers and associations of employees of employment opportunities to such persons solely because of their race, creed, color, national origin or ancestry deprives large segments of the population of the state of the earnings which are necessary to maintain a just and decent standard of living; and,

147

"WHEREAS it is the policy of the state that opportunity to obtain employment without discrimination because of race, color, creed, national origin or ancestry be protected as a right and privilege of citizens of the State of Indiana; and,

"WHEREAS. It is the public policy of the state to encourage all of its citizens to engage in gainful employment, regardless of race, creed, color, national origin or ancestry, and to encourage the full utilization of the productive resources of the state to the benefit of the state, the family and to all the people of the state;"]

40-2301. [1948 Cum. Supp.] **Definitions.** — When used in this act:
1. The term "person" includes one [1] or more individuals, partnerships, associations, corporations, legal representatives, trustees or receivers.
2. The term "associations of employees" means any organization of any kind, or any agency or employee representation committee or plan, in which employees participate and which exists for the purpose, in whole or in part, of dealing with employers concerning grievances, labor disputes, wages, rates of pay, hours of employment or conditions of work.

3. The term "employees" shall not include any individual employed by his parents, spouse, or child, or in the domestic service of any person in his home.

4. The term "employer" shall not include a social club, or a fraternal, charitable, educational or religious association, organization, board or body, not operating for private profit.

5. The term "division" means the division of labor of the department of labor of the state of Indiana.

6. The term "commissioner" means the commissioner of labor of the State of Indiana. [Acts of 1945, Chap. 325, §1, p. 1499.]

40-2302. [1949 Cum. Supp.] **Division of labor — Removal of discriminations.** — There is hereby conferred upon the division of labor the power and duty, in addition to the powers and duties now vested in it, to cooperate with or utilize other agencies and to utilize voluntary and uncompensated services, in connection with the efforts of said division to aid in removing discrimination with respect to employment because of race, creed, color, national origin or ancestry. [Acts of 1945, Chap. 325, §2, p. 1499.]

40-2303. [1947 Cum. Supp.] **Functions of Commissioner.** — There is hereby conferred upon the commissioner of labor, in addition to the functions now vested in him, the following functions, viz:

1. To appoint such employees and fix such salaries or other compensation therefor as he may from time to time find necessary for the proper performance of his functions under this act. The reasonable and necessary traveling and other expenses incurred by the commissioner, his agents or employees, while actually engaged in the performance of such functions, outside of the city of Indianapolis, and all salaries and expenses in administering this act (which salaries and expenses shall not exceed

$15,000 annually), shall be paid from the state treasury as expenses of ocers and employees and other expenses of departments of the state government are paid and the sum of $30,000 is hereby appropriated to pay such salaries and expenses for the fiscal years beginning June 1, 1945, and July 1, 1946.

2. To aid in bringing about the removal of discrimination in regard to hire or tenure terms or conditions of employment because of race, creed or color: by making comprehensive studies of such discrimination in different metropolitan districts and sections of the state, and of the effect of such discrimination, and of the best method of eliminating it; by formulating, in cooperation with other interested public or private agencies, comprehensive plans for the elimination of such discrimination as rapidly as possible in cities or areas where such discrimination may be found to exist; by conferring, cooperating with and furnishing technical assistance to employers and private or public agencies, organizations and associations in formulating and executing policies and programs for the elimination of such discrimination; by receiving and investigating meritorious written complaints charging any such discrimination and by investigating other cases where he has reason to believe that such discrimination is practiced; and by making specific and detailed recommendations to the interested parties in any such case as to ways and means for the elimination of any such discrimination. [Acts of 1945, Chap. 325, §3, p. 1499.]

40-2304. [1947 Cum. Supp.] **Study of Discrimination — Recommendation to general assembly.** — The commissioner shall make a study and investigation of discrimination in regard to hire, or tenure, terms or conditions of employment, in the departments and agencies of the state because of race, creed, or color, and may recommend to the general assembly a specific plan to eliminate it and such legislation as he deems necessary to eliminate it. [Acts of 1945, Chap. 325, §4, p. 1499.]

40-2305. [1947 Cum. Supp.] **Complaints — Investigations — Recommendation to legislature.** — The commissioner is authorized and empowered to receive written complaints of violation of the civil rights law or other discriminatory practices based upon race, creed, color, national origin or ancestry and to investigate such complaints as he deems meritorious, or to conduct such investigation in the absence of complaint whenever he deems it in the public interest. He may transmit to the legislature his recommendations for legislation designed to aid in the removing of such discrimination. [Acts of 1945, Chap. 325, §5, p. 1499.]

40-2306. [1947 Cum. Supp.] **Advisory Board — Members — Term — Qualifications — Functions — Expenses.** — There is hereby created an advisory board of nine [9] members, eight [8] of whom shall be appointed by the governor. Four [4] of the members appointed by the governor shall at the time of their appointment be members of the state senate and four [4] shall at the time of their appointment be members of the house of representatives of the state. The lieutenant governor shall be the ninth [9th] member of said board, by virtue of his office as lieutenant governor and he shall serve as chairman. Vacancies shall be filled in the same manner as original appointments. Such board shall advise and assist the division of labor and the commissioner in administering and carrying out the provisions of this Act. Members of said board shall be paid their expenses reasonably and necessarily incurred. [Acts of 1945, Ch. 325, §6, p. 1499.]

[Note: Sec. 7 of Acts 1945, Ch. 325, p. 1499, contained a separability clause providing that in the event any part of the act should be declared unconstitutional, such judgment would not affect the rest of the act. The separability section is not included in the code.]

Housing — Redevelopment Act of 1945

48-8503. [1949 Cum. Supp.] Definitions.— ... (b) ... Provided that no provision of this act shall authorize the exclusion of any citizen from a zoned area because of his or her race, creed or national origin. [Acts 1945, ch. 276, §3, p. 1219.]

Jurors

10-903. Jurors — Race or color no disqualification — Penalty. — No citizen of the state of Indiana, possessing all other qualifications which are or may be prescribed by law, shall be disqualified to serve as [a] grand or petit juror in any court of said state on account of race or color, and any officer or other person charged with any duty in the selection or summoning of jurors who shall exclude or fail to summon any citizen for the cause aforesaid, shall, on conviction thereof, be deemed guilty of a misdemeanor and be fined not more than one hundred dollars [$100], or imprisoned not more than thirty [30] days, or both. [Acts 1885, ch. 47, §3, p. 76.]

Military

See National Guard below.

Miscegenation

44-104. Void Marriages. — [Provides that "when one of the parties is a white person and the other possessed of one-eighth or more of Negro blood," a marriage between them is void.] [1 Rev. Stat. 1852, Ch. 67, §2, p. 361.]

44-105. Marriages void without legal proceedings. — [Provides that marriages prohibited by law on account of "difference of color . . . shall be absolutely void without any legal proceedings".] [Acts 1873, Ch. 43, §1, p. 107.]

10-4222. Miscegenation or amalgamation. — No person having one-eighth part or more of negro blood shall be permitted to marry any white woman of this state, nor shall any white man be permitted to marry any negro woman or any woman having one-eighth part or more of negro blood, and every person who shall knowingly marry in violation of the provisions of this section shall, on conviction, be fined not less than one hundred dollars [$100] nor more than one thousand dollars [$1,000], and imprisoned in a state prison not less than one [1] year nor more than ten [10] years. [Acts 1905, Ch. 169, §638, p. 584.]

10-4223. Miscegenation or amalgamation — Counseling or assisting in. — Whoever, knowingly counsels or assists in any manner in any marriage between any person having one-eighth part or more of negro blood and any white person, shall, on conviction, be fined not less than one hundred dollars [$100] nor more than one thousand dollars [$1,000]. [Acts 1905, Ch. 169, §639, p. 584.]

National Guard

45-113. Battalion of negro infantry — The adjutant-general shall provide for the organization, maintenance and discipline of a battalion of colored infantry of the Indiana national guard, in accordance with the provisions of law for the organization, maintenance and discipline of the Indiana national guard. [Acts 1909, Ch. 123, §1, p. 315.]

45-114. [1949 Cum. Supp.] National Guard — Proportional Racial Representation. — [Made provision "to permit the enlistment and induction of able-bodied citizens of each and all racial groups in the State of Indiana into any and all branches and departments of the Indiana National Guard and of any other military, naval, air and armed forces . . . to the end that each and all racial groups in the State of Indiana shall be entitled to that representation in each branch or department of military, naval, air and armed forces which is at least proportionate to said group or groups of the population of the state of Indiana."] [Acts 1941, ch. 191, §1, p. 579.]

Public Accommodation

See under Civil Rights above.

Public Works

53-103. Hiring of labor — Race Discrimination Penalty. — Every contract for or on behalf of the state of Indiana or any of the municipal corporations thereof, for the construction, alteration, or repair of any public building or public work in the state of Indiana shall contain provisions by which the contractor agrees:

(a) That in the hiring of employees for the performance of work under this contract or any subcontract hereunder, no contractor, subcontractor, nor any person acting on behalf of such contractor or subcontractor, shall, by reason of race or color, discriminate against any citizen of the state of Indiana who is qualified and available to perform the work to which the employment relates;

(b) That no contractor, subcontractor, nor any person on his behalf, shall, in any manner, by reason of race or color, discriminate against or intimidate any employee hired for the performance of work under this contract on account of race or color;

(c) That there may be deducted from the amount payable to the contractor by the state of Indiana or by any municipal corporation thereof, under this contract, a penalty of five dollars [$5.00] for each person for each calendar day during which such person was discriminated against or intimidated in violation of the provisions of the contract; and

(d) That this contract may be canceled or terminated by the state of Indiana or by any municipal corporation thereof, and all money due or to become due hereunder may be forfeited, for a second or any subsequent violation of the terms or conditions of this section of the contract. [Acts 1933, Ch. 270, §1, p. 1228.]

Race Hate

10-904. [1947 Cum. Supp.] **Public policy of state — Protection of people — Hatred — Race, color, and/or religion.** — It is hereby declared to be the public policy of the State of Indiana and of this Act [§§ 10-904 - 10-914] to protect the economic welfare, health, peace, domestic tranquility, morals, property rights and interests of the state of Indiana and the people thereof, to protect the civil rights and liberties of the people, to effectuate the Bill of Rights, to prevent racketeering in hatred and to prohibit persons from agreeing, combining, uniting, confederating, conspiring, organizing, associating or assembling for the purpose of creating, advocating, spreading or disseminating hatred by reason of race, color or religion. [Acts 1947, ch. 56, §1, p. 157.]

[Note: See *Christopher v. American News Co.* (1948) 171 Fed. (2d) 275.

10-905 [1947 Cum. Supp.] **Association for propagation of malicious hatred — Malicious dissemination causing or threatening disorder — Both unlawful by reason of race, color or religion.** — (A) It shall be unlawful for any person or persons to combine, unite, confederate, conspire, organize, or associate with any other person or persons for the purpose of creating, advocating, spreading or disseminating malicious hatred by reason of race, color, or religion not prohibited by law, for or against any person, persons, or group of persons, individually or collectively, not alien enemies of the United States.

(B) It shall be unlawful for any person or persons acting with malice to create, advocate, spread, or disseminate hatred for or against any person, persons or group of persons, individually or collectively, by reason of race, color or religion which threatens to, tends to, or causes riot, disorder, interference with traffic upon the streets or public highways, destruction of property, breach of peace, violence, or denial of civil or constitutional rights. [Acts 1947, ch. 56, §2, p. 157.]

10-906. [1947 Cum. Supp.] **Racketeering in hatred — Penalty.** — Any person violating any of the provisions of Section 2 [§10-905] of this act shall be deemed guilty of racketeering in hatred, and upon conviction, shall be disfranchised and rendered incapable of holding any office of profit or trust for any determinate period not exceeding ten [10] years, and shall be fined in any sum not exceeding ten thousand dollars [$10,000], to which may be added imprisonment in the state prison for any determinate period not exceeding two [2] years. [Acts 1947, ch. 56, §3, p. 157.]

10-907. [1947 Cum. Supp.] **Restraint of crime in relation of prosecuting attorney or attorney-general — Contempt for violation.** — Any of the acts prohibited by Section 2 [§10-905] may be restrained and enjoined by any court having equitable jurisdiction in an action brought by the state of Indiana either on the relation of any prosecuting attorney of any judicial circuit or the attorney general of Indiana. The state either on the relation of any prosecuting attorney or the attorney general may bring proper actions for contempt of court for the violation of any restraining order or injunction. [Acts 1947, ch. 56, §4, p. 157.]

10-908. [1947 Cum. Supp.] **Corporations to promote race, color, or creed hatred — Refusal to issue charter or certificate — Unlawful acts of members or officers deemed acts of corporation.** — No corporate charter shall be issued for any domestic corporation, nor shall any corporation organized under the laws of another state be admitted to do business within Indiana if said domestic or foreign corporation be organized for the purpose of doing any of the acts prohibited by section 2 [§10-905] or which shall do any of the acts prohibited by section 2, and the acts prohibited by section 2 of any two [2] or more of its members or officers purporting to be pursuant to or for said corporation, or as a part of its activities, whether authorized by the corporate charter or not, shall be deemed to be the acts of said corporation. [Acts 1947, ch. 56, §5, p. 157.]

10-909. [1947 Cum. Supp.] **Forfeiture of corporate charter. — Procedure —foreign corporations, loss of authority to do business.** — Any corporation organized for the purpose of doing any of the acts prohibited by section 2, [§10-905], or which shall do any of the acts prohibited by said section, shall have its corporate charter forfeited and terminated by an action brought by the State of Indiana on the relation of the attorney general of Indiana in any circuit or superior court and the acts prohibited by Section 2 of any two [2] or more of its members or officers purporting to be pursuant to or for said corporation, or as a part of its activities, whether authorized by the corporate charter or not, shall be deemed to be acts of said corporation and subject its charter to forfeiture. If any corporation organized under the laws of another state shall do any of the acts herein prohibited and shall have been admitted to do business within this state, such authority to do business within Indiana shall be forfeited and terminated in the same manner as in this section provided for domestic corporations. [Acts 1947, ch. 56, §6, p. 157.]

10-910. [1947 Cum. Supp.] **Civil provisions supplemental to common law or statutes.** — The civil provisions of this act [§§10-904 - 10-914] shall be deemed supplemental to any and all existing common law or statutory rights and remedies of the state of Indiana. [Acts 1947, ch. 56, §7, p. 157.]

10-911. [1947 Cum. Supp.] **No bond required — Not liable for costs.** — Neither the state nor the attorney general nor any prosecuting attorney shall be required to give bond or undertaking or be liable for any costs in any proceedings brought or defended pursuant to any provisions of this act. [§§10-904 - 10-914]. [Acts 1947, ch. 56, §8, p. 157.]

10-912. [1947 Cum. Supp.] **Definitions — "Hatred" — "Person".** — The term "hatred" as used in this act [§§10-904 - 10-914] shall mean and include malevolent ill will, animosity, odium, detestation or rancor. The term "person" shall mean any person, firm, association or corporation. [Acts 1947, ch. 56, §9, p. 157.]

10-913. [1947 Cum. Supp.] **Rights under state or federal constitution unimpaired by this act.** — No provision of any section of this act shall be construed to prohibit any right protected by the federal constitution or the constitution of the state of Indiana, including but not limited to rights of freedom of speech, freedom of the press and freedom of religion. [Acts 1947, ch. 56, §10, p. 157.]

10-914. [1947 Cum. Supp.] **Designation of groups in civil or criminal actions.** — In any action, either criminal or civil, it shall be sufficient to designate and identify a group of persons by stating such group is composed of members of a race, color or religion. [Acts 1947, ch. 56, §11, p. 157.]

[Note: Sec. 12, containing a separability clause, and Sec. 13 making the act effective from the date of its passage, are not included in the code. The act was approved on February 27th, 1947.]

Real Property

56-101. Who may convey. — No person except a citizen of the United States, or an alien who shall be at the time a bona fide resident of the United States, an Indian, a negro, or a mulatto or other person of mixed blood, shall take, hold, convey, devise, or pass by descent lands, except in such cases of descent or devise as are provided for the law . . . [1. R.S. 1852, ch. 23, §1, p. 232; Acts 1861, ch. 79, §1, p. 153.]

Voters — Enumeration of

65-619 - 65-621 [Enumeration of Voters] [Provides for the separate listing and enumeration of colored males over the age of 21.] [Acts 1877, ch. 38, §§1, 2, 3, p. 59.]

IOWA

CONSTITUTION

Article I. Rights of Persons — Sec. 1. — All men are, by nature, free and equal, and have certain inalienable rights — among which are those of enjoying and defending life and liberty, acquiring, possessing and protecting property, and pursuing and obtaining safety and happiness.

[Note: The Iowa Constitution of 1789, required that voters be "white" and "male" (Art. II, Sec. 1.), that members of the State House of Representatives be "free white and male" (Art. III, Sec. 4), and limited the state militia to "white male" citizens (Art. VI, Sec. 1.). By amendments of 1868 and 1880, the words "white" were removed and by 1926 amendment, the word "male" was struck out from the constitutional provision setting forth qualifications of state House of Representatives.]

Education

Art. IX, Sec. 12. Common Schools. — The Board of Education shall provide for the education of all the youths of the State, through a system of Common Schools . . . [Cons't. 1857.]

[Note: By judicial decision it has been established that the above constitutional provision and the statutes in force effectuating it prohibit the exclusion of children from the public schools on account of race or color, nor can a colored child be compelled to attend a separate school for colored children. See *Clark v. Board of Directors* (1868) 24 Iowa 266; *Smith v. The Directors of the Ind. Sch. Dist. of Keokuk,* (1875) 40 Iowa 518; *Dove v. The Independent School District of Keokuk et. al.* (1875) 41 Iowa 689.]

Slavery

Art. I, Sec. 23. Slavery — involuntary servitude. — There shall be no slavery in this State; nor shall there be involuntary servitude, unless for the punishment of crime. [Const. 1846, Art. I, sec. 23; Const. 1857, Art. I, sec. 23.]

STATUTES

CODE OF IOWA 1946

Aliens

567.1. Acquisition of real estate. — [Limits to 320 acres the amount of real estate within the state which may be acquired by aliens.] [C. 73, §§1908, 1909; C. 97, §2889; C. 24, 27, 31, 35, 39, §10214.]

567.2. Holders of liens — escheat. — [Provides for escheat to the state of land held by aliens in excess of 320 acres as provided in 567.1 and not disposed of.] [C. 97, §2890; C. 24, 27, 31, 35, 39, §10215; 50 GA, ch. 257, §1.]

[Note: The above two sections are similar to the Indiana law (Ind. Ann. Stats., Burns 1933, §56-505.); the prohibition applies to all aliens. The Alien Land Laws of the western states are directed particularly

155

against Japanese and other Orientals ineligible to citizenship under the laws of the United States.]

Civil Rights

Public Accomodation

735.1. Civil Rights defined. — All persons within this state shall be entitled to the full and equal enjoyment of the accommodations, advantages, facilities, and privileges of inns, restaurants, chophouses, eating houses, lunch counters, and all other places where refreshments are served, public conveyances, barber shops, bathhouses, theaters, and all other places of amusement. [C. 97, §5008; C. 24, 27, 31, 35, 39, §13251.]

735.2. Punishment. — Any person who shall violate the provisions of 735.1 by denying to any person, except for reasons by law applicable to all persons, the full enjoyment of any of the accommodations, advantages, facilities, or privileges enumerated therein, or by aiding or inciting such denial, shall be guilty of a misdemeanor and shall be punished by a fine not to exceed one hundred [$100.00] dollars or imprisonment in the county jail not to exceed thirty [30] days. [C. 97, §5008; C. 24, 27, 31, 35, 39, §13252.]

Indians

732.5. Disposing of liquor to Indians. — If any person give, sell, or dispose of any spiritous or intoxicating drinks to any Indian within this state, he shall be fined not exceeding two hundred [$200.00] dollars, or be imprisoned in the county jail not exceeding one [1] year, or both. [C. 51, §2735; R. 60, §4378; C. 73, §4044; C. 97, §5001; C. 24, 27, 31, 35, 39, §13241.]

303.6. [Department of History and Archives] **Duties of the curator of the department of history and archives.** — The curator shall . . .

(2) *Custody, display, and publication of material.* Under the direction of the board, collect, preserve, organize, arrange, and classify . . . objects and materials illustrative of . . . traditions and history of the Indian tribes and prior occupants of the region, and publish such matter and display such material as may be of value and interest to the public . . . [C. 97, §§2875 - 2878; S. 13, §2881-b; C. 24, 27, 31, 35, §4525; C. 39, §4541.06.]

Ku Klux Klan — Anti-Mask Laws

690.7. Assault while masked. — Any person within this state, masked or in disguise, who shall assault another with a dangerous weapon shall be deemed guilty of assault with intent to commit murder and shall be punished by imprisonment in the penitentiary for a term not to exceed twenty [20] years. [C. 24, 27, 31, 35, 39, §12916.]

694.3. Intimidation while masked. — Any person masked, or in disguise, who shall prowl, travel, ride or walk within this state to the disturbance of the people or to the intimidation of any person, shall be guilty of a misdemeanor and on conviction thereof shall be punished by a fine of not less than one hundred [$100.00] dollars nor more than five hundred [$500.00] dollars, or by imprisonment in the county jail of the county for not less than thirty

[30] days nor more than six [6] months, or by both such fine and imprisonment. [C. 24, 27, 31, 35, 39, §12931.]

694.4. Assault while masked. — Any person, masked or in disguise, who shall enter upon the premises of another or demand admission into the house of inclosure of another with intent to inflict bodily injury or injury to property, shall be deemed guilty of assault with intent to commit a felony and such entrance or demand for admission shall be *prima facie* evidence of such intent, and upon conviction thereof, such person shall be punished by imprisonment in the penitentiary for a term of not more than ten [10] years. [C. 24, 27, 31, 35, 39, §12932.]

KANSAS

CONSTITUTION

Slavery

Bill of Rights. §6. Slavery prohibited. — There shall be no slavery in this state; and no involuntary servitude except for the punishment of crime, whereof the party shall have been duly convicted. [Const. 1859.]

Suffrage

[Note: Art. 5, §1 of the Constitution of 1859 restricted the right to vote to white male citizens. This restriction was removed by amendment (L. 1917, ch. 353), adopted by the people at the general election November 8, 1918.]

STATUTES

General Statutes of Kansas Annotated, 1935.

Aliens

Alien Land Law

§§67-701 - 67-711. [This act provides that all aliens eligible to citizenship under the laws of the United States may acquire, hold or transfer real property in the state to the same extent as citizens of the United States. [67-701]. An ineligible alien may acquire or transfer real property only to the extent permitted in any treaty now existing between the United States and the county of which such alien is a subject or a citizen, and not otherwise. [67-702]. A similar prohibition applies to companies, associations or corporations of which the majority of the members are ineligible aliens or the majority of issued capital stock is owned by such aliens. [67-703].

The act forbids the appointment of an ineligible alien or company, etc., as described in 67-702 as guardian for that portion of the estate of a minor which such alien or company, etc. is barred from holding under the act, and requires the removal of such guardian. [67-704]. Any trustee having title, custody or control of property belonging to an ineligible alien or minor child of such alien must file an annual report on or about December 31st of each year showing the amount of property thus held by the trustee on behalf of such alien or minor child, the date each item was acquired or came into his possession or control and an itemized account of all expenditures, investments, rents and profits. The report must be filed with the secretary of state and the county clerk of the county in which the property is located. [67-707.] Violation of this section is a misdemeanor punishable by a fine up to $1,000.00 or by imprisonment up to 1 year or both. [67-705].

When an heir or devisee is not permitted to take property because of ineligibility under this act, the court shall direct the property to be sold and the cash proceeds of the sale distributed to such heir or devisee. [67-706].

The sale or transfer of real property to an ineligible alien, or company, etc., described in 67-702 is made unlawful and any real property acquired in violation of the provisions of this act shall escheat to the State of Kansas. [67-707]. Similarly, the conveyance of a leasehold interest

158

to an ineligible alien or company, etc., is unlawful and the property shall escheat to the state. [67-708].

A transfer of real property made with intent to avoid or evade escheat is void, and a *prima facie* presumption of intent to evade the statute arises where the property is taken in the name of one other than an ineligible alien or company, etc. where such alien or company, etc., pays the consideration for the property. [67-709].

A conspiracy to transfer real property in violation of the act is punishable by imprisonment up to 2 years or by fine up to $5,000.00, or both. [67-710.] [L. 1925, ch. 209, §§1-11; March 21.]

[Note: The Kansas Alien Land Law is almost identical to the Idaho Alien Land Law. See the California Alien Land Law and notes, *supra*.]

City Zoning

12-713. Race discriminations. — Nothing herein contained shall be construed as authorizing the governing body to discriminate against any person by reason of race or color. [L. 1921, ch. 100, §8; May 25; R.S. 1923, §13-1107.]

Civil Rights

Public Accommodation

21-2424. Denying civil rights on account of race or color; penalty. — That if any of the regents or trustees of any state university, college, or other school of public instruction, or the state superintendent, or the owner or owners, agents, trustees or managers in charge of any inn, hotel or boarding house, or any place of entertainment or amusement for which a license is required by any of the municipal authorities of this state, or the owner or owners or person or persons in charge of any steamboat, railroad, stage coach, omnibus, streetcar, or any other means of public carriage for persons or freight within the state, shall make any distinction on account of race, color, or previous condition of servitude, the person so offending shall be deemed guilty of a misdemeanor, and upon conviction thereof in any court of competent jurisdiction shall be fined in any sum not less than ten [$10.00] nor more than one thousand [$1,000.00] dollars, and shall also be liable to damages in any court of competent jurisdiction to the person or persons injured thereby. [L. 1874, Ch. 49, §1; Apr. 25; R.S. 1923, §21-2424.]

21-2425. Disposition of fines collected under §21-2424. — All fines collected under and by virtue of this act shall be paid over to the public-school fund of the county in which the offense was committed. [L. 1874, Ch. 49, §2; Apr. 25; R.S. 1923, §21-2425.]

Commission Against Employment Discrimination

L. 1949, Ch. 289, p. 523,
House Joint Resolution No. 1,
[Approved April 5, 1949.]

A joint Resolution creating a temporary commission to study and make a report on acts of employment discrimination against citizens because of race, creed, color, religion or national origin, prescribing its powers and duties and making appropriations therefor.

WHEREAS, It has been brought to the attention of the legislature of the state of Kansas that probable cause exists for the belief that acts of discrimination in employment are being perpetrated against some of the citizens of the United States because of race, creed, color, religion or national origin; and

WHEREAS, The state of Kansas is traditionally and historically opposed to discrimination against any of its citizens in employment; and

WHEREAS, It is the public policy of this state that all of the citizens of this state are entitled to work without restrictions or limitations based on race, religion, creed or national origin; and

WHEREAS, The legislature does not have sufficient information upon which to enact adequate and proper laws and there is a difference of opinion as to whether the alleged discriminatory employment conditions actually exist: Now, therefore

Be it resolved by the House of Representatives of the State of Kansas, the Senate agreeing thereto:

§1. There is hereby created a temporary commission, hereinafter referred to as the commission, to be known as the "Kansas commission against employment discrimination" consisting of five (5) members to be appointed by the governor.

§2. The commission shall organize and elect a chairman, vice-chairman and secretary on or before June 1, 1949, and is hereby authorized to hold such meeting at such times and places within this state as may be necessary to carry out the provisions of this resolution. The commission shall complete its duties as speedily as possible and shall submit its report to the governor and to the members of the Kansas legislative council on or before October 15, 1940.

§3. The commission shall have full power and authority to receive and investigate complaints and to hold hearings relative to alleged discrimination in employment of persons because of race, creed, color or national origin.

§4. The commission is hereby authorized to employ such clerical and other assistants as may be necessary to enable it to properly carry out the provisions of this resolution and to fix their compensation.

§5. The members of the commission shall receive as compensation for their services the sum of fifteen dollars ($15) per diem and their actual and necessary expenses for time actually spent in carrying out the provisions of this resolution: *Provided,* That in no case shall any member receive more than a total of five hundred dollars ($500) as per diem allowance.

§6. The commission shall have all the powers of the legislative committee as provided by law, and shall have power to do all things necessary to carry out the intent and purposes of this resolution and the preamble thereto.

§7. There is hereby appropriated to the Kansas commission against discrimination, out of any moneys in the state treasury not otherwise appropriated, the sum of five hundred dollars ($500) for the fiscal year ending June 30, 1949, and the sum of three thousand five hundred dollars ($3,500) for the fiscal year ending June 30, 1950, for the purpose of carrying out the provisions of this resolution: *Provided,* That any unexpended and unemcumbered balances of said appropriations as of June 30, 1949, and June 30, 1950, respectively, are hereby reappropriated for the same purposes for the next succeeding fiscal year.

§8. The auditor of state shall draw his warrants upon the state treasurer for the purposes provided for in this resolution upon duly itemized vouchers, executed as now or may hereafter be provided for by law, assigned in his office and approved by the chairman of the Kansas commission against discrimination.

§9. This act shall take effect and be in force from and after its publication in the official state paper.

Education

Public Schools

72-1724. Powers of board; separate schools for white and colored children; manual training. — The board of education shall have power . . . to organize and maintain separate schools for the education of white and colored children, including the high schools of Kansas City, Kansas; no discrimination on account of color shall be made in high schools, except as provided herein; . . . [L. 1862, Ch. 46, art. 4, §§3, 18; L. 1864, Ch. 67, §4; L. 1865, Ch. 46, §1; G.S. 1868, Ch. 18, §75; L. 1879, Ch. 81, §1; L. 1905, Ch. 414, §1; Feb. 28; R.S. 1923, §72-1724.]

[Note: The above section applies to schools in cities of the First Class, (cities with a population of over 15,000 inhabitants. See Kansas Gen. Stats. Sec. 13-101.) The provision authorizing racial segregation of school children in cities of the First Class was upheld in *Reynolds v. Board of Education* (1903), 66 Kansas 672, 72 P. 274. Sec. 72-1809, which applies to cities of the Second Class (cities with a population under 15,000), provides that the "Board of Education shall have power . . . to organize and maintain a system of graded schools, to establish a high school," and contains no provision authorizing the segregation of Negro school children. Thus, it was held in *Board of Education v. Tinnon* (1881), 26 Kansas 1, 16,20, that without clear legislative authority boards of education in cities of the Second Class have no power to establish separate schools for white and colored children and cannot exclude Negro children from the public schools.]

72-1747. [1947 Supp.] [Provides for the building of high-school buildings for Negro school children in Kansas City, Kansas.] [L. 1937, Ch. 309, §1, March 25.]

State University

76-307. Tuition and fees; persons not debarred on account of age,

161

race, sex or religion.—. . .No person shall be debarred from membership of the university on account of age, race, sex, or religion. [L. 1889, ch. 258, §11; L. 1895, ch. 226, §1; May 27; R.S. 1923, §76-307.]

Employment

See Commission Against Employment Discrimination, Labor Organizations and Public Works.

Housing

See City Zoning above.

Indians

21-2170. Indians, selling or giving liquor to; penalty. — If any person shall, directly or indirectly, sell, exchange, give, barter or dispose of any spirituous liquors, wine or other intoxicating liquors to any Indian within this state, under any circumstances, unless directed by a physician for medical purposes, such person upon conviction thereof shall be punished by fine not less than five dollars [$5.00] nor more than five hundred dollars, [$500.00] or imprisoned for not less than one [1] month nor more than six [6] months in the county jail, or both such fine and imprisonment. [G.S. 1868, ch. 50, §1; Oct. 31; R.S. 1923, §21-2170.] [Repealed, L. 1949, ch. 242, §115. Appvd. March 9, 1949.]

21-2171. Indictment or information therefor. — It shall not be necessary to aver, in an indictment or information for an offense under this act, the kind or character of the liquor alleged to have been sold, exchanged, given, bartered or disposed of, but it shall be sufficient, in that particular, if the indictment or information allege that such liquor was intoxicating. [G.S. 1868, ch. 50, §1; Oct. 31; R.S. 1923, §21-2170.] [Repealed, L. 1949, ch. 242, §115. Appvd. March 9, 1949.]

21-2172. Indians as witnesses. — Upon any trial under this act, Indians shall be deemed competent witnesses. [G.S. 1868, ch. 50, §3; Oct. 31: R.S. 1923, §21-2172.] [Repealed, L. 1949, ch. 242, §115, Appvd. March 9, 1949.]

21-2173. Act not to apply to Indians who are citizens. — This act shall not apply to sales of liquor to Indians who are citizens of the United States or of the state of Kansas. [G.S. 1868, ch. 50, §4; Oct. 31; R.S. 1923, §21-2173.] [Repealed, L. 1949, ch. 242, §115, Appvd. March 9, 1949.]

Labor Organizations

44-801. [1947 Supp.] Certain labor organizations prohibited from being representative unit for the purpose of collective bargaining. — No labor organization of any kind, agency or representative committee or plan, in which employees participate and which exists for the purpose, in whole or in part, of dealing with employers concerning grievances, labor disputes, wages, rates of pay, hours of employment, or any other conditions of work, shall be the representative unit for the purpose of collective bargaining in the state of Kansas in any of the trades, crafts, skilled and unskilled, work, labor or employment of any kind or capacity, which in any manner discriminates against, or bars, or excludes from its membership any person because of his race or color: *Provided,* That the provisions of this act shall not apply to labor organizations within the provisions of 48 U.S. Statutes 1186 and 49 U.S. Statutes 1189, title 45, Sections 151 to 188, both inclusive. [L. 1941, ch. 265, §1; June 30.]

[Note: The unions excepted from the operation of the above statute are those under the federal Railway Labor Act.]

Public Accommodation
See under Civil Rights above.

Public Works

21-2461. [1947 Supp.] **Denying public work employment on account of race or color.** — No person a citizen in the United States shall be refused or denied employment in any capacity on the ground of race or color, nor be discriminated against in any manner by reason thereof, in connection with any public work, or with the contracting for or the performance of any work, labor or service of any kind on any public work by or on behalf of the state of Kansas, or of any department, bureau, commission, board, or official thereof, or by or on behalf of any county, city, township, school district or other municipality of said state. [L. 1937, Ch. 257, §1; June 30.]

21-2462. [1947 Supp.] **Same; act is part of contracts.** — The provisions of this act shall apply to and become a part of any contract hereafter made by or on behalf of the state, or of any department, bureau, commission, board or official thereof, or by or on behalf of any county, city, township, school district, or other municipality of said state, with any corporation, association or person or persons, which may involve the employment of laborers, workmen, or mechanics on any public work; and shall apply to contractors, subcontractors, or other persons doing or contracting to do the whole or a part of any public work contemplated by said contract. [L. 1937, Ch. 257, §2; June 30.]

21-2463. [1947 Supp.] **Same; penalty.** — Any officer of the state of Kansas or of any county, city, township, school district, or other municipality, or any person acting under or for such officer, or any contractor, sub-contractor, or other person violating the provisions of this act shall for each offense be punished by fine of not less than fifty [$50.00] dollars nor more than one thousand [$1,000.00] dollars, or by imprisonment of not more than six [6] months or by both fine and imprisonment. [L. 1937, Ch. 257, §3; June 30.]

KENTUCKY

CONSTITUTION

Education — Segregation

§187. White and colored to share without distinction; separate schools. — In distributing the school fund no distinction shall be made on account of race or color, and separate schools for white and colored children shall be maintained. [Const. 1891.]

Definition of "Colored Children"

[Note: "Colored children", within the meaning of Section 187 of Kentucky Constitution, include all children wholly or in part of Negro blood, or having any appreciable admixture thereof; and a child having one-sixteenth Negro blood may not attend a school for white children.

Thus, a child whose mother's grandmother was a slave and about one-fourth Negro was a "colored child", within the meaning of the constitutional and statutory provisions requiring maintenance of separate schools for white and colored children, and was not entitled to attend a public school conducted exclusively for white children. *Asher v. Huffman*, (1943) 925 Ky. 312, 174 S.W. 2nd. 424; *Mullins v. Belcher*, (1911) 142 Ky. 673, 134 S.W. 1151, Ann. Cas. 1912D 456.]

Militia

[Note: The Kentucky Constitution of 1799 prohibited Negroes, Mulattoes and Indians from serving in the state militia (Art. III, §28.). The 1891 Constitution omitted this restriction (KRS §219.).]

Slavery

§25. Slavery. — Slavery and involuntary servitude in this state are forbidden, except as a punishment for crime, whereof the party shall have been duly convicted. [Const. 1891.]

Suffrage

[Note: The Kentucky Constitution of 1792 contained no racial restriction on the right to vote (Art. 3, §1.). The Constitution of 1799 excepted "negroes, mulattoes and Indians" from those free male citizens entitled to vote (Art. II, §8.). The Constitution of 1850 restricted suffrage to "free white male" citizens (Art. II, §8.). The Constitution of 1891 eliminated the racial restriction (KRS §145.).]

STATUTES

KENTUCKY REVISED STATUTES 1948

Aliens

[Note: KRS. 243.100 prohibits aliens from holding licenses to manufacture or sell alcoholic beverages.

KRS. 244.090 prohibits the employment of aliens in business of persons holding alcoholic beverages licenses.

KRS. 381.290 permits an alien to hold or transfer real property after declaration of intention to become a citizen.

KRS. 381.300 provides that unless an alien becomes a citizen within 8 years after he acquires real property it may be escheated to the state.

KRS. 381.320 provides that a resident alien may hold property for residence or business purposes within the state for a period not longer than 21 years.

While these statutes restrict the rights of aliens within the state of Kentucky, they are not directed against aliens ineligible for citizenship, i.e. Japanese and certain Oriental groups, and therefore are not included in this compilation.]

Defamation

See Race Prejudice below.

Education

Public Schools

§158.020. [4363-8; 4399-49] Separate schools for white and colored children. —

(1) Each board of education shall maintain separate schools for the white and colored children residing in its district.

(2) No person shall operate or maintain any college, school or institution where persons of both the white and colored races are received as pupils.

(3) No instructor shall teach in any college, school, or institution where persons of both the white and colored races are received as pupils.

(4) No white person shall attend any college, school or institution where colored persons are received as pupils or receive instruction.

(5) No colored person shall attend any college, school or institution where white persons are received as pupils or receive instruction.

(6) The provisions of this section do not apply to any penal institution or house of reform. [1934, c. 65, Art. I, §8; 1934, c. 65, Art. V, §44.]

[Note: *Johnson v. Board of Trustees* 83 F. Supp. 707, (U. S. District Court, E. D. Kentucky, decided, April 27, 1949) *Held* - Qualified Negroes are, upon proper application, entitled to be admitted to graduate and professional schools of State University of Kentucky until the commonwealth makes available graduate and professional training at a separate institution of learning located within the state equal or substantially equal to that provided at the university, and applicants cannot be compelled to accept substitute classes at Negro college conducted by itinerant instructors and requiring students to travel great distances for library facilities and to do so without benefit of graduate seminars. [KRS 164.100, 164.120, 164.130.]]

Exception to Sec. 158.020

§158.025. Hospital Courses in medicine, surgery or nursing not restricted by KRS 158.020. — The provisions of KRS 158.020 shall not be construed to prohibit the giving of instruction in nursing, medicine, surgery, or other related courses of graduate grade or on the professional level, within any hospital, if the governing body of the hospital, by a majority vote of its members, so elects. [1948, c. 112, effective June 17, 1948.]

School for Colored Deaf

§167.080. [282; 283; 283a] Colored deaf; provisions concerning school for.—(1) An institution for the education of the colored deaf is recognized as established and maintained at Danville, Kentucky. The school for the colored deaf shall be under the control of the same board of commissioners and superintendent as the school for the white deaf but the two schools shall be maintained and operated as separate and distinct institutions. The colored deaf shall be admitted on the same terms as the white deaf, and the colored deaf shall receive the same per capita for support as the white deaf receive.

(2) The school for the white deaf is entitled to all appropriations made for the benefit of The Kentucky School for the Deaf unless the appropriation is designated as being for the benefit of the school for the colored deaf. The school for the colored deaf is entitled only to appropriations made under Acts in which the word "colored" is used to distinguish the school from that of the white deaf. The funds of the two schools shall be kept and spent separately. [1883. c. 1491, §§1, 3; 1910, c. 99, §2.]

School for Colored Blind

§167.180. [311] Colored Blind. — Colored blind children are entitled to receive on equal terms per capita all rights, benefits and privileges secured to the white blind children of the state. The blind children of both races shall be under the same general management and the same superintendent. [1884, c. 462, §2.]

Higher Education for Negroes

[See Sec. 166.010 to Sec. 166.180; Sec. 164.520; Sec. 156.020.]

§166.010. Negro institutions recognized. — [Recognizes the following institutions for Negroes: Kentucky State College for Negroes, located at Frankfort and the West Kentucky Vocational Training School for Negroes, located at Paducah, Ky.] [1938, 1st Ex. S., c. 29, §§1, 2, 5, 7, 25.]

§166.020. Functions of Kentucky State College for Negroes. — [Provides functions of Kentucky State College for Negroes shall be "to train teachers for schools for colored children, and to give such industrial and general college training to young colored men and women as the State Board of Education deems advisable.] [1938, 1st Ex. S., c. 29, §2.]

§166.03. [Agricultural and Trade School] — Provides that the Kentucky State College for Negroes shall maintain department of agriculture and mechanical arts.] [Ibid., §3.]

166

§166.040. Functions of West Kentucky Vocational Training School.—
[Provides functions of West Kentucky Vocational Training School for
Negroes shall be "to make available facilities for vocational training for
colored children."] [Ibid., §7.]

§166.160. Tuition paid in schools outside Kentucky. — All bona
fide residents of this State who have been such residents continuously for
five years next preceding·application for aid pursuant to this section, and
who are duly qualified to pursue courses of study offered at state institutions that they cannot attend because of §187 of the Constitution and
not offered at other state institutions, shall have their tuition and fees
paid by the Commonwealth of Kentucky at educational institutions outside of Kentucky which they attend for purposes of pursuing such
courses. [1936, c. 43, §1.]

§166.170. Rules concerning tuition; amount allowed. — [Provides
maximum out-of-state tuition of $500 allowed under KRS 166.160
during any one school year of nine months.] [1936, ch. 43, §§2, 3;
1946, c. 67; 1948, c. 23 effective June 17, 1948.]

[Note: This amount was increased in 1948 from $175.00 to $500.00.]

Reform Schools

§198.030. [2095b-24; 2095b-28] . . . **white and colored races sepa-
parated** . . .—

(2) The children of white and colored races committed to the
houses of reform shall be kept entirely separate from each other. [1916,
c. 85, §§2, 6.]

[Note: See also §201.130 below.]

Hospitals

Mental Hospitals

§203.180. Distribution of patients . . .—[Provides that white and colored
patients shall not be kept in the same building.] [1928, c. 16, §46;
1938, 2d. Ex. S., c. 1., §12.]

Tuberculosis Sanatoria

§215.078. Acceptance and transfer of patients . . . Negroes. — . . . (6)
Provision shall be made at each sanatorium for the receipt and furnishing of adequate facilities for the treatment of paying and pauper patients
of the Negro race who are residents of the district. [1944, c. 97, §9;
1948, c. 190, §4, effective June 17, 1948.]

Lynching

§435.070. Lynching or mob viblence. — (1) As used in subsections (2),
(3) and (4) of this section, "mob" means any number of persons more
than three, assembled to do violence or injury to or lynch any person in the
custody of a peace officer or jailer in this state.

(2) Any person who takes part in and with any mob shall be punished
by confinement in the penitentiary for life, or by death, if the person in
custody meets death at the hands of the mob.

(3) Any person who takes part in and with a mob shall be confined in the penitentiary for not less than two [2] years nor more than twenty-one [21] years, if the person in custody does not meet death at the hands of the mob.

(4) Any person not standing in the relationship of husband or wife, parent, grandparent, child, grandchild, brother or sister, by consanguinity or affinity, who, after subsections (2) and (3) of this section have been violated, harbors, conceals or aids any member of the mob who participated in the offense, with the intent that that member of the mob shall escape arrest or punishment, shall be confined in the penitentiary for not less than two [2] nor more than twenty-one [21] years. [1920, c. 41, §§1, 2.]

[Note: See KRS 437.110, with reference to Conspiracy.]

Marriage

§391.110. [1399a; 139b-1; 1399b-2] **Slave marriages valid; issue legitimate.**— [Provides for the validation of marriages of all Negroes and mulattoes who lived and cohabitated together as man and wife prior to Feb. 14, 1866, and continued to live together since that time up to the death of either of them or until June 13, 1910. Provides that the issue of such marriages shall be legitimate.] [1898, c. 39; 1910, c. 70, §§1, 2.]

Miscegenation

§402.020. **Other prohibited marriages.** — [Prohibits marriage between a white person and a Negro or mulatto and declares such marriages are void.] [1928, c. 156; 1893, c. 205, §2.]

§391.100. [2098] **Children of void marriage.** — . . . (1) The issue . . . of a marriage between a white person and a negro or mulatto is not legitimate. [1893, c. 205, §3.]

§402.990. **Penalties.** — (1) Any party to a marriage prohibited by KRS 402.010 or between a white person and a Negro or a mulatto shall be fined not less than five hundred [$500.00] nor more than five thousand [$5,000.00] dollars. If the parties continue after conviction to cohabit as man and wife, either or both of them shall be imprisoned in the penitentiary for not less than three[3] nor more than twelve [12] months . . .

(3) [Any authorized person who knowingly performs a marriage ceremony of a marriage prohibited by Sec. 402.020 is liable to fine up to $1,000.00 or imprisonment from one to twelve months or both.] . . .

(8) [Any clerk who knowingly issues a marriage license to persons prohibited from marrying shall be fined from $500 to $1000.00 and removed from office.] [1928, c. 16, §50; 1893, c. 182, §82, 83; 1893, c. 205, §8; 1918, c. 41; 1914, c. 74, §§1, 2; 1893, c. 205, §9; 1940, c. 151, §1; 1893, c. 205, §§12, 14, 15, 16, 17, 19.]

[Note: Mulatto is defined as one having one-fourth or more Negro blood — *McGoodwin v. Shelby*, 182 Ky. 377; 206 S.W. 625.]

Orphans — Jefferson County Children's Home

§201.130. [938b - 12] **Classification and segregation of children.** — (1) The board shall cause all inmates of the home to be carefully and appropriately classified, segregated, maintained, and trained. The classification and segregation shall be made according to race, sex, and conditions or facts as to the delinquency or conviction for the commission of offenses, or bad conduct. The board may make such further classification of such children as the judgment and experience of the board proves to be wise . . . [1920, c. 92, §12.]

Race Prejudice

§437.100. Presentation of play based on master-slave antagonism of exciting race prejudice. — Any person who presents or participates in the presentation of, or permits to be presented in any theatre or other building under his control, any play that is based upon antagonism between master and slave or that excites race prejudice shall be fined not less than one hundred [$100.] dollars, or imprisoned for not less than one nor more than three months, or both. [1906, c. 59, §§1, 2.]

Transportation
Railroads — Segregation

Sec. 276.440. Separate coaches or compartments for white and colored passengers. — (1) Every company operating railroad cars or coaches on any railroad line within this state, and every railroad company doing business in this state upon lines of railroad leased or wholly or partly owned by it, shall furnish separate coaches or compartments for the transportation of the white and colored passengers on its lines of railroad. Where separate compartments are used, the compartments shall be separated by a good and substantial partition, with a door therein. Each separate coach or compartment shall bear in some conspicuous place, appropriate words in plain letters indicating the race for which it is set apart. The company shall make no difference or discrimination in the quality, convenience or accommodations in the coaches or compartments set apart for white and colored passengers.

(2) The conductor or manager of each train carrying passengers shall assign each white or colored passenger to his respective coach or compartment. If any passenger refuses to occupy the coach or compartment to which he is assigned, the conductor or manager may refuse to carry such passenger on his train, and may put such passenger off the train. Neither the conductor, manager nor railroad company shall be liable for damages for refusing to carry such passenger or putting him off the train.

(3) This section does not apply to the transportation of employees of railroads, or nurses in charge of other persons, or of officers in charge of prisoners, nor does it apply to the transportation of passengers in any caboose car attached to a freight train. [1892, c. 40, §§1, 2, 5; 1894, c. 61; 1892, c. 40, §7.]

Sec. 276.990. Penalties. — [(22) Any railroad company that violates provisions of Sec. 276.440 (1) shall be fined from $500 to $1500 for each offense. (23) Any conductor or manager of train carrying passenger who violates Sec. 276.440 (2) shall be fined $50 to $100 for each offense. [As last amended 1948 c. 162, eff. 6-17-48.]

LOUISIANA

CONSTITUTION

LOUISIANA CONSTITUTIONS (DART) ANNOTATED [1932]

Education

Art. 12, §1. [1947 Supp.] Schools — Separation of races — School age — Kindergartens. — The educaitonal system of the State shall consist of all public schools, and all institutions of learning, supported in whole or in part by appropriation of public funds. Separate public schools shall be maintained for the education of white and colored children between the ages of six and eighteen years; provided, that children attaining the age of six within four months after the beginning of any public school term or session may enter such schools at the beginning of the school term, and provided, further, kindergartens may be authorized for children between the ages of four and six years. [Const. 1845, Art. 134; 1852, Art. 136; 1864, Art. 141; 1868 Arts. 135, 136; 1879, Art. 224; 1898, Art. 248; 1913, Art. 248; 1921, Art. 12, §1, as amended; Acts 1932, No. 141, §1, adopted November 8, 1932; 1944, No. 320, §1, adopted November 7, 1944.]

Art. 12, §9. Higher educational institutions listed — Annual appropriation. — Northwestern State College of Louisiana heretofore known as the Louisiana State Normal College, the Louisiana Polytechnic Institute, heretofore known as the Louisiana Industrial Institute, the Southwestern Louisiana Institute of Liberal and Technical Learning heretofore known as the Southwestern Louisiana Industrial Institute, Southeastern Louisiana College, the State School for the Blind, the State School for the Deaf, the Southern University, the State School for Blind Negroes, the State School for Deaf Negroes, and such others as may hereafter be created by the Legislature, are declared to be the higher institutions of learning now embraced in the educational system subject to the direct supervision of the State Board of Education . . . [Const. 1879, Art. 231; 1898, Arts. 256, 257; 1913, Art. 257; 1921, Art. 12, §9, as amended, Acts. 1938, No. 388, adopted November 8, 1938; 1944, No. 326, §1, adopted November 7, 1944.]

STATUTES

LOUISIANA GENERAL STATUTES (DART) 1939

Adoption

§4839.58. [1948 Cum. Supp.] — Right to petition for adoption. — A single person over the age of twenty-one years or any married couple jointly, may petition to adopt any child of his or their race . . . [Acts 1948, No. 228, §1.]

Aged — Homes for — Separation

§6539.39. [1947 Cum. Supp.] — Indigent, aged or infirm person defined — Separate accommodations for different races — Compelling support. — An indigent, aged or infirm person is hereby declared to be a person who, because of age or because of being indigent and in necessitous circumstances or because of infirmity, is unable to care for himself or herself properly or to supply himself or herself with the necessities of life or needed medical care. This shall apply to all such persons, regardless of race, creed or color, but the Board of Trustees shall provide separate, equal accommodations for different races . . . [Acts 1942, No. 236, §5.]

Circuses, Tent Shows

§9791. Circuses and tent exhibitions — Segregation of races. — All circuses, shows and tent exhibitions, to which the attendance of the public of more than one race is invited or expected to attend shall provide for the convenience of its patrons not less than two ticket offices with individual ticket sellers, and not less than two entrances to the said performance, with individual ticket takers and receivers, and in the case of outside or tent performances, the said ticket offices shall not be less than twenty-five [25] feet apart; that one of the said entrances shall be exclusively for the white race, and another exclusively for persons of the colored races. [Acts 1914, No. 235, §1; 1916, No. 118, §1.]

§9792. Penalty. — Any proprietor, manager, ticket seller, or employee connected with any show, tent exhibition or circus violating the provisions of this act, or found admitting and receiving persons of several races in one and the same entrance, shall upon conviction suffer a fine of not more than twenty-five [$25.00] dollars and in the default of the payment of said fine imprisonment for 30 days. [Acts 1914, No. 235, §1; 1916, No. 118, §2.]

Civil Rights — Places of Public Accommodation

§1070. Carriers of passengers for hire — Racial discrimination prohibited. — All persons engaged within this State in the business of common carriers of passengers shall have the right to refuse to admit any person to their railroad cars, street cars, steam boats or other water crafts, coaches, omnibuses, or other vehicles, or to expel any person therefrom after admission, when such person shall, on demand, refuse or neglect to pay the customary fare, or when such person shall be of infamous character, or shall be guilty, after admission to the conveyance of the carrier, of gross, vulgar or disorderly conduct, or shall commit any act tending to injure the business of the carrier, prescribed for the management of his business after such rules and regulations shall have been made known; provided, said rules and regulations make no discrimination on account of race or color, and they shall have the right to refuse any person admission to such conveyance when there is not room or suitable accommodations; and except in cases above enumerated, all persons engaged in the business of common carriers of passengers are forbidden to refuse admission to their conveyance, or expel any person therefrom whomsoever. [Acts, 1869, p. 37, §1; R. S. §456.]

[Note: See Dart's Stat. §§8130-8135; §§8188-8190 requiring separation of races in railroad accommodations and in street cars and street railroads. *See Hall v. De Cuir*, 95 U.S. 485, 24 L. ed. 547 (1877), in which the United States Supreme Court ruled that the above section and the following three sections, "to the extent that it required those engaged in the transportation of passengers among the States to carry colored passengers in the same cabin with whites, is unconstitutional and void . . .

171

We confine our decision to the statute in its effect upon foreign and inter-state commerce, expressing no opinion as to its validity in any other respect." (pp. 490-491).

The Supreme Court reiterated the principle that States may not regulate interstate commerce in its decision of *Morgan v. Virginia*, 328 U.S. 373 (1946), in which that Court held unconstitutional a Virginia statute requiring racial segregation on motor buses, as it applied to passengers traveling in interstate commerce.

In short, the Supreme Court has ruled that a State statute is invalid to the extent that it regulates or burdens interstate commerce, whether the purpose of the statute be to enforce or to prohibit segregation.

Thus it would appear that §§1070, 1071, 1072 and 1073 are valid as applied to intra-state activities, although Louisiana has enacted segregation statutes, and the public officials refuse to enforce the civil rights statutes still on the Statute books.]

§1071. Discrimination at place of public resort. — Except in the cases enumerated in section four hundred and fifty-six of this act [§1070], no person shall be refused admission to or entertainment at any public inn, hotel or place of public resort within the state. [Acts, 1869, p. 37, §2; R. S. §457.]

§1072. Conditions embodied in licenses. — All licenses hereafter granted by this state, and by all parishes and municipalities therein, to persons engaged in business or keeping persons of public resort, shall contain the express condition that the place of business or public resort shall be open to the accommodation and patronage of all persons without distinction or discrimination on account of race or color, and any person who shall violate the condition of such license shall, on conviction thereof, be punished by forfeiture of his license, and his place of business or of public resort shall be closed; and, moreover, he shall be liable at the suit of the person aggrieved, to such damages as he shall sustain thereby, before any court of competent jurisdictions. [Acts, 1869, p. 37, §3; R. S. §458.]

§1073. Damages recoverable. — For a violation of any of the provisions of the four hundred and fifty-sixth and four hundred and fifty-seventh [§§1070, 1071] sections of this act, the party injured shall have a right of action to recover any damages, exemplary as well as actual, which he may sustain before any court of competent jurisdiction. [Acts, 1869, p. 37, §4, R. S. §459.]

Cohabitation

DART'S LOUISIANA CODE OF CRIMINAL PROCEDURE ANNOTATED (1932).

Art. 1128. Concubinage, white and colored person — Penalty. — [Acts 1910, No. 206, §1. Repealed by Acts 1942, No. 43, §2.]

Art. 1129. Proof of violation of act — Concubinage defined. — [Acts 1910, No. 206, §2. Repealed by Acts 1942, No. 43, §2.]

Art. 1130. Charging grand jury concerning act. — [Acts 1910, No. 206, §3. Repealed by Acts 1942, No. 43, §2.]

Art. 1131. Concubinage — Indians and colored persons. — [Acts 1920, No. 230, §1. Repealed by Acts 1942, No. 43, §2.]

Art. 1132. Proof of violation of act — Concubinage defined. — [Acts 1920, No. 230, §2. Repealed by Acts 1942, No. 43, §2.]

Art. 1133. Effective date of act — Act not retroactive. — Acts 1920, No. 230, §3. Repealed by Acts 1942, No. 43, §2.]

Art. 1134. Duty to charge grand jury concerning act. — [Acts 1920, No. 230, §4. Repealed by Acts 1942, No. 43, §2.]

LOUISIANA CRIMINAL CODE (DART) 1932.

Art. 740-79. [1942 Cum. Supp.] Miscegenation. — Miscegenation is the marriage or habitual cohabitation with knowledge of their difference in race between a person of the Caucasian or white race and a person of the colored or negro race.

Whoever commits the crime of miscegenation shall be imprisoned, with or without hard labor, for not more than five [5] years. [Acts 1942, No. 43, Art. 79.]

[Note: The compiler of the Louisiana Criminal Code (1942) comments that the above quoted article covers Louisiana Statutes (Dart's. Crim. Stats. [1932]), Secs. 1128 - 1130 [Acts 1910, No. 206, §§1-3] but that the former Louisiana Statute prohibiting cohabitation between Indians and Negroes [Dart's Crim. Statutes (1932) Secs. 1131-1134 (Acts 1920, No. 230, §§1-5)] "had little social utility; and its subject matter was not included". All statutes relating to concubinage between Indians and Negroes or Negroes and white persons have now been repealed. See Arts. 1128 — 1134 above. See also *Miscegenation* below.]

Courts

Racial Conditions

DART'S LOUISIANA CODE OF CRIM. PROC. ANNOT. 1932

Art. 422. Judicial notice of specific matters. — Judicial cognizance is taken of the following matters:

6 . . . *the political, social and racial conditions prevailing in this State: . . .* (italics added.)

[Note: *See State v. Bessa*, 115 La. 259, 38 So. 985 (1905).]

Right to sue

DART'S LA. CODE OF PRACTICE ANNOT. 1942 (Second Edition)

Art. 103. Right to Sue in general. — No disqualifications to bring actions can arise on account of race, color, or previous condition.

Definition of "Negro" or "Colored"

[No statutory definition, but see *Lee v. New Orleans Great Northern R. Co.*, (1910) 125 La. 236, 239, 51 So. 182, which defines "colored persons" as "all persons with any appreciable mixture of negro blood." See also *State v. Treadway*, (1910) 126 La. 300, 52 So. 500, for an exhaustive discussion of the definition of "Negro."]

Education

Public Schools

[Note: See Const., Art. 12, §1, above.]

2282.1. [1949 Cum. Supp.] — Parish school board in city with population in excess of 300,000 — Prohibited from changing [racial] classification of school without permission of property owners in the adjacent area. — It shall be unlawful for any parish school board in any city having a population in excess of three hundred thousand [300,000] to change the use or classification of any school building from negro to white or from white to negro, without first having obtained the written consent of at least seventy [70%] per cent of the property owners in the area within lines drawn parallel to and six hundred (600') feet distant from the property wherein a change in use or classification is proposed. [Acts 1948, No. 463, §1.]

2282.2. [1949 Cum. Supp.] — Procedure for obtaining consent for change of classification. — At least thirty (30) days prior to the circulation of the petition, there shall be posted for a period of not less than twenty (20) consecutive days, a printed notice in bold type on signs not less than one and one-half (1½) square feet in area on each block on each street in the area in which the use or status of the school is to be changed, and there shall be published in the official journal of the city a notice on three (3) separate days within ten (10) days prior to the circulation of a written consent, and this notice shall be extra heavy box and captions, setting forth the proposed change, the location and name of the school and the date the board will start circulating the petition for consent.

The written consent shall set forth clearly the proposed change, the name and location of the school, and it shall be executed in duplicate original and filed with the clerk of the council or other governing body of the city where it shall be open to inspection by the public. [Acts 1948, No. 463, §2.]

2282.3. [1949 Cum. Supp.] — Maps of property within area — Filed with clerk of the council. — [Provides that maps of the property within the area with the names of the property owners thereon and the written consent must be filed with the clerk of the local governing body within 90 days after the notices are posted in the area.] [Acts 1948, No. 463, §3.]

2282.4. [1949 Cum. Supp.] — Verification of signatures of persons consenting to change in classification. — [Provides that the clerk of the local governing body shall verify the signatures of all persons signing the written consent by sending them notice by registered mail. Unless the property owner denies he has signed the consent within 10 days from the date of mailing the notice, it shall be *prima facie* evidence that he has given consent.] [Acts 1948, No. 463, §4.]

2282.5. [1949 Cum. Supp.] — Clerk of council to determine if necessary consent has been obtained. — [Provides that clerk of local governing body, within 20 days after the notice has been sent in accordance with §2282.4, must determine if necessary consent of 70% of the property owners in the area has been obtained, and must notify all persons in writing within the 600′ area as defined of such findings.] [Acts 1948, No. 463. §5.]

2282.6. [1949 Cum. Supp.] — Appeal from findings of the clerk of the council. — [Provides any taxpayer of the city may appeal from the clerk's findings to the district court of the local parish within 30 days after the clerk has declared that the necessary 70% of the property owners have given their consent.] [Acts 1948, No. 463, §6.]

Blind and Deaf — Separation

LOUISIANA GENERAL STATUTES ANNOTATED (DART) 1939

State School for the Blind

§§2470-2482. — [Provides for the establishment and maintenance of a State School for the blind at Baton Rouge, La., known as "Louisiana Institute for the Blind."] [Acts 1898, No. 145, §§1-13.]

Institute for the Blind

§2476. Term for which pupils admitted — Separation of races. — . . . The board of trustees shall, with such appropriations as may be made for such purpose from time to time by the general assembly, construct and maintain a separate building or buildings on separate ground for the admission, care, instruction and support of all blind persons of the colored or black race who shall be received, maintained and retained in such separate department under the same provisions, conditions and limitations as are prescribed in this act for all blind persons, and persons of defective vision, as set forth in this act and with such appropriations made from time to time by the general assembly. [Acts 1898, No. 145, §7; 1920, No. 67, §1.]

State School for the Deaf

§§2483-2493. — [Provides for establishment and maintenance of "Louisiana Institute for the Deaf and Dumb" at Baton Rouge, La. No statutory provision for separation of races, nor does the statute by its terms limit admission to whites only, but see §§2498-2502.] [Acts 1898, No. 166, §§1-13.]

[Note: See comparable sections and §§7789-51-7789.56 in 1940 Supplement for administrative changes.]

Blind and Deaf Children — Separation

§§2498-2502. — [Establishes a "state school for the benefit of deaf and blind children of the negro race whose condition is such that they can not profitably attend the regular public schools." Provides that the school be administered by the state board of education.] [Acts 1920, No. 159, §§1-5.]

[Note: The Constitution of 1921, Art. 12, §9, enumerates the State School for Blind Negroes and the State School for Deaf Negroes among the State institutions of higher learning.]

§7789.52. — [1940 Supp.] — [Transfers the function of the board of education to State department of education and vests the duties of the executive committees of the state schools for blind and deaf Negroes in the State department of education: [Acts 1940, No. 47, Title 8, §2.]

[Note: See also §§7789.51 — 7789.56; Acts 1940, No. 47, Title 8, §§1-6.]

Juvenile Delinquents

DART'S LOUISIANA CODE OF CRIMINAL PROCEDURE ANNOTATED (1932)

Art. 1424. Colored Juveniles. — The governing authority of said prison district is hereby further authorized to maintain at said prison farm, a special department where colored juveniles may be held, and the juvenile judges shall have the power to order colored juveniles held at said place on said prison farm until a state reformatory for colored juveniles is built. Any colored juveniles duly committed to said farm by the juvenile court shall be managed and controlled by the authorities in charge of the prison farm, under the same rules and regulations as the Louisiana Training Institute, the state reformatory for white male juveniles. [Acts 1926, No. 203, §17; 1928, No. 189, §17.]

Art. 1425.1. [1942 Cum Supplement] — Sentence to imprisonment at hard labor. — [Provides that a district judge within his discretion may sentence a person convicted of a crime to imprisonment at hard labor on any prison farm instead of imprisonment in the state penitentiary and contains the following proviso, *inter alia*:

"Provided further, that if the governing authority of a prison district, operates a prison farm and maintains at said farm a special department where negro juveniles may be held, then the juvenile judge of the judicial district in which said prison farm is located shall be vested with the authority to order the commitment to said prison farm, of any negro juvenile from any parish comprising said judicial district, who has been sentenced as a delinquent or neglected child for violating any law, the punishment prescribed for which may be, or is necessarily, punishable at hard labor or for any other reason. Said negro juveniles shall be held at said place on said prison farm until discharged by the court, or until attaining the age of twenty-one years, or until a state reformatory is in operation. All negro juveniles shall be managed and controlled by the authorities in charge of the prison farm, under the same rules and regulations in force at the Louisiana training institute. [Acts 1938, No. 127, §1.]

Industrial School for Colored Youths

Arts. 1476-1484. — [1949 Cum. Supp.] — [Provides for the creation maintenance and supervision of The State Industrial School for Colored Youths (male).] [Acts 1928, No. 150, §§1-9; 1948, No. 21, §1.]

Arts. 1484.1 — 1484.10.—[1942 Supplement]—[Authorizes the establishment in each parish of an industrial school for colored male youths of the age of seventeen years, and under, convicted in the juvenile court of the parish for juvenile offenses. The school is to be known as the "Parish Industrial School for Colored Youths." This statute expressly provides that nothing contained therein shall affect the provisions of Act 150 of 1928 [§§1476-1484] which shall remain in full force and effect.] [Acts 1938, No. 226, §§1-10.]

Industrial School for Girls — White

Arts. 1492.1 - 1492.9. [Dart's Crim. Stats. Annot., 1943.] — State Industrial for Girls. — [Provision is made for the State Industrial Schools for Girls, "for white female children under seventeen years of age, who have been or shall be legally adjudged delinquent or neglected juveniles as defined by law . . ." [Acts 1942, No. 128, §§1-9. Repeals and replaces Acts 1926, No. 175; Acts 1940, No. 206.]

Louisiana Training Institute — white males

§§1475.1 - 1475.9. — [1942 Cum. Supp. C. Cr. Proc.] — [Provision for a training school for white male juveniles under 17 years of age and repeals Act 173 of 1904, Act 293 of 1908, Act 285 of 1926 and Act 178 of 1940.] [Acts 1942, No. 127, §§1-9.]

[Note: See also §§1492.3 - 1492.8 [Acts 1948, No. 20, §1.]]

State Industrial School for Girls

§1492.1 — [1942 Cum. Supp. C. Cr. Proc.] — [Provision for the establishment of The State Industrial School for Girls, "for white female children under seventeen years of age." Repeals Act 175 of 1926 and Act 206 of 1940.] [Acts 1942, No. 128, §1.]

[Note: See also §§1492.3 — 1942.8 (Acts 1948, No. 20, §1).]

Negro girls

[Appears to be no provision.]

Trades Schools — for whites only

LOUISIANA GENERAL STATUTES ANNOTATED (DART) 1939

§§2420.4 - 2420.7. — [Provides for establishment of Sullivan Memorial Trades School "for the education of the white people of the State of Louisiana" to be located at Bogalusa, Washington Parish, La.] [Acts 1934, No. 215, §§1-4.]

§§2420.8 - 2420.11. — [Provides for creation of Shreveport Trades School for whites only to be located at Shreveport, Caddo Parish, La.] [Acts 1936, No. 265, §§1-4.]

§§240.12 - 2420.16. — [Provides for establishment of Huey P. Long Memorial Trades School of Winnfield, Louisiana, for whites only.] [Acts 1938, No. 14, §§1-3.]

§§2420.15 - 2420.16. — [Provides for establishment of T. H. Harris Trades School at Opelousas, Louisiana, for whites only. [Acts 1938, No. 15, §§1-2.]

§§2420.17 - 2420.19. — [Provides for establishment of Southwest Louisiana Trades School to be located at Crowley, Acadia Parish, Louisiana, for whites only.] [Acts 1938, No. 25, §§1-3.]

§§2420.20 - 2420.22. — [Provides for establishment of Southwest Louisiana Trades School of Lake Charles, Louisiana, for whites only.] [Acts 1938, No. 62, §§1-3.]

§§2420.23 - 2420.25. — [Provides for establishment of Thibodaux Trades School for whites only at Thibodaux, Lafourche Parish, La.] [Acts 1938, No. 309, §§1-3.]

§§2420.26 - 2420.27. — [Provides for establishment of St. Bernard Parish Agricultural and Trades High School "for the education of white students in the parish of St. Bernard."] [Acts 1938, No. 314, §§1-2.]

§§2420.28 - 2420.30. — [Provides for establishment of Alexandria Trades School and Lafayette Trades School for white people in the State, to be located at Alexandria Rapides Parish, La., and in the city of Lafayette, Lafayette Parish, Louisiana.] [Acts 1938, No. 315, §§1-3.]

§§2420.32 - 2420.36. — [1947 Cum. Supp.] — [Provides for establishment of trades schools at New Iberia, Iberia Parish, La., and at Natchitoches at Natchitoches Parish, La., to be known as the New Iberia Trades School and the Natchitoches Trades School respectively. Both schools are for white persons only.] [Acts 1940, No. 53, §§1-5.]

§§2420.37 - 2420.39.—[1947 Cum. Supp.]—[Provides for establishment of Northeast Center Trades School in connection with the Northeast Center of the Louisiana State University and Agricultural and Mechanical College, at Monroe, Ouachita Parish, Louisiana, for whites only.] [Acts 1940, No. 25, §§1-3.]

§§2420.40. — [1947 Cum. Supp.] — **Aviation trades school.** — The governor of the State is hereby authorized, subject to the conditions of this act, to create and establish no more than three [3] free trade schools for the education of the white people of the State of Louisiana, giving instructions in flying, rapairs, alterations, maintenance and overhauling of air craft, air craft engines, propellers and appliances. [Acts 1940, No. 333, §1.]

§§2420.41 - 2420.45. — [1947 Cum. Supp.] — [Provides for an appropriation of $100,000.00 to effect the purposes of §2420.40 above; provided further that the governor might obtain such financial or advisory aid as might be available from the United States of America, or any agency thereof, in the construction and maintenance of such a project.] [Acts 1940, No. 333, §§2-6.]

[Note: No provision is made for similar training for Negroes.]

§§2420.46 - 2420.47. — [1947 Cum. Supp.] — [Creates Avoyelles Parish Trades school for whites only at Cottonport, La.] [Acts 1942, No. 109, §§1, 2.]

§§2420.48 - 2420.49. — [1947 Cum. Supp.] — [Creates Florida Parishes

Trades School for white only at Hammond, La.] [Acts 1942, No. 234, §§1, 2.]

§§2420.50 - 2420.52. — [1947 Cum. Supp.] — [Create Ouachita Valley Vocational School in West Monroe, La. for education of whites only.] [Acts 1944, No. 30, §§1-3; Acts 1946, No. 321, §1.]

§§2420.53 - 2420.55. — [1947 Cum. Supp.] — [Establishe Baton Rouge Trade School of Baton Rouge, La. for the education of white people. [Acts 1944, No. 263, §§1-3.]

§§2420.57 - 2420.59. — [1949 Cum. Supp.] — Provides for establishment of South Louisiana Trade School "for the education of white people of the State of Louisiana" to be located at Houma, Terrabonne Parish, La.] [Acts 1948, No. 69, Sec. 1.]

§§2420.60 - 2420.62.—[1949 Cum. Supp.]—[Provides for the establishment of Jefferson Davis Trade School "for the people of the State of Louisiana" to be located at Jennings, Parish of Jefferson Davis, La.] [Acts 1948, No. 347, sec. 1.]

§§2420.63 - 2420.64. — [1949 Cum. Supp.] — [Provides for the establishment of the Jefferson Parish Trade School "for the education of the white people of the State of Louisiana" to be located at Gretna, Jefferson Parish, La.] [Acts 1948, No. 349, sec. 1.]

Colleges and Universities
Louisiana State Normal College

§2421. Who admitted. — The State Normal School located at Natchitoches, in the parish of Natchitoches, in conformity with sections 4 and 8 of Act No. 51 of 1884, shall have for its object to train teachers for the public schools of Louisiana, and shall be open to white persons of either sex of such age and qualifications as may be hereinafter prescribed. [Acts 1884, No. 51, §1; 1886, No. 61, §1; 1892, No. 73, §1.]

[Note: See §§2421-2431 for provisions on supervision and administration of the school.]

Louisiana Polytechnic Institute

§§2432-2438. — [Establishes an "industrial institute and college for the education of the white children of the State of Louisiana in the arts and sciences." The institute is to be known as "The Industrial Institute and College of Louisiana and is to be located at Ruston, Lincoln parish, La. [Acts 1894, No. 68, §§1-7.]

[Note: The name was changed to Louisiana Polytechnic Institute by Const. 1921, Art. 12, §19. For administrative changes see 1940 Supplement, §§2433, 2434.]

Southwestern Louisiana Institute of Liberal and Technical Learning

§§2439-2445. — [Provides for the establishment of a "state industrial institute . . . for the education of the white children of the state of Louisiana, in the arts and sciences." The institute is to be known as

179

"Southwestern Louisiana Industrial Institute." [Acts 1898, No. 162, §§1-7.]

Southeastern Louisiana College

§§2449-2952. — [Provides for the creation and maintenance of the Southeastern Louisiana College at Hammond, Tangipahoa parish, Louisiana, for the higher education in the arts and sciences of white children of the State.] [Acts 1928, No. 136, §§1-4.]

Colleges and Universities — for Negroes
Southern University

§§2453 - 2464. — [Provides for the establishment and maintenance of Southern University, as a university for Negroes.] [Acts 1880, No. 87, §§1, 2, 3, 4, 6, 7; Acts 1882, No. 65, §1; Acts 1888; No. 90; Acts 1912, No. 118; §§1-5; Acts 1914, No. 207, §1.]

§2453. Establishment and name. — There shall be established in the City of New Orleans a university for the education of persons of color, to be named and entitled the "Southern University." [Acts 1880, No. 87, §1.]

§2454. Appointment of board of trustees. — [Provision for a governing body of twelve trustees, appointed for four-year terms by the governor with the advice and consent of the senate, with the proviso that at least four members of the board be Negroes.] [Acts 1880, No. 87, §2; 1882, No. 65, §1.]

[Note: See §2464. Powers and duties of the board of trustees and of the executive committee were transferred to the department of education. See Dart's Stat., §§7789.51 - 7789.56.]

§§2455-2456. — [Superseded. See §§7789.51 - 7789.56.]

§2457. — [Defines powers of board of trustees.] [Acts 1880, No. 87, §§4, 5.]

§2458. — [Provides for corporate status of Southern University.] [Acts 1880, No. 87, §6.]

§2459. Departments of arts and letters, law and medicine. — There shall be established by said board of trustees a faculty of arts and letters, which shall be competent to instruct in every branch of a liberal education, and under rules of and in concurrence with the board of trustees, to graduate students and grant all degrees appertaining to letters and arts known to universities and colleges in Europe and America, on persons competent and deserving the same

There may be also established by said board of trustees a department of law and medicine. The department of law shall consist of three (3) or more learned professors, learned and skilled in the practice of law in this state, who shall be required to give a full course of lectures on international, constitutional, commercial and municipal or civil law and instruction in the practice thereof. The medical department of the university shall consist of not less than three professors.

They shall be appointed by the board of trustees from regular practicing physicians of the State. The degree of bachelor of law and doctor of medicine, granted by them, shall authorize the person on whom it is conferred to practice law and physic and surgery in this State. [Acts 1880, No. 87, §7; 1888, No. 90.]

§§2460-2461. — [Provides for the acquisiiton of a new site and relocation of the institution thereon.] [Acts 1912, No. 118, §§1-2; 1914, No. 207, §1.]

§2462. **Industrial and Agricultural Normal School.** — In addition to carrying out the university purposes set forth in section 7 of Act No. 87, of 1880 [§2459], said board of trustees shall have power and it shall be their duty to establish a department of said Southern University, which shall be known as "The Industrial and Agricultural Normal School;" that said "Industrial and Agricultural Normal School" shall be equipped in such manner and provided with such teachers, so as to instruct persons of color, male and female, to be teachers, so they can teach industrial and agricultural subjects in schools for youths of both sexes of the colored race. [Acts 1912, No. 118, §3.]

§2463. **Model Industrial and Agricultural School.** — It shall be the duty of the said board of trustees of the Southern University, as soon as practicable after the establishment of the university upon the new site contemplated in this act, to establish a department of the university, which shall be known as "The Model Industrial and Agricultural School," and at least eight grades shall be created in said school, in which to assign pupils, and said grades and the course of teaching to be taught therein, shall be set forth in proper regulations to be formulated by the said board of trustees, provided that all teachers in the said "Model Industrial and Agricultural School", shall be persons of the colored race. [Acts 1912, No. 118, §4.]

§2464. **Powers of trustees.** — The said board of trustees shall be empowered to enact general rules and by-laws for the said university in all its departments, whether said departments appertain to industrial and agricultural subjects, or to the arts and letters, and to elect a president of the faculty, the professors and teachers and determine their compensation; also all officers and employees that may be necessary, and prescribe their duties and compensation; providing that the president of the faculty, the professors, teachers and all other employees except only the board of trustees, themselves shall be persons of the colored race. All members of the board of trustees shall be of the white race, and the board shall consist of one member from each of the congressional districts, appointed for a term of four years, by the governor of the state, and the state superintendent of public education and the governor, the governor to be chairman of the board. [Acts 1912, No. 118, §5.]

[Note: Acts 1912, No. 118, §6, repealed all laws or parts of laws in conflict therewith; thus, §2454 above, was apparently repealed to the extent that it provided that four of the members of the board of trustees should be Negroes.]

Grambling College of Louisiana (formerly Louisiana Negro Normal and Industrial School)

§§2465 - 2469. — [Provides for the establishment of a State Normal and Industrial School at Grambling, Lincoln Parish, Louisiana, for the training of Negro Youth. The school was formerly called "Louisiana Negro Normal and Industrial School", but the name was changed to "Grambling College of Louisiana" by Acts 1946, No. 33, §1.] [Acts 1928, No. 161, §§1-5, Acts 1946, No. 33, §1.]

[Note: The State department of education is vested with power to supervise the school. See Dart's Stat., §§7789.51 - 7789.56.]

Higher Education for Negroes — Out-of-State Aid

ACTS 1946. No. 142

§1. — Be it enacted by the Legislature of Louisiana, That there is hereby appropriated from the General Fund of the State of Louisiana to the State Department of Education the sum of Fifty Thousand Dollars ($50,-000.00) for the fiscal year beginning July 1, 1946, and ending June 30, 1947 or so much thereof as may be necessary, and the sum of Fifty Thousand Dollars ($50,000.00) for the fiscal year beginning July 1, 1947, and ending June 30, 1948, or so much thereof as may be necessary, for the purpose of providing, in schools and colleges located outside the State of Louisiana, educational opportunities for the specialized, professional, or graduate education of Negro physicians, dentists, veterinarians, public health workers, nurses, agriculturists, home economists, teachers, and others requiring specialized or advanced education.

§2. — That these funds when received by the State Department of Education shall be used for the purposes set forth in Section 1 of this Act, under rules and regulations recommended by the State Department of Education and approved by the State Board of Education . . . [Approved by the Governor, July 15, 1946.]

[Note: Acts 1948, No. 350, p. 885, increased the fund for out of state scholarships for Negro residents of Louisiana to obtain graduate training to $100,000.00 each year for the fiscal years 1948-1949 and 1949-1950.]

ACTS 1948, p. 981

ACT No. 366.

Senate Bill No. 126.

By Messrs. Richardson, Downs and Hennigan.

AN ACT

To permit institutions of higher learning which receive all or part of their support from the State of Louisiana to engage in interstate and intrastate education agreements with other state governments, agencies of other state governments, institutions of higher learning of other state governments, and private institutions of higher learning within or outside state boundaries.

Section 1. Be it enacted by the Legislature of Louisiana, That any institution of higher learning which receives all or part of its support from the State of Louisiana, subject to approval and under such rules and regulations as the State Board of Education and the Board of Supervisors of Louisiana State University shall determine, may contract with other state governments, agencies of other state governments, or institutions of higher learning of other state governments, to provide educational facilities at such Louisiana institution of higher learning to residents of such other states.

Section 2. Any institution of higher learning which receives all or part of its support from the State of Louisiana, subject to approval and under such rules and regulations as the State Board of Education and the Board of Supervisors of Louisiana State University shall determine, may contract with other state governments, institutions of higher learning of other state governments, or private institutions of higher learning within or outside state boundaries, to provide educational facilities to residents of Louisiana at an expense to such residents of Louisiana not exceeding the probable cost to them if the facilities were provided at such Louisiana institution of higher learning.

Section 3. All laws and parts of laws in conflict with this act are hereby repealed.

Section 4. If any part of this act is declared invalid in its general or specific application, such declaration shall not affect the validity of other parts or applications.

Section 5. This act shall take effect immediately upon its passage and approval by the Governor or upon its otherwise becoming a law.

Approved by the Governor: July 6, 1948.

A true copy:

WADE O. MARTIN, JR.,
Secretary of State.

Regional Education

ACTS 1948, p. 982
ACT No. 367.

Senate Bill No. 127.

By Messrs. Richardson, Downs and Hennigan.

AN ACT

Providing that the State of Louisiana may enter into a compact with any of the United States for co-operative regional education purposes and providing for the ratification thereof.

Section 1. Be it enacted by the Legislature of Louisiana, That the action of the Governor of this State in entering into a compact on behalf of the State of Louisiana with the states joining therein for co-operative regional education purposes is hereby authorized and ratified subject to the approval of said compact by the Congress of the United States, which compact is substantially as follows:

A COMPACT

Whereas, the States who are parties hereto have during the past several years conducted careful investigation looking towards the establishment and maintenance of jointly owned and operated regional educational institutions in the Southern states in the professional, technological, scientific, literary and other fields, so as to provide greater educational advantages and facilities for the citizens of the several States who reside within such region, and

Whereas, Meharry Medical College of Nashville, Tennessee, has proposed that its lands, building, equipment, and the net income from its endowment to be turned over to the Southern States, or to an agency acting in their behalf, to be operated as a regional institution for medical, dental and nursing education upon terms and conditions to be hereafter agreed upon between the Southern states and Meharry Medical College, which proposal, because of the present financial condition of the institution, has been approved by the said States who are parties hereto, and

Whereas, the said States desire to enter into a compact with each other providing for the planning and establishment of regional educational facilities;

Now therefore, in consideration of the mutual agreements, covenants and obligations assumed by the respective states who are parties hereto (hereinafter referred to as "States"), the said several States do hereby form a geographical district or region consisting of the areas lying within the boundaries of the contracting States which, for the purposes of this compact, shall constitute an area for regional education supported by public funds derived from taxation by the constituent States for the establishment, acquisition, operation and maintenance of regional education schools and institutions for the benefit of citizens of the respective States residing within the region so established as may be determined from time to time in accordance with the terms and provisions of this compact.

The States do further hereby establish and create a joint agency which shall be known as the Board of Control for Southern Regional Education (hereinafter referred to as the "Board"), the members of which Board shall consist of the Governor, of each State, ex officio, and two additional citizens of each State to be appointed by the Governor thereof, at least one of whom shall be selected from the field of education. The Governor shall continue as a member of the Board during his tenure of office as Governor of the State[,] but the members of the Board appointed by the Governor shall hold office for a period of five years except that in the original appointment one Board member so appointed by the Governor shall be designated at the time of his appointment to serve an initial term of three years, but thereafter his successor shall serve the full term of five years. Vacancies on the Board caused by death, resignation, refusal or inability to serve, shall be filled by appointment by the Governor for the unexpired portion of the term. The officers of the Board shall be a Chairman, a Vice Chairman, a Secretary, a Treasurer, and such additional officers as may be created by the Board from time to time. The Board shall meet annually and the officers shall be elected to hold office until the next annual meeting. The board shall have the right to formulate and establish by-laws not inconsistent with the provisions of this compact to govern its own actions in the performance of the duties delegated to it including the right to create and appoint an Executive Committee and a Finance Committee with such powers and authority as the Board may delegate to them from time to time.

It shall be the duty of the Board to submit plans and recommendations to the States from time to time for their approval and adoption by appropriate legislative action for the development, establishment, acquisition, operation and maintenance of educational schools and institutions within the geographical limits of the regional area of the States, of such character and type and for such educational purposes, professional, technological, scientific, literary, or otherwise, as they may deem and determine to be proper, necessary or advisable. Title to all such educational institutions when so established by appropriate legislative actions of the states and to all properties and facilities used in connection therewith shall be vested in said Board as the agency of and for the use and benefit of the said States and the citizens thereof, and all such educational institutions shall be operated, maintained and financed in the manner herein set out, subject to any provisions or limitations which may be contained in the legislative acts of the States authorizing the creation, establishment and operation of such educational institutions.

The Board shall have such additional and general power and authority as may be vested in it by the States from time to time by legislative enactments of the said States.

Any two or more States who are parties of this compact shall have the right to enter into supplemental agreements providing for the establishment, financing and operation of regional educational institutions for the benefit of citizens residing within an area, which constitutes a portion of the general region herein created, such institutions to be financed exclusively by such States and to be controlled exclusively by the member of the Board representing such states provided such agreement is submitted to and approved by the Board prior to the establishment of such institutions.

Each State agrees that, when authorized by the Legislature, it will from time to time make available and pay over to said Board such funds as may be required for the establishment, acquisition, operation and maintenance of such regional educational institutions as may be authorized by the States under the terms of this compact, the contribution of each State at all times to be in the proportion that its population bears to the total combined population of the States who are parties hereto as shown from time to time by the most recent official published report of the

Bureau of Census of the United States of America; or upon such other basis as may be agreed upon.

This compact shall not take effect or be binding upon any State unless and until it shall be approved by proper legislative action of as many as six or more of the States whose Governors have subscribed hereto within a period of eighteen months from the date hereof. When and if six or more States shall have given legislative approval to this compact within said eighteen months period, it shall be and become binding upon such six or more States 60 days after the date of legislative approval by the sixth State and the Governors of such six or more States shall forthwith name the members of the Board from their States as hereinabove set out, and the Board shall then meet on call of the Governor of any State approving this compact, at which time the board shall elect officers, adopt by-laws, appoint committees and otherwise fully organize. Other States whose names ar subscribed hereto shall thereafter become parties hereto upon approval of this compact by legislative action within two years from the date hereof, upon such conditions as may be agreed upon at the time.

After becoming effective this compact shall thereafter continue without limitation of time provided, however, that it may be terminated at any time by unanimous action of the States and provided further that any State may withdraw from this compact if such withdrawal is approved by its legislature, such withdrawal to become effective two years after written notice thereto to the Board accompanied by a certified copy of the requisite legislative action, but such withdrawal shall not relieve the withdrawing State from its obligations hereunder accruing up to the effective date of such withdrawal. Any State so withdrawing shall ipso facto cease to have any claim to or ownership of any of the property held or vested in the Board or to any of the funds of the Board held under the terms of this compact.

If any State shall at any time become in default in the performance of any of its obligations assumed herein or with respect to any obligation imposed upon said State as authorized by and in compliance with the terms and provisions of this compact, all rights, privileges and benefits of such defaulting State, its members on the Board and its citizens shall ipso facto be and become suspended from and after the date of such default. Unless such default shall be remedied and made good within a period of one year immediately following the date of such default this compact may be terminated with respect to such defaulting State by an affirmative vote of three-fourths of the members of the Board (exclusive of the members representing the State in default), from and after which time such State shall cease to be a party to this compact and shall have no further claim to or ownership of any of the property held by or vested in the Board or to any of the funds of the Board held under the terms of this compact, but such termination shall in no manner release such defaulting State from any accrued obligations or otherwise effect this compact or the rights, duties, privileges or obligations of the remaining States thereunder.

IN WITNESS WHEREOF this compact has been approved and signed by the Governors of the several States, subject to the approval of their respective legislatures in the manner hereinabove set out, as of the ....day of..1948.

STATE OF FLORIDA,
By..
      Governor

STATE OF MARYLAND,
By..
      Governor

STATE OF GEORGIA,
By..
      Governor

STATE OF LOUISIANA,
By..
      Governor

STATE OF ALABAMA,
By..
      Governor

STATE OF MISSISSIPPI,
By..
      Governor

COMMONWEALTH OF KENTUCKY,
By..
      Governor

STATE OF TENNESSEE,
By..
      Governor

COMMONWEALTH OF VIRGINIA,
By..
      Governor

STATE OF ARKANSAS,
By..
      Governor

STATE OF NORTH CAROLINA,
By..
      Governor

STATE OF SOUTH CAROLINA,
By..
      Governor

STATE OF TEXAS,
By..
      Governor

STATE OF OKLAHOMA,
By..
      Governor

STATE OF WEST VIRGINIA,
By..
      Governor

Section 2. That all laws or parts in conflict herewith be and the same are hereby repealed.

Approved by the Governor: July 6, 1948.

A true copy:

WADE O. MARTIN, JR.,
Secretary of State.

[Note: The foregoing statute has been codified as §9583.57 [1949 Cum. Supp.], Dart's Louisiana General Statutes (1939). The text of the Regional Compact as adopted by Louisiana differs slightly from the text of the Compact as amended. See under Maryland for amended text. See also Note On Regional Compact — Education, Appendix 6.]

Hospitals
Mental

§3896. Colored asylum. — Nothing contained in this act [§§3880 — 3897 which provide for the establishment of the Central Louisiana State Hospital in the parish of Rapides] shall change the organization of, nor impair the obligation of any contract entered into by and with the board of administrators of the Colored Asylum of the State of Louisiana as provided for by Act No. 92 of 1902. [Acts 1904, No. 143, §2.]

Housing — Segregation in Dwellings

CODE OF CRIMINAL PROC. (DART.) 1932

Art. 1315. Whites and negroes — Housing in same dwelling — Penalty. — Any person or the agent of any person; any firm or the agent of any firm, and any corporation or the agent or officer of any corporation in any city owning or having in charge any apartment-house, tenement-house, or other building used for dwelling purposes, who shall rent any part of any such building to a negro person or negro family when such building is already in whole or in part in occupancy by a white person or white family, or vice versa when the building is in occupancy by a negro person or negro family, shall be guilty of a misdemeanor and on conviction thereof shall be punished by a fine of not less than twenty-five [$25.00] nor more than one hundred [$100.00] dollars or be imprisoned not less than 10, or more than 60 days, or both such fine and imprisonment in the discretion of the court. [Acts 1921, (E.S.) No. 106, §1.]

Art. 1316. Whites and negroes — Separate entrances or partitions insufficient defense. — It shall not be a defense that in such building there have been provided partitions, or separate entrances, or other features of separation between the races. [Acts 1921, (E.S.) No. 106, §2.]

Art. 1371. Exceptions from act. — This act shall not apply to white and negro employees in hotels, lodging houses, boarding houses or private homes, or otherwise where it can be shown to the satisfaction of the court that the housing under the same roof of the two races is a necessary part of the requirements of the employment. [Acts 1921, (E.S.) No. 106, §3.]

Ku Klux Klan — Anti-Mask Laws

LOUISIANA CODE OF CRIMINAL PROCEDURE (DART 1932)

871. Wearing disguise, hood or mask in public place prohibited — Penalty. — If any person shall use or wear upon any public highway, public road, public by-path, public street, public passage way or any public place of any character whatsoever, or in any open place in view thereof, in the state of Louisiana, a hood and mask, or a hood or a mask, or anything in the nature of either, or any facial disguise of any kind or description whatsoever, calculated to conceal or hide the identity of said person, or to prevent his being readily recognized, he shall be deemed guilty of a misdemeanor and upon conviction thereof shall be punished by imprisonment in the parish prison for not less than six [6] months nor more than three [3] years. [Acts 1924, No. 3, §1.]

872. Hallowe'en and other exceptions. — This act shall not apply to activities of children on Hallowe'en, or to persons participating in any public parade or exhibition of an educational, religious or historical character given by any school or church, or by any public governing authority, or to persons in any private residence, club or lodge room. [Acts 1924, No. 3, §2.]

873. Mardi Gras and other entertainments excepted. — This act shall not apply to persons participating in masquerade balls or entertainments or to persons participating in carnival parades or exhibitions during the period of Mardi Gras festivities, or to persons participating in the parades or exhibitions of minstrel troupes, circuses or other dramatic or amusement shows, or to promiscuous masking on Mardi Gras, when such masquerades balls or entertainments, carnival parades or exhibition, or parades or exhibitions of minstrel troupes, circuses or other dramatic or amusement shows, or promiscuous masking on Mardi Gras, are duly authorized by the governing authorities of the municipalities in which they are held or by the sheriff of the parish if the same are held outside of an incorporated municipality. [Acts 1924, No. 3, §3.]

874. Permit required. — It shall be the duty of all persons having charge or control of any of the festivities set out in section 3 [873] hereof in order to bring the persons participating therein within the exceptions contained in said section 3 [873], to make written application for and to obtain in advance of said festivities, from the mayor of the city, town or village in which the festivities are to be held, or when the festivities are to be held outside of an incorporated city, town or village, from the sheriff of the parish in which same are to be held, a written permit to conduct such festivities, and said authorities may issue said permit; provided, however, that a general public proclamation by such officer authorizing such festivities shall be equivalent to an application and permit as hereinbefore required. [Acts 1924, No. 3, §4.]

875. Constitutionality of Act. — If any clause, sentence, paragraph, or part of this act shall for any reason be adjudged by any court of competent jurisdiction to be invalid, such judgment shall not affect, impair, or invalidate the remainder of this act, but shall be confined in its operation to the clause, sentence, paragraph, or any part thereof, directly involved in the controversy in which such judgment has been rendered. [Acts 1924, No. 3, §5.]

876. Entering premises disguised — Penalty. — If any person using a hood and mask or a mask or a hood or anything in the nature thereof of any kind or description whatsoever as a disguise calculated to conceal his identity, or using anything to conceal his face or features or any part thereof as a disguise calculated to conceal his identity, shall enter upon the premises of another or inclosure of another, or demand admission into the house or inclosure of another with intent to inflict bodily injury or injury to property or to intimidate or threaten any one therein, or any one residing therein, or customarily residing therein, he shall be deemed guilty of a felony and upon conviction thereof shall be imprisoned at hard labor for not less than one [1] nor more than ten [10] years. [Acts 1924, No. 4, §1.]

[Note: §§877-884 (Acts 1924, No. 4, §§2-9), which also dealt with criminal activities such as assault, beating, kidnapping and carrying concealed weapons while using a hood or mask to conceal identity, were repealed by Acts 1942, No. 43, §2.]

Miscegenation

CIVIL CODE OF LA. (DINOW) (1947); LOUISIANA REVISED CIVIL CODE OF 1870

Art. 94 . . . Miscegenation. — . . . Marriage between White persons and persons of Color is prohibited, and the celebration of all such marriages is forbidden and such celebration carries with it no effect and is null and void. [As amended, Acts 1894, No. 54.]

Art. 95 . . . That no marriage contracted in contravention of the above provisions in another State by citizens of this State, without first having acquired a domicile out of this State, shall have any legal effect in this State. [As amended Acts 1900, No. 120; 1902, No. 9.]

DART'S LOUISIANA GENERAL STATUTES ANNOTATED (1932)

§2185. Miscegenation prohibited. — Marriage between persons of the Indian race and persons of the colored and black race is prohibited, and the celebration of all such marriages is forbidden and such celebration carries with it no effect, and is null and void. [Acts 1920, No. 220, §1.]

[See Civ. Code Art. 94. above.]

§2186. Marriages in other states of persons domiciled in Louisiana — Validity. — If any person residing and intending to continue to reside in this state who is disabled or prohibited from contracting marriage under the laws of this state shall go into another state, territory, district, possession, or country and there contract a marriage prohibited and declared void by the laws of this state, such marriage shall be null and void for all purposes in this state with the same effect as though such prohibited marriage had been entered into in this state. [Acts 1914, No. 151, §1.]

§2189. Penalties imposed. — Any official issuing a license with the knowledge that the parties are thus prohibited from inter-marrying and any person authorized to celebrate marriage who shall knowingly celebrate such marriage shall be deemed guilty of a misdemeanor, and shall be punished by fine or imprisonment or both in the discretion of the court. [Acts 1914, No. 151, §4.]

§2196. No distinction of color or race. — The said right of making private or religious marriages legal, valid and binding, as aforesaid, shall apply to marriages of all persons of whatever race or color . . . [Acts 1868, No. 210, §4; R. S. §2215.]

§2212. Statistics of divorce proceedings. — [Clerk of court having jurisdiction over divorce proceedings must make annual report of all annulment, divorce and separation actions, and must specify the color of the plaintiff and defendant in each suit reported.] [Acts 1908, No. 307 §1.]

Prisons

LOUISIANA CODE OF CRIMINAL PROCEDURE (DART) 1932.

Art. 1495. Separate apartments and other requirements and necessities.

— Each and every municipal, parish or state prison, lockup or camp must be of sufficient size and strength to hold and keep securely the prisoners contained therein; and if used for both sexes and the white and negro races, must contain at least four separate apartments, one for white men, one for white women, one for negro men, and one for negro women, with separate apartments for communicable contagious diseases. The building shall be fireproof, screened, properly ventilated, sufficiently lighted, by day and night, adequately heated, and connected with water and sewer, where water and sewer connections are to be had in the town or city, including separate bathing facilities for whites and negroes. [Acts 1918, No. 251, §2.]

State Penitentiary
Art. 1432 — Penitentiary regulations. — The board of control shall make such rules and regulations as are necessary for the government of the penitentiary, . . . , said regulations to provide for the separation of . . . , as far as practicable, the whites and blacks . . . [Acts 1900, No. 70, §6.]

Public Accommodation
See under **Civil Rights** above.

Transportation
Motor Vehicles

§5307. Separate accommodations for white and colored races. — All bus companies, corporations, partnerships, persons or associations of persons carrying passengers for hire in their busses, carriages or vehicles in this state shall provide equal but separate accommodations for the white and colored races by designating separate seats or compartments so as to secure separate accommodations for the white and colored races; no person or persons shall be permitted to occupy seats or compartments other than the ones assigned to them on account of the race they belong to. [Acts 1928, No. 209, §1.]

§5308. Violation by passenger or operator — Penalty. — The person in charge of such busses, carriages or vehicles shall have power and is hereby required to assign each passenger to a seat or compartment used for the race to which such passenger belongs; any passenger insisting upon going into a seat or compartment to which by race he or she does not belong, shall be liable to a fine of twenty-five dollars ($25.00) or in lieu thereof, be imprisoned for the period of not more than thirty [30] days in the parish prison, and any person in charge or officer of any bus, carriage or vehicle insisting on assigning a person to a seat or compartment other than the one set aside for the race to which said passenger belongs, shall be liable to a fine of twenty-five dollars ($25.00), or in lieu thereof to imprisonment for a period of not more than thirty [30] days in the parish prison; and should any passenger refuse to occupy the seat or compartment to which he or she is assigned by the person in charge or officer of such bus, carriage or vehicle, said person in charge or officer shall have the power to refuse to carry such passenger on his car or cars, and for such refusal neither he nor the bus company, corporaiton, partnership, person or association of persons which he represents shall be held for damages in any of the courts in this state. [Acts 1928, No. 209, §2.]

§5309. Violation by companies and officers — Penalty. — All officers and directors of bus companies, corporations, partnerships, persons or associations carrying persons for hire over the public highways of the state, who shall refuse or neglect to comply with the provisions and requirements of this act, shall be deemed guilty of a misdemeanor and shall, upon conviction before any court of competent jurisdiction, be fined not less than fifty dollars ($50.00), nor more than three hundred dollars ($300.00), or be imprisoned in the parish jail for not less than ten [10] days nor more than sixty [60] days, or both fined and imprisoned at the discretion of the court. [Acts 1928, No. 209, §3.]

Railroads

§8130. Accommodations for white and colored races on trains — Provision — Use. — All railway companies carrying passengers in their coaches in this State, shall provide equal but separate accommodations for the white, and colored races, by providing two or more passenger coaches for each passenger train, or by dividing the passenger coaches by a partition, so as to secure separate accommodations; provided, that this section shall not be construed to apply to street railroads. No person or persons, shall be permitted to occupy seats in coaches, other than, the ones, assigned, to them on account of the race they belong to. [Acts 1890, No. 111, §1.]

[Note: Act No. 111 of Acts 1890 [§§8131-8133 herein] was reviewed by the United States Supreme Court in the famous case of *Plessy v. Ferguson* (1896), 163 U.S. 537, 41 L. ed. 256, 16 Sup. Ct. 1138. In that case a Negro was arrested and fined for violation of the Louisiana Statute by refusing to occupy a seat assigned in the coach set aside for Negroes. The court ruled that a State statute requiring the separation of the races, as applied to the internal commerce of the State, was not a violation of the equal protection clause of the Fourteenth Amendment, where provision was made for "separate but equal" accommodations.

The decision in the *Plessy* case was the legal foundation for segregation by law. Most of the original segregation statutes in this compilation were enacted following the *Plessy* decision.

Associate Justice Harlan wrote a forceful dissent in the *Plessy* case, in the course of which he declared:

"The arbitrary separation of citizens, on the basis of race, while they are on a public highway, is a badge of servitude wholly inconsistent with the civil freedom and equality before the law established by the Constitution. It cannot be justified upon any legal grounds.

"If evils will result from the commingling of the two races upon public highways established for the benefit of all, they will be infinitely less than those that will surely come from state legislation regulating the enjoyment of civil rights upon the basis of race. We boast of the freedom enjoyed by our people above all other peoples. But it is difficult to reconcile that boast with a state of the law which, practically, puts the brand of servitude and degradation upon a large class of our fellow-citizens, our equals before the law. The thin disguise of 'equal' accommodations for passengers in the railroad coaches will not mislead any one, nor atone for the wrong this day done." (p. 562)

The *Plessy* case has not been overruled.]

8131. Assignment of Compartments — Enforcement — Penalties. — The officers of such passenger trains shall have power and are hereby required to assign each passenger to the coach or compartment used for the race to which such passenger belongs; any passenger insisting on going into a coach or compartment to which by race he does not belong, shall be liable to a fine of twenty-five dollars ($25.00), or in lieu thereof to imprisonment for a period of not more than twenty (20) days in the parish prison, and any officer of any railroad insisting on assigning a passenger to a coach or compartment other than the one set aside for the race to which said passenger belongs shall be liable to a fine of twenty-five dollars ($25.00), or in lieu thereof to imprisonment for a period of not more than twenty (20) days in the parish prison; and should any passenger refuse to occupy the coach or compartment to which he or she is assigned by the officer of such railway, said officer shall have power to refuse to carry such passenger on his train, and for such refusal neither he nor the railway company which he represents shall be liable for damages in any of the courts of this state. [Acts 1890, No. 111, §2.]

[Note: See note to §8130, *supra.*]

§8132. Disobedience of law by railroad employees — Penalties Posting of law — Limits on application of law. — All officers and directors of railway companies that shall refuse or neglect to comply with the provisions and requirements of this act shall be deemed guilty of a misdemeanor and shall upon conviction before any court of competent jurisdiction be fined not less than one hundred dollars ($100.00) nor more than five hundred dollars ($500.00); and any conductor or other employees of such passenger train, having charge of the same, who shall refuse or neglect to carry out the provisions of this act shall on conviction be fined not less than twenty-five dollars ($25.00) nor more than fifty dollars ($50.00) for each offense. All railroad corporations carrying passengers in this State other than street railroads shall keep this law posted up in a conspicuous place in each passenger coach and ticket office; provided that nothing in this act shall be construed as applying to nurses attending children of the other race; or prisoners in charge of sheriffs or their deputies, or other officers. [Acts 1890, No. 111, §3; 1894, No. 177§1.]

[Note: See note to §8130, *supra.*]

§8133. Separate waiting rooms — Construction — Use. — All railway companies carrying passengers in this state shall upon the construction or renewal of depots at regular stations provide equal but separate waiting rooms in their depots for the white and colored races by providing two waiting rooms in each depot, provided that the requirements of this act shall be fully complied with by the first day of January, A.D. 1896, no person or persons shall be permitted to occupy seats or remain in waiting room other than the one assigned to them on account of the race to which they belong. [Acts 1894, No. 98, §1.]

§8134. Assignment of waiting rooms — Enforcement — Penalties. — All depot agents shall have power and are hereby required to assign each person entering the depots to the waiting room used for the race to which such passenger belongs, and any person insisting on going into a waiting room to which by race he or she does not belong shall be liable to a fine of twenty-five ($25.00) or in lieu thereof to imprisonment for a period of not more than thirty (30) days in the parish prison; and any depot agent or his subordinate knowingly insisting or assigning any person to a waiting room other than the one set aside for the race to which said person belongs shall be liable to a fine of twenty-five dollars ($25.00), or in lieu thereof to imprisonment of not more than thirty (30) days in the parish prison; and shall any person using the depots of any railway companies, refuse to occupy the waiting room to which he or she is assigned by the depot agents or their subordinates, of such railway companies, said agents or subordinates shall have power to eject such person from said depot and for such ejectment neither he nor the railway company, which said agent or subordinate represents, shall be liable for damages in any of the courts of this state. [Acts 1894, No. 98, §2.]

§8135. Disobedience of law by depot employees — Penalties — Posting of law — Limits on application of law. — All depot agents and their subordinates that shall neglect or refuse to comply with the provisions and requirements of this act shall be deemed guilty of a misdemeanor and shall upon conviction before any court of competent jurisdiction, be fined not less than twenty-five dollars ($25.00), nor more than fifty dollars ($50.00) for each offense. All railroad companies carrying passengers in this state shall keep this law posted in a conspicuous place in such depot, provided that nothing in this act shall be construed as applying to nurses attending children of the other race, or sheriffs having prisoners in their charge. [Acts 1894, No. 98, §3.]

Street Railways

§8188. Accommodations for white and colored races on street cars — Provision — Use. — All street railway companies carrying passengers in their cars in this state shall provide equal but separate accommodations for the white and colored races by providing two or more cars or by dividing their cars by wooden or wire screen partitions so as to secure separate accommodations for the white and colored races, no person or persons shall be permitted to occupy seats in cars or compartments other than the ones assigned to them on account of the race they belong to. [Acts 1902, No. 64, §1.]

§8189. Assignment of compartments — Enforcement — Penalties. — The officers of such street cars shall have power and are hereby required to assign each passenger to the car or compartment used for the race to which such passenger belongs; any passenger insisting upon going into a car or compartment to which by race he or she does not belong shall be liable to a fine of twenty-five dollars ($25.00), or in lieu thereof be imprisoned for a period of not more than thirty (30) days in the parish prison, and any officer of any street railway insisting on assigning a passenger to a car or compartment other than the one set aside for the race to which such passenger belongs, shall be liable to a fine of twenty-five dollars ($25.00) or in lieu thereof, to imprisonment for a period of not more than thirty (30) days in the parish prison; and should any passenger refuse to occupy the car or compartment to which he or she is assigned by the officer of such street railway, said officer shall have the power to refuse to carry such passenger on his car or cars, and for such refusal neither he nor the street railway company which he represents shall be liable for damages in any of the courts of this state. [Acts 1902, No. 64, §2.]

§8190. Disobedience of act by street railway employees — Penalties — Posting act — Limits on application. — All officers and directors of street railway companies that shall refuse or neglect to comply with the provisions and requirements of this act shall be deemed guilty of a misdemeanor, and shall upon conviction before any court of competent jurisdiction be fined not less than one hundred dollars ($100.00) or be imprisoned in the parish jail not less than sixty (60) days and not more than six (6) months; and any conductor or other employee of such street car having charge of the same, who shall refuse or neglect to carry out the provisions of this act shall, on conviction, be fined not less than twenty-five dollars ($25.00), or be imprisoned in the parish jail for not less than ten (10) days, nor more than thirty (30) days for each and every offense. All street railway corporations carrying passengers in this state shall keep this law posted up in a conspicuous place in each and every car and at their transfer stations; provided that nothing in this act shall be construed as applying to nurses attending children of the other race. [Acts 1902, No. 64, §3.]

MAINE

CONSTITUTION

[No constitutional provisions.]

STATUTES

REVISED STATUTES OF MAINE, 1944

Discriminatory Publication

Notices Discriminating Against Persons

Chap. 124, Sec. 44. Discrimination against persons and classes by printed notices and distribution by operators of places of accommodation, prohibited; definition; exception; penalty. — No person, being the owner, lessee, proprietor, manager, superintendent, agent, or employee of any place of public accommodation, resort, or amusement shall directly or indirectly, by himself or another, publish, issue, circulate, distribute, or display, in any way, any advertisement, circular, folder, book, pamphlet, written or painted or printed notice or sign, of any kind or description, intended to discriminate against or actually discriminating against persons of any religious sect, class, creed, denomination, or nationality, in the full enjoyment of the accommodations, advantages, facilities, or privileges offered to the general public by such places of public accommodation, resort, or amusement.

A place of public accommodation, resort, or amusement within the meaning of this section shall be deemed to include any inn, whether conducted for the entertainment, housing, or lodging of transient guests, or for the benefit, use, or accommodation of those seeking health, recreation, or rest, any restaurant, eating-house, public conveyance on land or water, bath-house, barbershop, theatre and music-hall.

Nothing in this section contained shall be construed to prohibit the mailing of a private communication in writing, sent in response to a specific written inquiry.

Any person who shall violate any of the provisions of this section, or who shall aid in or incite, cause, or bring about, in whole or in part, the violation of the provisions of this section, shall, for each and every violation, be punished by a fine of not more than $100, or by imprisonment for not more than 30 days, or by both such fine and imprisonment. [(1917), R.S.c. 134, §§7, 8, 9, 10.]

Education

Ch. 37, Sec. 126. Instructors of Colleges, etc., to inculcate certain virtues ... — [Provides it shall be the duty of instructors in all private and public schools to impress upon minds of children committed to their care "the principles of morality and justice, and a sacred regard for truth; love of country, humanity and a universal benevolence . . . also to teach the tendency of opposite vices "to slavery, degradation, and ruin . . . " as well as "the great principles of humanity as illustrated by kindness to birds and animals and regard for all factors which contribute to the well-being of man."] [R.S. c. 19, §124.]

Ch. 37, §39. School age; Kindergartens. [R. S. c. 19, §32, 1943, c. 240.]—The age of pupils allowed to attend the public schools of the state is fixed between the ages of 5 and 21 years; and every child between the said ages shall have the right to attend the public schools in the town in which his parent or guardian has a legal residence, . .

[Note: See also Ch. 37, §93, with reference to high schools. As a practical matter there is no segregation of school children in Maine public schools although no statute expressly forbids it. It may be argued that the above section forbids segregation on the grounds of race, color or creed where there is only one public school in a town.]

Innkeepers and Victualers

Ch. 88, Sec. 29. Duty of innkeepers to provide entertainment. [R.S. c. 36, §5; 1935, c. 17.] — Every innkeeper shall, at all times be furnished with suitable provisions and lodging for strangers and travelers, and he shall grant such reasonable accommodations as occasion requires to travelers and others.

Ch. 88, Sec. 30. Duties of victualers. [R.S. c. 36, §6.] — Every victualer has all the rights and privileges and is subject to all the duties and obligations of an innkeeper, except furnishing lodging for travelers.

Ch. 88, Sec. 34. Prosecutions. [R.S. c. 36, §10.] — The licensing board shall prosecute for any violations of sections 26 to 33 [includes Sections 29 and 30 above] that come to its knowledge, by complaint, indictment, or action of debt; and all penalties recovered shall inure to the town where the offense is committed. Any citizen of the state may prosecute for any violation of the said sections in the same manner as the licensing board may prosecute.

[Note: While the above statutes make no mention of race or color, it may be argued that these statutes may be used in cases of racial discrimination.]

Insurance

Ch. 56, Sec. 130.

[Note: This section prohibits life insurance companies from making any distinction or discrimination "between individuals of the same class of insurance risk and of equal expectation of life . . . " Most state insurance codes contain a similar clause. It may be argued that such clauses may be invoked to prevent discrimination because of race, color, etc.] [R.S., c. 60, §137.]

MARYLAND

CONSTITUTION

Slavery

(Declaration of Rights)

Art. 24. That slavery shall not be re-established in this State; but having been abolished, under the policy and authority of the United States, compensation, in consideration thereof, is due from the United States. [Const. 1867.]

Witnesses (Legislative Department)

Art. 3, Sec. 53. — No person shall be incompetent as a witness, on account of color, unless hereafter so declared by Act of the General Assembly. [Const. 1867.]

ANNOTATED CODE (1939) (FLACK)

Cohabitation

See Fornication with Negroes below.

Education

Public Schools

Art. 77, Sec. 111. — [Provides that all white youths between 6 and 21 shall be admitted to the public schools of state.] [An. Code, 1924, Sec. 114. 1912, sec. 63. 1904, sec. 59. 1888, sec. 54. 1872, ch. 377. 1916, ch. 506, sec. 63.]

Art. 77, Secs. 192-193 — [Provides for establishment of schools for colored youths between ages of 6 and 20 and management of these schools under direction of the county board of education.] [An. Code 1924, §§200, 201; 1912, §§131, 132; 1904, §§124, 125; 1888, §§96, 97; 1870, ch. 311; 1872, ch. 377, sub-ch. 18, §2; 1874, ch. 463; 1916, ch. 506, §132; 1904, ch. 584; 1916, ch. 506, §131; 1922, ch. 382, §131; 1937, ch. 552.]

Art. 77, Sec. 194-195. — [Repealed and replaced by Laws 1941, ch. 515, p. 872.]

Art. 77, Sec. 75. — Elementary schools shall be kept open for not less than one hundred and eighty (180) actual school days and for ten months in each year, if possible, and shall be free to all white youths, between six and twenty years of age. [An. Code, 1924, sec. 72. 1912, sec. 43; 1904, sec. 42; 1888, sec. 38; 1872, ch. 377; 1916, ch. 506, sec. 43.]

STATUTES

Education

Equalization of teachers' salaries in elementary and high schools of state for white and colored children.

Art. 77, 93. — [1947 Cum. Supp.] — [Repeals and re-enacts with amendments Art. 77, Sec. 93 of Annot. Code of Md. (1939 edition), Art. 77, Secs. 194 and 195 and provides for the equalization of salaries of principals and teachers in the elementary and high schools of the State for white and colored children.] Laws 1941, Ch. 515, p. 872, as amended 1945, ch. 543; 1947, ch. 535.]

Art. 77, Sec. 35. — The state department of education shall hereafter be provided with the following professional assistants . . .

(4) A white supervisor of colored schools, who shall have supervision of all colored schools, and shall perform such other duties as may be assigned to him by the state superintendent of schools . . .

[An. Code, 1924, sec. 35. 1912, sec. 21 A. 1916, ch. 506, sec. 21A.]

Normal and Industrial Schools

L. 1945, ch. 596. p. 645. — [Repealed Art. 77, Secs. 203, 204, 205, 206 of Annotated Code of Md. (1939 edition) relating to "Colored Industrial Schools" as obsolete.]

Art. 77, Sec. 252. — [Provides for the establishment of a "state normal school for the instruction and practice of colored teachers."] [An. Code, 1924. sec. 256. 1912, sec. 193. 1908, ch. 599.]

Art. 77, Sec. 207. — [Provides for the division of funds granted to the University of Maryland by the United States Government under the Morrill Act, on a percentage basis, so that funds equal to the percentum of the Negro population may be used for scholarship at Morgan College or at institutions outside of the state for Negro students who wish to take courses which are offered to white students at University of Maryland.] [1933, ch. 234.]

Art. 77, Sec. 253A. Morgan State College. — [new section]. — One student from each senatorial district of the State shall be educated free of charge for tuition, room and board at Morgan State College, provided, however, that the value of any such scholarship may be divided between two or more students upon the approval of the College and the appointing authority. The appointments for such scholarship shall be made after a competitive examination of the candidate and according to the general procedure provided in this sub-title. Nothing in this section shall, however, be construed to affect tuition scholarships already established to attract outstanding students without regard to geographical restrictions.

Sec. 2. *And be it further enacted;* That this act shall take effect June 1, 1949. [Laws 1949, ch. 420, p. 981. Approved April 29, 1949.]

Colleges — Negro Scholarship

Acts. 1935, ch. 577. — [Created a Commission on Higher Educaiton of Negroes, to make a study and survey of the needs of higher education in Maryland, including Morgan College, and to submit recommendations to the Governor and General Assembly. The Commission is also to administer the appropriation of $10,000 a year for 1936 and 1937 for

199

scholarships to Negroes to attend college outside of Maryland. Limit per person is $200.]

Art. 49B. Sec. 4. — The sum of thirty thousand dollars ($30,000) provided in the 1938-1939 Budget for scholarships and partial scholarships for negroes and expenses of awarding same, and all sums hereafter appropriated for such purpose shall be used to provide educational facilities and opportunities for negroes of this State equal to those now provided for white persons and especially to equip such negroes for the professions, such as Medicine, Law, Dentistry and Pharmacy, or any other profession or branch of education for which the State of Maryland provides opportunities for white students and for which it does not provide opportunities for negro students. [1937, ch. 506, sec. 4.]

Art. 49B, Sec. 5. — Whenever any *bona fide* negro resident, and citizen of this State, possessing the qualifications of health, character, ability and preparatory education required for admission to the University of Maryland, desires to obtain an education not provided for either in Morgan College or Princess Anne College, he may make application for a scholarship provided by the funds mentioned in the foregoing section, so that he may obtain aid to enable him to attend a college or university where equal educational facilities can be provided and furnished, whether or not such an agency or institution is operated by the State or under some other arrangement, and whether or not such facilities are located in Maryland or elsewhere. Under such conditions, it shall be provided that out of the scholarship funds mentioned in the foregoing section, the applicant, if he possesses the proper qualifications, may have paid to him or direct to the institution which he is to attend, such sum, if any, as may be necessary to supplement the amount which it would cost him to attend the University of Maryland, so that such person will be enabled to secure educational facilities, training and opportunities equal to those provided otherwise for white students, without additional cost to such person. Be it provided, however that the Commission [Commission on Scholarships for Negroes] hereinafter established, shall, in its discretion, have authority, in exceptional cases, to allow a grant for a scholarship in reasonable excess of the differential above referred to. In determining the comparative costs of attending any of the institutions to which scholarships may be provided, there shall be taken into consideration tuition charges, living expenses and costs of transportation. [1937, ch. 506, sec. 5.]

Art. 49B, Sec. 6. — [Sets up a nine member "Commission on Scholarships for Negroes "to be composed of the President of Morgan College, The Principal of Princess Anne College, the Director of Admissions of the University of Maryland, who shall serve ex-officio, and six other citizens of state to be appointed by the Governor for four-year terms. The Commission is to receive no salaries, but expenses for clerical help and other necessary expenditures to effect its duties.] [1937, ch. 506, sec. 6.]

Art. 49B, Sec. 7. — Sets forth the powers and duties of the Commission.] [1937, chap. 506, sec. 7.]

Art. 49B, Sec. 8.—The appropriation of sixty-thousand dollars ($60,000) provided in the 1938-1939 Budget for Morgan College, and all sums hereinafter appropriated to such institution, shall be used for the purpose of providing for Negroes both undergraduate education in the Arts and Sciences and education in the field of graduate studies. [1937, chap. 506, sec. 8.]

Art. 49B, Sec. 9. — All funds now or hereafter appropriated to Princess Anne College shall be used for the purpose of conducting there a four-year college or institute of agriculture and the mechanical arts, including home economics and two years of basic work in the arts and sciences. [1937, chap. 506, sec. 9.]

Art. 49B, Sec. 10. — As far as possible, consistent with the funds appropriated, Morgan and Princess Anne Colleges in their respective fields, shall offer such instruction as will provide competent teachers for the negro high schools of the State. [1937, Ch. 506, Sec. 10.]

[Note: Sec. 11 of Ch. 506 of Acts of 1937 repealed all acts inconsistent therewith.]

Regional Compact
LAWS OF MARYLAND 1949
CHAPTER 282, p. 706. [SENATE BILL 432]

AN ACT to approve, confirm and ratify a certain Compact entered into by the State of Maryland and other Southern States by and through their respective Governors on February 8, 1948, as amended, relating to the development and maintenance of regional educational services and schools in the Southern States in the professional, technological, scientific, literary and other fields, so as to provide greater educational advantages and facilities for the citizens in the several States here recited in such region, and to declare that the State of Maryland is a party to said Compact, as amended, and that the agreements, covenants and obligations therein are binding upon said State.

WHEREAS, on the 8th day of February, in the Year of Our Lord One Thousand Nine Hundred and Forty-eight, the State of Maryland, and the States of Florida, Georgia, Louisiana, Alabama, Mississippi, Tennessee, Arkansas, Virginia, North Carolina, South Carolina, Texas, Oklahoma, and West Virginia, through and by their respective Governors, entered into a written Compact relative to the development and maintenance of regional educational services and schools in the Southern States in the professional, technological, scientific, literary and other fields, so as to provide greater educational advantages and facilities for citizens of the several States who reside within such region; and

WHEREAS, the said Compact has been amended in certain respects, a copy of which Compact as amended is as follows:

THE REGIONAL COMPACT
(As Amended)

WHEREAS, The States who are parties hereto have during the past several years conducted careful investigation looking toward the establishment and maintenance of jointly owned and operated regional educational institutions in the Southern States in the professional, technological, scientific, literary and other fields, so as to provide greater educational advantages and facilities for the citizens of the several States who reside in such region; and

WHEREAS, Meharry Medical College of Nashville, Tennessee, has proposed that its lands, buildings, equipment and the net income from its endowment be turned over to the Southern States, or to an agency acting in their behalf, to be operated as a regional institution for medical, dental and nursing education upon terms and conditions to be hereafter agreed upon between the Southern States and Meharry Medical College, which proposal, because of the present financial condition of the institution, has been approved by the said States who are parties hereto; and

WHEREAS, The said States desire to enter into a compact with each other providing for the planning and establishment of regional educational facilities;

NOW THEREFORE, in consideration of the mutual agreements, covenants and obligations assumed by the respective States who are parties hereto (hereinafter referred to as "States"), the said several States do hereby form a geographical district or region consisting of the areas lying within the boundaries of the contracting States which, for the purposes of this compact, shall constitute an area for regional education supported by public funds derived from taxation by the constituent States and derived from other sources for the establishment, acquisition, operation and maintenance of regional educational schools and institutions for the benefit of citizens of the respective States residing within the region so established as may be determined from time to time in accordance with the terms and provisions of this compact.

The States do further hereby establish and create a joint agency which shall be known as the Board of Control for Southern Regional Education (hereinafter referred to as the "Board"), the members of which Board shall consist of the Governor of each State, *ex officio,* and three additional citizens of each State to be appointed by the Governor thereof, at least one of whom shall be selected from the field of education. The Governor shall continue as a member of the Board during his tenure of office as Governor of the State, but the members of the Board appointed by the Governor shall hold office for a period of four years except that in the original appointments one Board member so appointed by the Governor shall be designated at the time of his appointment to serve an initial term of two years, one Board member to serve an initial term of three years, and the remaining Board member to serve the full term of four years, but thereafter the successor of each appointed Board member shall serve the full term of four years. Vacancies on the Board caused by death, resignation, refusal or inability to serve shall be filled by appointment by the Governor for the unexpired portion of the term. The officers of the Board shall be a Chairman, a vice-chairman, a Secretary, a Treasurer, and such additional officers as may be created by the

Board from time to time. The Board shall meet annually and officers shall be elected to hold office until the next annual meeting. The Board shall have the right to formulate and establish by-laws not inconsistent with the provisions of this compact to govern its own actions in the performance of the duties delegated to it including the right to create and appoint an Executive Committee and a Finance Committee with such powers and authority as the Board may delegate to them from time to time. The Board may, within its discretion, elect as its Chairman a person who is not a member of the Board, provided such person resides within a signatory State, and upon such election such person shall become a member of the Board with all the rights and privileges of such membership.

It shall be the duty of the Board to submit plans and recommendations to the States from time to time for their approval and adoption by appropriate legislative action for the development, establishment, acquisition, operation and maintenance of educational schools and institutions within the geographical limits of the regional area of the States, of such character and type and for such educational purposes, professional, technological, scientific, literary, or otherwise, as they may deem and determine to be proper, necessary or advisable. Title to all such educational institutions when so established by appropriate legislative actions of the States and to all properties and facilities used in connection therewith shall be vested in said Board as the agency of and for the use and benefit of the said States and the citizens thereof, and all such educational institutions shall be operated, maintained and financed in the manner herein set out, subject to any provisions or limitations which may be contained in the legislative acts of the States authorizing the creation, establishment and operation of such educational institutions.

In addition to the power and authority heretofore granted, the Board shall have the power to enter into such agreements or arrangements with any of the States and with educational institutions or agencies, as may be required in the judgment of the Board, to provide adequate services and facilities for the graduate, professional, and technical education for the benefit of the citizens of the respective States residing within the region, and such additional and general power and authority as may be vested in the Board from time to time by legislative enactment of the said States.

Any two or more States who are parties of this compact shall have the right to enter into supplemental agreements providing for the establishment, financing and operation of regional educational institutions for the benefit of citizens residing within an area which constitutes a portion of the general region herein created, such institutions to be financed exclusively by such States and to be controlled exclusively by the members of the Board representing such States provided such agreement is submitted to and approved by the Board prior to the establishment of such institutions.

Each State agrees that, when authorized by the legislature, it will from time to time make available and pay over to said Board such funds as may be required for the establishment, acquisition, operation and maintenance of such regional educational institutions as may be authorized by the States under the terms of this compact, the contribution of each State at all times to be in the proportion that its population bears to the total combined population of the States who are parties hereto as shown from time to time by the most recent official published report of the Bureau of the Census of the United States of America; or upon such other basis as may be agreed upon.

This compact shall not take effect or be binding upon any State unless and until it shall be approved by proper legislative action of as many as six or more of the States whose Governors have subscribed hereto within a period of eighteen months from the date hereof. When and if six or more States shall have given legislative approval to this compact within said eighteen months period, it shall be and become binding upon six or more States 60 days after the date of legislative approval by the Sixth State and the Governors of such six or more States shall forthwith name the members of the Board from their States as hereinabove set out, and the Board shall then meet on call of the Governor of any State approving this compact at which time the Board shall elect officers, adopt by-laws, appoint committees and otherwise fully organize. Other States whose names are subscribed hereto shall thereafter become parties hereto upon approval of this compact by legislative action within two years from the date hereof, upon such conditions as may be agreed upon at the time. Provided, however, that with respect to any State whose constitution may require amendment in order to permit legislative approval of the Compact, such State or States shall become parties hereto upon approval of this Compact by legislative action within seven years from the date hereof, upon such conditions as may be agreed upon at the time.

After becoming effective this compact shall thereafter continue without limitation of time; provided, however, that it may be terminated at any time by unanimous action of the States and provided further that any State may withdraw from this compact if such withdrawal is approved by its Legislature, such withdrawal to become effective two years after written notice thereof to the Board accompanied by a certified copy of the requisite legislative action, but such withdrawal shall not relieve the withdrawing State from its obligations hereunder accruing up to the effective date of such withdrawal. Any State so withdrawing shall *ipso facto* cease to have any claim to or ownership of any of the property held or vested in the Board or to any of the funds of the Board held under the terms of this compact.

If any State shall at any time become in default in the performance of any of its obligations assumed herein or with respect to any obligations imposed upon said State as authorized by and in compliance with the terms and provisions of this compact, all rights, privileges and benefits of such defaulting State, its members on the Board and its citizens shall *ipso facto* be and become suspended from and after the date of such default. Unless such default shall be remedied and made good within a period of one year immediately following the date of such default this compact may be terminated with respect to such defaulting State by an affirmative vote of three-fourths of the members of the Board (exclusive of the members representing the State in default), from and after which time such State shall cease to be a party to this compact and shall have no further claim to or ownership of any of the property held by or vested in the Board or to any of the funds of the Board held under the terms of this compact, but such termination shall in no manner release such defaulting State from any accrued obligation or otherwise affect this compact or the rights, duties, privileges or obligations of the remaining States thereunder.

IN WITNESS WHEREOF this Compact has been approved and signed by Governors of the Several States, subject to the approval of their respective Legislatures in the manner hereinabove set out, as of the 8th day of February, 1948. [Signed by the Governors of the States of Florida, Maryland, Georgia, Louisiana, Alabama, Mississippi, Tennessee, Arkansas, Virginia, North Carolina, South Carolina, Texas, Oklahoma, West Virginia.] now therefore,

SECTION 1. *Be it enacted by the General Assembly of Maryland,* That the said Compact is hereby approved, confirmed and ratified, and that as soon as the said Compact shall be approved, confirmed and ratified by the Legislatures of at least six of the States signatory hereto in accordance with the provisions of the Compact, thereupon and immediately thereafter, every paragraph, clause, provision, matter and thing in the said Compact contained shall be obligatory on this State and the citizens thereof, and shall be forever faithfully and inviolably observed and kept by the government of this State and all of its citizens according to the true intent and meaning and provisions of the said Compact.

SEC 2. *And be it further enacted,* That, upon the approval of this Compact by the minimum requisite number of States, as provided in said Compact, the Governor is hereby authorized and directed to sign an engrossed copy of the Compact and sufficient copies thereof, so as to provide that each and every State approving the Compact shall have an engrossed copy thereof.

SEC 3. *And be it further enacted,* That this Act shall take effect on June 1, 1949.

Approved April 22, 1949.

[Note: See Note on Regional Compact — Education Appendix 6. Note also that in the first test case brought to challenge a state's use of the Regional Compact to enforce segregation of Negro students, Maryland's Court of Appeals has directed the University of Maryland to admit Esther McCready, 19-year old Baltimore Negro, to its School of Nursing. Reversing a lower court decision, the Maryland Court of Appeals held that Maryland could not deny a Negro applicant admission to an institution within the state solely because of race. The University of Maryland had rejected Miss McCready's application to enter its School of Nursing and had offered her admission to Meharry Medical College, Nashville, Tennessee, under the regional education compact. See *New York Times,* April 15, 1950.]

Deaf, Dumb, Blind

Art. 30, §9. [1947 Cum. Supp.] [Makes provision for blind minors or colored deaf minors at Maryland School for the Blind.] [An. Code. 1924, Sec. 14, 1924, Ch. 376, An. Code 1939, Sec. 9; 1947, ch. 133.]

Juvenile Delinquents

Art. 27, Secs. 684-692. — [Provides that House of the Good Shepherd in Baltimore is authorized to receive white female delinquents under 18 years of age.] [An. Code, 1924, Secs. 580-588; 1912, secs. 540-548; 1904, secs. 477-485; 1888, secs. 321-329; 1878, ch. 442, secs. 1-9.]

Art. 27, Secs. 693-694 — [Provides for the House of the Good Shepherd for Colored Girls in Baltimore to receive Negro female juvenile delinquents.] [An. Code 1924, §§589, 590; 1912, §549, 550; 1904, §§486, 487; 1894, ch. 187, §§329A, 329B.]

Art. 27, Secs. 696-697A. [1947 Cum. Supp.] — [Provision made for the establishment and maintenance of Cheltenham School for Boys at Cheltenham, Md., for the care and reformation of colored male minors.] [1937, ch. 70, secs. 611A-611B; 1947, ch. 189; 1941, ch. 645.]

Art. 27, Sec. 707. — [Provides for the Maryland School for Boys, as a reformatory for white male minors.] [An. Code, 1924, ch. 24, §612; 1918, ch. 300, §1, 1943, ch. 797, §17.]

1943 Supplement, Annot. Code of Md.

Art. 78A, Sec. 8A. — [The Board of Public Works is authorized to set up (a) a new training school for non-defective, colored juvenile delinquents, under the Supervision of the State Department of Public Welfare, to take the place of Cheltenham School for Boys, which institution shall then be converted into an institution exclusively for defective colored juvenile delinquents, under the supervision, direction and control of the Board of Mental Hygiene; . . . (c) a separate institution, or a division of an existing institution, midway between a training school and an adult prison, for incorrigible offenders, both white and colored, between the ages of 16 and 20, under the direct supervision and control of the State Department of Correction. [1943, ch. 797, sec. 8A.]

[Note: See 1947 Cum. Supp., Art. 88A, secs. 17-22.]

Fornication with Negroes

Art. 27, Sec. 493. — Any white woman who shall suffer or permit herself to be got with child by a negro or mulatto, upon conviction thereof in the court having criminal jurisdiction, either in the city or county where such child is begotten or where the same was born, shall be sentenced to the penitentiary for not less than eighteen months nor more than five years. [An. Code, 1924, sec. 415. 1912, sec. 370. 1904, sec. 337. 1888, sec. 218. 1715, ch. 44, sec. 25.]

Hospitals

Mental Patients

Art. 59, Secs. 61-63. — [Provides for the establishment of a state hospital for Negro insane called Crownsville State Hospital.] [An. Code 1924,

Secs. 60-66. 1912, sec. 54-58A. 1910, Ch. 250, secs. 9-13 (pp. 238-240). 1918, Ch. 443, sec. 58A; 1947, ch. 111, secs. 62-63.]

Tuberculosis Patients

Art. 43, Secs. 285-286. — [Provides for the establishment of facilities for care and treatment of colored persons by the Board of Managers of the Maryland Tuberculosis Sanatorium.] [An. Code, 1924, sec. 250, 1912, sec. 199A, 1918, ch. 148, sec. 1A, 1937, ch. 126.] [Repealed by 1947, ch. 583.]

[Note: Under the 1947 law, the Maryland Tuberculosis Sanatorium is abolished and its property and powers transferred to the State Board of Health.]

Interracial Commission — Commission to study problems affecting the colored population.

1943 Supp. Annot. Code of Maryland

Art. 49B, Sec. 1. [Creates a Commission for Colored Problems of 18 members appointed by the Governor. The first 18 members were named in the act. Successors to present members are named for a term of 9 years each.] [An. Code, 1939, Sec. 1. 1927, Ch. 559, Sec. 1. 1933, Ch. 280, 1943, Ch. 431, Sec. 1.]

Sec. 2. — [Members of the Commission not to receive any compensation, but reasonable and necessary expenses while engaged in their official duties are provided. Commission may appoint a salaried executive secretary.] [An. Code 1939, sec. 2. 1927, ch. 559, sec. 2. 1943, ch. 431, sec. 2.]

Sec. 3. — The said Commisson shall have power to make such surveys and studies concerning colored problems and inter-racial conditions as it may determine and shall have full power and authority to promote, in every way possible, the welfare of the colored race and the betterment of inter-racial relations. In making said studies and surveys, it shall be authorized to expend any funds which may be provided. [An. Code, 1939, Sec. 3. 1927, ch. 559, sec. 3. 1943, ch. 431, sec. 3.]

[Note: The Commission receives an annual appropriation of $8,000.00. See L. 1945, ch. 893, p. 1312; L. 1947, ch. 514, 1227; L. 1949, ch. 193, 512.]

Miscegenation

Art. 27, Sec. 445. — All marriages between a white person and a negro, or between a white person and a person of negro descent, to the third generation, inclusive, or between a white person and a member of the Malay race; or between the negro and a member of the Malay race; or between a person of Negro descent, to the third generation, inclusive, and a member of the Malay race, are forever prohibited, and shall be void; and any person violating the provisions of this Section shall be deemed guilty of an infamous crime, and punished by imprisonment in the penitentiary not less than eighteen [18] months nor more than ten [10] years: provided, however, that the provisions of this Section shall not apply to marriages between white persons and members of the Malay race, or between Negroes and members of the Malay race, or between persons of Negro descent, to the third generation, inclusive, and members of the Malay race, existing prior to June 1, 1935. [An. Code, 1924, sec. 365. 1912, sec. 330. 1904, sec. 305. 1888, ch. 200. 1884, ch. 264. 1935, ch. 60.]

Art. 27, Sec. 440. — If any minister, pastor or other person who, according to the laws of this State do usually join people in marriage, shall upon any pretense join in marriage any negro with any white person, he shall on conviction be fined one hundred dollars. [An. Code, 1924, sec. 358. 1912, sec. 324. 1904, sec. 299. 1888, sec. 194. 1715, ch. 44, sec. 24.]

Transportation — Segregation

Railroads

Art. 27, 510. — All railroad companies and corporations, and all persons running or operating cars or coaches by steam on any railroad line or track in the State of Maryland, for the transportation of passengers, are hereby required to provide separate cars or coaches for the travel and transportation of the white and colored passengers on their respective lines of railroad; and each compartment of a car or coach, divided by a good and substantial partition, with a door or place of exit from each division, shall be deemed a separate car or coach within the meaning of this section, and each separate car, coach or compartment shall bear in some conspicuous place appropriate words, in plain letters, indicating whether it is set apart for white or colored passengers. [An. Code, 1924, sec. 432. 1912, sec. 387. 1904, sec. 346. 1904, ch. 109, sec. 1.]

[Note: This and the following sections have been held valid in so far as they apply to intra-state passengers, but invalid as to inter-state passengers. It has been held, however, that the state has power to adopt reasonable police regulations to secure the safety and comfort of passengers on interstate trains while within its borders. *Hart. v. State,* 100 Md. 595, 600 (1905); *State v. Jenkins,* 124 Md. 376, 379 (1914).]

Art. 27, Sec. 511. — The railroad companies and corporations and persons aforesaid shall make no difference or discrimination in quality of or convenience or accommodation in the cars, coaches or compartments set apart for white and colored passengers. [An. Code, 1924, sec. 433, 1912, sec. 388. 1904, sec. 347. 1904, ch. 109, sec. 2.]

Art. 27, Sec. 512. — [Makes it a misdemeanor for railroad company or person to fail to comply with provisions of Sec. 510 and 511, punishable by $300.00 to $1,000.00 for each offense, upon conviction.] [An. Code, 1924, sec. 434. 1912, sec. 389. 1904, sec. 348. 1904, ch. 109, sec. 3.]

Art. 27, Sec. 513. — The conductors and managers on all railroads shall have power and are hereby required to assign to each white or colored passenger his or her respective car, coach or compartment, and, should any passenger refuse to occupy the car, coach or compartment to which he or she may be assigned by the conductor or managers, shall have the right to refuse to carry such passenger on his train, and may put such passenger off his train, and for such refusal or putting off the train neither the conductor, manager nor railroad company or corporation, or person owning or operating the same shall be liable for damages in any court; and the passenger so refusing to occupy the car, coach or compartment to which he or she may be assigned by the conductor or manager shall be deemed guilty of a misdemeanor, and, on indictment and conviction thereof, shall be fined not less than five [$5.00] dollars nor more than fifty [$50.00] dollars, or be confined in jail not less than thirty [30] days, or both, in the discretion of the court, for each offense. [An. Code, 1924, sec. 435. 1912, sec. 390. 1904, sec. 349. 1904, ch. 109, sec. 4.]

Art. 27, Sec. 514. — [Any conductor or manager of any railroad who fails to perform duties imposed by sec. 513 shall be deemed guilty of misdemeanor, punishable by fine of $25.00 to $50.00 for each offense, upon indictment and conviction.] [An. Code. 1924, sec. 436. 1912, sec. 391. 1904, sec. 350, 1904, ch. 109, sec. 5.]

Art. 27, Sec. 515. — [Special provisions for cars running in counties of Prince George's, Charles, St. Mary's Calvert and Anne Arundel, so that in those counties separate cars are not necessary, but separation may be achieved by having a combination car of which one-third is used for baggage and mail, the balance of which is divided by compartment. This section not to apply to trains making no scheduled intermediate service stops between their termini.] [An. Code, 1924, sec. 437. 1912, sec. 392. 1904, sec. 351. 1904, ch. 109, sec. 6. 1908, ch. 292.]

Art. 27, Sec. 516. — [Exceptions: Provisions: of sections 510 - 515 do not apply to (1) persons employed as nurses, (2) officers in charge of prisoners, whether said prisoners are white or colored, or both white and colored, or to the prisoners in their custody, (3) transportation of passengers in any caboose car attached to a freight train, (4) parlor or sleeping cars, (5) through express trains that do no local business.] [An. Code 1924, sec. 438. 1912, sec. 393. 1904, sec. 352. 1904, ch. 109, sec. 7.]

Steamboats

Art. 27, Sec. 517. — [Captains, pursers, or other officers in command of steamboats carrying passengers in Maryland waters are required "to assign white and colored passengers on said boats to the respective locations they are to occupy as passengers while on said boat," and "to separate, as far as the construction of his boat and due consideration for the comfort of the passengers will permit, the white and colored passengers on said boat in the sitting, sleeping and eating apartments; provided however, that no discrimination shall be made in the quality and convenience of accommodation afforded passengers in said locations; and provided, that this section and the two succeeding sections shall not apply to nurses or attendants traveling with their employers, nor to officers in charge of prisoners, whether the said prisoners are white or colored, or both white and colored, or to prisoners in their custody." [An. Code, 1924, sec. 439. 1912, sec. 394. 1904, sec. 353. 1904, ch. 110, sec. 1.]

Art. 27, Sec. 518. — [Failure of captain, purser, or other commanding officer of steamboat to carry out provisions of Sec. 517 is misdemeanor punishable, upon indictment and conviction, by fine of $25.00 to $50.00 for each offense.] [An. Code, 1924, sec. 440. 1912, sec. 395. 1904, sec. 354. 1904, ch. 110, sec. 2.]

Art. 27, 519. — Any passenger traveling on any steamboat plying in the waters within the jurisdiction of this State who shall wilfully refuse to occupy the location, whether of sitting, sleeping or eating, set apart or assigned by the captain, purser or other officer in command of such boat, shall be deemed guilty of a misdemeanor, and on indictment in any court having jurisdiction, and conviction thereof, shall be fined not less than five [$5.00] dollars nor more than fifty [$50.00] dollars, or be confined in jail not less than thirty [30] days, in the discretion of the court, for each offense; and such passenger may be ejected from the said boat by the officers thereof at any wharf or landing place of said boat, and, if necessary, such assistance may be invoked by the person in charge of said boat as he may require to eject such passenger; and provided, that in case of such ejectment neither the captain nor other person in charge of such boat, nor the steamboat company or corporation or person owning or operating such boat shall be liable in damages in any court. [An. Code, 1924, sec 441. 1912, sec. 396. 1904, sec. 355. 1904, ch. 110, sec. 3.]

Art. 27, Sec. 520. — [Requires owners and operators of steamboats operating on Chesapeake Bay between City of Baltimore and other points along the bay "to provide separate toilet or retiring rooms, and separate sleeping cabins on their respective steamboats . . . for white and colored passengers, under a penalty of a fine of fifty [$50.00] dollars for each and every day said steamboats may be operated upon the waters aforesaid in violation of this section." Provisions of four preceding sections shall apply in the assigning of passengers to the use of the toilet, or retiring rooms, and the sleeping quarters set apart for the respective white and colored passengers. [An. Code, 1924, sec. 442. 1912, sec. 397. 1908, ch. 617.]

Electric Cars

Art. 27, Sec. 521. — Conductors or managers of all railway companies and corporations, and all persons running or operating cars or coaches by electricity, running twenty miles beyond the limits of any incorporated city or town of the State for the transportation of passengers, are hereby authorized and required to designate separate seats for white and colored passengers, without any difference in the quality of or convenience or accommodation of the seats in such cars or coaches. The ordinary seat for two passengers shall be deemed a separate seat within the meaning of sections 521 to 526. [An. Code, 1924, sec. 443. 1912, sec. 398, 1908, ch. 248.]

[Note: The section applies to intra-state passengers only; thus held to be constitutional. *State v. Jenkins*, 124 Md. 376, 378 (1914). Statute held inapplicable to a passenger traveling from Annapolis, Md., to Washington, D.C., even though he had to change cars at Baltimore.

Passenger was traveling interstate. *Washington, B & A Electric R. Co. v. Waller*, 289 Fed. (1923) (C. Apps. D.C.) 598.]

Art. 27, Sec. 522. — [Discrimination by railway companies, etc. in quality of or convenience or accommodations offered is prohibited, and "no white person shall force himself or be permitted to force himself or herself in a seat designated for a colored person, and no colored person shall force himself or herself or be permitted to force himself or herself in a seat designated for a white person."] [An. Code, 1924, sec. 444. 1912, sec. 399. 1908, ch. 248.]

Art. 27, Sec. 523. — [This section is almost identical to sec. 513, *supra.*] [An. Code, 1924, sec. 445. 1912, sec. 400. 1908, ch. 248.]

Art. 27, Sec. 524. — [Violation of sections 521 to 526 by conductor or manager of railway, punishable as misdemeanor by fine of not more than $20.00 for each offense.] [An. Code, Sec. 446, 1912, sec. 401. 1908, ch. 248.]

Art. 27, Sec. 525. — When the seats in any car, coach or compartment shall all be occupied, but not filled, and the increased number of passengers cannot be accommodated with separate seats, the conductor or manager in charge of such car or coach is hereby authorized to assign passengers of the same color to the vacant seats, and he can, with the permission and consent of the occupant, assign a passenger of the other color to the unoccupied seats, but not otherwise. [An. Code, 1924, sec. 447. 1912, sec. 402. 1908, ch. 248.]

Art. 27, Sec. 526. — The provisions of sections 521 to 526 shall not apply to persons employed as nurses or valets when accompanying those needing their attention. [Ano. Code, 1924, sec. 448. 1912, sec. 403. 1908, ch. 248.]

MASSACHUSETTS

CONSTITUTION

[No constitutional provisions on race or color.]

STATUTES

ANNOTATED LAWS OF MASSACHUSETTS (MICHIE)

Aliens

[Note: It appears that Massachusetts has enacted no laws directed against any racial group. It is of interest to note, however, that *Ch. 266, §116* prohibits the picking of wild berries and flowers by aliens between April 1st and December 1st in Barnstable and Plymouth Counties, without a written permit from the owners of the land. *Ch. 140, §129A* [1948 Cum. Supp.] prohibits aliens from possessing firearms without first obtaining a permit. *Ch. 140, §130* [1948 Cum. Supp.] makes it a punishable offense for any person to sell or furnish an alien without a permit with any firearm. *Ch. 69, §11*, provides for the education and protection of aliens.]

Displaced Persons

Laws 1949, p....................

RESOLUTIONS MEMORIALIZING CONGRESS TO MAKE CERTAIN CHANGES IN THE DISPLACED PERSONS ACT OF NINETEEN HUNDRED AND FORTY-EIGHT, SO CALLED.

[H.B. No. 2222, Senate 114.]

WHEREAS, The present federal law, known as the Displaced persons Act of 1948, allowing the admission into the United States of certain displaced persons, is manifestly discriminatory against members of the Catholic and the Jewish faiths; and

WHEREAS, Said law discriminates against persons because of their land of origin, religion and occupations; therefore be it

RESOLVED, That the General Court of Massachusetts strongly urges the Congress of the United States and the leaders therein of the Democratic and Republican parties to lend their strongest efforts for the enactment of legislation to end such discrimination, and to liberalize said law by removing therefrom in the definition of "eligible displaced person" the restrictive admittance date of December twenty-second, nineteen hundred and forty-five, and by removing the preference granted to those eligible displaced persons who have previously been engaged in agricultural pursuits; and be it further

RESOLVED, That copies of these resolutions be sent forthwith by the state secretary to the President of the United States, to the presiding officer of each branch of Congress and to the members thereof from this Commonwealth.

In House of Representatives, adopted, March 10, 1949

LAWRENCE R. GROVE, Clerk

In Senate, adopted, in concurrence, March 16, 1949

IRVING N. HAYDEN, Clerk

A true copy. Attest:

EDWARD J. CRONIN (Signed)
Secretary of the Commonwealth

Civil Rights — Ch. 272

§92.A. [1948 Cum. Supp.] Places of Accommodation or Resort Not to Discriminate Because of Sect, Creed, Class, Race, Color or Nationality. — No owner, lessee, proprietor, manager, superintendent, agent or employee of any place of public accommodation, resort or amusement shall, directly or indirectly, by himself or another, publish, issue, circulate, distribute, or display, or cause to be published, issued, circulated distributed or displayed, in any way, any advertisement, circular, folder, book, pamphlet, written, or painted or printed notice or sign, of any kind or description, intended to discriminate against or actually discriminating against persons of any religious sect, creed, class, race, color, denomination or nationality, in the full enjoyment of the accommodations, advantages, facilities or privileges offered to the general public by such places of public accommodation, resort or amusement; provided, that nothing herein contained shall be construed to prohibit the mailing to any person of a private communication in writing, in response to his specific written inquiry.

A place of public accommodation, resort or amusement within the meaning hereof shall be defined as and shall be deemed to include any inn, whether conducted for the entertainment, housing or lodging of transient guests, or for the benefit, use or accommodation of those seeking health, recreation or rest, any restaurant, eating house, public conveyance on land or water or in the air, bathhouse, barber shop, theatre, and music hall.

Any person who shall violate any provision of this section, or who shall aid in or incite, cause or bring about, in whole or in part, such a violation shall be punished by a fine of not more than one hundred [$100] dollars, or by imprisonment for not more than thirty [30] days, or both. [1933, 117, Appvd. April 6, 1933.]

§98. [1948 Cum. Supp.] Color or Race Discrimination. — Whoever makes any distinction, discrimination or restriction on account of color or race, except for good cause applicable alike to all persons of every color and race, relative to the admission of any person to, or his treatment in, a theatre, skating rink, or other public place of amusement, licensed or unlicensed, or in a public conveyance or public meeting, or in an inn, barber shop or other public place kept for hire, gain or reward, licensed or unlicensed, or whoever aids or incites such distinction, discrimination, or restriction, shall be punished by a fine of not more than three hundred [$300.00] dollars or by imprisonment for not more than one [1] year, or both, and shall forfeit to any person aggrieved thereby not less than one hundred [$100.00] nor more than five hundred [$500.00] dollars; but such person so aggrieved shall not recover against more than one person by reason of any one act of distinction, discrimination or restriction. [1865, 277; 1866, 252; P.S. 207, §69; 1885, 316; 1893, 436; 1895. 461; R.L. 212, §89; 1934, 138, appvd. April 6, 1934.]

Sec. 98B. [1948 Cum. Supp.] **Discrimination in Employment on Public Works and in Dispensing of Public Welfare Because of Race, Color, Religion or Nationality.** — Whoever, knowingly, and wilfully, employs discriminatory practices in the administration of giving of employment on public works or projects, or in the dispensing or giving of public relief or public welfare or any public benefit, because of race, color, religion or nationality, shall be punished by a fine of not more than one hundred [$100.00] dollars. [1941, 170, appvd. April 9, 1941.]

Sec. 98C. [1948 Cum. Supp.] **Libel of Groups of Persons because of Race, Color or Religion.** — Whoever publishes any false written or printed material with intent to maliciously promote hatred of any group of persons in the commonwealth because of race, color or religion shall be guilty of libel and shall be punished by a fine of not more than one thousand [$1000.00] dollars or by imprisonment for not more than one [1] year, or both. The defendant may prove in defense that the publication was privileged or was not malicious. Prosecutions under this section shall be instituted only by the attorney general or by the district attorney for the district in which the alleged libel was published. [1943, 222, appvd. April 30, 1943.]

Defamation

See under Civil Rights above.

Discriminatory Publication

See under Civil Rights above.

Education

FAIR EDUCATIONAL PRACTICES
ACTS 1949, CH. 726
[House Bill No. 2721]

AN ACT to secure fair educational practices, equality of educational opportunity, and to eliminate and prevent discrimination in education because of race, religion, color or national origin.

Be it enacted by the Senate and House of Representatives in General Court assembled, and by the authority of the same, as follows:

SECTION 1. *Declaration of Policy.* — It is hereby declared to be the policy of the commonwealth that the American ideal of equality of opportunity requires that students, otherwise qualified, be admitted to educational institutions without regard to race, color, religion, creed or national origin, except that, with regard to religious or denominational educational institutions, students, otherwise qualified, shall have the equal opportunity to attend therein without discrimination because of race, color, or national

214

origin. It is a fundamental American right for members of various religious faiths to establish and maintain educational institutions exclusively or primarily for students of their own religious faith or to effectuate the religious principles in furtherance of which they are maintained. Nothing contained in this act shall impair or abridge that right.

SECTION 2. The General Laws are hereby amended by inserting after chapter 151B the following new chapter:-

CHAPTER 151C.
FAIR EDUCATIONAL PRACTICES.

Section 1. As used in this chapter:-

(a) The word "board" means the board of education established by section one A of chapter fifteen.

(b) The term "educational institution" means any institution for instruction or training, including but not limited to secretarial, business, vocational, trade schools, academies, colleges, universities, primary and secondary schools, which accepts applications for admission from the public generally and which is not in its nature distinctly private, except that nothing herein shall be deemed to prevent a religious or denominational educational institution from selecting its students exclusively from adherents or members of such religion or denomination or from giving preference in such selection to such adherents or members.

(c) The term "religious or denominational educational institution" shall include any educational institution, whether operated separately, or as a department of, or school within the university, and which is operated, supervised or controlled by religious or denominational organizations, or in which the courses of instruction lead primarily to the degree of bachelor, master or doctor of theology, and which has so certified to the board that it is so operated, supervised or controlled.

Section 2. It shall be an unfair educational practice for an educational institution:-

(a) To exclude or limit or otherwise discriminate against any United States citizen or citizens seeking admission as students to such institution because of race, religion, creed, color or national origin.

(b) To penalize any of its employees or students or any applicant for admission because he has testified, participated or assisted in any proceeding under this section.

(c) To cause to be made any written or oral inquiry concerning the race, religion, color or national origin of a person seeking admission, except that a religious or denominational educational institution which certified to the board that it is a religious or denominational educational institution may inquire as to the religious or denominational affiliations of applicants for admission. This section is not intended to limit or prevent an educational institution from using any criteria other than race, religion, color or national origin in the admission of students.

Section 3. (a) Any person seeking admission as a student, who claims to be aggrieved by an alleged unfair educational practice, hereinafter referred to as the petitioner, may himself, or by his parent or guardian, make, sign and file with the board a verified petition which shall set forth the particulars thereof and contain such other information as may be required by the board. The board shall thereupon make an investigation in connection therewith; and after such investigation, if the board shall determine that probable cause exists for crediting the allegations of the petition, it shall attempt by informal methods of persuasion, conciliation or mediation to induce the elimination of such unfair educational practice.

(b) Where the board has reason to believe that an applicant or applicants have been discriminated against, except that preferential selection by religious or denominational institutions of students on the grounds of religious or denominational affiliations shall not be considered an act of discrimination, the board may on its own motion make an investigation.

(c) The board shall not disclose what takes place during such informal efforts at persuasion, conciliation or mediation, and there shall not be offered in evidence in any proceeding the facts adduced in such informal efforts.

(d) A petition pursuant to this section must be filed with the board within six months after the alleged unfair educational practice was committed.

(e) If such informal methods fail to induce the elimination of the alleged unfair educational practice, the board may issue and cause to be served upon such institution, hereinafter called the respondent, a complaint setting forth the alleged unfair educational practice charged and a notice of hearing before the board, at a place therein fixed, to be held not less than twenty days after the service of said complaint. Any complaint issued pursuant to this section must be issued within one year after the alleged unfair educational practice was committed.

(f) The respondent shall have the right to answer the original and any amended complaint, and to appear at such hearing by counsel, present evidence and examine and cross-examine witnesses.

(g) The board shall have the power to subpoena witnesses, compel their attendance, administer oaths, take testimony under oath and require the production of evidence relating to the matter in question before it. The testimony taken at the hearing, which shall be public, shall be under oath and shall be reduced to writing and filed with the board.

(h) After the hearing is completed, the board shall file an intermediate report which shall contain its finding of fact and conclusions upon the issues in the proceeding. A copy of such report shall be served on the parties to the proceeding. Any such party, within twenty days thereafter, may file with the board exceptions to the findings of fact and conclusions, with a brief in support thereof, or may file a brief in support of such findings of fact and conclusions.

(i) If, upon all the evidence, the board shall determine that the respondent has engaged in an unfair educational practice, the board shall state its findings of fact and conclusions, and shall issue and cause to be served upon such respondent a copy of such findings and conclusions and an order requiring the respondent to cease and desist from such unfair educational practice, or such other order as it may deem just and proper.

(j) If, upon all the evidence, the board shall find that a respondent has not engaged in any unfair educational practice, the board shall state its findings of fact and conclusions and shall issue and cause to be served on the petitioner and respondent a copy of such findings and conclusions and an order dismissing the complaint as to such respondent.

Section 4. (a) Any party aggrieved by a final order of the board may obtain a judicial review thereof, and the board may obtain an order of the court for the enforcement thereof by a proceeding described in this section. Such proceeding shall be brought in the superior court within the county wherein any respondent is located.

(b) Upon the filing of a bill of complaint and the service of said bill, the court shall have equitable jurisdiction of the proceeding and of all the questions determined therein. Thereupon the board shall file with the court a transcript of the record of the hearing. The court after hearing and argument shall have power to make and enter upon such record and order annulling or confirming wholly or partly; or modifying the determination reviewed, as to any or all of the parties, and directing appropriate action by any party to the proceeding.

(c) The findings of the board as to the facts shall be conclusive if supported by evidence on the record considered as a whole.

(d) The jurisdiction of the superior court shall be exclusive and its judgment and order shall be final, subject to review by the supreme judicial court, upon appeal by the board or any party to the proceedings, in the same manner provided by general law for appeal from the equity jurisdiction of the superior court.

Section 5. The board shall have the power, after public hearing, to adopt, promulgate, amend or rescind rules and regulations concerning proceedings at hearings and other investigations under this chapter, which rules and regulations shall be not inconsistent with the provisions of said chapter.

Approved August 22, 1949.

Employment — Fair Employment Practices

Ch. 6, §17. Certain Officers to Serve Under Governor and Council. — [This section was amended by Laws 1946, Ch: 368, §2 to include among the various commissions and boards serving under and subject to the supervision of the governor and council the Massachusetts fair employment practice commission.] [1945, 393, §1, as amended 1946, §2, appvd. May 23, 1946; 612, §1, appvd. June 15, 1946, and 1948 amendments.]

Ch. 6, §56. Fair Employment Practice Commission. — There shall be a commission to be known as the Massachusetts Fair Employment Practice Commission. Such commission shall consist of three members, to be known as commissioners, who shall be appointed by the governor, by and with the advice and consent of the council, and one of whom shall be designated as chairman by the governor. The term of office of each member of the commission shall be for three years, provided, however, that of the commissioners first appointed, one shall be appointed for a term of one year, one for a term of two years one for a term of three years. Any member chosen to fill a vacancy occurring otherwise than by expiration of term shall be appointed for the unexpired term of the member whom he is to succeed. Two members of the commission shall constitute a quorum for the purpose of conducting the business thereof. A single vacancy in the commission shall not impair the right of the remaining members to exercise all the powers of the commission.

The chairman of the commission shall receive a salary of five thousand dollars per year, and each of the other members shall receive a salary of four thousand dollars per year, and each member shall also be entitled to his expenses actually and necessarily incurred by him in the performance of his duties, and shall be eligible for reappointment. Any member may be removed by the governor, with the consent of the council, for inefficiency, neglect of duty, misconduct or malfeasance in office, after being given a written statement of the charges and an opportunity to be heard thereon.

All employees of the commission, except an executive secretary, the heads of divisions, and attorneys, shall be subject to chapter thirty-one and the rules and regulations made thereunder. [1946, 368, §3, appvd. May 23, 1946; 1948, 411, appvd. May 27, 1948, effective 90 days thereafter.]

[Note: Laws 1946, Ch. 368 was entitled "An Act Providing for a Fair Employment Practice Law and Establishing a Commission, to be known as the Massachusetts Fair Employment Practice Commission, and Defining its Powers and Duties."

§1 of the Act provided: "The right to work without discrimination because of race, color, religious creed, national origin or ancestry is hereby declared to be a right and privilege of the inhabitants of the commonwealth." This section has not been included in the codified act as it appears in Chapter 151B.]

CHAPTER 151B [1948 Cum. Supp.]

Unlawful Discrimination Against Race, Color, Religious Creed, National Origin or Ancestry.

§1. Definitions. — As used in this chapter:

1. The term "person" includes one or more individuals, partnerships, associations, corporations, legal representatives, trustees, trustees in bankruptcy, receivers, and the commonwealth and all political subdivisions, boards, and commissions thereof.

2. The term "employment agency" includes any person undertaking to procure employees or opportunities to work.

3. The term "labor organization" includes any organization which exists and is constituted for the purpose, in whole or in part, of collective bargaining or of dealing with employers concerning grievances, terms or

conditions of employment, or of other mutual aid or protection in connection with employment.

4. The term "unlawful employment practice" includes only those unlawful employment practices specified in section four.

5. The term "employer" does not include a club exclusively social, or a fraternal, charitable, educational or religious association or corporation, if such club, association or corporation is not organized for private profit, nor does it include any employer with fewer than six persons in his employ, but shall include the commonwealth and all political subdivisions, boards, departments, and commissions thereof.

6. The term "employee" does not include any individual employed by his parents, spouse or child, or in the domestic service of any person.

7. The term "commission", unless a different meaning clearly appears from the context, means the Massachusetts fair employment practice commission created by section fifty-six of chapter six. [1946, 368, §4, appvd, May 23, 1946.]

§2. Commission to Formulate Policies and Make Recommendations. — The commission, as established by section fifty-six of chapter six, shall formulate policies to effectuate the purposes of this chapter and may make recommendations to agencies and officers of the commonwealth or its political subdivisions in aid of such policies and purposes. [1946, 368, §4, appvd. May 23, 1946.]

§3. Functions, Powers and Duties of Commission. — The commission shall have the following functions, powers and duties:

1. To establish and maintain its principal office in the city of Boston, and such other offices within the commonwealth as it may deem necessary.

2. To meet and function at any place within the commonwealth.

3. To appoint such attorneys, clerks, and other employees and agents as it may deem necessary, fix their compensation within the limitations provided by law, and prescribe their duties.

4. To obtain upon request and utilize the services of all executive departments and agencies.

5. To adopt, promulgate, amend, and rescind rules and regulations suitable to carry out the provisions of this chapter, and the policies and practice of the commission in connection therewith.

6. To receive, investigate and pass upon complaints alleging discrimination in employment because of race, color, religious creed, national origin, or ancestry.

7. To hold hearings, subpoena witnesses, compel their attendance, administer oaths, take the testimony of any person under oath, and in connection therewith, to require the production for examination of any books or papers relating to any matter under investigation or in question before the commission. The commission may make rules as to the issuance of subpoenas by individual commissioners.

No person shall be excused from attending and testifying or from producing books, records, correspondence, documents or other evidence in obedience to the subpoena of the commission, on the ground that the testimony or evidence required of him may tend to incriminate him or subject him to a penalty or forfeiture; but no individual shall be prosecuted or subjected to any penalty or forfeiture for or on account of any transaction, matter or thing concerning which he is compelled, after having claimed his privilege against self-incrimination, to testify or produce evidence, except that such individual so testifying shall not be exempt from prosecution and punishment for perjury committed in so testifying.

8. To create such advisory agencies and conciliation councils, local regional or state-wide, as in its judgment will aid in effectuating the purposes of this chapter, and the commission may empower them to study the problems of discrimination in all or specific fields of human relationships or in specific instances of discrimination, because of race, color, religious creed, national origin, or ancestry, in order to foster, through community effort or otherwise, good will, co-operation and conciliation among the groups and elements of the population of the commonwealth, and make recommendations to the commission for the development of policies and procedures in general and in specific instances, and for programs of formal and informal education which the commission may recommend to the appropriate state agency. Such advisory agencies and conciliation councils shall be composed of representative citizens, serving without pay, but with reimbursement for actual and necessary traveling expenses; and the commission may make provision for technical and clerical assistance to such agencies and councils and for the expenses of such assistance.

9. To issue such publications and such results of investigations and research as in its judgment will tend to promote good will and minimize or eliminate discrimination because of race, color, religious creed, national origin or ancestry.

10. To render each year to the governor and to the general court a full written report of its activities and of its recommendations.

11. To adopt an official seal. [1946, 368, §4, appvd. May 23, 1946.]

§4. Unlawful Employment Practices. — It shall be an unlawful employment practice:

1. For an employer, by himself or his agent, because of the race color, religious creed, national origin, or ancestry of any individual, to refuse to hire or employ or to bar or to discharge from employment such individual or to discriminate against such individual in compensation or in terms, conditions or privileges of employment, unless based upon a bona fide occupational qualification.

2. For a labor organization, because of the race, color, religious creed, national origin, or ancestry of any individual to exclude from full membership rights or to expel from its membership such individual or to discriminate in any way against any of its members or against any employer or any individual employed by an employer, unless based upon a bona fide occupational qualification.

3. For any employer or employment agency to print or circulate or cause to be printed or circulated any statement, advertisement or publication, or to use any form of application for employment or to make any inquiry or record in connection with employment, which expresses, directly or indirectly, any limitation, specification or discrimination as to race, color, religious creed, national origin or ancestry or any intent to make any such limitation, specification or discrimination, or to discriminate in any way on the ground of race, color, religious creed, national origin or ancestry, unless based upon a bona fide occupational qualification.

4. For any person, employer, labor organization or employment agency to discharge, expel or otherwise discriminate against any person because he has opposed any practices forbidden under this chapter or because he has filed a complaint, testified or assisted in any proceeding under section five.

5. For any person, whether an employer or an employee or not, to aid, abet, incite, compel or coerce the doing of any of the acts forbidden under this chapter or to attempt to do so.

Notwithstanding the foregoing provisions of this section, it shall not be an unlawful employment practice for any person, employer, labor organization or employment agency to inquire of an applicant or membership as to whether or not he or she is a veteran or a citizen. [1946, 368, §4, appvd. May 23, 1946; 1947, 424, appvd. May 20, 1947.]

§5. Complaint Alleging Unlawful Employment Practice; Proceedings before Commission. — Any person claiming to be aggrieved by an alleged unlawful employment practice may, by himself or his attorney, make, sign and file with the commission a verified complaint in writing which shall state the name and address of the person, employer, labor organization or employment agency alleged to have committed the unlawful employment practice complained of and which shall set forth the particulars thereof and contain such other information as may be required by the commission. The attorney general may, in like manner, make, sign and file such complaint. The commission, whenever it has reason to believe that any person has been or is engaging in an unlawful employment practice, may issue such complaint. Any employer whose employees, or some of them, refuse or threaten to refuse to co-operate with the provisions of this chapter, may file with the commission a verified complaint asking for assistance by conciliation or other remedial action.

After the filing of any complaint, the chairman of the commission shall designate one of the commissioners to make, with the assistance of the commission's staff, prompt investigation in connection therewith; and if such commissioner shall determine after such investigation that probable cause exists for crediting the allegations of the complaint, he shall immediately endeavor to eliminate the unlawful employment practice complained of by conference, conciliation and persuasion. The members of the commission and its staff shall not disclose what has occurred in the course of such endeavors, provided that the commission may publish the facts in the case of any complaint which has been dismissed, and the terms of conciliation when the complaint has been disposed of. In case of failure so to eliminate such practice, or in advance thereof if in his judgment circumstances so warrant, he may cause to be issued and served in the name of the commission, a written notice, together with a copy of such complaint, as the same may have been amended, requiring the person, employer, labor organization or employment agency named in such complaint, hereinafter referred to as respondent, to answer the charges of such complaint at a hearing before the commission, at a time and place to be specified in such notice. The place of any such hearing shall be the office of the commission or such other place as may be designated by it. The case in support of the complaint shall be presented before the commission by one of its attorneys or agents, and the commissioner who shall have previously made the investigation and caused the notice to be issued shall not participate in the hearing except as a witness, nor shall he participate in the deliberations of the commission in such case; and the aforesaid endeavors at conciliation shall not be received in evidence. The respondent may file a written verified answer to the complaint and appear at such hearing in person or otherwise, with or without counsel, and submit testimony. In the discretion of the commission, the complainant may be allowed to intervene and present testimony in person or by counsel. The commission or the complainant shall have the power reasonably and fairly to amend any complaint, and the respondent shall have like power to amend his answer. The commission shall not be bound by the strict rules of evidence prevailing in courts of law or equity. The testimony taken at the hearing shall be under oath and be transcribed at the request of any party. If, upon all the evidence at the hearing the commission shall find that a respondent has engaged in any unlawful employment practice as defined in section four, the commission shall state its findings of fact and shall issue and cause to be served on such respondent an order requiring such respondent to cease and desist from such unlawful employment practice and to take such affirmative action, including (but not limited to) hiring, reinstatement or upgrading of employees, with or without back pay, or restoration to membership in any respondent labor organization, as, in the judgment of the commission, will effectuate the purposes of this chapter, and including a requirement for report of the manner of compliance. If, upon all the evidence, the commission shall find that a respondent has not engaged in any such unlawful employment practice, the commission shall state its findings of fact and shall issue and cause to be served on the complainant an order dismissing the said complaint as to such respondent. A copy of its order shall be delivered in all cases to the attorney general and such other public officers as the commission deems proper. The commission shall establish rules of practice to govern, expedite and effectuate the foregoing procedure and its own actions thereunder. Any complaint filed pursuant to this section must be so filed within six months after the alleged act of discrimination. [1946, 368, §4, appvd. May 23, 1946.]

§6. Judicial Review of Order of Commission. — Any complainant, respondent or other person aggrieved by such order of the commission may obtain judicial review thereof, and the commission may obtain an order of court for its enforcement, in a proceeding as provided in this section. Such proceeding shall be brought in the superior court of the commonwealth within any county wherein the unlawful employment practice which is the subject of the commission's order occurs or wherein any person required in the order to cease and desist from an unlawful employment practice or to take other affirmative action resides or transacts business. such proceedings shall be initiated by the filing of a petition in such court, together with a written transcript of the record upon the hearing before the commission, and issuance and service of an order of notice as in proceedings in equity. The court shall have power to grant such temporary relief or restraining order as it deems just and proper, and to make and enter upon the pleadings, testimony and proceedings set forth in such transcript an order or decree enforcing, modifying, and enforcing as so modified, or setting aside in whole or in part the order of the commission with full power to issue injunctions against any respondent and to punish for contempt hereof. No objection that has not been urged before the commission shall be considered by the court, unless the failure or neglect to urge such objection shall be excused because of extraordinary circumstances. Any party may move the court to remit the case to the commission in the interests of justice for the purpose of adducing additional specified and material evidence and seeking findings thereon, provided he shows reasonable grounds for the failure to adduce such evidence before the commission. The findings of the commission as to the facts shall be conclusive if supported by sufficient evidence on the record considered as a whole. All such proceedings shall be heard and determined by the court as expeditiously as possible and shall take precedence over all other matters before it, except matters of like nature. The jurisdiction of the superior court shall be exclusive and its final order or decree shall be subject to review by the supreme judicial court in the same manner and form and with the same effect as in appeals from a final order or decree in proceedings in equity. The commission's copy of the testimony shall be available at all reasonable times to all parties for examination without cost and for the purposes of judicial review of the order of the commission. The review shall be heard on the record without requirement of printing. The commission may appear in court by one of its attorneys. A proceeding under this section when instituted by any complainant, respondent or other person aggrieved must be instituted within thirty days after the service of the order of the commission. [1946, 368, §4, appvd. May 23, 1946.]

§7. Posting Notices Setting Forth Excerpts of Chapter and Relevant Information; Penalty. — Every employer, employment agency and labor union subject to this act, shall post in a conspicuous place or places on his premises a notice to be prepared or approved by the commission, which shall set forth excerpts of this chapter and such other relevant information which the commission deems necessary to explain the act. Any employer, employment agency or labor union refusing to comply with the provisions of this section shall be punished by a fine of not less than ten dollars nor more than one hundred dollars [1946, 368, §4, appvd. May 23, 1946.]

§8. Penalty for Interfering with Commission, etc., Violating Final Order or Filing False Complaint. — Any person, employer, labor organization or employment agency, who or which shall wilfully resist, prevent, impede or interfere with the commission or any of its members or representatives in the performance of duty under its chapter, or shall wilfully violate a final order of the commission, or who shall wilfully file a false complaint shall be punished for each offense by imprisonment for not more than one year, or by a fine of not more than five hundred dollars, or by both; but procedure for the review of the order shall not be deemed to be such wilful conduct. [1946, 368, §4, appvd. May 23, 1946.]

§9. Chapter Construed Liberally; Inconsistent Laws; Procedure Exclusive. — The provisions of this chapter shall be construed liberally for the accomplishment of the purposes thereof, and any law inconsistent with any provision hereof shall not apply, but nothing contained in this chapter shall be deemed to repeal section ninety-eight of chapter two hundred and seventy-two or any other law of this commonwealth relating to discrimination because of race, color, religious creed, national origin, or ancestry; but, as to acts declared unlawful by section four, the procedure provided in this chapter shall, while pending, be exclusive; and the final determination therein shall exclude any other action, civil or criminal, based on the same grievance of the individual concerned. If such individual institutes any action based on such grievance without resorting to the procedure provided in this chapter, he may not subsequently resort to the procedure herein. [1946, 368, §4, appvd. May 23, 1946.]

§10. Invalidity in Part. — If any provision of this chapter or the application thereof to any person or circumstance, shall, for any reason, be held invalid, the remainder of this chapter or the application of such provision to persons or circumstances other than those as to which it is held invalid shall not be affected thereby. [1946, 368, §4, appvd. May 23, 1946.]

Housing

Low Rent Housing Projects — (Housing Authority Law)

Ch. 121, §26FF [1948 Cum. Supp.] — Maintenance and Operation; Tenant Selection; Rentals.— . . . (e) There shall be no discrimination; provided, that it the number of qualified applicants for dwelling accommodations exceeds the dwelling units available, preference shall be given to inhabitants of the city or town in which the project is located, and to the families who occcupied the dwellings eliminated by demolition, condemnation and effective closing as part of the project as far as is reasonably practicable without discrimination against persons living in other sub-standard areas within the same city or town. For all purposes of this chapter, no person shall, because of race, color, creed or religion, be subjected to any discrimination . . . [1946, 574, §1; 1948, 51, appvd. Feb. 11, 1948, effective 90 days thereafter.]

Innkeepers and Victuallers

Ch. 140, §5. Innholders, etc. to Have Suitable Accommodations for Travelers. — Every innholder and every common victualler shall at all times be provided with suitable food for strangers and travelers. Every innholder shall also have upon his premises suitable rooms, with beds and bedding, for the lodging of his guests. [C.L. 82, §10; 1698, 10, §1; 1786, 68, §3; 1832, 166, §10; R.S. 47, §5; G.S. 88, §8; 1878, 241, §§1, 2; P.S. 102, §§5, 6; R.L. 102, §5; 1931, 426, §35.]

Ch. 140, §7. Penalty for Refusing to Receive a Stranger. — Any innholder, who, upon request, refuses to receive and make suitable provision for a stranger or traveler shall be punished by a fine of not more than fifty [$50.00] dollars. [C.L. 82, §10; 1710-11, 11, §4; 1786, 68, §3; 1832, 166, §10; R.S. 47, §8; G. S. 88, §9; 1878, 241, §5; P.S. 102, §9; R.L. 102, §7; 1931, 426, §37.]

Ch. 140, §8. [1948 Cum. Supp.] Penalty for Refusing Food to a Stranger.— A common victualler who, upon request, on any day but Sunday, or on any day if he holds a license to sell alcoholic beverages on Sundays, refuses to supply food to a stranger or traveler shal be punished by a fine of not more than fifty [$50.00] dollars; provided, that nothing in this chapter shall be construed to permit or require a common victualler, who holds a license to keep a tavern under chapter one hundred and thirty-eight [Ch. 138] to admit a woman as a patron in such tavern. [1878, 241, §6; P.S. 102, §10; R.L. 102, §8; 1936, 368, §14, appvd. June 19, 1936, as amended 1943, 328, appvd. May 25, 1943.]

> [Note: The three statutes above are included in this compilation because, while making no reference to race or color, it has been held by the Supreme Judicial Court of Massachusetts that holders of licenses as common victuallers under these statutes are required on all secular days to supply food to a stranger or traveler without discrimination as to race or color. See *Liggett Drug Co. v. Board of License Com'rs.*, (1936) 296 Mass. 41, 4 N. E. (2d) 628, 635. This interpretation of Ch. 140, §8 was made by the court before the 1943 amendment which inserted the words "or on any day if he holds a license to sell alcoholic beverages on Sundays".]

Insurance

Ch. 175, §122. Discrimination on Account of Color Prohibited; Penalty. — No life insurance company shall make any distinction or discrimination between white persons and colored persons wholly or partly of African descent as to the premiums or rates charged for policies upon the lives of such persons, nor shall any such company demand or require greater premiums from such colored persons than are at that time required by such company from white persons of the same age, sex, general condition of health and prospect of longevity; nor shall any such company make or require any rebate, diminution or discount upon the amount to be paid on such policy in case of the death of such colored person insured, nor insert in the policy any condition, nor make any stipulation whereby such person insured shall bind himself or his heirs, executors, administrators or assigns to accept any amount less than the full value or amount of such policy in case of a claim accruing thereon, by reason of the death of such person insured, other than such as are imposed upon white persons in similar cases; and any such stipulation or condition so made or inserted shall be void.

Any such company which shall refuse the application of any such colored person for insurance upon such person's life shall furnish such person, on his request therefor, with the certificate of a regular examining physician of such company who made the examination, stating that the refusal was not because such applicant is a person of color, but solely on such grounds of the general health and prospect of longevity of such person as would be applicable to white persons of the same age and sex.

A company or an officer or agent thereof who violates any provision hereof shall be punished by a fine of not more than one hundred [$100.00] dollars. [1884, 235; 1887, 214, §§69, 109; 1894, 522, §§69, 109; R.L. 118, §§69, 109; 1907, 576, §§70, 118, 122.]

Military

Ch. 33, §1A. [1949 Cum. Supp.] — Discrimination, Segregation, etc., Because of Race, etc., Forbidden. — No person shall be denied the enjoyment of any military right, or be discriminated against in the exercise of any military right, or be segregated in such militia, land forces or naval forces, because of race, color or national origin. [Added by Laws 1949, ch. 398, §1, appvd. June 7, 1949.]

[Note: Section 2 of Laws 1949, ch. 398 provides that the act shall take effect on March 31st, 1950.]

Public Accommodation

See under Civil Rights above.

Public Relief, Public Works

See under Civil Rights above.

Public Utilities

Ch. 149, §43. Equal Opportunity of Certain Employment for All Citizens. — The application of a citizen of the commonwealth for employment in any department of the commonwealth or of any political subdivision thereof or in any department of a street railway company operated, owned, controlled or financially aided in any way by the commonwealth, or by any political subdivision thereof, shall not be affected by the applicant's national origin, race or color. [1920, 376.]

MICHIGAN

CONSTITUTION

Civil Service

[By amendment approved at Nov. 5, 1940, election, Art. VI, §22 on Civil Service was added to the Michigan Constitution of 1908. The section contained the following clause:

. . . "No removals from or demotions in the State civil service shall be made for partisan, racial or religious considerations."]

Electors

[In the Michigan Constitution of 1835 qualified electors were limited to "white male citizens" (Art. II, §1.). The word "white" was eliminated in the Constitution of 1850 (Art. VII, §1.).]

Slavery

Art. II, §8. Slavery prohibited. — Neither slavery nor involuntary servitude, unless for the punishment of crime shall ever be tolerated in this state. [Const. 1850, Art. XVIII, §11; Const. 1908, Art. II, §8.]

STATUTES

MICHIGAN COMPILED LAWS 1948

Civil Rights

750.146. **Civil Rights, equal accommodations, etc., at restaurants, etc.—Sec. 146.**—All persons within the jurisdiction of this State shall be entitled to full and equal accommodations, advantages, facilities and privileges of inns, hotels, restaurants, eating houses, barber shops, billiard parlors, stores, public conveyances on land and water, theatres, motion picture houses, public educational institutions, in elevators, on escalators, in all methods of air transportation and all other places of public accommodation, amusement, and recreation, where refreshments are or may hereafter be served, subject only to the conditions and limitations established by law and applicable alike to all citizens and to all citizens alike, with uniform prices. [As Am. 1937, Act. 117, p. 185 Eff. Oct. 29. Reenactment of §1 of Act 130 of 1885; C.L. 1897, 11759; C.L. 1915, 15570; Am. 1919, p. 657, Act. 375, eff. Aug. 14; C.L. 1929, 16809.]

750.147 **Same; Penalty.—Sec. 147.**—Any person being an owner, lessee, proprietor, manager, superintendent, agent or employe of any such place who shall directly or indirectly refuse, withhold from or deny to any person any of the accommodations, advantages, facilities and privileges thereof or directly or indirectly publish, circulate, issue, display, post or mail any written or printed communications, notice or advertisement to the effect that any of the accommodations, advantages, facilities and privileges of any such places shall be refused, withheld from or denied to any person on account of race, creed or color or that any particular race, creed or color is not welcome, objectionable or not acceptable, not desired or solicited, shall for every such offense be deemed guilty of a'misdemeanor and upon conviction thereof shall be fined not less than 25 [$25.00] dollars or imprisoned for not less than 15 days or both such fine and imprisonment in the discretion of the court; and every person being an owner, lessee, proprietor, manager, superintendent, agent or employee of any such place, and who violates any of the provisions of this section, shall be liable to the injured party, in treble the damages sustained, to be recovered in a civil action: Provided, however, that any right of action under this section shall be unassignable. [Act 130 of 1885, §2, as superceded and amended 1937, Act. 117, Eff. Oct. 29.]

750.148. Same; race or color not to disqualify for jury service. — Sec. 148. — No citizen of the state of Michigan, possessing all other qualifications which are or may be prescribed by law, shall be disqualified to serve as grand or petit juror in any court of said state on account of race, creed or color, and any officer or other person charged with any duty in the drawing, summoning, and selection of persons who shall exclude from, fail, neglect and/or refuse, by words, trick and/or artifice, to draw the name of, summon and/or select any citizen for jury service because of his or her race, creed and/or color, shall be guilty of a misdemeanor and upon conviction shall be fined not less than 50 [$50.00] dollars or shall be imprisoned for a period of not less than 30 days, or both such fine and imprisonment in the discretion of the court. [Act 130 of 1885, §3, as superceded and amended 1937, Act. 117, Eff. Oct. 29.]

Civil Service

38.424. Discrimination prohibited. — Sec. 24. — No person in the classified civil service or seeking admission thereto, shall be appointed, reduced or removed, or in any way favored or discriminated against because of his political, racial or religious opinions or affiliations, except for membership in any organization which has advocated or does advocate disloyalty to the government of the United States or any subdivision thereof. [Act 370, 1941, p. 711, Eff. Jan. 10, 1942.]

Education

344.26. School term; discrimination. — Sec. 26. — . . . (1) All persons, residents of any township school district and 5 years of age, shall have an equal right to attend any school therein, and no separate school or department shall be kept for any person on account of race or color . . . [C.L. 1929, 7156.]

352.9. Persons attending school; discrimination. — Sec. 9. — All persons residents of any school district, and 5 years of age, shall have an equal right to attend any school therein; and no separate school or department shall be kept for any person on account of race or color: Provided, that this shall not be construed to prevent the grading of schools according to the intellectual progress of the pupil, to be taught in separate places as may be deemed expedient. [C.L. 1929, 7368.]

Indians

750.348. Inciting Indians. — Sec. 348. — Inciting Indians to violate treaty, etc. — Any person who shall incite, or attempt to incite any Indian nation, tribe, chief or individual to violate any treaty of peace with any other Indian nation, tribe, chief or individual to violate any treaty of peace with any other Indian nation or tribe, or with the United States, or to disturb the peace and tranquility existing between any Indian nation or tribe, and any other Indian nation or tribe, or the people of the United States, or who shall incite or attempt to incite any Indian nation, tribe, chief or individual to violate any law of the United States, or of this state, shall be guilty of a felony. [C. L. 1857, 5855; C.L. 1871, 7689; How. 9272; C.L. 1897, 11342; C.L. 1915, 15009; C.L. 1929, 16606.]

Insurance

522.30. Race discrimination; forfeiture, penalty. Sec. 30. — That no life insurance company doing business in this state shall make any distinction or discrimination between white persons and colored persons, wholly or partially of African descent, as to the premiums or rates charged for policies upon the lives of such persons, or in any manner whatever; nor shall any such company demand or require a greater premium from such colored persons than is at that time required by such company from white persons of the same age, sex, general condition of health and prospect of longevity; nor make or require any rebate, diminution or discount upon the amount to be paid on such policy in case of death of such colored person insured; nor insert in the policy any condition, nor make any stipulation whereby such person insured shall bind himself, his heirs, executors, administrators and assigns to accept any sum less than the full amount or value of such policy in case of a claim accruing thereon by reason of the death of such person insured, other than such as are imposed on white persons in similar cases; and any such stipulations or conditions so made or inserted shall be void. Any company which shall violate any of the provisions of this section shall forfeit to the state the sum of 500 dollars [$500.00] for each violation, to be recovered by the attorney general by appropriate action in any court of competent jurisdiction, and any judgment therefor may be collected in the same manner as is herein provided for collecting judgments rendered in favor of policy holders. And any officer or agent who shall violate any of the provisions of this section shall be deemed guilty of a misdemeanor, and upon conviction thereof shall be punished by imprisonment in the county jail not exceeding 1 year, or by fine of not less than 50 [$50.00] dollars and not exceeding 500 dollars [$500.00], or by both such fine and imprisonment, in the discretion of the court. fflAct 77 of 1869, §32, as amended 1893, p. 60, reen., C.L. 1897, 7220; C.L. 1915, 9354, C.L. 1929, 12457.]

[Note: For action for forfeiture, see Compiled Laws, Michigan, 1948, §635.1, et. seq.]

Ku Klux Klan — Masks and Disguises

750.396. Wearing masks or face coverings in public. — Sec. 396. Wearing masks or face coverings in public. — Any person who shall assemble, march or parade on any street, highway or public place in this state while wearing a mask or covering which conceals in whole or in part, the face of the wearer, shall be guilty of a misdemeanor: Provided, This chapter shall not apply to the pranks of children on Hallowe'en, to those going to and from masquerade parties, to those participating in any public parade of an educational, religious or historical character and to those participating in the parades of minstrel troupes, circuses, or other amusement or dramatic shows. [C. L. 1929, 16609; C.L. 1929, 16610.]

Miscegenation

551.6. Legalization of white-African marriages. — . . . Sec. 6 — . . . All marriages heretofore contracted between white persons and those wholly or in part of African descent are hereby declared valid and effectual in law for all purposes; and the issues of such marriages shall be deemed and taken as legitimate as to such issue and as to both of the parents . . . [C.L. 1857, 3209; C.L. 1871, 4724; amended, 1883, p. 16, Act 23; C.L. 1929, 12695.] [Note: Prior to 1883, the above section prohibited and made void marriages between a Negro and a white person. The 1883 amendment eliminated the prohibition.]

MINNESOTA

CONSTITUTION

Slavery

Art. I, §2. — ... There shall be neither slavery nor involuntary servitude in the state otherwise than the punishment of crime, whereof the party shall have been duly convicted. [Minn. Const. 1857.]

Suffrage

Art. VII, §1. Elective franchise. — [Extended to (1) "citizens of the United States who have been such for the period of three (3) months next preceding any election," (2) "Persons of mixed white and Indian blood who have adopted the customs and habits of civilization," and (3) "Persons of Indian blood residing in this State, who have adopted the language, customs and habits of civilization, after an examination before any district court of the State, in such manner as may be provided by law, and shall have been pronounced by said court capable of enjoying the rights of citizenship within the State."] [Minn. Const. 1857, as amended Nov. 3, 1868; Nov. 3, 1896.]

> [Note: Negro voters were enfranchised by the amendment adopted Nov. 3, 1868, which eliminated the restriction of voting to "white" citizens and "white" persons as originally provided for in the Constitution of 1857.]

STATUTES

MINNESOTA STATUTES ANNOTATED (1946)

Aliens

[Note: §500.22 as amended April 13, 1945, c. 280, §1; L. 1947, ch. 153, §1.] provides for certain restriction upon the ownership of land by aliens who have failed to declare their intention to become citizens of the United States or by foreign corporations or by corporations more than 20 per cent of whose stock is owned by aliens. [Stat. 1927, §§8076-8080]. §5508 [Stat. 1927], Laws 1919, c. 400, §14, which prohibited the hunting of wild animals by aliens who had not declared intention to become citizens or who failed to effect citizenship within the necessary legal period after declaration, was repealed by Laws 1945, c. 248, §7. These statutes are directed against aliens generally and not against a particular racial group, hence they are not set forth in detail here.]

Beauticians

155.11. Schools of beauty culture. — ... (9) No school, duly approved under this chapter, shall refuse to teach any student, otherwise qualified, on on account of race, creed or color. [Laws 1943, c. 573, §3; Laws 1941, c. 490, §9; Laws 1933, c. 264, §3; St. 1927, §5846-36; Laws 1927, c. 245, §10.]

Education

Public Schools

126.07. Exclusion or Expulsion of Pupils. — Any member of any public school board or board of education of any district who, without

231

sufficient cause or on account of race, color, nationality, or social position, shall vote for, or being present, shall fail to vote against, the exclusion, expulsion, or suspension from school privileges of any person entitled to admission to the schools of such district, shall forfeit to the party aggrieved $50.00 for each such offense, to be recoverd in a civil action. [R.L. 1905, s. 1402; St. 1927, §2998 1941 c. 169 Art. 7, s. 7.]

126.08. Improper classification of pupils. — No district shall classify its pupils with reference to race, color, social position, or nationality, nor separate its pupils into different schools or departments upon any of such grounds. Any district so classifying or separating any of its pupils, or denying school privileges to any of its pupils upon any such ground shall forfeit its share in all apportioned school funds for any apportionment period in which such classification, separation, or exclusion shall occur or continue. The state commissioner of education, upon notice to the offending district and upon proof of the violation of the provisions of this section, shall withhold in the semiannual apportionment the share of such district and the county auditor shall thereupon exclude such district from his apportionment for such period. [R.L. 1905, §1403; St. 1927, §2999; 1941 c. 169, art. 7, §8.]

Housing — (Redevelopment Law)

MINN. LAWS, 1947, CH. 487
(Coded as Sections 462.411 to 462.711)

462.641. [1949 Cum. Supp.] — **Use of projects. —** . . . There shall be no discrimination in the use of projects, because of religious, political, or other affiliation . . . [L. 1947, ch. 487, §47.]

462.481. [1949 Cum. Supp.]—**Discrimnation prohibited; displaced families.** — . . . There shall be no discrimination in the selection of tenents because of religious, political, or other affiliations . . . [L. 1947, ch. 487, §15.]

[Note: Neither of the two above sections includes a prohibiiton against discrimination in redevelopment housing projects because of race or color.]

Indians

Intoxicating Liquors

340.73. [1949 Cum. Supp.] — **Persons to whom sales are illegal. —** Subdivision 1. It shall be unlawful for any person except a licensed pharmacist as aforesaid, to sell, give, barter, furnish or dispose of, in any manner, either directly or indirectly, any spirituous, vinous, malt or fermented liquors in any quantity, for any purpose, whatever, to any minor person, or to any pupil or student of any school or other educational institution in this state, or to any intoxicated person, or to any person of Indian blood who has not adopted the language, customs, and habits of civilization, or to any public prostitute . . . [L. 1861, c. 53, §1; R.L. '05, §1534; amended '11, c. 83; '13, c. 538, §1; St. 1927, §5238-4; as amended L. 1947, c. 87, §1.]

[Note: The 1947 amendment inserted the words "who has not adopted the language, customs, and habits of civilization."]

340.82. Sale, etc., to Indians. — Whoever sells or in any way furnishes liquor to any person of Indian blood, except as hereinbefore provided is guilty of a felony, and shall be punished by imprisonment in the state prison for not more than two [2] years, and a fine of not more than $300. [L. 1862, Ex. Sess., c. 11, §1; R.L. '05, §1560; G.S. '13, §3182; St. 1927, §3238-13, as amended L. 1947, c. 87, §2.]

Insurance

Automobile Insurance

72.17. Discrimination in policies and risks forbidden. — No insurance company, or its agent, shall refuse to issue any standard policy of automobile liability insurance or make any discrimination in the acceptance of risks, in rates, premiums, dividends, or benefits of any kind, or by means of rebate between persons of the same class, nor on account of race. Every company or agent violating any of the foregoing provisions shall be fined not less than $50.00, nor more than $100.00, and every officer, agent, or solicitor violating the same shall be guilty of a misdemeanor. [1941 c. 283.]

Life Insurance

61.05. Discrimination in accepting risks. — No company or agent, all other condiitons being equal, shall make any discrimination in the acceptance of risks, in rates, premiums, dividends, or benefits of any kind, or by way of rebates, between persons of the same class, or on account of race; and upon request of any person whose application has been rejected, the company shall furnish him in writing, the reasons therefor, including a certificate of the examining physician that such rejection was not for any racial cause. Every company violating either of the foregoing provisions shall forfeit not less than $500.00, nor more than $1,000, and every officer, agent, or solicitor violating the same shall be guilty of a gross misdemeanor; and the commissioner shall revoke the license of such company and its agents, and grant no new license within one year thereafter. [1895, c. 175, §§66, 67; R.L. '05, s. 1689; St. 1927, §3376.]

Ku Klux Klan — Wearing Masks

§615.16. Wearing of masks prohibited. — Subdivision 1. Prohibition. — It shall be unlawful for any person either alone or in company with others, to appear on any street or highway, or in other public places or any place open to view by the general public, with his face or person partially or completely concealed by means of a mask or other regalia or paraphernalia, with intent thereby to conceal the identity of such person. The wearing of any such mask, regalia or paraphernalia by any person on any street or highway or in other public places or any place open to view by the general public, shall be presumptive evidence of wearing the same with intent to conceal the identity of such person; this subdivision shall not be construed to prohibit the wearing of such means of concealment in good faith for purposes of amusement or entertainment.

Subdivision 2. Penalty. — Every person violating any of the provisions of this section shall be deemed guilty of a misdemeanor. [L. 1923, c. 160, §§1, 2; St. 1927, §§10300, 10301.]

Military

Laws 1949, p. 1584,
1949 Resolution No. 6
S. F. No. 10

A Concurrent Resolution

Memorializing the Congress of the United States to enact legislation securing to all citizens, and particularly to its Negro citizens, the right to serve in the National Guard of the United States without segregation in separate units.

WHEREAS, equality of opportunity, responsibility and privilege of all its people is a matter of vital importance to the people of the State of Minnesota; and

WHEREAS, it is the policy of the State of Minnesota that there shall be no discrimination between its people by reason of race, color, religion or national origin; and

WHEREAS, the regulations prescribed by the Department of the Army require that all Negro manpower subject to its authority except Negro manpower with special skills or qualifications be employed in Negro units which will conform in general to other units of the army; and

WHEREAS, these regulations control the employment of Negro manpower in the National Guard of the United States; and

WHEREAS, these regulations of the Department of the Army, in denying to Negro citizens of this state equality of opportunity and service in the National Guard, are in derogation of the public policy of the State of Minnesota;

NOW, THEREFORE, BE IT RESOLVED, By the Senate of the State of Minnesota, the House of Representatives concurring therein, that the Congress of the United States, at its present sitting, be and is urgently petitioned and requested to enact such legislation as will secure to all citizens of the United States, and particularly to its Negro citizens, the right to serve in the National Guard of the United States in the same units with all other members without segregation of Negro manpower or any other manpower by reason of race, color, religion or national origin; and

BE IT FURTHER RESOLVED, that a duly authenticated copy of this resolution be transmitted to the President of the United States, to the presiding officers of the Senate and the House of Representatives of the Congress of the United States, and to each of the Senators and Representatives from the State of Minnesota in the Congress of the United States.

App. 4-2-49

State National Guard — no segregation

[Note: By executive order signed on November 22, 1949 by Gov. Luther Youngdahl, Negroes were permitted to enlist in the Minnesota National Guard for the first time in the history of the state. The order decreed: "There shall be equality of opportunity and treatment for all, including

Negro citizens, who shall serve in the Military and naval forces of the State without segregation into separate units." The text of the order follows:

WHEREAS, the Minnesota National Guard, in time of war and peace, has achieved a most distinguished record of devoted and heroic service to the state and nation; and

WHEREAS, it seems highly fitting that the Minnesota National Guard, as an outstanding example of the noblest attributes of patriotism in a democracy, should accord all citizens, duly qualified, an equal opportunity to serve in its units; and

WHEREAS, the policy of the State of Minnesota has long set forth the conviction that there shall be no discrimination between its people by reason of race, color, religion or national origin; and

WHEREAS, this attitude was expressed by the Minnesota Legislature in 1885 when it enacted a civil rights statute, which to this day prevents discrimination in public places; and

WHEREAS, opposition to discrimination was again stated when the 1949 session of the Minnesota Legislature memorialized the Congress of the United States to permit all citizens, and particularly Negro citizens, to serve in the National Guard, without segregation into separate units; and

WHEREAS, Minnesota Negro citizens, in accordance with our philosophy of justice and fair play, merit the right to membership in the National Guard, without the humiliation of segregation;

NOW, THEREFORE, I, LUTHER W. YOUNGDAHL, Governor and commander-in-chief of the military and naval forces of the State of Minnesota, do hereby establish as the policy of the military and naval forces of the State of Minnesota including the Minnesota National Guard, that there shall be therein equality of opportunity and treatment for all, including Negro citizens who shall serve therein without segregation into separate units, and I hereby order the Adjutant General of Minnesota to forthwith issue all necessary directives to carry into effect in the military and naval forces of the State of Minnesota, including the Minnesota National Guard, the policy herein established.

IN WITNESS WHEREOF, I have hereunto set my hand and caused the great seal of the State of Minnesota to be affixed at the State Capitol in Saint Paul this twenty-second day of November in the year of our Lord one thousand nine hundred and forty-nine and of the state, the ninety-second.

LUTHER W. YOUNGDAHL,
Governor and Commander-in-Chief.

Attest:

MIKE HOLM
Secretary of State.]

Public Accommodations

327.09. Equal rights in hotels. — No person shall be excluded, on account of race, color, national origin, or religion from full and equal enjoyment

235

of any accommodation, advantage, or privilege furnished by public conveyances, theaters, or other public places of amusement, or by hotels, barber shops, saloons, restaurants, or other places of refreshments, entertainment, or accommodations. Every person who violates any provision of this section, or aids or incites another to do so, shall be guilty of a gross misdemeanor, and, in addition to the penalty therefor, shall be liable in a civil action to the person aggrieved for damage not exceeding $500. [L. 1885, c. 224, §§1, 2,; R.L. '05, §2812; St. 1927, §7321; 1943, c. 579, §1.]

Public Contracts

181.59. Discrimination on account of race, creed and color prohibited in contract — violation a misdemeanor. — Every contract for, or on behalf of the state of Minnesota, or any county, city, borough, town, township, school, school district, or any other district in the state, for materials, supplies, or construction, shall contain provisions by which the contractor agrees:

(1) That, in the hiring of common or skilled labor for the performance of any work under any contract, or any subcontract hereunder, no contractor, material supplier, or vendor, shall by reason of race, creed, or color, discriminate against the person or persons who are citizens of the United States who are qualified and available to perform the work to which such employment relates.

(2) That no contractor, material supplier, or vendor, shall in any manner, discriminate against, or intimidate, or prevent the employment of any such person or persons, or on being hired, prevent, or conspire to prevent, any such person or persons from the performance of work under any contract on account of race, creed or color.

(3) Any violation of this section shall be a misdemeanor; and

(4) That this contract may be canceled or terminated by the state, county, city, borough, town, school board, or any other person authorized to grant contracts for such employment, and all money due, or to become due hereunder, may be forfeited for a second or subsequent violation of the terms or conditions of this contract. [1941, c. 238, §1.]

Public Works

See under **Public Contracts** above.

Restrictive Covenants

[507.18 prohibits restrictive covenants in any instrument relating to or affecting real estate, where such restrictions are directed toward any person of a specified religious faith or creed. Such provision shall be void and every person who violates the prohibition shall be liable in a civil action to the person aggrieved in damages not exceeding $500.00. This provision does not include race or color as a ground of prohibition.] [1919, c. 188, ss. 1, 2, 3, 4.]

MISSISSIPPI

CONSTITUTION

Definition of Negro and "Colored"

[Note: Art. 14, section 263 of the Constitution of Mississippi which prohibits marriage of a white person with a Negro or mulatto, or a person having one-eighth or more Negro blood, does not determine the status of a person as to whether he is white or colored under Art. 8, section 207 of the Constitution which provides for separate schools for children of the white and colored races. The word "white" under Section 207 means a member of the Caucasian race and word "colored" includes not only Negroes but persons of mixed blood having any appreciable amount of Negro blood. *Moreau v. Grandich*, (1917) 114 Miss. 560, 75 So. 434.]

Education

Art. 8, §207. — Separate schools shall be maintained for the children of the white and colored races. [Const. 1890.]

[Note — Application to races other than Negro race. — The word "white race" used in this section is limited to the Caucasian race, and the term "colored races" is used in contradistinction of the white race and embraces all other races. See *Rice v. Gong Lum*, 139 Miss. 760, 104 So. 105 (affirmed by the U.S. Sup. Court in (1927) 275 U.S., 73, 72 L. ed 172, 48 S.C. 91).

The *Rice* case held that the constitutional convention used the word "colored" in the broad sense rather than the restricted sense; its purpose being to preserve the purity and integrity of the white race and its social policy. This case was decided by the United States Supreme Court in 1927 and that high court held that Mississippi might assign a child of Chinese blood, even though a citizen of the United States, to public schools separate from those provided for the whites, since he was classified by the State among the colored races.]

Art. 8, §213-A — The State institutions or Higher Learning now existing in Mississippi, to-wit: University of Mississippi, Mississippi State College, Mississippi State College for Women, Mississippi Southern College, Delta State Teacher's College, Alcorn Agricultural and Mechanical Colleges and Mississippi Negro Training School, and any others of like kind which may hereafter be organized or established by the State of Mississippi, shall be under the management and control of a Board of Trustees to be known as the Board of Trustees of State Institutions of Higher Learning, the members thereof to be appointed by the Governor of the State with the advice and consent of the Senate . . . [New section ratified November, 1942; inserted by Legis. House Concurrent Resolution No. 13, Laws 1944, ch. 344.]

Miscegenation

Art. 14, Sec. 263. — The marriage of a white person with a negro or mulatto or person who shall have one-eighth or more of negro blood, shall be unlawful and void. [Const. 1890.]

[Note: See below §§459, 2339.]

Prisons

Art. 11, Sec. 225. — [Provides for "the separation of white and black convicts as far as practicable" on state farms.] [1869, Art. XII, §28.]

Slavery

Art. 3, Sec. 15. — There shall be neither slavery nor involuntary servitude in this state, otherwise than in the punishment of crime, whereof the party shall have been duly convicted. [1869, Art. I, §19.]

STATUTES

MISSISSIPPI CODE (1942), ANNOTATED

Aliens

§842. Aliens holding land. — [Non-resident aliens are prohibited from holding land for more than 20 years, but may retain the land by becoming citizens within that period]. [Codes, 1892, §2439; 1906, §2768; Hemingway's 1917, §2272; 1930, §2121; Laws 1924, ch. 165; 1938, ch. 354; 1940, ch. 237.]

[Note: While this statute does not appear to be directed against a specific alien group, aliens ineligible for citizenship may not hold land for longer than 20 years.]

§1120. [Quo Warranto] To what cases applicable.—Tenth.—[Provides that quo warranto proceedings in the name of the state shall be used as the remedy "whenever any non-resident alien or corporation shall acquire or hold lands contrary to law."] [Codes, 1857, ch. 35; art. 12; 1871, §1490; 1880, §§2585-2587; 1892, §3520; 1906, §4017; Hemingway's 1917, §3012; 1930, §3053.]

§4109. Who may not purchase public lands. — [Bars non-resident aliens or corporations or associations composed in part of non-resident aliens from purchasing public lands.] [Codes, 1892, §2563; 1906, §2901; Hemingway's 1917, §5236; 1930, §6027; Laws 1938, Ex. ch. 79.]

Education

Public Schools

§6276. Separate districts for the races . . . — [Provides for separate districts for the schools of the white and colored races.] [Codes, 1930, §6586; Laws, 1924, ch. 283; 1930, ch. 278.]

Schools for Indians and Other Races

§6632. Counties establishing — licensing teachers. — In a county where there are Indian children, or children of any race not otherwise provided for by law with educational advantages, sufficient to form a school, the county board may locate one or more schools exclusively for Indians, or children of such other race, and pay salaries of teachers for same, and provide for the transportation of the children under rules and regulations prescribed by the State Board of Education. Special license may be provided by the State Board of Examiners for teachers of Indian schools and other schools mentioned in this section. [Codes 1930, §6789; Laws 1924, ch. 283; 1930, ch. 278; 1934, ch. 264.]

§6633. **Municipal separate schools districts — establishing.** — Trustees of municipal separate school districts are authorized and empowered to provide schools for Indian children living within the district in the same manner and under the same regulations as schools are provided for the children of other races. [Codes, 1930, §6790; Laws, 1924, ch. 283; 1930, ch. 278.]

Juvenile Delinquents — Negro and White Separate

§§6801-6807. [Repealed, Laws 1948, ch. 429, §12.] [This statute provided that a state reformatory be created and erected on the state farm at Oakley, in Hinds County, Mississippi for the proper training of delinquent Negro youth.] [Laws, 1940, ch. 172; 1942, ch. 285.]

§6744-01. [1948 Cum. Supp.] **Columbia Training School.** — [Provides for erection and maintenance of "Columbia Training School" at Columbia, Marion County, Mississippi, for the "care, education, training and rehabilitation of delinquent children ages ten through eighteen years inclusive." Presumably, this institution is for white juvenile delinquents.] [Laws, 1948, ch. 429, §1.]

§6744-02. [1948 Cum. Supp.] **Oakley Training School.** — [Provides for the erection of "Oakley Training School" at Oakley, Hinds County, Mississippi, for the "care, education, training and rehabilitation of delinquent negro children ages ten through eighteen years inclusive. [Laws, 1948, ch. 429, §2.]

§§6744-03 — 6744-13. [1948 Cum. Supp.] [Provision for joint regulation and control of the two above institutions by a joint board of trustees.] [Laws, 1948, ch. 429, §§3-13.]

[Note: See also §§6744-21; Laws 1946, ch. 434, §§1-5.]

Schools for Deaf and Blind — Segregation

§6785-10. [1948 Cum. Supp.] [Provides for the erection of a new plant for the use and housing of the Mississippi School for the Blind and the Mississippi School for the Deaf in Hinds County, Mississippi. Further provides, "The state building commission is hereby authorized and empowered, in its discretion, to select, as the site for the buildings to be used and occupied by the schools for the deaf and blind for members of the colored race, such part of the land in the city of Jackson, Hinds County, Mississippi, which is now owned and occupied by the Mississippi School for the Deaf, as the state building commission may deem suitable for such purposes, and to erect and equip such additional buildings and other facilities as the commission may deem necessary for the use and housing of the schools for the deaf and blind for members of the colored race."] [Laws 1946, ch. 374, §§1-3, as amended, Laws 1948, ch. 302, §§1-3.]

Colleges and Universities

§6719. [1948 Cum. Supp.] — **Board of Trustees.** — The state institutions of higher learning now existing in the state, to-wit:

University of Mississippi,

239

Mississippi State College,
Mississippi State College for Women,
Mississippi Southern College,
Delta State Teachers College,
Alcorn Agricultural & Mechanical College,
Mississippi Negro Training School, and any other of like kind which may hereafter be established by the state, shall be under the management and control of a board of trustees to be known as the board of trustees of state institutions of higher learning. [As amended, Laws 1944, ch. 262, §2.]

Alcorn Agricultural and Mechanical College

§6703. **Recognized and continued.** — The Alcorn Agricultural and Mechanical College of Mississippi, created by act approved February 28, 1878, for the education of the colored youth of the State, shall continue as a body-politic and corporate for that purpose. [Codes, 1880, §776; 1892, §28; 1906, §29; Hemingway's 1917, §3439; 1930, §7195.]

Mississippi State College for Women

§§6710-6711. [Provision for Mississippi State College for Women, the declared purpose of which is "the moral and intellectual advancement of the white girls of the State".] [Codes 1892, §§2295, 2296; 1906, §§2523, 2524; Hemingways 1917, §§4948, 4949; Hemingway's 1921 Supp. §5729; 1930, §§7204, 7205; Laws, 1920, ch. 256.]

Negro Teacher Training School — Jackson College for Negro Teachers

§6808. — [Creates the Mississippi Negro Training School.] [Laws, 1940, ch. 185.]

§6808-01. [1948 Cum. Supp.] — **Change of Name.** — The Corporate name of the Mississippi Negro Training School as created and established by chapter 185 of the laws of 1940 [this article], be hereby changed to the Jackson College for Negro Teachers. [Laws, 1944, ch. 159, §1.]

§6809. **Object and purposes of the Mississippi Negro Training School.** — [Provides that the objects and purposes of the training school shall be to qualify Negro teachers for the Negro public schools of Mississippi "by giving instruction in the art and practice of teaching in all branches of study" which pertain to industrial training, health, and rural and elementary education, and such other studies as the board of trustees of state institutions of higher learning, in cooperation with the state department of education, may, from time to time, prescribe. [Laws, 1940, ch. 185.]

§§6810 - 6814. — [Additional provisions for regulation of training school.] [Laws 1940, ch. 185.]

Vocational College

§§6814-01 - 6814-07. [1948 Cum. Supp.] [Provides for establishment of the Mississippi Vocational College to train Negro teachers for teaching in the Negro public schools of the state "by giving instruction in the art and practice of teaching in the elementary and high school grades and in all branches of study which pertain to industrial training, health, and rural and elementary education, and to provide instruction and training in such other subjects as the board of trustees of state institutions of higher learning may from time to time, prescribe." Further provision that an object of the school shall be "to establish and conduct schools, classes or courses, for preparing, equipping and training" Negro citizens of Mississippi "for employment in gainful occupations, in trade, industrial and distributive pursuits whether such students are qualified by educational requirements or not."] [Laws, 1946, ch. 327, §§1 - 7.]

Higher Education for Negro Students Outside State

§6726.5. [1948 Cum Supp.] **Trustees may provide instruction for negro students in graduate and professional schools outside state.** — The board of trustees of state institutions of higher learning, under such rules and regulations as it shall determine, may provide instruction in graduate and professional schools for qualified negro students, who are residents of Mississippi, in institutions outside the state boundaries, when such instruction is not available for them in the regularly supported institutions of higher learning. The board of trustees shall, by its rules and regulations, determine the qualifications of such students as may be aided by this act, and the decision by the board as to the qualifications of such students shall be final. The board of trustees shall provide such graduate and professional instruction, within the limits of the funds available for this purpose, at a cost to students, not exceeding the cost as estimated by the board, of such instruction, if it were available at a state supported institution of higher learning in the state of Mississippi. [Laws, 1948, ch. 282, §1.]

§6800.5. [1948 Cum. Supp.] **Compact for the operation of regional educational institutions in the southern states.** — [Laws 1948, ch. 284, §§1-3]

SENATE BILL NO. 612

AN ACT to ratify and approve the proposed compact of southern states for the purpose of operating regional educational institutions in the southern states as set out; to authorize the board of trustees of state institutions of higher learning to expend a sum not to exceed five thousand dollars ($5,000.00) out of any funds available or made available to carry out the purposes of this act during the biennium commencing on July 1, 1948 and ending on June 30, 1950, and to authorize said board of trustees to administer such funds, properties and facilities as may hereafter be made available from donations, grants, appropriations, from any source, to carry out the provisions of this act and the said compact hereby approved.

Be it enacted by the Legislature of the State of Mississippi:

Section 1. That the following compact of the southern states for the purpose of operating regional educational institutions in the southern states be, and the same, is hereby ratified and approved:

Whereas, the states who are parties hereto have during the past

241

several years conducted careful investigation looking toward the establishment and maintenance of jointly owned and operated regional educational institutions in the southern states in the professional technological, scientific, literary and other fields, so as to provide greater educational advantages and facilities for the citizens of the several states who reside within such region, and

Whereas, Meharry Medical College of Nashville, Tennessee, has proposed that its lands, building, equipment, and the net income from its endowment be turned over to the southern states, or to an agency acting in their behalf, to be operated as a regional institution for medical, dental and nursing education upon terms and conditions to be hereafter agreed upon between the southern states and Meharry Medical College, which proposal, because of the present financial condition of the institution, has been approved by the said states who are parties, hereto, and

Whereas, the said states desire to enter into a compact with each other providing for the planning and establishment of regional educational facilities;

Now therefore, in consideration of the mutual agreements, covenants and obligations assumed by the respective states who are parties hereto (hereinafter referred to as "States"), the said several states do hereby form a geographical district or region consisting of the areas lying within the boundaries of the contracting states which for the purposes of this compact, shall constitute an area for regional education supported by public funds derived from taxation by the constituent states for the establishment, acquisition, operation and maintenance of regional educational schools and institutions for the benefit of citizens of the respective states residing within the region so established as may be determined from time to time in accordance with the terms and provisions of this compact.

The states do further hereby establish and create a joint agency which shall be known as the board of control for southern regional education (hereinafter referred to as the "Board"), the members of which board shall consist of the governor of each state, ex-officio, and two additional citizens of each state to be appointed by the governor thereof, at least one of whom shall be selected from the field of education. The governor shall continue as a member of the board during his tenure of office as governor of the state but the members of the board appointed by the governor shall hold office for a period of five years except that in the original appointment one board member so appointed by the governor shall be designated at the time of his appointment to serve an initial term of three years, but thereafter his successor shall serve the full term of five years. Vacancies on the board caused by death, resignation, refusal or inability to serve, shall be filled by appointment by the governor for the unexpired portion of the term. The officers of the board shall be a chairman, a vice chairman, a secretary, a treasurer, and such additional officers as may be created by the board from time to time. The board shall meet annually and officers shall be elected to hold office until the next annual meeting.

The board shall have the right to formulate and establish by-laws not inconsistent with the provisions of this compact to govern its own actions in the performance of the duties delegated to it including the right to create and appoint an executive committee and a finance committee with such powers and authority as the board may delegate to them from time to time.

It shall be the duty of the board to submit plans and recommendations to the states from time to time for their approval and adoption by appropriate legislative action for the development, establishment, acquisition, operation and maintenance of educational schools and institutions within the geographical limits of the regional area of the states, of such character and type and for such educational purposes, professional, technological scientific, literary, or otherwise, as they may deem and determine to be proper, necessary or advisable. Title to all such educational institutions when so established by appropriate legislative actions of the states and to all properties and facilities used in connection therewith shall be vested in said board as the agency of and for the use and benefit of the said states and the citizens thereof, and all such educational institutions shall be operated, maintained and financed in the manner herein set out, subject to any provisions or limitations which may be contained in the legislative acts of the states authorizing the creation, establishment and operation of such educational institutions.

The board shall have such additional and general power and authority as may be vested in it by the states from time to time by legislative enactments of the said states.

Any two or more states who are parties of this compact shall have the right to enter into supplemental agreements providing for the establishment, financing and operation of regional educational institutions for the benefit of citizens residing within an area which constitutes a portion of the general region herein created, such institutions to be financed exclusively by such states and to be controlled exclusively by the members of the board representing such states provided such agreement is submitted to and approved by the board prior to the establishment of such institutions.

Each state agrees that, when authorized by the legislature, it will from time to time make available and pay over to said board such funds as may be required for the establishment, acquisition, operation and maintenance of such regional educational institutions as may be authorized by the states under the terms of this compact, the contribution of each state at all times to be in the proportion that its population bears to the total combined population of the states who are parties hereto as shown from time to time by the most recent official published report of the bureau of census of the United States of America or upon such other basis as may be agreed upon.

This compact shall not take effect or be binding upon any state unless and until it shall be approved by proper legislative action of as many as six or more of the states whose governors have subscribed hereto within a period of eighteen months from the date hereof. When and if

243

six or more states shall have given legislative approval to this compact within said eighteen months period, it shall be and become binding upon such six or more states 60 days after the date of legislative approval by the sixth state and the governors of such six or more states shall forthwith name the members of the board from their states as hereinabove set out, and the board shall then meet on call of the governor of any state approving this compact, at which time the board shall elect officers, adopt by-laws, appoint committees and otherwise fully organize. Other states whose names are subscribed hereto shall thereafter become parties hereto upon approval of this compact by legislative action within two years from the date hereof, upon such conditions as may be agreed upon at the time.

After becoming effective this compact shall thereafter continue without limitation of time provided, however, that it may be terminated at any time by unanimous action of the states and provided, further, that any state may withdraw from this compact if such withdrawal is approved by its legislature, such withdrawal to become effective two years after written notice thereof to the board accompanied by a certified copy of the requisite legislative action, but such withdrawal shall not relieve the withdrawing state from its obligations hereunder accruing up to the effective date of such withdrawal. Any state so withdrawing shall ipso facto cease to have any claim to or ownership of any of the property held or vested in the board or to any of the funds of the board held under the terms of this compact.

If any state shall at any time become in default in the performance of any of its obligations assumed herein or with respect to any obligation imposed upon said state as authorized by and in compliance with the terms and provisions of this compact, all rights, privileges and benefits of such defaulting state, its members on the board and its citizens shall ipso facto be and become suspended from and after the date of such default. Unless such default shall be remedied and made good within a period of one year immediately following the date of such default this compact may be terminated with respect to such defaulting state by an affirmative vote of three-fourths of the members of the board (exclusive of the members representing the state in default), from and after which time such state shall cease to be a party to this compact and shall have no further claim to or ownership of any of the property held by or vested in the board or to any of the funds of the board held under the terms of this compact, but such termination shall in no manner release such defaulting state from any accrued obligation or otherwise effect this compact or the rights, duties, privileges or obligations of the remaining states thereunder.

In witness whereof this compact has been approved and signed by the governors of the several states, subject to the approval of their respective legislatures in the manner hereinabove set out, as of the.................... day of... 1948.

State of Florida,   State of Tennessee,
By..   By..
      Governor   Governor

State of Maryland,	Commonwealth of Virginia,
By..	By..
Governor	Governor
State of Georgia,	State of Arkansas,
By..	By..
Governor	Governor
State of Louisiana,	State of North Carolina,
By..	By..
Governor	Governor
State of Alabama,	State of South Carolina,
By..	By..
Governor	Governor
State of Mississippi,	State of Texas,
By..	By..
Governor	Governor
Commonwealth of Kentucky,	State of Oklahoma,
By..	By..
Governor	Governor
State of West Virginia	
By..	
Governor	

Section 2. That the board of trustees of state institutions of higher learning is authorized and empowered to expend a sum not to exceed five thousand dollars ($5,000.00) out of any funds available, or made available, to carry out the purposes of this act during the biennium commencing on July 1, 1948, and ending on June 30, 1950

Section 3. That the said board of trustees of state institutions of higher learning is authorized and empowered to administer such funds, properties and facilities as may be made available from donations, grants, appropriation from any source, to carry out the provisions of this act, and the said compact hereby approved.

Section 4. That this act take effect and be in force from and after its passage.

Approved April 13, 1948.

[Note: See Note on Regional Compact — Education, Appendix 6.]

Hospitals

Mental Hospitals

§6766. **Plan of the Ellisville State School** (for feeble-minded). — [Provides for separate maintenance of white and colored races.] [Codes, Hemmingway's 1921 Supp. §5728i; 1930, §7275; Laws, 1920, ch. 210.

§6882. **The annex — colored patients.** — The annex [of the State Insane Hospital] shall be devoted to the care of lunatic and insane

245

colored persons, who shall be admitted therein to its full capacity, except that such as are not dangerous, and are not needing special treatment, and to whom the light work at the East Mississippi Insane Hospital might be beneficial, may in the discretion of the governor, be kept there. [Codes, 1892, §2808; 1906, §3188; Hemingway's 1917, §5705; 1930, §4541.]

§6883. The races kept separate. — The white and colored races shall be kept separate in the hospital. [Codes 1892, §2809; 1906, §3189; Hemingway's 1917, §5706; 1930, §4542.]

State Charity Hospitals
Mississippi State Charity Hospital

§6927. Races to be separated. — The white and colored races shall be kept separately in said hospital and suitable provisions made for their care and comfort by the board of trustees. [Codes, Hemingway's 1917, §3949; 1930, §4594; Laws, 1910, ch. 115.]

§6973. Separate entrances for races. — There shall be maintained by the governing authorities of every hospital maintained by the state for treatment of white and colored patients separate entrances for white and colored patients and visitors, and such entrances shall be used by the races only for which they are prepared. [Codes, 1930, §4618; Laws, 1928, Ex. ch. 95.]

§6974. Separate nurses for different races. — In all such institutions it shall be the duty of the superintendent and others in authority to furnish a sufficient number of colored nurses to attend colored patients, such colored nurses to be under the supervision of such white supervisors as the head of the institution may determine. A failure to comply with this and the next preceding section shall authorize the governor to remove the person in authority responsible for such violation. [Codes, 1930, §4619; Laws, 1928, Ex. ch. 95.]

Indians
See under Education, §6632.

Marriage and Divorce

§2748. — [Provides that all bills of divorce shall specify the race of the parties to the suit.] [Codes, 1906, §1671; Hemingway's 1917, §1413; 1930, §1426; Laws 1928, ch. 132.]

Miscegenation

§459. Unlawful marriages — between white person and negro or Mongolian prohibited. — The marriage of a white person and a negro or mulatto or person who shall have one-eighth or more of negro blood, or with a Mongolian or a person who shall have one-eighth or more of Mongolian blood, shall be unlawful, and such marriage shall be unlawful and void; and any party thereto, on conviction, shall be punished as for marriage within the degrees prohibited by the last two sections by marrying out of this state and returning to it shall be within them. [Codes 1880, §1147; 1892, §2859; 1906, §3244; Hemingway's 1917, §2551; 1930, §2361.]

[Note: Intermarriage is placed on the same level as incestuous marriages and marriages within certain degrees of kinship. The penalty for such marriages is a fine of $500.00 or imprisonment up to 10 years in the state penitentiary, or both. See §§2002, 2234, 2339.]

Prisons

§4259 . . . Separate rooms in jail for races . . . — [Requires the sheriff who is jailor of his county to keep in the county jail separate rooms for the races.] [Codes, Hutchinson's 1848, ch. 28, art. 3(15); 1857, ch. 6, art. 131; 1871, §237; 1880, §343; 1892; §4136; 1906, §4687; Hemingway's 1917, §3104; 1930, §3334; Laws 1896, p. 153.]

§7913 . . . races to be segregated . . . it shall be unlawful for those [convicts] of the colored races and those of the white races to be confined or worked together. Those of each race shall have like treatment. [Laws, 1908, chs. 109, 169.]

§7965. [1948 Cum. Supp.] [Penitentiary] Separation of races and sexes . . . — The warden shall see that the white convicts shall have separate apartments for both eating and sleeping from the negro convicts . . . [Supercedes §7965, Code of 1942; Laws 1944, ch. 332, §29, as amended, Laws, 1948, ch. 498, §1.]

§7971. [1948 Cum. Supp.] Prison Hospital. — [Provides for separate wards for white and Negro convicts.] [Supercedes §7971, Code of 1942; Laws, 1944, ch. 332, §35.]

Social Equality

§2339. Races — social equality, marriages between — advocacy of punished. — Any person, firm or corporation who shall be guilty of printing, publishing or circulating printed, typewritten or written matter urging or presenting for public acceptance or general information, arguments or suggestions in favor of social equality or of intermarriage between whites and negroes, shall be guilty of a misdemeanor and subject to a fine not exceeding five hundred [$500.00] dollars or imprisonment not exceeding six [6] months or both fine and imprisonment in the discretion of the court. [Codes, Hemingway's 1921 Supp. §1142e; 1930, §1103; Laws, 1920, ch. 214.]

Transportation

Depots

§7848. Regulations for passenger depots. — [Requires passenger depots in cities of 3,000 or more inhabitants to maintain in connection with reception room for whites, two closets labeled respectively "Closet, white; females only," "Closet, white; males only," and similarly in the waiting room for Negroes, closets labelled respectively substituting the word "colored" for "white".] [Codes, 1892, §4303; 1906, §4855; Hemingway's 1917, §7640; 1930, §7072.]

Railroads

§2351. Railroads — not providing separate cars. — If any person or corporation operating a railroad shall fail to provide two or more pass-

247

enger cars for each passenger train, or to divide the passenger cars by a partition, to secure separate accommodations for the white and colored races, as provided by law, or if any railroad passenger conductor shall fail to assign each passenger to the car or compartment of the car used for the race to which the passenger belongs, he or it shall be guilty of a misdemeanor, and, on conviction shall be fined not less than twenty [$20.00] dollars nor more than five hundred [$500.00] dollars. [Codes, 1892, §1276; 1906, §1351; Hemingway's 1917, §1085; 1930, §1115.]

[Note: This provision applies to sleeping cars. See *Alabama & V. R. Co. v. Morris*, (1912) 103 Miss. 511, 60 So. 11, Ann. Cas. 1915B 613.]

§7784. **Equal but separate accommodations for the races.**—Every railroad carrying passengers in this state shall provide equal but separate accommodations for the white and colored races by providing two or more passenger cars for each passenger train, or by dividing the passenger cars by a partition to secure separate accommodations; and the conductor of such passenger train shall have power, and is required, to assign each passenger to the car, or the compartment of a car, used for the race to which such passenger belongs; and should any passenger refuse to occupy the car to which he or she is assigned by the conductor, the conductor shall have power to refuse to carry such passenger on the train, and for such refusal neither he nor the railroad company shall be liable for damages in any court. [Codes, 1892, §3562; 1906, §4059; Hemingway's 1917, §6687; 1930, §6132; Laws, 1904, ch. 99.]

Street Railways and Busses

§7785. [1948 Cum. Supp.] — **Separate accommodaitons for races in street cars and busses — common carriers by motor vehicle.** — All persons or corporations operating street railways and street or municipal buses, carrying passengers in this state, and every common carrier by motor vehicle of passengers in this state as defined by section 3 (e) of Chapter 142 of the laws of 1938 [§7634, Code of 1942] shall provide equal, but separate, accommodations for the white and colored races.

Every common carrier by motor vehicle of passengers in this state, as defined by section 3 (e) of chapter 142 of the laws of 1938 [§7634, Code of 1942], by buses or street cars operated entirely within the corporate limits of a municipality, or within a radius of 5 miles thereof, shall divide its passengers by the use of an appropriate sign 4 x 9 inches, for the purpose of, and in a manner that will suitably provide for, a separation of the races, and all other buses and motor vehicles carrying passengers for hire in the state of Mississippi shall use a latticed movable partition extending from the top of the seat to the ceiling of the vehicle, said partition not to obstruct the view of the driver of the vehicle to secure such separate accommodations; provided, however, that this act shall not apply to buses operated exclusively for the carrying of military personnel, and the operators of such passenger buses shall have power, and are required, to assign each passenger to the compartment of the bus used for the race to which such passenger belongs; and in no case shall any passenger be permitted to stand in the aisle of the compartment in which he does not belong and is not so assigned; and should any passenger refuse to occupy the compartment to which he or she belongs and is assigned, the operator shall have power to refuse to carry such passenger on the bus; or should either compartment become so loaded in transit as not to permit the taking on of any further passengers for that compartment, then the bus operator shall not be required and shall refuse to take on any further passengers in violation of this act. Even though such additional passengers may have purchased and may hold tickets for transportation on the said bus, the only remedy said passengers shall have for failure or refusal to carry them under such circumstances is the right to a refund of the cost of his ticket, and for said refusal in either case neither the operator nor the common carrier shall be liable for damages in any court. Such partition may be made movable so as to allow adjustment of the space in the bus to suit the requirements of traffic. [Amends §7785, Code of 1942.] [Codes, 1906, §4060; Hemingway's, 1917, §7558; 1930, §6133; 1942, §7785; Laws 1904; ch. 99; 1940, ch. 169; 1944, ch. 267, §1.]

[Note: §7634, Code of 1942, Subsection (e): The term "common carrier by motor vehicle" means any person who or which undertakes, whether directly or by a lease or by any other arrangement, to transport passengers or property for the general public by motor vehicle for compensation, over regular routes, including such motor vehicle operation of carriers by rail or water, and of express or forwarding companies under this Act. [Laws 1938, ch. 142]]

§7786. [1948 Cum. Supp.] — Passengers required to occupy compartments to which they are assigned. — The operators of such street cars and street buses and motor vehicles, as defined by chapter 142 of the laws of 1938 [§§7632 - 7687, Code of 1942] shall have the power and are required to assign each passenger to the space or compartment used for the race to which such passenger belongs. Any passenger undertaking or attempting to go into the space or compartment to which by race he or she does not belong shall be guilty of a misdemeanor, and, upon conviction, shall be liable to a fine of twenty-five dollars ($25.00) or, in lieu thereof, by imprisonment for a period of not more than thirty (30) days in the county jail; and any operator of any street car or street bus or motor vehicle as herein defined, assigning or placing a passenger to the space or compartment other than the one set aside for the race to which said passenger belongs shall be guilty of a misdemeanor and, upon conviction, shall be liable to a fine of twenty-five dollars ($25.00) or, in lieu thereof, to imprisonment for a period of not more than thirty (30) days in the county jail. [Amends §7786, Code of 1942.] [Codes 1906, §4061; Hemingway's 1917, §7559; 1930, §6134; 1942, §7786; Laws, 1904, ch. 99; 1940, ch. 169; 1944, ch. 267, §1.]

§7786-01. [1948 Cum. Supp.] — Penalty for Violation. — Every person or corporation operating street railways and street or municipal buses carrying passengers in this state, and every common carrier of passengers in this state by motor vehicle, as defined by section 3 (e) of

Chapter 142 of the laws of 1938 [§7634, Code of 1942], guilty of wilful and continued failure to observe or comply with the provisions of this act shall be liable to a fine of twenty-five dollars ($25.00) for each offense, and each day's violation of the provision hereof shall constitute a separate violation of this act; provided, however, that in the case of persons or corporations operating street railways and street or municipal buses, the fine shall be ten dollars ($10.00) instead of twenty-five dollars ($25.00). [Laws 1944, ch. 267, §2.]

§7787. Penalty for refusal of street railway officers and employees to comply with this provision. — [Officers and directors who neglect or refuse to comply with §§7785, 7786, 7787, Code of 1942 are punishable by fine of not less than $100 or 60 days to 6 months in prison in the county jail. Conductors and other employees who have charge of vehicles to which this section applies are punishable by fine of not less than $25.00 or imprisonment of 10 to 30 days for each and every offense; *provided,* however, chapter is not to apply to nurses attending children of the other race.] [Codes, 1906, §4062; Hemingway's 1917, §7560; 1930, §6135; Laws 1904, ch. 99.]

MISSOURI

CONSTITUTION

Aliens

Art. VII, Sec. 8. No person shall be elected or appointed to any civil or military office in this state who is not a citizen of the United States, and who shall not have resided in this state one year next preceding his election or appointment, except that the residence in this state shall not be necessary in cases of appointment to administrative positions requiring technical or specialized skill or knowledge. [Const. 1875, Art. 8, §10, as amended by Const. of 1945, Laws 1945, p. 48, eff. March 30, 1945.]

Education

Art. IX, Sec. 1. — [Separate Schools] . . . Separate schools shall be provided for white and colored children, except in cases otherwise provided for by law. [Const. 1945, went into effect, March 30, 1945. Laws, 1945 p. 50.]

Art. IX, Sec. 3. [Teachers' Salaries] . . . No school district which permits differences in wages of teachers having the same training and experience because of race or color, shall receive any portion of said revenue or [Public School] fund . . . [Const. 1945, went into effect March 30, 1945. Laws 1945, p. 50.]

Slavery

Art. II, Sec. 31.—Slavery prohibited.—That there cannot be in the State either slavery or involuntary servitude, except as a punishment for crime, whereof the party shall have been duly convicted. [Const. 1875. This section apparently was omitted from the Missouri Constitution revised and readopted in 1945.]

STATUTES

MISSOURI REVISED STATUTES (1939)

Aliens

§§15228-15232. [Acquisition of real property by aliens.] [Provides that aliens may acquire real property by inheritance or will in the same manner as if they were citizens of the United States. [15228.] Female citizens of the United States owning an interest in real property who marry aliens may convey such property or devise it by will. [15229.] Except as provided by treaty provisions between the United States and the foreign countries of which aliens are citizens or subjects, persons who are not citizens of the United States or who have not declared their intention to become citizens are prohibited from acquiring or owning real estate within the state of Missouri. An exception is made in case of property acquired by will or inheritance or in the collection of debts. [15230]. The same prohibition applies to a corporation or association in which aliens own more than 20 per cent of the stock. Real property acquired in the enforcement of a lien or mortgage may be held for six years only. [15231.] All property acquired in violation of this act shall be for-

251

feited to the state of Missouri in a proceeding brought by the attorney general of the state. [15232.] [R.S. 1929, §§14011-14015.]

[Note: While the sections set forth above are directed against aliens generally, in effect aliens ineligible for citizenship in the U.S., i.e. Japanese and certain Oriental groups, are barred from holding or owning real property in Missouri.]

Dentists

§10065 . . . examinations, fees, qualifications, etc.—[Requires all applicants to furnish correct name, age, place of residence, color and nationality.] [R.S. 1929, §13560. Reenacted, Laws 1937, p. 479.]

Education

Public Schools

10349. Separate schools for white and colored children. — Separate free schools shall be established for the education of children of African descent; and it shall be unlawful for any colored child to attend any white school, or any white child to attend a colored school. [R.S. 1929, §9216.]

10350. [Board of Directors of school districts authorized to establish schools for colored children.] [R.S. 1929, §9217.] [Repealed and replaced by laws 1945, p. 1700, Sec. 10350, appvd. April 16, 1946.]

§§10488, 10489, 10490, 10491, 10492. — [Provision for the establishment and regulation of high schools for Negro children.]

[Note: Sections 10491, 10492 repealed by laws of Missouri, 1945, p. 1649 which enacted new sections. See Laws, 1945, pp. 1649-1650, Sections 10491, 10492. Appvd. Jan. 18, 1946.]

Colleges and Universities
Agricultural School

§10780. — [Agricultural School and demonstration farm at Dalton, Mo., turned over to board of curators for Lincoln University for supervision and control.] [R. S. 1929, §9623.]

§§10773-10781.—[Provision for organization and control of Lincoln University for Negroes.] [R.S. 1929, §§9616-9624.]

§10779.—[Provides for out-of-state tuition for Negro students who wish to take courses provided for at the State University of Missouri, and are not taught at Lincoln University, and authorizes the Board of Curators "to arrange for . . . attendance at a college or university in some other state . . . and to pay the reasonable tuition fees for such attendance."] [R.S. 1929, §9622. Reenacted, L. 1939, p. 685.]

[Note: In 1948, $20,000.00 was appropriated by Missouri legislature for the tuition of Negro residents attending institutions of higher education outside the state for the school year 1948-1949. See Laws, 1947, p. 152.]

[Note: Laws of Missouri, 1945, p. 1639, Sec. 14, provides that 1/16 of all funds appropriated to Missouri by the "Morrill Act" of

Congress, approved August, 30, 1890, shall be paid for the benefit of Lincoln University. Approved Dec. 12, 1945.]

School for Feeble-Minded

§9390 . . . The board of managers shall also establish and maintain a separate cottage or cottages for colored inmates [of Missouri State School.] [R.S. 1929, §8694.]

Juvenile Delinquents

§9021. State Industrial Home for Negro Girls. — There shall continue to be maintained at Tipton in the county of Moniteau, in this state an institution to be known as the "State Industrial Home for Negro Girls". [R.S. 1929, §8375.] [Repealed. Laws 1947, p. 320.]

§§9022 - 9033. — [Provides for supervision of Industrial Home and for the commitment of Negro girls.] [R.S. 1929, §§8376-8388 as amended L. 1945, p. 1333.] [Repealed. Laws 1947, p. 320.]

[Note: Laws 1947, p. 320, repealed §§8993 -9033 inclusive, and. enacted new sections numbered Sections 8893 to 9012, inclusive. Under the 1947 law, no statutory provision is made for segregation of Negro and white juvenile delinquents. The 1947 law provides that any boy over 12 years and under 17 years of age and any girl over 12 years and under 21 years of age who has been convicted of a crime or found by the juvenile or circuit court to be in need of training school education and discipline may be committed to the State Board of Training Schools. Juvenile delinquents under the age of 12 years may be committed to the Division of Welfare of the State Department of Public Health and Welfare. [new section 8994.]

Physical Education

§10521. [1949 Cum. Supp.] L. 1945, p. 1655, §1. Laws Missouri, 1945, pp. 1656-1657. — [Requires all teachers training institutions to provide courses in physical education. Section 10521, p. 1657 provides . . . "These provisions shall apply alike to schools for white and colored children.] [Appvd. Jan. 16, 1946.]

Negro Teachers

[Sec. 10632 of Revised Statutes (1939) repealed and replaced by Laws, 1945, p. 1698, Section 10632.]

§10632. [1949 Cum. Supp.] — State Board of Education to outline work of institutes and summer schools for Negro teachers. — The state board of education shall prepare or cause to be prepared outlines of work to be done in institutes for colored teachers, and outlines for minimum requirements for work done in approved summer schools and accepted on county certificates as provided in Section 10633. [Laws of Missouri, 1945, p. 1698. Appvd. July 6, 1946.] [Repealed Laws 1947, Vol. 2, p. 365, §1.]

Libraries, Parks and Playgrounds — Separation

§10474 . . . the board of education shall have power to establish and main-maintain separate libraries, and public parks and playgrounds for the use of white and colored persons in such school district . . . [R.S. 1929, §9333.]

Miscegenation

§3361. — Certain marriages prohibited . . . — . . . All marriages between . . . white persons and negroes or white persons and Mongolians, . . . are prohibited and declared absolutely void; and it shall be unlawful for any city, county or state official having authority to issue marriage licenses to issue such marriage licenses to the persons heretofore designated, and any such official who shall issue such licenses to the persons aforesaid knowing such persons to be within the prohibition of this section shall be deemed guilty of a misdemeanor; and this prohibition shall apply to persons born out of lawful wedlock as well as those in lawful wedlock. [R.S. 1929, §2974.]

§4651. Illegal marriages. — No person having one-eighth part or more of negro blood shall be permitted to marry any white person, nor shall any white person be permitted to marry any negro or person having one-eighth part or more of negro blood; and every person who shall knowingly marry in violation of the provisions of this section, shall, upon conviction, be punished by imprisonment in the penitentiary for two [2] years, or by fine not less than one hundred [$100.00] dollars, or by imprisonment in the county jail not less than three [3] months, or by both such fine and imprisonment; and the jury trying any such case may determine the proportion of negro blood in any party to such marriage from the appearance of such person. [R.S. 1929, §4263.]

MONTANA

CONSTITUTION

Aliens

Art. III, sec. 25. [Mining Property] [Provides that aliens and denizens shall have the same right as citizens to own or hold mining property or real property used in the business of mining.] [Const. 1889.]

Education

Art. XI. Section 1. It shall be the duty of the legislative assembly of Montana to establish and maintain a general, uniform and thorough system of public, free, common schools. [Const. 1889].

Art. XI, Section 7. The public free schools of the state shall be open to all children and youth between the ages of six and twenty-one years. [Const. 1889.]

Ordinance No. 1.

Fourth. That provision shall be made for the establishment and maintenance of a uniform system of public schools, which shall be open to all the children of said state of Montana and free from sectarian control. [Const. 1889.]

Slavery

Art. III, Sec. 28. — There shall never be in this state either slavery or involuntary servitude, except as punishment for crime, whereof the party shall have been duly convicted. [Const. 1889.]

STATUTES

Revised Codes of Montana (1935)

Adoption

§5856. Who may adopt minor child. — Any minor child may be adopted by any adult person who is a citizen, or who, under the laws of the United States, may become a citizen of the United States, *and is of the same race as the child to be adopted,* in the cases, and subject to the rules prescribed in this chapter. [italics supplied] [Ap. Sec. 1, 5th Div. Comp., Stat. 1887; reen. Sec. 310, Civ. C. 1895; amd. Sec. 1, ch. 140, L. 1907; reen. Sec. 3761, Rev. C. 1907; reen. Sec. 5856, R.C.M. 1921.] [R.C.M. 1947, 61-127.]

Aliens

§1088. Examination and certificates — certificates of qualification required of teachers. — 1. No certificate to teach in the public schools of Montana shall be granted to any person who is not a citizen of the United States. This requirement shall not apply to such persons who are not citizens of the United States but who are approved annually by the state board of education for employment as exchange teachers from foreign countries or who are approved annually for employment for special instruction, study or research in the public high schools, the public junior colleges and the units of the university of Montana. During no school or university year may the number of persons so approved for employment by the state board of education exceed a total of one hundred (100) persons for both the public high schools and the units of the university of Montana [Ap. p. Sec. 900, Ch. 76, L. 1913; and Sec. 20, Ch. 196, L. 1919; reen. Sec. 1088, R. C.M. 1921; amd. Sec. 8, Ch. 131, L. 1923; amd. Sec. 1, Ch. 147, L. 1931, Sec. 1, ch. 90, L. 1947.] [R.C.M. 1947, 75-2501.]

§§6802.2 - 6802.8. [Restriction on Ownership of Real Property.] [Aliens are barred from owning or taking title to real property in the state and land conveyed to aliens in violation of the statute shall be forfeited to the state. [§6802.2] Aliens are not qualified to be trustees, executors, administrators, or guardians of estates which include land. [§6802.3] Aliens acquiring land by inheritance or in the enforcement of a mortgage must dispose of the land within 12 years from the date title was taken. Failure to do so within the required period shall cause the land to be forfeited to the state. [§6802.4] Where an alien is in possession or control of land claiming under a mortgage, the mortgage is deemed matured and shall be foreclosed. If the land is not sold under foreclosure within three years after the alien obtained control, the mortgage obligation shall be forfeited to the state. [6802.5]. Penalties of $100 to $1000 or 6 months in prison, or both, are provided for violations of the act. [§6802.6]. Property forfeited to the state under this act shall inure to the benefit of the common school fund. [6802.7]. The act shall not affect the title of land acquired in good faith from an alien. [§6802.8]. [L. 1923, Ch. 58, §§1-8.] [R.C.M. 1947, 67-1001 — 67-1008.]

[Note: This act applies to all aliens and does not by its terms specify aliens ineligible for citizenship in the United States. The effect of the act, however, is that alien groups ineligible for citizenship, i.e. Japanese and certain Oriental groups, are barred from owning land in Montana.]

Indians

§1808. Same. Children permitted to attend public schools. — The Crow Indian children residing in the state of Montana shall be hereafter permitted to attend public schools of the state of Montana on the same conditions as the children of white citizens of the said state. [En. Sec. 2, Ch. 119, L. 1921; reen. Sec. 1808, R.C.M. 1921.] [R.C.M. 1947, 81-2103.]

§11314. Prohibiting the carrying of firearms by Indians while off reservation. — Any Indian while off, or away from, any Indian reservation carries or bears, or causes to be carried or borne by any member of any party with which he may travel or stop, any pistol, revolver, rifle, or other firearm, or any ammunition for any firearm, shall be guilty of a misdemeanor. And such arms shall be seized, confiscated and sold by the officer making the arrest, and the proceeds from such sale shall be disposed of as follows: When seized and sold by an officer of the stock association the proceeds shall be sent to the state treasurer and by him placed to the credit of the stock inspector and detective fund; when seized and sold by a game warden the proceeds shall be placed to the credit of the fish and game fund; and when seized and sold by any other peace officer the proceeds shall be turned over to the county treasurer and placed to the credit of the general fund in which county the arrest and seizure is made. [En. Sec. 1, Ch. 84, L. 1903; reen. Sec. 8590, Rev. C. 1907; reen. Sec. 11314, R.C.M. 1921.] [R.C.M. 1947, 94-35-102.]

§11259. Selling firearms and ammunition to Indians.—Every person who sells or furnishes to any Indian any firearm or ammunition therefor, is guilty of a misdemeanor. [En. Sec. 696, Pen. C. 1895; reen. Sec. 8527, Rev. C. 1007; reen. Sec. 11259, R.C.M. 1921.] [R.C.M. 1947, 94-35-103.]

Indians

4-413. [R. C. M. 1947] Persons to whom liquor may not be sold or given. — No licensee or his or her employee or employees shall sell, deliver, or give away or cause or permit to be sold, delivered or given away any liquor, beer or wine to; . . .

5. Any minor, Indian or other person who knowingly misrepresents his or her qualifications for the purpose of obtaining liquor from such licensee shall be equally guilty with said licensee and shall, upon conviction thereof, be subject to the penalty provided in section 4-439. [En. Sec. 11, ch. 84, L. 1937; amd. Sec. 3, ch. 221, L. 1939.]

[Note: R.C.M. 1947, 4-439 makes violation of the above section a misdemeanor, punishable by fine or imprisonment or both, and suspension or revocation of license upon conviction. Laws, 1937, ch. 226, Sec. 2; Laws 1937, ch. 84, Sec. 38.]

80-216 - 80-217. [R.C.M. 1947] — [Empowers the state board of examiners in charge of tubercular institutions to grant to the Federal Government a 2-acre tract of state land near Galen in Deer Lodge County, Montana, as a site for the erection of a federal hospital and sanatarium for the treatment of Montana Indians suffering with tuberculosis or allied afflictions. The grant is to be made on condition that the Federal hospital is erected within 5 years from the date of the grant.] [En. Secs. 1, 2, ch. 76, L. 1947.]

79-1601 - 79-1602. [R.C.M. 1947] — [Empowers state agencies to administer federal appropriations of funds for welfare of Indians.] [En. Secs. 1, 2, ch. 65, L. 1927; R.C. 1935, Secs. 5668.14, 5668.15.]

80-920. [R.C.M. 1947] — [Provision for commitment to state vocational school for girls delinquent Indian girls who are wards of the United States.] [En. Sec. 20, ch. 101, L. 1919; reen. Sec. 12537, R.C.M. 1921; amd. Sec. 1, ch. 214, L. 1947.]

Innkeepers and Carriers

Ch. 35, §11218. [Penal Code] Innkeepers and carriers refusing to receive guests.—Every person, and every agent or officer of any corporation, carrying on business as an innkeeper, or as a common carrier of passengers, who refuses, without just cause or excuse, to receive and entertain any guest, or to receive or entertain any passenger, is guilty of a misdemeanor. [En. Sec. 655, Pen. C. 1895; reen. Sec. 8466, Rev. C. 1907; reen. Sec. 11218, R.C.M. 1921.] [R.C.M. 1947, 94-35-104.]

Miscegenation

§5700. Marriage between a white person and negro void. — Every marriage hereafter contracted or solemnized between a white person and a negro or a person of negro blood or in part negro, shall be utterly null and void. [L. 1909, Ch. 49, Sec. 1, R.C.M. 1921, Sec. 5700.] [R.C.M. 1947, 48-106.]

§5701. **Marriage between white and Chinese person void.** — Every marriage hereafter contracted or solemnized between any white person and a Chinese person shall be utterly null and void. [L. 1909, Ch. 49, Sec. 2, R.C.M. 1921, Sec. 5701.] [R.C.M. 1947, 49-107.]

§5702. **Marriage between white and Japanese void.**—Every marriage hereafter contracted or solemnized between a white person and a Japanese person shall be utterly null and void. [L. 1909, Ch. 49, Sec. 3, R.C.M. 1921, Sec. 5702.] [R.C.M. 1947, 48-108.]

§5703. **Such marriages contracted outside side shall be void, when.** — Every such marriage mentioned in either of the foregoing sections [5700-5702], which may be hereafter contracted or solemnized without the state of Montana by any person who has, prior to the time of contracting or solemnizing said marriage, been a resident of the state of Montana, shall be null and void within the state of Montana. [L. 1909, Ch. 49, Sec. 4, R.C.M. 1921, Sec. 5703.] [R.C.M. 1947, 48-109.]

§5704. **Penalty for solemnizing such marriages.** — Any person or officer who shall solemnize any such marriage within the state of Montana shall be guilty of a misdemeanor, and upon conviction thereof, be punished by a fine of five hundred [$500.00] dollars, or imprisonment in the county jail for one months, or both. [L. 1909, Ch. 49, Sec. 5, R.C.M. 1921, Sec. 5704.] [R.C.M. 1947, 48-110.]

[Note: §§5700, 5701 above were copied by Montana from the California Civil Code, Sec. 60.]

NEBRASKA

CONSTITUTION

Aliens

Art. I., Sec. 25, Rights of property; no discrimination; aliens. — There shall be no discrimination between citizens of the United States in respect to the acquisition, ownership, possession, enjoyment or descent of property. The rights of aliens in respect to the acquisition, enjoyment and descent of property may be regulated by law. [Const. 1875, as amended, 1920.]

[Note: See 76-402 -76-415 below.]

Slavery

Art. I, Sec. 2. Slavery prohibited. — There shall be neither slavery nor involuntary servitude in this state, otherwise than for punishment of crime, whereof the party shall have been duly convicted. [Const. 1875.]

STATUTES

REVISED STATUTES OF NEBRASKA (1943)

Aliens

28-1008. — [Forbids aliens to have possession of firearms.] [*Source*: Laws 1921, c. 140, §1, p. 606; C.S. 1922, §9836; C.S. 1929, §28-1008.]

[Note: Directed to all aliens. Does not specify particular groups of aliens.]

28-1009. — [Violation of 28-1008 is punishable by fine from $50 to $100 or imprisonment in county jail from 30 to 90 days.] [*Source*: Laws 1921, c. 140, §2, p. 606; C.S. 1922, §9837; C. S. 1929, §28-1009.]

[Note: See Rev. Stats. Nebraska (1943) §§9894-9894.02 (1931-1941 Supp.) in connection with inheritance rights of aliens.]

4-101. Aliens; appointment to public office unlawful; penalty. — [Prohibits appointment of aliens to any public office or official position and any person, commission or official agency so doing may be punished by a fine of up to $500 or 90 days in prison, or both. [*Source*: Laws 1919, c. 170, §1, p. 382; C.S. 1922, §5076; C.S. 1929, §4-101.]

4-102. [1949 Cum. Supp.] **Aliens; holding of public office unlawful; penalty; exception.** — [An alien who holds public office in violation of this section may be punished by a fine of up to $200 or by 60 days in prison, or both, with the following proviso: "Nothing in this section shall be construed as a prohibition or limitation upon the right of colleges and universities to exchange teachers or research scientists with educational institutions or research agencies in other countries or to engage teachers or research scientists whose residence in the United States has not been of a duration long enough to have permitted them to become citizens of the United States."] [*Source*: Laws 1919, c. 171, §1, p. 383; C.S. 1922, §5077; C.S. 1929, §4-102; Laws 1947, c. 10, §1; eff. Sept. 7, 1947.]

79-1405. Public or private schools; teachers; aliens ineligible. — No person shall be qualified, licensed, or permitted to teach in any public, private or parochial school in the State of Nebraska unless such person is a natural born or duly and fully naturalized citizen of the United States. [*Source*: Laws 1919, c. 250, §1, p. 1020; C.S. 1922, §6456; C.S. 1929, §79-1419.] [Repealed. Laws 1947, c. 10, §2.]

79-1267. [1949 Cum. Supp.] Teachers; citizenship required; exception; exchange of teachers. — No person shall be qualified, licensed, or permitted by the state or county superintendents of public instruction to teach in any public, private, or parochial school in the State of Nebraska unless such person is a natural born or duly and fully naturalized citizen of the United States: *Provided*, in the case of an exchange of teachers between the United States and a foreign country, an authorized teacher may be issued a temporary certificate by the Superintendent of Public Instruction. [*Source*: Laws 1949, c. 256, §357, eff. Aug. 27, 1949.]

79-1247.01. [1949 Cum. Supp.] Teachers' certificates; alien; temporary certificate. — The Superintendent of Public Instruction may issue a temporary certificate for an alien to teach in any public school in the State of Nebraska; *Provided*, no such certificate shall be issued to a person who is an alien and whose residence in the United States has been of a duration sufficient to have permitted him to become a citizen of the United States. [*Source*: Laws 1949, c. 255, §1, eff. April 1, 1949.]

[Note: Former Section 79-1405 which barred aliens from teaching in public or private schools in Nebraska was repealed by Laws 1947, c. 10, §2. The 1949 statutes (79-1267, 79-1247.01) relax the rigid prohibition somewhat.]

76-402 - 76-415. — [Ownership of Property]

[Note: These sections place restrictions upon the period of time real property within the state may be held by aliens or foreign corporations, and provide for escheat to the state where the requirements are not met. The statutes apply to all aliens and are not directed specifically against a particular national or racial group, thus they are not included here. The effect of such statutes, however, is that in most instances aliens who are ineligible for citizenship in the United States, i.e. Japanese and certain Oriental groups, are barred from ownership of land in Nebraska for a period longer than 5 years.]

Civil Rights

20-101. Civil Rights of persons, enumerated. — All persons within this State shall be entitled to a full and equal enjoyment of the accommodations, advantages, facilities and privileges of inns, restaurants, public conveyances, barber shops, theatres and other places of amusement, subject only to the conditions and limitations established by law and applicable alike to every person. [*Source*: Laws 1893, c. 10, §1, p. 141; R.S. 1913, §547; C.S. 1922, §439; C.S. 1929, §23-101.]

20-102. Violations; penalty. — Any person who shall violate the provisions of section 20-101 by denying to any person, except for reasons by law applicable to all persons, the full enjoyment of any of the accommodations, advantages, facilities or privileges enumerated in said section, or by aiding or inciting such denials, shall for each offense be deemed guilty of a misdemeanor, and be fined in any sum not less than twenty-five [$25.00] dollars nor more than one hundred [$100.00] dollars, and pay the costs of the prosecution. [*Source*: Laws 1893, c. 10, §2, p. 141; R.S. 1913, §548; C.S. 1922, §440; C.S. 1929, §23-102.]

Civil Service

19-660. Civil service employees; politics, race, religion; discrimination forbidden; political activity. — No person in the classified service or seeking admission thereto, shall be appointed, reduced or removed, or in anyway favored or discriminated against because of race, color or religious belief . . . [*Source*: Laws 1917, c. 208, §61, p. 514; C.S. 1922, §4598; C.S. 1929, §19-661.]

Defense Contracts

See under Employment.

Education — University of Nebraska

85-116. Students; equal privileges. — No person shall be deprived of the privileges of this institution because of age, sex, color or nationality. [*Source*: Laws, 1869, §18, p. 177; R.S. 1913, §7097; C.S. 1922, §6729, C.S. 1929, §85-115.]

Elections

32-1305. Registration . . . . [Requires registration of voters in cities of 40,000 to 100,000 to include on registration card "Color" and to show whether the voter is "White" or "Black."] [Laws 1915, c. 188, §5, p. 385. Repealed by laws 1947, c. 117, §4.] [Repealed. Laws 1947, c. 117, §4.]

32-1417. [Similar requirement in cities of 7,000 to 40,000.] [Laws 1903, c. 72, §8, p. 377; R.S. 1913, §2257; C.S. 1922, §2224; C.S. 1929, §32 — 1517.]

32-1720. [Election Commissioner required to record color of all registered voters.] [Laws 1913, c. 36, §12, p. 124; R.S. 1913, §2322; C.S. 1922, §2263; C.S. 1929, §32-1811.]

Employment

48-214. Collective bargaining; race discrimination prohibited. — It is hereby declared to be the policy of this state that no representative agency of labor, in collective bargaining with employers concerning grievances, labor disputes, wages, rates of pay, hours of employment or other conditions of work, shall, in such collective bargaining, discriminate against any person because of his race or color. The Department of Labor shall be and hereby is charged with the duty of enforcement of this policy in conformity with Article I of the Constitution of Nebraska and section 1 of the 14th Amendment of the Constitution of The United States of America. [*Source*: Laws 1941, c. 96, §1, p. 406, C.S. Supp. 1941, §48-801.]

Unfair Employment Practices

LEGISLATIVE RESOLUTION 25, APRIL 29, 1949

WHEREAS, legislation should be enacted to regulate fair employment practices in this state; and

WHEREAS, a study should be made to determine what are unfair employment practices.

NOW, THEREFORE, BE IT RESOLVED BY THE MEMBERS OF THE NEBRASKA LEGISLATURE IN SIXTY-FIRST SESSION ASSEMBLED:

1. That the Nebraska Legislative Council be directed to study and examine into the unfair employment practices in Nebraska and suggest changes which are necessary to prevent discrimination in employment.

2. That the Nebraska Legislative Council report its findings, together with recommendations for regulating unfair employment practices in Nebraska, to the Nebraska State Legislature in January, 1951.

Approved May 3, 1949.

[Note: Resolutions passed by the Nebraska Legislature are not laws and do not appear in the Session Laws of Nebraska.]

Defense Contracts

48-215. Military supplies; production; distribution; discriminaton prohibited. — It shall be unlawful for any person, firm or corporation, engaged to any extent whatsoever in the State of Nebraska in the production, manufacture or distribution of military or naval material, equipment or supplies for the State of Nebraska or the government of the United States, to refuse to employ any person in any capacity, if said person is a citizen and is qualified, on account of the race, color, creed, religion or national origin of said person. [*Source*: Laws 1943, c. 114, §1, p. 400.]

48-216. Violation; penalty. — Any person, firm or corporation, violating any of the provisions of this act, shall be deemed guilty of a misdemeanor and, upon conviction thereof, shall be subject to a fine of not less than five hundred [$500.00] dollars nor more than one thousand [$1,000.00] dollars and such person so offending may in addition be imprisoned in the county jail not less than thirty [30] days nor more than ninety [90] days. Each violation of this act shall be deemed a separate offense. [*Source*: Laws, 1943, c. 114, §2, p. 400.]

Indians

42-401 — 42-408. [Regulates Indian marriages and divorces.] [*Source*: Laws 1913, c. 68, §§1-8; pp. 201-203; R.S. 1913, §§1607-1614; C.S. 1922, §§1556-1563; C.S. 1929, §§42-401 — 42-408.]

28-1002. Firearms or ammunition; sale to Indians; penalty. Whoever shall sell or give away under any pretext whatsoever, to any Indian not a citizen, any firearms, ammunition or other munitions of any kind which can be used in firearms, shall be deemed guilty of a felony, and upon conviction thereof shall be imprisoned in the penitentiary for a term not less than two [2] years nor more than five [5] years, or fined not less than one hundred [$100.00] dollars nor more than one thousand [$1,000.00] dollars. [*Source*: Laws 1891, c. 29, §1, p. 267; R.S. 1913, §8834; C.S. 1922, §9830; C.S. 1929, §28-1002.]

53-181. Sale to Indians; penalties. — It shall be unlawful for any person to sell, give away, dispose of, exchange, or barter any alcoholic liquor to any

Indian, a ward of the United States of America, under charge of any Indian superintendent or agent, or any Indian including mixed bloods, over whom the United States of America through its departments exercises guardianship. Any person who shall violate any of the provisions of this section shall be deemed guilty of a misdemeanor, and upon conviction thereof shall be punished by imprisonment in the county jail for not less than thirty [30] days nor more than sixty [60] days and by a fine of not less than ten [$10.00] dollars nor more than one hundred [$100.00] dollars for the first offense; and, for any second or subsequent offense, the person so convicted shall be fined not less than two hundred [$200.00] dollars nor more than five hundred [$500.00] dollars, and shall be imprisoned in the county jail for not less than sixty [60] days nor more than six [6] months; and a person so convicted shall stand committed to the county jail until such fine and costs are paid. [*Source*: Laws 1935, c. 116; §38, p. 400; Laws 1937, c. 125, §1, p. 437; C.S. Supp. 1941, §53-338; Laws 1943, c. 121, §1, p. 420.]

Miscegenation

42-103. Marriages, when void. — Marriages are void (1) when one party is a white person and the other is possessed of one-eighth or more negro, Japanese or Chinese blood . . . [*Source*: R.S. p. 254; Laws 1911, c. 76, §1, p. 322, Laws 1913, c. 72, §1, p. 216; R.S. 1913, §1542; C.S. 1922, §1491; C.S. 1929, §42-103.]

42-328. Decree of divorce, annulment; when issue deemed born out of wedlock. — Upon the dissolution by decree or sentence of nullity . . . of any marriage between a white person and a negro, the issue of the marriage shall be deemed to be born out of wedlock. [*Source*: R.S. p. 134; R.S. 1913, §1594; C.S. 1922, §1543; C.S. 1929, §42-328.]

NEVADA

CONSTITUTION

Slavery

§38. [Art. I, §17.] Slavery prohibited. — §17. Neither slavery nor involuntary servitude, unless for the punishment of crimes, shall ever be tolerated in this state. [Const. 1880].

Suffrage

§204. [Art. XVIII., §1.] — Rights of suffrage not to be withheld. — The rights of suffrage and office-holding shall not be withheld from any male citizen of the United States by reason of his color or previous condition of servitude. [Ratified 1880].

STATUTES

NEVADA COMPILED LAWS (1929)

Aliens

§3302. [1943-1949 Supp.] — [Prohibits aliens from procuring licenses for gambling and gambling devices.] [1931, 165, Appvd. March 19, 1931, as amended, Stats. 1949, 114.]

§2302. — [Prohibits aliens from possessing firearms capable of being concealed upon the person. Violation of this section is punishable as a felony by imprisonment from 1 to 5 years.] [1925, 54, appvd. March 5, 1925.]

[Note: The above sections 3302 and 2302 are directed against all aliens.]

§6365. Persons who may hold and own property — Chinese excepted. — §1. Any non-resident alien, person or corporation, except subjects of the Chinese empire, may take, hold, and enjoy any real property, or any interest in lands, tenements, or hereditaments within the State of Nevada, as fully, freely, and upon the same terms and conditions as any resident citizen, person, or domestic corporation. [1879, 51, appvd. February 28, 1879.]

§6365. [1943-1949 Supp.] — [Amends §6365 to eliminate the words *"except subjects of the Chinese empire."*] [As amended, Stats. 1947, 270.]

Indians

§§3060, 3063, 3150. — [1931-1941 Supp.] [Grants Indian residents right to sell fish in certain districts. These statutes appear to be of purely local significance and not included here.] [As amended, Stats. 1941, 241; Stats. 1945, 233 (1941 Supp.; 1945 Supp.); Stats. 1925, 241; Stats. 1933, 19; 1937, 253; 1939, 172; 1941, 11, 242.]

§3149. Resident Nevada Indians to have free hunting and fishing licenses. — [Exempts resident Indians from paying of fishing and hunting licenses and provides that county clerks shall issue such licenses free of charge to resident Indians upon application therefore.] [1923, 353, Appvd. March 21, 1923.]

§9954. Indians amenable to criminal law. — §5. All the laws of this state concerning crimes and punishments, or applicable thereto, are extended to and over Indians in this state, whether such Indians be on or off an Indian reservation, and all of said laws are hereby declared to be applicable to all crimes committed by Indians within this state, whether committed on or off an Indian reservation, save and except an offense committed upon an Indian reservation by one Indian against the person or property of another Indian. [Act appvd. March 17, 1911, eff. January 1, 1912.]

Intoxicating Liquors

§10189. Providing Indian Liquor, Felony. [1943-1949 Supp.] — §242. It shall be unlawful for any person to sell, barter, give or in any manner dispose of ardent, spirituous or malt liquors, or any intoxicating liquors, liquids, drug or substance whatsoever, to any Indian within this state; and any such person or persons so unlawfully disposing of such intoxicants, within this state, to an Indian who is not a ward of the government of the United States shall be deemed guilty of a felony, and upon conviction thereof, shall be fined in any sum not less than five hundred dollars [$500.00], nor more than one thousand dollars [$1,000.00], or be imprisoned in the state prison for a term not less than one [1] year nor more than five [5] years, or both. [Added, Stats. 1915, 355.] [Repealed. Stats. 1947, 456.]

> [Note: The introduction of intoxicating liquors into Indian reservations, or the selling or giving of the same to Indians who are wards of the government, is prohibited by the United States. — See U.S. Rev. Stats. (1878), §2139; 27 U.S. Stat. L. 260, 29 U.S. Stat. L. 506.]

§10190. Indian Punished for Soliciting Purchase of Liquor. — §242A. Any Indian soliciting any person to purchase any intoxicating liquor or substance as set out in the next preceding section of this act shall be guilty of a misdemeanor, and, upon conviction thereof, shall be fined in a sum not exceeding five hundred dollars [$500.] nor less than one hundred [100] days. [Added, Stats. 1915, 355.] [Repealed Stats. 1947, 24.]

§10191. Federal Government to Prosecute — Terms Defined. — §243. Any person who shall, within this state, so unlawfully dispose of any such intoxicants, as set forth in section 242, to any Indian who shall be a ward of the government of the United States, and for which offense the government has enacted, or may hereafter enact, laws against, with punishments therefor, may be arrested by any peace officer and delivered to the United States authorities, for punishment under the laws of the United States . . . The term "ward of the government of the United States" for the purposes of this and the preceding section, shall be construed to mean any Indian over whose tribe or person the government of the United States assumes any superintendency, guardianship or wardship, whether the same arises from government of Indian reservation, holding lands in allotment, or from any other cause. [Added, Stats. 1915, 355.]

> [Note: See also Nevada Compiled Laws 1929, §10192.]

§§4072.03 - 4072.05. [1943-1949 Supp.] [Validates Indian marriages consummated in accordance with tribal customs, and regulates the form of proof of such marriages.] [Stats. 1945, 152, appvd. March 21, 1945.]

Miscegenation

§10197 — Mixed marriages of Caucasians with Certain Races Prohibited — 249. It shall be unlawful for any person of the Caucasian or white race to intermarry with any person of the Ethiopian or black race, Malay or brown race, or Mongolian or yellow race, within the State of Nevada. [Act appvd. March 17, 1911, §249, as amended. Stats. 1919, 124.]

§10198. Penalty for Contracting Parties. — §250. All persons marrying contrary to the provisions of the last preceding section shall be guilty of a gross misdemeanor. [Act appvd. March 17, 1911, §250.]

§10199. Penalty for Minister. — §251. Any officer, minister, priest or other person authorized by the laws of the State of Nevada to perform ceremonies of marriage, who shall knowingly perform, or knowingly assist in the performance within the State of Nevada of any ceremony of marriage between any person of the Caucasian or white race and any person of any other race contrary to the provisions of section 249, shall be guilty of a gross misdemeanor. [Act appvd. March 17, 1911, §251.]

§10200. Fornication Between Certain Races Prohibited; Penalty. — §252. If any white person shall live and cohabit with any black person, mulatto, Indian, or any person of the Malay or brown race or of the Mongolian or yellow race, in a state of fornication, such person so offending shall, on conviction thereof, be fined in any sum not exceeding five hundred [$500.00] dollars, and not less than one hundred [$100.00] dollars, or be imprisoned in the county jail not less than six [6] months or more than [1] year, or both. [Act appvd. March 17, 1911, §252.]

Slavery

§10607. Involuntary servitude. §1. The imigration to this state of slaves and other people bound by contract to involuntary servitude for a term of years is hereby prohibited. [1879, 105, appvd. March 8, 1879.]

[Note: This statute was directed against the practice of importing Chinese laborers into the state under contracts binding them to labor for a term of years, and was enacted to enforce the provisions of §17, Art. 1, of the Nevada Constitution. See above.]

§10608. To pay wages, unlawful. — It shall be unlawful for any corporation, company, person or persons, to pay any owner or agent of the owner of any such persons mentioned in section 1· [§10607] of this act, any wages or compensation for the labor of such slaves or persons so bound by said contract to involuntary servitude. [1879, 105, appvd. March 8, 1879.]

10610. Penalty. — §4. Any violation of any of the provisions of this act shall be deemed a misdemeanor, and shall be punished by a fine of not less than three hundred dollars [$300.00], nor more than one thousand dollars [$1,000.00], or by imprisonment in the county jail for a term of not less than three [3] months or more than six [6] months, or by both such fine and imprisonment. [1879, 105, appvd. March 8, 1879.]

NEW HAMPSHIRE

CONSTITUTION

[No provisions]

STATUTES

REVISED LAWS OF NEW HAMPSHIRE (1942)

Aliens

Ch. 43, §4. Right to Hold Public Office — Aliens. — No person is eligible to hold any municipal office, elective or appointive, who is not a citizen of the United States. [Added, Laws 1949, ch. 214, §2. Appvd. May 26, 1949.]

Discriminatory Advertising or Publication

Hotels and Other Public Places

Ch. 208, §3. Discrimination. — No person shall directly or indirectly issue or cause to be issued any circular, publication, advertisement or notice intended or calculated to discriminate against any religious sect, class or nationality, or against any members thereof, as such, in the matter of board, lodging or accommodation, privilege, or convenience offered to the general public at places of public accommodation. [1919, 27:1. P.L. 171:3.]

Ch. 208, §4 — Definition. — A place of public accommodation, within the meaning hereof, shall include any inn, tavern or hotel, whether conducted for entertainment, the housing or lodging of transient guests, or for the benefit, use or accommodation of those seeking health, recreation or rest, any restaurant, eating house, public conveyance on land or water, bathhouse, barber shop, theater, and music or other public hall. [1919, 27:2. P.L. 171:4.]

Ch. 208, §6. Penalty. —

[Violators subject to fine of $10 to $100, or imprisonment of 30 to 90 days.] [1919, 27:3. P.L. 171:6.]

Employment

Ch. 212, Sec. 21. [as amended by Laws 1947, ch. 195, Sec. 21-a, III.] [Requires contracts negotiated by labor unions to "contain a clause, which shall be as binding on the labor organization as if in its by-laws, providing that such labor organizaiton shall impose no discriminatory qualifications for membership in such organizaion based on race, color, religious creed, sex, age, national origin, ancestry or numerical restriction of total membership, unless based upon a *bona fide* occupational qualification; and a further clause, which shall also be as binding on the labor organization as if in its by-laws, providing that such labor organizaiton shall grant to all members equal voting rights in such organization."]

Labor Organizations

See under Employment.

NEW JERSEY

CONSTITUTION

Civil and Military Rights

Article I, sec. 5. Denial of rights; discrimination; segregation. — No person shall be denied the enjoyment of any civil or military right, nor be discriminated against in the exercise of any civil or military right, nor be segregated in the militia or in the public schools, because of religious principles, race, color, ancestry or national origin. [New Const. adopted November 4, 1947.]

STATUTES

NEW JERSEY STATUTES ANNOTATED (1939)

Air Raid Shelter — Discrimination.

N.J.S.A. [1948 Supp.]

2:122A-1. Air raid shelter; refusal to admit or permit to remain. — It shall be unlawful for any person to refuse to another person access to a place of safety or shelter, or to refuse to permit a person to remain in a place of safety or shelter, during an air-raid or an air-raid practice alarm, by reason of race, creed, or color. [L. 1942, c. 298, p. 1126, §1.]

2:122A-2. Violation as misdemeanor; punishment. — Any person who violates this act shall be guilty of a misdemeanor and punishable by a fine of not less than one hundred dollars ($100.00) nor more than five hundred dollars ($500.00) or imprisonment for not more than six [6] months, or both. [L. 1942, c. 298, p. 1126, §2.]

2:122A-3. Person defined. — "Person" as used in this act includes an individual, a corporation or partnership. [L. 1942, c. 298, p. 1126, §3.]

Aliens

[Note: 46:3-18 (1948 Cum. Supp.) as amended by L. 1943, c. 145, p. 395, §1, grants alien friends the same rights and privileges with respect to ownership of real estate within the state as native-born citizens, but the section bars aliens from being elected into any office of public trust. 34:9-1 forbids the employment of aliens on public works.]

2:122-.1. [Misdemeanor for alien to work as a detective.] [L. 1918, c. 97, §1, p. 233.]

Anti-Hate Law

[Chapter 157B of New Jersey Statutes Annotated, L. 1935, c. 151, §§1-8. — (Secs. 2:157B-1-2:157B-8) — making it a misdemeanor to utter any statement inciting, promoting, or advocating hatred, abuse, violence of hostility against any group residing in the state, by reason of race, color, religion or manner of worship was held void for uncertainty and as a violation of free speech in *State v. Klappratt*, 127 N.J.L. 3 95,22A. 2d. 877 (1941).]

Attorney General, — Duties of

52:17A-4. [1948 Supp.] — Powers and duties of department. — The powers and duties of the Department of law shall be the powers and duties now or hereafter conferred upon or required of the Attorney-General, either by the Constitution or by the common and statutory law of the State, and as specifically but not exclusively as detailed herein, to wit:

. . . d. Carry out and enforce the provisions of the New Jersey securities law; *also the civil rights law* . . . (emphasis added.) [L. 1944, c. 20, p. 51, §4.]

Cemeteries

8:3-1. [1948 Cum. Supp.] — **Limitation on number; exception.** — No more than five cemeteries shall be located or placed under and by virtue of this Title in any one city, township, borough or town in any county of this State, except that any religious society duly incorporated pursuant to the laws of this State, may establish a cemetery, to be used exclusively for the burial of persons of its religious faith, in any municipality of this State in which it does not maintain a cemetery, notwithstanding there are five or more cemeteries located in such municipality, and except that any society, duly incorporated pursuant to the laws of this State whose membership is limited to persons of any color, may establish a cemetery to be used exclusively for the burial of persons of said color in any municipality of this State in which no cemetery limited to the burial of persons of said color is maintained, not withstanding there are five or more cemeteries located in any such municipality . . . [As amended L. 1942, c. 45, p. 256 §1.]

[Note: See 10: 1-9 below.]

Civil Rights

Law Against Discrimination (Freeman Law)

18:25-1. Short Title. — [1949 Supp.] — This Act shall be known as "Law Against Discrimination." [L. 1945, c. 169, p. 589.]

[Note: Title of Act. "AN ACT to protect all persons in their civil rights; to prevent and eliminate practices of discrimination against persons because of race, creed, color, national origin or ancestry; to create a division in the Department of Education to effect such prevention and elimination; and making an appropriation therefor." [L. 1945, c. 169, p. 589, as amended, L. 1949, c. 11, p. 37, §1, eff. April 5, 1949.]]

18:25-2. Police power, enactment deemed exercise of. — The enactment hereof shall be deemed an exercise of the police power of the State for the protection of the public safety, health and morals and to promote the general welfare and in fulfillment of the provisions of the Constitution of this State guaranteeing civil rights. [L. 1945, c. 169, p. 589, §2.]

18:25-3. Finding and declaration of legislature. — The Legislature finds and declares that practices of discrimination against any of its inhabitants, because of race, creed, color, national origin or ancestry are a matter of concern to the government of the State, and that such discrimination threatens not only the rights and proper privileges of the inhabitants of the State but menaces the institutions and foundation of a free democratic State. [L. 1945, c. 169, p. 589, §3.]

18:25-4. [1949 Supp.] Employment without discrimination declared a civil right.—All persons shall have the opportunity to obtain employment and to obtain all the accommodations, advantages, facilities and privileges of any place of public accommodation, without discrimination because of race, creed, color, national origin or ancestry, subject only to conditions and limitations applicable alike to all persons. This opportunity is recognized as and declared to be a civil right. [L. 1945, c. 169, p. 589, §4, as amended, L. 1949, c. 11, p. 38, §2, eff. April 5, 1949.]

18:25-5. [1949 Supp.] Definitions. — As used in this act, [Sec. 18:25-1 to 18:25-28] unless a different meaning clearly appears from the context:

a. "Person" includes one or more individuals, partnerships, associations, labor organizations, corporations, legal representatives, trustees, trustees in bankruptcy, receivers, and fiduciaries.

b. "Employment agency" includes any person undertaking to procure employees or opportunities for others to work.

c. "Labor organization" includes any organization which exists and is constituted for the purpose, in whole or in part, of collective bargaining or of dealing with employers concerning grievances, terms or conditions of employment, or of other mutual aid or protection in connection with employment.

d. "Unlawful employment practice" and "unlawful discrimination" includes only those unlawful practices and acts specified in section eleven of this act [18:25-12]

e. "Employer" does not include a club exclusively social or a fraternal, charitable, educational or religious association or corporation, if such club, association or corporation is not organized and operated for private profit nor does it include any employer with fewer than six persons in his employ.

f. "Employee" does not include any individual employed by his parents, spouse or child, or in the domestic service of any person.

g. "Division" means the State "Division Against Discrimination" created by this act.

h. "Commissioner" means the State Commissioner of Education.

i. "Commission" means the Commission on Civil Rights created by this act.

j. "A place of public accommodation" shall include any tavern, roadhouse, or hotel, whether for entertainment of transient guests or accommodation of those seeking health, recreation or rest; any retail shop or store; any restaurant, eating house, or place where food is sold for consumption on the premises; any place maintained for the sale of ice cream, ice and fruit preparations or their derivatives, soda water or confections, or where any beverages of any kind are retailed for consumption on the premises; any garage, any public conveyance operated on land or water, or in the air, and stations and terminals thereof; any public bathhouse, public boardwalk, public seashore accommodation; any auditorium, meeting place, or public hall, any theatre, or other place of public amusement, motion-picture house, music hall, roof garden, skating rink, swimming pool, amusement and recreation park, fair, bowling alley, gymnasium, shooting gallery, billiard and pool parlor; any comfort station; any dispensary, clinic or hospital; and any public library, any kindergarten, primary and secondary school, trade or business school, high school, academy, college and university, or any educational institution under the supervision of the State Board of Education, or the Commissioner of Education of the State of New Jersey. Nothing herein contained shall be construed to include, or to apply to, any institution, bona fide club, or place of accommodation, which is in its nature distinctly private; nor shall anything herein contained apply to any educational facility operated or maintained by a bona fide religious or sectarian institution, and the right of a natural parent or one in *loco parentis* to direct the education and upbringing of a child under his control is hereby affirmed; nor shall anything herein contained be construed to bar any private secondary or post-secondary school from using in good faith criteria other than race, creed, color, national origin or ancestry, in the admission of students. [L. 1945, c. 169, p. 589, §5, as amended L. 1949, c. 11, p. 38, §3.]

18:25-6. Division against discrimination in State Department of Education created; powers. — There is created in the State Department of Education a division to be known as "The Division against Discrimination" with power to prevent and eliminate discrimination in employment against persons because of race, creed, color, national origin or ancestry by employers, labor organizations, employment agencies or other persons and to take other actions against discrimination because of race, creed, color, national origin or ancestry, as herein provided; and the division created hereunder is given general jurisdiction and authority for such purposes. [L. 1945, c. 169, p. 589, §6.]

18:25-7. [1949 Supp.] Composition of division; commission; membership; appointment; term; vacancies; compensation. — The said division shall consist of the Commissioner of Education and the commission. The commission shall consist of seven members; each member shall be appointed by the Governor, with the advice and consent of the Senate, for a term of five years and until his successor is appointed and qualified, except that of those first appointed, one shall be appointed for a term of one year, one for a term of two years, one for a term of three years and two for a term of four years. Vacancies caused other than by expiration of term shall be filled in the same manner but for the unexpired term only. Members of the commission shall serve without compensation but shall be reimbursed for necessary expenses incurred in the performance of their duties. The first chairman of the commission shall be designated by the Governor and thereafter, the chairman shall be elected by the members, annually. [L. 1945, c. 169, p. 590, §7, as amended L. 1949, c. 11, p. 40, §4.]

18:25-8. [1949 Supp.] Powers and duties of Commissioner of Education. — The commissioner shall

a. Exercise all powers of the division not vested in the commission.

b. Administer the work of the division.

c. Organize the division into two sections, one of which shall receive, investigate, and act upon complaints alleging discrimination in employment against persons because of race, creed, color, national origin or ancestry, and the other of which shall receive, investigate, and act upon complaints alleging other unlawful acts of discrimination against persons because of race, creed, color, national origin or ancestry; prescribe the organization of said sections and the duties of his subordinates and assistants.

d. Subject to the approval of the commission and the Governor, appoint an assistant Commissioner of Education, who shall act for the commissioner, in his place and with his powers, and such other directors, field representatives and assistants as may be necessary for the proper administration of the division and fix their compensation within the limits of available appropriations. The assistant commissioner, directors, field representatives, and assistants shall not be subject to the civil service act [Sec. 11:1-1 et seq.] and shall be removable by the commissioner at will.

e. Appoint such clerical force and employees as he may deem necessary and fix their duties, all of whom shall be subject to the civil service act.

f. Maintain liaison with local and State officials and agencies concerned with matters related to the work of the division.

g. Subject to the approval of the commission adopt, promulgate, amend, and rescind suitable rules and regulations to carry out the provisions of this act. [Secs. 18:25-1 — 18:25-28].

h. Receive, investigate, and pass upon complaints alleging acts in violation of the provisions of this act.

i. Hold hearings, subpoena witnesses, compel their attendance, administer oaths, take the testimony of any person, under oath, and, in connection therewith, require the production for examination of any books or papers relating to any subject matter under investigation or in question before the commissioner. The commissioner may make rules as to the issuance of subpoenas by the assistant commissioner.

j. Issue such publication and such results of investigations and research tending to promote good will and to minimize or eliminate discrimination because of race, creed, color, national origin or ancestry, as the commission shall direct.

k. Render each year to the Governor and Legislature a full written report of all the activities of the division. [L. 1945, c. 169, p. 591, §8, as amended L. 1947, c. 155, p. 690, §1; L. 1949, c. 11, p. 40, §5.

18:25-9. [Derived from L. 1945, c. 169, p. 592, §8a, and related to appointment of assistant commissioner of education.] Repealed L. 1947, c. 155, p. 692, §2, Eff. May 13, 1947.]

18:25-10. [1949 Supp.] **Council's powers and duties.** — The commission shall

a. Consult with and advise the commissioner with respect to the work of the division.

b. Approve or disapprove the appointment of officers, employees and agents, and the fixing of their compensation by the commissioner.

c. Survey and study the operations of the division.

d. Report to the Governor and the Legislature with respect to such matters relating to the work of the division and at such times as it may deem in the public interest.

e. The mayors or chief executive officers of the municipalities in the State may appoint local commissions on civil rights to aid in effectuating the purposes of this act. Such local commissions shall be composed of representative citizens serving without compensaiton. Such commissions shall attempt to foster through community effort or otherwise good will, co-operation and conciliation among the groups and elements of the inhabitants of the community, and they may be empowered by the local governing bodies to make recommendations to them for the development of policies and procedures in general and for programs of formal and informal education that will aid in eliminating all types of discrimination based on race, creed, color, national origin, or ancestry. The State commission may make provision for technical and clerical assistance to municipal officials to aid in organizing such commissions in all of the municipalities in this State. [L. 1945, c. 169, p. 592, §9, as amended L. 1949, c. 11, p. 42, §6.]

18:25-11. Evidence in obedience to summons; immunity of witnesses.— No person shall be excused from attending and testifying or from producing records, correspondence, documents or other evidence in obedience to the subpoena of the commissioner or assistant commissioner, on the ground that the testimony or evidence required of him may tend to incriminate him or subject him to a penalty or forfeiture, but no person shall be prosecuted or subjected to any penalty or forfeiture for or on account of any transaction, matter or thing concerning which he is compelled, after having claimed his privilege against self-incrimination, to testify or produce evidence, except that such person so testifying shall not be exempt from prosecution and punishment for perjury committed in so testifying. The immunity herein provided shall extend only to natural persons so compelled to testify. [L. 1945, c. 169, p. 593, §10.]

18:25-12. [1949 Supp.] **Unlawful employment practice or unlawful discrimination.** — It shall be an unlawful employment practice, or, as the case may be, an unlawful discrimination:

a. For an employer, because of the race, creed, color, national origin or ancestry of any individual, to refuse to hire or employ or to bar or to discharge from employment such individual or to discriminate against such individual in compensation or in terms, conditions or privileges of employment.

b. For a labor organization, because of the race, creed, color, national origin or ancestry of any individual, to exclude or to expel from its membership such individual or to discriminate in any way against any of its members or against any employer or any individual employed by an employer.

c. For any employer or employment agency to print or circulate or cause to be printed or circulated any statement, advertisement or publication, or to use any form of application for employment or to make an inquiry in connection with prospective employment, which expresses, directly or indirectly, any limitation, specification or discrimination as to race, creed, color, national origin or ancestry or any intent to make any such limitation, specification or discrimination, unless based upon a bona fide occupational qualification.

d. For any employer, labor organization or employment agency to discharge, expel or otherwise discriminate against any person because he has opposed any practices or acts forbidden under this act or because he has filed a complaint, testified or assisted in any proceeding under this act. [Secs. 18:25-1 — 18:25-28].

e. For any person, whether an employer or an employee or not, to aid, abet, incite, compel or coerce the doing of any of the acts forbidden under this act, or to attempt to do so.

f. For any owner, lessee, proprietor, manager, superintendent, agent, or employee of any place of public accommodation directly or indirectly to refuse, withhold from or deny to any person any of the accommodations, advantages, facilities or privileges thereof, or to discriminate against any person in the furnishing thereof, or directly or indirectly to publish, circulate, issue, display, post or mail any written or printed communication, notice, or advertisement to the effect that any of the accommodations, advantages, facilities, or privileges of any such place will be refused, withheld from, or denied to any person on account of the race, creed, color, national origin, or ancestry of such person, or that the patronage or custom thereat of any person of any particular race, creed, color, national origin or ancestry is unwelcome, objectionable or not acceptable, desired or solicited, and the production of any such written or printed communication, notice or advertisement, purporting to relate to any such place and to be made by any owner, lessee, proprietor, superintendent, or manager thereof, shall be presumptive evidence in any action that the same was authorized by such person. [L. 1945, c. 169, p. 594, §11, as amended L. 1949, c. 11, p. 42, §7.]

18:25-13. [1949 Supp.] Remedies; complaint, persons entitled to file. — Any person claiming to be aggrieved by an unlawful employment practice or an unlawful discrimination may, by himself, or his attorney-at-law, make, sign and file with the commissioner a verified complaint in writing which shall state the name and address of the person, employer, labor organization, employment agency, owner, lessee, proprietor, manager, superintendent, or agent alleged to have committed the unlawful employment practice or unlawful discrimination complained of and which shall set forth the particulars thereof and shall contain such other information as may be required by the commissioner. The Commissioner of Labor or Attorney-General may, in like manner, make, sign and file such complaint. Any employer whose employees, or some of them, refuse or threaten to refuse to co-operate with the provisions of this act, may file with the commissioner a verified complaint asking for assistance by conciliation or other remedial action. [L. 1945, c. 169, p. 594, §12, as amended L. 1949, c. 11, p. 44, §8.]

18:25-14. [1949 Supp.] Investigation of complaint; commissioner's duties. — After the filing of any complaint, the commissioner shall cause prompt investigation to be made in connection therewith; and if the commissioner shall determine after such investigation that probable cause exists for crediting the allegations of the complaint, he shall immediately endeavor to eliminate the unlawful employment practice or the unlawful discrimination complained of by conference, conciliation and persuasion. Neither the commissioner nor any officer or employee of the division shall disclose what has transpired in the course of such endeavors. [L. 1945, c. 169, p. 595, §13, as amended L. 1949, c. 11, p. 44, §9.]

18:25-15. [1949 Supp.] Notice requiring respondent to answer charges; place of hearing. — In case of failure so to eliminate such practice or discrimination, or in advance thereof if in his judgment circumstances so warrant, the commissioner shall cause to be issued and served in the name of the division, a written notice, together with a copy of such complaint, as the same may have been amended, requiring the person, employer, labor organization, employment agency, owner, lessee, proprietor, manager, superintendent, or agent named in such complaint, hereinafter referred to as respondent, to answer the charges of such complaint at a hearing before the commissioner at a time and place to be specified in such notice. The place of any such hearing shall be the office of the commissioner or such other place as may be designated by him. [L. 1945, c. 169, p. 595, §14, as amended L. 1949, c. 11, p. 45, §10.]

18:25-16. Practice and Procedure. — The case in support of the complaint shall be presented before the commissioner by the attorney for the division and evidence concerning attempted conciliation shall not be received. The respondent may file a written verified answer to the complaint and appear at such hearing in person or representative, with or without counsel, and submit testimony. In the discretion of the commissioner, the complainant may be allowed to intervene and present testimony in person or by counsel. The commissioner or the complainant shall have the power reasonably and fairly to amend any complaint, and the respondent shall have like power to amend his answer. The commissioner shall not be bound by the strict rules of evidence prevailing in courts of law or equity. The testimony taken at the hearing shall be under oath and be transcribed. [L. 1945, c. 169, p. 595, §15.]

18:25-17. [1949 Supp.] Findings and order of commissioner; failure to file findings and serve order. — If, upon all the evidence at the hearing the commissioner shall find that the respondent has engaged in any unlawful employment practice or unlawful discrimination as defined in this act, the commissioner shall state his findings of fact and shall issue and cause to be served on such respondent an order requiring such respondent to cease and desist from such unlawful employment practice or unlawful discrimination and to take such affirmative action, including, but not limited to, hiring, reinstatement or upgrading of employees, with or without back pay, or restoration to membership in any respondent labor organization, or extending full and equal accommodations, advantages, facilities, and privileges to all persons, as, in the judgment of the commissioner, will effectuate the purpose of this act, and including a requirement for report of the manner of compliance. If, upon all the evidence, the commissioner shall find that the respondent has not engaged in any such unlawful employment practice or unlawful discrimination, the commissioner shall state his findings of fact and shall issue and cause to be served on the complainant an order dismissing the said complaint as to such respondent. The failure of the commissioner to file his findings of fact and to issue and serve an order as in this section provided, within ninety days after the filing of the verified complaint, with him in the manner provided by section twelve of this act [Sec. 18:25-13], or within such additional period as may, for good cause shown, be granted by the commission, may, at the election of the complainant, be deemed to be the equivalent of an order of the commissioner dismissing the complaint, from which an appeal shall lie as hereinafter provided. [L. 1945, c. 169, p. 596, §16, as amended L. 1949, c. 11, p. 45, §11.]

18:25-18. Rules of practice; limitations. — The commissioner shall establish rules of practice to govern, expedite and effectuate the foregoing procedure and his own actions thereunder. Any complaint filed pursuant to this section must be so filed within ninety days after the alleged act of discrimination. [L. 1945, c. 169, p. 596, §17.]

18:25-19. [1949 Supp.] Enforcement of orders; review. — Observance of an order of the commissioner may be enforced by proceedings in the County Court to compel the specific performance of the order or of the duties imposed by law upon the respondent named in the order. Such proceedings shall be brought in the County Court to which an appeal from the order would lie as hereinafter provided. [L. 1945, c. 169, p. 597, §18, as amended L. 1949, c. 11, p. 46, §12.]

18:25-20. Stay of order. — An appeal from any order of the commissioner shall not supersede or stay such order unless the County Court to which such appeal is taken shall so direct. [L. 1945, c. 169, p. 597, §19, as amended L. 1949, c. 11, p. 46, §13.]

18:25-21. [1949 Supp.] Appeal to County Court; procedure. — Any person aggrieved by a final order of the commissioner may take an appeal therefrom to the County Court of the county in which the alleged unlawful employment practice or unlawful discrimination took place; *provided,* that notice of such appeal be filed in such County Court within thirty days after the making of such order, together with an affidavit or an acknowledgement of service of copies of the notice of appeal upon the commissioner and all other parties to the proceeding or their attorneys. Within twenty days after the service of such notice of appeal, the commissioner shall file in the County Court the original or a certified copy of the record of the proceedings under review, including such testimony as shall have been taken stenographically, and shall serve notice of the filing of such record upon the appellant. By order of the County Court or upon stipulation of the parties, the record may be shortened by eliminating any portion thereof, or by the submission of an agreed statement of facts. Within twenty days after service of the notice by the commissioner that the record has been filed in the County Court, the appellant shall move the appeal to the County Court in the manner provided by law and the rules of court in respect to the making of motions in the County Court, and thereafter the matter shall proceed in the same manner as in other motions in the County Court. [L. 1945, c. 169, p. 597, §20, as amended L. 1949, c. 11, p. 46, §14.]

18:25-22. [1949 Supp.] **Harmless errors in proceedings.** — No order of the commissioner shall be set aside upon appeal in whole or in part for any irregularity or informality in the proceedings of the commissioner unless the irregularity or informality tends to defeat or impair the substantial right or interest of the appellant. [L. 1945, c. 169, p. 597, §21, as amended L. 1949, c. 11, p. 47, §15.]

18:25-23. [1949 Supp.] **Disposition by the county court; review.** — Upon appeal, the County Court may affirm, reverse or modify any such order or may make such other order as shall appear equitable and just. Any final order or judgment of the County Court shall be subject to appeal by the commissioner or by any party as in other causes in such court. [L. 1945, c. 169, p. 597, §22, as amended L. 1949, c. 11, p. 47, §16.]

18:25-24. [1949 Supp.] **Commissioner's copy of testimony to be available.** — The commissioner's copy of the testimony shall be available at all reasonable times to all parties for examination without cost. [L. 1945, c. 169, p. 598, §23, as amended L. 1949, c. 11, p. 48, §17.]

18:25-25. Attorney for Division. — The Attorney-General shall be the attorney for the division. [L. 1945, c. 169, p. 598, §24.]

18:25-26. [1949 Supp.] **Resisting or impeding commissioner or representatives unlawful; punishment.** Any person who shall willfully resist, prevent, impede, or interfere with the commissioner or any representative of the division in the performance of duty under this act, or shall willfully violate an order of the commissioner, shall be guilty of a misdemeanor and shall be punishable by imprisonment for not more than one year, or by a fine of not more than five hundred dollars [$500.00] or by both; but procedure for the review of the order shall not be deemed to be such willful conduct. [L. 1945, c. 169, p. 598, §25, as amended L. 1949, c. 11, p. 48, §18.]

18:25-27. [1949 Supp.] **Fair construction: other laws not effected; procedure herein while pending; exclusive other remedies.** — The provisions of this act shall be construed fairly and justly with due regard to the interests of all parties. Nothing contained in this act shall be deemed to repeal any of the provisions of the civil rights law or of any other law of this State relating to discrimination because of race, creed, color, national origin or ancestry; except that, as to practices and acts declared unlawful by section eleven of this act [Sec. 18:25-12], the procedure herein provided shall, while pending, be exclusive; and the final determination therein shall exclude any other action, civil or criminal, based on the same grievance of the individual concerned. Nothing herein contained shall bar, exclude, or otherwise affect any right or action, civil or criminal, which may exist independently of any right to redress against or specific relief from any unlawful employment practice or unlawful discrimination. [L. 1945, c. 169, p. 598, §26, as amended L. 1949, c. 11, p. 48, §19.]

18:25-28. Partial Invalidity. — If any clause, sentence, paragraph, or part of this act or the application thereof to any person or circumstances, shall, for any reason, be adjudged by a court of competent jurisdiction to be invalid, such judgment shall not affect, impair, or invalidate the remainder of this act. [L. 1945, c. 169, p. 598, §27.]

Right to Hold Office or Employment

10:1-1. [1949 Supp.] Right of citizens to hold office or employment; no discrimination because of sex or marital status. The right of citizens of this State to hold office or employment shall be co-extensive with their right to vote, shall be equal as to all citizens and shall not be denied or abridged on account of sex or marital status. Such equal rights and privileges shall extend to all offices, boards, commissions or other public service in the State and its political subdivisions of whatever nature or kind.

There shall be no discrimination based on sex or marital status in the compensation, appointment, assignment, promotion, transfer, dismissal or other matters pertaining to such office or employment of persons referred to in this section. [L. 1921, c. 299, §1, p. 866 (1924 Supp. §236-1), as amended L. 1941, c. 247, p. 668, §1.]

Public Accommodation

10:1-2. Equal rights and privileges of all persons in public places. — All persons within the jurisdiction of this state shall be entitled to the full and equal accommodations, advantages, facilities and privileges of any places of public accommodation, resort or amusement, subject only to the conditions and limitations established by law and applicable alike to all persons. [L. 1884, c. 219, §1, p. 339 (C. S. p. 1442, §1), as am. by L. 1917, c. 106, §1, p. 220, L. 1921, c. 174, §1, p. 468 (1924 Supp. §39-1.)]

[Note: See *Valle v. Stengel,* (1949) 176 F. 2d. 697 (U.S.C.A. Third Circuit).]

10:1-3. [1948 Supp.] Exclusion because of race, creed, color, national origin, or ancestry unlawful. — No owner, lessee, proprietor, manager, superintendent, agent or employee of any such place shall directly or indirectly refuse, withhold from, or deny to, any person any of the accommodations, advantages, facilities or privileges thereof, or directly or indirectly publish, circulate, issue, display, post, or mail any written or printed communication, notice or advertisement to the effect that any of the accommodations, advantages, facilities and privileges of any such place shall be refused, withheld from, or denied to, any person on account of race, creed or color, national origin, or ancestry, or that the patronage or custom thereat of any person belonging to or purporting to be of any particular race, creed, color, national origin, or ancestry is unwelcome, objectionable or not acceptable, desired or solicited. [L. 1884, c. 219, §1, p. 339 (C.S. p. 1442, §1), as am. by L. 1917, c. 106, §1, p. 220; L. 1921 c. 174, §1, p. 468 (1924 Supp. §39-1.), as amended L. 1945, c. 168, p. 587, §1, (1948 Supp. 10:1-3.)].

Discriminatory Publication

10:1-4. Written announcement of discrimination; presumption. — The production of any such written or printed communication, notice or advertisement, purporting to relate to any such place and to be made by any owner, lessee, proprietor, superintendent or manager thereof, shall be presumptive evidence in any civil or criminal action that the same was authorized by such person. [L. 1884, c. 219, §1, p. 339 (C. S. p. 1442, §1), as am. by L. 1917, c. 106, §1, p. 220, L. 1921, c. 174, §1, p. 468 (1924 Supp. §39-1.)]

10:1-5. Place of public accommodations, resort or amusement defined. — A place of public accommodation, resort or amusement within the meaning of this chapter shall be deemed to include any inn, tavern, road house or hotel, whether for entertainment of transient guests or accommodation of those seeking health, recreation or rest; any restaurant, eating house, or place where food is sold for consumption on the premises; any place maintained for sale of ice cream, ice and fruit preparations or their derivatives, soda water or confections, or where any beverages of any kind are retailed for consumption on the premises; any garage, any public conveyance operated on land or water, and stations and terminals thereof; any public bathhouse, public boardwalk, public seashore accommodation; any theater, or other place of public amusement, motion-picture house, airdrome, music hall, roof garden, skating rink, amusement and recreation park, fair, bowling alley, gymnasium, shooting gallery, billiard and pool parlor; any dispensary, clinic, hospital, public library, kindergarten, primary and secondary school, high school, academy, college and university, or any educational institution under the supervision of the regents of the state of New Jersey. Nothing contained in sections 10:1-2 to 10:1-7 of this title shall be construed to include, or to apply to, any institution, club, or place of accommodation which is in its nature distinctively private, or to prohibit the mailing of a private communication in writing sent in response to a specific written inquiry. [L. 1884, c. 219, §1, p. 339 (C. S. p. 1442, §1), as am. by L. 1917, c. 106, §1, p. 220, L. 1921, c. 174, §1, p. 468 (1924 Supp. §39-1.)]

10:1-6. [1948 Cum. Supp.] **Penalty and Punishment.**—Any person who shall violate any of the provisions of sections 10:1-2 to 10:1-5 of this title by denying to any citizen, except for reasons applicable alike to all citizens of every race, creed, color, national origin, or ancestry, and regardless of race, creed, color, national origin, or ancestry, the full enjoyment of any of the accommodations, advantages, facilities or privileges in said sections enumerated, or by aiding or inciting such denial, or who shall aid or incite the violation of any of the said provisions shall, for each and every violation thereof, forfeit and pay the sum of not less than one hundred dollars ($100.00) nor more than five hundred dollars ($500.00), to the State, to be recovered in an action at law, with costs, and shall also, for every such violation, be deemed guilty of a misdemeanor, and upon conviction thereof, shall be subject to a fine of not more than five hundred dollars ($500.00), or imprisonment of not more than ninety [90] days, or both. [L. 1884, c. 219, §2, p. 339 (C. S. p. 1442, §2], as am. by L. 1917, c. 106, §2, p. 220, L. 1921, c. 174, §2, p. 469 (1924 Supp. §39-2), L. 1935, c. 247, §1, p. 762., as amended L. 1945, c. 168, p. 587, §2, (1948 Supp. 10:1-6.)]

.10:1-7. Action for penalty; costs and attorney's fee; taxation and determination; payment out of judgment. — The aggrieved party or parties in any action authorized by section 10:1-6 of this title may institute said action in the name of the state of New Jersey. If judgment is awarded in favor of the plaintiff in such action, the aggrieved party shall be paid out of the judgment so recovered, the costs incurred in prosecuting such action, according to a bill of costs to be taxed as hereinafter provided, and also an attorney's fee of not less than twenty [$20.00] dollars nor more than one hundred [$100.00] dollars to be determined and fixed as hereinafter provided.

The bill of costs shall be taxed by the clerk of a district court if the action is brought in any district court of the state, or by the clerk of the court of common pleas if the action is brought in any county where there is no district court, such costs to be taxed as in civil action for tort within the jurisdiction of either of said courts. The amount of the attorney's fee shall be determined and fixed by an order of the judge of said district court or judge of the court of common pleas where such action is brought at the time of entry of said judgment. [L. 1884, c. 219, §2, p. 339 (C. S. p. 1442, §2), as am. by L. 1917, c. 106, §2, p. 220, L. 1921, c. 174, §2, p. 469 (1924 Supp. §39-2), L. 1935, c. 247, §2, p. 763.]

Jurors

10:1-8. [1948 Cum. Supp.] Jurors not disqualified for race, color, creed, national origin, or ancestry; penalty. — No citizen possessing all other qualifications prescribed by law shall be disqualified for service as a grand or petit juror in any court on account of race, color, creed, national origin, or ancestry, and any officer or other person charged with any duty in the selection or summoning of jurors who shall exclude or fail to summon any citizen for the cause aforesaid shall, on conviction thereof, be deemed guilty of a misdemeanor, and be fined not more than five thousand dollars ($5,000.00). [1884, c. 219, §3, p. 340 (C. S. p. 1442, §3), as amended L. 1945, c. 168, p. 588, §3.]

Burial of Dead

10:1-9. Discrimination in burial of dead, misdemeanor. — No cemetery corporation, association or company, organized under any law of this State, owning or having control of any cemetery or place for the burial of the dead, shall refuse to permit the burial of any deceased person therein because of the color of such deceased person, and any cemetery corporation, association or company offending against this section shall be guilty of a misdemeanor. [L. 1898, c. 235, §213, p. 853 (C. S. p. 1810, §213.)]

[Note: See **Cemeteries** above.]

Defense Contracts

10:1-10 [1948 Cum. Supp.] Defense industries; discrimination in employment because of race, color, creed, national origin, or ancestry. — It shall be unlawful for any employer engaged to any extent whatsoever in the production, manufacture or distribution of military or naval material, equipment or supplies for the State of New Jersey, or for the Federal Government, or for any subsidiary or agency of either the State or Federal Government, or who is engaged on any defense contract whatsoever, to refuse to employ any person in any capacity on account of the race, color, creed, national origin, or ancestry of such person. [L. 1942, c. 114, p. 387, §1, as amended L. 1945, c. 174, p. 603, §2.]

10:1-11. [1948 Cum. Supp.] Misdemeanor.—Any employer or person who

(1) Excludes a citizen by reason of race, color, creed, national origin, or ancestry, from any public employment, or employment in any capacity, in industries engaged on defense contracts, or

(2) Denies, or aids or incites another to deny, to any person, because of race, color, creed, national origin, or ancestry, public employment or employment in any capacity, in industries engaged on defense contracts, shall be guilty of a misdemeanor and punishable by a fine of not less than one hundred dollars ($100.00), nor more than five hundred dollars ($500.00), or imprisonment for not more than six [6] months or both. [L. 1942, c. 114, p. 387, §2, as amended L. 1945, c. 174, p. 604, §3.]

10:1-12. [1948 Cum. Supp.] — "Employer" and "Industry" defined. — (a) "Employer" includes any individual, partnership, association, corporation, business trust, legal representative or any organized group of persons acting directly or indirectly in the interest of any employer in its relations to employees.

(b) "Industry" refers to any trade, business, industry, or branch thereof, or group of industries, in which individuals are employed. [L. 1942, c. 114, p. 387, §3.]

Public Works

10:2-1. [1948 Cum. Supp.] Discrimination in employment on public works; contract provisions. — Every contract for or on behalf of the State or any county or municipality for the construction, alteration or repair of any public building or public work shall contain provisions by which the contractor agrees that:

a. In the hiring of laborers, workmen and mechanics for the performance of work under this contract or any subcontract hereunder, no contractor, nor any person acting on behalf of such contractor or subcontractor, shall, by reason of race, creed, color, national origin, or ancestry, discriminate against any citizen of the State of New Jersey who is qualified and available to perform the work to which the employment relates;

b. No contractor, subcontractor, nor any person on his behalf shall, in any manner, discriminate against or intimidate any employee hired for the performance of work under this contract on account of race, creed, color, national origin, or ancestry;

c. There may be deducted from the amount payable to the contractor by the State of New Jersey or by any municipal corporation thereof, under this contract, a penalty of five dollars ($5.00) for each person for each calendar day during which such person is discriminated against or intimidated in violation of the provisions of the contract; and

d. This contract may be cancelled or terminated by the State of New Jersey or by any county or municipality thereof; and all money due or to become due hereunder may be forfeited, for a second or any subsequent violation of the terms or conditions of this section of the contract. [L. 1933, c. 277, §1, p. 747, as amended L. 1945, c. 171, p. 600, §1.]

10:2-2. Complaint of violation; decision of labor commissioner final. — Complaint of violation of Section 10:2-1 of this title shall be made to the commissioner of labor or his representative within the department of labor authorized by him to act in the matter, within fifteen days from the date the violation occurred.

In case of a dispute as to the facts set forth in the complaint, the matter shall be heard by the commissioner of labor or his representative within the department of labor and his decision thereon shall be conclusive. [L. 1933, c. 277, §2, p. 748.]

10:2-3. Notice of complaint and hearing. — The commissioner of labor shall notify the state agency or county or municipality whenever complaint of violation of section 10:2-1 of this title shall be filed with him on the proper form prescribed by him and shall notify them of the date and place of any hearing on disputed facts. [L. 1933, c. 277, §3, p. 748.]

10:2-4. Notice of decision; fixing penalty. — On rendering his decision under section 10:2-2 of this title, the commissioner of labor shall notify the state agency, or county or municipality as to his decision, directing them to apply the penalty set forth in paragraph "c" of section 10:2-1 of this title for a first violation and to apply the penalty set forth in paragraph "d" of said section 10:2-1 for a second or subsequent violation [L 1933, c. 277, §4, p. 748.]

Redevelopment and Regional Development Agencies

40:55C-27. [1949 Cum. Supp.] Laws governing. — In the exercise of the functions, powers and duties conferred upon it hereunder, any agency shall be governed by the provisions of . . . chapter two of Title 10 of the Revised Statutes of New Jersey [Secs. 102-1 et seq.], in the same manner as if such agency were specifically named therein. [L. 1949, c. c. 306, p. 992, §27.]

Commission on Urban Colored Population

[N. J. S. A. (1948 Supp.) 52:9F-1 - 52:9F-4, L. 1941, c. 192, pp. 582-583, §§1-4. Established a 3-member unpaid commission to examine and report on the economic, cultural, health and living conditions of the urban colored population of New Jersey.]

Defense Contracts

See under **Civil Rights** above.

Discriminatory Publication

See under **Civil Rights** above.

Education

[Note: In addition to the provisions set forth below, see **Law Against Discrimination** (Freeman Law) under **Civil Rights** for provisions relating to fair educational practices.]

Public Schools

18:14-2. [1948 Cum. Supp.] — Exclusion on account of religion, nationality or color a misdemeanor. — No child between the ages of four and twenty years shall be excluded from any public school on account of his race, creed, color, national origin, or ancestry. A member of any board of education who shall vote to exclude from any public school any child, on account of his race, creed, color, national origin or ancestry shall be guilty of a misdemeanor, and punished by a fine of not less than fifty dollars ($50.00) no more than two hundred fifty dollars ($250.00), or by imprisonment in the county jail, workhouse, or penitentiary of the county in which the offense has been committed for not less than thirty [30] days nor more than six [6] months, or by both such fine and imprisonment in the discretion of the court. [L. 1903 (2d. Sp. Sess.), c. 1, §125, p. 48 (C. S. p. 4767, §125.) as amended L. 1945, c. 172, p. 601, §1.]

[Note: See *Patterson v. Board of Education*, (1933) 11 N.J. Misc. Rep. 179, affirmed (1934) 112 N.J. L. 99; *Hedgepeth v. Board of Education*, (1944) 131 N.J.L. 153, 35 A. 2d. 622.]

Teachers

18:13-19. [1948 Cum. Supp.] — Tenure provisions not to prevent reduction in force; seniority; preferred list. — Nothing contained in Sections 18:13-16 to 18:13-18 of this Title shall be held to limit the right of any school board to reduce the number of supervising principals, principals or teachers employed in the school district when the reduction is due to a natural diminution of the number of pupils in the district. Dismissals resulting from such reduction shall not be by reason of residence, age, sex, marriage, race, religion or political affiliation . . . [L. 1909, c. 243, §3, p. 399 (C. S. p. 4764, §106c), as am. by L. 1935, c. 126, p. §1 p. 331, supp. to L. 1903 (2d. Sp. Sess.) c. 1, p. 5, as amended L. 1942, c. 269, p. 713, §1.]

Employment

See **Law Against Discrimination, Defense Contracts, Public Works, and Redevelopment and Regional Development Agencies** under **Civil Rights.**

Fair Educational Practices

See **Law Against Discrimination** under **Civil Rights.**

Fair Employment Practices

See **Law Against Discrimination** under **Civil Rights.**

Hospitals

30:9-17. [1948 Cum. Supp.] — **Management of hospitals for indigent sick and disabled . . . ; No discrimination in admission or treatment of patient.** — . . . [Vests power to make rules and regulations for the management of all hospitals for the indigent sick and disabled in the local boards of health but provides "no rule or regulation so made shall allow any preference to be shown in the admission of patients to such hospitals or in granting relief to the sick or distressed on account of difference in race, creed, color, national origin or ancestry of applicants for admission to or treatment in such hospitals . . . " [L. 1883, c. 44, §§5, 6, pp. 48, 49 [C. S. p. 2760, §§40, 41.] L. 1893, c. 19, §§1, 2, pp. 32, 33 [C. S. p. 2760, §§43, 44], Supp. to L. 1883, c. 44, p. 47, as amended L. 1945, c. 173, p. 602, §1.]

Housing

New Jersey Veteran's Housing Law (1946)

[N.J.S.A. 1948 CUM. SUPP.]

55:14G-21. Discrimination because of race, creed, color or national origin prohibited. — For all the purposes of this act, [§§55:14G-1 to §55:14G-26] no person shall because of race, creed, color, national origin or ancestry be subject to any discrimination. [L. 1946, Second Sp. Sess. c. 323, p. 1361, §21.]

[Note: See *Seawell v. MacWithey*, (1949), 2. N.J. 255, 63 A. 2d. 542, reversed in part on other grounds and affirmed in part, 2 N.J. 563, 67 A. 2d. 309 (1949). In this case it was held that a municipality charged with the management of public housing projects furnished in part by the state and in part by the municipality could not exclude Negroes from three of the projects and segregate them within a fourth, notwithstanding the housing project made available to Negro applicants was of like character and equal quality as the other three projects. Such segregation was held to be unlawful discrimination in violation of the Fourteenth Amendment to the Federal Constitution and of N.J.S.A. 55:14G-21, Laws of 1946, 2d. Sp. Sess., 322, sec. 21.

Thus, it would appear that although the above section and the following eight amendments to the New Jersey housing laws does not specifically prohibit segregation, the *Seawell* decision suggests that any segregation because of race in public or publicly-assisted housing projects will be held to be discrimination prohibited under the amendments.]

Local Housing Authorities Law

55:14A-39.1. [1950 Supp.] Discrimination because of race, creed, color or national origin prohibited. — For all of the purposes of the act to which this act is a supplement [55:14-A-31 to 55:14A-48], no person shall because of race, religious principles, color, national origin or ancestry be subject to any discrimination. [Law 1949, c. 300, as amended L. 1950, c. 105, S. No. 178. Approved and effective May 5, 1950.]

[Title of Act: A supplement to "An act to authorize housing authorities to clear blighted areas and prevent blight; to acquire real property and make it available for redevelopment by private enterprise or by public agencies in accordance with approved redevelopment plans; and to confer necessary powers on housing authorities, cities and other public bodies, and to make obligations issued by housing authorities in connection with redevelopment projects legal investments and security for deposits; to enable the advance preparation of projects so they can provide jobs and stimulate industry when necessary in the period of reconversion; and to authorize the creation of an advisory board to housing authorities composed of representatives of business, real estate, home financing and other interests," approved June fourteenth, one thousand nine hundred and forty-nine (P.L. 1949, c. 300).]

[Note: The purpose of the above section and the following seven sections is to prohibit discrimination by reason of race, creed, color, national origin or ancestry in housing built with public funds or public assistance. The eight amendments to existing New Jersey housing laws were introduced by Senator Clapp and were sponsored by the Joint Council for Civil Rights and the following organizations:

Americans for Democratic Action, New Jersey Council.
American Jewish Committee, Trenton and Essex Chapters.
American Jewish Congress, New Jersey State Region.
American Legion, Guyton-Callahan Post, No. 152.
American Veterans Committee, New Jersey State Council.
B'nai Brith Councils of New Jersey.
Burlington County Council for Civil Rights.
Camden County Council for Civil Rights.
Essex County Intergroup Council.
Essex County Republican Council, Inc.
Gloucester County Civil Liberties Council.
Jewish Community Council of Essex County.
Lambda Kappa Mu, Delta and Epsilon Chapters.
Morris County Committee for Civil Rights.

National Conference of Christians and Jews.
National Council of Jewish Women, New Jersey Conference.
New Jersey State C.I.O. Council.
New Jersey State Conference of N.A.A.C.P. Branches.
New Jersey State Federation of Colored Women's Clubs, Inc.
New Jersey State Federation of Labor, A.F.L.
New Jersey State Federation of Teachers.
Newark Teachers Union.
North Jersey Civil Liberties League.
Trenton Council on Human Relations.
Union County Council for Civil Rights.
Urban League of Essex County.
Urban League Guild of New Jersey.

See New Jersey Session Law Service, 1950, No. 3, pp. 148-156. See also note under 55:14G-21 above.]

National Defense Housing Projects

55:14C-7.1. [1950 Supp.] **Discrimination because of race, creed, color or national origin prohibited.** — For all of the purposes of the act to which this act is a supplement [55:14C-1 to 55:14C-10], no person shall because of race, religious principles, color, national origin or ancestry be subject to any discrimination. [L. 1941, c. 213, p. 19, as amended L. 1950, c. 106, S. No. 179, approved and effective May 5, 1950.]

[Note: See note under 55:14A-39.1 above.]

Redevelopment Companies Law

55:14D-6.1. [1950 Supp.] **Discrimination because of race, creed, color or national origin prohibited.** — For all of the purposes of the act to which this act is a supplement [55:14D-1 to 55:14D-28], no person shall because of race, religious principles, color, national origin or ancestry be subject to any discrimination. [L. 1944, c. 169, as amended L. 1950, c. 107, S. No. 180. Approved and effective May 5, 1950.]

State Housing Law of 1949

55:14H-9.1. [1950 Supp.] **Discrimination because of race, creed, color or national origin prohibited.** — For all of the purposes of the act to which this act is a supplement [55:144H-1 to 55:14H-37], no person shall because of race, religious principles, color, national origin or ancestry be subject to any discrimination. [L. 1949, c. 303, as amended L. 1950, c. 108, S. No. 181, Approved and effective May 5, 1950.]

[Note: See note under 55:14A-39.1 above.]

Local Housing Authorities Law

55:14A-7.5. [1950 Supp.] **Discrimination because of race, creed, color or national origin prohibited.** — For all of the purposes of the act to which this act is a supplement [55:14A-1 to 55:14A-26], no person shall because of race, religious principles, color, national origin or ancestry be subject to any discrimination. [L. 1938, c. 19, as amended L. 1950, c. 109, S. No. 182. Approved and effective May 5, 1950.]

[Note: See note under 55:14A-39.1 above.]

Housing Co-operation Law

55:14B-5.1. [1950 Supp.] **Discriminaiton because of race, creed, color or national origin prohibited.** — For all of the purposes of the act to which this act is a supplement [55:14B-1 to 55:14B-8], no person shall because of race, religious principles, color, national origin or ancestry be subject to any discrimination. [L. 1938, c. 20, as amended L. 1950, c. 110, S. No. 183. Approved and effective May 5, 1950.]
[Note: See note under 55:14A-39.1 above.]

Urban Redevelopment Law

55:14E-7.1. [1950 Supp.] **Discrimination because of race, creed, color or national origin prohibited.** — For all of the purposes of the act to which this act is a supplement [55:14E-1 to 55:14E-19], no person shall because of race, religious principles, color, national origin or ancestry be subject to any discrimination. [L. 1946, c. 52, as amended L. 1950, c. 111, S. No. 184. Approved and effective May 5, 1950.]

[Note: See note under 55:14A-39.1 above.]

Limited Dividend Housing Corporations Law

55:16-8.1. [1950 Supp.] **Discrimination because of race, creed, color or national origin prohibited.** — For all of the purposes of the act to which this act is a supplement [55:16-1 to 55:16-21], no person shall because of race, religious principles, color, national origin or ancestry be subject to any discrimination. [L. 1949, c. 184, as amended L. 1950, c. 112, S. No. 185. Approved and effective May 5, 1950.]

[Note: See note under 55:14A-39.1 above.]

Insurance

17:34-44. Discrimination on account of color prohibited. — No life insurance company doing business in this state shall:

a. Make any distinction or discrimination between white persons and colored persons, wholly or partially of African descent, as to the premiums or rates charged for policies upon their lives, or in any other manner;

b. Demand or require a greater premium from the colored person than is, at that time, required by the company from white persons of the same age, sex, general condition of health and prospect of longevity;

c. Make or require any rebate, diminution or discount upon the amount to be paid on the policy in case of death of the colored person insured; or

d. Insert in the policy any condition, or make any stipulation whereby the person insured shall bind himself or his heirs, executors, administrators or assigns to accept a sum less than the full value or amount of the policy in case of a claim accruing thereon by reason of the death of the insured, other than such as are imposed on white persons in similar cases. Any such stipulation shall be void.

This section shall apply only to contracts of insurance issued on the lives of persons resident in this state at the time the application for insurance is made. Nothing in this subtitle shall be construed to require any agent or company to take or receive the application for insurance of any person or to issue a policy of insurance to any person. [L. 1902, c. 134, §83, p. 441; C.S. p. 2865, §83.]

[Note: See also 17:34-35 — 17:34-37.]

Jurors

See under **Civil Rights** above.

Law Against Discrimination (Freeman Law)

See under **Civil Rights** above.

Public Accommodation

See under **Civil Rights** above.

Public Works

See under **Civil Rights** above.

Relief

2:160 - 13. — [Forbids inquiry into the religion, creed, politics or party affiliation of any applicant for relief or work relief. Violation is made a misdemeanor.] [L. 1936, c. 169, §§1, 2, p. 404.]

NEW MEXICO

CONSTITUTION

Aliens

Art. 2, §22. [Alien land-ownership.] — Until otherwise provided by law no alien, ineligible to citizenship under the laws of the United States, or corporation, copartnership or association, a majority of the stock or interest in which is owned or held by such aliens, shall aquire title, leasehold or other interest in or to real estate in New Mexico. [Const. 1911, as amended September 20, 1921.]

[Note: But see 75-121 New Mexico Stat. 1941 (Ann.) which provides foreigners shall have full rights to acquire or hold real estate. The Opinions of Attorney-General 1929-30, p. 11, indicate however, that 75-121, enacted 1871, has been modified by the Const., Art. 2, §22, as amended in 1921.]

Education

Art. 12, §1. [Free public schools] — A uniform system of free public schools sufficient for the education of, and open to, all the children of school age in the state shall be established and maintained. [Const. 1911].

[Note: But see 55 — 1201 below.]

Art. 21, §4. [Public Schools.] — Provision shall be made for the establishment and maintenance of a system of public schools which shall be open to all children of the state and free from sectarian control, and said school shall always be conducted in English. [Const. 1911.]

Art. 12, §10. [Educational rights of Children of Spanish descent.]. — Children of Spanish descent in the state of New Mexico shall never be denied the right and privilege of admission and attendance in the public schools or other public educational institutions of the state, and they shall never be classed in separate schools, but shall forever enjoy perfect equality with other children in all public schools and educational institutions of the State, and the legislature shall provide penalties for the violation of this section. This section shall never be amended except upon a vote of the people of this state, in an election at which at least three-fourths of the electors voting in the whole state and at least two-thirds of those voting in each county in the State shall vote for such amendment. [Const. 1911].

Indians

Art. 21. §1. [. . . Intoxicating liquor for Indians.] — [Prohibits forever "the sale, barter or giving of intoxicating liquors to Indians" or the introduction of such liquors into the Indian country. [Const. 1911.]

Suffrage

Art. 21, §5. [Suffrage.] — This state shall never enact any law restricting or abridging the right of suffrage on account of race, color or previous condition of servitude. [Const. 1911 as amended Nov. 5, 1912.]

STATUTES

New Mexico Statutes (1941 Annot.)

Aliens

[Note: 43-234 - 43-239. [Prohibits aliens from hunting, provides penalty for the possession of shot guns or rifles and sets up procedure for the search, seizure and forfeiture of rifles or shotguns possessed by aliens in violation of this statute. Section 43-234 was amended in 1945 [Laws 1945, ch. 127] by excepting diplomatic representatives and aliens who have resided in New Mexico five years.] [Laws 1921, Ch. 113, §1, p. 201; Laws 1945, ch. 127, §1, p. 220.]

51-303. [Chiropractice] — [Aliens barred from receiving license to practice chiropractice in the state.] [Laws 1921, ch. 110, §3, p. 195; C.S. 1929, §23-103.]

51-216. [Chiropody] — [Aliens barred from the practice of chiropody within the state.] [Laws 1939, ch. 17, §16, p. 34.]

51-404. [Dentistry] — [Aliens are prohibited from practicing dentistry in the state.] [Laws 1919, ch. 35, §4, p. 78; C.S. 1929, §37-104; Laws 1939, ch. 201, §1, p. 492.]

51-504. [Physicians] — [Bars aliens from receiving license to practice medicine.] [Laws 1923, ch. 44, §3, p. 61; C.S. 1929, §110-104; Laws 1939, ch. 80, §1, p. 150.]

Education — Segregation in Public Schools

55-1201. . . . Separate Schools for colored pupils — Restriction. — Pupils who are residents of a district shall be permitted to attend school in the same regardless of the time when they acquired such residence, whether before or after the enumeration. Provided, that where, in the opinion of the country school or municipal school board and on approval of said opinion by the state board of education, it is for the best advantage of the school that separate rooms be provided for the teaching of pupils of African descent, and said rooms are so provided, such pupils may not be admitted to the school rooms occupied and used by pupils of Caucasian or other decent. Provided, further that such rooms set aside for the teaching of such pupils of African decent shall be as good and well kept as those used by pupils of Caucasian or other decent, and teaching therein shall be as efficient. Provided, further, that pupils of Caucasian or other decent may not be admitted to the school rooms so provided for those of African descent. [Laws 1923, ch. 148, §1201, p. 290; 1925, ch. 73, §21, p. 99, C. S. 1929, §120-1201.]

55-3001 - 55-3007. [1949 Cum. Supp.] [State Supervisor of Spanish.] [Creates the position of State Supervisor of Spanish "in order to bring about an improvement in the teaching of Spanish in the schools of the state, and in order to insure the retainment and the development of the Spanish language, with a view of future Inter-American relations." Provides for duties, qualifications, appointment, term of office, supervision of work and compensation for such position.] [Laws 1943, ch. 81, §§1-7, p. 123.]

Defamation

[Note: 41-2725 provides "Any person who, with intent to injure, publishes or circulates any malicious statement in writing, with reference to or concerning any fraternal or religious order or society, shall be guilty of criminal libel." Laws 1915, ch. 6, §1, p. 21; C.S. 1929, §35-3527. See also New Mexico Statutes 1941, §§41-2726-41-2728.]

Employment —

Equal Employment Opportunities Act
Laws 1949, Chapter 161
Senate Bill No. 45
Approved March 17, 1949

AN ACT relating to the prevention and elimination of practices of discrimination in employment and otherwise against persons because of race, creed, color or national origin, creating in the Executive Department the State Fair Employment Practices Commission, defining its functions, powers and duties and providing for the appointment of its officers and employees.

BE IT ENACTED by the Legislature of the State of New Mexico:

§1. Purposes and Declaration of Policy. — (a) The practice or policy of discrimination against individuals by reason of their race, color, religion, national origin or ancestry is a matter of state concern. Such discrimination foments domestic strife and unrest, threatens the rights and privileges of the inhabitants of the state and undermines the foundations of a free democratic state. The denial of equal employment opportunities because of such discrimination and the consequent failure to utilize the productive capacities of individuals to their fullest extent deprive large segments of the population of the state of earnings necessary to maintain decent standards of living, necessitates their resort to public relief and intensifies group conflicts, thereby resulting in grave injury to the public safety, health and welfare.

(b) It is hereby declared to be the public policy of this state to foster the employment of all persons in accordance with their fullest capacities, regardless of their race, color, religion, national origin or ancestry, and to safeguard their right to obtain and hold employment without such discrimination.

(c) This article shall be known as "Equal Employment Opportunities Act". It shall be deemed an exercise of the police power of the state for the protection of the public welfare, prosperity, health and peace of the people of the state. [N.M.S.A., 1949 Cum. Supp., §57-1201.]

§2. Opportunity for Employment Without Discrimination A Civil Right. — The opportunity to obtain employment without discrimination because of race, color, religion, national origin or ancestry is hereby recognized as and declared to be a civil right. [N.M.S.A., 1949 Cum. Supp., §57-1202.]

§3. **Definitions.** — When used in this article: (a) The term "person" includes one [1] or more individuals, partnerships, associations, organizations, corporations, legal representatives, trustees, receivers, or other organized groups of persons.

(b) The term "employment agency" includes any person undertaking with or without compensation to procure opportunities to work or to procure, recruit, refer or place employees.

(c) The term "labor organization" includes any organization which exists and is constituted for the purpose, in whole or in part, of collective bargaining or of dealing with employers concerning grievances, terms or conditions of employment, or for other mutual aid or protection in relation to employment.

(d) The term "employer" includes the State, or any political or civil subdivision thereof, any person employing four [4] or more persons in same kind of employment within the state, and any person acting in the interest of any employer, directly or indirectly, but does not include a religious corporation or association, or a social or fraternal club not organized for private profit.

(e) The term "employee" does not include any individual employed by his parents, spouse or child or in the domestic service of any person.

(f) The term "Commission" means the State Commission Against Discrimination created by this article.

(g) The term "unlawful employment practice" includes only those unlawful employment practices specified in Section 4 [57-1204] of this article.

(h) The term "discriminate" includes segregate or separate. [N.M.S.A., 1949 Cum Supp., §57-1203.]

§4. **Unlawful Employment Practices** — (a) It shall be unlawful employment practice: For an employer, by himself or his agent, because of the race, color, religious creed, national origin, or ancestry of any individual, to refuse to hire or employ or to bar or to discharge from employment such individual or to discriminate against such individual in compensation or in terms, conditions or privileges of employment, unless based upon a bona fide occupational qualification.

(b) For a labor organization hereafter to directly or indirectly, by ritualistic practice, constitutional or by-law prescription, by tacit agreement among its members, or otherwise, deny a person or persons membership in its organization by reason of his race, color or creed, or by regulations practice or otherwise, deny to any of its members, by reason of race, color or creed, equal treatment with all other members in any designations of members to any employer for employment, promotion or dismissal by such employer.

(c) For any employer or employment agency to print or circulate or cause to be printed or circulated any statement, advertisement or publication, or to use any form of application for employment or to make any inquiry or record in connection with employment, which expresses, directly or indirectly, any limitation, specification or discrimination as to race, color, religious creed, national origin or ancestry or any intent to make any such limitation, specification or

292

discrimination, or to discriminate in any way on the ground of race, color, religious creed, national origin or ancestry, unless based upon a bona fide occupational qualification.

(d) For any person, employer, labor organization or employment agency to discharge, expel or otherwise discriminate against any person because he has opposed any practices forbidden under. this chapter or because he has filed a complaint, testified or assisted in any proceeding under section five [§57-1205].

(e) For any person, whether an employer or an employee or not, to aid, abet, incite, compel or coerce the doing of any of the acts forbidden under this chapter or to attempt to do so. [N.M.S.A., 1949 Cum. Supp., §57-1204.]

§5. Government Contracts. — Every contract to which the state or any of its political or civil subdivisions is a party shall contain a provision requiring the contractor and his sub-contractors not to discriminate against any employee or applicant for employment, to be employed in the performance of such contract, with respect to his hire, tenure, terms, conditions, or privileges of employment or any matter directly or indirectly related to employment, because of his race, color, religion, national origin or ancestry. Breach of this covenant may be regarded as a material breach of the contract [N.M.S.A., 1949 Cum. Supp., §57-1205.]

§6. State Fair Employment Practice Commission. — (a) There is hereby created a commission to be known as New Mexico fair employment practice commission consisting of five (5) members to be known as commissioners, one of whom shall be the duly elected and qualified attorney general of the state of New Mexico and one of whom shall be the duly appointed and qualified and acting labor commissioner of the state of New Mexico, each of whom shall serve ex-officio, and three (3) members who shall be appointed by the governor by and with the advice and consent of the senate. One of such commissioners shall be designated as chairman by the governor. The term of office of each appointive member of the commission shall be for three (3) years. Provided, however, that of the commissioners first appointed, one [1] shall be appointed for a term of one [1] year, one [1] for a term of two [2] years, one [1] for a term of three [3] years. Any member chosen to fill a vacancy occurring otherwise than by expiration of term shall be appointed for the unexpired term of the member whom he is to succeed. A majority of said commissioners shall constitute a quorum to transact business and for the exercise of any of the powers or authority conferred by this article. A vacancy in the commission shall not impair the right of the remaining members to execute all the powers of the commission.

(b) The members of the commission shall receive no salary.

(c) Within ninety (90) days after the passage of this article the commission shall meet and organize in the manner herein provided.

(d) The commission shall appoint as director the labor commissioner of the state of New Mexico whose duties shall be, to keep a full and correct record of all proceedings of the commission, to issue all necessary processes, writs, warrants, orders, awards and notices and to perform all other duties as the commission may prescribe. He shall also have supervision of the collection of data, information concerning matters covered by the provisions of this article and make such reports and investigations as the commission shall be open to the public and shall stand and be adjourned without further notice thereof on its record.

(e) The commission shall have power the approval of the governor to employ during its pleasure such deputies, experts, examiners and other employees as may be deemed necessary to carry out the provisions of this article [§§57-1201 - 57-1214] or to perform the duties and exercise the powers conferred by law upon the commission. [N.M.S.A., 1949 Cum. Supp. §57-1206.]

§7. General Policies of the Commission — The commission shall formulate policies to effectuate the purposes of this act and make recommendations to agencies or officers of the State or local subdivisions of government in aid of such policies and purposes. [N.M.S.A., 1949 Cum. Supp., §57-1207.]

§8. Powers and Duties of the Commission — (a) To establish and maintain a principal office in the city and county of Santa Fe and such other offices within the State as it may deem necessary and to avail itself where deemed necessary of the offices, furniture, appliances, supplies, equipment of the labor and industrial commission of New Mexico or to hold sessions at the offices of the labor and industrial commission of New Mexico.

(b) To meet and function at any place within the State.

(c) To appoint with the approval of the governor and attorney general such attorneys, hearing examiners and other employees and agents as it may deem necessary, fix their compensation within the limitations provided by law and prescribe their duties.

(d) To adopt, promulgate, amend and rescind rules and regulations to effectuate the provisions of this act and the policies and practice of the commission in connection therewith.

(e) To formulate policies to effectuate the purposes of this act and make recommendations to agencies and officers of the state or local subdivisions of government to effectuate such policies.

(f) To receive, investigate and pass upon charges of unfair employment practices.

(g) To hold hearings, subpoena witnesses, compel their attendance, administer oaths, take the testimony of any person under oath and require the production for examination of any books and papers relating to any matter under investigation or in question before the commission. The commission may make rules as to the issuance of subpoenas by individual commissioners or the director. Contumacy or refusal to obey a subpoena issued pursuant to this section shall constitute a contempt punishable, upon the application of the commission, by the district court in which the witness resides, transacts business or is found. No person shall be excused from attending or testifying or from producing books, records, correspondence, documents or other evidence in obedience to the subpoena of the commission, on the ground that the testimony or evidence required of him may tend to incriminate him or subject him to a penalty or a forfeiture; but no individual shall be prosecuted or subjected to any penalty or forfeiture for or on account of any transaction, matter or thing concerning which he is compelled, after having claimed his privilege against self-incrimination, to testify or produce evidence, except that such individual so testifying shall not be exempt from prosecution and punishment for perjury committed in so testifying.

(h) To create such advisory agencies and conciliation councils, local, regional or state-wide, as in its judgment will aid in effectuating the purposes of this chapter, and the commission may empower them to study the problems of discrimination in all or specific fields of human relationships or in specific instances of discrimination, because of race, color, religious creed, national origin, or ancestry, in order to foster, through community effort or otherwise, good will, cooperation and conciliation among the groups and elements of the population of the state and make recommendations to the commission for the development of policies and procedures in general and in specific instances, and for programs of formal and informal education which the commission may recommend to the appropriate state agency. Such advisory agencies and conciliation councils shall be composed of representative citizens, serving without pay, but with reimbursement for actual and necessary traveling expenses; and the commission may make provision for technical and clerical assistance to such agencies and councils and for the expenses of such assistance.

(i) To issue such publications and such results of investigations and research as in its judgment will tend to promote good will and minimize or eliminate discrimination because of race, color, religious creed, national origin or ancestry.

(j) From time to time, but not less than once a year, to report to the Legislature and the governor, describing in detail the investigations, proceeding and hearings it has conducted and their outcome, the decisions it has rendered and the other work performed by it and make recommendations for such further legislation concerning abuses and discrimination because of race, color, religion, national origin or ancestry as may be desirable.

(k) To adopt an official seal. [N.M.S.A., 1949 Cum. Supp., §57-1208.]

§9. Educational Program — (a) In order to eliminate prejudice among the various racial, religious and ethnic groups in this state and to further good-will among such groups, the commission in cooperation with other departments of government is directed to prepare a comprehensive educational program, designed for the students of the public schools of this state and for all other residents thereof, designed to emphasize the origin of prejudice against such minority groups, its harmful effects, and its incompatibility with American principles of equality and fair play.

(b) The commission is hereby authorized to accept contributions from any person to assist in the effectuation of this section and may seek and enlist the cooperation of private charitable, religious, labor, civic and benevolent organizations for the purposes of this section. [N.M.S.A., 1949 Cum. Supp., §57-1209.]

§10. Prevention of Unfair Employment Practices — Procedure. — (a) The Commission is empowered and directed, as hereinafter provided, to prevent any person from engaging in unfair employment practices, provided that before instituting the formal hearing authorized by this section it

295

may attempt, by informal methods of persuasion and conciliation, to induce compliance with this act.

(b) Any person claiming to be aggrieved by an alleged unlawful employment practice or any associate or person on his behalf, may by himself or his attorney-at-law, make, sign and file with the commission a verified complaint in writing which shall state the name and address of the person, employer, labor organization or employment agency alleged to have committed the unlawful employment practice complained of and which shall set forth the particulars thereof and contain such other information as may be required by the commission. The industrial commissioner or attorney general may, in like manner, make, sign and file such complaint. Any employer whose employees, or some of them, refuse or threaten to refuse to cooperate with the provisions of this article, may file with the commission a verified complaint asking for assistance by conciliation or other remedial action. After the filing of any complaint, the director of the commission shall designate one of the commissioners to make, with the assistance of the commission's staff, prompt investigation in connection therewith; and if such commissioner shall determine after such investigation that probable cause exists for crediting the allegations of the complaint, he shall immediately endeavor to eliminate the unlawful employment practice complained of by conference, conciliation and persuasion. The members of the commission and its staff shall not disclose what has transpired in the course of such endeavors. In case of failure so to eliminate such practice, or in advance thereof if in his judgment circumstances so warrant, he shall cause to be issued and served in the name of the commission, a written notice, together with a copy of such complaint, as the same may have been amended, requiring the person, employer, labor organization or employment agency named in such complaint, hereinafter referred to as respondent, to answer the charges of such complaint at a hearing before any member of the commission or any qualified examiner designated in writing by the commission to conduct such hearings and receive evidence, sitting as the commission, at a time and place to be specified in such notice. The place of any such hearing shall be the office of the commission or such other place as may be designated by it. The case in support of the complaint shall be presented before the commission by one of its attorneys or agents or by an attorney for the complainant and the commissioner who shall have previously made the investigation and caused the notice to be issued shall not participate in the hearing except as a witness, nor shall he participate in the deliberations of the commission in such case; and the aforesaid endeavors at conciliation shall not be received in evidence. The respondent may file a written verified answer to the complaint and appear at such hearing in person or otherwise, with or without counsel, and submit testimony. In the discretion of the commission, the complainant may be allowed to intervene and present testimony in person or by counsel. The commission or the complainant shall have the power reasonably and fairly to amend any complaint, and the respondent shall have like power to amend his answer. The commission shall not be bound by the strict rules of evidence prevailing in courts of law or equity. The testimony taken at the hearing shall be under oath and be transcribed. If, upon all the evidence at the hearing the commission shall find that a respondent has engaged in any unlawful employment practice as defined in this article [§§57-1201-57-1214], the commission shall state its findings of fact and shall issue and cause to be served on such respondent an order requiring such respondent to cease and desist from such unlawful employment practice and to take such affirmative action, including (but not limited to) hiring, reinstatement or upgrading of employees, with or without back pay, or restoration to membership in any respondent labor organization, as, in the judgment of the commission, will effectuate the purposes of this article, and including a requirement for report of the manner of compliance. If, upon all the evidence, the commission shall find that a respondent has not engaged in any such unlawful employment practice, the commission shall state its findings of fact and shall issue and cause to be served on the complainant an order dismissing the said complaint as to such respondent. A copy of its order shall be delivered in all cases to the labor commissioner, the attorney general, and such other public officers as the commission deems proper, until a transcript of the record in a case shall be filed in a court as hereinafter provided, the commission may, at any time, upon reasonable notice, and in such manner as it shall deem proper, modify or set aside, in whole or in part, any finding or order made by it. [N.M.S.A. 1949 Cum. Supp., §57-1210.]

§11. Judicial Review and Enforcement. — (a) Any complainant, intervenor, or respondent claiming to be aggrieved by a final order of the commission, including a refusal to issue a complaint, may obtain judicial review thereof, and the commission may obtain an order of court for its enforcement, in a proceeding as provided in this section. Such proceeding shall be brought in the district court of the state within any county wherein the unfair employment practice which is the subject of the commission's order was committed or wherein any respondent required in the order to cease and desist from any unfair employment practice or to take other affirmative action resides or transacts business. Such proceedings shall without exception be by trial *de novo.*

(b) Such proceeding shall be initiated by the filing of a petition in such court and the service of a copy of the said petition upon the commission and upon all parties who appeared before the commission. Thereupon the commission shall file a transcript of the record upon the hearing before it. The court shall have jurisdiction of the proceeding and of the questions determined therein and shall have power to grant such temporary relief or restraining order as it deems just and proper. The court in its discretion, may consider the matter, solely upon the transcript filed by the commission or may order a new trial upon the merits as if no trial had been had or may consider such portions of the transcript as it considers admissible and as ordered by the court. Findings of the commission shall not be binding on the court but may be altered and modified as the court, shall in its discretion deem advisable. The court shall make and enter its order enforcing, modifying and or order of the commission or substituting its own findings and its own order. The court of its own motion or on motion of any party may remand the case to the commission in the interest of justice for the purpose of adducing additional specified and material evidence and the making of findings thereon.

297

(c) The jurisdiction of the court shall be exclusive and its judgment and order shall be final, subject to review by the supreme court as provided by law.

(d) The commission's copy of the testimony shall be available at all reasonable times to all parties without cost for examination and for the purposes of judicial review of the order of the commission. The petition shall be heard on the transcript of the record without requirement of printing.

(e) The commission may appear in court by its own attorney.

(f) Unless otherwise directed by the commission, tribunal or court, commencement of review proceedings under this section shall operate as a stay of any order.

(g) Petitions filed under this section shall be heard expeditiously and determined upon the transcript filed, without requirement of printing.

(h) If no proceeding to obtain judicial review is instituted by a complainant, intervenor, or respondent within thirty days from the service of an order of the commission pursuant to section 10 [§57-1210] hereof, the commission may obtain a decree of the court for the enforcement of such order upon showing that respondent is subject to the commission's jurisdiction and resides or transacts business within the county in which the petition for enforcement is brought. [N.M.S.A., 1949 Cum. Supp., §57-1211.]

§12. Construction.—The provisions of this act shall be construed liberally for the accomplishment of the purposes thereof and any law inconsistent with any provision hereof shall not apply. Nothing contained in this act shall be deemed to repeal any of the provisions of any law of this state relating to discrimination because of race, color, religion, national origin or ancestry. [N.M.S.A., 1949 Cum. Supp., §57-1212.]

§13. Severability. — If any clause, sentence, paragraph or part of this Act or the application thereof to any person or circumstances shall for any reason be adjudged by a court of competent jurisdiction to be invalid, such judgment shall not affect, impair or invalidate the remainder of this Act or its application to other persons or circumstances. [N.M.S.A., 1949 Cum. Supp., §57-1213.]

§14. Short Title — This Act may be cited as the "FAIR EMPLOYMENT PRACTICES ACT". [N.M.S.A., 1949 Cum. Supp., §57-1214.]

Indians

[Note: 25-1401 relates to recovery of property sold by Indians. 41-2122 - 41-2124 provides penalties for sale of imitation Indian articles as genuine, or falsely representing articles to be of Indian make. 42-2105 makes the civil and criminal laws of the state applicable to Indians for acts and misdemeanors committed off the reservation. See also 42-2106, 42-2107.]

43-233. Indians hunting off reservations — Hunting on reservations — Application of laws. — [Makes hunting and fishing laws applicable to Indians hunting off the reservation and to persons hunting on any Indian reservation within the state, but exempts Indians from requirement of license to hunt or fish within the reservation where the Indian resides.] [Laws 1912, ch. 85, §7; Code 1915, §2430; Laws 1919 ch. 133, §1, p. 285; C. S. 1929, §57-212.]

55-2304. [1949 Cum. Supp.] [Provides Indian children shall be admitted to the state school for deaf and dumb.] [Laws 1899, c. 42, §3; Code 1915, §5103; C. S. 1929, §130-405; Laws 1945, ch. 80, §1, p. 130.]

55-2901. [1949 Cum. Supp.] — **Preservation and development of Indian arts and crafts — Dissemination of knowledge of traditional Indian rites.** — [Designates the Inter-Tribal Indian Ceremonial Association as an official agency of the state "for the purpose of encouraging the preservation and development of the Indian arts and crafts among the Indian Tribes and Pueblos of the state of New Mexico, and for the further purpose of encouraging the preservation of the tradiitonal rites and ceremonials of the said Indian Tribes and Pueblos, and for the further purpose of affording an opportunity for the development of knowledge and appreciation of such arts, crafts, rites and ceremonials among other people."] [Laws 1939, ch. 42, §1, p. 80.]

*Suffrage

56-248. **Qualifications of electors.** — [Indians not taxed are not eligible to vote.] [Laws 1927, ch. 41, §210, p. 62, C. S. 1929, §41-210.]

Intoxicating Liquors

61-1013. **Sale to Indians, drunkards, and lunatics.** — It shall be a violation of this act for any person to sell, serve, give or deliver any alcoholic liquors to, or to procure or aid in the procuration of any alcoholic liquors for, any Indian, who is a ward of the United States government, habitual drunkard or person of unsound mind knowing that the person buying, receiving, or receiving service of, such alcoholic liquors is an Indian and a ward of the United States government, habitual drunkard or lunatic. [Laws 1939, ch. 236, §1203, p. 566.]

Ku Klux Klan — Masks

41-2901. **Disguise — Wearing with intent — Penalty.** — Every person who shall in any manner disguise himself, with intent to obstruct the due execution of the law, or with intent to intimidate, hinder or interrupt any officer, or any other person, in the legal performance of his duty, or the exercise of his rights under the law of the United States or of this state, whether such intent shall be effected or not, shall be punished by imprisonment for not more than one [1] year, or by fine not exceeding one hundred dollars [$100]. [Laws 1853-54, p. 122; C.L. 1865, ch. 54, §13; C.L. 1884, §810; C.L. 1897, §1205; Code 1915, §1819; C.S. 1929, §35-4628.]

41-2902. **Mask, wearing in street or other public way prohibited.** — It shall be unlawful for any person to appear or be upon any public street, alley, road, highway or thoroughfare in this state, wearing a mask, hood, robe or other covering upon his face, head or body, or disguised in any manner, so as to conceal the identity of the wearer thereof. [Laws 1923, ch. 4, §1, p. 6; C.S. 1929, §35-4629.]

41-2903. **Entering or being upon private property while masked prohibited.** — It shall be unlawful for any person, wearing a mask, hood, robe or other covering upon his face, head or body, or disguised in any manner, so as to conceal the identity of the wearer thereof, to enter or be upon the private property of any other person in this state, without the consent of the owner, lessee or occupant of such property. [Laws 1923, ch. 4, §2, p. 6; C.S. 1929, §35-4630.]

41-2904. Threats against person, family, or property. — Any person who shall transmit or cause to be transmitted to any other person any communication in writing or otherwise threatening injury to such other person, his or her family or property, or commanding or requiring of such other person to do or not to do anything in derogation of his or her lawful or constitutional rights or privileges, shall be punished as herein provided. [Laws 1923, ch. 4, §3. p. 6; C.S. 1929, §35-4631.]

41-2905. Penalty for violating §§41-2902 - 41-2904. — Any person violating sections 1 [§41-2902], 2[§41-2903], or 3[§41-2904] of this act, shall be punished by a fine of not more than $2,500, or by imprisonment in the .county jail or state penitentiary, for a period of not more than three [3] years, or by both such fine and imprisonment in the discretion of the court. [Laws 1923, ch. 4, §4, p. 5; C.S. 1929, §35-4632.]

41-2906. Assault while masked — Penalty. — Any person who, while wearing a mask, hood, robe or other covering upon his face, head or body or disguised in any manner, so as to conceal his identity, shall commit an assault upon another, or threaten another with bodily injury, upon conviction, shall be punished by imprisonment in the state penitentiary for not less than one [1], nor more than ten [10] years. [Laws 1923, ch. 4, §5, p. 6; C.S. 1929, §35-4633.]

Public Works
See FAIR EMPLOYMENT PRACTICES ACT, subtitle Government Contracts under Employment.

*[Note: Art. 7, §1, Const. of New Mexico excludes "Indians not taxed" from qualified electors. Cf. Art. 7, §3. Indian suffrage was established in New Mexico in 1948 when a special federal court ruled that the clause in the Mexico Constitution which prohibited Indians from voting was invalid as a violation of the Fourteenth and Fifteenth Amendments to the Constitution of the United States. See New York Times, October 8, 1950.]

NEW YORK

CONSTITUTION

Civil Rights

Art. 1, §11. [Equal protection of laws; discrimination in civil rights prohibited.] No person shall be denied the equal protection of the laws of this state or any subdivision thereof. No person shall, because of race, color, creed or religion, be subjected to any discrimination in his civil rights by any other person or by any firm, corporation, or institution, or by the state or any agency or subdivision of the state. [Newly adopted by Constitutional Convention of 1938 and approved by vote of the people November 8, 1938; McKinney's Consolidated laws of New York Annotated, Book 2.]

Education

Art. 11, §1. [Common schools.] The legislature shall provide for the maintenance and support of a system of free common schools, wherein all the children of this state may be educated. [Formerly §1 of Art. 9. Renumbered by Constitutional Convention of 1938 and approved by vote of the people November 8, 1938.]

[Note: As recently as 1900, it was held in the case of *People v. School Board*, 161 N.Y. 598, 56 N.E. 81, affirming 44 App. Div. 469, 61 N.Y.S. 330, that the above section did not prevent the legislature from authorizing the school board of Queens from maintaining separate schools for colored children, and from excluding them from the schools for white children. (Laws, 1894, Ch. 556). The effect of this decision was negated by the enactment of Sec. 3201 of the Education Law (L. 1945, c. 292, §7.). See below.]

Indians

Art. 1, §13. [Purchase of lands of Indians.] No purchase or contract for the sale of lands in this state, made since the fourteenth day of October, one thousand seven hundred seventy-five; or which may hereafter be made of, or with the Indians, shall be valid unless made under the authority, and with the consent of the legislature. [Formerly §15. Renumbered and amended by Constitutional Convention of 1938 and approved by vote of the people November 8, 1938.]

[Note: A contract made with an Indian for the sale of lands in violation of the above provision is punishable as a misdemeanor. See *Penal Law*, §2030.]

STATUTES

McKinney's Consolidated Laws of New York Annotated.

Alcoholic Beverage Control Law

§65. Prohibited Sales. — No person shall sell, deliver or give away or cause or permit or procure to be sold, delivered or given away any alcoholic beverages to

    1. Any minor, actually or apparently, under the age of eighteen years;

2. Any intoxicated person or to any person, actually or apparently, under the influence of liquor;

3. Any habitual drunkard known to be such to the person authorized to dispense any alcoholic beverages.

Neither such person so refusing to sell or deliver under this section nor his employer shall be liable in any civil or criminal action or for any fine or penalty based upon such refusal, except that such sale or delivery shall not be refused, withheld from or denied to any person on account of race, creed, color or national origin. [As amended L. 1937, c. 521; L. 1943, c. 276; L. 1945, c. 292, §1, eff. March 27, 1945.]

§118. Revocation of Licenses for cause. — Any license or permit issued pursuant to this chapter may be revoked, cancelled or suspended for cause . . . [As amended L. 1935, c. 162, §2; L. 1938, c. 329, §§2, 3; L. 1944, c. 203; L. 1945, c. 522. eff. April 4, 1945.]

§126. [Aliens are forbidden to traffic in alcoholic beverages.] [L. 1939, c. 267; L. 1942, c. 792; L. 1945, c. 94; L. 1945, c. 722, §1, 2; L. 1946, c. 259, eff. March 26, 1946.]

Aliens

Real Property Law

§10. Capacity to hold real property — . . . 2. Aliens empowered to take, hold, transmit, and dispose of real property within this state in the same manner as native-born citizens and their heirs and devisees take in the same manner as citizens. [As amended L. 1913, c. 152, §1; L. 1944, c. 272, eff. March 22, 1944.]

§15. Title through alien. — The right, title or interest in or to real property in this state now held or hereafter acquired by any person entitled to hold the same can not be questioned or impeached by reason of the alienage of any person through whom such title may have been derived. Nothing in this section affects or impairs the right of any heir, devisee, mortgagee, or creditor by judgment or otherwise. [Section derived from L. 1896, c. 547, §7.]

§16. Liabilities of alien holders of real property. — Every alien holding real property in this state is subject to duties, assessments, taxes and burdens as if he were a citizen of the state. [Section derived from L. 1896, c. 547, §8.]

[Note: See Alcoholic Beverage Control Law, §126 above.]

Attorney-General

Executive Law

§62. General duties.—

9. Bring and prosecute or defend, upon request of the industrial commission or of the state commission against discrimination, any civil action or proceeding, the institution or defense of which, in his judgment, is necessary for effective enforcement of the laws of the state against discrimination by reason of race, creed, color or national origin, or for enforcement of an order or determination of such commissioner or commission made pursuant of such laws.

10. Prosecute every person charged with the commission of a criminal offense in violation of any of the laws of this state against discrimination because of race, creed, color or national origin, in any case where in his judgment, because of the extent of the offense, such prosecution cannot be effectively carried on by the district attorney of the county wherein the offense or a portion thereof is alleged to have been committed, or where in his judgment the district attorney has erroneously failed or refused to prosecute. In all such proceedings, the attorney-general may appear in person or by his deputy or assistant before any court or any grand jury and exercise all the powers and perform all the duties in respect of such actions or proceedings which the district attorney would otherwise be authorized or required to exercise or perform. [Added by L. 1945, c. 813, Sec. 1, effective July 1, 1945.]

Attorneys

See under Judiciary Law.

Civil Rights

Civil Rights Law

§13 — **Right to serve on juries** — No citizen of the state possessing all other qualifications which are or may be required or prescribed by law, shall be disqualified to serve as a grand or petit juror in any court of this state on account of race, creed, color, national origin or sex, and any person charged with any duty in the selection or summoning of jurors who shall exclude or fail to summon any citizen for any of these causes aforesaid shall, on conviction thereof, be deemed guilty of a misdemeanor and be fined not less than one hundred dollars nor more than five hundred dollars or imprisoned for not less than thirty days, nor more than ninety days, or both such fine and imprisonment. [L. 1895, c. 1042, §3, as amended L. 1938, c. 163; L. 1945, c. 292, §2, eff. March 27, 1945.]

§40. **Equal rights in places of public accommodation, resort or amusement.** — All persons within the jurisdiction of this state shall be entitled to the full and equal accommodations, advantages, facilities and privileges of any places of public accommodations, resort or amusement, subject only to the conditions and limitations established by law and applicable alike to all persons. No person, being the owner, lessee, proprietor, manager, superintendent, agent or employee of any such place shall directly or indirectly refuse, withhold from or deny to any person any of the accommodations, advantages, facilities or privileges thereof, or directly or indirectly publish, circulate, issue, display, post or mail any written or printed communication, notice or advertisement, to the effect that any of the accommodations, advantages, facilities nd privileges of any such place shall be refused, withheld from or denied to any person on account of race, creed, color or national origin, or that the patronage or custom thereat, of any person belonging to or purporting to be of any particular race, creed, color or national origin is unwelcome, objectionable or not acceptable, desired or solicited. The production of any such written or printed communication, notice or advertisement, purporting to relate to any such place and to be made by any person being the owner, lessee, proprietor, superintendent or manager thereof, shall be presumptive evidence in any civil or criminal action that the same was authorized by such person. A place of public accommodation, resort or amusement within the meaning of this article, shall be deemed to include inns, taverns, road houses, hotels, whether conducted for the entertainment of transient guests or for the accommodation of those seeking health, recreation or rest, or restaurants, or eating houses, or any place where food is sold for consumption on the premises; buffets, saloons, barrooms, or any store, park or enclosure where spirituous or malt liquors are sold; ice cream parlors, confectioneries, soda fountains, and all stores where ice cream, ice and fruit preparations or their derivatives, or where beverages of any kind are retailed for consumption on the premises; retail stores and establishments, dispensaries, clinics, hospitals, bath-houses, barber-shops, beauty parlors, theatres, motion picture houses, air-dromes, roof gardens, music halls, race courses, skating rinks, amusement and recreation parks, fairs, bowling alleys, golf courses, gymnasiums, shooting galleries, billiard and pool parlors, public libraries, kindergartens, primary and secondary schools, high schools, academies, colleges and universities, extension courses, and all educational institutions under the supervision of the regents of the state of New York; and any such public library, kindergarten, primary and secondary school, academy, college, university, professional school, extension course, or other educational facility, supported in whole or in part by public funds or by contributions solicited from the general public; garages, all public conveyances, operated on land or water, as well as the stations and terminals thereof; public halls and public elevators of buildings and structures occupied by two or more tenants, or by the owner and one or more tenants. With regard to institutions for the care of neglected and/or delinquent children supported directly or indirectly, in whole or in part, by public funds, no accommodations, advantages, facilities and privileges of such institutions shall be refused, withheld from or denied to any person on account of race or color. Nothing herein contained shall be construed to modify or supersede any of the provisions of the children's court act, the social welfare law or the domestic relations court act of New York city in regard to religion of custodial persons or agencies or to include any institution, club, or place of accommodation which is in its nature distinctly private, or to prohibit the mailing of a private communication in writing sent in response to a specific written inquiry.

No institution, club, organization or place of accommodation which sponsors or conducts any amateur athletic contest or sparring exhibition and advertises or bills such contest or exhibition as a New York state championship contest or uses the words "New York state" in its announcements shall be deemed a private exhibition within the meaning of this section. [As amended L. 1918, c. 196; L. 1935, c. 737; L. 1939, c. 810, §1; L. 1942, cc. 764, 765; L. 1943, c. 554; L. 1944, c. 226, §1; L. 1945, c. 292, §3, eff. March 27, 1945.]

[Note: See *Camp of the Pines v. N.Y. Times Co.* (1945) 53 N.Y.S. (2d) 475.]

[Note: §40-a forbids inquiry concerning religion or religious affiliations of any person seeking employment or official position in the public schools of the state of New York. This section, added by L. 1932, c. 234, does not mention race or color.]

§40-b. Wrongful refusal of admission to and ejection from places of public entertainment and amusement. — No person, agency, bureau, corporation or association, being the owner, lessee, proprietor, manager, superintendent, agent or employee of any place of public entertainment and amusement as hereinafter defined shall refuse to admit to any public performance held at such place any person over the age of twenty-one years who presents a ticket of admission to the performance a reasonable time before the commencement thereof, or shall eject or demand the departure of any such person from such place during the course of the performance, whether or not accompanied by an offer to refund the purchase price or value of the ticket of admission presented by such person; but nothing in this section contained shall be construed to prevent the refusal of admission to or the ejection of any person whose conduct or speech thereat or therein is abusive or offensive or of any person engaged in any activity which may tend to a breach of the peace.

The places of public entertainment and amusement within the meaning of this section shall be legitimate theatres, burlesque theatres, music halls, opera houses, concert halls and circuses. [Added L. 1941, c. 893. §1, eff. April 30, 1941.]

§41. Penalty for violation. — Any person who or any agency, bureau, corporation or association which shall violate any of the provisions of sections forty, forty,-a, forty-b, or forty-two or who or which shall aid or incite the violation of any of said provisions and any officer or member of a labor organization, as defined by section forty-three of this chapter, or any person representing any organization or acting in its behalf who shall violate any of the provisions of section forty-three of this chapter or who shall aid or incite the violation of any of the provisions of such sections shall for each and every violation thereof be liable to a penalty of not less than one hundred dollars nor more than five hundred dollars, to be recovered by the person aggrieved thereby or by any resident of this state, to whom such person shall assign his cause of action, in any court of competent jurisdiction in the county in which the plaintiff or the defendant shall reside; and such person and the manager or owner of or each officer of such agency, bureau, corporation or association, and such officer or member of a labor organization or person acting in his behalf, as the case may be shall, also, for every such offense be deemed guilty of a misdemeanor, and upon conviction thereof shall be fined not less than one hundred dollars nor more than five hundred dollars, or shall be imprisoned not less than thirty days nor more than ninety days, or both such fine and imprisonment. [L. 1913, c. 265; as amended L. 1918, c. 196; L. 1932, c. 234, §2; L. 1940, c. 9, §2; L. 1941, c. 893; L. 1942, c. 478, eff. April 17, 1942.]

Publicly-Aided Housing

Laws 1950, Ch. 287

AN ACT

To amend the civil rights law, in relation to prohibiting discrimination and segregation because of race, color, religion, national origin or ancestry in housing accommodations acquired, constructed, repaired or maintained, in whole or in part, with the assistance or support of the state or any of its political subdivisions.

The People of the State of New York, represented in Senate and Assembly, do enact as follows:

Section 1. The civil rights law is hereby amended by inserting therein a new article, to be article two-A, to read as follows:

ARTICLE 2-A

EQUAL RIGHTS TO PUBLICLY-AIDED HOUSING

Section 18-a. Findings and declarations of policy.

18-b. Definitions.

18-c. Discrimination prohibited.

18-d. Restraint of discrimination; damages for violations.

18-e. Applicability.

§18-a. Findings and declarations of policy.—1. This article shall be deemed an exercise of the police power of the state for the protection of the welfare, health and peace of the people of this state and the fulfillment and enforcement of the provisions of the constitution of this state concerning civil rights.

2. The practice of discrimination because of race, color, religion, national origin or ancestry in any publicly assisted housing accommodations is hereby declared to be against public policy.

§18-b. Definitions. — When used in this article:

1. The term "person" includes one or more individuals, partnerships, associations, corporations, legal representatives, trustees, trustees in bankruptcy and receivers or other fiduciaries.

2. The term "housing accommodation" includes any building, structure, or portion thereof which is used or occupied or is intended, arranged or designed to be used or occupied, as the home, residence or sleeping place of one or more human beings, but shall not include any accommodations operated by a religious or denominational organization as part of its religious or denominational activities.

3. The term "publicly assisted housing accommodation" includes any housing accommodation to be constructed within the state of New York

(a) which is to be exempt in whole or in part from taxes levied by the state or any of its political subdivisions;

(b) which is to be construed on land sold below cost by the state or any of its political subdivisions or any agency thereof, pursuant to the federal housing act of nineteen hundred forty-nine;

(c) which is to be construed in whole or in part on property acquired or assembled by the state or any of its political subdivisions or any agency thereof through the power of condemnation or otherwise for the purpose of such construction; or

(d) for the acquisition, construction, repair or maintenance of which the state or any of its political subdivisions or any agency thereof supplies funds or other financial assistance.

4. The term "owner" includes the lessee, sub-lessee, assignee, managing agent, or other person having the right of ownership or possession or the right to rent or lease housing accommodations and includes the state and any of its political subdivisions and any agency thereof.

5. The term "discriminate" includes to segregate or separate.

§18-c. **Discrimination prohibited.** — It shall be unlawful:

1. For the owner of any publicly assisted housing accommodation to refuse to rent or lease or otherwise to deny to or withhold from any person or group of persons such housing accommodation because of the race, color, religion, national origin or ancestry of such person or persons.

2. For the owner of any publicly assisted housing accommodation to discriminate against any person because of the race, color, religion, national origin or ancestry of such person in the terms, conditions or privileges of any publicly assisted housing accommodations or in the furnishing of facilities or services in connection therewith.

3. For any person to cause to be made any written or oral inquiry concerning the race, color, religion, national origin or ancestry of a person seeking to rent or lease any publicly assisted housing accommodation.

§18-d. **Restraint of discrimination; damages for violations.** —

1. Any person aggrieved by a violation of section eighteen-c of this chapter and any person whose assessment shall amount to more than one thousand dollars and who shall be liable to pay taxes on such assessment in any county, town, village or municipal corporation in the state or who has been assessed or who has paid taxes upon any assessment of the above-named amount within one year previous to the initiation of an action under this section shall have a right of action in any court of appropriate jurisdiction for restraint of such violation and for other equitable remedies including such affirmative relief as may be necessary to undo the effects of such violation.

2. Any person aggrieved by a violation of section eighteen-c of this chapter shall in addition have a right of action in any court of appropriate jurisdiction for damages caused by such violation.

§18-e. **Applicability.** — The provisions of this section shall not apply to privately owned housing accommodations which are not publicly assisted within the meaning of section eighteen-b (3) of this chapter.

§2. This act shall take effect July first, nineteen hundred fifty. [Appvd. March 29, 1950.]

Civil Service Law

§14. [1949 Cum. Supp.] **The competitive class. —**

3. Application for examination. (b) [This subsection was amended by Laws of New York, 1949, c. 384, effective April 5, 1949, to eliminate from par. (b) the requirement that an applicant for competitive civil service exams state his place of birth in his application.] [Added L. 1948, c. 70; amended L. 1949, c. 384, eff. April 5, 1949.]

§14-b. Discrimination on account of race, creed, color or national origin prohibited. —

1. No person, having authority or control over, or discretion in, the selection or appointment of persons for employment in the civil service of the state, or of any of its civil divisions or cities, or over the promotion, or fixation of compensation, or dismissal of persons in such service, shall, solely by reason of the race, creed, color, or national origin of any person, deny to such person any employment, promotion or increase of salary, or dismiss or suspend such persons from employment.

2. Any person who shall be denied appointment to any employment in the classified service of the state or of any of its civil divisions or cities, or, who, being so employed in such service, shall be denied promotion or increase in salary, or shall be dismissed or suspended from service, such dismissal or suspension being stated to be due to reduction in the number of positions of the kind occupied by such person, or to the lack of work in such position, and who believes such denial of employment, promotion or salary increase, or such dismissal or suspension, to have been made solely by reason of his race, creed, color or national origin, may file a verified petition with the state civil service commission, if the position be in the state, county or village service, and if the service of a city, with the municipal civil service commission of such city, setting forth the facts, and his reasons for such belief, and praying for such redress as the said commission may deem proper.

3. Upon such petition being filed with such civil service commission, the commission shall if satisfied a prima facie showing of discrimination has been made by proper evidence in this petition promptly order a hearing to be held for the purpose of inquiring into the truth of such allegation, due notice of such hearing being given to the petitioner and to the officer who shall have made the appointment or promotion or who shall have ordered the salary increase or the suspension or dismissal referred to in the said petition, as well as to any person who it may be alleged in such petition was appointed or promoted or given a salary increase or retained in service in violation of the provisions of subdivision one of this section. If upon such hearing the commission shall find that the petitioner was denied appointment, promotion or increase of salary, or was dismissed or suspended solely by reason of his race, creed, color or national origin, the commission shall cause such finding to be entered of record in its office and shall transmit a certified copy of such finding to the petitioner and to the officer or board by whom he was denied appointment, promotion or increase of salary, or was so dismissed or suspended, and it shall thereupon be the duty of the said officer or board to rescind, if necessary, the aforesaid unlawful appointment, promotion or

salary increase, and to appoint, promote or increase the salary of said petitioner, or to restore the said petitioner to service, as the case may be. .

4. If, upon the hearing of a petition filed with it pursuant to subdivision two of this section, a municipal civil service commission shall find that the allegations of the petition are unfounded, and shall dismiss the same, but one or more members of the said commission shall dissent from such finding and such order of dismissal, the petitioner may file a petition with the state civil service commission praying for a review of such finding and a reversal or modification of such order. Upon such petition the state civil service commission shall proceed in the same manner and shall have the same power as in the case of a petition filed with it under the preceding section hereof. [Formerly §14-c, added L. 1939, c. 811; renumbered 14-b, L. 1940, c. 649, §2; amended L. 1945, c. 292, §6, eff. March 27, 1945.]

Defense Contracts

See §514 under Penal Law. See also Defense Industries.

Discriminatory Publication

See Civil Rights Law, §40.

Education Law

§3201. No exclusion on account of race, creed, color or national origin. — No person shall be refused admission into or be excluded from any public school in the state of New York on account of race, creed, color or national origin. [From Education Law of 1910, §920, as amended by L. 1945, c. 292, §7. Similar provisions were contained in Education Law of 1909, §980, which was derived from L. 1900, c. 492, §1.]

Fair Educational Practices

§313. [1948 Cum. Supp.] [Discrimination in admission of applicants to educational institutions.] (1) *Declaration of policy.* — It is hereby declared to be the policy of the state that the American ideal of equality of opportunity requires that students, otherwise qualified, be admitted to educational institutions without regard to race, color, religion, creed or national origin, except that, with regard to religious or denominational educational institutions, students, otherwise qualified, shall have the equal opportunity to attend therein without discrimination because of race, color or national origin. It is a fundamental American right for members of various religious faiths to establish and maintain educational institutions exclusively or primarily for students of their own religious faith or to effectuate the religious principles in furtherance of which they were maintained. Nothing herein contained shall impair or abridge that right.

(2) *Definitions.* — (a) Educational institution means any educational institution of post-secondary grade subject to the visitation, examination or inspection by the state board of regents or the state commissioner of education.

(b) Religious or denominational educational institution means an educational institution which is operated, supervised or controlled by a religious or denominational organization and which has certified to the state commismissioner of education that it is a religious or denominational educational institution.

(3) *Unfair educational practices.* — It shall be an unfair educational practice for an educational institution after September fifteenth, nineteen hundred forty-eight:

(a) To exclude or limit or otherwise discriminate against any person or persons seeking admission as students to such institution because of race, religion, creed, color, or national origin; except that nothing in this section shall be deemed to affect, in any way, the right of a religious or denominational educational institution to select its students exclusively or primarily from members of such religion or denomination or from giving preference in such selection to such members or to make such selection of its students as is calculated by such institution to promote the religious principles for which it is established or maintained.

(b) To penalize any individual because he has initiated, testified, participated or assisted in any proceedings under this section.

(c) It shall be an unfair educational practice for any educational institution to use criteria other than race, religion, creed, color or national origin in the admission of students.

(4) *Certification of religions and denominational institutions.* — An educational institution operated, supervised or controlled by a religious or denominational organization may, through its chief executive officer, certify in writing to the commissioner that it is so operated, controlled or supervised, and that it elects to be considered a religious or denominational educational institution, and it thereupon shall be deemed such an institution for the purposes of this section.

(5) *Procedure.* — (a) Any person seeking admission as a student who claims to be aggrieved by an alleged unfair educational practice, hereinafter referred to as the petitioner, may himself, or by his parent or guardian, make, sign and file with the commissioner of education a verified petition which shall set forth the particulars thereof and contain such other information as may be required by the commissioner. The commissioner shall thereupon cause an investigation to be made in connection therewith; and after such investigation if he shall determine that probable cause exists for crediting the allegations of the petition, he shall attempt by informal methods of persuasion, conciliation or mediation to induce the elimination of such alleged unfair educational practice.

(b) Where the commissioner has reason to believe that an applicant or applicants have been discriminated against, except that preferential selection by religious denominational institutions of students of their own religion or denomination shall not be considered an act of discrimination, he may initiate an investigation on his own motion.

(c) The commissioner shall not disclose what takes place during such informal efforts at persuasion, conciliation or mediation nor shall he offer in evidence in any proceeding the facts adduced in such informal efforts.

(d) A petition pursuant to this section must be filed with the commissioner within one year after the alleged unfair educational practice was committed.

(e) If such informal methods fail to induce the elimination of the alleged unfair educational practice, the commissioner shall have power to refer the matter to the board of regents which shall issue and cause to be served upon such institution, hereinafter called the respondent, a complaint setting forth the alleged unfair educational practice charged and a notice of hearing before the board of regents, at a place therein fixed to be held not less than twenty days after the service of said complaint.

Any complaint issued pursuant to this section must be issued within two years after the alleged unfair educational practice was committed.

(f) The respondent shall have the right to answer the original and any amended complaint and to appear at such hearing by counsel, present evidence and examine and cross-examine witnesses.

(g) The commissioner and the board of regents shall have the power to subpoena witnesses, compel their attendance, administer oaths, take testimony under oath and require the production of evidence relating to the matter in question before it or them. The testimony taken at the hearing, which shall be public shall be under oath and shall be reduced to writing and filed with the board of regents.

(h) After the hearing is completed the board of regents shall file an intermediate report which shall contain its findings of fact and conclusions upon the issues in the proceeding. A copy of such report shall be served on the parties to the proceeding. Any such party within twenty days thereafter, may file with the regents exceptions to the findings of fact and conclusions, with a brief in support thereof, or may file a brief in support of such findings of fact and conclusions.

(i) If, upon all the evidence, the regents shall determine that the respondent has engaged in an unfair educational practice, the regents shall state their findings of fact and conclusions and shall issue and cause to be served upon such respondent a copy of such findings and conclusions and an order requiring the respondent to cease and desist from such unfair educational practice, or such other order as they deem just and proper.

(j) If, upon all the evidence, the regents shall find that a respondent has not engaged in any unfair educational practice, the regents shall state their findings of fact and conclusions and shall issue and cause to be served on the petitioner and respondent, a copy of such findings and conclusions, and an order dismissing the complaint as to such respondent.

(6) *Judicial review and enforcement.* — (a) Whenever the board of regents has issued an order as provided in this section it may apply to the supreme court for the enforcement of such order by a proceeding brought in the supreme court within the third judicial district. The board of regents shall file with the court a transcript of the record of its hearing, and the court shall have jurisdiction of the proceeding and of the questions determined therein, and shall have power to make an order annulling or confirming, wholly or in part, or modifying the determination reviewed. The order

of the supreme court shall be subject to review by the appellate division of the supreme court and the court of appeals, upon the appeal of any party to the proceeding, in the same manner and with the same effect as provided on an appeal from a final judgment made by the court without a jury.

(b) Any party to the proceeding, aggrieved by a final order of the board of regents, may obtain a judicial review thereof by a proceeding under article seventy-eight of the civil practice act, which shall be brought in the appellate division of the supreme court for the third judicial department.

(7) *Regents empowered to promulgate rules and regulations.* — The regents from time to time may adopt, promulgate, amend or rescind rules and regulations to effectuate the purposes and provisions of this section.

(8) The commissioner shall include in his annual report to the legislature (1) a resume of the nature and substance of the cases disposed of through public hearings, and (2) recommendations for further action to eliminate discrimination in education if such is needed. [Added L. 1948, c. 753, eff. July 1, 1948.]

Elections

See under **Penal Law** below.

Employment — (Civil Rights Law)

Utilities Companies

§42. Discrimination by utility companies. — It shall be unlawful for any public utility company, as defined in the public service law, to refuse to employ any person in any capcity in the operation or maintenance of a public service on account of the race, creed, color or national origin of such person. [Added L. 1933, c. 511; amended L. 1945, c. 292, §4, eff. March 27, 1945.]

Labor Organizations

§43. Discrimination by labor organizations. — As used in this section, the term "labor organization" means any organization which exists and is constituted for the purpose, in whole or in part, of collective bargaining, or of dealing with employers concerning grievances, terms or conditions of employment, or of other mutual aid or protection. No labor organization shall hereafter, directly or indirectly, by ritualistic parctice, constitutional or by-law prescription, by tacit agreement among its members, or otherwise, deny a person or persons membership in its organization by reason of his race, creed, color or national origin, or by regulations, practice or otherwise, deny to any of its members, by reason of race, creed, color or national origin, equal treatment with all other members in any designation of members to any employer for employment, promotion or dismissal by such employer. [Added L. 1940, c. 9, §1; amended L. 1945, c. 292, §5, eff. 27, 1945.]

[Note: The constitutionality of the above section was upheld by the United States Supreme Court in *Railway Mail Ass'n v. Corsi* (1945) 326 U.S. 88, 65 S. Ct. 1483, 89 L. Ed. 2072, affirming 293 N.Y. 315, 56 N.E. (2) 721.]

Defense Industries

§44. Discrimination by industries involved in defense contracts. — It shall be unlawful for any person, firm or corporation engaged to any extent whatsoever in the production, manufacture or distribution of military or naval material, equipment or supplies for the state of New York or for the federal government to refuse to employ any person in any capacity on account of the race, color, creed or national origin of such person. [Added L. 1941, c. 478, §1; amended L. 1942, c. 676, §1, eff. May 6, 1942.]

Industrial Commissioner

§45. Powers of administration vested in industrial commissioner. — The industrial commissioner may enforce the provisions of sections forty-two, forty-three and forty-four of this chapter. For this purpose he may use the powers of administration, investigation, inquiry, subpoena, and hearing vested in him by the labor law; he may require submission at regular intervals or otherwise of information, records and reports pertinent to discriminatory practices in industries. [Added L. 1942, c. 677, eff. May 6, 1942.]

Fair employment Practices (Executive Law [1948 Cum. Supp.])

Law Against Discrimination.

§125. Purposes of article. This article shall be known as the "Law Against Discrimination." It shall be deemed an exercise of the police power of the state for the protection of the public welfare, health and peace of the people of this state, and in fullfilment of the provisions of the constitution of this state concerning civil rights; and the legislature hereby finds and declares that practices of discrimination against any of its inhabitants because of race, creed, color or national origin are a matter of state concern, that such discrimination threatens not only the rights and proper privileges of its inhabitants but menaces the institutions and foundation of a free democratic state. A state agency is hereby created with power to eliminate and prevent discrimination in employment because of race, creed, color or national origin, either by employers, labor organizations, employment agencies or other persons, and to take other actions against discrimination because of race, creed, color or national origin, as herein provided; and the commission established hereunder is hereby given general jurisdiction and power for such purposes. [L. 1945, c. 118, §1, eff. July 1, 1945.]

§126. Opportunity for employment without discrimination a civil right. — The opportunity to obtain employment without discrimination because of race, creed, color or national origin is hereby recognized as and declared to be a civil right. [L. 1945, c. 118, §1, eff. July 1, 1945.]

§127. Definitions. — When used in this article: 1. The term "person" includes one or more individuals, partnerships, associations, corporations, legal representatives, trustees, trustees in bankruptcy, or receivers.

2. The term "employment agency" includes any person undertaking to procure employees or opportunities to work.

3. The term "labor organization" includes any organization which exists and is constituted for the purpose, in whole or in part, of collective bargaining or of dealing with employers concerning grievances, terms or conditions of employment, or of other mutual aid or protection in connection with employment.

4. The term "unlawful employment practice" includes only those unlawful employment practices specified in section one hundred thirty-one of this article.

5. The term "employer" does not include a club exclusively social, or a fraternal, charitable, educational or religious association or corporation, if such club, association or corporation is not organized for private profit, nor does it include any employer with fewer than six persons in his employ.

6. The term "employee" and this article do not include any individual employed by his parents, spouse or child, or in the domestic service of any person.

7. The term "commission," unless a different meaning clearly appears from the context, means the state commission against discrimination created by this article.

8. The term "national origin" shall, for the purposes of this article, include "ancestry." [L. 1945, c. 118, §1, eff. July 1, 1945.]

§128. State commission against discrimination. — There is hereby created in the executive department a state commission against discrimination. Such commission shall consist of five members, to be known as commissioners, who shall be appointed by the governor, by and with the advice and consent of the senate, and one of whom shall be designated as chairman by the governor. The term of office of each member of the commission shall be for five years, provided, however, that of the commissioners first appointed, one shall be appointed for a term of one year, one for a term of two years, one for a term of three years, one for a term of four years, and one for a term of five years.

Any member chosen to fill a vacancy occurring otherwise than by expiration of term shall be appointed for the unexpired term of the member whom he is to succeed. Three members of the commission shall constitute a quorum for the purpose of conducting the business thereof. A vacancy in the commission shall not impair the right of the remaining members to exercise all the powers of the commission.

Each member of the commission shall receive a salary of ten thousand dollars a year and shall also be entitled to his expenses actually and necessarily incurred by him in the performance of his duties.

Any member of the commission may be removed by the governor for inefficiency, neglect of duty, misconduct or malfeasance in office, after being given a written statement of the charges and an opportunity to be heard thereon. [L. 1945, c. 118, §1, eff. July 1, 1945.]

§129. General policies of commission. — The commission shall formullate policies to effectuate the purposes of this article and may make recommendations to agencies and officers of the state or local subdivisions of government in aid of such policies and purposes. [L. 1945, c. 118, §1, effective July 1, 1945.]

§130. **General powers and duties of commission.** — The commission shall have the following functions, powers and duties: 1. To establish and maintain its principal office in the city of Albany, and such other offices within the state as it may deem necessary.

2. To meet and function at any place within the state.

3. To appoint such attorneys, clerks, and other employees and agents as it may deem necessary, fix their compensation within the limitations provided by law, and prescribe their duties.

4. To obtain upon request and utilize the services of all governmental departments and agencies.

5. To adopt, promulgate, amend, and rescind suitable rules and regulations to carry out the provisions of this article, and the policies and practice of the commission in connection therewith.

6. To receive, investigate and pass upon complaints alleging discrimination in employment because of race, creed, color or national origin.

7. To hold hearings, subpoena witnesses, compel their attendance, administer oaths, take the testimony of any person under oath, and in connection therewith, to require the production for examination of any books or papers relating to any matter under investigation or in question before the commission. The commission may make rules as to the issuance of subpoenas by individual commissioners.

No person shall be excused from attending and testifying or from producing records, correspondence, documents or other evidence in obedience to the subpoena of the commission or of any individual commissioner, on the ground that the testimony or evidence required of him may tend to incriminate him or subject him to a penalty or forfeiture, but no person shall be prosecuted or subjected to any penalty or forfeiture for on account of any transaction, matter or thing concerning which he is compelled, after having claimed his privilege against self-incrimination, to testify or produce evidence, except that such person so testifying shall not be exempt from prosecution and punishment for perjury committed in so testifying. The immunity herein provided shall extend only to natural persons so compelled to testify.

8. To create such advisory agencies and conciliation councils, local, regional or state-wide, as in its judgment will aid in effectuating the purposes of this article and of section eleven of article one of the constitution of this state, and the commission may empower them to study the problems of discrimination in all or specific fields of human relationships or in specific instances of discrimination because of race, creed, color or national origin, and to foster through community effort or otherwise goodwill, cooperation and conciliation among the groups and elements of the

population of the state, and make recommendations to the commission for the development of policies and procedures in general and in specific instances, and for programs of formal and informal education which the commission may recommend to the appropriate state agency. Such advisory agencies and conciliation councils shall be composed of representative citizens, serving without pay, but with reimbursement for actual and necessary traveling expenses; and the commission may make provision for technical and clerical assistance to such agencies and councils and for the expenses of such assistance.

9. To issue such publications and such results of investigations and research as in its judgment will tend to promote goodwill and minimize or eliminate discrimination because of race, creed, color or national origin.

10. To render each year to the governor and to the legislature a full written report of all its activities and of its recommendations.

11. To adopt an official seal. [L. 1945, c. 118, §1, eff. July 1, 1945.] [Note: RE: §130 — Advisory agencies on conciliation councils — Surrogates, county judges, judges of the court of general sessions of the county of N.Y., and justices of the peace, are eligible to serve as members of advisory agencies or conciliation councils under L. 1945, c. 118, Law against discrimination. 1946, Op. Atty Gen. 82.]

§131. Unlawful employment practices. — It shall be an unlawful employment practice: 1. For an employer, because of the race, creed, color or national origin of any individual, to refuse to hire or employ or to bar or to discharge from employment such individual or to discriminate against such individual in compensation or in terms, conditions or privileges of employment.

2. For a labor organization, because of the race, creed, color or national origin of any individual, to exclude or to expel from its membership such individual or to discriminate in any way against any of its members or against any employer or any individual employed by an employer.

3. For any employer or employment agency to print or circulate or cause to be printed or circulated any statement, advertisement or publication, or to use any form of application for employment or to make an inquiry in connection with prospective employment, which expresses, directly or indirectly, any limitation, specification or discrimination as to race, creed, color or national origin, or any intent to make any such limitation, specification or discrimination, unless based upon a bona fide occupational qualification.

4. For any employer, labor organization or employment agency to discharge, expel or otherwise discriminate against any person because he has opposed any practices forbidden under this article or because he has filed a complaint, testified or assisted in any proceeding under this article.

5. For any person, whether an employer or an employee or not, to aid, abet, incite, compel or coerce the doing of any of the acts forbidden

316

under this article, or to attempt to do so. [L. 1945, c. 118, §1, effective July 1, 1945.]

§132. Procedure. — Any person claiming to be aggrieved by an alleged unlawful employment practice may, by himself or his attorney-at-law, make, sign and file with the commission a verified complaint in writing which shall state the name and address of the person, employer, labor organization or employment agency alleged to have committed the unlawful employment practice complained of and which shall set forth the particulars thereof and contain such other information as may be required by the commission. The industrial commissioner or attorney-general may, in like manner, make, sign and file such complaint. Any employer whose employees, or some of them, refuse or threaten to refuse to cooperate with the provisions of this article, may file with the commission a verified complaint asking for assistance by conciliation or other remedial action.

After the filing of any complaint, the chairman of the commission shall designate one of the commissioners to make, with the assistance of the commission's staff, prompt investigation in connection therewith; and if such commissioner shall determine after such investigation that probable cause exists for crediting the allegations of the complaint, he shall immediately endeavor to eliminate the unlawful employment practice complained of by conference, conciliation and persuasion. The members of the commission and its staff shall not disclose what has transpired in the course of such endeavors. In case of failure so to eliminate such practice, or in advance thereof if in his judgment circumstances so warrant, he shall cause to be issued and served in the name of the commission, a written notice, together with a copy of such complaint, as the same may have been amended, requiring the person, employer, labor organization or employment agency named in such complaint, hereinafter referred to as respondent, to answer the charges of such complaint at a hearing before three members of the commission, sitting as the commission, at a time and place to be specified in such notice. The place of any such hearing shall be the office of the commission or such other place as may be designated by it. The case in support of the complaint shall be presented before the commission by one of its attorneys or agents, and the commissioner who shall have previously made the investigation and caused the notice to be issued shall not participate in the hearing except as a witness, nor shall he participate in the deliberations of the commission in such case; and the aforesaid endeavors at conciliation shall not be received in evidence. The respondent may file a written verified answer to the complaint and appear at such hearing in person or otherwise, with or without counsel, and submit testimony. In the discretion of the commission, the complainant may be allowed to intervene and present testimony in person or by counsel. The commission or the complainant shall have the power reasonably and fairly to amend any complaint, and the respondent shall have like power to amend his answer. The commission shall not be bound by the strict rules of evidence prevailing in courts of law or equity. The testimony taken at the hearing shall be under oath and be transcribed. If, upon all the evidence at the hearing the commission shall find that a respondent has engaged in any unlawful employment practice as defined in this article, the commission shall state its findings of fact and shall issue and cause to be served on such respondent an order requiring such respondent to cease and desist from such unlawful employment practice and to take such affirmative action, including (but not limited to) hiring, reinstatement or upgrading of employees, with or without back pay, or restoration to membership in any respondent labor organization, as, in the judgment of the commission, will effectuate the purposes of this article, and including a requirement for report of the manner of compliance. If, upon all the evidence, the commission shall find that a respondent has not engaged in any such unlawful employment practice, the commission shall state its findings of fact and shall issue and cause to be served on the complainant an order dismissing the said complaint as to such respondent. A copy of its order shall be delivered in all cases to the industrial commissioner, the attorney-general, and such other public officers as the commission deems proper. The commission shall establish rules of practice to govern, expedite and effectuate the foregoing procedure and its own actions thereunder. Any complaint filed pursuant to this section must be so filed within ninety days after the alleged act of discrimination. [L. 1945, c. 118, §1, eff. July 1, 1945.]

§133. Judicial review and enforcement. — Any complainant. respondent or other person aggrieved by such order of the commission may obtain judicial review thereof, and the commission may obtain an order of court for its enforcement, in a proceeding as provided in this section. Such proceeding shall be brought in the supreme court of the state within any county wherein the unlawful employment practice which is the subject of the commission's order occurs or wherein any person required in the order to cease and desist from an unlawful employment practice or to take other affirmative action resides or transacts business. Such proceeding shall be initiated by the filing of a petition in such court, together with a written transcript of the record upon the hearing before the commission, and the issuance and service of a notice of motion returnable at a special term of such court. Thereupon the court shall have jurisdiction of the proceeding and of the questions determined therein, and shall have power to grant such temporary relief or restraining order as it deems just and proper, and to make and enter upon the pleadings, testimony, and proceeding set forth in such transcript an order enforcing, modifying, and enforcing as so modified, or setting aside in whole or in part the order of the commission. No objection that has not been urged before the commission shall be considered by the court, unless the failure or neglect to urge such objection shall be excused because of extraordinary circumstances. Any party may move the court to remit the case to the commission in the interests of justice for the purpose of adducing additional specified and material evidence and seeking findings thereon, provided he shows reasonable grounds for the failure to adduce such evidence before the commission. The findings of the commission as to the facts shall be conclusive if supported by sufficient evidence on the record considered as a whole. All such proceedings shall be heard and determined by the court and by any appellate court as expeditiously as possible and with lawful precedence over other matters. The jurisdiction of the supreme court shall be exclusive and its judgment and order shall be final, subject to review by the appellate division of the supreme court and the court of appeals in the same manner and form and with the same effect as provided in the civil practice act for appeals from a final order in a special proceeding. The commission's copy of the testimony shall be available at all reasonable times to all parties for examination without cost and for the purposes of judicial review of the order of the commission. The appeal shall be heard on the record without requirement of printing. The commission may appear in court by one of its attorneys. A proceeding under this section when instituted by any complainant, respondent or other person aggrieved must be instituted within thirty days after the service of the order of the commission. [L. 1945, c. 118, §1, eff. July 1, 1945.]

§134. Penal provision. — Any person, employer, labor organization or employment agency, who or which shall wilfully resist, prevent, impede or interfere with the commission or any of its members or representatives in the performance of duty under this article, or shall wilfully violate an order of the commission, shall be guilty of a misdemeanor and be punishable by imprisonment in a penitentiary, or county jail, for not more than one year, or by a fine of not more than five hundred dollars, or by both; but procedure for the review of the order shall not be deemed to be such wilful conduct. [L. 1945, c. 118, §1, eff. July 1, 1945.]

§135. Construction. — The provisions of this article shall be construed liberally for the accomplishment of the purposes thereof. Nothing contained in this article shall be deemed to repeal any of the provisions of the civil rights law or of any other law of this state relating to discrimination because of race, creed, color or national origin; but, as to acts declared unlawful by section one hundred thirty-one of this article, the procedure herein provided shall, while pending, be exclusive; and the final determination therein shall exclude any other action, civil or criminal, based on the same grievance of the individual concerned. If such individual institutes any action based on such grievance without resorting to the procedure provided in this article, he may not subsequently resort to the procedure herein. [L. 1945, c. 118, §1, eff. July 1, 1945.]

§136. Separability. — If any clause, sentence, paragraph or part of this article or the application thereof to any person or circumstances, shall, for any reason, be adjudged by a court of competent jurisdiction to be invalid, such judgment shall not affect, impair, or invalidate the remainder of this article. [L. 1945, c. 118, §1, eff. July 1, 1945.]

Housing

See under Public Housing Law below. See also under Civil Rights Law, Art. 2-A.

Indian Law

[Note: No attempt is made here to outline the numerous laws relating to Indians and Indian tribes in New York State. For a collection of the special statutes relating to Indian tribes remaining in the state see McKinney's Consolidated Laws of New York Annotated, Book 25, Indian Law. A few statutes are set forth below to indicate the general status of Indians in New York state.]

§2. Power to contract. — An Indian shall be liable on his contracts not prohibited by law; and a native Indian may take, hold and convey real property the same as a citizen. Upon becoming a freeholder to the value of one hundred dollars he shall be subject to taxation. No person shall maintain an action on a contract against any Indian of the Tonawanda nation, the Seneca nation or Onondaga tribe, nor against any of their Indian friends residing with them on their reservations in this state, and every person who prosecutes such an action shall be liable to treble costs to the party aggrieved. [Derived from Indian Law of 1892, ch. 679, §2, as amended by L. 1893, ch. 229.]

[See also Const., Art. 1, §15 above.]

§3. Marriage and Divorce. — [Laws of the state relating to the capacity to contract marriage, the solemnization of marriage, the annulment of the marriage contract, and divorce are made applicable to Indians.] [Indian Law 1892, ch. 679, §3.]

§4. Pawns or pledges for liquor. — [Provides for the recovery of a penalty of ten times the value of any property or article given by an Indian to any person for intoxicating liquor or drink.] [Indian Law 1892, ch. 679, §5.]

Innkeepers and Carriers

See under Penal Law, §513.

Insurance Law — Art. 9-A

Life, Accident and Health Insurance Companies

§209. Discrimination and rebating; prohibited: inducements. —

1. No life insurance company doing business in this state shall make or permit any unfair discrimination between individuals of the same class and of equal expectation of life, in the amount or payment or return of premiums, or rates charged by it for policies of life insurance or annuity contracts, or in the dividends or other benefits payable thereon, or in any of the terms and conditions thereof; and no such company shall knowingly permit, and no agent thereof shall offer to make or make, any contract of life insurance or annuity contract or agreement as to such contract, other than as plainly expressed in the policy issued hereon; and no such company and no officer, agent solicitor or representative thereof, shall pay, allow or give, or offer to pay, allow or give, directly or indirectly, as an inducement to any person to insure, or shall give, sell or purchase, or offer to give, sell or purchase, as such inducement, or in connection with any policy of life insurance or annuity contract, any stocks, bonds, or other securities of any insurance company or other corporation or business unit, or any dividends or profits accruing or to accrue thereon, or any valuable consideration or inducement whatever not specified in such policy or contract; nor shall any person in this state knowingly receive as such inducement, any rebate of premium or any special favor or advantage in the dividends or other benefits to accrue on any such policy or

contract, or knowingly receive any paid employment or contract for services of any kind, or any valuable consideration or inducement whatever which is not specified in such policy or contract. In the case of life insurance policies issued on the industrial debit plan, the insurer may make an allowance to policyholders who have continuously for a specified period made premium payments directly to an office of the insurer, in an amount which fairly represents the saving in collection expense. This section shall not be deemed to prohibit the giving by any company, in its discretion, of medical examinations and diagnoses and of nursing services to all or any part of its policyholders, under reasonable rules and regulations.

2. No insurer doing in this state the business of accident or health insurance, as specified in paragraph three of section forty-six, and no officer or agent of such insurer, shall make or permit any unfair discrimination between individuals of the same class in the amount of premiums, policy fees, or rates charged for any policy or contract of accident or health insurance, or in the benefits payable thereunder, or in any of the terms or conditions of such contract, or in any other manner whatsoever; and no such company shall knowingly permit, and no agent thereof shall offer to make or make, any policy or contract of accident or health insurance, other than as plainly expressed in the policy or contract issued thereon; and no such company and no officer, agent, solicitor or representative thereof, shall pay, allow or give, or offer to pay, allow or give, directly or indirectly, as an inducement to any person to insure, or shall give, sell or purchase, or offer to give, sell or purchase, as such inducement, or in connection with any policy or contract of accident or health insurance, any stocks, bonds, or other securities of any insurance company or other corporation or business unit, or any dividends or profits accruing or to accrue thereon, or any valuable consideration or inducement whatever not specified in such policy or contract; nor shall any person in this state knowingly receive as such inducement, any rebate of premium or policy fee or any special favor or advantage in the dividends or other benefits to accrue on any such policy or contract, or knowingly receive any paid employment or contract for services of any kind, or any valuable consideration or inducement whatever which is not specified in such policy or contract. [Subdiv. 2 amended by L. 1948, c. 359, eff. March 22, 1948.]

3. No life insurance company doing business in this state shall make any distinction or discrimination between white persons and colored persons, wholly or partially of African descent, as to the premiums or rates charged for policies upon the lives of such persons, or in any other manner whatever; nor shall any such company demand or require a greater premium from such colored persons than is at that time required by such company from white persons of the same age, sex, general condition of health and prospect of longevity, nor shall any such company make or require any rebate, diminution or discount upon the amount to be paid on such policy in case of the death of such colored persons insured, nor insert in the policy any condition, nor make any stipulation, whereby such person insured shall bind himself, or his heirs, executors, administrators

or assigns, to accept any sum less than the full value or amount of such policy in case of a claim accruing thereon by reason of the death of such person insured, other than such as are imposed upon white persons in similar cases; and any such stipulation or condition so made or inserted shall be void. No life insurance company doing business in this state shall reject any application for a policy of life insurance issued and sold by it, or refuse to issue such policy after appropriate application therefor, nor shall any lower rate be fixed or discrimination be made by it in the fees or commissions of its agents for writing such a policy solely by reason of the applicant being wholly or partially of African descent. [As amended L. 1930, c. 802; L. 1945, c. 649, §205; L. 1946, c. 241, §20, March 22, 1948).]

[Note: See also under Penal Law, §1191.]

Judiciary Law — Article 14.

Attorneys and Counsellors

§460. **Examination and admission of attorneys.** — A citizen of this state, or any resident native born Filipino, of full age, applying to be admitted to practice as an attorney or counsellor in the courts of record of this state, must be examined and licensed to practice as prescribed in this chapter. Race, creed, color, national origin or sex shall constitute no cause for refusing any person examination or admission to practice. [As amended L. 1930, c. 802; L. 1945, c. 649, §205; L. 1946, c. 241, §20, eff. March 26, 1946.]

Jurors

See under Civil Rights Law, §13.

Ku Klux Klan

See under Penal Law §§710-713.

Labor Law — Article 8

Public Works

§220-e. **Provisions in contracts prohibiting discrimination on account of race, creed, color or national origin in employment of citizens upon public works.** — Every contract for or on behalf of the state or a municipality for the construction, alteration or repair of any public building or public work shall contain provisions by which the contractor with the state or municipality agrees:

(a) That in the hiring of employees for the performance of work under this contract or any subcontract hereunder, no contractor, subcontractor, nor any person acting on behalf of such contractor or subcontractor, shall by reason of race, creed, color, or national origin discriminate against any citizen of the state of New York who is qualified and available to perform the work to which the employment relates;

(b) That no contractor, subcontractor, nor any person on his behalf shall, in any manner, discriminate against or intimidate any employee hired for the performance of work under this contract on account of race, creed, color or national origin;

(c) That there may be deducted from the amount payable to the contractor by the state or municipality under this contract a penalty of five dollars for each person for each calendar day during which such person was discriminated against or intimidated in violation of the provisions of the contract; and

(d) That this contract may be cancelled or terminated by the state or municipality, and all moneys due or to become due hereunder may be forfeited, for a second or any subsequent violation of the terms or conditions of this section of the contract. [Added L. 1935, c. 158; amended L. 1945, c. 292, §9, eff. March 27, 1945.]

Labor Organizations

See under Employment, Civil Rights Law, §43; Law Against Discrimination.

Law Against Discrimination

See under Employment.

Military Law

§1-a. Equality of treatment and opportunity without regard to race, creed, color or national origin. — It is hereby declared to be the policy of the state of New York that there shall be equality of treatment and opportunity for all persons in the national guard, naval militia and the New York guard without regard to race, creed, color or national origin. Such policy shall be put into effect in the national guard, naval militia and New York guard by rules and regulations to be issued pursuant to section two hundred fifty-four of this chapter as soon as possible, it being necessary to give due regard to the powers of the federal government which are or may be exercised over all the militia of the state and to the time required to effectuate changes without impairing the efficiency or morale of the militia. [Added L. 1949, c. 497, §1, eff. April 11, 1949.]

§33. Colored regiment of infantry. — [Repealed by laws of New York 1949, Chapter 497, p. 810, §2 effective April 11, 1949. This section which was formerly §40, added L. 1913, c. 793, renumbered 33, L. 1917, c. 644, §42, eff. May 24, 1917, provided for a separate colored regiment of infantry in the city of New York to become a part of the national guard of New York.]

Penal Law
General Provisions

§29. Violation of statute which imposes no penalty is a misdemeanor. — Where the performance of any act is prohibited by a statute, and no penalty for the violation of statute is imposed by any statute, the doing such act is a misdemeanor. [L. 1909, c. 88, Sec. 29, effective March 12, 1909.]

Civil Rights — Art. 46

§513. Innkeepers and carriers refusing to receive guests and passengers. — A person, who, either on his own account or as agent or officer of a corporation, carries on business as innkeeper, or as common carrier of passengers, and refuses, without just cause or excuse, to receive and entertain any guest, or to receive and carry any passenger, is guilty of a misdemeanor. [L. 1909, c. 88, Sec. 513, effective March 12, 1909.]

§514. Protecting civil and public rights. — A person who:

1. Excludes a citizen of this state, by reason of race, color, creed, national origin or previous condition of servitude, from any public employment in any capacity in industries engaged in defense contracts or from the equal enjoyment of any accommodation, facility or privilege furnished by innkeepers or common carriers, or by owners, managers or lessees of theatres or other places of amusement, or by teachers and officers of common schools and public institutions of learning; or

2. Excludes a citizen of this state by reason of race, color, national origin or previous condition of servitude from the equal enjoyment of any accommodation, facility or privilege furnished by a cemetery association or associations;

3. Denies or aids or incites another to deny to any other person because of race, creed, color or national origin public employment or employment in any capacity in industries engaged in war contracts or the full enjoyment of any of the accommodations, advantages, facilities and privileges of any hotel, inn, tavern, restaurant, public conveyance on land or water, theatre or other place of public resort or amusement;

Is guilty of a misdemeanor, punishable by fine of not less than fifty dollars nor more than five hundred dollars. [As amended L. 1918, c. 380; L. 1941, c. 478, §2; L. 1942, c. 438; L. 1942, c. 676, §2; L. 1943, c. 105, §5, eff. March 12, 1943.]

[Note: See also Civil Rights Law §40 *et seq.*]

§515. Discrimination against person or class in price for admission. — If a person who owns, occupies, manages or controls a building, park, inclosure or other place, opens the same to the public generally at stated periods or otherwise, he shall not discriminate against any person or class of persons in the price charged for admission thereto. A person violating the provision of this section is guilty of a misdemeanor. [L. 1909, c. 88, Sec. 515, eff. March 12, 1909.]

Discrimination — Article 67

§700 — Discrimination — All persons within the jurisdiction of this state shall be entitled to the equal protection of the laws of this state or any subdivision thereof. No person shall, because of race, creed, color or national origin, be subjected to any discrimination in his civil rights by any other person or by any firm, corporation or institution, or by the state or any agency or subdivision of the state. [Added L. 1941, c. 910; as amended L. 1945, c. 292, §10, eff. March 27, 1945.]

§701. Penalty. — Any person who shall violate any of the provisions of the foregoing section, or who shall aid or incite the violation of any of said provisions shall for each and every violation thereof be liable to a penalty of not less than one hundred dollars nor more than five hundred dollars, to be recovered by the person aggrieved thereby in any court of competent jurisdiction in the county in which the defendant shall reside; and shall, also, for every such offense be deemed guilty of a misdemeanor, and upon conviction thereof shall be fined not less than one hundred dollars nor more than five hundred dollars, or shall be imprisoned not less than thirty days nor more than ninety days, or both such fine and imprisonment. [Added L. 1941, c. 910.]

Elective Franchise — Article 74

§772-a. Pernicious political activities. — It shall be unlawful for any person to:

* * *

3. Deprive, attempt to deprive or threaten to deprive, by any means, any person of any employment, position, work, compensation or other benefit provided for or made possible in whole or in part by any act of congress or of the legislature appropriating funds for work relief or relief purposes, on account of race, creed, color, national origin, or any political activity or on account of support for or opposition to any candidate or any political party in any nominating convention or election; . . . [Added L. 1940, c. 667; as amended L. 1945, c. 292, §11, eff. March 27, 1945.]

[Note: Subdiv.: 3. Amended by L. 1945, c. 292, §11. Inserted "national origin".]

Insurance — Article 112

§1191. Discrimination and rebates by life insurance companies prohibited. — Any life insurance corporation or corporation transacting the business of life insurance on the co-operative or assessment plan doing business in this state, or any officer or agent thereof, who:

1. Makes any discrimination in favor of individuals of the same class or of the same expectation of life either in the amount of the premium charged or in any return of premiums, dividends or other advantages; or,

2. Makes any contract for insurance or agreement as to such contract other than that which is plainly expressed in the policy issued; or,

3. Pays or allows, or offers to pay or allow as an inducement to any person to insure, any rebate or premium, or any special favor or advantage whatever, in the dividends to accrue thereon or any inducement whatever not specified in the policy; or,

4. Makes any distinction or discrimination between white persons and colored persons, wholly or partially of African descent, as to the premiums or rates charged for policies upon the lives of such persons, or in any other manner whatever; or demands or requires a greater premium

from such colored persons than is at that time required by such company from white persons of the same age, sex, general condition of health and prospect of longevity; or makes or requires any rebate, diminution or discount upon the amount to be paid on such policy in case of the death of such colored persons insured, or inserts in the policy any condition, or makes any stipulation whereby such person insured shall bind himself, or his heirs, executors, administrators and assigns to accept any sum less than the full value or amount of such policy in case of a claim accruing thereon by reason of the death of such person insured, other than such as are imposed upon white persons in similar cases, is guilty of a misdemeanor. Nothing in this section shall be construed to require any corporation doing business under articles nine-B or fourteen of the insurance law, which limits and confines its business or membership to the members of a secret or fraternal order or body, to insure or accept any individual who is not a member of such secret or fraternal order or body. [As amended L. 1913, c. 180; L. 1940, c. 435, §3, eff. April 13, 1940.]

Punishment — Article 174

§1937. Punishment of misdemeanors when not fixed by statute. — A person convicted of a crime declared to be a misdemeanor, for which no punishment is specially prescribed by this chapter, or by any other statutory provision in force at the time of the conviction and sentence, is punishable by imprisonment in a penitentiary, or county jail, for not more than one year, or by a fine of not more than five hundred dollars, or by both. [L. 1909, c. 88, Sec. 1967, effective March 12, 1909.]

Disguises — Article 69. [Ku Klux Klan]

§710. Disguised and masked persons; masquerades. — An assemblage in public houses or other places of three or more persons disguised by having their faces painted, discolored, colored or concealed, is unlawful, and every individual so disguised, present thereat, is guilty of a misdemeanor; but nothing contained in this section shall be construed as prohibiting any peaceful assemblage for a masquerade or fancy dress ball or entertainment, or any assemblage therefor of persons masked, or as prohibiting the wearing of masks, fancy dresses, or other disguise by persons on their way to or returning from such ball or other entertainment; if, when such masquerade, fancy dress ball or entertainment is held in any of the cities of this state, permission is first obtained from the police authorities in such cities respectively for the holding or giving thereof, under such regulations as may be prescribed by such police authorities. [Derived from Penal Code, §452, L. 1881, c. 676.]

§711. Allowing masquerades to be held in places of public resort. — A person being a proprietor, manager or keeper of a theater, circus, public garden, public hall, or other place of public meeting, resort or amusement, for admission to which any price or payment is demanded, who permits therein any assemblage of persons masked, prohibited in this article, is guilty of a misdemeanor, punishable by imprisonment in a state prison not exceeding two [2] years, or in a county jail not exceeding one [1] year, or by a fine not exceeding five thousand dollars [$5,000.00] and not less than one thousand dollars [$1,000.00], or by both such fine and imprisonment. [Derived from Penal Code, §453, L. 1881, c. 676.]

§712. Leaving state with intent to elude provisions of this article. — A person who leaves the state, with intent to elude any provision of this article, or to commit any act without the state, which is prohibited by this article, or who, being a resident of this state, does any act without the state, which would be punishable by the provisions of this article, if committed within the state, is guilty of the same offense and subject to the same punishment, as if the act had been committed within this state. [Derived from Penal Code, §461, L. 1881, c. 676.]

§713. Witnesses' privilege. — No person shall be excused from giving evidence upon an investigation or prosecution for any of the offenses specified in this article, upon the ground that the evidence might tend to convict him of a crime; but no person shall be prosecuted or subjected to any penalty or forfeiture for or on account of any transaction, matter or thing concerning which he may so testify or produce evidence, documentary or otherwise, and no testimony so given or produced shall be received against him upon any criminal investigation or proceeding. [Derived from Penal Code, §469, L. 1881, c. 676. As amended L. 1938, c. 108, §6, eff. March 14, 1938.]

Public Accommodation
See under **Civil Rights** above.

Public Housing Law — Art. 9-A
Emergency Housing for Veterans and Others
§201. [1948 Supp.] — **Prohibition against discrimination.** — For all purposes of this article, no person shall because of race, creed, color, or national origin, be subjected to any discrimination. [Added L. 1946, c. 3, Sec. 1, effective January 29, 1946.]

Defense Housing
§223. [1948 Supp.] — **Prohibiiton against discrimination.** — For all the purposes of this chapter, no person shall, because of race, creed, color or national origin, be subjected to any discrimination. [L. 1939, c. 808, §223 as amended L. 1945, c. 292, §12, eff. March 27, 1945.]

[Note: See also **Civil Rights Law, Art. 2-A** above.]

Public Utilities
See under **Employment** above.

Public Works
See under **Labor Law** above.

Tax Law
Taxable Property and Place of Taxation [1948 Supp.]
§4. Exemption from taxation. — The following property shall be exempt from taxation:

* * *

6. The real property of a corporation or association organized exclusively for the moral or mental improvement of men and women, or for religious, bible, tract, charitable, benevolent, missionary, hospital, infirmary, educational, public playground, scientific, literary, bar association, library, patriotic, historical or cemetery purposes, or for the enforcement of laws relating to children or animals, for two or more such purposes, and used exclusively for carrying out thereupon one or more of such purposes either by the owning corporation or by another such corporation as hereinafter provided ... *No education or corporation or association that holds itself out to the public to be non-sectarian and exempt from taxation pursuant to the provisions of this section shall deny the use of its facilities to any person otherwise qualified, by reason of his race, color or religion.* (italics supplied) [As amended L. 1914, c. 278; L. 1916, cc. 411, 412; L. 1917, c. 42; L. 1917, c. 707, §5; L. 1918, c. 288; L. 1920, c. 413; L. 1921, cc. 168, 169, 446; L. 1923, cc. 535, 679, 792; L. 1924, cc. 489, 595; L. 1925, c. 99, L. 1926, cc. 673, 708; L. 1927, cc. 260, 475, 565; L. 1929, c. 382; L. 1930, c. 340; L. 1931, cc. 339, 433; L. 1932, c. 328; L. 1933, c. 396; L. 1933, c. 470, §§3-14; L. 1934, cc. 460, 472; L. 1935, cc. 740, 852; L. 1936, cc. 578, 694; L. 1937, c. 568; L. 1939, cc. 291, 853; L. 1941, c. 786; L. 1942, c. 878; L. 1943, c. 636; L. 1944, cc. 18, 529; L. 1945, c. 232; L. 1946, cc. 86, 123, 139, 474, 556, 641; L. 1947 c. 24; L. 1947, c. 247; L. 1948, c. 548; L. 1948, c. 622, eff. March 30, 1948, L. 1949, c. 723, eff. April 20, 1949.]

[Note: The original statute (italicized portion) reads "*No education or corporation.*" It has been suggested that this is a typographical error and that the probable correct reading is "*No educational corporation*" etc.]

NORTH CAROLINA

CONSTITUTION

Education

Art. IX, §2. — General Assembly shall provide for schools; separation of the races.—The General Assembly at its first session under this Constitution, shall provide by taxation and otherwise a general and uniform system of public schools, wherein tuition shall be free of charge to all children of the State between the ages of six and twenty-one years. And the children of the white race and the children of the colored race shall be taught in separate public schools; but there shall be no discrimination in favor of, or to the prejudice of, either race. [Const. 1868, Convention 1875.]

Miscegenation

Art. XIV, §8. — Intermarriage of whites and Negroes prohibited. — All marriages between a white person and a Negro, or between a white person and a person of Negro descent to the third generation inclusive, are hereby forever prohibited. [Convention 1875.]

[Note: Every person who has one-eighth Negro blood in his veins is within the prohibited degree set out in this section and §51-3. *State vs. Miller*, (1944) 224 N.C. 228, 29 S.E.(2d) 751.]

Slavery Prohibited

Art. I, §33. — Slavery prohibited. — Slavery and involuntary servitude, otherwise than for crime, whereof the parties shall have been duly convicted, shall be, and are hereby forever prohibited within this State. [Const. 1868.]

STATUTES

GENERAL STATUTES OF N.C. (1943)

Aliens

§64.1. Rights as to real property. — It is lawful for aliens to take both by purchase and descent, or other operation of law, any lands, tenements or hereditaments, and to hold and convey the same as fully as citizens of this state can or may do, any law or usage to the contrary notwithstanding. [Rev., s. 182; Code, s. 7; 1870-1, c. 255; 1935, c. 243; 1939, c. 19; C.S. 192.]

[Note: §64-2 validates contracts to purchase or sell real estate made by or with Aliens.

Cemeteries

§65-38. [1947 Cum. Supp.] Racial restrictions as to use of cemeteries for burial of dead. — In the event said property [Municipal Cemeteries] has been heretofore used exclusively for the burial of members of the negro race, then said cemetery or burial ground so established shall remain and be established as a burial ground for the negro race. In the event said property has been heretofore used exclusively for the burial of members of the white race, then said

329

cemetery or burial ground so established shall remain and be established as a burial ground for the white race. [1947, c. 821, §2.]

Education — Segregation

Public Schools

§115-2. Separation of Races. — The children of the white race and the children of the colored race shall be taught in separate public schools, but there shall be no discrimination in favor of or to the prejudice of either race. All white children shall be taught in the public schools provided for the white race, and all colored children shall be taught in the public schools provided for the colored race, but no child with negro blood, or what is generally known as Croatan Indian blood, in his veins, shall attend a school for the white race, and no such child shall be considered a white child. The descendants of Croatan Indians, now living in Robeson, Sampson, and Richmond counties, shall have separate schools for their children. [1923, c. 136, §1; C.S. 5384.]

§115-3. Schools provided for both races; taxes. When the school officials are providing schools for one race it shall be a misdemeanor for the officials to fail to provide schools for the other races, and it shall be illegal to levy taxes on the property and polls of one race for schools in a district without levying it on all property and polls for all races within said district. [1923, c. 136, §1; C. S. 5385.]

§115-30. Division of negro education. — To secure better supervision of negro education in all normal schools, training schools, high schools, elementary schools, and teacher training departments in all colleges for negroes over which the state now or hereafter may have any control, the state board of education is authorized, upon the recommendation of the superintendent of public instruction to employ a director of negro education, and such supervisors assistants, both clerical and professional, as may be necessary to carry out the purposes of this section not inconsistent with the amount of the appropriation, and to define the duties of the same. [1921, t. 146, §17; C.S. 5405.]

§115-66. Board shall provide schools for Indians in certain counties. — It shall be the duty of the county board of education to provide separate schools for Indians as follows:

The persons residing in Robeson and Richmond counties, supposed to be descendants of a friendly tribe once residing in·the eastern portion of the state, known as Croatan Indians, and who have heretofore been known as "Croatan Indians," or "Indians of Robeson County," and their descendants, shall be known and designated as the "Cherokee Indians of Robeson County"; and the persons residing in Person county supposed to be descendants of a friendly tribe of Indians and "White's Lost Colony," once residing in the eastern portion of this state, and known as "Cubans," and their descendants, shall be known and designated as the "Indians of Person County".

The Indians mentioned above and their descendants shall have separate schools for their children, school committees of their own race and color, and shall be allowed to select teachers of their own choice, subject to the same rules and regulations as are applicable to all teachers in the general school law, and there shall be excluded from such separate schools all children of the negro race to the fourth generation. The County Superintendent in and for Robeson County shall keep in his office a record of schools for the Cherokee Indians of Robeson County, which said record shall disclose the operation of such schools, separate and apart from the record of the operation of schools for the other races. [1923, c. 136, s. 42, 1931, c. 141; C.S. 5445.]

§115-97. School districts. — The state board of education, with the advice of the county board of education, shall maintain in each county a convenient number of school districts.

There may be one district and one school committee for both races, or the races may have separate districts and separate school committee . . . [1923, c. 136, s. 73; 1943, c. 721, s. 8; C.S. 5480.]

Textbooks — Separate

§115-294. — Books not interchangeable between white and colored schools. — Books shall not be interchangeable between the white and colored schools, but shall continued (sic.) to be used by the race first using them. [1935, c. 422, s. 2.]

Teachers' Colleges

§116-101. Power of State board of education to establish. — the state board of education is hereby empowered to establish normal schools at any place it may deem most suitable, either in connection with one of the colored schools of high grade in the state, or otherwise, for teaching and training young men and women of the colored race, from the age of fifteen to twenty-five years, for teachers in the common schools of the state for the colored race. A preparatory department may be established in connection with the colored normal schools. And such board shall have the power to remove or close any of the existing state normal schools for the colored race. [Rev., s. 4180; Code, ss. 2651, 2652; 1881, cc. 91, 141, s. 5; 1879, c. 54, ss. 1, 2; 1876-7, c. 234, s. 2; 1901, c. 565, s. 1; C.S. 5850.]

§116-102. State board of education to control and manage Negro State Teachers Colleges. — The state board of education shall have supervision, and shall prescribe rules and regulations for the control, management and enlargement of each of the following normal schools: the Elizabeth City State Teachers College, Elizabeth City; Fayetteville State Teachers College, Fayetteville; Winston-Salem Teachers College, Winston-Salem.

The state board of education shall make all needful rules and regulations concerning the expenditure of funds, the selection of principals, teachers and employees. [1921, c. 61, s. 8; 1925, c. 306, s. 9; 1925 (Pr.), c. 170; 1931, c. 276, s. 1; 1939, cc. 178, 253; C.S. 5775.]

§116-103. **Trustees for Negro State Teachers Colleges.** — [Provides for appointment by governor of board of nine trustees each for four institutions named in preceding section.] [1925, c. 306, ss. 9, 13, 14.]

§116-104. **Four-year courses; granting of degrees.** — [Provides for "four-year courses in the field of elementary education to train elementary teachers qualified to obtain grammar grade and primary Class A certificates, and to train elementary school principals for rural and city schools," and the granting of degrees by the four institutions mentioned in §116-102, subject to provisions §§115-322 to 115-324 which give the State Board of Education authority to regulate degrees.] [1925 (Pr.), c. 170; 1939, cc. 178, 253.]

Colleges and Graduate Schools

Negro Agricultural and Technical College of North Carolina (Greensboro, N.C.)

§§116-92 - 116-98. [Provision for the establishment of a college of agricultural and mechanical arts for Negroes to teach "practical agriculture and the mechanical arts and such branches of learning as relate thereto, not excluding academical and classical instruction."] [Rev. ss. 4221-4227; 1891, c. 549, ss. 1-7; 1899, c. 389, ss. 1-3; 1915, c. 267; 1943, c. 132; 1949, c. 549, s. 5; C.S. 5826-5832.]

North Carolina College at Durham

§§116-99—116-100, as amended by Sess. Laws 1947, Ch. 190, p. 204.— [Provide for appointment of 12 trustees for North Carolina College at Durham [for Negroes] and empowers board of trustees to establish from time to time such graduate courses in the liberal arts field as the demand may warrant, and the funds of the said North Carolina College at Durham may justify. Such courses must be standard."

Board of trustees also empowered "to establish departments of law, pharmacy and library science at the above named institution whenever there are applicants desirous of such courses. Said board of trustees . . . may add other professional courses from time to time as the need for the same is shown, and the funds of the State will justify."

Provide further that graduates and professional courses may be added in agricultural and technical lines at A. & T. College at Greensboro, where need is shown and state funds will justify.

Provide for out-of-state tuition and other student expenses where qualified Negro students cannot obtain professional courses at the established Negro colleges. This section of the statute reads:

"In the event there are Negroes resident in the state properly qualified who can certify that they have been duly admitted to any reputable graduate or professional college and said graduate or professional courses are not being offered at the North Carolina College for Negroes [North Carolina College at Durham], then the board of trustees of the North Carolina College for Negroes when said certification has been presented to them by the president and faculty of the North Carolina College for

Negroes [North Carolina College at Durham], may pay tuition and other expenses for said student or students at such recognized college in such amount as may be deemed reasonably necessary to compensate said resident student for the additional expense of attending a graduate or professional school outside of North Carolina, and the budget commission may upon such presentaton reimburse the North Carolina College for Negroes [North Carolina College at Durham] the money so advanced. It is further provided that the student applying for such admission must furnish proof that he or she has been duly admitted to said recognized professional college. In the case of agricultural and technical subjects such students desiring graduate courses should apply to the Agricultural and Technical College at Greensboro, North Carolina. The general provision covering students in the liberal arts field as stated in this section shall apply. In no event shall there be any duplication of courses in the two institutions.

"Said board of trustees are authorized upon satisfactory completion of prescribed courses, to give appropriate degrees . . . " [1925, c. 306, ss. 9a, 13, 14; 1939, c. 65; 1947, c. 189.]

[Note: Before the 1947 amendment, the North Carolina College at Durham was designated North Carolina College for Negroes.]

Regional Education

LAWS 1949, p. 1716

S.R. 204, RESOLUTION 26

A Joint resolution giving Legislative approval to a certain compact entered into by the State of North Carolina and other Southern States by and through their respective Governors on February 8, 1948, as amended, relative to the development and maintenance of regional educational services in schools in the Southern States in the professional, technological, scientific, literary and other fields, so as to provide greater educational advantages and facilities for the citizens in the several States who reside in such region; to declare that the State of North Carolina is a part of the State compact as amended, and that the agreements, covenants and obligations therein are binding upon said state.

WHEREAS, on the 8th day of February, in the year of Our Lord, One Thousand Nine Hundred and Forty-eight, the State of Georgia, and the States of Florida, Maryland, Louisiana, Alabama, Mississippi, Tennessee, Arkansas, Virginia, North Carolina, South Carolina, Texas, Oklahoma, West Virginia, through and by their respective governors, entered into a written compact relative to the development and maintenance of regional educational services and schools in the Southern States in the professional, technological, scientific, literary, and other fields, so as to provide greater educational advantages and facilities for the citizens of the several States who reside within such region; and

WHEREAS, the said Compact has been amended in certain respects, a copy of which Compact as amended is as follows:

THE REGIONAL COMPACT
(As amended)

WHEREAS, The States who are parties hereto have during the past several years conducted careful investigation looking toward the establishment and maintenance of jointly owned and operated regional educational institutions in the Southern States in the professional, technological, scientific, literary and other fields, so as to provide greater educational advantages and facilities for the citizens of the several States who reside within such region, and

WHEREAS, Meharry Medical College of Nashville, Tennessee, has proposed that its lands, buildings, equipment, and the net income from its endowment be turned over to the Southern States, or to an agency acting in their behalf, to be operated as a regional institution for medical, dental and nursing education upon terms and conditions to be hereafter agreed upon between the Southern States and Meharry Medical College, which proposal, because of the present financial condition of the institution, has been approved by the said States who are parties hereto; and

WHEREAS, The said States desire to enter into a compact with each other providing for the planning and establishment of regional educational facilities;

Now, therefore, in consideration of the mutual agreements, covenants and obligations assumed by the respective States who are parties hereto (hereinafter referred to as "States"), the said several States do hereby form a geographical district or region consisting of the areas lying within the boundaries of the contracting States which, for the purposes of this compact, shall constitute an area for regional education supported by public funds derived from taxation by the constituent States and derived from other sources for the establishment, acquisition, operation and maintenance of regional educational schools and institutions for the benefit of citizens of the respective States residing within the region so established as may be determined from time to time in accordance with the terms and provisions of this compact.

The States do further hereby establish and create a joint agency which shall be known as the Board of Control for Southern Regional Education (hereinafter referred to as the "Board"), the members of which Board shall consist of the Governor of each State, ex-officio, and three additional citizens of each State to be appointed by the Governor thereof, at least one of whom shall be selected from the field of education. The Governor shall continue as a member of the Board during his tenure of office as Governor of the State, but the members of the Board appointed by the Governor shall hold office for a period of four years except that in the original appointments one Board member so appointed by the Governor shall be designated at the time of his appointment to serve an initial term of two years, one Board member to serve an initial term of three years, and the remaining Board member to serve the full term of four years, but thereafter the successor of each appointed Board member shall serve the full term of four years. Vacancies on the Board caused by death, resignation, refusal or inability to serve, shall be filled by appointment by the Governor for the unexpired portion of the term. The officers of the Board shall be a Chairman, a Vice Chairman, a Secretary, a Treasurer, and such additional officers as may be created by the Board from time to time. The Board shall meet annually and officers shall be elected to hold office until the next annual meeting. The Board shall have the right to formulate and establish by-laws not inconsistent with the provisions of this compact to govern its own actions in the performance of the duties delegated to it including the right to create and appoint an Executive Committee and a Finance Committee with such powers and authority as the Board may delegate to them from time to time. The Board may, within its discretion, elect as its Chairman a person who is not a member of the Board, provided such person resides within a signatory State, and upon such election such person shall become a member of the Board with all the rights and privileges of such membership.

It shall be the duty of the Board to submit plans and recommendations to the States from time to time for their approval and adoption by appropriate legislative action for the development, establishment, acquisition, operation and maintenance of educational schools and institutions within the geographical limits of the regional area of the States, of such character and type and for such educational purposes, professional, technological, scientific, literary, or otherwise, as they may deem and determine to be proper, necessary or advisable. Title to all such educational institutions when so established by appropriate legislative actions of the States and to all properties and facilities used in connection therewith shall be vested in said Board as the agency of and for the use and benefit of the said States and the citizens thereof, and all such educational institutions shall be operated, maintained and financed in the manner herein set out, subject to any provisions or limitations which may be contained in the legislative acts of the States authorizing the creation, establishment and operation of such educational institutions.

In addition to the power and authority heretofore granted, the Board shall have the power to enter into such agreements or arrangements with any of the States and with educatonal institutions or agencies, as may be required in the judgment of the Board, to provide adequate services and facilities for the graduate, professional, and technical education for the benefit of the citizens of the respective State residing within the region, and such additional and general power and authority as may be vested in the Board from time to time by legislative enactment of the said States.

Any two or more States who are parties of this compact shall have the right to enter into supplemental agreements providing for the establishment, financing and operation of regional educational institutions for the benefit of citizens residing within an area which constitutes a portion of the general region herein created, such institutions to be financed exclusively by such States and to be controlled exclusively by the members of the Board representing such States provided such agreement is submitted to and approved by the Board prior to the establishment of such institutions.

Each State agrees that, when authorized by the legislature, it will from time to time make available and pay over to said Board such funds as may be required for the establishment, acquisition, operation and maintenance of such regional educational institutions as may be authorized by the States under the terms of this compact, the contribution of each State at all times to be in the proportion that its population bears to the total combined population of the States who are parties hereto as shown from time to time by the most recent official published report of the Bureau of the Census of the United States of America; or upon such other basis as may be agreed upon.

This compact shall not take effect or be binding upon any State unless and until it shall be approved by proper legislative action of as many as six or more of the States whose Governors have subscribed hereto within a period of eighteen months from the date hereof. When and if six or more States have given legislative approval to this compact within said eighteen months period, it shall be and become binding upon such six or more States 60 days after the date of legislative approval by the Sixth State and the Governors of such six or more States shall forthwith name the members of the Board from their States as hereinabove set out, and the Board shall then meet on call of the Governor of any State approving this compact, at which time the Board shall elect officers, adopt by-laws, appoint committees and otherwise fully organize. Other States whose names are subscribed hereto shall thereafter become parties hereto upon approval of this compact by legislative action within two years from the date hereof, upon such conditions as may be agreed upon at the time. Provided, however, that with respect to any State whose constitution may require amendment in order to permit legislative approval of the compact, such State or States shall become parties hereto upon approval of this compact by legislative action within seven years from the date hereof, upon such conditions as may be agreed upon at the time.

After becoming effective this compact shall thereafter continue without limitation of time; provided, however, that it may be terminated at any time by unanimous action of the States and provided further that any State may withdraw from this compact if such withdrawal is approved by its legislature, such withdrawal to become effective two years after written notice thereof to the Board accompanied by a certified copy of the requisite legislative action, but such withdrawal shall not relieve the withdrawing State from its obligations hereunder accruing up to the effective date of such withdrawal. Any State so withdrawing shall *ipso facto* cease to have any claim to or ownership of any of the property held or vested in the Board or to any of the funds of the Board held under the terms of this compact.

If any State shall at any time become in default in the performance of any of its obligations assumed herein or with respect to any obligation imposed upon said State as authorized by and in compliance with the terms and provisions of this compact, all rights, privileges and benefits of such defaulting State, its members on the Board and its citizens shall *ipso facto* be and become suspended from and after the date of such default. Unless such default shall be remedied and made good within a period of one year immediately following the date of such default this compact may be terminated with respect to such defaulting State by an affirmative vote of three-fourths of the members of the Board (exclusive of the members representing the State in default), from and after which time such State shall cease to be a party to this compact and shall have no further claim to or ownership of any of the property held by or vested in the Board or to any of the funds of the Board held under the terms of this compact, but such termination shall in no matter release such defaulting State from any accrued obligation or otherwise affect this compact or the rights, duties, privileges or obligations of the remaining States thereunder.

IN WITNESS WHEREOF this compact has been approved and signed by Governors of the several States, subject to the approval of their respective legislatures in the manner hereinabove set out, as of the 8th day of February, 1948.

STATE OF FLORIDA
By Millard F. Caldwell
Governor

STATE OF ARKANSAS
By Ben Laney
Governor

STATE OF MARYLAND
By Wm. Preston Lane, Jr.
Governor

COMMONWEALTH OF VIRGINIA
By Wm. M. Tuck
Governor

STATE OF GEORGIA
By M. E. Thompson
Governor

STATE OF NORTH CAROLINA
By R. Gregg Cherry
Governor

STATE OF LOUISIANA
By J. H. Davis
Governor

STATE OF SOUTH CAROLINA
By J. Strom Thurmond
Governor

STATE OF ALABAMA
By James E. Folsom
Governor

STATE OF TEXAS
By Beauford H. Jester
Governor

STATE OF MISSISSIPPI
By F. L. Wright
Governor

STATE OF OKLAHOMA
By Roy J. Turner
Governor

STATE OF TENNESSEE
By Jim McCord
Governor

STATE OF WEST VIRGINIA
By Clarence W. Meadows
Governor

Now, therefore, be it

Resolved by the Senate, the House of Representatives concurring:

SECTION 1. That the said Compact as amended, be and the same is hereby approved and the State of North Carolina is hereby declared to be a party hereto, and agreements, covenants, and obligations therein are binding upon the State of North Carolina.

SEC. 2. That upon the approval of this Compact as amended by the requisite number of States, the Honorable W. Kerr Scott, Governor of the State of North Carolina, is authorized to sign an engrossed copy of the Compact as amended, and provide sufficient copies thereof so that every State approving the same shall have an engrossed copy.

SEC. 3. This Resolution shall take effect from and after its ratification. [Ratified on the 17th day of March, 1949.]

[Note: See Note on Regional Compact—Education, Appendix 6.]

Medical Training for Negroes

§131-124. [1947 Cum. Supp.] — Medical Training for Negroes. — The North Carolina medical care commission shall make careful investigation of the methods for providing necessary medical training for negro students, and shall report its findings to the next session of the general assembly. In addition to the benefits provided by §116-110, the North Carolina medical care commission is hereby authorized to make loans to negro medical students from the fund provided in §131-121, subject to such rules, regulations, and conditions as the commission may prescribe. [1945, c. 1096.]

Feeble Minded

§§116-142.1 - 116.142.9. [1947 Cum. Supp.] [Provision for the establishment of an institution for the care of feeble-minded Negro children in North Carolina under the management and control of the North Carolina Hospital Board of Control, to be built near the State Hospital for Negroes at Goldsboro, N. C., and to be called the "Negro Training School for Feeble Minded Children."] [1945, c. 459, §§1-10.]

Juvenile Delinquents — Negro Boys
Morrison Training School

§§134-79 - 134-84. [Provision for the establishment and maintenance of The Morrison Training School for the care, discipline and training of Negro boys.] [1921, c. 190; 1937, c. 146; 1943, c. 776; C.S. 5912 (a) to 5912 (f).]

Juvenile Delinquents — Negro Girls

§§134-84.1 - 134.84.9. [Provision for the establishment of an institution for the care of delinquent Negro girls in North Carolina known as the State Training School for Negro Girls under management and control of North Carolina Board of correction and training.] [1943, c. 381, §§1-9.]

Blind, Deaf and Dumb — State School for the Blind and Deaf in Raleigh

§ 116 - 09. Admission of pupils; how admission obtained. — The board of directors shall, on application, receive in the institution for the purpose of education, in the main department, all white blind children, and in the department for the colored all colored deaf-mutes and blind children, residents of this state, . . . who are between the ages of seven and twenty-one years: . . . [Rev., s, 4191; Code, s. 2231; 1881, c. 211, s. 5; 1917, c. 35, s. 1; C.S. 5876.]

§116-84. [Provides for a department in the Pembroke State College for Indians for the teaching of deaf, dumb and blind Indian children of Robeson County.] [1935, c. 435; 1941, c. 323, s.1.]

Employment

See under Labor.

Firemen's Relief Fund

§118-11. No discrimination on account of color. — Inasmuch as there are in a number of towns and cities of this State fire companies composed exclusively of colored men, it is expressly provided that the local boards of trustees shall make no discrimination on account of color in the payment of benefits. [1905, c. 831, S. 10; C.S. 6073 as amended 1925, cc. 41, 309.]

Fraternal Orders and Societies

§58-267 . . . Separation of races. — . . . No fraternal order or society or beneficiary association shall be authorized to do business in this State under the provisions of this article, whether incorporated under the laws of this or any other state, province, or territory, which associates with, or seeks in this State to associate with, as members of the same lodge, fraternity, society, association, the white and colored races with the objects and purposes provided in this article. [Rev. s. 4797; 1899, c. 54, s. 91; 1913, c. 46; C.S. 6494.]

Hospitals for Insane

§122-3. [1947 Cum. Supp.] — Division of patients among the several institutions under the North Carolina hospitals board of control. — The state hospital at Raleigh and the state hospital at Morganton shall be exclusively for the accommodation, maintenance, care and treatment of the white mentally disordered persons of the state, and the state hospital at Goldsboro shall be exclusively for the accommodation, maintenance, care and treatment for the colored mentally disordered, epileptic, feebleminded, and inebriate of the State . . . [1929, c. 265, s. 1; 1933, c. 342, s. 1; 1943, cc. 32, 164; 1945, c. 952, s. 9; 1947, c. 537, s. 5; C.S. 6153 (a).]

122-5. [1947 Cum. Supp.] — Care and treatment of Indians in mental hospitals. — The authorities of the State hospital at Raleigh and the state hospital at Morganton may also receive for care and treatment mentally disordered, epileptic, and inebriate Indians who are resident within the State, and who may, within the discretion of the superintendent, be assigned to any of the wards of the hospitals. [1919, c. 211; 1945, c. 952, s. 10; 1947, c. 537, s. 7; C.S. 6154.]

§122-83. [1947 Cum. Supp.] — Mentally disordered persons charged with crime to be committed to hospital. — [Provides that mentally disordered persons charged with crime be sent to the state hospital at Raleigh, if white or if an Indian from Robeson county; if a Negro, he shall be sent to the state hospital at Goldsboro. [1945, c. 952, s. 53.]

Indians

§71-1. Cherokee Indians of Robeson County — rights and privileges. —

The persons residing in Robeson, Richmond, and Sampson counties, who have heretofore been known as "Croatan Indians" or "Indians of Robeson County," together with their descendants, shall hereafter be known and designated as "Cherokee Indians of Robeson County." . . . [Rev. s. 4168, 1885, c. 51, s. 2; 1911, c. 215; P.L. 1911, c. 263; 1913, c. 123; C.S. 6257.]

§71-2. Separate privileges in schools and institutions. — Such Cherokee Indians of Robeson county and the Indians of Person county, defined in the chapter Education, §115-66, shall be entitled to the following rights and privileges:

1. Separate schools, with the educational privileges provided in the chapter Education.

2. Suitable accommodations in the State hospital for the insane at Raleigh, as provided in the chapter Hospitals for the Insane, in the article entitled Organization and Management.

3. The sheriffs, jailers, or other proper authorities of Robeson and Person counties shall provide in the common jails of said counties, and in the homes of the aged and infirm thereof, separate cells, wards, or apartments for such Indians in all cases where it shall be necessary under the laws of this State to commit any of said Indians to such jails or county homes. [1911, c. 215, s. 6; 1913, c. 123; P.L. 1913, c. 22; C.S. 6258.]

[Note: See also under Education, §115-66; under Hospitals for Insane, §122-5.]

§71-3. Chapter not applicable to certain bands of Cherokees. — [Above provisions do not apply eastern band of Cherokee Indians residing in Cherokee, Graham, Swain, Jackson and other adjoining counties in North Carolina.] [1913, c. 123, s. 5; C.S. 6259.]

§71-4. [1947 Cum. Supp.] Rights of eastern band of Cherokee Indians to inherit, acquire, use and dispose of property. — Subject only to restrictions and conditions now existing or hereafter imposed under federal statutes and regulations, or treaties, contracts, agreements, or conveyances between such Indians and the federal government, the several mmbers of the eastern band of Cherokee Indians residing in Cherokee, Graham, Swain, Jackson and other adjoining counties in North Carolina, and the lineal descendants of any bona fide member of such eastern band of Cherokee Indians, shall inherit, purchase, or otherwise lawfully acquire, hold, use, encumber, convey and alienate by will, deed, or other lawful means, any property whatsoever as fully and completely in all respects as any other citizen of the State of North Carolina is authorized to inherit, hold, or dispose of such property. [1947, C. 978, s. 1.]

§71-5. [1947 Cum. Supp.] . . . Eligibility of members of members of eastern band of Cherokee Indians to hold office in tribal organization. — Any person who is a lineal descendant of any bona fide member of such eastern band of Cherokee Indians who is a member of said band and who is domiciled on the lands of said eastern band of Cherokee Indians shall be eligible to hold any elective or appointive office or position within the tribal organization, including the position of chief, and may be elected or appointed and shall thereafter serve in such manner and for such time as a majority of the accredited membership of such eastern band of Cherokee Indians may decide at any election held for such purpose or appointment made by the accredited officials of said eastern band of Cherokee Indians. [1947, c. 978, s. 2.]

Separate College

§§116-79 - 116-86. [1949 Cum. Supp.], Pembroke State College for Indians. — [Provide for establishment and maintenance of Pembroke State College for Indians "for the purpose of the education of the Cherokee Indians of Robeson" . . .] [Rev. s. 4236, 4237, 4241; 1887, c. 400, §§1, 2; 1911, x. 168, §§1-3; c. 215, §4; 1913, c. 123, §§4-6; 1941, c. 323, s. 1; 1945, c. 817, §§1-3; C.S. 5843, 5845, 5847, 1949, c. 58, §2.]

Name changed to "Pembroke State College."

Laws 1949, ch. 58, p. 49. [S.B. 77.] [Amends G.S. 116-79, 116-80, 116-83, 116-84, 116-85 to strike the words "Pembroke State College for Indians" wherever such words occur and substitute therefor the words "Pembroke State College."] [Effective July 1, 1949.]

§§116-87 - 116-91. Vocational and normal school for Indians in certain counties — [Provides for establishment of vocational and normal schools for training of young Indian men and women where deemed suitable.] [1941, c. 370, s. 1-5.]

§22-3. Contracts with Cherokee Indians. — All contracts and agreements of every description made with any Cherokee Indian, or any person of Cherokee Indian blood within the second degree, for an amount equal to ten dollars [$10.00] or more, shall be void, unless some note or memorandum thereof be made in writing and signed by such Indian or person of Indian blood, or some other person by him authorized, in the presence of two witnesses, who shall subscribe the same; Provided, that this section shall not apply to any person of Cherokee Indian blood or any Cherokee Indian who understands the English and who can speak and write the same intelligently. [Rev., s. 975; code, s. 1553; R.C., c. 50, s. 16; 1907, c. 1004, s. 1; C.S. 989.]

Insurance

§58-44.3 [1947 Cum. Supp.] Discrimination forbidden. — No company doing the business of insurance . . . nor its agents, shall make any discrimination in favor of any person . . . [Rev. s. 4766; 1903, c. 488, s. 2; 1905, c. 170, s. 2; 1923, c. 4, s. 70; 1925, c. 70, s. 6; 1945, c. 458; C.S. 6430.]

[Note: Race or color not mentioned.]

Labor

§95.48. When separate toilets required; penalty. — All persons and corporations employing males and females in any manufacturing industry, or other business employing more than two males and females in towns and cities having a population of one thousand persons or more, and where such employees are required to do indoor work chiefly, shall provide and keep in a cleanly condition separate and distinct toilet rooms for such employees, said toilets to be lettered and marked in a distinct manner, so as to furnish separate facilities for white males, white females, colored males and colored females: Provided, that the provisions of this section shall not apply to cases where toilet arrangements or facilities are furnished by said employer off the premises occupied by him. [1913, c. 83, s. 1; C.S. 6559.]

§95-49. Location; intruding on toilet misdemeanor. — It shall be the duty of the persons or corporations mentioned under this article to locate their toilets for males and females, white and colored, in separate parts of their buildings or grounds in building hereafter erected, and in those now erected all closets shall be separated by substantial walls of brick or timber, and any employee who shall wilfully intrude upon or use any toilet not intended for his or her sex or color shall be guilty of a misdemeanor and upon conviction shall be fined five [$5.00] dollars. [1913, c. 83, s. 4; C.S. 6560.]

§95-50. Punishment for violation of article. — If any person, firm or corporation refuses to comply with the provisions of this article, he or it shall be guilty of a misdemeanor, and upon conviction shall be fined or imprisoned, or both, in the discretion of the court. [1913, c. 83, s. 2; 1919, c. 100, s. 12; C.S. 6561.]

[Note: See also §§95-51 - 95-53, Gen. Stats., providing for enforcement of the above provision by local sheriffs, police and department of labor.]

Libraries

§125-10. Separate reading room for colored people. — [State Library] — The state librarian is directed to fit up and maintain a separate place for the use of the colored people who may come to the library for the purpose of reading books or periodicals. [Rev. s. 5080; 1901, c. 503, s. 2; C.S. 6585.]

Militia

§127-6. White and colored enrolled separately. — The white and colored militia shall be separately enrolled, and shall never be compelled to serve in the same organization. No organization of colored troops shall be permitted where white troops are available, and while permitted to be organized, colored troops shall be under command of white officers. [1917, c. 200, s. 6; C.S. 6796.]

Miscegenation

§51-3. [1949 Cum. Supp.] . . . Void and voidable marriages.—All marriages between a white person and a negro or Indian, or between a white person and person of negro or Indian descent to the third generation, inclusive, or between a Cherokee Indian of Robeson county and a negro, or between a Cherokee Indian of Robeson county and a person of negro descent to the third generation, inclusive, . . . shall be void: Provided . . . that no marriage followed by cohabitation and the birth of issue shall be declared void after the death of either of the parties for any of the causes stated in this section, except for that one of the parties was a white person and the other a negro or Indian, or of negro or Indian descent to the third generation, inclusive . . . [Rev., s. 2083; Code, s. 1810; R.C., c. 68, s.s. 7, 8, 9; 1871-2, c. 193, s. 2; 1887, c. 245; 1911, c. 215, s. 2; 1913, c. 123; 1917, c. 135; 1947, c. 383, s. 3; 1949, c. 1022; C.S. 2495.]

§14-181. **Miscegenation.** — All marriages between a white person and a negro, or between a white person and a person of negro descent to the third generation inclusive, are forever prohibited, and shall be void. Any person violating this section shall be guilty of an infamous crime, and shall be punished by imprisonment in the county jail or state's prison for not less than four months nor more than ten years, and may also be fined, in the discretion of the court. [Rev., 3369; Code, s. 1084; Const., Art. XIV, s. 8; R.C., c. 68, s. 7; 1834, c. 24; 1838-9, c. 24; C.S. 4340.]

> [Note: Under this section the North Carolina Courts have held that where the parties are not residents of North Carolina and marry in a State permitting mixed marriages, the marriage will be valid in North Carolina, (*State v. Ross,* 76 N.C. 242), but that where the parties leave the State for the purpose of intermarriage and to evade the North Carolina anti-miscegenation law with the intent to return to the State, the marriage is not valid in N.C. (*State v. Kennedy,* 76 N.C. 251; *State v. Ross,* 76 N.C. 251; *State v. Ross,* 76 N.C. 242)]

§14-182. **Issuing license for marriage between white person and negro; performing marriage ceremony.**—If any register of deeds shall knowingly issue any license for marriage between any person of color and a white person; or if any clergyman, minister of the gospel or justice of the peace shall knowingly marry any such person of color to a white person, the person so offending shall be guilty of a misdemeanor. [Rev. s. 3370; Code, s. 1085; R.C., c. 34, s. 1830; c. 4, s. 2; C.S. 4341.]

Orphanages

§§116-138 - 116-142. — [Provides for establishment and maintenance of The Colored Orphanage of North Carolina for the training and care of Negro orphan children of the state.] [1927, c. 162, ss. 1-5.]

Prisons and Jails
County Jails

§153-51. **Jail to have five apartments.** — The common jails of the several counties shall be provided with at least five separate and suitable apartments, one for confinement of white male criminals; one for white female criminals; one for the colored male criminals; one for colored female criminals; and one for other prisoners. [Rev., s. 1336; Code, s. 783; R.C., c. 30, s. 2; 1795, c. 433, s. 4; 1816, c. 911; C.S. 1318.]

State Prisons

§148 - 43. **Prisoners of different races kept separate.** — White and colored prisoners shall not be confined or shackled together in the same room of any building or tent, either in the State prison or at any State or county convict camp, during the eating or sleeping hours, and at all other times the separation of the races shall be as complete as practicable. Any officer or employee of either the State or any county in the State having charge of convicts or prisoners who shall violate or permit the violation of this section shall be guilty of a misdemeanor, and upon conviction shall be fined not more than fifty dollars

[$50.00] or imprisoned not more than thirty [30] days. [1909, c. 832, ss. 1, 2; 1917, c. 286, s. 24; 1925, c. 163; C.S. 7740.]

§148 - 44. Segregation as to race, sex and age. — The commission shall provide separate sleeping quarters and separate eating space for the different races and the different sexes; and, in so far as it is practical to do so, shall provide for youthful convicts to segregate themselves. [1933, c. 172, s. 25.]

[Note: See also under Indians, §71-2(3) above.]

Transportation

Separate Waiting Rooms

§62-44. To provide for separate waiting rooms for races. — The [North Carolina Utilities Commission] commission is empowered and directed to require the establishment of separate waiting rooms at all stations for the white and colored races. [Rev., s. 1097; 1899, c. 64, s. 2, subsec. 14; 1933, c. 134, s. 8; 1941, c. 97; C.S. 1043.]

Railroads and Other Carriers

§60-94. Separate accommodations for different races. — All railroad and steamboat companies engaged as common carriers in the transportation of passengers for hire, other than street railways, shall provide separate but equal accommodations for the white and colored races at passenger stations or waiting-rooms, and also on all trains and steamboats carrying passengers. Such accommodations may be furnished by railroad companies either by separate passenger cars or by compartments in passenger cars, which shall be provided by the railroads under the supervision and direction of the utilities commission: Provided, that this shall not apply to relief trains in cases of accident, to Pullman or sleeping cars, or through express trains that do not stop at all stations and are not used ordinarily for traveling from station to station, to negro servants in attendance on their employers, to officers or guards transporting prisoners, nor to prisoners so transported. [Rev., s. 2619; 1899, c. 384; 1901, c. 213; 1933, c. 134, s. 8; 1941, c. 97, s. 5; C.S. 3494.]

§60-95. Certain carriers may be exempted from requirement. — The utilities commisson is hereby authorized to exempt from the provisions of §60-94 steamboats, branch lines and narrow-gauge railroads and mixed trains carrying both freight and passengers, if in its judgment the enforcement of the same be unnecessary to secure the comfort of passengers by reason of the light volume of passenger traffic, or the small number of colored passenger travelers on such steamboats, narrow-guage railroads, branch lines or mixed trains. [Rev. s. 2620; 1899, c. 384, s. 2; 1901, c. 213; 1933, c. 134, s. 8; 1941, c. 97, s. 5; C.S. 3495.]

§60-96. Use of same coach in emergencies. — When any coach or compartment car for either race shall be completely filled at a station where no extra coach or car can be had, and the increased number of passengers could not be foreseen, the conductor in charge of such train may assign and set apart a portion of a car or compartment assigned for passengers of one race to passengers of the other race. [Rev. s. 2621; 1899, c. 384, s. 3; C.S. 3496.]

§60-97. Penalty for failing to provide separate coaches. — Any railroad or steamboat company failing to comply in good faith with the provisions of §§60-94 to §§60-96 shall be liable to a penalty of one hundred dollars per day, to be recovered in an action brought against such company by any passenger on any train or boat of any railroad or steamboat company which is required by this chapter to furnish separate accommodations to the races, who has been furnished accommodations on such railroad train or steamboat only in a car or compartment with a person of a different race in violation of law. [Rev. s. 2622; 1899, c. 384, s. 5; C.S. 3497.]

§60-98. Exceptions to requirement of separate coaches and toilets. — As to trains consisting of not more than one passenger car unit, operated principally for the accommodation of local travel although operated both intrastate and interstate and irrespective of the motive power used, the utilities commission is authorized to make such rules and regulations for the separation of the races and with regard to toilet facilities as in its best judgment may be feasible and reasonable in the circumstances, and the rules and regulations established pursuant to this authority shall be exceptions to the provisions of §§60-94 and 60-107. [1935, c. 270; 1941, c. 97, s. 5.]

[Note: See also §§60.5, 60.6.]

Motor Carriers

§62-109. Regulatory powers of [Utilities] Commission; Separation of races. — [1925, c. 50, s. 4; 1927, c. 136, s. 7; 1929, c. 216, s. 1; 1933, c. 134, s. 8; 1941, c. 97.] [Repealed, L. 1949, c. 1132, §38.]

§60-139. Sections 60-135 to 60-138 extended to motor busses used as common carriers. — The provisions of §§60-135 to §60-138 are hereby extended to motor busses operated in the urban, interurban or suburban transportation of passengers for hire, and to the operator or operators thereof, and the agents, servants, and employees of such operators. [1933, c. 489.]

§62-121.71. [1949 Cum. Supp.] Separation of races. — The commission [North Carolina Utilities Commission] shall require every common carrier by motor vehicle to provide separate but substantially equal accommodations for the white and colored races at passenger stations or waiting rooms where the carrier receives passengers of both races, and on all common carriers by motor vehicles operating on a route or routes over which such carrier transports passengers of both races. **Provided,** that any requirement as to separate accommodation for the races shall not apply to specifically chartered motor vehicles or to negro servants and attendants and their employers, or to officers or guards transporting prisoners. [1949, c. 1132, s. 29.]

[Note: §62-121.71 replaces former section 62-109. See the following cases for a discussion of North Carolina's policy of racial segregation on motor vehicles: *State v. Brown* (1945), 225 N.C. 22, 33 S.E.(2d) 121; *Pridgen v. Carolina Coach Co.* (1948), 229 N.C. 46, 47 S.E. (2d) 609; *State v. Johnson* (1949), 229 N.C., 701, 51 S.E. (2d) 186.

The *Pridgen* case was decided two years after the Supreme Court of the United States held in *Morgan v. Virginia* (1946), 328 U.S. 373, 90 Law Ed. 1317, that provisions of a Virginia statute which required the separation of Negro and White passengers on both interstate and intrastate motor carriers were invalid as applied to *interstate* passengers in vehicles moving *interstate*, because they constituted a burden on interstate commerce in violation of the interstate commerce clause of the Constitution of the United States. The North Carolina court held, however, that the interstate commerce clause does not prevent private carriers from adopting reasonable rules and regulations for the government of their business and declared, "We know of nothing that makes segregation per se unconstitutional or violative of any act of Congress." (48)

In view of the recent decision of the Supreme Court in *Henderson v. United States*, 339 U.S. 816,70 S. Ct. 843, (decided June 5, 1950) which held that the rules and practices of the Southern Railway, which allotted ten tables exclusively to white passengers and one table exclusively to Negro passengers and which provided for a curtain or partition between that table and the other tables, violated section 3(1) of the Interstate Commerce Act (49 U.S.C.A., §3(1), the ruling of the *Pridgen* case would seem to be erroneous and not controlling in North Carolina, at least insofar as *interstate* passengers are concerned.

Furthermore, the language of §62-121.71 requires segregation of Negro and white passengers on all common carriers without reference to whether the statute applies to interstate or intrastate passengers. It would seem clear that this statute is invalid as applied to interstate passengers in vehicles moving interstate through North Carolina.

See *Legal Case Against Segregation*, Appendix 7, for complete text of the Supreme Court decision in *Henderson v. United States*.]

§62-121.72. [1949 Cum. Supp.] Unlawful operation. — (1) Any person, whether carrier, or any officer, employee, agent or representative thereof, knowingly and wilfully violating any provision of this article [§§62-121.1 - 62-121.79] or any rule, regulation, requirement, or order thereunder, or any term of [or] condition of any certificate or permit, for which a penalty is not otherwise herein provided, shall be guilty of a misdemeanor, and upon conviction thereof be fined not more than one hundred dollars ($100.00) for the first offense and not more than five hundred dollars ($500.00 for any subsequent offense.

(2) If any carrier, or any other person or corporation, shall operate a motor vehicle for the transportation of passengers for.compensation in violation of any provision of this article [§§62-121.1 - 62-121.79], except as to reasonableness of rates or charges and the discriminatory character thereof,

or shall operate in violation of any rule, regulation, requirement or order of the commission, or of any term or condition of any certificate or permit, the commission or any holder of a certificate or permit duly issued by the commission may apply to the resident superior court judge of any judicial district where such motor carrier or other person or corporation so operates, or to any superior court judge holding court in such judicial district, for the enforcement of any provision of this article, or of any rule, regulation, requirement, order, term or condition of the commission. Such court shall have jurisdiction to enforce obedience to this article or to any other rule, order, or decision of the commission by a writ of injunction or other process, mandatory or otherwise, restraining such carrier, person or corporation, or its officers, agents, employees and representatives from further violation of this article or of any rule, order, regulation, or decision of the commission. [1949, c. 1132, s. 30.]

Street and Interurban Railways

§60-135. Separate accommodations for different races; failure to provide misdemeanor. — All street, interurban and suburban railway companies, engaged as common carriers in the transportation of passengers for hire in the State of North Carolina, shall provide and set apart so much of the front portion of each car operated by them as shall be necessary, for occupation by the white passengers therein, and shall likewise provide and set apart so much of the rear part of such car as shall be necessary, for occupation by the colored passengers therein, and shall require as far as practicable the white and colored passengers to occupy the respective parts of such car so set apart for each of them. The provisions of this section shall not apply to nurses or attendants of children or of the sick or infirm of a different race, while in attendance upon such children or such sick or infirm persons. Any officer, agent or other employee of any street railway company who shall wilfully violate the provisions of this section shall be guilty of a misdemeanor, and upon conviction shall be fined or imprisoned in the discretion of the court. [1907, c. 850, ss. 1, 5, 7; 1909, C. 851; C.S. 3536.]

§60-136. Passengers to take certain seats; violation of requirement misdemeanor. — Any white person entering a street car or other passenger vehicle or motor bus for the purpose of becoming a passenger therein shall, in order to carry out the purposes of §60-135, occupy the first vacant seat or unoccupied space nearest the front thereof, and any colored person entering a street car or other passenger vehicle or motor bus for a like purpose shall occupy the first vacant seat or unoccupied space nearest the rear end thereof, provided, however, that no contiguous seat on the same bench shall be occupied by white and colored passengers at the same time, unless and until all the other seats in the car have been occupied. Upon request of the person in charge of the street car or other passenger vehicle or motor bus, and when necessary in order to carry out the purpose of providing separate seats for white and colored passengers, it shall be the duty of any white person to move to any unoccupied seat toward or in front of the car, vehicle or bus, and the duty of any colored person to move to any unoccupied seat toward or in the rear thereof, and the failure of any such person to so move shall constitute *prima facie* evidence of an intent to violate this section. Any person violating the provisions of this section shall be guilty of a misdemeanor and upon conviction, shall be fined not more than fifty [$50.00] dollars or imprisoned not exceeding thirty [30] days. Any such person may also be ejected from the car, vehicle or bus by the person charged with the operation thereof. Each person now or hereafter charged with the operation of any such street car, passenger vehicle or motor bus is hereby invested with police powers and authority to carry out the provisions of this section. [1907, c. 850, ss. 2, 6; 1939, c. 147, C.S. 3537.]

§60-137. No liability for mistake in assigning passengers to wrong seat. — No street, suburban or interurban railway company, its agents, servants or employees, shall be liable to any person on account of any mistake in the designation of any passenger to a seat or part of a car set apart for passengers of the other race. [1907, c. 850, s. 8; C.S. 3538.]

NORTH DAKOTA

CONSTITUTION

Education

Art. VIII. Section 147.— [Provides for the " . . . *establishment and maintenance of a system of public schools which shall be open to all children of the State of North Dakota and free from sectarian control."*] [Const. 1889] [Italics added]

Indians

Article V, Section 121. — [Provides that "civilized persons of Indian descent who have severed their tribal relations two years next preceding such election" shall be qualified electors.] [Constitution 1889 as amended by Article 2 and Article 37 of the amendments to the constitution, approved and ratified on November 8, 1898, and November 2, 1920 respectively.]

Slavery

Art. I., Section 17. — Neither slavery nor involuntary servitude, unless for the punishment of crime, shall ever be tolerated in this state. [Const. 1889.]

STATUTES

North Dakota Revised Code (1943)

Aliens

§20-0110. Aliens Not to Hunt or Take Wild Birds or Animals; When. — [Prohibits aliens who have not declared intention to become citizens of the United States from hunting or trapping wild birds or animals, except in defense of person or property.] [Source: S.L. 1915, c. 161, s. 67; 1925 Supp., s. 10322a70, am'd., S.L. 1931, c. 148, s. 43.]

47-0111. Private ownership; Persons Qualified; Citiden; Alien. — Any person whether citizen or alien, may take, hold and dispose of property, real or personal, within this State. [Source: R.C. 1895, s. 3277; R.C. 1899, s. 3277; R.C. 1899, s. 3277; R.C. 1905, s. 4713; C.L. 1913, s. 5256]

56-0116. Aliens May Take by Succession. — Aliens may take in all cases by succession as well as citizens. No person capable of succeeding under the provisions of this chapter is precluded from such succession by reason of the alienage of any relative. [Source: R. C. 1895, s. 3758; R.C. 1899, s. 3758; R.C. 1905, s. 5203; C.L. 1913, s. 5759.]

Indians

5-0210. [1947 Supp.] Sales to Certain Persons Unlawful; Penalty. — No person shall sell or deliver any beer, alcohol or alcoholic beverages to any person under the age of twenty-one [21] years, incompetent person, Indian as defined by federal law, or a person who is an inebriate, or habitual drunkard . . . [Violations punishable by 10 to 30 days in prison or a fine of $20 to $100, or both for the first offense; and for a second or subsequent offense 30 to 90 days in prison or $50 to $500, or both] [Source: I.M.

Sept. 22, 1933, s.9; S.L. 1935, p. 495, am'd. S.L. 1945, c. 52, s. 1, am'd. S.L. 1947, c. 8, s. 1., appvd. March 20, 1947.]

Laws 1949
Chapter 324, Page 426

North Dakota Indian Affairs Commission

§1. — [Creates a North Dakota Indian affairs commission to consist of the governor, commissioner of agriculture and labor, superintendent of public instruction, executive director of the public welfare board of North Dakota, State Health officer, and the chairman of the board of county commissioners of Sioux, Mercer, McLean, McKenzie, Dunn, Rolette, Benson and Eddy counties. The governor to act as chairman. The commission is to receive mileage and expenses.

§2. — [Provides for employment of an executive director and other necessary technical and professional personnel.]

§3. — In order that the state may be prepared and have the factual information needed to deal effectively with Indian affairs, provide aid and protection for Indians as needed, prevent undue hardships, assist in the integration of Indian citizens into modern economy, and coordinate state, local and federal programs relating to Indian affairs, the commission shall have the power and it shall be its duty,

1. To study, consider, accumulate, compile and assemble information on any phase of Indian affairs;

2. To formulate and develop proposals for the benefit of Indians who may be in need of assistance in securing employment in agriculture, business or other usual occupation, on a self-supporting basis;

3. To cooperate with and secure the assistance of the federal government or any agencies thereof, in formulating any such program, and coordinate such program, as nearly as maybe possible, with any program regarding Indian affairs adopted or planned by the federal government to the end that the state may secure the full benefit of such federal program;

4. To investigate relief needs of Indians in North Dakota and to prepare plans for the alleviation of such needs;

5. To confer with officials and agencies of other governmental units and congressional committees with regard to Indian needs and the coordination of state, local and federal programs in regard thereto.

§4. — [All state and local public officers required to furnish the commission with available information upon request.]

§5. — [Provision for meetings of commission. A majority of members of commission shall constitute a quorum and a majority of such quorum shall have power to act.]

§6. — [Commission is required to submit and make public a report to the legislative assembly on or before December 1, 1950, setting forth its findings, conclusions and recommendations. "It may submit recommendations in the form of proposed legislation or resolutions and may publish such additonal reports from time to time as it may deem necessary."]

§7. — [$20,000 is appropriated to carry out the provisions of this Act.]

§8. — [This Act is declared to be an emergency measure.]

Approved March 19, 1949.

Ku Klux Klan — Masks

12-4202. Wearing Masks in Public Prohibited; Misdemeanor. — Any person over the age of fifteen years who appears outside of any building in this state wearing a mask, regalia or other head covering worn so as to conceal the features and prevent recognition of the person, is guilty of a misdemeanor and shall be punished by a fine of not less than twenty-five dollars [$25.00] nor more than one hundred dollars [$100.00], or by imprisonment in the county jail for not less than ten [10] days nor more than thirty [30] days, or by both such fine and imprisonment. [Source: S.L. 1923, c. 240, ss. 1, 2; 1925 Supp., ss. 1024a1, 10241a2.]

Miscegenation

14-0304. Marriage Between White Person and Negro Person Void; Penalty. — No white person residing or being in this state shall intermarry with any negro person. Every such marriage shall be void. Each of the contracting parties, upon conviction, shall be punished by imprisonment in the penitentiary for a term of not more than ten [10] years, or by a fine of not more than two thousand [$2,000.00] dollars, or by both such fine and imprisonment. [Source: S.L. 1909, c. 164, s. 1; C.L. 1913, s. 9582.]

14-0305. Definition of a Negro Person. — Every person who shall have one-eighth or more of negro blood shall be deemed and held to be a colored person or negro. [Source: S.L. 1909, c. 164, s. 2; C.L. 1913, s. 9583.]

14-0326. Issuing License of Marriage Between Negroes and Whites; Penalty. — If any county judge knowingly shall issue a marriage license for a white person to marry a negro person, he shall be punished by imprisonment in the penitentiary for a term of not more than two [2] years, or by a fine of not more than two thousand dollars [$2,000.], or by both such fine and imprisonment. [Source: S.L. 1909, c. 164, s. 3; C.L. 1913, s. 9584.]

14-0327. Performing Marriage Ceremony Between Negroes and Whites; Penalty. — If any judge, justice of the peace, priest, or any person authorized to solemnize the rites of matrimony knowingly shall perform the ceremony of marriage for any white person with a negro person, he shall be punished by imprisonment in the penitentiary for a term of not more than two [2] years, or by a fine of not more than two thousand [$2000.00] dollars, or by both such fine and imprisonment. [Source: S.L. 1909, c. 164, s. 4; C.L. 1913, s. 9585.]

OHIO

CONSTITUTION

Militia

Art. IX, §1. Who shall perform military duty. — All white male citizens, residents of this state, being eighteen years of age, and under the age of forty-five years, shall be enrolled in the militia, and perform military duty, in such manner, not incompatible with the constitution and laws of the United States, as may be prescribed by law. [Const. 1851.]

> [Note: The racial restriction contained in the above constitutional provision appears never to have been repealed. Yet, Sec. 5176 of the Ohio Code provides "The militia of the State of Ohio shall consist of all able-bodied male citizens of the state, etc." and contains no racial restriction.]

Slavery

Art. I, §6. [Slavery and involuntary servitude.] — There shall be no slavery in this state; nor involuntary servitude, unless for the punishment of crime. [See Const. 1802, Art. VIII, §2, Const. 1851.]

Suffrage

> [Note: Art. IV, §1 of the Constitution of Ohio, 1802, restricted the right ot vote to "white male" inhabitants. The Constitution of 1851, Art. V, §1, as amended November 6, 1923, eliminates the restriction on race and sex.]

STATUTES

THROCKMORTON'S OHIO CODE ANNOTATED; BALDWIN'S 1948 REVISION

Aliens

§10503-13. Heirs of aliens may inherit; aliens may hold lands. — No person who is capable of inheriting shall be deprived of the inheritance by reason of any of his ancestors having been aliens. Aliens may hold, possess and enjoy lands, tenements and hereditaments, within this state, either by descent, devise gift or purchase, as fully and completely as any citizen of the United States or of this state can do. [114v. 320 (342). Eff. 1-1-32.]

Civil Rights

§12940. Penalty for denial of privileges at inns and other places by reason of color or race. — Whoever, being the proprietor or his employe, keeper or manager of an inn, restaurant, eating house, barber shop, public conveyance by air, land or water, theater, store or other place for the sale of merchandise, or other place of public accommodation or amusement, denies to a citizen, except for reasons applicable alike to all citizens and regardless of color or race, the full enjoyment of the accommodations, advantages, facilities or privileges thereof, or, being a person who aids or incites the denial thereof, shall be fined not less than fifty [$50.00] dollars nor more than five hundred [$500.00] dollars or imprisoned not less than thirty [30] days nor more than

352

ninety [90] days, or both. [R.S. §§4426-1, 4426-2; 91 v. 17, §2; 81 v. 15; 81 v. 90; 117 v. S. 31, §1. Eff. 7-31-37.]

§12941. Further penalty. — Whoever violates the next preceding section shall also pay not less than fifty [$50.00] dollars nor more than five hundred [$500.00] dollars to the person aggrieved thereby to be recovered in any court of competent jurisdiction in the county where such offense was committed. (91 v. 17 §2.) [R.S. §4426-2; 91 v. 17, §2; 81 v. 15.]

Insurance

§9401. Discrimination against persons of African descent prohibited. — No life insurance company organized or doing business, or that may be organized and do business within this state, shall make any distinction or discrimination between white persons and colored, wholly or partially of African descent, as to premiums or rates charged for policies upon the lives of such persons nor demand or require greater premiums from such colored persons than are at that time required by the company from white persons of the same age, sex, general condition of health and hope of longevity; nor make or require any rebate, diminution or discount upon the sum to be paid on such policy in case of the death of such colored person insured, nor insert in the policy any condition, nor make any stipulation whereby such person insured binds himself, his heirs, executors, administrators or assigns to accept any sum less than the full value or amount of such policy in case of a claim accruing thereon by reason of the death of the person insured, other than such as are imposed upon white persons in similar cases. Any such stipulation or condition so made or inserted shall be void. [86 v. 163 §1) [R.S. §3631-1; 86 v. 163, §1.]

§9402. Procedure, when application of such persons refused. — Any such company, which refuses the application of a colored person for insurance upon his life, shall furnish him with the certificate of some regular examining physician of the company who has made examination of such person, stating that his application has been refused, not because he is a person of color, but solely upon such grounds of his general health and hope of longevity as would be applicable to white persons of the same age and sex. (86 v. 164 §2.) [R.S. §3631-2; 86 v. 163, 164, §2.]

§12954. Life insurance company discriminating against colored persons. — Whoever, being a life insurance company organized or doing business in this state, or an officer or agent thereof, violates any provision of law relating to the distinction or discrimination between white persons and colored persons, wholly or partially of African descent, by demanding or receiving from a colored person a different or greater premium than from a white person, or by allowing a discount or rebate upon a premium paid or to be paid by a white person of the same age, sex, general condition of health and hope of longevity of any colored person, or by making or requiring a rebate, diminution or discount from the sum to be paid upon a policy in case of an insured colored person, or by failing to furnish a certificate of a regular examining physician of such company to such colored person as required by law, shall be fined not less than one hundred [$100.00] dollars nor more than two hundred [$200.00] dollars. (86 v. 164 §3.) [R.S. 3631-3; 86 v. 164, §3.]

§12955. Exceptions. — The next preceding section shall not require a life insurance company, or an agent thereof, to take or receive an application for insurance from any person. (86 v. 164 §3) [R.S. §3631-3; 86 v. 164, §3.]

Jurors

§12868. Race or color shall not disqualify to act as juror. — Whoever, being an officer or other person charged with a duty in selecting or summoning jurors, excludes or fails to summon a citizen as a grand or petit juror on account of his race or color, provided such citizen possesses all other qualifications required by law for jurors, shall be fined not less than fifty [$50.00] dollars nor more than five hundred [$500.00] dollars or imprisoned not less than thirty [30] days nor more than ninety [90] days, or both. [R.S. §4426-3; 91 v. 18, §3; 81 v. 15.]

Ku Klux Klan — Masks

§12810. Riotous conspiracy. — Whoever, being one of three or more persons who unite or combine together to commit a misdemeanor while wearing white caps, masks or other disguise, shall be imprisoned in the penitentiary not less than two [2] years nor more than ten [10] years and fined not more than two thousand [$2,000.00] dollars. [86 v. 169, §1; R.S. §6895-1.]

Public Accommodation

See under Civil Rights above.

Public Works

§2366-1. [Discrimination and intimidation on account of race, creed or color in employment under public contracts prohibited.] — That every contract for or on behalf of the state of Ohio or any townships, villages, counties or municipal corporations thereof, for the construction, alteration, or repair of any public building or public work in the State of Ohio shall contain provisions by which the contractor agrees:

(a) That in the hiring of employees for the performance of work under this contract or any subcontract hereunder, no contractor or subcontractor, nor any person acting on behalf of such contractor, subcontractor, shall, by reason of race, creed or color discriminate against any citizen of the state of Ohio in the employment of labor or workers, who is qualified and available to perform the work to which the employment relates;

(b) That no contractor, subcontractor, nor any person on his behalf shall, in any manner, discriminate against or intimidate any employee hired for the performance of work under this contract on account of race, creed or color. [116 v. 151, s. 1, Eff. July 24, 1935.]

§2366-2. Penalties. — Be it further provided as a penalty for any breach of said provisions against discrimination:

(a) That there shall be deducted from the amount payable to the contractor by the State of Ohio or by any village, township, county or municipal corporation thereof, under this contract, a penalty of twenty-five ($25.00) dollars for each person who is discriminated against or intimidated in violation of the provisions of this contract;

(b) and, that the contract shall be cancelled or terminated by the State of Ohio, or by any village, township, county or municipal corporation thereof, and all money to become due hereunder may be forfeited, for a second or any subsequent violation of the terms or conditions of this section of the contract. [116 v. 151 (152), §2. Eff. July 24, 1935.]

[Note: See FEPC ordinances of Cleveland and Youngstown, *infra*, Appendix 5.]

OKLAHOMA

CONSTITUTION

Aliens

Art. XXII, §1. Aliens — Ownership of land prohibited — Disposal of lands acquired. — No alien or person who is not a citizen of the United States, shall acquire title to or own land in this State, and the Legislature shall enact laws whereby all persons not citizens of the United States, and their heirs, who may hereafter acquire real estate in this State by devise, descent, or otherwise, shall dispose of the same within five years upon condition of escheat or forfeiture to the State: Provided, this shall not apply to Indians born within the United States, nor to aliens or persons not citizens of the United States who may become bona fide residents of this State: And Provided Further, that this section shall not apply to lands now owned by aliens in this State. [Const. 1907, as amended Stats. 1931, §13712.]

[Note: Under the above constitutional provision and Okla. Stats. 1941 Title 60, §§121-127, non-resident aliens are barred from owning land in Oklahoma, but aliens who are bona fide residents of the State may acquire title to land. It would appear that these provisions are not directed against any particular class of aliens and are therefore not racially restrictive.]

Definition of Races

Art. XXIII, §11. Colored race — Negro race — White race. — Wherever in this Constitution and laws of this State, the word or words, "colored" or "colored race", "negro" or "negro race", are used, the same shall be construed to mean or apply to all persons of African Descent. The term "white race" shall include all other persons. [Const. 1907 as amended Stat. 1931, §13724.]

Education

Art. XIII, §3. Separate schools for white and colored children. — Separate schools for white and colored children with like accommodation shall be provided by the Legislature and impartially maintained. The term "colored children," as used in this section, shall be construed to mean children of African descent. The term "white children" shall include all other children. [Const. 1907 as amended Stat. 1931, 13676.]

[Note: In the case of *Sipuel v. Board of Regents of University of Oklahoma*, 332 U.S. 631, 68 S. Ct. 299, 92 L. Ed. 247, (decided by the United States Supreme Court on January 12, 1948) it was held that the State of Oklahoma, in conformity with the equal protection clause of the Fourteenth Amendment, must provide a qualified Negro applicant with legal education afforded by a state institution and provide such education as soon as it does for applicants of any other group. When the applicant's admission was denied solely because of her race and color, the court indicated that *mandamus* to compel admission was the proper remedy. On June 18, 1949, Ada Lois Sipuel, the Negro applicant who sought admission, was permitted to enroll in the University of Oklahoma

Law School, although Acting President Carl M. Franklin allegedly reported that some means of segregation would be used in the classes which Mrs. Sipuel attended. (New York Times, June 19, 1949.) See Notes following Title 70, §5-5 below.]

Elections

Art. I, §6. Right of suffrage. — The State shall never enact any law restricting or abridging the right of suffrage on account of race, color, or previous condition of servitude. [Const. 1907 as amended Stat. 1931, §13411.]

Indians

Suffrage

Art. III, §1. Qualifications of electors . . . — [The right to vote is extended to Indians who are citizens of Oklahoma.] [Const., as amended by Referendum adopted Nov. 5, 1918.]

Art. I, §7. Intoxicating liquors in former Indian Territory and Indian Reservations. — [Barred the manufacture, sale, barter, giving away or otherwise furnishing intoxicating liquors within Indian Territory or Indian reservations. Violations of this provision made punishable by fine of $50.00 and by imprisonment of 30 days.] [Const. 1907, St. 1931, §13412.]

Art. I, §3. . . . Indian Lands . . . — [Disclaimer by the people of Oklahoma to all right and title to Indian lands.] [Const. 1907, Stats. 1931, §13408.]

OKLAHOMA STATUTES 1941

STATUTES

Aliens

Attorneys

Tit. 5, §1. Persons disqualified to practice law — Aliens. — [Bars aliens who have not declared intention to become citizens from practicing law.] [L. 1910, p. 81, §5. R. L. 1910, §240.]

[Note: Under this statute aliens ineligible to become United States citizens are barred permanently from practicing law in Oklahoma.]

State Officers and Employees

Title 74, §255. Appointments and Tenure. — . . . it shall be unlawful for the heads of any Department, or any Departments to employ in any way, any person who is not a citizen of the United States. [Laws 1919, ch. 211, p. 302, §2.]

Property — Successions

Title 84, §229. Aliens may take. — [Provides aliens may take property by succession as well as citizens.] [R.L. 1910, §8434.]

Education

Public Schools — Separate Schools

ARTICLE 5

Title 70, §5-1. Separation of Races — Impartial Facilities. — The public schools of the State of Oklahoma shall be organized and maintained upon a complete plan of separation between the white and colored races, with impartial facilities for both races. [Laws 1949, p. 536, art. 5, §1.]

Title 70, §5-2. Definitions. — The term "colored," as used in the preceding section, shall be construed to mean all persons of African descent who possess any *quantum* of negro blood, and the term "white" shall include all other persons. The term "public school," within the meaning of this article, shall include all schools provided for, or maintained, in whole or in part, at public expense. [Laws 1949, p. 536, art. 5, §2.]

Title 70, §5-3. County separate school defined — Designation — Race of members of district school board. — The county separate school in each district is hereby declared to be that school in said school district of the race having the fewest number of children in said school district. Provided the county superintendent of schools of each county shall have authority to designate what school or schools in each school district shall be the separate school and which class of children either white or colored shall have the privilege of attending such separate school or schools in said school district. Members of the district school board shall be of the same race as the children who are entitled to attend the school of the district, not the separate school. [Laws, 1949, p. 537, art. 5, §3.]

Title 70, §5-4. Teacher permitting child to attend school of other race. — Any teacher in this State who shall willfully and knowingly allow any child of the colored race to attend the school maintained for the white race or allow any white child to attend the school maintained for the colored race shall be deemed guilty of a misdemeanor, and upon conviction thereof shall be fined in any sum not less than ten dollars ($10.00) nor more than fifty dollars ($50.00), and his certificate shall be cancelled and he shall not have another issued to him for a term of one (1) year. [Laws 1949, p. 537, art. 5, §4.]

Title 70, §5-5. Maintaining or operating institution for both races. — It shall be unlawful for any person, corporation or association of persons to maintain or operate any college, school or institution of this State where persons of both white and colored races are received as pupils for instruction, and any person or corporation who shall operate or maintain any such college, school or institution in violation hereof shall be deemed guilty of a misdemeanor, and upon conviction thereof shall be fined not less than one hundred dollars ($100.00) nor more than five hundred dollars ($500.00), and each day such school, college or institution shall be open and maintained shall be deemed a separate offense. [*Provided, that the provisions of this Section shall not apply to programs of instruc-*

tion leading to a particular degree given at State owned or operated colleges or institutions of higher education of this State established for and/ or used by the white race, where such programs of instruction leading to a particular degree are not given at colleges or institutions of higher education of this State established for and/or used by the colored race; provided further, that said programs of instruction leading to a particular degree shall be given at such colleges or institutions of higher education upon a segregated basis. Segregated basis is defined in this Act as classroom instruction given in separate classrooms, or at separate times. The provisions of this section are subject to Section Four (4) hereof] [Laws 1949, p. 537, art. 5, §5. as amended by Laws 1949, ch. 15, p. 608, §1, H.B. No. 405, appvd. June 9, 1949.] (italics supplied)

[Note: The italicized portions in brackets in Title 70, §§5-5, 5-6, and 5-7 were added to former Title 70, §§455-457, by Laws 1949, ch. 15, p. 608-609, H.B. No. 405, approved June 9, 1949. The 1949 Oklahoma School Code enacted by Laws 1949, ch. 1-A, pp. 517-607, approved June 7, 1949, repealed former Title 70, Chapter 15 of Oklahoma Statutes, 1941 which contained §§455, 456 and 457. The School Code reenacted with slight modification §§455, 456 and 457, but without the *proviso* contained in the italicized material, as Laws 1949, p. 537, art. 5, §§5, 6, 7. (codified under Title 70, §§5-5, 5-6, 5-7 in the Oklahoma Statutes, 1949 Supp.). It is not clear whether the new School Code contains the italicized amendments, but it is reasonable to believe that since the amendments to former §§455-457 went into effect on June 9, 1949, two days after the 1949 School Code went into effect, they amend the new school code accordingly. Hence they are included here as amendments rather than as a separate statute.]

[Note: Following the *Sipuel* decision (see note to Art. XIII, §3 above), the 1949 Oklahoma Legislature amended Oklahoma Statutes, Title 70, §§455, 456, 457, to provide for admission of Negro students on a segregated basis to Oklahoma state institutions of higher education in cases where courses leading to higher degrees were not available in Negro colleges of the State (see italicized portions of Title 70, §§5-5, 5-6, 5-7 herein).

In accordance with the amended statutes, G. W. McLaurin, a Negro citizen of Oklahoma, was admitted to the University of Oklahoma in order to pursue courses of study leading toward a Doctorate in Education. McLaurin was required to receive instruction on a segregated basis, to sit at a desk in an ante-room apart from the other students in the main classroom, to use a separate desk in the library and to eat at a special table in the university cafeteria.

McLaurin brought suit against the Oklahoma State Regents charging that these restrictions violated his rights under the Fourteenth Amendment to the Constitution of the United States. The Supreme Court of the United States upheld McLaurin's contention in *McLaurin v. Oklahoma State Regents*, 339 U.S. 637, 94 L. ed. 787, 70

S. Ct. 851, decided June 5, 1950. The Court ruled that McLaurin, having been admitted to a state-supported graduate school, "must receive the same treatment at the hands of the state as students of other races." Thus, under the recent decision of the Supreme Court, it would appear that a state may not segregate a student solely because of race, once having admitted him to its graduate schools, and that Title 70, §§455, 456, 457, as amended, are unconstitutional and void.

For complete text of the opinion in *McLaurin v. Oklahoma State Regents*, see *post*, Appendix 7. See also *Sweatt v. Painter*, 339 U.S. 629, 94 L. ed. 783, 70 S. Ct. 848, decided on the same day as the McLaurin case, *post*, Appendix 7.]

Title 70, §5-6. Teaching [in] an institution receiving both races. — Any instructor who shall teach in any school, college or institution where members of the white and colored race are received and enrolled as pupils for instruction shall be deemed guilty of a misdemeanor, and upon conviction thereof, shall be fined in any sum not less than ten dollars ($10.00) nor more than fifty dollars ($50.00) for each offense, and each day any instructor shall continue to teach in any such college, school or institution shall be considered a separate offense. [*Provided, that the provisions of this Section shall not apply to programs of instruction leading to a particular degree given at State owned or operated colleges or institutions of higher education of this State established for and/or used by the white race, where such programs of instruction leading to a particular degree are not given at colleges or institutions of higher education of this State established for and/or used by the colored race; provided further, that said programs of instruction leading to a particular degree shall be given at such colleges or institutions of higher education upon a segregated basis, as defined in this Act. The provisions of this Section are subject to Section Four (4) [Title 70, §4, 57.1 hereof.]* [Laws 1949, p. 537, art. 5, §6, as amended by Laws 1949, ch. 15, p. 608, §2, H.B. No. 405, appvd. June 9, 1949.] (italics supplied)

[Note: See Title 70, §457.1 below.]

Title 70, §5-7. White person attending institution receiving colored pupils. — It shall be unlawful for any white person to attend any school, college, or institution where colored persons are received as pupils for instruction, and any one so offending shall be fined not less than five dollars ($5.00), nor more than twenty ($20.00) for each offense, and each day such person so offends as herein provided shall be deemed a distinct and separate offense: Provided, nothing in this Article shall be construed as to prevent any private school, college or institution of learning from maintaining a separate or distinct branch thereof in a different locality. [*Provided, that the provisions of this Section shall not apply to programs of instruction leading to a particular degree given at State owned or operated colleges or institutions of higher education of this State established for and/or used by the white race, where such programs of instruction leading to a particular degree are not given at colleges or* *institutions of higher education of this State established for and/or used by the colored race; provided further, that said programs of colleges or institutions or higher education upon a segregated basis, as defined in this Act. The provisions of this Section are subject to Section Four (4)* [Title 70, §457.1] hereof.] [Laws 1949, p. 537, art. 5, §7, as amended by Laws 1949, ch. 15, p. 609, §3, H.B. No. 405, appvd. June 9, 1949.] (italics supplied)

[Note: See Title 70, §457.1 below.]

Title 70, §5-8. Taxes for separate schools. — In all cases where county separate schools for white and colored children are maintained, the county excise board shall annually levy a tax on all taxable property in their respective counties sufficient to maintain such separate schools as hereinafter provided . . . [Laws 1949, p. 537, art. 5, §8.]

Title 70, §5-9. Management and control of separate school property in independent districts. — [Power vested in the board of education to manage separate school property "in such manner and on such terms as will be to the best interests of the children of the separate race."] [Laws 1949, p. 538, art. 5, §9.]

Title 70, §5-10. Separate schools not maintained when pupils can be transferred. — In any school district in such county having both white and colored children of school age where the number of such children, either white or colored, of school age, does not exceed ten, and they can be transferred to schools of their own color in adjoining districts, as hereinafter provided, no separate school shall be maintained. [Laws, 1949, p. 538, art. 5, §10.]

§5-11. Transfer of pupils to adjoining district. — When either the white children or colored children of school age in any said school district having both white and colored children of school age do not exceed ten (10) in number, the county superintendent of schools in such county shall transfer the white or colored children to the nearest school of their own color in some adjoining district when the same can be done with consent of their parents, guardian or custodian or without such consent when any such children can be transferred without compelling them to walk more than two and one half (2½) miles to attend such school, and when any such county superintendent shall apportion the per capita of all school revenue except local district taxes and per capita of all school revenues, except local school district taxes and county separate school fund, to the school district to which it is transferred, that are enjoyed by children resident in such district; provided the county superintendent may have authority to require the children of the separate races to travel more than two and one-half (2½) miles when proper provision is made for the transportation of such children, and the consent of the parents, guardian or custodian of any such child being required to travel more than two and one-half miles shall not be required when such transportation is furnished. The county superintendent and board of county commissioners of any county having separate school fund in the manner now provided by law for the payment of other necessary expenditures in maintaining such

361

separate schools and such transfer and transportation shall not be limited by the confines of any school district. [Laws 1949, p. 538, art. 5, §11.]

Title 70, §5-12. Ascertainment and report of facts to board of county commissioners. — [County superintendent required to report to board of county commissioners what districts in county have separate schools, the number of children of each color, and those districts maintaining separate schools which have not erected school houses for both white and colored children. Independent districts excepted from this section.] [Laws 1949, p. 539, art. 5, §12.]

Title 70, §5-13. School buildings for children entitled to attend separate school.—[If, upon receipt of the county superintendent's report, the board of county commissioners of local counties find there are no separate school buildings for white and colored children entitled to attend separate schools, then the board shall require the local county superintendent to file a statement of plans and specification for the kind of school needed, and contracts for the building of the schools are to be awarded to the lowest bidder.] [Laws 1949, p. 539, art. 5, §13.]

Title 70, §5-14. Teachers for separate schools. — It shall hereafter be the duty of all county superintendents of schools to contract with and employ all teachers for the county separate schools, except those in independent districts, now maintained or hereafter to be established in their respective counties: Provided the board of education in all independent districts shall contract with, and employ all teachers in the separate schools of such independent districts. Teachers so employed shall possess all the qualifications which are now required by law, and the county superintendent of schools shall have the power to prescribe rules and regulations for the government of all county separate schools in his county except independent districts. [Laws 1949, p. 539, art. 5, §14.]

Title 70, §5-15. Negro truancy officers in certain counties.—The county superintendent of schools of each county in the State having a population exceeding sixty thousand (60,000) inhabitants, according to the Federal Cunsus [Census], in which county twenty per cent (20%) or more of the total enrollment in the public or common schools during the school year ending June 30, 1946, were "colored children" as defined by Section 3, Art. XIII of the Constitution of the State of Oklahoma, is hereby authorized to appoint a Negro truancy officer for the schools of the county attended by said children, at an annual salary of not to exceed Twenty-four Hundred Dollars ($2400.00). Said officer shall have the same authority as that provided for regular truancy officers by 70 O. S. 1941 S. 402 [O. S. Supp. 1949, Tit. 70, §10-11.]. It shall be the mandatory duty of the county commissioners of the county to include in the appropriations thereof an item sufficient to pay the salary of said truancy officer and his actual and necessary traveling expenses while engaged in the performance of his official duties. This Article does not affect any county which already has a Negro truancy officer established in such county. [Laws 1949, p. 540, Art. 5, §15.]

[Note: Title 70, §§5-16, 5-17, 5-18, 5-19, 5-20, 5-21 and 5-22 (Laws

1949, pp. 540-541, §§16-22) deal with disbursements on account of separate schools, location of separate school buildings, and sale of county property for purpose of maintaining a county separate school.]

Title 70, §457. 1. [1949 Supp.] **Certificate of State Regents for Higher Education as conclusive proof.** — For the purposes of this Act, a certificate to the President of any college or institution of higher education by the Oklahoma State Regents for Higher Education or by the executive Officer of said Board, certifying that any course or courses given at such college or institution of higher education established for and/or used by the white race are not given at colleges or institutions of higher education of this State established for and/or used by the colored race shall be deemed conclusive proof of such fact in any criminal proceeding in the Courts of Oklahoma against the administrative officers of such college or institution, or against the faculty or against the students thereof for the violation of the provisions of any of the three (3) preceding Sections hereof [Title 70, §§5-5, 5-6 and 5-7.]. [Laws 1949, p. 609, §4.]

[Note: See Title 70, §§5-5, 5-6 and 5-7 above]

Agricultural and Technical School

Title 70, §§1451-1509. — [Provisions relating the establishment and operation of Langston University for the "instruction of both male and female colored persons in the art of teaching, and the various branches which pertain to a common school education; and in such higher education as may be deemed advisable by such board and in the fundamental laws of this State and of the United States, in the rights and duties of citizens, and in the agricultural, mechanical and industrial arts.] [R.L. 1910, §8018 et seq.]

Title 70, §1451b — §1451c. [1949 Supp.] [Operation, management and control of Langston University is vested in the Board of Regents for Oklahoma Agricultural and Mechanical Colleges created by Section 31a, Art. 6, Oklahoma Constitution, adopted July 11, 1944. Said Board of Regents is authorized to elect a President of the said University and to employ necessary faculty and other personnel. Said Board required to make an annual report to the Governor and Oklahoma State Regents for Higher Education concerning the progress of the University.] [Laws 1945, p. 345, §§1, 2.]

Regional Compact

Laws 1949, p. 790
House Joint Resolution No. 10

A joint resolution giving legislative approval to that certain compact entered into by the State of Oklahoma and other Southern States by and through their respective governors on February 8, 1948, as amended, relative to the development and maintenance of regional educational services and schools in the Southern States in the professional, technological, scientific, literary and other fields, so as to provide greater educational advantages and facilities for the citizens in the several states who reside in such region; to declare that the State of Oklahoma is a party to said compact, as amended, and that the agreements, covenants and obligations therein are binding upon said state; and declaring an emergency.

WHEREAS, on the 8th day of February, in the year of our Lord One Thousand Nine Hundred and Forty-eight (1948), the States of Florida, Maryland, Georgia, Louisiana, Alabama, Mississippi, Tennessee, Arkansas, Virginia, North Carolina, South Carolina, Texas, Oklahoma, and West Virginia, through and by their respective Governors, entered into a written compact relative to the development and maintenance of regional educational services and schools in the Southern States in the professional, technological, scientific, literary, and other fields, so as to provide greater educational advantages and facilities for the citizens of the several states who reside within such region; and

WHEREAS, the said compact has been amended in certain respects, a copy of which compact as amended is as follows:

THE REGIONAL COMPACT
(As amended)

WHEREAS, the states who are parties hereto have during the past several years conducted careful investigation looking toward the establishment and maintenance of jointly owned and operated regional educational institutions in the Southern States in the professional, technological, scientific, literary and other fields, so as to provide greater educational advantages and facilities for the citizens of the several states who reside within such region; and

WHEREAS, Meharry Medical College of Nashville, Tennessee, has proposed that its lands, buildings, equipment, and the net income from its endowment be turned over to the Southern States, or to an agency acting in their behalf, to be operated as a regional institution for medical, dental and nursing education upon terms and conditions to be hereafter agreed upon between the Southern States and Meharry Medical College, which proposal, because of the present financial condition of the institution, has been approved by the said states who are parties hereto; and

WHEREAS, the said states desire to enter into a compact with each other providing for the planning and establishment of regional educational facilities;

NOW, THEREFORE, in consideration of the mutual agreements, covenants and obligations assumed by the respective states who are parties hereto (hereinafter referred to as "states"), the said several states do hereby form a geographical district or region consisting of the areas lying within the boundaries of the contracting states which, for the purposes of this compact, shall constitute an area for regional education supported by public funds derived from taxation by the constituent states and derived from other sources for the establishment, acquisition, operation and maintenance of regional educational schools and institutions for the benefit of citizens of the respective states residing within the region so established as may be determined from time to time in accordance with the terms and provisions of this compact.

The states do further hereby establish and create a joint agency which shall be known as the Board of Control for Southern Regional Education (hereinafter referred to as the "Board"), the members of which Board shall consist of the Governor of each state, ex officio, and three (3) additional citizens of each state to be appointed by the Governor thereof, at least one (1) of whom shall be selected from the field of education. The Governor shall continue as a member of the Board during his tenure of office as Governor of the State, but the members of the Board appointed by the Governor shall hold office for a period of four (4) years except that in the original appointments one (1) Board member so appointed by the Governor shall be designated at the time of his appointment to serve an initial term of two (2) years, one (1) Board member to serve an initial term of three (3) years, and the remaining Board member to serve the full term of four (4) years, but thereafter the successor of each appointed Board member shall serve the full term of four (4) years. Vacancies on the Board caused by death, resignation, refusal or inability to serve, shall be filled by appointment by the Governor for the unexpired portion of the term. The officers of the Board shall be a Chairman a Vice-Chairman, a Secretary, a Treasurer, and such additional officers as may be created by the Board from time to time. The Board shall meet annually and officers shall be elected to hold office until the next annual meeting. The Board shall have the right to formulate and establish by-laws not inconsistent with the provisions of this compact to govern its own actions in the performance of the duties delegated to it including the right to create and appoint an Executive Committee and a Finance Committee with such powers and authority as the Board may delegate to them from time to time. The Board may, within its discretion, elect as its Chairman a person who is not a member of the Board, provided such person resides within a signatory state, and upon such election such person shall become a member of the Board with all the rights and privileges of such membership.

It shall be the duty of the Board to submit plans and recommendations to the states from time to time for their approval and adoption by appropriate legislative action for the development, establishment, acquisition, operation and maintenance of educational schools and institutions within the geographical limits of the regional area of the state, of such character and type and for such educational purposes, professional, technological, scientific, literary, or otherwise, as they may deem and determine to be proper, necessary or advisable. Title to all such educational institutions when so established by appropriate legislative actions of the states and to all properties and facilities used in connection therewith shall be vested in said Board as the agency of and for the use and benefit of the said states and the citizens thereof, and all such educational institutions shall be operated, maintained and financed in the manner herein set out, subject to any provisions or limitations which may be contained in the legislative acts of the states authorizing the creation, establishment and operation of such educational institutions.

In addition to the power and authority heretofore granted, the Board shall have the power to enter into such agreements or arrangements with any of the states and with educational institutions or agencies, as may be required in the judgment of the Board, to provide adequate services and facilities for the graduate, professional, and technical education for the benefit of the citizens of the respective states residing within the region, and such additional and general power and authority as may be vested in the Board from time to time by legislative enactment of the said states.

Any two (2) or more states who are parties of this compact shall have the right to enter into supplemental agreements providing for the establishment, financing and operation of regional educational institutions for the benefit of citizens residing within an area which constitutes a portion of the general region herein created, such institutions to be financed exclusively by such states and to be controlled exclusively by the members of the Board representing such states provided such agreement is submitted to and approved by the Board prior to the establishment of such institutions.

Each state agrees that, when authorized by the Legislature, it will from time to time make available and pay over to said Board such funds as may be required for the establishment, acquisition, operation and maintenance of such regional educational institutions as may be authorized by the states under the terms of this compact, the contribution of each state at all times to be in the proportion that its population bears to the total combined population of the states who are parties hereto as shown from time to time by the most recent official published report of the Bureau of the Census of the United States of America; or upon such other basis as may be agreed upon.

This compact shall not take effect or be binding upon any state unless and until it shall be approved by proper legislative action of as many as six (6) or more of the states whose Governors have subscribed hereto within a period of eighteen (18) months from the date hereof. When and if six (6) or more states shall have given legislative approval to this compact within said eighteen (18) months' period, it shall be and become binding upon such six (6) or more states sixty (60) days after the date of legislative approval by the sixth state and the Governors of such six (6) or more states shall forthwith name the members of the Board from their states as hereinabove set out, and the Board shall then meet on call of the Governor of any state approving this compact, at which time the Board shall elect officers, adopt by-laws, appoint committees and otherwise fully organize. Other states whose names are subscribed hereto shall thereafter become parties hereto upon approval of this compact by legislative action within two (2) years from the date hereof, upon such conditions as may be agreed upon at the time. Provided, however, that with respect to any state whose constitution may require amendment in order to permit legislative approval of the compact, such state or states shall become parties hereto upon approval of this compact by legislative action within seven (7) years from the date hereof, upon such conditions as may be agreed upon at the time.

After becoming effective this compact shall thereafter continue without limitation of time; provided, however, that it may be terminated at any time by unanimous action of the states and provided further that any state may withdraw from this compact if such withdrawal is approved by its Legislature, such withdrawal to become effective two (2) years after written notice thereof to the Board accompanied by a certified copy of the requisite legislative action, but such withdrawal shall not relieve the withdrawing state from its obligations hereunder accruing up to the effective date of such withdrawal. Any state so withdrawing shall *ipso facto* cease to have any claim to or ownership of any of the property held or vested in the Board or to any of the funds of the Board held under the terms of this compact.

If any state shall at any time become in default in the performance of any of its obligations assumed herein or with respect to any obligation imposed upon said state as authorized by and in compliance with the terms and provisions of this compact, all rights, privileges and benefits of such defaulting state, its members on the Board and its citizens shall *ipso facto* be and become suspended from and after the date of such default. Unless such default shall be remedied and made good within a period of one (1) year immediately following the date of such default this compact may be terminated with respect to such defaulting state by an affirmative vote of three-fourth ($\frac{3}{4}$) of the members of the Board (exclusive of the members representing the state in default), from and after which time such state shall cease to be a party to this compact and shall have no further claim to or ownership of any of the property held by or vested in the Board or to any of the funds of the Board held under the terms of this compact, but such termination shall in no manner release such defaulting state from any accrued obligaiton or otherwise affect this compact or the rights, duties, privileges or obligations of the remaining states thereunder.

IN WITNESS WHEREOF this compact has been approved and signed by Governors of the several states, subject to the approval of their respective Legislatures in the manner hereinabove set out, as of the 8th day of February, 1948.

STATE OF FLORIDA By Millard F. Caldwell Governor	STATE OF GEORGIA By M. E. Thompson Governor
STATE OF MARYLAND By Wm. Preston Lane, Jr. Governor	STATE OF LOUISIANA By J. H. Davis Governor
STATE OF ALABAMA By James E. Folsom Governor	STATE OF NORTH CAROLINA By R. Gregg Cherry Governor

STATE OF MISSISSIPPI
By F. L. Wright
Governor

STATE OF SOUTH CAROLINA
By J. Strom Thurmond
Governor

STATE OF TENNESSEE
By Jim McCord
Governor

STATE OF TEXAS
By Beauford H. Jester
Governor

STATE OF ARKANSAS
By Ben Laney
Governor

STATE OF OKLAHOMA
By Roy J. Turner
Governor

COMMONWEALTH OF
VIRGINIA
By Wm. M. Tuck
Governor

STATE OF WEST VIRGINIA
By Clarence W. Meadows
Governor

BE IT RESOLVED BY THE HOUSE OF REPRESENTATIVES AND THE SENATE OF THE TWENTY-SECOND LEGISLATURE OF THE STATE OF OKLAHOMA:

SECTION 1. That the said compact be and the same is hereby approved and the State of Oklahoma is hereby declared to be a party hereto, and agreements, covenants, and obligations therein are binding upon the State of Oklahoma.

SECTION 2. That upon the approval of this compact by the requisite number of states the Governor sign an engrossed copy of the compact and sufficient copies be provided so that every state approving the compact shall have an engrossed copy.

SECTION 3. It being immediately necessary for the preservation of the public peace, health and safety, an emergency is hereby declared to exist, by reason whereof this Resolution shall take effect and be in full force from and after its passage and approval.

Passed the House of Representatives the 24th day of March, 1949.

WALTER BILLINGSLEY
Speaker of the House of Representatives

DON BALDWIN
Acting President of the Senate

Passed the Senate the 20th day of April, 1949.

APPROVED by the Governor of the State of Oklahoma the 26 day of April, 1949.

ROY J. TURNER
Governor of the State of Oklahoma

[Note: The text of the Regional Compact is also found in Oklahoma Statutes (Official Edition) 1949 Cumulative Supplement, under Title 70, §§2120-2122. See Note on Regional Compact — Education, Appendix 6.]

Normal Institutes

Title 70, §363. **Separate institutes for negroes and whites.** — All teachers of the negro race shall attend separate institutes from those for teachers of the white race, and in all counties where the number of teachers of either race is less than twenty-five [25], desiring to attend such institute, they shall have the right and privilege to attend any institute for their race or to unite with the teachers of their race in any other county under the provisions of the preceding section, and they shall be given equal facilities with the other race in such county or counties, and their conductor or instructor shall be of their own race only; provided that all moneys and fees paid by them shall be used to pay their own conductor and instructors and they shall receive their *pro rata* of all appropriations made by the county commissioners for institute funds in their county or counties, according to the actual attendance thereof. [Laws 1913, ch. 219, p. 558, Art. 11, §13.] [Repealed, Laws 1949, p. 607, Art. 20, §9.]

Negro Blind and Deaf, and Orphans

Title 10, §206. [1949 Cum. Supp.] **Consolidation of institutions—Designation of Consolidated Institutions.** — The Institute for Colored Deaf, Blind and Orphans, The State Hospital for Negro Insane, and the State Training School for Negro Girls, all located at or near Taft, Oklahoma, are hereby consolidated and shall be designated as the Consolidated Negro Institution at Taft. [Laws 1945, p. 25, §1.]

Title 10, §§201-205. [Provision for the establishment and operation of the Institute for the Deaf, Blind and Orphans of the Colored Race, at Taft, in Muskogee County, Oklahoma.] [Laws 1909, p. 546; C.S. 1921, §§9078-82; St. 1931, §§5249-5253.]

Juvenile Delinquents

Title 10, §§211-221. [Provision for the establishment and maintenance of the "State Industrial School for White Girls"] [Laws 1917, ch. 255, pp. 467-469, §§1-10.]

Title 10, §212.1. [1949 Supp.] [Changes the name of State Industrial School for White Girls to "Girls Town".] [Laws 1947, p. 42, §1.]

Title 10, §§291-296. — [Provision for the establishment and maintenance of the State Training School for delinquent Colored Boys.] [Laws 1915, ch. 252, §§1-5.]

Title 10, §§231-261. [Provision for State Training School for White Boys (now Paul's Valley State Hospital).] [L. 1909, p. 477; R. L. 1910, §§7087-7116; C.S. 1921, §§9159-9193; St. 1931, §§5154-5240, as modified by L. 1945, p. 491, (Tit. 35, §§291-302.]

Title 10, §§301-304. — [Provide for the establishment and maintenance of the State Training School for "delinquent and incorrigible" Negro Girls.] [Laws 1917, p. 116, ch. 66, §§1-4.]

Elections

Title 26, §162a. **Statement of race in notification and declaration and on ballot.** — **Identification of candidate on ballot.** — **Application to primary**

369

and general elections. — Every candidate shall state in his notification and declaraiton his race. Any candidate who is other than of the White race, shall have his race designated upon the ballots in parenthesis after his name. This provision shall apply both to Primary and General Elections or either of them . . . [Laws 1937, p. 138, §5.]

Title 26, §77. [1949 Supp.] Elector required to furnish information under oath . . . — [Each voter is required to state his race and color upon registration. Upon failure to give information required, a certificate of registration shall not be issued to him.] [As amended Laws 1949, p. 214, §2.]

Fishing, Boating, Bathing — Segregation

Title 82, §489. Public use of waters and structures — Segregation of races authorized. — All structures herein provided for are declared to be public property and public necessities . . . The [Conservation] Commission shall have the right to make segregation of the white and colored races as to the exercise of rights of fishing, boating and bathing. [Laws, 1935, p. 349, §12.]

Hospitals

Consolidated Negro Institution

Title 10, §206.1 [1949 Supp.] [Consolidates the Institute for Colored Deaf, Blind and Orphans, The State Hospital for Negro Insane and the State Training School for Negro Girls, all located at or near Taft, Oklahoma, into a single institution.] [Laws 1945, p. 25, §1.]

Title 10, §206.2. [1949 Supp.] Jurisdiction and Control. [Provides for eclusive control over the institution by the State Board of Public Affairs.] [Laws 1945, p. 25, §2.]

Title 10, §206.3. [1949 Supp.] Functions — Admission of Inmates. — [The functions of the consolidated institution and the regulations regarding admissions shall be the same as they were for the three separate institutions before consolidation.] [Laws 1945, p. 25, §3.]

Mental Hospitals

Title 35, §§251-256. [Provides for the establishment and maintenance of a hospital for Negro insane at Taft, Oklahoma, under the control of the State Board of Public Affairs.] [Laws 1931, p. 79, §1, 3; Laws 1933, ch. 102, p. 198, §1; Laws 1935, pp. 99, 100, §§1, 2; Laws 1939, p. 116, §1.]

Mental Defectives

Title 35, §1.69. [1949 Supp.] Admission of mental defectives. — White mentally defective persons shall be admitted to the Enid State School, while colored (Negro) mentally defective persons . . . shall be admitted to the similar school on the grounds of Taft State Hospital . . . [Laws 1949, p. 244, §29.]

Title 35, §1.50. [1949 Supp.] Taft State Hospital, functions. — The Taft State Hospital shall receive the mentally ill persons of the colored (negro) race. On the grounds of the Taft State Hospital there shall be maintained a separate building or buildings for care, treatment, and schooling of negro mentally defective persons, with mental age of nine (9) years or less, such persons to be admitted by the same procedure as used for admission to the Enid State School [for white mental defectives]. Also on the grounds of Taft State Hospital there shall be maintained separate facilities for colored epileptic persons, such persons to be admitted by the same procedure as used for admission to the Pauls Valley State Hospital [for white epileptics]. Laws 1949, p. 234, §10.]

[Note: Title 35, §1.51 provides for care of white epileptics at Paul's Valley State Hospital. Title 35, §1.52 provides for care of white mental defectives at Enid State School.]

Tuberculosis Hospitals — Negro Patients

Title 63, §§531, 532. [Provision made for the erection of a ward building for the care of Negro patients at Clinton, Oklahoma State tubercular sanitarium.] [Laws 1925, ch. 152, p. 242, §1; Laws 1925, ch. 152, p. 359, §1.]

Indians

Title 25, §82.2. [1949 Supp.] [Designates the first Saturday after the full moon in September of each year as "Indian Day".] [Laws 1947, p. 235, §2.]

Ku Klux Klan — Masks

Title 21, §1301. Masks and hoods — Unlawful to wear — Exceptions. — It shall be unlawful for any person in this State to wear a mask, hood or covering, which conceals the identity of the wearer; provided, this Act shall not apply to the pranks of children on Hallowe'en, to those going to, or from, or participating in masquerade parties, to those participating in any public parade or exhibition of an educational, religious or historical character, to those participating in any meeting of any organization within any building or inclosure wholly within and under the control of said organization, and to those participating in the parades or exhibitions of minstrel troupes, circuses or other amusements or dramatic shows. Any person, or persons, violating the provisions of this Section of this Act, shall be deemed guilty of a misdemeanor, and upon conviction thereof, shall be punished by a fine of not less than Fifty ($50.00) Dollars nor more than Five Hundred ($500.00) Dollars, or by imprisonment in the county jail for a period of not exceeding (1) year, or by both such fine and imprisonment. [Laws 1923-24, ch. 2, p. 2, §1. St. 1931, §2366.]

Title 21, §1302. Trespass — Masked person demanding admission to premises. — Any person, masked or in disguise, who shall enter upon the premises or another or demand admission into the house or enclosure of another (with intent to inflict bodily injury, or injury to property) shall be deemed guilty of assault with intent to commit a felony and such entrance or demand for admission shall be *prima facie* evidence of such intent, and upon conviction thereof, such persons shall be punished by a fine of not less than Fifty ($50.00) Dollars nor more than Five Hundred ($500.00) Dollars, and by imprisonment in the penitentiary for a term of not less than (1) year nor more than five (5) years. [Laws 1923-24, ch. 2, p. 2, §2. St. 1931, §2367.]

Title 21, §1303. Assaults while masked or disguised. — Any person, while masked or in disguise, who shall assault another with a dangerous weapon, or other instrument of punishment, shall be deemed guilty of a felony, and upon conviction thereof shall be punished by a fine of not less than One Hundred ($100.00) Dollars nor more than Five Hundred ($500.00) Dollars, and by imprisonment in the penitentiary for a term of not less than five (5) years nor more than twenty (20) years. [Laws 1923-24, ch. 2, p. 2, §3. St. 1931, §2368.]

Mines

Title 45, §231. . . . Separate baths and lockers for negroes. — . . . The baths and lockers for the negroes shall be separate from the white race, but may be in the same building . . . [Laws 1929, ch. 251, p. 3404, Art. 17, §1. St. 1931, §11097.]

Miscegenation

Title 43 §12. Miscegenation prohibited. — The marriage of any person of African descent, as defined by the Constitution of this State, to any person not of African descent, or the marriage of any person not of African descent to any person of African descent, shall be unlawful and is hereby prohibited within this State. [R.L. 1910, §3894. L. 1907-08, p. 556; C.S. 1921, §7499; St. 1931, §1677.]

[Note: See Const. Art. XVIII, §11 above.]

Title 43 §13. Penalty for miscegenation. — Any person who shall marry in violation of the preceding section, shall be deemed guilty of felony, and upon conviction thereof shall be fined in any sum not exceeding five hundred [$500.00] dollars, and imprisonment in the penitentiary not less than one nor more than five [5] years. [R.L. 1910, §3895. L. 1907-08, p. 556; C.S. 1924, §7500; St. 1931, §1678.]

Parks, Playgrounds, Pools — Segregation

Title 74, §351j. [Oklahoma Planning and Resources Board.] . . . Segregation of white and colored races. — . . . The Board shall have the right to make segregation of the white and colored races as to the exercises of recreational rights, including boating, fishing and bathing. [Laws, 1937, p. 79, §16.]

Telephone Booths — Separate

Title 17, §135. Separate telephone booths for white and colored patrons. — The Corporation Commission is hereby vested with power and authority to require telephone companies in the State of Oklahoma to maintain separate booths for white and colored patrons when there is a demand for such separate booths. That the Corporation Commission shall determine the necessity for said separate booths only upon complaint of the people in the town and vicinity to be served after due hearing as now provided by law in other complaints filed with the Corporation Commission. [Laws, 1915, ch. 262, §1. C.S. 1921, §3461; St. 1931, §3718.]

Transportation — Separation of Races
Motor Carriers — Busses

Title 47, §201. Carriers to provide separate compartments. — Every bus or transportation company, corporation, individual, lessee, manager or receiver thereof, doing business in this state as a common carrier of passengers for hire between fixed termini, shall provide separate compartments, as hereinafter provided, for the accommodation of the white and negro races, which separate compartments shall be equal in points of comfort and convenience. [Laws, 1931, p. 184, §1.]

Title 47, §202. Separate waiting rooms at stations or depots. — Every bus or transportation company, corporation, individual, lessee, manager or receiver thereof, doing business in this State as a common carrier between fixed termini shall provide for and maintain separate waiting rooms at their stations or depots for the accommodation of white and negro races, which separate waiting rooms shall be equal in all points of comfort and convenience. Each waiting room shall bear in a conspicuous place words in plain letters indicating the race for which it is set apart. It shall be unlawful for any person to use, occupy, or to remain in any waiting room, toilet room, or in any depot or station in this state set apart to the race to which he does not belong. [Laws, 1931, p. 184, §2.]

Title 47, §203. Persons regarded as negroes. — The term "negro", as used herein includes every person of African descent, as defined by the Constitution. [Laws, 1931, p. 185, §3.]

Title 47, §204. Separate compartment, what constitutes. — Each compartment of a bus or motor vehicle divided by, or indicated by a board or marker placed in a conspicuous place bearing words in plain letters indicating the race for which it is set apart shall be deemed a separate compartment within the meaning of this Act. [Laws, 1931, p. 185, §4.]

Title 47, §205. Motor vehicle defined. — The term "motor vehicle" when used in this Act shall mean any automobile, motor bus or any other self propelled vehicle carrying passengers for hire between fixed termini not operated or driven upon fixed rails, or track. [Laws, 1931, p. 185, §5.]

Title 47, §206. Failure to comply with act— Punishment. — Any bus company, motor vehicle company, transportation company, lessee, manager or receiver thereof, who shall fail to provide its vehicles under the provisions of this Act, with separate coaches or compartments, as above provided, or fail to provide and maintain separate waiting rooms as provided herein, shall be liable for each and every failure to a penalty of not less than One Hundred ($100.00) Dollars, nor more than Five Hundred ($500.00) Dollars, to be recovered by suit in the name of the State in any court of competent jurisdiction, and each trip run with such vehicle or motor bus, as defined herein, without such separate compartment shall be deemed a separate and distinct offense. [Laws, 1931, p. 185, §6.]

Title 47, §207. Violations by passengers — Refusal to carry — Ejection from waiting room. — If any passenger upon motor bus or vehicle, as defined in this Act, provided with separate compartment as above provided, shall ride in any compartment not designated for his race after having been forbidden to do so by the driver or person in charge of said vehicle or bus, or shall remain in any waiting room not set apart for the race to which he belongs, he shall be guilty of a misdemeanor and upon conviction thereof shall be fined not less than Ten ($10.00) Dollars nor more than Twenty-five ($25.00) Dollars. Should any passenger refuse to occupy the compartment or room to which he is assigned by the officer or employee of such motor vehicle or bus company, said officer or employee shall have the power and the authority to refuse to carry said passenger on his motor vehicle, and should any passenger or any other person not a passenger, for the purpose of occupying or waiting in such waiting room not assigned to his race, enter said room, said agent or employee shall have the power and it is made his duty to eject such person from such room, and for such neither they nor the motor vehicle or bus company which they represent shall be liable for damage in any of the courts of this State. [Laws, 1931, p. 185, §7.]

Title 47, §208. Persons excepted from application of Act. — The provisions of this Act shall not be so construed as to extend to officers having in custody any person or persons, or employees, upon motor vehicles in the discharge of their duties. [Laws, 1931, p. 186, §8.]

Title 47, §209. Exclusion from compartment or removal from vehicle by driver. — Drivers or persons in charge of any motor bus or vehicle provided with separate compartments shall have the authority to refuse any passenger admittance to any compartment in which they are not entitled to ride under the provisions of this Act, and the person in charge of such motor vhicle or bus shall have authority, and it shall be his duty to remove from said vehicle any passenger not entitled to ride therein under the provisions of this Act and upon refusal to do so shall be guilty of a misdemeanor and upon conviction shall be fined in a sum of not less than Ten ($10.00) Dollars nor more than Two Hundred and Fifty ($250.00) Dollars, and the company, corporation, individual, manager, agent, employee or other officer, shall not be held for damages for any lawful removal of a passenger as herein provided. [Laws, 1931, p. 186, §9.]

Title 47; §210. Disposition of fines. — All fines collected under the provisions of this Act shall go to the Court fund of the county in which conviction is had. [Laws, 1931, p. 186, §10.]

[Note: It would appear that under recent federal decisions, Tit. 47, §§201-210 *supra,* and Tit. 13, §§181-191, *infra,* §§181-191, are unconstitutional as applied to inter-state passengers traveling on carriers moving interstate. See *Morgan v .Virginia* (1946), 328 U.S. 273; *Matthews v. Southern* Railway (1946), 157 F. 2d. 609; *Henderson v. United States* (1950), 70 S. Ct. 843. For text of *Henderson* case see Appendix 7, *infra.*]

Railroads — Separate Coaches or Compartments and Waiting Rooms

Title 13, §181. Separate coaches or compartments. — Every railway company, urban or suburban car company, street car or interurban car, railway company, lessee, manager or receiver thereof, doing business in this State, as a common carrier of passengers for hire, shall provide separate coaches or compartments, as hereinafter provided, for the accommodation of the white and negro races, which separate coaches or cars shall be equal in all points of comfort and convenience. [L. 1907-08, p. 201; R.L. 1910, §860.]

Title 13, §182. Separate waiting rooms. — Every railroad company, street car company, urban, suburban or interurban car company shall provide for and maintain separate waiting rooms at all their passenger depots for the accommodation of the white and negro races, which separate waiting rooms shall be equal in all points of comfort and convenience. Each waiting room shall bear in a conspicuous place words in plain letters indicating the race for which it is set apart. It shall be unlawful for any person to use, occupy or to remain in any waiting room, toilet room, or at any water tank in any passenger depot in this State, set apart to a race to which he does not belong. [L. 1907-08, p. 202; R.L. 1910, §861.]

Title 13, §183. Negro defined. — The term negro, as used herein, includes every person of African descent, as defined by the Constitution. L. 1907-08, p. 202; R.L. 1910, §862.]

[Note: See Const. Art. XXIII, §11 above.]

Title 13, §184. Separate coach and separate compartment defined. — Each compartment of a railway coach, divided by a good and substantial wooden partition, with a door therein shall be deemed a separate coach within the meaning of this Article, and each separate coach shall bear in some conspicuous place appropriate words in plain letters indicating the race for which it is set apart; and each compartment of an urban or suburban car company, interurban car or railway company, or street car company, divided by a board or marker, placed in a conspicuous place, bearing appropriate words in plain letters, indicating the race for which it is set apart, shall be sufficient as a separate compartment within the meaning of this Article. [L. 1907-08, p. 202; R.L. 1910, §863.]

Title 13, §185. Penalty — Separate offenses. — Any railway company, street car company, urban or suburban car company, or interurban car or railway company, lessee, manager or receiver thereof, which shall fail to provide its cars bearing passengers, with separate coaches or compartments as above provided, or fail to provide and maintain separate waiting rooms as provided herein, shall be liable for each and every failure to a penalty of not less than one hundred nor more than one thousand dollars, to be recovered by suit in the name of the State, in any court or competent jurisdiction, and each trip run with such railway train, street car, urban, suburban or interurban car without such separate coach or compartment shall be deemed a separate offense. [L. 1907-08, p. 202; R. L. 1910, §864.]

Title 13, §186. Passengers violating Statute — Penalty — Refusal to carry — Ejection. — If any passenger upon a railway train, street car, urban, suburban or interurban car provided with separate coaches or compartments as above provided shall ride in any coach or compartment not designated for his race, after having been forbidden to do so by the conductor in charge of the train or car, or shall remain in any waiting room not set apart for the race to which he belongs, he shall be guilty of a misdemeanor, and upon conviction shall be fined not less than five [$5.00] nor more than twenty-five [$25.00] dollars.

Should any passenger refuse to occupy the coach or compartment or room to which he or she is assigned by the officer of such railway company, said officer shall have the power to refuse to carry such passenger on his train and should any passenger or any other person not a passenger, for the purpose of occupying or waiting in such sitting or waiting room not assigned to his or her race, enter said room, said agent shall have the power and it is made his duty to eject such person from such room, and for such neither they nor the railroad company which they represent shall be liable for damages, in any of the courts of this State. [L. 1907-08; p. 203; R. L. 1910 §865.]

Title 13, §187. Exceptions to application of Act. — The provisions of this act shall not be so construed to extend to officers having in custody any person or persons, or employees upon trains or cars in the discharge of their duties, nor shall it be construed to apply to such freight trains as carry passengers in cabooses, provided that nothing herein contained shall be construed to prevent railway companies in this state from hauling sleeping cars or dining cars or chair cars attached to their trains for use exclusively for either white or negro passengers separately but not jointly and, provided further, that the Corporation Commission shall have power and authority to exempt any station or depot from the requirements of this Act, for such period of time as may be ordered in any city or town where no negroes reside. [L. 1907-08, p. 203; R.L. 1910, §866; Laws 1910-11, ch. 119, p. 262, §1.]

Title 13, §188. Duty to post law. — Every railway company carrying passengers in this State shall keep this law posted in a conspicuous place in each passenger depot and in each passenger coach provided in this law. [L. 1907-08, p. 203; R.L. 1910, §867.]

Title 13, §189. Extra or special trains. — Nothing in this Article shall be construed to prevent the running of extra or special trains or cars for the exclusive accommodation of either white or negro passengers, if the regular trains or cars are operated as required by this Act and upon regular schedule. [L. 1907-08, p. 203; R.L. 1910, §868.]

Title 13, §190. Conductor — Authority — Penalty for refusal to remove passenger — Exemption from liability. — Conductors of passenger trains, street cars, urban, suburban or interurban lines provided with separate coaches or compartments shall have the authority to refuse any passenger admittance to any coach or compartment in which they are not entitled to ride under the provisions of this Article, and the conductor in charge of the train, street car, urban, suburban, or interurban car shall have authority, and it shall be his duty to remove from the train, coach, street car, urban, suburban or interurban car, any passenger not entitled to ride therein under the provisions of this Article; upon his refusal to do so knowingly shall be guilty of a misdemeanor and upon conviction shall be fined in any sum of not less than fifty [$50.00] nor more than five hundred [$500.00] dollars, and the company, manager, agent, conductor, receiver or other officer, shall not be held for damages of any lawful removal of a passenger as provided herein. [L. 1907-08; p. 204; R.L. 1910, §869.]

Title 13, §191. Fines to County School fund — Venue of prosecutions — All fines collected under the provisions of this article shall go to the available common school fund of the county in which conviction is had. Prosecutions under the provisions of this Article may be instituted in any court of competent jurisdiction, in any county through or into which said railroad, urban, suburban, or interurban railway may be run or have an office. [L. 1907-08, p. 204; R.L. 1910, §870.]

[Note: See note following Title 47, §210 above.]

377

OREGON

CONSTITUTION

Aliens

Art. I, §31. Aliens: Property rights thereof: Immigration of persons not qualified to be citizens. — White foreigners who are or may hereafter become residents of this State shall enjoy the same rights in respect to the possession, enjoyment, and descent of property as native-born citizens. And the legislative assembly shall have power to restrain and regulate the immigration to this state of persons not qualified to become citizens of the United States. [Const. 1859.]

Slavery

Art. I, §34. Slavery or involuntary servitude: Prohibition thereof: Punishment for crime. — There shall be neither slavery nor involuntary servitude in the state, otherwise than as punishment for crime, whereof the party shall have been duly convicted. [Const. ratified November 1857, effective Feb. 14, 1859.]

STATUTES

OREGON COMPILED LAWS ANNOTATED (1940)

Aliens

Firearms

§25-112. Aliens and convicts forbidden to possess firearms . . . Penalty. — [Persons convicted of a felony and unnaturalized foreign-born persons forbidden to own or possess firearms. Violation a felony punishable by imprisonment in state penitentiary from 1 to 5 years.] [L. 1925, ch. 260, §2, p. 468; O.C. 1930, §72-202; L. 1933, ch. 315, §2, p. 488.]

Ownership of Property — Alien Land Law

Laws 1949, ch. 350, p. 503

AN ACT.

To repeal sections 61-101, 61-102, 61-103, 61-104, 61-105, 61-106, 61-108, 61-109, 61-110, 61-111 and 61-112 O.C.L.A., relating to the property rights of aliens not eligible for citizenship and confirming titles to property conveyed by aliens.

BE IT ENACTED BY THE PEOPLE OF
THE STATE OF OREGON:

Section 1. That sections 61-101, 61-102, 61-103, 61-104, 61-105, 61-106, 61-108, 61-109, 61-110, 61-111 and 61-112, O.C.L.A. be and the same hereby are repealed.

Section 2. The title to any lands heretofore conveyed shall not be questioned, nor in any manner affected, by reason of the alienage of any person from or through whom such title may have been derived.

Approved by the governor April 11, 1949.

378

Filed in the office of the secretary of state April 11, 1949.
Effective July 16, 1949

Laws 1949, ch. 28, p. 33

[Repeals chapter 436, Oregon Laws 1949 (O.C.L.A. 1947 Supp., §§61-201-61-204), a law restricting the right of ineligible aliens to lease property in the state.] [Appvd. February 10, 1949; eff. July 16, ch. 448; p. 737.

[Note: The two 1949 statutes set forth above repealed the Alien Land Law of Oregon directed against aliens ineligible for citizenship, i.e. Japanese, and certain groups of Orientals.]

Indians

Intoxicating Liquors. [Title 24, Intoxicating Liquors and Narcotics.]

§24-103. Meaning of words:... "Indian". — ... (9) An Indian within the meaning of this act shall be any person of whole or part Indian blood residing on or in the immediate vicinity of an Indian reservation; or, in the case of a person not residing on or in the vicinity of an Indian reservation, shall mean any person having more than 50 per cent of Indian blood. [L. 1933, ch. 17, §3, p. 38; O.C. 1935 Supp., §15-1003; L. 1937, ch. 448, p. 737.]

§24-511. Supplying liquor to Indian: Punishment. — If any person shall sell, barter or give to any Indian, or mixed blood, being more than one-eighth Indian, who lives and associates with Indians, any spiritous, malt or vinous liquor, such person, upon conviction thereof, shall be punished by imprisonment in the county jail not less than one [1] month nor more than one [1] year, or by fine not less than $100 or more than $500, or both such fine and imprisonment, in the discretion of the court. [L. 1931, ch. 74, §1, p. 108; O.C. 1935 Supp., §15-709.]

§24-137. Offenses: Penalties . . . — It shall be unlawful: . . . For any person to sell alcoholic liquor to any person under the age of twenty-one (21) years, . . . or to an Indian . . . , or

For an Indian to possess alcoholic liquor . . .

[Punishment for violations of this section are First offense: fine up to $500 or 6 months imprisonment, or both; Second offense: Fine up to $1,000, or 1 year in the county jail, or both, in the discretion of the court.] [L. 1933 (2d. S.S.), ch. 17, §33, p. 56, L. 1935, ch. 428, §15, p. 773; O.C. 1935 Supp., §15-1031; L. 1937, ch. 448, §22, p. 758.]

Marriage

See under Miscegenation, §23-1010.

Civil Service

§91-1314. [1947 Supp.] **Entrance and promotion tests . . .** — 3. . . . No discrimination shall be exercised, threatened or promised by any person in the employ of any division of the commission against or in favor of any applicant, eligible or employe because of his race or religious or political opinions or affiliations; provided, however, that the foregoing shall not prevent any inquiry as to whether the applicant, employe or eligible has any beliefs inimical to the government or who advocates or is a member of any organization which advocates the overthrow or resistance by force of our form of government. [Laws 1945, ch. 400, p. 670, §14.]

Elections

§81-2502. [1947 Supp.] [Art. II — Campaign Pamphlets.] **Filing of statement of reason why he should be nominated.** — [Amended to provide "Any statement or other matter favoring or opposing any candidate and offered for filing and printing in the voters' pamphlet, which, in the opinion of the secretary of state contains any . . . language which in any way incites, counsels, promotes or advocates hatred, abuse, violence or hostility toward, or which tends to cast ridicule or shame upon any person or group or groups of persons by reason of race, color, religion or manner of worship, . . . shall be refused and rejected by the secretary of state and shall not be filed or printed in the voters' pamphlet; nor shall any candidate be entitled to display in such pamphlet any cut showing the uniform or insignia of any organization which advocates or teaches racial or religious intolerance; provided that within five days after such refusal and rejection the person or persons submitting such statement for filing may appeal to a board of review, consisting of the governor, attorney general and state superintendent of public instruction, and the decision of such board shall be final upon the acceptance or rejection of the statement or matter in controversy." . . .] [Am. Laws 1945, ch. 50, sec. 14, p. 65.]

2505a. [1947 Supp.] **Portrait cuts of nominees and statements . . .** — [Amended to include a similar provision.] [Am. Laws, 1945, Ch. 50, Sec. 17, p. 68.]

Fair Employment Practices

Laws 1949, Ch. 221, p. 314.

AN ACT Relating to and providing for the elimination of certain practices of discrimination because of race, color, religion or national origin; providing penalties; and repealing chapter 508, Oregon Laws 1947.

Be It Enacted by the People of the State of Oregon:

§1. — It hereby is found and declared to be the public policy of Oregon that practices of discrimination against any of its inhabitants because of race, religion, color or national origin are a matter of state concern and that such discrimination threatens not only the rights and privileges of its inhabitants but menaces the institutions and foundation of a free democratic state.

§2. — The bureau of labor hereby is empowered to eliminate and prevent discrimination in employment because of race, religion, color or national origin or by employers, employes, labor organizations, employment agencies or other persons and to take actions against discrimination because of race, religion, color, or national origin as herein provided, and the bureau of labor hereby is given general jurisdiction and power for such purposes.

The commissioner of labor hereby is given authority to employ such personnel as may be necessary to carry into effect the provisions of this act, and to prescribe the duties and responsibilities of such employes.

§3. — The opportunity to obtain employment without discrimination because of race, religion, color or national origin hereby is recognized as and declared to be a civil right.

§4. — When used in this act: —

1. The term "person" includes one or more individuals, partnerships, associations, corporations, legal representatives, trustees, trustees in bankruptcy or receivers.

2. The term "employment agency" includes any person undertaking to procure employes or opportunities to work.

3. The term "labor organization" includes any organization which exists or may hereafter exist and which is constituted for the purpose, in whole or in part, of collective bargaining or in dealing with employers concerning grievances, terms or conditions of employment or of other mutual aid or protection in connection with employes.

4. The term "unlawful employment practice" includes only those unlawful employment practices hereafter specified and defined in this act.

5. The term "employer" does not include a club exclusively social, or a fraternal, charitable, educational or religious association or corporation, if such a club, association or corporation is not organized for private profit, nor does it include any employer with less than six persons in his employ.

6. The term "employe" does not include any individual employed by his or her parents, spouse or child or in the domestic service of any person.

7. The term "bureau" means the bureau of labor of Oregon.

8. The term "commissioner," unless a different meaning clearly appears in the context, means the commissioner of labor of Oregon.

9. The term "national origin" for the purposes of this act shall include ancestry.

§5. — For the purposes of this act it shall be an unlawful employment practice:

1. For an employer, because of the race, religion, color or national origin of any individual, to refuse to hire or employ or to bar or discharge from employment such individual or to discriminate against such individual in compensation or in terms, conditions or privileges of employment.

2. For a labor organization, because of the race, religion, color or national origin of any individual to exclude or to expel from its membership such individual or to discriminate in any way against any of its members or against any employer or any individual employed by an employer.

3. For any employer or employment agency to print or circulate or

cause to be printed or circulated any statement, advertisement or publication, or to use any form of application for employment or to make any inquiry in connection with prospective employment which expresses directly or indirectly any limitation, specification or discrimination as to race, religion, color or national origin, or any intent to make any such limitation, specification or discrimination, unless based upon a bona fide occupational qualification.

4. For any employer, labor organization or employment agency to discharge, expel or otherwise discriminate against any person because he has opposed any practices forbidden under this act or because he has filed a complaint, testified or assisted in any proceeding under this act.

5. For any person, whether an employer or an employe, or not, to aid, abet, incite, compel or coerce the doing of any of the acts forbidden under this act or to attempt to do so.

§6. — Any person claiming to be aggrieved by an alleged unlawful employment practice, may, by himself or his attorney at law, make, sign and file with the commissioner a verified complaint in writing which shall state the name and address of the person, employer, labor organization or employment agency alleged to have committed the unlawful employment practice complained of and which complaint shall set forth the particulars thereof. The complainant may be required to set forth in the complaint such other information as the commissioner may deem pertinent. Any employer whose employes, or any of them, refuse or threaten to refuse to abide by the provisions of this act or to cooperate in carrying out its purposes may file with the commissioner a verified complaint requesting assistance by conciliation or other remedial action.

§7. — After the filing of any complaint, the commissioner shall cause prompt investigation to be made in connection therewith; and if the commissioner shall determine that the allegations of the complaint are supported by any substantial evidence he immediately shall endeavor to eliminate the unlawful practice complained of by conference, conciliation and persuasion.

In case of failure to so eliminate such practice, the commissioner shall cause to be issued and served a written notice, together with a copy of the complaint, requiring the person, employer, labor organization or employment agency named in the complaint, hereinafter referred to as respondent, to answer such charges at a hearing before the commissioner at a time and place which shall be specified in said notice. Such hearing may be held at any public place within the state of Oregon designated by the commissioner. The respondent may file a verified answer to the allegations of the complaint and may appear at such hearing in person and with or without counsel. Testimony or other evidence may be introduced by either party. All evidence shall be under oath and a record thereof shall be made and preserved. If, after considering all the evidence, the commissioner shall find that the respondent has engaged in an unlawful employment practice as alleged in the complaint, he shall serve a certified copy of such finding on the respondent, together with an order requiring respondent to cease and desist from such unlawful employment practice. If, on the other hand, the commissioner shall find that the respondent has not engaged in an unlawful employment practice as alleged in the complaint, he shall serve a certified copy of his finding on the complainant, together with an order dismissing such complaint.

§8. — Any order issued by the commissioner as aforesaid may be enforced by *mandamus* or injunction or by a suit in equity to compel specific performance of such order.

§9. — Any party aggrieved by an order of the commissioner issued after hearing, as provided herein, may appeal from such order to the circuit court of the state of Oregon for the county in which the unlawful employment practice is alleged to have occurred, within 20 days after receipt of service of such order. Such appeal may be taken by serving upon the commissioner and filing with clerk of said county a notice of appeal, together with a copy of the order appealed from, a copy of the notice of hearing and an undertaking in the sum of five hundred dollars ($500), conditioned to pay all costs that may be awarded against appellant on such appeal. Upon the motion of either the commissioner or the appellant, the court shall determine whether or not the filing of the appeal shall operate as a stay of the order appealed from. Upon a notice of an appeal being filed in the office of the commissioner, a certified transcript of the entire record taken at the hearing shall promptly be filed with the clerk of said court.

§10. — The appeal shall be determined and tried *de novo* in the manner provided by law for the trial of suits in equity. Such appeal shall have precedence over other causes and shall be heard promptly. Either party aggrieved by order or decree of the circuit court may appeal therefrom to the supreme court of the state of Oregon in the same manner that appeals may be taken from a decree in a suit in equity.

§11. — Any person, employer, labor organization or employment agency who or which shall wilfully resist, prevent, impede or interfere with the commissioner or any of his authorized agents in the performance of duty under this act, or shall wilfully violate an order of the commissioner, shall be guilty of a misdemeanor and be punishable by imprisonment in the county jail for not more than one year, or by a fine of not more than five hundred dollars ($500), or by both such imprisonment and fine; but an appeal or other procedure for the review of any such order shall not be deemed to be such wilful conduct.

§12. — The governor shall appoint seven persons who shall constitute an advisory committee, which committee shall act in an advisory capacity to the commissioner of labor concerning all matters referred to in this act. On such committee, there shall be two representatives of labor organizations, one to be chosen from each of the two major labor organizations in this state. Two members shall be representatives of business and industrial management and the remaining three members shall be representative of the public at large. The term of office of the members of the original advisory committee shall be as follows: Two shall serve for one year, two for two years, two for three years and one for four years, such terms to be decided by lot as the first order of business at the first meeting of such advisory committee. Subsequently, the term of each member of the committee shall be for four years. The representation on such committee herein provided for shall be maintained by the governor in making reappointments to fill vacancies caused by the expiration of tenure or otherwise.

The advisory committee shall:

1. Investigate the existence, character, causes and extent of discrimination in this state and the extent to which the same is susceptible of elimination.

2. Study the best and most practicable ways of eliminating any discrimination found to exist, and formulate plans for the elimination thereof by education or other practicable means.

3. Publish and disseminate reports embodying its findings and the results of its investigations and studies relating to discrimination and ways or means of reducing or eliminating it.

4. Confer, cooperate with and furnish technical assistance to the commissioner of labor and to employers, labor unions, educational institutions and other public or private agencies in formulating plans for the elimination of discrimination.

5. Transmit to the governor and to the legislature recommendations as to procedure, plans and legislation which such committee may deem desirable as a result of its findings as to the existence, character and causes of any discrimination.

§13. — The members of the advisory committee originally appointed shall meet in the office of the commissioner of labor in Salem within 20 days after their appointment for the purpose of organization and the adoption of a procedural program; thereafter, such committee shall meet at least once each three months at such place within the state of Oregon as the committee shall designate. At its initial meeting and annually thereafter the committee shall elect one of its own members to act as chairman and another to act as secretary. Four members of the committee shall constitute a quorum.

The members of the committee shall receive no compensation but each shall be reimbursed actual expenses incurred in and incident to attendance at meetings of the committee:

§14. — That chapter 508, Oregon Laws 1947, be and the same hereby is repealed. [Approved by governor March 25, 1949.]

Military — National Guard

§103-272. Enlistment of non-commissioned personnel: Period of enlistment: Qualifications: . . . . — Hereafter the period of enlistment in the national guard shall be for such a period as may be prescribed by act of congress; if no period is prescribed by congress, the period shall be for two years; and the qualifications for enlistment shall be the same as those prescribed for admission to the regular army . . . [L. 1921, ch. 207, §42, p. 381; O.C. 1930, §52-142.]

[Note: While the above section makes no specific reference to race or color, it has been clarified by administrative policy to mean, "Any male citizen, regardless of race or religion, may enlist in the Oregon National Guard, provided he is acceptable by Department of Army Regulations." Such policy "is an interpretation of Sections 103-272 and 103-274, Oregon Code, in conjunction with Oregon's Fair Employment Practice Act. Governor [Douglas] McKay and myself [Adjutant General Thomas E. Rilea] have conferred on this interpretation and are in complete agreement." (From letter signed by Thomas E. Rilea, Major General, Office of the Adjutant General, Military Department, State of Oregon, dated June 1, 1950.)

Major General Rilea further declares, "Since the outset, there never has been either racial segregation or discrimination within the ranks of the Oregon National Guard. Prior to the last war, we had few Negro applicants due to the fact that comparatively few Negroes lived in Oregon. However, the ranks of the Oregon National Guard were sprinkled with members of Japanese, Chinese, Spanish and Indian descent." (From letter signed by Major General Rilea, dated April 20, 1950. See also *Oregon Statesman*, Salem, Oregon, January 1, 1950.)]

Miscegenation

§63-102. What marriages are prohibited. — The following marriages are prohibited: . . .

. 3. When either of the parties is a white person and the other a negro, or Mongolian, or a person of one-fourth or more of negro or Mongolian blood. [L. 1862, D. p. 783, §2; H. §2853; L. 1893, p. 41, §1; B. & C. §5217; L. O. L. §7017; O.L. §9721; O. C. 1930, §33-102.]

§23-1010. Miscegenation: Unlawfulness of intermarriage of races: Validity of purported marriage. — Hereafter it shall not be lawful within this state for any white person, male or female, to intermarry with a negro, Chinese, or any person having one-fourth or more negro, Chinese, Kanaka blood, or any person having more than one-half Indian blood; and all such marriages, or attempted marriages, shall be absolutely null and void. [L. 1866, §1, p. 10; D. & L. §689; H. §1927; B. & C. §1999; L. O. L. §2163; O. L. §2163; O. C. 1930, §14-840.]

§23-1011. Violation of law: Punishment. — If any white person, negro, Chinese, Kanaka, or Indian, within the degrees forbidden in section 23-1010, shall knowingly intermarry, or attempt the same, by procuring a solemnization of marriage, under any of the forms or ceremonies legalized in this state, such person or persons, upon conviction thereof, shall be punished by imprisonment in the penitentiary or county jail not less than three [3] months nor more than one [1] year. [L. 1866, §2, p. 10, D. & L. §690; H. §1928; B. & C. §2000; L. O. L. §2164; O. L. §2164; O. C. 1930, §14-841.]

§23-1012. **Licensing or solemnizing marriage: Punishment.** — If any person authorized to license marriages or to solemnize marriages within this state shall wilfully or knowingly license, marry, or attempt to marry any of the persons forbidden to marry by section 23-1010, such person or persons, upon conviction thereof, shall be imprisoned in the penitentiary or county jail not less than three [3] months nor more than one [1] year, and be fined not less than $100, nor more than $1,000. [L. 1866, §3, p. 10; D. & L. §691; H. §1929; B. & C. §2001; L. O. L. §2165; O.L. §2165; O. C. 1930, §14-842.]

Public Employment

Laws 1947, Ch. 508. [Repealed by Laws 1949, c. 221, p. 314.]

[Note: The statute repealed by the Oregon Fair Employment Practices law declared it to be against the public policy of the State of Oregon for any political or other representative of the State or any political subdivision thereof to discriminate against any individual with respect to hire, tenure, terms, conditions and privileges of employment or any other matter directly related to employment, because of race, color, religion, sex, union membership, national origin or ancestry of the individual involved. In view of the fact that Oregon has now enacted a fair employment practices act, and that the Fourteenth Amendment prohibits a state or any agency thereof from discriminating against an individual because of race, color or religion, it was apparently thought by the Oregon legislature that the statute directed toward public officials was unnecessary.]

Public Works

§98-401. [Repealed by laws 1945, ch. 235, p. 351. — This section prohibited the employment of Chinese laborers on any street or part of street of any city or incorporated town, or any public works or public improvement of any character except as a punishment for crime.]

PENNSYLVANIA

CONSTITUTION

Suffrage

[The Constitution of 1838, art. 3, §1, limited suffrage to "white" freemen. This racial restriction was eliminated from the Constitution of 1874. Art. 8, §1 of the Constitution of 1874 was amended on November 7, 1933 to remove the restriction of sex on the right to vote.]

STATUTES

PURDON'S PENNSYLVANIA STATUTES ANNOTATED (1940)

Aliens

Hunting

Title 34, §§1311.1001, 1311.1002. — [Makes it unlawful for any un-naturalized foreign-born resident to hunt game, and to that end to own or possess a firearm of any make or a dog of any kind. [1937, June 3, P.L. 1225, art. X, §§1001, 1002.]

[Note: See §1311.1004 for penalties; see also §1311.1206 with reference to search warrants.]

Property

Title 68, §25. [Provides that aliens who have announced their intention to become citizens of the U.S. may purchase and hold up to 500 acres of land.] [1807, Feb. 10, P.L. 23, 4 Sm. L. 362, §1.]

Title 20, §1.4. [1948 Supp.] Rules of descent. — . . . (7) Alienage. Real and Personal estate shall descend without regard to whether the decedent or any person otherwise entitled to take under this act is or has been an alien . . . [1947, April 24, P.L. 80, §4.]

Title 20, §180.17. [1948 Supp.] Alienage. — Real and personal estate shall pass without regard to whether the testator or any divisee or legatee is or has been an alien. [1947, April 24, P.L. 89, §17.]

Public Works

Title 43, §151. — [Provides that citizens of U.S. only (with certain exceptions) shall be employed on public works or public building within the state.] [1895, June 25, P.L. 269, §1.]

Civil Rights

Discriminatory Publication

Title 18, Sec. 4653. Discrimination on account of religion, creed or nationality. — (a). Whoever, being the owner, lessee, proprietor, manager, superintendent, agent or employe of any place of public accommodation, resort or amusement, directly or indirectly, by himself or anybody else, publishes, issues, circulates, sends, distributes, gives away, or displays (except as hereinafter provided), any communication, paper, poster, folder, manuscript, book, pamphlet, writing, print, letter, notice or advertisement, of any kind, nature or description, intended or calculated to discriminate, or actually discriminating, against any religious sect, creed, class, denomination, or nationality, or against any of the members thereof, in the matter of furnishing, or neglecting or refusing to furnish, to them, or any one of them, any lodging, housing, schooling, tuition, or any accommodation, right, privilege, advantage, or convenience, offered to or enjoyed by the general public or to the effect that any of the accommodations, rights, privileges, advantages, or conveniences of any such place of public accommodation, resort, or amusement, shall or will be refused, withheld from, or denied to any person or persons or class of persons, on account of religion, sect, creed, class, denomination, or nationality, or that the patronage, custom, presence, frequenting, dwelling, staying, or lodging at such place of any person, persons or class of persons, belonging to or purporting to be of any particular religion, sect, creed, denomination, or nationality is unwelcome, objectionable, or not acceptable, desired, or solicited, is guilty of a misdemeanor, and upon conviction thereof, shall be sentenced to pay a fine of not more than one hundred dollars ($100), or undergo imprisonment of not more than ninety (90) days, or both.

(b) The production of any such communication, paper, poster, folder, manuscript, book, pamphlet, writing, print, letter, notice of advertisement, purporting to relate to any such place, and to be made by any person being the owner, lessee, proprietor, agent, superintendent, manager, or an employe thereof, shall be presumptive evidence in any civil or criminal action or prosecution that the same was authorized by such person.

(c) A place of public accommodation, resort, or amusement, within the meaning of this section shall be deemed to include any inn, tavern, or hotel, whether conducted for the entertainment, housing or lodging of transient guests, or for the benefit, use or accommodation of those seeking health, recreation or rest; any restaurant, eating-house, public conveyance, on land or water, bathhouse, barber shop, theatre, and music hall.

(d) Nothing in this section contained shall be construed to prohibit the mailing of a private communication, in writing, sent in response to specific written inquiry. [1939, June 24, P.L. 872, §653.]

Public Accommodation

Title 18, §4654. Discrimination on account of race and color. —

(a) All persons within the jurisdiction of this Commonwealth shall be entitled to the full and equal accommodations, advantages, facilities, and privileges of any places of public accommodation, resort or amusement, subject only to the conditions and limitations established by law and applicable alike to all persons. Whoever, being the owner, lessee, proprietor, manager, superintendent, agent or employe of any such place, directly or indirectly refuses, withholds from, or denies to, any person, any of the accommodations, advantages, facilities or privileges thereof, or directly or indirectly publishes, circulates, issues, displays, posts or mails any written or printed communication, notice or advertisement to the effect that any of the accommodations, advantages, facilities and privileges of any such places, shall be refused, withheld from, or denied to, any person on account of race, creed, or color, or that the patronage or custom thereat of any person belonging to, or purporting to be of, any particular race, creed or color is unwelcome, objectionable or not acceptable, desired or solicited, is guilty of a misdemeanor, and upon conviction thereof, shall be sentenced to pay a fine of not more than one hundred dollars ($100), or shall undergo imprisonment for not more than ninety (90) days, or both.

(b) The production of any such written or printed communication, notice or advertisement, purporting to relate to any such place and to be made by any person being the owner, lessee, proprietor, superintendent or manager thereof, shall be presumptive evidence in any civil or criminal action that the same was authorized by such person.

(c) A place of public accommodation, resort, or amusement, within the meaning of this section shall be deemed to include inns, taverns, roadhouses, hotels, whether conducted for the entertainment of transient guests, or for the accommodation of those seeking health, recreation or rest, or restaurants or eating houses, or any place where food is sold for consumption on the premises, buffets, saloons, bar-rooms, or any store, park, or inclosure where spiritous or malt liquors are sold, ice cream parlors, confectionaries, soda fountains, and all stores where ice cream, ice and fruit preparations, or their derivatives, or where beverages of any kind, are retailed for consumption on the premises, drug stores, dispensaries, clinics, hospitals, bath-houses, theatres, motion-picture houses, airdromes, roof gardens, music-halls, race-courses, skating rinks, amusement and recreation parks, fairs, bowling alleys, gymnasiums, shooting gallaries, billiard and pool parlors, public libraries, kindergartens, primary and secondary schools, high schools, academies, colleges and universities, extension courses, and all educational institutions under the supervision of this Commonwealth, garages and all public conveyances operated on land or water, as well as the stations and terminals thereof.

(d) Nothing contained in this section shall be construed to include any institution, club or place or places of public accommodation, resort or amusement, which is or are in its or their nature distinctly private, or to prohibit the mailing of a private communication in writing sent in response to a specific written inquiry. [1939, June 24, P.L. 872, §654.]

Civil Service

Classified Civil Service

Title 71, §741.502. [1948 Cum. Supp.] **Nature of examinations.** — . . . No question in any examination shall relate to the race, religion, or political or labor union affiliation of the candidate. [As amended 1945, June 1, P.L. 1366, §1; 1947, June 21, P.L. 835, §1.]

Title 71, §741.807. [1948 Cum. Supp.] **Removal.** — (a) No person in the classified service shall be removed except for just cause which shall not be his race, religion or political, partisan or labor union affiliation.

To all persons in the classified service, except provisional, temporary and emergency employes, or probationary employes, written notice of removal, setting forth the reasons for such action and effective date thereof, must be furnished. They shall have ten [10] days from the receipt of such written notice to give the appointing authority such written answer as the person removed may desire. In every case of removal, a copy of the statement of reasons therefor, with the full written answer thereto, if any, shall be furnished to the commission by the appointing authority within ten [10] days from the receipt of the written answer, and shall be made a part of the public records of the commission. Within thirty [30] days after receipt of such notice of removal from an appointing authority the commission upon the request of the appointing authority or of the removed employe or upon its own behalf shall initiate an investigation which shall include a public hearing. Such investigation and hearing may be conducted by the commission or by anyone designated by the commission. The investigation and hearing shall be for the purpose of fairly determining whether the employe merits continuance in his position or should be removed therefrom or otherwise disciplined for the good of the service. At the hearing the commission, or those acting for the commission, shall not be required to follow technical rules of evidence or court precedure, but shall diligently seek all the evidence and information hearing on the merits of the case. Where an investigation is conducted at the request of the removed employe, the commission, within ten [10] days after the completion of such investigation and hearing, or sooner, if practicable, shall make it findings and conclusions which shall be forthwith certified to the appointing authority. If the commission finds that the action complained of was taken by the appointing authority for any political, partisan, religious or racial reason, or because of labor union affiliation, the employe shall be reinstated to his position without loss of pay. In all other cases the final decision shall not be reviewable by any court, but if such final decision is in favor of the employe the appointing authority shall reinstate him with the payment of so much of the salary or wages lost by him as the commission may, in its discretion, order . . .

[As amended 1945. June 1, P.L. 1366, §1; 1947, June 21, P.O. 835, §1.]

[Note: In *State Civil Service Comm. v. Swann,* 59 Dauph. 290, (1948) it was held that an appeal may be taken from the action of the Commission where an employee is removed for any political, partisan or racial reason, or because of labor union affiliation, but that the action of the Commission is final in all other cases.]

Police Force [1948 Cum. Supp.]

Title 53, §351.23. Discrimination on account of political or religious affiliations. — . . . No discrimination shall be exercised, threatened or promised by any person against or in favor of any applicant or employe because of political or religious opinions or affiliations or race . . . [1941, June 5, P.L. 84, §23.]

Fire Department [1948 Cum. Supp.]

Title 53, §355.23. Discrimination on account of political or religious affiliations. — . . . No discrimination shall be exercised, threatened or promised against, or in favour of, any applicant or employe because of racial, political or religious opinions, or race . . . [1945, June 1, P.L. 1232, §23.]

Education [1948 Cum. Supp.]

Title 24, §1377. Subdivision of district; assignment of pupils to; distinction on account of race or color prohibited. — . . . Provided, further, that hereafter it shall be unlawful for any school director, superintendent, or teacher to make any distinction whatever, on account of, or by reason of, the race or color of any pupil or scholar who may be in attendance upon, or seeking admission to, any public school maintained wholly or in part under the school laws of the Commonwealth. [As amended 1945, May 29, P. L. 1112, §4.]

Housing

Urban Redevelopment Law

Title 35, §1711. [1948. Cum. Supp.] Provisions of the redevelopment contract. —

(a) The contract between the Authority and a redeveloper shall contain . . . the following provisions:

(1) A legal description of the redevelopment area covered by the contract, and a covenant running with the land to the effect that no person shall be deprived of the right to live in the redevelopment project, or to use any of the facilities . . . by reason of race, creed, color, or national origin . . . [1945, May 24, P.L. 991, §11.]

Housing and Redevelopment Assistance Law (1949)

Title 35, §1664. [1949 Cum. Supp.] Grant authorization.

AN ACT

Providing and regulating State assistance FOR HOUSING including slum clearance and redevelopment and making an appropriation.

. . . Section 4 . . . There shall be no discrimination against any person because of race, color, religion or national origin in the rental or occupancy of any housing constructed under the provisions of this act. [1949, May 20, P.L. 1633, §4.]

Veteran's Housing Authority Act (1947)

Title 35, §1590.12. Operation and maintenance of emergency dwellings. — Any real property, acquired by an Authority under the provisions of this act, shall be rented only to veterans of World War II and their families, at such a rent and upon such terms and conditions as such Authority, by regulation, shall prescribe. In renting any such real property, it shall be unlawful to make any discrimination whatsoever on account of race, creed or color . . . [1947, July 7, P.L. 1414, §12.]

Indians

Title 12, §148. [Provides Indians may sue or be sued.] [1901, April 4, P.L. 70, §1.]

Labor Relations [1948 Cum. Supp.]

Title 43, §211.3. Definitions. — . . .

(f) The term "labor organization" means any organization of any kind or any agency or employe representation committee or plan in which employes participate, and which exists for the purpose, in whole or in part, of dealing with employers concerning grievances, labor disputes, wages, rates of pay, hours of employment, or conditions of work, *but shall not include any labor organization which, by ritualistic practice, constitutional or by-law proscription, by tacit agreement among its members, or otherwise, denies a person or persons membership in its organization on account of race, creed, color, or political affiliation.* [As amended, 1943, May 27, P.L. 741, §1.] (emphasis added).

Military

Title 51, §1-104. [1949 Cum. Supp.] **Equality of Treatment and Opportunity without Regard to Race, Creed, Color or National Origin.** — It is hereby declared to be the policy of the Commonwealth of Pennsylvania that there shall be equality of treatment and opportunity for all persons in the Pennsylvania National Guard, the Pennsylvania Guard, the Naval Militia, Pennsylvania Naval Militia and the unorganized militia without regard to race, creed, color or national origin. Such policy shall be put into effect giving due regard to the powers of the Federal Government which are or may be exercised over all the militia of the Commonwealth and to the time required to effectuate changes without impairing the efficiency or morale of the militia. [1949, May 27, P.L. 1903, §104.]

Public Relief and Assistance

Title 62, §2513 (c). [1948 Cum. Supp.] **Penalties.** — (c) . . . It shall be unlawful for any person, directly or indirectly, to deprive, attempt to deprive or threaten to deprive by any means any 'person of any employment, position, work, compensation or other benefit provided for in clause (1) section four of this act [Title 62, §2504] on account of race, creed, color or any support of, or opposition to, any candidate or any political party in any election . .

Any person violating the provisions of this subsection shall be immediately removed from any position or office, if any, held under the provisions of, clause (1) of section four of this act, and in addition thereto, he shall be sentenced to pay a fine, not to exceed one thousand dollars ($1,000), and to imprisonment, not to exceed one (1) year, or both. [Added, 1941, July 25, P. L. 509, §3.]

[Note: "Clause 1, section four" refers to Title 62, §2504.]

Public Works

Title 43, §153. Discrimination on account of race prohibited. — Every contract for, or on behalf of the Commonwealth of Pennsylvania or of any county, city, borough, town, township, school district, and poor district, for the construction, alteration or repair of any public building or public work, shall contain provisions by which the contractor agrees.

(a) That, in the hiring of employes for the performance of work under this contract or any subcontract hereunder, no contractor, subcontractor, nor any person acting on behalf of such contractor or subcontractor, shall by reason of race, creed or color discriminate against any citizen of the Commonwealth of Pennsylvania who is qualified and available to perform the work to which the employment relates.

(b) That no contractor, subcontractor, nor any person on his behalf, shall, in any manner, discriminate against or intimidate any employe hired for the performance of work under his contract on account of race, creed or color;

(c) That there may be deducted, from the amount payable to the contractor under this contract, a penalty of five [$5.00] dollars for each person for each calendar day during which such person was discriminated against or intimidated in violation of the provisions of the contract; and

(d) That this contract may be cancelled or terminated by the Commonwealth or the city, borough, town, township, school district or poor district, and all money due, or to become due hereunder may be forfeited for a second or any subsequent violation of the terms or conditions of this portion of the contract. [1935, July 18, P.L. 1173, §1.]

[Note: Repealed, 1949, May 27, P.L. 1955, 2131, Sec. 3501, so far as it relates to townships of the first class.]

Municipal and Quasi-municipal Corporations

Title 53, §13417. [1948 Supp.] Discrimination between employees. —
Every contract for, or on behalf of any borough, for the construction, alteration or repair of any public building or public work, shall contain provisions by which the contractor agrees —

(a) That, in the hiring of employes for the performance of work under this contract or any subcontract hereunder, no contractor, subcontractor, nor any person acting on behalf of such contractor or subcontractor, shall by reason of race, creed or color discriminate against any citizen of the Commonwealth of Pennsylvania who is qualified and available to perform the work to which the employment relates;

(b) That no contractor, subcontractor, nor any person on his behalf, shall, in any manner, discriminate against or intimidate any employe hired for the performance of work under his contract on account of race, creed or color;

(c) That there may be deducted, from the amount payable to the contractor under this contract, a penalty of five dollars for each person for each calendar day during which such person was discriminated against or intimidated in violation of the provision of the contract; and

(d) That this contract may be cancelled or terminated by the borough and all money due, or to become due hereunder may be forfeited for a second or any subsequent violation of the terms or conditions of this portion of the contract.

[1927, May 4, P.L. 519, art. XIII.I sec. 1321, added 1947, July 10, P.L. 1621, sec. 42.]

Railroads

Title 67, §651. Discrimination on account of race or color prohibited. — On or after the passage of this act, any railroad or railway corporation, within this Commonwealth, that shall exclude, or allow to be excluded, by their agents, conductors, or employes, from any of their passenger cars, any person or persons on account of color or race, or that shall refuse to carry in any of their cars, thus set apart, any person or persons, on account of color or race, or that shall, for such reason, compel, or attempt to compel, any person or persons, to occupy any particular part of any of their cars, set apart for the accommodation of people as passengers, shall be liable, in an action of debt, to the person thereby injured or aggrieved, in the sum of five hundred [$500] dollars, the same to be recovered in an action of debt, as like amounts in law are recoverable. [1867, March 22, P.L. 38, §1.]

Title 18, §4655. Discrimination by railroad and railway agents. — Whoever, being an agent, conductor, or employe of any railroad or railway corporation, excludes, allows to be excluded, or assists in the exclusion, from any of their cars, set apart for the accommodation of passengers, or refuses to carry thereon any person on account of color or race, or throws any car from the track, thereby preventing such person from riding, is guilty of a misdemeanor, and upon conviction thereof, shall be sentenced to pay a fine not exceeding five hundred dollars [$500], or undergo imprisonment for a term not exceeding three (3) months, or both. [1939, June 24, P.L. 872, §655.]

RHODE ISLAND

CONSTITUTION

Art. I, §4. Slavery shall not be permitted in this state. [1842]

STATUTES

GENERAL LAWS OF RHODE ISLAND (1938)

Aliens

Ch. 432, §1. — [Aliens have the right to hold, take, transmit and convey real estate with the same effect as if they were citizens. [General Laws 1923, ch. 296.]

Civil Rights

Ch. 606, §28. — No person within the jurisdiction of this state shall be debarred from the full and equal enjoyment of the accommodations, advantages, facilities and privileges of any licensed inns, restaurants, eating houses, bath houses, music-halls, skating rinks, theatres, public conveyances, on land or water, or from any licensed places of public accommodation or amusement, except upon conditions and limitations lawfully established and applicable alike to all citizens, or as provided by law. [P.L. 1925, Ch. 658.]

Ch. 606, §29. — Every person who shall violate the provisions of the foregoing section shall be fined not exceeding $100.00. [P.L. 1925, ch. 658.]

Civil Service

R. I. Acts 1939. Ch. 661, p. 117

§21. Political, Racial and Religious Considerations. — ... (1) The determinations of eligibility for, appointments, promotions and demotions in and dismissals from the classified service shall be based solely upon merit and shall in all cases be made without regard to political, religious or racial considerations.

Commission on Employment Problems of Negro

R. I. Acts 1941, p. 549

RESOLUTION creating a commission on the employment problems of the Negro

Resolved, That a commission, to be known as the "Commission on the employment problems of the Negro" be and the same hereby is created, consisting of 14 members to be appointed by the governor, and to serve at his pleasure, two of whom shall be representatives of the National Association for the Advancement of Colored People, one, a representative of the Providence Urban League, one a repreesntative of the national youth administration, one a representative of the unemployment compensation board, one a representative of the consumer's league of Rhode Island, one a representative of the state branch of the American Federation of Labor, one a representative of the state council of the Congress of Industrial Organization, three of whom to be well-known representatives of business, two of whom shall represent the manufacturing industry and one to represent the retail trade.

It shall be the purpose and duty of said commission to continue the study of the employment problems of the Negro, in order to obtain factual information with respect to the employment status and employment opportunities of the Negro in Rhode Island as designated in the four following schedules, namely:

Schedule I, *Family Schedule,* the object of which is to ascertain the social and economic status of Negro families, and also the difficulties which confront gainful workers in these families in obtaining employment;

Schedule II, *Information Concerning the Negro in Industry and Business in Rhode Island,* the object of which is to ascertain, in so far as possible, the employment policies of employers in Rhode Island with respect to Negroes;

Schedule III, *Employers of Domestic and Personal Servants,* the object of which is to obtain the attitude of a special group of employers with respect to Negroes; namely, housewives who employ domestic servants either for full-time or part-time work;

Schedule IV, *Labor Unions,* the object of which is to ascertain the attitude of such unions with respect to taking into membership Negroes who have adequate skills in the particular trades of such unions.

Said commission shall proceed with its study immediately upon its appointment and shall report to the governor, on or before March 1, 1942, the result of its survey with recommendations for remedial legislation in order to advance the economic status of the Negro people in Rhode Island.

[Provision for appropriation of $3,000.00 to facilitate commission's fact-finding program.]

[No. 54, H. 683, Approved April 28, 1941]

R. I. Acts 1942, p. 579
[Extended time of Commission's Study to Feb. 1, 1943.]

Education

Ch. 198, §1. — No person shall be excluded from any public school on account of race or color, or for being over 15 years of age, nor except by force of some general regulation applicable to all persons under the same circumstances. [Gen. Laws, 1923, ch. 77.]

Fair Employment Practices

R. I. Acts, 1949, Ch. 2181
H. 539 Approved April 1, 1949.

AN ACT to Prohibit Discriminatory Employment Practices and Policies Based Upon Race or Color, Religion, or Country of Ancestral Origin: To Create a Commission for Fair Employment practices, and Defining its Functions, Powers, and Duties.

396

§1. — Findings and Declaration of Policy. —

(A) The practice or policy of discrimination against individuals because of their race or color, religion, or country of ancestral origin is a matter of state concern. Such discrimination foments domestic strife and unrest, threatens the rights and privileges of the inhabitants of the state, and undermines the foundations of a free democratic state. The denial of equal employment opportunities because of such discrimination and the consequent failure to utilize the productive capacities of individuals to their fullest extent deprive large segments of the population of the state of earnings necessary to maintain decent standards of living, necessitates their resort to public relief, and intensifies group conflicts, thereby resulting in grave injury to the public safety, health, and welfare.

(B) It is hereby declared to be the public policy of this state to foster the employment of all individuals in this state in accordance with their fullest capacities, regardless of their race or color, religion, or country of ancestral origin, and to safeguard their right to obtain and hold employment without such discrimination.

(C) This act shall be deemed an excercise of the police power of the state for the protection of the public welfare, prosperity, health, and peace of the people of the state.

§2. — Right to Equal Employment Opportunities. —

The right of all individuals in this state to equal employment opportunities, regardless of race or color, religion, or country of ancestral origin, is hereby recognized as, and declared to be a civil right.

§3. — Definitions. —

When used in this act

(A) the term "person" includes one or more individuals, partnerships, associations, organizations, corporations, legal representatives, trustees, trustees in bankruptcy, or receivers.

(B) the term "employer" includes any person in this state employing four or more individuals, and any person acting in the interest of an employer directly or indirectly, but does not include a religious, charitable, fraternal, social, educational, or sectarian corporation or association not organized for private profit, other than labor organizations and non-sectarian corporations or organizations engaged in social service work.

(C) the term "employee" does not include any individual employed by his parents, spouse, or child, or in the domestic service of any person.

(D) the term "labor organization" includes any organization which exists for the purpose, in whole or in part, of collective bargaining or of dealing with employers concerning grievances, terms or conditions of employment, or of other mutual aid or protection in relation to employment.

(E) the term "employment agency" includes any person undertaking with or without compensation to procure opportunities to work, or to procure, recruit, refer, or place employees.

(F) the term "commission" means the commission for fair employment practices created by this act.

(G) the term "discriminate" includes segregate or separate.

§4. — Unlawful Employment Practices. —

It shall be an unlawful employment practice:

(A) for any employer (1) to refuse to hire any applicant for employment because of his race or color, religion, or country of ancestral origin, or (2) because of such reasons, to discharge an employee or discriminate against him with respect to hire, tenure, compensation, terms, conditions or privileges of employment, or any other matter directly or indirectly related to employment, or (3) in the recruiting of individuals for employment or in hiring them, to utilize any employment agency, placement service, training school or center, labor organization, or any other employee-referring source which such employer knows, or has reasonable cause to know, discriminates against individuals because of their race or color, religion, or country of ancestral origin;

(B) for any employment agency (1) to fail or refuse to classify properly or refer for employment or otherwise discriminate against any individual because of his race or color, religion, or country of ancestral origin, or (2) for any employment agency, placement service, training school or center, labor organization, or any other employee-referring source to comply with an employer's request for the referral of job applicants if such request indicates either directly or indirectly that such employer will not afford full and equal employment opportunities to individuals regardless of their race or color, religion, or country of ancestral origin;

(C) for any labor organization (1) to deny full and equal membership rights to any applicant for membership because of his race or color, religion, or country of ancestral origin, or (2) because of such reasons, to deny a member full and equal membership rights, expel him from membership, or otherwise discriminate in any manner against him with respect to his hire, tenure, compensation, terms, conditions or privileges of employment, or any other matter directly or indirectly related to membership or employment, whether or not authorized or required by the constitution or by-laws of such labor organization or by a collective labor agreement or other contract, or (3) to fail or refuse to classify properly or refer for employment, or otherwise to discriminate against any member because of his race or color, religion, or country of ancestral origin;

(D) except where based on a bona fide occupational qualification certified by the commission, for any employer or employment agency, labor organization, placement service, training school or center, or any other employee-referring source, prior or subsequent to employment or admission to membership of any individual, to

(1) elicit or attempt to elicit any information directly or indirectly pertaining to his race or color, religion, or country of ancestral origin;

(2) make or keep a record of his race or color, religion, or country of ancestral origin;

398

(3) use any form of application for employment, or personnel or membership blank containing questions or entries directly or indirectly pertaining to race or color, religion, or country of ancestral origin;

(4) print or publish or cause to be printed or published any notice or advertisement relating to employment or membership indicating any preference, limitation, specification, or discrimination based upon race or color, religion, or country of ancestral origin;

(5) establish, announce, or follow a policy of denying or limiting, through a quota system or otherwise, employment or membership opportunities of any group because of the race or color, religion, or country of ancestral origin of such group;

(E) for any employer or employment agency, labor organization, placement service, training school or center, or any other employee-referring source to discriminate in any manner against any individual because he has opposed any practice forbidden by this act, or because he has made a charge, testified, or assisted in any manner in any investigation, proceeding, or hearing under this act.

(F) for any person, whether or not an employer, employment agency, labor organization, or employee, to aid, abet, incite, compel, or coerce the doing of any act declared by this section to be an unlawful employment practice, or to obstruct or prevent any person from complying with the provisions of this act or any order issued thereunder, or to attempt directly or indirectly to commit any act declared by this section to be an unlawful employment practice.

§5. — State Commission for Fair Employment Practices. —

(A) There is hereby created a state commission for fair employment practices to consist of five members to be appointed by the governor, with the advice and consent of the senate, one of whom shall be designated by the governor as chairman.

(B) Of the members first appointed, one shall be appointed for a term of one year, one for a term of two years, one for a term of three years, one for a term of four years, and one for a term of five years, but their successors shall be appointed for terms of five years each, except that any member chosen to fill a vacancy occurring otherwise than by expiration of term shall be appointed only for the unexpired term of the member whom he shall succeed.

(C) Three members of said commission shall constitute a quorum for the purpose of conducting the business thereof. A vacancy in said commission shall not impair the right of the remaining members to exercise all the powers of the commission.

(D) Each member of the commission shall receive a salary of not more than $2,500.00 a year and shall also be entitled to his expenses actually and necessarily incurred by him in the performance of his duties. All members of the commission shall be eligible for reappointment.

(E) Any member of the commission may be removed by the governor

399

for inefficiency, neglect of duty, misconduct or malfeasance in office, after being given a written statement of the charges and an opportunity to be heard publicly thereon.

§6. — Powers and Duties of the Commission. —

The commission shall have the following powers and duties:

(A) to establish and maintain a principal office in the city of Providence, Rhode Island, and such other offices within the state as it may deem necessary;

(B) to meet and function at any place within the state;

(C) to appoint a full-time executive secretary to the commission and determine his remuneration. The executive secretary shall be selected on the basis of being exceptionally well qualified by education, training, and experience impartially to enforce the provisions of this act so as to reduce and eliminate unlawful employment practices. The commission is also empowered to appoint such personnel as it shall deem necessary to effectuate the purposes of the act. Provided, however, that the provisions of chapter 661, of the public laws of 1939, as amended, shall not apply to the act.

(D) to adopt, promulgate, amend, and rescind rules and regulations to effectuate the provisions of this act, and the policies and practice of the commission in connection therewith;

(E) to formulate policies to effectuate the purposes of this act;

(F) to receive, investigate, and pass upon charges of unlawful employment practices;

(G) to hold hearings, subpoena witnesses, compel their attendance, administer oaths, take the testimony of any person under oath, and, in connection therewith, to require the production for examination of any books and papers relating to any matter under investigation or in question before the commission. The commission may make rules as to the issuance of subpoenas by individual commissioners. Contumacy or refusal to obey a subpoena issued pursuant to this section shall constitute a contempt punishable, upon the application of the commission, by the superior court in the country in which the hearing is held or in which the witness resides or transacts business.

(H) to utilize voluntary and uncompensated services of private individuals and organizations as may from time to time be offered and needed.

(I) to create such advisory agencies and conciliation councils, local or state-wide, as will aid in effectuating the purposes of this act. The commission may itself, or it may empower these agencies and councils to (1) study the problems of discrimination in all or specific fields of human relationships when based on race or color, religion, or country of ancestral origin, and (2) foster through community effort or otherwise good will among the groups and elements of the population of the state. Such agencies and councils may make recommendations to the commission for the development of policies and procedure in general. Advisory agencies and conciliation councils created by the commission shall be composed of representative citizens serving without pay, but with reimbursement for actual and necessary traveling expenses.

(J) to issue such publications and such results of investigations and research as in its judgment will tend to promote good will and minimize or eliminate discrimination based on race or color, religion, or country of ancestral origin.

(K) from time to time, but not less than once a year, to report to the legislature and the governor, describing the investigations, proceedings, and hearings the commission has conducted and their outcome, the decisions it has rendered, and the work performed by it, and make recommendations for such further legislation, concerning abuses and discrimination based on race or color, religion, or country of ancestral origin, as may be desirable.

§7. — Educational Program. —

(A) In order to eliminate prejudice among the various ethnic groups in this state and to further goodwill among such groups, the commission and the state department of education are jointly directed to prepare a comprehensive educational program, designed for the students of the public schools of this state and for all other residents thereof, calculated to emphasize the origin of prejudice against minority groups, its harmful effects, and its incompatibility with American principles of equality and fair play.

(B) The commission is hereby authorized to accept contributions from any person to assist in the effectuation of this section and may seek and enlist the cooperation of private charitable, religious, labor, civic, and benevolent organizations for the purposes of this section.

§8. — Prevention of Unlawful Employment Practices. —

(A) The commission is empowered and directed, as hereinafter provided, to prevent any person from engaging in unlawful employment practices, provided that before instituting the formal hearing authorized by this section it shall attempt, by informal methods of conference, persuasion, and conciliation, to induce compliance with this act.

(B) Upon the commission's own initiative or whenever an aggrieved individual or an organization chartered for the purpose of combating discrimination or racism, or of safeguarding civil liberties, or of promoting full, free or equal employment opportunities, such individual or organization being hereinafter referred to as the complainant, makes a charge to the commission that any employer, employment agency, labor organization, or person, hereinafter referred to as the respondent, has engaged or is engaging in unlawful employment practices, the commission may initiate a preliminary investigation and if it shall determine after such investigation that it is probable that unlawful employment practices have been or are being engaged in, it shall endeavor to eliminate such unlawful employment practices by informal methods of conference, conciliation, and persuasion. Nothing said or done during such endeavors may be used as evidence in any subsequent proceeding. If, after such investigation and conference, the commission is satisfied that any unlawful employment practice of the respondent will be eliminated, it may, with the consent of the complainant, treat the complaint as conciliated, and entry of such disposition shall be made on the records of the commission. If the commission fails to effect the elimination of such unlawful employment practices and to obtain voluntary compliance with this act, or, if the circumstances warrant, in advance of any such preliminary investigation or endeavors the commission shall have the power to issue and cause to be served upon any person or respondent a complaint stating the charges in that respect and containing a notice of hearing before the commission, a member thereof, or a hearing examiner at a place therein fixed to be held not less than ten days after the service of such complaint. Any complaint issued pursuant to this section must be so issued within one year after the alleged unfair employment practices were committed.

(C) The commission, member thereof, or hearing examiner conducting the hearings shall have the power reasonably and fairly to amend any written complaint at any time prior to the issuance of an order based thereon. The respondent shall have like power to amend its answer to the original or amended complaint at any time prior to the issuance of such order. The commissioner assigned to the preliminary hearing of any complaint shall take no part in the final hearing except as a witness upon competent matters and will have no part in the determination or decision of the case after hearing.

(D) The respondent shall have the right to file an answer to such complaint, and shall appear at such hearing in person, or otherwise, with or without counsel to present evidence and to examine and cross-examine witnesses.

(E) In any such proceeding the commission, its member, or its agent shall not be bound by the rules of evidence prevailing in the courts of law or equity.

(F) The commission shall in ascertaining the practices followed by the respondent, take into account all evidence, statistical or otherwise, which may tend to prove the existence of a pre-determined pattern of employment or membership; provided that nothing herein contained shall be construed to authorize or require any employer or labor organization to employ or admit applicants for employment or membership in the proportion which their race or color, religion, or country of ancestral origin bears to the total population or in accordance with any criterion other than the individual qualifications of the applicant.

(G) The testimony taken at the hearing shall be under oath and shall be reduced to writing and filed with the commission. Thereafter, in its discretion, the commission upon notice may take further testimony or hear argument.

(H) If upon all the testimony taken the commission shall determine that the respondent has engaged in or is engaging in unlawful employment practices, the commission shall state its findings of fact and shall issue and cause to be served on such respondent an order requiring such respondent to cease and desist from such unlawful employment practices, and to take such further affirmative or other action as will effectuate the purposes of this act, including, but not limited to hiring, reinstatement, or upgrading of employees with or without back pay, or admission or restoration to union membership, including a requirement for reports of the manner of compliance. Upon the submission of such reports of compliance the commission, if satisfied therewith, may issue its findings that the respondent has ceased to engage in unlawful employment practices.

(I) If the commission shall find that no probable cause exists for crediting the charges, or, if upon all the evidence, it shall find that a respondent has not engaged in unfair employment practices, the commission shall state its findings of fact and shall issue and cause to be served on the complainant an order dismissing the said complaint as to such respondent. A copy of the order shall be delivered in all cases to the attorney general and such other public officers as the commission deems proper.

(J) Until a transcript of the record in a case shall be filed in a court as hereinafter provided, the commission may at any time, upon reasonable notice, and in such manner as it shall deem proper, modify or set aside, in whole or in part, any of its findings or orders.

(K) Until the commission shall determine that a cease and desist order shall be issued, no publicity shall be given to any proceedings before the commission, either by the commission or any employee thereof, the complainant, or the respondent, provided that the commission may publish the facts in the case of any complaint which has been dismissed.

If any individual, prior to resorting to the procedures established by this fact, shall willfully make available for publication information purporting to establish an unlawful employment practice against him, he may not subsequently resort to the procedures established by this act.

§9. — Judicial Review and Enforcement. —

(A) Any complainant, intervener, or respondent claiming to be aggrieved by a final order of the commission may obtain judicial review thereof, and the commission may obtain an order of court for its enforcement, in a proceeding as provided by this section. Such proceeding shall be brought in the superior court of the state within any county wherein the unlawful employment practices which are the subject of the commission's order were committed or wherein any respondent, required in the order to cease and desist from unfair employment practices or to take other affirmative action, resides or transacts business.

(B) Such proceeding shall be initiated by the filing of a petition in such court, together with a transcript of the record upon the hearing before the commission, and the service of a copy of the said petition upon the commission and upon all parties who appeared before the commission. Thereupon the court shall have jurisdiction of the proceeding and of the questions determined therein, and shall have power to grant such temporary relief or restraining order as it deems just and proper, and to make and enter upon the pleadings, testimony, and proceedings set forth in such transcript an order enforcing, modifying and enforcing as so modified, or setting aside in whole or in part the order of the commission.

(C) An objection that has not been urged before the commission, its member, or agent shall not be considered by the court, unless the failure or neglect to urge such objection shall be excused because of extraordinary circumstances.

(D) If either party shall apply to the court for leave to adduce additional evidence and shall show to the satisfaction of the court that such additional evidence is material and that there were reasonable grounds for the failure to adduce such evidence in the hearing before the commission, its member, or agent, the court may order such additional evidence to be taken before the commission, its member, or agent and to be made a part of the transcript.

(E) The commission may modify its findings as to the facts, or make new findings, by reason of additional evidence so taken and filed. The commission shall file such modified or new findings and its recommendations, if any, for the modification or setting aside of its original order.

(F) The jurisdiction of the court shall be exclusive and its judgment and order shall be, when necessary, subject to review by the supreme court as provided by law, to which court appeal from such judgment and order may be made as provided by law.

(G) The commission's copy of the testimony shall be available at all reasonable times to all parties without cost for examination and for the purposes of judicial review of the order of the commission. The petition shall be heard on the transcript of the record without requirement of printing.

(H) The commission may appear in court by its own attorneys.

(I) If no proceeding to obtain judicial review is instituted by a complainant, intervener, or respondent within thirty days from the service of an order of the commission pursuant to section 8 (H) hereof, the commission may obtain a decree of the court for the enforcement of such order upon showing that respondent is subject to the commission's jurisdiction, and resides or transacts business within the county in which the petition for enforcement is brought.

§10. — Notices to be Posted. —

Every employer, employment agency, and labor union subject to this act shall post in a conspicuous place or places on his premises a notice to be prepared or approved by the commission, which shall set forth excerpts of this act and such other relevant information which the commission deems necessary to explain the act. Any employer, employment agency, or labor union refusing to comply with the provisions of this section shall be punished by a fine of not less than one hundred dollars nor more than five hundred dollars.

§11. — Construction.

The provisions of this act shall be construed liberally for the accomplishment of the purposes thereof, and any law inconsistent with any provision hereof shall not apply. Nothing contained in this act shall be deemed to repeal any of the provisions of any law of this state relating to discrimination because of race or color, religion, or country of ancestral origin.

§12. — Separability.

If any clause, sentence, paragraph, or part of this act or the application thereof to any person or circumstance, shall, for any reason, be adjudged by a court of competent jurisdiction to be invalid, such judgment shall not affect, impair, or invalidate the remainder of this act or its application to other persons or circumstances.

§13. — Short Title. —

This act may be cited as the state fair employment practices act.

§14. — Appropriation. —

For the purpose of carrying this act into effect during the fiscal year ending June 30, 1950, the sum of $40,000.00 is hereby appropriated, out of any money in the treasury not otherwise appropriated; and the state controller is hereby authorized and directed to draw his orders upon the general treasurer for the payment of such sum, or so much thereof as may be required from time to time, upon the receipt by him of properly authenticated vouchers.

§15. — Effective Date. —

This act shall take effect July 1, 1949, and thereupon all acts and parts of acts inconsistent herewith shall stand repealed.

Indians

Ch. 646, §2. — [Provides for an annual Indian Day "with appropriate exercises in the public schools and otherwise commemorative of the Indian tribes of Rhode Island, including the Narragansetts, Wampanogs, Nipmucs, Acquednecks and Niantics."] [Added by P.L. 1936, ch. 2331.]

Jurors

Ch. 506, §2. — No citizen, possessing all other qualifications which are or shall be prescribed by law, shall be disqualified for service as grand or petit juror in any court of this state on account of race, color, or previous condition of servitude; and any officer or other person, charged with any duty in the selection or summoning of jurors, who shall wilfully exclude or fail to select or summon any citizen for any of the causes aforesaid shall, on conviction thereof, be fined not exceeding $1,000.00. [Gen. Laws, 1923, ch. 329; Pub. Laws, 1920, ch. 1948.]

Public Accommodation

See under Civil Rights.

SOUTH CAROLINA

CONSTITUTION

Aliens

Art. 3, Section 35. **Lands owned by aliens.** — It shall be the duty of the General Assembly to enact laws limiting the number of acres of land which any alien or any corporation owned by aliens may own within this State. [Const. 1895.]

Education

Art. 11, Section 7. **Separate schools.** — Separate schools shall be provided for children of the white and colored races, and no child of either race shall ever be permitted to attend a school for children of the other race. [Const. 1868, II, §7; Const. 1895, Art. 11, §7.]

Education

Art. 11, Section 8. — . . . **Provided,** That the General Assembly shall, as soon as practicable, wholly separate Claflin College from Claflin University, and provide for a separate corps of professors and instructors therein, representation to be given to men and women of the negro race; and it shall be the Colored Normal, Industrial Agricultural and Mechanical College of this State. [See Const. 1868, X, 9; Const. 1895, Art. 11, §8.]

Equal Protection of the Laws

Art. 1, Section 5. **Privileges and immunities — protection of laws.** — The privileges and immunities of citizens of this State and of the United States under this Constitution shall not be abridged, nor shall any person be deprived of life, liberty or property without due process of law, nor shall any person be denied the equal protection of the laws. [See Const. 1868, I, 12; Const. 1895, Art. I, §5.]

Lynching

Art. 6, Section 6. **Prisoner lynched through negligence of officer — penalty on officer — county liable for damages.** — In the case of any prisoner lawfully in the charge, custody or control of any officer, State, County or municipal, being seized and taken from said officer through his negligence, permision or connivance, by a mob or other unlawful assemblage of persons, and at their hands suffering bodily violence or death, the said officer shall be deemed guilty of a misdemeanor, and, upon true bill found, shall be deposed from his office pending his trial, and upon conviction shall forfeit his office, and shall, unless pardoned by the Governor, be ineligible to hold any office of trust or profit within this State. It shall be the duty of the prosecuting Attorney within whose Circuit or County the offense may be committed to forthwith institute a prosecution against said officer, who shall be tried in such County, in the same circuit, other than the one in which the offence [offense] was committed, as the Attorney General may elect. The fees and mileage of all material witnesses, both for the State and for the defence [defense], shall be paid by the State Treasurer, in such manner as may be provided by law: *Provided,* In all cases of lynching when death ensues, the County where such lynching takes place shall, without regard to the conduct of the officers, be liable in exemplary damages of not less than two thousand dollars [$2,000.00] to the legal representatives of the person lynched: *Provided, further,* That any County against which a judgment has been obtained for damages in any case of lynching shall have the right to recover the amount of said judgment from the parties engaged in said lynching in any Court of competent jurisdiction. [Const. 1895]

[Note: See §3041 below.]

Miscegenation

Art. 3, Section 33. Marriages of whites and negroes. — . . . The marriage of a white person with a negro or mulatto, or person who shall have one-eighth or more of negro blood, shall be unlawful and void . . . [Const. 1895.]

Suffrage, Right of

Art. 2, Section 1. Elections by ballot. — All elections by the people shall be by ballot, and elections shall never be held or the ballots counted in secret. [Const. 1868, VIII, 1; Const. 1895, Art. 2, §1.]

[Note: See important case of *Elmore v. Rice* (1947), 72 F. Supp. 516, *affirmed* 165 F. 2d. 387, *cert. denied,* (1948) 333 U.S. 875, 685 S. Ct. 905. Federal District Judge J. Waties Waring held in this case that Article 2 of the Constitution of South Carolina shows that the State recognized a primary as an integral part of the elective process and that qualified Negroes were entitled to enroll and vote in primaries conducted by the Democratic Party of South Carolina.]

STATUTES

SOUTH CAROLINA CODE (1942)

Aliens

§3077-1. Employ only American citizens with public funds . . . [Only American citizens may be employed with public funds, unless employing officer files a signed sworn statement that it is not practicable to find an American citizen who is available for such employment. [1937 (40) 181.]

§7790. Aliens can hold only 500 acres land. — . . . [With certain exceptions prohibits aliens from owning or controlling more than 500 acres of land within the State.] [1932 Code, §7790; Civ. C. '22, §4053; Civ. C. '12, §2689; Civ. C. '02; §1795; 1896 (22) 114; 1897 (22) 514; 1945 (44) 51.]

§8687. Aliens and foreign corporations entitled to same property as natural born citizens. — [Subject to the limitations of §7790, aliens may acquire, hold and dispose of real and personal property to the same extent as a natural born citizen. [1932 Code, §8687; Civ. C. '22, §5209; Civ. C. '12, §3466; §2360; G. S. 1768; R. S. 1880; 1872 (15) 72; 1873 (15) 488.]

§8686. — [Legalizes titles derived through aliens.] [1932 Code, §8686; Civ. C. '22, §5208; Civ. C. '12, §3445; Civ. C. '02, §2359; G. S. 1767; R. S. 1879; 1807 (5) 547.]

§8907. — [Provides aliens may inherit in the same manner as natural born citizens.] [1932 Code, §8907; Civ. C. '22, §5328; Civ. C. '12, §3556; Civ. C. '02, §2469; G.S. 1847; R.S. 1981; 1872(15) 73.]

[Note: See also §8908.]

Billiards and Pool Rooms

§6338. Application for license — conditions. — ... No license shall be issued to any person of the white Caucasian race to operate a billiard room to be used by, frequented or patronized by, persons of the negro race; or to any person of the negro race to operate a billiard room to be used by, frequented or patronized by persons of the white or Caucasian race. [1932 Code, §6388; 1924 (33) 895.]

Circuses — Separation

§1271. Tent shows to maintain separate entrances for races. — Any circus or other such traveling show exhibiting under canvas or out of doors for gain shall maintain two main entrances to such exhibition, and one shall be for white people and the other entrance shall be for colored people, and such main entrances shall be plainly marked "For White People," and the other entrance shall be marked "For Colored People," and all white persons attending such show or traveling exhibition other than those connected with the said show shall pass in and out of the entrance provided for white persons, and all colored persons attending such show or traveling exhibition shall pass in and out of the entrance provided for colored persons. Any circus or other such traveling show exhibiting under canvas and failing to comply with the provisions of this section shall be deemed guilty of a misdemeanor, and, upon conviction, shall be fined not more than $500.00 The sheriffs of the counties in which such circus or traveling show shall exhibits [exhibit] shall be charged with the duty of enforcing the provisions of this section. [1932 Code, §1271; Cr. C. '22, §166; 1917 (30) 48.]

Custody of White Child by Negro

§1446. Misdemeanor to give negro permanent custody of white child. — It shall be unlawful for any parent, relative, or other white person in this State, having the control or custody of any white child, by right of guardianship, natural or acquired, or otherwise, to dispose of, give or surrender such white child permanently into the custody, control, maintenance, or support, of a negro. Any person violating the provisions of this section shall be deemed guilty of a misdemeanor, and, on conviction, shall be fined or imprisoned, in the discretion of the presiding judge: *provided*, the provisions of this section shall not be construed so as to prevent the offices of a negro in the family of any white person as a nurse. [1932 Code, §1446; Cr. '22, §387; Cr. C. '12, §395; 1910 (26) 702.]

Education

Public Schools

§5377. Mixed schools unlawful. — It shall be unlawful for pupils of one race to attend the schools provided by boards of trustees for persons of another race. [1932 Code, §5406; Civ. C. '22, §2648; Civ. C. '12, §1780; Civ. C. '02, §1231; 1896 (22) 170.]

[Note: See *Wrighten v. Board of Trustees* (1947), 72 F. Supp. 948, in which Federal District Judge J. Waties Waring ruled that the State of South Carolina affording legal education to white residents was bound to furnish Negro residents facilities for legal education equal to those afforded persons of the white race either at the University of South Carolina itself, or South Carolina State College, or any other satisfactory institution in the State, or else furnish no law school education to any person of either race.]

South Carolina Institution for the Deaf, Dumb and Blind

[No statutory provision for segregation.]

§5494. **Deaf mutes and blind persons admit.** — All deaf mutes and blind of the State who are of proper age and mental capacity (each case to be decided by the board of commissioners) shall be admitted to the benefits of the institution. [1932 Code, §5690; Civ. C. '22, §2874; Civ. C. '12, §1924; Civ. C. '02, §1332; G. S. 1059; R.S. 1142; 1878 (16) 707.]

Juvenile Delinquent and Reform Schools

§§2014 - 2020. — [Provides for establishment and maintenance of South Carolina Industrial School for white juvenile delinquent boys.] [1932 code, §§2014-2020; Cr. C. '22, §§998, 1000, 1001, 1003, 1004; Cr. C. '12, §§990, 993, 994, 997; 1906 (21) 133; 1906 (25) 133; 1910 (26) 756; 1912(27) 530; 1914 (28) 666; 1916 (29) 884-886; 1926(34) 1728; 1939(41) 107; 1940(41) 1706; 1946(44) 1430; 1946 Supp., §§2016, 2017.]

§§2021 - 2023. — [Provides for establishment and operation of John G. Richards Industrial Training School for Negro Boys] [1932 Code, §§2021-2023; Cr. C. '22, §§1005-1007; Cr. C. '12, §§989, 996; Cr. C. '02, §700; 1900(23) 443; 1906(24) 133; 1918(30) 890; 1926(34) 1728; 1930(36) 2160; 1939(41) 107; 1940(41) 1706; 1946(44) 1430; 1946 Supp. §2021.]

§§2024 - 2037-1. — [Provides for establishment and operation of State Industrial School for Girls (white).] [1932 Code, §§2024-2025, 2027, 2029-2037; Cr. C. '22, §§1008, 1009; 1009, 1011, 1013-1021; 1918(30) 853; 1920(31) 999; 1923(33) 174; 1926(34) 1728; 1938(40) 1608; 1939(40) 107; 1940(41) 1706; 1946(44) 1430.]

Acts 1949, No. 224, p. 367. (appvd. June 1, 1949) — [Provided for the establishment of a training school exclusively for negro girls to be known as "The South Carolina Industrial School for Negro Girls."]

Feeble-Minded — State Training School

§6258. — [Admits white persons only.] [1932 Code, §6258; Civ. C. '22, §5121; 1918 (30) 729.]

Colleges

§§5800 - 5805. — [Provide for operation and maintenance of Colored

Normal Industrial, Agricultural and Mechanical College of South Carolina.] [1932 Code, §§5800-5805; Civ. C. '22, §§2819-2824; Civ. C. '12, §§1879-1884; Civ. C. '02, §§1293-1298; 1896 (22) 173, 174; 1909 (26) 213.7.]

[Note: See Note under §5377 above. See also §5748.]

Winthrop College (The South Carolina College for Women)

§5785. — [Provides for the establishment of "an institution for the practical training and higher education of white girls, which shall be known as 'Winthrop College' (The South Carolina College for Women)."] [1932 Code, §5785; Civ. C. '22, §2804; Civ. C. '12, §1870; Civ. C. '02, §1284; 1891 (20) 1102; 1920 (31) 968.]

Graduate Schools for Negro Students

S. C. Statutes at Large, 1945, Section 16, p. 401 . . . Provided, Further, That the Board of Trustees of the Colored Normal Industrial, Agricultural, and Mechanical College of South Carolina is hereby authorized to establish graduate Law and Medical departments and such other departments as may be necessary to provide training in all lines of college activities for students attending this College, and to fix tuition fees for such courses commensurate with the costs thereof and in line with similar tuition charges at other state institutions.

[Note: The above provision is a rider attached to the 1945 appropriation of $130,000.00 for maintenance of the Colored N.I.A. and M. College.]

S.C. Statutes at Large, 1947 Sec. 18, p. 622. [Appropriated $60,000 for Graduate and Law School at Colored Normal Industrial, Agricultural and Mechanical College of South Carolina.]

S.C. Statutes at Large 1948, Sec. 18, p. 2115. [Appropriated $125,000.00 for Graduate Work, Law, Medicine, Pharmacy etc., at Colored N.I.A. & M. College.]

S.C. Statutes at Large, Sec. 18, p. 669. [Appropriated $140,000.00 for Graduate Work, Law, Medicine, Pharmacy, etc., at Colored N.I.A. & M. College. But see Note under §5377 above. See also *Sweatt v. Painter* (1950) 339 U.S. 629, 70 S. Ct. 848, 94 L. ed. (Adv. Op.) 783; full text of opinion, *post,* Appendix 7.]

Regional Compact

Acts 1948, p. 2221, No. 860

(R846, S1259, H1533)

No. 860

A JOINT RESOLUTION. Giving Legislative Approval To that Certain Compact Entered Into by The States Of South Carolina, Georgia, Florida, Alabama, Tennessee And Other Southern States, By And Through Their Respective Governors On February 8, 1948, Relative To The Planning Acquisition, Establishment And

Maintenance Of Jointly Owned And Operated Regional Educational Institutions; To Declare That South Carolina Is A Party To Said Compact And That The Agreements, Covenants And Obligations Therein, Are Binding Upon Said State And To Appropriate Money To Be Used In Carrying Out The Purposes Thereof.

WHEREAS, on the 8th day of February in the Year of Our Lord One Thousand Nine Hundred and Forty-Eight, the States of South Carolina, Georgia, Florida, Alabama, Tennessee and other Southern States, through and by their respective Governors, entered into a written compact relative to planning, acquisition, establishment and maintenance of jointly owned and operated regional educational institutions, a copy of which compact is as follows:

"WHEREAS, the States who are parties hereto have during the past several years conducted careful investigation looking towards the establishment and maintenance of jointly owned and operated regional educational institutions in the Southern states in the professional, technological, scientific, literary and other fields, so as to provide greater educational advantages and facilities for the citizens of the several States who reside within such region, and

WHEREAS, Meharry Medical College of Nashville, Tennessee, has proposed that its lands, buildings, equipment, and the net income from its endowment be turned over to the Southern States, or to an agency acting in their behalf, to be operated as a regional institution for medical, dental and nursing education upon terms and conditions to be hereafter agreed upon between the Southern States and Meharry Medical College, which proposal, because of the present financial condition of the institution, has been approved by the said states who are parties hereto; and

WHEREAS, the said States desire to enter into a compact with each other providing for the planning and establishment of regional educational facilities;

NOW, THEREFORE, in consideration of the mutual agreements, covenants and obligations assumed by the respective states who are parties hereto (hereinafter referred to as "States"), the said several States do hereby form a geographical district or region consisting of the areas lying within the boundaries of the contracting States which, for the purposes of this compact, shall constitute an area for regional education, supported by public funds derived from taxation by the constituent States and derived from other sources for the establishment, acquisition, operation and maintenance of regional educational schools and institutions for the benefit of citizens of the respective States residing within the region so established as may be determined from time to time in accordance with the terms and provisions of this compact.

The States do further hereby establish and create a joint agency which shall be known as the Board of Control for Southern Regional Education (hereinafter referred to as the "Board"), the members of which Board shall consist of the Governor of each State ex-officio and two additional citizens of each State to be appointed by the Governor thereof, at least one

411

of whom shall be selected from the field of education. The Governor shall continue as a member of the Board during his tenure of office as Governor of the State but members of the Board appointed by the Governor shall hold office for a period of five (5) years except that in the original appointment one Board member so appointed by the Governor shall be designated at the time of his appointment to serve an initial term of three (3) years, but thereafter his successor shall serve the full term of five (5) years. Vacancies on the Board caused by death, resignation, refusal or inability to serve, shall be filled by appointment by the Governor for the unexpired portion of the term. The officers of the Board shall be a Chairman, a Vice Chairman, a Secretary, a Treasurer, and such additional officers as may be created by the Board from time to time. The Board shall meet annually and officers shall be elected to hold office until the next annual meeting. The Board shall have the right to formulate and establish by-laws not inconsistent with the provisions of this compact to govern its own actions in the performance of the duties delegated to it including the right to create and appoint an Executive Committee and a Finance Committee with such powers and authority as the Board may delegate to them from time to time.

It shall be the duty of the Board to submit plans and recommendations to the States from time to time for their approval and adoption by appropriate legislative action for the development, establishment, acquisition, operation and maintenance of educational schools and institutions within the geographical limits of the regional area of the States, of such character and type and for such educational purposes, professional, technological, scientific, literary, or otherwise, as they may deem and determine to be proper, necessary or advisable. Title to all such educational institutions when so established by appropriate legislative actions of the States and to all properties and facilities used in connection therewith shall be vested in said Board as the agency of and for the use and benefit of the said States and the citizens thereof, and all such educational institutions shall be operated, maintained and financed in the manner herein set out, subject to any provisions or limitations which may be contained in the legislative acts of the States authorizing the creation, establishment and operation of such educational institutions.

The Board shall have such additional and general power and authority as may be vested in it by the States from time to time by legislative enactments of the said States.

Any two or more States who are parties to this compact shall have the right to enter into supplemental agreements providing for the establishment, financing and operation of regional educational institutions for the benefit of citizens residing within an area which constitutes a portion of the general region herein created, such institutions to be financed exclusively by such States and to be controlled exclusively by the members of the Board representing such States provided such agreement is submitted to and approved by the Board prior to the establishment of such institutions.

Each State agrees that, when authorized by the Legislature, it will from time to time make available and pay over to said Board such funds as may be required for the establishment, acquisition, operation, and maintenance of such regional educational institutions as may be authorized by the States under the terms of this compact, the contribution of each State at all times to be in the proportion that its population bears to the total combined population of the States who are parties hereto as shown from time to time by the most recent official published report of the Bureau of Census of the United States of America, or upon such other basis as may be agreed upon. This compact shall not take effect or be binding upon any State unless and until it shall be approved by proper legislative action of as many as six or more of the States whose governors have subscribed hereto within a period of eighteen months from the date hereof. When and if six or more States shall have given legislative approval to this compact within said eighteen months' period, it shall be and become binding upon such six or more States sixty (60) days after the date of legislative approval by the sixth State and the Governors of such six or more States shall forthwith name the members of the Board from their States as hereinabove set out, and the Board shall then meet on call of the Governor of any State approving this compact, at which time the Board shall elect officers, adopt by-laws, appoint committees and otherwise fully organize. Other States whose names are subscribed hereto shall thereafter become parties hereto upon approval of this compact by legislative action within two years from the date hereof, upon such conditions as may be agreed upon at the time.

After becoming effective this compact shall thereafter continue without limitation of time provided, however, that it may be terminated at any time by unanimous action of the States, and PROVIDED, FURTHER, that any State may withdraw from this compact if such withdrawal is approved by its legislature, such withdrawal to become effective two years after written notice thereof to the Board accompanied by a certified copy of the requisite legislative action, but such withdrawal shall not relieve the withdrawing State from its obligations hereunder accruing up to the effective date of such withdrawal. Any State so withdrawing shall *ipso facto* cease to have any claim to or ownership of any of the property held or vested in the Board or to any of the funds of the Board held under the terms of this compact.

If any State shall at any time become in default in the performance of any of its obligations assumed herein or with respect to any obligation imposed upon said State as authorized by and in compliance with the terms and provisions of this compact, all rights, privileges and benefits of such defaulting State, its members on the Board and its citizens shall *ipso facto* be and become suspended from and after the date of such default. Unless such default shall be remedied and made good within a period of one year immediately following the date of such default, this compact may be terminated with respect to such defaulting State by an affirmative vote of three-fourths of the members of the Board (exclusive of the members representing the State in default,) from and after which time such State shall cease to be a party to this compact and shall have no further claim to or ownership of any of the property held by or vested in the Board or to any of the funds of the Board held under the terms of this compact, but such termination shall in no manner release such defaulting State from any accrued obligation or otherwise affect this compact or the rights, duties, privileges or obligations of the remaining States thereunder.

IN WITNESS WHEREOF, this compact has been approved and signed by the Governors of the several States, subject to the approval of their respective legislatures in the manner hereinabove set out, as of the 8th day of February, 1948; and

WHEREAS, it is desired that the said compact be given legislative approval by the State of South Carolina; NOW, THEREFORE,

BE IT RESOLVED by the General Assembly of South Carolina:

SECTION 1: Compact entered into by Southern States February 8, 1948, providing for jointly owned and operated regional educational institutions approved — State party thereto — terms binding on State. — That the said compact be, and the same is hereby, approved and the State of South Carolina is hereby declared to be a party thereto, and the agreements, covenants and obligations therein are binding upon the State of South Carolina.

SECTION 2: Appropriation. — That there is hereby appropriated the sum of Thirty-five Thousand ($35,000.00) Dollars from the general funds of this State, to be paid to the Board of Control for Southern Regional Education, if and when such Board is established under the provisions of said compact. Said money to be expended by said Board in carrying out the powers, duties and authorities as outlined in said compact.

SECTION 3: Time effective. — This Resolution shall take effect upon its approval by the Governor.

Approved the 3rd day of April, 1948

[Note: See Note on Regional Compact—Education, Appendix 6.]

Employment — Separation

§1272. Separation of employees of different races in cotton textile factories. — It shall be unlawful for any person, firm or corporation engaged in the business of cotton textile manufacturing in this State to allow or permit operatives, help and labor of different races to labor and work together within the same room, or to use the same doors of entrance and exit at the same time, or to use and occupy the same pay ticket windows or doors for paying off its operatives and laborers at the same time, or to use the same stairway and windows at the same time, or to use at any time the same lavatories, toilets, drinking water buckets, pails, cups, dippers or glasses: provided, equal accommodations shall be supplied and furnished to all persons employed by said person, firm or corporation engaged in the business of cotton textile manufacturing as aforesaid, without distinction [as] to race, color or previous conditions. Any firm, person, or corporation engaged in cotton textile manufacturing violating the provisions of this section shall be liable to a penalty of not over one hundred ($100.00) dollars for each and every offense,

414

to be recovered in suit by any citizen of the county in which the offense is committed and to be paid to the school fund of the district in which offending textile manufacturing establishment is located. Any firm, person or corporation engaged in cotton textile manufacturing violating the provisions of this section shall be punished by a fine not to exceed one hundred [$100.00] dollars for each offense or imprisonment at hard labor for a period not to exceed thirty [30] days or both at the discretion of the judge. This section shall not apply to employment of firemen as subordinates in boiler rooms, or to floor scrubbers and those persons employed in keeping in proper condition lavatories and toilets, and carpenters, mechanics and others engaged in the repair or erection of buildings. [1932 Code, §1272; Cr. C. '22, §167; 1915 (29) 79; 1916 (29) 706.]

Hospitals — Training School for Negro Nurses

§6223. — [The board of Regents of the South Carolina State Hospital is "authorized and empowered to establish at State Park a training school for Negro nurses at the Negro department of the South Carolina state hospital." The said board is also authorized to prescribe and promulgate rules and regulations for the conduct of such training school.] [1932 Code, §6223; Civ. C. '22, §5074; Civ. C. '12, §3355; Civ. C. '02, §2248; G.S. 1585; R.S. 1780; 1827 (11) 322; 1871 (14) 672; 1915 (29) 147; 1920 (31) 704; 1938 (40) 1665.]

Indians

§9332. [1944 Supp.] Catawba Indians, otherwise qualified, citizens. — All Cawtawba Indians, otherwise qualified, are hereby declared to be citizens of the State of South Carolina, and shall enjoy and have all the rights and privileges belonging to other citizens of the state. [1944(43) 1208.]

See under Miscegenation below.

Ku Klux Klan — Masks

§1131. [1944 Supp.] Assault, etc. by Masked Person.—It shall be unlawful for any person, individually or as a group of individuals, assembled under any pretext whatsoever, while wearing a mask or otherwise disguised, to assault or offer to assault, any other person or persons, and any person convicted of same shall be deemed guilty of a felony and be punished by a penalty of not less than one [1] year nor more than ten (10) years at hard labor upon the chaingang of the county wherein the crime is committed or for a like period in the State penitentiary. [1928(35) 1232; 1932 Code, §1131; 1943(43) 218.]

Lynching

§3041. When county liable for damages for lynching — may recover from guilty parties. — In all cases of lynching when death ensues the county where such lynching takes place shall, without regard to the conduct of the officers, be liable in exemplary damages of not less than two thousand [$2,000.00], to be recovered by action instituted in any court of competent jurisdiction by the legal representatives of the person lynched, and they are hereby authorized to institute such action for the recovery of such exemplary damages. A county against which judgment has been obtained for damages in any case of lynching shall have the right to recover the amount of said judgment from the parties engaged in said lynching in any court of competent jurisdiction, and is hereby authorized to institute such action. [1932 Code, §3041; Civ. C. '22, §5601; Civ. C. '12, §3947; Civ. C. '02. §2844; 1896 (22) 214.]

[Note: See Const. Art. 6, §6 above.]

§1952. Sheriff may impress a guard and call out posse comitatus — penalty for refusing to assist. — When any person accused of a capital offense shall be in custody and the sheriff acting by himself or his regular deputy, shall have cause to suspect that such person may be unlawfully taken from his custody, or will probably effect his escape, he may impress a sufficient guard for securing and keeping safely such prisoner, so long as it may be his duty to keep said prisoner in jail or in his custody. And the sheriff, by himself, or his regular deputy, shall have power to call out the *posse comitatus** to his assistance, whenever he is resisted, or has reasonable grounds to suspect and believe that such assistance will be necessary in the service or execution of such process in any criminal case; and any person refusing to act as such guard, or to assist as one of the *posse comitatus* in the service or execution of such process, when required by the sheriff, shall be liable to be indicted therefor, and upon conviction shall be fined and imprisoned, at the discretion of the court. 1932 Code, §1952; Cr. C. '22; §934; Cr. C. '12, §936; Cr. C. '02, §650; G.S. 2072; R.S. 537; 1839 (11) 52.]

[*Posse comitatus is defined as "the power of the county. A phrase signifying the rank and file of the citizens of a district or county who may be called to assist a sheriff or other officer in enforcing the laws, or in the execution of process." Chadman's Legal Dictionary.]

§1128. Penalty upon officer from whom prisoner is taken. — In the case of any prisoner lawfully in the charge, custody or control of any officer, state, county or municipal, being seized and taken from said officer through his negligence, permission or connivance, by a mob or other unlawful assemblage of persons, and at their hands suffering bodily violence or death, the said officer shall be deemed guilty of a misdemeanor, and, upon true bill found, shall be deposed from his office pending trial, and upon conviction shall forfeit his office, and shall unless pardoned by the Governor, be ineligible to hold any office of trust or profit within this State. It shall be the duty of the prosecuting attorney within whose circuit or county the offense may be committed to worthwith [forthwith] institute a prosecution against said officer, who shall be tried in such county in the same circuit, other than the one in which the offense was committed, as the attorney general may elect. The fees and mileage of all material witnesses, both for the State and the defense, shall be paid by the county treasurer of the county in which the case originated, on a certificate issued by the clerk and signed by the presiding judge, showing the amount of said fee due the witnsess. [1932 Code, §1128; Cr. C. '22, §27; Cr. C. '12, §173; Cr. C. '02, §142; 1896 (22) 213; 1908 (25) 1019.]

Miscegenation

§1438. Miscegenation — punishment for — penalty for performing ceremony. — It shall be unlawful for any white man to intermarry with any woman of either the Indian or negro races, or any mulatto, mestizo, or half-breed, or for any white woman to intermarry with any person other than a white man, or for any mulatto, half-breed, Indian, negro or mestizo to intermarry with a white woman; and any such marriage or attempted marriage, shall be utterly null and void and of none effect; and any person who shall violate this section, or any one of the provisions thereof, shall be guilty of a misdemeanor, and, on conviction thereof, shall be punished by a fine of not less than five hundred dollars [$500.00], or imprisonment for not less than twelve months, or both, in the discretion of the court. Any clergyman, minister of the gospel, magistrate or other person authorized by law to perform the marriage ceremony, who shall knowingly [knowingly] and wilfully unite in the bonds of matrimony any persons of different races, as above prohibited, shall be guilty of a misdemeanor and, upon conviction thereof, shall be liable to the same penalty or penalties as provided in this section. [1932 Code, §1438; Cr. C. '22, §378; Cr. C. '12, §385; Cr. C. '02, §293; R.S. 517. G.S. 2032, 2033, 2034; 1879 (17) 3; Const. Art. 2, §6.]

> [Note: Mestizo is defined, "Any one of mixed blood; specif., in Mexico, the western United States, and the Philippines, a person of mixed Spanish and Indian blood; also, a person of mixed Chinese and Philippine blood." Funk & Wagnall's New Standard Dictionary.]

§8571. Intermarriage of races prohibited. — It shall be unlawful for any white man to intermarry with any woman of either the Indian or negro races, or any mulatto, mestizo, or half-breed, or for any white woman to intermarry with any person other than a white man, or for any mulatto, half-breed, negro, Indian or mestizo to intermarry with a white woman; and any such marriage, or attempted marriage, shall be utterly null and void and of none effect. [1932 Code, §8571; Civ. C. '22, §5536; Civ. C. '12, §3757; Civ. C. '02, §2664; G.S. 2032; R.S. 2163; 1879 (17) 3.]

Parks, Playgrounds and Beaches

§9316. Joint use of parks, amusements or recreation centers and bathing beaches by white and colored races prohibited in counties with city over 60,000. — In all counties containing a city of a population in excess of 60,000, according to the 1930 census, it shall be unlawful to maintain public parks, public recreation centers, public amusements centers, and public bathing beaches for the joint use and enjoyment of both the white and colored races. Each such park, recreation center, amusement place, amusement center and bathing beach shall be publicly posted and designed by signs at the entrance to show whether the same is dedicated and maintained for the use and enjoyment of the white or the colored race, as the case may be. It shall be unlawful for any person of the white race to enter, use or attempt to use any such place which is duly posted to be dedicated and maintained for the use of the colored race; and it shall be unlawful for any person of the colored race to enter, use or attempt to use any such place which is duly posted to be dedicated and maintained for the use of the white race; *provided*, that the provisions hereof shall not apply to domestic servants accompanying their employers in the course of their employment, nor shall it apply to nurses accompanying the children of the opposite race in their charge, nor shall it apply to employees of such places. Any person, firm or corporation violating the provisions hereof shall be guilty of a misdemeanor and upon conviction thereof shall be punished by a fine of not less than ten ($10.00) dollars, nor more than one hundred ($100.00) dollars, or imprisonment for not less than ten (10) days nor more than thirty (30) days. [1934 (38) 1536.]

Pensions (Negroes in Civil War)

§4983. Certain faithful negroes entitled to pensions — limit.—Such negroes as were engaged for at least six months in the service of the State in the war between the states as body servants or male camp cooks on the side of the Confederacy, and proved faithful throughout said war, and whose conduct since then has recommended them to the county board of pensions for any of the counties of the State, are each entitled to receive out of any appropriation made for pensions for Confederate soldiers and sailors by the State, such an amount, annually, as a pension, as may be fixed by the state board of ensions . . . [Provides for maximum annual pension of $25.00 and applies only to such Negroes as went to war from South Carolina and now reside in the state.] [1932 Code, §4983; 1923 (33) 107; 1924 (33) 936.]

[Note: This statute is mainly of historical interest now.]

Prisons

Convicts on Chain Gangs

§1035. — [Provides that "separation of the sexes and races be at all times observed."] [1932 Code, §1035; Cr. P. '22, §125; Cr. C. '12, §104; 1911 (27) 169; 1912 (27) 553; 1914 (28) 515; 1917 (30) 265.

Transportation

Electric Railways

§1269. Separation of races in electric cars. — Electric railways outside of the corporate limits of cities and towns shall have authority to separate the races in their cars, and the conductors in charge of said cars are hereby authorized and directed to separate the races in said cars under their charge and control. Any conductor who shall fail or refuse to separate the races as herein provided, shall, upon conviction, be fined not more than one hundred [$100] dollars, or be imprisoned for not exceeding thirty [30] days for each offense. [1932 Code, §1269; Cr. C. '22, §164; Cr. C. '12, §315; 1905 (24) 954.]

§1270. — [Conductors and other employees of electric railways are given powers of peace officers and authorized to make arrests while in charge of cars on electric railways.] [1932 Code, §1270; Cr. C. '22, §165; Cr. C. '12, §316; 1905 (24) 954.]

Motor Busses

§8530-1. Passenger motor vehicle carriers separate white and colored passengers.

(1) Required — penalties. — All passenger motor vehicle carriers,

418

operating in the State of South Carolina shall separate the white and colored passengers in their motor buses and set apart and designate in each bus or other vehicle, a portion thereof, or certain seats therein, to be occupied by white passengers, and a portion thereof, or certain seats therein, to be occupied by colored passengers, and such company or corportation, person or persons that shall fail, refuse or neglect to comply with the provisions of this sub-section shall be guilty of a misdemeanor, and upon indictment and conviction, shall be fined not less than fifty [$50.00] dollars nor more than two hundred and fifty [$250.00] dollars for each offense.

(2) **Accommodations.** — The said companies, corporations or persons so operating motor vehicle carriers shall make no difference or discrimination in the quality or convenience of the accommodations provided for the two races under the provisions of subsection 1 hereof.

(3) **Duties and powers of person in charge of vehicle—penalty.** — The driver, operator, or other person in charge of any motor vehicle above mentioned, shall have the right, and he is hereby directed and required at any time when it may be necessary or proper for the comfort and convenience of passengers to do so, to change the designation so as to increase or decrease the amount of space or seats set apart for either race; but no contiguous seats on the same bench shall be occupied by white and colored passengers at the same time; and said driver, operator or other person in charge of the vehicle, may require any passenger to change his or her seat as it may be necessary or proper; the driver, operator or other person in charge of said vehicle who shall fail or refuse to carry out the provisions of this subsection shall be deemed guilty of a misdemeanor, and upon conviction thereof be fined not less than five [$5.00] dollars nor more than twenty-five [$25.00] dollars for each offense.

(4) **Driver, operator or person in charge of vehicle special policeman—powers.**—Each driver, operator or person in charge of any vehicle, in the employment of any company operating the same, while actively engaged in the operation, of said vehicle, shall be a special policeman and have all the powers of conservators of the peace in the enforcement of the provisions of this section, and in the discharge of his duty as special policeman, in the enforcement of order upon said vehicles; and such driver, operator or person in charge of said vehicle shall likewise have the powers of conservators of the peace and of special policeman while in pursuit of persons for disorder upon said vehicles, for violating the provisions of this section, and until such persons as may be arrested by him shall have been placed in confinement or delivered over to the custody of some other conservator of the peace or police officer; and, acting in good faith, he shall be for the purposes of this section, the judge of the race of each passenger whenever such passenger has failed to disclose his or her race.

(5) **Duties of passengers — violations — penalty — eject passengers — liability.** — All persons who fail while on any motor vehicle carrier, to take and occupy the seat or seats or other place assigned to them by the driver, operator or other person in charge of such vehicle, or by

the person whose duty it is to take up tickets or collect fares from passengers therein, or who fail to obey the directions of any such driver, operator, or other person in charge as aforesaid, to change their seats from time to time as occasions require, pursuant to any lawful rule, regulation or custom in force by such lines as to assigning separate seats or other space to white and colored persons, respectively, having been first advised of the fact of such regulation and requested to conform thereto, shall be deemed guilty of a misdemeanor and upon conviction thereof shall be fined not less than five [$5.00] dollars nor more than twenty-five [$25.00] dollars for each offense. Furthermore, such persons may be ejected from such vehicle by any driver, operator or person in charge of said vehicle, or by any police officer or other conservator of the peace; and in case such person ejected shall have paid their fares upon said vehicle, they shall not be entitled to the return of any part of same. For the refusal of any such passenger to abide by the request of the person in charge of said vehicle, as aforesaid, and his consequent ejection from said vehicle, neither the driver, operator, person in charge, owner, manager, nor bus company operating said vehicle shall be liable for damages to any court. [1937 (40) 376.]

Railroads — Steam Ferries.

§8396. Separate coaches for white and colored — toilet compartments. — All railroads and steam ferries and railroad companies engaged in this State as common carriers of passengers for hire, shall furnish separate coaches or cabins for the accommodation of white and colored passengers: *provided*, equal accommodations shall be supplied to all person without distinction of race, color or previous condition, in such coaches or cabins. ... [1932 Code, §8396; Civ. C. '22, §4944; Civ. C. '12, §3249; Civ. C. '02, 2158; 1898 (22) 777; 1900 (23) 457; 1904 (24) 438; 1912 (27) 563; 1937 (40) 154.]

§8397. Penalty for officer or employee violating provision as to white and colored. — It shall be unlawful for the officers or employees having charge of such railroad cars as are provided by this chapter to allow or permit white and colored passengers to occupy the same car except as herein permitted and allowed. [1932 Code, §8397; Civ. C. '22, §4945; C. '12, §3250; Civ. C. '02, §2160; 1898 (22) 777; 1900 (23) 457.]

§8398. White and colored allowed in the same coach when unavoidable. — In case the coach for either white or colored passengers should be full of passengers, and another coach cannot be procured at the time, then the conductor in charge of the train shall be, and he is hereby, authorized to set apart so much of the other coach as may be necessary to accommodate the passengers on said train. [1932 Code, §8398; Civ. C. '22, §4946; Civ. C. '12, §3251; Civ. C. '02, §2161; 1898 (22) 777; 1900 (23) 457.]

§8399. Exceptions to section 8396 to 8398. — The provisions of sections 8396 to 8398 shall not apply to nurses on trains, nor to narrow gauge roads, or branch lines, nor roads under forty miles in length, or to relief trains in case of accident, or to through vestibule trains not intended or used for local travel, nor to regular freight trains with a passenger coach attached for local travel, nor to officers or guards transporting prisoners, nor to prisoners or lunatices being so transported: *provided* that all railroads operated by steam under forty miles in length shall furnish separate apartments for white and colored passengers: *provided, further* that where said railroads under forty miles in length operate both a daily passenger train and a freight train, with or without a coach attached, said railroad shall be required to furnish separate apartments for white and colored passengers only on the said passenger trains: *provided*, also, that the provisions hereof shall not apply to electric railroads. *Provided, further,* that as to train consisting of not more than one passenger car unit, operated principally for the accommodation of local travel, although operated both intrastate and interstate, and irrespective of the motive power used, the public service commission is hereby authorized to make such modifications, changes and exceptions in and to the requirements of sections 8396 to 8398, inclusive, as in its best judgment may be feasible and reasonable in the circumstances, and the regulation established by the commission pursuant to this authority shall constitute exceptions to the provisions of sections 8396 to 8398, inclusive. [1932 Code, §8399; Civ. C. '22, §4947; Civ. C. '12, §3252; Civ. C. '02, §2159; 1898 (22) 777; 1900 (23) 457; 1903 (24) 84; 1935 (39) 203.]

§8400. Penalty for violation of provisions as to separate accommodations. — Should any railroad or railroad company, its agents or employees, violate the provisions of sections 8396, 8397, 8398, and 8399, such railroad or railroad company shall be liable to a penalty of not more than five hundred [$500.00] dollars nor less than three hundred [$300.00] dollars for each violation, to be collected by suit of any citizen of this State, and the penalty recovered shall, after paying off proper fees and costs, go into the general fund of the State treasury. [1932 Code, §8400; Civ. C. '22, §4948; Civ. C. '12, §3253; Civ. C. '02, §2162; 1898 (22) 777; 1900 (23) 457.]

§8400-1. Penalty for officer or employee violating the law as to separate cars for each race. — It shall be unlawful for the officers or employees having charge of such railroad cars as are provided for by sections 8396 to 8399, to allow or permit white and colored passengers to occupy the same car, except as herein permitted and allowed; and for a violation of this section any such officer or employee shall be guilty of a misdemeanor, and on conviction thereof, shall be punished by a fine of not less than twenty-five [$25.00] nor more than one hundred [$100.00] dollars. [1932 Code, §1702; Cr. C. '22, §648; Cr. C. '12, §673; Cr. C. '02, §479; 1898 (22) 777; 1900 (23) 457.]

§8400-2. Penalty for passenger refusing to obey law as to separate cars. — Any passenger remaining in a car other than that provided for him, after request by the officer or employee in charge of said car to remove into the car provided by him, shall be guilty of a misdemeanor, and, on conviction thereof, shall be fined not less than twenty-five [$25.00] dollars nor more than one hundred [$100.00] dollars. Jurisdiction of such offenses shall be in the county in which the same occurs. The conductor and any and all employees on such cars are hereby clothed with power to eject from the train or car any passenger who refuses to remain in such car as may be assigned and provided for him, or to remove from a car not so assigned and provided. [1932 Code, §1703; Cr. C. '22; §649; Cr. C. '12, §674; Cr. C. '02, §480; 1898 (22) 777; 1900 (23) 457.]

§8403. Meals to be furnished white and colored passengers apart. — No persons, firms, or corporations, who or which furnish meals to passengers at station restaurants or station eating houses, in times limited by common carriers of said passengers, shall furnish said meals to white and colored passengers in the same room, or at the same table, or at the same counter. Any person, firm or corporation violating the provisions of this section, shall, upon conviction, be deemed guilty of a misdemeanor, and subject to a fine of not less than twenty-five [$25.00] dollars nor to exceed one hundred [$100.00] dollars, or to imprisonment not to exceed thirty [30] days for each offense. [1932 Code, §§1268, 8403; Civ. C. '22, §4951, Civ. C. '12, §3256; Cr. C. '22, §163; Cr. C. '12, §314; 1906 (25) 76.]

Waiting Rooms

§8413. To keep rooms for passengers. — Every railroad company owning or operating a railroad in this State shall erect and keep at every office where tickets are sold for travel over its road, two good rooms or apartments of reasonable size for the amount of travel at such office, which shall be furnished with comfortable seats for the accommodation of passengers. Such rooms to be in charge of an employee of such company, and kept open at such hours as to accommodate passengers traveling over such road an any of its passenger trains; and it shall be the duty of the public service commissioners to enforce the provisions of this section. [1932 Code, §8413; Civ. C. '22, §4961; Civ. C. '12, §3266; Civ. C. '02, §2168; G.S. 1494; R. S. 1712; 1935 (39) 25.]

Rules Promulgated By The Public Service Commission Governing Common Carriers By Rail And Express Companies Under §8413. (filed secretary state's office June 30, 1937.)

Rule No. 8. Waiting rooms. A separate room for white and colored passengers, sufficient for their comfort and convenience, shall be provided at all stations where passenger tickets are offered for sale, and these waiting rooms shall be furnished with adequate lights, and when the inclemency of the weather requires, with fire, and at all times kept clean and comfortable for passengers . . .

SOUTH DAKOTA

CONSTITUTION

Aliens

Bill of Rights

Art. VI, §14. — No distinction shall ever be made by law between resident aliens and citizens, in reference to the possession, enjoyment and descent of property. [Const. 1889.]

Indians

[See Art. XXII and Art XXVI, §18 with reference to Indian lands being excluded from apportionment.]

Education

Art. VIII., §1. — . . . it shall be the duty of the legislature to establish and maintain a general and uniform system of public schools wherein tuition shall be without charge, and equally open to all; . . . [Const. 1889]

STATUTES

SOUTH DAKOTA CODE OF 1939

Aliens

25.0425. Hunting by aliens. — [No alien who has not declared his intention to become a citizen of the United States is entitled to a hunting license.] [1921, ch. 243, §1.]

Indians

65.0801. Rights of Indians, disabilities. — Indians resident within this state have the same rights and duties as other persons, except that while maintaining tribal relations:

(1) They cannot vote or hold office; and

(2) They cannot grant, lease, or incumber Indian lands, except in the cases provided by special laws. [Rev. Code 1919, §92.]

15.3501 et seq. — [Provision for compulsory attendance of Indian children at federal schools (with certain exceptions).] [1931, ch. 138, §§290, 291, 293.]

Laws 1949, Chapter 65, (H.B. 259) p. 67

RELATING TO EDUCATION OF INDIAN CHILDREN

AN ACT Entitled, An Act to Authorize and Empower the State Superintendent of Public Instruction to Contract with the U. S. Department of Interior as to the Education of Indian Children; To Receive Federal Aid Grants for Such Purpose and to Expend Such Funds.

Be It Enacted by the Legislature of the State of South Dakota:

Section 1. The State Superintendent of Public Instruction is hereby authorized to enter into contracts with the United States Department of the Interior for the education of Indian children, to receive grants of federal

423

funds for that purpose, and to expend such funds under such laws and regulations as the State Superintendent of Public Instruction may establish.

Approved February 23, 1949.

Laws 1949, Chapter 66, (H.B. 337) p. 67

PROVIDING SCHOLARSHIPS FOR INDIANS

AN ACT Entitled, An Act Creating Scholarships in State Educational Institutions for Persons of Indian Blood and Providing Qualifications therefore and an Appropriation for payment of same.

Be It Enacted by the Legislature of the State of South Dakota:

Section 1. The State Board of Regents shall provide thirty (30) Scholarships each year for persons of at least one-fourth Indian blood, which will entitle the persons to enter the State Educational Institutions upon compliance with all of the requirements required by such educational institution for admission, and be entitled to attend and pursue any course or courses in such institution. Such scholarship shall provide for free tuition and fees required in the completion of such course or courses.

Section 2. The eligibility of persons to such scholarship shall be determined by a board of examiners established by the Board of Regents. Such Board of examiners shall adopt such rules and regulations as may be necessary to establish eligibility for such scholarships.

Section 3. The institutions receiving enrollments under such scholarships shall be reimbursed from the general fund upon vouchers approved by Board of Regents. For the purposes of providing funds for the scholarships herein provided, there is hereby appropriated from the General Fund the sum of Five Thousand Dollars ($5,000.00) annually for the next biennium.

Approved March 7, 1949.

Commission of Indian Affairs
Laws 1949, ch. 244, p. 280

AN ACT

ENTITLED, An Act Creating a State Commission of Indian Affairs, Providing for Membership, Prescribing Duties and Powers and Providing an Appropriation therefore.

BE IT ENACTED BY THE LEGISLATURE OF THE STATE OF SOUTH DAKOTA:

Section 1. The State Commission of Indian Affairs is hereby established to consider and study living conditions among the Indians residing within the state, with the purpose in view of establishing a method of absorbing the Indian people into the economy of the state. Such study shall be made with reference to education, employment, housing, betterment of living conditions, medical care, hospitalization and promotion of the general welfare of the Indian population of the state. The members of the Commission may confer with any official of the Indian Bureau of the federal government in order to secure cooperation between the federal and state government in the promotion of the welfare of the Indian people residing within the state.

Section 2. The State Commission of Indian Affairs shall be composed of seven members, namely

(1) The Director of the State Board of Health, the State Director of the Department of Public Welfare, the Superintendent of Public Instruction, and the Attorney General.

(2) One member at large to be appointed by the Governor for a term of three years.

(3) Two persons of at least one-fourth Indian blood, to be appointed by the Governor for a term of three years each.

(4) The Governor shall be an honorary member of the Commission.

(5) Such terms of appointive officers shall begin on the first of May of the year of appointment and shall be so arranged and continued that only one term will expire each consecutive year. The appointive members shall hold office until their successors are appointed.

Section 3. The Commission shall adopt rules and regulations for the conduct of its meetings and provide for the appointment of its chairman and secretary who shall be active members of the commission, and may hold hearings or investigations to secure information to carry out the purposes of this Act. Such commission shall meet at least two times a year at such time and place as the Commission shall provide and may hold meetings upon the call of its chairman when necessity may require. Such Commission shall keep a record of all its transactions.

Section 4. All members serving by virtue of their office shall serve without compensation but shall receive necessary expenses for attending meetings. The appointive members shall receive $5.00 per diem for attending meetings in addition to actual expenses. The Commission shall report to the legislature at its next session and from time to time thereafter as said Commission may deem proper, give an account of its transactions and findings and advice and recommendations for legislation. This report shall be prepared for presentation to each legislature and members thereof.

Section 5. The sum of One Thousand Dollars ($1,000.00), for the purpose of this chapter, annually appropriated out of any money in the state treasury not otherwise appropriated belonging to the general fund, and the money herein appropriated shall be drawn from and become payable out of the state treasury by requisition upon the State Treasurer by said Commission after the approval of such requisition by the State Auditor.

Section 6. Whereas, this Act is necessary for the immediate support of the State government and its existing public institutions, therefore an emergency is hereby declared to exist, and this Act shall be in full force and effect from and after its passage and approval.

APPROVED MARCH 7, 1949.

Miscegenation

14.0106. Void marriages . . . mixed race marriages . . . void from the beginning. — The following marriages are null and void from the beginning: (4) The intermarriage or illicit cohabitation of any person belonging to the African, Korean, Malayan, or Mongolian race with any person of the opposite sex belonging to the Caucasian or white race. [Rev. Code 1919, §§106, 108, parts of §§107, 128.]

14.9901. Mixed race marriages: felony; penalty. — Whoever shall enter into any mixed race marriage or indulge in any such illicit cohabitation as is described in section 14.0106 (4) shall be guilty of a misdemeanor and punished by a fine not exceeding one thousand dollars or by imprisonment in the State Penitentiary not exceeding ten years or by both. [Part of §128 Rev. Code, 1919, revised for separate statement of penal provision.]

TENNESSEE

CONSTITUTION

Education — Segregation

Art. 11, Sec. 12. — . . . The State taxes derived hereafter from polls shall be appropriated to educational purposes, in such manner as the General Assembly shall, from time to time, direct by law. No school established or aided under this section shall allow white and negro children to be received as scholars together in the same school . . . [Const. 1870.]

Intermarriage

Art. 11, Sec. 14. — The intermarriage of white persons with negroes, mulattoes, or persons of mixed blood, descended from a negro to the third generation, inclusive, or their living together as man and wife, in this State, is prohibited. The legislature shall enforce this section by appropriate legislation. [Const. 1870.]

Slavery

Art. 1, Sec. 33. — That slavery and involuntary servitude, except as a punishment for crime, whereof the party shall have been duly convicted, are forever prohibited in this State. [Const. 1870.]

STATUTES

WILLIAMS TENNESSEE CODE ANNOTATED, 1934

Aliens

1191.10. [1948 Supp.] . . . [Forbids the employment of aliens in the manufacture of alcoholic beverages.] [1933, ch. 69, sec. 9a; 1935, ch. 170, sec. 3, 1943, ch. 53, secs. 2, 5.]

1191.11. [Aliens not permitted to engage in business of alcoholic beverages within the State.] [1933, ch. 69, sec. 9b.]

7187. 3659. Aliens may hold and dispose of property.—An alien, resident or non-resident of the United States, may take and hold property, real and personal, in this State and dispose of or transmit the same as a native citizen. [1875, ch. 2, secs. 1, 2, Modified.]

7188. 3660. Heirs of aliens may inherit. — The heir or heirs, devisee or devisees, of such an alien may take any lands, so held by descent or otherwise, as if a citizen or citizens of the United States. [Ib., sec. 3, Modified.]

7190. 3622. Heirs and distributees of aliens may sell and convey. — Any alien, to whom property, personal or real, shall descend under the provisions of the next preceding section, shall have the right to hold, sell, alienate, and convey the same in as full and ample a manner as if he were a citizen of the United States. [1883, ch. 250, sec. 2.]

Art. XXXIV. Unlawful to Employ Aliens as Teachers. 2513. [1948 Cum. Supp.] In what public schools; advocating overthrow of American form of government; violation is a misdemeanor; fine; forfeiture of office. — It shall be unlawful for the trustees of the University of Tennessee, the state board of education, or any county or city board of education, or any other person to employ any superintendent, principal, teacher, tutor, supervisor, or other person to have in any way the custody and care of students of the public educational institutions of this state who is not a citizen of the United States of America; provided that nothing in this section shall be construed to prohibit arrangements whereby professors and teachers who are citizens of other nations may be employed on a temporary basis on the faculties of colleges, universities or public schools in Tennessee; provided, however, that no person who advocates the overthrow of the American form of government or who is a member of a political party subscribing to a political faith which advocates the overthrow of the American form of government shall be employed in either a temporary or permanent basis in any school in this State financed in whole or in part with public funds. Any person who shall violate any of the provisions of this section shall be guilty of a misdemeanor, punishable by a fine of not less than fifty dollars ($50.00) nor more than one hundred dollars ($100.00), and shall forfeit his office. [1925, ch. 115, sec. 31; 1947, ch. 130, sec. 1., appvd. March 10, 1947.]

[Note: This section as amended by 1947, ch. 30, sec. 1, now provides that it shall be unlawful to employ any person to have "custody and care of students of the public educational institutions of this state who is not a citizen of the United States of America; provided nothing in this section shall be construed to prohibit arrangements whereby professors and teachers who are citizens of other nations may be employed on a temporary basis on the faculties of colleges, universities or public schools in Tennessee . . . "

The section, as originally passed in 1925 prohibited the employment of any person "to teach or have custody over white pupils except persons of the Caucasian race who were born in the United States, and whose parents could speak the English language and who have themselves spoken the English language since childhood". The 1947 amended action eliminated this strict requirement.]

Definition of Negro

25. Same. — The word "negro" includes mulattoes, mestizos and their descendants, having any blood of the African race in their veins.

8396. 417a1 (2745a). Persons of color defined. — All negroes, mulattoes, mestizos, and their descendants, having any African blood in their veins, shall be known as "persons of color." [1865 - 66, ch. 40, sec. 1, Modified.]

Descent and Distribution Among Persons of Color. —

[§§8397 - 8401 provide for inheritance of children of slaves and their collateral kindred. These laws were passed between the years 1865 - 1870 to provide for the descent of property held by slaves.| [1865-66, ch. 40, sec. 1, 2, 5; 1929, ch. 133, Modified.|

Education — Segregation
Public Schools

2376. Elementary schools for all the children. — There shall be established and maintained in each county as many elementary schools as may be necessary for the instruction of all the children of the county. [1925, ch. 115, sec. 13.]

2377. Schools Designated for Children; Separate Schools for White and Negro Children. — The county board of education shall designate the schools which the children shall attend; provided, that separate schools shall be established and maintained for white and for negro children. [Ib.]

2393.9. Pupils Admissible; Separate Schools for Negroes and Whites. — Junior high schools sharing in the state and county high school funds shall be open without tuition to all children of the county; provided, that only those who have completed the eight grades of the elementary school or their equivalent shall be admitted to junior high schools of Form I; and that those who have completed the six grades of the elementary school, or their equivalent shall be admitted to junior high schools of Form II or of Form III, senior high schools of four grades shall be open to all children of the county who have completed the eight grades of the elementary school or their equivalent; and senior high schools of three grades shall be open to all children of the county who have completed the ninth grade, or its equivalent, in a junior high school; provided, that separate schools shall be maintained for white pupils and negro pupils. [1925, ch. 115, sec. 14; 1931, ch. 71, sec. 1 in part.]

11395. (6888a37.) Unlawful for white and colored persons to attend same school. — It shall be unlawful for any school, academy, college, or other place of learning to allow white and colored persons to attend the same school, academy, college, or other place of learning. [1901, ch. 7, sec. 1.]

11396. (6888a38.) Unlawful for teacher to allow such mixed attendance or to teach them in the same class. — It shall be unlawful for any teacher, professor, or educator in any college, academy, or school of learning, to allow the white and colored races to attend the same school, or for any teacher or educator, or other person to instruct or teach both the white and colored races in the same class, school, or college building, or in any other place or places of learning, or allow or permit the same to be done with their knowledge, consent, or procurement. [Ib., sec. 2.]

11397. (6888a39) Violation is a misdemeanor; fine and imprisonment. — Any person violating any of the provisions of this article, shall be guilty of a misdemeanor, and, upon conviction, shall be fined for each offense fifty dollars, and imprisonment not less than thirty days nor more than six months. [Ib. sec. 4, Modified.]

Blind — Segregation

4545. (2656) 1575). Traveling expenses; terms of admission of colored students. — ... the terms of admission [to Tennessee School for Blind at Nashville] for colored students given separate accommodations, shall be the same as prescribed for white students. [1915, ch. 20, secs. 5, 9.]

Deaf — Segregation

4561. (2669). Colored students. — The terms of admission for colored students [to the Tennessee Deaf School at Knoxville], who shall be given separate accommodations, shall be the same as the terms prescribed for white students. [1881 ch. 109, sec. 3.]

Feeble-Minded

4523. Races and sexes and felons separated; . . . — The Tennessee home and training school for feeble-minded persons shall provide for the separate maintenance of white and colored races, and for the confinement and separation of persons convicted of felony. It shall also be arranged for the complete segregation of the sexes of both races . . . [1919, ch. 150, §19.]

Juvenile Delinquents

4658. (Tennessee Industrial School) (4429). Races separated; separate apartments for sexes. — The children of the white and colored races which may be committed to said school shall be kept entirely separate and apart from each other in every way, and they shall not be associated together on any pretense whatever, and the sexes shall have separate apartments. [1891, Ch. 195, sec. 12.]

4696 - 4707. [Provides for the establishment and control of the Tennessee Vocational School for Colored Girls under the supervision and control of the Commissioner of institutions. Instruction for delinquent Negro girls is to include "common school branches, and in the arts or trades suitable and adaptable to the several inmates . . . The inmates shall receive training in household and domestic work, serving and other needle work, and otherwise have a practical education to fit them for the duties of life . . . " [1921, ch. 127, secs. 1, 2, 6 - 9. 1923, ch. 7, secs. 12, 42.]

4708. Colored woman superintendent. — Said institution shall be under the direct supervision and immediate control of a superintendent to be appointed by the commissioner for a term of four years, which superintendent shall be a colored woman of education and experience in such work. She shall appoint, subject to the approval of the said commissioner, such colored women as teachers, and assistants as may be necessary to the proper management and conduct of the institution . . . [1921, ch. 127, sec. 10.]

Colleges

2398. [1948 Cum. Supp.] **Teacher colleges and other colleges to be maintained; functions to prepare teachers.** — There shall be maintained a state teachers' college in each grand division of the state, a polytechnic institute at Cookeville, the Austin Peay State College at Clarksville, and an agricultural and industrial normal college for negroes at Nashville . . . [1925, ch. 115, sec. 16; 1927, ch. 50; 1941, c. 82, sec. 1; 1943, ch. 19, sec. 1; 1943, ch. 57, sec. 1.]

2399. Admission to teacher college or normal school, without tuition. — White persons who are not under sixteen years of age and who have completed the full four year course of an approved high school shall be admitted to the teacher college or state normal school, without tuition . . . Residents of the state over twenty-one years of age who have not completed a four year high school course may be admitted as special students, without tuition. [1925, ch. 115, sec. 16; 1927, ch. 50; 1941, c. 82, sec. 1; 1949, ch. 286, sec. 1.]

2403. Function of agricultural and normal school for negroes; tuition is free to whom; but not to non-residents. — The function of the agricultural and industrial normal college for negroes shall be to train negro students in agricultural home economics, trades, and industry, and to prepare teachers for the elementary and high schools for negroes in the state. All the curricula of said college shall conform to the federal statute providing for land grant colleges; and the state board of education is also authorized to maintain a high school department in connection with said college. Negro persons, residents of the state, who are not under sixteen years of age, may be admitted to the college, without tuition; that all students admitted to the regular college courses shall have completed a standard four year high school course.

Negro persons over twenty-one years of age who do not meet the foregoing requirements may be admitted as special students.

Nonresidents of the state who meet the conditions for entrance to any of these institutions as prescribed in this section may be admitted on payment of such tuition rates as the state board of education may prescribe. [Ib.]

2403.1. Scholarships for colored students. — The state board of education is hereby authorized and directed to establish scholarships for colored students, payable out of the state appropriations made for the agricultural and industrial college for negroes, under the terms and conditions hereinafter set forth. Such scholarships shall be granted to colored students to take professional courses not offered in said agricultural and industrial college for negroes, or other state-maintained institution for negroes, but which are offered for white students at the University of Tennessee.

Such scholarships shall be granted only to bona fide residents and citizens of this state who possess the qualifications, the health, character, and ability and preparatory education required for admission to the University of Tennessee. Such scholarships shall be in an amount sufficient to give the recipient thereof educational facilities equal to those provided by the University of Tennessee, without cost to the recipients in excess of the cost which would be required to attend the University of Tennessee. [1937, ch. 256, sec. 1.]

2403.2. Amount and payment of scholarships. — The scholarships herein provided for shall be granted to the nearest university or institution of learning which the recipient can lawfully attend and which offers educational facilities equal to those of the University of Tennessee, whether such university or institution is located in Tennessee or elsewhere. In determining the amount of each scholarship the state board of education shall take into consideration the living expenses, the cost of transportation and the tuition charges at the institution to be attended as compared with such expenses and charges at the University of Tennessee. The state board of education shall pay the amount of such scholarships to the recipient or to the institution attended by him as and when needed. Such payment shall be made out of the funds appropriated by the state for the agricultural and industrial college for negroes, but in no event shall the total expenditure for such scholarships exceed that proportion of the appropriation for the agricultural and industrial college for negroes which the expenditure of state funds for professional courses at the University of Tennessee bears to the total state appropriation for the University of Tennessee.

Provided, that the total expenditures under this act shall not exceed the sum of twenty-five hundred dollars ($2,500) per annum.

The state board of education, acting as the board of trustees for the agricultural and industrial college for negroes, is hereby authorized to make such rules and regulations as may be necessary for the purpose of carrying this act into effect. [1937, ch. 256, sec. 2.]

2403.3. Educaional facilities for negro citizens equivalent to those provided for white citizens. — The state board of education and the commissioner of education are hereby authorized and directed to provide educational training and instruction for negro citizens of Tennessee equivalent to that provided at the University of Tennessee by the State of Tennessee for white citizens of Tennessee. Such training and instruction shall be made available in a manner to be prescribed by the state board of education and the commissioner of education; provided, that members of the negro race and white race shall not attend the same institution or place of learning. The facilities of the Agricultural and Industrial State College, and other institutions located in Tennessee, may be used when deemed advisable by the state board of education and the commissioner of education, insofar as the facilities of same are adequate. [1941, ch. 43, sec. 2.]

2403.4. Payment for educational facilities. — The cost of providing such facilities shall be paid out of appropriations made to the state board of education or from any other available funds. [1941, ch. 43, sec. 2.]

2404. General management and control of these schools shall be vested in the state board of education. — The general management and control of the teacher colleges, state normal school, polytechnic institute, and agricultural and industrial normal college for negroes shall be vested in the state board of education and the curricula and rules and regulations for the government of said institutions shall be fixed by said board; . . . [1925, ch. 115, sec. 16; 1939, ch. 33, sec. 1; 1949, ch. 148, sec. 1.]

Regional Compact

2404.3. [1949 Cum. Supp.] Form and terms of Compact. — WHEREAS, on the 8th day of February, in the Year of our Lord One Thousand Nine Hundred and Forty-eight, the State of Tennessee and the States of Florida, Maryland, Georgia, Louisiana, Alabama, Mississippi, Arkansas, North Carolina, South Carolina, Texas, Oklahoma, West Virginia, and the Commonwealth of Virginia, through and by their respective Governors, entered into a written compact relative to the development and maintenance of regional educational services and schools in the Southern States in the professional, technological, scientific, literary, and other fields, so as to provide greater educational advantages and facilities for the citizens of the several States who reside within such region; and

WHEREAS, the said compact, as amended, is as follows:

THE REGIONAL COMPACT
(As Amended)

WHEREAS, the States who are parties hereto have during the past several years conducted careful investigation looking toward the establishment and maintenance of jointly owned and operated regional educational institutions in the Southern States in the professional, technological, scientific, literary and other fields, so as to provide greater educational advantages and facilities for the citizens of the several States who reside within such region; and

WHEREAS, Meharry Medical College, of Nashville, Tennessee, has proposed that its lands, buildings, equipment, and the net income from its endowment be turned over to the Southern States, or to an agency acting in their behalf, to be operated as a regional institution for medical, dental and nursing education upon terms and conditions to be hereafter agreed upon between the Southern States and Meharry Medical College, which proposal, because of the present financial condition of the institution, has been approved by the said States who are parties hereto; and

WHEREAS, the said States desire to enter into a compact with each other providing for the planning and establishment of regional educational facilities;

NOW, THEREFORE, in consideration of the mutual agreements, covenants and obligations assumed by the respective States who are parties hereto (hereinafter referred to as "States"), the said several States do hereby form a geographical district or region consisting of the areas lying within the boundaries of the contracting States which, for the purposes of this compact, shall constitute an area for regional education supported by public funds derived from taxation by the constituent States and derived from other sources for the establishment, acquisition, operation and maintenance of regional educational schools and institutions for the benefit of citizens of the respective States residing within the region so established as may be determined from time to time in accordance with the terms and provisions of this compact.

The States do further hereby establish and create a joint agency which shall be known as the Board of Control for Southern Regional Education (hereinafter referred to as the "Board"), the members of which Board shall consist of the Governor of each State, ex officio, and three additional citizens of each State to be appointed by the Governor thereof, at least one of whom shall be selected from the field of education. The Governor shall continue as a member of the Board during his tenure of office as Governor of the State, but the members of the Board appointed by the Governor shall hold office for a period of four years except that in the original appointments one Board member so appointed by the Governor shall be designated at the time of his appointment to serve an initial term of two years, one Board member to serve an initial term of three years, and the remaining Board member to serve the full term of four years, but thereafter the successor of each appointed Board member shall serve the full term of four years. Vacancies on the Board caused by death, resignation, refusal or inability to serve, shall be filled by appointment by the Governor for the unexpired portion of the term. The officers of the Board shall be a Chairman, a Vice Chairman, a Secretary, a Treasurer, and such additional officers as may be created by the Board from time to time. The Board shall meet annually and officers shall be elected to hold office until the next annual meeting. The Board shall have the right to formulate and establish by-laws not inconsistent with the provisions of this compact to govern its own actions in the performance of the duties delegated to it including the right to create and appoint an Eecutive Committee and a Finance Committee with such powers and authority as the Board may delegate to them from time to time. The Board may, within its discretion, elect as its Chairman a person who is not a member of the Board, provided such person resides within a signatory State, and upon such election such person shall become a member of the Board, with all the rights and privileges of such membership.

It shall be the duty of the Board to submit plans and recommendations to the States from time to time for their approval and adoption by appropriate legislative action for the development, establishment, acquisition, operation and maintenance of educational schools and institutions within the geographical limits of the regional area of the States, of such character and type and for such educational purposes, professional, technological, scientific, literary, or otherwise as they may deem and determine to be proper, necessary or advisable. Title to all such educational institutions when so established by appropriate legislative actions of the States and to all properties and facilities used in connection therewith shall be vested in said Board as the agency of and for the use and benefit of the said States and the citizens thereof, and all such educational institutions shall be operated, maintained and financed in the manner herein set out, subject to any provisions or limitations which may be contained in the legislative acts of the States authorizing the creation, establishment and operation of such educational institutions.

In addition to the power and authority heretofore granted, the Board shall have the power to enter into such agreements or arrangements with any of the States and with educational institutions or agencies, as may be required in the judgment of the Board, to provide adequate services and facilities for graduate, professional, and technical education for the benefit of the citizens of the respective States residing within the region, and such additional and general power and authority as may be vested in the

Board from time to time by legislative enactment of the said States.

Any two or more States who are parties of this compact shall have the right to enter into supplemental agreements providing for the establishment, financing and operation of regional educational institutions for the benefit of citizens residing within an area which constitutes a portion of the general region herein created, such institutions to be financed exclusively by such States and to be controlled exclusively by the members of the Board representing such States provided such agreement is submitted to and approved by the Board prior to the establishment of such institutions.

Each State agrees that, when authorized by the legislature, it will from time to time make available and pay over to said board such funds as may be required for the establishment, acquisition, operation and maintenance of such regional educational institutions as may be authorized by the States under the terms of this compact, the contribution of each State at all times to be in the proportion that its population bears to the total combined population of the States who are parties hereto as shown from time to time by the most recent official published report of the Bureau of Census of the United States of America; or upon such other basis as may be agreed upon.

This compact shall not take effect or be binding upon any State unless and until it shall be approved by proper legislative action of as many as six or more of the States whose Governors have subscribed hereto within a period of eighteen months from the date hereof. When and if six or more States shall have given legislative approval to this compact within said eighteen months' period, it shall be and become binding upon such six or more States 60 days after the date of legislative approval by the sixth State and the Governor of such six or more States shall forthwith name the members of the Board from their States as hereinabove set out, and the Board shall then meet on call of the Governor of any State approving this compact, at which time the Board shall elect officers, adopt by-laws, appoint committees and otherwise fully organize. Other States whose names are subscribed hereto shall thereafter become parties hereto upon approval of this compact by legislative action within two years from the date hereof, upon such conditions as may be agreed upon at the time. Provided, however, that with respect to any State whose constitution may require amendment in order to permit legislative approval of the compact, such State or States shall become parties hereto upon approval of this compact by legislative action within seven years from the date hereof, upon such conditions as may be agreed upon at the time.

After becoming effective this compact shall thereafter continue without limitation of time provided, however, that it may be terminated at any time by unanimous action of the States and provided further that any State may withdraw from this compact if such withdrawal is approved by its legislature, such withdrawal to become effective two years after written notice thereof to the Board accompanied by a certified copy of the requisite legislative action, but such withdrawal shall not relieve

435

the withdrawing State from its obligations hereunder accruing up to the effective date of such withdrawal. Any State so withdrawing shall *ipso facto* cease to have any claim to or ownership of any of the property held or vested in the Board or to any of the funds of the Board held under the terms of this compact.

If any State shall at any time become in default in the performance of any of its obligations assumed herein or with respect to any obligation imposed upon said State as authorized by and in compliance with the terms and provisions of this compact, all rights, privileges and benefits of such defaulting State, its members on the Board and its citizens shall *ipso facto* be and become suspended from and after the date of such default. Unless such default shall be remedied and made good within a period of one year immediately following the date of such default this compact may be terminated with respect to such defaulting State by an affirmative vote of three-fourths of the members of the Board (exclusive of the members representing the State in default), from and after which time such State shall cease to be a party to this compact and shall have no further claim to or ownership of any of the property held by or vested in the Board or to any of the funds of the Board held under the terms of this compact, but such termination shall in no manner release such defaulting State from any accrued obligation or otherwise affect this compact or the rights, duties, privileges or obligations of the remaining States thereunder.

IN WITNESS WHEREOF this compact has been approved and signed by the Governors of the several States, subject to the approval of their respective legislatures in the manner hereinabove set out, as of the 8th day of February, 1948. [1949, ch. 82.]

2404.4. [1949 Cum. Supp.] **Compact ratified.**—The aforesaid compact be and the same is hereby ratified and approved and the State of Tennessee is hereby declared to be a party thereto in accordance with the terms, provisions, covenants, obligations and conditions thereof. [1949, ch. 82, sec. 1.]

2404.5. [1949 Cum. Supp.] **Annual appropriation.** — There is hereby appropriated per annum the sum of $50,000.00 to be expended for the operation and maintenance of Meharry Medical College, at Nashville, Tennessee, as a regional institution, and for other regional institutions for veterinary medical training, and for general expenses, as provided and in accordance with the aforesaid Compact for Southern Regional Education, such funds to be paid over, disbursed and expended under the direction and supervision of the Department of Education of the State of Tennessee. [1949, ch. 82, sec. 2.]

[SECTION 3. Acts 1949, ch. 82, provides, "That this Act take effect from and after its passage, the public welfare requiring same, but the appropriations herein made shall not be available until the scholastic year beginning July 1, 1949." Passed: April 1, 1949. Approved: April 1, 1949.]

[See also **Note on Regional Compact — Education**, Appendix 6.]

Employment — Coal Mines

5653. Separate wash rooms for whites and blacks. — All wash houses erected as herein described shall be so arranged as to provide separate compartments or buildings for whites and blacks, in the discretion of the chief mine inspector. [1921, ch. 24, sec. 5, Modified.]

Hospitals

Insane

4434. (2638). For Colored insane. — There are separate buildings on the grounds of the several hospitals for the insane for the colored insane, in which they shall be kept. [   ]

Ku Klux Klan — Masks and Disguises

11031. 668 (4770a). Penalty for going about masked or in disguise. — Any person or persons, masked or in disguise, who shall prowl or travel, or ride, or walk through the country or any town to the disturbance of the peace, or to the alarming of the citizens of any portion of this state, they shall be guilty of a misdemeanor and fined not less than one hundred dollars [$100.00] nor more than five hundred dollars [$500.00], and imprisoned in the county jail of the county wherein convicted, in the discretion of the jury trying the case. [1869-70, ch. 54, sec. 1.]

11032. 6669 (4770b). Entering upon the premises of another in disguise. — If any person or persons, disguised or in mask, by day or by night, shall enter upon the premises of another, or demand entrance or admission into the house or inclosure of any citizen of this state, it shall be considered *prima facie* that his or her intention is to commit a felony, and such demand shall be deemed an assault with intent to commit a felony, and the person or persons so offending, shall, upon conviction, be punished by imprisonment in the penitentiary not less than ten [10] years nor more than twenty [20] years. [Ib., sec. 2].

11033. 6670 (4770c). Assaulting another with deadly weapon in disguise. — If any person, so prowling, traveling, riding, or walking through the towns or country of this state, masked or in disguise, shall assault another with a deadly weapon, he shall be deemed guilty of an assault with intent to commit murder in the first degree, and, on conviction thereof, shall suffer death by electrocution; provided, the jury trying the cause may substitute imprisonment in the penitentiary for a period of not less than [10] years nor more than twenty-one [21] years. [Ib., sec. 3.]

11034. 6673 (4770f). Governor may offer two hundred and fifty dollars reward. — The governor is hereby authorized to offer a reward of two hundred and fifty dollars [$250.00], for the apprehension and delivery to the sheriff or jailer of any county, any person who may be guilty of a violation of section 11032 or 11033. [Ib., sec. 6].

11035. 6673a1. Misdemeanor to ride or travel through the county or towns, to the disturbance of the peace, damage of property, or intimidation of citizens; fine and imprisonment. — Any person or persons who shall wilfully prowl or travel or ride or walk through the country or towns, to the disturbance of the peace or the alarming of the citizens of any portion of the state, or for the purpose of damaging or destroying property, or for the purpose of intimidating or terrorizing any citizen or citizens of this state, or for the purpose of causing, through threats or intimidation or other improper means, any citizen or citizens of this state to do or not to do any lawful thing or to do any unlawful thing, shall be guilty of a misdemeanor, and, upon conviction, shall be fined not less than fifty dollars [$50.00] nor more than one hundred dollars [$100.00], and imprisoned in the county jail for not less than six [6] months nor more than twelve [12] months, said imprisonment to be within the discretion of the judge trying the case. [1907, ch. 427, §1.]

11036. 6673a4. Felony for night rider or other lawless person to attempt to prevent disposal of farm products: imprisonment in penitentiary. — It shall be a felony for any night rider or other lawless person, by threats, written or verbal, or by intimidation in any form, to attempt to prevent one having the disposal of farm products from selling and delivering such products, at such time and to such market as he may prefer. Any person convicted under this section shall be punished by imprisonment in the penitentiary for not less than three [3] nor more than fifteen [15] years. [1915, ch. 15, sec. 1].

11037. 6673a5. Felony for night rider or other person to seek to compel dismissal of laborers, share croppers, or tenants, or to compel them to vacate: imprisonment in penitentiary. — It shall be a felony for any night rider, or other person by threats, written or verbal, or by intimidation in any form, to compel or seek to compel one having hired laborers, share croppers, or tenants on his place to dismiss them or any of them from employment without due cause, or for any night rider or other person by threats, written or verbal, or by intimidation in any form, to compel or seek to compel hired laborers, sharecroppers, or tenants or their families to vacate, under fear or compulsion, the premises they have occupied. Any person convicted under this section shall be punished by imprisonment in the penitentiary for not less than three [3] nor more than fifteen [15] years. [Ib., sec. 2, Modified.]

11038. 6673a6. Felony to advise or incite, or to conspire to commit, such offenses; imprisonment in penitentiary. — Any person advising or inciting others, or conspiring with others to commit the offense mentioned in the two preceding sections shall be guilty of felony, and on conviction, shall be punished by imprisonment in the penitentiary for not less than three [3] nor more than fifteen [15] years. [Ib.]

Miscegenation

8409. (4186) 2437 2437a). White, negroes, etc. not to intermarry or cohabit. — The intermarriage of white persons with negroes, mulattoes, or persons of mixed blood descended from a negro, to the third generation inclusive, or their living together as man and wife in this state, is prohibited. [1822, ch. 19, sec. 1, 1870, ch. 39, sec. 1; Const. Art. 11, sec. 14.]

8410. (4187) (2437bu). Felony, imprisonment. — The person knowingly violating the provisions of the last section shall be guilty of a felony, and undergo imprisonment in the penitentiary not less than one [1] nor more than five [5] years; and the court may, on the recommendation of the jury, substitute, in lieu of punishment in the penitentiary, fine and imprisonment in the county jail. [1822, ch. 19, sec. 1 and 3; 1870 ch. 39, sec. 2.]

Orphans

4581. (4352), Colored asylums. — All houses for the support of destitute colored orphans, or indigent colored children, or children of indigent colored parents, incorporated under the laws of the state, may receive and take charge of any destitute colored orphan or indigent colored child of either sex, or children of indigent colored parents, under eighteen years of age, from part of the state under the provisions of this chapter. [1885, ch. 92, Sec. 9.]

Prisons

12040. Washing and Cleaning. — The jailers . . . shall provide bathing facilities separate for negroes and whites . . .

12119. (7522) (5503). Males and females apart. — The male and female white and colored convicts shall, at all times and on all occasions, be kept separate and apart from each other. [1829, ch. 38. sec. 25, subsec. 1.]

Public Places

5257 - 5259. — [Provide that there shall be no discrimination by owners and operators of places of public amusement in the admission of persons to such places of equal terms, and violation subjects offenders to damages and injunction.] [1885, ch. 68, sec. 1, Modified, secs. 2 and 3.]

5260. (3044). Separate accommodations for colored persons. — Nothing herein contained shall be construed as interfering with the existing rights to provide separate accommodations and seats for colored and white persons at such places. [Ib., sec. 4.]

[See also sections 5261, 5262.]

Transportation

Busses and Motor Carriers

[Note: While there appears to be no statutory provision expressly requiring separation of the races on motor vehicles and busses, §5501.4 vests power in the railroad and public utilities commission to "supervise and regulate every motor carrier in this state." Presumably segregation can be and is effected by regulation of the commission.]

Railroads

5518. 3074. Separate coaches or apartments for white and colored races. — All railroads carrying passengers in the state (other than street railroads) shall provide equal but separate accommodations for the white and colored races, by providing two or more passenger cars for each passenger train, or by dividing the passenger cars by a partition, so as to secure separate accommodations; but any person may be permitted to take a nurse in the car or compartment set aside for such persons. This law shall not

439

appply to mixed and freight trains which only carry one passenger or combination passenger and baggage car, but in such cases, the one passenger car so carried shall always be partitioned into apartments, one apartment for the white and one for the colored. [1891, ch. 52, sec. 1.]

5519. 3075. Conductors must separate passengers. — The conductors of such passenger trains shall have power, and are required, to assign passengers to the car or compartments of the car when it is divided by a partition, used for the race to which such passengers belong, and, should any passenger refuse to occupy the car to which he is assigned by such conductor, said conductor shall have power to refuse to carry such passenger on this train; and, for such refusal, neither he nor the railroad company shall be liable for any damages in any court [Ib., sec. 2.]

5520. 3076. Failure of companies and conductors to comply; penalties. — All railroad companies that shall fail, refuse, or neglect to comply with the requirements of section 5518 shall be guilty of a misdemeanor, and be fined not less than one hundred nor more than five hundred dollars; and any conductor who shall fail, neglect, or refuse to carry out the provisions of this law shall be fined not less than twenty-five nor more than fifty dollars for each offense. [Ib., sec. 3.]

Street Cars

5527. 309a1. Portions of car to be set apart and designated for each race. — All persons, companies, or corporations operating any street car line in the state are required, where white and colored passengers are carried or transported in the same car or cars, to set apart and designate in each car or coach, so operated, a portion thereof or certain seats therein to be occupied by white passengers, and a portion thereof or certain seats therein to be occupied by colored passengers; but nothing in this article shall be construed to apply to nurses attending children or other helpless persons of the other race. [1905, ch. 150, sec. 1.]

5528. 3097a2. Printed sign to indicate cars or parts of cars for each race. — Large printed or painted signs shall be kept in a conspicuous place in the car or cars, or the parts thereof set apart or designated for the different races, on which shall be printed or painted, if set apart or designated for the white people, and it being a car so designated or set apart, "This car for white people." If a part of a car is so designated, then this sign, "This part of the car for white people." If set apart or designated for the colored race, this sign to be displayed in a conspicuous place as follows, "This car for the colored race." If any part of a car is set apart or designated for said race then this sign as follows, "This part of the car for the colored race." [Ib.]

5529. 3079a3. Conductor may increase or diminish space for either race, or require change of seats. — The conductor or other person in charge of any car or coach so operated upon any street car line shall have the right at any time, when in his judgment it may be necessary or proper for the comfort or convenience of passengers so to do, to change the said designation so as to increase or decrease the amount of space or seats set apart for either race, or he may require any passenger to change his seat when or so often as the change in the passengers may make such change necessary. [Ib., Sec. 2.]

5530. 3079a4. **Passengers to take seats assigned by conductor and designated for their race; refusal and remaining on car is a misdemeanor.** — All passengers on any street carline shall be required to take the seats assigned to them, and any person refusing so to do shall leave the car or remaining upon the car shall be guilty of a misdemeanor, and upon conviction shall be fined in any sum not to exceed twenty-five dollars [$25.00]; provided, no conductor shall assign any person or passenger to a seat except those designated or set apart for the race to which said passenger belongs. [Ib., sec. 3.]

5531. 3079a5. **Failure to set apart portions of car for each race is a misdemeanor.** — Any person, company, or corporation failing to set apart or designate separate portion of the cars operated for the separate accommodation of the white and colored passengers, as provided by this article, shall be guilty of a misdemeanor and fined in any sum not to exceed twenty-five [$25.00] dollars. [Ib., sec. 4.]

5532. 3079a6. **Special cars for exclusive accommodations of either race.** — Nothing in this article shall be construed to prevent the running of extra or special cars for the exclusive accommodation of either white or colored passengers, if the regular cars are operated as required by this article. [Ib., sec. 5.]

TEXAS

CONSTITUTION

Education

Art. VII, Sec. 7. — Separate schools shall be provided for the white and colored children, and impartial provision shall be made for both. [Const. 1876]

Art. VII, Sec. 14. — The Legislature shall also when deemed practicable, establish and provide for the maintenance of a College or Branch University for the instruction of the colored youths of the state . . . [Const. 1876.]

STATUTES

VERNON'S STATUTES ANNOTATED (1947)
(Revision of 1925)

Aliens

Alien Land Law

Art. 166. [15] [19] Ownership of land prohibited. — No alien or alien corporation shall acquire any interest, right or title either legal or equitable in or to any lands in the State of Texas, except as hereinafter provided. [Acts 1854, p. 98, Acts C. S. 1892, p. 6, Acts 1921, p. 261.]

Art. 167. [16] [10] Exceptions. — [This title shall not apply to aliens eligible for citizenship in the United States who shall become bona fide residents of the State and who have declared their intention to become citizens; aliens who are natural born citizens of nations which have a common boundary line with the United States [Mexicans and Canadians]; aliens who are citizens of the state of Texas to own land in such country.] [Id.]

Art. 168. [168] [10] Time to alienate. — [Any alien acquiring land under the preceding sections must dispose of the land within 5 years after he ceases to be a bona fide resident of the State.] [Id.]

Art. 169. [17] [11] Liens, loans and debts. — [Aliens permitted to lend money secured by liens on real estate and may enforce such liens.] [Id.]

Art. 170. [18] [12] Term of title. — [Aliens prohibited from owning land in this State who acquire real estate by inheritance or will may hold it for a period of 5 years only.] [Id.]

Art. 171. [19] [13], Art. 172. [20] [14].—[Provisions relating to escheat the State and proceedings for escheat where land is held contrary to provisions of this act. An alien, however, may sell his land at any time before escheat so long as it is not done with intention to evade this act. Where a sale is made with intention to evade this act, the conveyance is void and the land may be forfeited to the State.] [Id.]

Art. 173. Qualifications as guardian. — [Aliens ineligible to own land under this act are prohibited from acting as guardian of the estate of minors or incompetent persons, or from becoming the administrator or executor of any decedent's estate in the State.] [Id.]

Art. 174. Corporations controlled by aliens. — [No corporation in which a majority of the capital stock is owned by aliens prohibited by law from owning land in the State shall acquire any interest in lands in the State.] [Id.]

Art. 175. Land owned in trust. — [Prohibits the holding in trust of land for the benefit of aliens barred from owning land under this act.] [Id.]

Art. 176. Report and record of ownership.—[Requires all aliens or alien corporations owning land or hereafter acquiring land to file detailed "Report of Alien Ownership" with local county clerk.] [Id.]

Art. 177. [15] [9] Personal Property. — Aliens shall have and enjoy in this State such rights as to personal property as are or shall be accorded to citizens of the United States by the laws of the Nation to which such alien shall belong or by the treaties by such Nation with the United States. [Id.]

Art. 2583. [2474] [1701] [1658] Alienage no bar to inheritance. — [Fact that an ancestor is or has been an alien is no bar to taking title to land by descent.] [P. D. 44, 45, 46.]

Art. 2880a. Certificates to aliens prohibited. — [Prohibits issuing of teachers certificates to teach in the elementary or secondary public schools to any alien who has failed to declare his intention to become a citizen.] [Acts 1929, 41 Leg., p. 72, ch. 38, §1.]

Labor Organizations

Art. 5154a. [1943 Supp.] Labor unions.—. . . sec. 4a It shall be unlawful for any alien or any person convicted of a felony charge to serve as an officer or official of a labor union or as a labor organizer as defined in this Act . . . [Acts 1943, 48th Leg., 180, ch. 104.]

Adoption of Children

Revised Civil Statutes

Art. 46a, Sec. 8. Restrictions as to white persons and negroes. — No white child can be adopted by a negro person, nor can a negro child be adopted by a white person. [Acts 1931, 42nd. Leg., p. 300, ch. 177.]

Boxing

Penal Code, Art. 614 - 11. Matters prohibited. — No individual, firm, club, copartnership, association, company or corporation shall . . .

(f) knowingly permit any fistic combat match, boxing, sparring or wrestling contest or exhibition between any person' of the Caucasian or "White" race and one of the African or "Negro" race . . . [Acts 1933, 43rd Leg. p. 843, ch. 241, §11.]

Penal Code, Art. 614 - 14. Penalty.—[Violation is a misdemeanor punishable by a fine of $25.00 to $250.00 and by the revocation of the license of the violator.] [Acts 1933, 43rd. Leg. p. 843, ch. 241, §14.]

Definition of Negro

Art. 2900. [2897-8] — . . . The terms "colored race" and "colored children," as used in this title, include all persons of mixed blood descended from negro ancestry. [Acts 1905, p. 263.]

[Note: This definition is found in the statute relating to separate schools.] Acts 1947, 50th Leg. Ch. 29, p. 36, Sec. 12. — [Defines "colored person" to mean "a negro or person of African descent."]

Penal Code [1943 Supp.] Art. 1661.1, Sec. 2. **"Negro" Defined.** — The term "Negro" as used herein includes every person of African descent as defined by the Statutes of the State of Texas, and all persons not included in the definition of "Negro" shall be termed "white persons" within the meaning of this Act . . . [Acts 1943, 48th Leg., p. 651, ch. 370.]

[Note: Relates to Motor buses.]

Penal Code, Art. 493. [484] [347] [327] **"Negro" and "white person".** — The term "negro" includes also a person of mixed blood descended from negro ancestry from the third generation inclusive, though one ancestor of each generation may have been a white person. Any person not included in the foregoing definition is deemed a white person within the meaning of this law. [[Penal Code 1911, Art. 484, Acts 1887, p. 37.]

[Note: Relates to miscegenation statutes.]

Education

Title 49, Vernon's Ann. Civ. Stats.

Art. 2755 [2848]. **Separate schools.** — A school house constructed in part by voluntary subscription of colored parents or guardians, and for a school for colored children, shall not be used for white children without the consent of the trustees of the district, and a like rule shall protect the use of school houses erected in part by voluntary subscription of white parents or guardians for the benefit of white children. [Acts 1905, p. 263.]

Public Schools

Art. 2900 [2897 - 8]. **Separate schools.** — All available public school funds of this State shall be appropriated in each county for the education alike of white and colored children, and impartial provisions shall be made for both races. No white children shall attend schools supported for colored children, nor shall colored children attend schools supported for white children. The terms "colored race" and "colored children," as used in this title, include all persons of mixed blood descended from negro ancestry. [Acts 1905, p. 263.]

Art. 2719. To provide separate schools. — Said board [County board of education] shall provide schools of two kinds; those for white children and those for colored children . . . [Acts 1923, p. 237.]

Art. 2819 [2776]. **Duty of county superintendent.** — . . . The county superintendent shall make, on prescribed forms, separate consolidated rolls for the white and colored children of his county, . . . showing the number of children of each race, of the different years of school age and the total number of children of each race, and the total of both races in his county . . . [Acts 1911, p. 201.]

Deaf, Dumb and Blind and Orphans

Arts. 3221, 3221a, 3221b, 3222. [1939 Supp.]—[Provides for supervision and control of Deaf, Dumb and Blind Asylum for Colored Youth at Austin, Texas, and for the admission of colored orphans at such school.

Name changed to Texas Blind, Deaf and Orphan School by Acts, 1947, Ch. 292, p. 497 (Vernon's Ann. Civ. St. Art. 3221b.)] [Acts 1921, 41 St. Leg. 3rd. C. S. p. 523, Ch. 21; Acts 1937, 45 Leg. p. 879, Ch. 434, Acts 1947, Ch. 292, p. 497.]

Juvenile Delinquents

Art. 3259a - 3259b [1945 Supp.]. Colored Girls Training School. — [Provides for location and establishment of a colored girls' training school for the education and training of delinquent and dependent colored girls. Superintendent of such school shall be a Negro woman of previous experience and training.] [Acts 1927, 40th Leg. p. 441, Ch. 293, Acts 1945, 49th Leg. p. 136, Ch. 92.]

Colleges and Universities

Art. 2628a - 1. — [Establishes a co-educational college at Kingsville, Texas for white youth, to be known as Texas College of Arts and Industries and provides for merger of South Texas State Teachers College into said institution.] [Acts 1929, 41st Leg. p. 627, Ch. 286, §1.]

Art. 2624 (2682) [1948 Cum. Supp.]. — [Provides for the Texas State College for Women "for the education of white girls in the arts and sciences."] [As amended, Acts 1945, 49th Leg., p. 203, Ch. 156; Ch. 171, §1.]

Art. 2638 - 2643. — [Provides for the establishment of Prairie View State Normal and Industrial College for colored teachers.] [Acts, 1879, p. 181; G.L. vol. 8, p. 1481; Acts 1899, p. 325; Acts 1901, p. 35.]

Art. 2643a [1945 Supp.]. — [Name of Prairie View State Normal Industrial College for colored teachers changed to Prairie View University. Board of Directors authorized to establish "courses in law, medicine, engineering, pharmacy, journalism, or any other generally recognized college course taught at the University of Texas, in said Prairie View University, which courses shall be substantially equivalent to those offered at the University of Texas." [Acts 1945, 49th Leg. p. 506, Ch. 308.] [Repealed by Acts, 1947, 50th Leg., Ch. 29, p. 36.]

State University and College for Negroes

Laws, 1947, 50th Leg., ch. 29, p. 36, Art. 2643b. (Approved Mar. 3, 1947.)

§1. — [Declares the purpose of the Act is to "establish an entirely separate and equivalent university [from the University of Texas] of the first class for negroes with full rights to the use of tax money and the general revenue fund for establishment, maintenance, erection of buildings and operation of such institution . . . "]

§2. — [Provides that "to provide instruction, training, and higher education for colored people there is hereby established a university of the first class in two divisions:" (1) "The Texas State University for Negroes at Houston, and (2) "The Prairie View Agricultural and Mechanical College of Texas" (formerly Prairie View University) at Prairie View.

The Texas State University for Negroes shall provide courses in agriculture, the mechanic arts, engineering, and the natural sciences, and any other courses authorized at the time of passage of this Act, "all of which shall be equivalent to those offered at The Agricultural and Mechanical College of Texas" (white).

The Texas State University for Negroes "shall offer all other courses of higher learning, including but without limitation . . . arts and sciences, literature, law, medicine, pharmacy, dentistry, journalism, education, and other professional courses, all of which shall be equivalent to those offered at the University of Texas. Upon demand being made by any qualified applicant for any present or future course of instruction offered at the University of Texas, or its branches, such course shall be established or added to the curriculum of the appropriate division of the schools hereby established in order that the separate universities for negroes shall at all times offer equal educational opportunities and training as that available to other persons of this state . . . ."]

§§3 - 5. — [Provide for the appointment, powers at duties of the Board of Directors of the Texas State University for Negroes.]

§§6 - 8. — [Provides for the location of the site of the institution, establishment of departments, professorships and salaries, powers of directors and acceptance of gifts for the use of the school.]

§9. — [Appropriates $2,000,000.00 for acquisition of land, buildings and equipment for the institution.]

§10. — [Provides that in the interim between effective date of this Act and actual erection of Texas State University for Negroes, courses demanded by qualified applicants (except law) which are now given at the University of Texas or any of its branches, are authorized to be given at Prairie View Agricultural and Mechanical College of Texas. $100,000.00 is appropriated for this purpose.

§11. — [Authorizes the establishment of a separate school of law at Austin for Negroes known as the "School of Law of the Texas State University for Negroes" to "provide instruction in law equivalent to the same instruction being offered in law at the University of Texas." Appropriates emergency appropriation of $100,000.00 for this purpose. "Students of the interim School of Law of the Texas State University for Negroes shall have use of the State Law Library in the Capital Building in addition to other special library facilities which shall be made available, but the entire school shall be operated separately and apart from the campus of the University of Texas as provided in the Texas constitutional requirement of separate schools for white and colored youths."]

§12. — [Defines "qualified applicant" as "any colored person who meets the educational requirements for entrance to the same course or courses in the University of Texas or any of its branches." Defines "colored person" to mean "a negro or person of African descent."

§13. — [Repeals Acts, 1945, Ch. 308. and all laws or parts of laws in conflict herewith to the extent of such conflict.]

§14. — [Declares this statute to be emergency legislation.] [See also Acts 1947, 50th Leg. p. 470, Ch. 278, (Vernon's Ann. Civ. St. Art. 2634c.)]

[Note: See Note under Art. 2587 below.]

Laws 1949, ch. 144 [H.B. No. 545]

[Authorizes and empowers the Board of Directors of Texas State University for Negroes to erect and equip buildings and fixtures including but not limited to student dormitories, faculty dormitories, dining halls, libraries, student activity buildings, stadia and gymnasia, and grounds therefor.] [Appvd. May 10, 1949 Vernon's Ann. Civ. St., Art. 2643d.]

Laws 1949, ch. 145 [H.B. No. 546.]

[Authorizes Texas State University for Negroes to charge, use and appropriate to its own use fees, receipts, gifts and institutional funds.] [Vernon's Ann. Civ. St., Art. 2643c.]

Laws 1949, ch. 584.

[Appropriates to Texas State University for Negroes $1,527,000.00 for the year ending August 31, 1950 and $1,407,500.00 for the year ending August 31, 1951.] [Appvd. July 22, 1949, eff. September 1, 1949.]

University of Texas

Art. 2587 (2641) (3849) Admission [requirements]. — . . . It shall be open to all persons of both sexes in this state on equal terms, without charge for tuition, under the regulation prescribed by the regents, and to all others under such regulation as the board of regents may prescribe. [Acts 1913, p. 131.]

[Note: By its terms, the statute governing admission to the University of Texas does not exclude Negroes, but declares that the university "shall be open to all persons of both sexes in this state on equal terms." Yet, a separate State University and College for Negroes was created by Laws 1947, ch. 29, p. 36, as summarized above. Until recently the State of Texas barred all Negroes from attendance at the University of Texas. In the case of *Sweatt v. Painter*, (1948) 210 S.W. 2d. 442, Herman Marian Sweatt, a Negro brought mandamus proceedings to compel the officials of the University of Texas to admit him to its law school. The respondent school officials contended that adequate and equal facilities had been established at a separate law school for Negroes. Sweatt contended that segregation itself was inherently discriminatory. The Texas Court of Civil Appeals held that the constitutionality of the policy of segregation "was not open to question" and rejected Sweatt's contention that

447

segregation is inherently discriminatory and contravenes his right to equal protection of the laws under the Fourteenth Amendment to the Constitution of the United States.

On appeal to the United States Supreme Court, the *Sweatt* case was decided on June 5, 1950. (339 U.S. 629, 70 S. Ct. 848, 94 Law. Ed. 783). The Court held that "the petitioner may claim his full and constituitonal right: legal education equivalent to that offered by the State to students of other races. Such education is not available to him in a separate law school as offered by the State . . . We hold that the Equal Protection Clause of the Fourteenth Amendment requires that petitioner be admitted to the University of Texas Law School." For complete text of the opinion see Appendix 7.

Following the Supreme Court decision, the Associated Press reported on June 7, 1950 that the University of Texas accepted two Negro students. [See *New York Times,* June 8, 1950.]}

Out of State Aid

Laws 1949, ch. 584

[Appropriations — Educational Institutions — General Provisions] **Subsection (26).** — The amounts appropriated for Out-Of State Scholarship Aid to the Texas State University for Negroes for each year of the biennium shall be used as scholarship aid to qualified negro students who have been residents of Texas for more than eight (8) years for graduate or professional study in approved colleges or universities outside of Texas until such time, in the biennium, as the State Colleges or universities for negro students offer programs considered by the Board of Directors of the Texas State University for Negroes as equivalent to those in institutions for white students; the out-of-state schools to be approved by, and the students to be selected by, the Directors of the Texas State University for Negroes. [Appvd. July 22, 1949, eff. Sept. 1, 1949.]

Teachers' Salaries

Acts 1947, 50th Leg. Ch. 228, p. 401, Art. III.

[Provides salary schedules for Negro and white teachers.]

Employment
See under Mines.

Hospitals
Tuberculosis

Art. 3254a. State Tuberculosis Sanatorium for Negroes. — [Provision for the creation and establishment of a State Tuberculosis Sanatorium for Negroes.] [Acts 1935, 44th Leg. p. 359, ch. 131.]

Art. 3254c. [1948 Supp.] — [Provides for the removal of the State Tuberculosis Sanatorium for Negroes from Kerrville, Texas and its reestablishment at a new location, and authorizes the establishment of the "Texas State School for Cerebral Palsied on the property now occupied by the State Tuberculosis Sanatorium for Negroes at Kerrville, Texas.] [Acts 1947, 50th Leg., p. 679, ch. 344.]

Art. 3254d. [1948 Supp.] — [Provision for the establishment of the "East Texas State Tuberculosis Sanatorium" for tubercular white persons. The Board of Control, under which the sanatorium is to be operated, is authorized to provide for and admit "white persons only," under the same laws, rules and regulations as are now provided for the State Tuberculosis Sanatorium at Carlsbad, Texas.] [Acts 1947, 50th Leg., p. 679, ch. 344.]

Art. 3254a-1. [1949 Supp.] — [Provides for the transfer of Negro patients from the Texas State Tuberculosis Sanatorium for Negroes at Kerrville, Texas to the East Texas State Tuberculosis Sanatorium and for the use of the buildings, equipment and grounds of the State Tuberculosis Sanatorium for Negroes as a tuberculosis sanatorium for care of mentally ill.] [Laws 1949, ch. 207, eff. May 14, 1949.]

Ku Klux Klan — Masks [Penal Code]

Art. 454a. Wearing mask in public. — If any person shall go into or near any public place masked or disguised in such manner as [to] hide his identity or render same difficult to determine, he or she shall be guilty of a misdemeanor, and upon conviction fined in any sum not exceeding $500.00 or imprisonment in the county jail not exceeding twelve [12] months, or by both such fine and imprisonment, provided this article shall not apply to private or public functions, festivals or events not fostered, caused or presented by any secret society or organization. [Acts 1925, 39th Leg., ch. 63, p. 213, §1.]

Art. 454b. "Public Place" defined. — Any "public place" as used in the preceding article is any public road, street, or alley of a town, city, or any store, garage, workshop, or any place at which people are assembled or to which people commonly resort for purposes of business, amusement, or other lawful purposes, other than a church or other place where people are assembled for religious services or purposes. [Acts 1925, 39th Leg., ch. 63, p. 213, §2.]

Art. 454c. Masked person entering house. — If any person who is masked or disguised in such manner as to hide his or [her] identity, or as to render same difficult to determine shall go into or near any private house, or shall demand or seek entrance therein or disturb any of the inhabitants thereof, he shall be guilty of a felony and upon conviction thereof shall be punished by confinement in the penitentiary for a term of not less than one [1] nor more than ten [10] years; provided this article shall not apply to persons attending social gatherings in private homes where social custom sanctions the wearing of a mask or disguise. [Acts 1925, 39th Leg., ch. 63, p. 213, §3.]

Art. 454d. Masked person entering church. — If any person masked or disguised in such manner as to hide his identity or make same difficult of determination shall go into any church or other place where people are assembled for religious services or purposes, he shall be punished by confinement in the penitentiary for a term of years not less than two [2] nor more than ten [10]; provided this article shall not apply to any entertainments or service solely under the auspices of such church or religious gathering, and not fostered, caused or presented by any secret society or organization. [Acts 1925, 39th Leg., ch. 63, p. 213, §4.]

Art. 454e. Masked persons assaulting: "masked" defined. — If any two or more persons acting in concert, or aiding and abetting each other, when either or all of whom are masked, or in disguise, shall assault or shall falsely imprison any other person, each of such persons so offending shall be guilty of a felony and upon conviction shall be punished by confinement in the penitentiary for any term of years not less than five [5]. The terms "masked" or "in disguise" used in this article mean that such person by artificial means has so changed or obscured his usual appearance as to render his identification impossible, or more difficult than it would have been if such mask or disguise has [had] not been used. [Acts 1925, 39th Leg., ch. 63, p. 214, §5.]

Art. 454f. Masked individuals parading on public highways. — It shall be unlawful for any secret society or organization, or a part of the members thereof, masked or in disguise, to parade upon or along any public road or any street or alley of any city or town in this State, and all members of such society or organization so parading or other members of such, who aid, abet or encourage such parade, shall be guilty of an offense and upon conviction shall be fined in any sum not less than one hundred [$100.00] nor more than five hundred [$500.00] dollars or imprisonment in the county jail not more than six [6] months, or by both such fine and imprisonment. [Acts 1925, 39th Leg., ch. 63, p. 214, §6.]

Art. 545g. Partial invalidity not to affect other parts. — Should any article or part of this Act be held invalid it shall not affect or invalidate any other article or part thereof. [Acts 1925, 39th Leg., ch. 63, p. 214, §7.]

Libraries

Art. 1688. [County Free Libraries] Use of library. — Any white person of such county may use the county free library under the rules and regulations prescribed by the commissioners court and may be entitled to all the privileges thereof. Said court shall make proper provision for the negroes of said county to be served through a separate branch or branches of the county free library, which shall be administered by custodian of the negro race under the supervision of the country librarian. [Acts 2d C.S. 1919, p. 219.]

Lynching

Acts 1949, Ch. 582, H.B. No. 83

AN ACT

defining mobs and lynching and defining lynching in the first degree and lynching in the second degree; prescribing penalties therefor; providing the duties of the District Attorneys with respect to the Act; protecting the rights of civil liability: providing that this Act shall not repeal existing laws relating to unlawful assemblies, rioting, and offenses against the person; and declaring an emergency.

BE IT ENACTED BY THE LEGISLATURE OF THE STATE OF TEXAS:

Sec. 1. Any collection of persons assembled without authority of law for the purpose and with the intention of committing an assault and battery upon any person or who shall form the intention of committing an assault and battery after so assembling upon any person shall be deemed a "mob" for the purpose of this Act; and any act of violence by a mob upon the body of any person which shall result in the death of such person, shall constitute lynching in the first degree within the meaning of this Act; and each person constituting such mob committing such lynching shall be deemed guilty of lynching in the first degree and each and every person composing a mob and any and every accessory thereto by which any person is lynched in the first degree, shall upon conviction be punished by death or confinement in the penitentiary for life or for any term of years not less than five (5).

Sec. 2. Any collection of persons assembled without authority of law for the purpose and with the intention of committing an assault and battery upon any person, or who shall form the intention of committing an assault and battery after so assembling upon any person shall be deemed a "mob" for the purpose of this Act, and any act of violence by a mob upon the body of any person, which shall not result in the death of such person, shall constitute a lynching in the second degree within the meaning of this Act, and any and every person composing a mob which shall commit assault and battery or which shall unlawfully shoot, stab, cut, maim, or wound any person or by any means cause him bodily injury with intent to injure, maim, stab, disfigure, or kill him, if said assault shall not result in the death of the assaulted person, shall be guilty of lynching in the second degree and upon conviction shall be confined in the penitentiary for not less than one (1) year nor more than ten (10) years.

Sec. 3. It shall be the duty of the District Attorney for any county in which a lynching, either of the first or second degree, may occur to promptly and diligently endeavor to ascertain the identity of the person who in any way participated therein or who composed the mob perpetrating the same and have them apprehended and to promptly proceed with the prosecution of any and all persons so found, to the end that such offenders may not escape punishment. The District Attorney may be assisted in all such endeavors and prosecutions by the Attorney General or other prosecutors designated by the Governor for the purpose.

Sec. 4. Nothing herein contained shall be construed to relieve any member of any such mob from civil liability to the victim or to the personal representative of the victim of such lynching.

Sec. 5. Nothing in this Act shall repeal any existing laws relating to offenses against the person and nothing herein shall repeal existing laws relating to unlawful assemblies and rioting but the provisions of this Act shall be cumulative to these Statutes.

Sec. 6. The fact that the State of Texas has no specific laws to punish mobs committing lynching and the crowded condition of the calendar, create an emergency and an imperative public necessity requiring that the Constitutional Rule providing that bills should be read on three separate days in each House be suspended, and said Rule is hereby suspended, and this Act shall take effect and be in force from and after its passage, and it is so enacted. Approved: July 22, 1949.

[Note: The above statute is codified Vernon's Ann. P.C. Art. 1260a.]

Mines

Separate bath facilities.

Art. 5920. Bath facilities. — . . . The baths and lockers [required to be kept by mine employers for use of mine employees] for negroes shall be separate from those for whites, but may be in the same building . . . [Acts 1915, p. 100.]

Penal Code Art. 1612. — [Similar to Art. 5920 except, adds the following clause:

"Any operator, owner, lessee or superintendent of any coal mine violating any provision of this article shall be fined not less than twenty-five [$25.00] nor more than two hundred [$200.00] dollars, or be imprisoned in jail for not more than sixty [60] days, or both. Every two weeks of such violation shall be considered a separate offense."] [Acts 1915, p. 100.]

Miscegenation

Art. 4607. [4613] [2959] [2843] — Certain intermarriages prohibited. — It shall not be lawful for any person of Caucasian blood or their descendants to intermarry with Africans or the descendants of Africans. If any person shall violate any provision of this article, such marriage shall be null and void. [P.D. 4670; P.C. 346.]

Penal Code, Art. 492. [483] [346] [326] — Miscegenation. — If any white person and negro shall knowingly intermarry with each other in this State, or having so intermarried in or out of the State shall continue to live together as man and wife within this State, they shall be confined in the penitentiary not less than two [2] years nor more than [5] years.

Penal Code, Art. 493. [484] [347] [327] — "Negro" and "white person". — [See Definition of Negro, above

Penal Code, Art. 494. [485] [348] [388] — Proof of Marriage. — In trials for any offense included in this chapter, proof of marriage by mere reputation shall not be sufficient.

[Note: Not repealed. Ex Parte Copeland (Cr. App.) 91 S.W. (2d) 700.]

Ordinances for Segregation

Art. 1015b. Ordinances for segregation of races.

Sec. 1. — That the power and authority is hereby conferred upon the Cities of Texas to provide by suitable ordinance for the segregation of negroes and whites in any such city and to withhold permits to build or construct a house to be occupied by white people in negro communities inhabited by negroes as defined by ordinance and to withhold building permits to any negro to establish a residence on any property located in a white community inhabited by white people as defined by ordinance.

Sec. 2. — That it shall be lawful for negroes and whites to enter into mutual covenants or agreements concerning their respective residence and the power and authority is conferred upon the governing body of any city to pass suitable ordinances requiring the observance of any such agreement.

Sec. 3. — That the governing authorities of any such city shall have the full power to define the negro race, negro community, white race and white community.

Sec. 4. — That the governing authorities of any such city shall have full power to enforce the observance of any ordinance passed leading to or providing for the segregation of the races and to require the observance thereof by appropriate penalties. [Acts 1927, 40th Leg., p. 154, ch. 103.]

[Note: This statute is unconstitutional, yet it remains on the Texas statute books. The United States Supreme Court has declared ordinances which sought to segregate the races in residence to be invalid as violative of the Fourteenth Amendment. See *Buchanan v. Warley* (1917) 245 U.S. 60, *Harmon v. Tyler* (1927) 273 U.S. 668; *Richmond v. Deans*, (1930) 281 U.S.704.]

Transportation
Railroads

Art. 6417. [6746 to 6753] Separate coaches. —

1. — Every railway company, street car company, and interurban railway company, lessee, manager, or receiver thereof, doing business in this State as a common carrier of passengers for hire, shall provide separate coaches or compartments, as hereinafter provided, for the accommodation of white and negro passengers, which separate coaches and compartments shall be equal in all points of comfort and convenience.

2. — "Negro" defined. — The term "negro" as used herein, includes every person of African descent as defined by the statutes of this State.

3. — "Separate coach" defined. — Each compartment of a railroad coach divided by good and substantial wooden partitions with a door therein shall be deemed a separate coach within the meaning of this law, and each separate coach shall bear in some conspicuous place appropriate words in plain letters indicating the race for which it is set apart; and each compartment of a street car or interurban car divided by a board or marker placed in a conspicuous place, bearing appropriate words in plain letters indicating the race for which it is set apart, shall be sufficient as a separate compartment within the meaning of this law.

4.— Penalty. — Any railway company, street car company, or interurban railroad company, lessee, manager or receiver thereof, which shall fail to provide its cars bearing passengers with separate coaches or compartments, as above provided for, shall be liable for each failure to a penalty of not less than one hundred [$100.00] nor more than one thousand [$1,000.00] dollars, to be recovered by suit in the name of the State; and each trip run with such train or street car or interurban car without such separate coach or compartment shall be deemed a separate offense.

5. — Exceptions. — This article shall not apply to any excursion train or street car as such for the benefit of either race, nor to such

freight trains as carry passengers in cabooses, nor be so construed as to prevent railroad companies from hauling sleeping cars, dining or cafe cars or chair cars attached to their trains to be used exclusively by either race, separately but not jointly, or to prevent nurses from traveling in any coach or compartment with their employer, or employes upon the train or cars in discharge of their duty.

6. — Law to be posted. — Every railroad company carrying passengers in this State shall keep this law posted in a conspicuous place in each passenger depot and each passenger coach provided in this law.

7. — Duty of conductor. — Conductors of passenger trains, street cars, or interurban lines provided with separate coaches shall have the authority to refuse any passenger admittance to any coach or compartment in which they are not entitled to ride under the provisions of this law, and the conductor in charge of the train or street car or interurban car shall have authority, and it shall be his duty, to remove from a coach or street car, or interurban car, any passenger not entitled to ride therein under the provisions of this law. [Acts 1891, p. 44; Acts 1907, p. 58; G.L. vol. 10, p. 46.]

Sleeping Cars

Art. 4477, Rule 71. Separate compartment for porter. — Sleeping car companies shall provide compartments and bedding for their negro porters separate from those provided for their white passengers. [Acts 1911, p. 173; Acts 1917, p. 328.]

Art. 4477, Rule 72. Negro porter not to sleep in berth. — Negro porters shall not sleep in sleeping car berths nor use bedding intended for white passengers. [Acts 1911, p. 173; Acts 1917, p. 328.]

Passenger Stations (Railroads)

Art. 6498 [6693]. Suitable depots. — Each railroad in this State shall provide and maintain adequate, comfortable, and clean depots and depot buildings at their several stations for the accommodation of passengers, and keep said depot buildings well lighted and warmed for the comfort and accommodation of the traveling public. They shall keep and maintain separate apartments in such depot buildings for the use of white passengers . . . [Acts 1909, 2d. C.S., p. 401.]

Separate Coach Law

Penal Code, Art. 1659 [1523] [1010]. Separate coaches. —

1. Every railway company, street car company and interurban railway company, or any person or the agent of any person, firm or corporation who operates an interurban, commercial motor vehicle in carrying passengers for hire between any cities, towns, or villages of this State, lessee, manager, or receiver thereof doing business in this State as a common carrier of passengers for hire shall provide separate coaches or compartments for the accommodation of white and negro passengers.

2. "Negro" defined. The term negro as used herein includes every person of African descent as defined by the Statutes of this State.

3. (a) "**Separate Coach**" defined. Each compartment of a railroad coach divided by good and substantial wooden partitions with a door therein, shall be deemed a separate coach within the meaning of this law, and each separate coach shall bear in some conspicuous place appropriate words in plain letters indicating the race for which it is set apart. (b) Separate compartments for street car, interurban car and commercial motor vehicle defined. Each street car, interurban car or commercial motor vehicle having a board or marker placed in a conspicuous place bearing appropriate words in plain letters indicating the race for which space is set apart, shall be sufficient as a separate compartment within the meaning of this law.

4. **Violating separate coach law.** — If any passenger upon a train or street car, interurban car or commercial motor vehicle provided with separate coaches or compartments as above provided shall ride in any coach or compartment not designated for his race after having been forbidden to do so by the conductor in charge of the train, he shall be fined not less than Five Dollars ($5) nor more than Twenty-five Dollars ($25).

5. **Duty of Conductor.** Conductors of passenger trains, street cars, interurban lines, or commercial motor vehicle provided with separate coaches shall have the authority to refuse any passenger admittance to any coach or compartment in which they are not entitled to ride under the provisions of this law, and the conductor in charge of the train or street car, interurban car or commercial motor vehicle shall have authority, and it shall be his duty, to remove from a coach or street car, or interurban car or commercial motor vehicle any passenger not entitled to ride therein under the provisions of this law, and upon his refusal to do so knowingly he shall be fined not less than Five Dollars ($5) nor more than Twenty-five Dollars ($25).

6. **Fines to go to School Fund.**—All fines collected under the provisions of this law shall go to the available common school fund of the county in which conviction is had. Prosecutions under this law may be instituted in any county through or into which said railroad may be run or have an office. [As amended Acts 1935, 44th Leg., p. 387, ch. 147, §1.]

Art. 1660. Exceptions. — The preceeding article shall not apply to any excursion train or street car or interurban car as such for the benefit of either race, nor to such freight trains as carry passengers in cabooses, nor be so construed as to prevent railroad companies from hauling sleeping cars, dining or cafe cars or chair cars attached to their trains to be used exclusively by either race. separately but not jointly, or to prevent nurses from traveling in any coach or compartment with their employer, or employes upon the train or cars in the discharge of their duty. [Penal Code 1911, art. 1523, sub. 6, 8.]

Motor Buses

Vernon's Texas Statutes, 1948 Supp.

Penal Code
Art. 1661.1.

§1. Separation of Races in Motor Buses. — That every transportation company, lessee, manager, receiver and owner thereof, operating motor buses in this State as a carrier of passengers for hire shall provide and require that all White passengers boarding their buses for transportation or passage shall take seats in the forward or front end of the bus, filling the bus from the front end, and that all Negro passengers boarding their buses for transportation or passage shall take seats in the back or rear end of the bus, filling the bus from the back or rear end.

§2. "Negro" Defined. — The term "Negro" as used herein includes every person of African descent as defined by the Statutes of the State of Texas, and all persons not included in the definition "Negro" shall be termed "White persons" within the meaning of this Act.

§3. Authority of Bus Operator. — The operators of all passenger motor buses in this State shall have authority to refuse any passenger or person the right to sit or stand in any motor bus unless such passenger or person shall comply with the provisions of this Act, and such operator shall have the right and it shall be his duty to call any peace officer of the State of Texas for the purpose of removing from any bus any passenger who does not comply with the provisions of this Act, and any such peace officer shall have the right and it shall be his duty to remove from said bus, and to arrest any such passenger violating this Act, the same as if such person were committing a breach of the peace in the presence of such officer.

§4. Penalty. — If any passenger upon any bus in this State shall ride or attempt to ride on said bus in a place prohibited under the provisions of this Act, he shall be guilty of a misdemeanor and upon conviction thereof shall be fined not less than Five Dollars ($5) nor more than Twenty-five Dollars ($25).

§5. Exceptions. — The provisions of this Act shall not be construed so as to prohibit nurses from riding in the same end of the bus with their employers or when actually in charge of a child or children of such employers, even though of different races, and shall not prohibit officers from riding with prisoners at the same end of the bus, even though of different races.

§6. Excursions, Chartered or Special Busses. — The provisions of this Act shall not apply to any chartered bus or special bus run directly as such for the exclusive benefit of either race, but in all such cases said buses shall be plainly marked "Chartered" or "Special." [Acts 1943, 48th Leg. p. 651, ch. 370.]

Witnesses

Art. 3714. [3688] [2300] [2246] **Color or interest does not disqualify.** — No person shall be incompetent to testify on account of color, nor because he is party to a suit or proceeding or interested in the issue tried. [Acts 1871, p. 108; P.D. 6826.]

UTAH

CONSTITUTION

Education

Art. X, Section 1. [Free non-sectarian schools.] — The Legislature shall provide for the establishment and maintenance of a uniform system of public schools, which shall be open to all children of the State, and be free from sectarian control. [Const. adopted November 5, 1895.]

Slavery

Art. I, Sec. 21. — [Slavery Forbidden]

Neither slavery nor involuntary servitude, except for punishment for crime, whereof the party shall have been duly convicted, shall exist within this State. [Constitution adopted Nov. 5, 1895.]

UTAH CODE ANNOTATED, 1943

Aliens

Alien Land Law

[Note: in 1943, the legislature of Utah enacted a strong alien land law directed against aliens ineligible for citizenship, i.e. Chinese, Japanese and certain other Oriental groups. See Laws 1943, ch. 85, p. 127, S.B. 216, eff. March 16, 1943, Utah Code, Secs. 78-6a-1 to 78-6a-10. The 1943 statute was repealed by Laws 1947, ch. 98, p. 383, S.B. No. 122, effective May 13, 1949. Thus, it would appear that aliens ineligible for citizenship may own and control real estate in Utah to the same extent as if they were citizens.]

Americanization Schools

75-28-1. — [Provision made for Americanization program in the public schools.] [L. 19, p. 285, §4.]

75-28-3. — [Requires all aliens between ages of 16 and 35 who cannot speak, read or write the English language to the degree required to complete the 5th grade of the public schools to attend Americanization schools or their equivalent.] [L. 21, p. 301, §2.]

Certified Public Accountants

79-2-1. Qualifications. — [To be eligible must be a citizen of the United States or have declared intention to become a citizen.] [L. 23, p. 84, §3.]

Pharmacists

79-12-1. Qualifications. — [Must be a citizen of the United States.] [L. 25, p. 123, §4406.]

Property

101-4-24. Aliens May Take by Succession. — Aliens as well as citizens may take by succession; and no person capable of succeeding under the provisions of this title is precluded from such succession by reason of the alienage of any relatives. [C.L. 17, §6427.]

Hunting — Fishing

30-0-56. Aliens — Hunting or Carrying Arms — Forbidden. — [Makes it unlawful for any unnaturalized foreign-born person to hunt wild game or to own or possess a firearm of any make, except under certain special conditions. Violation of this section is a misdemeanor, punishable by a fine of $25.00 for each offense, or by imprisonment for not less than 15 days, or both, together with a forfeiture of the firearm found in his possession. [C.L. 17, §2600.]

[See also 30-057 and 30-058.]

30-0-21. Aliens — License. — Any person who is not a citizen of the United States, upon applying to any license agent and paying $12, may receive a license to angle for any kind of fish; provided, that any alien who is ineligible to citizenship, but who has resided in the State of Utah for fifteen years prior to application for a license, may receive a license to angle for any kind of fish, or hunt for any kind of game, bird or animal as provided by law upon the payment of the same fee required for a resident citizen.

Section 2. Id. Residence 15 Years.

Aliens ineligible for citizenship, after they have been domiciled in the state for a period of 15 years shall be allowed to carry and use fire arms in order to hunt as provided in Section 1. [L. 27, p.37, §7[1], as amended by Laws 1947, Ch. 42, Laws 1949, Ch. 40, p. 79, H.B. No. 59, appvd. February 24, 1949, eff. May 10, 1949.]

Mining and Fire Bosses

55-2-15. Mining and Fire Bosses . . . — No person shall be granted a certificate as a mining boss or fire boss who is not a citizen of the United States unless he shall produce satisfactory evidence of good moral character and has declared his intention to become a citizen under the naturalization laws. [L. 23, p. 17, §3925.]

Indians

30-0-65. — [Fish and Game laws apply to all Indians and halfbreed Indians when outside an Indian reservation.] [L. 23, p. 47, §38.]

Intoxicating Liquors

103-32-1. Sales, etc. to Indians, a Felony. — Every person who sells, exchanges, gives, barters or disposes of any intoxicating drink to any Indian of the whole or half blood, or to any person living or cohabiting with an Indian woman, is guilty of a felony, and shall be punished by imprisonment in the state prison for a period of not more than three years or by a fine of not more than $300, or by both. [C.L. 17, §8208.]

Hotels and Restaurants

103-29-2. Innkeepers Wrongfully Refusing Entertainment. — Every person and every agent or officer of any corporation carrying on business as an innkeeper who refuses, without just cause or excuse, to receive and entertain any guest is guilty of a misdemeanor. [C.L. 17, §8445.]

[Note: A restaurant is not an "inn" within the meaning of this section, and a person operating a restaurant is not an innkeeper. *Nance v. Mayflower Tavern Inc.* (1944) 106 U 517, 150 P. 2nd 773.]

Miscegenation

40-1-2. Marriages Prohibited and Void. — The following marriages are prohibited and declared void; . . .

(5) Between a negro and a white person.

(6) Beetween a Mongolian, member of the malay race or a mulatto, quadroon, or octoroon, and a white person . . . [C. L. 17, §2967 as amended by L. 39, c. 50; L. 41, Ch. 35.]

40-1-4. Foreign — Valid. — Marriages solemnized in any other country, state or territory, if valid where solemnized, are valid here. [C. L. 17, § 2969.]

40-1-15. Solemnization of Prohibited Marriage —Penalty. — If any authorized person knowingly, with or without license, solemnizes a marriage such as is herein prohibited, he shall be imprisoned in the state prison not exceeding three [3] years, or fined not exceeding $1,000, or be both so fined and imprisoned. [C. L. 17, §2979.]

40-1-16. Misconduct of County Clerk — Penalty. — Every clerk or deputy clerk who knowingly issues a license for any prohibited marriage shall be punished by confinement in the State prison for a term not exceeding two [2] years, or by fine in any sum not exceeding $1,000, or by both such fine and imprisonment, and upon conviction shall be removed from his office by the judgment of the court before which his conviction is had; and if he willingly issues a license contrary to his duty as herein prescribed, he shall be fined not exceeding $1,000. [C. L. 17, §2980.]

VERMONT

CONSTITUTION

Slavery

Ch. I, Article 1st. — [Slavery Forbidden.] That all men are born equally free and independent, and have certain natural, inherent, and unalienable rights, amongst which are the enjoying and defending life and liberty, acquiring, possessing and protecting property, and pursuing and obtaining happiness and safety; therefore no person born in this country, or brought from over sea, ought to be holden by law, to serve any person as a servant, slave, or apprentice, after he arrives at the age of twenty-one years, unless he is bound by his own consent, after he arrives to such age, or bound by law for the payment of debts, damages, fines, costs or the like. [Const. 1777, Ch. 1, Art.1; Const. 1786, Ch. 1, Art. I., Proposal 1, 1924.]

STATUTES

VERMONT STATUTES (REVISION OF 1947)

Aliens

534. State employees, aliens. — No department or commission of the state government shall regularly employ an alien, provided however, a person who has made application for naturalization may be considered as eligible for employment. [1941, No. 208, §1.]

1720. — [Aliens are not qualified to act as jurors.] [P.L., §1679. 1933, No. 157, §1519, G.L. §6899. P.S. §5788. V.S. 4971. R.L. 4161. G.S. 114, §14. G.L. 6913. P.S. 5803. V.S. 4988. R.L. §4178. G.S. 114, §1.]

VIRGINIA

CONSTITUTION

Education

§140. **Mixed schools prohibited.** — White and colored children shall not be taught in the same school. [Const. 1902, as amended, Art. IX.]

[Note: See §680 below.]

Inheritance — Children of Slaves

§195. **Heirs of property; children of slaves.** — The children of parents, one or both of whom were slaves at and during the period of cohabitation, and who are recognized by the father as his children, and whose mother was recognized by such father as his wife, and was cohabitated with as such, shall be as capable of inheriting any estate whereof such father may have died seized or possessed, or to which he was entitled, as though they had been born in lawful wedlock. [Const. 1902, as amended, Art. XIV.]

[See below §§5091, 5268.]

Poll Tax Lists

§38. **Duties of treasurers, clerks of circuit and corporation courts and sheriffs in regard to making, filing, delivering and posting list of poll taxes; not corrected.** — The treasurer of each county and city shall, at least five months before each regular election, file with the clerk of the circuit court of his county, or of the corporation court of his city, a list of all persons in his county or city who have paid not later than six months prior to such election, the State poll taxes required by this Constitution during the three years next preceding that in which such election is held; which list shall be arranged alphabetically, by magisterial districts in the counties, and in such manner as the general assembly may direct in the cities, *shall state the white and colored persons separately*, and shall be certified by the oath of the treasurer . . . (emphasis added.) [Const. 1902 as amended, Art. II.]

STATUTES

CODE OF VIRGINIA, 1950

Aliens

§55-1. **Aliens may acquire, hold and transmit real estate.**—Any alien, not an enemy, may acquire by purchase or descent and hold real estate in this State; and the same shall be transmitted in the same manner as real estate held by citizens. [Code 1887, §43; Code 1919, §66; Michie Code 1942, §66.]

§64-4. **When alienage of ancestor not to bar.** — In making title by descent; it shall be no bar to a party that any ancestor (whether living or dead), through whom he derives his descent from the intestate, is or hath been an alien. [Code 1887, §2551; Code 1919, §5267; Michie Code 1942, §5267.]

Attorneys at Law

§54-61.1. **Preliminary certificate of character and age required of applicant; beneficiary studying law under provisions of §§23-10 to 23-13.** — In

461

the case of any beneficiary studying law at a law school under the provisions of §23-10 to §23-13, a certificate signed by any two professors of such law school that he is a person of honest demeanor, and of good moral character, is over the age of twenty-one years, and within the preceding three years has studied law at such school for a period of two collegiate years, may be accepted in lieu of the court certificate required by §54-61. [1948, p. 905; Michie Suppl. 1948, §3419a.]

> [Note: This section applies to Negro students who are denied admission to Virginia State institutions of higher learning but receive out-of-state scholarship aid in lieu thereof. See §§23-10 to 23-13 below.]

Birth, Death and Marriage Records

§32-351. Certificate to contain certain items. — The certificate of birth shall contain the following items: . .

    (8) Color or race of father . . .
    (14) Color or race of mother . . .
[1912, p. 440; Code 1919, §1574; Michie Code 1942, §1574.]

§32-337.2. [1950 Cum. Supp.] When correctness of record subject to question as to race. — Whenever the State Registrar is requested to furnish a certified copy of a birth, death or marriage certificate of a person and the records in his office or other public records concerning such person or his parents are such as to cause the Registrar to doubt the correctness of the racial designation or designations contained in the certificate, a copy of which is requested, it shall be the duty of the State Registrar to enter upon the backs of the original certificate and certified copy an abstract of such other certificates or records, showing their contents so far as they are material in determining the true races of the person or persons named in the original certificate copy, with specific reference to the records, indicating where same are to be found open to public inspection. [1944, p. 53; Michie Suppl. 1946, §1580; Code 1950, §32-337; 1950, p. 485.]

Conspiracy to Incite Insurrection

§18-353. Conspiring to incite the colored population to insurrection against the white population or the white against the colored. — If any person conspire with another to incite the colored population of the State to acts of violence and war against the white population or to incite the white population of the State to acts of violence and war against the colored population, he shall, whether such acts of violence and war be made or not, be punished by confinement in the penitentiary not less than five [5] nor more than ten [10] years. Code 1887, §3661; Code 1919, §4392; Michie Code 1942, §4392.]

Definitions

§1-14. Colored persons and Indians defined. — Every person in whom there is ascertainable any Negro blood shall be deemed and taken to be a colored person, and every person not a colored person having one-fourth or more of American Indian blood shall be deemed an American Indian; except that members of Indian tribes living on reservations allotted them by the Commonwealth of Virginia having one-fourth or more of Indian blood and less than one-sixteenth of Negro blood shall be deemed tribal Indians so long as they are domiciled on such reservations. [Code 1887, §49; 1910, p. 581; 1930, p. 97; Michie Code 1942, §67.]

§20-54. Intermarriage prohibited; meaning of term "white persons". — For the purpose of this chapter, the term "white person" shall apply only to such person as has no trace whatever of any blood other than Caucasian; but persons who have one-sixteenth or less of the American Indian and have no other non-Caucasic blood shall be deemed to be white persons . . . [1924, p. 534; Michie Code, 5099a.]

[Note: See under Miscegenation.]

Divorce

§20-101. Decree to show race of parties. — Any interlocutory or final decree granting a divorce a *mensa et thoro* or a *vinculo matrimonii*, as the case may be, shall contain a recital showing the race of the husband and wife; but the failure of such decree to contain such recital shall not affect the validity of such decree or divorce. [Code 1887, §2260; 1902, 3, 4, p. 98; 1920, p. 503; 1928, p. 535; 1938, p. 202; Michie Code 1942, §5106.]

20-123. Report of divorces by clerk to State Registrar of Vital Statistics. — The clerk of every court authorized to grant divorces in Virginia shall on or before the tenth day of each month forward to the State Registrar of Vital Statistics a report of each divorce and of each annulment of a marriage granted in his court during the preceding month . . .

The reports shall include alleged cause, sex, occupation and color of plaintiff and defendant, date and place of marriage, number of children in family, and time of separation, provided, however, the record discloses such information . . . [1918, p. 397; 1938, p. 188; Michie Code 1942, §5116a.]

Education

Public Schools

§22 221. White and colored persons.—White and colored persons shall not be taught in the same school, but shall be taught in separate schools, under the same general regulations as to management, usefulness and efficiency. [Code 719, 1928, p. 1213; Michie Code 1942, §680.]

Deaf, Dumb and Blind — Separate Schools

§§23-156 to 23-164. — [Provision for maintenance of Virginia School for the Deaf and the Blind for blind and·deaf white children.] [Code 1919, §§970-977; Michie Code 1942, §§970-977, 978b-978h.]

§23-175. Name of school. — The institution heretofore established under the name of the Virginia State School for Colored Deaf and Blind Children shall be, and hereby is continued under the name of Virginia State School at Newport News. All statutes relating to the Virginia State School for Colored Deaf and Blind Children shall be construed as relating to Virginia State School at Newport News. [1906, p. 248; 1940, p. 274; Michie Code 1942, §525; 1946, c. 311.]

§23-176. Departments. — In such institution there shall be two departments, each separate and distinct from the other. In one of these departments there shall be received such deaf and dumb children of the colored race whose parents or guardians are residents of the Commonwealth, as cannot be educated in the ordinary public schools of the State. In the other departments there shall be received such blind children of the colored race, residents as above described, as cannot be educated in the public schools. [1906, p. 248; Code 1919, §980; Michie Code 1942, §980.]

§23-177. No charge for education. — There shall be no charge for the education of colored children, afflicted as above described, whose parents or guardians are residents of the State of Virginia. [1906, p. 248; Code 1919, §981; Michie Code 1942, §981.]

§23-178. Board of visitors abolished; powers, etc. conferred on State Board of Education. — The Board of Visitors of the institution is abolished, and all the rights, powers, authority and duties formerly conferred and imposed by law upon the said board of visitors are hereby transferred to, vested in, and imposed upon the State Board of Education. [1906, p. 248; Code 1919, §982; 1940, p. 274; Michie Code 1942, §982.]

§23-179. Superintendent, professors, officers and agents. — [Provision is made for the appointment thereof.] [Code 1919, §985; Michie Code 1942, §985.]

§23-180. Institution under control of General Assembly; reports.—The Virginia State School shall in all things and all times be subject to the control of the General Assembly; and it shall be the duty of the State Board of Education to make an annual report to the General Assembly and make such other reports as may be provided by law. Each fiscal year of the school shall end on the thirtieth day of June, to which time its accounts shall be made; and the State Board of Education shall annually, on the first day of October, deliver to the Governor, for transmission to the General Assembly, its report showing the condition of the school, and its receipts and disbursements for the said fiscal year. [1906, p. 248; Code 1919, §983; 1940, p. 274; Michie Code 1942, §983.]

Juvenile Delinquents

§63-370. Acts concerning Negro Reformatory Association of Virginia continued in force. — The following acts are continued in effect in so far as presently applicable:

(1) Chapter 273 of the Acts of 1899-1900, approved February 5, 1900, as amended by chapter 371 of the Acts of 1908, approved March 14, 1908, and chapter 34 of the Acts of 1916, approved February 17, 1916, relating to the former Negro Reformatory Association of Virginia and to the minors committed thereto.

(2) Chapter 206 of the Acts of 1910, approved March 15, 1910, relating to the establishment of a public free school on the grounds of such association.

(3) Chapter 344 of the Acts of 1920, approved March 19, 1920, relating to the conveyance of the property of the Negro Reformatory Association of Virginia to the Commonwealth and providing for the Common-

wealth to assume possession and control of the Virginia Manual Labor School for Colored Boys. [1899-1900, p. 301; 1908 p. 653; 1910, p. 35; 1916, p. 41; Code 1919, §§1961; Michie Code 1942, §1961; R.P. 1948, §63-370.]

§63-369. Virginia Manual Labor School for Colored Boys. — The Virginia Manual Labor School for Colored Boys shall be continued under the control of the Department, and colored boys may be committed to such School for the same reasons and with the same effect as they were formerly committed to the Negro Reformatory Association of Virginia. [1920, p. 516; R.P. 1948, §63-369.]

[Note: See also §63-371; Michie Code 1942, §585(88).]

§63-372. Transfers to State farms. — Whenever, in the opinion of the superintendents of the Virginia Industrial School for Boys or of the Virginia Manual Labor School for Colored Boys and of the Department, a ward of the school is dangerous to the morals of the school because of his behavior and advanced age, he may be transferred to the State farm for defective misdemeanants or other farm or farms and when so transferred a per diem allowance of sixty cents [60c] shall be allowed out of the criminal fund. [1926, pp. 399, 400; 1930 p. 825; Michie Code 1942, §5058(10); R.P. 1948, §63-372.]

63-367. [1950 Cum. Supp.] Janie Porter Barrett School for Girls. — The Virginia School for Colored Girls, formerly the Industrial School for Wayward Colored Girls, shall be after February twenty, nineteen hundred fifty [February 20, 1950], known as the Janie Porter Barrett School for Girls and is continued under the control of the Department. The Governor and the State Board may sell the property of the school and locate the school elsewhere if, in their judgment, the same shall be deemed advisable; provided, that the Commonwealth shall maintain the school until the sale of the property, and that the proceeds of the sale shall be reinvested in a school of like character.

Colored girls may be committed to the Janie Porter Barrett School for Girls for the same reasons and with the same effect as they were formerly committed to the Virginia Industrial School for Colored Girls and to the Industrial School for Wayward Colored Girls. [1920, p. 63; Michie Code 1942, §1961a; R.P. 1948, §63-367; 1950, p. 33.]

§63-373. [1950 Cum. Supp.] Transfers to Virginia Industrial for Women. — Whenever, in the opinion of the superintendent of the Janie Porter Barrett School for Girls or of the Virginia Home and Industrial School for Girls and of the Department, a ward of the school is dangerous to the morals of the school because of her behavior and advanced age, she may be transferred to the State Industrial Farm for Women, and when so transferred a per diem allowance of sixty cents [60c] shall be allowed out of the criminal fund. [1942, p. 24; Michie Code 1942, §5058(16); R.P. 1948, §63-373; 1950, p. 634.]

63-368. Virginia Industrial School for Boys [White]. — [Provision for Industrial School for "the care and training of incorrigible or delinquent white boys."] [1918, p. 532; 1920, p. 64; R.P. §63-368.]

63-366. Virginia Home and Industrial School for Girls [White]. — [Provision for Industrial School for delinquent "white females" from 12 to 30 years of age.] [1920, p. 68; 1922, pp. 290, 344; 1924, pp. 183, 228; Michie Code 1942, §§1961b, 1961c; R.P. 1948, §63-366.]

Colleges and Universities

§23-47. [William and Mary College] Normal course to be maintained. — The College shall maintain in connection with its collegiate course, which shall be continued, a system of normal instruction and training for the purpose of educating and training white teachers for the public free schools of the State. [1887, p. 512; 1906, p. 94; Code 1919, §934; Michie Code 1942, §934.]

§23-54. State teachers colleges for white women continued. — The State teachers colleges for the training and education of white female teachers for public schools established at Farmville and at Harrisonburg, shall be continued as provided by law, and under the supervision and management and government of the State Board of Education as provided for in this chapter. [1902-3-4, pp. 411, 840; 1908, p. 427; 1910, p. 176; Code 1919, §939; 1924, p. 14; 1944, p. 345; Michie Code 1942, §939.]

§23-147. State Teachers College at Radford consolidated with Virginia Polytechnic Institute. [Limited to education of white women.] [1944, c. 240, p. 341; Michie Supp., 1948, §925a.]

Virginia State College

§23-165. Name of School; curriculum. — The school for Negro students near Petersburg formerly known as the Virginia Normal and Industrial Institute, shall hereafter be known as the Virginia State College. The curriculum of the College shall embrace such branches of learning as relate to teacher training, agriculture and the mechanic arts without excluding other scientific and classical studies. [Code 1887, §1613; 1887, p. 415; 1889-90, p. 151; 1893-94, p. 87; 1901-2, p. 397; 1902-3-4, p. 548; 1930, p. 768; 1946, p. 74; Code 1919, §947; Michie Code 1942, §947.]

[Note: The 1946 amendment rewrote this section and changed the title of the chapter from "Virginia State College for Negroes" to its present designation.]

§23-166. Body corporate under control of State Board of Education; board of visitors abolished. — The institution shall continue to be a body corporate under the name and style of the "Virginia State College. It shall be under the management, supervision and control of the State Board of Education; and the board of visitors of the institution is hereby abolished. [Code 1919, §948; 1930, p. 768; Michie Code 1942, §948; 1946, p. 74.]

[The 1946 amendment substituted the words "Virginia State College" for "Virginia State College for Negroes."]

§23-167. Powers and duties of the State Board of Education. — The powers and duties of the State board of education shall be to direct and do all things not inconsistent with the laws of this State which to the Board shall seem best adapted to accomplish the legitimate objects of the College; to designate depositories, provide for the proper bonding of financial officers and depositories, and provide for the disbursing of the funds of the College consistent with the laws of the State; to grant to such as excel in any field of knowledge or complete a prescribed course of study, such certificates, diplomas or degrees as shall be deemed expedient and proper. All of which several functions they shall be free to exercise rules, by-laws, resolutions, orders, instructions, or otherwise. [Code 1919, §951; 1930, p. 768; Michie Code 1942, §951.]

§23-169. Notice of vacancies in case of State students; filling vacancies. — Due notice shall be given by the president of the College to the division superintendents of schools of all vacancies existing, in the College in the case of State students; whereupon the division superintendents of schools may proceed to nominate person to fill the vacancies and officially notify the president of the College of the nominations. If, in due time after such notice, no nomination be made, the vacancy indicated may be filled by the president of the College at the discretion of the State Board of Education from the State at large. [Code 1919, §954; 1930, p. 769; Michie Code 1942, §954; 1946, p. 74.]

§23-170. Bequests and gifts; governmental aid. — Any person may deposit in the treasury of the State, or bequeath money, stocks, or bonds to be deposited, or grant, devise, or bequeath property, real or personal, to be sold, and the proceeds so deposited, which shall be invested as the donor may indicate, or the State Board of Education may see proper, for the benefit of the College, and in such case the interest or dividends accruing on such deposits shall be placed to the credit of the College to be used for the purpose hereof, unless some particular appropriation shall have been designated by the donor or testator; in which case such particular use or appropriation shall be respected.

The College shall receive the governmental aid designated in §§23-136 and 23-137. [Code 1919, §957; 1930, p. 769; Michie Code 1942, §957.]

[Note: §23-136 provides that two-thirds of the interest from a fund set up by the State through sale of lands donated to Virginia by Act of Congress, July 2, 1862, shall be paid to Virginia Polytechnic Institute (for white students) and one-third of such interest shall be paid to the Virginia State College (for Negro students). §23-137 provides that of the funds allotted to Virginia under Act of Congress, approved August 30, 1890, two-thirds shall go to the treasurer of Virginia Polytechnic Institute and one-third shall go to the treasurer of Virginia State College.]

§23-171. Additional pay to professors. — The Superintendent of Public Instruction may, in his discretion, supplement the salary of any professor or teacher for teaching during the summer normal from any funds at his disposal for the purpose of conducting normal institutes. [Code 1887, §1628; Code 1919, §966; Michie Code 1942, §966.]

§23-172. Use of funds by Superintendent of Public Instruction.—Nothing in this chapter shall be construed as limiting or affecting the authority of the Superintendent of Public Instruction to use any funds at his disposal, other than State funds, to promote and encourage a system of normal instruction among colored teachers in other parts of the State. [Code 1887, §1633; Code 1919, §967; Michie Code 1942, §967.]

§23-168. Division of College in City of Norfolk. — [Provision for a division of Virginia State College to be located at Norfolk. See amendment, Acts 1950, c. 108, p. 128.] [1946, p. 74; Michie Suppl. 1946, §969b.]

§23-174. Control by General Assembly. — The College, and all its property and funds, shall, at all times and in all things, be under the control of the General Assembly. [Code 1887, §1636; Code 1919, §969; 1930, p. 769; Michie Code 1942, §969.]

Medical and Dental Education

§23-173. Contributing to cost of education of medical and dental students. — In order to provide for the education in medicine and dentistry of properly qualified Negroes of Virginia, the State Board of Education, as the governing board of the Virginia State College, is authorized to contribute to the cost of the education of medical students and dental students at Meharry Medical College, located at Nashville, Tennessee, the amount of the contribution to be five hundred [$500.00] dollars a year for each medical student, and four hundred [$400.00] dollars a year for each dental student. These contributions shall be made in such manner and for such students as determined by the Board and out of funds appropriated to the Board for equalization of higher education opportunities. [1946, p. 74: Michie Suppl. 1946, §969a.]

> [Note: The act inserting this section repealed Acts 1944, C. 72. of similar import. Also note this act is a forerunner of the Regional Compact plan of education.]

Aid to Persons Denied Admission

§23-10. Amount payable to persons denied admission. — Whenever any bona fide resident and citizen of this State, regardless of race, possessing the qualifications of health, character, ability and preparatory education customarily required for admission to any Virginia State institution of higher learning and education, or any branch or department thereof, upon application, is denied admission thereto, for any reason, by the board which constitutes the governing authority of such institution, or whenever any Negro, who is a bona fide resident and citizen of this State and possesses the qualifications of health, character, ability and preparatory education customarily required for admission to any such State institution of higher learning and education, or any branch or department thereof, applies to the Virginia State college for admission and enrollment in any graduate or professional course or course of study not offered in such College but offered at one or more of the other State institutions of higher learning and education, if it appear to the satisfaction of the State Board of Education that such resident and citizen, regardless of race, or such Negro, is unable to obtain from some other State institution of higher learning and education, other than the one in which he seeks or sought admission, educational facilities equal to those applied for, and that such equal educational facilities can be provided and furnished to the applicant by a college, university or institution, not operated as an agency or institution of the State, whether such other facilities are located in Virginia or elsewhere in the United States, the State Board of Education is hereby authorized, out of the funds appropriated for such purpose, to pay to such person, or the institution attended by him and approved by the Board, as and when needed, an amount equal to the amount, if any, by which the cost to such person to attend such college, university or institution, not operated as an agency or institution of the State exceeds the amount it would have cost such person to attend the State institution of higher education and learning to which admission was denied or in which the graduate or professional course or course of study desired is offered. In determining the comparative costs of attending the said respective institutions the Board shall take into consideration tuition charges, living expenses and costs of transportation. [1936, p. 561; 1938, p. 191; 1940, p. 60; Michie Code 1942, §10031(b).]

26-11. Payment in lieu of sum authorized by preceding section. — The State Board of Education may, in lieu of paying to any Negro or any institution attended by him the sum authorized to be paid such person pursuant to the provisions of the preceding section, pay to such Negro or the institution attended by him a sum equal to the amount appropriated, for the then current year, by the State per student to the State institution of higher learning and education to which such admission was sought and denied or in which the graduate or professional course or course of study desired is offered. To determine the amount appropriated per student by the State, there shall be deducted from the total State appropriation to such State institution all fees, rents, and charges collected by the institution, and all gifts, grants and other sums originally received by the institution from sources other than the State, included in such total appropriation; the sum then remaining shall be divided by the total number of students attending the State institution. [1940, p. 61; Michie Code 1942, §10031(b).]

§23-12. Certificate of denial of admission, etc. — Whenever any person has been denied admission to any Virginia State institution of higher learning and education, or any branch or department thereof, or whenever any Negro is unable to secure from the Virginia State College any graduate or professional course or course of study, as specified in section 23-10, if such person possesses the qualifications, health, character, ability and preparatory education customarily required for admission thereto, the president of such institution, or a dean or department head designated by the president for that purpose, shall issue a certificate addressed to the State Board of Education certifying the fact of the applicant's denial of admission and his qualification for admission and forward same to the Board.

The certificate shall be prima facie evidence of the facts therein stated. Nothing in the certificate contained, however, shall prevent the State Board of Education from making such further investigation of any application for money to provide equal educational facilities as the Board may deem proper. [1938, p. 192; 1940, p. 61; Michie Code 1942, §10031(b).]

§23-13. Refusal of payment for failure to meet minimum requirements. — The State Board of Education is authorized to refuse or withhold the payment of any moneys under the provisions of this chapter to or from any person, or to or from any institution attended by any person, who fails or refuses to meet such minimum requirements as shall be prescribed by the Board with reference to the studies, course or course of study pursued or taken by such person. [1940, p. 62; Michie Code 1942, §10031(b).]

Medical and Nursing Scholarships

§23-35.1. [1950 Cum. Supp.] Medical scholarships authorized. — The governing boards of the Medical College of Virginia and of the University of Virginia, and of Virginia State College [for Negroes] are authorized to establish, as to the former two, twenty [20] annual medical scholarships, and as to the last, ten [10] annual medical scholarships, to be awarded to Virginia students attending Meharry Medical College, Nashville, Tennessee, each of the value of one thousand [$1,000.00] dollars to be awarded and paid subject to the conditions and restrictions set out in the following sections. [1950, p. 1289.]

[Note: See also §§23-35.2 to 23-35.8, (1950 Cum. Supp.). Note also that §23-36(8) which authorized the governing board of Virginia State College to establish 5 annual medical scholarships to be awarded to Virginia students attending Meharry Medical College, Nashville, Tenn. as provided by §23-173, was repealed by Acts 1950, p. 1292.]

§23-35.9. [1950 Cum. Supp.] Nursing scholarships authorized. — There are established six [6] annual scholarships for each congressional district of the value of one hundred fifty [$150.00] dollars. These awards shall be made by the State Board of Health and the recipients of such scholarships shall be allowed to attend any accredited nursing school in this state operated by any nonprofit institution. If any of the above created scholarships for any congressional district are not awarded for any year they shall be awarded from the State at large.

There are established twenty [20] annual nursing scholarships for Negroes to be awarded from the State at large of the value of one hundred fifty [$150.00] dollars. These awards shall be made by the State Board of Health and the recipients of such scholarships shall be allowed to attend any accredited Negro nursing school in this State. [1950, p. 1291.]

[Note: See also §§23-35.10 to 23-35.13. Note also that §23.36.1 authorized the governing board of the Medical College of Virginia to establish 20 annual nursing scholarships, 5 of which were to be made available to members of the Negro race, for residents of Virginia to be awarded on a competitive basis. This act was repealed and replaced by Acts 1950, p. 1292.]

Regional Compact

Acts 1950, p. 1648.

SENATE JOINT RESOLUTION NO. 22

Giving legislative approval to that certain Compact entered into by the Commonwealth of Virginia and other Southern States by and through their respective Governors on February 8, 1948, as amended, relative to the development and maintenance of regional educational services and schools in the Southern States in the professional, technological, scientific, literary and other fields, so as to provide greater educational advantages and facilities for the citizens in the several States who reside in such region, to declare that, if and when the Constitution of Virginia is so amended as to remove any constitutional limitations now existing which prohibit full participation by the Commonwealth of Virginia in the program of development and maintenance of regional educational services and schools for such region as provided in said Compact, the Commonwealth of Virginia shall be a party to said Compact, as amended, and the agreements, covenants and obligations therein contained shall be binding upon the Commonwealth of Virginia.

Agreed to by Senate, March 2, 1950

Agreed to by House, March 10, 1950

Whereas, on the 8th day of February, Nineteen Hundred and Forty-eight, the Commonwealth of Virginia and the States of Florida, Maryland, Georgia, Louisiana, Alabama, Mississippi, Tennessee, Arkansas, North Carolina, South Carolina, Texas, Oklahoma and West Virginia, through and by their respective governors, entered into a written Compact relative to the development and maintenance of regional educational services and schools in the Southern States in the professional, technological, scientific, literary, and other fields, so as to provide greater educational advantages and facilities for the citizens of the several States who reside within such region; and

Whereas, the said Compact has been amended in certain respects, a copy of which Compact as amended is as follows:

THE REGIONAL COMPACT

(As amended)

Whereas, the States who are parties hereto have during the past several years conducted careful investigation looking toward the establishment and maintenance of jointly owned and operated regional educational institutions in the Southern States in the professional, technological, scientific, literary and other fields, so as to provide greater educational advantages and facilities for the citizens of the several States who reside within such region; and

Whereas, Meharry Medical College of Nashville, Tennessee has proposed that its lands, buildings, equipment, and the net income from its endowment be turned over to the Southern States, or to an agency acting in their behalf, to be operated as a regional institution for medical, dental and nursing education upon terms and conditions to be hereafter agreed upon between the Southern States and Meharry Medical College, which proposal, because of the present financial condition of the institution, has been approved by the said States who are parties hereto; and

Whereas, the said States desire to enter into a compact with each other providing for the planning and establishment of regional educational facilities;

Now, therefore, in consideration of the mutual agreements, covenants and obligations assumed by the respective States who are parties hereto (hereinafter referred to as "States"), the said several States do hereby form a geographical district or region consisting of the areas lying within the boundaries of the contracting States which, for the purposes of this compact, shall constitute an area for regional education supported by public funds derived from taxation by the constituent States and derived from other sources for the establishment, acquisition, operation and maintenance of regional educational schools and institutions for the benefit of citizens of the respective States residing within the region so established as may be determined from time to time in accordance with the terms and provisions of this compact.

The States do further hereby establish and create a joint agency which shall be known as the Board of Control for Southern Regional Education (hereinafter referred to as the "Board"), the members of which Board shall consist of the Governor of each State, *ex officio,* and three additional citizens of each State to be appointed by the Governor thereof, at least one of whom shall be selected from the field of education. The Governor shall continue as a member of the Board during his tenure of office as Governor of the State, but the members of the Board appointed by the Governor shall hold office for a period of four years except that in the original appointments one Board member so appointed by the Governor shall be designated at the time of his appointment to serve an initial term of two years, one Board member to serve an initial term of three years, and the remaining Board member to serve the full term of four years, but thereafter the successor of each appointed Board member shall serve the full term of four years. Vacancies on the Board caused by death, resignation, refusal or inability to serve, shall be filled by appointment by the Governor for the unexpired portion of the term. The officers of the Board shall be a Chairman, a Vice-Chairman, a Secretary, a Treasurer, and such additional officers as may be created by the Board from time to time. The Board shall meet annually and officers shall be elected to hold office until the next annual meeting. The Board shall have the right to formulate and establish by-laws not inconsistent with the provisions of this compact to govern its own actions in the performance of the duties delegated to it including the right to create and appoint an Executive Committee and a Finance Committee with such powers and authority as the Board may delegate to them from time to time. The Board may, within its discretion, elect as its Chairman a person who is not a member of the Board, provided such person resides within a signatory State, and upon such election such person shall become a member of the Board with all the rights and privileges of such membership.

It shall be the duty of the Board to submit plans and recommendations to the States from time to time for their approval and adoption by appropriate legislative action for the development, establishment, acquisition, operation and maintenance of educational schools and institutions within the geographical limits of the regional area of the States, of such character and type and for such educational purposes, professional, technological, scientific, literary, or otherwise, as they may deem and determine to be proper, necessary or advisable. Title to all such educational institutions when so established by appropriate legislative actions of the States and to all properties and facilities used in connection therewith shall be vested in said Board as the agency of and for the use and benefit of the said States and the citizens thereof, and all such educational institutions shall be operated, maintained and financed in the manner herein set out, subject to any provisions or limitations which may be contained in the legislative acts of the States authorizing the creation, establishment and operation of such educational institutions.

In addition to the power and authority heretofore granted, the Board shall have the power to enter into such agreements or arrangements with any of the States and with educational institutions or agencies, as may be required in the judgment of the Board, to provide adequate services and facilities for the graduate, professional, and technical education for the benefit of the citizens of the respective States residing within the region, and such additional and general power and authority as may be vested in the Board from time to time by legislative enactment of the said States.

Any two or more States who are parties of this compact shall have the right to enter into supplemental agreements providing for the establishment, financing and operation of regional educational institutions for the benefit of citizens residing within an area which constitutes a portion of the general region herein created, such institutions to be financed exclusively by such States and to be controlled exclusively by the members of the Board representing such States provided such agreement is submitted to and approved by the Board prior to the establishment of such institutions.

Each State agrees that, when authorized by the legislature, it will from time to time make available and pay over to said Board such funds as may be required for the establishment, acquisition, operation and maintenance of such regional educational institutions as may be authorized by the States under the terms of this compact, the contribution of each State at all times to be in the proportion that its population bears to the total combined population of the States who are parties hereto as shown from time to time by the most recent official published report of the Bureau of the Census of the United States of America; or upon such other basis as may be agreed upon.

This compact shall not take effect or be binding upon any State unless and until it shall be approved by proper legislative action of as many as six or more of the States whose governors have subscribed hereto within a period of eighteen months from the date hereof. When and if six or more States shall have given legislative approval to this compact within said eighteen months period, it shall be and become binding upon such six or more States 60 days after the date of legislative approval by the sixth State and the governors of such six or more States shall forthwith name the members of the Board from their States as hereinabove set out, and the Board shall then meet on call of the governor of any State approving this compact, at which time the Board shall elect officers, adopt by-laws, appoint committees and otherwise fully organize. Other States whose names are subscribed hereto shall thereafter become parties hereto upon approval of this compact by legislative action within two years from the date hereof, upon such conditions as may be agreed upon at the time. Provided, however, that with respect to any State whose constitution may require amendment in order to permit legislative approval of the compact, such State or States shall become parties hereto upon approval of this compact by legislative action within seven years from the date hereof, upon such conditions as may be agreed upon at the time.

After becoming effective this compact shall thereafter continue without limitation of time; provided however, that it may be terminated at any time by unanimous action of the States and provided further that any State may withdraw from this compact if such withdrawal is approved by its legislature, such withdrawal to become effective two years after written notice thereof to the Board accompanied by a certified copy of the requisite legislative action, but such withdrawal shall not relieve the withdrawing State from its obligations hereunder accruing up to the effective date of such withdrawal. Any State so withdrawing shall *ipso facto* cease to have any claim to or ownership of any of the property held or vested in the Board or to any of the funds of the Board held under the terms of this compact.

If any State shall at any time become in default in the performance of any of its obligations assumed herein or with respect to any obligation imposed upon said State as authorized by and in compliance with the terms and provisions of this compact, all rights, privileges and benefits of such defaulting State, its members on the Board and its citizens shall *ipso facto be* and become suspended from and after the date of such default. Unless such default shall be remedied and made good within a period of one year immediately following the date of such default this compact may be terminated with respect to such defaulting State by an affirmative vote of three-fourths of the members of the Board (exclusive of the members representing the State in default), from and after which time such State shall cease to be a party to this compact and shall have no further claim to or ownership of any of the property held by or vested in the Board or to any of the funds of the Board held under the terms of this compact, but such termination shall in no manner release such defaulting State from any accrued obligation or otherwise affect this compact or the rights, duties, privileges or obligations of the remaining States thereunder.

In witness whereof this compact has been approved and signed by governors of the several States, subject to the approval of their respective legislatures in the manner hereinabove set out, as of the 8th day of February, 1948.

STATE OF FLORIDA
By Millard F. Caldwell, Governor

STATE OF ARKANSAS
By Ben Laney, Governor

STATE OF MARYLAND
By Wm. Preston Lane, Jr., Governor

COMMONWEALTH OF VIRGINIA
By Wm. M. Tuck, Governor

STATE OF GEORGIA
By M. E. Thompson, Governor

STATE OF NORTH CAROLINA
By R. Gregg Cherry, Governor

STATE OF LOUISIANA
By J. H. Davis, Governor

STATE OF SOUTH CAROLINA
By J. Strom Thurmond, Governor

STATE OF ALABAMA
By James E. Folsom, Governor

STATE OF TEXAS
By Beauford H. Jester, Governor

STATE OF MISSISSIPPI
By F. L. Wright, Governor

STATE OF OKLAHOMA
By Roy J. Turner, Governor

STATE OF TENNESSEE
By Jim McCord, Governor

STATE OF WEST VIRGINIA
By Clarence W. Meadows, Governor

Now, therefore, be it resolved by the Senate, the House of Delegates concurring,

1. That the said Compact be and the same is hereby approved and that, if and when the Constitution of Virginia is so amended as to remove any constitutional limitations now existing which prohibit full participation by the Commonwealth of Virginia in the program of development and maintenance of regional educational services and schools by the participating Southern States as provided in said Compact, the Commonwealth of Virginia shall be a party to said Compact, as amended, and the agreements, covenants and obligations therein contained shall be binding upon the Commonwealth of Virginia.

2. That upon the approval of the Compact by the requisite number of States the Governor sign an engrossed copy of the Compact and sufficient copies be provided so that every State approving the Compact shall have an engrossed copy.

3. This Resolution shall take effect upon its approval by the Governor.

[Note: See Note on Regional Compact—Education, Appendix 6.]

Fraternal Organizations

§38-281. Prohibition of fraternal beneficiary associations with both white and colored members.—Fraternal beneficiary associations, companies, orders and societies which admit both white and colored persons to membership, and fraternal beneficiary associations, companies, orders and societies which have white officers and colored members or colored officers and white members, shall not be licensed to do business in this State, and shall not maintain an office in this State or receive dues or make disbursements or carry on any other business pertaining thereto from or at any point within this State. Any person acting for or in behalf of such organization in violation of this section or aiding or advising or assisting in its violation shall be guilty of a misdemeanor, and on conviction thereof, shall be fined not less than five hundred [$500.00] nor more than five thousand [$5000.00] dollars, or imprisoned in jail for not less than six [6] months nor more than twelve months, or both such fine and imprisonment. [1926, p. 853; Michie Code 1942, §4302a.]

Hospitals

§37-1. State hospitals for insane continued. — [Provision for the continued maintenance under the management of the State Hospital Board of the following State hospitals: Eastern State Hospital at Williamsburg, Va., Western State Hospital at Staunton, Va., Southwestern State Hospital at Marion, Va., and Central State Hospital [for Negroes] at Petersburg, Va. [Code 1887, §1660; 1893-94, p. 397; 1899-1900, p. 1036; Code 1919, §§1004, 1005, 1920, p. 376; 1940, p. 163; Michie Code 1942, §§1004, 1005; 1944, p. 290.]

§37-4. Lynchburg State Colony continued. — [Provision for care of (white) mentally deficient (feeble-minded) and epileptic patients at the Lynchburg State Colony located at Madison Heights, Amherst County.] [Code 1887, §1660; 1906, p. 36; 1910, p. 491; Code 1919, §1004; 1920, p. 376; Michie Code 1942, §1004; 1944, p. 290.]

[Note: See also §§37-186, 37-189 (1950 Cum. Supp.).]

§37-5. Petersburg State Colony continued. — [Provision for the care of colored mentally deficient (feeble-minded) patients at the Petersburg State Colony, located partly in Prince George and partly in Dinwiddie Counties.] [Code 1887, §1600; 1906, p. 36; 1910, p. 491; 1920, p. 376; Michie Code 1942, §1004; 1944, p. 290.]

[Note: See also §37-191 and §§37-183, 37-192 (1950 Cum. Supp.).]

§37-7. [1950 Cum. Supp.] Transfer of patients from one institution to another. — A patient committed to any such hospitals or colonies, except one committed by court order to one of the departments for the criminal mentally-ill, may be transferred by order of the Commissioner [of Mental Hygiene and Hospitals] to any other of the hospitals or colonies and when so transferred is hereby declared to be a lawfully committed patient of the hospital or colony to which he is transferred, provided no white person shall be transferred to an institution used exclusively for colored persons or vice versa. [Code 1887, §1600; 1906, p. 36; 1910, p. 491; Code 1919, §1004; 1920, p. 376; Michie Code 1942, §1004; 1944, p. 290; 1950, p. 900.]

§37-18. [De Jarnette State Sanatorium.] Purposes of Sanatorium. — ... The purpose of the DeJarnette State Sanitorium [a special unit of the Western State Hospital, for voluntary pay patients] shall be to furnish to white residents of Virginia, affected with nervous diseases, mental diseases, alcohol or drug addiction, modern sanitorium care and treatment at the approximate cost and maintenance and operation of the Sanitorium. [1946, p. 194; Michie Supp. 1946, §1005a.]

§37-19. [De Jarnette State Sanatorium.] Persons admitted as patients. — Any white person applying for admission to the DeJarnette State Sanitorium may be received therein as a patient . . . [1946, p. 194; Michie Supp., 1946; §1005a.]

§37-182. [1950 Cum. Supp.] **Where epileptics committed; temporary detentions; white and colored persons.**—Whenever an epileptic person is adjudged to be such, as defined in §37-178, by any commission held for that purpose, if he be a white person he shall be committed to the Lynchburg State Colony at Madison Heights, Amherst County, and if he be a colored person he shall be committed to a department for epileptics in the Central State Hospital at Petersburg. Nothing in this title shall be construed to forbid the necessary and temporary detention of any epileptic or mentally-deficient white person in any of the hospitals nor of any mentally-ill person in the colony until he can be transferred to the proper hospital or colony. Nothing in this title shall be construed to authorize or permit a white person to be sent to or received at the Central State Hospital or a colored person to be sent to or received in any other hospital or colony than said Central State Hospital. [Code 1919, §1067; 1920, p. 382; Michie Code 1942, §1067; 1950, p. 726.]

§37-185. [1950 Cum. Supp.] **Provisions apply to colored and white persons alike.** — All the provisions of this chapter relating to the commitment, care, training and treatment of mentally-deficient white persons shall be applicable to the commitment, care, training and treatment of mentally-deficient colored persons when legally committed to the Petersburg State Colony. [Code 1919, §1093; Michie Code 1942, §1093; 1950, p. 926.]

Indians

§4968. [Michie Code 1942] **Proceedings against Indians.** — In a criminal case against an Indian, or a person of Indian descent, the proceeding shall be as against a white person. [Code 1887, §4090; Michie Code 1942, §4968.] [Omitted from Code 1950.]

Legitimation of Slave Marriages: Inheritance

§20-56. **Certain colored persons not married to be deemed husband and wife; children legitimated.** — Where colored persons prior to the twenty-seventh day of February, eighteen hundred and sixty-six, agreed to occupy the relation to each other of husband and wife, and were cohabiting together as such at that date, whether the rites of marriage had been celebrated between them or not, they shall be deemed husband and wife, and be entitled to the rights and privileges, and subject to the duties and obligations of that relation in like manner, as if they had lawfully married; and all their children shall be deemed legitimate, whether born before or after said date. And where the parties had ceased to cohabit before the twenty-seventh day of February, eighteen hundred and sixty-six, in consequence of the death of the woman, or from any other cause, all the children of the woman, recognized by the man to be his, shall be deemed legitimate. [Code 1887, §2227; Code 1919, §5091; Michie Code 1942, §5091.]

§64-5. **When bastards take; when children of former slaves take.** — Bastards shall be capable of inheriting and transmitting inheritance on the part of their mother as if lawfully begotten. And the children of parents, one or both of whom were slaves at and during the period of cohabitation, and who were recognized by the father as his children, and whose mother was recognized by such father as his wife, and was cohabited with as such, and their descendants, shall be as capable of inheriting any estate whereof such father may have died seized or possessed, or to which he was entitled, as though such children had been born in lawful wedlock. [Code 1887, §2552; 1902-3-4, p. 664; Code 1919, §5268; Michie Code 1942, §5268.]

Miscegenation

§20-50. Certificates of racial composition. — The State Registrar of Vital Statistics may prepare a form whereon the racial composition of any individual, as Caucasian, Negro, Mongolian, American Indian, Asiatic Indian, Malay, or any mixture thereof, or any other non-Caucasic strains, and if there be any mixture, then the racial composition of the parents and other ancestors, in so far as ascertainable, so as to show in what generation such mixture occurred, may be certified by such individual, which form shall be known as a registration certificate. The State Registrar of Vital Statistics may supply to each local registrar a sufficient number of such forms for the purpose of this chapter; each local registrar may, personally or by deputy, as soon as possible after receiving the forms, have made thereon in duplicate a certificate of the racial composition, as aforesaid, of each person resident in his district, who so desires, born before June fourteenth, nineteen hundred twelve [June 14, 1912], which certificate shall be made over the signature of such person, or in the case of children under fourteen [14] years of age, over the signature of a parent, guardian, or other person standing in loco parentis. One of such certificates for each person thus registering in every district shall be forwarded to the State Registrar of Vital Statistics for his files; and the other shall be kept on file by the local registrar.

Every local registrar may, as soon as practicable, have such registration certificate made by or for each person in his district who so desires, born before June fourteenth, nineteen hundred twelve [June 14, 1912], for whom he has not on file a registration certificate, or a birth certificate. [1924, p. 534; Michie Code 1942, §5099a.]

§20-51. False registration or certificate. — It shall be a felony for any person wilfully or knowingly to make a registration certificate false as to color or race. The wilful making of a false registration or birth certificate shall be punished by confinement in the penitentiary for one [1] year. [1924, p. 534; Michie Code 1942, §5099a.]

§20-52. Fees for certificate. — For each registration certificate properly made and returned to the State Registrar of Vital Statistics, the local registrar returning the same shall be entitled to a fee of twenty-five cents, to be paid by the registrant. Application for registration and for transcript may be made direct to the State Registrar, who may retain the fee for expenses of his office. [1924, p. 534; Michie Code 1942, §5099a.

§20-53. License not to issue until clerk assured statements are correct. —
No marriage license shall be granted until the clerk or deputy clerk has reasonable assurance that the statements as to color of both man and woman are correct.

If there is reasonable cause to disbelieve that applicants are of pure white race, when that fact is stated, the clerk or deputy culerk shall withhold the granting of the license until satisfactory proof is produced that both applicants are "white persons" as provided for in this chapter.

The clerk shall use the same care to assure himself that both applicants are colored, when that fact is claimed. [1924, p. 634; Michie Code 1942, §5099a.]

§20-54. Intermarriage prohibited; meaning of "white person". — It shall hereafter be unlawful for any white person in this State to marry any save a white person, or a person with no other admixture of blood than white and American Indian. *For the purpose of this act, the term "white person" shall apply only to the person who has no trace whatsoever of any blood other than Caucasian; but persons who have one-sixteenth or less of the blood of the American Indian and have no other non-Caucasic blood shall be deemed to be white persons.* All laws heretofore passed and now in effect regarding the inter-marriage of white and colored persons shall apply to marriages prohibited by this chapter. [1924, p. 535; Michie Code 1942, §5099a.] (italics supplied)

§20-55. Fees received by Bureau of Vital Statistics. — For carrying out the purposes of this chapter and to provide the necessary clerical assistance, postage and other expenses of the State Registrar of Vital Statistics, twenty per cent of the fees received by local registrars under this act shall be paid to the State Bureau of Vital Statistics, which may be expended by the said bureau for the purposes of this chapter. [1924, p. 535; Michie Code 1942, §5099a.]

§50-57. Marriages void without decree. — All marriages between a white person and a colored person shall be absolutely void, without any decree of divorce or other legal process. [Code 1887, §2252; Code 1919, §5087; Michie Code 1942, §5087.]

§20-58. Leaving State to evade law. — If any white person and colored person, shall go out of this State for the purpose of being married, and with the intention of returning, and be married out of it, and afterwards return to and reside in it, cohabiting as man and wife, they shall be punished as provided in §20-59, and the marriage shall be governed by the same law as if it had been solemnized in this State. The fact of their habitation here as man and wife shall be evidence of their marriage. [Code 1887, §3783; Code 1919, §§4540, 5089; Michie Code 1942, §§4540, 5089.]

§20-59. Punishment for marriage. — If any white person intermarry with a colored person, or any colored person intermarry with a white person, he shall be guilty of a felony and shall be punished by confinement in the penitentiary for not less than one [1] nor more than five [5] years. [Code 1887, §3788; Code 1919, §4546; 1932, p. 68; Michie Code 1942, §4546.]

§20-60. Punishment for performing ceremony. — If any person perform the ceremony of marriage between a white person and a colored person, he shall forfeit two hundred [$200.00] dollars, of which the informer shall have one-half. [Code 1887, §3789; Code 1919, §4547; Michie Code 1942, §4547.]

Poll Tax Lists

[See Const. §38 above.]

§24-120. Treasurer to file with clerk list of persons who have paid. — The treasurer of each county and city shall, at least five months before the second Tuesday in June in each year in which a regular June election is to be held in such county or city, and at least five months before each regular election in November, file with the clerk of the circuit court of his county or the corporation court of his city a list of all persons in his county, or city, who have paid not later than six months prior to each of said dates the State poll taxes required by the Constitution of this State during three years next preceding that in which such election is to be held, *which list shall state the white and colored persons separately;* and shall be verified by the oath of the treasurer. [1904, p. 131; 1908, p. 162; Code 1919, §109 1924, p. 57; 1926, p. 525; 1928, pp. 713, 714; 1934, p. 73; Michie Code 1942, §109.] [emphasis added.]

Prisons

§53-42. Separation of the races and of youthful from old criminals. — The races shall be kept separate, and youthful convicts from old and hardened criminals in sleeping quarters, as far as possible. [1918, p. 476; Michie Code 1942, §5048n; R.P. 1948, §53-42.

Public Halls and Public Places

§18-327. Duty to separate races at public assemblage. — Every person, firm, institution, or corporation operating, maintaining, keeping, conducting, sponsoring or permitting, any public hall, theatre, opera house, motion picture show or any place of public entertainment or public assemblage which is attended by both white and colored persons, shall separate the white race and the colored race and shall set apart and designate in each public hall, theatre, opera house, motion picture show or place of public entertainment or public assemblage certain seats therein to be occupied by white persons and a portion thereof, or certain seats therein, to be occupied by colored persons, and any such person, firm, institution or corporation that shall fail, refuse or neglect to comply with the provisions of this section shall be guilty of a misdemeanor and upon conviction thereof shall be fined not less than one hundred [$100.00] dollars nor more than five hundred [$500.00] dollars for each offense. [1926, p. 945; Michie Code 1942, §1796a.]

[Note: See Nash v. Terminal Air Services (1949), 85 F. Supp. 545. See also Civil Aeronautics Administration regulation, *post* Appendix 3, p. 608.]

§18-328. Failure to take space assigned in pursuance of preceding section. —Any person who fails, while in any public hall, theatre, opera house, motion picture show or any place of public entertainment or public assemblage, to take and occupy the seat or other space assigned to them in pursuance of the provisions of the preceding section by the manager, usher, or other person in charge of such public hall, theatre, opera house, motion picture show or place of public entertainment or public assemblage or whose duty is to take up tickets or collect the admission from the guests therein, or who shall fail to obey the request of such manager, usher or other person, as aforesaid, to change his seats from time to time as occasion requires, in order that the preceding section may be complied with, shall be deemed guilty of a misdemeanor and upon conviction thereof shall be fined not less than ten [$10.00] dollars nor more than twenty-five [$25.00] dollars for each offense. Furthermore such person may be ejected from such public hall, theatre, opera house, motion picture show or other place of public entertainment or public assemblage, by any manager, usher or ticket taker, or other person in charge of such public hall, theatre, opera house, motion picture show or place of public entertainment or public assemblage, or by a police officer or any other conservator of the peace, and if such person ejected shall have paid admission into such public hall, theatre, opera house, motion picture show or other place of public entertainment or public assemblage, he shall not be entitled to a return of any part of the same. [1926, p. 946; Michie Code 1942, §1796b.]

Segregation Districts

[Note: §§3043-3053, Michie Code 1942, (1912, p. 330, 1916, p. 60.) were omitted from the Code of Virginia 1950. These omitted sections authorized local councils of cities and towns to adopt segregation ordinances dividing such cities and towns into racial residential districts and making it unlawful for Negroes to reside in districts designated as white districts and vice versa. The compiler of the Code of Virginia, 1950, explains that certain sections have been omitted because they have been repealed by implication or have been declared unconstitutional. Although these sections apparently have not been expressly repealed, the United States Supreme Court and the Supreme Court of Appeals of Virginia have declared that such segregation ordinances are unconstitutional. See *Buchanan v. Warley*, 245 U.S. 60 (1917); *Harmon v. Tyler*, 273 U.S. 668 (1928); *Richmond v. Deans*, 281 U.S. 704 (1930); *Irvine v. City of Clifton Forge*, 124 Va. 781, 97 S.E. 310 (1918.).]

Tax Assessments and Land Books

§58-790. Assessment of values and notation whether owner white or colored. — [Provides that tax assessors shall examine all lands assessable by them, with improvements and buildings thereon, "and at the same time shall note whether the owner is white or colored."] [Code 1919, §2244; 1920, p. 34; 1924, p. 409; 1928, pp. 169, 1349; 1930, p. 871; 1932, p. 119; Tax Code, §244.]

§58-804. Form of land book; what matters to be shown separately. — . . . The land book on which levies are to be assessed on city lots shall be prepared so that lots owned by white persons and lots owned by colored persons will be assessed separately . . . [Code 1919, §2279; 1928, p. 171; 1930, p. 872; 1932, p. 415; Tax Code, §253.]

§58-880. Books to assess separately white and colored persons. — The personal property book shall be so arranged that personal property owned by white persons shall be assessed with taxes and levies in one part of the book and personal property owned by colored persons shall be assessed with taxes and levies in another part of the book. [Code 1919, §2300; 1928, p. 191; Tax Code §317.]

Transportation
Air Carriers

§56-196. Waiting rooms and other public facilities. — The [State Corporation] Commission may require the establishment of separate waiting rooms at stations or depots [of aircraft carriers] for the white and colored races by the operators of such stations or depots. [1944, p. 383; Michie Suppl. 1946, §3915(18).

Motor Buses

§56-324.1. Motor bus operators, etc., to be conservators of the peace. — The operators of motor buses operated as common carriers of persons, and station depot agents, shall be conservators of the peace, and they and each of them shall have the same power to make arrests that other conservators of the peace have, except that the agents shall have such power only at their respective places of business, and the said operators of motor buses and agents may cause any person so arrested by them to be detained, and delivered to the proper authorities for trial as soon as practicable. [1902-3-4, ch. 4, §10; 1904, p. 293; Code 1919, §3944; 1930, p. 788; Michie Code 1942, §3944.]

§56-325. Waiting rooms and other public facilities. — . . . The Commission [State Corporation Commission] may require the establishment by passenger motor carriers of separate waiting rooms at stations or depots for the white and colored races. [1936, p. 244; Michie Code 1942, §4097y(13e).]

§56-326. Segregation of white and colored passengers. — All motor vehicle carriers of passengers operating under the provisions of this chapter shall separate the white and colored passengers in their motor vehicles and set apart and designate in each motor vehicle a portion thereof or certain seats therein to be occupied by white passengers and a portion thereof or certain seats therein to [be] occupied by colored passengers.

Any such motor carrier that shall fail, refuse, or neglect to comply with the provisions of this section shall be guilty of a misdemeanor, and upon indict-ment and conviction, shall be fined not less than fifty [$50.00] dollars nor more than two hundred and fifty [$250.00] for each offense. [1930, p. 343; Michie Code 1942, §4097z.]

[Note: §§56-326 - 56-329 have replaced §§4097z to 4097dd, Michie Code 1942. These sections have been declared invalid as applied to inter state passengers moving interstate on the ground that the requirement of segre-gation of Negro and white interstate passengers is a burden upon inter-state commerce contrary to Art. I, §8, ch. 3, of the Constitution of the United States. *Morgan v. Virginia* (1946), 328 U.S. 373, 66 S. Ct. 1050, 90 L. Ed. 1317, 165 A.L.R. 574, reversing 184 Va. 24, 34 S.E. 2d. 491.

The United States Supreme Court has also invalidated the rule of inter-state railroads requiring segregation of Negro and white passengers in dining cars. *Henderson v. U.S.* (1950), 339 U.S. 816. For complete text of *Henderson* decision, see *post*, Appendix 7. Cf. *Day v. Atlantic Greyhound Corp.* (1948), 171 F. 2d. 59.

See recent Virginia Court decisions on the issue of segregation on public transportation facilities: *New v. Atlantic Greyhound Corp.* (1947), 186 Va. 726, 43 S.E. (2d) 872; *Davis v. Commonwealth* (1947), 182 Va. 760, 30 S.E. (2d) 700; *Lee v. Commonwealth* (1949), 189 Va. 890, 54 S.E. (2d) 888.]

§56-327. Discrimination prohibited. — The motor carriers subject to the pre-ceding section shall make no difference or discrimination in the quality or convenience of the accommodations provided for the two races under the provisions of the preceding section. [1930, p. 343; Michie Code 1942, §4097aa.]

§56-328. May increase or decrease space for either race; contiguous seats; changing seats; offenses. — The driver, operator or other person in charge of any motor vehicle of a motor carrier of passengers shall, at any time when it may be necessary and proper for the comfort and convenience of passengers so to do, change the designation so as to increase or decrease the amount of space or seats set apart for either race; but no contiguous seats on the same bench shall be occupied by white and colored passengers at the same time; and such driver, operator or other person in charge of the vehicle may require any passenger to change his or her seat as it may be necessary or proper. Any such driver, operator or other person in charge of such a vehicle who shall fail or refuse to carry out the provisions of this section shall be deemed guilty of a misdemeanor, and upon conviction thereof shall be fined not less than five [$5.00] dollars nor more than twenty-five [$25.00] dollars for each offense. [1930, p. 343; Michie Code 1942, §4097bb.]

§56-329. Violation by passengers; misdemeanor; ejection. — All persons who fail while on any motor vehicle carrier, to take or occupy the seat or seats or other space assigned to them by the driver, operator or other person in charge of such vehicle, or by the person whose duty it is to take up tickets or collect fares from passengers therein, or who fail to obey the directions of any such driver, operator or other person in charge, as aforesaid, to change their seats from time to time as occasion may require, pursuant to any lawful rule, regulation or custom in force by such lines as to assigning separate seats or other space to white and colored persons, respectively, having been first advised of the fact of such regulation and requested to conform thereto, shall be deemed guilty of a misdemeanor, and upon conviction thereof shall be fined not less than five [$5.00] dollars nor more than twenty-five [$25.00] dollars for each offense. Furthermore, such persons may be ejected from any such vehicle by any driver, operator or person in charge of such vehicle, or by any police officer or other conservator of the peace; and in case such persons ejected shall have paid their fares upon such vehicle, they shall not be entitled to the return of any part of the same. For the refusal of any such passenger to abide by the request of the person in charge of such vehicle as aforesaid and his consequent ejection from such vehicle, neither the driver, operator, person in charge, owner, manager nor bus company operating such vehicle shall be liable for damages in any court. [1930, p. 344; Michie Code 1942, §4097dd.]

§56-330. Operators are special policemen to enforce §§56-326, 56-328 and 56-329; other powers. — Each driver, operator or other person in charge of any motor vehicle of any motor carrier of passengers in the employment of any such motor carrier, while actively engaged in the operation of such vehicle, shall be a special policeman and have all the powers of conservators of the peace in the enforcement of provisions of §§56-326, 56-328 and 56-329, and in discharge of his duty as special policeman, in the enforcement of order upon such vehicle; and such driver, operator or person in charge of any such vehicle shall likewise have the powers of conservators of the peace and of special policemen while in pursuit of persons for disorder upon such vehicle or for violating the provisions of either of the two preceding sections, and until such persons as may be arrested by him shall have been placed in confinement or delivered over to custody of some other conservator of the peace or public officer; and, acting in good faith, he shall be for the purposes of this chapter, the judge of the race of each passenger whenever such passenger has failed to disclose his or her race. [1930, p. 344; Michie Code 1942, §4097cc.]

Electric Railways

§56-390. Electric railway companies to separate white and colored passengers. — All urban, interurban, and suburban electric railway companies or other persons operating trains, cars or coaches by electricity for the carriage of passengers, shall separate the white and colored passengers in their cars and set apart and designate in each car or coach a portion thereof, or certain seats therein to be occupied by white passengers, and a portion thereof, or certain seats therein, to be occupied by colored passengers, and such company or person that shall fail, refuse or neglect to comply with the provisions of this section shall be guilty of a misdemeanor, and upon indictment and conviction shall be fined not less than fifty [$50.00] dollars nor more than two hundred and fifty [$250.00] dollars for each offense. [1902-3-4, p. 968, ch. 4, §41; 1906, p. 92; Code 1919, §3978; Michie Code 1942, §3978.]

§56-391. Discrimination as to accommodation not permitted. — Any such company or person as is mentioned in the preceding section shall make no difference or discrimination in the quality and convenience of the accommodations provided for the two races, under the provisions of the preceding section. [1902-3-4, p. 968; ch. 4, §42; 1906, p. 92; Code 1919, §3979; Michie Code 1942, §3979.]

§56-392. May decrease or increase space for either race; contiguous seats; changing seats; penalty. — The conductor, manager or other person in charge of any car or coach operated upon any such line of railroad or railway as is mentioned in §56-390 shall, at any time when it may be necessary or proper for the comfort and convenience of passengers so to do, change the designation so as to increase or decrease the amount of space or seats set apart for either race; but no contiguous seats on the same bench shall be occupied by white and colored passengers at the same time (unless or until all the other seats in such car shall be occupied); and such conductor or manager may require any passenger to change his or her seat as often as it may be necessary or proper. Any such conductor, manager or other person in charge of any such car or coach who shall fail or refuse to carry out the provisions of this section shall be deemed guilty of a misdemeanor, and upon conviction thereof shall be fined not less than five [$5.00] dollars nor more than twenty-five [$25.00] dollars for each offense. [1902-3-4, ch. 4, §43; 1906 p. 92; Code 1919, §3980; Michie Code 1942, §3980.]

56-393. Penalty for failure to obey conductor in respect to seats assigned; ejection. — All persons who fail, while on any coach or car used for the carriage of passengers for hire by any company or person on any railway line, whether the motive power thereof be steam or electricity, or other motive power or whether such coach or car be on a street railway or interurban railway or a steam railway, to take and occupy the seat or seats or other space assigned to them by the conductor, manager or other person in charge of such car or coach, or whose duty it is to take up tickets or collect fares from passengers therein, or who fail to obey the direction of any such conductor, manager or other person, as aforesaid, to change their seats from time to time, as occasions require, pursuant to any lawful rule, regulation, or custom in force on such lines as to assigning separate seats or compartments, or other space, to white and colored passengers, respectively, being first advised of the fact of such regulation and requested to conform thereto, shall be deemed guilty of a misdemeanor, and upon conviction thereof shall be fined not less than five [$5.00] nor more than twenty-five [$25.00] dollars for each offense. Furthermore, such persons may be ejected from any such car, and from the right of way of such company by any conductor, motorman or manager of such company, or by any police officer or other conservator of the peace; and in case such persons ejected shall have paid their fares upon said car, they shall not be entitled to a return of any part of same. [1910, p. 335; Code 1919, §3983; Michie Code 1942, §3983.]

[Note: See *Lee v. Commonwealth* (1949) 189 Va. 890, 54 S.E. (2d) 888, holding §56-393 invalid as applied to interstate passengers.]

56-394. Conductor and motorman conservators of the peace; other powers. — Each conductor and motorman in the employment any such company as mentioned in §56-390, and upon the cars of such company, shall be a special policeman, and have all the powers of conservators of the peace in the enforcement of the provisions of this chapter, and in the discharge of his duty as special policeman in the enforcement of order upon such cars and such right of way; and such conductors and motorman shall likewise have the powers of conservators of the peace and of special policemen while in pursuit of persons for disorder upon said cars and right of way for violating the provisions of this chapter, and until such persons as may be arrested by such conductor or motorman shall have been placed in confinement, or delivered over to the custody of some other conservator of the peace or police officer; and, acting in good faith, he shall be for the purposes of this chapter, the judge of the race of each passenger, whenever such passenger has failed to disclose his or her race. [1902-3-4, p. 968, ch. 4, §45; 1906, p. 92; Code 1919, §3981 Michie Code 1942, §3981.]

§56-395. Provisions not to apply to employees, nurses, etc. — The provisions of §§56-390, 56-392 and 56-394 shall not apply to employees engaged in conducting, managing or operating the trains, cars or coaches therein mentioned or to persons employed as nurses, or officers of prisoners or lunatics. [1902-3-4, Ch. 4, §47; 1906, p. 92; Code 1919, §3982; Michie 1942, §3982.]

Steam Railroads

§56-396. Separate cars for white and colored passengers on steam railroads. — All persons engaged in running or operating any railroad in this State by steam for the transportation of passengers are hereby required to furnish separate cars or coaches for the travel of the white and colored passengers on their respective lines of railroad. Each compartment of a coach divided by a good and substantial partition, with a door therein, shall be deemed a separate coach within the meaning of this section, and each separate coach or compartment shall bear in some conspicuous place appropriate words in plain letters indicating the race for which it is set apart. [1902-3-4, p. 968, ch. 4, §28; Code 1919, 3962; Michie Code 1942, §3962.]

§56-397. No discrimination in quality of accommodations for each race permitted. — No difference or discrimination shall be made in the quality, convenience or accommodation in the cars or coaches or partitions set apart for white and colored passengers under the preceding section. [1902-3-4, Ch. 4, §29; Code 1919, §3963; Michie Code 1942, §3963.]

§56-398. Liability for failure to comply with two preceding sections. — Any railroad company or person, that shall fail, refuse, or neglect to comply with the provisions of the two preceding sections shall be deemed guilty of a misdemeanor, and upon indictment and conviction thereof shall be fined not less than three hundred [$300.00] nor more than one thousand [$1,000.00] dollars for each offense. [1902-3-4, Ch. 4, §30; Code 1919, §3964; Michie Code 1942, §3964.

[Note: §§56-396 to 56-398 (Michie Code 1942, §§3962-3964) were held invalid as applied to interstate passengers in *Matthews v. Southern Railway* (1946), 157 F. 2d. 609.]

§56-399. Conductors to assign white and colored passengers to cars. — The conductors or managers on all such railroads shall have power, and are hereby required, to assign to each white or colored passenger his or her respective car, coach or compartment. If the passenger fails to disclose his race, the conductor and managers, acting in good faith, shall be the sole judges of his race; and if any passenger refuse to occupy the car, coach, or compartment to which he or she may be assigned by the conductor or manager, said conductor or manager shall have the right to refuse to carry such passenger on his train, and may put him off his train. For such refusal and putting off of the train, neither the manager, conductor, nor railroad company shall be liable for damages in any court. [1902-3-4, ch. 4, §31; Code 1919, §3965; Michie Code 1942, §3965.]

[Note: For penalty for failure to obey conductor in respect to seats assigned on steam railroads, see §56-393 above.

§56-400. Penalty for failure to carry out provisions of preceding section. — Any conductor or manager on any such railroad who shall fail or refuse to carry out the provisions of the preceding section shall be deemed guilty of a misdemeanor, and upon indictment and conviction thereof shall be fined not less than twenty-five [$25.00] nor more than fifty [$50.00] dollars for each offense. [1902-3-4-, ch. 4, §326; Code 1919, §3966; Michie Code 1942, §3966.]

§56-401. When portion of car may be assigned to passengers of another race. — When any coach or compartment of a car for either race shall be completely filled, and no extra coaches or cars can be had, and the number of passengers is larger than could have been foreseen, the conductor in charge of such train is hereby authorized to assign and set apart a portion of the car or compartment asigned to passengers of one race to passengers of another race. [1902-3-4, Ch. 4, §33; Code 1919, §3967; Michie Code 1942, §3967.]

§56-402. Application of preceding sections. — The provisions of §§56-397 to 56-400 inclusive, shall not apply to employees on railroads, or to persons employed as nurses, or to officers in charge of prisoners, or lunatics, whether the prisoners or lunatics are white or colored, or both white and colored, or to prisoners or lunatics in his custody, nor shall the same apply to the transportation of passengers in any caboose car attached to a freight train, nor to Pullman cars, nor to through or express trains that do no local business. [1902-3-4, ch. 4, §34; Code 1919, §3968; Michie Code 1942, §3968.]

§ 56-403. Circuit courts to have jurisdiction for violation of certain preceding sections. — The circuit courts of the counties in which such railroads are operated shall have jurisdiction over offenses committed within the limits of their respective counties in violation of §§56-396 to 56-398; and 56-401 of this chapter, and the corporation courts of the cities in which such railroads are opperated shall have jurisdiction of all offenses in violation of such sections committed within the corporate limits of such cities. [1902-3-4, ch. 4, §35; Code 1919, §3969; Michie Code 1942, §3969.]

§56-404. Exclusion of persons from sleepers, dining cars, etc. — Any corporation, its agents, conductors, or employees, operating in this State sleeping, dining, palace, or compartment cars on the railroads in this State may reject and refuse admittance to any and all persons to enter and ride in such sleeping, dining, palace, parlor, chair, or compartment cars, when in the discretion of such corporation, its conductors, agents or employees, it may be advisable to do so. [1904, p. 129; Code 1919, §4007; Michie Code 1942, §4007.]

[Note: Exclusion from or segregation of Negro passengers in dining car of interstate railroad held unlawful in *Henderson v. United* (1950)339 U.S. 816. See Appendix 7.]

Steamboats

§56-452. Separation of white and colored passengers; discrimination. — The captain, purser, or other officer in command of any steamboat carrying passengers and plying in the waters within the jurisdiction of the Commonwealth, shall assign white and colored passengers on such boat to the respective location they are to occupy as passengers while on such boat, and to separate the white and colored passengers on said boats in the sitting, sleeping, and eating apartments. But no discrimination shall be made in the quality and convenience of accommodation afforded passengers in respective locations. This section shall not apply to nurses or attendants traveling with their employers, nor to officers in charge of prisoners or lunatics. [1902, 3-4, p. 968, ch. 6, §1; Code 1919, §4023, Michie Code 1942, §4022.]

§56-453. Penalty for violation of preceding section. — Any captain, purser, or other officer in command of such boat as mentioned in the preceding section who shall fail or refuse to carry out the provisions of such section shall be deemed guilty of a misdemeanor and upon conviction thereof shall be fined not less than twenty-five [$25.00] dollars nor more than one hundred [$100.00] dollars for each offence. [1902-3-4, ch. 6, §2; Code 1919, §4023; Michie Code 1942, §4023.]

§56-454. Passenger to occupy space assigned; penalty for disorderly conduct; ejection. — Any passenger traveling on any steamboat plying in the waters within the jurisdiction of the Commonwealth, who shall wilfully refuse to occupy the location, whether of sitting, sleeping, or eating, set apart or assigned by the captain, purser, or other officer in command of such boat, or behaves in a riotous or disorderly manner, shall be deemed guilty of a misdemeanor, and on conviction thereof shall be fined not less than five [$5.00] dollars nor more than fifty [$50.00], or confined in jail not less than thirty [30] days, or both, in the discretion of the court; and any such person may be ejected from such boat by the officers thereof at any landing place of such boat; and, if necessary, such assistance may be invoked by such person in charge of such boat as he may require to eject such passenger. [1902-3-4, p. 968, ch. 6, §3; Code 1919, §4024; Michie Code 1942, §4024.]

§56-456. Masters, etc., to be conservators of the peace. — Masters of steamships or steamboats, and wharf or landing agents, shall be conservators of the peace, and they, and each of them, shall have the same power to make arrests that other conservators of the peace have, except that the masters of steamships and steamboats shall only have such power on board their respective vessels, and the agents at their respective places of business; and the masters and agents may cause any person so arrested by them to be detained and delivered to the proper authorities for trial as soon as practicable. [1902-3-4, ch. 6, §4; Code 1919, §4025; Michie Code 1942, §4025.]

Waiting Rooms

§56-114. Separate waiting rooms for white and colored races. — The [State Corporation] Commission may require the establishment by transportation companies of separate waiting rooms at all stations, wharves, or landings for the white and colored races. [1902-3-4, p. 137, §16; Code 1919, §3716; 1932, p. 448; Michie Code 1942, §3716.]

Riotous Conduct — Penalty

§18-131. Riotous or disorderly conduct in other public places; disturbance in public conveyance; local ordinances. — If any person behaves in a riotous and disorderly manner . . . or causes any unnecessary disturbance in any street car, railroad car, omnibus or other public conveyance, by . . . failing to move to another seat when lawfully requested to so move by the operator, or otherwise annoying passengers and employees therein, he shall be guilty of a misdemeanor.

Cities and towns are authorized and empowered to adopt ordinances or resolutions prohibiting and punishing the above acts, or any of them, when committed in such cities, towns, or counties, and such ordinances or resolutions shall provide the same punishment for a violation thereof as is provided by this section, anything in the charters of such cities to the contrary notwithstanding. All fines imposed for the violation of such ordinances or resolutions shall be paid to and retained by such cities, towns and counties, and the Commonwealth shall not be chargeable with any costs in connection with any prosecution for the violation of any such ordinances or resolutions. [1946, p. 494; Michie Suppl. 1946, §4533a; 1950, p. 36.]

[Note: This statute has been invoked in cases where Negroes have contested segregation practices of public carriers in Virginia. See *Taylor v. Commonwealth* (1948)), 187 Va. 214, 46 S.E. (2d) 384.]

Chapter 569, Acts of Assembly, 1950*

ACTS OF ASSEMBLY

23-35.9. Nursing scholarships authorized. — There are established six annual scholarships for each Congressional District of the value of one hundred fifty dollars. These awards shall be made by the State Board of Health and the recipients of such scholarships shall be allowed to attend any accredited nursing school in this State operated by any non-profit institution. If any of the above created scholarships for any Congressional District are not awarded for any year they shall be awarded from the State-at-large.

There are established twenty annual nursing scholarships for Negroes to be awarded from the State-at-large of the value of one hundred fifty dollars. These awards shall be made by the State Board of Health and the recipients of such scholarships shall be allowed to attend any accredited Negro nursing school in this State.

23-35.10. Must be bona fide resident. — Each applicant for such scholarship must be a bona fide resident of the State of Virginia when such scholarship is awarded. Awards shall be made upon such basis, competitive or otherwise, as determined by the State Board of Health, with due regard for scholastic attainments, character, and adaptability of the applicant for the service contemplated in such award; provided no award shall be made if the applicant fails to possess the requisite qualifications.

23-35.11. Contract to be signed before award. — Before any such scholarship is awarded, the applicant must sign a written contract, under the terms of which the applicant agrees to pursue the nursing course of the school awarding the scholarship until completion, and thereupon to promptly begin and thereafter engage continuously in nursing work in the State of Virginia for a period of years equal in number to the years she has been a beneficiary of such scholarship or scholarships. The contract shall contain such other provisions as are necessary, in the opinion of the State Board of Health, to accomplish the purposes of the scholarship.

23-35.12. Scholarship may be from year to year. — Each said scholarship shall be awarded for a single year, but the same student shall, after making satisfactory progress toward the completion of her training in the school, receive such award for any succeeding year or years, provided no student shall receive any such scholarship for more than a total of three years.

23-35.13. How payments made. — The funds making up each scholarship shall be paid to the recipient thereof or applied toward the payment of her expenses at the school in such a manner and at such a time during the school year as determined by the superintendent or other proper officer of the nursing school attended, provided no recipient shall receive for any such scholarship less than one hundred fifty dollars.

23-35.14. To whom payable. — The funds making up each scholarship shall be paid to the recipient thereof or applied toward the payment of his expenses at the school, in such manner and at such times during the school year as

---

*Sections 23-35.1 through 23-35.8 deal with scholarships for the study of medicine.

determined by the president or other proper officer of the school, provided no recipient shall receive for any such scholarship less than one thousand dollars. 2. There is appropriated to the Medical College of Virginia and to the University of Virginia and to the Virginia State College and the State Board of Health, respectively, the sums sufficient for each year of the biennium beginning July one, nineteen hundred fifty. All payments out of this appropriation shall be made by the Treasurer of Virginia on warrants issued by the Comptroller and signed by the president or other authorized officer of the particular institution, or by the Chairman of the State Board of Health, respectively.

WASHINGTON

CONSTITUTION

Aliens

Art. 2, §33. Ownership of land by aliens, prohibited — Exceptions. — The ownership of land by aliens, other than those who in good faith have declared their intention to become citizens of the United States, is prohibited in this state, except where acquired by inheritance, under mortgage or in good faith in the ordinary course of justice in the collection of debts; and all conveyances of lands hereafter made to any alien directly, or in trust for such alien shall be void: Provided, that the provisions of this section shall not apply to lands containing valuable deposits of minerals, metals, iron, coal, or fire clay, and the necessary land for mills and machinery to be used in the development thereof and the manufacture of the products therefrom. Every corporation, the majority of the capital stock of which is owned by aliens, shall be considered alien for the purposes of this prohibition. [Const. 1889.]

[Note: See §10581 *et seq.* below.]

Education

Art. 9, §1. Preamble. — It is the paramount duty of the state to make ample provision for the education of all children residing within its borders, without distinction or preference on account of race, color, caste, or sex. [Const. 1889.]

STATUTES

Remington's Revised Statutes of Washington Annotated (1931)

Aliens

Alien Land Law

§10581. Aliens — Rights and Disabilities — Definition. — . . . (a) "Alien" does not include an alien who has in good faith declared his intention to become a citizen of the United States, but does include all other aliens and all corporations and other organized groups of persons a majority of whose capital stock is owned or controlled by aliens or a majority of whose members are aliens . . . [L. '21, p. 156, §1.]

[Note: Under the definition in §10581, aliens ineligible for citizenship (Japanese, and certain Oriental groups) are the groups against which this statute is directed. Subsection (b) of this section expressly excepts mining and metallurgical lands from the prohibitions contained in this act.]

§10582. Aliens — Restrictions as to land. — An alien shall not own land or take or hold title thereto. No person shall take or hold land or title thereto for an alien. Land now held by or for aliens in violation of the constitution of the state is forfeited to and declared to be the property of the state. Land hereafter conveyed to or for the use of aliens in violation of the constitution or of this act shall thereby be forfeited to and become the property of the state. [L. '21, p. 157, §2.]

§10582b. Minor child of alien — Presumption. — If a minor child of an alien hold title to land either heretofore or hereafter acquired, it shall be presumed that he holds in trust for the alien. [L. '23, p. 220, §2.]

§10583. Fiduciary restrictions. — [Prohibits an alien from acting as trustee under a will, guardian, executor or administrator, if any part of an estate is land.] [L. '21, p. 157, §3.]

§10584. Land acquired by aliens by inheritance, etc. — [Land acquired by inheritance or in good faith through the enforcement of a lien or the collection of a debt must be disposed of within 12 years, or the land shall be forfeited to the state. [L. '21, p. 157, §4.]

§10585. Limitations as to mortgagee. — [Provision for forfeiture to the state of land now in possession or control of an alien as mortgagee unless the land is sold under foreclosure within 3 years.] [L. '21, p. 158, §5.]

§10586. Citizenship — Presumption of bad faith. — Unless an alien who has declared his intention to become a citizen of the United States be admitted to citizenship within seven years after his declaration was made, it shall be presumed that he declared his intention in bad faith. [L. '21, p. 158, §6.]

§10587. Violations of Act — Offenses enumerated. — Whoever

(a) Knowingly transfers or conveys land or title to land to an alien; or

(b) Knowingly takes land or title to land in trust for an alien; or

(c) [Fails to notify attorney general or local prosecuting attorney that he holds or has acquired title to land in trust for an alien;] or

(d) [If an alien, refuses to disclose to attorney general or local prosecuting attorney the nature, extent and location of any land within the state which he owns or controls;] or

(e) [If an officer of an alien corporation or organized group, refuses to disclose to the attorney general pertinent facts about any land owned or controlled by the corporation or group;] or

(f) [If an officer of a corporation or organized group which holds land in trust for an alien, refuses to disclose pertinent facts about the land to the attorney general or local prosecuting attorney;], or

(g) Wilfully counsels, aids or abets another in violating or evading this act,

Is guilty of a gross misdemeanor. [L. '21, p. 158, §7.]

[Note: See §§10582a, 10588, 10589, §10590, §10591 for provisions relating to enforcement, scope and validity of the act. See also §10592 which confirms the titles of all lands conveyed to or acquired by aliens prior to the date of the adoption of the state Constitution (Oct. 1, 1889).]

Firearms

§2517-1. Aliens — Firearms without license prohibited. — [Unlawful for an alien who has not declared his intention to become a citizen of the United States to own or possess firearms without a license or to hunt and fish without a license. Violation of this section is punishable as a misdemeanor.] [L. '11, p. 303, §1.]

> [Note: Under the above section the alien must pay $15.00 for a license to carry firearms. Under former §§5902, 5903, (repealed by L. '47, ch. 275, §118, p. 1242) an alien was required to pay $25.00 for a license to hunt and fish. §5897-1 and §5897-2 (1947 Supp.) require citizens or aliens who have declared intention of becoming citizens to pay $2.50 for a county hunting and fishing license and $5.00 for a state hunting and fishing license. See L. '47, ch. 128, §§1, 2, p. 673, effective January 1, 1948. Presumably non-eligible aliens must pay a higher fee.]

§5711. Right to take fish for sale limited to citizens. — [L. '23, p. 266, §4.] [Repealed L. '49, ch. 112, §87.]

Teachers

§4845. [1949 Supp.] Aliens not to teach in public schools — Exceptions — Oath — Revocation of permit. — No person, who is not a citizen of the United States of America, shall teach or be permitted or qualified to teach in the public schools in this State: *Provided, however,* That the Superintendent of Public Instruction may grant to an alien a permit to teach in the public schools of this state; providing such teacher has all the other qualifications required by law, has declared his or her intention of becoming a citizen of the United States of America, and that five years and six months have not expired since such declaration was made. *Provided, further,* That the Superintendent of Public Instruction may grant to an alien teacher whose qualifications have been approved by the State Board of Education a temporary permit to teach as an exchange teacher in the public schools of this state, irrespective of requirements respecting citizenship and oath of allegiance. Before such alien shall be granted a temporary permit he or she shall be required to subscribe to an oath or affirmation in writing that such alien applicant is not a member of or affiliated with a Communist or Communist-sponsored organization or a Fascist or Fascist-sponsored organization. The form of such oath or affirmation shall be prepared by the State Superintendent of Public Instruction. All oaths or affirmations subscribed as herein provided shall be filed in the office of the Superintendent of Public Instruction and shall be there retained for a period of five (5) years. Such permits shall at all times be subject to revocation by and at the discretion of the Superintendent of Public Instruction. [L. 1919, ch. 38, p. 82, §1 as amended by Laws 1949, ch. 32, p. 86, §1. Appvd. March 4, 1949.]

Civil Rights

§2686. Protecting civil rights. — Every person who shall deny to any other person because of race, creed or color, the full enjoyment of any of the accommodations, advantages, facilities or privileges of any place of public resort, accommodation, assemblage or amusement, shall be guilty of misdemeanor. [L. '09, p. 1027, §434.]

Education

[See Constitution, Art. 9, §1 above.]

Employment — Discrimination in Employment

[See under Fair Employment Practices.]

Fair Employment Practices

[1949 Supp.]

§7614-20. Citation of act — Declaration of policy — Agency created — Jurisdiction and power. — This law shall be known as the "Law Against Discrimination in Employment." It shall be deemed an exercise of the police power of the state for the protection of the public welfare, health and peace of the people of this state, and in fulfillment of the provisions of the constitution of this state concerning civil rights; and the legislature hereby finds and declares that practices of discrimination against any of its inhabitants because of race, creed, color or national origin are a matter of state concern, that such discrimination threatens not only the rights and proper priviliges of its inhabitants but menaces the institutions and foundation of a free democratic state. A state agency is hereby created with powers with respect to elimination and prevention of discrimination in employment because of race, creed, color or national origin, as herein provided; and the Board established hereunder is hereby given general jurisdiction and power for such purposes. [L. '49, ch. 183, §1.]

> [Note: Title of Act: "AN ACT To prevent and eliminate discrimination in employment against persons because of race, creed, color or national origin, creating in the executive department a state board against discrimination, defining its functions, powers and duties and providing for the appointment and compensation of its officers and employees." L. 49, ch. 183.]

§7614-21. Opportunity to obtain employment recognized and declared a civil right. — The opportunity to obtain employment without discrimination because of race, creed, color or national origin is hereby recognized as and declared to be at civil right. [L. '49, ch. 183, §2.]

§7614-22. Definitions. — As used herein: (a) The term "person" includes one or more individuals, partnerships, associations, corporations, legal representatives, trustees in bankruptcy, receivers, or any group of persons, and includes any political or civil subdivision of the state and any agency or instrumentality of the state or of any political or civil subdivision thereof;

(b) The term "employer" includes any person acting in the interest of an employer, directly, or indirectly, who has eight (8) or more persons in his employ, and does not include any religious, charitable, educational, social or fraternal association or corporation, not organized for private profit;

(c) The term "employee" does not include any individual employed by

494

his parents, spouse or child, or in the domestic service of any person;

(d) The term "labor organization" includes any organization which exists for the purpose, in whole or in part, of dealing with employers concerning grievances or terms or conditions of employment, or for other mutual aid or protection in connection with employment;

(3) The term "employment agency" includes any person undertaking with or without compensation to recruit, procure, refer, or place employees for an employer;

(f) The term "national origin" shall, for the purposes of this act, include "ancestry." [L. '49, ch. 183, §3.]

§7614-23. State Board Against Discrimination in Employment — Creation — Members — Chairman — Terms — Compensation and expenses — Seal — Filling Vacancies — Offices — Reports — Removal of members. — (a) There is hereby created a Board to be known as the Washington State Board Against Discrimination in Employment, which shall be composed of five members to be appointed by the Governor, one of whom shall be designated as chairman by the Governor.

(b) One of the original members shall be appointed for a term of one year, one for a term of two years, one for a term of three years, one for a term of four years, one for a term of five years, but their successors shall be appointed for terms of five years each, except that any individual chosen to fill a vacancy shall be appointed only for the unexpired term of the member whom he shall succeed.

(c) Each member of the Board while in session or on official business shall receive the sum of twenty dollars ($20.00) per day in lieu of subsistence and shall receive reimbursement for actual and necessary travelling expenses incurred during such time. Such reimbursement to be made in the manner provided by law for similar reimbursements for state employees. A member shall be eligible for reappointment.

(d) The Board shall have an official seal which shall be judicially noticed.

(e) A vacancy in the Board shall be filled within thirty days, the remaining members to exercise all powers of the Board.

(f) The principal office of the Board shall be in the City of Seattle, but it may meet and exercise any or all of its powers at any other place in the state and may establish such district offices as it deems necessary.

(g) The Board, at the close of each six months period, shall report to the Governor, describing in detail the investigations, proceedings, and hearings it has conducted and their outcome, the decisions it has rendered, the recommendations it has issued, and the other work performed by it, and shall make such recommendations for further legislation as may appear desirable. The Board shall present its reports to each regular session of the Legislature; the Board's reports shall be published and made available upon request.

(h) Any member of the Board may be removed by the Governor for inefficiency, neglect of duty, misconduct or malfeasance in office, after being given a written statement of the charges and an opportunity to be heard thereon. [L. '49, ch. 183, §4.]

§7614-24. Policies and recommendations. — The Board shall formulate policies to effectuate the purpose of this act and may make recommendations to agencies and officers of the state or local subdivisions of government in aid of such policies and purposes. [L. 49, ch. 183, §5.]

§7614-25. Functions, powers and duties. — The Board shall have the following functions, powers and duties:

(a) To establish and maintain its principal office in the City of Seattle, and such other offices within the state as it deems necessary.

(b) To meet and function at any place within the state.

(c) To appoint an Executive Secretary and Chief Examiner, and such investigators, examiners, clerks, and other employees and agents as it may deem necessary, fix their compensation within the limitations provided by law, and prescribe their duties.

(d) To obtain upon request and utilize the services of all governmental departments and agencies.

(e) To adopt, promulgate, amend, and rescind suitable rules and regulations to carry out the provisions of this act, and the policies and practices of the Board in connection therewith.

(f) To receive, investigate and pass upon complaints alleging discrimination in employment because of race, creed, color or national origin.

(g) To hold hearings, subpoena witnesses, compel their attendance, administer oaths, take the testimony of any person under oath, and in connection therewith, to require the production for examination of any books or papers relating to any matter under investigation or in question before the Board. The Board may make rules as to the issuance of subpoenas by individual members as to service of complaints, decisions, orders, recommendations and other process or papers of the Board, its member, agent, or agency, either personally or by registered mail, return receipt requested, or by leaving a copy thereof at the principal office or place of business of the person required to be served. The return post office receipt, when service is by registered mail, shall be proof of service of the same.

No person shall be excused from attending and testifying or from producing records, correspondence, documents or other evidence in obedience to the subpoena of the Board or of any individual member, on the ground that the testimony or evidence required of him may tend to incriminate him or subject him to a penalty or forfeiture, but no person shall be prosecuted or subjected to any penalty or forfeiture for or on account of any transaction, matter or thing concerning which he is compelled, after having claimed his privilege against self-incrimination, to testify or produce evidence, except that such person so testifying shall not be exempt from prosecution and punishment for perjury committed in so testifying. The immunity herein provided shall extend only to natural persons so compelled to testify.

In case of contumacy or refusal to obey a subpoena issued to any person, the Superior Court of any county within the jurisdiction of which the investigation,

496

proceeding, or hearing is carried on or within the jurisdiction of which said person guilty of contumacy or refusal to obey is found or resides or transacts business, upon application by the Board shall have jurisdiction to issue to such person an order requiring such person to appear before the Board its member, agent, or agency, there to produce evidence if so ordered, or there to give testimony touching the matter under investigation or in question, and any failure to obey such order of the Court may be punished by said Court as a contempt thereof.

(h) To create such advisory agencies and conciliation councils, local, regional or statewide, as in its judgment will aid in effectuating the purposes of this article, and the Board may empower them to study the problems of discrimination in all or specific fields of human relationships or in specific instances of discrimination because of race, creed, color or national origin, and to foster through community effort or otherwise good-will, cooperation and conciliation among the groups and elements of the population of the state, and make recommendations to the Board for the development of policies and procedures in general and in specific instances, and for programs of formal and informal education which the Board may recommend to the appropriate state agency. Such advisory agencies and conciliation councils shall be composed of representative citizens, serving without pay, but with reimbursement for actual and necessary travelling expenses, and the Board may make provision for technical and clerical assistance to such agencies and councils and for the expenses of such assistance; the Board may use organizations specifically experienced in dealing with questions of discrimination.

(i) To issue such publications and such results of investigations and research as in its judgment will tend to promote good-will and minimize or eliminate discrimination because of race, creed, color or national origin.

(j) To adopt an official seal.

(k) To make such technical studies as are appropriate to effectuate the purposes and policies of this act and to publish and distribute the reports of such studies.

(l) Witnesses before the Board, its member, agent, or agency, shall be paid the same fees and mileage that are paid witnesses in the Courts of this state. Witnesses whose depositions are taken and the person taking the same shall be entitled to same fees as are paid for like services in the Courts of the state. [L. '49, ch. 183, §6.]

§7614-26. Unfair employment practices. — (1) It shall be an unfair employment practice for any employer:

(a) To refuse to hire any person because of such person's race, creed, color, or national origin, unless based upon a bona fide occupational qualification.

(b) To discharge or bar any person from employment because of such person's race, creed, color, or national origin.

(c) To discriminate against any person in compensation or in other terms or conditions of employment because of such person's race, creed, color or national origin.

(2) It shall be an unfair employment practice for any labor union or labor organization:

(a) To deny full membership rights and privileges to any person because of such person's race, creed, color, or national origin.

(b) To expel from membership any person because of such person's race, creed, color or national origin; or

(c) To discriminate against any member, employer, or employee because of such person's creed, color, or national origin.

(3) It shall be an unfair employment practice for any employment agency, except in the case of a *bona fide* occupational qualification or need, to fill or refuse to classify property or refer for employment, or otherwise to discriminate against, any individual because of his race, color, religious creed, national origin or ancestry.

(4) It shall be an unfair employment practice for any employer, employment agency, or labor union to discharge, expel, or otherwise discriminate against person because he has opposed any practices forbidden by this act, or because he has filed a charge, testified, or assisted in any proceeding under this act.

(5) It shall be an unlawful employment practice for any person to aid, abet, encourage, or incite the commission of any unlawful employment practice, or to attempt to obstruct or prevent any other person from complying with the provisions of this act or any order issued thereunder. [L. '49, ch. 183, §7.]

§7614-27. Proceeding where complainant claims to be aggrieved by unfair employment practice.—Any person claiming to be aggrieved by an alleged unfair employment practice may, by himself or his attorney, make, sign and file with the Board a complaint in writing under oath, which shall state the name and address of the person, employer, labor organization or employment agency alleged to have committed the unfair employment practice, and which shall set forth the particulars thereof and contain such other information as may be required by the Commission. The Board, whenever it has reason to believe that any person has been engaged or is engaging in an unfair employment practice may issue a complaint. An employer whose employees, or any of them, refuse or threaten to refuse to comply with the provisions of this act may file with the Board a written complaint under oath asking for assistance by conciliation or other remedial action. After the filing of any complaint, the chairman of the Board shall refer the same to a member or investigator to make prompt preliminary investigation of such complaint, and, if such member or investigator determines after such preliminary investigation that there is reasonable cause for believing that an unfair employment practice has been or is being committed as alleged in such complaint, he shall immediately endeavor to eliminate the unfair employment practice complained of by conference, conciliation and persuasion. No member or investigator shall disclose what has occurred in the course of such endeavors, provided the Board may publish the facts in the case of any complaint which has been dismissed and the terms of conciliation when a complaint has been adjusted. In case of failure to eliminate such practice, the investigator or investigating member shall certify the complaint and the results of his investigation to the Chairman of the Board. The Chairman of the Board shall thereupon appoint a hearing tribunal of three persons who shall be members of the Board or panel of hearing examiners to hear such complaint and shall cause to be issued and served in the name of the Board a written notice, together with a copy of such complaint, as the same may have been amended, requiring the person, employer, labor organization or employment agency named in such complaint, hereinafter referred to as the respondent, to answer the charges of such complaint at a hearing before such tribunal, at a time and place to be specified in such notice. The place of any such hearing may be the office of the Board or another place designated by it. The case in support of the complaint shall be presented at the hearing by counsel for the Commission; and no member of the Board who previously made the investigation or caused the notice to be issued shall participate in the hearing except as a witness, nor shall he participate in the deliberations of the tribunal in such case. Any endeavors or negotiations for conciliation shall not be received in evidence. The respondent may file a written answer to the complaint and appear at such hearing in person or otherwise, with or without counsel, and submit testimony and be fully heard. The tribunal conducting any hearing may permit reasonable amendment to any complaint or answer and the testimony taken at each hearing shall be under oath and be transcribed at the request of any party. If, upon all the evidence, the tribunal finds that a respondent has engaged in any unfair employment practice as defined in section 7 [§7614-26], it shall state its findings of fact and shall issue and file with the Board and cause to be served on such respondent an order requiring such respondent to cease and desist from such unfair employment practice. If, upon all the evidence, the tribunal finds that the respondent has not engaged in any alleged unfair employment practice, it shall state its findings of fact and shall similarly issue and file an order dismissing the complaint. The board shall establish rules of practice to govern, expedite and effectuate the foregoing procedure. Any complaint filed pursuant to this section must be so filed within six months after the alleged act of discrimination. [L. '49, ch. 183, §8.]

§7614-27A. Court enforcement of order — Review of order — Restraining orders and injunctions — Orders against state subdivisions. — (a) The Board may petition the court within the county wherein any unfair employment practice occurred or wherein any person charged with unlawful employment practice resides or transacts business, for the enforcement of any order issued by a tribunal under the provisions of this act and for appropriate temporary relief or a restraining order, and shall certify and file in Court a transcript of the entire record of the proceedings, including the pleadings and testimony upon which such order was made and the findings and orders of the hearing tribunal. Within five days after filing such petition in the Court the Board shall cause a notice of such petition to be sent by registered mail to all parties or their representatives. The Court shall have jurisdiction of the proceedings and of the questions determined thereon, and shall have the power to grant such relief by injunction or otherwise, including temporary relief, as it deems just and suitable and to make and enter, upon the pleadings, testimony and proceedings set forth in such transscript, a decree enforcing, modifying and enforcing as so modified, or setting aside in whole or in part any order of the Board or hearing tribunal.

(b) The findings of the hearing tribunal as to the facts, if supported by substantial and competent evidence, shall be conclusive. The Court, upon its own motion or upon motion of either of the parties to the proceeding, may permit each party to introduce such additional evidence as the court may believe necessary to a proper decision of the cause.

(c) The jurisdiction of the Court shall be exclusive and its judgment and decree shall be final, except that the same shall be subject to review by the Supreme Court, on appeal, by either party, irrespective of the nature of the decree or judgment. Such appeal shall be taken and prosecuted in the same manner and form and with the same effect as is provided in other cases of appeal to the Supreme Court, and the record so certified shall contain all that was before the lower Court.

(d) Any respondent aggrieved by a final order of a hearing tribunal may obtain a review of such order in the Superior Court for the county where the unfair employment practice is alleged to have occurred or in the county wherein such person resides or transacts business by filing with the Clerk of said court, within two weeks from the date of such order, a written petition in duplicate praying that such order be modified or set aside. The clerk shall thereupon mail the duplicate copy to the Board. The board shall then cause to be filed in said court a certified transcript of the entire record in the proceedings, including the pleadings, testimony and order. Upon such filing said court shall proceed in the same manner as in the case of a petition by the Board under this section and shall have the same exclusive jurisdiction to grant to the respondent such temporary relief or restraining order as it deems just and suitable, and in like manner to make and enter a decree enforcing or modifying and enforcing as so modified or setting aside, in whole or in part, the order sought to be reviewed.

(e) Unless otherwise directed by the Board tribunal or Court, commencement of review proceeding under this section shall operate as a stay of any order.

(f) Petitions filed under this section shall be heard expeditiously and determined upon the transcript filed, without requirement of printing. Hearings in the Court under this act shall take precedence over all other matters, except matters of the same character.

(g) No Court of this state shall have jurisdiction to issue any restraining order or temporary or permanent injunction preventing the Board from performing any function vested in it by this act, nor shall any Court have any jurisdiction to issue any order relating to the administration of this act, except as provided by Sections 10 and 11 [§§7614-28, 7614-29] hereof.

(h) This section shall not be applicable to orders issued against any political or civil subdivision of the state, or any agency, office, or employee thereof. [L. '49, ch. 183, §9.]

§7614-28. Interference with board, etc., a misdemeanor — Procedure for review.—Any person, employer, labor organization or employment agency, who or which shall willfully resist, prevent, impede, or interfere with the Board or any of its members or representatives in the performance of duty under this article, or shall wilfully violate an order of the Board, shall be guilty of a misdemeanor; but procedure for the review of the order shall not be deemed to be such wilful conduct. [L. '49, ch. 183, §10.]

§7614-29. Orders against state subdivisions — Transmission of copy to Governor. — In any case in which the Board shall issue an order against any political or civil subdivision of the state, or any agency, or instrumentality of the State or of the foregoing, or any officer or employee thereof, the Board shall transmit a copy of such order to the Governor of the state who shall take such action as he deems appropriate to secure compliance with such order. [L. '49, ch. 183, §11.]

§7614-30. Construction of act. — The provisions of this act shall be construed liberally for the accomplishment of the purposes thereof. Nothing contained in this act shall be deemed to repeal any of the provisions of any other law of this state relating to discrimination because of race, color, creed or national origin. [L. '49, ch. 183, §12.]

[Note: Laws 1949, ch. 183, also provides:

"§13. — If any provision of this act or the application of such provision to any person or circumstance shall be held invalid, the remainder of such act or the application of such provision to person or circumstances other than those to which it is held invalid shall not be affected thereby.

"§14. — There is hereby appropriated from the General Fund the sum of twenty-five thousand dollars ($25,000) to carry out the purpose of this act."]

Indians

§§10593, 10594. — [Provisions enabling the Puyallup Indians to lease or sell lands of the Puyallup Indian reservation, upon the consent of the United States government to the removal of restrictions upon conveyances by the Indians.] [L. '90, p. 500, §§1, 2; 1 H.C., §§2957, 2958.]

§10595. Indians may sell stone, timber, etc., from land. — Any Indian who owns within this state any land or real estate allotted to him by the government of the United States may with the consent of congress, either special or general sell and convey by deed made, executed and acknowledged before any officer authorized to take acknowledgments to deeds within this state, any stone, mineral, petroleum or lumber contained on said land or the fee thereof and such conveyance shall have the same effect as a deed of any other person or persons within this state; it being the intention of this section to remove from Indians residing in this state all existing disabilities relating to alienation of their real estate. [L. '99, p. 155, §1.]

§5391. Inducing certain Indians to vote. — [If any person induces or attempts to induce any Indian to vote, he is punishable by a fine up to $500, and imprisonment in the county jail up to 3 months or both, but this section does not include Indians who are citizens and entitled to vote under the amendments to the Constitution of the United States and the laws of Congress.] Cd. '81, §910; 2.H.P.C., §129.]

§5694. — [Restrictions against fishing do not apply to Indians fishing on reservations.] [L. '15, p. 82, §42.]

§7347. **Sale to Indians prohibited Penalty.** — Any person who shall sell, give away, dispose of, exchange, or barter any malt, spiritous or vinous liquor of any kind whatever, or any essence, extract, bitters, preparation, compound, composition, or any article whatsoever, under any name, label or brand, which produces intoxication, to any Indian, either of the whole or mixed blood to whom allotment of land has been made while the title to the same shall be held in trust by the government of the United States, or to any Indian of the whole or mixed blood, a ward of the government of the United States, under the charge of any Indian superintendent or agent, or of any Indian of the whole or mixed blood. over whom the government of the United States, through its departments, superintendent or agent exercises or assumes to exercise guardianship, or to any Indian of the whole or mixed blood the subject of any foreign nation, or to any Indian of the whole or mixed blood a member of any tribe of Indians, or to any Indian whatsoever, or a mixed blood Indian being more than one-eighth Indian, shall be guilty of a felony and punished therefor by imprisonment in the penitentiary for a period of not less than one [1] or more than two [2] years, or by imprisonment in the county jail not less than thirty [30] days nor more than six [6] months or by fine of not less than one hundred dollars ($100) nor more than one thousand dollars ($1,000) or by both such fine and imprisonment in the discretion of the court. [L. '09, p. 537, §1. Cf. L. '67, p. 95, §1; L. '69, p. 228, §133; Cd. '81, §942; 2 H. C., §137; Bal. Code, §7316.]

§3207-10. [1941 Supp.] **Mutilation, etc. of graves and records of ancient peoples. — Penalty. —** Any person who shall wilfully remove, mutilate, deface, injure or destroy any cairn or grave of any native Indian, or any glyptic or painted record of any prehistoric tribes or peoples, shall be guilty of a gross misdemeanor. [L. '41, ch. 216, §1.]

Ku Klux Klan — Masks

§2553. **Disguised and masked persons. —** Any assemblage of three or more persons, disguised by having their faces painted, discolored, colored or concealed, shall be unlawful; and every person so disguised present thereat, shall be guilty of a gross misdemeanor; but nothing herein shall be construed as prohibiting any peaceful assemblage for a masquerade or fancy dress ball or entertainment. [L. '09, p. 982, §301.]

§2554. **Owner of premises allowing masqueraders. —** Every person, being the owner, lessee or occupant of any building, boat or part thereof, who shall knowingly permit therein any unlawful assemblage of masked persons, shall be guilty of a gross misdemeanor. [L. '09, p. 982, §302.]

Military

§8462. **Classes of militia.** The militia of the state of Washington shall consist of all able-bodied male citizens of the United States and all other able-bodied males who have or shall have declared their intention of becoming a citizen of the United States, residing in this state, [between 18 and 45 years of age inclusive] ... [L. '17, p. 354, §1.]

[Note: The American Council on Race Relations reports that on May 15, Brigadier General Lilburn H. Stevens, after conferences with the Seattle Civic Unity Committee, issued an order stating there shall be "complete equality of treatment and opportunity regardless of race or color" in the Washington National Guard. See Report, June, 1950, p. 3.]

WEST VIRGINIA

CONSTITUTION

Aliens

Art. II, §5. No distinction shall be made between resident aliens and citizens as to the acquisition, tenure, disposiiton or descent of property. [Const. 1872.]

Education

Art. XII, §8. — White and colored persons shall not be taught in the same school. [Const. of 1872.]

[See §1775, below.]

STATUTES

West Virginia Code 1943 (Annotated)

Aliens

§3541. [21] Alien May Own Land. — Any alien make may take by devise, inheritance, gift or purchase, and hold, convey, devise or otherwise dispose of land within this State as if he were a citizen, and if an alien owner of land within this State shall die, his land shall descend in the same manner as if he were a citizen. [Code 1849, c. 115, §§1, 2; Code 1860, c. 115, §§1, 2; Code 1868, c. 70, §§1, 2; 1872, c. 48; 1882, c. 56; Code 1923, c. 70, §§1, 2.]

§4083. [4] Alienage of Ancestor Not to Bar. — In making title by descent, it shall be no bar to a party that any ancestor, whether living or dead, through whom he derives his descent from the intestate, is or has been an alien. [Code 1849, c. 123, §4; Code 1860, c. 123, §4; Code 1868; c. 78, §4; 1882, c. 94, §4; Code 1923, c. 78, §4.]

§2918. [3] [1945 Supp.] . . . Registered Nurse. — [Licenses for registered nurses may be issued to a person who is not a citizen of the United States but who has declared his or her intention of becoming a citizen. Unless citizenship is perfected within 7 years of such declaration the license shall terminate.] [1945, c. 96, §3.]

§6051. . . . Sale [of Weapon] to unnaturalized Person; Penalties.—[Unlawful to sell, rent, give or lend any type of firearm or dangerous weapon to an unnaturalized person. Punishable by a fine of $50 to $300 or imprisonment of 30 days to 6 months, or both.] [1925, Ex. Sess., c. 3.]

Bureau of Negro Welfare and Statistics

§2830. [1] Director. — The bureau of negro welfare and statistics, heretofore established, shall be continued. It shall be in charge of a director who shall be a member of the negro race, to be appointed by the governor, by and with the advice and consent of the senate, and shall hold office for four years, unless sooner removed according to law. [1921, C. 146, §1; Code 1923, C. 15 T., §1.]

§2831. [2] Duties. — The duties of the director shall be to study the economic condition of the negro throughout the State; to inspect negro hotels, restaurants, pool rooms and barber shops and to report to responsible officials conditions that are not conducive to the health and morals of the community; to encourage the ownership of homes and farms in this State by negroes, and to furnish such information to persons and corporations interested in securing homes and farms for negroes in this State as may be requested; to stimulate and encourage thrift, industry and economy among negroes and to promote the general welfare and uplift of the negro race in this State; to consider all questions pertaining to the negro that may be referred to him by any and all departments of the state government and recommend a solution of any and all problems so submitted; to prepare and keep records of the number of negroes employed in the several industries, trades, professions, and upon the farms of the State, of the number and location of industries, businesses, plants, homes and farms owned and operated by negroes, with the number and sex of persons employed by them; to promote and encourage friendly and harmonious relations between the white and negro races to report to the legislature, through the governor, all his acts and doings, and to make such recommendations for the solution of any problem or problems affecting the negro that he may deem advisable. [1921, C. 146, §2; Code 1923, C. 15 T, §2.]

§2832. [3] Salary. — The salary of the director shall be three thousand six hundred [$3600.00] dollars per annum and actual necessary traveling expenses, to be paid in the same manner as other State officials are paid. [1921, C. 146, §3; 1923, C. 15 T, §3; 1937, C. 82, §15.]

§2833. [4] Office of Bureau. — The board of public works shall provide an office for the bureau and provide such clerical assistants as may be necessary. [1921, C. 146, §4; Code 1923, C. 15 T. §4.]

Discriminatory Publication

See under Race Hate.

Education

Public Schools — Segregation

§1775. [14] Schools for Colored Pupils. — White and colored pupils shall not receive instruction in the same school, or in the same building. The board [county board of education] shall establish one free school, or more if necessary, in any part of the county where there are ten or more colored children of school age living within two miles of a point where a school might be established. And when such schools are established for colored children, the teachers thereof shall be supplied from members of their own race. The board may if practical, establish a school in a part of the county where there are less than ten colored children of school age.

The board, for the purpose of carrying out the provision of this section, may transfer pupils from one county to another as provided in section sixteen (§1777) of this article.

Whenever, in any district, the benefit of a free school education is not secured to the colored children of school age residing therein in the manner mentioned in this section, the funds applicable to the support of the free schools in the district shall be divided by the board in the proportion which the number of colored children bears to the number of white children therein, according to the last enumeration made for school purposes, and the share of the former shall be set apart for the education of colored children of school age in the district, and applied for the purpose from time to time in such manner as the board may deem best. [1863, C. 137, §17; 1866, C. 74, §26; 1867, C. 98, §§19, 20; Code 1868, C. 45, §§19, 20; 1872-3, C. 123, §§17, 18; 1881, C. 15, §17, 18; 1901, C. 73, §17; 1908, C. 27, §§70, 71; 1919, C. 2, §67; Code 1923, C. 45, §67; 1929, C. 35, §67; 1933, Ex. Sess., C. 8.]

[Note: A board of education has no right under this section to exclude colored persons from a public library which is not a part of the public school system. See *Brown v. Board* (1928), 106 W. Va. 476, 483, 146 S.E. 389, 64 A.L.R. 297. See Const. of W. Va. Art. 12, §8 above.]

§1777. [16] [1947 Supp.] **Transfer of Pupils; Transportation and maintainance.**—. . . In any district where no high school for negro pupils is maintained the board shall provide for the payment of tuition fees, not to exceed ten [$10.00] dollars a month for each pupil, necessary to permit the enrollment of all qualified negro pupils in the nearest available negro high school, negro vocational high school, or in the high school department of a negro institution of higher education, and shall also pay the cost of the daily transportation of the pupils to such high school. If, however, the daily transportation of such pupils is impracticable, necessitating their absence from home overnight, the board shall pay in addition to the tuition fees a maintenance allowance of at least thirty [$30.00] dollars a month to each such pupil, and daily transportation involving a round trip of more than fifty [50] miles shall at the election of the pupil be considered impracticable for the purposes of this requirement . . . [1863, C. 137, §8; 1866, C. 74, §24; 1867, C. 98, §14; Code 1868, C. 45, §14; 1872-3, C. 123, §12; 1877, C. 77, §12; 1881, C. 15, §12; 1908, C. 27, §§66, 67; 1919, C. 2, §59; Code 1923, C. 45, §59; 1925, C. 51, §59; 1933, Ex. Sess., C. 8; 1935, C. 50; 1947, C. 90.]

Teachers Salaries

§1806. [2] [1947 Supplement] **Salaries for Teachers; Basic Salaries; Advanced Salaries.** — [This section provides a basic schedule of salaries for teachers based upon degree of certificates, amount of training and tenure of teaching. This statute was amended in 1947. The 1947 amendment changed the amounts and omitted a former provision relating to salaries of Negro teachers. The provision, now omitted from the Code, originally enacted in 1929 (1929, C. 35, pp. 167-168) read as follows:

"Salaries of colored teachers shall be the same as the salaries of other teachers in the same district with the same training and experience and holding similar credentials. Any board of education failing to comply with the provisions of this paragraph may be compelled to do so by *mandamus.*"] [1863, C. 137, §7; 1866, C. 74, §21; 1867, C. 98, §15; Code 1868, C. 45, §15; 1872-3, C. 123, §6; 1879, C. 74, §6; 1881, C. 15, §6; 1882, C. 101, §6; 1893, C. 26, §6; 1901, C. 70, §6; 1905, C. 69, §6; 1908, C. 26, §6; C. 27, §27½; 1915, C. 60, §28; 1919, C. 2, §55; 1921, C. 8, §55; Code 1923, C. 45, §55; 1929, C. 35, §67 (a); 1933, Ex. Sess., C. 11; 1933, 2nd. Ex. Sess., C. 40; 1939, C. 55; 1941, C. 37; 1945, C. 50; 1947, C. 75.]

§1726. [1] [1947 Supp.] **State Board of Education.** — There shall be a state board of education . . . The state board shall consist of ten members of whom one shall be the state superintendent of schools, ex officio, who shall not be entitled to vote. The other nine members shall be citizens of the state appointed by the governor, by and with the advice and consent of the senate, for overlapping terms of nine years, . . . and at least one member shall be of the Negro race. [1908, C. 27, §130; 1915, C. 56, §130; 1919, C. 2, §4; 1921, C. 1, §4; Code 1923, C. 45, §4; 1947, C. 72.]

[Note: The 1947 amendment increased the membership from seven to 10 and added the requirement that at least one member shall be of the Negro race. See §1727 [2] below.]

§1727. [2] **Negro Board of Education:** — [1933, Ex. Sess. C. 12.] [Repealed by Acts 1947, c. 72.]

[Note: This section provided for a separate board of education for Negroes to supervise the education of Negro Youth in the State. See §1726, above.]

§1740 (1). [16] **Joint Powers of State and Negro Boards of Education** — [1933, Ex. Sess., C. 12.] [Repealed by Acts 1947, C. 72. See 1947 Supp.]

§1740 (2). [17] **Report of Joint Boards of Education Concerning Negro Institutions.** — [1933, Ex. Sess. C. 12.] [Repealed by Acts 1947, C. 72. See 1947 Supp.]

§1749. [9] [1947 Supp.] **State Department of Public Schools; Supervisor of Colored Schools.** For carrying into effect the provisions of this chapter, the state superintendent of schools shall maintain a department of public schools at his office at the state capital, and he shall have authority to employ assistants and such other employees as may be necessary, including a state supervisor of colored schools. [1919, C. 2, §25; Code 1923, C. 45, §25; 1929, C. 89, §94; 1945, C. 54.]

Deaf and Blind — West Virginia School for Colored Deaf and Blind

§1904. [1] **Continuation; Management; Chief Executive Officer.** — The West Virginia School for the colored deaf and blind, heretofore established and located at Institute, in Kanawha County, shall be continued and shall be known as the "West Virginia school for the colored deaf and blind." The school shall be maintained for the care and training of the colored deaf and blind of the State, and its educational affairs shall be under the control, supervision and management of the said joint boards of education. The chief executive officer of this school shall be the principal, who shall be a member of the negro race, shall be a graduate of a reputable college, shall have had at least six years' experience as a teacher, and shall be a person of good executive ability. [1919, C. 11, §1; Code 1923, C. 45, §158a; 1933, Ex. Sess., C. 12.]

[Note: See also Laws 1947, ch. 78, pp. 297-299.]

Deaf and Blind — West Virginia Schools for the Deaf and Blind. {white} Laws 1949, c. 53, pp. 212-213. [Reenacts ch. 18, Art. 17, §2 of West Virginia Code of 1931 providing for the admission of white deaf and blind youths resident in the state between 6 and 25 years of age.]

§1905. [2] General Provisions [relating to eligibility for admission; appropriation.] [1943, C. 39.]

Juvenile Delinquents

Industrial School for White boys {1947 Supplement}

§2698 — [2] [Provides for commitment to West Virginia Industrial School for Boys "any white male youth between the ages of ten and eighteen years."] [1889, C. 3, §6; 1904, C. 22, §6; 1905, C. 68, §6; 1908, C. 27, §241; 1913, C. 70, §2; 1919, C. 2, §160; Code 1923, C. 45, §160; 1947, C. 149.] [See §2697 [1], §§2699 [3] - 2707 [11].]

Industrial School for Colored Boys

§2708. [1] **Continuation and Management.** — The West Virginia industrial school for colored boys, heretofore established, shall be continued and shall be exclusively charged with the care, training and reformation of colored male youths of the State committed to its custody . . . [Provision for management under state board of control, and for control of its educational policies by State board of education.] [1921, C. 155, §§1, 5; Code 1923, C. 45, §171a.]

§2709. [2] General Provisions. — [Makes applicable provisions for commitment, parole or discharge and transfer. See §§2699 [3] to 2707 [11].]

Industrial Home for Girls

§§2710. [1] to 2731. [22] [Provision for commitment, care, training and reformation of white girls.] [1897, C. 8, §1, 5, 6, 10, 11, 12; 1901, C. 47; 1908 C. 27, §§253, 258, 259, 262, 264, 265; 1919, C. 2, §§172, 173, 174, §177; 179, 180; 1921, C. 144, §§172, 173, 175, 175a, - 175m,; Code 1923, C. 45, §§172, 173, 175, 175a - 175m; 176, 180; 1947, C. 149.]

Industrial Home for Colored Girls {1947 Supplement}

§§2732 - 2733. — [Provision for West Virginia industrial home for colored girls "exclusively charged with the care, training and reformation of colored girls committed to its custody.] [1921, C. 154, §§1, 4, Code 1923, C. 45, §176a, 1947, C. 149.]

Colleges and Universities — West Virginia State College

§1893. [1] **Continuation and Management; Four-H. Camp.** — The institution for the instruction of colored students heretofore established and located at Institute, in Kanawha County, shall be continued and shall be known as the "West Virginia State College". The educational affairs of said college shall be under the control, supervision and management of the state board of education and the negro board of education, as provided in sections thirteen and sixteen [§§1738, 1740 (1)] article two of this chapter, and its financial and business affairs shall be under the charge and control of the State board of control as provided in section four (§2581), article one, chapter twenty-five of the Code.

The said joint boards of education shall establish and maintain in the West Virginia State College, in addition to the departments already established such professional and graduate schools and college courses of study as may be expedient and practicable, and shall prescribe the conditions for graduation therefrom and make rules for the conferring of degrees and for issuing the proper diplomas to those who complete such courses . . . [Provides for extension work in agriculture, home economics, mining, and for the establishment of a Four-H Camp, institute and state exhibit for Negroes.] [1891, C. 65; 1901, C. 50, §2; 1908, C. 27, §§204 - 210; 1915, C. 66, §§205a, 207a; 1919, C. 2, §150; Code 1923, C. 45, §150; 1929, C. 11; 1933, Ex. Sess., C. 12; 1937, C. 101.]

[Note: §1740 [1] providing for a Negro Board of Education, was repealed by Acts, 1947, C. 72. Presumably West Virginia State is now controlled by a single State Board of Education. See §1726 [1] above.]

§1894. [2] State Aid to Students Taking Advanced Courses Outside State. — All bona fide residents of this State who have been residents of this State for five years, and who have completed courses of study equivalent to two years of college grade preparatory to special courses to be pursued outside of the State, or who have otherwise qualified to enter such courses, and who are now pursuing or may hereafter pursue, courses of study in educational institutions outside of the State the same as those taught in the West Virginia university or other West Virginia schools, and, because of section eight, article twelve of the constitution of West Virginia, [Art. 12, §8 prohibiting mixed schools] cannot pursue such course in the West Virginia university, or other state schools, and no other courses are taught in state supported educational institutions provided for them, shall have their annual tuiton and fees paid by the State for the amount paid by a nonresident student of the State university or other state supported schools, over and above the amount of any tuition and fees paid by a resident student of the State University or other schools, such tuition cost to be ascertained by the state board of education for the preceding school year and paid upon recognition of the state superintendent of schools out of funds appropriated for that purpose. The negro board of education and the state board of education, acting jointly, shall prescribe rules and regulations governing the granting of aid under this section. [1927, C. 10, §§1-3; 1929, C. 34, §§1-3; 1933, Ex. Sess., C. 12.]

[See 1726 [1] above as amended providing for a single state board of education.]

Bluefield State College

§1895. [1] [Provision for maintenance and control of Bluefield State College, formerly known as "Bluefield State Teachers' College" for Negroes.] [1895, C. 40; 1908, C. 27, §§211-218; 1919, C. 2, §151; Code, 1923, C. 45, §151; 1931, C. 7; 1933, Ex. Sess., C. 12; 1943, C. 80.

Hospitals
Insane and Mental Defectives

§2649. [2] Segregation of Races. — The Weston, Spencer and Huntington state hospitals shall be used for the care and treatment of white persons, and the Lakin state hospital shall be used for the care and treatment of colored persons. [Code 1943, §2649.]

Tubercular Patients

§2635. [1] 2636 [2] [Provides for the admission of white residents of the State to Hopemont and Rutherford Sanitariums.] [1911, C. 6, §§1, 3; Code 1923, C. 15L, §§1, 3; 1927, C. 8; 1933, C. 83.]

§§2637. [1] 2638 [2] — Provides for the continuation and management of the State tuberculosis sanitarium for colored persons at Denmar Sanitarium. [1917, C. 38, §§1, 3; Code 1923, C. 15L; §4.]

Marriage

§4694. [16] Marriage of Colored Persons. — All marriages heretofore celebrated between colored persons under license issued by any recorder or clerk of a county court in this State, and all marriages between such persons, whether under such license or not, if the same were consummated in good faith on the part of the persons so married, and such persons were living together as husband and wife on the twenty-eighth day of February, eighteen hundred and sixty-six [Feb. 28, 1866], shall be deemed valid. Where colored persons prior to the twenty-eighth day of February, eighteen hundred and sixty-six, had undertaken and agreed to occupy the relation to each other of husband and wife, and were cohabiting as such at the time, whether the rites of marriage shall have been so solemnized between them or not, shall be deemed husband and wife, and be entitled to all the privileges, and subject to the duties and obligations of that relation, in like manner as if they had been duly married by law; and all their children shall be deemed legitimate, whether born before or after the said twenty-eighth day of February, eighteen hundred and sixty-six; and where the parties have ceased to cohabit before the said date, in consequence of the death of the woman, or from any other cause, all the children of the woman recognized by the man to be his, shall be deemed legitimate. [1866, C. 102, §1; Code 1868, C. 63, §8; 1872-3, C. 161, §8; 1882, C. 58, §8; Code 1923, C. 63, §8.]

Military
See under National Guard.

Miscegenation

§4697. [19] Miscegenation; Penalties. — Any white person who shall intermarry with a negro shall be guilty of a misdemeanor, and, upon conviction thereof, shall be fined not exceeding one hundred [$100.00] dollars, and confined in jail not more than one [1] year. Any person who shall knowingly perform the ceremony of marriage between a white person and a negro shall be guilty of a misdemeanor, and, upon conviction thereof, shall be fined not exceeding two hundred [$200.00] dollars. [Code 1849, C. 196, §§8, 9; Code 1860, C. 196, §§8, 9; Code 1868, C. 149, §§8, 9; 1882, C. 123, §§8, 9; Code 1923, C. 149, §§8, 9.]

§4701. [1] For What and When Marriages Void. — All marriages between a white person and a negro; . . . shall be void from the time they are so declared by a decree of nullity. [Code 1849, C. 109, §§1, 6; Code 1860, C. 109, §§1, 6; 1867, C. 17, §6, Code 1868, C. 64, §§1; 5; Code 1923, C. 64, §§1; 5; 1935, C. 35.]

[Note: Under this section an interracial marriage is not void *ab initio*, but only voidable, and is void only after a decree of nullity is obtained. *Stewart v. Vandevort* (1890), 34 W. Va. 524, 12 S. E. 736, L. R. A. 1916C, 714n, 4 A.L.R. 931n; *Hastings v. Douglas* (1918), 249 F. 378, 382.]

§4698. [20] Issuing Marriage License Contrary to Law; Penalties. — If any clerk of the county court shall knowingly issue a marriage license contrary to law, he shall be guilty of a misdemeanor, and upon conviction thereof, shall be fined not exceeding five hundred [$500.00] dollars, or confined in jail not more than one [1] year, or both, at the discretion of the Court. [Code 1849, C. 196, §4; Code 1860, C. 196, §4; Code 1868, C. 149, §4; 1872-3, C. 76, §1; 1875, C. 46, §1; 1882, C. 123, §4; Code 1923, C. 149, §4.]

§4695. [17] Marriage Out of State to Evade Law. — If any person resident of this state shall, in order to evade the law, and with an intention of returning to reside in this state, go into another state or country, and there intermarry in violation of section one, article two (§4701) of this chapter, and shall afterwards return and reside here, such marriage shall be governed by the same law, in all respects, as if it had been solemnized in this State. [Code 1849, C. 109, §2; Code 1860, C. 109, §2; Code 1868, C. 64, §3; Code 1923, C. 64, §3, 1941, C. 28.]

National Guard

§1152. [5] How National Guard Constituted and Organized. — . . . The governor . . . is hereby directed to organize a unit or units and equip same, composed of negro troops which unit or units shall be organized and equipped in accordance with the provisions of the U.S. Army regulations governing same . . . [1897, C. 61, §9; 1905, C. 47, §9; 1909, C. 62, §9; 1921, C. 117, §9; Code 1923, C. 18, §9; 1923, C. 62, §9; 1935, C. 112; 1949, C. 105, §5.]

[Note: The amendment of 1935 inserted the provisions relating to organization of a regiment of Negro troops.]

Orphans and Aged

§§2626. [1] to 2628. [3]—[Provides for the West Virginia children's home for the care and custody of white children. [1909, C. 80, §§1, 2; 1917, C. 23, §1; Code 1923, C. 15K; §1.]

§§2629. [1] to 2631. [3]—[Provides for management and control of the West Virginia colored children's home.] [1911, C. 24, §§1, 3, 4; Code 1923, C. 57B, §§1, 3, 4.]

§§2631(1). [1] to 2631(5). [5] [1947 Supp.].—[Provision for establishment, management and supervision of West Virginia Home for Aged and Infirm white men and women at Sweet Springs, Monroe County, West Virginia.] [1945, C. 135, §§1-5.]

§§2632. [1] 2634 [3] — Provision for continuation, location and management of West Virginia Home for aged and infirm colored men and women at McKendree, Fayette County, West Virginia. [1923, C. 64, §§1, 3, 4; 1943, C. 79.]

Race Hate

§6109. [16] Picture or Theatrical Act Reflecting upon Any Race or Class of Citizens; Penalty. — It shall be unlawful for any person, corporation or company to advertise, exhibit, display or show any picture or theatrical act in any theatre or other place of public amusement or entertainment within this State, which shall in any manner injuriously reflect upon the proper and rightful progress, status, attainment or endeavor of any race or class of citizens, calculated to result in arousing the prejudice, ire or feelings of one race or class of citizens against another race or class of citizens. Any person, corporation or company violating any of the provisions of this section shall be guilty of a misdemeanor, and upon conviction, shall be fined not less than one hundred [$100.00] nor more than one thousand [$1000.00] dollars, and may, in the discretion of the court, be confined in jail not more than thirty [30] days. [1919, C. 117; Code 1923, C. 151, §17.]

Witnesses

§5732. [7] Race or Color Not an Incompetency. — No person shall be incompetent as a witness on account of race or color. [Code 1849, C. 176, §19; Code 1860, C. 176, §20; 1866, C. 89, §1; Code 1868, C. 130, §24, 1882, C. 160, §24; Code 1923, C. 130, §24.]

WISCONSIN

CONSTITUTION

Aliens

Article II, Sec. 15. Equal rights for aliens and citizens.—No distinction shall ever be made by law between resident aliens and citizens, in reference to the possession, enjoyment or descent of property.

[Note: See also Wisconsin Statutes (1949), 234.22, 234.23, 234.24.]

Indians

Article III, Sec. 1. Electors. — [Right to vote extended to "persons of Indian blood, who have once been declared by Congress to be citizens of the United States, any subsequent law of congress to the contrary not withstanding".]

Slavery

Art. I, Sec. 2. Slavery Prohibited. — There shall be neither slavery, nor involuntary servitude in this State, otherwise than for the punishment of crime, whereof the party shall have been duly convicted.

WISCONSIN STATUTES (1949)

Aliens

234.22. Aliens may acquire lands. — Subject to the limitations of section 234.23 an alien may acquire and hold lands or any right thereto or interest therein by purchase, devise or descent, and he may convey, mortgage and devise the same; and if he shall die intestate the same shall descend to his heirs; and in all case such lands shall be held, conveyed, mortgaged or devised or shall descend in like manner and with like effect as if such alien were a native citizen of the state or of the United States.

234.23. Limitation on nonresident — aliens and corporations. — [Unlawful for nonresident aliens and alien corporations except as such land may be acquired by inheritance, will, or in the collection of debts. Land acquired or held in violation of this provision shall be forfeited to the state, and it shall be the duty of the attorney-general to enforce such forfeiture.]

[Note: See also §234.24.]

STATUTES

Civil Rights

See under **Public Accommodation.**

Civil Service

16.11. Examinations . . . (18) [Prohibits inquiry into political or religious opinions or affiliations of civil service applicants. Does not include race or color within protection against discrimination.]

16.14. Discrimination. — [Prohibits discrimination because of religious or political affiliations or opinions. Does not specify race or color.]

513

Education
Public Schools

40.777. Exclusion on account of religion, nationality or color a misdemeanor. — No child between the ages of 4 and 20 years shall be excluded from any public school on account of his religion, nationality or color. No separate school or department shall be kept for any person or persons on account of his religion, nationality or color. A member of any board of education who shall vote to exclude from any public school any child, on account of his religion, nationality or color shall be punished by a fine not to exceed $100 or by imprisonment for not less than 30 days, nor more than 6 months, or by both such fine and imprisonment. [Added by Laws 1949, Ch. 433, p. 403, appvd. July 7, 1949, entitled "An Act To create 40.777 of the statutes, relating to segregation and discrimination in the public schools and providing a penalty."]

Public School Teachers

40.775. Race, religious political discrimination as to teachers prohibited. — (1). No discrimination shall be practiced in the employment of teachers in public schools because of their race, nationality or political or religious affiliations, and no questions of any nature or form shall be asked applicants for teaching positions in the public schools relative to their race, nationality or political or religious affiliations, either by public school officials or employes or by teachers' agencies and placement bureaus

(2) Any person who shall violate the provisions of this section shall be punished by a fine of not less than twenty-five [$25.00] dollars nor more than fifty [$50.00] dollars, or by imprisonment in the county jail not less than five [5] days nor more than thirty [30] days. Violation of this section shall be cause for the removal of any superintendent, member of a board of education or school board, or other public·official. [1933, c. 12.

Employment

66.94. Metropolitan transit authority. — (28) *Supervision of officers and employees.* — .... No discrimination shall be made in any appointment or promotion because of race, creed, color, or political or religious affiliation . . .

Fair Employment Practices

111.31. Declaration of Policy. — (1) The practice of denying employment and other opportunities to, and discriminating against, properly qualified persons by reason of their race, creed, color, national origin, or ancestry, is likely to foment domestic strife and unrest, and substantially and adversely affect the general welfare of a state by depriving it of the fullest utilization of its capacities for production. The denial by some employers and labor unions of employment opportunities to such persons solely because of their race, creed, color, national origin, or ancestry, and discrimination against them in·employment, tends to deprive the victims of the earnings which are necessary to maintain a just and decent standard of living, thereby committing grave injury to them.

(2) It is believed by many students of the problem that protection by

law of the rights of all people to obtain gainful employment, and other privileges free from discrimination because of race, creed, color, national origin, or ancestry, would remove certain recognized sources of strife and unrest, and encourage the full utilization of the productive resources of the state to the benefit of the state, the family, and to all the people of the state.

(3) In the interpretation and application of this subchapter, and otherwise, it is declared to be the public policy of the state to encourage and foster to the fullest extent practicable the employment of all properly qualified persons regardless of their race, creed, color, national origin, or ancestry. All the provisions of this subchapter shall be liberally construed for the accomplishment of this purpose. [1945 c. 490.]

11.32. Definitions. — When used in this subchapter:

(1) The term "labor organization" shall include any collective bargaining unit composed of employes.

(2) The term "employes" shall not include any individual employed by his parents, spouse, or child.

(3) The term "employer" shall not include a social club, fraternal or religious association, not organized for private profit.

(4) The term "commission" means the industrial commission of the state of Wisconsin.

(5) The term "discrimination" means discrimination because of race, color, creed, national origin, or ancestry, by an employer individually or in concert with others against any employe or any applicant for employment in regard to his hire, tenure or term, condition or privilege of employment, and by any labor organization against any member or applicant for membership, and also includes discrimination on any of said grounds in the fields of housing, recreation, education, health and social welfare. [1945, c. 490.]

111.33. Industrial commission to administer. — Sections 111.31 to 111.37 shall be administered by the industrial commission. The commission shall have authority from time to time to make, amend and rescind such rules and regulations as may be necessary to carry out this subchapter. The commission may, by one or more of its members, or by such agents or agencies as it may designate, conduct in any part of this state any proceeding, hearing, investigation, or inquiry necessary to the performance of its functions. The commission shall at the end of every year make a report in writing to the government, stating in detail the work it has done and its recommendations, if any. [1945 c. 490.]

111.34. Advisory committee. — The governor shall appoint an advisory committee consisting of 7 members. Two shall be representatives of labor organizations, one to be chosen from each of the 2 major labor organizations of the state, 2 members shall be representatives of business and industrial management, and the remaining 3 members shall be representatives of the public at large. The term of members shall be 3 years. The members of the committee shall elect their own chairman. The commission may refer to such committee for study and advice on any matter relating to fair employment. Such committee shall give consideration for the practical operation and applicaiton of this subchapter and may report to the proper legislative committee its view on any pending bill relating to the subject matter of this subchapter. Members of the committee shall receive no salary or compensation for services on said committee, but shall be entitled to reimbursement for necessary expenses. [1945, c. 490.]

111.35. Investigation and study of discrimination. — The commission shall:

(1) Investigate the existence, character, causes and extent of discrimination in this state and the extent to which the same is susceptible of elimination.

(2) Study the best and most practicable ways of eliminating any discrimination found to exist, and formulate plans for the elimination thereof by education or other practicable means.

(3) Publish and disseminate reports embodying its findings and the results of its investigations and studies relating to discrimination and ways and means of reducing or eliminating it.

(4) Confer, co-operate with and furnish technical assistance to employers, labor unions, educational institutions and other public or private agencies in formulating programs, educational and otherwise, for the elimination of discrimination.

(5) Make specific and detailed recommendations to the interested parties as to the methods of eliminating discrimination.

(6) Transmit to the legislature from time to time, recommendations for any legislation which may be deemed desirable in the light of the commission's findings as to the existence, character and causes of any discrimination. [1945, c. 490.]

111.36. Commission Powers. — (1) The commission may receive and investigate complaints charging discrimination or discriminatory practices in particular cases, and give publicity to its findings with respect thereto.

(2) In carrying out the provisions of this subchapter the commission and its duly authorized agents are empowered to hold hearings, subpoena witnesses, take testimony and make investigations in the manner provided in chapter 101. The commission or its duly authorized agents may privilege witnesses testifying before them under the provisions of this subchapter against self-incrimination. [1945, c. 490.]

111.37. Separability. — It is the intent of the legislature that the provisions of this act are separable and if any provision shall be held unconstitutional, such decision shall not affect the remainder of this subchapter. [1945, c. 490.]

Housing

Chapter 592, Laws of 1949

Veteran's Housing Authorities

66.39(13). Tenant selection, Discrimination. — All tenants selected for veterans' housing projects shall be honorably discharged veterans of wars of the United States of America. Selection between veterans shall be made in accordance with rules and regulations promulgated and adopted by the Wisconsin department of veterans' affairs which regulation said department is authorized to make and from time to time change as it deems proper. Such rules and regulations, however, shall give veterans of World War II preference over veterans of all other wars. Notwithstanding such rules and regulations or any law to the contrary a veteran shall not be entitled to or be granted any benefits under sections 66.39 to 66.404 from a housing authority unless such veteran was at the time of his induction into military service a resident of the state of Wisconsin. *Veterans otherwise entitled to any right, benefit, facility or privilege under this section shall not, with reference thereto, be denied them in any manner for any purpose nor be discriminated against because of race, color, creed or national origin.* [1949, c. 592, §1.] (italics supplied)

Housing Authorities Law

66.40(2m). Discrimination. — Persons otherwise entitled to any right, benefit, facility or privilege under sections 66.40 to 66.404 shall not, with reference thereto, be denied them in any manner for any purpose nor be discriminated against because of race, color, creed or national origin. [1949, c. 592, §2.]

Urban Redevelopment Law

66.405(2m). Discrimination. — Persons otherwise entitled to any right, benefit, facility or privilege under section 66.405 to 66.425 shall not, with reference thereto, be denied them in any manner for any purpose nor be discriminated against because of race, color, creed or national origin. [1949, c. 592, §3.]

Blighted Area Law

66.43(2m). Discrimination. — Persons otherwise entitled to any right, benefit, facility or privilege under this section shall not, with reference thereto, be denied them in any manner for any purpose nor be discriminated against because of race, color, creed or national origin. [1949, c. 592, §4.]

Indians

40.766. Indian Rights Day. — [Designates July 4th as "Indian Rights Day" to be celebrated in conjunction with Independence Day, "in commemoration of the granting by congress of home rule and a bill of rights to the American Indians.] [1935, c. 277.]

40.71. Indian reservation schools. — [Compulsory attendance at federal schools for Indian children required. Penalties set forth for parents who refuse to comply.]

[Note: See also §40.47 (11).]

27.012. Indian antiquities on public lands. — [Makes it unlawful to deface or destroy historic Indian remains on state property. Subject to penalty as provided in 343.453 (fine of $10 to $100, or up to 90 days in prison, or both).] [1947, c. 549.]

29.09. Hunting, trapping, and fishing licenses. — (1) [Indians hunting, fishing or trapping off Indian reservation lands are subject to all provisions of Fish and Game laws requiring licenses.] [1931, c. 351 s. 2; 1933 c. 243; s. 1; 1933 c. 370; 1935 c. 213; 1939 c. 182; 1943 c. 343, 434; 1945 c. 49, 189; 1947, c. 168.]

142.07. (lm) (a). — Hospital charges. — [Provides for admission of Indian children to Wisconsin orthopedic hospital for children or Wisconsin general hospital where orthopedic hospital care for such children is to be provided from funds granted the office of Indian affairs, United States department of Interior.]

14.205. Federal donations for Indians. — [Authorizes governor on behalf of the state to accept funds made available by the United States government "for the education, the promotion of health, the relief of indigency, the promotion of agriculture or for any other purpose other than the administration of the tribal or individual funds of Wisconsin Indians." Provision is made for state administration of such funds.]

70.11. Property exempted from taxation. (19) [Exempts from taxation Indian mounts "or other works of ancient man."]

24.09. (1) [Provision is made for the sale of public lands within exterior boundaries of Indian reservations to Indian tribes located on such reservations or to the United States for the benefit and use of such Indian tribes.]

29.475. Wild life on Indian reservations protected. — [Prohibits the removal from any Indian reservation the carcass of any protected wild animal, bird or fish during the close season without a permit from the state conservation commission.]

Insurance

Automobile Insurance

See Sec. 340.75 under **Public Accommodation.**

Fire Insurance

203.32. Insurance rates and practices. — . . . (3) (a) (2) Rates shall not be excessive, inadequate or unfairly discriminatory. [1947, c. 487, p. 909.]

> [Note: No reference is made to race or color but it would appear that this section could be used to take legal action against discrimination in insurance rates because of race.]

Workmen's Compensation

205.20. Discrimination prohibited. — No company shall make or charge any rate for workmen's compensation insurance in this state which discriminates unfairly between risks or classes, or which discriminates unfairly between risks in the application of like charges and credits in the plan of schedule or merit rating in use; . . . [1933 c. 487, §181.]

> [Note: No reference to race or color.]

206.33. Discriminations. — (1) No life insurance company shall make or permit any distinction or discrimination between insurants of the same class and equal expectation of life in the amount of payment of premiums or in any return of premium, dividends or other advantages. [Stats. 1931, §207.01 (1), (7), (10); 1933 c. 487, §225.]

> [Note: No reference to race or color.]

Ku Klux Klan — Masks

359.17. Masking aggravates crime. — If the defendant committed the crime while masked, he may, in addition to the maximum punishment fixed for such crime, in case of conviction for a misdemeanor, be imprisoned not to exceed one [1] year in the county jail, and in case of a felony not to exceed 5 years in the state prison. [1923, c. 272; 1925 c. 4.]

Military

National Guard — Chapter 76 Laws of 1949

21.35. Federal laws and regulations; no discrimination. — The organization, armament and discipline of the Wisconsin national guard shall be the same as that which is now, or may hereafter be prescribed for the regular and volunteer armies of the United States; and the governor may by order perfect such organization, armament and discipline, at any time, so as to comply with the laws, rules and regulation that may be prescribed for the regular and volunteer armies of the United States; and the governor shall have power to fix and from time to time alter the maximum number of enlisted men which shall form part of any organization of the Wisconsin national guard; provided, that such maximum shall not exceed the statutory maximum prescribed for a like organization of the regular army. Notwithstanding any rule or regulation prescribed by the federal government or any officer or department thereof, no person, otherwise qualified, shall be denied membership in the Wisconsin national guard because of color, race or creed and no member of the Wisconsin national guard shall be segregated within the Wisconsin national guard on the basis of color, race or creed. [1949, c. 76.]

Motor Carriers

194.34. Contract motor carriers ... discrimination. — [Prohibits "any unjust or unreasonable discriminatory rate or practice" in the furnishing of service or charging of rates by contract motor carriers. This section does not mention race or color, but it may be argued that such a section may be invoked to protect against racial or religious discrimination.]

Public Accommodation

Sec. 340.75. Denial of rights. — Any person who shall deny to any other person, in whole or in part, the full and equal enjoyment of the accommodations, advantages, facilities and privileges of inns, restaurants, saloons, barber shops, eating houses, public conveyances on land or water, or any other place of public accommodation or amusement, except for reasons applicable alike to all persons of every race or color, or who shall aid or incite such denial, or require any person to pay a larger sum than the regular rate charged other persons for such accommodations, advantages, facilities, and privileges or any of them, or shall refuse to sell or furnish any type of automobile insurance or charge a higher rate for such insurance because of race or color, shall be liable to the person aggrieved thereby in damages not less than twenty-five [$25.00] dollars with costs, and shall also be punished for every such offense by fine of not more than one hundred [$100.00] dollars or be imprisoned in the county jail not exceeding six [6] months, or by both such fine and imprisonment; provided, that a judgment in favor of the party aggrieved or the imposition of a fine or imprisonment shall bar any other proceeding. [1931, c. 21; 1939 c. 392.]

Public Utilities

196.62. Discrimination, definition, penalty. — If any public utility shall give any unreasonable preference or advantage to any person or shall subject any person to any unreasonable prejudice or disadvantage, such public utility shall be deemed guilty of unjust discrimination which is hereby prohibited . . . Any public utility violating the provisions of this section shall forfeit not less than fifty [$50.00] dollars nor more than one thousand [$1,000.00] dollars for each offense.

[Note: No reference is made in the above section to race or color, but such statutes may be invoked to protect against discrimination generally. See also Sections 196.60 and 196.63. Section 196.64 provides that the public utility may be liable in treble damages to the aggrieved person.]

Railroads

195.12. Preference by carriers prohibited. — If any railroad shall make or give any undue or unreasonable preference or advantage to any person, firm or corporation, or shall subject any person, firm or corporation to any undue or unreasonable prejudice or disadvantage in any respect whatsoever, such railroad shall be deemed guilty of unjust discrimination which is hereby prohibited.

[Note: See also section 195.11. No reference is made to race or color, but such statutes may be invoked against discrimination generally.]

Telephone Companies

175.06. Discrimination by. — [Prohibits discrimination in furnishing of service and transmission of telephone calls by telephone companies and provides for monetary damages where discrimination is practiced. Does not refer to race or color, but may be invoked against discrimination generally.]

WYOMING

CONSTITUTION

Aliens

Art. I, §29. Alien's rights. — No distinction shall ever be made by law between resident aliens and citizens as to the possession, taxation, enjoyment and descent of property. [Const. 1889.]

Art. VI, §10. Alien suffrage. — Five year limit. — Nothing herein contained shall be construed to deprive any person of the right to vote who has such right at the time of the adoption of this constitution, unless disqualified by the restrictions of section six of this article. After the expiration of five (5) years from the time of the adoption of this constitution, none but citizens of the United States shall have the right to vote. [Const. 1889.]

Art. VI, §5. Must be citizens of United States.—No person shall be deemed a qualified elector of this state, unless such person be a citizen of the United States. [Const. 1889.]

Labor on Public Works

Art. XIX, §3. Who shall not be employed. — No person not a citizen of the United States or who has not declared his intention to become such, shall be employed upon or in connection with any state, county or municipal works or employment. [Const. 1889.]

Art. XIX, §4. Enforcement provided for. — The legislature shall, by appropriate legislation, see that the provisions of the foregoing section are enforced. [Const. 1889.]

Education

Art. VII, §10. No discrimination between pupils. — In none of the public schools so established and maintained shall distinction or discrimination be made on account of sex, race or color. [Const. of 1889 as amended.]

[Note: But see below Education, 67-624.]

Art. VII, §16. Tuition free. — The university [of Wyoming] shall be equally open to students of both sexes, irrespective of race or color; . . . [Const. of 1889 as amended.]

Equal Political Rights

Art. I, §3. Equal political rights. — Since equality in the enjoyment of natural and civil rights is only made through political equality, the laws of this state affecting the political rights and privileges of its citizens shall be without distinction of race, color, sex, or any circumstance or condition whatsoever other than individual incompetency, or unworthiness duly ascertained by a court of competent jurisdiction. [Constitution of 1889 as amended.]

Indians

Art. XXI, §26. Public lands—Ownership of disclaimed—Taxation of non-residents — Restrictions. — The people inhabiting this state do agree and declare that they forever disclaim all right and title to the unappropriated public lands lying within the boundaries thereof, and to all lands lying

521

within said limits owned or held by any Indian or Indian tribes, and that until the title thereto shall have been extinguished by the United States, the same shall be and remain subject to the disposition of the United States and that said Indian lands shall remain under absolute jurisdiction and control of the congress of the United States; that the lands belonging to the citizens of the United States residing without this state shall never be taxed at a higher rate than the lands belonging to residents of this state; that no taxes shall be imposed by this state on lands or property therein, belonging to, or which may hereafter be purchased by the United States, or reserved for its use. But nothing in this article shall preclude this state from taxing as other lands are taxed, any lands owned or held by any Indian who has severed his tribal relations, and has obtained from the United States or from any person, a title thereto, by patent or other grant, save and except such lands as have been or may be granted to any Indian or Indians under any acts of congress containing a provision exempting the lands thus granted from taxation, which last mentioned lands shall be exempt from taxation so long, and to such an extent, as is, or may be provided in the act of congress granting the same. [Const. 1889.]

STATUTES

Wyoming Compiled Statutes
1945 (Annotated)

Aliens
Alien Land Law

66-401. **Alien land law.** — There is hereby created an "Alien Land Law." [Laws 1943, ch. 35, §1.]

66-402. **Aliens ineligible to citizenship not to posses land.** — All aliens not eligible to citizenship under the laws of the United States are hereby prohibited from acquiring, possessing, enjoying, using, leasing, transferring, transmitting and inheriting real property, or any interest therein, in this State, or having in whole or in part the beneficial use therof. [Laws 1943, ch. 35, §2.]

[Note: See Const. Art. 1, §29.]

66-403. **Transfer to alien void.** — Any transfer of real property or any interest therein in this State, in whole or in part, to any alien not eligible to citizenship under the laws of the United States is absolutely void and of no effect whatsoever. [Laws 1943, ch. 35, §3.]

66-404. **Chinese excepted.** — Provided the Chinese nationals shall be excluded from the provisions of this Act. [§§66-401 - 66-407]. [Laws 1943, ch. 35, §4.]

66-405. **Violation of provisions by alien.** — Any alien, not eligible for citizenship under the laws of the United States, violating any of the provisions of this Act [§66-401 - 66-407] is deemed guilty of a felony. [Laws 1943, ch. 35, §5.]

66-406. **Violation of provisions by citizen.** — Any citizen of the United

States or any person eligible to citizenship under the laws of the United States who knowingly violates any of the provisions of this Act [§66-401 - 66-407] shall be guilty of a felony. [Laws 1943, ch. 35, §6.]

66-407. Penalty. — Any person violating any of the provisions of this Act [§§66-401 - 66-407] shall be subject to a fine of not more than five thousand dollars [$5,000.00] and sentenced to not more than five [5] years in the state penitentiary, either or both, at the discretion of the court. [Laws 1943, ch. 35, §7.]

6-2506. Alienage not to affect inheritance. — The alienage of the legal heirs shall not invalidate any title to real estate which shall descend or pass from the decedent. [C. L. 1876, ch. 42, §6; R. S. 1887, §2226; R. S. 1899, §4861; C. S. 1910, §5730; C. S. 1920, §7005; Laws 1931, ch. 73, §143; R. S. 1931, §88-4004.]

[Note: See §§66-401 - 66-407 above.]

54-613. Contracts for alien labor void. — No contract made for labor or services with any alien or foreigner previous to the time that such alien or foreigner may come into the state shall be enforced within this state for any period after six [6] months from the date of such contract. [C. L. 1876, ch. 37, §1; R. S. 1887, §1075; R. S. 1899, §2520; C. S. 1910, §3428; C. S. 1920, §4304; R. S. 1931, §63-117.]

[Note: See Const., Art. 19, §3.]

54-614. Alien may recover upon *quantum meruit*. — Any alien or foreigner who shall hereafter perform labor or services for any person or persons, company or corporation within this state, shall be entitled to recover from such person or persons, company or corporation, a reason-able compensation for such labor or services, notwithstanding such person or persons, company or corporation may have paid any other party or parties for the same; and in actions for the price of such labor or services, no defense shall be admitted to the effect that the defendant or defend-ants had contracted with other parties who had, or pretended to have, power or authority to hire out the labor or services of such party or parties, or to receive the pay or price for such labor or services. [C. L. 1876, ch. 37, §2; R. S. 1887, §1076; R. S. 1899, §2521; C. S. 1910, §3429; C. S. 1920, §4305; R. S. 1931, §63-118.]

54-615. Third party receiving pay for ailen's labor. — Any person, whether he or she acts for himself or herself, or as agent, attorney or em-ploye for another or others, who shall, in pursuance of, or by virtue of, any contract made with any alien or foreigner, made before such alien or foreigner came into this state, receive or offer to receive any money, pay or remuneration for the labor or services of any alien or foreigner, except-ing the person so performing such labor or services, shall be deemed guilty of a misdemeanor, and on conviction thereof, shall be fined not less than five hundred dollars [$500.00], and not more than five thousand dollars [$5,000.00], and imprisoned in the county jail for not less than three [3] nor more than twelve [12] months, for each and every offense. [C. L. 1876, ch. 37, §3; R. S. §32-410. 1887, §1077; R. S. 1899, §5125; C. S. 1910 §5976; C. S. 1920, §7272; R. S. 1931, §32-822.]

9-1205. Possession of weapons by aliens. Every person, not being a citizen of the United States, who shall own, possess, wear or carry any dirk, pistol, shot gun, rifle, or other fire arm, bowie knife, dagger, or any other dangerous or deadly weapon, shall upon conviction thereof, be adjudged guilty of a misdemeanor, and shall be fined in any sum not less than twenty-five dollars ($25.00) nor more than one hundred dollars ($100.00) or imprisoned in the county jail not more than six [6] months, or by both such fine and imprisonment. [Laws 1925, ch. 106, §1; R. S. 1931, §32-410.]

Education

67-624. Separate schools for colored children. — When there are fifteen [15] or more colored children within any school district, the board of directors thereof, with the approval of the county superintendent of schools, may provide for a separate school for the instruction of such colored children. [C.L. 1876, ch. 103, §34; R.S. 1887, §3947; R.S. 1899, §552; C.S. 1910, §1954; C.S. 1920, §2258; R.S. 1931, §99-332.]

Jews

3-4611. Persons privileged from arrest. — The following persons are privileged from arrest, viz: . . . . 6. Israelites and such persons as religiously observe the last or any other day of the week as a day of worship, on such day, within, going to, or returning from their places of worship, or during the time of services, and while [going] to our returning therefrom. [Laws 1886, ch. 60, §457; R. S. 1887, §2805; R. S. 1899, §3925; C. S. 1910, §4779; C. S. 1920, §6049; R. S. 1931, §89-3004.]

[Note: The word "going" in brackets is not found in the Compiled Statutes version of 3-4611.]

Miscegenation

§50-108. Intermarriage prohibited in certain cases. — All marriages of white persons with Negroes, Mulattoes, Mongolians or Malaya hereafter contracted in the State of Wyoming are and shall be illegal and void. [Laws, 1913 ch. 57, §1; C.S. 1920, §4972; R.S. 1931, §68-118.]

50-109. Penalty for violation. — Whosoever shall knowingly contract marriage in fact contrary to the prohibition in the preceding section, and whosoever shall knowingly solemnize any such marriage shall be deemed guilty of a misdemeanor, and upon being convicted thereof, shall be punished by a fine of not less than one hundred dollars [$1,00.00], nor more than one thousand dollars [$1,000.00], or imprisonment of not less than one year nor more than five [5] years, or both, at the discretion of the court which shall try the cause. [Laws 1913, ch. 57, §2; C.S. 1920, §4973, R.S. 1931, §68-119.]

50-118. Foreign Marriages. — All marriages contracts without this state, which would be valid by the laws of the country in which the same were contracted, shall be valid in all courts and places in this State. [C.L. 1876, ch. 81, §17; R.S. 1887, §1557; R.S. 1899, §2971; C.S. 1910, §3907; C.S. 1920, §4971; R. S. 1931, §68-117.]

APPENDIX 1.

International Documents

    A. Act of Chapultepec [Excerpts]

    B. Charter of the United Nations [Excerpts]

    C. Final Act of the United Nations Conference for the Establishment of an Educational, Scientific and Cultural Organization.

    D. Universal Declaration of Human Rights.

    E. Full Text of UNESCO Report on Race.

A. ACT OF CHAPULTEPEC

Agreement between the United States of America and Other American Republics
Contained in the Final Act of the Inter-American Conference on
Problems of War and Peace
Signed at Mexico City, March 8, 1945, Effective March 8, 1945.

RESOLUTION XLI
RACIAL DISCRIMINATION

Whereas: World peace cannot be consolidated until men are able to exercise their basic rights without distinction as to race or religion,

The Inter-American Conference on problems of War and Peace
Resolves: 1. To reaffirm the principle, recognized by all the American States, of equality of rights and opportunities for all men, regardless of race or religion.

2. To recommend that the Governments of the American Republics, without jeopardizing freedom of expression, either oral or written, make every effort to prevent in their respective countries all acts which may provoke discrimination among individuals because of race or religion. [Approved at the plenary session of March 7, 1945.]

LX

The Inter-American Conference on Problems of War and Peace **Condemns:** The procedures of cruel racial persecution employed by Hitlerism against the Jews. [Approved at the plenary session of March 8, 1945.]

B. CHARTER OF THE UNITED NATIONS

[Adopted at the United Nations Conference on International Organization at San Francisco, California, April 25th to June 26th, 1945.]

We, the peoples of the United Nations

* * *

To reaffirm faith in fundamental human rights, in the dignity and worth of the human person, in the equal right of men and women and of nations large and small, and

To promote social progress and better standards of life in larger freedom, and for these ends.

To practice tolerance and live together in peace with one another as good neighthese ends

* * *

Accordingly, our respective governments, through representatives assembled in the city of San Francisco, who have exhibited their full powers found to be in good and due form, have agreed to the present Charter of the United Nations and do hereby establish an international organization to be known as the United Nations.

CHAPTER I

PURPOSES AND PRINCIPLES

Article 1. — The purposes of the United Nations are:

* * *

3. To achieve international cooperation in solving international problems of an economic, social, cultural or humanitarian character, and in promoting and encouraging respect for human rights and for fundamental freedoms for all without distinction as to race, sex, language or religion;

* * *

CHAPTER IX

INTERNATIONAL ECONOMIC AND SOCIAL COOPERATION

Article 55. — With a view to the creation of conditions of stability and well-being which are necessary for peaceful and friendly relations among nations based on respect for the principle of equal rights and self-determination of peoples, the United Nations shall promote:

* * *

(c) Universal respect for, and observance of, human rights and fundamental freedoms for all without distinction as to race, sex, language, or religion.

Article 56. — All members pledge themselves to take joint and separate action in co-operation with the Organization for the achievement of the purposes set forth in Article 55.

C. FINAL ACT OF THE UNITED NATIONS CONFERENCE FOR THE ESTABLISHMENT OF AN EDUCATIONAL, SCIENTIFIC AND CULTURAL ORGANIZATION.*

London, 16th November, 1945.

THE Conference for the Establishment of an Educational, Scientific and Cultural Organisation of the United Nations was convened by the Government of the United Kingdom in association with the Government of France. The invitations were sent out in accordance with the recommendation of the Conference of San Francisco and upon the request of the Conference of the Allied Ministers of Education, in order to promote the aims set out in Article I, paragraph 3, of the Charter of the United Nations. The Conference met in London from the 1st to the 16th November, 1945.

The Governments of the following countries were represented at the Conference by Delegates and Advisers:—

Argentine Republic.	France.	Peru.
Australia.	Greece.	Philippines, The.
Belgium.	Guatemala.	Poland.
Bolivia.	Haiti.	Saudi Arabia.
Brazil.	India.	Syria.
Canada.	Iran.	Turkey.
Chile.	Iraq.	Union of South Africa.
China.	Lebanon.	United Kingdom of
Colombia.	Liberia.	Great Britain and
Cuba.	Luxembourg.	Northern Ireland.
Czechoslovakia.	Mexico.	United States of
Denmark.	Netherlands, The.	America.
Dominican Republic.	New Zealand.	Uruguay.
Ecuador.	Nicaragua.	Venezuela (represented
El Salvador.	Norway.	by an Observer).
Egypt.	Panama.	Yugoslavia.

The following international organisations were also represented by Observers:—

International Labour Organisation.
League of Nations Secretariat.
League of Nations Committee on Intellectual Co-operation.
International Institute of Intellectual Co-operation.
Pan-American Union.
United Nations Relief and Rehabilitation Administration (U.N.R.R.A.).
International Bureau of Education.

The Conference had before it, and adopted as its basis of discussion a draft Constitution prepared by the Conference of Allied Ministers of Education. It likewise had

*See *infra.*, E. Full Text of UNESCO Report on Race.

before it a draft Constitution prepared by the French Government. A number of proposals put forward by other Governments and by various bodies and organisations were also before the Conference.

After consideration of these drafts and proposals the Conference drew up a Constitution establishing an Educational, Scientific and Cultural Organisation and an Instrument establishing a Preparatory Educational, Scientific and Cultural Commission.

The Conference also adopted the following Resolution:—

"The seat of the United Nations Educational, Scientific and Cultural Organisation shall be in Paris.

"This Resolution shall not in any way affect the right of the General Conference to take decisions in regard to this matter by a two-thirds majority."

In faith whereof, the undersigned have signed this Final Act.

Done in London, the sixteenth day of November, 1945, in a single copy in the English and French languages, both texts being equally authentic. This copy shall be deposited in the archives of the Government of the United Kingdom, by whom certified copies will be sent to all the United Nations.

(See List of Signatories — page 12.) [*infra*, p. 538]

CONSTITUTION OF THE UNITED NATIONS EDUCATIONAL, SCIENTIFIC AND CULTURAL ORGANISATION

London, 16th November, 1945.

THE Governments of the States parties to this Constitution on behalf of their peoples declare,

that since wars begin in the minds of men, it is in the minds of men that the defences of peace must be constructed;

that ignorance of each other's ways and lives has been a common cause, throughout the history of mankind, of that suspicion and mistrust between the peoples of the world through which their differences have all too often broken into war;

that the great and terrible war which has now ended was a war made possible by the denial of the democratic principles of the dignity, equality and mutual respect of men, and by the propagation, in their place, through ignorance and prejudice, of the doctrine of the inequality of men and races; that the wide diffusion of culture, and the education of humanity for justice and liberty and peace are indispensable to the dignity of

528

man and constitute a sacred duty which all the nations must fulfil in a spirit of mutual assistance and concern;

that a peace based exclusively upon the political and economic arrangements of governments would not be a peace which could secure the unanimous, lasting and sincere support of the peoples of the world, and that the peace must therefore be founded, if it is not to fail, upon the intellectual and moral solidarity of mankind.

For these reasons, the States parties to this Constitution, believing in full and equal opportunities for education for all, in the unrestricted pursuit of objective truth, and in the free exchange of ideas and knowledge, are agreed and determined to develop and to increase the means of communication between their peoples and to employ these means for the purposes of mutual understanding and a truer and more perfect knowledge of each other's lives;

In consequence whereof they do hereby create the United Nations Educational, Scientific and Cultural Organization for the purpose of advancing, through the educational and scientific and cultural relations of the peoples of the world, the objectives of international peace and of the common welfare of mankind for which the United Nations Organisation was established and which its Charter proclaims.

ARTICLE I.
Purposes and Functions.

1. The purpose of the Organisation is to contribute to peace and security by promoting collaboration among the nations through education, science and culture in order to further universal respect for justice, for the rule of law and for the human rights and fundamental freedoms which are affirmed for the peoples of the world, without distinction of race, sex, language or religion, by the Charter of the United Nations.

2. To realise this purpose the Organisation will:

(a) collaborate in the work of advancing the mutual knowledge and understand- of peoples, through all means of mass communication and to that end recommend such international agreements as may be necessary to promote the free flow of ideas by word and image;

(b) give fresh impulse to popular education and to the spread of culture; by collaborating with Members, at their request, in the development of educational activities;

by instituting collaboration among the nations to advance the ideal of equality of educational opportunity without regard to race, sex or any distinctions, economic or social;

by suggesting educational methods best suited to prepare the children of the world for the responsibilities of freedom;

(c) maintain, increase and diffuse knowledge;

by assuring the conservation and protection of the world's inheritance of books, works of art and monuments of history and science, and recommending to the nations concerned the necessary international conventions;

by encouraging co-operation among the nations in all branches of intellectual activity, including the international exchange of persons active in the fields of education, science and culture and the exchange of publications, objects of artistic and scientific interest and other materials of information; by initiating methods of international co-operation calculated to give the people of all countries access to the printed and published materials produced by any of them.

3. With a view to preserving the independence, integrity and fruitful diversity of the cultures and educational systems of the States Members of this Organisation, the Organization is prohibited from intervening in matters which are essentially within their domestic jurisdiction.

ARTICLE II.
Membership.

1. Membership of the United Nations Organisation shall carry with it the right to membership of the United Nations Educational, Scientific and Cultural Organisation.

2. Subject to the conditions of the agreement between this Organisation and the United Nations Organisation, approved pursuant to Article X of this Constitution, States not members of the United Nations Organisation may be admitted to membership of the Organisation, upon recommendation of the Executive Board, by a two-thirds majority vote of the General Conference.

3. Members of the Organisation which are suspended from the exercise of the rights and privileges of membership of the United Nations Organisation shall, upon the request of the latter, be suspended from the rights and privileges of this organisation.

4. Members of the Organisation which are expelled from the United Nations Organisation shall automatically cease to be members of this Organisation.

ARTICLE III.
Organs.

The Organisation shall include a General Conference, an Executive Board and a Secretariat.

ARTICLE IV.
The General Conference.

A.—*Composition.*

1. The General Conference shall consist of the representatives of the States Members of the Organisation. The Government of each Member State shall appoint not more than five delegates, who shall be selected after consultation with the National Commission, if established, or with educational, scientific and cultural bodies.

B.—*Functions.*

2. The General Conference shall determine the policies and the main lines of work of the Organisation. It shall take decisions on programmes drawn up by the Executive Board.

3. The General Conference shall, when it deems it desirable, summon international conferences on education, the sciences and humanities and the dissemination of knowledge.

4. The General Conference shall, in adopting proposals for submission to the Member States, distinguish between recommendations and international conventions submitted for their approval. In the former case a majority vote shall suffice; in the latter case a two-thirds majority shall be required. Each of the Member States shall

submit recommendations or conventions to its competent authorities within a period of one year from the close of the session of the General Conference at which they were adopted.

5. The General Conference shall advise the United Nations Organisation on the educational, scientific and cultural aspects of matters of concern to the latter, in accordance with the terms and procedure agreed upon between the appropriate authorities of the two Organisations.

6. The General Conference shall receive and consider the reports submitted periodically by Member States as provided by Article VIII.

7. The General Conference shall elect the members of the Executive Board and, on the recommendation of the Board, shall appoint the Director-General.

C.—*Voting.*

8. Each Member State shall have one vote in the General Conference. Decisions shall be made by a simple majority except in cases in which a two-thirds majority is required by the provisions of this Constitution. A majority shall be a majority of the members present and voting.

D.—*Procedure.*

9. The General Conference shall meet annually in Ordinary Session; it may meet in Extraordinary Session on the call of the Executive Board. At each session, the location of its next session shall be designated by the General Conference. [As amended in Paris, February 18, 1949.]

10. The General Conference shall adopt its own rules of procedure. It shall at each session elect a President and other officers. '[As amended in Paris, February 18, 1949.]

11. The General Conference shall set up special and technical committees and such other subordinate bodies as may be necessary for its purposes.

12. The General Conference shall cause arrangements to be made for public access to meetings, subject to such regulations as it shall prescribe.

E.—*Observers.*

13. The General Conference, on the recommendation of the Executive Board and by a two-thirds majority, may subject to its rules of procedure, invite as observers at specified sessions of the Conference or of its commissions representatives of international organisations, such as those referred to in Article XI, paragraph 4.

14. When consultative arrangements have been approved by the Executive Board for such international non-governmental or semi-governmental organisations in the manner provided in Article XI (4), those organisations shall be invited to send observers to sessions of the General Conference and its Commissions. [Added at Paris, February 18, 1949.]

ARTICLE V.
Executive Board.

A.—*Composition.*

1. The Executive Board shall consist of eighteen members elected by the General Conference from among the delegates appointed by the Member States, together with the President of the Conference who shall sit *ex officio* in an advisory capacity.

2. In electing the members of the Executive Board the General Conference shall endeavour to include persons competent in the arts, the humanities, the sciences, education and the diffusion of ideas, and qualified by their experience and capacity to fulfill the administrative and executive duties of the Board. It shall also have regard to the diversity of cultures and a balanced geographical distribution. Not more than one national of any Member State shall serve on the Board at any one time, the President of the Conference excepted.

3. The elected members of the Executive Board shall serve for a term of three years, and shall be immediately eligible for a second term, but shall not serve consecutively for more than two terms. At the first election eighteen members shall be elected of whom one-third shall retire at the end of the first year and one-third at the end of the second year, the order of retirement being determined immediately after the election by the drawing of lots. Thereafter six members shall be elected each year.

4. In the event of the death or resignation of one of its members, the Executive Board shall appoint, from among the delegates of the Member State concerned, a substitute, who shall serve until the next session of the General Conference which shall elect a member for the remainder of the term.

B.—*Functions.*

5. The Executive Board, acting under the authority of the General Conference, shall be responsible for the execution of the programme adopted by the Conference and shall prepare its agenda and programme of work.

6. The Executive Board shall recommend to the General Conference the admission of new Members to the Organisation.

7. Subject to decisions of the General Conference, the Executive Board shall adopt its own rules of procedure. It shall elect its officers from among its members.

8. The Executive Board shall meet in regular session at least twice a year and may meet in special session if convoked by the Chairman on his own initiative or upon the request of six members of the Board.

9. The Chairman of the Executive Board shall present to the General Conference, with or without comment, the annual report of the Director-General on the activities of the Organisation, which shall have been previously submitted to the Board.

10. The Executive Board shall make all necessary arrangements to consult the representatives of international organisations or qualized persons concerned with questions within its competence.

11. The members of the Executive Board shall exercise the powers delegated to them by the General Conference on behalf of the Conference as a whole and not as representatives of their respective Governments.

ARTICLE VI.
Secretariat.

1. The Secretariat shall consist of a Director-General and such staff as may be required.

2. The Director-General shall be nominated by the Executive Board and appointed by the General Conference for a period of six years, under such conditions as the Conference may approve, and shall be eligible for reappointment. He shall be the chief administrative officer of the Organisation.

3. The Director-General, or a deputy designated by him, shall participate, without the right to vote, in all meetings of the General Conference, of the Executive Board, and of the committees of the Organisation. He shall formulate proposals for appropriate action by the Conference and the Board.

4. The Director-General shall appoint the staff of the Secretariat in accordance with staff regulations to be approved by the General Conference. Subject to the paramount consideration of securing the highest standards of integrity, efficiency and technical competence, appointment to the staff shall be on as wide a geographical basis as possible.

5. The responsibilities of the Director-General and of the staff shall be exclusively international in character. In the discharge of their duties they shall not seek or receive instructions from any Government or from any authority external to the Organisation. They shall refrain from any action which might prejudice their position as international officials. Each State Member of the Organisation undertakes to respect the international character of the responsibilities of the Director-General and the staff, and not to seek to influence them in the discharge of their duties.

6. Nothing in this Article shall preclude the Organisation from entering into special arrangements within the United Nations Organisation for common services and staff and for the interchange of personnel.

ARTICLE VII.
National Co-operating Bodies.

1. Each Member State shall make such arrangements as suit its particular conditions for the purpose of associating its principal bodies interested in educational, scientific and cultural matters with the work of the Organisation, preferably by the formation of a National Commission broadly representative of the Government and such bodies.

2. National Commissions or national co-operating bodies, where they exist, shall act in an advisory capacity to their respective delegations to the General Conference and to their Governments in matters relating to the Organisation and shall function as agencies of liaison in all matters of interest to it.

3. The Organisation may, on the request of a Member State, delegate, either temporarily or permanently, a member of its Secretariat to serve on the National Commission of that State, in order to assist in the development of its work.

ARTICLE VIII.
Reports by Member States.

Each Member State shall report periodically to the Organisation, in a manner to be determined by the General Conference, on its laws, regulations and statistics relating to educational, scientific and cultural life and institutions, and on the action taken upon the recommendations and conventions referred to in Article IV, paragraph 4.

ARTICLE IX.
Budget.

1. The budget shall be administered by the Organisation.

2. The General Conference shall approve and give final effect to the budget and to the apportionment of financial responsibility among the States Members of the

Organisation subject to such arrangement with the United Nations as may be provided in the agreement to be entered into pursuant to Article X.

3. The Director-General, with the approval of the Executive Board, may receive gifts, bequests, and subventions directly from Governments, public and private institutions, associations and private persons.

ARTICLE X.
Relations with the United Nations Organisation.

This Organisation shall be brought into relation with the United Nations Organisation, as soon as practicable, as one of the specialised agencies referred to in Article 57 of the Charter of the United Nations. This relation ship [relationship] shall be effected through an agreement with the United Nations Organisation under Article 63 of the Charter, which agreement shall be subject to the approval of the General Conference of this Organisation. The agreement shall provide for effective co-operation between the two Organisations in the pursuit of their common purposes, and at the same time shall recognise the autonomy of this Organisation, within the fields of its competence as defined in this Constitution. Such agreement may, among other matters, provide for the approval and financing of the budget of the Organisation by the General Assembly of the United Nations.

ARTICLE XI.
Relations with other specialised international Organisations and agencies.

1. This Organisation may co-operate with other specialised inter-governmental organisations and agencies whose interests and activities are related to its purposes. To this end the Director-General, acting under the general authority of the Executive Board, may establish effective working relationships with such organisations and agencies and establish such joint committees as may be necessary to assure effective co-operation. Any formal arrangements entered into with such organisations or agencies shall be subject to the approval of the Executive Board.

2. Whenever the General Conference of this Organisation and the competent authorities of any other specialised inter-governmental organisations or agencies whose purposes and functions lie within the competence of this Organisation, deem it desirable to effect a transfer of their resources and activities to this Organisation, the Director-General, subject to the approval of the Conference, may enter into mutually acceptable arrangements for this purpose.

3. This Organisation may make appropriate arrangements with other inter- governmental organisations for reciprocal representation at meetings.

4. The United Nations Educational, Scientific and Cultural Organisation may make suitable arrangements for consultation and co-operation with non-governmental international organisations concerned with matters within its competence, and may invite them to undertake specific tasks. Such co-operation may also include appropriate participation by representatives of such organisations on advisory committees set up by the General Conference.

ARTICLE XII.
Legal status of the Organisation.

The provisions of Articles 104 and 105 of the Charter of the United Nations Organisation concerning the legal status of that Organisation, its privileges and immunities shall apply in the same way to this Organisation.

ARTICLE XIII.
Amendments.

1. Proposals for amendments to this Constitution shall become effective upon receiving the approval of the General Conference by a two-thirds majority; provided, however, that those amendments which involve fundamental alterations in the aims of the Organisation or new obligations for the Member States shall require subsequent acceptance on the part of two-thirds of the Member States before they come into force. The draft texts of proposed amendments shall be communicated by the Director-General to the Member States at least six months in advance of their consideration by the General Conference.

2. The General Conference shall have power to adopt by a two-thirds majority rules of procedure for carrying out the provisions of this Article.

ARTICLE XIV.
Interpretation.

1. The English and French texts of this Constitution shall be regarded as equally authoritative.

2. Any question or dispute concerning the interpretation of this Constitution shall be referred for determination to the International Court of Justice or to an arbitral tribunal, as the General Conference may determine under its rules of procedure.

ARTICLE XV.
Entry into force.

1. This Constitution shall be subject to acceptance. The instruments of acceptance shall be deposited with the Government of the United Kingdom.

2. This Constitution shall remain open for signature in the archives of the Government of the United Kingdom. Signature may take place either before or after the deposit of the instrument of acceptance. No acceptance shall be valid unless preceded or followed by signature.

3. This Constitution shall come into force when it has been accepted by twenty of its signatories. Subsequent acceptances shall take effect immediately.

4. The Government of the United Kingdom will inform all members of the United Nations of the receipt of all instruments of acceptance and of the date on which the Constitution comes into force in accordance with the preceding paragraph.

In faith whereof, the undersigned, duly authorised to that effect, have signed this Constitution in the English and French languages, both texts being equally authentic.

Done in London the sixteenth day of November, 1945, in a single copy, in the English and French languages, of which certified copies will be communicated by the Government of the United Kingdom to the Governments of all the Members of the United Nations.

(See List of Signatories — page 12.) [infra, p. 538]

INSTRUMENT ESTABLISHING A PREPARATORY EDUCATIONAL, SCIENTIFIC AND CULTURAL COMMISSION.

London, 16th November, 1945.

THE Governments represented at the United Nations Educational and Cultural Conference in London,

Having determined that an international organisation to be known as the United Nations Educational, Scientific and Cultural Organisation shall be established, and

Having formulated the Constitution of the United Nations Educational, Scientific and Cultural Organisation,

Agree as follows:—

1. Pending the coming into force of the Constitution and the establishment of the Organisation provided for therein, there shall be established a Preparatory Commission to make arrangements for the first Session of the General Conference of the Organisation, and to take such other steps as are indicated below.

2. For this purpose the Commission shall:—

(*a*) Convoke the First Session of the General Conference.

(*b*) Prepare the provisional agenda for the First Session of the General Conference and prepare documents and recommendations relating to all matters on the agenda including such matters as the possible transfer of functions, activities and assets of existing international agencies, the specific arrangements between this Organisation and the United Nations Organisation, and arrangements for the Secretariat of the Organisation and the appointment of its Director-General.

(*c*) Make studies and prepare recommendations concerning the programme and the budget of the Organisation for presentation to the General Conference at its First Session.

(*d*) Provide without delay for immediate action on urgent needs of educational, scientific, and cultural reconstruction in devasted countries as indicated in Paragraph 6 and 7.

3. The Commission shall consist of one representative of each of the Governments signatory to this Instrument.

4. The Commission shall appoint an Executive Committee composed of fifteen members to be selected at the first meeting of the Commission. The Executive Committee shall exercise any or all powers of the Commission as the Commission may determine.

5. The Commission shall establish its own rules of procedure and shall appoint such other committees and consult with such specialists as may be desirable to facilitate its work.

6. The Commission shall appoint a special technical sub-committee to examine the problems relating to the educational, scientific and cultural needs of the countries devastated by the war, having regard to the information already collected and the work being done by other international organisations, and to prepare as complete a conspectus as possible of the extent and nature of the problems for the information of the Organisation at the First Session of the Conference.

7. When the technical sub-committee is satisfied that any ameliorative measures are immediately practicable to meet any educational, scientific or cultural needs it shall report to the Commission accordingly and the Commission shall, if it approves, take steps to bring such needs to the attention of Governments, organisations, and persons wishing to assist by contributing money, supplies or services in order that co-ordinated relief may be given either directly by the donors to the countries requiring aid or indirectly through existing international relief organisations.

8. The Commission shall appoint an Executive Secretary who shall exercise such powers and perform such duties as the Commission may determine, with such international staff as may be required. The staff shall be composed as far as possible of officials and specialists made available for this purpose by the participating Governments on the invitation of the Executive Secretary.

9. The provisions of Articles 104 and 105 of the Charter of the United Naitons Organisation concerning the legal status of that Organisation, its privileges and immunities shall apply in the same way to this Commission.

10. The Commission shall hold its first meeting in London immediately after the conclusion of the present Conference and shall continue to sit in London until such time as the Constitution of the Organisation has come into force. The Commission shall then transfer to Paris where the permanent Organisation is to be located.

11. During such period as the Commission is in London, the expenses of its maintenance shall be met by the Government of the United Kingdom on the understanding:

(1) that the amount of the expenses so incurred will be deducted from the contribution of that Government to the new Organisation until they have been recovered, and

(2) that it will be open to the Commission, if circumstances so warrant, to seek contributions from other Governments.

When the Commission is transferred to Paris, the financial responsibility will pass to the French Government on the same terms.

12. The Commission shall cease to exist upon the assumption of office of the Director-General of the Organisation, at which time its property and records shall be transferred to the Organisation.

13. The Government of the United Kingdom shall be temporary depositary and shall have custody of the original document embodying these interim arrangements in the English and French languages. The Government of the United Kingdom shall transfer the original to the Director-General on his assumption of office.

14. This Instrument shall be effective as from this date, and shall remain open for signature on behalf of the States entitled to be the original Members of the United Nations Educational, Scientific and Cultural Organisation, until the Commission is dissolved in accordance with paragraph 12.

In faith whereof, the undersigned representatives having been duly authorised for that purpose, have signed this Instrument in the English and French languages, both texts being equally authentic.

Done in London the Sixteenth day of November, 1945, in a single copy, in the English and French languages, of which certified copies will be communicated by the Government of the United Kingdom to the Governments of all the States Members of the United Nations.

(See List of Signatories — page 12.) [infra, p. 538]

UNITED NATIONS CONFERENCE FOR THE ESTABLISHMENT OF AN EDUCATIONAL, SCIENTIFIC AND CULTURAL ORGANISATION

LIST OF SIGNATORIES.

Country	Final Act	Constitution of Organisation	Instrument Establishing a Preparatory Commission.
Argentine Republic	X	X	X
Australia	X		
Belgium	X	X	X
Bolivia	X	X	X
Brazil	X	X	X
Canada	X	X	X
Chile	X	X	X
China	X	X	X
Colombia	X	X	X
Cuba	X	X	X
Czechoslovakia	X	X	X
Denmark	X	X	X
Dominican Republic	X	X	X
Ecuador	X	X	X
Egypt	X	X	X
France	X		
Greece	X	X	X
Guatemala	X	X	X
Haiti	X	X	X
India	X	X	X
Iran	X		X
Iraq	X		X
Lebanon	X	X	X
Luxembourg	X	X	X
Mexico	X	X	X
The Netherlands	X	X	X
New Zealand	X	X	X
Nicaragua	X	X	X
Norway	X	X	X
Panama	X	X	X
Peru	X	X	X
The Philippines	X	X	X
Poland	X	X	X
Saudi Arabia	X	X	X
Syria	X	X	X
Turkey	X	X	X
Union of South Africa	X		X
United Kingdom of Great Britain and Northern Ireland	X	X	X
United States of America	X		X
Uruguay	X	X	X
Venezuela	X	X	X

538

D. UNIVERSAL DECLARATION OF HUMAN RIGHTS*

THE UNIVERSAL DECLARATION OF HUMAN RIGHTS was approved by the United Nations General Assembly in Paris December 10, 1948, by a vote of 48 to 0. Eight countries abstained — the U. S. S. R., the Ukraine, Byelorussia, Poland, Czechoslovakia, Yugoslavia, Saudi Arabia, and the Union of South Africa.

The Declaration is a statement of principles approved as a common standard of achievement for all peoples and all nations. It is not a treaty and therefore imposes no legal obligations. It is, however, a challenge to all mankind to promote world-wide respect for human rights and fundamental freedoms.

An International Covenant on Human Rights is now being developed in the United Nations. This will be a treaty and will deal with certain of the basic civil and political rights embodied in the Declaration. The United Nations Commission on Human Rights expects to complete the drafting of this Covenant at its next session early in 1949. It will then be considered by the Economic and Social Council of the United Nations and later by the General Assembly. After it has been approved by the General Assembly, the Covenant will be submitted to individual countries for ratification and will become legally binding on the countries which ratify it.

The United States actively supported the approval of the Declaration of Human Rights in the General Assembly in Paris. Secretary of State Marshall called for its approval at the opening of the session. He began his address by urging the nations to approve "a new declaration of human rights for free men in a free world", and continued:

"Systematic and deliberate denials of basic human rights lie at the root of most of our troubles and threaten the work of the United Nations. It is not only fundamentally wrong that millions of men and women live in daily terror of secret police, subject to seizure, imprisonment, or forced labor without just cause and without fair trial, but these wrongs have repercussions in the community of nations. Governments which systematically disregard the rights of other nations and other people and are likely to seek their objectives by coercion and force in the international field."

---

*Reprinted from Department of State publication 3381, International Organisation and conference Series III, 20. Released January 20, 1949, U. S. Government Printing Office, Washington 25, D.C.

UNIVERSAL DECLARATION
OF HUMAN RIGHTS*

APPROVED BY THE GENERAL ASSEMBLY AT ITS PLENARY
MEETING ON 10 DECEMBER 1948

Preamble

WHEREAS recognition of the inherent dignity and of the equal and inalienable rights of all members of the human family is the foundation of freedom, justice and peace in the world,

WHEREAS disregard and contempt for human rights have resulted in barbarous acts which have outraged the conscience of mankind, and the advent of a world in which human beings shall enjoy freedom of speech and belief and freedom from fear and want has been proclaimed as the highest aspiration of the common people,

WHEREAS it is essential, if man is not to be compelled to have recourse, as a last resort, to rebellion against tyranny and oppression, that human rights should be protected by the rule of law,

WHEREAS it is essential to promote the development of friendly relations between nations,

WHEREAS the peoples of the United Nations have in the Charter reaffirmed their faith in fundamental human rights, in the dignity and worth of the human person and in the equal rights of men and women and have determined to promote social progress and better standards of life in larger freedom,

WHEREAS Member States have pledged themselves to achieve, in co-operation with the United Nations, the promotion of universal respect for and observance of human rights and fundamental freedoms,

WHEREAS a common understanding of these rights and freedoms is of the greatest importance for the full realization of this pledge,

Now therefore

The General Assembly,

Proclaims this Universal Declaration of Human Rights as a common standard of achievement for all peoples and all nations, to the end that every individual and every organ of society, keeping this Declaration constantly in mind, shall strive by teaching and eduction to promote respect for these rights and freedoms and by progressive measures, national and international, to secure their universal and effective recognition and observance, both among the peoples of Member States themselves and among the peoples of territories under their jurisdiction.

Article 1

All human beings are born free and equal in dignity and rights. They are endowed with reason and conscience and should act towards one another in a spirit of brotherhood.

Article 2

Everyone is entitled to all the rights and freedoms set forth in this Declaration, without distinction of any kind, such as race, colour, sex, language, religion, political

*Dept. of State publication 3381.

or other opinion, national or social origin, property, birth or other status.

Furthermore, no distinction shall be made on the basis of the political, jurisdictional or international status of the country or territory to which a person belongs, whether it be independent, trust, non-self-governing or under any other limitation of sovereignty.

Article 3

Everyone has the right to life, liberty and the security of person.

Article 4

No one shall be held in slavery or servitude; slavery and the slave trade shall be prohibited in all their forms.

Article 5

No one shall be subjected to torture or to cruel, inhuman or degrading treatment or punishment.

Article 6

Everyone has the right to recognition everywhere as a person before the law.

Article 7

All are equal before the law and are entitled without any discrimination to equal protection of the law. All are entitled to equal protection against any discrimination in violation of this Declaration and against any incitement to such discrimination.

Article 8

Everyone has the right to an effective remedy by the competent national tribunals for acts violating the fundamental rights granted him by the constitution or by law.

Article 9

No one shall be subjected to arbitrary arrest, detention or exile.

Article 10

Everyone is entitled in full equality to a fair and public hearing by an independent and impartial tribunal, in the determination of his rights and obligations and of any criminal charge against him.

Article 11

1. Everyone charged with a penal offence has the right to be presumed innocent until proved guilty according to law in a public trial at which he has had all the guarantees necessary for his defence.

2. No one shall be held guilty of any penal offence on account of any act or ommission which did not constitute a penal offence, under national or international law, at the time when it was committed. Nor shall a heavier penalty be imposed than the one that was applicable at the time the penal offence was committed.

Article 12

No one shall be subjected to arbitrary interference with his privacy, family, home or correspondence, nor to attacks upon his honour and reputation. Everyone has the right to the protection of the law against such interference or attacks.

Article 13

1. Everyone has the right to freedom of movement and residence within the borders of each state.

2. Everyone has the right to leave any country, including his own, and to return to his country.

Article 14

1. Everyone has the right to seek and to enjoy in other countries asylum from persecution.

2. This right may not be invoked in the case of prosecutions genuinely arising from non-political crimes or from acts contrary to the purposes and principles of the United Nations.

Article 15

1. Everyone has the right to a nationality.

2. No one shall be arbitrarily deprived of his nationality nor denied the right to change his nationality.

Article 16

1. Men and women of full age, without any limitation due to race, nationality or religion, have the right to marry and to found a family. They are entitled to equal rights as to marriage, during marriage and at its dissolution.

2. Marriage shall be entered into only with the free and full consent of the intending spouses.

3. The family is the natural and fundamental group unit of society and is entitled to protection by society and the State.

Article 17

1. Everyone has the right to own property alone as well as in association with others.

2. No one shall be arbitrarily deprived of his property.

Article 18

Everyone has the right to freedom of thought, conscience and religion; this right includes freedom to change his religion or belief, and freedom, either alone or in community with others and in public or private, to manifest his religion or belief in teaching, practice, worship and observance.

Article 19

Everyone has the right to freedom of opinion and expression; this right includes freedom to hold opinions without interference and to seek, receive and impart information and ideas through any media and regardless of frontiers.

Article 20

1. Everyone has the right to freedom of peaceful assembly and association.

2. No one may be compelled to belong to an association.

Article 21

1. Everyone has the right to take part in the Government of his country, directly or through freely chosen representatives.

2. Everyone has the right of equal access to public service in his country.

3. The will of the people shall be the basis of the authority of government; this will shall be expressed in periodic and genuine elections which shall be by universal and equal suffrage and shall be held by secret vote or by equivalent free voting procedures.

Article 22

Everyone, as a member of society, has the right to social security and is entitled to realization, through national effort and international cooperation and in accordance with the organization and resources of each State, of the economic, social and cultural rights indispensable for his dignity and the free development of his personality.

Article 23

1. Everyone has the right to work, to free choice of employment, to just and favourable conditions of work and to protection against unemployment.

2. Everyone, without any discrimination, has the right to equal pay for equal work.

3. Everyone who works has the right to just and favourable remuneration insuring for himself and his family an existence worthy of human dignity, and supplemented, if necessary, by other means of social protection.

4. Everyone has the right to form and to join trade unions for the protection of his interests.

Article 24

Everyone has the right to rest and leisure, including reasonable limitation of working hours and periodic holidays with pay.

Article 25

1. Everyone has the right to a standard of living adequate for the health and well-being of himself and of his family, including food, clothing, housing and medical care and necessary social services, and the right to security in the event of unemployment, sickness, disability, widowhood, old age or other lack of livelihood in circumstances beyond his control.

2. Motherhood and childhood are entitled to special care and assistance. All children, whether born in or out of wedlock, shall enjoy the same social protection.

Article 26

1. Everyone has the right to education. Education shall be free, at least in the elementary and fundamental stages. Elementary education shall be compulsory. Technical and professional education shall be made generally available and higher education shall be equally accessible to all on the basis of merit.

2. Education shall be directed to the full development of the human personality and to the strengthening of respect for human rights and fundamental freedoms. It shall promote understanding, tolerance and friendship among all nations, racial or religious groups, and shall further the activities of the United Nations for the maintenance of peace.

3. Parents have a prior right to choose the kind of education that shall be given to their children.

Article 27

1. Everyone has the right freely to participate in the cultural life of the community, to enjoy the arts and to share in scientific advancement and its benefits.

2. Everyone has the right to the protection of the moral and material interests resulting from any scientific, literary or artistic production of which he is the author. author.

Article 28

Everyone is entitled to a social and international order in which the rights and freedoms set forth in this Declaration can be fully realized.

Article 29

1. Everyone has duties to the community in which alone the free and full development of his personality is possible.

2. In the exercise of his rights and freedoms, everyone shall be subject only to such limitations as are determined by law solely for the purpose of securing due recognition and respect for the rights and freedoms of others and of meeting the just requirements of morality, public order and the general welfare in a democratice society.

3. These rights and freedoms may in no case be exercised contrary to the purposes and principles of the United Nations.

Article 30

Nothing in this Declaration may be interpreted as implying for any State, group or person any right to engage in any activity or to perform any act aimed at the destruction of any of the rights and freedoms set forth herein.

UNITED NATIONS

Department of Public Information
Press and Publications Bureau
Lake Success, New York

E. FULL TEXT OF UNESCO REPORT ON RACE*

(The following was received at UN Headquarters from UNESCO, Paris.)

1. Scientists have reached general agreement in recognizing that mankind is one: that all men belong to the same species, *Homo sapiens*. It is further generally agreed among scientists that all men are probably derived from the same common stock; and that such differences as exist between different groups of mankind are due to the operation of evolutionary factors of differentiation such as isolation, the drift and random fixation

---

*Reprinted from Press Release UNESCO/220/8dd. 1 18, July 1950.

of the material particles which control heredity (the genes), changes in the structure of these particles, hybridization, and natural selection. In these ways groups have arisen of varying stability and degree of differentiation which have been classified in different ways for different purposes.

2. From the biological standpoint, the species *Homo Sapiens* is made up of a number of populations, each one of which differs from the others in the frequency of one or more genes. Such genes, responsible for the heriditary differences between men, are always few when compared to the whole genetic constitution of man and to the vast number of genes common to all human beings regardless of the population to which they belong. This means that the likenesses among men are far greater than their differences.

3. A race, from the biological standpoint, may therefore be defined as one of the group of populations constituting the species *Homo sapiens*. These populations are capable of inter-breeding with one another but, by virtue of the isolating barriers which in the past kept them more or less separated, exhibit certain physical differences as a result of their somewhat different biological histories. These represent variations, as it were, on a common theme.

4. In short, the term "race" designates a group or population characterised by some concentrations, relative as to frequency and distribution, of hereditary particles (genes) or physical characters, which appear, fluctuate, and often disappear in the course of time by reason of geographic and/or cultural isolation. The varying manifestations of these traits in different populations are perceived in different ways by each group. What is perceived is largely preconceived, so that each group arbitrarily tends to misinterpret the variability which occurs as a fundamental difference which separates that group from all others.

5. These are the scientific facts. Unfortunately, however, when most people use the term "race" they do not do so in the sense above defined. To most people, a race is any group of people whom they choose to describe as a race. Thus, many national, religious, geographic, linguistic or cultural groups have, in such loose usage, been called "race", when obviously Americans are not a race, nor are Englishmen, nor Frenchmen, nor any other national group. Catholics, Protestants, Moslems, and Jews are not races, nor are groups who speak English or any other language thereby definable as a race, people who live in Iceland or England or India are not races; nor are people who are culturally Turkish or Chinese or the like thereby describable as races.

6. National, religious, geographic, linguistic and cultural groups do not necessarily coincide with racial groups; and the cultural traits of such groups have no demonstrated genetic connection with racial traits. Because errors of this kind are habitually committed when the term "race" is used in popular parlance, it would be better when speaking of human races to drop the term "race" altogether and speak of *ethnic groups*.

7. Now what has the scientist to say about the groups of mankind which may be recognized at the present time? Human races can be and have been differently classified by different anthropologists, but at the present time most anthropologists agree in classifying the greater part of present-day mankind into three major divisions, as follows:

The Mongoloid Division

The Negroid Division

The Caucasoid Division

The biological processess which the classifier has here embalmed, as it were, are dynamic, not static. These divisions were not the same in the past as they are at present, and there is every reason to believe that they will change in the future.

8. Many sub-groups or ethnic groups within these divisions have been described. There is no general agreement upon their number, and in any event most ethnic groups have not yet been either studied or described by the physical anthropologists.

9. Whatever classification the anthropologist makes of man, he never includes mental characteristics as part of those classificatitons. It is now generally recognized that intelligence tests do not in themselves enable us to differentiate safely between what is due to innate capacity and what is the result of environmental influences, training and education. Wherever it has been possible to make allowances for differences in environmental opportunities, the tests have shown essential similarity in mental characters among all human groups. In short, given similar degrees of cultural opportunity to realise their potentialities, the average achievement of the members of each ethnic group is about the same. The scientific investigations of recent years fully support the dictum of Confucius (551-478 B.C.) "Men's natures are alike; it is their habits that carry them far apart".

10. The scientific material available to us at present does not justify the conclusion that inherited genetic differences are a major factor in producing the differences between the cultures and cultural achievements of different peoples or groups. It does indicate, however, that the history of the cultural experience which each group has undergone is the major factor in explaining such differences. The one trait which above all others has been at a premium in the evolution of men's mental characters has been educability, plasticity. This is a trait which all human beings possess. It is indeed, a species character of *Homo sapiens*.

11. So far as temperament is concerned, there is no definite evidence that there exist inborn differences between human groups. There is evidence that whatever group differences of the kind there might be are greatly over-ridden by the individual differences, and by the differences springing from environmental factors.

12. As for personality and character, these may be considered raceless. In every human group a rich variety of personality and character types will be found, and there is no reason for believeing that any human group is richer than any other in these respects.

13. With respect to race-mixture, the evidence points unequivocally to the fact that this has been going on from the earliest times. Indeed, one of the chief processes of race-formation and race-extinction or absorption is by means of hybridization between races or ethnic groups. Furthermore, no convincing evidence has been adduced that race-mixture of itself produces biologically bad effects. Statements that human hybrids frequently show undesirable traits, both physically and mentally, physical disharmonies and mental degeneracies, are not supported by the facts. There is, therefore, no *biological* justification for prohibiting inter-marriage between persons of different ethnic groups.

14. The biological fact of race and the myth of "race" should be distinguished, for all practical social purposes "race" is not so much a biological phenomenon as a social myth. The myth of "race" has created an enormous amount of human and social damage. In recent years it has taken a heavy toll in human lives and caused untold suffering. It still prevents the normal development of millions of human beings and deprives civilization of the effective co-operation of productive minds. The biological differences between ethnic groups should be disregarded from the standpoint of social acceptance and social action. The unity of mankind from both the biological and social view points is the main thing. To recognize this and to act accordingly is the first

requirement of modern man. It is but to recognize what a great biologist wrote in 1875: "As man advances in civilization, and small tribes are united into larger communities, the simplest reason would tell each individual that he ought to extend his social instincts and sympathies to all the members of the same nation, though personally unknown to him. This point being once reached, there is only an artificial barrier to prevent his sympathies extending to the men of all nations and races". These are the words of Charles Darwin in "The Descent of Man" (2nd ed., 1875, pp. 187-188). And, indeed, the whole of human history shows that a co-operative spirit is not only natural to men, but more deeply rooted than any self-seeking tendencies. If this were not so we should not see the growth of integration and organization of his communities which the centuries and the millennia plainly exhibit.

15. We now have to consider the bearing of these statements on the problem of human equality. It must be asserted with the utmost emphasis that equality as an ethical principle in no way depends upon the assertion that human beings are in fact equal in endowment. Obviously individuals in all ethnic groups vary greatly among themselves in endowment. Nevertheless, the characteristics in which human groups differ from one another are often exaggerated and used as a basis for questioning the validity of equality in the ethical sense. For this purpose we have thought it worth while to set out in a formal manner what is at present scientifically established concerning individual and group differences.

(1) In matters of race, the only characteristics which anthropologists can effectively use as a basis for classifications are physical and physiological.

(2) According to present knowledge there is no proof that the groups of mankind differ in their innate mental characteristics, whether in respect of intelligence or temperament. The scientific evidence indicates that the range of mental capacities in all ethnic groups is much the same.

(3) Historical and sociological studies support the view that genetic differences are not of importance in determining the social and cultural differences between different groups of *homo sapiens,* and that the social and cultural *changes* in different groups have, in the main, been independent of *changes* in inborn constitution. Vast social changes have occurred which were not in any way connected with changes in racial type.

(4) There is no evidence that race mixture as such produces bad results from the biological point of view. The social results of race mixture whether for good or ill are to be traced to social factors.

(5) All normal human beings are capable of learning to share in a common life, to understand the nature of mutual service and reciprocity, and to respect social obligations and contracts. Such biological differences as exist between members of different ethnic groups have no relevance to problems of social and political organization, moral life and communication between human beings.

Lastly, biological studies lend support to the ethic of universal brotherhood; for man is born with drives toward co-operation, and unless these drives are satisfied, men and nations alikè fall ill. Man is born a social being who can reach his fullest development only through interaction with his fellows. The denial at any point of this social bond between men and man brings with it disintegration. In this sense, every man is his brother's keeper. For every man is a piece of the continent, a part of the main, because he is involved in mankind.

Original statement drafted at Unesco House, Paris, by the following experts:-

Professor Ernest Beaglehole, *New Zealand*.

Professor Juan Comas, *Mexico*.

Professor L. A. Costa Pinto, *Brazil*.

Professor Franklin Frazier, *United States*.

Professor Morris Ginsberg, *United Kingdom*.

Dr. Humayun Kabir, *India*.

Professor Claude Levi-Strauss, *France*.

Professor Ashley Montagu, *United States* (Rapporteur)

Text revised by Professor Ashley Montagu, after criticism submitted by Professors Hadley Cantril, E. G. Conklin, Gunnar Dahlberg, Theodosius Dobzhansky, L. C. Dunn, Donald Hager, Julian S. Huxley, Otto Klineberg, Wilbert Moore, H. J. Muller, Gunnar Myrdal, Joseph Needham.

APPENDIX 2.

Excerpts from
Declaration of Independence, Constitution and Laws of the United States.

THE DECLARATION OF INDEPENDENCE — 1776
In Congress, July 4, 1776

The unanimous Declaration of the thirteen United States of America.

. . . We hold these truths to be self-evident, that all men are created equal, that they are endowed by their Creator with certain unalienable Rights, that among these are Life, Liberty and the pursuit of Happiness. That to secure these rights, Governments are instituted among Men, deriving their just powers from the consent of the governed,—That whenever any Form of Government becomes destructive of these ends, it is the Right of the People to alter or to abolish it, and to institute new Government, laying its foundation on such principles and organizing its powers in such form, as to them shall seem most likely to effect their Safety and Happiness. * * *

CONSTITUTION
of the
UNITED STATES — 1787

(Preamble)

We The People of the United States, in Order to form a more perfect Union, establish Justice, insure domestic Tranquility, provide for the common defence, promote the general Welfare, and secure the Blessings of Liberty to ourselves and our Posterity, do ordain and establish this Constitution for the United States of America.

* * * *

ARTICLE IV

Section 2. The Citizens of each State shall be entitled to all Privileges and Immunities of Citizens in the several States.

[Note: See *Valle v. Stengel*, 176 F. 2d. 697 (U.S.C. App. Third Circuit, decided August 10, 1949.)]

* * * *

BILL OF RIGHTS
AMENDMENT V

No person shall be held to answer for a capital, or otherwise infamous crime, unless on a presentment or indictment of a Grand Jury, except in cases arising in the land or naval forces, or in the militia, when in actual service in time of war or public danger; nor shall any person be subject for the same offense to be twice put in jeopardy of life or limb; nor shall be compelled in any criminal case to be a witness against himself, nor be deprived of life, liberty, or property, without due process of law; nor shall private property be taken for public use without just compensation.

* * * *

AMENDMENT XIII.

Section 1. Neither slavery nor involuntary servitude, except as a punishment for crime whereof the party shall have been duly convicted, shall exist within the United States, or any place subject to their jurisdiction.

Section 2. Congress shall have power to enforce this article by appropriate legislation. [eff. Dec. 18, 1865.]

AMENDMENT XIV

Section 1. All persons born or naturalized in the United States, and subject to the jurisdiction thereof, are citizens of the United States and of the State wherein they reside. No State shall make or enforce any law which shall abridge the privileges or immunities of citizens of the United States; nor shall any State deprive any person of life, liberty, or property, without due process of law; nor deny to any person within its jurisdiction the equal protection of the laws. [Became effective July 21, 1868.]

AMENDMENT XV

Section 1. The right of citizens of the United States to vote shall not be denied or abridged by the United States or by any State on account of race, color, or previous condition of servitude.

Section 2. The Congress shall have power to enforce this article by appropriate legislation. [Became effective March 30, 1870.]

UNITED STATES CODE
[1946 Edition]
ALIEN OWNERSHIP OF LAND
[See United States Code, Title 8, Ch. 5, §§71-86]

* * *

TITLE 5.

EXECUTIVE DEPARTMENTS — OFFICERS — EMPLOYEES

§22. Departmental Regulations. — The head of each department is authorized to prescribe regulations, not inconsistent with law, for the government of his department, the conduct of its officers and clerks, the distribution and performance of its business, and the custody, use, and preservation of the records, papers, and property appertaining to it. [R.S. §161.]

[Note: See below Executive Order No. 9980.]

[1946 Edition, Supp. III]

TITLE 5

EXECUTIVE DEPARTMENTS — OFFICERS — EMPLOYEES.

Ch. 2-A.—Department of Defense

§171. Establishment and composition. — (a) There is established, as an Executive Department of the Government, the Department of Defense, and the Secretary of Defense shall be the head thereof.

(b) There shall be within the Department of Defense (1) the Department of the Army, the Department of the Navy, and the Department of the Air Force, and each such department shall on and after August 10, 1949, be military departments in lieu of their prior status as Executive Departments and (2) all other agencies created under sections 171, 171a, 171c-171i, 411a, 626 and 626c of this title. [July 26, 1947, ch. 343, title II, §201 (a), (b), 61 Stat. 499, amended Aug. 10, 1949, ch. 412, §4, 63 Stat. 579.]

[Note: The 1949 amendment changed the name of the National Military Establishment to the Department of Defense. See below **Executive Order No. 9981** and directives and statements issued by the **National Military Establishment** and the **Department of Defense** with reference to equality of opportunity in the armed forces.]

* * *

551

TITLE 5
EXECUTIVE DEPARTMENTS — OFFICERS — EMPLOYEES
Chapter 13
CLASSIFICATION OF CIVILIAN POSITIONS

* * *

§681. (e) Prohibition against racial, religious, or color discrimination. — [Repealed, Oct. 28, 1949, ch. 782, title XII, §1202(6-8), 63 Stat. 973.]

[1946 Ediiton, Supp. III.]

Chapter 21
Classification of Civilian Positions

§1074. Discrimination banned. — In the administration of this chapter, there shall be no discrimination with respect to any person, or with respect to the position held by any person on account of sex, marital status, race, creed, or color. [Oct. 28, 1949, ch. 782, title XI, §1103, 63 Stat. 972.]

[Note: The above section relates to classified civil service appointments, promotions, exemptions and compensation. See below Executive Order 9980, Regulations and Procedures for the Internal Operation of the Fair Employment Board of the United States Civil Service Commission and Instructions for Carrying Out the Fair Employment Program Under Executive Order 9980.]

TITLE 7
AGRICULTURE
Chapter 13
AGRICULTURAL AND MECHANICAL COLLEGES

§323. Racial discrimination by colleges restricted. — No money shall be paid out under Sections 321-328 of this title to any State and Territory for the support or maintenance of a college where a distinction of race or color is made in the admission of students, but the establishment and maintenance of such colleges separately for white and colored students shall be held to be a compliance with the provisions of said sections if the funds received in such State or Territory be equitably divided as hereinafter set forth: *Provided,* That in any State in which there has been one college established in pursuance of sections 301-308 of this title, and also in which an educational institution of like character has been established, or may be hereafter established, and is on August 30, 1890, aided by such State from its own revenue, for the education of colored students in agriculture and the mechanic arts, however named or styled, or whether or not it has received money prior to August 30, 1890, under sections 301-308 of this title, the legislature of such State may propose and report to the Secretary of the Interior a just and equitable division of the fund to be received under sections 321-328 of this title between one college for white students and one institution for colored students established as aforesaid, which shall be divided into two parts and paid accordingly, and thereupon such institution for colored students shall be entitled to the benefits of said sections and subject to their provisions, as much as it would have been if it had been included under sections 301-308 of this title, and the fulfillment of the foregoing provisions shall be taken as a compliance with the provision in reference to separate colleges for white and colored students. [Aug. 30, 1890, ch. 841, §1, 26 Stat. 417.]

[1946 Edition]

TITLE 8
ALIENS AND NATIONALITY

Chapter 2
ELECTIVE FRANCHISE

§31. Race, color, or previous condition not to affect right to vote. — All citizens of the United States who are otherwise qualified by law to vote at any election by the people in any State, Territory, district, county, city, parish, township, school district, municipality, or other territorial subdivision, shall be entitled and allowed to vote at all such elections, without distinction of race, color, or previous condition of servitude; any constitution, law, custom, usage, or regulation of any State or Territory, or by or under its authority, to the contrary notwithstanding. [As enacted by 16 Stat. 140, Act May 31, 1870, ch. 114, §1; R.S. §2004.]

CHAPTER 3 — CIVIL RIGHTS

§41. Equal rights under the law. — All persons within the jurisdiction of the United States shall have the same right in every State and Territory to make and enforce contracts, to sue, be parties, give evidence, and to the full and equal benefit of all laws and proceedings to the full and equal benefit of all laws and for the security of persons and property as is enjoyed by white citizens, and shall be subject to like punishment, pains, penalties, taxes, licenses, and exactions of every kind, and to no other. [R.S. §1977, derived from Act May 31, 1870, ch. 114, §16, 16 Stat. 144.]

[Note: See the highly important decision in *Valle v. Stengel et al.* 176 F. 2d. 697 (C.C.A. 3rd Cir., August 10, 1949.) Plaintiffs, some of whom were Negroes, were denied admission to Palisades Amusement Park, N. J. swimming pool open to the public upon the payment of admission price. Stengel, local chief of police, aided and abetted the private managers of the amusement park in refusing the plaintiffs admission and helped to eject them from the park. They brought suit charging the violation of U.S. Code, Title 8, §§41, 42, 43, the Fourteenth Amendment and Art. IV, Section 2, Cl. 1 of the Constitution of the United States. The court *held* that the plaintiffs were denied equal protection of the laws guaranteed by the Fourteenth Amendment and were denied the right to make and enforce contracts, within the protection of U.S. Code, Title 8, §41, *supra,* and §43, *infra.*

The Court declared, "If a man cannot make or enforce a contract already made because of the interference of a State officer he is being denied a civil right. He cannot support his family or earn a living under the system to which we adhere. The *liberty* involved is in fact the liberty of contract . . . To refuse an individual the liberty to contract is to put him beyond the pale of capitalism. Thus ostracized, he cannot engage in the acquisition of property or the pursuit of happiness . . ." (p. 703.)

"The right to enjoy 'privileges and immunities' of citizenship, for the violation of which Section 43 [see below] imposes civil sanctions, covers, as we think we have demonstrated, the wide field of activities ordinarily engaged in by citizens. We think Congress intended to confer on Negroes a civil status equivalent to that enjoyed by white people." (p. 703).]

§42. **Property rights of citizens.** — All citizens of the United States shall have the same right, in every State and Territory, as is enjoyed by white citizens thereof to inherit, purchase, lease, sell, hold, and convey real and personal property. [R. S. §1978, derived from Act April 9, 1866, ch. 31, §1, 14 Stat. 27.]

[Note: See note to §41 *supra.*]

§43. **Civil action for deprivation of rights.** — Every person who, under color of any statute, ordinance, regulation, custom, or usage, of any State or Territory, subjects, or causes to be subjected, any citizen of the United States or other person within the jurisdiction thereof to the deprivation of any rights, privileges, or immunities secured by the Constitution and laws, shall be liable to the party injured in an action at law, suit in equity or other proper proceeding for redress. [R. S. §1979, derived from Act April 20, 1871, ch. 22, §1, 17 Stat. 13.]

[Note: See note to §41 *Supra.*]

[1946 Edition, Supp. II]

§44. **Repealed, June 25, 1948, ch. 645, §21, 62 Stat. 862, eff. Sept. 1, 1948.**

[Note: See Title 18, §243.]

§45. **Repealed, June 25, 1948, ch. 645, §21, 62 Stat. 862 eff. Sept. 1 1948.**

[Note: This section which dealt with the exclusion of jurors on account of race or color was repealed as obsolete. See Title 18, §243.]

§47. **Conspiracy to interfere with civil rights.** —

(1) **Preventing officer from performing duties.**

If two or more persons in any State or Territory conspire to prevent, by force, intimidation, or threat, any person from accepting or holding any office, trust, or place of confidence under the United States, or from discharging any duties thereof; or to induce by like means any officer of the United States to leave any State, district, or place, where his duties as an officer are required to be performed, or to injure him in his person or property on account of his lawful discharge of the duties of his office, or while engaged in the lawful discharge thereof, or to injure his property so as to molest, interrupt, hinder, or impede him in the discharge of his official duties;

(2) Obstructing justice; intimidating party, witness, or juror.

If two or more persons in any State or territory conspire to deter, by force, intimidation, or threat, any party or witness in any court of the United States from attending such court, or from testifying to any matter pending therein, freely, fully, and truthfully, or to injure such party or witness in his person or property on account of his having so attended or testified, or to influence the verdict, presentment, or indictment of any grand or petit juror in any such court, or to injure such juror in his person or property on account of any verdict, presentment or indictment lawfully assented to by him, or of his being or having been such juror; or if two or more persons conspire for the purpose of impeding, hindering, obstructing, or defeating, in any manner, the due course of justice in any State or Territory, with intent to deny any citizen the equal protection of the laws, or to injure him or his property for lawfully enforcing, or attempting to enforce, the right of any person, or class of persons, to the equal protection of the laws;

(3) Depriving persons of rights or privileges.

If any two or more persons in any State or Territory conspire or go in disguise on the highway or on the premises of another, for the purpose of depriving, either directly or indirectly, any person or class of persons of the equal protection of the laws, or of equal privileges and immunities under the laws; or for the purpose of preventing or hindering the constituted authorities of any State or Territory from giving or securing to all persons within such State or Territory the equal protection of the laws; or if two or more persons conspire to prevent by force, intimidation, or threat, any citizen who is lawfully entitled to vote, from giving his support or advocacy in a legal manner, toward or in favor of the election of any lawfully qualified person and an elector for President, or Vice-President, or as a Member of Congress of the United States; or to injure any citizen in person or property on account of such support or advocacy; in any case of conspiracy set forth in this section, if one or more persons engaged therein do, or cause to be done, any act in furtherance of the object of such conspiracy, whereby another is injured in his person or property, or deprived of having and exercising any right or privilege of a citizen of the United States, the party so injured or deprived may have an action for the recovery of damages, occasioned by such injury or deprivation, against any one or more of the conspirators. [R.S. §1980. Derived from Acts July 31, 1861, ch. 33, 12 Stat. 284; Apr. 20, 1871, ch. 22, §2, 17 Stat. 13.]

[Note: See below Title 28, §1343.]

§48. Same; action for neglect to prevent. — Every person who, having knowledge that any of the wrongs conspired to be done, and mentioned in section 47 of this title, are about to be committed, and having power to prevent or aid in preventing, the commission of the same, neglects or refuses so to do, if such wrongful act be committed, shall be liable to the party injured, or his legal representatives, for all damages caused by such wrongful act, which such person by reasonable diligence could have prevented; and such damages may be recovered in an action on the case; and any number of persons guilty of such wrongful neglect or refusal may be joined as defendants in the action; and if the death of any party be caused by any such wrongful act and neglect the legal representatives of the deceased shall have such action therefor, and may recover not exceeding $5,000.00 damages therein, for the benefit of the widow of the deceased, if there be one, and if there be no widow, then for the benefit of the next of kin of the deceased. But no action under the provisions of this section shall be sustained which is not commenced within one [1] year after the cause of action has accrued. [R.S. §1981, derived from Act Apr. 20, 1871, ch. 22, §6, 17 Stat. 15.]

[1946 Edition, Supp. III.]

49a. Proceedings in vindication of civil rights. — The jurisdiction in civil and criminal matters conferred on the district courts by the provisions of this chapter and Title 18, for the protection of all persons in the United States in their civil rights, and for their vindication, shall be exercised and enforced in conformity with the laws of the United States, so far as such laws are suitable to carry the same into effect; but in all cases where they are not adapted to the object, or are deficient in the provisions necessary to furnish suitable remedies and punish offenses against law, the common law, as modified and changed by the constitution and statutes of the State wherein the court having jurisdiction of such civil or criminal cause is held, so far as the same is not inconsistent with the Constitution and laws of the United States, shall be extended to and govern the said courts in the trial and disposition of the cause, and, if it is of a criminal nature, in the infliction of punishment on the party found guilty. [R. S. §722, derived from Acts April 9, 1866, ch. 31, §3, 14 Stat. 27; May 31, 1870, ch. 114, §18, 16 Stat. 144.]

§56. Peonage abolished.

The holding of any person to service or labor under the system known as peonage is abolished and forever prohibited in any Territory or State of the United States; and all acts, laws, resolutions, orders, regulations, or usages of any Territory or State, which have heretofore established, maintained, or enforced, or by virtue of any attempt shall hereafter be made to establish, maintain, or enforce, directly or indirectly, the voluntary or involuntary service or labor of any persons as peons, in liquidation of any debt or obligation, or otherwise, are declared null and void. [R.S. §1990. Derived from Act Mar. 2, 1867, ch. 187, §1, 14 Stat. 546.]

Chapter 4. — FREEDMEN

§§61-65. [Relates to payment of bounty, prize money and other claims of colored soldiers, sailors and marines, or their heirs.] .[R.S. §§2032, 2033, 2037; 20 Stat. 402; 25 Stat. 9; 30 Stat. 640.]

Chapter 6.

SUBCHAPTER III.

QUOTA AND NON QUOTA IMMIGRANTS

§237. Admission of alien spouses and minor children of members of United States armed forces during Second World War; race of alien spouse. — The alien spouse of an American citizen by a marriage occuring before thirty [30] days after the enactment of sections 232-237 of this title, shall not be considered as inadmissible under said sections. [Dec. 28, 1945, ch. 591, §6, as added July 27, 1947, ch. 289, 61 Stat. 401.]

Chapter 7.

EXCLUSION OF CHINESE

§261. **Control or exclusion of Chinese.** [Obsolete.]

§§262-297. **[Repealed. Dec. 17, 1943, ch. 344, §1, 57 Stat. 600.]**
[Note: Until repealed in 1943, Chinese exclusion laws had existed in the United States since 1882. (Acts 1882, ch. 126, §§1, 3, 6-13, 15, 16, 22 Stat. 59-61 as amended.) See below U.S.C. Title 8, ch. 11; Subch. III, §703.]

Chapter 11.

SUBCHAPTER III.—NATIONALITY THROUGH NATURALIZATION.

§703. **Jurisdiction to naturalize; Race.**

(a) The right to become a naturalized citizen under the provisions of this chapter shall extend only to —

(1) White persons, persons of African nativity or descent, and persons who are descendants of races indigenous to the continents of North and South America or adjacent islands and Filipino persons or persons of Filipino descent;

(2) persons who possess, either singly or in combination, a preponderance of blood of one or more of the classes specified in clause (1);

(3) Chinese persons and persons of Chinese descent, and persons of races indigenous to India; and

(4) persons who possess, either singly or in combination, a preponderance of blood of one or more of the classes specified in clause (3) or, either singly or in combination, as much as one-half blood of those classes and some additional blood of one of the classes specified in clause (1).

(b) Nothing in the preceding subsection shall prevent the naturalization of former citizens of the United States who are otherwise eligible to naturalization under the provisions of section 717 of this title. [October 14, 1940, ch. 876, title I, subch. III, §303, 54 Stat. 1140, Dec. 17, 1943, ch. 344, §3, 57 Stat. 601; July 2, 1946, ch. 534, §1, 60 Stat. 416.]

TITLE 10

THE ARMY

Chapter 14. — CAVALRY

§253. **Negro regiments.**

The enlisted men of two regiments of Calvary shall be colored men. [R.S. §1104; derived from Act July 28, 1866, ch. 299, §3, 14 Stat. 332.]

Chapter 17. — INFANTRY

§282. Negro regiments.

The enlisted men of two regiments of Infantry shall be colored men. [R.S. §1108, derived from Act July 28, 1866, ch. 299, §4, 14 Stat. 332; Act Mar. 3, 1869, ch. 124, §2, 15 Stat. 318.]

Chapter 23. — ENLISTED FORCE

§621a. Enlistment of Negroes. — No Negro, because of race, shall be excluded from enlistment in the Army for service with colored military units now organized or to be organized for such service. [As enacted 54 Stat. 713, ch. 508, §2(b), Act July 2, 1940.]

TITLE 16

CONSERVATION

Chapter 3A

UNEMPLOYMENT RELIEF THROUGH PERFORMANCE OF USEFUL PUBLIC WORK

Civilian Conservation Corps

§584g. Qualifications of enrollees; term of enrollment; educational leaves; certificates of merit. — The enrollees in the Corps (other than war veterans, enrollees in the Territories and insular possessions, Indians not to exceed one mess steward, three cooks, five project assistants, and one leader per each company) shall be unmarried male citizens of the United States between the ages of seventeen and twenty-three years, both inclusive, and shall at the time of enrollment be unemployed and in need of employment: Provided, That the Director may exclude from enrollment such classes of persons as he may consider detrimental to the well-being or welfare of the Corps, except that no person shall be excluded on account of race, color, or creed: . . . [As last amended by Oct. 21, 1940, ch. 906, 54 Stat. 1206.]

[Note: The Civilian Conservation Corps was liquidated under provisions of Acts July 2, 1942, ch. 475, title II, 56 Stat. 569, and July 12, 1943, ch. 221, title II, 57 Stat. 499.]

[1946 Edition, Supp. III.]

TITLE 18.

CRIMES AND CRIMINAL PROCEDURE

Chapter 13. — CIVIL RIGHTS

§241. [formerly §51.] Conspiracy against rights of citizens. — If two or more persons conspire to injure, oppress, threaten, or intimidate any citizen in the free exercise or enjoyment of any right or privilege secured to him by the Constitution or laws of the United States, or because of his having so exercised the same; or

If two or more persons go in disguise on the highway, or on the premises of another, with intent to prevent or hinder his free exercise or enjoyment of any right or privilege so secured —

They shall be fined not more than $5,000 or imprisoned not more than ten [10] years, or both. [June 25, 1948, ch. 645, §1, 62 Stat. 696, eff. Sept. 1, 1948. Based on Title 18 U.S.C. 1940 ed., §51. (Mar. 4, 1909, ch. 321, §19, 35 Stat. 1092.)]

[Note: The former provision that the violator be ineligible for public office was eliminated by the 1948 revision as too severe a punishment.]

[1946 Edition, Supp. III.]

§242. [formerly §52.] Deprivation of rights under color of law. — Whoever, under color of any law, statute, ordinance, regulation, or custom, wilfully subjects, or causes to be subjected, any inhabitant of any State, Territory, or District to the deprivation of any rights, privileges, or immunities secured or protected by the Constitution or laws of the United States, or to different punishments, pains, or penalties, on account of such inhabitant being an alien, or by reason of his color, or race, than are prescribed for the punishment of citizens, shall be fined not more than $1,000 or imprisoned not more than one year, or both. [June 25, 1948, ch. 645, §1, 62 Stat. 696, eff. Sept. 1, 1948. Based on Title 18 U.S.C. 1940 ed., §52, (Mar. 4, 1909, ch. 321, §20, 35 Stat. 1092.]

§243. Exclusion of jurors on account of race or color. — No citizen possessing all other qualifications which are or may be prescribed by law shall be disqualified for service as grand or petit juror in any court of the United States, or of any State on account of race, color, or previous condition of servitude; and any officer or other person charged with any duty in the selection or summoning of jurors excludes or fails to summon any citizen for such cause, shall be fined not more than $5,000. [June 25, 1948, ch. 645, §1, 62 Stat. 696, eff. Sept. 1, 1948. Based on former Section 44 of title 8, U.S.C. 1940 ed., Aliens and Nationality (Mar. 1, 1875, ch. 114, §4, 18 Stat. 336.]

§244. Discrimination against person wearing uniform of armed forces. — Whoever, being a proprietor, manager, or employee of a theatre or other public place of entertainment or amusement in the District of Columbia, or any Territory, or Possession of the United States, causes any person wearing the uniform of any of the armed forces of the United States to be discriminated against because of that uniform, shall be fined not more than $500. [June 25, 1948, ch. 645, §1, 62 Stat. 697, eff. Sept. 1, 1948, amended May 24, 1949, ch. 139, §5, 63 Stat. 90. Based on title 18, U.S.C., 1940 ed.,

§523 (Mar. 1, 1911, ch. 187, 36 Stat. 963; Aug. 24, 1912, ch. 387, §1, 37 Stat. 512; Jan. 28, 1915, ch. 20, §1, 38 Stat. 800).]

[Note: There appears to be no case interpreting this statute, but the terms do not appear to apply to race or color as bases of discrimination, although this view is taken by Newman, The Law of Civil Rights and Civil Liberties, p. 88.]

Chapter 28 — ELECTIONS AND POLITICAL ACTIVITIES.

§601. Deprivation of employment or other benefit for political activity. — Whoever, except as may be required by law, directly or indirectly deprives, attempts to deprive, or threatens to deprive any person of any employment, position, work, compensation, or other benefit provided for or made possible by any Act of Congress appropriating funds for work relief or relief purposes, on account of race, creed, color, or any political activity, support of, or opposition to any candidate or any political party in any election, shall be fined not more than $1,000 or imprisoned not more than one year, or both. [June 25, 1948, ch. 645, §1, 62 Stat. 721, eff. Sept. 1, 1948. Based on title 18, U. S. C., 1940 ed., §§61c, 61g. (Aug. 2, 1939, ch. 410, §§4, 8, 53 Stat. 1147, 1148.]

TITLE 22
FOREIGN RELATIONS AND INTERCOURSE
Chapter 14. — FOREIGN SERVICE

§807. Prohibitions; political, racial, religious or color discrimination. — In carrying out the provisions of this chapter, no political test shall be required and none shall be taken into consideration, nor shall there be any discrimination against any person on account of race, creed or color. [Aug. 13, 1946, ch. 957, title X, §1005, 60 Stat. 1030.]

Chapter 17 — RELIEF AID TO WAR-DEVASTATED COUNTRIES

§1413. Conditions governing relief assistance. — No relief assistance shall be provided under the authority of this chapter to the people of any country unless the government of such country has given assurance satisfactory to the President that (a) the supplies transferred or otherwise made available pursuant to this chapter, as well as similar supplies produced locally or imported from outside sources, will be distributed among the people of such country without discrimination as to race, creed or political belief; . . . [May 31, 1947, Chapter 90 §3, 61 Stat. 126.]

[1946 Edition, Supp. III.]

TITLE 28

JUDICIARY AND JUDICIAL PROCEDURE
Chapter 85. — DISTRICT COURTS: JURISDICTION.

§1343. **Civil Rights.** — The district courts shall have original jurisdiction of any civil action authorized by law to be commenced by any person:

(1) To recover damages for injury to his person or property, or because of the deprivation of any right or privilege of a citizen of the United States, by any act done in furtherance of any conspiracy mentioned in section 47 of Title 8;

(2) To recover damages from any person who fails to prevent or to aid in preventing any wrongs mentioned in section 47 of Title 28 which he had knowledge were about to occur and power to prevent;

(3) To redress the deprivation, under color of any State law, statute, ordinance, regulation, custom or usage, of any right, privilege or immunity secured by the Constitution of the United States or by any Act of Congress providing for equal rights of citizens or of all persons within the jurisdiction of the United States. [June 25, ch. 46, §1, 62 Stat. 932, eff. Sept. 1, 1948; based on Title 28, U.S.C., 1940 ed., §41 (12), (13), and (14) (Mar. 3, 1911, ch. 231, §24, pars. 12, 13, 14, 36 Stat. 1092.]

[Note: See *Valle v. Stengel*, 176 F. 2d. 697, (U.S.C. App. Third Circuit, decided August 10, 1949.]

§1344. **Election disputes.** — The district courts shall have original jurisdiction of any civil action to recover possession of any office, except that of elector of President or Vice President, United States Senator, Representative in or delegate to Congress, or member of a state legislature, authorized by law to be commenced, wherein it appears that the sole question touching the title to office arises out of denial of the right to vote, to any citizen offering to vote, on account of race, color, or previous condition of servitude.

The jurisdiction under this section shall extend only so far as to determine the rights of the parties to office by reason of the denial of the right, guaranteed by the Constitution of the United States and secured by any law, to enforce the right of citizens of the United States to vote in all the states. [June 25, 1948, ch. 646, §1, 62 Stat. 932, eff. Sept. 1, 1948. Based on title 28 U.S.C., 1940 ed., §40(15) (Mar. 3, 1911, ch. 231, §24, par. 15, 36 Stat. 1092.]

Chapter 121 — JURIES

§1863. [formerly §415] — **Exclusion or excuse from service.** — . . .

(c) No citizen shall be excluded from service as grand or petit juror in any court in the United States on account of race or color. [June 25, 1948, ch. 646, §1, 62 Stat. 952, eff. Sept. 1, 1948. Based on title 28 U.S.C. 1940 ed., §415 (Mar. 3, 1911, ch. 231, §278, 36 Stat. 1165.)]

TITLE 32

NATIONAL GUARD

Chapter 1. — COMPOSITION, ORGANIZATION, AND CONTROL GENERALLY

§3. **Exemptions from militia duty.** — . . . and all persons who because of religious belief shall claim exemption from military service, if the conscientious holding of such belief by such person shall be established under such regulations as the President shall prescribe, shall be exempted from militia service in a combatant capacity; but no person so exempted shall be exempt from militia service in any capacity that the President shall declare to be noncombatant. [As enacted June 3, 1916, ch. 134, §59, 39 Stat. 197.]

[Note: This section deals with exemption from militia duty of religious objectors. It does not relate to race or color.]

TITLE 38.

PENSIONS, BONUSES, AND VETERANS' RELIEF

Chapter 3. — DISABILITY OR DEATH CAUSE DUE TO SERVICE SINCE MARCH 4, 1861.

§198. [Relates to pensions for widows of colored and Indian soldiers who enlisted prior to March 3, 1873.] [R.S. §4075; derived from Act March 3, 1873, ch. 234, §11, 17 Stat. 570.]·

TITLE 43

PUBLIC LANDS

Chapter 7. — HOMESTEADS

RIGHT OF PARTICULAR PERSONS TO MAKE ENTRY

§184. **No distinction on account of race or color.** — No distinction shall be made in the construction or execution of sections 161-164, 169, 171, 173, 175, 183, 184, 191, 201, 211, 239, 254, 255, 271, 272, 274, 277 and 278 of this title, on account of race or color. [R.S. Sec. 2302, Act June 21, 1866, ch. 127, §1, 14 Stat. 67]

[Note: The sections cited are concerned with homestead and mineral lands, generally, and with the rights to homesteads by veterans, their widows and children, and with Soldiers' and Sailors' Homesteads.]

TITLE 49.

TRANSPORTATION

Chapter I. — INTERSTATE COMMERCE ACT

§3. Preferences; interchange of traffic; terminal facilities.

(1) Undue preferences or prejudices prohibited. — It shall be unlawful for any common carrier, subject to the provisions of this chapter to make, give, or cause any undue or unreasonable preference or advantage to any particular person, company, firm, corporation, association, locality, port, port district, gateway, transit point, region, district, territory, or any particular description of traffic; in any respect whatsoever; or subject any particular person, company, firm, corporation, association, locality, port, port district, gateway, transit point, region, district, territory, or any particular description of traffic to any undue or unreasonable prejudice or disadvantage in any respect whatsoever: *Provided, however,* That this paragraph shall not be construed to apply to discrimination, prejudice, or disadvantage to the traffic of any other carrier of whatever discription. [Feb. 4, 1887, ch. 104, part. I, §3, 24 Stat. 380; Feb. 20, 1920, ch. 91, §405, 41 Stat. 479; Mar. 4, 1927, ch. 510, §1; 44 Stat. 1447; Aug. 9, 1935, ch. 498, §1, 49 Stat. 543; Aug. 12, 1935, ch. 509, 49 Stat. 607; Sept. 18, 1940, ch. 722, title I, §5, 54 Stat. 902.]

[Note: On June 5, 1950, the United States Supreme Court *held* that the rules and practices of an inter-state railroad which divide each dining car so as to allot ten tables exclusively to white passengers and one table exclusively to Negro passengers, and which require a curtain or partition separating the table for Negro passengers from the other tables, violate §3(1) of the Interstate Commerce Act, 49 U.S.C. §3(1), the above section, which makes it unlawful for such a railroad to subject any particular person to any undue or unreasonable prejudice or disadvantage in any respect whatsoever. *Henderson v. United States* (1950), 339 U.S. 816, 70 S. Ct. 843, 94 L. Ed. (Adv. Op.) 790. For complete text of the *Henderson* opinion, see *infra,* Appendix 7.]

Chapter 10. — TRAINING OF CIVIL AIRCRAFT PILOTS

Civilian Pilot Training Act of 1939

§752. Training programs; rules and regulations; racial, etc., discrimination; facilities and personnel. — The Civil Aeronautics Authority is authorized, within the limits of available appropriations made by the Congress, to train pilots and technicians and mechanics or to conduct programs for such training, including studies and researches as to the most desirable qualifications for aircraft pilots and technicians and mechanics.

Such training or programs shall be conducted pursuant to such regulations as such Administrator may from time to time prescribe, including regulations requiring students participating therein to maintain appropriate insurance and to pay such laboratory or other fees for ground-school training, not exceeding $40 per student, as the Administrator may deem necessary or desirable: *Provided*, That in the administration of this chapter none of the benefits of training or programs shall be denied on account of race, creed, or color . . . [As last amended by Act of June 10, 1943, ch. 121, §1, 57 Stat. 150.]

[Note: This act expired July 1, 1946.]

TITLE 50 APPENDIX

SELECTIVE TRAINING AND SERVICE ACT OF
1940, Act. Sept. 16, 1940, ch. 720, 54 Stat. 885.

§304. Manner of selecting men for training and service; quotas. — (a) . . . *Provided*, That in the selection and training of men under this Act, and in the interpretation and execution of the provisions of this Act, there shall be no discrimination against any person on account of race or color; . . . [Sept. 6, 1940, ch. 720, §4, 54 Stat. 887; Dec. 20, 1941, ch. 602, §3, 55 Stat. 815; June 29, 1946, ch. 522, §1, 60 Stat. 341.]

WAR TRAINING OF NURSES THROUGH GRANTS TO INSTITUTIONS

§1451. Appropriation to assure supply of nurses for armed forces and other needs; discrimination prohibitd. — For the purpose of assuring a supply of nurses for the armed forces, governmental and civilian hospitals, health agencies, and war industries, there are hereby authorized to be appropriated sums sufficient to carry out the purposes of this Act: *Provided*, That there shall be no discrimination in the administration of the benefits and appropriations made under the respective provisions of this Act, on account of race, creed, or color . . . [June 15, 1943, ch. 126, §1, 57 Stat. 153.]

[Note: This act terminated on the termination of hostilities of World War II, proclaimed at 12 o'clock noon of Dec. 31, 1946, by Proc. No. 2714.]

APPENDIX 3.

EXECUTIVE ORDERS, DEPARTMENTAL RULES, REGULATIONS AND DIRECTIVES — UNITED STATES GOVERNMENT.

EXECUTIVE ORDER No. 8802*

REAFFIRMING POLICY OF FULL PARTICIPATION IN THE DEFENSE PROGRAM BY ALL PERSONS, REGARDLESS OF RACE, CREED, COLOR, OR NATIONAL ORIGIN, AND DIRECTING CERTAIN ACTION IN FUTHERANCE OF SAID POLICY

Whereas it is the policy of the United States to encourage full participation in the national defense program by all citizens of the United States, regardless of race, creed, color, or national origin, in the firm belief that the democratic way of life within the Nation can be defended successfully only with the help and support of all groups within its borders; and

Whereas there is evidence that available and needed workers have been barred from employment in industries engaged in defense production solely because of consideration of race, creed, color, or national origin, to the detriment of workers' morale and of national unity:

Now, therefore, by virtue of the authority vested in me by the Constitution and the statutes, and as a prerequisite to the successful conduct of our national defense production effort, I do hereby reaffirm the policy of the United States that there shall be no discrimination in the employment of workers in defense industries or government because of race, creed, color, or national origin, and I do hereby declare that it is the duty of employers and of labor organizations, in furtherance of said policy and of this order, to provide for the full and equitable participation of all workers in defense industries, without discrimination because of race, creed, or national origin;

And it is hereby ordered as follows:

1. All departments and agencies of the Government of the United States concerned with vocational and training programs for defense production shall take special measures appropriate to assure that such programs are administered without discrimination because of race, creed, color, or national origin;

2. All contracting agencies of the Government of the United States shall include in all defense contracts hereafter negotiated by them a provision obligating the contractor not to discriminate against any worker because of race, creed, color, or national origin;

3. There is established in the Office of Production Management a Committee on Fair Employment Practice, which shall consist of a Chairman and four other members to be appointed by the President. The Chairman and members of the Committee shall serve as such without compensation but shall be entitled to actual and necessary transportation, subsistence, and other expenses incidental to performance of their duties. The Committee shall receive and investigate complaints of discrimination in violation

---

*See *Final Report,* Fair Employment Practice Committee, June 28, 1946, United States Government Printing Office, Washington; 1947.

of the provisions of this order and shall take appropriate steps to redress grievances which it finds to be valid. The Committee shall also recommend to the several departments and agencies of the Government of the United States and to the President all measures which may be deemed by it necessary or proper to effectuate the provisions of this order.

FRANKLIN D. ROOSEVELT.

The White House,
June 25, 1941
(F. R. Doc. 41-4544; Filed, June 25, 1941; 12:17 p.m.)

EXECUTIVE ORDER
No. 9346

8 F.R. 7183

FURTHER AMENDING EXECUTIVE ORDER No. 8802 BY ESTABLISHING A NEW COMMITTEE ON FAIR EMPLOYMENT PRACTICE AND DEFINING ITS POWERS AND DUTIES

In order to establish a new Committee on Fair Employment Practice, to promote the fullest utilization of all available manpower, and to eliminate discriminatory practices, Executive Order No. 8802 of June 25, 1941, as amended by Executive Order No. 8823 of July 18, 1941, is hereby amended to read as follows:

"WHEREAS the successful prosecution of the war demands the maximum employment of all available workers regardless of race, creed, color, or national origin; and

"WHEREAS it is the policy of the United States to encourage full participation in the war effort by all persons in the United States regardless of race, creed, color, or national origin, in the firm belief that the democratic way of life within the nation can be defended successfully only with the help and support of all groups within its borders; and

"WHEREAS there is evidence that available and needed workers have been barred from employment in industries engaged in war production solely by reason of their race, color, or national origin, to the detriment of the prosecution of the war, the workers' morale, and national unity:

"NOW, THEREFORE, by virtue of the authority vested in me by the Constitution and statutes, and as President of the United States and Commander in Chief of the Army and Navy, I do hereby reaffirm the policy of the United States that there shall be no discrimination in the employment of any person in war industries or in Government by reason of race, creed, color, or national origin, and I do hereby declare that it is the duty of all employers, including the several Federal departments and agencies, and all labor organizations, in furtherance of this policy and of this Order, to eliminate discrimination in regard to hire, tenure, terms or conditions of employment, or union membership because of race, creed, color, or national origin.

"It is hereby ordered as follows:

"1. All contracting agencies of the Government of the United States shall include in all contracts hereafter negotiated or renegotiated by them a provision obligating the contractor not to discriminate against any employee or applicant for employment because of race, creed, color, or national origin and requiring him to include a similar provision in all subcontracts.

"2. All departments and agencies of the Government of the United States concerned with vocational and training programs for war production shall take all measures appropriate to assure that such programs are administered without discrimination because of race, creed, color, or national origin.

"3. There is hereby established in the Office for Emergency Management of the Executive Office of the President a Committee on Fair Employment Practice, hereinafter referred to as the Committee, which shall consist of a Chairman and not more than six other members to be appointed by the President. The Chairman shall receive such salary as shall be fixed by the President not exceeding $10,000 per year. The other members of the Committee shall receive necessary traveling expenses, and unless their compensation is otherwise prescribed by the President, a per diem allowance not exceeding twenty-five dollars per day and subsistence expenses on such days as they are actually engaged in the performance of duties pursuant to this Order.

"4. The Committee shall formulate policies to achieve the purposes of this Order and shall make recommendations to the various Federal departments and agencies and to the President which it deems necessary and proper to make effective the provisions of this Order. The Committee shall also recommend to the Chairman of the War Manpower Commission appropriate measures for bringing about the full utilization and training of manpower in and for war production without discrimination because of race, creed, color, or national origin.

"5. The Committee shall receive and investigate complaints of discrimination forbidden by this Order. It may conduct hearings, make findings of fact, and take appropriate steps to obtain elimination of such discrimination.

• "6. Upon the appointment of the Committee and the designation of its Chairman, the Fair Employment Practice Committee established by Executive Order No. 8802 of June 25, 1941, hereinafter referred to as the old Committee, shall cease to exist. All records and property of the old Committee and such unexpended balances of allocations or other funds available for its use as the Director of the Bureau of the Budget shall determine shall be transferred to the Committee. The Committee shall assume jurisdiction over all complaints and matters pending before the old Committee and shall conduct such investigations and hearings as may be necessary in the performance of its duties under this Order.

"7. Within the limits of the funds which may be made available for that purpose, the Chairman shall appoint and fix the compensation of such personnel and make provision for such supplies, facilities, and services as may be necessary to carry out this Order. The Committee may utilize the services and facilities of other Federal departments and agencies and such voluntary and uncompensated services as may from time to time be needed. The Committee may accept the services of State and local authorities and officials, and may perform the functions and duties and exercise the powers conferred upon it by this Order through such officials and agencies and in such manner as it may determine.

"8. The Committee shall have the power to promulgate such rules and regulations as may be appropriate or necessary to carry out the provisions of this Order.

"9. The provisions of any other pertinent Executive order inconsistent with this Order are hereby superseded."

FRANKLIN D. ROOSEVELT

THE WHITE HOUSE,
     May 27, 1943.

EXECUTIVE ORDER No. 9664

CONTINUING THE WORK OF THE FAIR EMPLOYMENT PRACTICE COMMITTEE

By virtue of the authority vested in me by the Constitution and statutes, it is hereby ordered as follows:

The duties and responsibilities imposed upon the Committee on Fair Employment Practice by Executive Order 8802, dated June 25, 1941, as amended by Executive Order 8823 of July 18, 1941, and by Executive Order 9346 of May 27, 1943, shall be continued thereunder for the period and subject to the conditions stated in the National War Agencies Appropriation Act, 1946 (Public Law 156, 79th Congress, 1st Session, approved July 17, 1945).

As a part of its duties the Committee shall investigate, make findings and recommendations, and report to the President, with respect to discrimination in industries engaged in work contributing to the production of military supplies or to the effective transition to a peacetime economy.

HARRY S. TRUMAN.

THE WHITE HOUSE,
     December 20, 1945.

EXECUTIVE ORDER 9808*
December 5, 1946
11 F. R. 14153

ESTABLISHING THE PRESIDENT'S COMMITTEE ON CIVIL RIGHTS

WHEREAS the preservation of civil rights guaranteed by the Constitution is essential to domestic tranquility, national security, the general welfare, and the continued existence of our free institutions; and

WHEREAS the action of individuals who take the law into their own hands and inflict summary punishment and wreak personal vengeance is subversive of our democratic system of law enforcement and public criminal justice, and gravely threatens our form of government; and

WHEREAS it is essential that all possible steps be taken to safeguard our civil rights:

NOW, THEREFORE, by virtue of the authority vested in me as President of the United States by the Constitution and the statutes of the United States, it is hereby ordered as follows:

1. There is hereby created a committee to be known as the President's Committee on Civil Rights, which shall be composed of the following-named members, who shall serve without compensation:

Mr. C. E. Wilson, Chairman; Mrs. Sadie T. Alexander; Mr. James B. Carey; Mr. John S. Dickey; Mr. Morris L. Ernst; Rabbi Roland G. Gittelsohn; Dr. Frank P. Graham; The Most Reverend Francis J. Haas; Mr. Charles Luckman; Mr. Francis P. Matthews; Mr. Franklin D. Roosevelt, Jr.; The Right Reverend Henry Knox Sherrill; Mr. Boris Shishkin; Mrs. M. E. Tilley; Mr. Channing H. Tobias.

2. The Committee is authorized on behalf of the President to inquire into and to determine whether and in what respect current law enforcement measures and the authority and means possessed by Federal, State, and local governments may be strengthened and improved to safeguard the civil rights of the people.

3. All executive departments and agencies of the Federal Government are authorized and directed to cooperate with the Committee in its work, and to furnish the Committee such information or the services of such persons as the Committee may require in the performance of its duties.

4. When requested by the Committee to do so, persons employed in any of the executive departments and agencies of the Federal Government shall testify before the Committee and shall make available for the use of the Committee such documents and other information as the committee may require.

5. The Committee shall make a report of its studies to the President in writing, and shall in particular make recommendations with respect to the adoption or establishment, by legislation or otherwise, of more adequate and effective means and procedures for the protection of the civil rights of the people of the United States.

---

*See *To Secure These Rights*, The Report of the President's Committee on Civil Rights, United States Government Printing Office, Washington; 1947.

6. Upon rendition of its report to the President, the Committee shall cease to exist, unless otherwise determined by further Executive order.

HARRY S. TRUMAN

THE WHITE HOUSE
December 5, 1946.

STATEMENT BY THE PRESIDENT
in Issuing Executive Order 9808, December 5, 1946

Freedom From Fear is more fully realized in our country than in any other on the face of the earth. Yet all parts of our population are not equally free from fear. And from time to time, and in some places, this freedom has been gravely threatened. It was so after the last war, when organized groups fanned hatred and intolerance, until, at times, mob action struck fear into the hearts of men and women because of their racial origin or religious beliefs.

Today, Freedom From Fear, and the democratic institutions which sustain it, are again under attack. In some places, from time to time, the local enforcement of law and order has broken down, and individuals — sometimes ex-servicemen, even women — have been killed, maimed, or intimidated.

The preservation of civil liberties is a duty of every Government — state, Federal, and local. Wherever the law enforcement measures and the authority of Federal, state, and local governments are inadequate to discharge this primary function of government, these measures and this authority should be strengthened and improved.

The Constitutional guarantees of individual liberties and of equal protection under the laws clearly place on the Federal Government the duty to act when state or local authorities abridge or fail to protect these Constitutional rights.

Yet in its discharge of the obligations placed on it by the Constitution, the Federal Government is hampered by inadequate civil rights statutes. The protection of our democratic institutions and the enjoyment by the people of their rights under the Constitution require that these weak and inadequate statutes should be expanded and improved. We must provide the Department of Justice with the tools to do the job.

I have, therefore, issued today an Executive Order creating the President's Committee on Civil Rights and I am asking this Committee to prepare for me a written report. The substance of this report will be recommendations with respect to the adoption or establishment by legislation or otherwise of more adequate and effective means and procedures for the protection of the civil rights of the people of the United States.

The members of this Committee will be:

MR. C. E. WILSON, Chairman; President, General Electric Company; formerly Executive Vice-Chairman of the War Production Board.

MRS. SADIE T. ALEXANDER, lawyer, of Philadelphia, Pennsylvania; Assistant

City Solicitor, City of Philadelphia; member of the Board of Directors, National Urban League; member of the Inter-Racial Committee of Philadelphia.

RABBI ROLAND G. GITTELSOHN of New York City; Spiritual Leader of the Central Synagogue at Rockville, Long Island; recipient of the Navy Commendation Medal for his services as the Jewish Chaplain of the Fifth Marine Division at Iwo Jima.

DR. FRANK P. GRAHAM, President of the University of North Carolina; formerly member of the War Labor Board.

THE MOST REVEREND FRANCIS J. HAAS, Bishop of Grand Rapids, Michigan; formerly Chairman of the President's Committee on Fair Employment Practice.

MR. CHARLES LUCKMAN of Cambridge, Massachusetts; President of Lever Brothers; formerly consultant to the war Loan Division, United States Treasury.

MR. FRANCIS P. MATTHEWS of Omaha, Nebraska; Former Supreme Knight of the Knights of Columbus; Vice-President of the National War Fund; designated Papal Chamberlain by Pope Pius XII.

MR. FRANKLIN D. ROOSEVELT, JR., lawyer of New York City; Chairman of the Housing Committee of the American Veterans Committee.

THE RIGHT REVEREND HENRY KNOX SHERRILL of Boston, Massachusetts, Presiding Bishop of the Episcopal Church; member of the Governor of Massachusetts' Committee on Racial and Religious Understanding.

MR. BORIS SHISHKIN of Alexandria, Virginia, Economist for the American Federation of Labor; formerly a member of the President's Committee on Fair Employment Practice.

MRS. M. E. TILLEY of Atlanta, Georgia; Secretary, Department of Social Relations, Women's Society of Christian Service, Methodist Church.

MR. CHANNING H. TOBIAS of New York City, Director of the Phelps-Stokes Fund; formerly Senior Secretary of the National Council of the Young Men's Christian Association.

EXECUTIVE ORDER NO. 9980
July 27, 1948, 13 F.R. 4311
REGULATIONS GOVERNING FAIR EMPLOYMENT PRACTICES WITHIN THE FEDERAL ESTABLISHMENT.

1. All personnel actions taken by Federal appointing officers shall be based solely on merit and fitness; and such officers are authorized and directed to take appropriate steps to insure that in all such actions there shall be no discrimination because of race, color, religion, or national origin.

2. The head of each department in the executive branch of the Government shall be

personally responsible for an effective program to insure that fair employment policies are fully observed in all personnel actions within his department.

3. The head of each department shall designate an official thereof as Fair Employment Officer. Such officer shall be given full operating responsibility under the immediate supervision of the department head, for carrying out the fair-employment policy herein stated. Notice of the appointment of such Officer shall be given to all officers and employees of the department. The Fair Employment officer shall, among other things—

(a) Appraise the personnel actions of the department at regular intervals to determine their conformity to the fair-employment policy expressed in this order.

(b) Receive complaints or appeals concerning personnel actions taken in the department on grounds of alleged discrimination because of race, color, religion, or national origin.

(c) Appoint such central or regional deputies, committees, or hearing boards, from among the officers or employees of the department, as he may find necessary or desirable on a temporary or permanent basis to investigate, or to receive, complaints of discrimination.

(d) Take necessary corrective or disciplinary action, in consultation with, or on the basis of delegated authority from, the head of the department.

4. The findings or action of the Fair Employment Officer shall be subject to direct appeal to the head of the department. The decision of the head of the department on such appeal shall be subject to appeal to the Civil Service Commission, hereinafter provided for.

5. There shall be established in the Civil Service Commission a Fair Employment Board (hereinafter referred to as the Board) of not less than seven persons, the members of which shall be officers or employees of the Commission. The Board shall —

(a) Have authority to review decisions made by the head of any department which are appealed pursuant to the provisions of this order or referred to the Board by the head of the department for advice and to make recommendations to such head. In any instance in which the recommendation of the Board is not promptly and fully carried out the case shall be reported by the Board to the President, for such action as he finds necessary.

(b) Make rules and regulations, in consultation with the Civil Service Commission, deemed necessary to carry out the Board's duties and responsibilities under this order.

(c) Advise all departments on problems and policies relating to fair employment.

(d) Disseminate information pertinent to fair-employment programs.

(e) Coordinate the fair-employment policies and procedures of the several departments.

(f) Make reports and submit recommendations to the Civil Service Commission for transmittal to the President from time to time, as may be necessary to the maintenance of the fair-employment program.

6. All departments are directed to furnish to the Board all information needed for the review of personnel actions or for the compilation of reports.

7. The term "department" as used herein shall refer to all departments and agencies of the executive branch of the Government, including the Civil Service Commission. The term "personnel action", as used herein, shall include failure to act. Persons fail-

ing of appointment who allege a grievance relating to discrimination shall be entitled to the remedies herein provided.

8. The means of relief provided by this order shall be supplemental to those provided by existing statutes, Executive orders, and regulations. The Civil Service Commission shall have authority, in consultation with the Board, to make additional regulations, and to amend existing regulations, in such manner as may be found necessary or desirable to carry out the purposes of this order.

REGULATIONS AND PROCEDURES FOR THE INTERNAL OPERATION
of the
FAIR EMPLOYMENT BOARD OF THE U. S. CIVIL SERVICE COMMISSION

I. ORGANIZATION AND ADMINISTRATION

A. **OFFICIAL NAME** — This Board shall be known as the Fair Employment Board of the U. S. Civil Service Commission, hereafter referred to as the Board.

B. **OFFICIAL ADDRESS** — The official mailing address of the Board shall be "The Fair Employment Board, U. S. Civil Service Commission, Washington 25, D. C."

C. **MEMBERSHIP OF BOARD** — The Board shall be composed of not less than seven members selected and appointed by the U. S. Civil Service Commission.

D. **OFFICERS**

1. The permanent officers of the Board shall consist of a Chairman and an Executive Secretary. In the event of the absence of or the inability of the Chairman to act he may designate a member to act as Chairman pro-tem.

2. The Chairman shall perform all of the duties usually pertaining to the office of Chairman, including preparation of an agenda, the convening of the Board, presiding at Board meetings and exercising general supervision over the administrative work of the Board. He will appoint any necessary committees and may serve as ex-officio chairman of such committees; he will sign such correspondence and reports as he may elect, and will review publicity releases; he will represent the Board during the interim between meetings of the Board and perform such other duties as may be necessary to the proper functioning and administration of the Board.

3. The Executive Secretary, under the general direction of the Chairman, will be responsible for the supervision of the administrative work of the Board and the direction of the staff. He will aid and assist members of the Board as may be necessary in connection with the performance of their duties.

573

E. MEETINGS

1. The Board may arrange for meetings from time to time as may be required. Special meetings may be called either by the Chairman, or on request of three or more members.

2. A quorum of the Board shall be a majority of all the members of the Board.

3. The minutes of the Board shall be recorded in summary form by the Executive Secretary or under his direction and shall indicate the matters discussed, the conclusions and decisions made and, where necessary, the reasons therefor.

F. PUBLICITY

Publicity releases of the Board shall be issued, after review by the Chairman, through the Civil Service Commission's Information Officer. The Board as a whole shall decide upon the scope and nature of the publicity to be issued.

II. COVERAGE OF EXECUTIVE ORDER 9980

A. Executive Order 9980 shall apply to all departments and agencies in the executive branch of the Federal government.

B. The remedies provided under Executive Order 9980 shall be available to citizens of, and persons who owe allegiance to the United States who are employed by, or are applicants for employment in the Executive branch of the Federal government.

III. AUTHORITY AND RESPONSIBILITY OF THE BOARD

Executive Order 9980 places a two-fold obligation on the Board, namely,

(a) to entertain appeals involving discrimination and make recommendations thereon, and

(b) To advise with and assist the departments in carrying out a fair employment program directed toward the elimination of discrimination in the executive branch of the Federal service in the first instance.

To carry out its obligations the Board has authority and responsibility:

(1) To accept appeals involving discrimination from decisions made by heads of departments and to make recommendations thereon to the heads of the departments;

(2) To report to the President when the recommendations of the Board are not fully and promptly carried out;

(3) To make all necessary rules and regulations, consistent with Executive Order 9980, in consultation with the Civil Service Commission, for carrying out the Board's duties and responsibilities;

(4) To advise all departments on problems and policies relating to fair employment practices;

(5) To coordinate the fair-employment policies and procedures of the several departments;

(6) To disseminate information pertinent to the fair employment program;

(7) To secure from the departments all information needed for the review of personnel actions or for the compilation of reports;

(8) To make reports and recommendations from time to time to the Civil Service Commission for transmittal to the President as may be necessary to the maintenance of the fair employment program.

(9) To request the services of the various divisions and regions of the Civil Service Commission through the office of the Executive Director and Chief Examiner.

IV. EXPLANATION OF TERMS AS USED HEREIN

1. Department — All departments and agencies of the executive branch of the government, including the Civil Service Commission.

2. Personnel Action — Any action taken within a department which affects the equality of economic opportunity of an employee or applicant. The term "personnel action" shall include failure to act.

3. Employee — An individual appointed by a Federal officer, and who is engaged in the performance of Federal functions in the executive branch of the Federal service under authority of an Act of Congress or an Executive Order, and who, in the performance of such duties, is supervised and directed by a Federal officer.

4. Applicant — A person failing of appointment in the executive branch of the Federal service who alleges a grievance relating to discrimination.

5. Discrimination — An unfavorable personnel action affecting an employee or applicant based on race, color, religion or national origin, and not on merit and fitness. Preference in appointment and differences in conditions of employment such as pay, leave, hours of work, etc., based upon law or upon regulations under authority of law, do not constitute discrimination within the meaning of Executive Order 9980.

6. Federal appointing officer — A person having power by law, or by lawfully delegated authority, to make appointments in the Federal service.

7. Fair Employment Officer — The official designated by the head of each department for carrying out the fair employment policy stated in Executive Order No. 9980.

8. Complete file — All letters, notices, memoranda, reports, transcripts, affidavits or supporting documents in connection with the initiation, investigation, hearing, decision and closing of a case or cases.

V. PROCEDURES OF THE BOARD

A. APPEALS

1. Acceptance and Review

   a. An employee or applicant, as defined herein, who alleges discrimination on the basis of race, color, religion or national origin may file an appeal with the Board from an unfavorable decision of the head of a department under the privisions [provisions] of Executive Order 9980, and such appeal will be accepted by the Board, provided that;

   (1) He is an employee of, or applicant for employment, in a department as defined herein.

   (2) He has exhausted all administrative remedies provided by the department and has presented, or attempted to present, all his evidence to the department.

(3) He files his appeal, in writing, within 10 days from the date of receipt by him of notice of the adverse decision and within 20 days if he resides outside of the continental United States.

b. On receipt of an appeal the head of the department shall be requested to furnish the complete file of the case.

c. If the appellant's appeal is not accepted by the Board he shall be advised in writing of the reasons for its non-acceptance.

d. On acceptance of an appeal, the appellant shall be notified of his right to a hearing and advised that, if he desires, he may submit a statement outlining the grounds on which he bases his appeal.

e. If, upon a review of the appeal, the Board is of the opinion that the record should be clarified or additional evidence secured, the Board may remand the case to the head of the department for reconsideration or may utilize the investigative facilities of the Civil Service Commission to secure additional information.

2. Hearing

a. All appellants, whose appeals are accepted by the Board, shall be afforded an opportunity to appear before the Board in person, by representative or accompanied by a representative.

b. When an appellant is granted a hearing, the Executive Secretary, in consultation with the Chairman, shall make the necessary arrangements. In any case where appearance before the Board in Washington would be unduly burdensome to the appellant, the Board may arrange for a hearing at a place reasonably convenient to the appellant before a panel of the Board or before a representative or representatives designated by the Board. In the event a hearing is held before a panel of the Board or other persons designated by the Board a transcript of the hearing shall be made and transmitted to the Board for its consideration.

c. Attendance at hearings shall be limited to the appellant and/or his personal representative and representatives of the department. The appellant may testify orally or in writing and arguments by or in his behalf may be made under such limitations as the Board may impose. In unusual circumstances, the Board may permit the appellant or the department to call witnesses to testify or it may on its motion invite witnesses to give testimony before the Board.

d. Strict legal rules of evidence shall not be followed but reasonable bounds shall be maintained as to competency, relevancy and materiality.

e. Testimony before the Board shall be given under oath or affirmation.

f. If the appellant offers new evidence bearing upon a material issue, the Board shall remand the case to the department head for reconsideration.

g. Normally, *verbatim* transcripts of hearings before the Board will not be made. In lieu thereof, a summary of the material facts disclosed at the hearing may be incorporated in the record of the case. The Board in any case may depart from this practice.

3. Decisions and Recommendations

a. If, upon a review of the complete file, the Board finds that the appellant was not substantially accorded the procedural rights to which he was entitled, the Board may remand the case to the head of the department for appropriate action.

b. Decision on the merits of an appeal shall be made on the complete file including briefs and oral arguments. In any case in which the Board has received additional or new material evidence, not available to the head of the department, the Board shall refer the complete file together with the additional evidence to the department head for reconsideration before taking final action on the appeal.

c. The decision of the Board on an appeal shall be concurred in by a majority of Board members present.

d. If, after consideration of all the material facts in a case, the Board finds that there has been discrimination within the purview of Executive Order 9980 because of race, color, religion or national origin a recommendation shall be made to the head of the department that he take such corrective action as the Board deems advisable.

e. In all cases, the appellant and his representative and the head of the department shall be advised in writing of the decision and recommendation of the Board.

f. After the Board has taken final closing action on an appeal, the Executive Secretary shall transmit the file on the case received from the department along with the Board's recommendations to the appropriate department head.

VI. RECORDS AND REPORTS

From time to time the Board will request the heads of the departments to furnish statistical data and reports reflecting the progress and development of the Fair Employment Program in each department.

INSTRUCTIONS FOR CARRYING OUT
THE FAIR EMPLOYMENT PROGRAM UNDER EXECUTIVE ORDER 9980

I. INTRODUCTION

The President, in his Order 9980, calls for more effective application of the long established policy of employment in the Federal service on the basis of merit and fitness alone without regard to race, color, religion or national origin.

Paramount responsibility for the execution of this policy is placed squarely upon department heads and subordinate administrative officials.

The Fair Employment Board must act on individual appeals from departmental decisions in cases where discrimination is alleged. It has the duty of advising the departments on fair employment problems and policies. It is required to coordinate the fair employment policies and procedures of the several departments. In consultation with the Civil Service Commission it is to set up rules and regulations necessary to carry out its duties and responsibilities.

By setting out special assignments of duties and outlining the framework of procedure, the Order makes a clear distinction between cases in which discrimination is alleged and the common run of grievances arising in other phases of personnel management.

The Board has given first attention to procedures for handling complaints. Its aim is to insure (1) full ascertainment of the facts as a basis for action, (2) furtherance of good relationships between complainants and administrative officers concerned by means of informal discussion and negotiations, (3) easy access by complainants to officials specially designated to give attention to discriminatory acts, and (4) adjustment of complaints without unreasonable delay.

There are wide variations among departments, in structure, administrative practice and geographical spread. Therefore, it is not believed necessary or desirable that all departments be required to operate under regulations identical in every respect. There are certain procedures however which should be uniform throughout the service. The Board has consulted with the fair employment officers and personnel officers of the departments and with the Civil Service Commission and has prepared a statement of the provisions, with certain alternatives, which it believes should be incorporated into the regulations of each department. It is the view of the Board that these provisions represent the minimum required to achieve that degree of uniformity which is essential to effective administration.

The objectives of the Order can not be reached by the adjudication of complaints alone. There is need for a positive program to remove the causes of complaints.

Acting together, the departments, the Commission and the Board can achieve the objectives of the President's program. Through joint effort equality of economic opportunity in the Federal service can be more fully realized. As the concept of fair play becomes more dominant in the consciousness of officers and employees alike it will exert an impelling influence upon attitudes and actions. Within the Federal government one of the basic ideals to which the nation proudly lays claim will be more conclusively demonstrated in practice.

The Board expects to consult further with the departments in seeking out the reasons for deviations from the established non-discrimination policy, in exploring the problems involved and the successful experience in dealing with these situations, and in developing a continuing positive program of remedial action.

II. COVERAGE

A. Executive Order 9980 and these instructions apply to all departments and agencies in the executive branch of the Federal government.

B. The remedies provided under Executive Order 9980 and these instructions shall be advisable to citizens of, and persons who owe allegiance to the United States who are employed by, or are applicants for employment in the executive branch of the Federal government.

III. EXPLANATION OF TERMS AS USED HEREIN

A. Department — Any department or agency of the executive branch of the Federal government, including the Civil Service Commission.

B. Employee — An individual appointed by a Federal officer, and who is engaged in the performance of Federal functions in the executive branch of the Federal government under authority of an Act of Congress or an Executive Order, and who, in the performance of such duties, is supervised and directed by a Federal officer.

C. Applicant — A person failing of appointment in the executive branch of the Federal government who alleges a grievance relating to discrimination.

D. Discrimination — An unfavorable personnel action affecting an employee or applicant based on race, color, religion or national origin and not on merit and fitness. Preference in appointment and difference in conditions of employment, such as pay, leave, hours of work, etc., based upon law or upon regulations under authority of law do not constitute discrimination within the meaning of Executive Order 9980.

E. Personnel action — Any action taken within a department which affects the equality of economic opportunity of an employee or applicant. The term "personnel action" shall include failure to act.

F. Complete file — All letters, notices, memoranda, reports, transcripts, affidavits or supporting documents in connection with the initiation, investigation, hearing, decision and closing of a case or cases.

G. Deputy Fair Employment Officer — The term "Deputy Fair Employment Officer" shall include committees and boards.

IV. FAIR EMPLOYMENT OFFICER

The head of each department shall appoint a Fair Employment Officer who shall have full operating responsibility under the immediate supervision of the head of the department for carrying out the fair employment policies stated in Executive Order 9980. There shall be appointed, as necessary and desirable, at central or local levels of the department, Deputy Fair Employment Officers who shall have the responsibility for carrying out the fair employment policies in their respective offices. The name and official address of the Fair Employment Officer of each department shall be made known to all employees of the department. The name and official address of each Deputy Fair Employment Officer shall be made known to the employees of the respective field offices.

[Comment — It is the view of the Board that the best interests of the fair employment program would be served by the appointment of a permanent Deputy Fair Employment Officer at each field establishment of substantial size to handle complaints and also to assist the Fair Employment Officer to carry out his other responsibilities under the Order.]

V. INSTRUCTIONS FOR HANDLING COMPLAINTS AND APPEALS

A. Initiation of complaint

1. Procedures under Executive Order No. 9980 shall apply and be available only to an employee or to a person failing of appointment who alleges that

579

a personnel action, as defined herein, which affects him has been taken because of race, color, religion or national origin.

2. The complaint must be made within thirty days of the date the complainant learns of the alleged discrimination and not later than six months from the date of the personnel action complained of, unless failure to submit the complaint within these time limits was due to unusual circumstances beyond the control of the complainant.

3. It shall be optional with a department to require an *employee* to initiate his complaint (a) either with the first-line supervisor or the supervisor next higher in authority, (b) either with the first-line supervisor or the Deputy Fair Employment Officer, or (c) with the Deputy Fair Employment Officer. Complaints initiated with a supervisor may be oral or in writing. Those initiated with a Deputy Fair Employment Officer must be in writing. If no appropriate Deputy Fair Employment Officer has been appointed then the Fair Employment Officer may be substituted under (b) and (c) above.

4. It shall be optional with an *applicant* to file a complaint in writing, either with the head of the local office, with the Deputy Fair Employment Officer, or with the Fair Employment Officer of the department. If the complaint is filed with the head of the local office and he is superior to the Deputy Fair Employment Officer, or if it is filed with the Fair Employment Officer of the department, it may be referred to the appropriate deputy for handling as an initial complaint. In all other respects complaints of applicants will be handled in the same manner as complaints of employees.

5. All written complaints or appeals must be signed by the aggrieved employee or applicant. Any initial written complaint or appeal must include information regarding the specific personnel action complained of, the approximate date thereof, reasons in support of the allegation of discrimination, and a statement as to when the appellant first learned of the discrimination.

> [Comment — It is the view of the Board that where not inconsistent with administrative practices, an employee should first discuss a complaint with the first-line supervisor or the supervisor next higher in authority. Good relations between the supervisor and the employee will thus be furthered. Many incipient complaints can be eliminated by giving valid reasons for an action that is being brought into question. Where error has crept in, the supervisor will have opportunity to correct it on his own motion. Furthermore, with responsibility upon the supervisor for initial action on the complaint the problems involved will be more forcefully impressed upon him.]

B. Action on a complaint by the Supervisor

1. If complaint is made to a supervisor, immediate steps shall be taken to effect such adjustment as is warranted by the facts. If the complaint cannot be satisfactorily and promptly adjusted, the complainant shall be advised in writing that he may file an appeal within ten days with the

Deputy Fair Employment Officer. In addition, he shall be advised that if he appeals to the Deputy Fair Employment Officer, he shall furnish a copy of the letter of appeal to the supervisor to whom he presented his original complaint. On receipt of a copy of the appeal, the supervisor concerned shall forward to the Deputy Fair Employment Officer the complete file in the case through the channels prescribed by the department.

If the department prescribes that the file in the case be routed through an ascending chain of administrative authority, the administrative officer at any intermediate level may make an adjustment of the case satisfactory to the complainant. In such case, he should report the action taken to the Deputy Fair Employment Officer to whom the appeal is addressed and advise the subordinate administrative officers concerned. If no adjustment is made the file shall automatically be forwarded through the prescribed channels, each officer making whatever comment thereon he desires, with no further action required upon the part of the complainant.

C. **Action on a complaint (or appeal) by the Deputy Fair Employment Officer.**

1. **Investigation and adjustment by informal negotiation** — The Deputy Fair Employment Officer shall promptly make or cause to be made such investigation as is necessary to ascertain the facts at issue on the complaint. He should endeavor through informal negotiation to effect a satisfactory settlement of the complaint and, if necessary, shall take or cause to be taken corrective action. All interested parties shall be advised of the settlement of the complaint and any corrective action which may be taken.

2. **Failure of adjustment by informal negotiation** — In the event the Deputy Fair Employment Officer is not able to effect a satisfactory settlement of the complaint by informal negotiation, he shall furnish the complainant with a statement of the pertinent facts disclosed by the investigation of the complaint and shall afford him an opportunity to reply thereto in writing or personally, by authorized representative or accompanied by such representative. The complainant shall be permitted to present by witness or otherwise any pertinent facts not disclosed by the investigation. Where practicable, a transcript of testimony shall be made. If a *verbatim* transcript is not possible, a full summary of the oral testimony shall be made by the Deputy Fair Employment Officer. The summary may be agreed to and signed by the complainant and the Deputy Fair Employment Officer, or if the complainant does not agree with the summary, he may note and sign his exceptions which will become a part of the summary. Any transcript or summary shall be available for inspection by the complainant or his authorized representative and by interested agency officials.

3. **Decision** — On all the material facts disclosed by the investigation and the hearing, if held, the Deputy Fair Employment Officer shall make a decision or make a recommendation to appropriate authority. If the decision on the complaint is favorable to the complainant, the responsible official shall so notify him in writing and shall take or cause to be taken such corrective and disciplinary action as appears warranted by the facts in the case. In the event of an unfavorable decision, the complainant shall be

advised in writing of the decision and the reasons therefor and of his right to appeal to the Fair Employment Officer or the head of the department as the department may prescribe, within ten days (twenty days if outside the continental United States) from date of receipt of the unfavorable decision. Officials directly concerned should also be advised of any decision made.

D. Appeal to the Fair Employment Officer

1. The complainant shall be advised that if he appeals to the Fair Employment Officer of the department he shall furnish a copy of the letter of appeal to the Deputy Fair Employment Officer who handled his case.
2. On receipt of a copy of the appeal the Deputy Fair Employment Officer shall forward to the Fair Employment Officer of the department the complete file in the case through the channels prescribed by the department.

   If the department prescribes that the file be routed through an ascending chain of administrative authority, the administrative officer at any intermediate level may make an adjustment of the case satisfactory to the complainant. In such case, he should report the action taken to the Fair Employment Officer and advise the subordinate administrative officers concerned. If no adjustment is made the file shall automatically be forwarded through the prescribed channels, each officer making whatever comment thereon he desires, with no further action required upon the part of the complainant.

3. After reviewing the complete file in the case, the Fair Employment Officer shall make further investigation if necessary and shall, through informal negotiation attempt a solution satisfactory to all interested parties, who shall be granted the privilege of appearing personally or by an authorized representative, or accompanied by such representative, before the Fair Employment Officer. If a satisfactory solution cannot be accomplished by the foregoing means, the Fair Employment Officer shall either make a decision or make a recommendation to the head of the department based upon the material evidence in the file. If he makes a decision he shall notify the interested parties in writing of the decision reached and the reasons therefor.
4. If the Fair Employment Officer makes a decision favorable to the appellant, he shall, in consultation with or on the basis of delegated authority from, the head of the department, take such corrective and disciplinary action as the facts warrant.
5. If the decision of the Fair Employment Officer is unfavorable to the appellant, the Fair Employment Officer shall notify him in writing of his right to appeal to the head of the department within ten days (twenty days if outside the continental United States) from the date of receipt of the decision.

E. Appeal to the head of the department

1. In the event that a recommendation is made by the Fair Employment Officer to the head of the department, or an appeal is taken from a

decision of the Fair Employment Officer, the head of the department shall make a decision upon the facts of the case and notify the interested parties in writing of such decision.

2. If the decision is favorable to the appellant, the head of the department shall take, or cause to be taken, such corrective and disciplinary action as appears warranted.

3. If the decision is unfavorable to the appellant, the head of the department shall advise the appellant in writing, in duplicate, of the decision and of his right to appeal to the Fair Employment Board of the Civil Service Commission within ten days from the date of receipt of the decision, or within twenty days if he resides outside of the continental United States. In addition, he should be advised that if he appeals to the Fair Employment Board, a copy of the adverse decision should accompany his appeal.

VI. GENERAL PROVISIONS

A. The head of each department shall prescribe procedures consistent with Executive Order No. 9980 and these instructions for the prompt handling of complaints and appeals which are made under that Order.

B. All officers and employees of the department who occupy supervisory positions shall be instructed as to the meaning, spirit and requirements of Executive Order No. 9980.

C. The department's regulations and procedures for handling complaints and appeals shall be brought to the attention of all officers and employees of the department and shall be made available to applicants who lodge a complaint within the purview of Executive Order No. 9980.

D. Amendments in regulations and changes in procedures becoming effective while an appeal is being processed may be applied to such appeal at whatever stage it has then reached, provided that the appellant shall not be deprived of any substantive right or resource to which he would have been entitled under the regulations and procedures in effect at the time his complaint was initiated.

E. If no appropriate Deputy Fair Employment Officer has been appointed the Fair Employment Officer shall be designated to receive appeals under Section V-B-1.

If a complaint or appeal is filed initially with the Fair Employment Officer of the department, no appropriate Deputy Fair Employment Officer having been appointed, the Fair Employment Officer shall proceed directly or through designated representative to process the case in the manner prescribed for the Deputy Fair Employment Officer in Section V-C-1 and 2, and such parts of V-C-3 and V-D as are pertinent.

F. If a complaint of discrimination because of race, color, religion or national origin is denied on the ground that the action complained of is not a personnel action as defined herein, the complainant shall be advised that he may appeal this determination through the same channels as are prescribed under Section V herein. If, on appeal, it is determined that the action complained of is a personnel action as defined herein, the case may be remanded to the proper officers for further investigation or action on the issue of discrimination.

G. The means of relief provided by Executive Order 9980 or any regulations thereunder shall be supplemental to those provided by existing statutes, Executive Orders and regulations, such as appeals to the Civil Service Commission under Section 14 of the Veterans Preference Act of 1944 or the reduction-in-force regulations, etc.

VII. RECORDS AND REPORTS

Upon request the departments shall furnish to the Board all information needed for the review of personnel actions or for the compilation of reports. The complete file in each case or cases under Executive Order 9980 shall be maintained intact in each department at least until such time as all appeal rights have been exhausted and, upon request, shall be promptly forwarded to the Fair Employment Board of the Civil Service Commission.

VIII. THESE INSTRUCTIONS SUPERSEDE THE INTERIM PROCEDURES ISSUED BY THE CIVIL SERVICE COMMISSION UNDER DATE OF SEPTEMBER 28, 1948 AND FAIR EMPLOYMENT BOARD MEMORANDUM NO. 2, DATED NOVEMBER 4, 1948.

EXECUTIVE ORDER No. 9981*
July 27, 1948, 13 F.R. 4313

PRESIDENT'S COMMITTEE ON EQUALITY OF TREATMENT AND OPPORTUNITY IN THE ARMED FORCES.

* * * *

1. It is hereby declared to be the policy of the President that there shall be equality of treatment and opportunity for all persons in the armed services without regard to race, color, religion or national origin. This policy shall be put into effect as rapidly as possible having due regard to the time required to effectuate any necessary changes without impairing efficiency or morale.

---

*The following persons were appointed by the President to be members of the Committee: Charles Fahy, *Chairman,* Alphonsus J. Donahue, Lester B. Granger, Charles Luckman, Dwight R. G. Palmer, John H. Sengstacke, William E. Stevenson. See the report issued by the Committee on May 22, 1950, *Freedom to Serve,* Equality of Treatment and Opportunity in the Armed Forces, United States Government Printing Office, Washington; 1950.

2. There shall be created in the National Military Establishment an advisory committee to be known as the President's Committee on Equality of Treatment and Opportunity in the Armed Services, which shall be composed of seven members to be designated by the President.

3. The Committee is authorized on behalf of the President to examine into the rules, procedures and practices of the armed services in order to determine in what respect such rules, procedures and practices may be altered or improved with a view toward carrying out the policy of this order. The Committee shall confer and advise the Secretary of Defense, the Secretary of the Army, the Secretary of the Navy, and the Secretary of the Air Force, and shall make such recommendaitons to the President and to said Secretaries as in the judgment of the Committee will effectuate the policy hereof.

4. All executive departments and agencies of the Federal Government are authorized and directed to cooperate with the Committee in its work, and to furnish the Committee such information or the services of such persons as the Committee may require in the performance of its duties.

5. When requested by the Committee to do so, persons in the armed services or in any of the executive departments and agencies of the Federal Government shall testify before the Committee and shall make available for the use of the Committee such documents and other information as the Committee may require.

6. The Committee shall continue to exist until such time as the President shall terminate its existence by Executive order.

DEPARTMENT OF DEFENSE
(formerly National Military Establishment)

*DIRECTIVE ISSUED BY SECRETARY OF DEFENSE LOUIS JOHNSON ON APRIL 6, 1949 TO ARMY, NAVY, AND AIR FORCE TO REVIEW THEIR PERSONNEL PRACTICES.

THE SECRETARY OF DEFENSE
WASHINGTON

MEMORANDUM FOR THE SECRETARY OF THE ARMY
                    THE SECRETARY OF THE NAVY
                    THE SECRETARY OF THE AIR FORCE
                    CHAIRMAN, PERSONNEL POLICY BOARD

SUBJECT: Equality of Treatment and Opportunity in the Armed Services

    1. a. It is the policy of the National Military Establishment that there shall be

equality of treatment and opportunity for all persons in the Armed Services without regard to race, color, religion, or national origin.

b. To assist in achieving uniform application of this policy, the following supplemental policies are announced:

(1) To meet the requirements of the Services for qualified individuals, all personnel will be considered on the basis of individual merit and ability and must qualify according to the prescribed standards for enlistment, attendance at schools, promotion, assignment to specific duties, etc.

(2) All individuals, regardless of race, will be accorded equal opportunity for appointment, advancement, professional improvement, promotion and retention in their respective components of the National Military Establishment.

(3) Some units may continue to be manned with Negro personnel; however, all Negroes will not necessarily be assigned to Negro units. Qualified Negro personnel shall be assigned to fill any type of position vacancy in organizations or overhead installations without regard to race.

2. Each Department is directed to examine its present practices and determine what forward steps can and should be made in the light of this policy and in view of Executive Order 9981, dated July 26, 1948, which directs that this policy shall be put into effect as rapidly as possible with due regard to the time required to effectuate any necessary changes without impairing efficiency or morale.

3. Following the completion of this study, each Department shall state, in writing, its own detailed implementation of the general policy stated herein and such supplemental policies as may be determined by each Service to meet its own specific needs. These statements shall be submitted to the Chairman of the Personnel Policy Board, Office of the Secretary of Defense, not later than 1 May 1949.

/s/ LOUIS JOHNSON

*From release issued by National Military Establishment, Office of Public Information, Washington 25, D.C., April 20, 1949.

STATEMENT ISSUED BY NATIONAL MILITARY ESTABLISHMENT,
OFFICE OF PUBLIC INFORMATION,
WASHINGTON 25, D.C., MAY 11, 1949

SECRETARY JOHNSON APPROVES AIR FORCE POLICIES
FOR EQUALITY OF TREATMENT AND OPPORTUNITY

Secretary of Defense Louis Johnson today approved policies proposed by the Air Force to assure equality of treatment and opportunity for all members of its personnel.

Mr. Johnson also announced that he is studying statements from the Army and Navy concerning their personnel practices and policies, but had requested additional clarifying information before making a decision. He directed that this information be submitted to him, through Chairman Thomas R. Reid of the NME Personnel Policy Board, by May 25.

The statements were submitted by the Secretaries of the three military departments in response to a directive issued by Secretary Johnson on April 6. He asked them to examine their personnel practices and to suggest steps that should be made to attain the uniform equality of treatment and opportunity demanded by President Truman's Executive Order 9981.

The proposals to assure equality of treatment and opportunity for all persons in the Air Force, regardless of race, color, religion or national origin, provide for the assignment and utilization of Negro personnel on the basis of individual capacity. It permits general assignment of such individuals on an Air Force-wide basis. Heretofore, Negroes had been assigned only to special type units.

Initial step in the policy's implementation will be the deactivation of the 2,000-man 332nd Fighter Wing, an all-Negro tactical group based at Lockbourne Air Force Base, Columbus, Ohio. The majority of highly skilled Negro Air Force specialists are presently assigned to that unit. Members of the 332nd will be considered individually for reassignment throughout the Air Force and to training schools, consonant with the need of Air Force Commands and with individual capabilities.

Present Negro strength in the Air Force is 21,026, representing 7.0 per cent of the total figure. Of that number, 316 are officers, five are warrant officers, and the balance, 20,705, are enlisted personnel. Assigned at Lockbourne are approximately 1,800 enlisted men and women and 200 officers. Among this latter group are included 11 Army Nurses and four WAF officers.

Other Negro personnel throughout the Air Force will be screened by their respective commands and their capabilities re-evaluated with a view to possible assignment changes or additional training, as indicated by individual cases.

Prior policy has specified that 10 per cent of the Air Force strength be composed of Negroes, a figure taken from the general percentage of Negroes in the national population. The new policy will relieve the earlier, administratively difficult and expensive, effort to absorb the total Negro quota into a few specialized units and into certain selected vocational specialties. Some units may continue to be manned with Negro personnel; however, all Negroes will not necessarily be assigned to Negro units.

The policy statement provides that one standard shall govern the utilization of both Negro and white personnel in the Air Force.

The new policy, which began early in 1948 as a routine staff study, is effective immediately and, under present plan, is to be completely in operation on or about December 31, 1949.

Lockbourne Air Force Base will not be inactivated. It has not been determined what unit will replace the 332nd Fighter Wing at that station.

STATEMENT ISSUED BY
NATIONAL MILITARY ESTABLISHMENT
OFFICE OF PUBLIC INFORMATION
Washington 25, D. C.
JUNE 7, 1949

SECRETARY JOHNSON APPROVES NAVY PROPOSALS FOR
EQUALITY OF TREATMENT AND OPPORTUNITY

Secretary of Defense Louis Johnson today approved specific actions proposed by the Department of the Navy to assure equality of treatment and opportunity for all Navy personnel.

At the same time, Secretary Johnson asked the Department of the Army to restudy its position on the subject, to consider carefully informal suggestions received from the President's Committee on Equality of Treatment and Opportunity in the Armed Forces (Fahy Committee), and to submit its reconsideration of the matter by June 20.

Proposals of the Department of the Air Force to assure equality for all its personnel were approved by Secretary Johnson on May 11. He then asked the Departments of the Army and the Navy to furnish clarifying information through Chairman Thomas R. Reid of the National Military Establishment's Personnel Policy Board, before making a decision in their cases.

The Department of the Navy has proposed taking these specific additional actions:

1. To promulgate a statement of the Navy Department's policy regarding minority races.

2. To augment efforts to obtain Negroes to enlist in the Navy by the assignment of Negro petty officers to duty in the Navy Recruiting Service, ordering volunteer qualified Negro Reserve officers to active duty to assist in recruitment, and slanting advertisements, posters, films, and pamphlets to attract Negroes to the Navy by use of photographs showing whites and Negroes working together in the Naval Service.

3. To exert greater effort to attract qualified Negro students to participate in the Navy ROTC program.

4. To promulgate a directive to insure that all members of the steward branch who are in all respects qualified are given an opportunity to change their rate to another rating branch.

5. To change the status of chief stewards to that of chief petty officers.

6. To disestablish within the Marine Corps the present separate Negro recruit training facility and integrate the training of Negro recruits with that of whites.

The proposed directive to all ships and stations, setting forth the Navy's revised policy regarding minority races, states:

"It is the policy of the Navy Department that there shall be equality of treatment and opportunity for all persons in the Navy and Marine Corps without regard to race, color, religion, or national origin.

"In their attitude and day-to-day conduct of affairs, officers and enlisted personnel of the Navy and Marine Corps shall adhere rigidly and impartially to the Navy Regulations, in which no distinction is made between individuals wearing the uniform of these Services.

"All personnel will be enlisted or appointed, trained, advanced or promoted, assigned duty and administered in all respects without regard to race, color, religion, or national origin.

"In the utilization of housing, messing, berthing and other facilities, no special or unusual provisions will be made for the accommodation of any minority race."

In his memorandum to the Secretary of the Navy, Mr. Johnson said: "In my judgment, the specific actions you propose to undertake meet the spirit and intent of Executive Order 9981 of 26 July 1948 and are in accord with my memorandum of 6 April and my second memorandum on the same subject, dated 11 May. Therefore, I am pleased to approve your proposals and trust that you will begin their implementation without delay."

In asking the Department of the Army for reconsideration of its proposals for equality of treatment and opportunity, Secretary Johnson, in a memorandum to the Secretary of the Army, said:

"I have reviewed your comprehensive memorandum of 26 May concerning equality of treatment and opportunity in the Department of the Army and have noted with pleasure the significant progress made by the Army in this field in the last few years. I also note with pleasure the measures you propose in order to broaden still further the professional basis for the utilization of Negro manpower. I have read with understanding and sympathy the Army's contention that its current policies and practices are in accord with Executive Order 9981 of 26 July 1948 and my supplemental policy statement of 6 April 1949. I fully realize the grave problem presented by this question, and that it is of greater magnitude in the Army than in either the Navy or the Air Force. Nevertheless, I am forced to the conclusion that your proposals in reply to my second memorandum on this subject still fail to meet the basic intent of Executive Order 9981 and my memorandum of 6 April.

"Accordingly, I am asking you to restudy your position and your proposals and at the same time to consider very carefully the informal suggestions of the Fahy Committee which, I understand, have been made available to you. I would be pleased to have your reconsideration of this matter submitted to me by 20 June."

STATEMENT ISSUED BY
DEPARTMENT OF DEFENSE
OFFICE OF PUBLIC INFORMATION
Washington 25, D. C.
SEPTEMBER 30, 1949

ARMY PROGRAM FOR RACIAL EQUALITY
APPROVED BY SECRETARY OF DEFENSE

Secretary of Defense Louis Johnson today approved a program proposed by the Department of the Army to give greater assurance of equality of treatment and opportunity to all Army personnel without regard to race or color.

In submitting the new program to the Secretary of Defense, Secretary of the Army Gordon Gray pointed out that he had discussed with Charles Fahy, Chairman of the President's Committee on Equality of Treatment and Opportunity in the Armed Forces, the Committee's suggestions and the Army's proposed program.

Secretary Gray said that in order to insure a progressively more efficient utilization of manpower, including utilization of Negroes in each of the Army's career fields, the Army is taking these specific steps:

1. Military Occupational Specialties (MOS) will be open to qualified personnel without regard to race or color.

2. The present Negro quotas for selection to attend Army Schools will be abolished and selection will be made from the best qualified personnel without regard to race or color.

3. The promotion system of the enlisted career guidance program will be administered on an equal merit basis so that all promotions will be obtained by open competition on Army-wide examinations, against a single standard and without regard to race or color.

4. ROTC students attending summer training camps as members of school units to which they are regularly assigned will be trained with those units without regard to race or color.

5. A board of senior Army Officers will be convened from time to time to determine current progress under the program and to re-examine and review the fundamental policies for the utilization of Negro manpower in the light of changing conditions and experiences. The first board will be convened in the near future.

"This program," Mr. Gray said, "does not mean that existing Negro units will be broken up or that Negro personnel of these units will be scattered throughout the Army. It does mean that qualified Negroes, including members of these existing units, will have the opportunity to learn those skills previously unavailable to them. Hereafter, Negroes who acquire skills will be assigned to positions where their specialties may be applied in the manner most useful to the Army."

Under a new reenlistment policy, the Army has limited reenlistments to those who, during the first regular enlistment, qualify for promotion to Private First Class if unmarried, and to Corporal, if married. Since promotions to these grades may be made without regard to vacancies, all Army members are eligible to win these promotions. Mr. Gray said this policy is expected to produce greater economy and efficiency by gradually eliminating from Army service those who fail to demonstrate the capacity to advance. Its progressive application will also assure continuing opportunities to highly qualified individuals, both Negroes and others, to enlist in the Army.

Under the Army's new program Military Occupational Specialties will be open to all qualified personnel. No individual who qualifies for a Military Occupational Specialty will be denied the opportunity to follow it because of race or color. This will give greater significance and provide further implementation to the Army's policy and practice of using qualified persons without regard to race in filling the operating—or so-called overhead — positions at Army installations.

Formerly, Negroes were excluded from acquiring certain Military Occupational Specialties. Also, they were selected to attend schools on the basis of Negro distribution in the Army. They competed for promotion only among themselves. Now all non-commissioned officers will complete [compete] for promotion on an Army-wide equal merit basis, against a single standard, without regard to race or color.

Under the old policy, Negro ROTC students attending summer camps were placed in Negro units for their training. Now all personnel regularly assigned to an ROTC unit will remain together and be trained together.

Mr. Gray declared that the Army was continuing its study of the present policy of regulating Negro original enlistments in the Army, which is now based on the population ratio of Negroes to the total population — currently about 10 percent.

He pointed out that present policies concerning the utilization of Negro man-power in the Army are based on the recommendations of a board, headed by Lieutenant General A. C. Gillem, which made its report in 1946 and which itself recommended a periodic review of Army policies.

"Changing conditions and attitudes require and permit constant reexamining and testing of our policies and our practices," Mr. Gray said. "The new board, which I intend to appoint promptly, will help us in the performance of this duty."

STATEMENT ISSUED BY
DEPARTMENT OF DEFENSE
OFFICE OF PUBLIC INFORMATION
Washington 25, D.C.
OCTOBER 14, 1949

DEPARTMENT OF DEFENSE CIVILIAN PERSONNEL POLICY
ANNOUNCED BY SECRETARY JOHNSON

Secretary of Defense Louis Johnson today approved an over-all personnel policy for civilian employees throughout the Department of Defense.

The statement of policy, prepared by Personnel Policy Board, under the chairmanship of Hubert E. Howard, emphasizes the significant role of civilian employees in accomplishing the mission of the Department of Defense. It holds management responsible for leadership, the development of sound management-employee relationships, and the provision of opportunity for the individual development of employees. The policy expects of civilian employees that they discharge their assigned duties in the most effective manner possible, respect the administrative authority of those directing their work, and observe the spirit of the laws and regulations governing their official conduct.

Text of the statement signed by Secretary Johnson follows:

The Department of Defense is responsible for the security of our country. Civilian employees share fully in that responsibility. Use of civilian employees affords abilities not otherwise available, assures continuity of administration and operation, and provides a nucleus of trained personnel necessary for expansion in any emergency. Because civilian employees free military personnel for primarily military duties, they shall be utilized in all positions which do not require military skills or military incumbents for reasons of training, security or discipline.

The establishment of a work environment in which civilian employees will be able to contribute most effectively shall be the responsibility of every person who plans or directs the work of others. Supervisors will provide progressive and constructive leadership to individual employees and shall endeavor to create sound management-employee relationships. They will insure that every employee understands what is expected of him, to whom he is responsible, and his work relationships with his fellow-workers. Productive efficiency can be built only upon a recognition of the individual as the basis of the organization and through application of sound principles of human relations.

The following principles will guide the conduct of human relations in the Department of Defense:

1. There shall be no discrimination because of race, sex, color, religion, national origin, lawful political affiliation, or physical handicap.

2. Employees shall be placed in jobs for which they are best fitted and shall be given opportunities for advancement.

3. Training necessary to insure improved job performance and individual development shall be provided.

4. Appraisal of work performance shall be made fairly and objectively on a continuing basis and such appraisal shall be discussed with employees.

5. Within whatever compensation schedule is applicable, employees shall receive equal pay for work of equal difficulty and responsibility.

6. Working conditions shall be made as safe and healthful as possible.

7. Recognizing that a well-informed work force is a productive work force, employees shall be informed, insofar as possible, of plans and policies affecting them and their work.

8. Employees shall be encouraged to express themselves concerning improvement of work method and working conditions.

9. Employees shall have the right, without interference, coercion, restraint, or reprisal, to join or refrain from joining any lawful employee organization or association.

10. Any employee having a grievance shall be accorded a fair and prompt discussion with the supervisor immediately concerned and, failing prompt and satisfactory adjustment, he shall have a right to appeal, under established grievance procedure. In presenting a grievance, an employee shall be free from interference, restraint, or reprisal, and he may designate a representative of his own choice to assist him.

Maintenance of sound management-employee relations is not the responsibility of management alone. The Department of Defense recognizes its obligations to its employees. In return, it makes reasonable demands of employees to discharge conscientiously their assigned duties in the most effective manner possible, to respect administrative authority of those directing their work, and to observe the spirit as well as the letter of the laws and regulations governing their official conduct.

This policy is applicable throughout the Department of Defense. The Secretaries of the Army, the Navy, and the Air Force will assure that it is made effective within their respective departments.

Signed:

LOUIS JOHNSON

SR 600-629-1

SPECIAL REGULATIONS }   DEPARTMENT OF THE ARMY
No. 600-629-1   }   WASHINGTON 25, D. C., *16 January 1950*

PERSONNEL
UTILIZATION OF NEGRO MANPOWER IN THE ARMY

	Paragraph
Policy	1
Responsibility	2
Periodic review of utilization of Negro manpower	3
Enlisted personnel processing	4
Army school training	5
Eligibility for military occupational specialties	6
Enlisted promotions	7
Officer personnel management	8
ROTC students at summer training camps	9
Utilization and assignment	10

1. **Policy.** — The policy of the Department of the Army is that there shall be equality of treatment and opportunity for all persons in the Army without regard to

race, color, religion, or national origin. All manpower will be utilized to obtain maximum efficiency in the Army.

2. **Responsibility.** — *a.* Commanders of all echelons of the Army will insure that all personnel under their command are thoroughly oriented in the necessity for the unreserved acceptance of the provisions of these policies.

b. Commanders of organizations or installations containing Negro personnel will be responsible for the execution of these policies.

c. The planning, promulgation, implementation, and revision of these policies will be coordinated by the Director of Personnel and Administration, General Staff, United States Army.

3. **Periodic review of utilization of Negro manpower.** — A board of senior Army officers will be convened from time to time to determine current progress under the policies and implementation prescribed herein and to reexamine and review the fundamental policies for the utilization of Negro manpower.

4. **Enlisted personnel processing.** — All enlisted personnel without regard to race or color will be accorded the same reception processing through appropriate installations to insure proper initial classification.

5. **Army school training.** — Army school quotas for replacement stream personnel, and requests for and issuance of school quotas for assigned enlisted personnel will make no reference to race or color. Selection of personnel to attend Army schools will be made without regard to race or color. Graduates of Army schools will be used in positions where their school acquired skill may be utilized in accord with personnel management regulations equally applicable to all enlisted personnel.

870458°—50

SR 600-629-1

6. **Eligibility for military occupational specialties.** — Military occupational specialties will be open to qualified enlisted personnel without regard to race or color. Utilization of Negro personnel in military occupational specialties will be in accord with personnel management regulations equally applicable to all enlisted personnel.

7. **Enlisted promotions.** — The promotion system of the enlisted career guidance program will be administered on an equal merit basis so that all promotions will be obtained by open competition, on examinations uniform throughout the Army, against a single standard, without regard to race or color.

8. **Officer personnel management.** — *a.* Officers will be procured for the Regular Army and for the Officers' Reserve Corps without regard to race or color.

b. All officers, regardless of race or color, will be afforded equal opportunities for advancement, professional improvement, extended active duty, active duty training, promotion and retention in the Army.

9. **ROTC students at summer training camps.** — ROTC students attending summer training camps as members of school units to which they are regularly assigned will remain together and be trained together without regard to race or color.

10. **Utilization and assignment.** — *a.* In furtherance of the policy of the President as expressed in Executive Order 9981, dated July 26, 1948, that there shall be equality of treatment and opportunity for all persons in the armed services without regard to race, color, religion or national origin, it is the objective of the Department of the

Army that Negro manpower possessing appropriate skills and qualifications will be utilized in accordance with such skills and qualifications, and will be assigned to any T/D [overhead] or T/O&E [organized] unit without regard to race or color.

b. In consonance with the foregoing, and as additional steps towards its attainment:

(1) The Department of the Army will publish periodically to major commanders a list of the critical specialties in which vacancies exist within the Army. The first such list is being published concurrently herewith in DA AGO letter dated 16 Jan. 1950. Major commanders concerned will assign Negro personnel who possess any of such critical specialties to any T/D or T/O&E unit in their areas having such critical specialist vacancies, without regard to race or color.

(2) In addition to the provisions of subparagraph (1) above, to fill other vacancies requiring special skills, qualified Negro specialists may be assigned to any appropriate unit by order of the major commander concerned.

[AG 291.2 (25 Oct 49)]

By order of the Secretary of the Army:

OFFICIAL:

EDWARD F. WITSELL
Major General, USA
The Adjutant General

DISTRIBUTION:

A

J. LAWTON COLLINS
Chief of Staff, United States Army
U. S. Government Printing Office: 1950

Effective with the month of April all enlistments in the army within overall recruiting quotas will be open to qualified applicants without regard to race or color.

Staff Message to Army Commands
27 March 1950

[Note: The above regulation eliminated the 10 percent racial quota which formerly had been a part of Army policy toward the enlistment of Negroes.]

DEPARTMENT OF THE NAVY

49-447—Policy Regarding Minority Races
23 June 1949

ACTION: ALL SHIPS AND STATIONS

(Ref.: (a) Alnav 423-45.)

1. Reference (a) is canceled and superseded by this letter.

2. It is the policy of the Navy Department that there shall be equality of treatment and opportunity for all persons in the Navy and Marine Corps without regard to race, color, religion, or national origin.

3. In their attitude and day-to-day conduct of affairs, officers and enlisted personnel of the Navy and Marine Corps shall adhere rigidly and impartially to the Navy Regulations, in which no distinction is made between individuals wearing the uniform of these services.

4. All personnel will be enlisted or appointed, trained, advanced or promoted, assigned duty, and administered in all respects without regard to race, color, religion, or national origin.

5. In the utilization of housing, messing, berthing, and other facilities, no special or unusual provisions will be made for the accommodation of any minority race.

—SecNav. Francis P. Matthews.

CIRCULAR LETTER NO. 115-49
49-525—Chief Stewards
Pers-21-rwh, MB, 25 July 1949

ACTION: ALL SHIPS AND STATIONS

(Ref.: (a) BuPers Manual (1948).)

1. In accordance with a recent directive of the Secretary of the Navy, chief stewards are hereafter to be considered as chief petty officers and will be accorded the prerogatives of that status as prescribed by U. S. Naval Regulations and Bureau of Naval Personnel Manual. They shall take precedence immediately following chief dental technicans.

2. Appropriate changes to reference (a) will be promulgated.

—BuPers, T. L. Sprague.

CIRCULAR LETTER NO. 141-49
49-626—First-Class, Second-Class, and Third-Class Stewards
Pers-211-mf, MB, 30 August 1949

ACTION: ALL SHIPS AND STATIONS

1. Effective 1 January 1950, stewards, first-, second-, and third-class, will be considered petty officers of their appropriate pay grade and will be accorded the prerogatives of that status as prescribed by U. S. Navy Regulations and Bureau of Naval Personnel Manual. They shall take precedence immediately after dental technician, first-, second-, and third-class, respecively.

2. The Secretary of the Navy has authorized a change, effective on the above date, in the uniform prescribed for stewards, first-, second-, and third-class, which will require them to wear the same type of uniform as is prescribed for other petty officers. More detailed information concerning the uniform change will be published at a later date. In the meantime, commanding officers are requested to advise stewards, first-, second-, and third-class, under their commands of this prospective change in order that they may anticipate their needs in regard to uniforms.

3. Appropriate changes to Bureau of Naval Personnel Manual will be promulgated.

—BuPers, T. L. Sprague.

DEPARTMENT OF THE AIR FORCE

AIR FORCE LETTER⎰DEPARTMENT OF THE AIR FORCE
NO. 35-3　　　⎱　　WASHINGTON, 11 May 1949

MILITARY PERSONNEL
Air Force Personnel Policies

(Effective until 11 November 1950 unless sooner rescinded or superseded)

1. *Policy.*—It is the policy of the United States Air Force that there shall be equality of treatment and opportunity for all persons in the Air Force without regard to race, color, religion, or national origin.

2. *Supplemental policies.* — To insure uniform application of this policy, the following supplemental policies are announced.

a. There will be no strength quotas of minority groups in the Air Force troop basis.

b. Some units will continue to be manned with Negro personnel; however, all Negroes will not necessarily be assigned to Negro units. Qualified Negro personnel may be assigned to fill any position vacancy in any Air Force organization or overhead installation without regard to race.

c. To meet the requirements of the Air Force for qualified individuals, all Air Force personnel will be considered on the basis of individual merit and ability and must qualify according to the prescribed standards for enlistment, attendance at schools, promotion, assignment to specific duties, etc.

d. All individuals, regardless of race, will be accorded equal opportunity for appointment, advancement, professional improvement, promotion, and retention in all components of the Air Force of the United States.

e. Officers will be accepted into the Regular Air Force through the operation of existing programs and in accordance with their qualifications without regard to race.

f. All enlisted personnel will be accorded identical processing through appropriate installations to insure proper classification and assignment of individuals.

g. Directives pertaining to the release of personnel from the services shall be applied equally without reference to race.

3. *Rsponsibility.*

a. The planning, promulgation, and revision of this policy will be coordinated by the Director of Personnel Planning, Office of the Deputy Chief of Staff, Personnel, Headquarters USAF.

b. Commanding officers are hereby directly charged with the responsibility for implementation of the above policy.

c. Commanders of all echelons of the Air Force will insure that all personnel in their command are indoctrinated thoroughly with the necessity for the unreserved acceptance of the provisions of this policy.

4. *Army units and individuals.* — Army units and individuals with the Air Force will continue to be governed by the policies promulgated by the Army.

5. *Previous policy.*—All prior policy statements with regard to Negro Personnel which are contrary to the above are hereby rescinded and superseded by the policy enunciated herewith.

By Order of the Air Force:

Official:

L. L. JUDGE
Colonel, USAF
Air Adjutant General

Chief of Staff,
HOYT S. VANDENBERG
United States Air Force

FEDERAL HOUSING ADMINISTRATION

AMENDMENT TO RULES OF THE
FEDERAL HOUSING COMMISSIONER FOR
MUTUAL MORTGAGE INSURANCE
UNDER SECTION 203 OF THE
NATIONAL HOUSING ACT

Section III of the Administrative Rules under Section 203 of the National Housing Act, revised August 15, 1946, as amended, is hereby amended by adding at the end thereof the following new subsection:

"15. The mortgage shall contain a covenant by the mortgagor that until the mortgage has been paid in full, or the contract of insurance otherwise terminated, he will not execute or file for record any instrument which imposes a restriction upon the sale or occupancy of the mortgaged property on the basis of race, color, or creed. Such covenant shall be binding upon the mortgagor and his assigns and shall provide that upon violation thereof the mortgagee may, at its option, declare the unpaid balance of the mortgage immediately due and payable."

Section IV of said Administrative Rules is hereby amended by adding at the end thereof the following new subsection:

"5. A mortgagor must certify that until the mortgage has been paid in full, or the contract of insurance otherwise terminated, he will not file for record any restriction upon the sale or occupancy of the mortgaged property on the basis of race, color, or creed or execute any agreement, lease, or conveyance affecting the mortgaged property which imposes any such restriction upon its sale or occupancy."

Section V of said Administrative Rules is hereby amended by adding at the end thereof the following new subsection:

"5. A mortgagee must establish that no restriction upon the sale or occupancy of the mortgaged property, on the basis of race, color, or creed, has been filed of record at any time subsequent to February 15, 1950, and prior to the recording of the mortgage offered for insurance."

This amendment is effective as to all mortgages on which a commitment to insure is issued on or after February 15, 1950.

Issued at Washington, D. C., this 12th day of December, 1949.

Franklin D. Richards
Federal Housing Commissioner

AMENDMENT TO RULES OF THE
FEDERAL HOUSING COMMISSIONER FOR
FARM MORTGAGE INSURANCE UNDER SECTION 203(d)
OF THE NATIONAL HOUSING ACT

Section III of the Administrative Rules under Section 203(d) of the National Housing Act, revised January 1, 1949, is hereby amended by adding at the end thereof the following new subsection:

"14. The mortgage shall contain a covenant by the mortgagor that until the mortgage has been paid in full, or the contract of insurance otherwise terminated, he will not execute or file for record any instrument which imposes a restriction upon the sale or occupancy of the mortgaged property on the basis of race, color, or creed. Such covenant shall be binding upon the mortgagor and his assigns and shall provide that upon violation thereof the mortgagee may, at its option, declare the unpaid balance of the mortgage immediately due and payable."

Section IV of said Administrative Rules is hereby amended by adding at the end thereof the following new subsection:

"6. A mortgagor must certify that until the mortgage has been paid in full, or the contract of insurance otherwise terminated, he will not file for record any restriction upon the sale or occupancy of the mortgaged property on the basis of race, color, or creed or execute any agreement, lease, or conveyance affecting the mortgaged property which imposes any such restriction upon its sale or occupancy."

Section V of said Administrative Rules is hereby amended by adding at the end thereof the following new subsection:

"5. A mortgagee must establish that no restriction upon the sale or occupancy of the mortgaged property, on the basis of race, color, or creed, has been filed of record at any time subsequent to February 15, 1950, and prior to the recording of the mortgage offered for insurance."

This amendment is effective as to all mortgages on which a commitment to insure is issued on or after February 15, 1950.

Issued at Washington, D.C., this 12th day of December, 1949.

Franklin D. Richards
Federal Housing Commissioner

AMENDMENT TO THE ADMINISTRATIVE RULES OF THE
FEDERAL HOUSING COMMISSIONER FOR
MULTIFAMILY RENTAL HOUSING INSURANCE
UNDER SECTION 207
OF THE NATIONAL HOUSING ACT

Section II of the Administrative Rules under Section 207 of the National Housing

Act, revised August 26, 1948, as amended, is hereby amended by adding at the end thereof the following new subsection:

"15. The mortgage shall contain a covenant by the mortgagor that until the mortgage has been paid in full, or the contract of insurance otherwise terminated, he will not execute or file for record any instrument which imposes a restriction upon the sale or occupancy of the mortgaged property on the basis of race, color, or creed. Such covenant shall be binding upon the mortgagor and his assigns and shall provide that upon violation thereof the mortgagee may, at its option, declare the unpaid balance of the mortgage immediately due and payable."

Paragraph (c) of Subsection 3 of Section VI of said Administrative Rules, is hereby amended to read as follows:

"(c) Such dwelling and other improvements, if any, must not violate any zoning or deed restrictions applicable to the project site (other than race restrictions), and must comply with all applicable building and other governmental regulations."

Section VI of said Administrative Rules, is further amended by adding at the end thereof the following new subsection:

"4. A mortgagor must establish that no restriction upon the sale or occupancy of the mortgaged property, on the basis of race, color, or creed, has been filed of record at any time subsequent to February 15, 1950, and prior to the recording of the mortgage offered for insurance, and must certify that, until the mortgage has been paid in full or the contract of insurance otherwise terminated, he will not file for record any such restriction affecting the mortgaged property or execute any agreement, lease, or conveyance affecting the mortgaged property which imposes any such restriction upon its sale or occupancy."

This amendment is effective as to all mortgages on which a commitment to insure is issued on or after February 15, 1950.

Issued at Washington, D.C., this 12th day of December, 1949.

Franklin D. Richards
Federal Housing Commissioner

AMENDMENT TO RULES OF THE
FEDERAL HOUSING COMMISSIONER FOR
WAR HOUSING INSURANCE UNDER SECTION 603
OF THE NATIONAL HOUSING ACT

Section IV of the Administrative Rules under Section 603 of the National Housing Act, revised July 15, 1946, as amended, is hereby amended by adding at the end thereof the following new subsection:

"14. The mortgage shall contain a covenant by the mortgagor that until the mortgage has been paid in full, or the contract of insurance otherwise terminated, he will not execute or file for record any instrument which imposes a restriction upon the sale or occupancy of the mortgaged property on the basis of race, color, or creed. Such covenant shall be binding upon the mortgagor and his assigns and shall provide that upon violation thereof the mortgagee may, at its option, declare the unpaid balance of the mortgage immediately due and payable."

Section V of said Administrative Rules is hereby amended by adding at the end thereof the following new subsection:

"7. A mortgagor must certify that until the mortgage has been paid in full, or the contract of insurance otherwise terminated, he will not file for record any restriction upon the sale or occupancy of the mortgaged property on the basis of race, color, or creed or execute any agreement, lease, or conveyance affecting the mortgaged property which imposes any such restriction upon its sale or occupancy."

Section VI of said Administrative Rules is hereby amended by adding at the end thereof the following new subsection:

"4. A mortgagee must establish that no restriction upon the sale or occupancy of the mortgaged property, on the basis of race, color, or creed, has been filed of record at any time subsequent to February 15, 1950, and prior to the recording of the mortgage offered for insurance."

This amendment is effective as to all mortgages on which a commitment to insure is issued on or after February 15, 1950.

Issued at Washington, D. C., this 12th day of December, 1949.

Franklin D. Richards
Federal Housing Commissioner

AMENDMENT TO RULES OF THE FEDERAL HOUSING COMMISSIONER FOR RENTAL HOUSING INSURANCE UNDER SECTION 608 OF THE NATIONAL HOUSING ACT

Section III of the Administrative Rules under Section 608 of the National Housing Act, issued December 19, 1947, as amended, is hereby amended by adding at the end thereof the following new subsection:

"16. The mortgage shall contain a covenant by the mortgagor that until the mortgage has been paid in full, or the contract of insurance otherwise terminated, he will not execute or file for record any instrument which imposes a restriction upon the sale or occupancy of the mortgaged property on the basis of race, color, or creed. Such covenant shall be binding upon the mortgagor and his assigns and shall provide that upon violation thereof the mortgagee may, at its option, declare the unpaid balance of the mortgage immediately due and payable."

Subsection 3 of Section VI of said Administrative Rules, is hereby amended to read as follows:

"3. Such dwelling and other improvements, if any, must not violate any zoning or deed restrictions applicable to the project site (other than race restrictions), and must comply with all applicable building and other governmental regulations."

Section VI of said Administrative Rules, is further amended by adding at the end thereof the following new subsection:

"4. A mortgagor must establish that no restriction upon the sale or occupancy of the mortgaged property, on the basis of race, color, or creed, has, been filed of record at any time subsequent to February 15, 1950, and prior to the recording of the mortgage offered for insurance, and must certify that, until the mortgage has been paid in full or the contract of insurance otherwise terminated, he will not file for record any such restriction affecting the mortgaged property or execute any agreement, lease, or conveyance affecting the mortgaged property which imposes any such restriction upon its sale or occupancy."

This amendment is effective as to all mortgages on which a commitment to insure is issued on or after February 15, 1950.

Issued at Washington, D. C., this 12th day of December, 1949.

Franklin D. Richards
Federal Housing Commissioner

AMENDMENT TO RULES OF THE FEDERAL HOUSING COMMISSIONER FOR WAR HOUSING INSURANCE UNDER SECTION 603 OF THE NATIONAL HOUSING ACT PURSUANT TO THE PROVISIONS OF SECTION 610

Section IV of the Administrative Rules under Section 603 of the National Housing Act, pursuant to the provisions of Section 610, issued August 19, 1947, as amended, is hereby amended by adding at the end thereof the following new subsection:

"15. The mortgage shall contain a covenant by the mortgagor that until the mortgage has been paid in full, or the contract of insurance otherwise terminated, he will not execute or file for record any instrument which imposes a restriction upon the sale or occupancy of the mortgaged property on the basis of race, color, or creed. Such covenant shall be binding upon the mortgagor and his assigns and shall provide that upon violation thereof the mortgagee may, at its option, declare the unpaid balance of the mortgage immediately due and payable."

Section V of said Administrative Rules is hereby amended by adding at the end thereof the following new subsection:

"7. A mortgagor must certify that until the mortgage has been paid in full, or the contract of insurance otherwise terminated, he will not file for record any restriction upon the sale or occupancy of the mortgaged property on the basis of race, color, or creed or execute any agreement, lease, or conveyance affecting the mortgaged property which imposes any such restriction upon its sale or occupancy."

Section VI of said Administrative Rules is hereby amended by adding at the end thereof the following new subsection:

"4. A mortgagee must establish that no restriction upon the sale or occupancy of the mortgaged property, on the basis of race, color, or creed, has been filed of record at any time subsequent to February 15, 1950, and prior to the recording of the mortgage offered for insurance."

This amendment is effective as to all mortgages on which a commitment to insure is issued on or after February 15, 1950.

Issued at Washington, D. C., this 12th day of December, 1949.

Franklin D. Richards
Federal Housing Commissioner

AMENDMENT TO THE ADMINISTRATIVE RULES OF THE FEDERAL HOUSING COMMISSIONER FOR WAR HOUSING INSURANCE UNDER SECTION 608 OF THE NATIONAL HOUSING ACT PURSUANT TO THE PROVISIONS OF SECTION 610

Section III of the Administrative Rules under Section 608 of the National Housing Act, pursuant to the provisions of Section 610, issued August 19, 1947, as amended, is hereby amended by adding at the end thereof the following new subsection:

"16. The mortgage shall contain a covenant by the mortgagor that until the mortgage has been paid in full, or the contract of insurance otherwise terminated, he will not execute or file for record any instrument which imposes a restriction upon the sale or occupancy of the mortgaged property on the basis of race, color, or creed. Such covenant shall be binding upon the mortgagor and his assigns and shall provide that upon violation thereof the mortgagee may, at its option, declare the unpaid balance of the mortgage immediately due and payable."

Section VI of said Administrative Rules, is hereby amended by adding at the end thereof the following new subsection:

"3. A mortgagor must establish that no restriction upon the sale or occupancy of the mortgaged property, on the basis of race, color, or creed, has been filed of record at any time subsequent to February 15, 1950, and prior to the recording of the mortgage offered for insurance, and must certify that, until the mortgage has been paid in full or the contract of insurance otherwise terminated, he will not file for record any such restriction affecting the mortgaged property or execute any agreement, lease, or conveyance affecting the mortgaged property which imposes any such restriction upon its sale or occupancy."

This amendment is effective as to all mortgages on which a commitment to insure is issued on or after February 15, 1950.

Issued at Washington, D. C., this 12th day of December, 1949.

Franklin D. Richards
Federal Housing Commissioner

AMENDMENT TO THE ADMINISTRATIVE RULES OF THE FEDERAL HOUSING COMMISSIONER UNDER SECTION 611 OF TITLE VI OF THE NATIONAL HOUSING ACT

Section III of the Administrative Rules under Section 611 of the National Housing Act, issued August 23, 1948, is hereby amended by adding at the end thereof the following new subsection:

"16. The mortgage shall contain a covenant by the mortgagor that until the mortgage has been paid in full, or the contract of insurance otherwise terminated, he will not execute or file for record any instrument which imposes a restriction upon the sale or occupancy of the mortgaged property on the basis of race, color, or creed. Such covenant shall be binding upon the mortgagor and his assigns and shall provide that upon violation thereof the mortgagee may, at its option, declare the unpaid balance of the mortgage immediately due and payable."

Subsection 3 of Section V of said Administrative Rules, is hereby amended to read as follows:

"3. Such dwelling and other improvements, if any, must not violate any zoning or deed restrictions applicable to the project site (other than race restrictions), and must comply with all applicable building and other governmental regulations."

Section V of said Administrative Rules, is further amended by adding at the end thereof the following new subsection:

"4. A mortgagor must establish that no restriction upon the sale or occupancy of the mortgaged property, on the basis of race, color, or creed, has been filed of record at any time subsequent to February 15, 1950, and prior to the recording of the mortgage offered for insurance, and must certify that, until the mortgage has been paid in full or the contract of insurance otherwise terminated, he will not file for record any such restriction affecting the mortgaged property or execute any agreement, lease, or conveyance affecting the mortgaged property which imposes any such restriction upon its sale or occupancy."

This amendment is effective as to all mortgages on which a commitment to insure is issued on or after February 15, 1950.

Issued at Washington, D.C., this 12th day of December, 1949.

Franklin D. Richards
Federal Housing Commissioner

AMENDMENT TO THE ADMINISTRATIVE RULES OF THE FEDERAL HOUSING COMMISSIONER UNDER TITLE VII OF THE NATIONAL HOUSING ACT

Section III of the Administrative Rules of the Federal Housing Commissioner under Title VII of the National Housing Act, issued November 12, 1948, as amended, is hereby amended by adding at the end thereof the following new subsection:

"7. An investor must establish that no restriction upon the sale or occupancy of the project, on the basis of race, color, or creed, has been filed of record at any time subsequent to February 15, 1950, and must certify that so long as the insurance contract remains in force he will not file for record any restriction affecting the project or execute any agreement, lease, or conveyance affecting the project which imposes any such restriction upon its sale or occupancy."

This amendment is effective as to all projects on which a commitment is issued on or after February 15, 1950.

Issued at Washington, D. C., this 12th day of December, 1949.

Franklin D. Richards
Federal Housing Commissioner

AMENDMENT TO THE ADMINISTRATIVE RULES OF THE FEDERAL HOUSING COMMISSIONER FOR MILITARY HOUSING INSURANCE UNDER TITLE VIII OF THE NATIONAL HOUSING ACT

Section III of the Administrative Rules under Title VIII of the National Housing Act, issued August 22, 1949, is hereby amended by adding at the end thereof the following new subsection:

"16. The mortgage shall contain a covenant by the mortgagor that until the mortgage has been paid in full, or the contract of insurance otherwise terminated, he will not execute or file for record any instrument which imposes a restriction upon the sale or occupancy of the mortgaged property on the basis of race, color, or creed. Such covenant shall be binding upon the mortgagor and his assigns and shall provide that upon violation thereof the mortgagee may, at its option, declare the unpaid balance of the mortgage immediately due and payable."

Subsection 3 of Section VI of said Administrative Rules, is hereby amended to read as follows:

"3. Such dwelling and other improvements, if any, must not violate any zoning or deed restrictions applicable to the project site (other than race restrictions), and must comply with all applicable building and other governmental regulations."

Section VI of said Administrative Rules, is further amended by adding at the end thereof the following new subsection:

"4. A mortgagor must establish that no restriction upon the sale or occupancy of the mortgaged property, on the basis of race, color, or creed, has been filed of record at any time subsequent to February 15, 1950, and prior to the recording of the mortgage offered for insurance, and must certify that, until the mortgage has been paid in full or the contract of insurance otherwise terminated, he will not file for record any such restriction affecting the mortgaged property or execute any agreement, lease, or conveyance affecting the mortgaged property which imposes any such restriction upon its sale or occupancy."

This amendment is effective as to all mortgages on which a commitment to insure is issued on or after February 15, 1950.

Issued at Washington, D. C., this 12th day of December, 1949.

Franklin D. Richards
Federal Housing Commissioner

VETERANS ADMINISTRATION

Information Service

Washington 25, D. C.

RELEASE

December 16, 1949

Regulations to bar restrictive covenants based on race, creed or color in connection with home loan mortgages guaranteed for veterans under the GI Bill will go into effect next February, Veterans Administration announced today.

The new regulations will apply to all such covenants created and recorded subsequent to February 15, 1950, and to all GI mortgages guaranteed or insured by VA after that date. Loans guaranteed or covenants recorded prior to February 16 will not be affected, V-A said.

As applied to mortgage lenders, V-A said any guarantee issued for a loan on property subject to a recorded covenant barred by the regulations would be affected in the event of subsequent default and foreclosure. In such cases, the lender's option of transferring the property to V-A, which he normally has the right to do, would be nullified if the covenant was still effective of record at the time of the proposed transfer.

Also, with respect to mortgages guaranteed or insured by V-A after February 15, the borrower may be declared in default on his loan — with the entire unpaid balance immediately due and payable — if he thereafter records such a covenant on the property.

The type of covenants referred to are those designed to restrict the occupancy or use of the property as to race, creed or color. V-A said the new regulations are being issued to bring the agency's loan guaranty program into full accord with a recent decision of the United States Supreme Court. The Court held that such covenants are contrary to public policy and are not sustainable by action in the Federal courts.

The new regulations have been issued to the various V-A field offices which administer the loan guaranty program, and copies will be distributed to builders, lenders and others participating in the program.

CIVIL AERONAUTICS ADMINISTRATION
13 F. R. 8736
RULES AND REGULATIONS
TITLE 14 — CIVIL AVIATION

Chapter II — Civil Aeronautics Administration
[Amdt. 1]

PART 570—GENERAL REGULATIONS OF THE
WASHINGTON NATIONAL AIRPORT
DISCRIMINATION OR SEGREGATION

Acting pursuant to the authority vested in me by the act to provide for the Administration of Washington National Airport (54 Stat. 686-688), finding that compliance with the notice, procedures and effective date provisions of section 4 of the Administrative Procedure Act would be unnecessary and contrary to the public interest, since actual notice has been given and delay would permit continuance of the practices prohibited by this amendment, I hereby amend Part 570 of this chapter by adding a new §570.28 to read as follows:

§570.28 *Discrimination or segregation*. In the operation of all facilities of the Washington National Airport, services shall be rendered without discrimination or segregation as to race, color or creed.

This amendment shall become effective immediately. (Sec. 2, 54 Stat. 688)

[SEAL]   D. W. RENTZEL,
                                   Administrator of Civil Aeronautics.

DECEMBER 27, 1948.

[F. R. Doc. 48-11400; Filed, Dec. 29, 1948; 9:41 a. m.]

[Note: The above regulation was upheld by Federal District Judge Albert W. Bryan on January 3, 1949, who refused to grant an injunction sought by the Air Terminal Services, Inc., operator of the dining room at the Washington National Airport in Alexandria, Virginia. The court held that the C.A.A. had full authority to issue regulations banning segregation and discrimination. See New York Herald Tribune, Jan. 4, 1949, Associated Press report dated January 3, 1949.

But see *Nash v. Air Terminal Services, Inc.*, 85 F. Supp, 545. (Aug. 31, 1949.)]

APPENDIX 4.

Alaska Civil Rights Act

ALASKA

ORGANIC ACT

§3. [Extends the Constitution and laws of the United States to the Territory of Alaska.] [37 Stat. 512.]

STATUTES

Alaska Compiled Laws 1949

Civil Rights

Civil Code, §20-1-3. Citizens entitled to full and equal accommodations, facilities and privileges in places of public accommodation. — All citizens within the Territory of Alaska shall be entitled to the full and equal enjoyment of accommodations, advantages, facilities and privileges of public inns, restaurants, eating houses, hotels, soda fountains, soft drink parlors, taverns, roadhouses, barber shops, beauty parlors, bathrooms, resthouses, theaters, skating rinks, cafes, ice cream parlors, transportation companies, and all other conveyances and amusements, subject only to the conditions and limitations established by law and applicable alike to all citizens. [L. 1945, ch. 2, §1, p. 36.]

Civil Code, §20-1-4. Violation as a misdemeanor: Punishment. — Any person who shall violate or aid or incite a violation of said full and equal enjoyment; or any person who shall display any printed or written sign indicating a discrimination on racial grounds of said full and equal enjoyment, for each day for which said sign is displayed shall be deemed guilty of a misdemeanor and upon conviction thereof shall be punished by imprisonment in jail for not more than thirty (30) days or fined not more than two hundred fifty ($250.00) dollars, or both. [L. 1945, ch. 2, §2, p. 36.]

Education

§37-1-1. Legislative power as to schools. — The Legislature of Alaska is empowered to establish and maintain schools for white and colored children and children of mixed blood who lead a civilized life in said Territory and to make appropriations of Territorial funds for that purpose. [39 Stat. 1131; CLA 1933, §475; 48 U.S.C. §170.]

[Note: "Mixed blood" is held to mean "mixed Indian blood." *Davis v. Sitka School Board* (1908) 3 A. 481.

The Constitution of the United States does not prohibit establishment of separate schools for people not of the white race, provided such schools are on an equal plane with those maintained for the white race. *Sing v. Sitka School Board* (1927) 7 A. 616. But see *Jones v. Ellis* (1929) 8 A. 146, which held that the above section makes no provision as to segregation of races, and therefore a child of Indian blood was entitled to attend a city school established under section 37-1-1 although a school for Indian children was established under §37-8-1.]

610

§37-8-1. **Supervision of education of Eskimos and Indians: Appropriations for schools: Admission to Indian boarding schools.** The education of the Eskimos and Indians in Alaska shall remain under the direction and control of the Secretary of the Interior, and schools for and among the Eskimos and Indians of Alaska shall be provided for by an annual appropriation, and the Eskimo and Indian children of Alaska shall have the same right to be admitted to any Indian boarding school as the Indian children in the States or Territories of the United States. [33 Stat. 619; CLA 1933, §267; 48, U.S.C. §169.]

University of Alaska

§37-10-24. **Discrimination because of sex, color or nationality prohibted.** — No person shall, because of sex, color or nationality, be deprived of the privileges of this institution. [L. 1935, ch. 49, §24, p. 115, effective July 1, 1935].

APPENDIX 4A.

VIRGIN ISLANDS

Civil Rights Act

BILL No. 1

THE FIFTEENTH LEGISLATIVE ASSEMBLY OF THE VIRGIN ISLANDS OF THE UNITED STATES

First Session

AN ACT

To Provide Equal Rights in Places of Public Accommodations,
Resort or Amusement

BE IT ENACTED BY THE LEGISLATIVE ASSEMBLY OF THE VIRGIN ISLANDS IN SESSION ASSEMBLED:

SECTION 1. STATEMENT OF PUBLIC POLICY

WHEREAS, it is the cultural and democratic heritage of the people of the Virgin Islands to respect the human and civil rights of all people and to judge all men according to their individual merit without reference to race, creed, color, or national origin;

NOW, THEREFORE, it is hereby declared to be the public policy of the Virgin Islands that all natural persons within the jurisdiction of the Virgin Islands shall be entitled to the full and equal accommodations, advantages, facilities, and privileges of any place of public accommodations, resort, or amusement, subject only to the conditions and limitations established by law and applicable alike to all persons. In order to implement this public policy, it is the intent of this Act to prevent and prohibit discrimination in any form based upon race, creed, color, or national origin, whether practiced directly or indirectly, or by subterfuge in any and all places of public accommodation, resort, or amusement.

SECTION 2. CONSTRUCTION. The courts shall construe this Act liberally in furtherance of the above declarations.

SECTION 3. DEFINITIONS. As used in this Act —

(a) The term "person" shall mean any individual, partnership, corporation, institution, association, department or agency of the municipal governments of the Virgin Islands or the officers and employees thereof of any of the foregoing.

(b) "Places of public accommodation, resort, or amusement" shall be deemed to be any places where food or drink is sold, or rooms are rented, or any charge is made for admission or service, or occupancy or use of any property or facilities, including but not limited to inns, hotels (whether conducted for the entertainment of transient guests or for the accommodation of those seeking health, recreation, or rest), taverns, road houses, rooming houses, restaurants, eating houses, or any places where food is sold for consumption on the premises, buffets, saloons, barrooms, parks or enclosures where food, spirituous or malt liquors, wines, soft drinks or beer are sold; bathing houses, beaches, barber shops, beauty parlors, soda fountains, drink parlors of all kinds, shops, stores, gardens, amusement and recreation parks, theaters, golf courses, public and private schools, public conveyances operated on land or water or in the air as well as the stations or terminals threof, or any hospital, sanitarium, dispensary or clinic.

(c) "Discrimination" shall include segregation based on race, creed, color, or national origin.

SECTION 4. All natural persons within the jurisdiction of the Virgin Islands shall be entitled to the full and equal accommodations, advantages, facilities, and privileges of any place of public accommodations, resort, or amusement, subject only to the conditions and limitations established by law and applicable alike to all persons; and it shall be unlawful for any person, being the owner, manager, proprietor, lessee, superintendent, agent, or employee of any place of public accommodation, resort or amusement, directly or indirectly or by subterfuge, to withhold from or deny to any other person any of the accommodations, advantages, facilities, or privileges thereof, or to adopt or pursue any custom, policy or practice, requirement or secret understanding, or any custom or policy of non-membership discrimination or guest card requirement with respect to the operation or management of such place which is intended, calculated or designed to, or which shall have the effect of discriminating against any other person by reason of non-membership in a club or on account of race, creed, color or national origin.

SECTION 5. Hereafter, no later than January 5 of each year, any person or incorporated or unincorporated association of individuals, maintaining, owning, leasing, possessing or operating any club facilities consisting of physical property such as land, beaches, or buildings shall file with the Government Secretary a statement of what licenses he or it holds to sell liquor, food or drink, or to rent rooms, or to charge for any other use or occupancy of property or facility or service or beach together with a statement of what articles, if any, are sold, what rooms, if any, are rented and what other facilities or services are maintained for charge; and a copy of its constitution and by-laws including a list of all duly elected officers and directors and a list of all members of the association; all of which must be certified upon oath, and if any charge is made, either to members or non-members of clubs for any of the above, then the statement must also include an affidavit by the president and manager of the club certifying that there is no discrimination in such sales, renting, or use based upon race, creed, color, national origin or non-membership in said club; *provided, that* any person, or incorporated or unincorporated association of individuals charging in any manner for any article, or for the use or occupancy of any property, facility or service is expressly declared to be a place of public accommodation, resort or amusement within the spirit and meaning of this law and shall, upon determination thereof by the Government Secretary or the District Court, be registered as such in the Office of the Government Secretary; and provided further, that nothing contained in this Act shall be construed to prevent a reasonable difference in charges by parochial or denominational schools for tuition of members and non-members or preference in admission to members of the religious body maintaining the school.

SECTION 6. It shall be the duty of the Director of Police of each respective municipality, or his duly authorized representative, to make periodical inspections, at reasonable times, of all places of public accommodation, resort or amusement, in order to see that the provisions of this law are complied with.

SECTION 7. Whenever, in the opinion of the District Attorney, any person shall engage in any act, or adopt, or pursue any custom, policy, practice or requirement amounting in effect to a violation or evasion of this Act, it shall be his duty to procure a Rule to Show Cause to issue out of the District Court requiring such person to show cause before the District Court why the license of such person should not be revoked as against public policy; and if the Court shall find that the act, policy, custom, practice or requirement engaged in or adopted or pursued, violates any provision of this Act, the Court shall then order the license of such person revoked or suspended as against public policy.

SECTION 8. Any person, whether as owner, manager or employee, of a place of public accommodation, resort or amusement, who shall violate any of the provisions of this Act or who shall aid or incite the violation of any of the said provisions shall for each and every violation thereof be liable to a penalty of not more than five hundred dollars ($500) to be recovered by the person aggrieved thereby or by any resident of the Virgin Islands to whom such person shall assign his cause of action, and, in addition, shall also, for every such offense be deemed guilty of a misdemeanor and upon conviction thereof shall be fined not more than five hundred dollars ($500) or imprisoned for not more than ninety (90) days or both. Every day of violation shall constitute a separate offense.

SECTION 9. In addition to any other penalties provided for herein, the license to conduct a business, or to sell any articles or facilities or services, of any person who shall violate any of the provisions of this Act in connection with the said business may in the discretion of the Governor, after adequate notice and hearing, be revoked, suspended or its renewal denied.

SECTION 10. Should any section or sections or part of any section, or any single provision, or provisions of this Act be declared unconstitutional, illegal or void, by any competent court, it shall not affect the remaining provisions or sections or part of section or sections, as the case may be, which shall remain in full force and effect.

SECTION 11. This Act may be cited as the "Harris-Neazer-McFarlane Anti-Discrimination Act of 1950."

SECTION 12. All laws or Ordinances, or parts thereof, in conflict with this Act are hereby repealed.

Thus passed by the Legislative Assembly of the Virgin Islands of the United States on September 12, 1950.

* * * * *

[Approved by MORRIS F. de CASTRO, Governor, September 15, 1950.]

APPENDIX 5.

ORDINANCES

ALABAMA

CITY OF BIRMINGHAM

GENERAL CITY CODE (1944)

(SEGREGATION)

OFFENSES — MISCELLANEOUS

Sec. 859. **Separation of Races — Generally.** — (a) It shall be unlawful for any person in charge or control of any room, hall, theatre, picture house, auditorium, yard, court, ball park, public park, or other indoor or outdoor place, to which both white persons and negroes are admitted, to cause, permit or allow therein or thereon any theatrical performance, picture exhibition, speech, or educational or entertainment program of any kind whatsoever, unless such room, hall, theatre, picture house, auditorium, yard, court, ball park, or other place, has entrances, exits and seating or standing sections set aside for and assigned to the use of white persons, and other entrances, exits and seating or standing sections set aside for and assigned to the use of negroes, and unless the entrances, exits and seating or standing sections set aside for and assigned to the use of white persons are distinctly separated from those set aside for and assigned to the use of negroes, by well defined physical barriers, and unless the members of each race are effectively restricted and confined to the sections set aside for the use of each race.

(b) It shall be unlawful for any member of one race to use or occupy any entrance, exit or seating or standing section set aside for and assigned to the use of members of the other race.

(c) It shall be unlawful for any person to conduct, participate in or engage in any theatrical performance, picture exhibition, speech, or educational or entertainment program of any kind whatsoever, in any room, hall, theatre, picture house, auditorium, yard, court, ball park, public park, or other indoor or outdoor place, knowing that any provision of the two preceding sub-divisions has not been complied with.

(d) The chief of police and members of the police department shall have the right, and it shall be their duty, to disperse any gathering or assemblage in violation of this section, and to arrest any person guilty of violating the same. (1930, Sec. 5516)

DRUGS AND FOOD

Sec. 369. **Separation of Races** (Article III, Food Establishments). — It shall be unlawful to conduct a restaurant or other place for the serving of food in the city, at which white and colored people are served in the same room, unless such white and colored persons are effectually separated by a solid partition extending from the floor upward to a distance of seven feet or higher, and unless a separate entrance from the street is provided for each compartment. (1930, Sec. 5288)

GAMBLING

Sec. 597. **Negroes and White Persons Not to Play Together** (Art. I—Gambling).

— It shall be unlawful for a negro and white person to play together or in company with each other in any game of cards or dice, dominoes or checkers.

Any person, who, being the owner, proprietor or keeper or superintendent of any tavern, inn, restaurant or other public house or public place, or the clerk, servant or employee of such owner, proprietor, keeper or superintendent, knowingly permits a negro and a white person to play together or in the company with each other at any game with cards, dice, dominoes or checkers, in his house or on his premises shall, on conviction, be punished as provided in section 4. (1930, Sec. 5066, 5067)

[Sec. 4 makes violation of code punishable by fine up to $100.00 or imprisonment in the city jail, workhouse or house of correction or at hard labor upon the streets or public works up to 6 months, or both fine and imprisonment.]

POOL AND BILLIARD ROOMS AND BOWLING ALLEYS

Sec. 939. Separation of Races, Pool and Billiard Rooms. — It shall be unlawful for a negro and white person to play together or in company with each other at any game of pool or billiards.

Any person who, being the owner, proprietor or in charge of any poolroom, pool table, billiard room or billiard table, knowingly permits a negro and a white person to play together or in company with each other at any game of pool or billiards on his premises shall, on conviction, be punished as provided in Sec. 4. (1930, Sec. 5066, 5067)

RAILROADS AND STREET RAILWAYS

Sec. 1002. Separation of Races, Railroads and Street Railways. — Every common carrier engaged in operating street cars in the city for the carriage of passengers shall provide equal but separate accommodations for the white and colored races by providing separate cars or by clearly indicating or designating by physical visible marks the area to be occupied by each race in any streetcar in which the two races are permitted to be carried together and by confining each race to occupancy of the area of such streetcar so set apart for it.

Every common carrier engaged in operating street cars in the city for the carrying of passengers shall provide for each car used for white and colored passengers, separate entrances and exits to and from such cars in such manner as to prevent intermingling of the white and colored passengers when entering or leaving such car, but this provision for separate entrances and exits shall not apply to the cars operated on the following lines: The South Highlands, Idlewild and Rugby Highland lines or routes.

It shall be unlawful for any such common carrier to operate or cause or allow to be operated, or for any servant, employee or agent of any such common carrier to aid in operating for the carriage of white and colored passengers, any street car not equipped as provided in this section. And it shall be unlawful for any person, contrary to the provisions of this section providing for equal and separate accommodations for the white and colored races on street cars, to ride or attempt to ride in a car or a division of a car designated for the race to which such person does not belong.

Failure to comply with this section shall be deemed a misdemeanor. (1930, Sec. 5699)

TRAFFIC

Sec. 1413. Separation of Races, Public Service Automobiles. — Every owner or operator of any jitney, bus or taxicab in the city shall provide equal but separate accommodations for the white and colored races by providing separate vehicles or by clearly indicating or designating by visible markers the area to be occupied by each race in any vehicle in which the two races are permitted to be carried together and by confining each race to occupancy of the area of such vehicle so set apart for it.

It shall be unlawful for any person to operate or cause or allow to be operated or to aid in operating for the carriage of white and colored passengers any vehicle not equipped as provided in this section. And it shall be unlawful for any person, contrary to the provisions of this section providing for equal and separate accommodations for the white and colored races, to ride or attempt to ride in a vehicle or a division of a vehicle designated for the race to which such person does not belong.

Failure to comply with this section shall be deemed a misdemeanor.

Sec. 1110. Toilet Facilities, Male. — Every employer of white or negro males shall provide for such white or negro males reasonably accessible and separate toilet facilities in such number that there shall be available a separate water closet for each twenty-five or lesser number of white or negro males having access thereto during a single day. Such separate white and negro toilet facilities shall be clearly marked to distinguish each from the other and it shall be unlawful for any person to use any facility not designated for such person's comfort. (1930, Sec. 5210, 5212)

Sec. 1111. Toilet Facilities, Female. — Every employer of white or negro females shall provide for such white or negro females reasonable accessible and separate toilet facilities in such number that there shall be available a separate water closet for each twenty-five or lesser number of white or negro females having access thereto during a single day. Such separate white and negro toilet facilities shall be clearly marked to distinguish each from the other and it shall be unlawful for any person to use any facility not designated for such person's comfort. (1930, Sec. 5211, 5213)

ALABAMA

CITY OF BIRMINGHAM

ORDINANCE NO. 709-F

BE IT ORDAINED By the Commission of the City of Birmingham that:

Section 1. The commission finds as a matter of fact that:

(a) From the date of the original settlement of this City unto the present time it has been the invariable custom, supported for most of that time by municipal law and universally observed, to require white and colored residents to live in separate residential areas; and

(b) That when attempts have been made by members of one race to enter for purposes of a permanent residence into an area commonly recognized as set aside for members of the other race, violence, disturbances of the peace, destruction of property and life has resulted almost without exception; and

(c) This Commission further finds from its knowledge of present conditions and public sentiment in this City that in the event attempts shall now or in the fore-seeable future be made by members of one race to establish residences in areas here-tofore regarded as set apart for the residences of members of the other race, breaches of the peace, riots, destruction of property and life will follow; and

(d) That neither the City of Birmingham nor any other law enforcement agency is able so completely to police, supervise and safeguard the person and prop-erty of persons attempting to establish a residence in an area not commonly recog-nized as an area to be occupied by members of the race to which such person belongs, as to prevent injury to such person, members of his family, third parties in the area affected, and destruction of property; and

(e) That the zoning ordinances of the City of Birmingham now in effect do substantially and fairly well delineate those areas historically and generally regarded as available for residences and occupation by members of the white and colored races; and

(f) That this ordinance is necessary to preserve the peace of said City and to safeguard the property and safety of its citizens and of the public in general.

Now, therefore, BE IT FURTHER ORDAINED:

Section 2. That it shall be a misdemeanor for a member of the white race to move into, for the purpose of establishing a permanent residence, or, having moved into, to continue to reside in an area in the City of Birmingham generally and historically recognized at the time as an area for occupancy by members of the colored race; and

Section 3. That it shall be a misdemeanor for a member of the colored race to move into, for the purpose of establishing a permanent residence, or having moved into, to continue to reside in an area in the City of Birmingham generally and historically recognized at the time as an area for occupancy by members of the white race.

Section 4. The words "permanent residence" as used herein shall be construed as meaning the occupancy of a house or tenement for more than twenty-four hours, except a house or tenement which is appurtenant to, used in connection with, and a part of the curtilage of another house or tenement and occupied by a person who shall be in the employ of the person occupying the residence or tenement to which it is appurtenant.

Section 5. The moving into for the purpose of establishing a permanent resi-dence shall constitute a separate offense from remaining there, and remaining in resi-dence in a forbidden area for each twenty-four hour period shall constitute a separate offense.

Section 6. This Ordinance shall take effect immediately, the public welfare requiring.

STATE OF ALABAMA }
JEFFERSON COUNTY }

I, Eunice S. Hewes, City Clerk of the City of Birmingham, do hereby certify that the foregoing is a true and correct copy of an ordinance duly adopted by the

Commission of the City of Birmingham at its meeting held August 9, 1949, and as same appears of record in Minute Book A-32 of said City.

GIVEN UNDER MY HAND AND CORPORATE SEAL of the City of Birmingham, this the 22nd day of August, 1949.

EUNICE L. HEWES
City Clerk

[Seal]

[Note: This ordinance is reportedly invalidated by a federal district court decision. See NAACP Balance Sheet on Race Relations, 1949, issued Dec. 31, 1949.]

ALABAMA

CITY OF MOBILE

CHAPTER 20, ARTICLE 1.

BUSES, PASSENGERS ON, REGULATION OF.

224. DESIGNATIONS OF SEATS FOR WHITE AND COLORED PASSENGERS. — All passengers on buses operated within the City of Mobile and its police jurisdiction, shall, in taking seats in buses, take such seats as will separate the white persons from the negroes, by the white persons taking the front vacant seats and occupying the seats from the front end of the bus, toward the rear of the bus as they enter the bus, and the negro passengers taking the rear vacant seats and occupying the seats from the rear end of the bus towards the front of the bus, as they enter the bus. Negro nurses in charge of white children, or of sick or infirm white persons, may occupy seats amongst the white people.

225. ASSIGNMENT OF SEATS BY DRIVER. — All bus drivers or other employees, while in charge of buses, operated in the City of Mobile or its police jurisdiction, in order to carry out the provisions of this article, shall assign persons of each race to seats and require passengers who are already seated to change their seats by moving the white passengers further to the front and the negroes further to the rear of the bus, whenever it shall become necessary to do either in order to utilize to the utmost the seating capacity of the bus while keeping the races separated; provided that negro nurses having in charge while [white] children or sick or infirm white persons may be seated with their charges amongst the white people.

226. DRIVERS VESTED WITH POLICE POWER. — All drivers or other employees, while in charge of buses in the City of Mobile and its police jurisdiction, are hereby vested with the police power of police officers of the City of Mobile to carry out the provisions of this article, and any person failing or refusing to take a seat assigned to the race to which he or she belongs, if any such seat is vacant, or who fails or refuses to move from the seat which he or she is then occupying, to such other seat as may be assigned to him or her by the driver, or other person in charge of said bus, whenever it becomes necessary that he or she should change seats in order to keep the races separated or to utilize to the utmost the seating capacity of the bus, shall, under conviction, be fined in the sum of not more than fifty dollars.

227. ASSIGNMENT OF SEATS TO BE GOVERNED BY THE NUMBER OF WHITE PEOPLE AND COLORED PEOPLE. — Nothing in this article shall prevent white persons from occupying all of the seats of a bus, provided that the white passengers take the front seats until by so doing they fill all of the then vacant seats of the bus; and nothing in this article shall prevent negro persons from occupying all of the seats of a bus, provided that the negro passengers take the rear vacant seats until by so doing they fill all of the then vacant seats of the bus; provided further, that as passengers leave the bus, the driver or other person in charge of the bus, may assign passengers to seats and require them to change seats so as to keep the races separated and so as to utilize to the utmost the seating capacity of the bus.

228. PENALTY. — All drivers and other employees, in charge of buses, and all owners of buses, who shall fail or refuse to enforce such separation of the races as is herein provided, upon the buses of a bus company operating in the City of Mobile and its police jurisdiction, shall upon conviction be fined not more than fifty dollars for each time they fail to carry out the terms and provisions of this article. Each day's failure to comply with this article shall constitute a separate offense as to each separate bus.

229. SEPARATE BUSES MAY BE PROVIDED. — Nothing in this article shall be construed as prohibiting bus companies from separating the races by means of separate buses or trailers on such routes as they may see fit.

230. If any provision of this article shall be declared invalid by any court of competent jurisdiction, the remaining provisions shall not be affected thereby.

STATE OF ALABAMA}
COUNTY OF MOBILE}

I, S. H. Hendrix, being the duly appointed, qualified and acting City Clerk of the City of Mobile, hereby certify that the above and foregoing is a true and correct copy of Section 224 to 230, inclusive, of the Code of Ordinances of the City of Mobile adopted on May 6th, 1947.

IN WITNESS WHEREOF, I have hereunto set my hand and affixed the Seal of the City of Mobile, this, the 28th day of November, 1949.

Sig. P. Hendrix
City Clerk of the City of Mobile, Alabama.

ARIZONA

CITY OF PHOENIX

ORDINANCE NO. 4810

AN ORDINANCE RELATING TO THE HIRING OF AND THE APPLICATION FOR EMPLOYMENT OF PROSPECTIVE EMPLOYEES OF THE CITY OF PHOENIX.

BE IT ORDAINED BY THE COMMISSION OF THE CITY OF PHOENIX as follows:

SECTION 1. It shall be unlawful for any person, employee, department head, or other person acting in behalf of the City of Phoenix who has the authority to accept applications or hire employees on behalf of the City of Phoenix to discriminate against any applicant or prospective employee because of his or her race, creed, color or national origin, with respect to his or her hiring or application for employment.

SECTION 2. All contracting agencies of the City of Phoenix, or any department thereof, shall include in all contracts hereafter negotiated or renegotiated by them a provision obligating the contractor not to discriminate against any employee or applicant for employment because of race, creed, color or national origin and shall require him to include a similar provision in all sub-contracts.

SECTION 3. The provisions of Sections 1 and 2 shall not apply to applicants or prospective employees who individually or as a member of a group subscribe to a program that advocates the overthrow by force of the United States Government in a manner declared illegal by the appropriate courts.

PASSED by the Commission of the City of Phoenix this 27th day of April, 1948.

APPROVED by the Mayor this 27th day of April, 1948.

RAY BUSEY
M a y o r

Seal
ATTEST:

AARON KINNEY
City Clerk

Approved as to form:

JACK CHOISSER
City Attorney

621

CALIFORNIA

CITY OF RICHMOND

ORDINANCE NO. 1303

AN ORDINANCE DECLARING THE POLICY OF THE CITY OF RICHMOND
IN REGARD TO DISCRIMINATION IN EMPLOYMENT, AND
MAKING UNLAWFUL SUCH DISCRIMINATION BY
THE CITY OF RICHMOND AND PERSONS HEREAFTER
ACQUIRING CITY CONTRACTS OR FRANCHISES

The Council of the City of Richmond do ordain as follows:

Section 1. It is hereby declared to be the policy of the City of Richmond to promote and to encourage good will and understanding within the various racial, religious and national groups within the City, and to oppose discrimination based on race, creed, color, national origin or ancestry.

Section 2. It shall be unlawful for any department head, official, agent or employee of the City of Richmond, or any commission, department, division, board or agency thereof, acting for or on behalf of said City, in any matter involving employment by said City, to discriminate on the ground or because of race, color, creed, national origin or ancestry, against any person otherwise qualified, in employment or in tenure, terms or conditions of employment; or so to discriminate in promotion or increase in compensation; or to adopt or to enforce any rule or employment policy which so discriminates between employees or prospective employees; or to seek information relative to race, creed, color, national origin or ancestry, from any person or employee as a condition of employment, tenure, terms or conditions of employment, promotion or increase in compensation; or so to discriminate in the selection of personnel for training.

Section 3. Said City and all of its contracting agencies and departments shall include in all contracts and franchises hereafter negotiated, let or awarded by or on behalf of the City of Richmond, a provision obligating the contractor in the performance of such contract not to discriminate on the ground or because of race, creed, color, national origin or ancestry against any employee of, or applicant for employment with, such contractor, and shall require such contractor to include a similar provision in all sub-contracts let or awarded thereunder.

Section 4. This ordinance shall be deemed an exercise of the police power of this City for the protection of the public welfare and the peace and security of the inhabitants thereof.

Section 5. Any person violating any of the provisions of this ordinance shall be deemed guilty of a misdemeanor, and upon conviction thereof shall be punishable by a fine not exceeding $500.00, or by imprisonment in the city jail of the City of Richmond, or in the county jail of the County of Contra Costa for a period not exceeding six (6) months, or by both such fine and imprisonment.

Section 6. This ordinance shall take effect and be in force on and after its final passage and adoption.

First read at a regular meeting of the Council of the City of Richmond held

May 9, 1949, and finally passed and adopted as read at a regular meeting thereof held May 16, 1949, by the following vote:

Ayes: Councilmen Erickson, Bradley, Kenny, Massey,

Johnson, Hinkley, Tiller, Lee and Miller.

Absent: None.

Noes: None.

Clerk of the City of Richmond

C. A. PITCHFORD

Approved: (SEAL)

R. H. MILLER
   Mayor

CALIFORNIA

CITY OF SAN FRANCISCO

FILE NO. 4781 (Series of 1939)

RESOLUTION APPROVING APPLICATION OF HOUSING AUTHORITY OF THE CITY AND COUNTY OF SAN FRANCISCO TO THE PUBLIC HOUSING ADMINISTRATION FOR A PRELIMINARY LOAN IN AN AMOUNT NOT TO EXCEED $450,000.00 TO COVER THE COSTS OF SURVEYS AND PLANNING IN CONNECTION WITH THE DEVELOPMENT OF NOT TO EXCEED 3000 DWELLING UNITS OF LOW-RENT PUBLIC HOUSING IN THE CITY AND COUNTY OF SAN FRANCISCO; APPROVING THE DEVELOPMENT, CON-STRUCTION, ACQUISITION AND OWNERSHIP OF SAID DWELLING UNITS; APPROVING THE FORM OF COOPERATION AGREEMENT BETWEEN THE CITY AND COUNTY OF SAN FRANCISCO AND THE HOUSING AUTHORITY OF THE CITY AND COUNTY OF SAN FRANCISCO AND AUTHORIZING THE EXECUTION THEREOF.

WHEREAS, . . . It is the policy of the City and County of San Francisco that there shall be no discrimination or segregation in any form by reason of race, color, religion, national origin or ancestry in expenditure of public funds, in exercise of public powers, or in development or administration of any program entailing such funds or powers, whether through tax exemption or other forms of public contribution or cooperation;

NOW, THEREFORE, BE IT RESOLVED BY THE BOARD OF SUPERVISORS OF THE CITY AND COUNTY OF SAN FRANCISCO:

. . . 5. That the Board of Supervisors of the City and County of San Francisco declares that the best interests of the community will be served by an administration of all low-rent housing projects or developments which results in integrated or nonsegregated occupancy by families, otherwise eligible, of all groups comprising the City's popula-tion, and that in the development and/or administration of each and all housing projects or developments under the jurisdiction of the Housing Authority of the City and County of San Francisco said Housing Authority shall avoid or refrain from any policy or practice which results, directly or indirectly, in discrimination or any form of segregation by reason of race, color, religion, national origin or ancestry, provided that nothing herein would require the Authority to relocate any tenant presently occupying a dwelling unit.

[The "Cooperation Agreement" between the Housing Authority of the City and County of San Francisco and the City and County of San Francisco · contains the following clause:

"9. In respect to the development and/or administration of each Project the Local Authority shall avoid or refrain from any policy or practice which results, directly or indirectly, in discrimination or any form of segregation by reason of race, color, religion, national origin or ancestry."]

Approved .... 1949.

FLORIDA,

CITY OF JACKSONVILLE

ORDINANCE No. T-215

BILL No. T-220

AN ORDINANCE REGULATING the Operation of "For Hire" Cars in the City of Jacksonville, with Regard to Separation of White and Colored Passengers.

BE IT ORDAINED BY THE MAYOR AND CITY COUNCIL OF THE CITY OF JACKSONVILLE:

SECTION 1. All companies, persons, firms and corporations operating "For Hire" cars in the City of Jacksonville are hereby required to furnish separate cars for white and colored passengers, and passengers are required to occupy the respective cars provided for them, so that white passengers shall occupy only cars provided for white passengers, and colored passengers shall occupy only the cars provided for the accommodation of colored passengers. Provided, however, that colored passengers may ride in cars provided for white passengers when accompanied by a white person in the capacity of master, mistress or legal custodian.

SECTION 2. It is hereby made the duty of chauffeurs and others engaged in the operation of "For Hire" cars within the limits of the City of Jacksonville, to call the attention of passengers to the provisions of this ordinance, and to request white or colored passengers, who are about to enter or who have entered cars not intended for their accommodation; to occupy only the cars provided for their accommodation; and if any such passenger refuses or fails to leave the car, such chauffeur or other person operating such car shall notify the police department, or member thereof, as soon as possible.

SECTION 3. Any police officer of the City of Jacksonville seeing any white or colored passenger of chauffeur occupying a "For Hire" car not provided for his or her accommodation, shall arrest any such person and take him or her from such car and carry him or her to the police station as in case of any other person guilty of disorderly conduct.

SECTION 4. Any officer, agent or employe of any company, person or firm, who shall operate any "For Hire" car contrary to the provisions of this Ordinance on the streets of the City of Jacksonville; and any white person wilfully occupying as a passenger any "For Hire" car not set apart and provided for white passengers, and any colored person wilfully occupying as a passenger any "For Hire" car not set apart and provided for colored passengers, except as hereinabove provided, shall be deemed guilty of disorderly conduct, and shall, on conviction in the Municipal Court of the City of Jacksonville, be punished by fine not exceeding Fifty Dollars ($50.00), or by imprisonment not exceeding thirty (30) days or by both such fine and imprisonment in the discretion of the Judge of said Court.

Passed by City Council. February 26th, 1929.
Approved March 4th, 1929.

JOHN T. ALSOP, JR.,
Attest: Mayor.
R. T. SMOTHERMAN,
City Recorder.
(Seal)
(Published Florida Times-Union, March 6th, 1929).

FLORIDA

CITY OF MIAMI BEACH

ORDINANCE NO. 883

AN ORDINANCE OF THE CITY COUNCIL OF THE CITY OF MIAMI BEACH, FLORIDA, MAKING IT UNLAWFUL TO MAINTAIN OR DISPLAY ANY ADVERTISEMENT, NOTICE OR SIGN WHICH IS DISCRIMINATORY AGAINST PERSONS OF ANY RELIGION, SECT, CREED, RACE OR DENOMINATION IN THE ENJOYMENT OF PRIVILEGES AND FACILITIES OF PLACES OF PUBLIC ACCOMMODATION, AMUSEMENT OR RESORT; DEFINING PLACES OF PUBLIC ACCOMMODATION, AMUSEMENT OR RESORT; PROVIDING FOR A RULE OF PRESUMPTIVE EVIDENCE; PROVIDING FOR A PENALTY FOR THE VIOLATION OF THIS ORDINANCE.

BE IT ORDAINED BY THE CITY COUNCIL OF THE CITY OF MIAMI BEACH, FLORIDA:

SECTION 1: It shall be unlawful for any person, firm, association or corporation in the City of Miami Beach, Florida, as owner, lessee, operator, manager, superintendent, concessionaire, custodian, agent or employee of any place of public accommodation, resort or amusement, as hereinafter defined, to place, post, maintain or display, or

625

knowingly cause, permit or allow the placing, posting, maintenance or display of any written or printed advertisement, notice or sign of any kind or description, which said advertisement, notice or sign is intended to or tends to discriminate directly or indirectly against, or actually discriminates against any person or persons of any religion or of any religious belief, sect, race or denomination in the full enjoyment of any advantages, facilities or privileges offered to the general public by places of public accommodation, resort or amusement.

SECTION 2: A place of public accommodation, resort or amusement, within the meaning, intent and purpose of this ordinance, shall be deemed to include inns, taverns, road houses, hotels, apartment hotels, whether conducted for the entertainment of transient guests or for the accommodation of those seeking health, recreation or rest, and restaurants, or eating houses, or any place where food is sold for consumption on the premises; buffets, saloons, bar-rooms or any store, park or enclosure, where spirituous or malt liquors are sold; or where beverages of any kind are retailed for consumption on the premises; retail stores and establishments, dispensaries, clinics, hospitals, bath-houses, barber shops, beauty parlors, theatres, motion picture houses, air dromes, roof gardens, music halls, race courses, skating rinks, amusement and recreation parks, fairs, bowling alleys, golf courses, gymnasiums, shooting galleries, billiard and pool parlors; public libraries or educational facilities supported in whole or in part by public funds or by contributions solicited from the general public; and public conveyances operated on land, air or water as well as the stations and terminals thereof.

SECTION 3: In any prosecution for the violation of this ordinance, the production of, or proof of the display or maintenance of, any such written or printed notice or advertisement purporting to relate to any place of public accommodation, shall be presumptive evidence that such display or maintenance was authorized by the person, firm, association or corporation maintaining and operating such place of public accommodation.

SECTION 4: If any section, sentence, phrase, word or words of this ordinance shall be held or declared invalid or unconstitutional, such adjudication shall in no manner affect any other section, sentence, phrase, word or words of this ordinance which shall be and remain in full force and effect.

SECTION 5: Any person or persons violating this ordinance shall, upon conviction thereof, be punished by a fine not exceeding $500.00 or by imprisonment in the City Jail for a term not exceeding ninety (90) days, or by both such fine and imprisonment in the discretion of the Municipal Judge.

SECTION 6: That this ordinance shall go into effect immediately upon its passage and posting as required by law.

PASSED AND ADOPTED this 15th day of June   A. D. 1949.

ATTEST: (Signed) Harold Turk
(Signed) C. W. Tomlinson   Mayor
          City Clerk
(SEAL)

1st reading — June 1, 1949   3rd reading — June 15, 1949
2nd reading — June 1, 1949   POSTED — June 15, 1949

GEORGIA
CITY OF ATLANTA

CODE OF CITY OF ATLANTA (1942)

37-129. Barber Shops Must show on Signs Whether White or Colored Persons are Served Therein. — It shall be the duty of all persons conducting barber shops to show on their barber shop signs whether white persons only, colored persons only, or both races are served in such shops, excepting in buildings where no signs are displayed. A violation of this ordinance shall be punished upon conviction in the Recorder's Court by a fine not exceeding $100, or imprisonment not exceeding 30 days, in the discretion of the court.

37-130. Colored Barbers Forbidden to Serve White Women or Girls. — No colored barber shall serve as a barber white women or girls; meaning by this the doing of any of the work barbers ordinarily perform and as defined by the law of the State of Georgia. Any barber or the manager of any barber shop, violating this section shall be deemed guilty of an offense and on conviction thereof in the Recorder's Court shall be punished by a fine not exceeding $200, or sentenced to work on the public works of the city for not exceeding 30 days, either or both penalties to be inflicted in the discretion of the Recorder. (Feb. 16, 1926)

[Note: The ordinance from which this section is codified also forbade colored barbers to work for white children under the age of 14 years. That part of the ordinance was held unconstitutional in *Chaires v. Atlanta,* 164 Ga. 755, 139 S.E. 559. The part of the ordinance here codified was not attacked in the Chaires case, and the court made no ruling on its constitutionality.]

42-302. Burial of Colored Persons on Ground Set Apart for White Persons Prohibited. — The officer in charge shall not bury, or allow to be buried, any colored persons upon ground set apart or used for the burial of white persons.

53-603. Separate Restaurants for White and Colored People. — All persons licensed to conduct a restaurant, shall serve either white people exclusively or colored people exclusively and shall not sell to the two races within the same room or serve the two races anywhere under the same license; the purpose of this section being that each licensee shall serve either one race or the other and that no license shall authorize sale to the two races at or near the same place.

53-604. License Shall Designate Race to Be Served. — The Clerk of Council in issuing licenses for restaurants shall designate therein the character of the trade authorized to be served under such license, as "for white people only" or "for colored people only."

53-605. Restaurants to Display Signs Showing Race Served. — Each license shall display prominently in front of his place of business a notice as follows: "Licensed to serve colored people only," so that the public may be informed of the character of trade served at each such place.

53-606. Penalties for Violation of Sections Respecting Separation of races. — Any person violating any of the provisions of section 53-603 to 53-605, inclusive, shall be deemed guilty of an offense and on conviction thereof in the Recorder's Court shall be fined not exceeding $100, or sentenced to work on the public works for not exceeding 30 days, either or both penalties to be inflicted in the discretion of the Recorder. A violation of the said provisions, or a conviction for any such violation in the Recorder's Court, shall *ipso facto* work a forfeiture of the license. Any sales or business done after such forfeiture shall constitute an offense punishable as herein provided.

Taxicabs and Hired Automobiles

62-121. Races To Be Separated in Cabs and Hired Automobiles. — It shall be the duty of all owners and operators of taxicabs or autos for hire within the City of Atlanta to indicate on the sides of such vehicles whether the taxicab or auto for hire is to be used by and shall serve white or negro passengers. The sign so indicating shall be painted under the owner's name and shall be in letters not less than one inch in height. The sign shall read, "For White Passengers Only" or "For Colored Passengers Only," as the case may be. This sign, as well as the "auto for hire" or "taxi" sign, shall be painted on both sides of the vehicle in an oil paint of contrasting color to the vehicle, and in paint that cannot be rubbed or washed off. Such sign shall remain on said car so long as the operator holds a permit and license to operate that machine. No such taxicab or auto for hire owner or operator shall carry both white and negro passengers in the same vehicle, but shall serve one or the other of said races to the exclusion of the other. There shall be white drivers for carrying white passengers and colored drivers for carrying colored passengers. Applicants filing their petitions for permits shall state on their applications whether the taxicab or auto for hire is to be used for hauling white or colored passengers. (May 7, 1940)

62-122. Penalties. — Any person violating any of the provisions of this Article shall, at the option of the Mayor and General Council, have his permit or license, or both, revoked and shall be fined not less than $50 nor more than $200 for each offense or imprisoned not less than 30 nor more than 60 days, or both, within the discretion of the Recorder. (April 30, 1939; May 7, 1949)

66-1005. Amateur Baseball Prohibited on Grounds Within Two Blocks of Playground Devoted to Other Race. — It shall be unlawful for any amateur white baseball team to play baseball on any vacant lot or baseball diamond within two blocks of a playground devoted to the Negro race, and it shall be unlawful for any amateur colored baseball team to play baseball in any vacant lot or baseball diamond within two blocks of a playground devoted to the white race. The playgrounds referred to in this section are the playgrounds set apart by the city surrounding public schools and given over to athletic purposes during the summer. (June 21, 1932)

68-126. Separation of Races in Parks. — It shall be unlawful for colored people to frequent any park owned or maintained by the city for the benefit, use and enjoyment of white persons, excepting so much of Grant Park as is occupied by the zoo, and unlawful for any white person to frequent any park owned or maintained by the city for the use and benefit of colored persons. (June 4, 1940)

68-134. [Penalty for violation $100 fine and 30 days or both.]

55-217. Sale of Wine and Beer to White and Colored People in the Same Room Forbidden. — All persons licensed to conduct the business of selling beer or wine or either of them shall serve either white people exclusively or colored people exclusively and shall not sell to the two races within the same room at any time; it being the purpose of this section that each dealer in wine and beer or either of them shall serve only one race and that if the two races are served there must be two separate and distinct rooms for that purpose and the licensee must procure separate licenses therefor. Each dealer in wine and beer or either of them shall display prominently in front of his place of business a notice as follows: "Licensed to serve white people only;" or "Licensed to serve colored people only;" so that the public may be informed of the character of trade served in such place. When an application for license is filed, the applicant shall state in the application the class or character of people to be served, namely, whether or not he proposes to sell to white people only or colored people only. Any person selling wine or beer or either of them in violation of any of the terms of this section shall be deemed guilty of an offense against the City of Atlanta and on conviction thereof in the Recorder's Court shall be fined not exceeding $100, or sentenced to work on public works not exceeding 30 days, either or both penalties to be inflicted in the discretion of the Recorder. It is further provided that a violation of the provisions of this section by any dealer in wine and beer, or either of them, either personally or through agents or employees, shall *ipso facto* work a forfeiture of the license; it being the purpose of this provision that a conviction of any such dealer in the Recorder's Court shall immediately work a forfeiture of the license. Any person continuing to sell beer or wine or either of them after the forfeiture of the license, as herein above provided, shall be deemed guilty of an offense against the City of Atlanta and upon conviction thereof shall be fined not exceeding $100, or sentenced to work on the public works for not exceeding 30 days, either or both penalties to be inflicted in the discretion of the Recorder. (November 16, 1937)

Street Railroads

85-138. Passengers to Observe State Laws Respecting Separate Seating of Races. — Passengers on street cars operated in the limits of the City of Atlanta, and in territory outside the city limits which has been incorporated as a part of said city for police purposes, must observe and obey the requirements of the penal laws of the State as to the separate seating of the races in such cars; and any passenger failing to obey the directions of the conductor or person in charge of the car in this respect, in so far as it is practicable to do so, shall be guilty of an offense and punishable as hereinafter provided.

[Police jurisdiction over street railways and line of transportation is extended beyond city limits and to limits of Fulton County by Sections 3-109 and 77-119]

85-139. Duty of Police to See That Conductors Enforce State Laws Requiring Separation of Races. — It shall be the duty of the policy to give special attention to ascertain whether conductors or other employees in charge of street and other railroad cars, require passengers in their trains or cars to comply with the provisions of the laws of Georgia respecting separate seating of races in such cars; and in case of the violation of the said laws by conductors or other employees of railroad or street railroad companies, to arrest such persons so violating said laws, and prosecute them in the proper State court for such offenses.

85-142. Penalties. — [Violation punishable by fine up to $100 and costs, or by imprisonment up to 30 days, or both.]

ILLINOIS

CITY OF CHICAGO

CHICAGO FAIR EMPLOYMENT PRACTICES ORDINANCE

Municipal Code of Chicago Chapter 198.7A

Section 1. Whereas, it is the policy of the United States Government in furtherance of the successful winning of the peace to insure the maximum participation of all available workers in production, regardless of race, creed, color or national origin, in the firm belief that the democratic way of life within the nation can be defended successfully only with the help and support of all groups within its borders, the City of Chicago, to cooperate with the United States Government, by eliminating possible discrimination in public and private employment, enacts this ordinance to be known as the Fair Employment Practices Ordinance.

Section 2. It shall be unlawful for any department of the city of Chicago, or any city official, his agent or employee, for or on behalf of the City of Chicago, involving any public works of the City of Chicago to refuse to employ or to discharge any person, otherwise qualified, on account of race, color, creed, national origin, or ancestry; to discriminate for the same reasons in regard to tenure, terms or conditions of employment; to deny promotion or increase in compensation solely for these reasons, to publish offer of employment based on such discrimination; to adopt or enforce any rule, or employment policy which discriminates between employees on account of race, color, religion, national origin, or ancestry; to seek such information as to any employee as a condition of employment; to penalize any employee or discriminate in the selection of personnel for training, solely on the basis of race, color, religion, national origin, or ancestry.

Section 3. All contracting agencies of the city of Chicago, or any department thereof, shall include in all contracts hereafter negotiated or renegotiated by them a provision obligating the contractor not to discriminate against any employee or applicant for employment because of race, creed, color or national origin and shall require him to include a similar provision in all sub-contracts.

Section 4. It shall be unlawful for any person to discriminate against any other person by reason of race, creed, color or national origin, with respect to the hiring, application for employment, tenure, terms or conditions of employment.

Section 5. Any person, firm or corporation who shall violate or fail to comply with any of the provisions of this ordinance shall be guilty of a misdemeanor, and shall be punished by a fine in any sum not exceeding two hundred dollars ($200.00).

Section 6. If any part of this ordinance shall be declared invalid the balance of the ordinance shall remain in full force and effect.

The following ordinance was passed unanimously by the City Council on December 12, 1947, establishing the Commission on Human Relations as an integral part of the Municipal Government of the City of Chicago:

BE IT ORDAINED BY THE CITY COUNCIL OF THE CITY OF CHICAGO:

COMMISSION ON HUMAN RELATIONS

Section 21-49. Declaration of Policy — Establishment of Commission. The city council finds that prejudice and the practice of discrimination against any individual or group because of race, color, creed, national origin or ancestry menace peace and public welfare; that to eliminate such prejudice and discrimination an instrumentality should be established through which the citizens of Chicago may be kept informed of developments in human relations, the officers and departments of the City may obtain expert advice and assistance in ameliorative practices to keep peace and good order and private persons and groups may be officially encouraged to promote tolerance and good will toward all people.

There is hereby established a commission to be known as the Commission on Human Relations consisting of fifteen members, one of which members shall be designated as Chairman, to be appointed by the Mayor by and with the advice and consent of the City Council. They shall serve without compensation but may be reimbursed for any personal expense incurred in the performance of their duties. The commission shall appoint, according to law, an executive director and such other persons as are provided for in the annual appropriation ordinance to direct its activities.

Section 21-50. (Duties and Functions.) The commission shall cooperate with the Mayor, City Council, city departments, agencies and officials in: securing the furnishing of equal services to all residents, and where the need is greater, in meeting that need with added services; training city employees to use methods of dealing with intergroup relations which develop respect for equal rights and which result in equal treatment without regard to race, color, creed, national origin or ancestry; assuring fair and equal treatment under the law to all citizens; protecting the rights of all persons to enjoy public accommodations and facilities and to receive equal treatment from all holders of licenses, contracts or privileges from the city; and maintaining equality of opportunity for employment and advancement in the city government.

The services of all city departments and agencies shall be made available by their respective heads to the Commission at its request, and information in the hands of any department or agency shall be furnished to the Commission when requested. Upon receipt of recommendations in writing from the Commission, each department or agency shall submit a reply in writing indicating the disposition of and action taken with regard to such recommendations.

The Commission shall advise and consult with the Mayor and City Council on all matters involving racial, religious or ethnic prejudice or discrimination and recommend such legislative action as it may deem appropriate to effectuate the policy of this ordnance [ordinance]. The Commission shall render an annual report to the Mayor and City Council which shall be published.

Section 21-51. (Cooperation with Civic Groups and Governmental Agencies.) The Commission shall invite and enlist the cooperation of racial, religious and ethnic groups, community organizations, labor and business organizations, fraternal and benevolent societies, veterans organizations, professional and technical organizations, and other groups in the City of Chicago in carrying on its work. The Commission may aid in the formation of local community groups in such neighborhoods as it may deem necessary or desirable to carry out specific programs designed to lessen tensions or improve understanding in the community.

The Commission shall cooperate with State and Federal agencies whenever it deems such action appropriate in effectuating the policy of this ordinance.

Section 21-52. (Investigations, Research and Publications.) The Commission shall receive and investigate complaints and initiate its own investigations of tensions, practices of discrimination and acts of prejudice against any person or group because of race, religion or ethnic origin and may conduct public hearings with regard thereto; carry on research, obtain factual data and conduct public hearings to ascertain the status and treatment of racial, religious and ethnic groups in the city, and the best means of progressively improving human relations in the entire city; and issue such publications and such results of investigations and public hearings and make such recommendations to the Mayor and City Council as in its judgment will effectuate the policy of this ordinance.

INDIANA

CITY OF EVANSVILLE

ORDINANCE NO. 1824

AN ORDINANCE ESTABLISHING THE MAYOR'S COMMISSION OF HUMAN RELATIONS, PROVIDING FOR THE APPOINTMENT OF ITS MEMBERS AND DEFINING ITS DUTIES AND FUNCTIONS

WHEREAS, there exists a need in the City of Evansville for the establishment of a body of citizens to study the problems of the relationships of the various races, colors, creeds and nationalties [nationalities] living within the community and to advise with and assist the Department of the City Government on problems involving differing racial groups.

NOW, THEREFORE, be it ordained by the Common Council of the City of Evansville:

Section 1. There is hereby established in the City Government of the City of Evansville a commission to be known as the Mayor's Commission on Human Relations, which Commission shall consist of not less than forty-five (45) nor more than sixty (60) representative citizens to be appointed by the Mayor of the City of Evansville and to serve at his pleasure for a term of four (4) years. It being provided, however, that the first appointments to said Commission shall be divided into four (4) groups, one (1) group to be appointed for a term of one (1) year, one group (1) to be appointed for a term of two (2) years, one (1) group to be appointed for a term of three (3) years, and one (1) group to be appointed for a term of four (4) years. The Mayor of the City of Evansville shall also appoint a Chairman of said Commission, a Vice-Chairman of said Commission, and a Secretary for said Commission, each of which said officers shall serve in his respective office for a term of (1) year or until his successor shall have been appointed and qualified. The officers and members of said Commission shall serve without compensation.

Section 2. It shall be the duty of the Commission to study problems of race relationships within the City, particularly as such problems may affect, or be affected by, the Government of the City and to advise with and cooperate with the Mayor, the City Council and all other City Departments, agencies and officials with relation to any such problems. The Commission shall further make recommendations to the Mayor, the City Council, City Departments, agencies and officials, for the betterment of intergroup relationships within the community and for the education and training of City employees where such education and training may be beneficial. The services of all City Departments and Agencies shall be made available by their respective heads to the Commission at its request and information in the hands of any City Department or Agency shall be furnished to the Commission when requested. Upon receipt of recommendations in writing from the Commission each City Department or Agency shall submit a reply within a reasonable time indicating the disposition of and action taken with regard to such recommendations.

The Commission shall render an annual report of its doings to the Mayor and to the City Council.

Section 3. The Commission shall invite and enlist the cooperation of all racial, religious and ethnic groups and all other community organizations in carrying on its work and shall act as a coordinating agency among such other groups in the establishment and maintenance of educational programs in the community with a view to bringing about better intergroup and racial relationships. The Commission shall also cooperate with State and Federal agencies wherever such cooperation is appropriate in effectuating the policy of this Ordinance.

Section 4. This ordinance shall be in full force and effect from and after its passage by the Common Council and its approval by the Mayor.

Passed by the Common Council of the City of Evansville, Indiana, on this 1st day of March, 1948, and on said day signed by the President of the Common Council and attested by the City Clerk.

Fred C. Fischer
President

ATTEST:
Thomas P. Toon
City Clerk

Presented by me, the undersigned, City Clerk of the City of Evansville, Indiana, to the Mayor of said City, this 2nd day of March, 1948, at 11:00 o'clock A.M., for his consideration and action.

Thomas P. Toon
City Clerk

Having examined the foregoing ordinance, I do now, as Mayor of said City of Evansville, Indiana, approve said ordinance, and return the same to the Clerk this 2nd day of March, 1948, at 11:00 A.M.

William H. Dress
Mayor of the City of Evansville, Ind.

LOUISIANA

CITY OF NEW ORLEANS

MAYORALTY OF NEW ORLEANS,
City Hall, Sept. 18, 1924.
Calendar No. 8347.

NO. 8037 COMMISSION COUNCIL SERIES.

AN ORDINANCE relative to Negro and White Communities.

Whereas, Act 117 of 1912 authorizes municipalities to withhold permits for white or negro houses, under certain circumstances; and

Whereas, Act 118 of 1924 prohibits white persons from establishing a home residence in a negro community and prohibits negroes from establishing a home residence in a white community and,

Whereas, in the interest of public peace and welfare, it is advisable to foster the separation of white and negro residential communities; therefore,

SECTION 1. Be it ordained by the Commission Council of the City of New Orleans, That whenever the City Engineer shall have notice or information that any person whatsoever proposes to construct a house for negroes in a white community or portion of the municipality inhabited by white people, or a house for white persons in a negro community, or portion of the municipality inhabited principally by negroes, he shall not issue a building permit for said house except on the written consent of a majority of the persons of the opposite race inhabiting such community or portion of the City to be affected.

SECTION 2. Be it further ordained, etc., That it shall be unlawful for any white person to hereafter establish a home residence on any property located in a negro community or portion of the municipality inhabited principally by negroes, or for any negro to establish a home residence on any property located in a white community, or portion of the municipality inhabited principally for white people, except on the of a majority of the persons of the opposite race inhabiting such community or portion of the city to be effected [affected], the aforesaid portion of the municipality inhabited principally for white people, except on the written consent to be filed of record with the Mayor.

SECTION 3. Be it further ordained, etc., That it shall be unlawful to maintain any home residence established in violation of Section (2) of this ordinance.

SECTION 4. Be it further ordained, etc., That each seven days' maintenance of any home, residence established in violation of Section (2) of this ordinance shall be deemed to be a separate and distinct offense.

SECTION 5. Be it further ordained, etc., That the terms "white community" and "negro community" as used in this ordinance shall be taken and held to mean and embrace every residence fronting on either side of any street within three hundred feet of the location of the property involved, measured along the middle of the streets in any and all directions.

SECTION 6. Be it further ordained, etc., That any person violating any of the provisions of this ordinance shall on conviction be punished for each offense by a fine not exceeding twenty-five dollars, or by imprisonment not exceeding thirty days, or by such fine and such imprisonment in default of payment of the fine, or by both such fine and such imprisonment in the discretion of the court having jurisdiction.

SECTION 7. Be it further ordained, etc., That should any provision of this ordinance be invalid, its invalidity shall not annul the other provisions of this ordinance, which shall nevertheless have the fullest effect possible in such case.

Adopted by the Commission Council of the City of New Orleans, September 16, 1924.

GEORGE FERRIER, JR.
Clerk of Commission Council.

A true copy:
F. C. FONT,
Secretary to the Mayor.

Approved September 18, 1924.
ANDREW J. McSHANE,
Mayor.

[Note: This ordinance was declared unconstitutional by the Supreme Court of the United States in the case of *Harmon v. Tyler*, 273 U.S. 668, 47 Sup. Ct. 471, 71 L. Ed. 831 (1927). One further ordinance, City Ordinance No. 4418, Commission Council Series, at one time segregated and delimited the areas of the City within which colored and white prostitutes respectively might reside; however this ordinance was declared unenforceable on other than segregation grounds and has been a dead issue since the prohibition of legal prostitution in this City. See *City of New Orleans vs. Miller*, 142 La. 163, 76 So. 596, LRA 1918B, 331.]

MINNESOTA

CITY OF MINNEAPOLIS

AN ORDINANCE

To Prohibit Discriminatory Practices in employment and in membership in labor unions based upon Race, Color, Creed, National Origin, or Ancestry; to Create a Commission on Job Discrimination, Prescribing its Duties and Powers; and for other Purposes; and Providing Penalties for Violations hereof.

The Council of the City of Minneapolis does hereby ordain:

Section 1. FINDINGS AND DECLARATION OF POLICY:

a) Discrimination in public and private employment on the grounds of race, creed, color, national origin, or ancestry, with consequent arbitrary denial of job opportunities to large groups of inhabitants of this City, foments strife, creates unrest, disturbances, disorders and group tensions, and substantially and adversely affects the general welfare and good order of this City.

b) Such job discrimination tends unjustly to condemn large groups of inhabitants of this City to depressed living conditions, which breed vice, ignorance, disease, degeneration, juvenile delinquency and crime, thereby causing grave injury to the public safety, general welfare and good order of this City, and endangering the public health thereof.

c) Such job discrimination and the resulting effects on the community and the inhabitants thereof tend to impose substantial financial burdens on the public revenues for the relief and amelioration of conditions so created.

d) Experience has proved that legislative enactment prohibiting such job discrimination removes some of the sources of strife, unrest, poverty, disease, juvenile delinquency and crime, and would directly promote the general welfare and good order of this City.

e) The right of every inhabitant of this City to job opportunities without being subjected to such job discrimination is hereby declared to be a civil right.

f) This Ordinance shall be deemed an exercise of the police power of this City, for the protection of the public welfare and the health and peace of the inhabitants thereof.

Section 2. DEFINITIONS

a) The word "discriminate", discriminates", or "discrimination" wherever used in this Ordinance, is hereby defined and declared to mean and include discrimination on the ground or because of race, creed, color, national origin or ancestry.

b) The word "employee", wherever used in this Ordinance is hereby defined and declared not to include an employee in domestic service, or an employee of an organized religious congregation or an institution limited in its membership to persons of a single religious faith.

c) The word "employer" wherever used in this Ordinance is hereby defined and declared to include only employers of two or more employees within the City of Minneapolis.

Section 3

It shall be unlawful for any head of department, official, or agent or employee of the City of Minneapolis, or of any department thereof, acting for or on behalf of said City, in any manner involving employment by said City, to discriminate against any person otherwise qualified, in employment or in tenure, terms or conditions of employment; or to discriminate in promotion or increase in compensation; or to publish offers of or to offer employment based upon such discrimination; or to adopt or enforce any rule or employment policy which discriminates between employees or prospective employees; or to seek information relative to race, creed, color, national origin or ancestry from any person or any employee, as a condition of employment, tenure, terms, or in connection with conditions of employment, promotion or increase in compensation; or to discriminate in the selection of personnel for training.

*Section 4

Said City and all of its contracting agencies and departments thereof shall include in all contracts hereafter negotiated, a provision obligating the contractor not to discriminate against any employee of, or applicant for employment with, such contractor *in the City of Minneapolis*, and shall require such contractors to include a similar provision in all sub-contracts *to be performed in the City of Minneapolis*.

Section 5

a) It shall be unlawful for any employer within said City to discriminate against any person in connection with any hiring, application for employment, tenure, terms or conditions of employment.

*b) It shall be unlawful for any person, firm or corporation engaged in the business of or acting as an employment, referral, or vocational placement agency or bureau within said City, to discriminate against any person in connection with any application for employment, referral for employment, hiring, tenure, terms or conditions of employment.

*c) It shall be unlawful for any employer covered by this Ordinance or labor union or any person, firm or corporation engaged in the business of or acting as an employment, referral or vocational placement agency or bureau with respect to employees covered by this Ordinance within said City to include in an application form or biographical statement relating to employment any questions or statements designed to elicit or record information concerning the race, creed, color, national origin or ancestry of the applicant.

Section 6

It shall be unlawful for any labor union within said City to discriminate against any person with respect to membership in labor union.

Section 7

There is hereby created a permanent Commission on Job Discrimination, which shall consist of a chairman and four other members, to be appointed by the Mayor and to be confirmed by the City Council. The first chairman shall be appointed for a term of five years, and the remaining four members shall be first appointed for terms respectively of four years, three years, two years and one year. Each of said appointees shall serve for his respective term and until his respective successor has been appointed, and has assumed office. After the expiration of the initial term each of the members shall be appointed and shall serve for a five-year term, and until his respective successor has been appointed, and has assumed office. They shall serve without compensation. Said Commission shall be charged with the duties of:

a) Effectuating the purpose and policies of this Ordinance.

b) Receiving complaint of violations of this Ordinance, and investigating into the merits thereof.

c) Promoting cooperation among all groups for the purpose of effectuating the purposes and policies of this Ordinance.

d) Conducting studies, surveys, and projects and disseminating information concerning job discrimination and related problems.

e) Aiding in the enforcement of this Ordinance.

f) Make reports of its activities to the City Council annually or more often, as requested by said City Council.

The Commission shall hear all complaints on violations and shall after said hearing certify and recommend to the City Attorney for prosecution those complaints which in the judgment of said Commission are deemed to be violations of this Ordinance.

Nothing in this section contained shall be construed to limit the right of a complainant to make and file a complaint without such certificate or recommendation by said Commission.

Section 8

Any person, whether acting in an official capacity, or in a private capacity, who shall violate or fail to comply with any of the provisions of this Ordinance shall be guilty of a misdemeanor, and shall be punished by fine not exceeding $100.00 or by imprisonment in the Workhouse for a period of not to exceed ninety (90) days.

Section 9

If any provisions of this Ordinance or the application of such provision to any person or circumstance shall be held invalid, the remainder of such Ordinance or the application of such provision to persons or circumstances other than those to which it has been held invalid shall not be affected thereby.

Section 10

This Ordinance shall be in force and effect from and after its publication.

*[Note: This Minneapolis Fair Employment Practice Ordinance was originally passed by the Minneapolis City Council by a vote of 21 to 3 on Friday, January 31, 1947. The Ordinance was published and put into effect on Wednesday, February 5, 1947.

On Friday, October 29, 1948, the City Council passed amendments which added the words underlined in Section 4 and added Paragraphs b and c to Section 5.]

AN ORDINANCE

PROHIBITING THE PRINTING, PUBLISHING, OR DISTRIBUTING OF ANONYMOUS HANDBILLS, DODGERS, CIRCULARS, BOOKLETS, PAMPHLETS, LEAFLETS, CARDS, STICKERS, PERIODICALS, LITERATURE OR PAPERS WHICH TEND TO EXPOSE ANY INDIVIDUAL OR ANY RACIAL OR RELIGIOUS GROUP TO HATRED, CONTEMPT, RIDICULE OR OBLOQUY. The City Council of the City of Minneapolis do ordain as follows:

Section 1. The word "person", when used in this ordinance, shall mean any person, individual, firm, partnership, corporation, organization or any officer or agent thereof.

Section 2. It shall be unlawful for any person to print, publish, distribute, or cause to be printed, published or distributed, by any means, or in any manner whatsoever, any handbill, dodger, circular, booklet, pamphlet, leaflet, card, sticker, periodical, literature or paper which tends to expose any individual or any racial or religious group to hatred, contempt, ridicule or obloquy, unless the same has clearly printed or written thereon:

  (a) The true name and post office address of the firm, partnership, corporation, or organization causing the same to be printed, published or distributed; and

  (b) If such name is that of a firm, corporation or organization, the name and post office address of the individual acting in its behalf in causing such printing, publication, or distribution.

Section 3. This ordinance shall not be construed to relieve the author, distributor or person who causes to be printed, published or distributed any of the matter herein set forth, from any civil or criminal liability now or hereafter imposed by law or ordinance.

Section 4. Every person who shall violate any provision of this ordinance shall be guilty of a misdemeanor, and, upon conviction therefor, shall be punished by a fine not exceeding One Hundred Dollars, or imprisonment for a period not exceeding ninety days.

Section 5. This ordinance shall take effect and be in force from and after its publication.

  Passed March 28, 1947. Eric G. Hoyer, President of the Council.
  Approved March 28, 1947. Eric G. Hoyer, Acting Mayor.
  Attest: Chas. C. Swanson, City Clerk.

MISSOURI

CITY OF ST. LOUIS

St. Louis Charter Amendment to Outlaw Racial Discrimination in City Employment

Ordinance 43548

An ordinance submitting a proposed amendment to the Charter of the City of St. Louis, to the qualified voters of the City, providing for an election to be held therefor, and the manner of voting thereat, and for the publication of this ordinance.

Be it ordained by the City of St. Louis, as follows:

Section One. That the following amendment to the Charter of the City of St. Louis is hereby proposed and submitted to the qualified voters of the City of St. Louis which shall be voted upon at an election to be held as hereinafter provided. Said amendment is denominated and referred to as Amendment No. 2, and is in words and figures as follows: Amendment No. 2 to the City Charter. That Article XVIII of the Charter of the City of St. Louis be and the same is hereby amended by striking out Section 16 and enacting in lieu thereof a new Section 16 so that said section as amended shall read as follows:

Section 16. *No recommendation or question under the authority of this Article shall relate to the race, political or religious opinions, affiliations, or service, of any person. No person shall be appointed to a position in the classified service hereunder, nor be demoted, reemployed, promoted, removed, increased or reduced in compensation, nor in any other way be favored or discriminated against in any matter within the purview of this Article, because of his race, political or religious opinions, affiliations, or service.* (italics supplied.)

Section Two. At the Primary Election to be held in the City of St. Louis Missouri, on Tuesday, the 6th day of August, 1946, the foregoing amendment to the Charter of the City of St. Louis shall be submitted to the qualified voters of the City, and if said amendment shall receive in its favor the votes of three-fifths of the qualified voters voting at said election for or against said amendment, it shall be adopted and become a part of the Charter of the City of St. Louis from the date of said election. The qualified voters of the City of St. Louis may, at the election aforesaid, deposit a printed ballot substantially in the following form:

Amendment No. 2. Amendment to Section 16 of Article XVIII of the City Charter so as to prohibit discrimination in the classified service because of race, political or religious opinions, affiliations or service. The voters at said election who favor the adoption of said amendment proposed, shall erase from their ballot the word "NO" following the statement of said amendment, and those of the voters who do not favor the adoption of said amendment proposed shall erase from their ballot the word "YES" following the statement of said amendment. The Board of Election Commissioners shall provide the ballots and conduct the election, and shall ascertain and certify the result thereof according to law.

Section Three. Upon the approval of this ordinance, it shall be published in the paper doing the City printing. Proof of the publication of this ordinance shall be made by affidavit of the publishers of said paper, and such affidavit shall be filed with the City Register, and a copy of said publication attached thereto.

Approved: April 8, 1946.

NEW YORK

CITY OF BUFFALO
ORDINANCES
Chapter 3 of 1945

PUBLISHING ANONYMOUS SCURRILOUS LITERATURE

Chapter IX of the Ordinances of the City of Buffalo is hereby amended by adding thereto the following section, to be known as Section 50 and to read as follows:

Section 50. Prohibition on the printing, publishing or distributing of certain anonymous circulars, pamphlets, etc. It shall be unlawful for any person to print, publish, distribute, or cause to be printed, published or distributed, by any means, or in any manner whatsoever, whether printed, typewritten or handwritten, any handbill, dodger, circular, booklet, pamphlet, leaflet, card, paper sticker, periodical or literature which tends to expose any individual or any racial or religious group to hatred, contempt, ridicule or obloquy, unless the same has clearly printed or written thereon:

(a) The true name and post office address of the person, firm, partnership, corporation or organization causing the same to be printed, published or distributed, or the true name and address of the distributor thereof.

(b) If such name is that of a firm, partnership, corporation or organization, the true name and post office address of the individual acting in its behalf, in causing such printing, writing, publication or distribution.

It is hereby certified, pursuant to section 34 of the Chapter, that the immediate passage of this ordinance is necessary.

(Approved effective April 25, 1945.)

_____

Chapter 96 of 1945

"BOARD OF COMMUNITY RELATIONS"

The Common Council of the City of Buffalo do ordain as follows:

The Ordinances of the City of Buffalo are hereby amended by adding thereto a new chapter to be known as Chapter XCVI, to read as follows:

CHAPTER XCVI

Section 1. A board of fifteen members to be known as "Board of Community Relations" is hereby created to be appointed by the Mayor for terms of five years each, beginning August 1, 1945, except that of the members first appointed the terms of five members shall expire on July 31, 1948, five on July 31, 1949 and five on July 31, 1950, and their successors shall be appointed for terms of five years each; provided, however, that any appointment made to fill a vacancy caused by the death, resignation or removal of a member shall be for the balance of said member's term. The mayor shall designate the chairman of said board from among its members and may, from time to time, change said designation. Any member of said board may be removed by the mayor for reasons stated in writing after an opportunity to be heard. The board shall hold at least one meeting in each calendar month, except the months of July and August, on such dates at [as] it shall determine. Other meetings of the board shall be held upon the call of the chairman, or as determined by the board.

Section 2. It shall be the duty of the board to inquire into the causes of inter-group tensions which may exist and to recommend to the mayor and common council the enactment of such ordinances and other legislation, and that such other actions be taken as, in the judgment of the board, will tend:

(1) To eradicate or lessen those irritations which threaten social harmony.

(2) To promote amicable relations among racial, religious and cultural groups of the city.

(3) To encourage and foster the spirit of American democracy in keeping with the traditions which have made this country great.

It shall also be the duty of the Board to assemble and analyze factual data relating to inter-group relationships. It shall also make such other studies concerning discriminations against groups or races and related subjects as may be referred to said board by the mayor or the common council, and to make a report thereon without unnecessary delay.

Section 3. The mayor shall appoint an executive director of said board and such other employes as the common council shall provide by ordinance. The executive director shall act as secretary of said board and perform such other duties as shall be assigned to him. The compensation of the executive director and other employes of said board shall be fixed by the common council.

It is hereby certified pursuant to Section 34 of the Charter that the immediate passage certified pursuant to Section 34 of the Charter that the immediate passage of the foregoing ordinance is necessary.

(Approved, effective August 1, 1945.)

ADMINISTRATIVE CODE
of the
CITY OF NEW YORK

Chapter 13
CONTRACTS AND PURCHASES
Title A

Section 343-8.0. **Discrimination in employment.** — a. It shall be unlawful for any person engaged in the construction, alteration or repair of buildings or engaged in the construction or repair of streets of highways pursuant to a contract with the city, or engaged in the manufacture, sale or distribution of materials, equipment or supplies pursuant to a contract with the city to refuse to employ or to refuse to continue in any employment any person on account of the race, color or creed of such person.

b. It shall be unlawful for any person or any servant, agent or employee of any person, described in subdivision a to ask, indicate or transmit orally or in writing, directly or indirectly, the race, color or creed or religious affiliation of any person employed or seeking employment from such person, firm or corporation.

c. The wording of section 343-8.0 subdivisions a and b, shall appear on all contracts entered into by the city, and disobedience thereto shall be deemed a violation of a material provision of the contract.

d. Any person, or the employee, manager or owner of or officer of such firm or corporation who shall violate any of the provisions of this section shall, upon conviction thereof, be punished by a fine of not more than one hundred dollars or by imprisonment for not more than thirty days, or both. [As added by L. L. 1942, No. 44, September 9.]

OFFICE OF THE MAYOR

Text of Mayor F. H. LaGuardia's Sunday Broadcast to
People of New York from the Mayor's House, February
27, 1944. Broadcast over WNYC at 1:00 P.M.

I have appointed a City-wide Committee on Unity. The purpose of this Committee is to promote understanding and mutual respect among all the racial and religous groups in our city . . .

* * *

The Commission's purpose is to observe and study unfavorable conditions and dangerous trends, and analyze objectively their causes and what steps may be taken to combat them; to further amity and religious harmony in our City . . . The Commission will not seek to supplant or supersede existing organizations having similar purpose or interest in avoiding conflict between racial and religious groups. It will seek through its influence to correct racial and religious prejudice and devolop the common interest of the community in mutual understanding and respect.

CHAPTER 32
DEPARTMENT OF LICENSES
Title B
ARTICLE XXXII

ADVERTISING BY EMPLOYMENT AGENCIES

Section B32-240.0. Manner of advertising. — It shall be unlawful for any person carrying on the business of an employment agency to place in any newspaper, magazine or other publication any advertisement offering employment but restricting such offer to a person or persons of a particular race, creed or color or excluding from such offer of employment persons of any race, creed or color unless the prospective employer of such person shall have specified in writing such limitations and restrictions with respect to race, creed or color hereinbefore set forth. [As added by L. L. 1942, No. 11, May 9.]

Section B32-241.0. **Publication of name of prospective employer in certain cases.** — No advertisement shall be inserted in, or caused to be published in, any newspaper, magazine or other publication by any person carrying on the business of an employment agency offering employment, but restricting such offer to a person or persons of a particular race, creed or color, or excluding from such offer of employment persons of any race, creed or color, unless such advertisement shall also state the name of the prospective employer. [As added by L. L. 1942, No. 11, May 9.]

Section B32-242.0. **Maintenance of records.** — It shall be the duty of every person licensed to conduct an employment agency to receive and keep on file for a period of one year from the date of receipt thereof the written request specified in the preceding section B32-240.0 and to submit it upon demand to the commissioner of licenses or his duly authorized representative for examination. [As added by L. L. 1942, No. 11, May 9.]

Section B32-243.0. **Penalty for violation.** — A violation of any provision of this article shall constitute a misdemeanor and in addition thereto, in the direction [discretion] of the commissioner of licenses, subject the violator to a revocation or suspension of his license. [As added by L. L. 1942, No. 11, May 9.]

Chapter 41 [1948 Cum. Supp.]

TRANSITORY PROVISIONS
Title J
TAXATION OF REAL ESTATE

Article I — Exemptions

Section J41-1.2. **Discrimination in tax exempt projects.** — No exemption from taxation, for any project, other than a project hitherto agreed upon or contracted for, shall be granted to a housing company, insurance company, redevelopment company or redevelopment corporation, which shall directly or indirectly, refuse, withhold from, or deny to any person any of the dwelling or business accommodations in such project or property, or the privileges and services incident to occupancy thereof, on account of the race, color or creed of any such person.

Any exemption from taxation hereafter granted shall terminate sixty days after a finding by the supreme court of the state of New York that such discrimination is being or has been practiced in such project or property; if within said sixty days such discrimination shall have been ended, then the exemption shall not terminate. [As added by L. L. 1944, No. 20, July 3, 1944, as amended by L. L. 1947, No. 45 June 23.]

LOCAL LAWS
OF
THE CITY OF NEW YORK
FOR THE YEAR 1949

No. 111

A LOCAL LAW

To amend the administrative code of the city of New York, in
relation to discrimination in housing.

Be it enacted by the Council as follows:

Section 1. Title A of chapter fifteen of the administrative code of the city of New
York is hereby amended by adding thereto a new section, to follow section 384-15.0,
to be section 384-16.0, to read as follows:

§384-16.0. **Discrimination in housing.** — Every deed, lease or instrument
made or entered into by the city, or any agency thereof, for the conveyance, lease or
disposal of real property or any interest therein for the purpose of housing construction
pursuant to the provisions of section seventy-two-k of the general municipal law and
laws supplemental thereto and amendatory thereof shall provide that no person seeking
dwelling accomodations in any structure erected or to be erected on such real property
shall be discriminated against because of race, color, religion, national origin or
ancestry.

§2. This local law shall take effect immediately.

THE CITY OF NEW YORK, OFFICE OF THE CITY CLERK, SS.:

I hereby certify that the foregoing is a true copy of a local law passed by the
Council of The City of New York, concurred in by the Board of Estimate and approved by the Acting Mayor on December 23, 1949, on file in this office.

MURRAY W. STAND, City Clerk, Clerk of the Council.

OHIO

CITY OF CINCINNATI

AN ORDINANCE No. 196-1946

To prohibit discrimination in the appointment promotion or grading of employees, and
in recommendations for increases or reductions in compensation by ordaining supple-
mentary Section 308-19 of the Code of Ordinances.

Be It Ordained by the Council of the City of Cincinnati, State of Ohio:

Section 1. That the Code of Ordinances is hereby supplemented by ordaining Section 308-19 to read as follows:

Sec. 308-19. **Fair Employment Practices.** In the appointment, promotion or grading of employees, and in recommendations for increases or reductions in compensation, there shall be no discrimination for or against any person because of race, color, creed or national origin. A violation of this section by any officer charged with the duty of appointing, promoting or grading any employee or employees, or making recommendations as to employment or compensation, shall be considered a failure of good behavior, justifying his dismissal from city employment.

Section 2. This ordinance shall take effect and be in force from and after the earliest period allowed by law.

Passed June 5, A. D. 1946.

JAMES G. STEWART, Mayor.

Attest: AL J. BECHTOLD, Clerk.

A copy of this ordinance is on file in the office of the Clerk of Council for public inspection. 6-18-1t-50

OHIO

CITY OF CLEVELAND

ORD. No. 2139-49

An emergency ordinance providing for the cooperation of the City of Cleveland with the Cleveland Metropolitan Housing Authority in the elimination of unsafe and insanitary dwellings and the development of housing for low-income families and authorizing the execution of an agreement with respect thereto.

. . . 10. Within any project undertaken under this agreement, or any amendment, modification or extension of this agreement, or any new agreement for a like purpose, there shall be no discrimination or segregation in the selection of tenants, the fixing of rentals, or in the construction, maintenance and operation of any such project, because of race, color, creed, religion or national origin . . .

Passed December 19, 1949.
Effective December 22, 1949.

OHIO

CITY OF CLEVELAND

Ord. No. 1579-48.

An ordinance to supplement the Municipal Code of Cleveland of 1924 by enacting new Sections 2999-2 to 2999-9 inclusive, prohibiting discrimination in employment because of race, color, religious creed, national origin, or ancestry by employers, employment agencies, or labor organizations.

Whereas, the Community Relations Board has heretofore made and filed with this Council a report and recommendations on legislation to prohibit employment discrimination in Cleveland in which the practice of discrimination was found to exist in Cleveland and,

Whereas, subsequent to this report this Council has held public hearings on employment discrimination in Cleveland, and,

Whereas, experience has proved that legislative enactment prohibiting employment discrimination removes some of the sources of economic inequality and would directly promote the general welfare and good order of this city; now, therefore,

Be it ordained by the Council of the City of Cleveland:

Section 1. That this Council hereby determines that discriminatory employment practices exist in the City of Cleveland which are inimical to the public welfare and good order of the City of Cleveland and require the exercise of the police power residing in the Council to prevent the continuation of such discriminatory employment practices, and therefore the Municipal Code of Cleveland of 1924 be and the same is hereby supplemented by enacting new Sections 2999-2 to 2999-9 inclusive, to read respectively as follows:

Section 2999-2. Definitions.

(a) The words "discriminate", "discriminates", or "discrimination" wherever used in this ordinance are hereby defined and declared to mean and include discrimination solely on the ground or because of race, religious creed, color, national origin or ancestry.

(b) The word "employe" wherever used in this ordinance is hereby defined to include all persons except those engaged in domestic service, personal service or an employe of an organized religious congregation or an employe of an organization or institution limited to members of a single religious faith.

(c) The word "employer" wherever used in this ordinance is hereby defined as a person, one or more individuals, a partnership, association, or corporation hiring employes unless exemption is provided in Section 2999-5.

(d) The term "labor organization" wherever used in this ordinance is hereby defined as any organization which exists and is constituted for the purpose, in whole or in part, of collective bargaining or of dealing with employers concerning grievances, terms or conditions of employment, or of mutual aid or protection in connection with employment.

(e) The term "employment agency" wherever used in this ordinance is hereby defined as any person, company, partnership, association, or corporation, which undertakes with or without compensation, to procure opportunities to work, or to procure, recruit, refer, or place employees.

Section 2999-3. Discrimination in Employment Practices Prohibited.

It shall be unlawful for employers, employes, labor unions, employment agencies or others subject to this ordinance to:

(a) Discriminate against any person with regard to hire, discharge, tenure, up-grading, terms or conditions of employment or union membership solely on grounds of race, religious creed, color, national origin or ancestry.

(b) Publish or cause to be published any notice or advertisement relating to employment or membership which contains any specification or limitation as to race, religious creed, color, national origin or ancestry.

(c) Require of any applicant as a condition of employment or membership any information concerning his race, religious creed, color, national origin or ancestry.

(d) Aid, abet, encourage or incite the commission of any discrimination in employment practice prohibited by this ordinance.

Section 2999-4. Discrimination in Employment Practices Prohibited in City Employment and Public Works Contracts.

The City of Cleveland shall prohibit all of the discriminatory practices set forth in Section 2999-3 in all of its departments, divisions, boards, and commissions; or the commission of said discriminatory practices by any city officials their agents or employees acting for or on behalf of said city.

The City of Cleveland and all of its contracting agencies and departments shall include in all public works contracts hereafter negotiated a provision obligating the public works contractor not to commit any of the discriminary [discriminatory] practices set forth in Section 2999-3 and shall require such contractor to include a similar provision in all sub-contracts

This provision shall apply to all public works contracts and said sub-contracts carried on by said city on property under its ownership or control.

Section 2999-5. Authorized Exemptions.

Exemptions from the requirements of this ordinance shall be:

(a) Any employer of less than twelve persons; nor shall members of the immediate family of an employer be included in determining the number of employes.

(b) Any religious organization or institution whose membership or service is limited to persons of a single religious faith.

(c) Any private organization having a purely social or fraternal purpose.
(d) Any type of employment where religion, religious creed, or nationality would usually and normally be considered an essential qualification of employment.

Section 2999 6. Administration.

The administration of this ordinance shall be the responsibility of the Community Relations Board.

In addition to any powers heretofore conferred in this board, said board shall have the power to:

a. Formulate a plan of education to promote fair employment practices by employers, employees, employment agencies and the general public to eliminate employment discrimination based on race, religious creed, color, national origin or ancestry.

b. To confer and co-operate with and furnish technical·assistance to employers, labor unions, employment agencies and other public and private agencies in formulating educational programs for elimination of employment discrimination based on race, religious creed, color, national origin or ancestry. In connection herewith, the Board may stimulate the establishment of committees in industry, labor and other areas.

c. To make technical studies and prepare and disseminate educational material relating to discrimination and ways and means of reducing and eliminating it.

d. To make specific and detailed recommendations to the interested parties as to the method of eliminating discrimination in employment.

e. Receive, investigate and seek to adjust all complaints of discriminatory employment practices prohibited by this ordinance. Such complaints shall be properly verified and filed by the person discriminated against within 30 days after the alleged discriminatory act is committed.

f. Render to City Council and the Mayor from time to time or upon request, but not less than annually a report of its activities.

g. Adopt such reasonable rules and procedures as are necessary to effect the broad purposes of this ordinance.

Section 2999-7. Compliance and Enforcement.

a. In the consideration of a complaint, the Board shall determine the facts and if there appears to be probable cause for the complaint, the Commission shall use its offices to attempt an adjustment by education, persuasion, conciliation and conference. A reasonable time shall be allowed for this purpose.

b. If in the opinion of a majority of the members of the Board, the efforts to settle any complaint by education, persuasion, conciliation and conference have not adjusted the specific complaint the Board may certify the complaint to the Mayor who shall make a further effort to adjust said complaint. If the Mayor is unable to adjust the complaint to the satisfaction of the Board, the Board shall cause a public hearing to be held. A notice of the particulars of the complaint shall be sent to the respondent by registered mail not less than ten days prior to the day set for the hearing. The hearing shall be held before the Community Relations Board.

c. The respondent shall have the right to file an answer to the complaint and appear at such hearing to testify in his own behalf, or be represented by counsel or otherwise, and to examine and cross-examine witnesses.

If upon all the testimony taken, the Board by a majority vote of the members thereof shall determine that the respondent committed the discriminatory practice set forth in the complaint, the Board shall issue an order directing the respondent to cease such discriminatory employment practice so found to be engaged in. The Board shall have power to require proof of compliance.

d. In the event respondent fails or refuses to comply with the order of said board, the fact of said refusal together with the verified complaint and the record of the proceedings of the public hearing shall be certified to the director of law for prosecution. No prosecution under this ordinance shall be brought except after certification to the director of law.

Section 299-8. Any person violating the provisions of this ordinance shall be guilty of a misdemeanor and upon conviction thereof shall be fined in a sum not to exceed one hundred dollars or imprisoned for not more than ten days if said fine is not paid within 30 days or the execution thereof stayed by appeal or order of the court.

Section 2999-9. Severability.

Sections 2999-2 to 2999-8, inclusive, and each part of such sections, are hereby declared to be independent sections and parts of sections, and notwithstanding any other evidence of legislative intent it is hereby declared to be the controlling legislative intent that if any provision of said sections, or the application thereof to any person or circumstance is held invalid, the remaining sections of parts of sections, and the application of such provision to any person or circumstances, other than those as to which it is held invalid, shall not be affected thereby, and it is hereby declared that this ordinance would have been passed independently of such section, sections or parts of a section so held to be invalid.

Section 2. That this ordinance shall take effect and be in force from and after the earliest period allowed by law.

Passed January 30, 1950.
Effective March 12, 1950.

OHIO

CITY OF TOLEDO

AN ORDINANCE No. 229-46

Creating a Board of Community Relations and providing for the functioning thereof.

Be it ordained by the Council of the City of Toledo:

Section 1. A Board of Community Relations of the City of Toledo is hereby created and the Mayor is hereby authorized and directed to appoint to said Board not less than fifteen (15) nor more than twenty-five (25) persons. The membership of said Board shall contain representatives of the following interests or groups:

Employers, labor, religious, racial, national origin, law enforcement, social, health, housing, governmental instrumentalities and such others as to the Mayor shall deem advisable. In the original appointments of members, approximately one-third of those appointed shall serve respectively for one (1) year, two (2) year and three (3) year terms. Thereafter appointments shall be for a three (3) year term.

Section 2. It shall be the duty of the Community Relations Board to promote amicable relations among the racial and cultural groups within the community; to take appropriate steps to deal with conditions which strain relationships; to aid in the coordination of the activities of private organizations concerned with these relationships; to assemble, analyze and disseminate authentic and factual data relating to interracial and other group relationships. It shall have the power to publish and distribute such factual material as it deems necessary or desirable and to make such investigations, studies and surveys as are necessary for the performance of its duties. The Board shall meet not less than once a month and shall adopt, by majority vote, such rules as to it shall seem expedient for the conduct of its business. It shall annually report its activities to the Council of the City of Toledo.

Section 3. The position of Secretary to the Board of Communnty [Community] Relations is hereby created and appointment to said position shall be made by the Mayor on the recommendation of the Board. Such Secretary shall serve until removed by the Mayor on the concurrence of the majority of the Board. Such clerical and other employees of the Board, as Council shall approve, shall be appointed by the City Manager in accordance with the provisions of the Charter of the City of Toledo. The salary of the Secretary and other employees shall be fixed by Council.

Section 4. Under the direction of the Board, it shall be the duty of the Secretary to maintain contacts with groups in the community which are concerned with interracial and inter-cultural understanding; to report to the Board regarding the activities of these groups; to serve as a source of accurate and reliable data on the problems in the above mentioned fields; to implement the decisions of the Board; work in cooperation with the directors of all municipal departments and other governmental divisions in the improvement of services; to eliminate whatever source of inter-racial friction may exist; to work to remove inequalities which pertain to minority group status on such problems as housing, recreation, education, employment, law enforcement, vocational guidance and related matters, and to do and perform such other and further acts and things as may be directed by the Board.

Section 5. The City Manager shall assign to the Board of Community Relations, adequate office space and facilities for the fulfillment of its duties.

Section 6. The expenses of the aforesaid Board shall be met by such appropriations as are made by Council for such purpose.

Section 7. This ordinance shall take effect and be in force from and after the earliest period allowed by law.

Passed July 1, 1946, Recess session.

LLOYD E. ROULET,
Mayor.

Attest: C. F. DIEFENBACH,
Clerk of Council.

[Toledo City Journal, July 6, 1946, pp. 358-359.]

OHIO

CITY OF YOUNGSTOWN

51948

AN ORDINANCE

DEFINING UNFAIR EMPLOYMENT PRACTICES; PROHIBITING THE SAME; AND PROVIDING A PENALTY FOR THE VIOLATION THEREOF.

WHEREAS, the Council of the City of Youngstown finds that the population of this City is composed of peoples of many diverse racial, religious and ethnic groups, and

WHEREAS, the practice of discrimination in employment against members of these groups has in the past endangered the continued peace, safety and welfare of the whole community which it is the power and duty of the City to protect, and

WHEREAS, discrimination in employment because of race, color, religion, ancestry or national origin by officials of this City or by persons enjoying licenses, franchises, contracts, or subcontracts, or other authorizations issued by this City, constitutes an abuse of power and benefits derived from all the people of the City and a perversion of the democratic principles which govern its administration.

NOW, THEREFORE, BE IT ORDAINED BY THE COUNCIL OF THE CITY OF YOUNGSTOWN, STATE OF OHIO:

SECTION 1

That the unfair employment practices hereinafter defined and established are hereby prohibited.

SECTION 2

DEFINITIONS. When used herein:

(a) The term "person" includes one or more individuals, partnerships, associations, corporations, legal representatives, or other organized groups of persons.

(b) The term "employer" means (1) all departments, officials, agents, or employees of this City and its instrumentalities; (2) all persons operating enterprises which solicit or accept the custom of the public generally and which are operated under a privilege granted by this City; (3) all contractors and their subcontractors engaged in the performance of any contract entered into with this City or any of its contracting agencies; and (4) all private employers having ten or more employees in this City, exclusive of the parents, spouse or children of such employer. The term, however, shall not include religious, charitable, fraternal or sectarian organizations.

(3) The term "employee" does not include any individual employed in the domestic service of any person.

(d) The term "labor organization" means any organization in this City which exists for the purpose, whole or in part, or [of] collective bargaining or of dealings with employers concerning grievances, terms or conditions of employment or of other mutual aid or protection in relation to employment.

(e) The term "employment agency" means any person regularly undertaking in this City, with or without compensation, to procure opportunities to work or to procure, recruit, refer, or place employees.

(f) The term "privilege granted by this City" means any franchise, license, permit, tax exemption, authorization or other permission granted by this City.

SECTION 3

UNFAIR EMPLOYMENT PRACTICES. It shall be an unfair employment practice:

(a) For any employer, because of the race, color, religion, ancestry or national origin of any individual, to refuse to hire or otherwise to discriminate against him with respect to hire, tenure, terms, conditions or privileges of employment or any matter directly or indirectly related to employment.

(b) For any employer, employment agency or labor organization to establish, announce or follow a policy of denying or limiting through a quota system or otherwise, employment or membership opportunities to any group because of its race, color, religion, ancestry or national origin.

(c) Except where based on a bona fide occupation qualification for any employer, employment agency or labor organization prior to employment or admission to membership to

(1) make any inquiry concerning, or record of, the race, color, religion, ancestry or national origin of an applicant for employment or membership;

(2) use any form of application for employment or personnel or membership blank containing questions or entries regarding race, color, religion, ancestry or naitonal origin;

(3) cause to be printed, published or circulated any notice or advertisement relating to employment or membership indicating any preference, limitation, specification or discrimination, based upon race, color, religion, ancestry or national origin.

(d) For any employment agency to fail or refuse to classify properly, refer for employment or otherwise to discriminate against any individual because of his race, color, religion, ancestry or national origin.

(e) For any labor organization to discriminate against any individual or to limit, segregate or classify its membership in any way which would tend to deprive such individual of employment opportunities or would limit his employment opportunities or otherwise adversely affect his status as an employee or as an applicant for employment or would affect adversely his wages, hours or employment conditions, because of such individual's race, religion, color, ancestry or national origin.

(f) For any employer, employment agency or labor organization to penalize or discriminate in any manner against any individual because he has opposed any practice forbidden by this ordinance.

(g) For any persons to aid, abet, incite, compel or coerce the doing of any act declared herein to be an unfair employment practice or to obstruct or prevent any person from complying with the provisions of this ordinance or to attempt directly or indirectly to commit any act declared by this section to be an unfair employment practice.

SECTION 4

PENALTY. Any person who shall commit any unfair employment practice as herein defined shall be guilty of a misdemeanor and shall be punished by a fine of not less than FIFTY ($50.00) DOLLARS nor more than FIVE HUNDRED ($500.00) DOLLARS. For any violation committed after a prior conviction, such persons shall, in addition, be liable to imprisonment for not more than thirty (30) days.

SECTION 5

SEPARABILITY. If any provision of this ordinance or the application of such provision to any person or circumstance shall be held invalid, the remainder of such ordinance or the application of such provision to persons or circumstances other than those to which it is held invalid shall not be affected thereby.

SECTION 6

That this ordinance shall take effect and be in force from and after the earliest period allowed by law.

Passed in Council this 15th day of May, 1950.

FRANK X. KRYZAN
PRESIDENT OF COUNCIL

ATTEST:
JNO. H. LEMON
CLERK

Approved: This 16th day of May, 1950.

CHARLES P. HENDERSON
MAYOR

FILED WITH THE MAYOR THIS 16TH DAY OF MAY, 1950.

OREGON

CITY OF PORTLAND

ORDINANCE NO. 91214*

An ordinance amending the Police Code by adding a new section relating to discrimination in certain places and by certain types of business on account of race, color, religion or national origin.

The City of Portland does ordain as follows:

Section 1. The Council finds that to further the objectives contained in the

Constitution of the United States and the Constitution of the State of Oregon, and as an exercise of the police power of the City of Portland, provision should be made against discrimination on account of race, color or religion in public or quasi-public places; that in the interest of public health and as an exercise of the police power of the City such regulations should also extend to hospitals, ambulances, mortuaries, funeral conveyances and cemeteries; that civil rights of all persons within the police jurisdiction of the City should be safeguarded as provided herein; now, therefore, Article 27 of Ordinance No. 76339 (Police Code) hereby is amended by adding thereto a new section to be numbered, entitled and to read as follows:

Section 16-2703. PLACES OF PUBLIC ACCOMODATION SHALL BE OPENED TO ALL PERSONS WITHOUT DISCRIMINATION BECAUSE OF RACE, COLOR, RELIGION, ANCESTRY OR NATIONAL ORIGIN. All persons within the police jurisdiction of the City of Portland shall be entitled to full and equal accommodation advantages, facilities and privileges in all places or businesses offering or holding out services or facilities to the general public, including but not limited to hotels, lodging houses and rooming houses as defined in the License and Business Code of the City of Portland, restaurants or other places where food or drink are offered to the public generally for consumption upon the premises, theaters or other places of amusement, public transportation carriers, public facilities in office buildings or other places open to the general public, retail stores, hospitals, ambulances, mortuaries, funeral conveyances and cemeteries. It shall be unlawful for the owner, lessee, manager, or proprietor of a place of business within the City offering or holding itself out as affording services or facilities to the general public including but not limited to the businesses mentioned in this section to discriminate against any person in such service or sale of privilege, facility or commodity on account of race, color, religion, ancestry or national origin.

Passed by the Council Feb. 21, 1950.

DOROTHY McCULLOUGH LEE
Mayor of the City of Portland
Attest WILL GIBSON.
Auditor of the City of Portland

Mayor Lee
1-23-50
MCR: gm/y

*The above Ordinance will be submitted to the voters of Portland, Oregon, for approval by referendum on November 7, 1950.

PENNSYLVANIA

CITY OF PHILADELPHIA

CITY OF PHILADELPHIA

FAIR EMPLOYMENT
PRACTICE COMMISSION
ORDINANCE

Approved March 12, 1948

CLERK'S OFFICE, CITY COUNCIL
Room No. 492, City Hall

This is to certify that the following is a true and correct copy of the original Ordinance passed by City Council and approved by the Mayor on the twelfth day of March, 1948.

AN ORDINANCE

Prohibiting discrimination in employment because of race, color, religion, national origin or ancestry by employers, employment agencies, labor organizations and others; providing for the creation of the Philadelphia Fair Employment Practice Commission; prescribing its duties and powers; and providing penalties.

WHEREAS, Discrimination in employment due to race, color, religion, national origin or ancestry has prevented and threatens to prevent the gainful employment of large segments of the people of Philadelphia and has created and tends to create breaches of the peace; and has been and will continue to be detrimental to the health, welfare and safety of the City of Philadelphia and its inhabitants.

SECTION 1. *The Council of the City of Philadelphia ordains,* That this ordinance shall be known as "The Philadelphia Fair Employment Practice Ordinance."

SECT. 2. *Declaration of Policy.*

It is hereby declared to be the policy of the City in the exercise of its police power for the protection of the public welfare, health, safety and peace of the City and the inhabitants thereof, to prohibit unfair employment practices as hereinafter defined and to establish the Philadelphia Fair Employment Practice Commission as an administrative agency charged with the duty of effectuating the provisions and purposes of this ordinance.

SECT. 3. *Definitions.*

The term "person" as used in this ordinance, shall include an individual, partnership, corporation, union or association, including those acting in a fiduciary or representative capacity, whether appointed by a court or otherwise. Whenever used in any clause prescribing and imposing a penalty, the term "person," as applied to partnerships, unions or associations, shall mean the partners or members thereof and as applied to corporations, the officers thereof. The singular shall include the plural and the masculine shall include the feminine and neuter.

The term "employer," as used in this ordinance shall include every person, as hereinabove defined, who employs one or more employees, exclusive of parents, spouse or children of such person. The term, however, shall not include fraternal, sectarian, charitable or religious organizations, but shall include any governmental unit, agency or employee as to which the City has the power to legislate.

The term "labor organization" shall include any organization which exists for the purpose, in whole or in part, of collective bargaining or of dealing with employers concerning grievances, terms or conditions of employment or of other mutual aid or protection in relation to employment.

The term "employment agency" shall include every person, as hereinabove defined, regularly undertaking in this City, with or without compensation, to procure opportunities to work or to procure, recruit, refer, or place employees.

The term "employment" shall not include the employment of individuals as domestic servants nor the employment of individuals to serve in personal confidential positions.

The term "commission" means the Philadelphia Fair Employment Practice Commission created herein.

SECT. 4. *Unfair Employment Practices Prohibited.*

Unfair employment practices are hereby prohibited.

It shall be an unfair employment practice, except where based on a bona fide occupational qualification certified by the commission:

(a) For any employer, because of the race, color, religion, national origin or ancestry of any individual, to refuse to hire, or otherwise to discriminate against him with respect to hire, tenure, promotions, terms, conditions or privileges of employment or any matter directly or indirectly related to employment.

(b) For any employer, employment agency or labor organization to establish, announce or follow a policy of denying or limiting through a quota system or otherwise, employment or membership opportunities of any group or individual because of race, color, religion, national origin or ancestry.

(c) For any employer, employment agency or labor organization prior to employment or admission to menbership to:

1. Make any inquiry concerning, or record of, the race, color, religion, national origin or ancestry of any applicant for employment or membership.

2. Use any form of application of employment of personnel or membership blank containing questions or entries regarding race, color, religion, national origin or ancestry.

3. Cause to be printed, published or circulated any notice or advertisement relating to employment or membership indicating any preference, limitation, specification or discrimination, based upon race, color, religion, national origin or ancestry.

(d) For any employment agency to fail or refuse to classify properly, refer for employment or otherwise discriminate against any individual because of his race, color, religion, national origin or ancestry.

(e) For any labor organization to discriminate against any individual or to limit, segregate or classify its membership in any way which would deprive or tend to deprive such individual of employment opportunities or would limit his employment opportunities or otherwise adversely affect his status as an employee or as an applicant for employment or would affect adversely his wages, hours or employment conditions, because of such individual's race, religion, color, national origin or ancestry.

(f) For any employer, employment agency or labor organization to penalize or discriminate in any manner against any individual because he has opposed any practice forbidden by this ordinance or because he has made a charge, testified or assisted in any manner in any investigation, proceeding or hearing thereunder.

(g) For any person to aid, abet, incite, compel or coerce the doing of any act declared herein to be an unfair employment practice or to obstruct or prevent any person from complying with the provisions of this ordinance or any order issued thereunder or to attempt directly or indirectly to commit any act declared by this ordinance to be an unfair employment practice.

(h) It is specifically provided, that if the provisions of this ordinance are not otherwise violated, it shall not be an unfair employment practice for any employer to select for employment or employ any person who possesses qualifications, training or experience which best adapts him for the welfare and interest of such employer's business or profession.

SECT. 5. *Fair Employment Practice Commission.*

(a) There is hereby established the Philadelphia Fair Employment Practice Commission which shall consist of five members, three of whom shall be appointed by the Mayor and two of whom shall be appointed by the President of Council. Any three members of the commission shall constitute a quorum. They shall serve without compensation but shall be reimbursed for all expenses necessarily incurred. Each member of the commission shall serve for a period of three years, and until his successor is duly appointed and qualified. The members of the commission shall annually elect a chairman and secretary. Any member of the commission may be removed by the appointing power.

(b) The commission shall appoint such personnel at such compensation as may from time to time be authorized by Council.

SECT. 6. *Duties of the Commission.*

The commission is authorized to and shall:

(a) Receive and investigate and seek to adjust all complaints of unfair employment practices forbidden by this ordinance, but no complaint shall be received unless made to the commission within sixty days of such alleged unfair practice.

(b) Make and publish appropriate findings as a result of its investigation.

(c) From time to time but not less than once a year, render to the Mayor and Council a written report of its activities and recommendations.

(d) Formulate and carry out a comprehensive educational program designed to eliminate and prevent prejudice and discrimination based upon race, color, religion, national origin or ancestry.

(e) Adopt such rules and regulations as may be necessary to carry out the functions of the commission and effectuate the purposes and provisions of this ordinance.

SECT. 7. *Investigations, Hearings and Enforcement.*

(a) Upon its own initiative or whenever a charge has been made either by an aggrieved individual or by an organization which has as one of its purposes the combatting of discrimination or of promoting full, free or equal employment opportunities, that any person has engaged or is engaging in any unfair employment practice, the commission shall have power to issue and cause to be served on such person a complaint stating the charges in that respect and containing a notice of public hearing before the commission at a place therein fixed, to be held not less than ten days after the service of said complaint. The respondent shall have the right to file an answer to the complaint and to appear at such hearing in person or by attorney or otherwise to examine and cross-examine witnesses. If upon all the testimony taken the commission shall determine that the respondent has engaged or is engaging in any unfair employment practices, the commission shall state its findings of fact and shall render such decision or enter such order as the facts warrant.

(b) In the event the respondent refuses or fails to comply with any such order issued by the commission, the commission shall certify the case and the entire record of its proceedings to the City Solicitor who shall invoke the aid of an appropriate court to impose the penalties provided in Section 8 of this ordinance and by appropriate action secure enforcement of the order.

(c) Whenever the commission finds that any official, agent, or employee of this City, or any contractor or subcontractor doing work for this City, has engaged in any unfair employment practice, it shall make a report thereof to the Mayor for appropriate action.

SECT. 8. *Penalty.*

Any person who shall violate any of the provisions of this ordinance or any of the rules and regulations adopted thereunder or who shall fail, refuse, or neglect to comply with any decision or order of the Philadelphia Fair Employment Practice Commission shall be subject for each violation to a fine not exceeding one hundred (100) dollars together with judgment of imprisonment not exceeding thirty days if the amount of said fine and costs shall not be paid within ten days from the date of the imposition thereof: *Provided,* That prosecutions under this ordinance shall be brought only by the City Solicitor, and such prosecutions shall be brought only after certification of a case to him by the commission.

SECT. 9. *Severability.*

The provisions of this ordinance are severable and if any provision, sentence, clause, section or part thereof shall be held illegal, invalid or unconstitutional or inapplicable to any person or circumstance such illegality, invalidity, unconstitutionality or inapplicability shall not affect or impair any of the remaining provisions, sentences, clauses, sections or parts of the ordinance or their application to other persons and circumstances. It is hereby declared to be the legislative intent that this ordinance would have been adopted if such illegal, invalid or unconstitutional provision, sentence, clause, section or part had not been included therein and if the person or circumstances to which the ordinance or any part thereof is inapplicable had been specifically exempted therefrom.

Attest:

WILLIAM W. FELTON,
Clerk of City Council.

CLERK'S OFFICE, CITY COUNCIL
Room No. 492, CITY HALL
Philadelphia, May 19, 1950

This is to certify that the following is a true and correct copy of the original Ordinance passed by City Council and approved by the Mayor on the nineteenth day of May, 1950.

AN ORDINANCE

Authorizing and directing the execution of a co-operation agreement among The Philadelphia Housing Authority, the City of Philadelphia and the School District of Philadelphia, in connection with the construction, maintenance and operation of ten thousand [10,000] low-rent homes in the City of Philadelphia by The Philadelphia Housing Authority.

Section 1. *The Council of the City of Philadelphia ordains,* That the Mayor of the City of Philadelphia be and he is hereby authorized and directed to enter into, execute and deliver, on the part of the City, an agreement with The Philadelphia Housing Authority and the School District of Philadelphia, in form substantially as follows:

[Terms and conditions of agreement to enter into contracts with the Public Housing Administration for loans and annual contributions in connection with the development and administration of low-rent housing in the City of Philadelphia.]

10. That there shall be no discrimination or segregation in the selection of tenants the fixing of rentals, conditions of occupancy, or in the construction, maintenance and operation of any housing project because of race, color, creed, religion or national origin.

* * * *

Attest: *William W. Felton,*
                                     Clerk of City Council.

TEXAS

CITY OF DALLAS

DALLAS CITY CODE (1941) (SEGREGATION)
[Intraurban Motor Busses]

Art. 76-22. **Separate Spaces for Colored People; Penalty for Refusal to Ride in Such Space.** — Every person who operates motor busses or other commercial motor vehicles (other than motor vehicles having a passenger capacity of six or less), or all or any of the same, upon the streets of the city of Dallas, Texas, as common carriers of passengers for hire, or any agent, lessee, manager or receiver thereof, shall provide separate spaces in such vehicles for the accommodation of white and negro passengers, which shall be designated by signs showing the division between the white and the negro spaces. If any passenger upon a motor bus, or commercial motor vehicle, provided with separate spaces, as above provided, and operating upon any or all of the streets of the city of Dallas, Texas, shall ride in any space not so designated for his or her race, after having been forbidden to do so by the operator in charge of the vehicle, he shall, upon conviction thereof, be fined not less than five dollars nor more than twenty-five dollars. (1, 2 Ord. 2904, Bk. 31, p. 48.)

Art. 77-14. [Identical provision applicable to interurban busses]

* * * * * * *

Art. 136-1 (1926) (475) **White Passengers to Occupy Seats Near Front.** — It shall be the duty of white persons upon street cars in the city of Dallas to occupy the vacant seats nearest to the front of the car.

Art. 136-2 (1927) 476) **Negroes to Occupy Seats Near Rear.** — It shall be the duty of negroes upon street cars in the city of Dallas to occupy the vacant seats nearest to the rear of the car.

Art. 136-3 (1928) (476a) **Passengers to Occupy Nearest Vacant Seat to Left.** — It shall be the duty of any passenger, regardless of race, entering an open car to occupy the nearest vacant seat to the left side of the car.

Art. 136-4 (1929) (477) **Obstructing Platform.** — Persons, regardless of race, shall not stand upon the rear platform of a closed car in such manner as to interfere with other passengers getting on or off of car.

Art. 136-5 (1930) (478) **When Seat Deemed Vacant.** — A seat shall be deemed vacant under the provisions of this chapter until it is occupied by the number of persons for which it is intended, or by a person of the opposite race.

Art. 136-6 (1931) (479) **"Negro" Defined.** — The term "negro" as used herein, includes every person of African descent, as the same is defined by the statutes of the State of Texas. All persons not included in said definition of negro shall be deemed white persons within the meaning of this chapter.

Art. 136-7 (1932) (480) **Posting of Signs Concerning Occupancy of Seats.** — It shall be the duty of every person, firm or corporation owning and operating street cars in the city of Dallas to keep posted in the front and rear of each car a sign in plain letters containing these words: "City ordinance requires white persons to occupy nearest vacant seat to the front, and colored persons the nearest vacant seat to the rear of car."

Art. 136-8 (1933) (481) **Penalty.** — Any person who shall violate any of the provisions of this chapter or who shall wilfully fail to comply with the provisions thereof shall be deemed guilty of a misdemeanor and shall, upon conviction, be fined not less than one dollar nor more than fifty dollars.

Art. 136-9 **Persons excepted from provisions of Chapter.** — The provisions of this chapter shall not be so construed as to prohibit nurses from riding upon the same seat with their employer or with the child in their charge even though of a different race, or to prohibit officers from riding with prisoners in their charge, nor shall its provisions extend to any other case of imperative necessity.

Art. 136-10 **Excursion Cars Excepted.** — The provisions of this chapter shall not apply to any excursion car or special run strictly for the exclusive benefit of either race, but in all such cases said cars shall be plainly marked "excursion car" or "special car,"

and it shall be unlawful for any person of a different race from that which said "excursion car" or "special car" is intended, to enter and ride upon said car.

TEXAS

CITY OF HOUSTON

CITY CODE OF HOUSTON (1942)

Sec. 1387. Use of Public Buildings for Promotion of Religious or Racial Antagonism. — The rental or use of the Sam Houston Coliseum, the City Auditorium or any other city-owned building, park, or property used as a place of public assembly, for any purpose which will tend, by speech or otherwise, to engender racial or religious antagonism.

The manager of the coliseum, with respect to the use of the coliseum, the auditorium or other city-owned building, and the superintendent of parks, with respect to the use of park property, are authorized and directed to investigate all applicants for the rental or use of such buildings, property or parks with respect to the nature of the proposed use thereof by way of lectures, speeches, debates and otherwise, and to deny the use thereof, if, in their opinion, the use will tend to engender religious or racial antagonism. The determination of the manager of the coliseum, or of the superintendent of parks, as the case may be, shall be final, except that an appeal from their decision may be taken to the city council for capricious or arbitrary action. The manager of the coliseum, or the superintendent of parks, as the case may be, shall act upon applications within ten days of receipt thereof and the applicant shall have ten days in which to appeal, and the city council shall act upon appeals within ten days of the filing thereof with the city secretary.

Sec. 1434. Emancipation Park to be used Exclusively by Colored People. — There is hereby set aside for the exclusive use of the colored people of the city, the park known as Emancipation Park, which park shall be under the jurisdiction and control of the department of public parks of the city. All other parks in the city now or hereafter existing and not set aside exclusively for the use of colored people shall be used exclusively by white people.

Sec. 1348. Cohabitation Between Races. — It shall be unlawful for any white person and any negro to have sexual intercourse with each other, within the corporate limits of the city. Each act of sexual intercourse between said persons shall constitute a separate and distinct offense.

The term "negro", as used herein, is hereby defined to be any person of African descent or any person who has any negro blood in his veins of whatsoever quantity.

Any person violating any of the terms of this section shall be fined not less than twenty-five nor more than two hundred dollars.

Art. III — Segregation of Races in Busses

Sec. 2207. Bus Companies Must Provide Separate Compartments. — Every company, lessee, manager, receiver or owner thereof, operating motor busses in the city as common carriers of passengers for hire, shall provide separate compartments for the accommodation of white and for the accommodation of negro passengers, which separate compartments shall be equal in all points of comfort and convenience.

Sec. 2208. What Deemed Separate Compartment; Designation. — Each division of a motor bus divided or designated by a sign plainly indicating the separate portion of the motor bus to be used by each race shall be deemed a separate compartment within the meaning of Section 2207, and each separate compartment shall have in some conspicuous place appropriate words in plain letters indicating the race for which it is set apart.

Sec. 2209. **Term "Negro" Defined.** — The term "Negro" as used in this article, includes every person of African descent, as the same is defined by the Statutes of the State of Texas. All persons not included in the definiton of "Negro" as above defined shall be deemed white persons within the meaning of this article.

Sec. 2210. **Penalty for Failure to Provide Separate Compartments.** — Any company, lessee, manager or receiver thereof which fails to equip and operate its motor busses with separate compartments for passengers as above provided for, shall be liable, for each and every failure, to a penalty of not less than twenty-five dollars nor more than one hundred dollars to be recovered by the city in a suit to be brought in the name of the city in any court having competent jurisdiction, and each trip run with any such bus, or string of busses, without separate compartments as herein defined, shall be deemed a separate offense.

Sec. 2211. **Right to Refuse Permission to Sit in Compartment; Right to Remove Passenger From Compartment.** — The conductor or person in charge of any motor bus operating in the city, shall have the authority to refuse any passenger or person the right to sit or stand in any separate compartment of a motor bus in which said passenger is not entitled to ride under the provisions and within the meaning of this article, and such conductor or other such person in charge of such motor bus shall have the right to remove from a separate compartment of a motor bus any passenger not entitled to ride therein under the provisions of this article, and such person so removed shall not be entitled to return of any fare paid.

Sec. 2212. **Penalty for Riding in Compartment After Having Been forbidden To Do So.** — If any passenger upon any motor bus provided with separate compartments within the meaning of this article shall ride in any separate compartment not designated for his race after having been forbidden to do so by the conductor or other person in charge of said motor bus, he shall be guilty of a misdemeanor and shall be fined, upon conviction, not less than five dollars nor more than twenty-five dollars.

Sec. 2213. **Article inapplicable to Nurses and Officers.** — The provisions of this article shall not be so construed as to prohibit nurses from riding in the same separate compartment of any motor bus with their employer, even though of a different race, and shall not prohibit officers from riding with prisoners in their charge.

Sec. 2214. **Article inapplicable to Special or Excursion Busses.** — The provisions of this article shall not apply to any excursion motor busses or special motor busses strictly as such for the exclusive benefit of either race, but in all such cases, said motor busses shall be plainly marked "special" or "excursion:"

Sec. 2215. **Shifting Signs That Separate Compartments.** — It shall be the duty of the person in charge of any motor bus, in his discretion, to shift the signs that separate the two separate compartments for the white and for the black races, and any person other than said person in charge of said motor bus who shall shift or change from one place to another the signs separating the two separate compartments of any motor bus shall be guilty of an offense and, upon conviction thereof in the corporation court, shall be fined not less than five dollars nor more than two hundred dollars.

It is hereby made the duty of the person in charge of any motor bus, whereon or in which any person other than himself shall shift or change from one position to another any signs separating the two separate compartments of said motor bus, to report said person so offending to the corporation court and to file complaint against the said offender, and any conductor who shall fail to refuse to report such violation shall be guilty of offense and, upon conviction of the same in the corporation court, shall be fined not more than fifty dollars.

Sec. 2216. **Powers of person in Charge of Bus Over Signs and Passengers.** — The person in charge of any motor bus in which there are signs separating and designating the separate compartments for the white and for the Negro races, is hereby authorized, in his discretion, to shift and change said signs, and to require passengers to occupy seats in the proper compartment designated by such signs, or to occupy space, whether seated or standing room space, in the proper separate compartments designated by such signs, and any person who shall fail or refuse to move to the seat or space proper for his own race when directed to do so by the person in charge of said motor bus, shall be guilty of an offense and, upon conviction in the corporation court, shall be fined not less than five dollars nor more than two hundred dollars.

WISCONSIN

CITY OF MILWAUKEE

CERTIFIED COPY OF ORDINANCE
22 — AN ORDINANCE

To create Sections 106-24, 106-25, 106-26, 106-28 and 106-29 of the Millwaukee Code, relating to fair employment practices.

Whereas, The State of Wisconsin, through its duly elected representatives, has set forth a policy against discrimination in public and private employment; and

Whereas, The City of Milwaukee, desiring to grant to all its citizens the basic democratic right of earning their livelihood without being discriminated against because of race, creed, color or national origin, enacts this ordinance to be known as the Fair Employment Practices Ordinance:

The Mayor and Common Council of the City of Milwaukee do ordain as follows:

Part 1. There are hereby created six new sections of the Milwaukee Code to read:

Section 106-24. It shall be unlawful for any department of the City of Milwaukee; or any city official, his agent or employe, for or on behalf of the City of Milwaukee; or any private employer performing work within the City of Milwaukee, involving any public works of the City of Milwaukee; to wilfully refuse to employ or to discharge any person otherwise qualified because of race, color, creed, national origin, or ancestry; to discriminate for the same reasons in regard to tenure, terms or conditions of employment; to deny promotion or increase in compensation solely for these reasons; to publish offer of employment based on such discrimination; to adopt or enforce any rule or employment policy which discriminates between employes on account of race, color, religion, national origin, or ancestry; to seek such information as to any employe as a condition of employment; to penalize any employe or discriminate in the selection of personnel for training, solely on the basis of race, color, religion, national origin, or ancestry.

Section 106-25. All contracting agencies of the City of Milwaukee, or any department thereof, shall include in all contracts hereafter negotiated or renegotiated by them a provision obligating the contractor not to discriminate against any qualified employe or qualified applicant for employment because of race, creed, color or national origin and shall require him to include a similar provision in all sub-contracts.

Section 106-26. No person properly qualified shall be wilfully discriminated against by reason of race, creed, color, or national origin in the hiring, receiving of applications for employment or in tenure, terms or conditions of employment.

Section 106-27. It shall be unlawful for any employment agency operating in the City of Milwaukee to wilfully refuse to refer any person properly qualified for employment because of his race, creed, color or national origin.

Section 106-28. Any person, firm or corporation who shall wilfully violate or fail to comply with any of the provisions of this ordinance shall be punished by a fine not exceeding $10.00, and in default of payment thereof, by imprisonment in the House of Correction for not exceeding five days.

Section 106-29. If any part of this ordinance shall be declared invalid, the balance shall remain in full force and effect.

Part 2. All ordinances or parts of ordinances contravening the provisions of this ordinance are hereby repealed.

Part 3. This ordinance shall take effect and be in force from and after its passage and publication.

August 10, 1949
Office of the City Clerk
Milwaukee, Wis.

I hereby certify that the foregoing is a copy of an Ordinance passed by the Common Council of the City of Milwaukee on

May 13, 1946

STANLEY J. WITKOWSKI
City Clerk
Form CC 6 5M 10-48

APPENDIX 6.

*NOTE ON REGIONAL COMPACT — EDUCATION

On February 8, 1948, the governors of fourteen Southern states — Alabama, Arkansas, Florida, Georgia, Louisiana, Maryland, Mississippi, North Carolina, Oklahoma, South Carolina, Tennessee, Texas, Virginia and West Virginia — entered into an interstate compact for regional education subject to ratification by their respective state legislatures. The compact inaugurated what is now known as the Southern Regional Education Program. By September 1, 1949, at least ten state legislatures[1] had ratified the compact. Arkansas, Texas, Virginia and West Virginia have not yet formally approved the plan.

Under the terms of the compact the states who are parties thereto agree to cooperate toward the "establishment and maintenance of jointly owned and operated regional educational institutions in the Southern States in the professional, technological, scientific, literary and other fields, so as to provide greater educational advantages and facilities for the citizens of the several States who reside within such region". A Board of Control for Southern Regional Education is set up to consist of the governor of each member state, ex officio, and three additional citizens from each state to be appointed by the governor, at least one of whom shall be chosen from the field of education. Regional educational institutions are to be developed under the control of the Board and the participating states agree to turn over such funds, when authorized by their respective legislatures, as may be required for the establishment and maintenance of regional institutions. States may enter into agreements with the Board of Control and with other states to provide adequate educational facilities for the residents of the particular region.

The Southern Regional Education Program is based upon the assumption that no single southern state is financially able to provide a complete first-class program of professional and specialized education on graduate levels for all of its citizens. It is a matter of common knowledge that inadequate state educational facilities in the Southern states have compelled many graduates of Southern universities to continue their training in Northern and Eastern schools. Very often these graduates settle outside of the South, robbing that region of much needed professional and technical leadership. To rectify this situation each participating state in the regional program may strengthen existing facilities in certain specialized fields within the state while entering into regional compacts to purchase much needed educational facilities in other fields from a neighboring state.

For example, the program envisions that students of the fourteen southern states will be able to obtain training in veterinary medicine in the four existing accredited institutions in that field — Alabama Polytechnic Institute, University of Georgia, Oklahoma A. & M. and Tuskeegee Institute (for Negroes). Similarly, under the plan, Mississippi and Florida which have no accredited medical schools, could arrange through scholarships to enroll white medical students in any Southern medical school of their choice. Southern state legislatures would also contribute to the development of Meharry College at Nashville, Tennessee to provide for the education of Negro

---

[1]ALA. Acts 1949, p. 327; Act No. 227; FLA. Spec. Acts 1949, ch. 25017; GA. Laws 1949, p. 56; LA. 1948 Act No. 367, p. 982; MD. Laws 1949, ch. 282; MISS. Laws 1948, ch. 284, S.B. No. 612; N.C. Laws 1949, Res. No. 26; OKLA. Laws 1949, p. 790; S.C. Acts 1948, No. 860, p. 2221; TENN. Pub. Acts 1949, ch. 82, p. 280.

students in the fields of medicine, dentistry, nursing and related subjects. As the plan has developed, medical students will be trained at seven universities — Duke, Emory, Louisiana State, Meharry Medical College, at Nashville, Tennessee, Tulane, and Vanderbilt. Training for dental students will be provided at six institutions—Emory, Loyola of Louisiana, Maryland, Medical College of Virginia, Meharry, and Tennessee. Under the regional arrangements these institutions will accept students upon the payment of scholarships by the several states ranging from $1,000 to $1,500 for each student.[2]

On the surface the Southern Regional Education Program would appear to offer a constructive solution to the chronic problem of education in the Southern states. Indeed, the principle involved is sound educationally and eleven Western states are now reported to have adopted the concept of interstate collaboration to further higher education.[3] It is generally conceded that the Southern states which maintain segregation are unable to provide equal educational facilities for both Negro and white residents. Yet, under a line of recent Supreme Court decisions in the field of education, the Southern states are required by the Constitution of the United States to furnish equal educational opportunities to their Negro residents.

Coming as it did on the heels of the Supreme Court decision in the *Sipuel* case, the regional compact has been attacked as an attempt to maintain racial segregation in higher education while at the same time meeting the constitutional requirements of equal educational facilities for Negro students. Edward N. Savath declares, "The rather innocently named Southern Regional Education Program . . . is actually the last stand by the South in defense of segregated education. Confronted by the carefully developed legal campaign of the National Association for the Advancement of Colored People, based upon the Supreme Court ruling in the Gaines case, southern segregationists have responded with a regional plan, one of the results of which would be to root segregation even more firmly in the educational system of the South."[4]

Against the background of litigation surrounding the efforts of Negroes to obtain equality of opportunity in education, Mr. Savath's criticism carries considerable weight. In 1938, the Supreme Court ruled that if a State furnishes higher education to white residents, it is bound to furnish substantially equal advantages to Negro residents. Failure to do this was held to be a denial of equal protection of the laws. *Missouri ex rel Gaines v. Canada* 305 U.S. 337 (1938).

Prior to the *Gaines* decision a number of Southern states had attempted to forestall court actions by appropriating funds to be used for out-of-state scholarships for Negro students who were denied admission to the existing state professional and graduate schools. The Court declared in the *Gaines* decision that the obligation of a state to give equal protection of its laws to all residents was not fulfilled by affording opportunity to its Negro citizens to obtain higher education in other states. The *Gaines* decision left the Southern states with two alternatives: to admit Negro students into the existing state institutions where no graduate school facilities existed for them, or

[2]For detailed discussions of the Southern Regional Education Program see Saveth, *Jim Crow and the Regional Plan,* Survey Graphic, September, 1949, pp. 476-480; Lesesne, *Regional Education in Dixie,* New York Herald Tribune, January 3, 1949; *Regionalism in Education,* New York Herald Tribune, December 3, 1949; American Council on Race Relations, "Recent Developments in Regional Education," Release No. 44, Oct. 20, 1949.

[3]New York Times, November 21, 1949.

[4]Survey Graphic, September, 1949 p. 476.

to establish separate institutions substantially equal to those provided for white residents.

Ten years later the case of Ada Lois Sipuel reached the Supreme Court. In this case Miss Sipuel, a Negro, sued the Board of Regents of the University of Oklahoma to compel her admission into the law school. In deciding this case, the Supreme Court made it clear that a state must not only provide its Negro applicants with facilities for graduate education equal to that provided for other applicants but must provide such education "as soon as it does for applicants of any other group." *Sipuel v. Board of Regents of University of Oklahoma,* 332 U. S. 631 (1948). In neither of these two decisions, however, did the Supreme Court rule directly on the question of segregation *per se.*

The reaction to the latest Supreme Court ruling has been varied. The University of Delaware announced on January 31, 1948 that Negroes would henceforth be enrolled at that institution for any courses not provided by the Delaware State College for Negroes.[4a] On February 26, 1948, the University of Arkansas announced the enrollment of Silas Hunt, a Negro student, in its School of Law,[4b] and on August 24, 1948, a young Negro woman, Edith May Irby, was admitted to the University of Arkansas School of Medicine.[4c] For some time Negroes have been admitted to the University of Maryland School of Law under a decision of the Maryland Supreme Court, *University of Maryland v. Murray,* 169 Md. 478, 182 A. 590, (1935).

The 1948 Kentucky legislature amended its segregation statutes in the field of education to permit the training of Negro nurses and doctors in existing institutions, provided that the majority of the governing board of such institutions registered approval.[5] In October 1948, the Board of Regents of the University of Oklahoma was ordered to admit G. W. McLaurin, a Negro student, to the Graduate College. Mr. McLaurin was admitted to classes but compelled to receive instruction from an anteroom physically separated from the other students although he could see and hear the instructor. It is reported, however, that Mrs. Opherita Daniels was admitted to the University of Oklahoma graduate school of social work on a non-segregated basis early in 1949.[6] The Oklahoma 1949 legislature also amended its educational laws to provide for the admission of Negro students on a segregated basis to institutions of higher learning where the programs of instruction sought are not available at the separate schools provided for Negroes.[6a]

In an opinion dated April 27, 1949, Judge H. Church Forde of the United States District Court, Eastern District, Kentucky, ruled that qualified Negroes are entitled to be admitted to the graduate schools of the University of Kentucky until such time as the Commonwealth of Kentucky provides and makes available substantially equal professional training for qualified Negroes at a separate institution located within the state. *Johnson v. Board of Trustees of the University of Kentucky,* 83 F. Supp. 707 (1949). On June 17, 1949, Dr. H. L. Donovan of that institution announced that

---

[4a]Associated Press, Jan. 31, 1948; New York Herald Tribune, February 1, 1948.

[4b]United Press, February 26, 1948; New York Herald Tribune, February 27, 1948.

[4c]Associated Press, August 24, 1948; New York Post Home News, August 24, 1948.

[5]Kentucky Rev. Stats. §158.025; Laws 1948, c. 112; effective June 17, 1948.

[6]Afro American, February 2, 1949.

[6a]See Okla. Laws 1949, ch. 15, p. 609, H.B. 405, appvd. June 9, 1949, amending Okla. Stats. 1941, Sections 455, 456, 457.

Negroes would be permitted to attend classes with whites, but intimated that maximum segregation would be maintained wherever possible.[6b] On June 21, 1949, the Dean and Registrar of the University of Kentucky announced that 12 qualified Negroes had been enrolled in summer classes for subjects necessary to obtain higher degrees.[6c] Mr. Saveth reports, "The professional divisions of engineering, law, pharmacy, commerce and agriculture at the University of Kentucky are also open to qualified Negro applicants, on the same terms as to white students."[7]

The University of Texas is reported to have admitted a Negro applicant to its School of Medicine at Galveston in September, 1949, on a "temporary" basis until such time as a separate medical school is constructed for Negroes. It was announced that the medical degree would be conferred upon the Negro applicant by the Texas State University for Negroes.[8] Recent indications are that the University of Florida may admit Negroes.

For some time the University of West Virginia has quietly enrolled Negro students in its graduate school and in some undergraduate departments.[8a] Furthermore, a few private colleges and universities in the District of Columbia, Missouri, North Carolina and Virginia have admitted Negroes in recent years.[8b] Thus, it would appear that in at least eleven Southern and border jurisdictions — Arkansas, Delaware, District of Columbia, Kentucky, Maryland, Missouri, North Carolina, Oklahoma, Texas, Virginia and West Virginia — Negroes have made limited inroads upon the rigid barriers of segregation in higher education and are attending white institutions without difficulty.

Two recent surveys conducted among faculty members of Southern colleges and universities indicate that there is considerable favorable opinion for nonsegregation in graduate education. One survey among faculty members of eleven Southern State universities showed that 69 per cent favored opening the graduate schools to Negroes without segregation.[9] In seven of the universities — Arkansas, Florida, North Carolina, Oklahoma, Tennessee, Texas and Virginia — a majority of the faculty was in favor of the elimination of segregation in graduate and professional schools. The faculty of the University of Alabama divided evenly on this issue. In only three of the eleven state institutions — Georgia, Mississippi and South Carolina — did a majority of the faculty members favor the continuation of segregation through the establishment of regional schools for Negroes.[10]

The second survey was conducted among the teachers and professors of 155 institutions of higher learning in the Southern and border states.[11] With the excep-

[6b]Associated Press, June 17, 1949, New York Post Home News, June 17, 1949.

[6c]United Press, June 21, 1949; N.Y. Times, June 22, 1949.

[7]Survey Graphic, September 1949, p. 477.

[8]Pittsburgh Courier, September 3, 1949.

[8a]Journal of Negro Education, Vol. 19, No. 1, Winter 1950, p. 4.

[8b]Ibid., p. 5.

[9]See report of Southern Educational Fund cited in article by Harry Lesesne, New York Herald Tribune, January 3, 1949, "Regional Education in Dixie."

[10]Survey Graphic, September 1949, p. 480.

[11]"Current Trends and Events of National Importance in Negro Education, Vol. 19, No. 1, Winter 1950, p. 118," and report entitled "Attitudes of Southern University Professors Toward the Elimination of Segregation in Graduate and Professional Schools in the South," by James A. Dombrowski, discussed therein.

tion of the University of West Virginia, no state universities were included. 15,000 instructors were circularized and 3,422 answers were received. Only 288 answers came from teachers in Negro colleges. The survey showed that 70.5 per cent of those answering favored the opening of existing graduate institutions, although 596 of those who took this point of view conditioned it upon situations where there are no presently available facilities for Negro graduate students. 3 per cent, or 88, favored opening the existing graduate schools to Negroes on a segregated basis, while 2 per cent, or 80, favored new graduate schools for Negroes. 842 professors or 24.5 per cent of those who answered, voted in favor of setting up regional segregated schools for Negroes.[12]

Student opinion in Southern state universities also indicates growing approval of the admission of Negro students without segregation to the existing institutions. A poll of 1,461 graduate students of the University of North Carolina showed that two-thirds of these students were in favor of the admission of Negro students to that institution.[12a] During the litigation surrounding the *Sweatt* case, a poll of students of the University of Texas revealed that a majority either favored Sweatt's admission to the University or were indifferent to his presence.[12b] The students of the University of Missouri voted, 4,156 to 1,847 in favor of a proposal to change the state laws to permit the enrollment of qualified Negro students to that institution.[12c]

In addition to this climate of changing opinion, the President's Committee on Civil Rights and the President's Commission on Higher Education have recommended the elimination of segregation.[13]

Mr. Savath's argument that the Southern Regional Education Program is intended by its sponsors to bolster segregation in education received additional support when the validity of the Regional Compact was questioned in the Maryland courts. Six students of Baltimore, Maryland, have begun mandamus actions to compel their admission into the University of Maryland in the fields of nursing, dentistry, engineering and home economics.[14] Although the University of Maryland Law School admits Negroes without difficulty, that institution has refused to enroll Negroes in other departments. The action of Esther McCready, Negro applicant to the University of Maryland School of

---

[12]Ibid.

[12a]Savath, "Jim Crow and the Regional Plan", Survey Graphic, September 1949, p. 480.

[12b]Ibid.

[12c]Ibid.

[13]"The separate but equal doctrine has failed in three important aspects. First, it is inconsistent with the equalitarianism of the American way of life in that it marks groups with the brand of inferior status. Secondly, where it has been followed, the results have been separate and unequal facilities for minority peoples. Finally, it has kept people apart despite incontrovertible evidence that an environment favorable to civil rights is fostered whenever groups are permitted to live and work together. There is no adequate defense of segregation." *To Secure These Rights*, The Report of the President's Committee on Civil Rights, (1947), p. 166.

"Another expedient which has received consideration is the establishment of regional centers of study, attached to strong colleges and open to both white and Negro students, with broad curricular offerings and high standards of scholarship and research. This fails to meet the legal issue of providing equality of educational opportunity within each State, but it has the immediate practical merit that it would be economically feasible and be conducive to a more nonsegregated approach to regional educational problems." *Higher Education for Democracy*, Equalizing and Expanding Individual Opportunity, Vol. II, p. 36, A Report of the President's Commission on Higher Education.

[14]New York Times, August 27, 1949.

Nursing after she had rejected an exchange scholarship to Meharry College under Maryland's Regional Compact, was dismissed by the Baltimore Superior Court after hearing on October 10, 1949.[15] Similar actions brought by Donald W. Stewart, Richard Williams and Richard Tyson are pending before the Maryland courts.[16] Undoubtedly these cases will be appealed to the federal courts.

The issue of segregation in regional education is bound up in the issue of segregation *per se*. At present two cases are pending before the United Supreme Court in which the basic question is whether segregation is discrimination *per se*. In *Sweatt v. Painter*,[17] Herman Marion Sweatt has appealed from a Texas state court decision that the refusal of the University of Texas Law School to admit him does not deny equal protection of the laws. Sweatt was refused admission to the University of Texas Law School on the ground that the state had provided adequate and equal facilities at a separate law school for Negroes. In *McLaurin v. Board of Regents of University of Oklahoma*,[18] a Negro graduate student has appealed from a decision of a federal district court dismissing his action to compel his admission to the State University on a nonsegregated basis, to enjoin the Oklahoma statutes making it a misdemeanor to maintain schools for both white and colored races,[19] and to enjoin the enforcement of an order of the Regents permitting him to register under such rules of segregation as to require him to participate in classes through an open doorway, maintaining a special segregation from other students.

In both of these cases the Supreme Court will be called upon to reconsider the doctrine of "separate but equal" facilities enunciated in the case of *Plessy v. Ferguson*, 163 U.S. 537 (1896). Should the court overrule the *Plessy* case, it would seem clear that segregated regional education would also be unconstitutional. Certainly, under the *Gaines* case, supra., it would appear that regional education which establishes a pattern of out-of-state segregated education does not meet constitutional requirements.

NOTE *

Since this note was written in January, 1950, a number of significant events have occurred which have changed considerably the picture as described in the note and which will hasten the trend toward nonsegregated education on graduate and professional levels in Southern state-supported universities.

On June 5, 1950, the United States Supreme Court unanimously decided the Sweatt *and* McLaurin *cases discussed* supra. *The Court held that the equal protec-*

[15]New York Times, October 10, 1949.

[16]New York Times, August 27, 1949.

[17]U.S. Supreme Court Docket, October 1948 Term No. 667, Filed March 23, 1949, on appeal from 210 S.W. 2nd. 442, (1948).

[18]U.S. Supreme Court Docket, October 1948 Term No. 614, Filed March 1, 1949, on appeal from U.S. District Court, W.D. Oklahoma, decision of November 22, 1948.

[19]70 Oklahoma Revised Statutes, 1941, Sections 455, 456, 457.

tion clause of the Fourteenth Amendment required that Herman Marion Sweatt be admitted to the University of Texas Law School, since the separate school for Negroes did not provide equal facilities. In the McLaurin case, the Court ruled that G. W. McLaurin, having been admitted to the University of Oklahoma graduate school, must receive the same treatment at the hands of the state as students of other races. The McLaurin decision thus invalidated segregation at the University of Oklahoma. [See Appendix 7, infra, for complete texts of the Sweatt and McLaurin decisions.]

The Supreme Court refused to affirm or overrule the decision of Plessy v. Ferguson, 163 U.S. 537 (1896), which held that separate but equal facilities for Negroes were valid under the Thirteenth and Fourteenth Amendments. The issue of segregation per se is left often. Nevertheless, it seems clear that these two decisions together with the Henderson decision decided on the same day, have struck a severe blow to legally enforced racial segregation.

The following developments took place during the first eight months of 1950 in the seventeen Southern states with reference to equal educational facilities:

Alabama: — The Alabama State Supreme Court rejected the petition of four Negro lawyers seeking to be licensed without taking the state bar examination. The petitioners contended that since they were barred from attending the state-supported law school, they were entitled to be admitted to practice by diploma courtesy in the same manner as white students graduating from the Alabama state law school. [Pittsburgh Courier, July 8, 1950.]

Arkansas: — Negroes have been admitted to the graduate schools of law and medicine since 1948.

Delaware: — On August 9, 1950, the Delaware Court of Chancery ruled that the University of Delaware must admit Negro citizens of Delaware to that institution on the same basis as white students because the educational facilities at Delaware State College for Negroes were "grossly inadequate." The court's opinion did not consider the question of segregation. [Associated Press, August 9, 1950; New York Times, August 10, 1950.]

Florida: — The Florida Supreme Court ruled in August, 1950, that Negroes must be admitted to the University of Florida and other state colleges for white students on a temporary basis until courses not now available can be established at Florida A. and M. College for Negroes. The court withheld a final order until the Board of Control gives evidence of furnishing or of having failed to furnish the constitutionally required equal educational facilities as set forth in the Gaines, Sweatt and McLaurin decisions. [Pittsburgh Courier, August 12, 1950.]

Georgia: Two suits demanding equal facilities in the public schools are reported to be pending. [Herald Tribune, June 7, 1950.] No suit involving a demand for admission into the existing graduate and professional schools has been reported. Georgia Democratic leaders, however, allegedly have expressed an intention to defy the recent Supreme Court rulings. [Associated Press, August 9, 1950; New York Times, August 10, 1950.]

Kentucky: — The Kentucky legislature enacted a new state law effective June 15, 1950, which permits Boards and Trustees of public and private educational institutions in that

state to admit Negro students for courses not available at existing institutions for Negroes.
[*1950 S.B. 100.*] *Kentucky also approved the Regional Compact, but provided that in
its participation in the regional plan, "the Commonwealth of Kentucky shall not erect,
acquire, develop or maintain in any manner any educational institution within its borders
to which Negroes will not be admitted on an equal basis with other races, nor shall any
Negro citizen of Kentucky be forced to attend any segregated institution to obtain instruction in a particular course of study if there is in operation within the Commonwealth at
the time an institution that offers the same course of study to students of other races."*
[*1950, S.R. No. 53, appvd. March 25, 1950; 1950, S.R. No. 62, eff. June 15, 1950.*]

*Since the enactment of the new state law, the University of Louisville has announced
that Negroes will be admitted to all graduate divisions during the 1950-51 school year and
to undergraduate schools the following year. The Louisville Municipal College, Negro
adjunct of the University of Louisville, will be closed after the 1950-51 school year. Ten
Negroes are reported to be enrolled in graduate departments in the University of Kentucky
and one in the undergraduate school. In the area of private colleges, Berea College has
established a policy under which Negro students will be admitted to both graduate and
undergraduate courses, and three Catholic colleges — Nazareth, Ursuline and Bellarmine
— have opened their doors to Negroes.* [**Report,** *American Council on Race Relations,
May, 1950, p. 3.*]

Louisiana: — *Four suits are pending in Louisiana in which Negroes demand equal
facilities in the public schools.* [*Associated Press, June 6, 1950. New York Herald
Tribune, June 7, 1950.*] *The application of a Negro for admission to the University
of Louisiana was rejected on July 28, 1950, and a court test is expected in that state.*
[*Associated Press, July 28, 1950; New York Times, July 29, 1950.*]

Maryland: — *Maryland's Court of Appeals has directed the University of Maryland
to admit Esther McCready, a young Negro woman, to its School of Nursing. Reversing
a lower court decision, the Court of Appeals ruled that Maryland could not deny an
applicant admission to a state institution solely because of race and held unlawful
Maryland's use of the regional compact to enforce Negro segregation. The University
of Maryland had rejected Miss McCready's application for admission following her
refusal to accept a scholarship to Meharry Medical College, Nashville, Tennessee,
under the regional plan approved by the Maryland legislature.* [*New York Times,
April 15, 1950.*] *The University of Maryland has announced its intention to appeal
the case to the United States Supreme Court.* [*Pittsburgh Courier, June 24, 1950.*]
*A suit brought by Parran J. Mitchell, a Negro of Baltimore, to compel the University
of Maryland to admit him to its graduate school to pursue courses leading to a Master's
degree in sociology, was filed in the Baltimore City Court in August, 1950.* [*Afro-
American, August 19, 1950.*]

*A spokesman for the Southern Regional Board which administers the Southern
Regional Education Program, has made it clear that the Board does not wish to be
involved in controversies with reference to racial policies. Dr. John E. Ivey, Jr.,
director of the Board, declared recently, "We are serving States which have relaxed
their segregation laws and those which are rigid about it. We feel that segregation
is a State issue and that the regional Compact should not be used as an instrument
to abolish or extend segregation."* [*Afro-American, June 17, 1950, p.3.*]

Mississippi: — *A suit brought on behalf of Negro teachers demanding equal salary scales where training, experience and responsibilities are similar to those of white teachers is now pending before a Federal District Court.* ["American Rights for American Citizens," Annual NAACP Report, 1949, p. 29.]

Missouri: — *Following a Missouri Circuit Court order of June 25, 1950, to admit qualified Negro students, the University of Missouri voted unanimously to admit Negro students to the five state-supported colleges of that institution.* [Afro-American. July 22, 1950.]

North Carolina: — *Three suits are pending in the United States Middle District Court involving equal facilities in the public schools.* [New York Herald Tribune, June 7, 1950.] *A suit has also been brought by two Negro students, Harold Epps and David Glass, who seek admission to University of North Carolina's School of Law. The plaintiffs contend that the separate law school facilities provided at the North Carolina College at Durham* [for Negroes] *are not equal to those at the University of North Carolina.* ["American Rights for American Citizens," Annual NAACP Report, 1949, p. 32.]

Oklahoma: — *The McLaurin decision has already been discussed, supra. In June, 1950, three Negro students were awarded graduate degrees by the University of Oklahoma. The three graduates were among twenty-five Negroes who have been enrolled at that institution following the United States ruling in the Sipuel case in 1948. Presumably, these students are attending courses on a nonsegregated basis.* [Pittsburgh Courier, June 17, 1950.]

South Carolina: — *A suit against the Trustees of School District No. 22 of Clarendon County, charging that unequal facilities are being provided for Negro school children of grammar school and high school level, is now pending before the United States District Court.* [Carolina Times, June 25, 1950, p. 1.]

Tennessee: — *No test cases with reference to admission of Negroes to graduate and professional institutions have been reported recently. State educators and officials have indicated, however, that under the recent Supreme Court decisions, the University of Tennessee could be compelled to admit Negroes to the graduate and professional departments.* [Pittsburgh Courier, June 17, 1950.]

Texas: — *Immediately following the Sweatt decision discussed supra, the University of Texas announced the enrollment of two Negro students. Mr. Sweatt has stated that he would enroll in the University of Texas School of Law in September, 1950.* [New York Times, June 9, 1950.]

Virginia: — *The 1950 legislature approved the Regional Compact, conditional upon an amendment to the Virginia Constitution to remove any existing limitations which prohibit full participation by the Commonwealth in the regional plan.* [Acts 1950, p. 1648; S.J.R. No. 22.]

In July, 1950, the University of Virginia rejected the application of Gregory Swanson, a Negro seeking admission to its School of Law, in spite of a warning by

State Attorney General J. Lindsay Almond Jr., that the action would not be upheld in a Federal Court. [*Pittsburgh Courier*, July 22, 1950, p. 5] Mr. Swanson has filed suit in the United States District Court for the Western District of Virginia, to compel his admission to the University of Virginia. [*Afro-American*, August 19, 1950, p. 6.]

West Virginia: — For some time the University of West Virginia has enrolled Negroes in its graduate schools. No new developments have been reported.

In conclusion, it would appear that sixteen Southern states have approved the Regional Compact. In two of these states, Kentucky and Maryland, the issue of segregation in regional education has been raised. Kentucky has decided the question by a state law prohibiting the use of the regional compact to compel Negro citizens to attend segregated regional institutions within or without the state. Maryland has been ordered by its highest court to refrain from using the regional plan to enforce Negro segregation. In view of this trend and in view of the United States Supreme Court's recent decisions, it seems quite probable that attempts of Southern states to bolster segregation in institutions of higher learning through the device of regional education will be invalidated by that Court.

IN THE SUPREME COURT OF THE UNITED STATES

ON APPEAL FROM THE UNITED STATES DISTRICT COURT FOR THE DISTRICT OF MARYLAND

BRIEF FOR THE UNITED STATES

APPENDIX 7.

THE LEGAL CASE AGAINST SEGREGATION

[NOTE: On June 5, 1950, the United States Supreme Court handed down unanimous decisions in the historic *Henderson*, *Sweatt* and *McLaurin* cases. These cases involved segregation in interstate transportation and higher education. The United States Government filed an exhaustive brief on behalf of the plaintiff in the *Henderson* case in which it urged the Court to re-examine and overrule the doctrine of "separate but equal" facilities as contained in the case of *Plessy v. Ferguson*, 163 U.S. 537, decided by that Court in 1896.

Although the Supreme Court did not expressly overrule the *Plessy* case, the effect of the three decisions is to deliver a decisive blow against legally enforced segregation. In view of the excellence of the Government's brief and the importance of the issue of segregation, excerpts from the brief and the complete text of the Court's decisions are set forth below.]

IN THE SUPREME COURT OF THE UNITED STATES

OCTOBER TERM, 1949

No. 25

ELMER W. HENDERSON, APPELLANT

v.

THE UNITED STATES OF AMERICA, INTERSTATE COMMERCE COMMISSION AND SOUTHERN RAILWAY COMPANY

ON APPEAL FROM THE UNITED STATES DISTRICT COURT FOR THE DISTRICT OF MARYLAND

BRIEF FOR THE UNITED STATES

* * * *

SUMMARY OF ARGUMENT

The order of the Interstate Commerce Commission approving the dining car regulations involved in this case is invalid on constitutional and statutory grounds. Both the Constitution and the Interstate Commerce Act give all persons traveling on interstate carriers the right to equal treatment, without being subject to governmentally-enforced discriminations based on race or color. Contrary to the holding below, the obligation of carriers to provide equality of treatment means equality as between individuals and not as between racial groups. The regulations are clearly unlawful in that they permit discrimination against individual passengers, white as well as colored, in situations where available accommodations are denied solely on grounds of race or color. Beyond that, however, the Commission's order is invalid because it attempts to place the sanction of law upon a system of compulsory racial segregation which denies colored passengers the equality of treatment to which they are entitled under the Constitution and the Interstate Commerce Act. This case does not involve segregation by private individuals. The decisive factor here is that the segregation regulations bear the approval of an agency of government.

Segregation as enforced by the regulations imports the inferiority of the Negro race. Enforced racial segregation in itself constitutes a denial of the right to equal treatment. Equal treatment means the same treatment. The issues before the Court in this case are not governed by the so-called "separate but equal" doctrine of *Plessy* v. *Ferguson,* 163 U. S. 537, and related cases. Even assuming, *arguendo,* that that doctrine retains some vitality for constitutional purposes, it does not establish the validity, under Section 3 of the Interstate Commerce Act, of the railroad's regulations. But if the Court should conclude that the issues here cannot be decided without reference to the "separate but equal" doctrine, the Government submits that the legal and factual assumptions upon which *Plessy* v. *Ferguson* was decided have been demonstrated to be erroneous, and that the doctrine of that case should now be re-examined and overruled. The notion that separate but equal facilities satisfy constitutional and statutory prohibitions against discrimination is obsolete. The phrase "equal rights" means the same rights.

* * * *

III

THE REGULATIONS ARE UNLAWFUL BECAUSE THEY COMPEL PASSENGERS TO BE SEGREGATED ACCORDING TO THEIR COLOR; SUCH ENFORCED RACIAL SEGREGATION, HAVING THE SANCTION OF AN AGENCY OF GOVERNMENT, DENIES COLORED PASSENGERS THE EQUALITY OF TREATMENT WHICH IS THEIR RIGHT UNDER THE LAW

In Point II, *supra,* we have argued that the dining car regulations here involved are unlawful because they permit discrimination against an individual passenger, whether white or colored, in a situation where an available seat is denied him simply because it is reserved for a person of another race. We agree with Judge Soper, dissenting below, that the regulations as applied in such a situation clearly contravene the requirements of Section 3 of the Interstate Commerce Act. But a fundamental infirmity inheres in these regulations which goes much deeper and requires their invalidation for all purposes. The regulations, which carry the endorsement of an agency of government, compel colored passengers to be segregated from other passengers solely because of their color. Such legally-enforced racial segregation in and of itself constitutes a discrimination and inequality of treatment prohibited by the Constitution and the Interstate Commerce Act.

A. *Racial segregation under compulsion of law is not equality*

Since these regulations bear the imprimatur of the Interstate Commerce Commission, they in effect lay down a rule of law that when a man travels on an interstate railroad, the color of his skin shall dictate where and with whom he is permitted to dine, no matter what his own desires may be. This case does not involve segregation by private individuals. These regulations establish a system of racial segregation enforced by and having the sanction of law. Cf. *Harmon* v. *Tyler,* 273 U. S. 668. The regulations

677

do not merely permit voluntary segregation in the sense that they allow a passenger, if his prejudices so require, to refuse to eat at the same table or even in the same car with a passenger of another color. They go much further: a white passenger who has no prejudice against Negroes, or indeed, one who affirmatively desires the company of a colored person or persons, is forbidden by the regulations to have company of his own choice. The regulations compel such a passenger to yield to the prejudices of others. Under the regulations here involved, persons traveling together, if they are of different color, cannot eat together regardless of their personal desires. Even if he so wishes, a white passenger is forbidden to sit at a colored table. In other words, the regulations do not merely carry out the prejudices of some members of the community; they compel everybody else to abide by such prejudices.

We do not argue that individuals do not, or should not have a legal privilege to exercise a personal preference against eating at the same table, or in the same section of the dining car, with Negroes. If the regulations are declared unlawful, that individual privilege would remain unimpaired. A passenger who prefers to forego or postpone a meal rather than take it while a person of another color is being served in the same car would be free to do so. A passenger who objects to dining at the same table with a person of another color would be free to decline a seat proffered at a table where such a person is being served. The decisive point here, however, is that it is one thing to permit an individual to act on his personal prejudices; it is something entirely different for the law to force such prejudices upon everyone else.

In *Plessy* v. *Ferguson,* 163 U. S. 537, the first case holding that segregation does not violate the equal protection clause of the Fourteenth Amendment, the Court expressed the view that the alternative to segregation is "an enforced commingling" of the white and colored races. This observation, as we shall argue in a later section of this brief, was irrelevant to the constitutional issue before the Court. In determining the validity of legislation alleged to involve an invidious racial discrimination, the inquiry is not whether the enactment will eradicate racial prejudice or solve problems of racial antagonism; the issue is simply whether it enforces, supports, or otherwise contributes to the denial of a constitutionally-protected right. But, in any event, the Court's dictum rests on an obviously false premise. If "Commingling" between white and colored persons comes about as a consequence of nullifying segregation ordinances or regulations, such commingling is not "enforced" by the law. It is the result of voluntary conduct of the individuals concerned, acting not under the coercion of the law but in response to their own desires.

The alternative to compulsory segregation, therefore, is *not* an "enforced" commingling of the races. With non-segregated service, the individual passenger is free to avoid any "commingling" which he considers objectionable. Some individuals may object to eating in the same car with a Negro. Others will "draw the line" at eating at the same table with a Negro. Still others will feel that it makes no difference what the color of their fellow-passengers may be. Whatever the individual's personal preferences or code of social behavior, no departure from it is "enforced" by anything except his own will.

It must be remembered, of course, that one who goes to a public place or rides in a public conveyance necessarily surrenders some freedom of choice as to those with whom he will mingle. What was said in *Ferguson* v. *Gies,* 82 Mich. 358, 367-368, deserves repetition:

The man who goes either by himself or with his family to a public place must expect to meet and mingle with all classes of people. He cannot ask, to suit his caprice or prejudice or social views, that this or that man shall be excluded because he does not wish to associate with them. He may draw his social line as closely as he chooses at home, or in other private places, but he cannot in a public place carry the privacy of his home with him, or ask that people not as good or great as he is shall step aside when he appears.

B. Segregation imports, and is designed to import, the inferiority of the Negro race

Segregation of Negroes, as practiced in this country, is universally understood as imposing on them a badge of inferiority.[16] It "brands the Negro with the mark of inferiority and asserts that he is not fit to associate with white people".[17] Forbidding this group of American citizens "to associate with other citizens in the ordinary course of daily living creates inequality by imposing a caste status on the minority group."[18]

More than fifty years of subsequent history confirm and give new emphasis to the views expressed by Mr. Justice Harlan in his dissent in Plessy v. Ferguson, 163 U. S. 537, 562. He declared that the "arbitrary separation" of members of the Negro race when traveling in a public conveyance "is a badge of servitude." He further said (p. 560):

What can more certainly arouse race hate, what more certainly create and perpetuate a feeling of distrust between these races, than state enactments, which, in fact, proceed on the ground that colored citizens are so inferior and degraded that they cannot be allowed to sit in public coaches occupied by white citizens? That, as all will admit, is the real meaning of such legislation as was enacted in Louisiana.

That the type of segregation imposed by the railroad's regulations is humiliating to those subjected to it is so obvious as scarcely to need documentation. Myrdal has noted that "the Jim Crow car is resented more bitterly among Negroes than most other forms of segregation."[19] Johnson has described the trend among Negroes towards travel by automobile which "is considered worth the extra cost" because of "the emotional satisfaction derived from escaping humiliating treatment."[20] Dollard has indicated that the Negro understands this type of segregation as marking him off as inferior, "of not being worthy to participate fully in American social life."[21] See also appellant's brief in the instant case, Appendix, pp. 94-106.

One who is compelled to live in a ghetto, because of his color or creed, does not enjoy "equality", no matter how luxurious his abode. Cf. Shelley v. Kraemer, 334 U. S. 1, and Hurd v. Hodge, 334 U. S. 24. The same principle applies here. A colored passenger who is set apart in a corner by himself is in no real sense being treated as an equal. The curtain or partition which fences Negroes off from all other diners exposes, naked and unadorned, the caste system which segregation manifests and fosters. A

---

[16]Myrdal, An American Dilemma, vol. I, pp. 615, 640; Johnson, Patterns of Negro Segregation, p. 3; Fraenkel, Our Civil Liberties, p. 201; Dollard, Caste and Class in a Southern Town, pp. 349-351; Note, 56 Yale L. J. 1059, 1060; Note, 49 Columbia L. Rev. 629, 634; Note, 39 Columbia L. Rev. 986, 1003.
[17]To Secure These Rights, Report of the President's Committee on Civil Rights, 79.
[18]Id., 82.
[19]Myrdal, An American Dilemma, vol. 1, p. 635.
[20]Johnson, Patterns of Negro Segregation, 270.
[21]Dollard, Caste and Class in a Southern Town, 350. See also Stouffer, et al., Studies in Social Psychology in World War II, The American Soldier, vol. I, p. 561.

Negro can obtain service only by accepting or appearing to accept, under the very eyes of his fellow passengers, white and colored, the caste status which the segregation signifies and is intended to signify.

The effect of the railroad's regulations and practice emphasizes that their single purpose is to foster maintenance of a caste system. One side of the segregated table adjoins the side of the car. Of the other three sides, the curtain shuts off only one. The table is exposed to the view of those passing in the aisle, to those sitting at the table immediately across the aisle,"[22] and to some extent to those sitting at other tables. One sociologist has commented that the table is "exposed only enough to indicate the intent to segregate."[23] Another commentator has described this type of separation as "merely a symbolic assertion of social superiority, a 'ceremonial' separation."[24]

Concerning the five-foot high wooden partition which the railroad proposed to erect as a substitute for the curtain, the remarks of Judge Soper in the course of the argument in the court below are pertinent and illuminating (R. 38):

> Why do you put up these absurd partitions? They don't conceal anything they simply call attention of the white passengers to the fact that the colored person is dining there. It seems to me that it is just unnecessary humiliation.

Counsel for the railroad answered the question as to the reason for the partition by saying: "Simply to separate the two races." (R. 39.) He added that "it satisfies the white people, and it certainly is much *less offensive* to the negroes" (*ibid.*, italics supplied).

Section 3 of the Interstate Commerce Act forbids "undue or unreasonable prejudice or disadvantage in any respect whatsoever." The prohibition applies to "any discriminatory action or practice of interstate carriers" which Congress had "authority to reach." *Mitchell* case, p. 94. Under the broad and inclusive language of the section, the "substantial equality of treatment" which it requires (*id.*, p. 97) is plainly not confined to the physical elements of dining car service, such as food, tableware, etc. Manifestly, colored passengers would be discriminated against if the railroad's rules required its waiters to say, when serving them: "Don't think, because we have to serve you, that we believe you're as good as whites." The wrong would be compounded if a loud-speaking device carried these words to every diner in the car. But in substance, although the form may have been less offensive, these were the conditions under which the railroad furnished dining car service to colored passengers.

If ex-convicts were given dining car service only at a table barred off from others, but open to view, and carrying a card, "Reserved for Ex-Convicts," we have no doubt that the courts would be quick to recognize the gross inequality of treatment. To make this analogy fit the facts of the present case, the traveling public would have to be

---

[22]When the change to a wooden partition is made, the space across the aisle will be occupied by the dining car steward rather than by white passengers (*supra*, p. 8).

[23]Johnson, *Patterns of Negro Segregation*, p. 321.

[24]McGovney, *Racial Residential Segregation by State Court Enforcement of Restrictive Agreements, Covenants or Conditions in Deeds Is Unconstitutional*, 33 Calif. L. Rev. 5, 27 at n. 94.

The Railroad's dining car steward testified that the curtain hangs on hooks on a rod and if it is not properly hooked up and gets only half drawn he "has done the technical thing" and will not take the trouble to draw the curtain fully (R. 160).

informed that not only were ex-convicts thus segregated but also all descendants of ex-convicts, to the third or fourth generation.[25]

The colored passenger, paying the same price for his meal as other passengers, does not receive the same thing in return. True, he receives the same food, but the condition which is attached to receiving it is that he submit to having his mind bombarded with the message that he and all members of his race are classified as inferior, as constituting a lower social caste.[26] This message of humiliation comes, not as a single voice, but with all the reverberations of the entire pattern of segregation and discrimination of which it is a part. And that is not a matter of small consequence. The segregation which isolates the Negro from others in the community and marks him as ostracized, a kind of "untouchable," gravely affects his personality and causes serious psychological difficulties and disturbances (infra pp. 50-54).

The Negro is plagued by the concept — evidence of which he constantly sees around him in his daily life — that he and his people are regarded as inferior.[27] It remains one of the most devastating frustrations of his life. Under its impact, he does not dare to be a person of his own distinct uniqueness and individuality.[28] The persistent effort of Negro leaders to develop attitudes aimed at maintaining the human dignity of the Negro tells its own story.[29]

It is bad enough for the Negro to have to endure the insults of individuals who look upon him as inferior. It is far worse to have to submit to a formalized or institutionalized enforcement of this concept, particularly when, as in this case, it carries the sanction of an agency of government and thus appears to have the seal of approval of the community at large. Such enforced racial segregation in and of itself consti-

---

[25]For the varying statutory and judicial definitions of "Negro" or "colored," see Morgan v. Virginia, 328 U. S. 373, 382-383; Mangum, The Legal Status of the Negro, ch. I; Note, 34 Cornell Law Quar. 246, 247-251; Note, 58 Yale L. J. 472, 480-481.

"Without any doubt there is also in the white man's concept of the Negro 'race' an irrational element which cannot be grasped in terms of either biological or cultural differences. It is like the concept 'unclean' in primitive religion. It is invoked by the metaphor 'blood' when describing ancestry. * * * The one who has got the smallest drop of 'Negro blood' is as one who is smitten by a hideous disease. It does not help if he is good and honest, educated and intelligent, a good worker, an excellent citizen and an agreeable fellow. Inside him are hidden some unknown and dangerous potentialities, something which will sooner or later crop up. This totally irrational, actually magical, belief is implied in the system of specific taboos * * *." Myrdal, An American Dilemma, vol. 1, p. 100

[26]"The fact that accommodations are identical in physical comfort does not make them really equal, since there is a social stigma attached to the position of the minority. To say that, since neither group can use the facilities reserved for the other, they are in an equal position is unrealistic; members of the minority know only too well the reasons for the segregation and are humiliated by it." Note, 39 Col. L. Rev. 986, 1003.

[27]"The word 'segregation' itself has come to represent to Negroes a crucial symbol of white attitudes of superiority." Stouffer, et al., Studies in Social Psychology in World War II, The American Soldier, vol. I, p. 566.

[28]Cooper, The Frustrations of Being a Member of a Minority Group: What Does It Do to The Individual and To His Relationships With Other People?, 29 Mental Hygiene 189, 190-191.

[29]"The pledge to myself which I have endeavored to keep through the greater part of my life is:
"I will not allow one prejudiced person or one million or one hundred million to blight my life. I will not let prejudice or any of its attendant humiliations and injustices bear me down to spiritual defeat. My inner life is mine, and I shall defend and maintain its integrity against all the powers of hell."
James Weldon Johnson, Negro Americans, What Now?, p. 103. See also Washington, The Future of the American Negro, p. 26.

tutes inequality.[30] In this situation the phrase "separate but equal" is a plain contradiction in terms.

C. The "separate but equal" doctrine does not control the issues before the Court in this case but that doctrine, if it be deemed applicable here, should be reexamined and discarded.

The segregated basis on which the railroad furnished dining car service to colored passengers clearly constituted inequality of treatment condemned by Section 3 of the Interstate Commerce Act, unless it is to be interpreted as requiring only the trappings, not the substance, of equality. Such a narrow construction could not easily be squared with the "sweeping prohibitions" of the Act. *Mitchell* case, 313 U. S. at p. 94.[81] The court below has held, however, that the enforced segregation of Negro passengers in railroad dining cars is not a denial of their right to equal accommodations, and in support of this holding has relied on several decisions of this Court regarded as establishing the rule that "separate but equal" facilities satisfy the requirements of the law. It is submitted, however, that (1) the authorities relied on do not control the issues presented by this case, and that (2) if the so-called "separate but equal" doctrine be deemed applicable here, it should be reexamined and overruled.

(1) *Hall* v. *DeCuir*, 95 U. S. 485, the earliest of the cases cited in support of the ruling below, held only that a state enactment infringes upon the federal commerce power when it regulates an interstate carrier with respect to separation or non-separation of white and colored passengers. This ruling obviously has no application to the issues here presented. Cf. *Morgan* v. *Virginia*, 328 U. S. 373. Similarly, *Chiles* v. *Chesapeake & Ohio Rwy. Co.*, 218 U. S. 71, merely held that when an interstate carrier provides separate cars or compartments for the exclusive use of white passengers and others for the exclusive use of colored passengers, it does not exceed the limits of its authority to establish reasonable regulations governing the transportation service which it performs. This was implicitly held in the *De Cuir* case, and the *Chiles* case was regarded as controlled by the earlier decision.[32] In the *Chiles* case the plaintiff did not at any stage of the proceeding rely upon any provision of the Interstate Commerce Act[33] and the briefs filed in this Court did not even mention Section 3 of the Act. The Court, in assuming that Congress had taken no action respecting segregation in interstate travel, referred to what was said and held on this point in the *De Cuir* case. See pp. 75-77. Since the Court's assumption as to nonaction by Congress was based on a

---

[30]"No argument or rationalization can alter this basic fact: a law which forbids a group of American citizens to associate with other citizens in the ordinary course of daily living *creates inequality* by imposing caste status on the minority group." [Italics supplied.] *To Secure These Rights*, Report of the President's Committee on Civil Rights, 82.

"The Court has never faced the reality that segregation necessarily implies inequality, for equals do not hesitate to mingle with each other in public places. Any traveler in lands where segregation is practiced, be it the South where the victim is the Negro, or Nazi Germany where it is the Jew, knows that segregation is a badge of one race's claim to superiority over the other." Fraenkel, *Our Civil Liberties*, p. 201.

[81]The prohibition of "any undue or unreasonable prejudice or disadvantage in any respect whatsoever" is certainly as broad as the prohibition of denial of "full and equal accommodations," the phrase generally used in state statutes prohibiting discrimination. This prohibition has been uniformly held to apply to segregation. See, e. g., *Jones* v. *Kehrlein*, 49 Cal. App. 646; *Ferguson* v. *Gies*, 82 Mich. 358, 363; *Joyner* v. *Moore-Wiggins Co.*, 136 N. Y. S. 578, affirmed without opinion, 211 N. Y. 522; *Anderson* v. *Pantages Theatre Co.*, 114 Wash. 24. See also Mangum, *The Legal Status of the Negro*, pp. 34-38; Note, 39 Col. L. Rev. 986, 1003. Cf. *Railroad Co.* v. *Brown*, 17 Wall. 445, 451-453.

case decided ten years before passage of the Interstate Commerce Act, and since it was made without giving any consideration to the anti-discrimination provisions of Section 3 of that Act, the decision cannot possibly be deemed a construction of the meaning or application of Section 3.

In *Mitchell* v. *United States*, 313 U. S. 80, the carrier had refused to give to the plaintiff, because of his race, any Pullman car accommodations. The case therefore presented, as this Court said (p. 94), "not a question of segregation but one of equality of treatment." To be sure, the Court's opinion appeared to agree with the view that the carrier's subsequent practice of furnishing a compartment to a colored passenger for the price of a Pullman seat "avoids inequality." See p. 96. This aspect of the decision is not however presently apposite. The type of segregation here involved is far more serious. When colored passengers are furnished dining car service only at a table partially screened off as a symbol and token of their separate and inferior status, the segregation is open, explicit, and humiliating.

Finally, reliance is placed most heavily on *Plessy* v. *Ferguson*, 163 U. S. 537, which ruled that state-enforced separation of white and colored persons under a statute requiring "equal" accommodations does not necessarily infringe the command of the Fourteenth Amendment that no State shall deny to any person the equal protection of the laws. We submit that, even assuming *arguendo* that the "separate but equal" doctrine retains some vitality for constitutional purposes, it does not establish the validity, under the Interstate Commerce Act, of the segregation enforced in the railroad's dining cars.

In the first place, the language of the statute provides a possible basis for distinction. The prohibition of Section 3, that no carrier shall subject any person to *"any undue or unreasonable prejudice or disadvantage in any respect whatsoever"*, is both precise and inclusive. This may conceivably be construed differently from the language of the "equal protection of the laws" clause of the Fourteenth Amendment, which has "a generality and adaptability * * * found to be desirable in constitutional provisions."[34]

In the second place, the statute and the constitutional provision differ in background and, to some extent, in purpose. In the *Plessy* case the Court gave as grounds for its ruling that the equal protection clause covers only "civil and political" rights and that enforced separation of the white and colored races does not infringe such rights. See 163 U. S. 537, at pp. 544, 551. As we have stated, we believe this holding to be erroneous. But, even if it be accepted, the same conclusion does not necessarily follow where the question is whether giving service to the members of a race under conditions which publicly stigmatize them as ostracized and inferior, when no such conditions attach to the service given others, is in conflict with the explicit statutory provision that no interstate carrier shall, in the course of the service which it renders, subject any person to "any undue or unreasonable prejudice or disadvantage in any respect whatsoever."

[32]Of the portion of the opinion in the *Chiles* case setting forth the grounds of decision (pp. 75-78), over two-thirds is devoted to a discussion of the *De Cuir* case and its application.

[33]The plaintiff had not filed a complaint with the Interstate Commerce Commission and therefore was probably barred from relying upon any claim of violation of the Interstate Commerce Act. If such a claim "necessarily involves a question of 'reasonableness,'" the Commission has "primary jurisdiction" and there can be no recovery in the absence of a ruling by the Commission on the question of violation. *United States* v. *Interstate Commerce Commission*, 337 U. S. 426, 437.

[34]See *Appalachian Coals, Inc.* v. *United States*, 288 U. S. 344, 360.

In the third place the present case comes within an exception to the "separate but equal" doctrine stated or plainly indicated in the *Plessy* opinion. The Court there said (p. 544) that laws requiring the separation of the white and colored races "do not *necessarily* imply the inferiority of either race to the other" (italics supplied). In other words if the separation required did imply the inferiority of one race, the accommodations would be "separate" but they would not be "equal." While the *Plessy* case held that enforced separation is not in and of itself inequality, it did not hold that, as a matter of law, similar but separate physical accommodations are always equal. And if the question is one of fact, the facts of the present case establish beyond all doubt that the segregation which is enforced here is the antithesis of equality (*supra*, pp. 28-34).

(2) If this Court should conclude that the issues presented by this case cannot be considered without reference to the "separate but equal" doctrine, the Government respectfully urges that, in the half-century which has elapsed since it was first promulgated, the legal and factual assumptions upon which that doctrine rests have been undermined and refuted. The "separate but equal" doctrine should now be overruled and discarded.

The decision in the *Plessy* case appears to rest on two major premises. One is that laws requiring separation of the white and colored races do not imply the inferiority of the colored race. The other is that segregation infringes only "social" rights and that these rights, as distinct from "civil" or "political" rights, are not within the ambit of the equal protection clause of the Fourteenth Amendment.

It is a question of fact what the community at large understands to be the meaning of singling out the members of the colored race for separation from all other citizens, whether it is in purchasing a bus ticket at the same ticket window, riding on the same street car or railroad coach, or going to the same restaurant, theatre or school. In the *Plessy* case the Court concluded that this minority race is not stigmatized as inferior, as constituting a lower social caste, when law decrees that it shall ride apart, eat apart, or stand in line for tickets apart. We submit that the Court's *a priori* conclusion cannot stand today in the face of a wealth of evidence flatly contradicting it.[35]

---

[35] In addition to the materials and authorities cited elsewhere in this brief, see Myrdal, *An American Dilemma*, 100, 628; Dollard, *Caste and Class in a Southern Town*, 62-63, 266; Heinrich, *The Psychology of a Suppressed People*, 57-61; Sutherland, *Color, Class, and Personality*, 42-59; Johnson, *Patterns of Negro Segregation*, 270; Bond, *Education of the Negro and the American Social Order*, 384; Moton, *What the Negro Thinks*, 12-13, 99; Bunche, *Education in Black and White*, 5 Journal of Negro Education 351; *To Secure These Rights*, *supra*, 79, 82; Fraenkel, *Our Civil Liberties*, 201.

See also McGovney, *Racial Residential Segregation by State Court Enforcement of Restrictive Agreements, Covenants or Conditions in Deeds is Unconstitutional*, 33 Calif. L. Rev. 5, 27, note, 94; Note, 39 Columbia L. Rev. 986, 1003; Note, 56 Yale L. J. 1059, 1060; Note, 49 Columbia L. Rev. 629, 634.

In *Collins* v. *Oklahoma State Hospital*, 76 Okla. 229, 231, the Court said: "In this state, where a reasonable regulation of the conduct of the races has led to the *establishment of separate schools and separate coaches*, and where conditions properly have erected insurmountable barriers between the races when viewed from a social and a personal standpoint, and where the habits, the disposition, and characteristics of the race *denominate the colored race as inferior* to the Caucasian, it is libelous per se to write of or concerning a white person that he is colored." [Italics supplied.]

In *Wolfe* v. *Georgia Railway & Electric Co.*, 2 Ga. App. 499, 505, the court said: "It is a

We likewise believe that there was error in the second premise of the "separate but equal" doctrine enunciated in the *Plessy* case, namely, that enforced separation of the races affects only "social" rights not within the purview of the Fourteenth Amendment. The Amendment strikes at inequality without qualification. Certainly its language furnishes no basis for the distinction which the Court drew between "social" rights and those which are "civil" or "political." Furthermore, the distinction drawn is, at best, nebulous and largely a matter of emphasis. "In reality it is not possible to isolate a sphere of life and call it 'social.' There is, in fact, a 'social' angle to all relations."[86]

It is one thing to define social equality in terms of integration into white social organizations; it is another to define as "social" the right to equality in the use and enjoyment of public facilities.[87] Travel is for business as well as for pleasure. This court has held that the Fourteenth Amendment requires "substantial equality of treatment" as to the facilities afforded to those who travel by railroad. *McCabe* v. *Atchison, T. &S. F. Ry. Co.,* 235 U. S. 151, 161.

In the *Plessy* case the Court also said (p. 551) that legislation is "powerless to eradicate" racial prejudice. This observation, even if true, was irrelevant to the constitutional issue before the Court. It might properly have been made before a legislative body considering the merits of a bill to penalize conduct manifesting racial prejudice. But the Court was not called upon to make a judgment of policy as to whether racial prejudice can be eradicated by legislation; the only question was whether a particular statute created, enforced, or supported the denial of a constitutionally protected right. Statutes and ordinances may not in themselves remove racial antagonisms, but it is clear that they cannot constitutionally magnify such antagonisms by giving the sanction of law to what would otherwise be a private, individual act of discrimination. That is the basic vice of the Commission's order in this case.

In any event, the Court's observation is, at best, a half-truth. Although legislation cannot "eradicate" racial prejudice, experience has shown that it can create conditions favorable to the gradual disappearance of racial prejudice; or it can, on the other hand, strengthen and enhance it. Civil-rights and antidiscrimination statutes have been shown to have the former effect, and so-called Jim Crow laws the latter. A Commissioner of the New York State Commission Against Discrimination has recently written:

> Critics of fair-employment laws used to claim that long-established habits of discrimination could not be changed by legislation. Their argument has been unmistakably answered today. Nearly four years' experience in New York — and similar experience in New Jersey, Massachusetts, Connecticut, Washington, Oregon, New Mexico and Rhode Island, all of which have

---

matter of common knowledge, that viewed from a social standpoint, the negro race is in mind and morals inferior to the Caucasian. The record of each from the dawn of historic time denies equality."

For other cases holding that applying the word "Negro" or "colored person" to a white man gives rise to an action for defamation see *Flood* v. *News & Courier Co.,* 71 S. C. 112; *Stultz* v. *Cousins* 242 Fed. 794 (C. A. 6). See also *Louisville & Nashville R. R. Co.* v. *Ritchel,* 148 Ky. 701, 706; *Missouri, K. & T. Ry. Co.* v. *Ball,* 25 Tex. Civ. App. 500, 503; *Chicago R. I. & P. Ry. Co.* v. *Allison,* 120 Ark. 54, 60-61.

[86]Myrdal, *An American Dilemma,* vol. 1, p. 642.
[87]Drake & Cayton, *Black Metropolis,* 121.

passed anti-discrimination legislation modeled after the New York law — indicates conclusively that wise legislation creates a climate of opinion in which discrimination tends to disappear.[88]

On the other side of the picture, "Jim Crow" laws, which govern important segments of every-day living, not only indoctrinate both white and colored races with the caste conception, but they solidify the segregation existing outside these laws and give it respectability and institutional fixity.[39] As the Supreme Court of California has pointedly said, the way to eradicate racial tension is not "through the perpetuation by law of the prejudices that give rise to the tension."[40] In fields which "Jim Crow" laws do not cover there has been "a slow trend toward a breakdown of segregation"; within the fields of their operation the laws "keep the pattern rigid."[41]

We submit, moreover, that the Fourteenth Amendment, considered in the light of its history and purposes, furnishes no support for the "separate but equal" doctrine. The Amendment was primarily designed to establish Negroes as citizens and to protect them in the full enjoyment of rights concomitant to such status. This Court has said that "the chief inducement to the passage of the Amendment was the desire to extend federal protection to the recently emancipated race from unfriendly and discriminating legislation by the States." *Buchanan* v. *Warley*, 245 U. S. 60, 76. It is "to be construed liberally, to carry out the purposes of its framers," and the effect of its prohibitions is to declare that "the law in the States shall be the same for the black as for the white; * * * and, in regard to the colored race, for whose protection the amendment was primarily designed, that no discrimination shall be made against them by law because of their color." *Strauder* v. *West Virginia*, 100 U. S. 303, 307. It was designed to forestall state legislation aimed at maintaining the subordinate status of those newly emancipated. When the Amendment was adopted, "it required little knowledge of human nature to anticipate that those who had long been regarded as an inferior and subject race would, when suddenly raised to the rank of citizenship, be looked upon with jealousy and positive dislike, and that State laws might be enacted or enforced to perpetuate the distinctions that had before existed." *Id.*, p. 306. See also the *Slaughter-House Cases*, 16 Wall. 36, 70-72, 81.

Segregation does not appear to have been specifically discussed in the debates on the Amendment itself. The apparent reasons for this were that the first section of the Fourteenth Amendment was designed to secure the analogous provisions of Section 1 of the Civil Rights Act of 1866, 14 Stat. 27, by incorporating them into the Constitution,[42] and that the question of segregation had been fully considered during the debates preceding passage of the Civil Rights Act of 1866. The opponents of the bill

---

[88]Simon, *Causes and Cure of Discrimination*, New York Times, May 29, 1949, section 6, p. 10, at p. 35. "Can this technique of eliminating discrimination by rooting out the fears that cause it be applied successfully on a large scale? Our New York experience insists that the answer is an unequivocal 'Yes.' * * * we have changed the entire pattern of employment of the most populous state in the union in less than four years." (Id., p. 36.) See *1948 Report of Progress*, New York State Commission Against Discrimination, pp. 11-12.

[39]Myrdal, *An American Dilemma*, vol. 1, pp. 579-580. See also Berger, *The Supreme Court and Group Discrimination Since 1937*, 49 Col. L. 201, 204-205.

[40]*Perez* v. *Sharp*, 32 Calif. 2d 711, 725.

[41]Myrdal, *An American Dilemma*, vol. 1, p. 635.
In the South, segregation in privately operated public services "is often less rigid than in those operated by government" (*id.*, p. 634).

[42]Flack, *Adoption of the Fourteenth Amendment*, 20, 81, 94-95.

had repeatedly argued that it would require the abolition of separate schools.[43] While a few advocates of the measure disputed this,[44] it is far from clear that a majority of the bill's supporters shared this view. Contemporaneous press comment reflects the general understanding that the bill would prohibit segregation.[45]

The debates preceding enactment of the Civil Rights Act of 1875, 18 Stat. 335, show even more clearly that the Amendment was understood to outlaw state-enforced segregation. The bill in its original form provided that all persons, without distinction as to race or color, should be entitled to "equal and impartial" enjoyment of any accommodation furnished by common carriers, public schools, innkeepers and the like.[46] Both supporters and opponents of the measure construed it as invalidating racial segregation.[47] Proposed amendments to permit local communities to provide equal but separate educational facilities were defeated in both branches of Congress.[48] While express reference to public schools was finally eliminated,[49] its elimination was not because of doubt of the power of Congress under the Fourteenth Amendment, since the "full and equal" requirement was retained as to other accommodations, advantages and facilities.

Since Section 5 of the Fourteenth Amendment authorizes Congress to enforce only the provisions of the Amendment, the passage of prohibitory legislation embracing racial segregation clearly shows that a majority of both branches of Congress thought that segregation came within the prohibitions of the Amendment.

D. *The harm to the public interest which has resulted from enforced racial segregation argues against the extension to the field of interstate transportation*

The effects of the segregation to which Negroes are subjected are not confined to those who are colored. They extend also to those who are white, and they bear vitally upon the interests of the Nation as a whole. We submit that the harmful effects to the public interest which have resulted from racial segregation furnish persuasive grounds for rejecting its extension to the field of interstate transportation. In addition, the materials referred to in this section of the brief conclusively refute the notion that facilities segregated on a racial basis can in any circumstances be regarded as equal.

1. Effect on Negroes

Segregation is a dominant factor in every aspect of the Negro's life. It limits his physical movements and economic opportunities, and adversely affects his personality and social development. It is much more than jim-crowism in vehicles and public

---

[43]Cong. Globe, 39th Cong., 1st Sess., 499, 500, 1268.

[44]*Id.*, 1117-1118, 1294.

[45]Flack, *supra*, at 41, 44-45, 53-54.

[46]Cong. Globe, 42d Cong., 2d Sess., 244 (1871). The bill was first introduced by Senator Sumner as an amendment to another measure on December 20, 1871. Each succeeding session it was reintroduced with immaterial variations until its passage in 1875. The change from "equal and impartial" to "full and equal" in the Act's final form appears to be without significance.

[47]Cong. Globe, 42d Cong., 2d Sess., 763, 843-845, 3258-3262 (1872); 2 Cong. Rec. 4116, 4143-4145, 4167-4169, 4171-4174 (1874). See also Flack, supra, 250-276.
The Civil Rights Act of 1875 was eventually declared unconstitutional upon the ground that it operated directly upon individuals, whereas the prohibitions of the Fourteenth Amendment run only against state action. *Civil Rights Cases*, 109 U. S. 3.

[48]Cong. Globe, 42d Cong., 2d Sess., 3258-3262 (1872); 2 Cong. Rec. 4167 (1864); 3 Cong. Rec. 1010 (1875).

[49]3 Cong. Rec. 1010.

places. It is an ostracism symbolizing inferiority which colors his thoughts and action at almost every moment.[50]

Professional opinion is almost unanimous that segregation has detrimental psychological effects on those segregated. A questionnaire addressed to 849 representative social scientists was answered by 61% of those to whom it was sent.[51] Of those replying, 90.4% believed that enforced segregation has "detrimental psychological effects" on those segregated if "equal facilities" are provided, 2.3% expressed the opposite opinion, and 7.4% did not answer the question or expressed no opinion.[52] Those who elaborated their position with comments (55% of those replying) stressed that segregation induced feelings of inferiority, insecurity, frustration, and persecution, and that it developed, on the one hand, submissiveness, martyrdom, withdrawal tendencies, and fantasy, and on the other hand, aggression.[53]

The resentment and hostility provoked by segregation find various means of psychological "accommodation," various forms of release.[54] Mediocrity is accepted as

---

[50]"Every time I think about it, I feel like somebody's poking a red-hot iron down my throat. Look! we live here and they live there. We black and they white. They got things and we ain't. They do things and we can't. It's just like living in jail. Half the time I feel like I'm on the outside of the world peeping in through a knothole in the fence." Cooper, *The Frustrations of Being a Member of a Minority Group: What Does It Do to the Individual and to His Relationships with Other People?* 29 Mental Hygiene 189, 193, quoting from *Native Son* by Richard Wright.

[51]Deutscher & Chein, *The Psychological Effect of Enforced Segregation: A Survey of Social Science Opinion*, 26 Journal of Psychology 259, 261, 262. The questionnaire was sent to all members of the American Ethnological Society, to all psychologists who were members of the Division of Social Psychology and Personality of the American Psychological Association, to all sociologists who were members of the American Sociological Society and listed race relations or social psychology as a major or dominant interest, and to sociologists who had published research on race relations during the period 1937-1947 (id., 260). Nearly two-thirds of those who replied gave personal professional experience as a basis for the opinion expressed (id., 271).

[52]Id., 261, 266.

[53]Id., 272-277.

[54]"A constant stream of stimuli bombarding the personality with feelings of humiliation, must inevitably produce among others a state of continuously existing hatred, which unable to discharge itself directly on the offending stimulus, remains floating, to be released in a greatly exaggerated form on the first suitable object." Prudhomme, *The Problem of Suicide in the American Negro*, 25 Psychoanalytic Review 187, 200;

"Accommodation involves the renunciation of protest or aggression against undesirable conditions of life and the organization of the character so that protest does not appear, but acceptance does. It may come to pass in the end that the unwelcome force is idealized, that one indentifies with it and takes it into the personality; it sometimes even happens that what is at first resented and feared is finally loved. In this case a unique alteration of the character occurs in the direction of masochism." Dollard, *Caste and Class in a Southern Town*, 255.

"Even though their personalities seem well accommodated to the caste system, it should not he thought that the Negroes are too stupid to realize the nature of the situation. They understand it quite well, in fact much better than do members of the white caste who naturally wish to disguise and extenuate it out of loyalty to our democratic theory which does not countenance caste and class gains. * * * We may believe, then, that Negroes will perceive the caste and class distinctions as a chronic frustration situation. In such a situation we should expect aggression from them. What, in fact, do they do?

"There seem to be five possibilities of action on the part of the Negroes in the face of these gains [since slavery].

They can:

"(1) Become overtly aggressive against the white caste; this they have done, though infre-

a standard because of the absence of adequate social rewards or acceptance.[55] Energy and emotion which might be constructively used are lost in the process of adjustment to the "Jim Crow" concept of the Negro's characteristics and his inferior status in society.[56] Psychosomatic disease is induced by the tensions engendered by segregation and other forms of racial discrimination.[57]

quently and unsuccessfully in the past.

"(2) Suppress their aggression in the face of the gains and supplant it with passive accommodative attitudes. This was the slavery solution and it still exists under the caste system.

"(3) Turn aggression from the white caste to individuals within their own group. This has been done to some extent and is a feature of present-day Negro life.

"(4) Give up the competition for white-caste values and accept other forms of gratification than those secured by the whites. This the lower-class Negroes have done.

"(5) Compete for the values of white society, raise their class position within the Negro caste and manage aggression partly by expressing dominance within their own group and partly by sheer suppression of the impulse as individuals. This is the solution characteristic of the Negro middle class." Dollard, *supra*, 252-253.

[55]"The middle-class Negro tries to maintain allegiance to the dominant American standards and then experiences the bitter fact that this allegiance is not rewarded as it is in the white caste; instead he is ignominiously lumped with persons in his own class whose behavior standards are inferior to his own." Dollard, *supra*, 424.

"In order for any individual to mature, that is, to be willing to assume responsibility in work and in personal relations, he must feel that there is some hope of attaining some of the satisfactions of maturity. * * * White society gives him [the Negro] little share in any of the mature gratifications of creative work, education, and citizenship. It would not be remarkable if, deprived of all mature gratifications, he lost zest for responsible action." McLean, *Group Tension*, 2 Journal of American Medical Women's Association 479, 482.

[56]"One of the most devastating frustrations that plague the Negro is the majority concept that the Negro people are inferior; that always they remain infantile or childlike; that their smiling, happy faces are but conclusive evidence that they are not capable of seriousness of purpose or of sustained intellectual participation. * * * All of us know the terrific impact that constant repetition has upon the psyche. * * * The Negro is born into a culture that stubbornly refuses to accept him as an equal. Custom and tradition force the majority concept of his inferiority into his consciousness and keep it there.

"Let us next consider the frustrations involved in the process of never being allowed to be one's self, never daring to be a person in one's own distinct uniqueness and individuality. * * * Negroes when in contact, casual or prolonged, with other Negroes, invariably turn the conversation to a discussion of race, its implications and methods of solving the problem, either through individual or through collective action. When Negroes are in the company of white persons, the conscious awkwardness, the studied carefulness, the restraint, the unconscious tones and undertones — all these are a constant reminder to the Negro that he is a Negro and that his status is that of a dispossessed minority. Imagine, if you will, the tremendous emotional energy expended in the process of never being able to be unaware of one's self. Imagine, if you can, the tragedy of the diffused and dissipated energy that is lost in the process of having constantly to think of one's designated and specifically limiting minority role." Cooper, *The Frustrations of Being a Member of a Minority Group: What Does It Do to the Individual and to His Relationships with Other People?*, 29 Mental Hygiene 189, 190-191.

[57]"The high incidence of hypertension among southern Negroes is probably one indication of an unconscious attempt at mastery of the hostility which must be controlled. The chronic rage of these individuals produces the hypertension which initially is fluctuating in character. Eventually the pathological changes resulting from this overload on the cardiovascular renal system lead to a consistently high blood pressure. All available evidence from clinicians indicates that functional (that is, psychosomatic) disease is markedly on the increase in the Negro." McLean, *Psychodynamic Factors in Racial Relations*, The Annals of the American Academy of Political and Social Science (March 1946), 159, 161.

"The psychology of the Negro developed in the repressive environment in which he lives might

The extensive studies made of Negro troops during the recent war furnished striking example of how racism, of which segregation is the sharpest manifestation, handicaps the Negro. The most important single factor affecting integration of the Negro into Army life was that he had to carry the burden of race prejudice in addition to all of the other problems faced by the white soldier.[58]

For a general discussion of the effects of the caste system, which segregation supports and exemplifies, on Negro personality and behavior, see Myrdal, *An American Dilemma*, vol. 2, pp. 757-767.

2. Effect on Whites

Segregation also detrimentally affects the dominant white group.[59] "Segregation and discrimination have had material and moral effect on whites, too. Booker T. Washington's famous remark, that the white man could not hold the Negro in the gutter without getting in there himself, has been corroborated by many white Southern and Northern observers." Myrdal, *An American Dilemma*, vol. I, pp. 643-644. The white person must adjust himself, consciously or unconsciously, to the hypocrisy of a double standard violating the American creed which he professes to follow. Feelings of guilt are generated and moral values weakened; the basic realities of the racial problem are diverted into the mechanism of segregation:

> Those who segregate others soon become frightened, insecure people forced to accept and invent prejudice to justify their actions. They become hypocrites who either close their eyes to stark reality or invent slogans to hide fundamental issues. The master classes, no less than the subjected, become victims of the system.[60]

Segregation and practices allied to it promote the master-race psychology, thus sowing the seeds for oppressive individual and collective action.

3. Effect on the Nation

Segregation is part of a vicious cycle. It prevents groups from knowing each other. This lack of knowledge engenders distrust and antagonism. They in turn stimulate the demand for sharp cleavage between races and maintenance of a system of segregation. Thus groups within the Nation are kept asunder.[61]

Experience and informed opinion are in agreement that normal contacts between

be described as the psychology of the sick * * *It is impossible to estimate what are the pathological results of the above outlook on life. It must certainly mean a reduction in that energy that characterizes healthy organisms." Frazier, *Psychological Factors in Negro Health*, Journal of Social Forces, vol. 3, p. 488.

[58]*Studies in Social Psychology in World War II*, vol. I, chap. 10. See particularly pp. 502, 504, 507.

[59]Deutscher & Chein, *supra*, 26 Journal of Psychology 261, 267.

[60]Weaver, *The Negro Ghetto*, 270.

[61]"From these natural causes the white man's knowledge of Negro life is diminishing and the rate is accelerated by the present-day policy of segregation. This operates practically to make an ever-widening gulf between the two races which leaves each race more and more ignorant of the other. Without contact there cannot be knowledge; segregation reduced the contacts, and so knowledge and understanding decrease. With decreasing knowledge comes increasing distrust and suspicion, and these in turn engender prejudice and even hatred. So a vicious circle is established whose ultimate effect, unless counteracted, must be a separation of the races into more or less opposing camps, with results as disastrous to the spirit of American institutions as to the genuine progress of both races." Moton, *What the Negro Thinks*, 5. See also Dollard, *Caste and Class in a Southern Town*, supra, 73.

the races diminish prejudice while enforced separation intensifies it.[62] Race relations are improved by living together,[63] working together,[64] serving together[65] going to school together.[66] The absence of a color line in certain countries goes far to show that racial prejudice is not instinctive or hereditary, but is rather kept alive by man-made barriers such as segregation.[67]

The experience of the Sperry Gyroscope Company is noteworthy. Its employment of Negroes began in 1941 and steadily progressed until, by 1944, one-third of its Negro employees were in highly skilled occupations, one-third in semi-skilled, and one-third in other jobs.[68] In the words of the president of the company:

> The initial employment of Negroes and each subsequent extension of their employment into new categories was received with doubt by the supervisors, and, in some cases, by rumblings and even threats of trouble from some groups of white workers. The threats never materialized, the doubts disappeared and were succeeded by friendliness and cooperation in helping the Negro to learn his new job and to progress to a better one. I know of no instance now where the Negro worker is not judged entirely on the basis of his competency and without consciousness of his race.

A marked change in attitude occurred in white soldiers who served in combat with Negro troops. Two out of three admitted that at first they had been unfavorable to serving with Negro troops. Three out of four stated their feelings had changed after service with them in combat. And a survey of opinion of white servicemen on the question of including Negro and white platoons in the same company showed that their willingness to accept such integration was in direct ratio to their closeness to actual combat experiences with Negro troops.[69]

Rebellion against constituted authority (parental, school or state) is, for the adolescent, a normal manifestation of growth toward independence. But, in the case of many, the apparent hypocrisy of a society professing equality but practicing segregation and other forms of racial discrimination furnishes justification and reason for the latent urge to rebel, and frequently leads to lasting bitterness or total rejection of the American creed and system of government.

Recently a Congressional committee summoned "Jackie" Robinson, the Negro baseball star, as a witness to rebut certain widely publicized statements which had

---

[62]Sancton, *Segregation: The Pattern of a Failure*, Survey Graphic (Jan. 1947), p. 10; Yarros, *Isolation and Social Conflicts*, 27 American Journal of Sociology, 211.

[63]*To Secure These Rights*, Report of the President's Committee on Civil Rights, 85-86. Lee & Humphrey, *Race Riot*, 17.

[64]Brophy, *The Luxury of Anti-Negro Prejudice*, 9 Public Opinion Quarterly 456; Oppenheimer, *Non-Discriminatory Hospital Service*, 29 Mental Hygiene 195.

[65]*Studies in Social Psychology in World War II*, vol. I, pp. 594-595; Nelson, *The Integration of the Negro into the United States Navy* (Navy Dept., 1948), 71-72.

[66]*Race Riot*, supra, p. 17; Ware, *The Role of Schools in Education for Racial Understanding*, 13 Journal of Negro Education, 421-424.

[67]Pierson, *Negroes in Brazil*, 336, 344-350.

[68]Gillmor (president of Sperry Gyroscope Co.), *Can the Negro Hold His Job?*, National Association for the Advancement of Colored People Bulletin (Sept. 1944) 3-4.

[69]Report No. ETO-82, Research Branch, European Theatre of Operations of the Army, as summarized in *To Secure These Rights*, supra, 83-85.

questioned the loyalty of large numbers of the Negro race. He testified:[70]

> Just because Communists kick up a big fuss over racial discrimination when it suits their purposes, a lot of people try to pretend that the whole issue is a creation of Communist imagination.
>
> But they are not fooling anyone with this kind of pretense, and talk about "Communists stirring up Negroes to protest," only makes present misunderstanding worse than ever. Negroes were stirred up long before there was a Communist Party, and they'll stay stirred up long after the party has disappeared — unless Jim Crow has disappeared by then as well.

In our foreign relations, racial discrimination, as exemplified by segregation, has been a source of serious embarrassment to this country. It has furnished material for hostile propaganda and raised doubts of our sincerity even among friendly nations. A letter from Mr. Dean Acheson, then Acting Secretary of State, to the Fair Employment Practice Committee on May 8, 1946, stated:[71]

> * * * the existence of discrimination against minority groups in this country has an adverse effect upon our relations with other countries. We are reminded over and over by some foreign newspapers and spokesmen, that our treatment of various minorities leaves much to be desired. While sometimes these pronouncements are exaggerated and unjustified, they all too frequently point with accuracy to some form of discrimination because of race, creed, color, or national origin. Frequently we find it next to impossible to formulate a satisfactory answer to our critics in other countries; the gap between the things we stand for in principle and the facts of a particular situation may be too wide to be bridged. * * *
>
> I think it is quite obvious * * * that the existence of discriminations against minority groups in the United States is a handicap in our relations with other countries.

Recent remarks of representatives of foreign powers in a subcommittee of the United Nations General Assembly typify the manner in which racial discrimination in this country is turned against us in the international field.[72] The references to this subject in the unfriendly foreign press are frequent and caustic.[73]

---

[70] *Hearings Regarding Communists Infiltration of Minority Groups, Part I,* House Committee on Un-American Activities, 81st Congress, 1st Sess., p. 479.

[71] Quoted in *To Secure These Rights, supra,* 146-147.

[72] In discussing a Bolivian proposal concerning aboriginal populations of the American continent, the Soviet representative said:

> Guided by the principles of the United Nations Charter, the General Assembly must condemn the policy and practice of racial discrimination in the United States and any other countries of the American continent where such a policy was being exercised. (United Nations, General Assembly, *Ad Hoc* Political Committee, Third Session, Part II, Summary Record of the Fifty-Third Meeting (May 11, 1949), p. 12.)

Another Soviet representative stated:

> In the southern states, the policy of racial discrimination was actually confirmed by law and most strictly observed in trains, restaurants, cinemas, and elsewhere (id., Summary Record of Fifty-Fourth Meeting (May 13, 1949), p. 3).

The Polish representative said:

> The representative of Poland did not, however, believe that the United States Govern-

Our opposition to racial discrimination has been affirmed in treaties and international agreements. The Charter of the United Nations has been approved as a treaty (59 Stat. 1213). By Article 55, the United Nations agree to promote "universal respect for, and observance of, human rights and fundamental freedoms for all without distinction as to race, sex, language, or religion" (59 Stat. 1046).

At the Inter-American Conference on Problems of War and Peace at Mexico City in 1945, this country joined with the other participants in adopting Resolution No. 41, which reaffirms the principle of equality of rights and opportunities for all men "regardless of race or religion" and recommends that the Governments of the American Republics make every effort to prevent in their respective countries "all acts which may provoke discrimination among individuals because of race or religion."[74]

Racial segregation enforced by law hardly comports with the high principles to which, in the international field, we have subscribed. Our position and standing before the critical bar of world opinion are weakened if segregation not only is practiced in this country but also is condoned by federal law.

Mr. Justice Harlan said in his memorable dissent in the *Plessy* case (163 U. S. at 562):

> We boast of the freedom enjoyed by our people above all other peoples. But it is difficult to reconcile that boast with a state of the law which, practically, puts the brand of servitude and degradation upon a large class of our fellow-citizens, our equals before the law. The thin disguise of "equal" accommodations for passengers in railroad coaches will not mislead any one, nor atone for the wrong this day done.

Various subterfuges have been employed during the years since the adoption of the Thirteenth and Fourteenth Amendments to evade and nullify the effects of their provisions. The emancipation of an entire race has proved a most complicated task. More than three-quarters of a century has not been enough time within which to break down the barriers surrounding the enslaved, and to bring them to the full dignity and stature of free citizens. Discrimination, political, economic, and social, is still widespread. However, there are indications that the process of education, of lessening the incidence of unreasoning prejudice, lagging for so many years, is increasing in momentum.

Racial antagonisms become acute in localities, and it is there that discriminatory

---

ment had the least intention to conform to the recommendations which would be made by the United Nations with regard to the improvement of living conditions of the coloured population of that country (id., p. 6).

[73]Thus an article in *The Bolshevik* (U. S. S. R.) No. 15, 1948 (Frantsov, *Nationalism — The Tool of Imperialist Reaction*), contain[s] the statement: "The theory and practice of racial discrimination against the Negroes in America is known to the whole world. The poison of racial hatred has become so strong in post-war America that matters go to unbelievable lengths; for example a Negress injured in a road accident could not be taken to a neighbouring hospital since this hospital was only for 'whites.'" Similarly, in the *Literary Gazette* (U. S. S. R.) No. 51, 1948, the article *The Tragedy of Coloured America*, by Berezko, states "It is a country within a country. Coloured America is not allowed to mix with the other white America, it exists within it like the yolk in the white of an egg. Or, to be more exact, like a gigantic ghetto. The walls of this ghetto are invisible but they are nonetheless indestructible. They are placed within cities where the Negroes live in special quarters, in buses where the Negroes are assigned only the back seats, in hairdressers where they have special chairs."

[74]Department of State Publication 2497 (Conference Series 85) p. 109.

acts are practiced, legislation is enacted and on occasion validated by courts unwittingly responding to their environment. And so this Court has been faced through the years with one controversy after another in which efforts were made to obtain approval of measures cleverly calculated to keep the Negro in bondage, to prevent him from enjoying his full rights as a citizen, and to pervert the true intent and meaning of the Thirteenth and Fourteenth Amendments. This Court has stricken down acts of local law-making bodies and officials depriving the Negro of the right to vote, to serve on petit and grand juries, and of the right to acquire and use property. More recently, it has restrained judicial enforcement of racial restrictive covenants on real property. In other fields, this Court has acted to compel local authorities to provide the Negro with opportunities for education previously denied him.

The evasions and violations of the Constitution are being gradually eliminated. One handicap is the approval, given in another day and generation, to the proposition that the Constitution could be satisfied and friction removed by the establishment of "separate but equal" facilities. Experience has shown that neither the Constitution, nor the laws enacted under its authority, nor the individuals affected, are given the required respect and status under such an arrangement. "Equal" facilities, if separate, are rarely if ever equal, even in a physical sense. In most situations they have been used to cloak glaring inequalities. And the very idea of separate facilities, or separate rights, is in itself a negation of the full and complete possession of privileges and immunities of citizenship.

So long as the doctrine of the *Plessy* case stands, a barrier erected not by the Constitution but by the courts will continue to work a denial of rights and privileges and immunities antagonistic to the freedoms and liberties on which our institutions and our form of government are founded. "Separate but equal" is a constitutional anachronism which no longer deserves a place in our law. The Court has said that "It is of the very nature of a free society to advance in its standards of what is deemed reasonable and right. Representing as it does a living principle, due process is not confined within a permanent catalogue of what may at a given time be deemed the limits or the essentials of fundamental rights." *Wolf* v. *Colorado*, 338 U. S. 25, 27. It is neither reasonable nor right that colored citizens of the United States should be subjected to the humiliation of being segregated by law, on the pretense that they are being treated as equals.

CONCLUSION

It is respectfully submitted that the judgment of the district court should be reversed and that the Interstate Commerce Commission should be directed to enter an order prohibiting the railroad from furnishing dining car service to passengers segregated on a basis of race or color.

PHILIP B. PERLMAN,
Solicitor General.

HERBERT A. BERGSON,
Assistant Attorney General.

CHARLES H. WESTON,

PHILIP ELMAN,
Special Assistants to the Attorney General.

OCTOBER 1949.

SUPREME COURT OF THE UNITED STATES

No. 25.—OCTOBER TERM, 1949.

*Elmer W. Henderson, Appelant, v. The United States of America, Interstate Commerce Commission, and Southern Railway Company.	On Appeal From the United States District Court for the District of Maryland.

[June 5, 1950.]

MR. JUSTICE BURTON delivered the opinion of the Court.

The question here is whether the rules and practices of the Southern Railway Company, which divide each dining car so as to allot ten tables exclusively to white passengers and one table exclusively to Negro passengers, and which call for a curtain or partition between that table and the others, violate § 3 (1) of the Interstate Commerce Act. That section makes it unlawful for a railroad in interstate commerce "to subject any particular person, . . . to any undue or unreasonable prejudice or disadvantage in any respect whatsoever: . . ." 54 Stat. 902, 49 U. S. C. § 3 (1). We hold that those rules and practices do violate the Act.

This issue grows out of an incident which occurred May 17, 1942. On that date the appellant, Elmer W. Henderson, a Negro passenger, was traveling on a first-class ticket on the Southern Railway from Washington, D. C., to Atlanta, Georgia, en route to Birmingham, Alabama, in the course of his duties as an employee of the United States. The train left Washington at 2 p. m. At about 5:30 p. m., while the train was in Virginia,[1] the first call to dinner was announced and he went promptly to the dining car. In accordance with the practice then in effect, the two end tables nearest the kitchen were conditionally reserved for Negroes. At each meal those tables were to be reserved initially for Negroes and, when occupied by Negroes, curtains were to be drawn between them and the rest of the car. If the other tables were occupied before any Negro passengers presented themselves at the diner then those two tables also were to be available for white passengers, and Negroes were not to be seated at them while in use by white passengers.[2] When the appellant reached the diner, the end

---

*339 U. S. 816, 70 S. Ct. 843, 94 L. ed. (Adv. Op.) 790.

[1] No reliance is placed in this case upon any action by any state.

[2] Rule of the Southern Railway Company issued July 3, 1941, and in effect May 17, 1942:

"DINING CAR REGULATIONS

"Meals should be served to passengers of different races at separate times. If passengers of one race desire meals while passengers of a different race are being served in the dining car, such meals will be served in the room or seat occupied by the passenger without extra charge. If the dining car is equipped with curtains so that it can be divided into separate compartments, meals may be served to passengers of different races at the same time in the compartments set aside for them." 258 I. C. C. 413, 415, 63 F. Supp. 906, 910.

Joint Circular of the Southern Railway System issued August 6, 1942:

tables in question were partly occupied by white passengers but at least one seat at them was unoccupied. The dining-car steward declined to seat the appellant in the dining car but offered to serve him, without additional charge, at his Pullman seat. The appellant declined that offer and the steward agreed to send him word when space was available. No word was sent and the appellant was not served, although he twice returned to the diner before it was detached at 9 p. m.

In October, 1942, the appellant filed a complaint with the Interstate Commerce Commission alleging especially that the foregoing conduct violated § 3 (1) of the Interstate Commerce Act.[3] Division 2 of the Commission found that he had been subjected to undue and unreasonable prejudice and disadvantage, but that the occurrence was a casual incident brought about by the bad judgment of an employee. The Commission declined to enter an order as to future practices. 258 I. C. C. 413. A three-judge United States District Court for the District of Maryland, however, held that the railroad's general practice, as evidenced by its instructions of August 6, 1942, was in violation of § 3 (1). Accordingly, on February 18, 1946, it remanded the case for further proceedings. 63 F. Supp. 906. Effective March 1, 1946, the company announced its modified rules which are now in effect. They provide for the reservation of ten tables, of four seats each, exclusively and unconditionally for white passengers and one table, of four seats, exclusively and unconditionally for Negro passengers. Between this table and the others a curtain is drawn during each meal.[4]

"Effective at once please be governed by the following with respect to the race separation curtains in dining cars:

"Before starting each meal pull the curtains to service position and place a 'Reserved' card on each of the two tables behind the curtains.

These tables are not to be used by white passengers until all other seats in the car have been taken. Then if no colored passengers present themselves for meals, the curtain should be pushed back, cards removed and white passengers served at those tables.

"After the tables are occupied by white passengers, then should colored passengers present themselves they should be advised that they will be served just as soon as those compartments are vacated.

" 'Reserved cards are being supplied you." 258 I. C. C. at p. 415, 63 F. Supp. at p. 910.

[3]"(1) *It shall be unlawful for any common carrier* subject to the provisions of this part *to make, give, or cause any undue or unreasonable preference or advantage to any particular person,* company, firm, corporation, association, locality, port, port district, gateway, transit point, region, district, territory, or any particular description of traffic, *in any respect whatsoever; or to subject any particular person,* company, firm, corporation, association, locality, port, port district, gateway, transit point, region, district, territory, or any particular description of traffic *to any undue or unreasonable prejudice or disadvantage in any respect whatsoever: . . . ."* (Emphasis supplied.) 54 Stat. 902, 49 U. S. C. § 3 (1).

The appellant sought an order directing the railroad not only to cease and desist from the specific violations alleged but also to establish in the future, for the complainant and other Negro interstate passengers, equal and just dining-car facilities and such other service and facilities as the Commission might consider reasonable and just, and requiring the railroad to discontinue using curtains around tables reserved for Negroes.

The appellant sought damages, but the Commission found no pecuniary damages and that issue has not been pressed further.

[4]"TRANSPORTATION DEPARTMENT CIRCULAR NO. 142. CANCELLING INSTRUCTIONS ON THIS SUBJECT DATED JULY 3, 1941, AND AUGUST 6, 1942.

"SUBJECT: SEGREGATION OF WHITE AND COLORED PASSENGERS IN DINING CARS.

"To: Passenger Conductors and Dining Car Stewards.

"Consistent with experience in respect to the ratio between the number of white and colored passengers who ordinarily apply for service in available diner space, equal but separate accommodations.

On remand, the full Commission, with two members dissenting and one not participating, found that the modified rules do not violate the Interstate Commerce Act and that no order for the future is necessary.[5] 269 I. C. C. 73. The appellant promptly instituted the present proceeding before the District Court, constituted of the same three members as before, seeking to have the Commission's order set aside and a cease and desist order issued. 28 U. S. C. §§ 41 (28), 43-48; 49 U. S. C. § 17 (9); see also, 28 U. S. C. (Supp. III) §§ 1336, 1398, 2284, 2321, 2325. With one member dissenting, the court sustained the modified rules on the ground that the accommodations are adequate to serve the average number of Negro passengers and are "proportionately fair." 80 F. Supp. 32, 39. The case is here on direct appeal. 28 U. S. C. (Supp. III) §§ 1253, 2101 (b). In this Court, the United States filed a brief and argued orally in support of the appellant.

It is clear that appellant has standing to bring these proceedings. He is an aggrieved party, free to travel again on the Southern Railway. Having been subjected to practices of the railroad which the Commission and the court below found to violate the Interstate Commerce Act, he may challenge the railroad's current regulations on the ground that they permit the recurrence of comparable violations. *Mitchell* v. *United States*, 313 U. S. 80, 92-93.

The material language in §3 (1) of the Interstate Commerce Act has been in that statute since its adoption in 1887. 24 Stat. 380. From the beginning, the Interstate Commerce Commission has recognized the application of that language to discrimina-

---

accommodations shall be provided for white and colored passengers by partitioning diners and the allotment of space, in accordance with the rules, as follows:

(1) That one of the two tables at Station No. 1 located to the left side of the aisle facing the buffet, seating four persons, shall be reserved exclusively for colored passengers, and the other tables in the diner shall be reserved exclusively for white passengers.

"(2) Before starting each meal, draw the partition curtain separating the table in Station No. 1, described above, from the table on that side of the aisle in Station No. 2, the curtain to remain so drawn for the duration of the meal.

"(3) A 'Reserved' card shall be kept in place on the left-hand table in Station No. 1, described above, at all times during the meal except when such table is occupied as provided in these rules. "(4) These rules become effective March 1, 1946.

"R. K. McClain,
"Assistant Vice-President."

269 I. C. C. 73, 75, 80 F. Supp. 32, 35.

Counsel for the railway company, at a subsequent hearing, corrected the above rules "to the extent of using the word 'negroes' in place of 'colored persons.' " Also, the evidence shows, and the Commission has stated, that "White and Negro soldiers are served together, without distinction." 258 I. C. C. 413, 415. 63 F. Supp. 906, 910. The rules, accordingly, are treated as applicable only to civilian passengers. The company further showed that it is now substituting a five-foot high wooden partition in place of the curtain. The steward's office is being placed in the table space opposite that reserved for Negro passengers and a similar wooden partition is being erected between that office and the rest of the car.

[5]The company was permitted to introduce two tabulations, covering about ten days each, showing the comparative numbers of meals served to white and Negro passengers on trips comparable to the one which the appellant had taken. These show that only about 4% of the total meals served were served to Negro passengers whereas four reserved seats exceed 9% of a total seating capacity of 44. On the other hand, the tabulations also show that at one meal 17 Negro passengers, and at each of 20 meals more than eight Negro passengers, were served. Similarly, the brief filed by the Commission states that, out of the 639 serving periods reported, on 15 occasions more than four times as many white passengers were served as there were seats reserved for them, and, on 541 occasions, there were two or more rounds of servings.

tions between white and Negro passengers. *Councill* v. *Western & Atlantic R. Co.*, 1 I. C. C. 339;[6] *Heard* v. *Georgia R. Co.*, 1 I. C. C. 428; *Heard* v. *Georgia R. Co.*, 3 I. C. C. 111; *Edwards* v. *Nashville, C. & St. L. R. Co.*, 12 I. C. C. 247; *Cozart* v. *Southern R. Co.*, 16 I. C. C. 226; *Gaines* v. *Seaboard Air Line R. Co.*, 16 I. C. C. 471; *Crosby* v. *St. Louis-San Francisco R. Co.*, 112 I. C. C. 239. That section recently was so applied in *Mitchell* v. *United States, supra.*

The decision of this case is largely controlled by that in the *Mitchell* case. There a Negro passenger holding a first-class ticket was denied a Pullman seat, although such a seat was unoccupied and would have been available to him if he had been white. The railroad rules had allotted a limited amount of Pullman space, consisting of compartments and drawing rooms, to Negro passengers and, because that space was occupied, the complainant was excluded from the Pullman car and required to ride in a second-class coach. This Court held that the passenger thereby had been subjected to an unreasonable disadvantage in violation of § 3 (1).[7]

The similarity between that case and this is inescapable. The appellant here was denied a seat in the dining car although at least one seat was vacant and would have been available to him, under the existing rules, if he had been white.[8] The issue before us, as in the *Mitchell* case, is whether the railroad's current rules and practices cause passengers to be subjected to undue or unreasonable prejudice or disadvantage in violation of § 3 (1). We find that they do.

The right to be free from unreasonable discriminations belongs, under § 3 (1), to each particular person. Where a dining car is available to passengers holding tickets entitling them to use it, each such passenger is equally entitled to its facilities in accordance with reasonable regulations. The denial of dining service to any such passenger by the rules before us subjects him to a prohibited disadvantage. Under the rules, only four Negro passengers may be served at one time and then only at the table reserved for Negroes. Other Negroes who present themselves are compelled to await a vacancy at that table, although there may be many vacancies elsewhere in the diner. The railroad thus refuses to extend to those passengers the use of its existing and unoccupied facilities. The rules impose a like deprivation upon white passengers whenever more than 40 of them seek to be served at the same time and the table reserved for Negroes is vacant.

We need not multiply instances in which these rules sanction unreasonable discriminations. The curtains, partitions and signs emphasize the artificiality of a difference in treatment which serves only to call attention to a racial classification of passengers holding identical tickets and using the same public dining facility. Cf. *McLaurin* v. *Oklahoma State Regents, ante*, p. 637, decided today. They violate § 3 (1).

Our attention has been directed to nothing which removes these racial allocations from the statutory condemnation of "undue or unreasonable prejudice or disadvantage

---

[6] "The Western and Atlantic Railroad Company will be notified to cease and desist from subjecting colored persons to undue and unreasonable prejudice and disadvantage in violation of section 3 of the Act to regulate commerce, and from furnishing to colored persons purchasing first-class tickets on its road accommodations which are not equally safe and comfortable with those furnished other first-class passengers." 1 I. C. C. at p. 347.

[7] The rules also denied access by Negroes to the dining car and observation car. The principles there announced applied equally to those facilities.

[8] That specific denial of service was condemned by the Commission and the District Court as a violation of § 3 (1). Review of that condemnation is not sought here.

. . . ." It is argued that the limited demand for dining-car facilities by Negro passengers justifies the regulations. But it is no answer to the particular passenger who is denied service at an unoccupied place in a dining car that, on the average, persons like him are served. As was pointed out in *Mitchell* v. *United States*, 313 U. S. 80, 97, "the comparative volume of traffic cannot justify the denial of a fundamental right of equality of treatment, a right specifically safeguarded by the provisions of the Interstate Commerce Act." Cf. *McCabe* v. *Atchison, T. & S. F. R. Co.*, 235 U. S. 151; *Missouri ex rel. Gaines* v. *Canada*, 305 U. S. 337.

That the regulations may impose on white passengers, in proportion to their numbers, disadvantages similar to those imposed on Negro passengers is not an answer to the requirements of § 3 (1). Discriminations that operate to the disadvantage of two groups are not the less to be condemned because their impact is broader than if only one were affected. Cf. *Shelley* v. *Kraemer*, 334 U. S. 1, 22.

Since § 3 (1) of the Interstate Commerce Act invalidates the rules and practices before us, we do not reach the constitutional or other issues suggested.

The judgment of the District Court is reversed and the cause is remanded to that court with directions to set aside the order of the Interstate Commerce Commission which dismissed the original complaint and to remand the case to that Commission for further proceedings in conformity with this opinion.

It is so ordered.

MR. JUSTICE DOUGLAS concurs in the result.

MR. JUSTICE CLARK took no part in the consideration or decision of this case.

SUPREME COURT OF THE UNITED STATES

No. 44.—OCTOBER TERM, 1949.

*Heman Marion Sweatt, Petitioner, v. Theophilis Shickel Painter, et al.	On Writ of Certiorari to the Supreme Court of the State of Texas.

[June 5, 1950.]

MR. CHIEF JUSTICE VINSON delivered the opinion of the Court.

This case and *McLaurin* v. *Oklahoma State Regents, post*, p. 637, present different aspects of this general question: To what extent does the Equal Protection Clause of the Fourteenth Amendment limit the power of a state to distinguish between students of different races in professional and graduate education in a state university? Broader issues have been urged for our consideration, but we adhere to the principle of

*339 U. S. 629, 70 S. Ct. 848, 94 L. ed. (Adv. Op.) 783

deciding constitutional questions only in the context of the particular case before the Court. We have frequently reiterated that this Court will decide constitutional questions only when necessary to the disposition of the case at hand, and that such decisions will be drawn as narrowly as possible. *Rescue Army* v. *Municipal Court*, 331 U. S. 549 (1947), and cases cited therein. Because of this traditional reluctance to extend constitutional interpretations to situations or facts which are not before the Court, much of the excellent research and detailed argument presented in these cases is unnecessary to their disposition.

In the instant case, petitioner filed an application for admission to the University of Texas Law School for the February, 1946 term. His application was rejected solely because he is a Negro.[1] Petitioner thereupon brought this suit for mandamus against the appropriate school officials, respondents here, to compel his admission. At that time, there was no law school in Texas which admitted Negroes.

The State trial court recognized that the action of the State in denying petitioner the opportunity to gain a legal education while granting it to others deprived him of the equal protection of the laws guaranteed by the Fourteenth Amendment. The court did not grant the relief requested, however, but continued the case for six months to allow the State to supply substantially equal facilities. At the expiration of the six months, in December, 1946, the court denied the writ on the showing that the authorized university officials had adopted an order calling for the opening of a law school for Negroes the following February. While petitioner's appeal was pending, such a school was made available, but petitioner refused to register therein. The Texas Court of Civil Appeals set aside the trial court's judgment and ordered the cause "remanded generally to the trial court for further proceedings without prejudice to the right of any party to this suit."

On remand, a hearing was held on the issue of the equality of the educational facilities at the newly established school as compared with the University of Texas Law School. Finding that the new school offered petitioner "privileges, advantages, and opportunities for the study of law substantially equivalent to those offered by the State to white students at the University of Texas," the trial court denied mandamus. The Court of Civil Appeals affirmed. 210 S. W. 2d 442 (1948). Petitioner's application for a writ of error was denied by the Texas Supreme Court. We granted certiorari, 338 U. S. 865 (1949), because of the manifest importance of the constitutional issues involved.

The University of Texas Law School, from which petitioner was excluded, was staffed by a faculty of sixteen full-time and three part-time professors, some of whom are nationally recognized authorities in their field. Its student body numbered 850. The library contained over 65,000 volumes. Among the other facilities available to the students were a law review, moot court facilities, scholarship funds, and Order of the Coif affiliation. The school's alumni occupy the most distinguished positions in the private practice of the law and in the public life of the State. It may properly be considered one of the nation's ranking law schools.

The law school for Negroes which was to have opened in February, 1947, would

---

[1] It appears that the University has been restricted to white students, in accordance with the State law. See Tex. Const. Art. VII, §§ 7, 14; Tex. Civ. Stat. §§ 2643b, 2719, 2900 (Vernon, 1925, Supp. 1949).

have had no independent faculty or library. The teaching was to be carried on by four members of the University of Texas Law School faculty, who were to maintain their offices at the University of Texas while teaching at both institutions. Few of the 10,000 volumes ordered for the library had arrived;[2] nor was there any full-time librarian. The school lacked accreditation.

Since the trial of this case, respondents report the opening of a law school at the Texas State University for Negroes. It is apparently on the road to full accreditation. It has a faculty of five full-time professors; a student body of 23; a library of some 16,500 volumes serviced by a full-time staff; a practice court and legal aid association; and one alumnus who has become a member of the Texas Bar.

Whether the University of Texas Law School is compared with the original or the new law school for Negroes, we cannot find substantial equality in the educational opportunities offered white and Negro law students by the State. In terms of number of the faculty, variety of courses and opportunity for specialization, size of the student body, scope of the library, availiability of law review and similar activities, the University of Texas Law School is superior. What is more important, the University of Texas Law School possesses to a far greater degree those qualities which as incapable of objective measurement but which make for greatness in a law school. Such qualities, to name but a few, include reputation of the faculty, experience of the administration, position and influence of the alumni, standing in the community, traditions and prestige. It is difficult to believe that one who had a free choice between these law schools would consider the question close.

Moreover, although the law is a highly learned profession, we are well aware that it is an intensely practical one. The law school, the proving ground for legal learning and practice, cannot be effective in isolation from the individuals and institutions with which the law interacts. Few students and no one who has practiced law would choose to study in an academic vacuum, removed from the interplay of ideas and the exchange of views with which the law is concerned. The law school to which Texas is willing to admit petitioner excludes from its student body members of the racial groups which number 85% of the population of the State and include most of the lawyers, witnesses, jurors, judges and other officials with whom petitioner will inevitably be dealing when he becomes a member of the Texas Bar. With such a substantial and significant segment of society excluded, we cannot conclude that the education offered petitioner is substantially equal to that which he would receive if admitted to the University of Texas Law School.

It may be argued that excluding petitioner from that school is no different from excluding white students from the new law school. This contention overlooks realities. It is unlikely that a member of a group so decisively in the majority, attending a school with rich traditions and prestige which only a history of consistently maintained excellence could command, would claim that the opportunities afforded him for legal education were unequal to those held open to petitioner. That such a claim, if made, would be dishonored by the State, is no answer. "Equal protection of the laws is not

---

[2] "Students of the interim School of Law of the Texas State University for Negroes [located in Austin, whereas the permanent School was to be located at Houston] shall have use of the State Law Library in the Capitol Building. . . ." Tex. Civ. Stat. Art. 2634b [2643b], § 11 (Vernon, Supp. 1949). It is not clear that this privilege was anything more than was extended to all citizens of the State.

achieved through indiscriminate imposition of inequalities." *Shelley* v. *Kraemer*, 334 U. S. 1, 22 (1948).

It is fundamental that these cases concern rights which are personal and present. This Court has stated unanimously that "The State must provide [legal education] for [petitioner] in conformity with the equal protection clause of the Fourteenth Amendment and provide it as soon as it does for applicants of any other group." *Sipuel* v. *Board of Regents*, 332 U. S. 631, 633 (1948). That case "did not present the issue whether a state might not satisfy the equal protection clause of the Fourteenth Amendment by establishing a separate law school for Negroes." *Fisher* v. *Hurst*, 333 U. S. 147, 150 (1948). In *Missouri ex rel. Gaines* v. *Canada*, 305 U. S. 337, 351 (1938), the Court, speaking through Chief Justice Hughes, declared that ". . . petitioner's right was a personal one. It was as an individual that he was entitled to the equal protection of the laws, and the State was bound to furnish him within its borders facilities for legal education substantially equal to those the State there afforded for persons of the white race, whether or not other Negroes sought the same opportunity." These are the only cases in this Court which present the issue of the constitutional validity of race distinctions in state-supported graduate and professional education.

In accordance with these cases, petitioner may claim his full constitutional right: legal education equivalent to that offered by the State to students of other races. Such education is not available to him in a separate law school as offered by the State. We cannot, therefore, agree with respondents that the doctrine of *Plessy* v. *Ferguson*, 163 U. S. 537 (1896), requires affirmance of the judgment below. Nor need we reach petitioner's contention that *Plessy* v. *Ferguson* should be reexamined in the light of contemporary knowledge respecting the purposes of the Fourteenth Amendment and the effects of racial segregation. See *supra*, p. 631.

We hold that the Equal Protection Clause of the Fourteenth Amendment requires that petitioner be admitted to the University of Texas Law School. The judgment is reversed and the cause is remanded for proceedings not inconsistent with this opinion.

Reversed.

SUPREME COURT OF THE UNITED STATES

No. 34.—OCTOBER TERM, 1949.

| *G. W. McLaurin, Appellant,*
v.
Oklahoma State Regents for Higher Education, Board of Regents of University of Oklahoma, et al. | On Appeal From the United States District Court for the Western District of Oklahoma. |

[June 5, 1950.]

MR. CHIEF JUSTICE VINSON delivered the opinion of the Court.

*339 U. S. 637, 70 S. Ct. 851, 94 L ed. (Adv. Op.) 787.

In this case, we are faced with the question whether a state may, after admitting a student to graduate instruction in its state university, afford him different treatment from other students solely because of his race. We decide only this issue; see *Sweatt v. Painter, ante,* p. 629.

Appellant is a Negro citizen of Oklahoma. Possessing a Master's Degree, he applied for admission to the University of Oklahoma in order to pursue studies and courses leading to a Doctorate in Education. At that time, his application was denied, solely because of his race. The school authorities were required to exclude him by the Oklahoma statutes, 70 Okla. Stat. §§ 455, 456, 457 (1941), which made it a misdemeanor to maintain or operate, teach or attend a school at which both whites and Negroes are enrolled or taught. Appellant filed a complaint requesting injunctive relief, alleging that the action of the school authorities and the statutes upon which their action was based were unconstitutional and deprived him of the equal protection of the laws. Citing our decisions in *Missouri ex rel. Gaines* v. *Canada,* 305 U. S. 337 (1938), and *Sipuel* v. *Board of Regents,* 332 U. S. 631 (1948), a statutory three-judge District Court held that the State had a constitutional duty to provide him with the education he sought as soon as it provided that education for applicants of any other group. It further held that to the extent the Oklahoma statutes denied him admission they were unconstitutional and void. On the assumption, however, that the State would follow the constitutional mandate, the court refused to grant the injunction, retaining jurisdiction of the cause with full power to issue any necessary and proper orders to secure McLaurin the equal protection of the laws. 83F. Supp. 526.

Following this decision, the Oklahoma legislature amended these statutes to permit the admission of Negroes to institutions of higher learning attended by white students, in cases where such institutions offered courses not available in the Negro schools. The amendment provided, however, that in such cases the program of instruction "shall be given at such colleges or institutions of higher education upon a segregated basis."[1] Appellant was thereupon admitted to the University of Oklahoma Graduate School. In apparent conformity with the amendment, his admission was made subject to "such rules and regulations as to segregation as the President of the University shall consider to afford to Mr. G. W. McLaurin substantially equal educational opportunities as are afforded to other persons seeking the same education at the Graduate College," a condition which does not appear to have been withdrawn. Thus he was required to sit apart at a designated desk in an anteroom adjoining the classroom; to sit at a designated desk on the mezzanine floor of the library, but not to use the desks in the regular reading room; and to sit at a designated table and to eat at a different time from the other students in the school cafeteria.

To remove these conditions, appellant filed a motion to modify the order and judgment of the District Court. That court held that such treatment did not violate the

---

[1]The amendment adds the following proviso to each of the sections relating to mixed schools: "Provided, that the provisions of this Section shall not apply to programs of instruction leading to a particular degree given at State owned or operated colleges or institutions of higher education of this State established for and/or used by the white race, where such programs of instruction leading to a particular degree are not given at colleges or institutions of higher education of this State established for and/or used by the colored race; provided further, that said programs of instruction leading to a particular degree shall be given at such colleges or institutions of higher education upon a segregated basis." Okla. Stat. Ann. tit. 70, §§ 455, 456, 457 (1950). Segregated basis is defined as "classroom instruction given in separate classrooms, or at separate times." *Id.* § 455.

provisions of the Fourteenth Amendment and denied the motion. 87 F. Supp. 528. This appeal followed.

In the interval between the decision of the court below and the hearing in this Court, the treatment afforded appellant was altered. For some time, the section of the classroom in which appellant sat was surrounded by a rail on which there was a sign stating, "Reserved For Colored," but these have been removed. He is now assigned to a seat in the classroom in a row specified for colored students; he is assigned to a table in the library on the main floor; and he is permitted to eat at the same time in the cafeteria as other students, although here again he is assigned to a special table.

It is said that the separations imposed by the State in this case are in form merely nominal. McLaurin uses the same classroom, library and cafeteria as students of other races; there is no indication that the seats to which he is assigned in these rooms have any disadvantage of location. He may wait in line in the cafeteria and there stand and talk with his fellow students, but while he eats he must remain apart.

These restrictions were obviously imposed in order to comply, as nearly as could be, with the statutory requirements of Oklahoma. But they signify that the State, in administering the facilities it affords for professional and graduate study, sets McLaurin apart from the other students. The result is that appellant is handicapped in his pursuit of effective graduate instruction. Such restrictions impair and inhibit his ability to study, to engage in discussions and exchange views with other students, and, in general, to learn his profession.

Our society grows increasingly complex, and our need for trained leaders increases correspondingly. Appellant's case represents, perhaps, the epitome of that need, for he is attempting to obtain an advanced degree in education, to become, by definition, a leader and trainer of others. Those who will come under his guidance and influence must be directly affected by the education he receives. Their own education and development will necessarily suffer to the extent that his training is unequal to that of his classmates. State-imposed restrictions which produce such inequalities cannot be sustained.

It may be argued that appellant will be in no better position when these restrictions are removed, for he may still be set apart by his fellow students. This we think irrelevant. There is a vast difference — a Constitutional difference — between restrictions imposed by the state which prohibit the intellectual commingling of students, and the refusal of individuals to commingle where the state presents no such bar. *Shelley* v. *Kraemer*, 334 U. S. 1, 13-14 (1948). The removal of the state restrictions will not necessarily abate individual and group predilections, prejudices and choices. But at the very least, the state will not be depriving appellant of the opportunity to secure acceptance by his fellow students on his own merits.

We conclude that the conditions under which this appellant is required to receive his education deprive him of his personal and present right to the equal protection of the laws. See *Sweatt* v. *Painter*, ante, p. 629. We hold that under these circumstances the Fourteenth Amendment precludes differences in treatment by the state based upon race. Appellant, having been admitted to a state-supported graduate school, must receive the same treatment at the hands of the state as students of other races. The judgment is

Reversed.

TABLE OF STATUTES PROHIBITING RELIGIOUS DISCRIMINATION IN THE EMPLOYMENT OF PUBLIC SCHOOL TEACHERS

Colorado
Constitution, Art. IX, §8 (1876).

Delaware
Delaware Revised Code 1935, §2630
(fixing of teachers' salaries only; includes racial discrimination).

Idaho
Idaho Code 1947, §§33-3009, 33-1113; 33-3214.

Illinois
Illinois Revised Statutes 1949, c. 122, §22-4.

Indiana
Burns' Indiana Annotated Statutes, §28-5161 (1943 Replacement, Supp. 1949) (includes racial discrimination).

Iowa
Constitution, Art. I., §4. Iowa Code 1950, §735.4.

Montana
Constitution, Art. XI, §9 (1889).

Nebraska
Constitution, Art. VII, §11 (as amended 1920). Nebraska Revised Statutes 1943, §§79-1268, 79-1269.

New Jersey
New Jersey Statutes Annotated 1939, 18:48, 18:5-49; 18:13-19 (dismissal; includes racial discrimination).

New Mexico
Constitution, Art. 12, §9(1912).

Pennsylvania
Purdon's Pennsylvania Statutes Annotated (1940 Perm. Ed.), Tit. 24, §§1-108, 20-2005.

Texas
Vernon's Texas Revised Civil Statutes 1936, Art. 2899a.

Washington
Laws 1937, c. 52.

Wisconsin
Wisconsin Statutes 1949, §40.775 (includes racial discrimination).

Wyoming
Wyoming Compiled Statutes 1945, §67-136.

TABLE OF STATUTES PROHIBITING RELIGIOUS DISCRIMINATION IN CIVIL SERVICE EMPLOYMENT

Alabama

Alabama Code 1940, Tit. 55, §317.

Arkansas

Arkansas Statutes Annotated 1947, 42-406 (state police).

California

California General Laws 1944, Act 1404 §201.5 (Deering) (includes racial discrimination).

Colorado

Constitution Art. XII, §13. Colorado Statutes Annotated 1935, c. 36, §4.

Connecticut

Connecticut General Statutes 1949 c. 14, §374 (includes racial discrimination).

Idaho

Idaho Code 1947, §50-213.

Illinois

Illinois Revised Statutes 1949, c. 24½, §8; c. 24½, §38b (Univ. of Ill. employees; includes racial discrimination); c. 105, §389.7 (park police).

Indiana

Burns' Indiana Annotated Statutes 1933, §§60-1316, 60-1336 (1943 Replacement, Supp. 1949) (includes racial discrimination).

Kansas

Kansas General Statutes 1935, §§75-2906, 75-2916.

Louisiana

Acts 1940, No. 171, §20; No. 172, §20; No. 253, §13.

Maine

Maine Revised Statutes 1944, C. 59, §13.

Maryland

Maryland Code Annotated 1939 (Flack), Art. 64A, §19.

Massachusetts

Massachusetts Annotated Laws 1944, c. 31, §10.

Michigan

Constitution, Art. VI, §22 (approved 1940; includes racial discrimination). Michigan Compiled Laws 1948, §§38.424, 38.512, 38.513.

Minnesota

Minnesota Statutes 1945, §§43.15, 43.24.

Missouri

Laws 1945, pp. 1157-1182, §§20, 38(e) (includes racial discrimination).

706

Nebraska

Nebraska Revised Statutes 1943, §19-1808; §81-899 (Reissue 1950).

New Jersey

New Jersey Statutes Annotated 1939, 11:22-11; 11:17-1; 11:10-8 (Cum. Supp. 1949) includes racial discrimination.

New York

New York Civil Service Law 1946, §14b (includes racial discrimination).

Ohio

Page's Ohio General Code 1946, §§486-10, 486-17.

Oregon

Oregon Compiled Laws Annotated 1940, §87-827; §93-1314 (Supp. 1944-1947) (includes racial discrimination).

Pennsylvania

Purdon's Pennsylvania Statutes Annotated 1941, Tit. 53, §§9383, 9386; Supp. 1949, Tit. 71, §741.502 (includes racial discrimination); Tit. 61, §331.13.

Rhode Island

Acts 1939, c. 661, §21 (includes racial discrimination).

Tennessee

Williams' Tennessee Code 1934, §423.24p (1943 Replacement).

Texas

Vernon's Texas Revised Civil Statutes 1936, Art. 4413(9).

Washington

Laws 1937, c. 13 (police department).

West Virginia

West Virginia Code 1943, §§546(13), 546(14), 525(13), 525(14) (police and fire departments).

Wisconsin

Wisconsin Statutes 1945, §§16.11(1), 16.15, 16.24(1)(a).

Wyoming

Wyoming Compiled Statutes 1945, §§29-1311, 29-1513.

TABLE OF COMPILATIONS AND LAWS CITED

Alabama
Alabama Code Annotated (1940).
Alabama Code Annotated (Cum. Supp. 1947).
Alabama Acts, 1945.
Alabama Acts, 1949.

Alaska
Alaska Compiled Laws (1949).

Arizona
Arizona Code Annotated (1939).
Arizona Code Annotated (Cum. Supp. 1947).

Arkansas
Arkansas Statutes Annotated (1947).

California
California Business and Professional Code (Deering, 1941).
California Business and Professional Code (Deering, Supp. 1947).
California Civil Code (Deering, 1949).
California Education Code (Deering, 1944).
California Education Code (Deering, Supp. 1949).
California Fish and Game Code (Deering, Supp. 1949).
California Health and Safety Code (Deering, Supp. 1949).
California General Laws (Deering, 1941).
California General Laws (Deering, Supp. 1947).
California Labor Code (Deering, 1941).
California Military and Veterans Code (Deering, Supp. 1949).
California Penal Code (Deering, Supp. 1947).
California Penal Code (Deering, 1949).
California Statutes, 1949.
California Welfare and Institutions Code, (Deering, Supp. 1947).

Colorado
Colorado Statutes Annotated (1935).
Colorado Statutes Annotated (Cum. Supp. 1947).

Connecticut
Connecticut General Statutes (Revision 1949).
Connecticut General Statutes (Revision, Supp. 1949).

Delaware
Delaware Revised Code (1935).
Delaware Laws, 1937.

District of Columbia
District of Columbia Compiled Statutes In Force (1894).
District of Columbia Code (1940).
District of Columbia Code (Supp. VI. 1948).
District of Columbia Code (Supp. VII. 1949).

708

Florida

Florida Acts, 1949.
Florida Statutes (1941).
Florida Statutes (Cum. Supp. 1948).
Florida Statutes (1949).
Florida Statutes Annotated.

Georgia

Georgia Code Annotated (1935).
Georgia Code Annotated (Cum. Supp. 1947).
Georgia Laws, 1949.

Idaho

Idaho Code (1947).

Illinois

Illinois Revised Statutes (1949).
Illinois Statutes, 1949.
Illinois Statutes Annotated (Jones).

Indiana

Indiana Annotated Statutes (Burns, 1933).
Indiana Annotated Statutes (Burns, Cum. Supp. 1947).
Indiana Annotated Statutes (Burns, Cum. Supp. 1948).
Indiana Annotated Statutes (Burns, Cum. Supp. 1949).
Indiana Laws, 1949.

Iowa

Iowa Code (1946).

Kansas

Kansas General Statutes Annotated (1935).
Kansas General Statutes Annotated (Cum. Supp. 1947).
Kansas Laws, 1949.

Kentucky

Kentucky Revised Statutes (1948).
Kentucky Revised Statutes (Legislative Supp. 1950).

Louisiana

Louisiana Civil Code (Dinow 1947).
Louisiana Code of Criminal Procedure Annotated (Dart 1932).
Louisiana Code of Criminal Procedure Annotated (Dart, Cum. Supp. 1942).
Louisiana Code of Criminal Procedure Annotated (Dart, Cum. Supp. 1949).
Louisiana Code of Practice Annotated (Dart 1942).
Louisiana Code of Practice Annotated (Dart, Cum. Supp. 1949).
Louisiana Constitutions Annotated (Dart 1932).
Louisiana General Statutes Annotated (Dart 1939).
Louisiana General Statutes Annotated (Dart, Cum. Supp. 1947).
Louisiana General Statutes Annotated (Dart, Cum. Supp. 1948).

Louisiana General Statutes Annotated (Dart, Cum. Supp. 1949).
Louisiana Revised Civil Code (1870).
Louisiana Acts, 1946.
Louisiana Acts, 1948.

Maine

Maine Revised Civil Code (1944).

Maryland

Maryland Annotated Code (Flack 1939).
Maryland Annotated Code (Flack, Supp. 1943).
Maryland Annotated Code (Flack, Supp. 1947).
Maryland Laws, 1949.

Massachusetts

Massachusetts Annotated Laws (Michie 1944).
Massachusetts Annotated Laws (Michie Cum. Supp. 1948).
Massachusetts Annotated Laws (Michie Cum. Supp. 1949).
Massachusetts Acts, 1949.

Michigan

Michigan Compiled Laws (1948).

Minnesota

Minnesota Statutes Annotated (1946).
Minnesota Statutes Annotated (Cum. Supp. 1949).
Minnesota Laws, 1949.

Mississippi

Mississippi Code Annotated (1942).
Mississippi Code Annotated (Cum. Supp. 1948).
Mississippi Laws, 1948.

Missouri

Missouri Revised Statutes (1935).
Missouri Laws, 1945.
Missouri Laws, 1947.

Montana

Montana Revised Codes (1935).
Montana Revised Codes (1947).

Nebraska

Nebraska Revised Statutes (1943).
Nebraska Revised Statutes (Cum. Supp. 1949).
Nebraska Laws, 1947.

Nevada

Nevada Compiled Laws (1929).
Nevada Compiled Laws (Supp. 1931-1941).
Nevada Compiled Laws (Supp. 1943-1949).

New Hampshire
New Hampshire Revised Laws (1942).
New Hampshire Laws, 1947.
New Hampshire Laws, 1949.

New Jersey
New Jersey Statutes Annotated (1939).
New Jersey Statutes Annotated (Cum. Supp. 1948).
New Jersey Statutes Annotated (Cum. Supp. 1949).
New Jersey Statutes Annotated (Supp. 1950).

New Mexico
New Mexico Statutes Annotated (1941).
New Mexico Statutes Annotated (Cum. Supp. 1949).
New Mexico Laws, 1949.

New York
McKinney's Constitution.
New York Alcoholic Beverage Control Law.
New York Civil Rights Law.
New York Civil Service Law (Cum. Supp. 1949).
New York Education Law (Cum. Supp. 1948).
New York Executive Law (Cum. Supp. 1948).
New York Indian Law.
New York Insurance Law.
New York Judiciary Law.
New York Labor Law.
New York Military Law (Supp. 1949).
New York Penal Law.
New York Public Housing Law.
New York Real Property Law (Supp. 1948).
New York Tax Law (Supp. 1948).
New York Laws, 1950.

North Carolina
North Carolina General Statutes (1943).
North Carolina General Statutes (Cum. Supp. 1947).
North Carolina General Statutes (Cum. Supp. 1949).
North Carolina Laws, 1949.

North Dakota
North Dakota Revised Code (1943).
North Dakota Revised Code (Supp. 1947).
North Dakota Laws, 1949.

Ohio
Ohio Code Annotated (Throckmorton, Baldwin's Revision, 1948).

Oklahoma
Oklahoma Statutes (1941).
Oklahoma Statutes (Supp. 1949).
Oklahoma Laws, 1949.

Oregon

Oregon Compiled Laws Annotated (1940).
Oregon Compiled Laws Annotated (Supp. 1947).
Oregon Laws, 1947.
Oregon Laws, 1949.

Pennsylvania

Pennsylvania Statutes Annotated (Purdon, 1940).
Pennsylvania Statutes Annotated (Purdon, Cum. Supp. 1948).
Pennsylvania Statutes Annotated (Purdon, Cum. Supp. 1949).

Rhode Island

Rhode Island General Laws (1938).
Rhode Island Acts, 1939.
Rhode Island Acts, 1941.
Rhode Island Acts, 1942.
Rhode Island Acts, 1949.

South Carolina

South Carolina Code (1942).
South Carolina Code (Supp. 1944).
South Carolina Statutes at Large, 1945.
South Carolina Statutes at Large, 1947.
South Carolina Statutes at Large, 1948.

South Dakota

South Dakota Code (1939).
South Dakota Laws, 1949.

Tennessee

Tennessee Code Annotated (Williams, 1934).
Tennessee Code Annotated (Williams, Cum. Supp. 1948).
Tennessee Code Annotated (Williams, Cum. Supp. 1949).

Texas

Texas Statutes Annotated (Vernon's 1947 Revision of 1925).
Texas Statutes Annotated (Vernon's, Supp. 1948).
Texas Laws, 1947.
Texas Laws, 1949.

Utah

Utah Code Annotated (1943).
Utah Laws, 1947.
Utah Laws, 1949.

Vermont

Vermont Statutes (Revision of 1947).

Virginia

Virginia Code (1950).
Virginia Code (Supp. 1950).

Washington

Washington Revised Statutes Annotated (Remington's, 1931).
Washington Revised Statutes Annotated (Remington's, Supp. 1949).

West Virginia

West Virginia Code Annotated (1943).
West Virginia Code Annotated (Supp. 1947).

Wisconsin

Wisconsin Statutes (1949).

Wyoming

Wyoming Compiled Statutes Annotated (1945).

United States

United States Code (1946 Edition).
United States Code (1946 Edition, Supp. III).

ADDENDA

STATES' LAWS ON RACE AND COLOR

The compiler would appreciate being notified of any typographical or other errors or omissions, as well as any further developments relating to the materials treated in this study. Interested readers are invited to communicate with Pauli Murray, 6 Maiden Lane, New York 7, N. Y.

SCOPE NOTE

Page 8.—Paragraph 4, sentence 1 should read: "In addition to criminal proceedings, Massachusetts, New Jersey and Connecticut permit the aggrieved individual to file a complaint before an administrative agency which has power to issue orders enforceable in the courts." [See 1950 amendment to the Massachusetts law; Acts 1950, c. 479; appvd. May 23, 1950.]

Page 9.—Last paragraph, sentences 1 to 3 should read: "Twenty-nine states have legislated against religious bias in the field of civil service. Eleven of these states include racial discrimination although coverage varies. Fourteen states bar discrimination on religious grounds in the employment of public school teachers, but only three of these prohibit racial discrimination. A fifteenth state, Delaware, prohibits discrimination. in the fixing of teachers' salaries on racial or religious grounds."

Note 20a should read: "California, Connecticut, Illinois, Indiana, Michigan, Missouri, New Jersey, New York, Oregon, Pennsylvania, Rhode Island."

Page 10.—Note 22 should read: "Indiana, New Jersey and Wisconsin."

Page 12.—Paragraph 3, sentence 1 should read: "Seven states have taken steps to eliminate discrimination in slum clearance and redevelopment housing. In addition to Illinois, Indiana, Minnesota and Pennsylvania, the legislatures of New Jersey, New York and Wisconsin have acted in this field."

Paragraph 4: By July 1950, 13 states were reported to have declared integration in the state National Guard without discrimination because of race, color or religion to be state policy. These states are: California, Connecticut, Illinois, Massachusetts, Michigan, Minnesota, New Hampshire, New Jersey, New York, Oregon, Pennsylvania, Wisconsin and Washington. Eight states have outlawed discrimination by legislative

714

action; five states —Michigan, Minnesota, New Hampshire, Oregon and Washington — by executive order or military regulation. [See *Report*, American Council on Race Relations, July, 1950, p. 2.]

Page 16.—Paragraph 5: For the U.S. Supreme Court decision in the *Henderson* case, see Appendix 7.

Page 19.—Paragraph 4, sentence 2 should read: "In fifteen states the furnishing of liquor to Indians is forbidden."

Note 81 should read: "Arizona, Colorado, Florida, Idaho, Iowa, Minnesota, Montana, Nebraska, New Mexico, New York, North Dakota, Oklahoma, Oregon, Utah and Washington. Kansas and Nevada recently repealed similar laws. See Kansas Laws 1949, c. 242, §115; Nevada Stats. 1947, 24, 456."

Paragraph 4, sentence 3 should read: "Arizona, Montana and Nebraska make it unlawful to furnish Indians with firearms. Idaho repealed a similar law in 1949. (See Idaho Laws 1949, c. 9, §1; c. 10, §1.)"

KENTUCKY

Page 166.—Insert following §158.025:

§158.021. Exceptions to requirement of separate schools for white and colored students. — The provisions of KRS 158.020 shall not be construed to prohibit the giving or receiving of instruction in any course of study, above high school level, in any institution of higher education, public or private, at the undergraduate or graduate grade or on the professional level, or in any course of instruction for adults conducted or sponsored by or under the auspices of public or private corporations, groups or bodies, providing the governing authorities of the institution, corporation, group or body so elect, and provided that an equal, complete and accredited course is not available at the Kentucky State College for Negroes. [1950, c. 155, eff. June 15, 1950.]

Regional Education

§164.530. Regional Compact of Southern States for educational services; approval and signature of. — [Approves Regional Compact. For text of Regional Compact see under *Maryland*, p. 201.] [1950, c. 252, §§2, 3, eff. March 25, 1950.]

§164.540. University of Kentucky designated agency of state for purposes of Regional Compact; restrictions concerning negroes. — . . . (2) In its participation in the regional compact, or in any other regional plan having a similar purpose, the Commonwealth of Kentucky shall not erect, acquire, develop or maintain in any manner any educational institution within its borders to which Negroes will not be admitted on an equal basis with other races, nor shall any Negro citizen of Kentucky be forced to attend any segregated regional institution to obtain instruction in a particular course of study if there is in operation within the Commonwealth at the time an institution that offers the same course of study to students of other races. [1950, c. 255, §§2, 3, eff. March 25, 1950.]

715

Page 213.—Insert in place of Ch. 272, §98.

§98. [1950 Amendment] Color, Race or Religious Discrimination. — Whoever makes any distinction, discrimination or restriction on account of religion, color or race, except for good cause applicable alike to all persons of every religion, color and race, relative to the admission of any person to, or his treatment in, any place of public accommodation, resort or amusement, as defined in section ninety-two A of chapter two hundred and seventy-two [Ch. 272, §92A], or whoever aids or incites such distinction, discrimination or restriction, shall be punished by a fine of not more than three hundred [$300] dollars or by imprisonment for not more than one [1] year, or both, and shall forfeit to any person aggrieved thereby not less than one hundred [$100] nor more than five hundred [$500] dollars; but such person so aggrieved shall not recover against more than one person by reason of any one act of distinction, discrimination or restriction. All persons shall have the right to the full and equal accommodations, advantages, facilities and privileges of any place of public accommodation, resort or amusement, subject only to the conditions and limitations established by law and applicable alike to all persons. This right is recognized and declared to be a civil right. [Acts 1950, c. 479, §3; appvd. May 23, 1950.]

Page 217.—Ch. 6, §§17, 56. — [Both sections are amended to change the name of the Massachusetts Fair Employment Practice Commission to "Massachusetts Commission Against Discrimination."] [Acts 1950, c. 479, §§1, 2; appvd. May 23, 1950.]

Page 221.—§5. — [This section is amended to permit any person claiming to be aggrieved by an alleged unlawful fair employment practice, or by a violation of Ch. 272, §§92A, 98 (public accommodations), or by a violation of Ch 121, §26FF(e) (housing) to file a complaint before the Massachusetts Commission Against Discrimination. For full text of this statute see Mass. Acts 1950, c. 479, §4, appvd. May 23, 1950.]

Page 224.—Ch. 121, §26FF(e). [This section is amended to prohibit segregation as well as discrimination in low rent housing projects. See Mass. Acts 1950, c. 479, §5, appvd. May 23, 1950.]

MISSOURI

Page 252.—Insert before *Dentists*:

Civil Service

Laws 1945, §38(e), p. 1178. [Provides that any regular civil service employee who is dismissed, demoted or suspended, may appeal in writing to the state Personnel Advisory Board within 30 days from the effective date of such removal, where such employee believes "the dismissal, suspension or demotion was for political, religious, or racial reasons." If the Board "finds the dismissal was based on political, social or religious reason," it is required to reinstate the employee with back pay.]

NEW JERSEY

Page 283.—Insert before *Commission on Urban Colored Population*:

Civil Service

11:10-8. **Discrimination against eligibles certified for appointments; statement of reasons for appointment.** — [Provides that where an appointing officer makes an appointment from the civil service list of any person graded lower than the person or persons passed over in making the appointment, he must file with the Civil Service Commission a statement certifying under oath that such acts were not not done by reason of race, color political faith or creed. Until such certified statement is filed, the Commission shall not include the name of the person so appointed or given employment in the payroll.] [As amended L. 1947, c. 123, p. 594, §1.]

PENNSYLVANIA

Page 390.—Insert before *Police Force*

Penal and Correctional Institutions

Tit. 61, §331.13. [1949 Cum. Supp.] **Competitive examination for positions.** — . . . no applicant for appointment shall be excluded from the examination conducted by the board [State Board of Parole] for political, racial or religious reasons, . . . [1941, Aug. 6, P.L. 861, §13.]

Insert after *Police Force*:

Title 53, §351.20. [1949 Cum. Supp.] **Removals, suspension or reduction in rank.** — . . . A person so employed shall not be removed for religious, racial or political reasons . . . [1941, June 5, P.L. 84, §20.]

Page 392.—Insert after text under *Military*

Orphans

Title 24, §2647. [Thaddeus Stevens Industrial School] **Boys admitted; no discrimination on account of race, color, etc.** — . . . In considering such admission [orphan boys under 14 years of age] no preference shall be shown on account of race or color or religion . . . [1905, May 11, P.L. 518, §8.]

APPENDIX 6.

Page 671.—See *New York Times*, Sunday, Sept. 3, 1950, p. 25, col. 1; Sunday, October 23, 1950, p. 29, col. 6, for latest developments in admission of Negroes to Southern colleges.

ERRATA

Page 22, line 8: *for* certatin *read* certain.

Page 30, line 36: *for* formication *read* fornication.

Page 59, line 5: *insert* **Education** as a title following line 5.

Page 88, line 26: *for* scure *read* secure.

Page 144, line 44: *for* Indian *read* Indiana.

Page 169, line 8: *for* of *read* or.

Page 232, line 26: *for* Discrimnation *read* Discrimination.

Page 248, line 26: *for* accommodaitons *read* accommodations.

Page 258, line 9: *for* side *read* state.

Page 261, line 31: *for* prohbited *read* prohibited.

Page 273, line 1: *for* Council's *read* Commission's.

Page 327, line 30: *for* Prohibiiton *read* Prohibition.

Page 349, line 24: *for* Citiden read *Citizen.*

Page 432, line 19: *for* Educaional *read* Educational.

Page 465, line 36: *insert* Farm *after* Industrial.

Page 523, line 35: *for* ailen's *read* alien's.

A SPECIAL NOTE ABOUT THIS EDITION

The three charts on states' laws on segregation and against discrimination that appeared in the first printing of States' Laws on Race and Color *were not reproduced in the University of Georgia Press edition. The first three footnotes on page six, referring to the first edition charts, were also omitted from the University of Georgia Press edition.*

INDEX

by P. A. I. Brown

Laws and Statutes passed by individual States are indexed under the name of each State. Other headings in the index refer to the comprehensive of legislation throughout the United States contained in the compiler's Scope Note and materials found in the Appendices.

Laws relating to Negroes are too numerous to classify under one heading. They may be found under such headings as "Employment," "Segregation", etc.

[References are to pages]

INDEX

744

CPSIA information can be obtained
at www.ICGtesting.com
Printed in the USA
LVHW030903110723
PP17810900002B/3